On the Air

On the Air

The Encyclopedia of Old-Time Radio

JOHN DUNNING

New York   Oxford
Oxford University Press
1998

Oxford University Press

Oxford   New York
Athens   Auckland   Bangkok   Bogotá   Bombay
Buenos Aires   Calcutta   Cape Town   Dar es Salaam
Delhi   Florence   Hong Kong   Istanbul   Karachi
Kuala Lumpur   Madras   Madrid   Melbourne
Mexico City   Nairobi   Paris   Singapore
Taipei   Tokyo   Toronto   Warsaw

and associated companies in
Berlin   Ibadan

Published by Oxford University Press, Inc.
198 Madison Avenue, New York, New York 10016

Library of Congress Cataloging-in-Publication Data
Dunning, John, 1942–
On the air : the encyclopedia of old-time radio / John Dunning.
p.   cm.   Includes index.
Rev. ed. of: Tune in yesterday. © 1976.
ISBN 0-19-507678-8
1. Radio programs—United States—Dictionaries.
I. Dunning, John, 1942-   Tune in yesterday.   II. Title.
PN1991.3.U6D8   1998   791.44'75'0973—DC20   96-41959

7 9 8
Printed in the United States of America
on acid-free paper

To the seven who read the manuscript and made
it a better book by far than it might have been.

Barrett Benson, collector and listener for two decades; member since 1979 of the Radio Historical Association of Colorado.

Frank Bresee, actor, radio man, show host: his *Golden Days of Radio* has been on the air continuously since 1949, including 29 years on Armed Forces Radio.

George Fowler, who initiated the author into old-time radio in 1969; one of the earliest collectors of taped radio material.

Terry Salomonson, expert on the WXYZ Trendle shows; compiler of detailed logs; holder of one of the largest collections of shows.

Chuck Schaden, Chicago radio show host, whose programs, *Those Were The Days* and *Old-Time Radio Classics*, have run since 1970.

Ray Stanich, who, in the words of radio historian Jay Hickerson, did more work dating shows than anyone. Ray died before this book was finished, but his research in libraries and network archives pinned down and corrected hundreds of elusive dates.

Barbara J. Watkins, collector, California radio show host, radio actress, historian, columnist, and active member of SPERDVAC, the California-based radio society.

And to

Helen Dunning, who coordinated the readers' comments, chased final dates and spellings, and argued with the author over points large and small.

Contents

Credits

*T*hanks to those, living or dead, who contributed in many ways to this or the first edition. Some read parts of the manuscript; some sent suggestions or corrections; many consented to lengthy on-air interviews.

Steve Allen
Elvia Allman
Dave Amaral
Andy Anderson
Arthur Anderson
Eve Arden
Hy Averback
Parley Baer
Bill Baldwin
George Balzer
Harry Bartell
Andre Baruch
John Behrens/CBS Program
  Information
Court Benson
Bernice Berwin
Curley Bradley
Terry Black
Ray Bradbury
Barry and Richard Brooks
Howard Brenner
The Broadcast Pioneers Library
Candy Candido
Carroll Carroll

Charles Collingwood
Whitfield Connor
Norman Corwin
Skip Craig
Mary Jane Croft
Dennis Day
Rosemary De Camp
John Dehner
Kenny Delmar
The Denver Public Library
Jerry Devine
Fred Dickey
Howard Duff
Mrs. Clarice Durham
Richard Durham
Sam Edwards
Al Ellis
Georgia Ellis
Alice Faye
Ruth Duskin Feldman
George Fenneman
Morton Fine
Sam Frank
Paul Frees

Jack French
Fred Friendly
Alice Frost
John Gassman
Larry Gassman
Art Gilmore
Roberta Goodwin
Gale Gordon
Martin Grams Jr.
Ken Greenwald
Virginia Gregg
Dan Haefele
William and Teresa Harper
Phil Harris
Clarence Hartzell
Richard K. Hayes
Joe Hehn
Catherine Heinz
Jay Hickerson
Tim Hollis
Dennis Horsford
John Houseman
Bill Idelson
Raymond Edward Johnson
Jack Johnstone
Jim Jordan
Dick Joy
Hal Kanter
Patrick King
Sheldon Leonard
Phil Leslie
Larry Lesueur
Elliott Lewis
John MacVane
Tyler McVey
Fletcher Markle
Grace Matthews
Jack Miller
Marvin Miller
Shirley Mitchell
Carlton E. Morse

The National Lum and Abner
   Society
Frank Nelson
E. Jack Neuman
Nelson Olmsted
John R. Olsen Jr.
Pacific Pioneer Broadcasters
Vic Perrin
Tom Price
Bob Proctor
Michael Raffetto
John Rayburn
Pat Rispole
Bill Sabis
John Scheinfeld
Barbara Schwarz
Anne Seymour
William L. Shirer
Penny Singleton
Society to Preserve and Encourage
   Radio Drama, Variety and
   Comedy (SPERDVAC)
Jay K. Springman
Andrew Steinberg
Berne Surrey
Glenhall Taylor
Irene Tedrow
Bill Thoennes
Cliff Thorsness
Anthony Tollin
Les Tremayne
Lurene Tuttle
Veola Vonn
Bea Wain
Janet Waldo
Bob Wallenberg
Peggy Webber
Marion Wedin
Paul Wesolowski
Anne Whitfield
Bob Wilkinson

Introduction

Twenty years have passed since the original edition of *Tune In Yesterday* appeared in bookstores. It was subtitled *The Ultimate Encyclopedia of Old-Time Radio*, its author slightly uncomfortable in such a huge hat. We are older now and hopefully wiser. We know that books are seldom, if ever, ultimate. And in radio history, the information that has come to light since the first edition appeared has some of the characteristics of a major flood.

The book quickly became the standard reference work. Frank Buxton and Bill Owen had compiled an earlier encyclopedia, *The Big Broadcast*. Vincent Terrace produced a later one, *Radio's Golden Years*. But *Tune In Yesterday*—possibly because it dealt with behind-the-mike folklore in addition to facts and dates—became one of the most-sought out-of-print books in America. Collectors routinely pay $150 to $200 for a copy, a gratifying experience to its slightly bewildered author.

But these books all failed the tests of comprehensiveness and accuracy. *The Big Broadcast* had been criticized by buffs for a few glaring errors, but Buxton and Owen went where none had gone before, and their book remains a valued reference tool. Terrace was more widely denounced. His book seemed a poor man's copy of *The Big Broadcast*, the mistakes compounded and enlarged. But Terrace too had his contributions: in his pages a reader will find dozens of arcane tidbits, intriguing facts that appear nowhere else.

Between Buxton and Terrace was my book, *Tune In Yesterday*. This was judged far less critically than either Buxton or Terrace. People were generally so delighted to have access to the material that they gladly overlooked the book's many problems. There were, of course, exceptions: a few reviewers pointed out errors; some wondered how an encyclopedia could neglect such important milestones as the Metropolitan Opera broadcasts; and the author still remembers a strong letter from radio actress Alice Reinheart, taking him to task for what then seemed like a Sears catalogue of mistakes. But the reaction from the sadly diminishing community of radio pioneers was positive; even when they had bones to pick, the people who worked in network radio seemed thrilled by the book. Dick Joy wrote a long letter from the Northwest: Dick had been the announcer on *The Adventures of Sam Spade*, among many others, and offered some gentle corrections to the author's faulty assumptions and "mistakes in judgment." He became a friend, as did Elliott Lewis, a true genius of the medium. The recollections of these and other radio pioneers have enriched the author's understanding of life behind the mike during the network years (1926–62), when the business was truly a big-time national force.

How big was it? People who grew up with television have no idea how much their parents and grandparents were affected by what they heard. Radio took the country by storm. Careers were made overnight, and a few were lost the same way. The shows that came out of the three national radio centers—New York, Chicago, and Hollywood—informed, entertained, and shaped the opinions of three generations. *On the Air*, a revised and vastly enlarged edition of *Tune In Yesterday*, will hopefully fill a gap even for the serious student of radio history. A week seldom passes when I am not asked for a copy of the old book: interest in big-time radio continues to grow as more people realize what a truly special art form it was. Like any popular medium, it was saturated with junk, but there were also shows that cannot be called anything less than wonderful, even from the critical and somewhat jaded distance of four decades. The tragedy of radio in America is unique. It's the only lost art, abandoned by its public at the very moment when (in the words of writer E. Jack Neuman) "radio was just starting to stand up and put on its long pants."

In this revision, readers will find full descriptive and factual details on hundreds of people and shows that were not covered in the first book. Some are of major importance. Richard Durham's powerful series on black history, *Destination Freedom*, was virtually unknown when the original book was published: today it would make this writer's list of the greatest radio shows of its day. The same can be said of *Words at War*, which had an unheralded run on NBC during World War II. There are also hundreds of little shows, important early series of which no recordings and little descriptive material was available. *The A&P Gypsies*, *The Palmolive Hour*, *The Clicquot Club Eskimos*, *The Gold Dust Twins*, *The Atwater-Kent Hour*, *The Majestic Theater of the Air*, and *The Eveready Hour* are a few of the important 1920s shows of which no accounting can be found in *Tune In Yesterday*. I wanted to do more than list the names of people who appeared: I wanted the life of each show, its essence. And the great days of collecting shows had only begun.

Everything on radio was done live, often with so little preparation that it defies belief today. Thankfully, these broadcasts were captured on cumbersome acetate records by network sound engineers, or by various transcription services that could be professionally engaged to "aircheck" any given program on the dial. It is now estimated that the number of shows saved on transcriptions might run into hundreds of thousands. Even at this writing, almost three decades into the collecting game, at least 100,000 shows are on tape and circulating among buffs. My own radio library has grown to around 40,000 shows. Most have received my full listening attention. For more than 20 years, I have produced and hosted a radio show in Denver, playing these wonderful recordings for anyone who wanted to listen. I interviewed 125 radio stars, writers, newscasters, and sound effects people. Some of them—Elliott Lewis, Eve Arden, Clarence Hartzell, Virginia Gregg, Frank Nelson, Howard Duff, Phil Harris, Charles Collingwood, Eric Sevareid, and Dennis Day are a few who come immediately to mind—have died. Others who gave their time generously, and whose memories I have preserved on tape, include Janet Waldo, Sam Edwards, Parley Baer, Steve Allen, Bill Idelson . . . the list does run on. These interviews also add to the revision.

It was a massive but simple research job. I spent months at the Denver Public Library, photocopying everything from every magazine or newspaper that had any reference to radio. At night, abetted by my wife, Helen, I stapled and collated this material and built it into a giant file, which eventually took up most of a filing cabinet. Each article was marked with the name of the show it covered: these were inserted in alphabetical order, encyclopedia-style. A gentleman named Roy Bright sent me 11 years of *Radio Life*; Terry Salomonson, who became one of my proofreaders, sent years of *Radio Guide*. When I came to, say, *The Adventures of Sam Spade*, I might find a dozen or more articles ranging from *Radio Stars* and *Tune In* to *Time, Life,* and *Newsweek*. I would read this material, check the dates through *Radio Guide* and *New York Times* microfilm, listen to a few shows, and write the entry. The question always remains—was the contemporary reportage reliable? Some accounts were obviously better than others; a few were heavily fictionalized, but *Radio Life* and *Radio Guide* had beat reporters on the scene and dealt in hard facts that could often be verified elsewhere. I still admit to some uneasiness when confronted with the memories of an aging radio star. Did it actually happen as he now remembers it, or was it the way *Radio Life* reported it 50 years ago? Reporters can be wildly inaccurate, but the memory does occasionally embellish. To guard against errors, I asked seven friends, each with at least 15 years of experience in the field—studying, researching, logging, and listening—to read the work and point out questionable material. They have been diligent and tireless, and each of them has saved me from mistakes and oversights. Naturally, any errors that remain are my own responsibility.

The author is also indebted to a trio of fine editors at Oxford. To India Cooper, a gentle copy editor and a wizard at formatting. Without her there'd be no organization. To Joellyn Ausanka, a cheerful and diligent production editor. Without her there'd have been no safety net. And to Sheldon Meyer, a good, tough editor-in-chief. Without him there'd be no book.

The new format should make this an easier book to use and read. At the top of each article, a reader will find all the factual material: who did what, when, what time it ran, who sponsored it. Then comes the narrative, the essence, which may run many pages, depending upon the importance of the entry. Occasionally, in postscript, I try to assess the show's impact today, when many episodes exist on tape. This is the happiest thing about radio drama—it is still with us, just as it was then. It is truly living history. Maybe we've changed, but radio is eternal. No matter how many comebacks radio might make, no matter how advanced our audio technology may become, scholars will always look to those three decades of American broadcasting as the prime force in shaping its generation. Much of it still plays well, as gripping and hilarious as ever it was. The best of it is simply sensational, and even the worst of it is interesting. As someone once said, discussing *The Romance of Helen Trent*, "That's so bad it's great."

This, I believe, eclipses the old book. Few are the articles that stand as written 20 years ago. Generalities have hardened into specifics as hundreds of new shows have been unearthed and added. That it can never be ultimate is a fact for which the writer apologizes, preferring not to carry that particular conceit this time around.

Ongoing research by many radio historians continues to turn up previously unknown programs, some heard for only a few broadcasts before dropping from schedules and disappearing. As this book was entering its final phase, Jay Hickerson of Hamden, Conn., issued a massive log containing thousands of series titles and dates, including many unfamiliar to this writer. What the author has tried to do here is describe and date all the significant shows, with enough intriguing unknowns to give a reader a comprehensive grasp of the depth, vitality, variety, and scope of the most important entertainment medium of its day.

John Dunning
Denver, Colorado
1969–1997

How to Use This Book

*F*irst, use the index. The book is heavily cross-referenced, and the index will lead to comparisons and mentions perhaps not to be found in the main entries on particular programs. The index will also point the way to programs that might not be arranged by the titles a reader remembers best. A look at *Ozzie and Harriet* or *Sam Spade* in the index will reveal that these programs may be found under *The Adventures of* in the main encyclopedia, and that *The Boston Symphony Orchestra* will be grouped with others of its ilk under the general article *Concert Broadcasts*. If all else fails, look for the people involved. The index listing for *Nelson, Ozzie* will not only lead to the program titled *The Adventures of Ozzie and Harriet* but will point out prior appearances by the stars that may have been significant in the eventual development of their own series. The Nelsons, for example, worked with Joe Penner in the 1930s, in a series titled not *The Joe Penner Show* but *The Baker's Broadcast.* The index will clear up these apparent lapses and inconsistencies.

All timeslots, with the exceptions here noted, refer to Eastern Time. A show that ran at 8 P.M. in the East could often be found one hour earlier for each time belt westward that a listener moved. But this was by no means reliable. Some shows were done on different days in the West. Far more common, especially on major programs, was the practice of having the casts do two live broadcasts so that both might play in prime time. A show originating in Hollywood and scheduled at 8 P.M. might be aired live to the east at 5 P.M., Pacific time, with the cast returning three hours later to do the identical show live for the West Coast. Shows originating in New York, of course, had this cycle reversed, with the "repeat show for the West" going out at 11 P.M. To avoid confusion, the eastern timeslot is used as the anchoring point for the majority of entries, the obvious exceptions being the regional broadcasts that were confined to the western states. These are clearly designated "Pacific time" within the entry.

A staunch attempt has been made to pin down exact starting and ending dates for each series. When dates are general (1927–31 rather than Dec. 14, 1927–Jan. 5, 1931), it is because the specifics remain elusive or are in doubt.

Most entries contain precise timeslots with the show's length abbreviated. An entry designated "60m, Wednesdays at 8" means an hour-long broadcast at 8 P.M. "Then at 9" means the show later moved to a 9 P.M. timeslot, still on Wednesday. Morning designations only are noted as A.M.

Confusion is bound to result from the fact that NBC owned two networks, the Red and the Blue, and that the Blue was sold in 1943 (with a little nudge from a federal government concerned about monopolies in broadcasting), to be renamed the American Broadcasting Company. For our purposes, references to NBC without a color indicates the main NBC Red Network. The confusion deepens during the transition period, 1942–44: references are made to the Blue Network through 1943 and into 1944, when the name change to ABC took place. In several instances during this time, the network is described as Blue/ABC.

Finally, the reader should avoid assuming facts not in evidence. The lists of personnel under *cast, announcers, directors, sound effects*, and the like are as complete as the author can make them within the scope of this book. That there may have been other announcers, directors, and even players for the roles described remains distinctly possible, though the goal has always been to list every major contributor. And though programs usually took summer vacations, these absences from the air are only noted when there was a significant change of format or network.

On the Air

THE A&P GYPSIES, exotic music with a no-madic motif; one of radio's earliest, most distinctive programs.

BROADCAST HISTORY: 1923–27, WEAF, New York. First heard as an unsponsored group in the winter of 1923; scheduled regularly beginning March 17, 1924, Monday nights. A&P Food Stores.

Jan. 3, 1927–Sept. 7, 1936, NBC. 60m initially, Mondays at 9 (8:30, 1928–31). Split into two half-hours, 1931–32: Red Network, Mondays at 9; Blue Network, Thursdays at 10. 1932–36, Red only, 30m, Mondays at 9. A&P.

CREATOR-LEADER: Harry Horlick. ANNOUNC-ERS: Phillips Carlin, Milton Cross. THEME: *Two Guitars.*

It arrived on the air at the dawn of broadcasting, its world a place that radio people today can hardly imagine. There was no direct advertising then. Even the concept of using the airwaves for commercial gain was controversial, the future far from certain. Continuity was spotty: much that went on the air was hit-or-miss, with programs penciled in as talent and scheduling became mutually available, often at the last minute.

By 1924 potential clients realized that radio could be an advertising powerhouse. But the rules were strict: "No merchandise could be offered," William Peck Banning wrote of WEAF in his comprehensive history of the station. "Not even the color of a can could be mentioned." Radio, which would later thrive on the hard sell, opened with the softest sell possible. The acts would simply bear the sponsor's name: if people liked the act, hopefully the sponsor would make new friends. Thus came the weekly radio variety show, with regular personalities performing in a consistent timeslot. The best of these shows were highly successful: their performers became stars, and their sponsors, with all the limitations, enjoyed national success.

The A&P Gypsies was created as a commercial entity when a sales executive from the Great Atlantic and Pacific Tea Company happened to hear a haunting gypsy melody as he was touring WEAF in 1923. Looking up, he saw the musicians beyond the control room glass, their melodies coming through an intercom. It was precisely what he had been looking for, a novelty act to link with the A&P. He approached the leader, Harry Horlick, and the six-piece ensemble was signed on the spot.

Horlick, born in a hamlet near Moscow, was pursuing a lifelong interest in the music of nomads. He had played in the Moscow Symphony before the war, but he found the "communized" music of the symphony's postwar years sterile and restricting. He went to Constantinople, where he began traveling with gypsy bands and learning their ancient folk music.

Much of the music he learned had never been written down: when he came to the United States and formed his group, his musicians had to learn it by hearing Horlick sing it. It had a sound that could be haunting, romantic, or fiery. Americans found it fascinating and appealing.

Success brought inevitable changes. The six-

1

man ensemble grew into an orchestra of more than 25. Top guests of the time, such singers as Jessica Dragonette and Frank Munn, appeared on the program. A singing quartet was added: its tenor, Frank Parker, went on to a successful radio career, including stints with Jack Benny and Arthur Godfrey. The musicians "dressed" for the show, performing in gypsy costume. For most of its run, *The A&P Gypsies* was among radio's elite. By the time it left the air, a new era was in full bloom.

A. L. ALEXANDER'S MEDIATION BOARD, advice to the hapless.

BROADCAST HISTORY: Jan. 11, 1943–April 11, 1952, Mutual. 30m though also heard in an unusual 45-m format; 15m, 1952. Mondays at 9:15 through mid-1943, then Sundays, often at 8 or 8:15. Serutan.

A. L. Alexander had achieved great success with *Goodwill Court*, breaking into radio's top ten in 1936. That series offered legal advice to defendants in real court cases, but it died on the vine when the New York Supreme Court barred lawyers from giving counsel on the air. Six years later, Alexander returned with a similar show, minus the legal problems. Here he used sociologists and educators on a panel that dissected and advised on personal problems. Marital discord, even infidelity and promiscuity, were frequent topics. Taped copies reveal a dated but interesting series, sometimes hilarious when the subjects were obviously coached—none too successfully—in microphone technique.

THE ABBOTT AND COSTELLO SHOW, comedy in the vaudeville style, often slapstick, with guest stars, variety, and an orchestra.

BROADCAST HISTORY: July 3–Sept. 25, 1940, NBC. 30m, Wednesdays at 9. Summer substitute for *The Fred Allen Show*. Sal Hepatica.

Oct. 8, 1942–June 27, 1947, NBC. 30m, Thursdays at 7:30 until 1943, then at 10. Camel Cigarettes.

Oct. 1, 1947–June 9, 1949, ABC. 30m, Wednesdays at 9, 1947–48; Thursdays at 8, 1948–49. Sustained.

Dec. 6, 1947–March 26, 1949, ABC. 30m, Saturdays at 11 A.M. *The Abbott and Costello Children's Show*. Sustained.

CAST: Bud Abbott and Lou Costello, Universal film stars, with support from Mel Blanc, Frank Nelson, Sid Fields, Iris Adrian, Martha Wentworth, Sharon Douglas, Verna Felton. ANNOUNCER: Ken Niles, who had regular roles in the comedy, with Elvia Allman as Mrs. Niles. VOCALISTS: Connie Haines, Marilyn Maxwell. ORCHESTRA: Leith Stevens (1942), Skinnay Ennis, Will Osborne, Jack Meakin. PRODUCER: Martin Gosch. WRITERS: Gosch, Howard Harris, Hal Fimberg, Don Prindle, Ed Cherkose, Len Stern, Martin Ragaway, Paul Conlan, Ed Forman (head writer from the mid-1940s). SOUND EFFECTS: Floyd Caton.

Bud Abbott and Lou Costello, remembered primarily as movie comics, got their start toward national fame in radio. For two seasons, beginning Feb. 3, 1938, they were regulars on *The Kate Smith Hour*; they also appeared on Edgar Bergen's *Chase and Sanborn Hour*. They had met in 1929, when Costello was booked with a vaudeville act into a neighborhood theater. Abbott worked in the box office and soon found himself onstage, serving as Costello's straight man. In 1936 they forged a permanent partnership, playing vaudeville and burlesque in the Depression. In 1938 they appeared at Loew's in New York, where they were seen by Ted Collins, architect of Kate Smith's career. Their slaphappy style was perfect for radio, and their rise to frontline stardom was rapid.

Their standup comedy consisted mainly of short skits with clever plays on words. The famous baseball spoof *Who's on First* was created for the stage but proved ideal for radio. The skits developed their images: Abbott was the stern taskmaster; Costello fumbled his way through life and shrugged off his bumbling with the memorable catchphrase "I'm a baaaaad boy!" Costello's shrieks were punctuated by flat sarcasm from Abbott, a simple formula that especially delighted children and kept the duo near the top of the entertainment world for a decade.

Together they made and lost a fortune. Signed by Universal in 1939, they pulled the financially troubled studio out of red ink with a string of low-budget hits. The radio show supplemented their screen success, boosting the gate for such films as *Buck Privates, In the Navy*, and *Hold That Ghost*. But their personal lives countered the happy image. William "Bud" Abbott was born Oct. 2, 1895—it is said in a circus tent—

to a family of circus performers. He earned millions in his film and radio career but died a pauper, April 24, 1974, after an eight-year audit of his back taxes left him penniless. Costello's life was marked by numerous tragedies, earning him the nickname "Hard-Luck Lou." Born March 6, 1908, in Paterson, N. J., Costello would also be plagued by the tax man. In March 1943, with the radio show at its peak, he was stricken with rheumatic fever and forced off the air. Abbott refused to carry on alone, so a new team, Jimmy Durante and Garry Moore, was hastily recruited to replace them. Costello returned in the fall to another cruel tragedy. In dress rehearsal for his first show, he was called home suddenly for the news that his year-old son had fallen into the family pool and drowned.

The news swept through Hollywood. Mickey Rooney was brought in to read his lines. Calls offering to help came from Durante, Bob Hope, and Red Skelton. But around 6 P.M. Costello called Abbott and said he was returning to the show. For 30 minutes he fought back tears and wisecracked with his partner. Abbott pushed the show at its usual pace, wrote Bob Thomas in his dual biography, but guest star Lana Turner "was so distraught she could scarcely deliver her lines above a whisper." As Ken Niles read the sign-off, Costello broke down: Abbott then stepped forward and explained to the stunned studio audience what had happened.

Costello never lost his interest in youth. *The Abbott and Costello Children's Show* featured top juvenile talent and awarded $1,000 savings bonds to "outstanding youngsters of the week." But the slapstick brand of comedy faded along with radio. Costello died March 3, 1959.

ABBOTT MYSTERIES, comedy-detective, following the formula established by *The Thin Man* and *Mr. and Mrs. North*.

BROADCAST HISTORY: June 10, 1945–Aug. 31, 1947, Mutual. 30m, Sundays at 6, 1945; 5:30, 1946–47. Summers only, substituting for *Quick as a Flash*. Helbros Watches. **CAST:** Julie Stevens and Charles Webster (1945, 1947) as Jean and Pat Abbott, a young married couple who regularly solved murders. Les Tremayne and Alice Reinheart as the Abbotts in 1946. **WRITERS:** Howard Merrill, Ed Adamson, from the novels of Frances Crane.

Oct. 3, 1954–June 12, 1955, NBC. 30m, Sundays at 8:30. *The Adventures of the Abbotts.* **CAST:** Claudia Morgan, Les Damon.

A *Radio Life* critic, writing in 1947, found the Abbotts "cute, brave, witty, and sophisticated"— all the attributes of the Norths and of Nick and Nora Charles. There was even an "at home with the Abbotts" bit at each episode's end—the same kind of thing Nick and Nora had been doing for years. Though the series got decent reviews, had a colorful locale (San Francisco), capitalized well on the lighthearted sleuth formula, and, in its 1954–55 revival, featured the same female lead as the earlier *Thin Man* series, it never enjoyed the success of the big two.

THE ABE BURROWS SHOW, sophisticated comedy, wit, satire: a small but highly regarded series with occasional guests and music by a quartet.

BROADCAST HISTORY: July 26, 1947–June 26, 1948, CBS. 15m, Saturdays at 7:30. Sustained until Jan. 1948, then Listerine.

July 4–Oct. 28, 1949, CBS. 30m, Mondays at 9:30 until Sept., then Fridays at 9:30. Satirically titled *Breakfast with Burrows*.

Manhattan-born and -reared, Abe Burrows moved to Hollywood in 1939 and found work writing for radio. His credits included *The Texaco Star Theater*, some of the John Barrymore skits on the Rudy Vallee Sealtest show, and *This Is New York*, for Ed Gardner. He helped create Archie, the sloppy manager of Gardner's *Duffy's Tavern*, and when *Duffy* became a regular series in April 1941, Burrows was hired as its head writer. He worked on a serial of his own, *Holiday and Company* (CBS, Feb.–April 1946) and later wrote the Joan Davis program. While he was with Davis, his career as a performer began.

One night after the broadcast, Davis invited the audience to stay around while she turned the stage over to Burrows, long known as the life of any party; his wit was admired by Robert Benchley, Groucho Marx, and Danny Kaye, among others. He satirized the songs of Tin Pan Alley to his own piano accompaniment. His after-hours performances with Davis led to his own show, which won a Radio Critics Circle Award and was promptly canceled. Highlights were Burrows's razor-sharp quips, his self-taught piano, and music by the Milton DeLugg Quartet. His later show, *Breakfast with Burrows*, was more of the same in a longer format. Burrows explained the title by saying, "I get up late." His career before the mike was brief, but he would have brighter days in other fields—a successful TV series, writing the book for the musical *Guys and Dolls*, and coauthorship of *How To Succeed in Business Without Really Trying*.

ABIE'S IRISH ROSE, situation comedy with a "marriage of two cultures" theme.

BROADCAST HISTORY: Jan. 24, 1942–Sept. 2, 1944, NBC. 30m, Saturdays at 8. Drene Shampoo. **CAST:** Sydney Smith and Betty Winkler as Abie and Rosemary Levy, a young married couple from Jewish and Catholic families. When rumors arose of a movie deal, the leads were recast with a camera in mind: the parts went to Richard Coogan and Mercedes McCambridge, but the movie was never made. Abie was also played during the run by Richard Bond and Clayton Collyer; Rosemary by Julie Stevens and Marion Shockley. Alan Reed and Walter Kinsella as the feuding fathers, Solomon Levy and Patrick Joseph Murphy (with Alfred White heard for a time as Solomon Levy). Menasha Skulnik and Anna Appel as Mr. and Mrs. Cohen. Carl Eastman as David Lerner. Ann Thomas as Casey, the secretary. Bill Adams as Father Whelan. Dolores Gillen as the Levy twins. Amanda Randolph as the maid. **DIRECTOR:** Joe Rines. **WRITER:** Anne Nichols. **THEME:** *My Wild Irish Rose.*

Abie's Irish Rose was one of the great hits of Broadway, closing in 1927 after 2,327 performances. The radio show was first heard as part of NBC's *Knickerbocker Playhouse*, a formula "theater" anthology in the *First Nighter* mode. The theater format disappeared in early 1942, leaving *Abie's Irish Rose* with the regular timeslot. Author Nichols gave it a "true love conquers all" flavor, opening with the elopement of Abie Levy and Rosemary Murphy. This set family against family until the couple became parents of twins, born on Christmas Day. Even then, disputes between the crusty old fathers were always brewing. The series drew solid ratings in 1942 but faded the following year and disappeared in 1944.

ACADEMY AWARD, an anthology of famous movie stories, using the original film stars whenever possible.

BROADCAST HISTORY: March 30–Dec. 18, 1946, CBS. 30m, Saturdays at 7 through June, then Wednesdays at 10. House of Squibb. **CAST:** top Hollywood stars: Ronald Colman, Gregory Peck, Henry Fonda, etc. **MUSIC:** Leith Stevens, composer-conductor. **PRODUCER-DIRECTOR:** Dee Engelbach. **WRITER-ADAPTER:** Frank Wilson. **SOUND EFFECTS:** Berne Surrey.

All of the plays on *Academy Award* had something in common: one or more of the players or the film on which the script was based had won or been nominated for the Oscar. The opening show was *Jezebel*, with Bette Davis; high spots included *Stagecoach* (Claire Trevor, Randolph Scott, May 4), *The Maltese Falcon* (Humphrey Bogart, Sydney Greenstreet, Mary Astor, July 3), and *Suspicion* (Cary Grant, Oct. 30). The House of Squibb, a drug firm, footed a stiff bill: up to $4,000 for the stars and $1,600 a week to the Academy of Motion Picture Arts and Sciences for use of the title. The production had all the class of a *Lux* or *Screen Guild* show. For *Stagecoach*, four soundmen (Gene Twombly, Jay Roth, Clark Casey, and Berne Surrey) were brought in to create the illusion of the racing coach. But the tariff took its toll, and after 39 weeks the series was scrapped.

THE ACADEMY AWARDS SHOW, the annual presentation of the Oscar, Hollywood's highest award for motion picture excellence. The first awards were given in 1927, and on April 30, 1930, KNX, Los Angeles, began radio's coverage of the event. It continued as a local broadcast in the '30s. The Academy of Motion Picture Arts and Sciences banned radio from the 1939 ceremony, but KNX reporter George Fisher defiantly opened a microphone and locked himself in the booth. Security guards broke in the door with axes, and the broadcast was halted after a few minutes.

CBS gave partial coverage in 1942 and 1943. By 1944 the event was on KFWB, with a short-wave hookup around the world. The master of ceremonies was Jack Benny, and the whole show took less than 30 minutes. *Casablanca*, the 1944 winning movie, received the first award of the evening, without melodramatic buildup. Acceptance speeches were brief, and only the major awards were broadcast.

On March 15, 1945, the affair went on the Blue Network. The ceremony, now 70 minutes long, included clips from the films, which had to be explained for the radio audience. Bob Hope, emcee, became closely identified with the show (20 appearances as host or cohost, 1940–78), always coveting the statuettes that went to others.

By 1946 the show had grown to 80 minutes. In 1947 it ballooned to three hours. Television coverage began in 1952. Radio dropped it after the 1968 awards, but it has continued as a TV extravaganza. Today it takes an entire evening and ends in the early hours.

THE ADMIRAL BYRD BROADCASTS, one of the earliest series of on-the-spot true adventures, broadcast from Antarctica and also heard under the titles *The Adventures of Admiral Byrd* and *The Byrd Expeditions*.

BROADCAST HISTORY: Nov. 11, 1933–Jan. 6, 1935, CBS. 30m, Saturdays at 10 until late May, then Wednesdays at 10. General Foods.

Feb. 2–May 24, 1940, NBC. 30m. Alternate Fridays at 11:30 *A Salute to the Byrd Expedition*.

When Admiral Richard E. Byrd announced his second trip to the South Pole, CBS explored the possibility of sending radio equipment and setting up a weekly news show. This concept soon expanded to include variety. A network executive discovered that the Byrd supply ship, the *Bear of Oakland*, contained a collapsible organ and a piano. Sgt. Al Carbone, the cook, could "do double tremolos on the harmonica," and Capt. Alan Innes-Taylor, the main dog-driver, "headed a mean quartet of Malemute-mushers" (*Radioland*). The news segments would be handled by announcer-director Charles J. V. Murphy, who would make the two-year trip with the expedition. The show would be shortwaved to Buenos Aires, 4,000 miles away, then relayed to New York and CBS.

Sponsor General Foods supplied the frozen vegetables taken on the journey and promoted its Grape Nuts cereal line on the air. The radio station, given the letters KFZ, was set up at Little America, the base camp established by Byrd in 1928. As Murphy told it: "At noon on Monday, KFZ was nothing but a pile of crates, boxes, and loose gear on the deck of the S. S.

Jacob Rupert"; this equipment was ferried across the ice on a Citroen tractor; "Thursday night it was in communication with New York, and Saturday it was broadcasting." In addition to the "Antarctic Antics," the show offered geologists, oceanographers, zoologists, and a generous slice of time for Admiral Byrd. A tense situation developed when Byrd departed to spend the winter (March to August) in a tiny hut alone, 120 miles from base camp. He was equipped with a radio but was severely hampered by frostbite and monoxide poisoning from his gasoline heater.

For the third Byrd expedition, in 1939, NBC used the concept of an oral mailbag. Each show consisted of mail readings and personal conversations between expedition members and their relatives at home. This series originated at WGEO, Schenectady, which had a powerful directional shortwave tower and was able to boost a signal at 20 times the norm. In Antarctica, the men often picked it up "just like a local program."

ADOPTED DAUGHTER, soap opera, telling of a "courageous young wife who fights for home and happiness."

BROADCAST HISTORY: 1939–41, NBC Midwest only. 15m. Transcribed for J. C. Penney.

Adopted Daughter was developed from a series of regional skits created by Jettabee Ann Hopkins. Originally titled *The Jangles*, it told of the Jangles family and their adopted daughter Jennie. Hopkins, in addition to writing the script, played the lead. In 1937 she joined station WOW, Omaha, where the serial was bought by a Penney's representative. In April 1939 it went on NBC.

ADULT EDUCATION SERIES, a blanket title covering three distinct CBS educational radio programs.

BROADCAST HISTORY: April 28, 1938–April 23, 1940: *Americans at Work*. 30m. Heard variously on Thursdays, Saturdays, and Tuesdays, late evenings.

May 4, 1938, then March 3–June 30, 1942; *Living History*. 15m, Tuesdays, early evenings.

March 17, 1938–Aug. 18, 1957: *Adventures in Science*. 15m, various days, mostly late afternoon.

The Adult Education Series, a landmark experiment in adult education by radio, was under the overall supervision of Sterling Fisher. *Americans at Work*, the most popular segment, offered interviews with executives and workers recorded in the field. One show followed animator Walt Disney through a typical day, but mostly the series was concerned with the "common man." By 1939 *Americans at Work* was being heard regularly on Thursday nights. Many of the shows were in-studio sessions, done live and without script. In *The Auctioneer*, the show of Sept. 21, 1939, announcer John Reed King hosted auctioneers in five widely disparate fields—livestock, furs, art and literary properties, real estate, and, "of all things, eggs." Listeners learned how auctions were conducted, the secrets of bidding signals, and even the pay scale, the fur auctioneer revealing a salary of $5,000–$10,000, to which King commented, "That's a very good salary." Brewster Morgan directed the later *Americans at Work* shows. Pamphlets of scripts, complete with directors' cues, were available to the public.

Living History dramatized famous moments of the past and, where possible, drew an illuminating parallel with the present. *Adventures in Science* came under the *Adult Education* banner May 6, 1938, after running as its own series for two months previous: historian Allan Nevins hosted the opening show, and the series dealt with such topics as medicine and atomic research.

ADVENTURE PARADE, juvenile serial, specializing in classics by installment.

BROADCAST HISTORY: 1946–49, Mutual. 15m, daily at 4:45. Sustained. **CAST:** John Drake, host and storyteller and source of all the voices in the dramas. **ANNOUNCER:** George Hogan. **MUSIC:** John Gart on organ. **PRODUCER-DIRECTORS:** Robert and Jessica Maxwell.

Action was the hallmark of this series: the goal was to convince young people that literature was an exciting alternative to comic books. Drake was cited by *Radio Life* for his ability to single-handedly maintain "compelling suspense." A chapter from *The Bells of Leyden Sing* (November 1948) sounds quite fully dramatized. Announcer Hogan called the club to order with "Adventurers atten-shun! Fall in for *Adventure Parade!*" Among the plays heard were *Moby-*

Dick, Swiss Family Robinson, and *Last of the Mohicans*. Each story lasted about a week and was transcribed.

ADVENTURE THEATER, a dramatic anthology of classics; a noble though futile attempt to resurrect radio drama long after its network demise.

BROADCAST HISTORY: Feb. 5, 1977–Jan. 29, 1978, CBS. 50m, Saturdays and Sundays at 6:07. Known also as *The General Mills Radio Adventure Theater* and *The CBS Adventure Theater.* General Mills, Feb.–Aug. **HOST:** Tom Bosley. **CAST:** Vintage-era New York radio people, including Robert Dryden, Evelyn Juster, Court Benson, Ralph Bell, Bill Griffis, Mason Adams, Teri Keane. **PRODUCER-DIRECTOR:** Himan Brown. **WRITERS:** Ian Martin, Elspeth Eric, and others who had been actors in the old days.

Adventure Theater joined Himan Brown's *CBS Radio Mystery Theater* on a 218-station network in an era when radio drama had long been relegated to the scrap heap. The series was designed for young people; the plays were classic fare (*Captains Courageous, The Black Arrow, Gulliver's Travels*, etc.). Brown produced them at an oldtime pace. A morning taping session of three hours would wrap up a show; then, after a short break, he would begin another show with another cast. Many young performers joined the oldtimers on the soundstage. But even the vast energy of Himan Brown and a major national sponsor couldn't keep it afloat.

THE ADVENTURER'S CLUB, a title given to two action series 15 years apart.

BROADCAST HISTORY: 1932, 15m. Transcribed syndication. *The World Adventurer's Club.*
Jan. 11, 1947–Jan. 3, 1948, CBS. 30m, Saturdays at 11:30 A.M. Sheaffer Pens. **HOST:** Ken Nordine.

The 1932 run comprised 32 shows, with such titles as Pancho Villa's Treasure and Land of the Black Hand; all survive on tape. The premise of the 1947–48 series was an adventure story told by the explorer, hunter, or traveler who experienced it.

ADVENTURES BY MORSE, adventure thriller.

BROADCAST HISTORY: 1944–45, transcribed syndication, intended for weekly play in 30m timeslots. **CAST:** Elliott Lewis, David Ellis, and Russell Thorson all serving stints as Capt. Bart Friday, a San Francisco detective who roamed the world looking for dangerous adventure. Jack Edwards as Skip Turner, Friday's Texas-talking sidekick. **WRITER-PRODUCER:** Carlton E. Morse.

It's no accident that *Adventures by Morse* bears a striking resemblance to *I Love a Mystery*: both were written and directed by Carlton E. Morse, who produced this syndication soon after his *ILAM* had been scrapped by NBC. The hero, Capt. Friday, sounded much like *ILAM* strongman Jack Packard; the sidekick, Skip Turner, was an *ILAM* Doc Long sound-alike. The stories bordered on the supernatural, though there was usually a near-rational explanation. Major stories of ten weeks alternated with shorter pieces of three chapters, accommodating the standard 13-week broadcasting contracts. The first show sent Friday and Turner to a graveyard in northern California, a fog-shrouded place where the dead walked, wolfmen prowled, and ghouls roamed at will. Later they went to Cambodia and confronted an ancient order of vampire priests inside a vast hollow mountain. The entire 52-week run exists on tape in splendid sound, giving a fine example of the kind of terror-chillers that Morse did better than anyone else.

ADVENTURES IN READING, educational series, an NBC alternative to the CBS shows that dominated this field.

BROADCAST HISTORY: May 2, 1938–Oct. 7, 1940, Blue Network. 30m, Mondays at 2. **PRODUCER-DIRECTOR:** James Church. **WRITERS:** Helen Walpole, Margaret Leaf.

Adventures in Reading gave insights into the works of writers great and obscure, classic and modern, by looking at how events in the authors' lives had shaped their books. It came to the air when Walpole and Leaf submitted a script on Mark Twain to Lewis Titterton, a network editor. The second script focused on Raymond Ditmars, snake expert at New York's Zoological Park. A show on John Milton was selected by Max Wylie as one of the best broadcasts of 1938. Originally scheduled for only six broadcasts, the series ran two years.

THE ADVENTURES OF BILL LANCE, detective drama, heard in two runs with separate casts and production people.

BROADCAST HISTORY: April 23, 1944–Sept. 9, 1945, CBS West Coast. 30m, Sundays at 9, Pacific time. Planters Peanuts. **CAST:** John McIntire as detective Bill Lance until March 1945; Pat McGeehan as Lance, March–Sept. 1945. Howard McNear as Ulysses Higgins, Lance's friend and assistant. Regular players: Mercedes McCambridge, Cathy Lewis, Joseph Kearns, Frank Graham. **ANNOUNCERS:** Dick Joy, occasionally Owen James. **MUSIC:** Milton Charles. **CREATOR-WRITER:** J. Donald Wilson. **PRODUCER:** Glan Heisch. **DIRECTOR:** Mel Williamson. **WRITERS:** Stewart Sterling, Sylvia Richards, Maurice Zimm, Martha Chapin.
June 14, 1947–Jan. 4, 1948, ABC. 30m, Saturdays at 9 until Aug.; Mondays at 9 until Sept.; then Sundays at 5. **CAST:** Gerald Mohr as Lance. **PRODUCER:** Dwight Hauser.

The opening signature in 1944 pegged Bill Lance as "that ace of criminologists, whose daring exploits and infallible accuracy have earned him, from the underworld, the nickname Fer de Lance, the deadliest of reptiles, so swift, so sure, that it never misses." Creator J. Donald Wilson, a crime show veteran, said of his hero: "He has the deductive type of mind and is very fond of music." Lance's assistant Higgins, said Wilson, "doesn't have the deductive mind and isn't fond of music." Producer Heisch had a weakness for exotic locales: circuses, waterfronts, morgues, South American cafes, and such places as North Africa."

THE ADVENTURES OF CAPTAIN DIAMOND, an early series of sea tales.

BROADCAST HISTORY: Oct. 5, 1932–March 29, 1934, Blue Network. 30m, Wednesdays at 8 until Jan. 1933, then Thursdays at 8. General Foods for Diamond Salt.
Nov. 15, 1936–April 18, 1937, Blue Network. 30m, Sundays at 3:15 until Jan., then at 3. General Foods for Diamond Salt. **CAST:** Al Swenson as Captain Diamond, an old salt who told stories in his lighthouse-home. Florence Malone as Mrs. Diamond. **ANNOUNCER:** Tiny Ruffner, who listened to the stories.

THE ADVENTURES OF CHAMPION, juvenile adventure serial.

BROADCAST HISTORY: 1949, Mutual. 15m. **CAST:** Unknown. **DIRECTOR:** William Burch.

"A series of fast, exciting stories about a boy named Ricky West, raised in the wilderness since childhood by his adopted Uncle Smoky, a German shepherd dog named Rebel, and a stockin'-legged chestnut stallion you know and love—*Champion*! . . . the world's wonder horse!" Uncle Smoky told stories of western mystery: Champion was presented as a king of wild horses who let only Ricky ride him. The series was subtitled *Gene Autry's Champion*, but it was not explained in the reviewed episode where Autry was or how the horse became wild again.

THE ADVENTURES OF CHRISTOPHER LONDON, crime drama with international flavor.

BROADCAST HISTORY: Jan. 22–April 30, 1950, NBC. 30m, Sundays at 7. **CAST:** Glenn Ford as Christopher London. Supporting players: Barton Yarborough, Joan Banks, Virginia Gregg, Ben Wright, Ted de Corsia, Alan Reed. **MUSIC:** Lyn Murray. **CREATOR:** Erle Stanley Gardner. **PRODUCER-DIRECTOR:** William N. Robson.

Christopher London was a globetrotting investigator-troubleshooter who tackled a weekly "excursion against crime."

THE ADVENTURES OF CHRISTOPHER WELLS, crime drama.

BROADCAST HISTORY: Sept. 28, 1947–June 22, 1948, CBS. 30m, Sundays at 10 through Jan., then Tuesdays at 9:30. DeSoto-Plymouth. **CAST:** Myron McCormick and Charlotte Lawrence as newspaperman Christopher Wells and his assistant Stacy McGill; beginning in Feb., Les Damon and Vicki Vola in the leads. **MUSIC:** Peter Van Steeden. **CREATOR-DIRECTOR:** Ed Byron. **WRITER AND "CHIEF ASSISTANT":** Robert Shaw.

Christopher Wells shared elements of the more successful *Mr. District Attorney*. Both were created and produced by Ed Byron, who had an almost uncanny knack of foreshadowing the news. Byron often went slumming through New York in search of plot material, and with *Mr. DA* he had earned a reputation of fictionalizing scoops before they happened. On a *Christopher Wells* smuggling case, a real incident with strong similarities occurred at the same time the episode aired. Wells also just happened to be in India at the time of Gandhi's assassination. These hot elements kept the show interesting, but the midseason shift into a Tuesday night timeslot (opposite NBC's *Fibber McGee and Molly* powerhouse) proved fatal.

Byron wrote out a complete biography of his hero, giving a thumbnail sketch to *Newsweek*. Wells was born Sept. 28, 1912, sold newspapers, started as a "sub-cub" reporter on a New York daily for $16 a week, and eventually became a bylined columnist with some of the trademarks of Walter Winchell, Nellie Bly, Richard Harding Davis, and any charming bachelor. It was a traveling show, with Wells in Shanghai one week and India the next.

THE ADVENTURES OF DICK COLE, juvenile adventure.

BROADCAST HISTORY: 1942, transcribed syndication for Bluebolt magazine and Foremost Comics, in whose pages the hero excelled. **CAST:** Leon Janney as Dick Cole, a cadet at Farr Military Academy.

With his Academy friends Ted and Simba, Dick Cole won football games, tracked down crooks, and covered his alma mater with glory.

THE ADVENTURES OF ELLERY QUEEN, mystery, combined with a panel of clue-sifters, alleged experts challenged to guess the murderer.

BROADCAST HISTORY: June 18, 1939–Sept. 22, 1940, CBS. 60m until Feb., then 30m. Sundays at 8 until Sept.; at 10 until April; then at 7:30. Sustained until late April, then supported by Gulf Oil in the summer slot for *The Screen Guild Theater*. **CAST:** Hugh Marlowe as Ellery Queen, deductive genius, a suave modern-day Sherlock in the William Powell mode: Santos Ortega as Inspector Queen, the detective's father: Marion Shockley as Nikki Porter, Queen's adventurous secretary: Howard Smith as Sergeant Velie until Sept. 1939, when Ted de Corsia took the role: Robert Strauss as Doc Prouty: later Arthur Allen in this role. **AN-NOUNCER**: Ken Roberts until April 1940, then Bert Parks. **MUSIC**: Bernard Herrmann, then Leith Stevens, then Lyn Murray. **PRODUCER-DIRECTOR**: George Zachary.

Jan. 10, 1942–Dec. 30, 1944, NBC. 30m, Saturdays at 7:30. Bromo Seltzer. **CAST**: Carleton Young as Ellery until Aug. 1943, then Sydney Smith. Santos Ortega, Marion Shockley, and Ted de Corsia returned as Inspector Queen, Nikki, and Sergeant Velie (Helen Lewis briefly as Nikki). **ANNOUNCER**: Ernest Chappell. **MUSIC**: Charles Paul (organ). **PRODUCER-DIRECTOR**: George Zachary.

Jan. 24, 1945–April 16, 1947, CBS. 30m, Wednesdays at 7:30. Anacin. **CAST**: Smith, Ortega, and de Corsia returned as Ellery, Inspector Queen, and Sergeant Velie. Barbara Terrell briefly as Nikki, then Gertrude Warner, then (Oct. 1946) Charlotte Keane. **ANNOUNCER**: Don Hancock.

June 1–Sept. 21, 1947, NBC. 30m, intermittently, Sundays at 6:30. Anacin. Production moved from New York to Hollywood. **CAST**: Lawrence Dobkin as Ellery. Bill Smith as Inspector Queen. Ed Latimer as Sergeant Velie. Charlotte Keane as Nikki. **ANNOUNCER**: Don Hancock. **MUSIC**: Chet Kingsbury (organ). **DIRECTOR**: Tom Victor.

Nov. 27, 1947–May 27, 1948, ABC. 30m, Thursdays at 7:30 until Feb., then at 8:30. Sustained. **CAST**: Lawrence Dobkin as Ellery until Jan. 1948; Howard Culver thereafter. Herb Butterfield as Inspector Queen. Alan Reed as Sergeant Velie. Virginia Gregg, later Kaye Brinker, as Nikki. **ANNOUNCER**: Paul Masterson. **MUSIC**: Rex Koury. **DIRECTORS**: Dick Woollen, Dwight Hauser.

Ellery Queen, perhaps as famous as any fictional detective after Sherlock Holmes, was created by cousins Frederic Dannay and Manfred Lee over lunch one day in 1929. This led to more than 40 popular novels, a film series, a long and convoluted run on radio, and various runs on TV. The radio series grew out of an appearance by Dannay and Lee on the Mutual quiz series *Author, Author*: radio director George Zachary thought an interesting format could be devised from the best qualities of the panel show and the melodrama. For a $350 fee, Dannay and Lee would write one mystery per week. Dannay left the series after the 1944 NBC run; Anthony Bou-

cher became coauthor with Lee. The action would be stopped near the end, and a panel of "armchair experts" would try to guess the solution. The experts would come from the worlds of entertainment and news broadcasting, hopefully adding a layer of glamor to the standard detective thriller. Early panelists included Deems Taylor, Ed "Archie" Gardner, photographer Margaret Bourke-White, and Princess Alexandra Kropotkin, who earned fees of $25–$50 for guessing the answers—generally wrong. In the first four months, only playwright Lillian Hellman correctly nailed the culprit. This caused the format to be reorganized, with the "experts" being solicited from the studio audience. It was a disaster: the people from the audience were not only *always* wrong, they were uniformly lifeless and boring on the air. In a later format, a panel of mystery writers was used: they enjoyed relative success in the guessing game without putting the audience to sleep in the process. The "armchair detective" format, despite its drawbacks, remained popular with listeners, especially when panelists were major celebrities. Among those who appeared were Dorothy Kilgallen, Gypsy Rose Lee, Norman Corwin, Guy Lombardo, Ed Sullivan, Fred Waring, John Wayne, Spike Jones, Jane Russell, Jack Dempsey, Orson Welles, Milton Berle, Bela Lugosi, Arthur Godfrey, and Mel Blanc.

THE ADVENTURES OF FATHER BROWN, detective drama.

BROADCAST HISTORY: June 10–July 29, 1945, Mutual. 30m, Sundays at 5. **CAST**: Karl Swenson as Father Brown, the detective priest created by G. K. Chesterton. Supporting players: Mitzi Gould, Robert Readick, Barry Thomson, Bill Griffis, Will Geer, Vinton Hayworth, Gretchen Davidson, Gladys Thornton. **ANNOUNCER**: John Stanley. **DIRECTOR**: William Sweets.

This summer series found the priest each week "at his desk in his modest parish house." He was watched over by a housekeeper named Nora but still found plenty of mystery and murder.

THE ADVENTURES OF FRANK MERRIWELL, juvenile adventure, based on the dime novels by Gilbert S. Patton under the name Burt L. Standish.

BROADCAST HISTORY: March 26–June 22, 1934, NBC. 15m continuation, three a week at 5:30. Dr. West's Toothpaste. **CAST:** Donald Briggs as Frank Merriwell, a super athlete who was usually deeply involved in mystery. **ANNOUNCER:** Harlow Wilcox.

Oct. 5, 1946–June 4, 1949, NBC. 30m, Saturdays at 10 A.M. (1946–48); then various Saturday times. **CAST:** Lawson Zerbe as Frank Merriwell, beloved hero of American fiction, super athlete at turn-of-the-century Yale. Elaine Rost as girlfriend Inza Burrage. Hal Studer as Bart Hodge. Patricia Hosley as Elsie Bellwood. Also: Lamont Johnson, Brad Barker, Grace Keddy. **ANNOUNCER:** Mel Brant. **MUSIC:** Paul Taubman at the organ. **DIRECTORS:** Ed King, Joseph Mansfield, Harry Junkin, Fred Weihe. **WRITERS:** Ruth and Gilbert Brann, with William Welch.

The two eras of Frank Merriwell are from widely diverse times in American radio. All the information on the early series comes from one scratchy disc. Frank gets drawn into a shameful poker game and later confesses to his enemy-turned-pal Bart Hodge an uncontrollable weakness for gambling. There are periodic, teary references to Frank's "dear, sweet mother," from whom he once stole money to support his despicable habit.

The later series was a complete-in-each-episode half-hour. It strived mightily for a nostalgic flavor, opening to the sounds of a trotting horse and a distinctive signature. "There it is, an echo of the past—an exciting past, a romantic past—the era of the horse and carriage, gas-lit streets and free-for-all football games: the era of one of the most beloved characters in American fiction, Frank Merriwell."

THE ADVENTURES OF FRANK RACE, adventure melodrama.

BROADCAST HISTORY: 1949–50, transcribed syndication by Bruce Ells Productions (began running in some markets May 1, 1949). **CAST:** Tom Collins as Frank Race, an attorney who took up a life of intrigue after the war; Paul Dubov assumed the led after 22 shows. **WRITER-DIRECTORS:** Joel Murcott, Buckley Angel. **MUSIC:** Ivan Ditmars, composer and performer (organ).

THE ADVENTURES OF NERO WOLFE, detective drama, based on the novels of Rex Stout.

BROADCAST HISTORY: July 5, 1943–July 14, 1944, Blue Network after a trial run on a regional northeastern network in early 1943. 30m, Mondays at 8:30 until late Sept.; off the air four months, then Fridays at 7. **CAST:** Santos Ortega as Nero Wolfe, "gargantuan gourmet, the detective genius who rates the knife and fork the greatest tools ever invented by man." Luis Van Rooten assumed the role in 1944. John Gibson as Archie Goodwin, Wolfe's legman, assistant, and secretary, who told the stories.

1946, Mutual Network. 30m, Sundays. *The Amazing Nero Wolfe.* Jergens Lotion. **CAST:** Francis X. Bushman as Nero. Elliott Lewis as Archie. **ANNOUNCER:** Jim Bannon. **PRODUCER-DIRECTOR:** Travis Wells. **WRITER:** Louis Vittes.

Oct. 20, 1950–April 27, 1951, NBC. 30m, Fridays at 8. *The New Adventures of Nero Wolfe.* Sponsored in part by Plymouth. **CAST:** Sydney Greenstreet as Wolfe (typecasting, as his greatest screen role is thought to be that of Guttman the fat man in *The Maltese Falcon*); a potpourri of actors as Archie, including Gerald Mohr, Wally Maher, Harry Bartell, Herb Ellis, and Lawrence Dobkin. **ANNOUNCER:** Don Stanley. **PRODUCER:** Edwin Fadiman. **DIRECTOR:** J. Donald Wilson.

The eccentricities of Rex Stout's Nero Wolfe were well known by the time the character came to radio. He was an orchid fancier world-class. He was a bon vivant by nature and a fat man by consequence. He waddled about and solved the most baffling murders from the comfort of his home, without ever visiting the scene. Wolfe grumbled whenever a potential client appeared, but usually took the case because high living had taken its toll on his bank account. It was Wolfe's assistant, Archie Goodwin, who actually got around, interviewing witnesses and gathering clues for interpretation by the great one later. It was also Archie whose appreciation of a well-shaped leg gave the show its token romance.

THE ADVENTURES OF OZZIE AND HARRIET, situation comedy.

BROADCAST HISTORY: Oct. 8, 1944–June 11, 1948, CBS. 30m, Sundays at 6 until Jan. 1948, then Fridays at 9:30. International Silver.

Oct. 3, 1948–July 10, 1949, NBC until April; season finished on CBS. 30m, Sundays at 6:30. International Silver.

Oct. 14, 1949–June 18, 1954, ABC. 30m, Fridays at 9. Heinz Foods until June 1952; various sponsors thereafter.

CAST: Ozzie and Harriet Nelson. Tommy Bernard and Henry Blair as their sons David and Ricky Nelson until April 1949, when the sons began playing themselves. Joel Davis as David Nelson, 1944–45. John Brown as "Thorny" Thornberry, the next-door neighbor. Lurene Tuttle as Harriet's mother (usually on the telephone). Janet Waldo as Emmy Lou, a breathless teenager who often gave Ozzie bad advice. **ANNOUNCER:** Verne Smith. **PRODUCER-DIRECTOR:** Glenhall Taylor, Dave Elton. **MUSIC:** Billy May. **SOUND EFFECTS:** Ed Ludes, Monty Fraser, David Light.

Ozzie and Harriet filled one decade with music and the next decade with laughs. They had two full, distinct careers. Harriet came out of Iowa, gave up her real name (Peggy Lou Snyder), and became a singer in the big band era. Ozzie was leading one of the best-known dance bands of the time and was looking for a girl singer when he happened to see Harriet in a short film she had made for Paramount in 1932. They arranged a meeting, and she agreed to give up her current billing—songstress at a New York restaurant—and sing with the band. Together they worked out the song-and-patter routine that would become their trademark: while the band played, Ozzie and Harriet would toss song lyrics back and forth in an almost conversational banter, developing a style that was distinctive in its time.

Ozzie (born Oswald George Nelson, March 20, 1906) formed his first orchestra at age 14. He worked his way through college and law school by playing ballrooms and proms. He graduated from Rutgers, then took a law degree in 1930. But his band was doing too well to give it up: a booking at the Glen Island Casino was giving him national exposure on the networks, and his orchestra was becoming one of the best-paid in the country.

After three years together in the band, Ozzie and Harriet were married Oct. 8, 1935. They had been signed as melodians for Joe Penner's *Baker's Broadcast*, an engagement they continued after Penner left the show and Robert "Believe It or Not" Ripley took it over. Their son David was born Oct. 24, 1936; another son, Eric, May 8, 1940. After the birth of Eric, who later became famous as Ricky, the Nelsons moved to Hollywood, where they joined *The Red Skelton Show* on NBC in 1941.

The Skelton job lasted three years, ending suddenly when Skelton was drafted. This led Nelson to develop his own situation comedy. *The Adventures of Ozzie and Harriet* would depict the Nelsons at home. They would be billed as "America's favorite young couple," living the good life but constantly entangled in amusing situations created by Ozzie. The plots were simple: Ozzie was the pivotal character, his tangents the vehicles to confusion. Once Ozzie had set his mind to something, nothing could dissuade him until disaster had run its inevitable course. This week it might be a "men are superior" kick; next week he'd get the notion that the boys were being neglected. Whatever the cause, Ozzie would take it to ridiculous lengths, Harriet would gently try to guide him back to reason, David and Ricky would get in a few wisecracks, and Ozzie would be further confused by the ill-timed advice of his next-door neighbor Thorny.

At first Nelson refused to allow his boys to portray themselves. He felt that the experience of big-time radio was too much for children of 8 and 4 to handle. In April 1949 he relented, and the real David and Ricky began playing themselves. The series made an almost painless transition to television and was one of TV's early success stories. The characters remained consistent: the voices were the same; the shows were always in good taste; the Nelsons looked like the Nelsons were supposed to look, even to those who had never seen them. It was a solid series, a radio staple, a cute show. But as the times changed, *Ozzie and Harriet* seemed a little too cute, too precious. Ozzie was a guy who never seemed to work: he lounged around his home ("1847 Rogers Road" during the years when 1847 Rogers Brothers Silver was the sponsor) in a sweater and slacks, his whole existence built around his weekly displays of flawed judgment. This even became a running gag for nightclub comics: the question "What does Ozzie Nelson do for a living?'' was prime trivia. For the record, he was a bandleader; because most of the action of *Ozzie and Harriet* was set on weekends when the boys were out of school, his occupation was never a factor. But the notion persisted as the times changed—here was a family from Neverland, far away from Real Life. Along with *Father Knows Best* and *Leave It to Beaver, Ozzie and Harriet* is most frequently cited as the epitome of sitcom fantasy. This undoubtedly led to Ricky's deepening discomfort with the old show, a distancing that was evident in the last years.

Nelson wrote much of the material himself, though many writers were used in the show's ten-year radio run. The TV series had an even longer life than the radio version, seen from 1952 through 1966. Ozzie and Harriet seemed an eternal part of the broadcasting scene, successful at everything they tried until the ill-fated TV series *Ozzie's Girls* in 1973.

On June 3, 1975, Ozzie Nelson died of cancer at his California home. Rick, who emerged as one of the major stars of rock and roll, was killed in a plane crash between engagements Dec. 31, 1985. David went into television production. Harriet lived in retirement in California until her death Oct. 2, 1994.

THE ADVENTURES OF PHILIP MARLOWE, detective drama, based on the novels of Raymond Chandler.

BROADCAST HISTORY: June 17–Sept. 9, 1947, NBC. 30m, Tuesdays at 10. Summer replacement for Bob Hope. Pepsodent. **CAST:** Van Heflin as Philip Marlowe, Los Angeles private detective. **ANNOUNCER:** Wendell Niles. **MUSIC:** Lyn Murray. **WRITER:** Milton Geiger. **PRODUCER:** Jim Fonda.

Sept. 26, 1948–Sept. 29, 1950, and a short summer run July 7–Sept. 15, 1951, CBS. 30m, various days and times. Ford Motors, briefly in 1950. **CAST:** Gerald Mohr as Marlowe, with support from top-line Hollywood players: Edgar Barrier, Gloria Blondell, Vivi Janiss, Lou Krugman, David Ellis, Wilms Herbert, Virginia Gregg, John Dehner, Lawrence Dobkin, Jack Moyles, Laurette Fillbrandt, Parley Baer, Howard McNear, among others. Jeff Corey as Lieutenant Ybarra. **ANNOUNCER:** Roy Rowan. **MUSIC:** Richard Aurandt. **PRODUCER-DIRECTOR:** Norman Macdonnell. **WRITERS:** Gene Levitt, Robert

Mitchell, Mel Dinelli, Kathleen Hite. **SOUND EFFECTS:** Cliff Thorsness.

Raymond Chandler was never fully thrilled with the treatment radio gave his hard-boiled detective Philip Marlowe. He allowed himself to be photographed with actor Van Heflin and producer Jim Fonda in 1947 but looked none too happy about it. ''It was thoroughly flat,'' he wrote to colleague Erle Stanley Gardner of the opening episode. Chandler's role was strictly ornamental: for both series, he was given pretitle or in-title billing, but he took no hand in the shows. The CBS series was somewhat more to his liking. A voice like Gerald Mohr's, he wrote to scripter Levitt, at least packed personality. Indeed, Mohr had one of the most distinctive voices on the air. This was not a cute series: it had little of the *Sam Spade* charm or the *Richard Diamond* flippancy. It was blood, guts, and thunder, and Mohr's bassy voice carried it. ''Get this and get it straight,'' he barked, opening the show. ''Crime is a sucker's road, and those who travel it end up in the gutter, the prison, or an early grave.'' The story titles were of the genre: *The Hard Way Out, The Last Laugh*, etc. The music was loud and stinging, containing the essence of hard-boiled action.

THE ADVENTURES OF SAM SPADE, DETECTIVE, detective drama, based on the character created by Dashiell Hammett.

BROADCAST HISTORY: July 12–Oct. 4, 1946, ABC. 30m, Fridays at 8. Wildroot Cream Oil.

Sept. 29, 1946–Sept. 18, 1949, CBS. 30m, Sundays at 8. Wildroot.

Sept. 25, 1949–Sept. 17, 1950, NBC. 30m, Sundays at 8. Wildroot.

Nov. 17, 1950–April 27, 1951, NBC. 30m, Fridays at 8:30. New series with change of male leads. Sustained.

CAST: Howard Duff as Sam Spade, a San Francisco private detective; Steve Dunne as Spade late in the NBC run, beginning Nov. 17, 1950. Lurene Tuttle as Effie Perrine, Spade's slightly breathless, addled and babbling secretary. John McIntire as Lieutenant Dundy; William Conrad as Dundy in the NBC series. Regulars from the Hollywood radio pool: Cathy and Elliott Lewis, June Havoc, Joseph Kearns, Jerry Hausner, Elliott Reid, Mary Jane Croft, Jeanette Nolan, Betty Lou Gerson. **ANNOUNCER:** Dick Joy. **MUSIC:** Lud Gluskin,

Rene and Pierre Garriguenc. **PRODUCER-DIRECTOR:** William Spier. **WRITERS:** Bob Tallman and Jo Eisinger until March 1947; then Tallman and Gil Doud until June 19, 1949; rotating group of writers thereafter including John Michael Hayes, E. Jack Neuman, Harold Swanton, and others. **SOUND EFFECTS:** Berne Surrey. **THEME:** *Goodnight, Sweetheart.*

The first thing Sam Spade wanted to know was "How much you got on you?"

Two hundred?

"Okay, I'll take that and you can pay me the rest later."

Spade was not in business for his health. He was a man for hire, though principle often came to bear in the cases he took. His appearance on the air was a marked departure from the old Humphrey Bogart image, though the early ABC series was based on creator Dashiell Hammett's original stories. Hammett had brought Spade to life in the 1930 crime classic *The Maltese Falcon*, and in 1946 he was the most striking detective on the air.

Director William Spier wanted an actor in the Bogart mold. Howard Duff, the man who got the part, was decidedly not that. Duff had earned his radio stripes with the Armed Forces Radio Service, arriving in Hollywood in 1945 a seasoned but unsung veteran. His reading for Spier was less than memorable: the only person impressed was Spier's wife Kay Thompson, who became such an advocate that Duff won the job. Thirteen weeks later, it would be difficult to remember that any other choice had been possible. Duff had become Spade, overcoming two intimidating handicaps—the image of Bogart and the power of the novel. Compared with Bogart's dour and straitlaced Spade, Duff's was a cutup: a hard-knuckled master of street-level whimsy and sarcastic comeback. His sense of burlesque was superb. *The Adventures of Sam Spade* on the air was its own entity, owing little to the forces that had created it.

"An audition record was made on May 1, 1946," wrote John Scheinfeld, a radio historian who spent years researching this and Spier's other series, *Suspense.* "The script was called *Sam and the Walls of Jericho* and was adapted by Bob Tallman and Jo Eisinger." But Tallman and Eisinger got no air credit: "ABC wanted to give the impression that Hammett was really involved with the show (he wasn't). Of the 13 shows broadcast on ABC, six were Tallman-Eisinger originals; the remainder were adaptations of Hammett short stories. Tallman and Eisinger were finally given credit with the first CBS broadcast on Sept. 29, 1946. But Eisinger was under contract to Columbia Pictures and was forced to employ a pseudonym, Jason James."

Spade was no spendthrift. His favorite mode of transportation was the streetcar, which took him anywhere for a dime. He had an aversion to cabs and a liking for cheap booze. A listener didn't have to be told: those clinking glasses as Sam opened his desk drawer and began dictating each week were enough. His clients got bumped off with startling regularity. But Spade had a code, one of his lingering endowments from Hammett, and it went like this: if a client dies in the course of things, a guy is supposed to do something about it.

His dictation was taken by Effie Perrine, who was always flustered and secretly in love with him. Each case unfolded as a report—a caper, if you will—dated with the actual air date, signed and delivered to the client, the client's widow, or the police. Spade's license number, 137596, was always included in the report, which unfolded chronologically, with the scene shifting between Sam and Effie in the office and the infield dramatization of Sam's dictation.

"March 16, 1947, was the last script cowritten by Tallman and James," wrote Scheinfeld. Tallman and Gil Doud wrote every subsequent episode through June 19, 1949, when, "written-out and going insane," they relinquished their duties. The writing was high-class if metaphorical, and the Wildroot commercials—imploring listeners in lively song to "Get Wildroot Cream Oil, Charlie!"—seemed to fit right in. By most accounts it was a happy show, until political pressure came to bear in 1950.

Dashiell Hammett's name had come up before the House Committee on Un-American Activities, and in June Howard Duff was listed in *Red Channels.* This may have been inevitable, for as early as 1947 the show had taken some not-so-subtle digs at Communist-hunting lawmakers. "The Constitution says every citizen shall have the right to bear arms," Sam said in one episode. "Even Parnell Thomas can't. . . ." Exactly what Rep. J. Parnell Thomas, whose thinking often ran with that of Sen. Joseph McCarthy, could or could not do was lost in the heat of the moment. Sharp-eared listeners got the point, and so, by 1950, did Wildroot. The sponsor had moved with Duff and the entire cast to NBC in 1949 but was having serious second thoughts nine months later. *Variety* reported that Wildroot would continue only if Hammett's name was removed from the credits, and the sponsor wasn't enthusiastic about Duff either. The shoe fell on September 9: *Billboard* announced that Wildroot was dumping *Spade* and putting its money into a new series, *Charlie Wild, Private Detective*. The report caused an avalanche of mail: 250,000 letters poured in protesting the decision, a powerful enough voice that NBC was persuaded, unwisely, to continue the series without Duff. Duff's last broadcast was *The Femme Fatale Caper*, Sept. 17, 1950. When the new show arrived November 17, the role was played by Steve Dunne, a boyish-sounding Spade laboring under a major handicap. Not even Bogart could have followed Howard Duff by then.

The show was loved in its time and still is. The plots were often run-of-the-mill radio fare, obviously hacked out in the heat of the deadline. No one cared if holes were patched in an obvious and sometimes careless way—this show had a style and class that the others all envied. Duff made the writing part of his own unique character. The wit and charm of the show has weathered four decades, and *The Adventures of Sam Spade* remains today the pinnacle of radio private eye broadcasts.

THE ADVENTURES OF SUPERMAN, juvenile adventure serial, based on the hero of DC Comics.

BROADCAST HISTORY: 1940–42, transcribed syndication, beginning Feb. 12, 1940, WOR, New York.

Aug. 31, 1942–Jan. 28, 1949, Mutual. 15m, initially three a week at 5:30; mostly five a week thereafter, sometimes at 5:15, sometimes 5:45. Kellogg's Pep, Jan. 1943–Dec. 1947.

Jan. 31–June 17, 1949, Mutual. 30m, three a week at 5.

Nov. 5, 1949–March 1, 1951, ABC. 30m, Saturdays at 8:30, then at 8; twice a week at 5:30 as of June 1950.

CAST: Clayton Bud Collyer as Clark Kent, reporter for the *Daily Planet* in Metropolis, who in reality was the strange being from another world known as Superman; Michael Fitzmaurice took the lead role in 1950. Joan Alexander as cynical reporter Lois Lane. Julian Noa as Perry White, *Daily Planet* editor. Jackie Kelk as cub reporter Jimmy Olsen. Gary Merrill, Stacy Harris, and Matt Crowley as Batman, another DC Comics superhero who often visited the show. Ronald Liss as Robin, Batman's sidekick. **ANNOUNCER:** Jackson Beck from ca. 1943. **DIRECTORS:** George Lowther, Robert and Jessica Maxwell, Mitchell Grayson, Allen Ducovny. **WRITERS:** Jack Johnstone, B. P. Freeman. **SOUND EFFECTS:** Jack Keane, Al Binnie, Keene Crockett, John Glennon.

The comic *Superman* was created by Jerry Siegel and Joe Shuster in 1938. It, and the subsequent radio serial, told of the destruction of the planet Krypton and how the scientist Jor-El and his wife Lara placed their infant son in a rocket headed for Earth. Here, the child had wondrous powers: he grew up disguised as Clark Kent, "mild-mannered reporter for a great metropolitan newspaper" who "leads a never-ending battle for truth, justice, and the American way." Kent wore glasses and took on a meek demeanor. He was bullied by his boss Perry White and barely tolerated by Lois Lane, the *Planet*'s star female reporter. Lois adored Superman even as she disdained the alter ego, Kent. Superman could fly through the air, a feat accomplished on radio with a gush of windy sound effects and a shout, "Up, up, and away!" The network opening signature was one of radio's best, setting the stage for those quarter-hour flights into fantasy with a cascade of voices, narration, and sound effects.

Faster than a speeding bullet!
More powerful than a locomotive!
Able to leap tall buildings at a single bound!
"Look! Up in the sky!"
"It's a bird!"
"It's a plane!"
"It's SUPERMAN!"

One month found Superman chasing train robbers; the next battling Nazis and "Japs" at the North Pole. During the war, Superman joined most other serial characters in the fight against tyranny. Only two things stopped him: his X-ray vision couldn't penetrate lead, and when confronted with the element Kryptonite he was rendered helpless. In 1945 he was joined briefly by Batman, the other great DC Comics hero, but Batman suffered in the inevitable comparison.

Could he fly? Could he see through brick walls? Could he dart in front of a bullet and save the day? The character faded from *The Adventures of Superman* and never did break away for a show of his own.

The producers went to great lengths to protect the identity of the hero, onstage and off. In the storyline, anyone who discovered Superman's secret identity was eliminated: the writer simply killed him off by accident or disaster. It was also insisted that the identity of Clayton Bud Collyer, the actor who gave voice to the man of steel, be kept secret. Only in 1946 did Collyer emerge in an interview with *Time* to promote a *Superman* campaign against racial and religious intolerance. The serial became the first of its kind to tackle such heavy themes. Collyer, who later became a well-known TV game show host, gave the series one of its trademarks—the ability to change characters in midsentence, from the mousy Clark ("This looks like a job for . . .") to the barrel-chested ("SUPERMAN!") man of steel.

THE ADVENTURES OF THE THIN MAN,
a comedy thriller, lighthearted mystery based on the novel by Dashiell Hammett.

BROADCAST HISTORY: July 2, 1941–Dec. 23, 1942, NBC. 30m, Wednesdays at 8. Woodbury Soap.

Jan. 8, 1943–Dec. 26, 1947, CBS. 30m, mostly Fridays at 8:30, some Sunday timeslots. General Foods for Post Toasties, Maxwell House Coffee, and Sanka.

June 22–Sept. 22, 1948, NBC. 30m, Tuesdays at 9 until mid-July, then Wednesdays at 10:30. *The New Adventures of the Thin Man.* Pabst Beer.

Oct. 28, 1948–Jan. 20, 1949, Mutual. 30m, Thursdays. Kaiser-Fraser.

June 23–Sept. 1, 1950, ABC. 30m, Fridays at 9. Heinz Foods.

CAST: Les Damon as suave New York sleuth Nick Charles until 1943; then Les Tremayne, David Gothard (1944–45), Tremayne (1945–46), Damon again (1946–47), Tremayne (1948–49), and Joseph Curtin as the last Nick, 1950. Claudia Morgan as Nora Charles throughout. Parker Fennelly as Sheriff Ebenezer Williams of Crabtree County. AN-NOUNCERS: Ed Herlihy, Nelson Case, Glenn Riggs, Tom Shirley, Ron Rawson, Jimmy Wallington, Joe Weeks, Ted Pearson, Dwight Weist. MU-SIC: Fred Fradkin. PRODUCER-DIRECTOR: Himan Brown. WRITERS: Ruth Hawkins, Denis Green, Milton Lewis, Louis Vittes, Robert Newman, Eugene Wang. SOUND EFFECTS: Hal Reid.

The Thin Man was a slick piece of high-hatted sophistication based on the 1934 film, which was based on the Hammett novel of the same year. Nick Charles, the hero, was a retired private eye who just couldn't stay away from murder. Abetted by his eccentric wife Nora, Nick ran a ten-year race with that other light thriller *Mr. and Mrs. North*, and for a time the Charleses were billed as "the happiest, merriest married couple in radio."

They certainly were the sexiest. *The Thin Man* gave its listeners all the censor would allow. Nick and Nora were cast in the screen images, with William Powell and Myrna Loy firmly in mind. Les Damon and Claudia Morgan learned to talk so much like the screen stars that some listeners refused to believe the credits, insisting that Powell and Loy were actually at the microphone. Morgan cooed invitingly: she mouthed long, drawn-out kisses and kidded Nicky-darling about his outlandish pajamas. One critic strongly objected to the "ooooohs" and "aaaaahs" and "mmmmmm's" during the "squeaky" kisses and love scenes. But as feminine and cozy as Nora was played, *Life* noted that "she can step across pools of blood with all the calm delicacy of a lady-in-waiting." Nick, the deductive genius, developed a distinctive, sexually suggestive purr. When she preened, he purred. This was pure radio, imagery carried through dialogue and sound with no narration necessary.

Nick became the top sleuth of the martini set while keeping a running acquaintance with such characters as Dippy Danny the Pickpocket, Charlie the Creep, and Big-Ears Benny. With the show well in progress, Parker Fennelly was added as Nick's old friend and partner Sheriff Ebeneezer Williams of Crabtree County. Fennelly played the same kind of Titus Moody character he had originated for Fred Allen. These three were the only regular characters, with the exception of Nick and Nora's famous wirehaired terrier Asta.

THE ADVENTURES OF TOPPER, situation
comedy, based on the novel by Thorne Smith

and the subsequent film series starring Roland Young.

BROADCAST HISTORY: June 7–Sept. 13, 1945, NBC. 30m, Thursdays at 8:30 (final two shows at 8). Post Toasties. **CAST:** Roland Young as Cosmo Topper. Hope Emerson as his wife Henrietta. Paul Mann and Frances Chaney as George and Marion Kerby, ghosts who appear only to Topper (Tony Barrett also heard as George).

Cosmo Topper was a banker whose life was complicated by two friendly spirits. The comedy ensued when Topper talked to his ethereal friends and, of course, seemed to be talking to people around him. "Go away," he would say, or, "That's a terrible suit you're wearing." This was the same dilemma faced by Donald O'Connor in the Francis (the talking mule) film series. *Topper* was done far more effectively on television, becoming one of that medium's early successes. In the TV series, George and Marion Kerby were killed in an avalanche while skiing. Also killed was Neal, the alcoholic St. Bernard who had come to rescue them. The TV roles were played by Leo G. Carroll (Topper), Lee Patrick (Henrietta), and Anne Jeffreys and Robert Sterling (George and Marion).

THE AFFAIRS OF ANN SCOTLAND, detective drama.

BROADCAST HISTORY: Oct. 30, 1946–Oct. 22, 1947, ABC. 30m, Wednesdays at 9. Hudnut. **CAST:** Arlene Francis as Ann Scotland. **MUSIC:** Del Castillo (organ). **DIRECTOR:** Helen Mack.

Ann Scotland was described in the memoir of Arlene Francis as "a sort of private eyelash." She was a satin-tongued cutie, quick on the uptake, the kind of role that was ideal for Francis. Arlene was pregnant when this series aired ("I could have been called Scotland Yard because that's how wide I was"), but it didn't matter in a medium where everything was done with the voice. Her friend Claire Trevor gave this assessment of her come-hither performance: "You don't sound the least bit pregnant, but you sound as though you might be at any moment."

THE AFFAIRS OF ANTHONY, soap opera.

BROADCAST HISTORY: May 29, 1939–March 22, 1940, Blue Network. 15m, daily at 3:15. Sustained. **CAST:** Henry Hunter as Anthony Marleybone Jr. Marvin Miller as Anthony Sr. Laurette Fillbrandt as Susan. Lenore Kingston as June. Bernardine Flynn as Alice McGinty. **DIRECTOR:** Axel Gruenberg. **WRITER:** Sandra Michael.

THE AFFAIRS OF PETER SALEM, detective drama.

BROADCAST HISTORY: May 7, 1949–April 18, 1953, Mutual. 30m. Heard most often on Sundays, but also Mondays and Saturdays. Sustained. **CAST:** Santos Ortega as Peter Salem, a small-town detective who used brainpower and wits to trip up sophisticated lawbreakers from the city. Jack Grimes as his sidekick Marty. Regulars from the New York radio pool: Everett Sloane, Luis Van Rooten, Ann Shepherd, etc. **PRODUCER:** Himan Brown. **DIRECTOR:** Mende Brown. **WRITER:** Louis Vittes. **SOUND EFFECTS:** Adrian Penner.

AFRICAN TREK, African folk music.

BROADCAST HISTORY: Oct. 13, 1939–Oct. 17, 1943, Blue Network. 30m, Fridays at 7:30 until Nov. 1940, then Sundays at 1:30.
July 13, 1946–March 15, 1947, ABC. 15m, Saturdays at 10:15 A.M.

The creator of *African Trek* was Josef Marais, who, with three companions, performed a vast repertoire of native African and Boer folksongs. Much as Harry Horlick had done with gypsy ballads a decade earlier, Marais gave his show an authentic sound, rooted in firsthand knowledge. Born near Cape Town, Marais was a symphony orchestra violinist in his teens and a longtime collector of Afrikaner and Hottentot music. His series drew so much fan mail that the Blue Network expanded it from 15 to 30 minutes. By 1941 it was being shortwaved to Africa. The campfire flavor of such Boer War numbers as *Brandy, Leave Me Alone* gave the series an exotic ambience that Americans found fascinating. There were also stories and folk yarns. The theme was *Sarie Marais*.

AGAINST THE STORM, serial drama.

BROADCAST HISTORY: Oct. 16, 1939–Dec. 25, 1942, NBC. 15m, daily, opened at 5:15 but was frequently moved. Procter & Gamble for Ivory Soap.

April 25–Oct. 21, 1949, Mutual. 30m, daily at 11:30 A.M. Philip Morris.

Oct. 1, 1951–June 27, 1952, ABC. 15m, daily at 10:45 A.M. Philip Morris.

CAST: Roger DeKoven as Professor Jason McKinley Allen of Harper College (DeKoven starred in the three runs, though years apart). May Davenport Seymour as his wife Margaret from 1939; also played by Katherine Anderson (1949) and Florence Malone. Gertrude Warner and Claudia Morgan as their daughter Christy. Joan Tompkins and Dolores Gillen as their daughter Siri. Arnold Moss and Alexander Scourby as Philip Cameron, who married Christy. Grant Richards as Siri's husband Hal Thomas. Chester Stratton as Mark Scott. Joan Alexander and Ruth Matteson as Nicole Scott. Charlotte Holland as Kathy Reimer. Philip Clarke as Dr. Reimer. Elliott Reid as Julian Browning (1949). Eddie Mayehoff as Professor Waldo Greentree (1949). DIRECTOR: Axel Gruenberg. WRITER: Sandra Michael. THEME: Theme from *Song of Bernadette*, by Alfred Newman.

Against the Storm was so highbrow that to call it a soap opera made its creator-writer "see red." Sandra Michael had long believed that daytime radio needed an antidote for the mindless formula of *Our Gal Sunday* and *Stella Dallas*. Michael disdained the cliffhanger, that well-worn device that made listeners wonder, "Will John's wife finally meet John's other wife, and what will happen then?"

Michael was born in Denmark. She wrote commercials and announced fashion shows in Milwaukee, then moved to Hollywood to write some of the quality nighttime shows. Her serial opened in wartime and quickly established its theme of resistance to that war, indeed to all wars. The central character, Professor Allen, taught at Harper University and lived at Deep Pool Farm, a setting taken from the 32-acre farm in Connecticut where Michael lived. Allen was a pacifist and an outspoken opponent of Hitler. Many episodes were solid philosophy: on Memorial Day 1941, the entire broadcast was a soliloquy about Allen's childhood pal Porky Mason, killed in France in the First War.

Against the Storm was lauded for originality. A *New York Times* critic, comparing it with its daytime neighbors, termed it "stratospheric." Whole broadcasts were given over to ballads or readings from Walt Whitman or Edna St. Vincent Millay.

Edgar Lee Masters appeared, reading from his *Spoon River Anthology*. John Masefield was shortwaved in from Britain, ostensibly lecturing to Professor Allen's class. President Roosevelt accepted a speaking part, an appearance shelved when the Japanese attacked Pearl Harbor. In 1942 the show won a Peabody Award, the only daytime serial ever thus honored. By the end of that year it was off the air.

Newsweek summed up the network line, saying the show "didn't click" with listening housewives. But ratings were respectable throughout the run. Sandra Michael gave a *Radio Life* reporter a different version years later. She wanted the show expanded to 30 minutes daily, a format unheard of in the soap schedule. When the network refused, she requested and received a release from the agency. She did get her half-hour, from Mutual, in 1949, but it lasted less than a year.

THE AIR ADVENTURES OF JIMMIE ALLEN, transcribed juvenile adventure serial.

BROADCAST HISTORY: 1933–37, 15m. Transcribed for Skelly Oil, a Midwest petroleum company, and aired by stations throughout the Skelly market area; syndicated by World Broadcasting to businesses outside the Skelly area. Though production ceased, repeats aired sporadically throughout the country through the early 1940s. CAST: John Frank as Jimmie Allen, 16-year-old boy pilot. Shelby Storck as his pal and mentor Speed Robertson. Also: Art Ellison, Al Christi.

1946–47, more than 400 new 15m episodes recorded and broadcast for International Shoe Company of Kansas City and other sponsors. CAST: Jack Schlicter as Jimmie. Shelby Storck as Speed. Twila Comer as Jimmie's girlfriend Barbara. CREATORS-WRITERS: Bob Burtt and Bill Moore.

Because *The Air Adventures of Jimmie Allen* was never on a network, its history has until recently remained vague. In 1980 *Jimmie Allen* advocate Walter House unearthed all the vital facts and published them in a detailed two-part article in the magazine *R/C Model Builder*.

The idea of a serial about a boy pilot was first suggested by a pair of World War I flying aces, Bob Burtt and Bill Moore, at a party in Kansas City. Burtt and Moore had become writers, and their scenario was met with enthusiasm by adman Russell C. Comer. Comer sold the package to Skelly Oil. Three stations carried the initial series: KDAF, Kansas City; KLZ, Denver; and KVOO, Tulsa. The first broadcast was aired Feb. 23, 1933. Soon seven more stations were added, and Skelly found itself involved in one of the great promotions of early radio.

A Jimmie Allen Flying Club was created: all a kid had to do was apply at any Skelly station. Applicants received many premiums, highly treasured today—a set of wings, a membership emblem, and a "personal letter" from Jimmie Allen. Other giveaways: a Jimmie Allen picture puzzle (a Skelly truck refueling a light airplane), a "secret service whistle," and a Jimmie Allen album. The club newspaper was sent out to 600,000 kids a week, and Jimmie Allen Air Races—attended by tens of thousands of people—were held in major Midwest cities where the show was heard. Skelly had to hire a special staff just to answer Jimmie Allen mail. Flying lessons, model plans, and other promotions were part of the mix, available to listeners who displayed their club credentials at their Skelly Oil station. Comer never sold the show to a network: by marketing it himself (to the Richfield Oil Company on the West Coast and to scores of individual businesses elsewhere), he kept control of it.

Throughout the 1930s, interest was high. Boys were fascinated by the adventures of Jimmie, his older pal Speed Robertson, and their mechanic Flash Lewis. Together they solved mysteries (even murder, unusual for juvenile fare at that time, when Jimmie's passenger Quackenbush died under mysterious circumstances), went on hunts for treasure, and raced in air shows around the country. Their enemies were Black Pete and Digger Dawson.

The original Jimmie Allen, John Frank, was more than 40 years old when the series opened. Murray McLean, then 16 and a son of radio actress Betty McLean, was hired to make personal appearances as Jimmie, but Frank continued the radio role throughout the original series. By 1936 the character was so popular that Paramount shot a Jimmie Allen movie, *The Sky Parade*. In 1937 Skelly dropped the show and began working with Burtt and Moore on a new air series, which would become the long-running classic *Captain Midnight*. The postwar revival was not success-ful: its day was the 1930s, when, as House tells us, "kids, radio, and aviation were growing up together."

THE AL JOLSON SHOW, musical variety spanning the years 1932–49, for various sponsors and under various titles. Jolson was a dominant personality whose appearance in any series inevitably made the public think of it as "the Jolson show," whatever its real title might have been.

BROADCAST HISTORY: Nov. 18, 1932–Feb. 24, 1933, NBC. 30m, Fridays at 10. *Presenting Al Jolson.* Chevrolet. ORCHESTRA: Ted Fio Rito.

Aug. 3, 1933–Aug. 16, 1934, NBC. 60m, Thursdays at 10. Joined Paul Whiteman's *Kraft-Phenix Program*, which had begun June 26, 1933, and became the long-running *Kraft Music Hall*. Jolson's appearances were erratic, with many absences. *KMH* continued long after Jolson's departure, with Bing Crosby as a star.

April 6, 1935–March 6, 1936, NBC. 60m, Saturdays at 9:30. *Shell Chateau.* Shell Oil. ORCHESTRA: Victor Young. DIRECTOR: Herb Polesie of J. Walter Thompson. WRITER-PRODUCER: Carroll Carroll of the Thompson agency. THEME: *Golden Gate.* Jolson left the show in progress; it ran with other hosts until June 26, 1937.

Dec. 22, 1936–March 14, 1939, CBS. 30m, Tuesdays at 8:30. *The Lifebuoy Program*, then *The Rinso Program*, then *The Tuesday Night Party*. Lever Brothers. COSTARS: Harry Einstein as Parkyakarkus; Martha Raye. ANNOUNCER: Tiny Ruffner. MUSIC: Lud Gluskin, Victor Young. Again, Jolson left the series in progress: Dick Powell took over (March 21, 1939), then Walter O'Keefe (Sept. 19), and it left the air Dec. 12, 1939.

Oct. 6, 1942–June 29, 1943, CBS. 30m, Tuesdays at 8:30. *The Colgate Program.* Colgate. CO-STAR: Monty Woolley. VOCALIST: Jo Stafford. ORCHESTRA: Gordon Jenkins, Ray Bloch. PRODUCER: William A. Bacher. DIRECTOR: Bill Lawrence.

Oct. 2, 1947–May 26, 1949, NBC. 30m, Thursdays at 9. *The Kraft Music Hall.* Kraft Foods. CO-STAR: Oscar Levant. ANNOUNCER: Ken Carpenter. ORCHESTRA: Lou Bring. THEME: *April Showers.*

Depending on the source, Al Jolson was either the world's greatest entertainer or the world's biggest ham. Some people would have said both.

His natural environment was the stage. He had buckets of charisma before anyone had ever heard of the word. Though Jolson loved performing before an audience, he was a formidable radio presence, fully able to project his dynamic, forceful nature over the air.

His name was Asa Yoelson; he was born May 26, 1886, son of a Russian rabbi. In his youth he considered becoming a cantor: instead he became a performer, a specialist in blackface vaudeville skits whose down-on-one-knee delivery of robust southern songs was as powerful in its way as Louis Armstrong was on trumpet.

His popularity grew quickly after 1909, when he first sang *Mammy* from a San Francisco stage. He so loved performing that he often kept his captive audience overtime. In 1927 he starred in *The Jazz Singer*, the world's first talking picture. He was on the air as early as 1928, in guest roles and cameos, but he seemed too busy to be tied down long in regular radio jobs.

Carroll Carroll described in his 1970 memoir (*None of My Business*) how the mid-1930s series *Shell Chateau* was put together. It was typical Depression fare, "five acts and Jolson," with much brainstorming put into the title. The sponsor wanted its name up front, and it was Carroll himself who came up with *Shell Chateau*. It was thought at the time that a variety show gained something by pretending to air from some exotic location, though some amusing (and justified, as the tapes reveal) fears were expressed over how Jolson might pronounce "chateau" on the air. The mix was predictable: greetings, a warmup and a song by Jolson, a comedy act, another song, a singing guest such as Dixie Lee, music, another Jolson number, station break, a dramatic skit, Jolson again, and so on. Among other guests, *Shell Chateau* drew John and Lionel Barrymore, Bette Davis, Ginger Rogers, Joe Penner, and such sports personalities as "Slapsie" Maxie Rosenbloom. When Jolson left the show in midstream, Shell tried to keep it on the air with such hosts as Wallace Beery and Edward Everett Horton. But the show was swamped in the ratings wars, proving that Jolson had been its one major draw.

Jolson's *Lifebuoy Program*, at 30 minutes, was not as well produced as *Shell Chateau*, but it soon gained a major share of the Tuesday night audience. This was Jolson's longest regular stint, but again he left before the run concluded. In many ways, his 1942–43 CBS series for Colgate was his most interesting show. Monty Woolley, ex–Yale professor turned actor, parlayed a single guest appearance into regular costar status. The writers had a fine time with this, pitting the lowbrow Jolson against the highbrow Woolley. "If you give your brain to the Smithsonian," Woolley said to Jolson on one broadcast, "I'll give them a magnifying glass."

Jolson's career went into a decline in the early '40s but was resurrected in 1946, when Columbia filmed *The Jolson Story*. Larry Parks played the young Jolson, but Jolson's voice was used in the soundtrack, and again he was a hot property. He was now doing so many radio guest spots that it became a running gag of comedians. It also led to a sequel, *Jolson Sings Again*, in 1949. Both stories were dramatized on *The Lux Radio Theater*, with Jolson playing himself. By then Bing Crosby had left *The Kraft Music Hall* in a format dispute, and Jolson was given the host's role, returning to the series that he had left 13 years before.

Shows are available on tape from each Jolson era after the 1934 *Kraft Music Hall*. Though his music lost favor for a time because of its "darky" lyrics, he remains one of the medium's giants. *Shell Chateau* offers a dated format, historically important but tired. *The Lifebuoy Program* is musically interesting, but the comedy is stale business. Perhaps Jolson's best series for modern listening is the later *Kraft Music Hall*. Many shows exist in good fidelity. Jolson is in good voice, and Oscar Levant adds significantly to the show, for those who appreciate his dry wit. This came at the end of Jolson's life, as he died Oct. 23, 1950.

THE AL PEARCE SHOW, comedy.

BROADCAST HISTORY: 1928–32, KFRC, San Francisco. *The Happy-Go-Lucky Hour.*

Jan. 13, 1934–March 29, 1935, Blue Network. 30m, Saturdays at 6 until Sept., then two 15m shows heard Mondays and Fridays at 5.

May 13, 1935–April 3, 1936, NBC, sometimes Blue Network. 30m. A schedule-bouncer, but often Fridays at 5. Pepsodent.

Jan. 5, 1937–June 28, 1938, CBS. 30m, Tuesdays at 9. *Watch the Fun Go By.* Ford Motors.

Oct. 10, 1938–July 31, 1939, NBC. 30m, Mondays at 8. Grape Nuts.

Oct. 11, 1939–April 3, 1940, CBS. 30m, Wednesdays at 8. Dole Pineapple.

May 3, 1940–Jan. 2, 1942, CBS. 30m, Fridays at 7:30. Camel Cigarettes.

Jan. 8–July 2, 1942, NBC. 30m, Thursdays at 7:30. Camel Cigarettes.

May 7–July 30, 1944, Blue Network. 30m, Sundays at 4. *Fun Valley.* Dr. Pepper.

Dec. 9, 1944–June 30, 1945, CBS. 30m, Saturdays at 10:15. *Here Comes Elmer* or *The Al Pearce Show.* Lewis-Howe.

Dec. 3, 1945–Sept. 6, 1946, ABC. 30m, five a week at 3.

July 26–Oct. 25, 1947, ABC. 60m, Saturdays at 9 A.M.

CAST: Al Pearce, often in the role of Elmer Blurt, self-conscious door-to-door salesman. Broadcasting often under the title *Al Pearce and His Gang,* the "gang" in 1929 included Pearce's brother Cal, Jean Clarimoux, Norman Nielsen, Hazel Warner, Abe Bloom, Monroe Upton as Lord Bilgewater, Tommy Harris, Charles Carter, Edna Fisher, and Cecil Wright. Mid-1930s gang included Arlene Harris, "the human chatterbox," who delivered mile-a-minute telephone monologues; Andy Andrews, the singing comic; tenor Harry Foster; Mabel Todd; Morey Amsterdam; Tony Romano; tenor Carlyle Bennett; Harry Stewart as Yogi Yorgesson; Bill Wright as Zeb of the Eb and Zeb skits (Pearce was Eb); Kitty O'Neil, "the laughing lady"; Jennison Parker as Yahbut of the team Yahbut and Cheerily (Bill Wright as Cheerily); Bill Comstock as Tizzie Lish, the show's expert in cooking and health. Others: Artie Auerbach, Arthur Q. Bryan, Orville Andrews, Marie Green and her Merry Men, the Three Cheers (Travis Hale, Phil Hanna, E. J. Derry). ANNOUNCERS: Bill Goodwin, Ken Roberts, Wendell Niles. ORCHESTRA: Harry Sosnik, Larry Marsh, Carl Hoff. SOUND EFFECTS: Ray Erlenborn.

Al Pearce was one of radio's earliest and most durable comics. He was singing and playing banjo at KFRC, San Francisco, when a writer offered him a character skit starring a timid traveling salesman named Elmer. Pearce was typecast, as he had once sold insurance door-to-door. He later sold real estate and, with his brother Cal, sang on the air in 1928 with the San Francisco Real Estate Glee Club.

He was moonlighting at KFRC when writer Jack Hasty gave him the Elmer skit. Elmer was a bashful salesman who'd rather miss a sale than confront a customer. He would knock distinctly—bump-bump-abump-bump . . . bump-bump—and mutter, "Nobody home, I-hope-I-hope-I-hope." Elmer became Elmer Blurt, and the phrase became a national slogan.

Many of his "gang" remained with Pearce across frequent changes of network, format, and sponsor. Arlene Harris, the human chatterbox, could gush 240 words a minute, talking to her friend Mazie on the phone. Bill Comstock developed his female Tizzie Lish character on a recipe show at a station where he'd once worked. Eb and Zeb were two geezers who ran a general store at the crossroads. Harry Stewart as Yogi Yorgesson sang nonsense songs with a Swedish accent, among the most popular being *Yingle Bells* and *I Yust Go Nuts at Christmas.*

Pearce faded quickly after the war. He had a brief stint on TV in the '50s, but his comedy was of an earlier day. He died June 3, 1961.

THE ALAN YOUNG SHOW, situation comedy.

BROADCAST HISTORY: June 28–Sept. 20, 1944, NBC. 30m, Wednesdays at 9. Summer substitute for Eddie Cantor. Sal Hepatica. CAST: Alan Young as himself, a bashful young man (he really was, said his wife Ginni), throughout the run of the show. VOCALIST: Bea Wain. MUSIC: Peter Van Steeden.

Oct. 3, 1944–June 28, 1946, ABC. 30m, Tuesdays at 8:30 until Sept., then Fridays at 8:30. Ipana. CAST: Jean Gillespie as Young's girlfriend Betty; also played by Doris Singleton. Ed Begley as Papa Dittenfeffer, Betty's crusty father. WRITERS: Jay Sommers, Will Glickman.

Sept. 20, 1946–May 30, 1947, NBC. 30m, Fridays at 8:30, then at 8. Ipana.

Jan. 11–July 5, 1949, NBC. 30m, Tuesdays at 8:30. Tums. CAST: Louise Erickson as Betty. Jim Backus as snooty playboy Hubert Updike III. With Nicodemus Stewart, Hal March, Ken Christy. ANNOUNCER: Don Wilson. VOCALISTS: The Regalaires (Sue Allen, Fay Reiter, Ginny Reese, and Ginni Young). MUSIC: George Wylie. PRODUCER-DIRECTOR: Helen Mack.

Alan Young was an English-born comic who learned the craft of radio in Canada. At CJOR he became friends with Fletcher Markle, who later became a force in American radio. Young's earliest Canadian show was called *Stag Party*: he was virtually the entire act, and when he asked for a raise (from $15 a week) he was fired. Soon he was earning $150 a week doing situation comedy at CBL, where he was heard by an agent who helped him break into American radio.

His summer show for Eddie Cantor was "routine situation comedy" laced with "rapid-fire gags," according to one trade journal. But it led to his own show, where he was typecast. *Newsweek* thought him a "meek, washed-down blond with saucer eyes and a perpetual woebegone manner . . . [with] flashes of Harold Lloyd and Charlie Chaplin." He was signed for *The Jimmy Durante Show* in 1948, and his new series for Tums premiered while he was still a Durante regular. He finished the year on both shows. But Young had a hot-and-cold career on radio. He was often thought to be the man about to make it big. He made some films to mixed critical notice; then he went into TV, where, perhaps, his humor was better placed. Today he is best remembered for his 1961–65 CBS-TV role of Wilbur Post, the man who talked to Mr. Ed, the talking horse.

THE ALDRICH FAMILY, teenage situation comedy.

BROADCAST HISTORY: July 2–Oct. 1, 1939, NBC. 30m, Sundays at 7. Summer replacement for *The Jack Benny Program*. General Foods for Jell-O.

Oct. 10, 1939–May 28, 1940, Blue Network. 30m, Tuesdays at 8. Jell-O.

July 4, 1940–July 20, 1944, NBC. 30m, Thursdays at 8:30. Jell-O.

Sept. 1, 1944–Aug. 30, 1946, CBS. 30m, Fridays at 8. General Foods for Jell-O and Grape Nuts.

Sept. 5, 1946–June 28, 1951, NBC. 30m, Thursdays at 8. Jell-O, Grape Nuts.

Sept. 21, 1952–April 19, 1953, NBC. 30m, Sundays at 7:30. Sustained.

CAST: Ezra Stone as Henry Aldrich, 16-year-old student at Central High School in the town of Centerville; Norman Tokar as Henry, 1942–43, when Stone went into the Army; Dickie Jones as Henry, 1943–44; Raymond Ives as Henry as of mid-1945; Ezra Stone resumed the role in Nov. 1945; Bobby Ellis as Henry in 1952–53. House Jameson as lawyer Sam Aldrich, Henry's father, for most of the run; also played by Clyde Fillmore and Tom Shirley. Katharine Raht as Henry's mother Alice (Lea Penman and Regina Wallace were also heard in the role). At least a dozen actresses over the years as Henry's sister Mary, among them Betty Field, Patricia Peardon, Charita Bauer, Ann Lincoln, Jone Allison, Mary Mason, and Mary Rolfe. Jackie Kelk almost all the way as Homer Brown, Henry's pal and companion in mischief, with Johnny Fiedler, Jack Grimes, and Michael O'Day in the Homer role in 1952–53. Ed Begley, Arthur Vinton, and Howard Smith as Will Brown, Homer's father. Agnes Moorehead and Leona Powers as Homer's mother. Mary Shipp as Henry's girlfriend Kathleen Anderson; also played by Ethel Blume, Jean Gillespie, and Ann Lincoln. Eddie Bracken as Henry's pal Dizzy Stevens. Charles Powers as Henry's rival George Bigelow. AN-NOUNCERS: Harry Von Zell, Dwight Weist, George Bryan, Dan Seymour, Ralph Paul. MUSIC: Jack Miller. CREATOR-WRITER: Clifford Goldsmith. DIRECTORS: Harry Ackerman, Edwin Duerr, Fran Van Hartesveldt, George McGarrett, Sam Fuller, Bob Welsh, Lester Vail, Joseph Scibetta, Day Tuttle. SOUND EFFECTS: Bill Brinkmeyer.

Henry Aldrich was described in the press of the time as "typical," "not at all typical," and with all the daffy adjectives that those two opposites suggest. He was described as the Penrod of the '40s, but his likeness to the hero of Booth Tarkington's 1914 classic was more imagined than real. Henry found more ways to turn the ordinary into complete chaos and disaster than Mack Sennett ever devised for his old two-reel chase films. With Henry, ordinary objects became lethal weapons. A telephone was a window to such bizarre convolution that its consequences tested the imagination. A bicycle with a flat tire led to much round-robin lunacy before the tire was patched and a sadder-but-no-wiser Henry Aldrich pedaled his way home.

Each week for 13 years, Henry was summoned into millions of living rooms to the wail of his long-suffering mother:"*Hen-reeeee! Henry Aldrich!*" And the cracking adolescent voice that answered, "Coming, Mother!" was the ticket to mayhem. If the show began with Henry tying up the family telephone, it was certain that within the half-hour he would somehow have every phone in town tied up, and calls would be coming into the Aldrich house for everything from plumbers to cab drivers.

The show was developed by Clifford Goldsmith from his Broadway play *What a Life*. Goldsmith drew his *Aldrich* ideas from his own teenage sons, who frequently left him bills for services rendered and good-natured complaints about "plagiarism" after the broadcast. By then Goldsmith had arrived at an enviable plateau in radio: at $3,000 a week, he was the highest-paid writer in the business, an overnight success after years of obscurity. His first attempts at writing had gone nowhere. As originally conceived, *What a Life* was a heavy problem piece, with Henry a minor character. Producer George Abbott advised him to make it a comedy. How little Goldsmith thought of its chances is revealed in a magazine interview: he was so skeptical that he considered selling half interest in the property to a clothier for a winter coat.

In the play, all the action takes place in the office of the high school principal. Rudy Vallee saw it and asked Goldsmith to work up some radio skits. These were performed on the Vallee program, and in 1938 the company (with Ezra Stone, who had played Henry onstage) was signed by Ted Collins for a 39-week run on *The Kate Smith Hour*. Bob Welsh, the director on the Smith show, devised the famed "Coming, Mother" signature, which became an indelible part of radio when *The Aldrich Family* opened in 1939.

It was a hit, and a big one. By 1941 the show had streaked to a Crossley rating of 33.4 and was nestled high in the top ten with Jack Benny, Bob Hope, and *Fibber McGee and Molly*. But this was wartime, and the young cast was soon depleted. When Stone went into the Army in 1942, his replacement was his understudy from the stage show, Norman Tokar. Tokar had been unable to find much radio work because producers thought he sounded too much like Henry Aldrich: his role of Willie Marshall, Henry's friend, had to be given a "marbles in the mouth" treatment to avoid confusion with Henry. But Tokar was called into the Signal Corps soon after getting the lead, and a frantic search went out for a new Henry. Dickie Jones, who got the part, was a radio veteran at 16: he had faced his first microphone at 5 and was the voice of Pinocchio in the 1940 Disney cartoon. Two years later, with Stone, Tokar, and Jones all in the Army, the role went to Raymond Ives. "Not a single member of the original cast is left," *Tune In* reported in 1943. The same magazine found Jackie Kelk (as Homer Brown) the actor most consistent with his role. "Always slightly in need of a haircut and inclined to rattle around in his clothes, Jackie actually looks like he sounds."

By all accounts it was a happy cast. Goldsmith believed in two things: family love and keeping the cast happy. There could be bickering at the Aldrich house, but at the root of it was love. Said *Tune In*: "If Norman Tokar reads a line to his mother with the barest annoyance, the director is quick to remind him, 'Be nice to your mother, Henry, when you say that.'" Such a stickler for Aldrich ambience was Goldsmith that he had Dickie Jones as his houseguest in the summer of 1943, immersed in the language of the character he would assume that fall.

But it was Ezra Stone who made the biggest impact as Henry. He became a TV director after the series ended and in later life was director of the David Library of the American Revolution. Even in middle age he could get his voice "up" on demand for that broken echo of a lost era. The show peaked during his run, in 1941–42, and its fade was slow throughout the decade. Tapes reveal a charming period piece, silly, frivolous, undeniably crazy: nostalgic even to the jingle that set off the commercials:

> *Oh, the big red letters stand for*
> *the Jell-O family!*
> *Oh, the big red letters stand for*
> *the Jell-O family!*
> *That's Jell-O!*
> *Yum-yum-yum!*
> *Jell-O pudding!*
> *Yum-yum-yum!*
> *Jell-O Tap-i-oca Pudding, yes sir-eee!*

ALEC TEMPLETON TIME, musical variety.

BROADCAST HISTORY: July 4–Aug. 29, 1939, NBC. 30m, Tuesdays at 9:30. Summer substitute for *Fibber McGee and Molly*. Johnson's Wax. **ANNOUNCER:** Conrad Nagel. **VOCALIST:** Edna O'Dell. **ORCHESTRA:** Billy Mills.

Sept. 25, 1939–April 25, 1941, NBC. 30m, Mondays at 9:30 until June 1940, then Fridays at 7:30. Miles Laboratories for Alka-Seltzer. OR-CHESTRA: Daniel Saidenberg, with a chorus of 16 voices. VOCALIST: Pat O'Malley, with Irish monologues and songs of the English North Country.

March 1–Aug. 27, 1943, Blue Network. 5m, Three a week. Dubonnet Wine.

June 2–Aug. 25, 1946, and June 1–Aug. 31, 1947, NBC. 30m, Sundays at 8. Summer series replacing *The Charlie McCarthy Show.*

Alec Templeton was a pianist, mimic, mnemonist, and satirist. Blind from birth, he came to the United States from Wales in 1936. His act was built around satire: with the Jack Hylton Orchestra, he created comic interpretations of the classics, and his first summer show highlighted this talent. He loved to dip in and out of classical pieces, mixing them, blending into new arrangements and current musical styles. He played popular songs in the manner of Strauss or Mozart to great effect.

Templeton had studied at London's Royal Academy and played with various American symphonies before his radio career began. His initial radio exposure came on *The Rudy Vallee Show, The Chase and Sanborn Hour, The Kraft Music Hall,* and *The Magic Key.* He was a voracious radio listener, "everything from *Vic and Sade* to Toscanini." He memorized his radio scripts by having them read to him 20 times. His longtime director and manager was Stanley North. They developed an intricate series of touch cues: North would squeeze Templeton's shoulder when the star was to speak or play; a finger across the back meant slow the tempo, and a squeeze with the forefinger meant pick it up. Templeton was clever and became popular with the so-called intellectual set.

ALIAS JANE DOE, adventure drama.

BROADCAST HISTORY: April 7–Sept. 22, 1951, CBS. 30m, Saturdays at 1:30. Toni Home Permanents, Gillette Super Speed Razor. CAST: Kay Phillips as Jane Doe, the "lovely magazine writer" who assumes various roles in order to get her stories. Hollywood players included Tudor Owen, Lamont Johnson, Eric Sinclair, etc. AN-NOUNCER: Frank Martin. PRODUCER: Rogers Brackett. DIRECTOR: Robert Shue. WRITERS:

Kay Phillips, E. Jack Neuman, John Michael Hayes.

ALIAS JIMMY VALENTINE, crime drama, based on the O. Henry story *A Retrieved Information.*

BROADCAST HISTORY: Jan. 18, 1938–Feb. 27, 1939, Blue Network. 30m, Tuesdays at 9:30 until April 1938 for Edgeworth Tobacco; Mondays at 7 beginning June 1938 for Dr. Lyons Tooth Powder. CAST: Bert Lytell as Jimmy Valentine, a safecracker; James Meighan also played the role. PRODUCERS: Frank and Anne Hummert.

ALICE JOY, THE DREAM SINGER, music and song; vaudevillian turned radio star.

BROADCAST HISTORY: Oct. 26, 1931–April 30, 1932, NBC. 15m, six a week at 7:30. Prince Albert Tobacco.

1932–34, Blue Network. 15m, various times.

Jan. 3, 1938–Feb. 25, 1938, NBC. 15m, three a week at 9:30 A.M.

ALMA KITCHELL, vocalist and interviewer.

BROADCAST HISTORY: Ca. 1927, WJZ, New York.

1928–1942, NBC, many formats and timeslots on Red and Blue Networks; also under titles *Let's Talk It Over, Women's Exchange,* and *Alma Kitchell's Brief Case.*

Alma Kitchell began as a singer of opera and later became an accomplished interviewer. She sang in NBC's first televised opera in 1939, and her programs on both radio and TV included family affairs, cooking, and chats with the famous. She died in 1996 at 103.

AMANDA OF HONEYMOON HILL, soap opera.

BROADCAST HISTORY: Feb. 5, 1940–April 26, 1946. Blue Network, 15m, daily at 3:15 until Aug. 1942; CBS thereafter, at 10:30 A.M. until 1943, then at 11 A.M. Cal Aspirin, Milk of Magnesia, Haley's MO. CAST: Joy Hathaway as Amanda Dyke Leighton, a "beauty of flaming red hair." Boyd Crawford, George Lambert, and Staats Cotsworth variously as Edward Leighton, "a handsome young southerner who lived in a mansion on the hill, married her, and took her away from her strict father, who kept her close to their Virginia valley.'' Jack MacBryde as Amanda's father, Joseph Dyke, a common baker of bricks. Muriel Starr and Irene Hubbard as Susan Leighton, Edward's mother, a snob, a women's clubber. Cecil Roy and Florence Edney as kind old Aunt Maisie, ''the wise old woman of the valley,'' who dispensed wisdom between puffs on her corncob pipe and helped Amanda weather emotional storms. John Connery as Colonel Leighton. Helen Shields as Sylvia Meadows. Jay Meredith as Marion Leighton. **ANNOUNCERS:** Howard Claney, Frank Gallop, Hugh Conover. **PRODUCERS:** Frank and Anne Hummert. **DIRECTOR:** Ernest Ricca.

Amanda of Honeymoon Hill worked a much-used Hummert theme, the common girl who marries into a rich, aristocratic family. Amanda ''had nothing in life except her own beauty, neither education nor background nor any real contact with the world.'' But ''in spite of the hatred of both their families, they seek happiness on Honeymoon Hill in Virginia, in a world that few Americans know.''

Edward was an artist who whiled away his days making portraits of Amanda. The war took him far away, to Abbeyville and the supervision of his factory, which had been converted to war production. Amanda stayed on the hill and helped in the nursery she had established for the children of war workers. Her father fretted that she would lose her common-folk heritage; his mother worried that Edward had married beneath his station. Overriding all else was a son, Robert Elijah, born to Amanda and dearly loved by all.

THE AMAZING MRS. DANBERRY, situation comedy.

BROADCAST HISTORY: April 21–June 16, 1946, CBS. 30m, Sundays at 8. Lewis-Howe for Tums.
CAST: Agnes Moorehead as Mrs. Jonathan Danberry, ''the lively widow of a department store owner who has a tongue as sharp as a hatpin and a heart as warm as summer.'' Also: Cathy Lewis, Dan Wolfe, Bill Johnstone. **ANNOUNCER:** Ken Niles. **DIRECTOR:** Helen Mack.

The Amazing Mrs. Danberry filled the slot held by *The Beulah Show* when Marlin ''Beulah'' Hurt died of a heart attack. First came a quickly assembled interim series, *Calamity Jane*, with Moorehead playing a bumptious newspaper reporter battling the rackets. *Calamity* ran only three weeks (CBS, March 30–April 14); then the cast, under *Beulah* director Helen Mack, regrouped and came up with *Danberry*. Mrs. D. tried to delegate the store to her son but couldn't stop meddling. Other characters were banker Tom Stephen and the Danberry servants Judd and Prunella Tuttle.

THE AMAZING MR. SMITH, comedy-mystery.

BROADCAST HISTORY: April 7–June 30, 1941, Mutual. 30m, Mondays at 8. American Can Company.
CAST: Keenan Wynn as Gregory Smith, ''a carefree young man who runs into trouble galore and becomes an involuntary detective.'' Charlie Cantor as Herbie, Smith's valet, chauffeur, and man Friday. Also: Elizabeth Reller, Santos Ortega, Cliff Carpenter, John Brown. **ANNOUNCER:** Harry Von Zell. **MUSIC:** Harry Salter. **CREATOR-WRITERS:** Howard Harris, Martin Gosch. **DIRECTOR:** George McGarrett.

THE AMAZING MR. TUTT, lighthearted legal drama, based on the *Saturday Evening Post* stories of Arthur Train.

BROADCAST HISTORY: July 5–Aug. 23, 1948, CBS. 30m, Mondays at 9:30. **CAST:** Will Wright as Ephraim Tutt, ''America's most beloved lawyer, the old gentleman attorney at law with the stovepipe hat and the stogie.'' John Beal as Bonnie Doon, Tutt's ''legal helper'' and narrator of the tales. Norman Field as Judge Babson. Joe Granby as District Attorney O'Brion. Herb Rawlinson as Edgar, the courthouse guard. **ANNOUNCER:** Roy Rowan. **MUSIC:** Lud Gluskin. **PRODUCER-DIRECTOR:** Anton M. Leader. **WRITER:** Arnold Perl.

AMERICA IN THE AIR, war drama.

BROADCAST HISTORY: Aug. 8, 1943–Oct. 13, 1945, CBS. 30m, Sundays at 6:30 until Sept. 1944, then Saturdays at 7:30. Wrigley's Gum. **PRODUCER-DIRECTOR:** Les Weinrott. **WRITER:** David Harmon.

America in the Air was billed as ''a tribute to the daring men of the United States Air Forces''; its purpose was ''to give the average man on the ground a clear understanding of the Air Forces—

its men, its equipment, and its operations.'' The first broadcast told of the Flying Fortress *Memphis Belle*. The series used both drama and interviews. It may have been an important show in the *Words at War* genre, but no broadcasts have been unearthed at this writing, and all known data comes from a CBS publicity release.

AMERICAN AGENT, spy drama.

BROADCAST HISTORY: Dec. 6, 1950–Sept. 26, 1951, ABC. 30m, Wednesdays at 8. Mars Candy. CAST: Jack McCarthy as Bob Barclay, globetrotting soldier of fortune. ANNOUNCER: Jay Michael. PRODUCER: George W. Trendle.

The American agent of the title led two lives. In real life, he was a foreign correspondent for "Amalgamated News"; under cover, he was an agent for the government. This premise was offensive to real newsmen, who flooded the network with angry mail. Their major complaint: that the series was hurting the case of real-life newsman William Oatis, who was being held in Czechoslovakia on a charge of espionage. Producer Trendle fired back from Detroit, where the series was produced, telling *Newsweek* that the press corps was "too serious about themselves." But by August 1951 Barclay had resigned from the wire service, and a month later he disappeared from the air.

THE AMERICAN ALBUM OF FAMILIAR MUSIC, traditional music by orchestra, soloists, and vocalists.

BROADCAST HISTORY: Oct. 11, 1931–Nov. 19, 1950, NBC. 30m, Sundays at 9 until 1933, then at 9:30. Bayer Aspirin.
Nov. 26, 1950–June 17, 1951, ABC. 30m, Sundays at 9:30. Bayer Aspirin.
COMPANY: Singers Frank Munn, Jean Dickenson, Elizabeth Lennox, Lucy Monroe, Evelyn MacGregor, Vivian della Chiesa, Virginia Rea, Donald Dame. ORCHESTRA: Gustave Haenschen. ANNOUNCERS: Andre Baruch, Howard Claney, Roger Krupp. PIANO DUO: Arden and Arden. VIOLIN SOLOIST: Bernard Hirsch: VOCAL GROUP: the 12-voice Buckingham Choir. PRODUCERS: Frank and Anne Hummert. DIRECTOR: James Haupt.

The American Album of Familiar Music was geared for mass appeal. Like the dozens of soap operas created by Frank and Anne Hummert, the taste was decidedly blue-collar. "Not a song is sung or a melody played that hasn't first been selected and okayed by Mr. and Mrs. Hummert," said *Radio Mirror* of the show in 1939. "The Hummerts have only one rule for the music they select, but that's a good one—it must be full of melody."

It was "old-fashioned radio," said *Mirror*, "without ballyhoo or studio audiences." The Hummerts had discontinued the audience in 1938, deciding that the music was more effective if the room wasn't filled with extra people. The cast alone was almost a roomful: the singers performed in full evening dress, a custom held over from the audience days, and rehearsal was long and arduous. Each Sunday the cast gathered at 5 P.M. Rehearsal consumed the evening, often lasting right up to air time.

Frank Munn, a barrel of a man, was one of radio's major early singing stars. His career began in 1923; he starred on *The Palmolive Hour* and was installed on *American Album* in its first season. Billed as "the golden voice of radio," Munn sang such favorites as *I'll Take You Home Again, Kathleen*; *Home Sweet Home*; and *When You and I Were Young, Maggie*. He left the show abruptly in 1945 and retired from the air. Let it merely be said here that Munn was a man of independent mind: his life and character are more fully described in *The Mighty Music Box* by Thomas A. DeLong. Tenor Frank Parker came in as his replacement.

THE AMERICAN FORUM OF THE AIR, public affairs panel discussion.

BROADCAST HISTORY: 1934–37, WOR-Mutual. *The Mutual Forum Hour.*
Dec. 26, 1937–Jan. 18, 1949, Mutual. Sundays until 1943, then Tuesdays; various timeslots, usually early evening; heard in 30m, 45m, and 60m seasons.
Oct. 30, 1949–March 11, 1956, NBC. 30m, Sundays, various timeslots, often midafternoon but as late as 10:30.
MODERATOR: Theodore Granik.

The roots of *The American Forum of the Air* were planted in New York's Gimbel's department store in 1928. Gimbel's owned a radio station, WGBS: Theodore Granik, a young law student who worked for Gimbel's, thus gravitated into radio. Granik did continuity, wrote dialogue, reported sports events, and once, when an act failed to arrive, gave a Bible reading. His law studies gave him an idea for a radio show: it would be called *Law for the Layman*, a panel discussion on all kinds of legal issues. When the station was sold, Granik was offered a similar job at WOR.

He expanded his show beyond the law, working up an adversary format. His breakthrough came when a heated debate—virtually unheard of in radio then—erupted on the topic of Prohibition. The opponents were Rep. Emanuel Celler of New York and Mrs. Ella Boole of the Woman's Christian Temperance Union. Mrs. Boole charged congressmen with illegal drunkenness, saying that "underground passages" ran directly from their offices to some of Washington's most notorious speakeasies. This caused a national sensation, and the show was off and running.

It was the first regular series of its kind. When the Mutual Network was formed in 1934, with WOR as a flagship station, the *Forum*—then called *The Mutual Forum Hour*—became the centerpiece of its public affairs programming. Granik by then was a practicing attorney, with his office in Washington, and in 1937 the show was moved there to begin broadcasting as *The American Forum of the Air*.

Guests included then-Sen. Harry Truman, New York mayor Fiorello La Guardia, Norman Thomas, Dorothy Thompson, William Allen White, and Sen. Robert A. Taft. Topics ran the gamut, from New Deal legislation to labor strife, civil liberties, isolationism, government controls, fascism, and Communism. Though a staunch advocate of free speech, Granik refused to let Communists on the show, even when Communism was the topic. Other than that he tried to remain neutral while being (in the opinion of *Radio Mirror*) "firm, hard-headed, and diplomatic." Much of his time was spent deflecting personal barbs between the guests and keeping panelists on the issues.

The format was tight. Proponents and opponents were each allowed an opening statement; a panel discussion followed, questions were taken from the audience, and closing summations wrapped it up. Granik admitted that he looked for hot issues: if a major story was "broken" on the air, so much the better. *Forum* was

the only radio show reprinted verbatim in the *Congressional Record*: it sparked many floor debates in Congress, as lawmakers continued on Monday discussions they had heard on the Sunday broadcast.

The show won a Peabody, radio's highest award, and a television version opened in 1949. In addition to his radio work, Granik became an assistant district attorney in New York and did consulting work for the Selective Service Administration, the War Production Board, and the U.S. Housing Authority. He received no salary for the show, once estimating that even the expense money paid him fell $250,000 short of out-of-pocket expenses over the duration.

AN AMERICAN IN ENGLAND, documentary drama, a landmark experiment produced under difficult wartime conditions.

BROADCAST HISTORY: Aug. 3–Sept. 7, 1942, CBS. 30m, Mondays at 10 via shortwave pickup from England. CAST: Joseph Julian as the "American in England." MUSIC: Royal Air Force Symphony Orchestra. COMPOSER: Benjamin Britten. CREATOR-WRITER-PRODUCER-DIRECTOR: Norman Corwin. COPRODUCER: Edward R. Murrow.

Dec. 1–Dec. 22, 1942, CBS. 30m, Tuesdays at 10 from New York. CAST: Joseph Julian. MUSIC: Lyn Murray. WRITER-PRODUCER-DIRECTOR: Norman Corwin.

An American in England was the story of Norman Corwin's visit to wartime Britain. He had been asked by CBS to observe and report on the character and hardships of a nation under siege. "The style suggested a fusing," wrote Erik Barnouw years later: "the drama of Corwin, the journalism of Murrow. They were, in fact, closely related forms of expression."

In his four months in England, wrote Corwin, "I did not once interview a high government official. The main objective of the series was to establish the character of the British *people* and not disseminate the handouts of the Ministry of Information. The people were soldiers, sailors, workers, miners, the theater manager, the elevator man, Police Officer Gilbert, the Everingtons, the Westerbys, Betty Hardy the actress, Henry Blogg the lifesaver, Mary Seaton the newspaperwoman, the RAF officer who handed me a dish in the mess and explained, 'This sausage is made of two ingredients—paper and sawdust'; the navigator, just returned from Wilhelmshaven, who said wistfully, 'Somehow we're always first in over the target'; the woman in Swansea who went to the Guildhall one morning following a severe blitz and turned in two suits of clothes, both nearly new, saying she had bought them for her two boys, killed in the raid.''

The series was scheduled to begin July 27, 1942. It would air live at 4 A.M. London time and be carried to the United States, weather permitting, by shortwave. This presented technical problems of an unprecedented nature. No one knew how the 60-piece Royal Air Force Orchestra would sound on the transoceanic signal; no one knew until Corwin tested it with CBS executive Davidson Taylor on a closed-circuit London-to-New York procedure that the sound of a door slamming was "like a bomb going off" on the air. "This sound effects test ruled out at least two-thirds of my intended repertoire of sound," Corwin wrote in his book *Untitled and Other Radio Dramas*. Then there was the problem of a voice for the show. Though Corwin himself was the "American," the two eyes through which the panorama unfolded, he needed a radio actor to carry the part. After auditioning British actors, he called New York, and Joseph Julian was dispatched on a bomber, arriving the day before the scheduled broadcast.

The first show was star-crossed. Corwin had written a pretitle scene in which Julian was having trouble making a telephone connection. At the words "Hello? . . . Hello? . . . What's the matter with this line?" an engineer assumed the show was not coming through and cut the broadcast off the air, going with alternate programming. "No one heard it, except maybe a lonely RAF pilot flying over London," Corwin recalled. Murrow broke the news after the show; Corwin was deflated but bounced back—they would do the same show the following week. In fact, the atmosphere was so oppressive that week that most of the show would have been lost anyway.

So the show premiered in the United States the following week. The Sept. 7 broadcast, in which Murrow had a small speaking role, was snuffed by atmosphere. The stormy season was now at hand, so Corwin returned home and produced four additional shows from the relative comfort of CBS New York. Joseph Julian re-

turned to find that his performance had been lauded in the press. He became one of Corwin's favored players.

AN AMERICAN IN RUSSIA, documentary drama, promoted as an extension of Norman Corwin's *An American in England*.

BROADCAST HISTORY: Jan. 16–Jan. 30, 1943, CBS. 30m, Saturdays at 6:15. **NARRATOR:** Larry Lesueur, CBS newsman who covered the Russian front in 1941–42. **MUSIC:** Composed and conducted by Bernard Herrmann. **PRODUCER:** Norman Corwin. **DIRECTOR:** Guy della Cioppa. **WRITER:** Sylvia Berger.

Though only three shows were produced in this series of Larry Lesueur's Russian war experiences, the scope, historical significance, and talent involved made it a major undertaking. At this writing, no shows have circulated on tape, but a sense of the series is conveyed by a CBS press release from January 1943. "The final broadcast presents a picture of Moscow's people living in the shadow of the German juggernaut as it hurled high explosives into the city from the air and from long-range guns. Veterans of the Soviet defending armies shuttled back and forth between the mud-holes of the first-line trenches and the Moscow ballet." The three half-hours were shortwaved to England and heard on the BBC.

A year later, Corwin again focused on the Russian front, in a one-shot broadcast, *Concerning the Red Army* (CBS, Feb. 22, 1944). This was written by Norman Rosten, narrated by Martin Gabel, and again scored and conducted by Herrmann. It ended with the morale-building announcement that "during the period of this broadcast, the Red Army killed 3,000 Nazis in the Cherkassy and Nikopol encirclements." Corwin produced and directed.

THE AMERICAN MELODY HOUR, music in the mode of *The American Album of Familiar Music*.

BROADCAST HISTORY: Oct. 22, 1941–April 15, 1942, Blue Network. 30m, Wednesdays at 10 until Feb., then at 9. Bayer Aspirin.

April 21, 1942–July 7, 1948, CBS. 30m, Tuesdays at 7:30 until mid-1947, then Wednesdays at 8. Bayer Aspirin.

SINGERS: Vivian della Chiesa, who also served as hostess for two seasons; Bob Hannon, Evelyn MacGregor, Conrad Thibault, Eileen Farrell, Frank Munn. PRODUCERS: Frank and Anne Hummert.

AMERICAN NOVELS, dramatic anthology.

BROADCAST HISTORY: 1947, 1948, NBC. 30m, Fridays and some Saturdays from Chicago. Premiere: July 4, 1947. CAST: Harry Elders, Harriet Allyn, Boris Aplon, Cliff Norton, Johnny Coons, Cliff Soubier, Jess Pugh, Charles Flynn, Sherman Marks, etc. MUSIC: Emil Soderstrom, Bernard Berquist. DIRECTOR: Homer Heck.

This was part of a larger series, *The World's Great Novels*, offering classics in single shows and in continuations. It was staged by the NBC University of the Air and offered a *Handbook of the World's Great Novels* to listeners. These shows were direct forerunners to *The NBC University Theater. American Novels* was heard during the summer months.

THE AMERICAN RADIO NEWSREEL, news and interviews, one of the early attempts at cut-and-edit syndication.

BROADCAST HISTORY: 1939, transcribed syndication. CREATOR-PRODUCER: Erich Don Pam. WRITER: Joseph Johnston.

The process was the problem when *American Radio Newsreel* went into production in the fall of 1939. The idea was to catch newsmakers and celebrities for recorded interviews, edit these into a smooth 15-minute show, then make these shows available to the 300 stations that had no network affiliation, at a rate these independents could afford. The subjects might be Hollywood stars, sports heroes, aviators, or witnesses to some disaster: their words were blended with music and sound effects on a transcription disc and shipped to subscriber stations. Rates were $12.50 per show ($7.50 for little 100-watters) and an even split of any sponsor monies that might accrue. The flavor was that of a movie newsreel, and the response was strong. Within a month, 150 stations had signed on for twice-a-week broadcast. Early shows included pieces on Babe Ruth, Jack Dempsey, and Dick Powell. Reporter Bill Harding is shown in one photograph interviewing Martha Raye. Recordings took place "in the field" and were edited in the stu-

dio. "By this process," said *Newsweek*, "isolated current events are joined in a diversified but unified table d'hôte for the ear." The day of canned radio had arrived.

THE AMERICAN REVUE, musical variety.

BROADCAST HISTORY: Oct. 22, 1933–Feb. 25, 1934, CBS. 30m, Sundays at 7. American Oil Company. CAST: Blues singer Ethel Waters. ORCHESTRA: Jack Denny.

THE AMERICAN SCENE, syndicated drama based on articles from *American* magazine and "authenticated" by the editors.

BROADCAST HISTORY: 1937, 15m transcription. CAST: Dunbar Bigelow, news editor of the magazine and "stage manager" of the broadcasts.

Typical features of this series were the life stories of Buck Jones and Paul Muni. A show called *Gun Crazy* pretended to be the story of the Brady gang "as presented by head G-man John Edgar Hoover," but Hoover did not appear on the broadcast.

THE AMERICAN SCHOOL OF THE AIR, perhaps the most outstanding show in educational radio, offered as a teaching supplement; the equivalent of a half-hour course, often dramatized by radio's top actors.

BROADCAST HISTORY: Feb. 4, 1930–April 30, 1948, CBS. 30m. Mostly five a week at 2:30; moved to 9:15 A.M. in 1939; to 5 in 1945. CAST: Parker Fennelly, Mitzi Gould, Ray Collins, Chester Stratton, and others from the New Rork radio pool. Gene Leonard and Betty Garde as mother and father of *The Hamilton Family*, a popular skit in the 1930s about a globetrotting family who enlightened the audience on geography; Walter Tetley, Ruth Russell, Albert Aley, and John Monks as their children. ANNOUNCERS: Robert Trout, John Reed King, etc. MUSICAL DIRECTION: Dorothy Gordon, one of the best-known children's programmers; Channon Collinge. SUPERVISORS: Dr. Lyman Bryson, Sterling Fisher. DIRECTORS: Most of the CBS New York staff worked the show, including Earle McGill, George Allen, Albert Ward, Brewster Morgan, Marx Loeb, John Dietz, Howard Barnes, and Richard Sanville. WRITERS: Hans Christian Adamson, Edward

Mabley, Howard Rodman, and others. **SOUND EFFECTS:** Walter Otto, Jerry McCarty.

So new was the concept of education by radio when *The American School of the Air* opened that few teachers were interested. But soon the show was required listening in classrooms around the country. Some states integrated it into their formal curricula, and network writers prepared teaching manuals to help blend the show into classwork.

By 1939 *School* was using this format: on Mondays its topic was *Frontiers of Democracy*, telling true stories of industry and agriculture; Tuesdays, *Folk Music of America* (retitled frequently to reflect different musical forms); Wednesdays, *New Horizons*, describing the feats of American explorers; Thursdays, *Tales from Near and Far*; and Fridays, *This Living World*, offering dramas and discussions of contemporary life. The *New Horizons* show of April 26, 1939, presented Dr. Roy Chapman Andrews, explorer, on a trip to "the fabled islands of spice and pearls" in the South Pacific. Discussion centered on weather, pearl diving, equipment, and sharks. Helen Lyon, a series regular, asked the questions a child might ask: How are pearls formed? How was it to trek through the jungles of Borneo?

The series was not offered for sponsorship, carried for 18 years as a CBS public affairs offering. The full resources of the network were available to the program: when Hitler invaded Austria in 1938, CBS found itself momentarily short of on-scene newsmen, as both Edward R. Murrow and William L. Shirer were helping set up a *School* music broadcast.

In 1940 Sterling Fisher expanded the scope, initiating *The American School of the Air of the Americas*, and by 1941 15 countries were receiving the broadcasts. An advisory board set the show's policy. The theme, *Lenore Overture Number 3*, by Beethoven, was set off by a distinctive trumpet call, played live from CBS in New York.

AMERICAN WOMEN, patriotic drama; stories of women in the war effort.

BROADCAST HISTORY: Aug. 2, 1943–June 23, 1944, CBS. 15m, daily at 5:45. Wrigley's Gum. **CAST:** Charlotte Manson and Eloise Kummer, narrators. **WRITERS:** Frank and Doris Hursley.

THE AMERICAN WOMEN'S JURY, human interest; advice in a mock trial setting.

BROADCAST HISTORY: May 15, 1944–March 16, 1945, Mutual. 15m, daily at 1:45. **CAST:** Dolly Springer as Judge Emily Williams. Evelyn Hackett as Jane Allen, defense attorney. Bill Syran as Robert Coulter, prosecutor and devil's advocate. **CREATOR-WRITER:** George Simpson. **PRODUCER:** Don Fitzgerald.

Listeners would write in with problems; a "jury" of 12 women was assembled to hear evidence on both sides and give a decision. *The American Women's Jury* was described by *Radio Life* as "a three-way parlay of courtroom drama, confession, and soap opera." Problems ranged from a husband's misery at the hands of his mother-in-law to the young wife forced to live with her husband's parents after the husband went into the service. Infidelity was a key ingredient, though *Time* noted that "no two-time divorcées or multiwidowed women are allowed."

Broadcast from Boston, the show came with a judge and opposing attorneys who all were impersonated by actors. It opened to three raps of a gavel and a call to order. Judge Emily Williams would read the letter describing the problem of the day; the jury—drawn from Boston-area women's clubs—could vote one of two possible solutions. As prosecutor Coulter, Bill Syran was surrounded by 14 female adversaries each day and hence was once called "the bravest man in radio." Some of the verdicts were surprising: real-life mothers-in-law often voted against their own kind, and in one case a jury unanimously voted that a woman should stay with her unfaithful husband.

AMERICANS ALL, IMMIGRANTS ALL, cultural documentary drama.

BROADCAST HISTORY: Nov. 13, 1938–May 7, 1939, CBS. 30m, Sundays at 2. **MUSICAL DIRECTOR:** Leon Goldman. **DIRECTORS:** Earle McGill, William N. Robson. **WRITER:** Gilbert Seldes.

This series highlighted the contributions of the many ethnic and cultural groups who helped build the nation. Twenty-six shows were produced by the Department of the Interior, with WPA assistance. Topics included *Our Hispanic*

Heritage, The Negro, The Irish, The Germans, and *The Jews.*

AMERICA'S HOUR, documentary drama.

BROADCAST HISTORY: July 14–Sept. 22, 1935, CBS. 60m, Sundays at 8. MUSIC: Howard Barlow. PRODUCERS: Dwight Cooke, Max Wylie.

America's Hour was a product of the Depression, created by CBS president William S. Paley to help lift the country out of the blues. It marked an important break with broadcasting tradition, the first time an American network devoted 60 minutes of prime entertainment programming to—as *Newsweek* put it—"editorialize on current conditions." The magazine called it "Paley's Invitation-to-Recovery Waltz," a full-hour melodrama with casts of up to 50 players, a large studio orchestra, and the network's full production staff. An unknown Orson Welles appeared with four players—Agnes Moorehead, Ray Collins, Joseph Cotten, and Betty Garde—who three years later would play significant roles in *The Mercury Theater on the Air.* The stories were of railroads, hospitals, mining, aviation, shipping: the shows praised the mutual worker-employer relationship and denounced "radicals who preach discontent."

The premiere was July 14. The *Newsweek* critic found it "replete with social wisdom," though producer Cooke denied any intention to boost a political agenda. "All we want to do is boost America." The importance of *America's Hour* was its style. It gave rise to the patriotic genre that so infused network broadcasting during World War II. Norman Corwin would bring this kind of radio to its zenith.

AMERICA'S TOWN MEETING OF THE AIR, public affairs discussion.

BROADCAST HISTORY: May 30, 1935–July 1, 1956, Blue Network/ABC. 60m, Thursdays at 9:30 until 1941, then in various timeslots—30m, 45m, and 60m: Thursdays, most often at 8:30, 1942–47; Tuesdays at 8:30, 1947–49; Tuesdays at 9, 1950–54; Sundays at 8, 1955–56. MODERATOR: George V. Denny Jr. ANNOUNCER: Ed Herlihy, Howard Claney, Milton Cross, Ben Grauer, George Gunn, Gene Kirby. PRODUCER: Marian Carter. DIRECTORS: Wylie Adams, Leonard Blair, Richard Ritter.

America's Town Meeting of the Air was broadcast from Town Hall, New York, at 123 West 43rd Street. The hall had opened Jan. 15, 1921. The League for Political Education, an outgrowth of the suffrage era, was established in 1894 and still met there. Its associate director, George V. Denny Jr., was interested in the idea of a Town Hall radio series. Mrs. Richard C. Patterson, League director, was the wife of an NBC executive, and the program was given a six-week trial run.

The six weeks became two decades. The mail sometimes ran to 4,000 pieces a week. More than 1,000 debate and discussion clubs were formed to listen to the broadcast and continue the debate on into the night. In 1936 *Radio Mirror* termed the show "a stupendous innovation for radio."

What made *Town Meeting* so different and volatile was its format. Other shows, even Theodore Granik's lively *American Forum of the Air,* discouraged hecklers. On *Town Meeting,* open condemnation of the speakers by the audience was expected. In each audience, said Max Wylie in choosing a *Town Meeting* show as one of the best broadcasts of 1938–39, was certain to be "a scattered but recurrent percentage of irresponsibles, drunks, and crackpots." Moderator Denny tried but couldn't weed them all out. On one show a questioner yelled, "I don't object to President Roosevelt using the radio to inform the country on the state of the nation, but I do object to his using it to propagate!"

And if this wasn't enough, the guests themselves often came to the edge of violence. Heywood Broun and Julian Mason seemed ready to do physical battle on the air. At least one libel suit was brought as a result of the verbal fireworks, and almost every kind of debating tactic was put into play. The guests were political and philosophical opposites, their causes heartfelt and of long standing. Most were at home with the microphone, but on *America's Town Meeting* even such radio veterans as Socialist Norman Thomas admitted to bouts of nerves. It wasn't the first half of the show that worried them: that was when the opposing guests were each given 10 to 20 minutes to make their best arguments. What drove Thomas, Dorothy Thompson, and others to distraction was the free-for-all with the studio audience. "The speakers heckle each other and the audience heckles everybody," *Time* reported in January

1938. "What a chance to make a fool of yourself on a national scale."

Moderator Denny loved it. The last thing he wanted was an orderly, polite meeting. He went into each show prepared, and hoping, for a verbal bloodbath.

A reading of titles and guests reveals the potential for heated disagreement. The opening show, May 30, 1935, was *Which Way America—Communism, Fascism, Socialism, or Democracy?* Listeners heard Eleanor Roosevelt debate Mrs. Eugene Meyer on the pros and cons of the New Deal, and noted black author Langston Hughes was a guest for *Let's Face the Race Question.* Other program titles included *Do We Have a Free Press?* and *Are Parents or Society Responsible for Juvenile Crime?* Denny often took the show on the road. A broadcast from Los Angeles in May asked, "Is America losing its morals?" Actress Irene Dunne and the Rev. J. Herbert Smith said yes; Eddie Cantor and historian Will Durant thought not.

The show opened to the sound of the town crier's bell and his voice calling people to an old-style town meeting. Denny was fond of displaying a small ball, black on one side, white on the other, and asking someone in the audience to tell him its color. There are two sides to everything, the people learned when Denny revealed the other hue. Denny also liked to say that his show had three basic ingredients—conflict, suspense, and fair play. "Everything possible is done to ensure a hearing for all points of view," Max Wylie wrote. As early as 1936, Denny had installed a remote system, which allowed people from all parts of the nation to be beamed in for their two cents worth. He loved having such intellects as Carl Sandburg, John Gunther, and Pearl Buck. "I would rather put on author Will Durant than philosopher John Dewey," he told *Time* in 1938. He admitted that his shows contributed little new information: their main function was to stimulate. His favorite guests were those with "fire and color," he told *Radio Life.*

Said Max Wylie: *Town Meeting* made it essential for a man to listen to all sides of an argument in order to hear his own. The Town Hall, which had such modest origins on 43rd Street, had "lengthened its shadow until it stretched to the Pacific Coast." The broadcasts were published in pamphlet form (by Columbia University Press), and in 1938–39 more than 250,000 copies were sold to people who wanted "a permanent record of what had been said." For many years Denny turned down offers of sponsorship, fearing that commercial interests would inhibit free talk. For only one season, 1944–45, was a sponsor, *Reader's Digest*, associated with the show.

AMOS 'N' ANDY, a comedy milestone that grew out of a prenetwork series, *Sam 'n' Henry*, and was heard in various formats, in many timeslots, and across several networks in a 34-year run.

BROADCAST HISTORY: As *Sam 'n' Henry*: Jan. 12, 1926–Dec. 18, 1927 (586 episodes), WGN, Chicago. 15m continuation, weekdays.

As *Amos 'n' Andy*: March 19, 1928–Aug. 16, 1929, WMAQ, Chicago. 15m continuation.

Aug. 19, 1929–Dec. 31, 1937, NBC, Blue Network until 1935, then Red Network. 15m continuation, initially at 10; at 7 after 1930. Pepsodent.

Jan. 3, 1938–March 31, 1939, NBC Red. 15m continuation, weekdays at 7. Campbell Soups.

April 3, 1939–Feb. 19, 1943, CBS. 15m continuation, weekdays at 7. Campbell Soups.

Oct. 8, 1943–June 1, 1945, NBC. Fridays at 10. Reorganized and heard as a 30m situation comedy with new characters, a new announcer, and an orchestra. Lever Brothers for Rinso.

Oct. 2, 1945–July 6, 1948, NBC. 30m, Tuesdays at 9. Rinso.

Oct. 10, 1948–May 22, 1955, CBS. 30m, Sundays at 7:30. Rinso until mid-1949, then Rexall.

Sept. 13, 1954–Nov. 25, 1960, CBS. 25, 30, 45m, weeknights at 9:30 until 1956, then at 7. Reorganized as *The Amos 'n' Andy Music Hall*, with the characters playing records, disc-jockey style, and talking among themselves or with guests between songs. Multiple sponsorship.

CAST: Freeman Gosden and Charles Correll as Amos Jones and Andrew H. Brown, blacks from the South who moved to Chicago. Gosden also as George Stevens, the conniving "Kingfish" of the Mystic Knights of the Sea lodge hall, and as Lightnin', the slow-talking janitor at the lodge hall. Correll also as Henry Van Porter and Brother Crawford. In the early serial days it was a two-man show, with Gosden and Correll playing any role required. *The cast after 1943*: Ernestine Wade as Sapphire Stevens, wife of the Kingfish. Amanda

Randolph as Mamma, the Kingfish's mother-in-law. Harriette Widmer as Madame Queen, Andy's most notorious flame. Elinor Harriot as Ruby Taylor, Amos's wife. Terry Howard as Arbadella, Amos's daughter. Madeline Lee as Miss Genevieve Blue, secretary of the Fresh Air Taxi company. Lou Lubin as Shorty the Barber. Eddie Green as Stonewall, the crooked lawyer. Johnny Lee as lawyer Algonquin J. Calhoun. **ANNOUNCERS:** Bill Hay until 1943: then Del Sharbutt for less than a year; then Harlow Wilcox; also, Art Gilmore. **MUSIC:** Gaylord Carter (organ throughout the serial days); Lud Gluskin, 1944–45, then Jeff Alexander's Orchestra and chorus. **VOCAL GROUP:** The Jubilaires (Theodore Brooks, John Jennings, George MacFadden, Caleb Ginyard). **WRITERS:** Gosden and Correll exclusively in the early series; Joe Connelly and Bob Mosher, head writers and producers of the sitcom, with Bob Fisher, Arthur Stander, Harvey Helm, Shirley Illo, Paul Franklin, Octavus Roy Cohen, etc. **THEME:** *The Perfect Song* from *Birth of a Nation*. **SOUND EFFECTS:** Frank Pittman and Ed Ludes (NBC); David Light and Gus Bayz (CBS).

It was perhaps the most popular radio show of all time. At its peak, *Amos 'n' Andy* held the hearts and minds of the American people as nothing did before or since.

Media analysts have picked at it for 60 years. Historians have marveled at the grip in which two white men, performing in black dialect, held the nation. Marquees on movie houses in early 1931 announced that the film would be stopped at 7 P.M., so the audience would not miss a word of *Amos 'n' Andy*. The show was piped into theaters, and newspapers published daily accounts of the serial's progress. When Amos was arrested and charged with murder, interest was at such a fever pitch that during the broadcast no one rode the buses, no one used the toilet ("Sanitary engineers finally figured out why the sewer pipes barely carried a flow between 7 and 7:15, then erupted with a roar immediately afterward," wrote Bart Andrews and Ahrgus Juilliard in *Holy Mackerel*, their biography of the show), no one visited, made plans, or was robbed. The listening audience was estimated at 40 million, almost one-third of Americans living at that time. In big-city neighborhoods and small midwestern towns, people could stroll down streets on warm spring nights and listen to the show as they walked. Every window was open; every radio was tuned to *Amos 'n' Andy*.

Why?

Radio itself was new then. It was the new national pastime, requiring no long drive to the ballpark or tedious waits in line. *Amos 'n' Andy* was a phenomenon waiting to happen. The country was in a desperate economic depression, and *Amos 'n' Andy* brought nightly relief from the fundamental worries of staying alive. Amos Jones and Andrew H. Brown were the commonest of common men: they symbolized the poor Joe with no money, no job, and no future.

People who couldn't afford the vaudeville acts of Eddie Cantor, Jack Benny, and Fred Allen got *Amos 'n' Andy* free of charge. Later all the major vaudevillians would invade radio, but *Amos 'n' Andy* had been there first. It is generally considered the first great radio show. Its format was original: it was the first significant serial, utilizing the surefire elements of sympathetic characters, comedy, and suspense. The cliffhanger endings gripped listeners at a primal level and held them for weeks.

Freeman Gosden was born May 5, 1899, in Richmond, Va. His family was rooted in Old South tradition: its sons had fought for the Confederacy in the Civil War. Gosden sold cars and tobacco as a young man and served as a Navy radio operator in World War I.

Charles Correll was born in Peoria, Ill., Feb. 2, 1890. He worked as a stenographer and a bricklayer while coveting a career in show business. About 1919 Gosden and Correll went to work for the Joe Bren Producing Company, which offered services to amateur, charity, and other small theatrical groups. Correll signed on in Peoria and was sent to Durham, N.C., where he met Gosden, who was working for another unit of the same company. In 1924 Bren added a circus division: Gosden and Correll were anchored in Chicago as managers and roomed together as pals.

In their apartment, they filled their spare time singing harmony: Gosden would play the ukelele and Correll the piano. They began accepting engagements, billing themselves as the Life of the Party. A friend suggested that they go into radio. One appearance on WQGA was all the encouragement they needed, wrote Andrews and Juilliard: they auditioned for Bob Boneil at WEBH, "a small station located in a tiny studio off the main dining room at the Edgewater Beach Hotel."

Literally, they played for their supper: the station could not pay them, except in meals. They did a six-a-week songfest at 11:30 P.M., which was well enough received that they decided to quit their jobs and go into radio. WGN, owned by the *Chicago Tribune*, offered $250 a week for a show that was eventually broadened to include impersonations and humorous chats between musical numbers. It was then suggested that they develop a "strip show," so called because the five skits each week were likened to an audio comic strip. The *Tribune* wanted a show patterned after one of its popular comic strips, but Gosden and Correll turned instead to their roots. Both knew what passed in those days for Negro dialect. They worked up a scenario that, within a week, was on the air as *Sam 'n' Henry*.

The characters were Sam Smith and Henry Johnson. The story, mirroring the real-life pattern of countless poor blacks at that time, followed two "boys" from Birmingham who came north to seek their fortune. In Chicago, Sam and Henry found a grim hand-to-mouth existence that listeners everywhere understood. The storylines—each about two weeks long—were about the perils of the times. After a slow start, Gosden and Correll signed a two-year contract at $300 a week, and the ratings continued to improve. Soon the show was so popular it became obvious they had undersold themselves. To capitalize on their own creation, Gosden and Correll proposed a novel idea: they would record the show on discs and sell them to stations outside the Chicago listening area. But WGN balked at this: the station owned the show and the names of its two characters and would grant no permissions for use in other markets. Gosden and Correll worked for wages until the contract expired, leaving the station after the broadcast of Dec. 18, 1927.

They found the deal at WMAQ more to their liking. They were allowed to record, and the transcribed version of their new show, *Amos 'n' Andy*, began to build a national audience. Legend has it that Gosden and Correll decided on the new names while riding up in an elevator for their first WMAQ broadcast. In fact, the decision followed weeks of hard thought: they wanted names typical of southern blacks; they wanted simple names with biblical undertones.

Everything about *Amos 'n' Andy* (except the music and the announcing) was done by Gosden and Correll. They wrote the scripts, often just before air time, and enacted all the voices. In a complicated scene, such as the courtroom sequences in the Amos murder trial, they might use as many as ten voice changes. They broadcast in solitude, sitting at a table in an otherwise empty studio. Even the placement of the single microphone they shared was done with great care. Correll, as Andy, would lean close, within an inch of the mike, and speak in a deep, mellow voice. As Amos, Gosden was about two feet away, delivering his lines in a high-pitched wail. Gosden used a different microphone position for the chiseling George "Kingfish" Stevens and yet another, very close, for the young boy Sylvester, who figured so prominently in the early shows. In the writing, Gosden would often dictate while Correll, using the shorthand he had learned as a stenographer, would transcribe and later type the script. Gosden would pace while he talked out the skit: he would flip coins as he talked, pouring them from hand to hand. The finished script was then placed on the table between them.

"The boys are in character every minute they are on the air," it was revealed in an early premium book, *All About Amos 'n' Andy*. If a line called for Andy to ask for a pencil, Gosden would hand him one. Cigarettes and cigars were lit, dishes and glasses broken, and food consumed during the broadcast. If either character was called upon to take off his shoes, the star did likewise, and "the listener hears a very lifelike grunt of relief."

They never looked at each other during the broadcast—the chance of breaking into laughter was too great. Once Gosden had to douse himself with a glass of water to keep from breaking up on the air. They did the show cold, with no rehearsal, believing in the spontaneity this gained them. They were so engrossed in the ten-minute sketches they created that, according to announcer Bill Hay, they often left the studio with tears in their eyes.

The new serial was an instant hit in Chicago,

and the syndicated recordings were beating NBC programming in markets where they played. Soon the network beckoned, and there success was massive and instantaneous. Gosden and Correll were now splitting a quarter-million-dollar annual paycheck. By 1931 they were listed along with Will Rogers as "public gods." That was their peak year: the show drew a CAB rating of more than 50 points, and listeners included Presidents Calvin Coolidge and Herbert Hoover. Gosden and Correll were guests at the White House, George Bernard Shaw issued his much-quoted tribute ("There are three things I'll never forget about America—the Rocky Mountains, Niagara Falls, and *Amos 'n' Andy*"), and the nation literally stopped for 15 minutes every night.

Amos 'n' Andy was an outgrowth of *Sam 'n' Henry*, with certain differences. Amos Jones and Andy Brown had come to Chicago from Atlanta, not Birmingham. Their struggle had a harder edge in 1929 than it had a few years earlier. The early shows revolved around money—how to get it, how to keep it: never, it seemed, was there enough. They lived in a State Street rooming house in a neighborhood populated with others like themselves. There was Fred the Landlord, who listened sympathetically to their woes. There were the Kingfish and other officers of the Mystic Knights of the Sea, people known only as "the Shad," "the Mackerel," "the Whale," and "the Swordfish." There was Ruby Taylor, love of Amos's life, described in *All About Amos 'n' Andy* as "pretty, sweet, and intelligent, daughter of a well-to-do owner of a local garage." There was the Widow Parker ("Snookems" to Andy), who was "practiced in the arts of love and a graduate of five marriages." Her breach of promise suit helped keep those vast early audiences hanging, the trial dragging on until, just as Andy was facing a certain guilty verdict, the widow screamed and fainted. Listeners had to wait until Monday to learn that she had spotted her husband in the courtroom crowd, a man everyone supposed had been lost at sea. A similar ruse had been played on the audience in the Amos murder trial. Just as Amos was being convicted, an alarm went off: listeners learned that the entire sequence had been a bad dream. If such a device seems crude and unfair today, it did not seem quite that way at the beginning of broadcasting.

Some of the early characters, such as George "Kingfish" Stevens, would be around for decades; others, like the urchin Sylvester, all but disappeared as the serial developed. Sylvester, who was described as a "loyal and lovable friend of the boys," helped solve a mystery in 1929 when he, Amos, and Andy captured the culprits who had robbed the garage safe. Sylvester also put the skids to the main rival in Amos's pursuit of lovely Ruby Taylor. Gosden claimed to have modeled the character on a childhood pal, a black kid identified only as "Snowball." By the early 1930s, the breakdown of minor parts went this way: Gosden played Sylvester, the Shad, the Mackerel, and Ruby Taylor's father; Correll was Fred the Landlord, the Whale, and the Swordfish. No women were heard on these early broadcasts. Ruby Taylor and the Widow Parker were characterized by being discussed and in one-sided telephone conversations. Only in one other show, Paul Rhymer's *Vic and Sade*, did characters come so fully to life in absentia.

In Chicago, the boys went into business. They sank $25 into a rattletrap automobile and formed the Fresh Air Taxi Company, "Incopolated," so named because the cab had no windshield. The abuses of language were memorable and deep. "I'se regusted" was a national catchphrase. "Ya doan mean tuh tell me," Amos would wail. Other well-knowns in his vocabulary were "Ain't dat sumpin' " and "I ain't-a-gonna-do-it." Andy was often "layin' down to think," "puttin' muh head to it," or "workin' on de books." This was the world that Amos and Andy created alone. It would change as the times changed: eventually Amos would be virtually dropped from the story, and in his place Andy would be supported by the Kingfish. The Kingfish was introduced when the show was still on WMAQ, on May 25, 1928, and in later years he would become the series' pivotal character.

By the mid-1930s the show was losing its audience. From a high of 53.4 in 1931, it fell to 22.6 in 1935, 11.6 in 1940, and 9.4 in 1943. New voices had been added: the Kingfish's wife Sapphire, who initially had simply been called "the Battleaxe," and Sapphire's truly abrasive Mamma. But the erosion continued, and even such old-style cliffhangers as the "Andy's wedding" episode, climaxing May 3, 1939, were not enough to save it. Still, the wedding show remains a prime example of the serial at its most polished. The ceremony took up the entire broadcast. At last the moment of truth is at hand. The minister turns to Andy. Will he take this woman? The answer is on his lips when suddenly a shot rings out! Andy falls wounded! Panic erupts throughout the church, while in the background we hear that famed cry of distress from Amos: "Ow-wah! ow-wah! ow-wah!"

A national debate ensued. Was Andy married or not? Lawyers and clergy wrote opinions, and it almost seemed like old times. But *Amos 'n' Andy* had slipped to 60th place in the ratings. By early 1943 tough choices had to be made.

The show would return that fall as a situation comedy, and the toughest choice was that of announcer. Bill Hay had been with Gosden and Correll for 15 years. His delivery was of the old school, low-key and simple. "Ladies and gentlemen, *Amos 'n' Andy*" was his entire announcement in the serial days. The new show would be half an hour, with a writing staff, a big band, a chorus, and a full supporting cast. Bill Hay was out, heartbroken. Among the new voices would come Shorty the Barber, who stuttered his way through every line and always ended up with a one-or two-word summary, often the opposite of what he'd been trying to say. Miss Genevieve Blue, secretary of the cab company, became fully realized: Andy's line "Buzz me, Miz Blue" was well known in this era. Amos's little daughter Arbadella was given voice, in the annual Christmas show that was an instant classic. Arbadella had her heart set on a doll for Christmas. Andy took a job as a department store Santa to earn the money, suffered abuse from children all day long, got the doll, and brought it to Amos's house as an anonymous gift. In the closing sequence, Amos explained to the child the true meaning of Christmas while on the radio the chorus sang the Lord's Prayer.

There were more new voices, notably the lawyer Stonewall, whose lines were funny and sharp. Andy would say, "Stonewall, is you tryin' to gits me to do sumpthin' as mean and crooked as dat?" And Stonewall, without a pause, would say, "Oh, man, yeah!" When actor Eddie Green moved on, actor Johnny Lee brought in a new lawyer-figure, the conniving eel Algonquin J. Calhoun. The show now thrived on funny one-liners. The Kingfish spoke of going to a fine restaurant and savoring the piece de resistance; Andy reckoned that, if he liked it enough, he

might have two pieces. The audience laughed anew: never mind that every show was a carbon of the one before. Now the plots revolved around the double-dealings of the Kingfish, with Andy the inevitable victim. If Kingfish wasn't selling Andy a piece of the moon, it was the Brooklyn Bridge or a car with no motor. The Kingfish always needed money: his crisis of the week would result in a scheme so outlandish that only Andy would fall for it. So slick was the Kingfish that, around 1929, Louisiana's most famous politician, Huey P. Long, had been nicknamed for the Gosden character.

Andy was the perfect fool, thick of voice, dense, single, and pudgy. He wore a derby, smoked old stogies, and made the chasing of women his life's work. He never worked for a living but usually had a little money, which kept him ripe for the con games of the Kingfish. As for Amos, he had come far from the character of the late twenties, when he was a stooge berated by Andy. He had achieved in the half-hour show an almost elder statesman status. Wise, pure of heart, he was always able to see a Kingfish scheme for what it was.

Like its predecessor, the half-hour show was resiliant. It immediately doubled the 1942 rating, leaping to a 17.1 and eventually edging into the low twenties. The show moved to CBS in 1948, when the chairman of that network, William S. Paley, raided the cream of NBC's comedy stock with deals involving vast tax breaks to the stars. This resulted in an outright sale of *Amos 'n' Andy* to CBS for more than $2 million. Just as it had been one of the first of its kind, *Amos 'n' Andy* was one of the last. It ran on CBS until 1955, but even then the characters lived on—*The Amos 'n' Andy Music Hall*, a watered-down disc jockey show, endured on the network until 1960.

A few shows from the '20s are on tape, a few more from the thirties. The best sample of the serial is the wedding episode of 1939. Long runs of the half-hour show are available in excellent sound quality. Listeners who have never liked this kind of humor will like it no better today. As comedy, the shows hold up well, and the lines can still be funny. There is little doubt that *Amos 'n' Andy* was one of radio's great shows: even the embarrassing *Music Hall* cannot diminish that. But the social history of the program is rocky. Such historians as William Manchester dismissed it as "a racial slur," and even in the early days battle lines were drawn. A petition by the *Pittsburgh Courier* to have *Amos 'n' Andy* removed from the air drew almost 750,000 names in 1931. The National Association for the Advancement of Colored People attacked the series in the '30s and was its bitter foe throughout, becoming especially vocal when the television show began in 1951. While the radio show continued relatively unscathed, the NAACP condemned the TV series, calling it a "national disgrace," and sued CBS. Ironically, black actors were used on television (with Alvin Childress, Spencer Williams Jr., and Tim Moore in the lead roles), but on TV, said the NAACP, the entire black race seemed crooked, stupid, or cowardly. The TV show was forced off the air in the outcry; after a period of syndication, the films were withdrawn and have not been seen in more than 40 years.

Gosden, Correll, and their sponsors countered the criticism by saying that their show was enjoyed by blacks as well as whites. Their entertainment was harmless fun, they said; they meant no real harm; they were quite fond of Negroes and would often play benefits for black children. In their behalf it was said that the blacks who complained were unreasonable and hypersensitive. In fact, many blacks did like the show: whether this approached a majority was never determined. One thing is certain: Gosden and Correll were on the defensive almost from the beginning. Their 1929 book has pictures of the pair backslapping and joking with "colored boys" in various locales. The "coloreds" look happy, delighted to have them there. It was a different world then. Gosden was especially stung by the criticism. He withdrew from public life when the show had finally run its last, refusing interview requests and seldom seen. He declined to comment when Correll died Sept. 26, 1972. Gosden died Dec. 10, 1982.

ANCHORS AWEIGH, wartime series of Navy music, talk, and variety.

BROADCAST HISTORY: Dec. 13, 1941–Feb. 28, 1943, Mutual. 30m, Saturdays, Sundays, usually early evenings. **CAST:** Tenor Glenn Burris, Lt. George O'Brien, Lt. Cmdr. Perry Wood. **ANNOUNCER:** Terry O'Sullivan: "Your Navy needs you!" **MUSIC:** Leon Leonardi with a 32-piece Navy band. **PRODUCER:** Dave Titus.

This series featured guest stars, interviews, and stories of the sea. Among the guests were George Burns and Gracie Allen, Freddie Bartholomew, and cowboy star Jimmy Wakely.

THE ANDREWS SISTERS, musical variety with popular tunes and guest stars.

BROADCAST HISTORY: Dec. 31, 1944–Sept. 23, 1945, ABC. 30m, Sundays at 4:30. *The Andrews Sisters' Eight-to-the-Bar Ranch.* Nash-Kelvinator for Norge.

Oct. 3, 1945–March 27, 1946, ABC. 30m, Wednesdays at 10:30. *The N-K Musical Showroom.* Nash-Kelvinator.

CAST: the Andrews Sisters (LaVerne, Maxene, and Patti), Curt Massey and the Ambassadors, Foy Willing and the Riders of the Purple Sage, and George "Gabby" Hayes, perennial sidekick of western B-picture heroes (all 1944–45 only, the second season featured the Andrews Sisters with guest stars). **ANNOUNCER:** Andre Baruch. **MUSIC:** Vic Schoen.

The Andrews Sisters came out of Minneapolis, where they had been performing since childhood. LaVerne was born in 1915, Maxene in 1917, and Patti in 1920. They had toured with a small band in the South and Midwest during the Depression and, after six years of it, were discouraged and ready to give up. Then Lou Levy, a promoter who became their manager and later Maxene's husband, introduced them to Sammy Cahn. Cahn had the sheet music to a Yiddish folk song, *Bei Mir Bist Du Schoen*, to which he added English lyrics. The trio recorded it for Decca for a flat fee of $50. It hit the top of the pop charts and was the first song by a girl trio to break the million mark in sales.

Other memorable records followed: *Rhumboogie, Beer Barrel Polka*, and *Rum and Coca-Cola*. It was bound to lead to radio. They were signed by CBS as part of the Dole Pineapple show, and in 1939 they received featured billing with Glenn Miller on his CBS quarter-hour Chesterfield broadcasts. By 1941 they had logged an estimated 700 hours on the air. "You'd have to be a hermit to escape them," said *Radio Life* that year. They were frequent guests with Fred Allen, Bing Crosby, and other headliners. Their own show, in its first year, was a standard musical variety half-hour in which the Andrews Sisters sang a few songs and had a regular supporting cast with a western flavor. The second season featured a top guest each week, who would step out of the "N-K Green Room" to do the routine that had made him or her famous. One week it might be Sophie Tucker singing *One of These Days*; the next, Abbott and Costello doing their *Who's on First?* routine.

The sister act dissolved after the war. LaVerne died of cancer May 8, 1967; Patti became a solo act; Maxene taught drama and speech at a small college in California and died Oct. 21, 1995.

THE ANSWER MAN, questions and answers, usually with intriguing or surprising elements.

BROADCAST HISTORY: 1937–56, 15m, often Mutual Network, but also syndicated and locally developed. CAST: Albert Mitchell as the Answer Man. CREATORS: Albert Mitchell and Bruce Chapman.

The listeners sent in questions; the Answer Man gave the answers. That's all there was to this program. But within the quarter-hour daily offering was enough exotic information to keep it running almost 20 years.

The Answer Man was sometimes sold as a concept and developed in individual markets. Joe Mansfield was the Answer Man in Los Angeles. Derivatives were heard in Europe via Radio Luxembourg, and local versions ran in Greece, Holland, Poland, and Germany.

The Answer Man took on everything. As many as 2,500 questions a day came to *Answer Man* headquarters in New York. Chapman and his staff answered almost a million pieces of mail a year. Every question was answered by mail, even the few that made the broadcast. "Is it true that only the male cricket chirps?" *Yes, the male cricket does all the chirping; the female remains silent and just listens.* "How many muscles are there in an elephant's trunk?" *There are 40,000 muscles in an elephant's trunk.* The questions were read deadpan; the answers given the same way, in a rapid-fire exchange. Chapman and his staff, including 40 helpers, trod a center road with controversial questions. They never gave legal advice except to read exactly what the law said, though they did settle thousands of bets and provided help on such household problems as getting rid of ants or removing stubborn stains. The Answer Man always seemed to have the answers at his fingertips. In fact, his headquarters were just across from the New York Public Library.

ARABESQUE, early series of music, drama, poetry, and desert philosophy.

BROADCAST HISTORY: Jan. 24, 1929–Dec. 29, 1931, CBS. 30m. Various timeslots, mostly mid- to late evening. CAST: Reynolds Evans as Achmed the Arab Chieftain. Also: Frank Knight, Georgia Backus, Geneva Harrison. ANNOUNCER: David Ross. MUSIC: Emery Deutsch. WRITER: Yolande Langworthy.

According to *The Big Broadcast* by Frank Buxton and Bill Owen, *Arabesque* opened with David Ross reading *Drifting Sands in the Caravan. Poems from Arabesque*, a 1930 premium book by Yolande Langworthy, gives some indication of the poetry and philosophy that fueled this desert series.

ARCH OBOLER'S PLAYS, dramatic anthology.

BROADCAST HISTORY: March 25, 1939–March 23, 1940, NBC. 30m, Saturdays, usually at 10 (also heard at 8, 9, and 9:30). CAST: Alla Nazimova, Geraldine Page, Elsa Lanchester, Ronald Colman, and other major personalities, with support from such radio people as Raymond Edward Johnson, Ray Collins, Martin Gabel, Frank Lovejoy, Betty Garde, Lurene Tuttle and Santos Ortega.

April 5–Oct. 11, 1945, Mutual. 30m, Thursdays at 10. CAST: Franchot Tone, Greer Garson, Eddie Cantor, Van Heflin, etc., supported by radio stars Lou Merrill, Elliott Lewis, Martin Gabel, etc. WRITER-PRODUCER-DIRECTOR: Arch Oboler.

Few people were ambivalent when it came to Arch Oboler. He was one of those intense personalities who are liked and disliked with equal fire. Assessments of his contributions to radio ran the gamut, from "genius" to "showoff." In 1939 *Time* called Oboler a "30-year-old horn-rimmed half-pint scrivener" and dwelled on his eccentricities. Years later Oboler said that the woman who had written it had seen his worst side because her questions, "superficial and impertinent," had irked him from the start. In 1943

Newsweek noted that, while some critics regarded Oboler as radio's top literary genius, "to others he is an objectionable little round-faced Sammy Glick with a flair for flashy writing and a knack for getting his name in the papers." His work was compared to that of Norman Corwin, the resident genius at CBS. Both men did what was then regarded as "radio literature." Both crusaded loudly against Hitler and wrote intimately, with a flair and style that radio had not heard before. Irene Tedrow worked with both. She remembered Oboler as a "fascinating, brilliant man" who in his writing liked to stretch the boundaries of reality, while Corwin "dealt with things as they are." Corwin she termed "a very dear, gentle man, such a loving person. Arch is a neurotic. He yells, and sometimes he's very difficult."

That Oboler may have been influenced by Corwin is interesting speculation, Tedrow said, though Oboler would never admit it. He was certainly no Corwin by-product: his use of stream-of-consciousness was evident in his days on the horror show *Lights Out*, two years before Corwin came on the scene, and in one of his books Oboler reveals a high regard for Corwin's talent. He had made his break with radio horror shows: he would return to the genre later and would always write the occasional fantasy, but his interest in other things was evident by 1938.

He was born Dec. 6, 1909, endowed with a generous helping of natural curiosity and imagination. In the early 1930s, while still in school, he began submitting plays to NBC in Chicago. By one account, he wrote 50 plays before his first, *Futuristics*, was produced. That play caught the attention of Clarence L. Menser, production chief at NBC Chicago, and was used to commemorate the opening of NBC at Radio City, New York, in 1934. Oboler was dismayed at the $50 he was paid, and he did one of the voices on the show to earn a few dollars more. He wrote short playlets for *Grand Hotel* in 1934–35, did similar work on *The Rudy Vallee Hour*, then got a year-long contract "writing plays for Don Ameche" on *The Chase and Sanborn Hour*. Here he wrote the scandalous "Adam and Eve" skit for Mae West, which caused one of the biggest uproars in radio history (see *The Edgar Bergen/Charlie McCarthy Show*).

He was given the job of writing *Lights Out* when its creator, Wyllis Cooper, departed for Hollywood. Soon he established his reputation and became a potent radio force. Much of what he learned on *Lights Out* would be put to good use in his later mainstream offerings. Oboler was quick to credit Cooper, who, despite a low-key radio career, is recognized today as a major talent. It was Cooper who pioneered the audio techniques that Oboler and perhaps Corwin would bring to a new art form. "To follow Mr. Cooper was a challenge," Oboler wrote.

But the challenge of producing horror shows was temporary. In Hitler, Oboler saw a real Frankenstein, more chilling than anything he could ever make up. He visualized a radio theater of his own, a forum that would give free reign to his imagination. He wrote a play about the world's ugliest man and decided to produce and direct it himself. Until then, he would write in his book, *Oboler Omnibus*, "I had never thought of directing my own plays, but this was one I wanted to have interpreted exactly as written." He hired three seasoned radio actors, Raymond Edward Johnson, Ann Shepherd, and Betty Caine, and "with the last of my assets I rented a studio and made a recording." His new career crystalized: directing, he wrote, would allow him to close "the gap between the author's conception and the actor's performance." Lewis Titterton, NBC script editor, listened to the record and bought the concept. It was a "young writer's dream," wrote Oboler: "the first series of varied radio plays ever given to the works of one radio playwright."

The first series of *Arch Oboler's Plays* ran a calendar year and was sustained. The problem, according to the NBC sales staff, was that his plays had more significance in Europe than in the United States, which was still torn by isolationist sentiment and was officially determined to stay out of the war. He could be staunchly anti-Nazi one week and bizarre the next. His play *The Word* was on the face of it straight fantasy, but the anti-fascist sentiment was there, for anyone who wanted to look. The theme was heavier in *The Ivory Tower*, which explored the tragic consequences of turning a blind eye to aggression. In the first year he used tried-and-true radio performers: their fees were only $21 per show, and he was dealing with known quality. Having seen movie stars perform on the big variety shows, he had concluded that most of them couldn't touch radio people for on-air competence. The microphone was a fierce taskmaster. On live radio, there was no retake.

But the stars began hearing about Oboler and asking for roles in his plays. Alla Nazimova became interested in radio, and in Oboler. She worked for union scale in the anti-Nazi play *The Ivory Tower* (July 2, 1939), which Oboler wrote especially for her. Joan Crawford, who might normally earn $5,000 for a single broadcast, appeared on the March 2, 1940, Oboler play, *Baby*. To calm her preshow jitters, Oboler let her broadcast in her bare feet. The problem with most film people, he would write, was inexperience. They existed to be adored, and when they did appear on the air they were not expected to take direction. No one dared dispute their readings, Oboler wrote: radio directors were "so paralyzed at the sight of a $5,000-per-broadcast star in front of the microphone that they confined their direction to apology and mentally crossed themselves before daring to point a cue." If this statement has a ring of truth, it still couldn't have made him many new friends in the business.

So Oboler directed. His direction was not done from a glassed-in booth: he got right down on the soundstage with his performers. Sometimes he would stand on a table, compensating for his short stature. In one contemporary photograph, Oboler is halfway up a large stepladder, looming over the cast. The stars took his direction, and most, he wrote, came to appreciate it. "Temperament was checked outside the studio door," and Oboler's reputation was further enhanced by the acquisition of these major names. On Aug. 26, 1939, the 110-piece NBC Symphony was recruited for his play *This Lonely Heart*, the story of Russian composer Piotr Ilich Tchaikovsky: it was the first time the symphony had been used in a dramatic show. James Cagney appeared in Dalton Trumbo's *Johnny Got His Gun*, which some critics considered the last word in anti-war stories. Trumbo was using stream-of-consciousness in book form: his story was of a First World War veteran who came home without legs, without arms, without eyes, a man whose face was gone, who could not speak, who had been reduced to a "block of flesh." The result startled millions, said *Radio Life*: the core of Oboler's technique was the ability to get deep into the human mind, "to assay the spiritual and psychological truth behind a smile, a scientist making marks in the sand during a seashore night, mysteries of birth and death, a shutter banging in the wind, the implications behind a sigh." These things were Oboler's stock in trade.

When *Plays* ended in March 1940, Oboler moved on. His work on *Everyman's Theater, Plays for Americans, The Treasury Star Parade*, and *Everything for the Boys* is covered under those titles in this book. His war years were full, turning out plays and sketches for the cause, often without pay. In 1945 he reopened *Plays*, again using a mix of radio and movie people: it ran on Mutual for six months. Throughout his career, he was controversial and colorful. Inevitably he worked in a sloppy T-shirt, unpressed pants, a sportcoat, and a porkpie hat. Historian Erik Barnouw reported that Oboler was capable of having a dozen friends over for a social evening, withdrawing around 11 P.M. and returning two hours later with a new play in hand. For a time he carried a pet toad, which died, he said, from eating too many worms. He had Frank Lloyd Wright build his house, which perched over a mountain and had a brook running through the living room.

Genius . . . or showoff?

That he loved radio and left his mark there is obvious. As early as 1945 he saw it all ending with the complete takeover by television. His "requiem for radio" at the end of *Oboler Omnibus* sees the end of "blind broadcasting" as he knew it and mourns its passing.

Oboler died March 19, 1987. Many of his *Lights Out* and *Plays* broadcasts have survived: probably most have, for Oboler was a saver, and radio people had easy access to such transcription services as Radio Recorders in Hollywood. His material is not so startling after half a century: listeners almost need the ability to project themselves back to that earlier time, when stream-of-consciousness was new and only Oboler was doing it. Some of his *Plays* remain interesting. *Johnny Got His Gun* is probably a classic of the medium. But an author who pioneers technique will always have problems with later generations. Someone will come along who does it better, and people will forget who did it first and the impact it had when it was fresh.

ARCHIE ANDREWS, teenage situation comedy, based on the comic strip by Bob Montana.

BROADCAST HISTORY: May 31–Dec. 24, 1943, Blue Network. Began as a five-a-week 15m strip show; as of Oct. 1, became a weekly 25m series, Fridays at 7:05.

Jan. 17–June 2, 1944, Mutual. 15m, daily at 5:15.

June 2, 1945–Sept. 5, 1953, NBC. 30m. Mostly Saturdays at 10:30 A.M., sponsored by Swift and Company 1947–48; also heard June–Aug. 1949, Wednesdays at 8:30, for *The Great Gildersleeve* and Kraft Foods; other brief evening timeslots. CAST: Charles Mullen, Jack Grimes, and Burt Boyar in the early series as Archie Andrews, a high school student in the town of Riverdale; Bob Hastings as Archie in the main NBC era. Harlan Stone (also Cameron Andrews) as Archie's pal Jughead Jones. Rosemary Rice as Archie's friend Betty Cooper (Joy Geffen and Doris Grundy in earlier versions). Gloria Mann and Vivian Smolen as Archie's girlfriend Veronica Lodge. Alice Yourman and Arthur Kohl (NBC) as Archie's parents Mary and Fred Andrews (Vinton Hayworth and Reese Taylor also heard as Fred; Peggy Allenby as Mary). Paul Gordon (NBC) as Reggie Mantle, Archie's rival. Arthur Maitland as Mr. Weatherbee, the high school principal. ANNOUNCER: Bob Sherry. MUSIC: George Wright on organ. PRODUCER (NBC): Kenneth W. MacGregor. SOUND EFFECTS: Agnew Horine.

Archie Andrews was obviously inspired by the success of Clifford Goldsmith's *The Aldrich Family*, but it displayed little of the *Aldrich* ratings muscle. It was B-grade teen fare, its plots outlandish even for its genre. It was a noisy show, with everyone frequently shouting at once and the juvenile NBC studio audience encouraged to cheer wildly. The character taglines were Veronica's "Hello, Archiekins, mmmmmm," Archie's inane giggle, and Mr. Andrews yelling, "Quiet! . . . *quiet*! . . . QUIIIIEEETTT!" over the din of everyone shouting at everyone else. In its sponsored year, it opened with four distinct whistles, corresponding to the pitch of the "Swift's Prem-yum Franks" jingle of the commercial. Archie would yell, "Come on down, Jughead, it's a matter of life or death!" Jughead would answer, "Relax, Archie, reeelax!" The kiddies in the studio audience would sing the Swift song ("Ten-der beef, juicy pork, known from the West Coast to New York . . . Swift's Prem-yum Franks!"), and another week's insanity would begin.

ARE THESE OUR CHILDREN?, crime drama, based on the 1931 RKO film of the same name.

BROADCAST HISTORY: Sept. 29, 1946–Jan. 22, 1948, ABC. 30m, Sundays at 4, then Thursdays at 10. CAST: Norma Jean Rose, Helen Kleeb, Herb Ellis. ANNOUNCER: John Galbraith. MUSIC: Composed and conducted by Phil Bovero. CREATOR-WRITER-DIRECTOR: Gilbert Thomas.

Are These Our Children? came from the San Francisco studios of ABC. It used "actual case histories taken from the files of juvenile delinquency courts." The names were changed, but the facts "occurred today and yesterday and the day before to people who didn't ask, are these our children?" Topics handled included parental neglect, divorce, racial prejudice, and the "mother complex." A discussion after each story usually hinted that "we" were all to blame as a society.

ARE YOU A GENIUS?, juvenile quiz show.

BROADCAST HISTORY: April 13, 1942–Jan. 8, 1943, CBS. 15m and 30m, weekdays. CAST: Ernest Chappell, host and quizmaster.

Ernest Chappell asked ten questions with point values of ten each. A score of 100 points was perfect, and the winning child was pronounced genius of the day. The questions were a better gauge of general knowledge than of genius, judging from the Christmas show in 1942: What gifts were brought by the three wise men? Where did the Christmas tree custom originate? It was the simplest of all possible formats.

ARMCHAIR ADVENTURES, dramatic anthology.

BROADCAST HISTORY: 1952, CBS. 15m. CAST: Marvin Miller in a one-man show, doing all voices and narration. PRODUCER-DIRECTORS: Ralph Rose, Gomer Cool.

Armchair Adventures was a novelty, utilizing Miller in both original dramas and adaptations. A few other one-man shows were done on radio: *Adventure Parade* (John Drake), *The Player* (Paul Frees), and the various formats of Nelson Olmsted.

THE ARMSTRONG THEATER OF TODAY, romantic drama.

BROADCAST HISTORY: Oct. 4, 1941–May 22, 1954, CBS. 30m, Saturdays at noon. Armstrong

Cork Company for Armstrong Quaker Rugs and Linoleum; Cream of Wheat 1953–54. CAST: Second-grade Hollywood stars in original dramas. Elizabeth Reller and Julie Conway as "the Armstrong Quaker Girl," who read the commercials. ANNOUNCERS: George Bryan, Tom Shirley. PRODUCER-DIRECTOR: Ira Avery. DIRECTOR: Al Ward. SOUND EFFECTS: James Rinaldi.

Theater of Today was typical Saturday boy-girl fluff. It followed the formula set by *Lincoln Highway* and *Stars over Hollywood*, proving that stars could be lured and audiences built even in timeslots that were the "ghetto of the schedule." The subtitle of one show aptly describes the series content: "the story of a girl who never stopped daring to dream." The opening signature featured the sounds of a busy street and the announcement "It's high noon on Broadway!" Then came a few minutes of world news with "Armstrong's news reporter, George Bryan." The drama followed the news.

THE ARMY HOUR, news and variety depicting the Army in wartime.

BROADCAST HISTORY: April 5, 1942–Nov. 11, 1945, NBC. 60m until July 1945, then 30m, Sundays at 3:30. ANNOUNCER: George Putnam. PRODUCER-WRITER-DIRECTOR: Wyllis Cooper.

The Army Hour gave Americans their first long look at the war and how it was being fought. On paper, the idea looked simple. The War Department wanted to boost homefront morale with a no-nonsense, authoritative radio show that told people what their Army was doing. Technically, however, it was far from simple: its problems were both technical and tactical, and it was a producer's nightmare.

The show would put its listeners right into the fields of battle, using shortwave pickups from far-flung theaters. Signals, almost certainly, would be lost, some would be jammed by the enemy. Remotes would have to be cued in advance, by synchronization. This was live radio: entire sequences might vanish while the show was in progress. Tactically, how would security be maintained? How could a nation be informed without giving away vital information to the enemy? Scheduling was another problem. Even a

major subject like Gen. Douglas MacArthur could get no preshow billing: a hint of his whereabouts would invite a rain of Japanese fire.

The show was conceived in the War Department's Radio Division, a unit made up mainly of people who had been broadcasters in civilian life. Its chief was Edward M. Kirby, a veteran of WSM, Nashville, who (with Jack W. Harris) assessed *The Army Hour* in his history of Armed Forces broadcasting, *Star-Spangled Radio*. The original idea was to include the Navy—an Army-Navy hour. But the Navy bowed out, its brass wary that the networks might resent the military getting into radio production. Perhaps there was truth in this: the idea was turned down at CBS, Mutual, and the Blue Network. At NBC, however, it was embraced eagerly.

Time found it "a skillful blend of Army and NBC talent." Wyllis Cooper, director-writer of the horror show *Lights Out* a decade earlier, was given the top job. An Army vet from World War I, Cooper told *Time* the series was to be "100 percent authentic." There would be no "inspirational stuff, no lush prose. This will be in language that everybody can understand." He vowed to tell the truth, "good, bad, or indifferent." Eddie Dunham would be studio director and later producer; Ed Byron, another major radio director, would be liaison between the military and the network.

The show was a masterpiece of cooperation, with networks and broadcast organizations around the world lending a hand: the Voice of Freedom, the BBC, the CBC, the Army Signal Corps; even the radio facilities of the Soviet Union were utilized. Listeners did hear MacArthur, broadcasting from Australia. They heard Joe Louis talking to his mother. They learned from a camp cook how the men were fed, and from privates what life was like in the trenches. There were descriptions of fighting on Bataan: Col. Warren Clear was reduced to tears as he told about it. The last message from Corregidor was heard on *The Army Hour*, a segment David Sarnoff thought "could find no rival in any radio drama." Frequently the remotes were backed by the roar of mortars and the chatter of machine guns. In one memorable show, the use of "gougers" was detailed. These were eight-inch steel blades, just right, said one young warrior, "to take some Jap's buck teeth out by the roots." *Time* thought the series had "information, guts, a good musical score, and the best dramatic material extant—the fighting fronts themselves—to draw from.'' Even NBC sportscaster Bill Stern was heard, interviewing pilots ''somewhere in the East,'' and describing the global conflict in football terms.

By 1943 *The Army Hour* had three million listeners. In the words of creator Kirby, it was ''three and a half years of triumphs, flubs, and escapes. . . . The uncertainty that any program would work out as planned filled the life of the radio reporter with suspense. From this broadcasting crucible emerged the battlefront radio reporters, officers and enlisted men, who did the actual field reporting. They reported on the Army in its darkest moments—the surrender of Corregidor, the bad days at Anzio, the Ardennes breakthrough. But they were also there to hail the Army in its brightest successes.''

ARNOLD GRIMM'S DAUGHTER, soap opera.

BROADCAST HISTORY: July 5, 1937–May 27, 1938, CBS. 15m, daily at 1:30. Softasilk.

May 30, 1938–June 26, 1942, NBC. 15m, daily at 2:15 until March 1941, then at 2:45. General Mills.

CAST: Margarette Shanna originally as Connie Tremaine, daughter of Arnold Grimm; Betty Lou Gerson as Connie as of mid-1938; also played by Luise Barclay. Ed Prentiss and Robert Ellis as Dal Tremaine, Connie's husband. Don Merrifield as Arnold Grimm. Genelle Gibbs as Sonia Kirkoff, Connie's loyal friend, ''blond but intelligent.'' Jeanne Juvelier as Madame Babette. Frank Dane as Jimmy Kent, designer in Babette's shop. Verne Smith as Bill Hartley, Arnold Grimm's business partner. Mento Everett as Judy, Connie's maid. Gertrude Bondhill as Dal's mother. Orson Brandon as Dal's father. Jeanne Dixon and Bonita Kay as Mrs. Gladys Grimm, wife of Arnold. Butler Mandeville as Mr. Tweedy. **ANNOUNCERS:** Roger Krupp, Harlow Wilcox. **PRODUCERS:** Frank and Anne Hummert, Ed Morse. **WRITER:** Margaret Sangster. **THEME:** *Modern Cinderella.*

Arnold Grimm was an old tyrant who opposed his daughter Connie's marriage to her childhood sweetheart Dal Tremaine and vowed to disinherit her. Dal's mother was a schemer who disliked Connie and plotted against her; Dal's father slowly came around to Connie's side. Dal was

an artist, irresponsible and often moody, but Connie gave him all her moral and financial help. She went into business with Madame Babette, a French lingerie dealer, opened a shop in Milford, and began to prosper. But Dal hated the poverty imposed upon them by their fathers, and he brooded frequently.

Among supporting characters in love with Connie were designer Jimmy Kent and Bill Hartley, Arnold Grimm's business partner. Connie's maid Judy was outspoken and added comic relief. Mr. Tweedy was described as a character out of Dickens, ''thoroughly good, lovable,'' and a lover of flowers.

The story changed dramatically when Dal was killed saving a child from a racing fire engine. His son Little Dal was born after his death, and Connie's life focused more upon the problems of her father, whose stove manufacturing firm had fallen on hard times.

ART BAKER'S NOTEBOOK, philosophical discourse.

BROADCAST HISTORY: 1938–58; transcribed syndication, heard on ABC briefly, Jan.–March 1950. 15m, weekdays at 1:45. First heard on KFI, Los Angeles, Sept. 8, 1938.

Art Baker was a quizmaster, commentator, and interviewer. His career began in 1936, when he announced *Tapestries of Life.* He hosted *Reunion of the States,* an audience participation show, the genre that later became his specialty. On CBS he hosted *Hollywood in Person,* a 1937–38 celebrity interview show. In 1938 he was host of *Pull Over, Neighbor,* a forerunner of *People Are Funny,* which he also hosted until producer John Guedel dropped him for Art Linkletter. He was heard on *Sing, America, Sing* on CBS in 1939. Baker's first national exposure came as host of *The Bob Hope Show.* He worked Hedda Hopper's Sunkist shows, 1939–41, and was West Coast announcer for the hit giveaway series *Pot o' Gold.* In 1943 he hosted the CBS audience show *Meet Joe Public.* In *Art Baker's Notebook,* he offered musings and tidbits on the ways of the world.

ART FOR YOUR SAKE, art appreciation through dramatized skits.

BROADCAST HISTORY: Oct. 7, 1939–April 27, 1940, NBC. 30m. Saturdays at 7:30. **HOST:** Dr. Bernard Myers.

In this series, the stories behind the world's great art masterpieces were dramatized. The dramas were based on the artists' letters and diaries or those of people who knew them. The National Art Society, which coproduced, offered a portfolio of 48 color reproductions of masterworks with a home study course. While studying the picture, a listener learned how Gauguin painted *Tahitian Woman* and what influenced Rubens in his execution of *Fox Hunt*.

ARTHUR GODFREY TIME, talk, variety, and music; best known in its early-morning CBS format that spanned 27 years, but a broadcast phenomenon that had many spinoffs. Godfrey had a fabled radio career, progressing from one-night stands to top network star status.

BROADCAST HISTORY: 1930, WFBR, Baltimore. First appearance on the air.

1930–33, NBC staff announcer.

1934–45, CBS staff announcer and personality. Heard on the Chesterfield program (1934), *Professor Quiz* (1937), and on both CBS and Mutual for Barbasol (1937–38); had shows of his own for Carnation Milk and Barbas-Cremo Cigars. His fortunes began to rise with his early-morning broadcasts over WJSV, the CBS station in Washington, D.C., which later became WTOP. This series ran 1933–45 and was relayed to New York 1941–45. Godfrey hit the network briefly as announcer of Fred Allen's *Texaco Star Theater* (CBS, Oct. 1942), but Allen dropped him after a few broadcasts.

April 30, 1945–April 30, 1972, CBS. *Arthur Godfrey Time.* Daily at midmorning (10, 10:15, or 11 A.M.) in timeslots of 30m, 45m, 60m, 75m. Sustained for two years, then an avalanche of sponsorship, notably Chesterfield Cigarettes. **ANNOUNCER:** Tony ("Here's that man himself") Marvin. **VOCALISTS:** Janette Davis, Bill Lawrence, Patti Clayton, Frank Parker, Julius LaRosa, Marion Marlowe, Hawaiian singer Haleloke, Pat Boone, Carmel Quinn, Lu Ann Simms. **VOCAL GROUPS:** The Mariners (Thomas Lockard, James O. Lewis, Martin Karl, Nathaniel Dickerson), the Chordettes (Virginia Osborn, Dorothy Schwartz, Janet Ertel, Carol Hagedorn), the McGuire Sisters (Christine, Dorothy, Phyllis).

ORCHESTRA: Hank Sylvern, Archie Bleyer.

July 2, 1946–Oct. 1, 1956, CBS. *Arthur Godfrey's Talent Scouts.* 30m, Tuesdays at 9 until mid-1947, then Fridays at 9:30 briefly, then Mondays at 8:30 after Aug. 1947. Lipton Tea, on radio and TV after 1947. **ANNOUNCER:** George Bryan. **VOCALISTS:** Peggy Marshall; the Holidays. **ORCHESTRA:** Archie Bleyer.

Jan. 28, 1950–Sept. 30, 1955, CBS. *Arthur Godfrey Digest*; also known as *The Arthur Godfrey Round Table.* Taped highlights from the weekday show. Mostly 30m timeslots initially Saturday nights, then Sunday afternoons (1950–53) and Friday nights (1953–55).

THEME (BOTH SHOWS): *Seems Like Old Times* (*Beautiful Dreamer* in the earliest days of *Arthur Godfrey Time*).

People trusted Arthur Godfrey. They liked his humor, which skirted the risqué but seldom went too far. They liked the fact that, as he himself would put it, he had no talent whatever.

They loved hearing him give the needle to a client. This was something new. When Godfrey chided the sponsor's ad copy, people laughed. Sometimes he would ball up the script noisily and throw it away. "Boy, the stuff they give me to read," he would moan, and the audience laughed. Network vice presidents who dared suggest that something might be done more effectively would find themselves ribbed by Godfrey on the air. When CBS chairman William S. Paley hinted that a certain Godfrey show lacked movement, Godfrey brought on a team of hula dancers. "That enough movement for you, Bill?" he asked at the end of the number.

By then he was the most powerful man in broadcasting. He was fond of saying that he made $400,000 before the average guy got up in the morning. In a parody of breakfast shows, Fred Allen once barked, "Six o'clock in the morning! Who's up to listen to us? A couple of burglars and Arthur Godfrey!" A lot of people were up—listening to Godfrey. CBS estimated that he was heard by 40 million people a week. In the loudest statistic of all, sales of Chesterfields and Lipton Tea soared during their sponsorship of Godfrey's shows. In the words of *Time* magazine: "He is the greatest salesman who ever stood before a microphone."

People discussed his red hair and his style, which boiled down to the fact that Godfrey did and said whatever occurred to him. Scriptwriters despaired: inevitably, a few minutes into the broadcast, Godfrey would cast aside prepared material. Instead, he might turn to bandleader Archie Bleyer and ask, "Hey, Archie, what's the name of this song?" He'd hum a few bars and ask the band to play a number that had not been rehearsed. People talked about Godfrey's habit of plugging such nonsponsors as Life Savers. If he liked it, he talked about it. And his voice was unique: adenoidal, briary, instantly identifiable in a room full of voices. He had a down-home way that made people think he might be their next-door neighbor. All this contributed to the bond he had with his audience. "He has a deep-rooted dislike for anything that is phony, stuffed-shirt, or highfalutin," *Radio Mirror* wrote in 1948.

He was born Aug. 31, 1903, in New York City. As a young man he led a colorful, nomadic life. He had many jobs but little formal education. He took some courses from International Correspondence School but learned most of what he knew in the "school of hard knocks." By 1921 he was in the Navy, taking sea duty as a radio operator. At sea he learned to plunk a banjo and play the ukelele, instruments that would later become part of his routine. In Detroit he sold cemetery lots and learned that selling was something he did well. He accumulated $10,000, lost it in a traveling vaudeville act, drove a cab, and rejoined the service, this time going into the Coast Guard.

He was in Baltimore in 1929, listening with some Guardsmen to an amateur show on WFBR. The usual "I can do better" challenges were issued, and the group showed up at the station. The manager put Godfrey on as "Red Godfrey, the Warbling Banjoist": this led to his first regular air job, a plunking-singing-talking gig at $5 per show for the Triangle Pet Shop. By 1930 he had joined NBC, but it was strictly a local job, announcing shows at the network's Washington station. The following year he was nearly killed in an automobile accident, a misfortune that became the watershed of his life. For months he lay in traction, with little to do but listen to the radio. He discovered a stiffness in the selling techniques of the announcers. He decided they were trying to appeal to large groups of people instead of to that one person who is all people. There were really only "two guys" involved in radio: "If there are more than two people in a room," he often said in later life, "they've got better things to do than listen to the radio."

He put this new informality into play when he returned to NBC, but it got him fired. He moved over to the CBS station in Washington, WJSV, where he was squirreled away in an all-night slot, playing records and chatting. His informality and natural humor helped him build an audience: sales on Godfrey-advertised products began to rise. One of his early successes was his commercial for a department store sale on ladies' black-lace panties. "Man, is my face red," Godfrey recalled telling his audience. The next day the store was mobbed by women looking for the underwear that had made Godfrey blush.

Godfrey's reputation grew quickly, though CBS still considered him a "local boy" whose appeal on a national hookup was unknown. Walter Winchell heard him and wrote a rave review: Godfrey was given a job on a network show sponsored by Chesterfield, but it bombed and Winchell (according to Godfrey's account years later) dropped him flat. In April 1941 WABC (the New York affiliate that later became WCBS) picked up his Washington show. On Oct. 4, 1942, he began announcing the new Fred Allen show, *The Texaco Star Theater*. In the 18 months that he had been carried in New York, Godfrey had become so popular that the Manhattan audience applauded loudly when his name was announced on the network. Allen was not so charmed: he dropped Godfrey after six weeks.

But his failures were minor. He continued appearing on isolated CBS broadcasts, and in April 1945 he was made the network's special reporter for the funeral of President Franklin D. Roosevelt. He wept at the microphone in a broadcast that has become a classic. Two weeks later, after a serious threat to quit and rejoin NBC, Godfrey was given his own network morning series.

Now, instead of playing records, he would use live talent. Thus were formed the "Little Godfreys," that wholesome, well-scrubbed group that rode the crest of his greatest success and would ultimately lead to his downfall. His rise on the network was meteoric, leading to an unprecedented concentration of power. He had two weekly shows in both television's and radio's top ten, a situation that may never be duplicated. By 1948 he could hire and fire in a single sentence, and his *Talent Scouts* broadcast was a perfect auditioning platform for his regular company. Godfrey was his own best talent scout: his sense of what would play in heartland America was almost flawless. On *Talent Scouts*, three or four acts were judged by the studio audience. The series followed the general format of all radio talent hunts, with two exceptions: this had Godfrey, and the winners were given continuing national exposure on Godfrey's morning show, Tuesday through Thursday the week following the competition. The few that Godfrey liked best were given further dates and might even be asked to join the Little Godfreys if an opening should occur. The McGuire Sisters and the Chordettes came out of *Talent Scouts*. But the other Little Godfreys were discovered when Godfrey caught their acts by happenstance, and was impressed.

One of the earliest was Janette Davis, a singer who had her own program briefly. Godfrey resurrected the career of tenor Frank Parker, who had been a favorite of early-day radio audiences. Godfrey found Marion Marlowe when he dropped into a hotel and heard her sing; he billed her with Parker in many memorable duets. When Godfrey went to Pensacola, Fla., for an appearance at a Navy enlisted men's club, he discovered Julius LaRosa, an aviation electronics technician. The key words for the Little Godfreys were "plain," "wholesome," and "humble." Godfrey wanted no stars on his show. He was the star, and a more unlikely one never came out of radio.

He couldn't sing, yet his recording of the *Too Fat Polka* ("I don't want her, you can have her, she's too fat for me") leaped onto pop charts in November 1947. He couldn't dance or act, but in time he would try. He wasn't even the cleverest ad-libber on the air. He made his reputation flaunting the sacred cows of broadcasting. Lipton Tea representatives cringed when Godfrey reached for the ad copy to begin his commercial. Perhaps, after a half-hearted attempt to read it, he'd end up by poking holes in it, but he always left his listeners with his personal promise that "the tea is the thing. Just try this stuff, and you're in for the best cuppa tea you ever tasted." This was the difference between Godfrey and Henry Morgan, the most notorious sponsor-drubber of the day. Godfrey never maligned a product: he'd rib the agency for its copy, but if he couldn't recommend a client wholeheartedly, he'd have no part of that company on his show.

By then he had as many as 63 clients on his morning programs, with many more waiting in the wings.

He ate breakfast between numbers, sometimes praising products that had never sponsored him. When Chesterfield took him on, he smoked Chesterfields. But when 4,000 people wrote in after a *Parade* profile, asking why that pack of Camels happened to be on Arthur's desk in the photograph, Godfrey explained on the air that it was an old picture, taken before he'd discovered how good Chesterfields were. This was one of broadcasting's strongest taboos: people never discussed competing products by name. Godfrey did. He also retained what *Newsweek* described as "a profane off-mike vocabulary that would startle a parrot." No one cared.

Sitting with him at his table during the broadcasts was Margaret "Mug" Richardson, a former North Carolina beauty queen who was his girl Friday. It was Richardson who handled the writers and the endless stream of salesmen wanting to get to Godfrey. In his later years, Godfrey often broadcast from his farm, an 800-acre estate in Virginia that was well known to listeners. CBS installed a mini-studio at the farm, where Godfrey would chat with his cast as they did their lines in New York. The farm, the horses, his love of flying, his mannerisms, all were part of the American landscape. His show had ambience and style. After Tony Marvin's opening announcement, trombonist Lou McGarity would ease into Godfrey's then-famous theme, *Seems Like Old Times*. The *Talent Scouts* opening was more elaborate, a jingle by Peggy Marshall and the Holidays:

Here comes Arthur Godfrey
Your talent scout MC
Brought to you by Lip-ton
Brisk Lipton Tea
You know it's Lipton Tea
If it's B-R-I-S-K
You know it's Arthur Godfrey
When you hear them play...

Up came McGarity's trombone, with Godfrey singing a few lines to get him into the show. McGarity was on the show 26 years, from the first broadcasts until he died in 1971. Others were not so lucky. Discord rippled through the ranks of the Little Godfreys, though fans initially heard none of it. Magazines inevitably referred to Godfrey as a "grand guy": seldom before

1950 was a disparaging word published about him. When the honeymoon ended, it ended badly, with a sourness that Godfrey would take to his grave.

He had begun treating his cast like children, almost like possessions. When Godfrey took up swimming, the cast could expect to do a lot of swimming. He had become a hard taskmaster, lecturing his cast on Navy pilots' equipment or some other front-burner Godfrey passion. No one could be interviewed without Godfrey's consent. It was ironic: Godfrey, who had reached fame and fortune simply by being unpretentious, was suddenly being seen as his own stuffed shirt.

The blowup came Oct. 19, 1953, when Julius LaRosa was fired on the air. A *Radio Life* reporter, Jack Holland, had visited a Godfrey rehearsal earlier in the week and found the studio "filled with a kind of tension you couldn't put your finger on." Godfrey was not there; Robert Q. Lewis was taking his part for the rehearsal. The McGuire Sisters went over their song repeatedly. LaRosa was sitting glumly in the theater. "You could feel his impatience, his trigger-like tension."

Holland said LaRosa had been ordered by Godfrey to take ballet lessons but had skipped the appointment. Godfrey was fuming but kept himself out of touch until air time. The ballet issue was a final straw: other reports indicated that Godfrey was unhappy with LaRosa's growing popularity. Young and good-looking, LaRosa seemed poised on the brink of a major career, and there were no stars on Arthur Godfrey's show.

Godfrey affirmed this on the air. He recapped LaRosa's career in a friendly, easy tone of voice. He had picked LaRosa, he said, because of his humility. But in his two years on the show, LaRosa had "gotten to be a great big name." He spoke these words deliberately, slowly, then he asked LaRosa to sing *I'll Take Manhattan*. At the end of the song, Godfrey said, "Thanks ever so much, Julie. That was Julie's swan song with us. He goes now out on his own, as his own star, soon to be seen in his own programs, and I know you wish him godspeed the same as I do." Godfrey then gave his own closing network ID and signed off to an audible "aaaahhh" from the surprised audience and cast.

Immediately after the show he fired Archie Bleyer. The bandleader had formed a recording company with LaRosa: the company had just made a recording for Don McNeill, star of *The Breakfast Club* and Godfrey's main rival for the affections of the wakeup crowd.

The story broke on front pages around the country. Godfrey, America's favorite radio man, suddenly found himself under attack.

He counterattacked, a mistake. Saying LaRosa had been guilty of a "lack of humility," he succeeded only in pinning that label on himself. LaRosa made it worse by his impeccable postshow conduct. The model of humility, he refused every opportunity to criticize Godfrey and told reporters he would always be grateful for the opportunities that Godfrey had given him. Among those who came to LaRosa's defense was the first lady, Mamie Eisenhower. Ed Sullivan invited LaRosa to his *Toast of the Town* TV show. Godfrey lashed out again. He called Sullivan "a dope" and said reporters covering the story were "a bunch of jerks."

Then, in the most amazing string of self-defeating acts ever seen in broadcasting, Godfrey dismantled everything he had created. He fired the Mariners, the Chordettes, Hawaiian singer Haleloke, and three writers. He refused to rehire Bill Lawrence when the singer returned from the Army. His excuse was that Lawrence and his bobby-soxed fans had driven him "haywire." Lawrence had a different version. Godfrey had given him "hell," Lawrence said, when he had begun dating Janette Davis. This, it turned out, was yet another heavy-handed Godfrey rule—no dating among the cast. The press reported that Archie Bleyer had also fallen into disfavor because of his backstage relationship with Chordette Janet Ertel. Producer Larry Puck was fired when he and Marion Marlowe began dating, then Marlowe too got the ax. What might have been an isolated incident stretched into six years of bitchy, bickering strife. At the end of it, Godfrey's popularity was a shambles.

Marlowe was replaced by Carmel Quinn, a young red-haired Irish woman. LaRosa's spot was taken by Pat Boone. But the effect of the controversy lingered. It was epitomized by the LaRosa incident, and two decades later the mention of LaRosa's name would still cause Godfrey to bristle. "You guys never forget," he complained to reporters. As for LaRosa, the stardom that seemed so inevitable in 1953 never worked out. He faded quickly from the national scene.

He made a film (a disaster, he said), and in 1969 he turned up as a disc jockey on WNEW, New York. He tried his hand at a Broadway play in 1978, but when the director fired him it made headlines reminiscent of 1953.

Godfrey's problems continued. He lost his pilot's license when he buzzed an airport tower. One by one his shows folded. Then he got lung cancer and later, pronouncing himself cured, devoted much of his time to the fight against the disease. He professed to be writing a book that would tell "the whole story" of his incredible life. He claimed to be working out a deal for a new TV show, but in the end CBS had no spot for him. He continued his network radio show until 1972, when he took it off the air himself.

He took up new causes, becoming an ecologist-conservationist and doing occasional commercials for Axion, a Procter & Gamble laundry product. But when he learned from congressional hearings the extent of the soap's polluting power, he dropped the job and publicly rebuked the product. In his 70s, he still talked occasionally about coming back. He died March 16, 1983, in the city of his birth, New York.

Godfrey's first and last network shows are on tape. The latter is especially interesting, a rambling exercise in nostalgia. *Arthur Godfrey Time* is quite topical: this, 40 years later, is its limitation. *Talent Scouts* exists in great quantity. It is easily the best of the talent shows, far surpassing the dated *Original Amateur Hour* in modern listenability. Godfrey attracted fine talent: with some of these youngsters, it remains amazing that major careers did not follow. *Talent Scouts* is Godfrey at his best—wisecracking, rambling, then rushing through the spot to get the last act in. The temptation is strong, listening to these, to think of Godfrey as a decent man who lost his way. Like Amos and Andy, but for different reasons, he was deified and discarded.

ARTHUR HOPKINS PRESENTS, dramatic anthology.

BROADCAST HISTORY: April 19, 1944–Jan. 3, 1945, NBC. 60m, Wednesdays at 11:30. **CAST:** Major Broadway stars. **PRODUCER:** Arthur Hopkins, one of Broadway's best-known figures of the 1910s and 1920s. **DIRECTOR:** Herb Rice.

Arthur Hopkins Presents was an attempt to counter the trend toward short theatrical road tours and longer runs on Broadway by bringing major drama to all parts of the country by radio. The first play was *Our Town*, with Frank Craven and Evelyn Varden. Other highlights: *Ah, Wilderness* (Montgomery Clift, May 24), *Lady with a Lamp* (Helen Hayes, July 26), and *The Letter* (Geraldine Fitzgerald, August 2).

ARTHUR'S PLACE, situation comedy.

BROADCAST HISTORY: June 20–Sept. 12, 1947, CBS. 30m, Fridays at 9. **CAST:** Arthur Moore as the owner of a cafe. Also: Jack Kirkwood, Sara Berner. **ORCHESTRA:** Jeff Alexander.

ASHER AND LITTLE JIMMY, country music.

BROADCAST HISTORY: 1931, WSM, Nashville; syndicated from there throughout the 1930s. **CAST:** Asher Sizemore and his son Little Jimmy.

This popular duo sang five songs within a quarter-hour format. Asher did mountain ballads; Jimmy sang novelties and cowboy classics. The show closed each night with Jimmy's prayer: "Now I lay me down to sleep." The Sizemores were also heard on WSM's *Grand Ole Opry*.

THE ASK-IT BASKET, quiz.

BROADCAST HISTORY: Oct. 5, 1938–April 10, 1941, CBS. 30m, Wednesdays at 7:30; Thursdays at 8 beginning Aug. 1939. Colgate. **HOST:** Jim McWilliams until Oct. 1940, then Ed East. **ANNOUNCER:** Del Sharbutt.

Jim McWilliams, the original host of *The Ask-It Basket*, was billed as "radio's original question-and-answer man," by virtue of having worked on one of the earliest quiz shows, *Uncle Jim's Question Bee* (Blue Network, 1936). The *Ask-It* format was simple. McWilliams chose four contestants from the audience and put them through a series of questions sent in by listeners. The levels of questions seemed to increase in difficulty. The first level might be multiple choice ("If you were told that your parsimonious proclivities predominate perceptively, would you be a mountain climber, a miser, or a music lover?"), the second level translations of poetry. Announcer Sharbutt kept a running total of points scored, and the winner got a $25 grand prize, with $10 to the runner-up and $5 for third.

The hapless contestant who finished out of the money was consoled with platitudes ("Gosh, it's too bad you got all the tough ones") and was given a final round of four questions for a chance to win $1 per correct answer. On the show auditioned by this writer, the contestant missed all four, to the great amusement of the studio audience.

ATLANTIC SPOTLIGHT, transatlantic short-wave talk.

BROADCAST HISTORY: Jan. 1, 1944–Feb. 2, 1946, NBC. 30m, Saturdays at 12:30. **HOST:** Ben Grauer, who chatted with British colleagues at the BBC in London. Interviews were done with such personalities as Eddie Cantor and Glenn Miller.

ATTORNEY AT LAW, crime drama, a title given to three distinct series, all of short duration.

BROADCAST HISTORY: Jan. 3–June 29, 1938, Blue Network. 15m serial, daily at 10:30 A.M. Johnson's Wax. **CAST:** Jim Ameche as Terry Regan, attorney. Fran Carlon as Sally Dunlap, his secretary. **ANNOUNCER:** Fort Pearson.

July 5–Aug. 30, 1938, NBC. 30m, Tuesdays at 9:30. Summer replacement for *Fibber McGee and Molly.* Johnson's Wax. **CAST:** Henry Hunter as Terry Regan. Betty Winkler as Sally Dunlap. **ANNOUNCER:** Harlow Wilcox. **PRODUCER:** Cecil Underwood. **WRITER:** Milton Geiger.

June 9–July 28, 1946, Mutual. 30m, Sundays at 5. **CAST:** Al Hodge as Roger Allen, attorney at law.

THE ATWATER-KENT HOUR, a pioneering series of concert music.

BROADCAST HISTORY: Oct. 4, 1925, first broadcast on WEAF, New York, and an 11-station pre-network hookup. Atwater-Kent.

1926–31, NBC. 60m, Sundays at 9:15, crossing the hour. Atwater-Kent.

Sept. 24–Dec. 17, 1934, CBS. 30m, Mondays at 8:30. Atwater-Kent. **ORCHESTRA:** Josef Pasternack. **THEME:** *Now The Day Is Over.*

The Atwater-Kent Hour set the standard for early concert music. Sponsored by a well-known radio manufacturer, *Atwater-Kent* featured stars of the Metropolitan Opera, backed by a large symphony orchestra. The obstacles to producing

such a show in radio's earliest days were political, economic, and personal. Stations were proliferating, and there was no real consensus as to how the airwaves should be used. The idea of commercial radio had many critics; others, pointing to the overall excellence of the Atwater-Kent, Eveready, and Palmolive hours, believed that only American capitalism could overcome the dreadful mediocrity that most stations offered. Major talent from the musical stage was needed, but many name performers found the prospect of entertaining for a cigar manufacturer or an oil company reprehensible. Politicians were deeply divided on the questions of regulations and constraints.

For a few years in the '20s, advertising was broadcasting's major problem. The sponsor's message had to be couched: it was subtle and sometimes sneaky. On *The Atwater-Kent Hour*, only two commercials a week were heard. But the show was its own commercial, and in the course of the hour a listener might hear 15 Atwater-Kent mentions. The singing quartet was "the Atwater-Kent Quartet"; the soloist was billed as "the tenor of the Atwater-Kent Quartet"; the orchestra was "the Atwater-Kent Symphony Orchestra." Repetition alone sold radios, said Thomas A. DeLong in *The Mighty Music Box.* "Many listeners firmly believed that they had to buy an Atwater-Kent receiver to tune in the program." But this was frustrating to listeners, who wanted to know the names of favored performers. Jennie Irene Mix, writing in *Radio Broadcast* in 1925, was a critic who wanted to know the identity of "the tenor of the Atwater-Kent Quartet." She guessed that the quartet comprised "paid professionals—and admirable ones at that—who do not want their names sent out as 'radio artists,' a position that can be understood considering the chaotic conditions prevailing in broadcasting."

By the time the advertising question was settled, *The Atwater-Kent Hour* had an established routine. Maestro Pasternack conducted an opening number; then the major artist would sing. Usually this was a performer from the Met's Golden Horseshoe. John McCormack and Lucrezia Bori were regulars. Both had openly disdained radio, but now they, and others, found that there was real money to be made. Atwater-Kent budgeted $120,000 for the show in its first prenetwork year. Later the figure climbed sharply, the budget reaching $250,000–500,000 a year. This meant that headliners like McCormack and Bori could overcome their disdain with $1,000 paychecks, for a few hours work.

Others who found their way to the air via *Atwater-Kent* were Frances Alda, Josef Hoffman, Louise Homer, and Albert Spalding. Fees to the Met alone ran $25,000 a year. By 1930 Frances Alda was the regular soloist. That year, the first that reliable ratings were compiled, *Atwater-Kent* had a 31.0, finishing third behind *Amos 'n' Andy* and *The Rudy Vallee Hour*. An offshoot of sorts was *Atwater-Kent Auditions*, the first talent scout show, heard in 1927 and culminating in December that year. Local competitions were initiated around the country: the five winners from each division (male and female) competed for $5,000 prizes in the finale. Donald Novis and Thomas L. Thomas came out of *Atwater-Kent Auditions*, but Kenny Baker— who also went on to a notable radio career— never got past the local level. Graham McNamee announced the show.

A further offshoot, *The Atwater-Kent Dance Orchestra*, aired on the Blue Network in a 60-minute timeslot, Thursdays at 10 P.M., in 1929–30. But it was *The Atwater-Kent Hour* that made radio history and was fondly remembered for years.

AUCTION GALLERY, human interest.

BROADCAST HISTORY: May 22, 1945–March 13, 1946, Mutual. 30m, Tuesdays at 8:30 until late June 1945. Reorganized as *Victory Auction* in August 1945, Mondays at 10. Revamped again in Dec. 1945 as *Radio Auction*, Wednesdays at 10. HOST-AUCTIONEER: Dave Elman. THEME: *You Are My Lucky Star.*

Dave Elman was a master of offbeat human interest radio. His *Hobby Lobby* had run on Mutual for seven years when *Auction Gallery* premiered. It was billed as "the first nationwide auction in radio history," but the items it handled were chosen as much for entertainment value as for cash value. Guest stars provided background on them in dramatic sketches. The studio audience was small and select, brought in by invitation only: it consisted of established antique dealers and collectors who were serious buyers.

Each item was described by Elman, then was featured in a dramatic skit. The studio audience was allowed just 30 seconds to bid; Elman then threw open the bidding to the nation, and the listeners had one week to top the high bid, by mail or wire.

Among the items offered were Mark Twain's writing desk, Adolf Hitler's dice, Robert Burns's notebook, Lincoln's draft of the 13th Amendment, a letter from George Gershwin to Irving Caesar, and Goering's Iron Cross decoration. A "surprise auction" was also held, wherein a bidder bought a trivial item and found a valuable bonus attached. A sack of barley beans, restricted to young couples in love, brought with it a $500 diamond ring; a collection of "Jap" battle souvenirs picked up in the Pacific by the son of New York furrier I. J. Fox earned the successful bidder a Fox patina fox fur as a rider.

The first broadcast, auditioned by this writer, is still viable after half a century. Lincoln's breakfast table was the first item, highlighted in a sketch by actor Walter Hampden. A dozen eggs, one broken, was offered. The audience, sensing a trick, bid the item seriously, but Elman called back everything over the ceiling price on eggs, then 56 cents a dozen. The trick was that the broken egg was a valuable dinosaur egg, supplied by explorer Roy Chapman Andrews. Diamond Jim Brady's piano was auctioned. Music critic Deems Taylor told the story: how Brady had ordered the piano at great cost ($60,000) especially for Lillian Russell, whose voice, Brady thought, had never been done justice by the usual piano accompaniment. Helen Jepson of the Metropolitan Opera then sang "one of the songs Lillian Russell used to sing," accompanied by the Brady piano. This was marvelous radio. The final item was George Washington's death robe. Washington's bloodstains were still in evidence, and the item was accompanied by letters of provenance from the Washington family. A fine show, highly entertaining, deserving of a better run than it got.

AUCTION QUIZ, quiz show with auction motif.

BROADCAST HISTORY: 1941–42, Blue Network, Midwest regional hookup. Fridays at 8. Esso Oil. QUIZMASTER: Chuck Acree. AUCTIONEER: Bob Brown. ANNOUNCER: Dan Donaldson.

Listeners sent in questions; the studio audience bid for chances to answer and win prizes.

AUNT JEMIMA, minstrel-type variety.

BROADCAST HISTORY: Jan. 17, 1929–June 5, 1953, heard in many brief runs and formats, in many timeslots over the years. First series was on CBS, 30m, Thursdays at 9, running until April 4, 1929. Also heard on CBS 1931–33 (15m, three a week at 2); Blue Network 1937–38 (15m, five a week at 9:45 A.M.; 10 A.M. in 1938); CBS 1943–44 (5m, early to mid-1943; 15m, Saturdays, Nov. 1943–Jan. 1944); Blue 1944–45 (5m, daily); and CBS 1952–53 (10m, weekdays at 3:45). Quaker Oats; Jad Salts, 1931–33.

CAST: Tess Gardella as Aunt Jemima, the good-natured mammy of pancake fame. Also in the role: Hariette Widmer, Vera Lane, Amanda Randolph.

The *Aunt Jemima* show consisted of minstrel music and exaggerated black dialect. With few blacks on the air in radio's early years, the title role was ironically carried for most of the run by white actresses Gardella, Widmer, and Lane, with Amanda Randolph (a well-known black actress) playing it later. Gardella, who had played a similar role on Broadway, was the first Jemima. Widmer starred in the five-minute 1943 run. This featured a couple of songs by the "Jemima Chorus" and some banter between Jemima and her announcer, Marvin Miller: "Do you have an oldtime saying for us, Aunt Jemima?" *Why a cose ah has—ovah worry hurts a lot mo folks den ovah work.* The theme in 1943 was *Dixie*.

AUNT JENNY'S REAL-LIFE STORIES, soap opera.

BROADCAST HISTORY: Jan. 18, 1937–Nov. 16, 1956, CBS. 15m, weekdays at 11:45 A.M. (12:15, 1946–55). Spry shortening. **CAST:** Edith Spencer and Agnes Young as Aunt Jenny. **ANNOUNCER:** Dan Seymour, who also played Danny in the scripts. **MUSIC:** Elsie Thompson on organ. **SOUND EFFECTS:** Jimmy Dwan. **THEME:** *Believe Me, If All Those Endearing Young Charms*, on strings.

Aunt Jenny, unlike most daytime serials, confined its tales to five-chapter, complete-each-week plotlines, with constantly shifting casts. The two continuing characters were Aunt Jenny

and announcer Dan Seymour, who dropped in each day to hear her tale.

Aunt Jenny lived on Indian Hill in the town of Littleton, USA, where she was well rooted as the philosopher of record. In her cozy kitchen, a listener could get a bit of home cooking, some positive wisdom, and a new installment of the running story. Early in the run, Jenny was married to a man named Calvin, editor of the *Littleton News*. When Seymour would ask for a "golden thought of the day," Jenny would say, "Yes, Danny, Calvin read these lines to me last night." What followed was inevitably a creaky platitude on the search for True Happiness. Jenny's cooking tips were likewise simple, all shamelessly linked to liberal use of her sponsor's product: "Brush with lemon juice, then with melted Spry, and broil to a golden brown." There were homey sound effects, largely sizzling pans and boiling pots, and Aunt Jenny had a canary, played by Henry Boyd. In her later days, Aunt Jenny was a widow.

AUNT MARY, soap opera.

BROADCAST HISTORY: Ca. 1942–51, NBC. 15m, West Coast. **CAST:** Jane Morgan as Mary Lane. Fred Howard as Lefty Larkin. Jane Webb as Peggy Douglas Mead. Patrick McGeehan as Ben Calvert. Josephine Gilbert and Vivi Janiss as Kit Calvert. Jack Edwards and Bob Bailey as Bill Mead. Irene Tedrow as Jessie Calvert. Jay Novello as David Bowman. Also: Tom Collins, Cy Kendall, Betty Lou Gerson, Ken Peters. **ANNOUNCERS:** Dick Wells, Hugh Brundage, Marvin Miller, Vincent Pelletier. **DIRECTORS:** George Fogle, Edwin H. Morse. **WRITERS:** Lee and Virginia Crosby, Gil South. **THEME:** *Dear Old Girl*.

Aunt Mary was heard on a regional West Coast hookup "and as far east [according to a later sales pitch for syndication] as El Paso and Dallas." The heroine was a wise old lady philosopher who lived on "Willow Creek Road" and displayed great character in the *Ma Perkins* mold.

AUNT SAMMY, recipes and household hints.

BROADCAST HISTORY: 1926–ca. 1935, various stations.

In the mid-1920s, the U.S. Department of Agriculture began using radio to communicate with farmers in distant corners of the nation. William A. Wheeler, USDA official charged with dispensing market reports, worked up several shows offering advice from county agents. By far the best known was *Aunt Sammy*. First heard as *Housekeeper's Half-Hour*, it was prepared for use by local stations in the summer of 1926. By October it had become *Aunt Sammy*. The first broadcast under that name was prepared for release Oct. 4, 1926. Fifty stations are believed to have carried it, with 50 women in stations around the country reading the same script. *Aunt Sammy* gave advice on pest control, floor care, laundry, and food. The recipes were simple and economical, and the program joined *Betty Crocker* (which started the same year on NBC) as one of the pioneering homemaker shows.

AUTHOR, AUTHOR, quiz derivative with literary guests.

BROADCAST HISTORY: April 7, 1939–Feb. 12, 1940, Mutual. 30m, Fridays at 8:30 initially, then Mondays at 9:30, then at 8. B. F. Goodrich, partial sponsor. **MODERATOR:** S. J. Perelman. **PLOT-SMITH:** Ellery Queen. **PANELISTS:** Dorothy Parker, Ludwig Bemelmans, Heywood Broun, Ruth McKenney, Carl Van Doren, Alice Duer Miller, etc.

The idea behind *Author, Author* was fascinating: assemble a panel of literati, have them match plotting skills with detective author Ellery Queen, and allow free reign for spontaneous wit. The situations were submitted by listeners and might be written as nonsense questions. The panel was expected to whip these into respectable scenarios. The show had the potential to be intellectually frisky at the level of *Information, Please*, which had begun on NBC the previous year. But *Time* found it "impaired by talkiness and the occasional complete blankness of literary minds." Panelists squaring off against Queen found themselves double-teamed, as Ellery was the pen name of Frederic Dannay and Manfred Lee.

AUTHOR MEETS THE CRITICS, literary confrontation.

BROADCAST HISTORY: June 12, 1946–April 2, 1947, Mutual. 30m, Wednesdays at 10:30.
May 25, 1947–Oct. 3, 1948, NBC. 30m, Sun-

days at 4:30 until late Feb.; returned in early July, Sundays at 5.
Nov. 24, 1949–April 22, 1951, ABC. 30m, Thursdays at 10 through Sept. 1950, then Sundays at 11:30 A.M.

MODERATOR: Barry Gray on Mutual; John K. M. McCaffrey, editor of the *American Mercury*, on NBC and ABC. **PRODUCER:** Martin Stone.

This lively show resulted when producer Martin Stone was asked to do a book review program on a local New York station. Stone thought a more interesting situation would grow out of face-to-face meetings between authors and their critics. Two critics of "unquestionable stature" were brought in to dissect a book. One show featured Basil Davenport, editor of the Book-of-the-Month Club, and Edith Walton of the *New York Times*. For 15 minutes the critics flailed away at James Caffee's *Poor Cousin Evelyn*. In the second half, the author criticized the critics. Often heated, the talk focused on character, style, and even the author's integrity. It was spontaneous, with no rehearsals. Among the books discussed was James Jones's controversial 1951 novel *From Here to Eternity*.

AUTHOR'S PLAYHOUSE, dramatic anthology.

BROADCAST HISTORY: March 5, 1941–June 4, 1945, NBC; Blue Network until mid-Oct. 1941, then Red. Many briefly held 30m timeslots, including Sundays at 11:30, 1941–42; Wednesdays at 11:30, 1942–44; Mondays at 11:30, 1944–45. Philip Morris, 1942–43. **CAST:** John Hodiak, Fern Persons, Arthur Kohl, Laurette Fillbrandt, Kathryn Card, Bob Jellison, Nelson Olmsted, Marvin Miller, Olan Soulé, Les Tremayne, Clarence Hartzell, Curley Bradley, etc. **ORCHESTRA:** Rex Maupin, Roy Shield, Joseph Gallicchio. **CREATOR:** Wynn Wright. **DIRECTORS:** Norman Felton, Fred Weihe, Homer Heck, etc.

Famous stories by celebrated authors: among them, *Elementals* (Stephen Vincent Benét), *The Piano* (William Saroyan), and *The Snow Goose* (Paul Gallico).

AVALON TIME, comedy-variety.

BROADCAST HISTORY: Oct. 1, 1938–May 1, 1940, NBC. 30m, Saturdays at 7 until mid-1939, then Wednesdays at 8:30. First-season title: *Avalon Variety Time*: Avalon Cigarettes. **CAST:** *1938*: Del King, Red Foley, Kitty O'Neil, "the Neighborhood Boys." *1939*: Red Skelton star comic as of Jan. 7; Curt Massey replacing Red Foley in July; singers Dick Todd and Janette Davis added in the fall, with comic Marlin Hurt and comedy team Tommy Mack and Bud Vandover. Skelton departed Dec. 20, 1939, and the show was reorganized again. *1940*: Cliff Arquette comic star as of Jan. 3; Don McNeill, host; Vandover and Todd in support. **ORCHESTRA:** Phil Davis (1938), Bob Strong (1939–40). **THEME:** *Avalon.*

Despite its many faces, *Avalon Time* is best known as Red Skelton's first regular comedy show. When Skelton joined the show in progress, it was mainly a vehicle for western music. Cliff Arquette brought another change in 1940. Immediately after *Avalon Time* left the air in May 1940, the cast, orchestra, and sponsor moved into a revamped version of *Show Boat*, which ran until April 1941 (see SHOW BOAT).

THE AVENGER, crime melodrama.

BROADCAST HISTORY: July 18, 1941–Nov. 3, 1942, WHN, New York. 30m, Fridays at 9 through mid-1941; later Tuesdays. **CAST:** Unknown New York actor as Richard Henry Benson, a crimefighter of super-strength known as the Avenger. Humphrey Davis as his sidekick, Fergus "Mac" MacMurdie. **DIRECTOR:** Maurice Joachim. **WRITER:** Paul Ernst, under the pseudonym Kenneth Robeson, with plotlines by Henry Ralston. Based on the Paul Ernst pulp stories in *The Avenger* magazine, by Street & Smith.

1945–46, transcribed syndication. **CAST:** James Monks as Jim Brandon, "famous biochemist," who fought crime as the Avenger. Dick Janaver also as the Avenger. Helen Adamson as his assistant, the beautiful Fern Collier, the only person who shared his secrets and knew that he was the man feared by the underworld as the Avenger. **PRODUCER:** Charles Michelson. **WRITERS:** Walter B. Gibson, Gil and Ruth Braun.

No shows were available from the first *Avenger* series at this writing. In the transcribed series, Jim Brandon perfected two inventions that aided him in the fight against crime: the "telepathic indicator" allowed him to pick up random thought flashes, and the "secret diffusion capsule" cloaked him in the "black light of invisibility." It was a poor man's version of *The Shadow*, despite scripting by *Shadow* author-creator Walter B. Gibson.

BABE RUTH, baseball commentary and patter.

BROADCAST HISTORY: April 16–July 13, 1934, Blue Network. 15m, three a week at 8:45. Quaker Oats.

April 14–July 9, 1937, CBS. 15m, twice a week at 10:30. Sinclair Oil.

June 5–July 10, 1943, NBC. 15m, Saturdays at 10:45 A.M.

Aug. 28–Nov. 20, 1943, and July 8–Oct. 21, 1944, NBC. 15m, Saturdays at 10:30 A.M. Spaulding.

George Herman ''Babe'' Ruth was an awkward radio novice who croaked his lines and had almost no sense of timing. But he was the biggest sports hero of his day. His radio shows consisted of chatter, interviews, stale jokes, analysis, and predictions of upcoming games. Ruth had done vaudeville tours as early as 1921: he was an old hand at working crowds but still suffered periodic bouts with mike fright. His biographer Ken Sobol described his role on the 1937 series as ''baseball dopester.'' The 1943 NBC series became a baseball quiz, a format that extended into 1944. Alternate titles to some of his programs were *The Adventures of Babe Ruth* (1934), *Here's Babe Ruth* (1943), and *Baseball Quiz* (1943–44). Ruth was a frequent guest with sportscasters Bill Stern and Red Barber and in 1937 played himself in the comedy-drama *Alibi Ike* on *The Lux Radio Theater*. Probably his finest moment before the microphone was his swan song when, dying of throat cancer, he gave an elegant, moving farewell speech on Mutual. The date was April 27, 1947. He died Aug. 16, 1948.

BABY ROSE MARIE, songs by radio's first genuine child star.

BROADCAST HISTORY: 1926, WGP, Atlantic City, first appearance on the air, at age 3; first sang on NBC later that same year.

1931, WJZ, New York, beginning in July.

1932–33, Blue Network. 15m, Sundays at noon beginning Christmas Day. Julius Grossman Shoes.

1933–34, Blue Network. 15m, Twice a week. Tastyeast.

March 21, 1938–Feb. 20, 1939, Blue Network. 15m, Mondays and Wednesdays at 7:30.

Born Rose Marie Curley in New York's Lower East Side on Aug. 15, 1923, Baby Rose Marie had a fully developed voice as a toddler, amazing the nation with its range and adult sound. By age 5, she was reportedly earning $100,000 a year as ''the child wonder of song.'' She appeared on *The Rudy Vallee Hour* in the '20s and usually sang four songs on quarter-hour broadcasts under her own name. She ''retired'' in 1935 but returned to the air in 1938. In later life she was an accomplished comedienne, taking the role of a wisecracking writer on TV's *Dick Van Dyke Show*.

THE BABY SNOOKS SHOW, situation comedy.

BROADCAST HISTORY: Feb. 29–June 6, 1936, CBS. 60m, Saturdays at 8. Part of *The Ziegfeld Follies of the Air*. Palmolive.

Dec. 23, 1937–July 25, 1940, NBC. 60m until March 1940, then 30m, Thursdays at 9. *Good News of 1938*; *Baby Snooks* routines joined series in progress; subsequent *Good News* editions of 1939, 1940. Maxwell House Coffee.

Sept. 5, 1940–June 15, 1944, NBC. 30m, Thursdays at 8. A curious half-hour divided equally between *Snooks* and comic Frank Morgan. Heard as *Maxwell House Coffee Time* after the sponsor.

Sept. 17, 1944–May 28, 1948, CBS. 30m, Sundays at 6:30 until fall 1946, then Fridays at 8. Initially titled *Toasties Time* but soon widely known as *The Baby Snooks Show*. General Foods for Post Toasties, Sanka, and Jell-O.

Nov. 8, 1949–May 22, 1951, NBC. 30m, Tuesdays at 8:30. Tums. Fanny Brice memorial broadcast May 29, 1951.

CAST: Fanny Brice as Baby Snooks, impish little girl of the air. Hanley Stafford as her father Lancelot "Daddy" Higgins, with Alan Reed as Daddy in earliest appearances on *The Ziegfeld Follies* broadcasts of 1936. Lalive Brownell as "Mommy" Higgins, a role also played by Lois Corbet (mid-1940s) and Arlene Harris, "the human chatterbox" (post-1945). Leone Ledoux as Snooks's little brother Robespierre, beginning in 1945. Danny Thomas as Jerry Dingle (1944–45), the "daydreaming postman" who, from week to week, imagined himself as Mr. District Attorney, a railroad conductor, the greatest dancer in the world, and a circus owner. Fanny Brice also as Irma Potts, the befuddled department store clerk (1944). Charlie Cantor as Uncle Louie (1945). Alan Reed as Daddy's boss Mr. Weemish; Ken Christy as Mr. Weemish, ca. 1951. Also: Irene Tedrow, Frank Nelson, Ben Alexander, Lillian Randolph, Elvia Allman, Earl Lee, Sara Berner, etc. ANNOUNCERS: John Conte (late 1930s, early 1940s), Tobe Reed (1944–45), Harlow Wilcox (mid-late 1940s), Dick Joy, Don Wilson, Ken Roberts. VOCALIST: Bob Graham (1945). MUSIC: Meredith Willson (ca. 1937–44), Carmen Dragon. PRODUCER-DIRECTORS: Mann Holiner (early 1940s), Al Kaye (1944), Ted Bliss, Walter Bunker, Arthur Stander. WRITERS: Phil Rapp, Jess Oppenheimer, Everett Freeman, Bill Danch, Sid Dorfman, Arthur Stander, Robert Fisher. SOUND EFFECTS: (CBS): Clark Casey, David Light. THEME: *Rockabye Baby*.

Baby Snooks was created by Fanny Brice at a party in 1921. But Brice was a middle-aged woman before the medium of "blind broadcasting" gave her a new career in the voice of a child.

Her original name was Borach, but in two separate and equally acclaimed careers she became known to the world as Fanny Brice. Years after she died, she was known by another name, "Funny Girl," when Barbra Streisand dramatized her early life in a successful film.

She was born Oct. 29, 1891, on Forsyth Street in New York's Lower East Side. As a child she ran away from school to play in the streets of Harlem. She begged nickels and dimes at Coney Island and sang sad songs, with real tears, for her coin-throwing crowds. She made the free lunches in her father's saloon, and on the streets she picked up the voices of European immigrants and learned to do dialect comedy.

She won an amateur night at Keeney's Theater in Brooklyn, singing *When You Know You're Not Forgotten by the Girl You Can't Forget*. Her prize was $10, and she gathered $23 in coins from the floor of the stage. She worked for George M. Cohan but was fired when Cohan learned that she couldn't dance. After singing with a road show, she appeared in New York musical revues. A struggling young songwriter, Irving Berlin, gave her a musical piece called *Sadie Salome* and suggested she sing it in Yiddish dialect at the Columbia Burlesque House, where she was working. In the audience that night was Florenz Ziegfeld, whose *Follies* were at the pinnacle of Broadway entertainment.

By 1917 she was a major *Follies* star. She had incredible range as a singer and a comic, recalled Eddie Cantor, who arrived in the *Follies* that year: Brice had the singular ability to make people laugh and cry at the same time. Her rendition of the haunting love song *My Man* was one of her trademarks. In the '20s she was singing *Secondhand Rose*, *Cooking Breakfast for the One I Love*, and *I'd Rather Be Blue over You* (than be happy with somebody else). She appeared in two plays and three films, divorced gambler Nicky Arnstein, married producer Billy Rose, and appeared in the Rose revue *Sweet and Low* in 1930.

Brice had been using her little-girl routine (originally called "Babykins") in sporadic stage routines in the '20s, and in *Sweet and Low* she introduced the character to Broadway. In 1932 she did a brief radio series, singing with George Olsen's band: one source calls this a "straight singing job," while another suggests that she may have done short comedy skits as Baby Snooks on this early program. Snooks was a definite entity by 1934, when the new Ziegfeld *Follies* opened on Broadway. Brice appeared onstage in her baby garb and brought down the house. The routine was revived for the 1936 *Follies*, with Eve Arden playing the mother figure, and in February that year it became a running part of *The Ziegfeld Follies of the Air* on CBS. Her December 1937 entry into *Good News of 1938* (which had been on the air almost two months before she arrived) gave *Snooks* its first long-running national exposure.

Fanny Brice was 46 years old. She was beginning her second career, playing the most notorious brat of the air.

Snooks had a real daddy now. Hanley Stafford won the part almost immediately. "He was perfect," Brice would recall years later; "we didn't need to hear anyone else." Stafford rivaled Gale Gordon and Hans Conried among the best stackblowers in radio, erupting at least once per show as he became the focus of all Snooks's mischief. If Daddy had insomnia, Snooks would make sure (of *course* she would) that he'd have a peaceful, quiet night. If Daddy wanted to paper a wall, Snooks would "help." If Snooks wasn't giving Daddy's suits to charity, she was making "atomic lotion" with her chemistry set. Snooks did her deeds and suffered the consequences: corporal punishment was the norm then, and listeners regularly heard Snooks getting her comeuppance across Daddy's knee.

Maxwell House Coffee Time, her first real series outside the variety show format, found her in an equal division of time with Frank "Wizard of Oz" Morgan. Morgan did tall-tales monologues, and Brice-Stafford and Company performed a quarter-hour Snooks skit. Occasionally there was crossover, as when Morgan—to his regret—decided to take Snooks to the zoo, but in the main it was like two distinct programs. Intense competition developed between Morgan and Brice: each kept trying to top the other for more than three years. The unusual pairing was an outgrowth of the *Good News* variety hour, where it had begun: Morgan and Brice had shared top billing on *Good News of 1940*, and

their routines were simply channeled into a more direct format.

When the *Maxwell House* series ended in 1944, *Snooks* moved into its own full half-hour sitcom timeslot. Snooks was the central character in the Higgins household in Sycamore Terrace. "Mommy" Higgins was now fully realized, to play against Daddy. The parents argued about everything, from Lancelot's old girlfriends to Mommy's burnt toast. Snooks played one against the other, ever finding ways to make bad situations worse. If Daddy came home with lipstick on his collar, Snooks threatened to tell. She could be bribed, of course: she was a shameless blackmailer and often a double-crosser as well, leaving the shirt, "by accident," exactly where Mommy would find it, even after she'd collected her ten-cent bribe to drop it in the wash and keep her mouth shut.

She was compared with Charlie McCarthy and with Junior, Red Skelton's "mean widdle kid." But she possessed neither the sophistication of Bergen's dummy nor the coarse meanness of Junior. Confronted, Snooks was the soul of little-girl innocence. A listener could see her, batting her eyes, looking at her feet, saying, full of remorse, "Whyyyy, Daddy. . . ."

Brice missed several episodes due to illness at the beginning of her 1945 season. Her absence was written in logically, as substitute star Eddie Cantor launched a search for Snooks. Robert Benchley, Sydney Greenstreet, Peter Lorre, and Kay Kyser joined the hunt. Snooks returned for the Oct. 7 episode, and the chaos continued anew. The most significant addition that year was the voice of Leone Ledoux as Snooks's brother Robespierre, who had existed as an off-mike character. Ledoux specialized in gibberish, playing many baby roles on the air: she had worked for Disney and done all the baby roles on *The Lux Radio Theater* for more than four years. On *Blondie*, she gave voice to Baby Dumpling and, in the words of one trade journal, "grew him into the articulate Alexander and then brought the prattling Cookie into the world."

The 1946 season sounded much the same, with Arlene Harris replacing Lois Corbet as Mommy, Ben Alexander brought in as a "utility man," and the rest of the cast continuing as before. Snooks was the constant, "the kid I used to be," Brice recalled. The role was such a natural it was "like stealing money," she told an interviewer. She was stealing, at that time, around $3,000 a week. As Snooks emerged, Brice's real personality faded. She all but abandoned her natural voice in public and was seldom seen out of character. After a performance, it could take as long as an hour for her to completely shed the Snooks characteristics. Onstage, she would mug for the microphone, jumping around in her little-girl costume and twisting her face into a broad, goofy grin. She rarely ad-libbed, but in interviews she referred to "Schnooks" almost as a living person. A new generation came of age without knowing Fanny Brice as anything other than Baby Snooks.

On May 24, 1951, she suffered a cerebral hemorrhage. She died five days later, at 59. Her show was still running strong at her death.

BACHELOR'S CHILDREN, soap opera.

BROADCAST HISTORY: 1935–36, WGN, Chicago.

Sept. 28, 1936–March 21, 1941, CBS. 15m, daily at 9:45 A.M. Old Dutch Cleanser.

March 24, 1941–Sept. 25, 1942, NBC. 15m, daily at 10:15 A.M. Colgate.

Sept. 28, 1942–Sept. 27, 1946, CBS. 15m, daily at 10:45 A.M. Wonder Bread.

CAST: Hugh Studebaker as Dr. Bob Graham, a bachelor who took in his dying friend's 18-year-old twin daughters; Art Kohl as Dr. Bob for five months in 1940, when a throat illness forced Studebaker off the air. Marjorie Hannan and Laurette Fillbrandt as Ruth Ann, the kind and gentle twin. Patricia Dunlap as her sister Janet, fiery and impulsive. Olan Soulé as Sam Ryder. Marie Nelson and Hellen Van Tuyl as Ellen Collins, the kindly housekeeper. Ginger Jones as Marjory Carroll. David Gothard as Don Carpenter. Peg Hillias as Allison Radcliffe. Dorothy Denvir as Margaret Gardner. Charles Flynn as Michael Kent. Jonathan Hole as Dr. Clifford. Arthur Van Slyke as Roy Conway. Don Thompson as Vincent Burke. Michael Romano as Clyde Fallon. Harry Elders as Frank Gardner. Chris Ford as Mr. Wilkes. Lenore Kingston and Allan Franklyn as the Carneys. ANNOUNCERS: Russ Young, Don Gordon. WRITER: Bess Flynn. SOUND EFFECTS: Ed Bailey. THEME: *Ah, Sweet Mystery of Life,* on the organ.

Dr. Bob Graham had lost his own mother as a child and was raised by his kindly house-keeper, Miss Ellen Collins. Now, 35 and still a bachelor as the story opens, Dr. Bob is visiting his best friend, Sam Ryder, when the letter arrives that will change his life. His old sergeant from the war, James Dexter, is on his deathbed. Dexter was his teacher on the responsibilities of manhood, Dr. Bob recalls, and may have saved his life as well. Graham vowed then that, should Dexter ever be in need, he (Graham) would "go all the way for him." Dexter's request: that Dr. Bob take in his soon-to-be-orphaned children.

Sam Ryder is aghast. How could Graham have made such a promise? Both men are surprised at the arrival of the "children," a matched set of lovely young ladies, identical in everything except temperament. Soon a four-way bond exists, with Sam Ryder taking to Janet first as her tormentor and later as her best friend. Dr. Bob tries to maintain an "older brother" demeanor, but it's soon evident that Ruth Ann has stronger feelings.

Among other plotlines, these unfolded: Sam falls in love with Janet; Ruth Ann falls in love with Dr. Bob. But Ruth Ann frets over the impropriety of this, and Sam hides his feelings under a cloak of banter; the girls open a tea room; the theme of unrequited love stretches its way through the '30s. Sam, teasing, makes up a name of a girl he says he really loves—Marjory Carroll. Then a real Marjory Carroll arrives, and they all become friends. Marjory, a musician, falls in love with Sam. Ruth runs away but returns when Dr. Bob gets blood poisoning and hovers for many episodes between life and death. There are many such hoverings: Ruth Ann herself was thus poised not long before with pneumonia. The staples were love, jealousy, and, always, misunderstanding.

Janet and Sam will find love after being quarantined for a month in a scarlet fever case: after years of denying him, Janet will see the light in a blinding instant when she takes a false step while hanging a picture and falls into Sam's arms. By then, Sam is engaged to Marjory Carroll. Dr. Bob will learn of Ruth Ann's love after an auto accident when, still only half-conscious, she confesses but later forgets, leading to a stretch of *Now I know but she must not know that I know* complications for Dr. Bob. Eventually they marry, but the union is haunted by a letter written by Dr. Bob long ago, denying his love. The letter, never mailed (and completely untrue), is played out for months before Ruth Ann finds it. Meanwhile, Allison Radcliffe, a beautiful patient, drives Ruth Ann to fits of jealousy. Outlaws kidnap Dr. Bob and go on a shooting spree. When Sam and Janet may finally marry after years of trouble, a new tragedy strikes: Sam's sister and her four children are left destitute, and Sam must take on their support. Bravely, Janet puts away her wedding dress.

Eventually they do marry, but it's touch and go all the way.

BACKSTAGE WIFE, soap opera.

BROADCAST HISTORY: 1935, WGN, Chicago.

Aug. 5, 1935–March 27, 1936, Mutual. 15m continuation, weekdays at 9:45 A.M. Sterling Drugs.

March 30, 1936–July 1, 1955, NBC. 15m, weekday mornings initially, then at 4:15; then, beginning in Sept. 1936, a 19-year run at 4. Sterling Drugs for Dr. Lyons Tooth Powder; Procter & Gamble as of mid-1951.

July 4, 1955–Jan. 2, 1959, CBS. 15m, weekdays at 12:15. Multiple sponsorship.

CAST: Vivian Fridell (1930s, early 1940s) and Claire Niesen as Mary Noble, a little Iowa girl who came to the big city and married into the theater. Ken Griffin, James Meighan, and Guy Sorel, over the years, as Larry Noble, Mary's husband, "matinee idol of a million other women." Betty Ruth Smith as the tempestuous Catherine Monroe. Henrietta Tedro and Ethel Wilson as kind, devoted Maud Marlowe. Frank Dane, Charles Webster, and Mandel Kramer as Tom Bryson. Helen Claire as the devious Virginia Lansing, with Andree Wallace as her sister, the charming Irene. Phil Truex as Cliff Caldwell. Anne Burr as the evil adventures Regina Rawlings. Eloise Kummer in many roles, including the calculating Marcia Mannering. Ethel Owen as Lady Clara, Larry's mother. John M. James as stage manager Arnold Carey. Alan MacAteer as the stage doorman Pop. ANNOUNCERS: Harry Clark, Ford Bond, Sandy Becker, Howard Claney, Roger Krupp. MUSIC: Chet Kingsbury on organ. PRODUCERS: Frank and Anne Hummert. DIRECTORS: Blair Walliser, Les Mitchel, Fred Weihe, Joe Mansfield, etc. WRITERS: Ned Calmer, Ruth Borden, Elizabeth Todd, etc. SOUND EFFECTS: Bob Graham, John Katulik, Frank Blatter, Ed Bailey, Michael Eisen-

menger, Tom Horan, Chet Hill. THEME: *Stay as Sweet at You Are* (1930s), *Rose of Tralee* (1940s).

There was one endless plot at the core of *Backstage Wife*: sweet Mary Noble stood in the wings as scores of Broadway glamor girls took dead aim at her sometimes fickle man. With Stella Dallas and Helen Trent, Mary was one of the most tortured creatures of the afternoon. The word "suffer" does no justice to Mary's life with Larry Noble. Mary endured.

She faced the most startling array of hussies, jezebels, and schemers ever devised in a subgenre that made an art form of such shenanigans. Add to this the common soap opera ingredients—arrogant foes in high places, misunderstandings that real people would correct in a moment, and festering resentment fueled by the refusal to communicate—then move on to the real meat of this agony of agonies: avarice, backbiting, hatred, amnesia, insanity, murder. Larry Noble may have been a "matinee idol of a million other women," but Mary too had her admirers. Most of them were psychotics, and this led *Backstage Wife* to a frantic level of melodrama touched by few other soaps in radio history.

Her marriage, according to one late-1930s fan magazine, "brought her the most complete happiness she had ever known. But soon she learned that she had to fight for her husband's love." Her rival then was Catherine Monroe, "the worst adversary Mary ever met." Listeners sent cards, hand-addressed to "Mary Noble," advising her to "watch out for Catherine Monroe." Catherine had come in the guise of a friend. She had agreed to fund Larry's return to the stage after an accident had felled him. This triangle deepened until Mary, in desperation, walked out.

She turned to Ken Paige, an artist who owned the Greenwich Theater where Larry's new play was scheduled to open. The Nobles were strapped for cash after Larry's accident, and Paige was offering a year's free rent, IF Mary would sit for a portrait, and IF the portrait won an award, and. . . . Mary agreed but did not tell Larry, who, when he found out, flew into a jealous rage. Larry was like that: he frequently bristled with jealousy.

The birth of little Larry Jr. had a calming effect, but this was confined to brief moments within the continuing chaos. "Each episode began and ended in trouble,'' wrote Erik Barnouw. ''Sunny stretches were in the middle. A Friday ending was expected to be especially gripping, to hold interest over the weekend. A serial was not conceived in terms of beginning or end; such terms had no meaning. It ended when sponsorship ended.''

Friends and enemies over the years included:

—Maud Marlowe, the character actress who befriended both Nobles and adored Larry Jr. A faithful and true companion, always ready to share their trouble and fun.

—Tom Bryson, Larry's theatrical manager. Gruff, unsentimental, wise in the ways of the world, Bryson took up writing and turned out the play *Blackout*, in which Mary was coaxed to play a starring role. Her emergence as an actress, coming at the precise moment when Larry was struggling professionally, led to a crisis-of-confidence plotline.

—Virginia Lansing, devious, unscrupulous, who did everything she could to undercut Larry's self-confidence, ''so that, consoling him, she can come to mean more to Larry than Mary does.''

—Irene, the charming young sister of Virginia Lansing, who thwarted her sister's attempts to pry Mary and Larry apart. Irene lived on Park Avenue with her sister, despite the fact that Virginia stole and married her first love.

—Cliff Cauldwell, ''handsome young actor'' in the new Tom Bryson play. Cliff loved Irene, but Virginia Lansing stood in the wings, ready to upset her sister's life again.

The characters were like paper dolls, flat and one-dimensional, bludgeoning each other with identifying names and traits. ''Well, Mary, what have you got to say for yourself?'' ''Oh, Larry!'' ''Never mind, Mary, I can see for myself what's going on.'' ''But, Larry, wait!'' The listener was never in doubt about what was being said, what was at stake, and, above all, who was speaking. Each character was given a catchphrase or a descriptive set of adjectives. Rupert Barlow became ''the unscrupulous Rupert Barlow''; Regina Rawlings ''the calculating, devious Regina Rawlings.'' This was the trademark of the husband-and-wife producing team Frank and Anne Hummert, whose shows were so heavy-handed that they were parodies of themselves.

Frank Hummert was a Chicago copywriter in the '20s. In 1930 he met Anne Ashenhurst, a former newspaperwoman who became his assistant and, five years later, his wife. The Hummerts had a formula that was surefire: appeal to the lowest common denominator, make it clear, grab the heartstrings, and reap the rewards. With writer Robert Hardy Andrews they created *The Stolen Husband*, one of radio's earliest soaps. Hummert went on to do the most notable serials of the daytime. His name was added to the agency Blackett & Sample, though he was never a partner and owned no part of it. He left Blackett-Sample-Hummert and moved to New York. His new company, Air Features, Inc., turned out (among many others) *Just Plain Bill, The Romance of Helen Trent, Ma Perkins, Our Gal Sunday, Lorenzo Jones*, and *Stella Dallas*. It was estimated that Hummert at his peak bought 12.5 percent of the entire network radio schedule, that he billed $12 million a year, that his fiction factory produced almost seven million words a season.

A factory it was, rivaling such earlier operations as Beadle & Adams (creators of Victorian-era novels by the dozens), the Stratemeyer syndicate (a powerhouse in juvenile thriller books, creators of Tom Swift, Nancy Drew, the Rover Boys, the Hardy Boys, The Bobbsey Twins, and others going strong today), and the system that enabled Alexandre Dumas to turn out more than 250 books in his lifetime. The Hummerts ''supervised writers,'' who filled in dialogue from broad, general sketches provided by Anne Hummert. As many as two dozen writers and 60 readers and assistants worked in the soap factory in New York. Writers were paid scale rates, $25 per episode: a writer who could handle two or three shows could make a fair living. The Hummerts communicated with this vast corps through detailed memoranda and by liaison. They were seldom seen outside their Greenwich, Conn., estate as their fortune grew ever larger. When they did come to New York, they had a regular table, hidden from view by a wall of ferns, at a favorite restaurant. They were not generous people—an actor could count on little overtime pay for rehearsals, and even associates of long standing got piddling gifts at Christmas—but neither were they swayed by political trends. They ignored the blacklists in the late '40s, employing writers and actors who gave them what they wanted. But, as

Mary Jane Higby remembered in her memoir *Tune In Tomorrow*, "any actor who was late to an Air Features rehearsal was in trouble."

Higby remembered the Hummerts well. "He was tall, thin, solemn-looking, and he stooped slightly. She was small, slim, cheerful-looking with light-brown hair. She wore no makeup except a light trace of lipstick. . . . She looked like a well-to-do Quaker lady." The scripts were done in lavender ink: "A radio actor could spot an Air Features script across the room," wrote Higby. The Hummerts brooked little in the way of suggestion or interference. The directors, said Higby, "were not allowed to introduce 'art' effects—unessential sound, background music— that might obscure one word of dialogue." And when Mrs. Hummert was dictating a change of direction, no one ventured an opinion. Vacation plans were shelved and work redone, and an errant remark might be met with instant dismissal.

The Hummerts perfected a soap formula that was best explained by Erik Barnouw. A series of narrative and dramatic hooks was woven into a three- or four-week main storyline. Before the main crisis was resolved, the next one was stirred in as a subplot, which was brought up to a full boil as the old story was resolved and dropped. It was the simplest kind of radio, ripe for satire: comics Bob Elliott and Ray Goulding had little to exaggerate in their *Mary Backstayge, Noble Wife* skits.

THE BAKER'S BROADCAST, a comedy-variety series, composed of three distinct radio acts, each of which existed as an entity apart from the series. Ozzie and Harriet Nelson were the linking performers through each era.

BROADCAST HISTORY: Oct. 8, 1933–June 30, 1935, Blue Network. 30m, Sundays at 7:30. Standard Brands for Fleischmann's Yeast. STAR: Joe Penner, comic.

Oct. 6, 1935–June 27, 1937, Blue Network. 30m, Sundays at 7:30. Fleischmann's Yeast. STAR: Robert "Believe It or Not" Ripley.

Oct. 3, 1937–June 26, 1938, Blue Network. 30m, Sundays at 7:30. Fleischmann's Yeast. STAR: Syndicated cartoonist Feg Murray.

The Baker's Broadcast was created for comic sensation Joe Penner. Born Jozsef Pinter (or Pinta) in a small village near Budapest in 1904,

Penner came to America around 1912, struggled to learn English, and worked his way into vaudeville in the 1920s. He often appeared in a derby hat and used a cigar as a prop. For almost a decade he toiled as a second-rate entertainer, rooted in obscurity until he hit upon a phrase in 1931 that made his fortune.

Faced with a cold audience in Birmingham, Ala., Penner ad-libbed the line "Wanna buy a duck?" The audience tittered, he recalled later, so he began to build on the gag. "Well, does your brother wanna buy a duck? . . . Well, if you *had* a brother, would he wanna buy a duck?" By then the audience was coming to life. Penner soon learned that this was no isolated accident. Soon crowds everywhere were responding to the one-liner, delivered in that unique Penner style.

He came to the attention of J. Walter Thompson, the agency handling *The Rudy Vallee Hour*, and in 1933 he was booked for a single appearance on Vallee's Thursday night NBC hour. The response was thunderous: literally overnight, Joe Penner was a national figure. He did a second Vallee show, and the agency booked him for his own regular half-hour. Ozzie and Harriet Nelson were brought in for musical hijinks, and *The Baker's Broadcast* went into the Sunday night Blue Network schedule as a new feature for Vallee's sponsor, Fleischmann's Yeast.

The ratings soared. For some reason that would be lost on later generations, Penner's silly duck joke became the American rage in the fall of 1933. By January the show was perched in fourth place at 35.2, just behind Eddie Cantor, the Maxwell House *Show Boat*, and Vallee himself. It was estimated that every word of the duck gag put $250,000 in Penner's pockets. His weekly income rose from $500-when-he-was-working to $7,000, and his duck became a better-known radio figure than most human acts on the air.

He named the duck Goo-Goo, and Mel Blanc gave it voice. Listeners sent him ducks, real and fake. Penner developed new lines that exaggerated words and reeked sarcasm. "You nah-sty man!" and "Don't ever doooo that!" and "Wo-o-oe is me!" joined the lexicon of topical catchphrases. In 1934 Penner was voted radio's outstanding comedian.

Then, as it so often happens with vast, rapid success, Penner grew unhappy. He criticized the writing on *The Baker's Broadcast* and demanded a change of format. The show was still nestled in the top ten: the agency took a "Don't argue with success" position, and Penner quit the show cold. He was out of radio for a year. By the time he returned with a new sponsor, the heat had cooled, and people were soon to find another overnight sensation, Edgar Bergen. "Joe was a terribly insecure little man who had an unfortunate knack for placing his trust in the wrong people," Ozzie Nelson wrote in his memoir. "As a result, his career was badly mishandled." By 1937 he was washed up and he knew it.

But *The Baker's Broadcast* went on. John Reber, head of radio production at J. Walter Thompson, liked the Nelsons and wanted to continue the show. Ozzie and Harriet had made great use of their exposure during the Penner days: they were young and attractive, and their music—lighthearted and melodious—was what America wanted in the Depression. Ozzie's talent was distinctive: not only was he a capable arranger and writer of novelty tunes, he also adapted the popular music of other writers to fit the Ozzie and Harriet style. It was breezy and fun, rich with '30s boy-girl frivolity. A number like *Am I Gonna Have Trouble with You?* was shot through with playful but unstated sex. He is frustrated, she seems aloof. She eats crackers in bed and is an expensive playmate. In counterpoint, she complains of his roving eye—"you're just a guy what won't behave." But in the end they agree on the main bit of business—"you're too darned sweet for me to have trouble with you." Here the Nelsons became stars. They batted lyrics back and forth in a style that had been utilized a few years earlier by Phil Harris and Leah Ray. The Nelsons owned that style by 1935.

Reber needed a new headliner, and he came up with the unlikeliest possible choice. Booked with Ozzie and Harriet for the new season was Robert Ripley and his collection of *Believe It or Not* oddities. This was just another radio job for Ripley, whose career on the air spanned two decades. He told of a "mouthless man" in China, able to talk despite having smooth unbroken skin where his mouth should be. His "armless pianist" could play concertos by hitting the keys with his chin. The world's fastest-talking woman could recite the Gettysburg Address in 26 seconds.

Ripley's dramatizations ran from merely strange to truly bizarre. Twice he had as guests men who had been executed (one by hanging, the other by firing squad) but failed to die. "The broadcasts with Ripley were interesting, challenging, often hilarious and occasionally frightening," Ozzie wrote in his memoir. Nelson remembered Ripley as a "gentle, kind person . . . painfully shy with strangers." The studio audience was a "terrible ordeal" for Ripley, so "he would usually fortify himself with a couple of drinks before the show." When he misjudged his capacity, Nelson recalled, "it was 'anything can happen' time."

Ozzie played the doubting Thomas, the devil's advocate who challenged Ripley to prove his claims. Ripley's reputation rested upon his alleged ability to back up every tale. When pressed by Ozzie, he cited authorities and witnesses chapter and verse, but in fact, wrote Ozzie, "Ed Gardner was the guy who dug up most of those *Believe It or Not* items we dramatized on the show." Gardner produced *The Baker's Broadcast* from 1935 until 1937, and "I often suspected that when Ed couldn't come up with a bona fide story, he either made one up or did a little embellishing."

Harriet continued her singing duties until she became pregnant with her first son, David. The announcer through this era was Ben Grauer. By 1937 Reber felt that the Ripley show had played itself out, but he still liked the Nelsons and proposed to continue *The Baker's Broadcast* under yet another format. The show was moved from New York to Hollywood, where it was decided to offer 30 minutes of music and backstage film-world chatter. Feg Murray hosted, and Ozzie helped with interviews. This never generated much excitement: it faded after a single season.

BAND REMOTES, live programs of popular music, heard on all networks often beginning at 11 P.M. Usually broadcast in half-hour timeslots from hotels, restaurants, ballrooms, dance halls, or Army camps, band remotes thrived in the period 1935–50.

The shows at their best were uninhibited and occasionally inspired. The musicians were loose and often happy, as free as their leaders allowed, sometimes fortified by the contents of the stainless steel hip flask. Remotes were sustained by the networks, and numbers could go on and on, unrestrained by commercial interruption or the three-minute limitations of studio recordings. Sidemen would long for the ability to capture the fire of a live performance in the studio, but it seldom happened. Only onstage, with a crowd rising to the occasion, could an Artie Shaw build a piece like *Carioca* to a feverish pitch, the powerhouse effect growing for five minutes or more; then, kicking his clarinet into a stratospheric mode, finish with an explosion that had the Blue Room patrons and the NBC announcer shouting with delight.

As early as 1921 stations were experimenting with band music over direct wires from remote locations. The first dance bands to broadcast were probably Paul Specht, Vincent Lopez, and the Coon-Sanders Nighthawks. Specht is believed by Thomas A. DeLong and others to have made the first studio broadcast of dance music, Sept. 14, 1920, on WWJ, Detroit. Lopez took his orchestra to WJZ on Nov. 27, 1921, and filled a 90-minute vacancy that had suddenly appeared on the schedule. Soon he was doing remotes from the Hotel Pennsylvania, his band becoming so identified with that location that by 1924 it had become known as the Hotel Pennsylvania Orchestra. Lopez was perhaps the best-known of the early maestros: his greeting, a simple "Lopez speaking," was the first famous catchphrase in the cradle of radio. His rivalry with Paul Whiteman and George Olsen was spirited and serious. These three bandmasters worked to secure the best talent of the time. They played what then passed for popular jazz. Whiteman defined it: his self-proclaimed moniker, "the king of jazz," would later be ridiculed and dismissed by real jazz artists, but in those first years of broadcasting it was the only exposure to such music that was available to mainstream America.

Speaking of Lopez, Erik Barnouw wrote: "It was decaffeinated jazz he sent to WJZ via Western Union lines from the Hotel Pennsylvania. A distant echo of New Orleans, yet it spoke to listeners." The '20s style was lively, rich with saxophone and violin and well-sprinkled with novelty tunes. Lopez was instantly identified by his theme, *Nola*, given a dexterous workout on the Lopez keyboard. Whiteman had Gershwin: his *Rhapsody in Blue* concert at Aeolian Hall on Feb. 12, 1924, established his reputation. And though Whiteman was slow to find his way into radio, he was a major force in band music of the

'20s. George Olsen was a master of popular music: his 1925 recording *Who* was a bestseller, followed by such period hits as *The Varsity Drag, Because My Baby Don't Mean Maybe Now*, and *Doin' the Raccoon*, a testament to the national passion for fur coats. Olsen employed a singing trio (Fran Frey, Bob Rice, and Jack Fulton) that instantly and forever stamped these novelty numbers with the flavor of the times. Also featured in Olsen's band was Rudy Wiedoeft, the best-known sax man of his day.

A thousand miles to the west, the Coon-Sanders Nighthawks had taken Kansas City by storm. There are those who believe that this was the first band of the air. It was a close call: by 1922 they were entrenched in the Muehlebach Hotel doing popular jazz on WDAF. The leaders, drummer Carleton Coon and pianist Joe Sanders, had met in a music store and formed their group in 1918. They sang duets through megaphones: hot, roaring numbers, and Sanders's bubbly greeting—"Howdja do, howdja do, you big ole raddio pooblic"—gave further evidence of the unstilting of America. The nation charged into the new era with music that had never been heard outside small bistros and smoky Harlem speakeasies. Radio was bringing these locations into thousands of homes, making such obscure regional groups as the Coon-Sanders Nighthawks national celebrities. Listeners with crystal sets were picking up WDAF from afar, and interest in the band spread well beyond the Midwest. Coon-Sanders took on road engagements: they were among the first bands to do one-night stands, engagements that were soon engrained in big band life. In 1924 they were playing the Congress Hotel in Chicago: two years later they were at the Blackhawk Restaurant, sharing the bandstand with Ted Weems and Wayne King and carried on the air via WGN. They were still going strong in 1932 when Coon became ill and died.

Quite a counterpoint they offered to Wayne King (soon dubbed "the Waltz King" for the kind of music he favored) and Ted Weems (whose style was always popular and safe). Weems and King were favorites at Chicago's Aragon and Trianon ballrooms: King had a long stint at the Aragon in the late '20s, broadcasting on KYW. The so-called jazz age was on the wane. Jean Goldkette had broken up his important group, a band that George Simon would remember 40 years later as "marvelous . . . full of spirit, musical kicks and such brilliant musicians as Bix Beiderbecke, Jimmy and Tommy Dorsey, Joe Venuti and Eddie Lang, Frankie Trumbauer, Pee Wee Russell, Russ Morgan, Don Murray, and many others." There were still exciting groups on the horizon: Ben Pollack, Isham Jones, Red Nichols, and Ted "Is Ev-rybody Happy?" Lewis provided an early training ground for many of the stars of the swing era, which was just around the corner. Fletcher Henderson, Louis Armstrong, Earl "Fatha" Hines, Jimmie Lunceford, and Chick Webb had started or were soon to start bands in the mid- to late 1920s, and Duke Ellington was already one of the most respected names in the industry. But the tide of American taste, thus the lion's share of radio air time, went to more traditional people.

By 1926 the technology was much advanced. There were still glitches, but remote broadcasting had made giant strides since the wing-and-a-prayer days of 1921. For NBC's grand opening on Nov. 15, 1926, the network was able to pull in the bands of George Olsen, Vincent Lopez, Ben Bernie, B. A. Rolfe, and Fred Waring from various locations. All were then nationally known. Bernie had been on the air intermittently in 1923. He was actually a "front man," a showman whose success was rooted more in personal charm than musicianship. His trademarks were the glib tongue, the cigar, and the nonsense phrase, widely imitated, "yowsah, yowsah, yowsah." Waring was also a showman, though less flamboyant than Bernie. Waring's career would span decades: his band, the Pennsylvanians, came of age in the '20s and was still viable in the '70s, long after most of his contemporaries had disbanded, retired, or died. His first broadcast is said to have been on WWJ, Detroit, in the early '20s, but it was for his elaborate musical shows that he was best known.

And then there were Irving Aaronson and his Commanders, Al Donahue, George Hall, Horace Heidt, Kay Kyser, and Will Osborne. The day of the sweet band had arrived. Guy Lombardo moved his orchestra down from Canada: his Royal Canadians developed (and never lost, over a span of five decades) a sound that was unique. Rich and mellow, it was copied but never duplicated. His first New Year's broadcast aired on WBBM, Chicago, in 1927. His theme song, *Auld Lang Syne*, was already a traditional year-ender,

and soon Lombardo became known as "the man who invented New Year's Eve."

What the public seemed to want above all else was melody. Clyde McCoy struck gold with *Sugar Blues* in 1928; Sammy Kaye was soon swinging and (primarily) swaying and announcing his numbers with singing song titles. Gimmicks were in. Shep Fields blew bubbles at the microphone and called it "Rippling Rhythm." These extraneous trappings caught attention and were temporarily popular, but they did nothing to enhance the music. It was a time of Hal Kemp, Jan Garber, and Freddy Martin. Ted Fio Rito had a stand of five years in Chicago; Gus Arnheim was a regular at the Ambassador Hotel in Los Angeles. Remotes of the late '20s and early '30s could be stuffy affairs, announced in wordy superlatives and near-perfect diction.

Themes were vital. A soft saxophone arrangement of *When My Baby Smiles at Me* made the masses think of only one leader. "Need we tell you, ladies and gentlemen, that this melody heralds the approach to the microphone of that high-hatted tragedian of song, Ted Lewis." Announcers now reached for that extra word, the colorful turn of phrase that burned up adjectives while saying nothing. "Isham Jones requests your listening attention," the announcer would say. The bands came elegantly wrapped, like an invitation to the White House. Formality had invaded the late hours on Radio Row. In a way it reflected the mood of the country, but on another level the reverse was true. These were hard times: the illusion of refinement was a strong lure to listeners in Wichita and Minneapolis. But there was a nervous energy that was yet untapped, a musical search for something new.

When it came, it came literally overnight.

Benny Goodman had had a long career for a young man of 26 years. His training ground was the mid-1920s band scenes in Chicago and Los Angeles. He had been playing clarinet for 16 years: his professional career had begun at age 11. He had been with Ben Pollack, Isham Jones, Red Nichols, and Ted Lewis, among others, and had formed his first band in 1934. Now, in mid-1935, the group seemed stagnated. Goodman had not been able to capitalize on a stroke of good luck that had landed him a regular NBC air job on a Saturday night music show, *Let's Dance*. First heard Dec. 1, 1934, this series aired at 10:30 in the East and spanned three full hours.

It was sponsored (National Biscuit Company) and ran six months, ending May 25, 1935. It featured three regular bands. Goodman found his group sandwiched between the Latin jazz of Xavier Cugat and the saccharine sounds of Kel Murray (real name Murray Kellner). The instant comparison, said George Simon, made Goodman's sound "downright thrilling."

Goodman had hired Fletcher Henderson to arrange his book. When *Let's Dance* went off the air, he had more than 70 choice swing charts in his pocket. He also had the men who could play them: drummer Gene Krupa, trumpets Pee Wee Erwin, Ralph Muzzillo, and Jerry Neary; trombones Red Ballard and Joe Harris; saxes Toots Mondello, Hymie Shertzer, Art Rollini, and Dick Clark; and pianist Jess Stacy. His singer was Helen Ward, warmly remembered by big band enthusiasts as one of the best. But the band was still largely unknown. Goodman opened at the Roosevelt Hotel, and the blast sent the Lombardo-primed patrons and staff into near-shock. He was fired on opening night. A long road trip followed. The band headed west for an August date at the Palomar, playing to small crowds in places like Jackson, Mich., and Columbus, Ohio. Bunny Berigan joined up on the road, but the reception remained lukewarm until, in July, the band reached Denver.

They were playing at Elitch's Gardens, an engagement that historian Simon would remember as "horrendous." Goodman described it simply: "the most humiliating experience of my life." The dancers at Elitch's wanted waltzes and fox trots. Many demanded refunds. To make matters worse, Kay Kyser was playing to packed houses at Lakeside Ballroom, a few blocks away. It was a striking contrast, sax man Shertzer told writer Mort Goode years later: Kyser was wowing his crowds with "hokum music" and funny hats while Goodman was dying with what was, at that moment, perhaps the best band in the nation.

But momentum picked up in Oakland. The fans had been primed—Goodman records were getting good West Coast air play, and the Oakland date was a boost for everyone. They drove into Los Angeles for the Aug. 21 date at the Palomar. This was the night swing was born: it was the watershed, critics would agree, that would change music for the next 15 years.

It began slowly. Goodman was still gun-shy from his Denver experience, and his opening numbers were conservative. At some point it was decided to kick the program into high gear. One story has it that Gene Krupa came over to Goodman and said, "If we're gonna die, let's die playing our thing." Goodman put into the third set some of the powerhouse Henderson swing arrangements. As Shertzer described it to Goode: "When Berigan stood up and blew *Sometimes I'm Happy* and *King Porter Stomp*, the place exploded."

Goodman was crowned "king of swing." His subsequent engagements at Chicago's Congress Hotel and New York's Paramount Theater were wild hits. Jitterbugs danced in the aisles at the Paramount, and Goodman—aided by red-hot radio lines almost everywhere he played—became a household word. With Krupa and black pianist Teddy Wilson (Goodman was the first major leader to cross the "color line" and hire black musicians) he formed a trio. In 1936, when Lionel Hampton was added on vibes, it became the Benny Goodman Quartet. The band played the Madhattan Room of the Hotel Pennsylvania: CBS was there in October 1936. Ziggy Elman and Harry James joined up; Helen Ward left, and in time Martha Tilton was signed as the regular singer. Goodman was at the vanguard of a musical wave that grew larger by the week. "For ten years," one old swing fan would lovingly recall decades later, "our music and the public taste were in complete agreement."

The key ingredient was radio. Careers were established in days, after years of struggle. Glenn Miller had formed his orchestra in 1937 but had no notable success until an engagement at the Glen Island Casino brought him to the NBC microphone. Soon he was doing eight or ten broadcasts a week. By 1940 he had signed with Chesterfield for a quarter-hour nightly run on CBS. This priceless exposure booted his career at a record pace until his was the nation's top orchestra. Tommy Dorsey, who came out of the same '20s bands that produced Goodman and Miller, developed a distinctive smoothness but could swing, almost with the best of them. Artie Shaw had a good date at the Hotel Lincoln in the fall of 1938, and his fans came along through NBC. Tony Pastor, Hank Freeman, George Arus, Harry Rodgers, Chuck Peterson, Johnny Best, Buddy Rich, and singer Helen Forrest gave Shaw a happy, exciting sound.

That all these leaders were temperamental and

difficult mattered little to the fans who loved them. Goodman was called "an ornery SOB" by more than one sideman. His icy stare, "the Goodman ray," was usually a prelude to termination. Miller was considered cold and distant. His demeanor kept his men at bay and uneasy. Dorsey could be openly combative. Some stories had it that he and his brother Jimmy sometimes settled disputes with fists in the old days of the Dorsey Brothers band. And Artie Shaw had serious bouts of nervous depression, walking out on his great 1939 band and escaping to Mexico.

Hundreds of bands were now at work across the land. Catchphrases and one-liners—some poking fun at the sweet "mickey mouse" bands—were heavy on the air. Listeners could "swing and sweat with Charlie Barnet" (whose group was described as the blackest-sounding white band of its day). The music of 52nd Street in New York was becoming known by way of radio. Club names—Onyx, Samoa, Three Deuces, Downbeat—were as familiar in Chicago and St. Louis as on the street that housed them. Through band remotes and on such series as *The Saturday Night Swing Club* (CBS, 1936–39) and *Young Man with a Band* (CBS, 1939–40) listeners came to know Jack Teagarden, Wingy Manone, Fats Waller, Coleman Hawkins, Hot Lips Page, and Louis Prima. The nightspots themselves, because of radio, took on exalted and exotic qualities in the minds of faraway listeners who would never see them. "The beautiful Cafe Rouge" opened in the Hotel Pennsylvania in 1937, an elegant contrast to the hotel's smaller, more intimate Madhattan Room. The Glen Island Casino was billed as "the mecca of music for moderns." Management needed no primer in economics to know that an NBC wire was as good for its business as it was for the bands that played there. Fans from coast to coast knew that the Glen Island Casino was "just off the shore road at New Rochelle, New York." Frank Dailey's Meadowbrook, where Tommy Dorsey, Frank Sinatra, and the Pied Pipers were featured in early 1940, was "located on Route 23, the Newark-Pompton Turnpike, at Cedar Grove, New Jersey."

And though there were far fewer radio opportunities for black bands than for their white counterparts, it was through remote broadcasts from the Cotton Club that the general public first heard of Duke Ellington and Cab Calloway. Earl Hines had become a radio favorite during a long stand at the Grand Terrace in Chicago in the mid-1930s. And it was on a radio broadcast from the Reno Club in Kansas City that Count (William) Basie was discovered by jazz critic John Hammond, who helped launch Basie's career.

Business was booming as the new decade came. In the ten years between Benny Goodman–Palomar and the end of the war, listeners heard the following among at least 50,000 remotes broadcast on the four national networks. On CBS: Bob Crosby from the Hotel New Yorker; Tommy Dorsey from the Blue Room of the Hotel Lincoln; Artie Shaw at the Silver Grill, Hotel Lexington; Red Norvo at the Hotel Pennsylvania; Sammy Kaye at the Palm Room, Commodore Hotel, New York; Harry James at Roseland. On NBC: Chick Webb and Ella Fitzgerald from the Savoy Ballroom in Harlem; Andy Kirk and his Clouds of Joy from the Savoy; Gene Krupa at the Steel Pier, Atlantic City; Larry Clinton at Glen Island Casino; Jimmie Lunceford at Southland, Boston; Jan Savitt at the Hotel Lincoln; Will Bradley at the Famous Door; Les Brown (with a young Doris Day on vocals), Glen Island Casino; Stan Kenton at the Casino in Balboa Beach, Calif.; Lionel Hampton and Lena Horne at the Savoy. On Mutual: Woody Herman and Count Basie at Roseland; Duke Ellington at the Cotton Club; Horace Heidt on the Moonlit Terrace, Hotel Biltmore; Cab Calloway from Club Zanzibar. The scene was rich and alive: to those who lived through it, as spectator or performer, the time of their lives, never to return.

Then, in 1942, a disastrous strike against the record companies disrupted the industry and upset the delicate balance of business. Though it hit directly at record producers, the real target was radio. James C. Petrillo, president of the American Federation of Musicians, was alarmed at the rapid proliferation of disc jockeys. He objected to the free use of recorded music on the air, charging that jocks had cost musicians their jobs at hundreds of radio stations. Petrillo wanted to impose fees at the source, the big companies like RCA and Columbia, where the records were produced. The final agreement, which was not accepted by the two biggest companies until 1944, created a union-supervised fund for indigent and aging musicians. Historian Erik Barnouw found this a "not unreasonable approach to a serious problem,'' though Petrillo's move was ''generally pictured by the broadcasting trade press as an act of gangsterism.'' The damage caused by the strike was incalculable. With the long silence in the record stores, the fickle public switched its interest to singers and vocal groups.

The bands continued to swing on the air. All through the two strike years the nights were filled with marvelous remotes and exciting live performances. The war brought in such shows as Coca-Cola's *Victory Parade of Spotlight Bands*, thought by many the final word in band remotes. Heard on various networks in nightly half-hours from 1941–46, *Spotlight* traveled to Army camps, hospitals, naval installations, and war-worker factories. The bands were hot and the boys were loud: even the commercials for Coke had a snappy patriotic flavor. ''As Charlie Spivak signs his musical signature in Coca-Cola's guest register, it's been night number 731 for the *Victory Parade of Spotlight Bands*,'' said the announcer, ''and we've marched 896,415 *Spotlight* miles.''

The end of the war marked the end of the bands. Glenn Miller had been lost over the English Channel in 1944. Artie Shaw had disbanded and regrouped and disbanded again. Though name leaders like Goodman and Basie and Harry James would always find work, the financial base eroded and the labor troubles lingered. When Petrillo called a second strike in 1948, the die was cast. Perhaps, as Barnouw said, the cause was just and the problem serious, but in the end the strikes hurt no one more than the union's own membership. As Pogo put it, ''We have met the enemy, and he is us.''

Roll Call

Major bands or band shows with regular time-slots on network radio.

ABC DANCING PARTY, Aug. 18, 1951–April 7, 1956, ABC. Saturday nights, various personnel and times.

ABE LYMAN, middle-of-road, his programs filled with old standards. According to George Simon, Lyman was uncomfortable as a leader, and his radio shows were often led by Jacques Renard or Victor Arden.

Sept. 1, 1931–Sept. 1, 1934, CBS. Various days and times for Sterling Drugs.

1936, Blue Network. 30m, Mondays at 8:30.

AL DONAHUE, violinist, arranger, leader of a popular ''society band.''

June 2–Oct. 5, 1937, NBC. Various days. Radio City's Rainbow Room.

May 15–Oct. 2, 1939, NBC. 30m, Mondays at 10:30.

ARTIE SHAW, one of the best swing outfits ever, led by an eccentric genius who couldn't stomach the harsh light of fame. Marvelous line checks exist of individual remotes, often from the Blue Room of the Hotel Lincoln. But Shaw had only one regular series of note.

Nov. 20, 1938–Nov. 14, 1939, CBS. 30m, Sundays at 10. Old Gold.

BANDSTAND USA, 1949–59, Mutual. 30m, variously Fridays, Saturdays, Sundays. Another poststrike dance party.

BENNY GOODMAN, innovative hot swing, at the cutting edge of popular music. Countless remotes between 1935–48, eagerly sought. Regular slots:

Dec. 1, 1934–May 25, 1935, NBC. 3 hours, Saturdays at 10:30. *Let's Dance*. National Biscuit Company.

June 30, 1936–June 20, 1939, CBS. 30m, Tuesdays at 9:30. *The Camel Caravan*, also titled *Benny Goodman's Swing School*. Camel Cigarettes.

July 8, 1939–Jan. 6, 1940, NBC. 30m, Saturdays at 10.

Feb. 10–May 5, 1941, Blue Network. 30m, Mondays at 7:30. *What's New*. Old Gold Cigarettes.

July 17–Aug. 28, 1941, NBC. 30m, Thursdays at 8. *Housewarming Time*. Holland Furnace.

Jan. 10–Feb. 21, 1942, Mutual. 30m, Saturdays at 2.

July 17–Aug. 14, 1943, CBS. 30m, Saturdays at 7:30.

July 3–Sept. 25, 1945, NBC. 30m, Tuesdays at 9:30. Paired with Danish comic Victor Borge as summer replacement for *Fibber McGee and Molly*. Johnson's Wax.

July 1–Sept. 2, 1946, NBC. 30m, Mondays at 9:30. *Music Festival*.

Sept. 9, 1946–June 30, 1947, NBC. 30m, Mondays at 9:30. Continuation of *Music Festival* timeslot with Victor Borge. *Victor Borge Show*.

BLUE BARRON ORCHESTRA, April 26–July 12, 1941, Blue Network. 30m, Saturdays/Sundays at 6.

CAB CALLOWAY, a showman who popularized the ballad *Minnie the Moocher* and took for his trademark the catchphrase "Heigh-de-ho."
July 6–Oct. 5, 1941, Mutual. 30m, Sundays at 9:30. Musical quiz from Harlem.
Feb. 18–June 24, 1942, Blue Network. 30m, Wednesdays at 9:30.

CARMEN CAVALLARO, "the poet of the piano;" popular, danceable music with his piano as the centerpiece.
Jan. 10–April 4, 1942, Blue Network. 30m, Saturdays at 10:30.
Dec. 16, 1945–Sept. 7, 1947, NBC. 30m, Sundays at 3. *The Sheaffer Parade.* Sheaffer Pens.
June 29–Sept. 21, 1948, NBC. 30m, Tuesdays at 8:30. Summer replacement for *A Date with Judy.* Tums.

CHARLIE SPIVAK, trumpet man with a gorgeous open-horn sound. Sweet style.
Nov. 12, 1940–March 8, 1941, NBC. 30m, daily at 6.
1952–53, CBS. 15m, Fridays/Saturdays at 10:45.

CHUCK FOSTER, "music in the Foster fashion," a full array of sweet arrangements, singing song titles, music by rote. A leader since the 1930s, his style was well-suited to the nostalgia of the 1950s. Regular runs, 1954–56, CBS. Various times.

DAVID ROSE, mainly a studio band (music for Red Skelton). Also:
April 11–Aug. 1, 1940, Mutual. 30m, Thursdays at 9. With pianist Art Tatum.
May 7, 1941–Feb. 4, 1942, Mutual. 30m, Wednesdays at 9:30.
June 26–Sept. 18, 1947, NBC. 30m, Thursdays at 10:30. Summer replacement for *The Eddie Cantor Show.* Pabst Beer.
Aug. 27–Sept. 24, 1950, CBS. 30m, Sundays at 8:30. Summer replacement for *The Red Skelton Show.* Tide.

DESI ARNAZ, primarily remembered for *I Love Lucy* on TV. One season on *The Bob Hope Show* and one brief run in his own name.
Jan. 21–Oct. 6, 1951, CBS. 30m, Sundays at 3:30, then Saturdays at 7.

DICK JURGENS, July 2–Sept. 24, 1948, CBS. 30m, Fridays at 10:30. *Summer Spotlight Revue.* Coca-Cola.

THE DORSEY BROTHERS, a good concept that seldom works—a single great band under two sometimes brilliant and often fiery leaders. Tommy and Jimmy Dorsey formed their first band as teenagers in 1922. They worked together in many big bands of the 1920s—the California Ramblers, Jean Goldkette, Paul Whiteman—and revived the Dorsey Brothers concept around 1927. It lasted until 1935, marked by frequent squabbles and sometimes fistfights. At the core of it were deep differences in musical taste: Jimmy liked an even balance of reeds and brass; Tommy wanted a heavier brass section. Tommy went on to great success as a sweet-and-swing trombonist; Jimmy to a hot-and-cold career on clarinet and saxophone. Both were first-rate musicians. They regrouped late in their careers for one final try as coleaders, and radio carried much of it. They died in 1956 and 1957, six months apart.
1953–55, CBS. 30m, twice a week at 10:30. *Those Fabulous Dorseys,* also *The Tommy Dorsey Orchestra Starring Jimmy Dorsey.*

DUKE ELLINGTON, who led what many jazz experts consider the most important band of the day, though sadly lacking in regular air time.
May 5–July 22, 1943, Mutual. 15m, various days at 10:15.
May 16–Sept. 19, 1943, Mutual. 30m, Sundays at 7.
March 31, 1945–Sept. 21, 1946, ABC. Variously 15 to 60m, Saturdays at 5 until Jan., returned Saturdays at 4 in April. *A Date with the Duke.* Singer Mel Tormé had these performances airchecked and issued most of the music on LPs in 1974. But the editing was poor and the sound just fair. Full transcriptions unearthed since then give a much better accounting of this great orchestra.

EDDY DUCHIN, pianist, a popular personality who peaked in the 1930s.
Jan. 2–June 23, 1934, Blue Network. 30m, three a week at 9:30. Pepsodent and Pepso Junis.
Nov. 5, 1936–Jan. 28, 1937, NBC. 30m, Thursdays at 4. Cadillac Motor Car Company for La-Salle.
Sept. 29–Dec. 22, 1937, Blue Network. 30m, Wednesdays at 8. Elizabeth Arden.
Sept. 24–Dec. 17, 1937, NBC. 30m, Fridays at 7:30. Koppers Coke.

Dec. 28, 1937–March 22, 1938, Mutual. 30m, Tuesdays at 10. Elizabeth Arden.

Sept. 5, 1938–May 29, 1939, NBC. 30m, Mondays at 9:30. Pall Mall Cigarettes.

Oct. 8, 1938–Feb. 1, 1941, CBS. 30m, Saturdays at 5:30; sporadic run.

Sept. 16–Nov. 25, 1940, Mutual. 30m, Mondays at 9:30.

July 14–Oct. 6, 1947, ABC. 15m, three a week at 4:30. *A Date with Duchin.* Kremel Shampoo.

EDDY HOWARD, a sweet band built around the leader's vocals on such numbers as *To Each His Own* and *Careless,* his theme.

Sept. 14, 1947–Sept. 5, 1948, NBC. 30m, Sundays at 3. *The Sheaffer Parade.* Sheaffer Pens.

1952–53, CBS. 15m, Thursdays at 10:45.

1955–56, CBS. 30m, Tuesdays at 10.

FRED WARING: See THE FRED WARING SHOW.

FRANKIE CARLE, pianist.

July 10–Oct. 9, 1946, ABC. 30m, Wednesdays at 9:30.

May 9–July 11, 1948, CBS. 30m, Sundays at 5:30.

FREDDY MARTIN, maestro of the sweet school; trained with Guy Lombardo, an experience that influenced his entire career.

Jan. 16–Sept. 29, 1933, CBS. 15m, three a week at 7:30. Tydol Oil.

Dec. 13, 1936–March 21, 1937, NBC. 30m, Sundays at 4. International Silver.

Feb. 9–Oct. 12, 1942, CBS. 30m, Mondays at 10. Lady Esther.

July 4–Sept. 5, 1942, NBC. 30m, Saturdays at 8:30. Substitute for *Truth or Consequences.* Duz.

April–May 1943, NBC. 15m, Saturdays at 10:15.

July 8–Nov. 4, 1956, CBS. 30m, Sundays at 12:30.

GEORGE OLSEN, popular novelty and dance band of the 1920s and 1930s.

1934–35, Blue Network. 30m, Saturdays at 8:30.

1939–40, Blue Network. 30m, Fridays at 10:30. Sohio Oil.

GLEN GRAY AND HIS CASA LOMA ORCHESTRA, one of the prime movers in the early swing era. Casa Loma was actually an incorporated business;

sax man Gray was the front, but the members themselves were the owners. It featured "sophisticated swing," with complicated charts requiring long rehearsals. A favorite of college students of the early 1930s. In 1933–34 Gray played Glen Island Casino in the summer and New York's Essex House in the winter. Aided by frequent CBS remote lines, the band soon had a regular sponsored network timeslot.

Dec. 7, 1933–June 25, 1936, CBS. 30m, Tuesdays and Thursdays at 10, later at 9. *The Camel Caravan.* Camel Cigarettes.

Jan. 2–July 17, 1943, Mutual. 60m, Saturdays at 5, later 45m at 5:15.

GLENN MILLER, the epitome of big bands, a group that burst on the scene in 1938, reached the heights, and spent its primary career in five years. Miller was a trombonist, unable to match the technical ability of Tommy Dorsey or the creativity of Jack Teagarden. But he was a superb arranger who knew what he wanted and how to find the men who could produce that esteemed sound. Miller disappeared over the English Channel in December 1944. Later editions of the Glenn Miller band were led by Ray McKinley, Buddy De Franco, and Tex Beneke. Like the airchecks of Benny Goodman, Miller programs have been issued on LP records, often with dubious results.

Dec. 27, 1939–Sept. 24, 1942, CBS. Mostly 15m, three times a week (Tuesday-Wednesday-Thursday) at 10. *Chesterfield Time,* also known as *Moonlight Serenade.* Miller replaced the Paul Whiteman Orchestra, running in the Wednesday half-hour for one week before moving to the shorter, more frequent format. Featured performers were the Andrews Sisters, themselves arriving at a crest of popularity. Regular singers: Marion Hutton, Ray Eberle. Announcer Paul Douglas extolled the virtues of "the cigarette that satisfies" in a long series of memorable commercials. Here Miller initiated his famous medley—"something old, something new, something borrowed, something blue."

Aug. 30, 1941–May 30, 1942, Blue Network. 60m, Saturdays at 5. Mutual Network as of Jan. 10. *Sunset Serenade.*

July 10, 1943–June 10, 1944, CBS (30m, Saturdays at 2) until Sept. 1943, then NBC (Saturdays at 11:30). *I Sustain the Wings,* featuring Miller's huge Army Air Force Band. The series continued after Miller left, running until Nov. 24, 1945.

GUY LOMBARDO, "the sweetest music this side of heaven," long associated with New York's Roosevelt Hotel, but heard for virtually the entire span of network radio. Lombardo formed his first band in Canada as a youth. In 1924 he came to the United States, where he believed fame and fortune could be achieved through the new medium, radio. His early broadcasts were in Cleveland and Chicago. Always prominent on his programs were members of his family—brothers Carmen, Lebert, and Victor, and sister Rose Marie, who sang.

December 25, 1928, first network broadcast, CBS, beginning a year of 60m shows, Tuesdays at 11. Wrigley's Gum. Wendell Hall, "the red-headed music-maker," was featured vocalist. Lombardo also began his New Year's broadcasts in 1928 from WBBM, the CBS affiliate in Chicago.

1929–34, CBS. 30m, Mondays at 10 until 1932, then Wednesdays at 9:30. George Burns and Gracie Allen, comics. Robert Burns Cigars.

July 11, 1934–July 3, 1935, NBC. 30m, Wednesdays at 10. Plough.

July 8, 1935–June 29, 1936, CBS. 30m, Mondays at 8. Esso.

1936–37, Mutual. 30m, Thursdays at 8:30.

Sept. 6, 1936–Aug. 14, 1938, CBS. 30m, Sundays at 5:30. Bond Bread.

Oct. 10, 1938–July 28, 1941, CBS. 30m, Mondays at 10. Lady Esther.

1938–40, NBC. 30m, Fridays at 10. Lady Esther.

Nov. 20, 1940–April 23, 1941, Mutual. 30m, Wednesdays at 9:30.

Aug. 2, 1941–July 11, 1942, CBS. 30m, Saturdays at 8. Colgate.

March 8–Dec. 20, 1943, CBS. 90m, Mondays at 10:30. Ogden Nash, resident wit. Ballantine.

Jan. 16, 1944–March 26, 1946, Blue/ABC. 30m, various days and times. *Musical Autographs*. Chelsea.

July 3–Sept. 11, 1949, NBC. 30m, Sundays at 7:30. Summer substitute for *The Phil Harris/Alice Faye Show*.

Oct. 30, 1948–May 19, 1957, Mutual. 30m, Saturday or Sunday nights. *Lombardoland USA*.

Nov. 27, 1955–July 1, 1956, CBS. 30m, Sundays at 12:30.

HAL KEMP, by most accounts an engaging sweet band with several regular radio slots before the death of its leader in an automobile accident in December 1940. Kemp could play almost every instrument but favored the saxophone. Notable Kemp sidemen Skinnay Ennis and John Scott Trotter later led their own radio bands, for the Bob Hope and Bing Crosby shows respectively.

April 3–July 24, 1935, Blue Network. 30m, Wednesdays at 8:30. Joined *Penthouse Party*, in progress. Eno Salt.

August 1936, NBC. 30m, Wednesdays at 8:30. Substitute for Wayne King. Lady Esther.

Jan. 1–Dec. 24, 1937, CBS. 30m, Fridays at 8:30. *Music from Hollywood*, with singers Alice Faye, Bob Allen, and Maxine Gray and comic vocalist Saxie Dowell. Phil Cohan, producer; Carlton KaDell, announcer. Chesterfield Cigarettes.

April 19–Oct. 11, 1938, and May 2–Oct. 24, 1939, CBS. 30m, Tuesdays at 10. Griffin Shoe Polish.

HAL MCINTYRE, a veteran of the Glenn Miller band who, according to George Simon, played music more in the Duke Ellington mode.

Jan. 16, 1943–Jan. 8, 1944, Mutual. 30m, Saturdays at 2.

Jan. 2–Jan. 30, 1945, ABC. 30m, Tuesdays at 10:30. Eversharp.

HARRY JAMES, as energetic and dynamic as any orchestra of the period. James joined Benny Goodman in 1937 and quickly became a thrilling force on trumpet. His first band, bankrolled with a loan from Goodman, failed to click, so he shifted the emphasis from hot swing to a sweeter sound and found success. His recording *You Made Me Love You* sold a million and made him a household name in 1942. His appearances at the Paramount Theater in New York were mobbed by jitterbugs, who danced in the aisles and even invaded the stage. His hot numbers too were in sudden demand: his playing was described by one critic as "aphrodisiacal."

Sept. 29, 1942–March 24, 1944, CBS. 15m, Tuesdays-Wednesdays-Thursdays at 7:15, with an 11:15 repeat. *Chesterfield Time* for the departing Glenn Miller. A fine 28-piece orchestra with a solid string section, vocalists Helen Forrest and Johnny McAfee, and "tenor sax wizard" Corky Corcoran.

June 8–Sept. 21, 1945, CBS. 30m, Fridays at 10:30. Substitute for *The Danny Kaye Show*, on which James was regular maestro. His theme was *Ciribiribin*. Featured vocalists were Kitty Kallen and Buddy Devito. Pabst Beer.

HARRY RESER, Dec. 9, 1934–June 2, 1935, NBC. 15m, Sundays at 4:30. Wrigley's Gum.

HENRY BUSSE, a novelty band featuring Busse's muted trumpet, well defined in his theme, *Hot Lips*.
Sept. 9, 1936–Nov. 28, 1937, NBC. 30m, Wednesdays at 4, then Sundays at 11:45 A.M. Maro-Oil.

ISHAM JONES, a sweet band full of rich melody; a launching pad for many major talents (first name pronounced "Eye-sham").
Oct. 9, 1934–April 2, 1935, CBS. 30m, Tuesdays at 9:30. Vocals by Tito Guizar. Chevrolet.
Jan.–March 1936, Mutual. 30m, Sundays at 6.

JACK HYLTON, British bandmaster of the smooth school. He arrived in the United States in 1935, but his British musicians were not allowed to play because of problems with the American Federation of Musicians. Hylton formed a new band, composed of Americans.
Oct. 13, 1935–June 28, 1936, CBS. 30m, Sundays at 10:30. Standard Oil.

JAN GARBER, diverse and enduring. His career ran from World War I well into the 1970s; his many sounds ranged from hot swing to sweet and low. But his regular radio stints were few and far between.
1933–34, Blue Network. 30m, Sundays at 3:30. *The Yeast Foamers*.
1934–35, Blue Network. 30m, Mondays at 8. *Jan Garber Supper Club*. Northwest Yeast.
1935–36, Mutual. 30m, Sundays at 6:30.
1954–56, CBS. 30m, Saturdays at 4 until 1955, then at 3:30.

JEAN GOLDKETTE, a trailblazing unit, filled with major performers at early stages of their careers.
1929–31, NBC. 30m, Sundays at 10:15. *The Studebaker Champions* for the car manufacturer. Goldkette disbanded in 1931, at the height of his fame. *Champions* resumed in 1934 with Richard Himber and a much different sound indeed.

JIMMY DORSEY, led by the older half of the Dorsey Brothers band. This good swing band had few reg-

ular air opportunities after a single season, 1936, on Bing Crosby's *Kraft Music Hall*.
Feb. 3–March 10, 1939, Mutual. 30m, Fridays at 8:30.
May–Oct. 1939, Blue Network. 30m, Sundays at 4:15, 5, or 5:15.
June 14–Aug. 2, 1940, Blue Network. 30m, Fridays at 7:30.

JOE REICHMAN, "the Pagliacci of the piano," an eccentric leader who played while standing. It was not uncommon, according to Leo Walker (*Big Band Almanac*) "to see him pitch a piano stool onto the dance floor" in a fit of temper. "He insisted that radio announcers bring him on the air by drawing out 'Joe' to 'J-o-o-o-e' in a manner supposedly achieved by an announcer one night when he was fighting the urge to sneeze." Commercial, midroad.
1954–55, CBS. 30m, Fridays at 10:30. Remotes from ca. 1940 on.

KAY KYSER, the master of novelty orchestration. See also KAY KYSER'S KOLLEGE OF MUSICAL KNOWLEDGE.
May–July 1937, Mutual. 30m, Sundays at 10. Willys.

THE KING COLE TRIO, a black jazz combo composed of Nat King Cole, piano; Oscar Moore, guitar; and Wesley Prince, bass. Reportedly the first black unit to gain sponsorship on network radio.
Oct. 26, 1946–April 10, 1948, NBC. 15m, Saturdays at 5:45. Wildroot.

LARRY CLINTON, a fine swing band with vocals by Bea Wain.
July 3, 1939–June 24, 1940, NBC. 30m, Mondays at 6:30, then at 7:30. *Larry Clinton's Musical Sensations*.

LAWRENCE WELK, the pinnacle of mickey mouse units, a saccharine polka group, heavy of accordion and much lampooned in the wake of great television success. Welk's career as a bandleader began in 1925 in South Dakota. He first appeared on radio there, at WNAX, Yankton, in 1927. For the next decade he played in near-total obscurity. By the mid-1930s, his band had gone through several sweeping changes, arriving at the "champagne music" style that he would play for the rest of his life.

June 1, 1949–March 28, 1951, ABC. 30m, Wednesdays at 9:30, then at 10. *The High-Life Review*. Miller Beer. This format continued, unsponsored, in various timeslots until Nov. 16, 1957.

LEO REISMAN, a top society band through the entire 1930s.

1931–33, NBC. 30m, Fridays at 9:30. With Eleanor Roosevelt, 1932–33. Ponds Cream.

1934–37, NBC. 30m, Tuesdays at 8. Philip Morris.

1937–38, NBC. 30m, Thursdays at 7:30. *The Sheaffer Revue*. With host Bud Collyer and baritone Ray Heatherton. Sheaffer Pens.

LET'S DANCE, Dec. 1, 1934–June 8, 1935, NBC. 3 hours, Saturdays at 10:30. Three orchestras: Benny Goodman, Xavier Cugat, Kel Murray. National Biscuit Company.

LYN MURRAY, a studio orchestra; regular series for two seasons.

Oct. 11, 1943–March 23, 1945, CBS. 15m, three a week at 6:15. *To Your Good Health*. House of Squibb.

MORTON GOULD, another studio band.

Dec. 6, 1936–Oct. 6, 1942, Mutual. Many timeslots briefly held, seldom more than a few months.

NAT SHILKRET, still another studio band, prominent in the earliest days of the networks.

1931–32, CBS. 15m, five a week at 10:30. *The Chesterfield Quarter Hour*, with Alexander Gray.

1933–34, CBS. 30m, Sundays at 8. *Songs You Love*. Smith Brothers.

Jan. 7–March 25, 1934, Blue Network. 15m, Sundays at 9:45. Bourjois.

1934–35, NBC. 30m, Saturdays at 9. *Songs You Love*. Smith Brothers.

PAUL WHITEMAN, the self-styled "king of jazz," the biggest name in band music in the 1920s. Whiteman focused on stage appearances and used radio sporadically in its earliest years, then made up for lost time.

Feb. 5, 1929–May 6, 1930, CBS. 60m, Tuesdays at 9. *The Old Gold Hour*.

Jan. 27, 1931–July 1, 1932, Blue Network. 30m, Tuesdays at 8, then Fridays at 10. Allied Paints (1931), Pontiac (1932).

July 8, 1932–March 27, 1933, NBC. 30m, Fri-

days at 10, then Mondays at 9:30. Pontiac (to Sept.), then Buick.

June 26, 1933–Nov. 28, 1935, NBC. 60m, Thursdays at 10. *The Kraft Music Hall*, often with Al Jolson.

Jan. 5–Dec. 27, 1936, Blue Network. 45m, Sundays variously at 9, 9:15, and 9:45. *Paul Whiteman's Musical Varieties*. Woodbury Soap. With Bob Lawrence, Johnny Hauser, Morton Downey, Durelle Alexander, songs by the King's Men, and announcer Roy Bargy. The show featured a children's amateur contest. Near the end of the run Whiteman introduced comedienne Judy Canova, who inherited timeslot and sponsor in the Woodbury *Rippling Rhythm Revue*.

Dec. 31, 1937–Dec. 20, 1939, CBS. 30m, Fridays at 8:30 until mid-July 1938, then Wednesdays at 8:30. *Chesterfield Time*, with Joan Edwards, Deems Taylor (musical commentary), and announcer Paul Douglas. Whiteman took over the slot vacated by Hal Kemp and two years later vacated it for the sensational new Glenn Miller orchestra.

Nov. 9–Dec. 28, 1939, Mutual. 30m, Thursdays at 9:30.

June 6–Aug. 29, 1943, NBC. 30m, Sundays at 8. *Paul Whiteman Presents*. Summer substitute for Edgar Bergen. Chase and Sanborn.

Dec. 5, 1943–April 28, 1946, Blue/ABC. 60m, Sundays at 6. *Paul Whiteman's Radio Hall of Fame*. Philco.

Sept. 5–Nov. 14, 1944, Blue Network. 30m, Tuesdays at 11:30. Music of current American composers.

Jan. 21–Sept. 23, 1946, ABC. 30m, Mondays at 9:30. *Forever Tops*.

Sept. 29–Oct. 27, 1946, ABC. 60m, Sundays at 8. *The Paul Whiteman Hour*. Extended until Nov. 17, 1947, as a 30m show, *The Paul Whiteman Program*, various days and times.

June 30, 1947–June 25, 1948, ABC. 60m, five a week at 3:30. *The Paul Whiteman Record Program*. Glorified disc-jockeyism.

Sept. 29, 1947–May 23, 1948, ABC. 30m, Mondays at 8, then at 9 after Oct. *On Stage America*, for the National Guard. Whiteman's orchestra with John Slagle, George Fenneman, etc. Producer: Roland Martini. Director: Joe Graham. Writer: Ira Marion.

June 27–Nov. 7, 1950, ABC. 30m, Tuesdays at 8. *Paul Whiteman Presents*.

Oct. 29, 1951–April 28, 1953, ABC. Various

times. *Paul Whiteman's Teen Club*. An amateur hour with the accent on youth.

Feb. 4–Oct. 20, 1954, ABC. 30m, Thursdays at 9 until July, then Wednesdays at 9:30. *Paul Whiteman Varieties*.

PERCY FAITH, primarily remembered for the theme from the film *A Summer Place*, but active in bands since the 1930s.

Oct. 5, 1938–April 24, 1940, Mutual. 30m, Wednesdays at 9:30.

1941–42, NBC. 30m, Mondays at 10. *The Carnation Contented Hour*.

1948–49, CBS. 30m, Fridays at 10:30. *The Pause That Refreshes on the Air*. With Jane Froman. Coca-Cola.

PHIL HARRIS, a light novelty band of the early 1930s, featuring vocalist Leah Ray in bouncy duets with Harris.

June 23, 1933–Dec. 14, 1934, Blue Network. 30m, Fridays at 9. Cutex.

RALPH FLANAGAN, a strong Glenn Miller copy: post-band-era nostalgia.

Jan.–July 1951, ABC. 30m, Mondays at 10.

1954–55, ABC, 30m, Thursdays at 9:30; CBS, 30m, Mondays at 10.

RAY ANTHONY, more Glenn Miller echoes.

1951–52, CBS. 30m, Fridays at 10:30.

RAY KINNEY, interpreter of Hawaiian rhythm; Alfred Apaka, vocalist. May 14, 1938–Sept. 29, 1941, Blue Network. Sporadic, briefly held timeslots; various days.

RAY NOBLE, a notable sweet band full of soon-to-be stars, among them trombonists Glenn Miller and Will Bradley. Noble was a British maestro who arrived in 1934.

Feb.–Oct. 1935, NBC. 30m, Wednesdays at 10:30. Coty Cosmetics.

1935–36, CBS. 30m, Wednesdays at 9:30. Coca-Cola.

RAYMOND SCOTT, a swing group that came to prominence in 1939.

Jan. 9, 1940–Dec. 24, 1944, CBS. Many brief stands, various days.

RICHARD HIMBER, a highly popular 1930s band, specializing in easy listening. Himber quickly assembled his orchestra to fill an air date he had cajoled out of NBC in 1932. He was on the air,

often daily, from the Essex House and later from the Ritz-Carlton Hotel. The NBC lines brought him to national prominence and led him to commercial work.

Aug. 1933, NBC. 30m, Saturdays at 7:30. *The Pure Oil Hour*, with Eddie Peabody.

Jan. 7–Feb. 11, 1934, NBC. 30m, Sundays at 3:30. *The Spartan Hour*, with Frances Langford. Spartan Radios.

June 13, 1934–June 26, 1936, CBS. Various days and times. *The Studebaker Champions*, a series resurrected by Studebaker from the Jean Goldkette days. Also on NBC Monday nights July 9, 1934–June 24, 1935, and June 29, 1936–May 31, 1937.

RUSS COLUMBO, a singer of the early 1930s who fronted an orchestra and was considered Bing Crosby's strongest rival until his death in a 1934 gunshot accident.

1931–32, Blue Network. 15m, three a week at 10.

1932–33, Blue Network. 15m, twice a week at 6:15.

RUSS MORGAN, master of the "wah-wah" trombone and leader of a soft, melodious group from 1935 on.

Feb. 13, 1937–Jan. 21, 1939, CBS. 30m, Saturdays at 8:30. Often as *Johnny Presents*. Philip Morris. Also: NBC, 30m, Tuesdays at 8.

SAMMY KAYE, the foremost example of mickey mouse music, wrote George Simon: "where the phrase came from I don't know, except perhaps that the music sounded as manufactured and mechanical as Walt Disney's famous character—and projected just about as much depth!" Kaye was on the networks for two decades, bringing all the usual sweet-music gimmicks (singing song titles, etc.). His slogan was "Swing and sway with Sammy Kaye."

1937–39, Mutual. Many brief timeslots.

Jan. 1–June 24, 1940, NBC. 30m, Mondays at 7:30. *Sensation and Swing*. Sensation Cigarettes.

1941–44, both NBC networks. Various slots.

Jan. 27, 1943–March 29, 1944, CBS. 30m, Wednesdays at 8. *The Old Gold Program*, with sportscaster Red Barber and later comic Monty Woolley.

Jan. 2–April 30, 1944, Blue Network. 30m, Sundays at 1:30. *Sunday Serenade*, a title used extensively by Kaye beginning with this date.

May 7, 1944–Aug. 26, 1945, shows on two networks for Tangee: ABC, 30m, Sundays at 1:30; Mutual, 30m, Thursdays at 8:30 (Aug.–Feb.).

Nov. 18, 1945–Jan. 25, 1948, ABC. 30m, Sundays at 1:30. Rayve Shampoo and Richard Hudnut.

Jan. 23, 1946–May 31, 1948, ABC. Various 30m timeslots. See also SO YOU WANT TO LEAD A BAND.

1949–50, CBS. 30m, Sundays at 1:30. Treasury Department.

1952–53, NBC. 30m, Sundays at noon.

1953–54, Mutual. 30m, Sundays at 2:30.

Jan. 6, 1947–Feb. 12, 1956, ABC. Many shows. 1951–52, 30m. Sundays at 5. Sylvania. 1953–54, *Sammy Kaye's Cameo Room*, 15m, five a week at 8:15. 1954–55, 25m, four a week at 9. 1955–56, 20m, Sundays at 9:35.

THE SATURDAY NIGHT SWING CLUB, a weekly jam session by America's best practitioners of hot jazz.

June 13, 1936–April 1, 1939, CBS. 30m, Saturdays at 8. Bunny Berigan, Red Nichols, Benny Goodman, Red Norvo, Tommy Dorsey, Duke Ellington, Jack Teagarden, and Fats Waller were a few of the jazz greats who appeared on this major series. The program was anchored by a house orchestra under the direction of CBS staff conductor Leith Stevens; in it were such players as bassist Lou Shoobe, guitarist Dick McDonough, trombonist Jack Jenney, pianist Walter Gross, and hot drummer Billy Gussak. The stars were often content to sit in with the band, though usually they were featured in freewheeling solos. Improvisation was the order of the day: a number might unexpectedly turn into a hot race between pianist Gross and drummer Gussak. Phil Cohan, Ed Cashman, creators; Al Rinker, Bob Smith, producers; Paul Douglas, Mel Allen, Ted Husing, announcers. Hormel Packing.

SHEP FIELDS, purveyor of "rippling rhythm," music to bubble accompaniment.

Jan. 3–Sept. 26, 1937, Blue Network. 30m, Sundays at 9:15. *The Rippling Rhythm Revue* with tenor Frank Parker and comics Judy Canova and, later, Bob Hope. Woodbury Soap.

1942, Mutual. 30m, Sundays at 10.

1943–44, Mutual. 30m, Saturdays at 4.

STAN KENTON, proponent of "progressive jazz."

1952–53, NBC. Various times. *Concert in Miniature*, some of the most unusual big band sounds

ever played. Kenton's music was praised and damned, and his *Concerts* were usually offered in the summer months.

TED FIO RITO, longtime leader of sweet music.

1935–36, Mutual. 30m, Saturdays at 8:30.

June–Sept. 1936, Blue Network. 30m, Fridays at 9:30. *Frigidaire Frolics*.

1938–40, Mutual. 30m, Mondays at 8.

TED WEEMS, a band made famous by one song, *Heartaches*, which was recorded by Weems three times and was a hit for two generations. The orchestra featured the whistling of Elmo Tanner and, in the late 1930s, the vocals of Marvel (Marilyn) Maxwell and Perry Como.

1933–34, Blue Network. 30m, Sundays at 7.

April 12, 1936–Nov. 28, 1937, Mutual. 30m, Sundays at 1:30, then at 2:30. Varady of Vienna.

TOMMY DORSEY ORCHESTRA, one of the smoothest outfits on the air, highlighted by the "sentimental gentleman of swing" on trombone. Vocalists included Jack Leonard and Edythe Wright and, by 1940, Frank Sinatra, Jo Stafford, and the Pied Pipers. The band was perhaps the scene's most versatile, capable of switching immediately from *Beale Street Blues* to the *Andante cantabile* from Tchaikovsky's Fifth Symphony.

May 1936, CBS. 30m, Sundays at 7.

Aug. 4–25, 1936, CBS. 30m, Tuesdays at 9. Replacing Fred Waring. Ford Motors.

Nov. 9, 1936–Sept. 20, 1939, NBC. See THE RALEIGH-KOOL PROGRAM.

June 1–Nov. 30, 1940, NBC. 55m, Saturdays at 5.

June 25–Sept. 17, 1940, NBC. 30m, Tuesdays at 10. Substitute for *The Bob Hope Show*. Pepsodent.

Oct. 17, 1940–April 10, 1941, Blue Network. 30m, Thursdays at 8:30. *Fame and Fortune*, a musical quiz with Sinatra, Connie Haines, and the Pied Pipers. Nature's Remedy.

March 8–July 5, 1942, Blue Network. 30m, Sundays at 8.

June 16–Sept. 8, 1942, NBC. 30m, Tuesdays at 10:30. Substitute for *The Red Skelton Show*. Raleigh Cigarettes.

Sept. 16, 1942–Sept. 8, 1943, NBC. 30m, Wednesdays at 8:30. Raleigh Cigarettes.

June 3–Sept. 30, 1945, NBC. 30m, Sundays at 8:30. Standard Brands.

July 22–Nov. 25, 1945, NBC. 30m, Sundays at 4:30. RCA.

March 20–Aug. 7, 1946, Mutual. 30m, Wednesdays at 10. *Endorsed By Dorsey.*

May 17–Sept. 30, 1946, Mutual. 30m, Fridays, then Mondays at 10. *Tommy Dorsey's Playshop.*

Aug. 30–Oct. 18, 1946, Mutual. 30m, Fridays at 8:30.

July 7–Sept. 29, 1946, NBC. 30m, Sundays at 8:30. *The Tommy Dorsey Show.* Substituting for Fred Allen. Tenderleaf Tea. A solid half-hour of postwar swing, with Charlie Shavers, Ziggy Elman, and Wendell Niles, announcer.

THE VICTORY PARADE OF SPOTLIGHT BANDS, a late-night wartime remote series, following the best-loved bands in the nation to the scenes of domestic war production: to camps and hospitals, to plants and factories. *The Victory Parade* was billed as the show "for the men and women on the victory march . . . wherever they are—Maine, Florida, California, or Oregon—we bring them the music they like best by the bands they like most." A different band was heard each night with the top band of the week determined by record sales and slotted in the coveted Saturday spotlight. The first week's lineup was composed of Kay Kyser, Guy Lombardo, Sammy Kaye, Tommy Dorsey, and Eddy Duchin. More than 1,200 shows were aired, covering every type of popular music. The shows had a rousing sound, the servicemen and war workers providing a vigorous cheering section. Each week a tabulation was given as to the number of shows done and the miles traveled on "the victory march." Also known simply as *Spotlight Bands*, the key word for the sponsor was "spotlight"; it was a Coca-Cola trademark, used constantly in the company's radio advertising.

Nov. 3, 1941–May 2, 1942, Mutual. 15m, five a week at 10:15, with the top band of the week heard Saturday night in a 30m finale. Coca-Cola.

Sept. 21, 1942–June 16, 1945, Blue Network. 30m, weeknights and some Saturdays at 9:30. Coca-Cola.

June 18, 1945–Nov. 22, 1946, Mutual. 30m, three a week at 9:30. Coca-Cola.

VINCENT LOPEZ, one of the original bands of the air, first heard on WJZ in 1921 and active throughout the prenetwork era.

Sept.–Nov. 1928, CBS. Wednesdays at 10. Kolster Radios.

Feb.–June 1933, Blue Network. 30m, Sundays at 10:15.

1934, CBS. Tuesdays at midnight.

1941–43, Blue Network. 30m, twice a week at 2.

1943–46, Mutual. 30m, four to six a week at 1:30.

1949–56, Mutual. 30m, five a week, usually at 1 or 1:30. *Luncheon with Lopez.*

1950–51, NBC. 30m, Saturdays at 12:30.

1951–56, ABC. 30m, Saturdays at 1:30.

WAYNE KING, "the waltz king," offering flowing dance music for the older crowd. Estimated to play more classics than any other two or three bands combined.

July 29, 1930–Jan. 27, 1931, NBC. 30m, Tuesdays at 8. Pure Oil.

Sept. 27, 1931–Jan. 26, 1940, NBC, CBS. Long runs with overlapping dates and various timeslots for Lady Esther cosmetics. King helped establish this struggling cosmetics company and made it one of radio's most potent advertisers.

Oct. 21, 1939–Jan. 25, 1941, CBS. 30m, Saturdays at 8:30. Colgate-Palmolive for Halo Shampoo, etc.

June 7, 1941–March 21, 1942, CBS. 30m, Saturdays at 7:30. Luxor.

June 3–Sept. 23, 1945, NBC. 30m, Sundays at 7. Substitute for *The Jack Benny Program.* Lucky Strike.

June 14–Sept. 6, 1946, CBS. 30m, Fridays at 9:30. Substitute for *The Jimmy Durante Show.* Rexall.

1947, Ziv syndication, 78 quarter-hour shows released.

WOODY HERMAN, a swinging outfit by almost any standard during the 1940s; prior to that his was known as "the band that plays the blues." Herman divided his swing bands into "herds": his "First Herd" rode in 1944–45. His radio opportunities were largely confined to remotes, with a few exceptions.

March 26–April 30, 1942, Mutual. 30m, Thursdays at 8:30.

1944, CBS. Summer series, 30m, Wednesdays at 8. Old Gold Cigarettes.

Oct. 13, 1945–July 5, 1946, ABC. 30m, Saturdays at 8, then Fridays at 8. *The Woody Herman Show.* Wildroot Cream Oil. Singer Frances Wayne and bassist Chubby Jackson got billing; Herman was billed as "the man behind the voice and the clarinet."

    July 13–Aug. 31, 1947, CBS. 30m, Sundays at 4:30.

    1955–56, CBS. 25m, Saturdays at 10:05.

XAVIER CUGAT, rhumbas and other music with a Latin beat.

    1933–35, NBC. 15m, five a week at 6.

    1940–41, NBC. 30m, Thursdays at 7:30.

    Jan. 9, 1941–July 7, 1942, NBC. 30m, Thursdays at 7:30 until Jan. 1942, then Blue Network, Tuesdays at 8. *Xavier Cugat's Rhumba Revue.* Camel Cigarettes.

    July 10, 1942–March 19, 1943, CBS. 30m, Fridays at 10. *The Camel Caravan.* Camel Cigarettes.

    Sept. 4–Nov. 27, 1943, Blue Network. 30m, Saturdays at 11 A.M. Dubonnet.

    Dec. 1, 1943–July 26, 1944, Mutual. 30m, Wednesdays at 8:30. Dubonnet.

    Aug. 3–Sept. 7, 1947, CBS. 30m, Sundays at 10. Eversharp.

    July 7–Sept. 22, 1948, ABC. 30m, Wednesdays at 8.

THE BARON AND THE BEE, quiz show with a spelling bee motif.

BROADCAST HISTORY: July 21, 1953–Jan. 16, 1954, NBC. 30m, Tuesdays at 9 until Sept., then Saturdays at 7, Nov.–Jan. **CAST:** Jack Pearl as Baron Munchhausen, teller of tall tales. Cliff Hall as Sharlie.

The Baron and the Bee was a comedy quiz in which teams of contestants competed for cash prizes in spelling bees conducted by one of radio's most outrageous characters. Jack Pearl had created radio's Baron Munchhausen in the early '30s, inspired by the real hunter, soldier, and yarnspinner of 18th-century Germany. Pearl's routine consisted of heavy dialect, peppered with verbal explosions when his straight man, Cliff Hall, refused to believe his exploits. But his classic punch line, "Vass you dere, Sharlie?" was virtually his entire act, and his spelling bee spelled the end of a career that had had such a sensational beginning, in 1932.

BARRIE CRAIG, CONFIDENTIAL INVESTIGATOR, detective drama.

BROADCAST HISTORY: Oct. 3, 1951–June 30, 1955, NBC. 30m, various times. Brief periods of sponsorship by Lewis-Howe (1952), Knomark, and Coleman (both 1953) but mostly sustained. Broadcast from New York 1951–54; from Hollywood 1954–55. **CAST:** William Gargan as Barrie Craig, private eye. Ralph Bell as Lt. Travis Rogers (ca. 1951–53). Also (from New York): Elspeth Eric, Parker Fennelly, Santos Ortega, Arnold Moss, etc. (from Hollywood): Betty Lou Gerson, Jack Moyles, Barney Phillips, Parley Baer, Virginia Gregg, Vivi Janiss, etc. **DIRECTORS:** Himan Brown (New York); Arthur Jacobson, Andrew C. Love (Hollywood). **WRITERS:** Louis Vittes, John Roeburt.

Barrie Craig operated out of a Madison Avenue office, worked alone, and seldom rose above B-grade detective fare. For William Gargan, who had originated the better-known Martin Kane character, it was an interesting bit of typecasting. As a young man he had worked in a real detective office and had once confessed amusement at the blunders of radio detectives.

BARRY CAMERON, soap opera.

BROADCAST HISTORY: April 16, 1945–Oct. 11, 1946, NBC. 15m continuation, weekdays at 11:30 A.M. Sweetheart Soap.

CAST: Spencer Bentley as Barry Cameron, a veteran returning from three years of war. Florence Williams as his wife Anna. Doris Rich as Vinnie, the maid. **ANNOUNCER:** Larry Elliott. **PRODUCER:** Duane Jones agency. **WRITERS:** Richard Leonard and Peggy Blake.

The original title of this serial was *The Soldier Who Came Home,* which was changed about three months into the show.

THE BARTONS, serial drama.

BROADCAST HISTORY: Dec. 25, 1939–Oct. 31, 1941, Blue Network. 15m continuation, weekdays at 5:30.

    Nov. 3, 1941–Sept. 11, 1942, NBC. 15m, weekdays at 11:30 A.M., later at 5:45. Duz.

CAST: Dick Holland as Bud Barton. Bill Bouchey and Les Damon as Henry "Pa" Barton. Fern Persons as Ma Barton. Kathryn Card as Grandma Barton. Jane Webb as Midge. Cliff Soubier as Police Chief Herman Branch. Ed Prentiss and Don Kraatz as Col. Francis Welch. Fred Sullivan as Judge Summerfield. **DIRECTOR:** Frank Papp. **WRITER:** Harlan Ware.

The Bartons began as a comedy serial for young people in the late afternoon, underwent several changes of title (*Those Bartons, The Story of Bud Barton, Bud Barton*), and, after its first two seasons, became part of the soap opera schedule.

BATTLE OF THE SEXES, quiz with a staunch male-female competition.

BROADCAST HISTORY: Sept. 20, 1938–Feb. 2, 1944, NBC. 30m Red Network, Tuesdays at 9 until Aug. 31, 1943, then Wednesdays at 8:30. Blue Network, Molle Shave Cream (Red), Energine (Blue).
HOSTS: Frank Crumit and Julia Sanderson, a husband-wife team, popular from the first years of network radio. **EMCEES:** Jay C. Flippen and Walter O'Keefe (after Crumit and Sanderson left in July 1942).

This series was "designed to prove once and for all" whether men or women were smarter. Crumit headed the male team; Sanderson was the female general. Each questioned the other, Sanderson interrogating the men while Crumit marshaled his forces and awaited his turn. The questions were prepared by editors from *Quiz Digest* magazine.

In 1942 the format changed. Flippen and O'Keefe were hosts, and men from the Armed Forces were thrown into battle against female war workers and women from USOs and canteens. It was spirited, but if it ever proved which sex is smarter, the evidence has remained hidden.

BEAT THE BAND, musical quiz.

BROADCAST HISTORY: Jan. 28, 1940–Feb. 23, 1941, NBC. 30m, Sundays at 6:30. Kix Cereal.
CAST: Garry Moore, master of ceremonies, with the 14-piece Ted Weems Orchestra, including Elmo ("the Whistling Troubador") Tanner, "Country" Washburne, comedic sax man Red Ingle, Orm Downes, Rosy McHargue, and vocalists Parker Gibbs, Marvel Maxwell, and Perry Como.
June 15, 1943–Sept. 6, 1944, NBC. 30m, beginning as a summer replacement for *The Red Skelton Show,* Tuesdays at 10:30 until Sept. 1943; then Wednesdays at 8:30. Raleigh Cigarettes until June 1944. **CAST:** "The Incomparable Hildegarde" (Hildegarde Loretta Sell), hostess until June 1944;

then Eddie Mayehoff, host. **ANNOUNCERS:** Marvin Miller, Tom Shirley, Fort Pearson. **MUSIC:** Harry Sosnik's band.

The two runs of *Beat the Band* were similar in title only. Originally aired from Chicago, it came on the heels of Horace Heidt's popular *Pot o' Gold* and offered a scaled-down quiz with cornpone roots. Questions were solicited from listeners and read to the band by a highly energetic Garry Moore. Listeners got $10 for submitting usable material; those who "beat the band" got at least $20 and a case of Kix cereal. The questions were usually posed as riddles. (Q: What song title tells you what Cinderella might have said if she awoke one morning and found that her foot had grown too large for the glass slipper? A: *Where, Oh Where Has My Little Dog Gone?*) Musicians who missed their answers had to "feed the kitty" by tossing half-dollars onto a big bass drum, a sound that came over the air like popcorn in a land of giants. The singer or player who scored the most points took home the kitty. Elmo Tanner added a distinctive touch with whistling interludes, Perry Como was on the verge of a major career, and Marvel Maxwell offered an almost innocent and shy counterpoint in her answers. The band mugged to the rafters. Never again would Garry Moore sound this young and pumped-up.

The 1943 revival was broadcast from New York. Listeners won $25 and a carton of Raleighs for sending in questions: for beating the band, the jackpot was $50. Packs of Raleighs were thrown on the bass drum and sent to servicemen in the war effort. *Radio Life* found the performance of femcee Hildegarde charming, feminine, and alluring: she joined wholeheartedly in the gags, laughed loudly, and shouted boisterously to the boys in the band. Her catchphrase, "Give me a little traveling music, Harry," was filched by Jackie Gleason and recycled for the first TV generation.

BEATRICE FAIRFAX, love drama and advice to the lovelorn.

BROADCAST HISTORY: March 10–June 30, 1934, NBC. 30m, Saturdays at 9:30. General Foods.
May 1936, CBS. 15m, Fridays.
Aug. 31, 1937–Feb. 25, 1938, Mutual. 15m, four a week at 2:45. Silver Dust.

Fairfax was a love-advice newspaper columnist: her shows usually offered two love dramas and a gamut of "heartthrob" problems each week.

THE BEATRICE LILLIE SHOW, musical variety, heard under several titles, all with the Toronto-born Lillie as centerpiece.

BROADCAST HISTORY: Jan. 4–June 28, 1935, NBC, Blue Network, then Red. 15m, Fridays at 9. Borden Milk. Lillie was backed by the Cavaliers Quartet and the music of Lee Perrin.

Feb. 7–May 22, 1936, CBS. 30m, Fridays at 8. *The Flying Red Horse Tavern.* Socony Oil. Walter Woolf King, master of ceremonies; Lennie Hayton Orchestra; vocals by "the Tavern Singers."

Jan. 6–July 28, 1937, Blue Network. 30m, Wednesdays at 8. *Broadway Merry-Go-Round.* Dr. Lyons Tooth Powder. Music by Al Rickey.

BEHIND THE FRONT PAGE and **A BRIGHTER TOMORROW,** dramas.

BROADCAST HISTORY: Oct. 13, 1946–Aug. 31, 1947, Mutual. 30m, Sundays at 10, 8:30 from July 20. *A Brighter Tomorrow,* also known as *The Gabriel Heatter Show.* Mutual of Omaha.

Sept. 7, 1947–July 25, 1948, Mutual. 30m, Sundays at 10: *Behind the Front Page,* a veritable continuation of *A Brighter Tomorrow* under a new title. Mutual of Omaha. Continued as *Gabriel Heatter Comments,* Sundays at 7:30, until Dec. 19, 1948.

CAST: Gabriel Heatter, host and narrator. **ANNOUNCER:** Cy Harrice. **MUSIC:** Charles Paul on organ. **DIRECTOR:** Ted Corday.

These series, though of different titles, were the same in almost every way. As *A Brighter Tomorrow,* stories had conflict but upbeat endings. Heatter put himself on the periphery of the action, as part of the audience, and at the end wrapped it up with a barrage of cheery and optimistic homilies: count your blessings, there's opportunity in this great land for everyone.

The change to *Behind the Front Page* seemed greater than it was. Now purporting to tell the stories behind the newspaper headlines, it was in fact the same show, with the same sponsor and, for much of the run, the same timeslot. Heatter now capitalized on his reputation as "America's ace commentator," rooting out the human tales

of people "behind the front page." He narrated in his usual husky style, telling tales of "love, hate, jealousy, and fear," but each proving in the end that every cloud had a silver lining.

BEHIND THE MIKE, interviews with radio people.

BROADCAST HISTORY: 1931–32, CBS. 15m, Mondays at 9:15. Frostilla.

Sept. 15, 1940–April 19, 1942, Blue Network. 30m, Sundays at 4:30. Continued until June 7, 1942, under new titles *This Is the Truth,* then *Nothing but the Truth.*

CAST (1940–42): Graham McNamee, host; also, Ben Grauer. **ANNOUNCER:** Gilbert Martin. **MUSIC:** Ernie Watson, Jimmy Lytell. **WRITER:** Mort Lewis.

Little is known of the first *Behind the Mike,* of 1931. The 1940 series was billed as "radio's own show, the stories behind your favorite programs, favorite personalities, and the radio people you never hear of." Guests included Lee De Forest, whose inventions of the audion and the "wireless telephone" made radio possible, and Walter Compton, who told of heartwarming listener response to the plight of an unfortunate on his *Double or Nothing* series. Graham McNamee told of announcer fluffs, revealed "what happens when a daytime serial needs firing up," described a "sound effect of the week," and read letters from listeners.

BELIEVE IT OR NOT, drama of freaks and strange facts, with Robert L. Ripley.

BROADCAST HISTORY: April 14, 1930–Jan. 26, 1931, NBC. 30m, Mondays at 7:30. Colonial Beacon Oil Company.

May 20, 1931–June 3, 1932, Blue Network. 15m, Wednesdays and Fridays at 7:15. Standard Oil, Esso.

Jan. 6–March 24, 1934, NBC. 60m, Saturday at 10. Joined the series *Saturday Party.* Hudson Motor Car Company. **ANNOUNCER:** Curt Patterson. **VOCALIST:** Linda Lee. **MUSIC:** B. A. Rolfe.

Oct. 6, 1935–June 27, 1937, Blue Network. 30m, Sundays at 7:30. *The Baker's Broadcast.* Fleischmann's Yeast. **VOCALISTS:** Ozzie and Harriet Nelson. **DIRECTOR:** Ed Gardner.

July 16, 1937–Oct. 3, 1938, NBC. 30m, Blue Network, Fridays at 9 until Oct. 1937; then Red

Network, Saturdays at 8 until April 1938, then Tuesdays at 10 until July, then Mondays at 8. General Foods. ANNOUNCERS: Ben Grauer, Graham McNamee. ORCHESTRA: B. A. Rolfe.

March 31, 1939–Dec. 6, 1940, CBS. 30m, Fridays at 10:30, then at 10. Subtitled *See America First with Bob Ripley.* Royal Crown Cola for Nehi. VOCALIST: Linda Lee. DIRECTOR: Herbert Sanford.

Jan. 17–July 25, 1942, Blue Network. 30m, Saturdays at 10. A tribute to Latin America under the subtitle "See All the Americas," with rhumba and samba music by the (Al) D'Artega orchestra, and overall musical direction by B. A. Rolfe.

Jan. 18–April 14, 1944, Mutual. 15m, five a week at 9:15. Pall Mall Cigarettes.

April 12–Oct. 4, 1945, CBS. 30m, Thursdays at 10:30. *Romance, Rhythm, and Ripley.* Bourjois.

May 12, 1947–Sept. 3, 1948, NBC. 15m, five a week, at 1:15. "Pages from Robert L. Ripley's Radio Scrapbook." ANNOUNCER: Bill Griffis. NARRATOR: Gregory Abbott, "the dean of newsreel commentators." DIRECTOR: Walter McGraw. WRITER: George Lefferts. STAR: Robert L. Ripley, the newspaper cartoonist who made a career out of chronicling the unusual. CREATOR-PRODUCER: Douglas F. Storer. DIRECTORS: Ed King, Eddie Dunham, etc.

Believe It or Not and radio were made for each other. The series adapted to any format and timeslot and proved itself time and again to be among the air's most durable concepts. In 1940 *Radio Guide* described Ripley's as "consistently the most interesting and thrilling program on the air."

"Never did so miscast a performer score so sweeping a success," wrote Ripley's biographer Bob Considine. Burdened by the twin handicaps of shyness and a stutter, Ripley rose above both and held the audience for two decades. He guaranteed the truth of his stories but was not above fudging his "authentication" for dramatic impact.

Ripley claimed Christmas as his birthday, but Considine said he was actually born Dec. 26, 1893. He added the name Robert to his real name, LeRoy, when he was about 20 years old. His career in journalism dates from around 1909, when he was hired as a cartoonist for the *San Francisco Bulletin.* In 1918 he began drawing a panel of sports oddities. Soon he was considered

a specialist on bizarre happenings, and in 1929 Simon & Schuster published his most startling cartoons in a book. He moved to King Features Syndicate, where within a year his income reached $100,000. Within a few years, his *Believe It or Not* enterprises extended to radio, movies, and vaudeville. He employed researchers, secretaries, and technical assistants. Nine people kept busy at King Features answering his mail.

Considine, who in preparing his biography had access to early transcriptions not generally available, describes Ripley's first radio shows as "mumbling, fumbling, stumbling . . . compounded of simple mike fright and gross ineptitude. The script shook in Ripley's hands. It fell to the floor, and in retrieving it, he almost [sent] the microphone hurtling into the audience."

His radio debut was nonetheless compelling. Invited to the Blue Network's *Collier Hour* in 1930, he opened with his "Marching Chinese" assertion. If all the Chinese marched four abreast past a given point, Ripley said, they'd never finish passing. This was widely disputed, but Ripley achieved such infinity with simple math: if U.S. Army marching regulations were followed, 26,280,000 Chinese would pass each year, but given a birth rate of 10 percent and figuring that half the children would die in infancy, there would still be 30 million new marchers each year. People were intrigued: not only did Ripley deal with nature's freaks, he was clever with everyday facts as well. Considine believed it impossible that Ripley could sit down to a steak dinner without calculating how many steaks were in the average steer and going on from there.

The response to his *Collier Hour* show was so strong that, on April 14, he was inserted into a Monday night NBC slot for his first regular series. This was very simple radio, as was his two-a-week 1931 show for Esso. He just told some of his adventures in travel, Considine said, and related "some of the weirder items from his voluminous *Believe It or Not* files." But his broadcasting career underwent vast improvement in 1933, when he was added to B. A. Rolfe's Saturday night variety program. Douglas F. Storer, producer of the Rolfe show, had caught Ripley's early broadcasts. Storer was able to see past the cartoonist's fumbling microphone demeanor to what might be possible with such a show, and he became Ripley's longtime guiding force on radio.

Dramatization was the key. If Ripley had only to introduce the drama, a real piece of dynamic radio might be achieved. On Rolfe's *Saturday Party*, Ripley's air time would be limited to brief introductions, less than a minute, and giving the authentication after the play. This was packaged with Rolfe's dance music, novelty tunes, and commercials for the new Hudson Terraplane. There was a male trio, a popular singing style of the time, and Ripley was introduced in a colorful bit of tongue-twisting that he would carry into later shows. "Radio's regal revealer of remarkable realities" he was called, setting up a *Baker's Broadcast* of mid-1937, and some of his copy, as reported by Considine, might have played well on *Fibber McGee and Molly*.

He took diction lessons to eliminate his stutter. For his mike fright, a few drinks would help, and sometimes, it was said, he had more than a few. His shows, done across 19 years for a variety of sponsors, fell into similar formats, Ripley being the centerpiece of longer shows featuring acts that had nothing to do with the unusual. By 1935 Ripley had become a national conduit for unusual happenings, and tips received by his staff accumulated by hundreds a day.

He was one of the first radio performers to make regular use of remote pickups. He spoke with rapids-runners on the Colorado River and with people trekking under Niagara Falls. He interviewed a polio victim in an iron lung and talked by shortwave with Douglas "Wrong Way" Corrigan, who set out in his small plane for California and managed to land in Dublin, Ireland. In 1938, in one of his most dramatic shows, he staged a firewalking event in the parking lot at Radio City, describing for his audience how Kuda Bux of India could traverse a bed of hot coals.

He was said to be the first person to broadcast from midocean. He claimed that his voice was heard from more distant places than any other speaker's. He broadcast live from Schenectady to Sydney, then went 10,000 miles to keep a blind date with the woman he had interviewed on the air. His shows combined mystery, suspense, and romance. When American GIs stormed the beaches of North Africa, one of the passwords they used to tell friend from foe was "believe it or not." On the air, Ripley was a strange mix of P. T. Barnum, Bill Stern, and Casper Milquetoast. He was "habitually blushing," said *Newsweek*, but his acts of daring could keep a listener on the edge of the seat. A notable example was the show in which Ripley and a snake handler were lowered into a pit of rattlesnakes. When a power failure plunged the pit into darkness, the snake man could clearly be heard saying, "Let's get the hell out of here!"

Storer believed that listeners were fascinated by radio's new ability to reach distant locales. Ripley's 1940 CBS Nehi show, *See America First with Bob Ripley*, went on the road. Accompanied by a vocalist, an agency representative, writers, and engineers, he roamed from the floor of the Grand Canyon to an underwater garden off the coast of Florida. His Mutual series of 1944 concentrated on "amazing new wonders culled from a world at war." This daily 15-minute offering had Ripley telling of amazing events—some from antiquity—that had occurred at the site of that day's headlines. A British patrol was trapped in the same valley where Israelites were surrounded by Philistines 3,000 years ago, and escaped through the same passage. A young American was almost hit by a piece of enemy shrapnel, then found his father's name cut into the metal—his father, a mechanic at Boeing Aircraft, had cut his name on the engine of his 1929 automobile but had no idea how the scrap fell into the hands of the "Japs" and nearly killed the son.

Throughout his life, Ripley was viewed by the press as an enigmatic figure. More than once he was described as his own kind of curiosity. He collected cars but did not drive; he had an almost superstitious fear of the telephone. In his last years he became ever more eccentric. He was a hard taskmaster to his crews and was said by biographer Considine to have a volatile, unpredictable temper. He died May 27, 1949.

BEN BERNIE, THE OLD MAESTRO, musical variety.

BROADCAST HISTORY: 1930–31, WJZ and Blue Network, beginning Jan. 17, 1930. 30m, Fridays at 8. Mennen.

June 2, 1931–July 26, 1932, CBS. 15m, Tuesdays at 10:15, then 30m, Tuesdays at 9. Pabst Beer.

Sept. 13, 1932–Oct. 22, 1935, NBC. 30m, Tuesdays at 9. Pabst Beer.

Oct. 29, 1935–Oct. 19, 1937, Blue Network. 30m, Tuesdays at 9. American Can Company.

Jan. 12–July 6, 1938, CBS. 30m, Wednesdays at 9:30, then at 8:30. U.S. Rubber.

Oct. 2, 1938–July 3, 1940, CBS. 30m, Sundays at 5:30. Musical quiz format. Half-&-Half Tobacco.

Oct. 1, 1940–April 1, 1941, Blue Network. 30m, Tuesdays at 8. Bromo Seltzer. Moved to Fridays at 9 as of April 11 and continued, sustained, until Aug. 1, 1941.

June 22, 1941–March 5, 1943 (intermittent, with long break Dec. 1941–June 1942), CBS. 15m, weekdays at 5:45. *The Ben Bernie War Workers' Program*. Wrigley's Gum.

CAST: Ben Bernie and "All the Lads," as his orchestra was known. Vocalists Jane Pickens, Buddy Clark, Mary Small, Pat Kennedy, Dinah Shore, Scrappy Lambert, Little Jackie Heller. Comics Lew Lehr, Fuzzy Knight. ANNOUNCERS: Jimmy Wallington (Pabst era), Harlow Wilcox, Harry Von Zell, Bob Brown.

Throughout his career, Ben Bernie was one of radio's most popular personalities. In 1933, when his show peaked well into the top ten at 34 points, Bernie had a style that was uniquely his. He wasn't a musician, though he did play the violin. He wasn't an expert leader or arranger, leaving baton duties to first violinist Mickey Garlock. He wasn't a good comic, his gags listing to stale warmed-overs. He wasn't a keen talent scout, though notables including Oscar Levant, trombonist Lou McGarity, sax man Dick Stabile, and singer Dinah Shore passed through his ensemble on their way somewhere else. What Bernie was, and he excelled at it, was a personality.

He blended words: he clipped his *g*'s, and still his voice managed to suggest influences of Europe as well as Brooklyn and the Old South. Bernie could refer to his audience as "youse guys and youse gals" and still hold an image of sophistication. His trademarks were the fat cigars he chainsmoked, the phrases "au revoir" and "yowsah, yowsah, yowsah," and his traditional closing, "pleasant dreeeaaaams." His plea in the depths of the Depression—"Come back, prosperity, all is forgiven!"—was a classic, remembered for years. His lingo was unique, "yowsah" being merely a cornerstone in the

"Bible of Berniana." He was a "radio natural," hotly pursued by sponsors, according to the trade press of the day. "His radio shows reflect serenity and harmony, edged possibly by just a trace of condescension," said his entry in the 1941 *Current Biography*.

He was born Bernard Anzelvitz May 30, 1891, and was considered by his mother the "infant wonder of the violin." But if Bernie had any real musical genius, it remained well hidden behind his gift of gab. "For most orchestra leaders, dialogue is the nexus between musical numbers," said *Current Biography*: "but for Ben Bernie, music is merely an interlude between snatches of talk." He came up through vaudeville, for a time teamed with Phil Baker in violin-accordion routines with comic undertones. His first band had been formed by Don Juelle: by one account, Juelle rented it to Bernie, who billed it "Ben Bernie's Orchestra." It was "an excellent stage band," one critic wrote, and Bernie "may have been the first [band] performer to adopt an informal, clowning style."

By the time of his first radio series in 1930, his act was complete. *Radio Stars* thought he projected a "smug air of assurance," but it was agreed that he had savior faire by the bucket. His opening theme was *It's a Lonesome Old Town*: to close, the "lads" would play *Au Revoir* while Bernie talked nonsense and fluff (remembered by his fans for decades) over the music. *And now, we've gotta leave you here . . . don't forget that good old Pabst Blue Ribbon beer . . . Yowsah! . . . Au revoir, a fond cheerio, a fond toodle-doo, a bit of a tweet-tweet . . . God bless you . . . and pleasant dreeeeeeaaaaaams. . . .*

Bernie's "feud" with Walter Winchell was more show business gimmickry. It had no more basis in true acrimony than the famous Fred Allen–Jack Benny feud a few years later. Bernie and Winchell, both coming from vaudeville, knew how to work a crowd, and, predictably, a large segment of the radio audience took the act at face value. Bernie insulted Winchell on the air; Winchell replied in kind, on his own radio show or in his newspaper column. When a joint appearance was arranged at the Paramount, they played to overflow crowds. Bernie finally called a truce after Pearl Harbor, when a woman in his audience stood and scolded him for criticizing such a good American as Walter Winchell.

Bernie's best commercial association was with

Pabst: he had a long remote run in the Pabst pavilion at the Chicago Century of Progress Exhibition in 1931; thereafter, his show was mostly heard from New York. The broadcasts highlighted such major guests as Fanny Brice and Sophie Tucker, and his own musical numbers usually ran to light comedy. When he did *Mamma Makes Me Practice*, one reporter wrote in 1936, "he talked it into the mike, and Mickey Garlock scraped a few discordant notes on his fiddle, like a kid practicing." He did not run by the clock: he seldom timed a show, his secretary Eleanor Smith told a reporter, preferring to judge the time instinctively and make up with medleys at the end. Thus his shows have a sound of patchworked closings—if a show is tight, it fades fast; otherwise, Bernie says goodnight, toodle-doo, and au revoir at his leisure. "Should you ever send in a request-a, why, we'll sho' try to do our best-a," he would sometimes say, closing a show.

He thrived in the '30s and in 1941 settled into a quarter-hour daily salute to war workers that *Radio Life* considered well suited to his style. His regulars included electric guitarist Les Paul, the King's Jesters vocal trio, and singers Jack Fulton, Russ Brown, and Gale Robbins. But Bernie became ill in 1943, leaving the show to his cast in mid-January. On Oct. 23, he died.

BENAY VENUTA, singer from the nightclub circuit.

BROADCAST HISTORY: March–June 1935, CBS. 15m, Fridays at 3; also, 30m with the Freddie Rich Orchestra, Thursdays at 7:30.

June 23, 1935–April 26, 1936, CBS. 30m, Sundays at 7. *Freddie Rich's Penthouse Party.*

Jan.–April 1938, Mutual. 60m, Saturdays at 2. Venuta was billed as "writer, producer, director, announcer, and singer."

1938–40, Mutual. Various brief timeslots, often on Sundays. Last noted in a regular 30m singing series Oct. 9, 1938–Feb. 9, 1940.

Benay Venuta became a network performer after a 1935 appearance on Al Jolson's *Shell Chateau*. In 1948, long after her retirement as a singer, she hosted a Saturday Mutual quiz show, *Keep Up with the Kids*. The game pitted children against their parents (Roddy McDowall and his father, Penny Singleton and her daughter, and Pat O'Brien and his son were some of the celeb-

rity contestants) for a prize that was donated to charity.

BEST PLAYS, dramatic anthology.

BROADCAST HISTORY: June 8, 1952–Sept. 27, 1953, NBC. Sundays at 9; Fridays at 9 beginning fall 1952; Sundays at 8:30 beginning June 1953; 60m and 30m series aired. **CAST:** Host John Chapman, drama critic of the New York *Daily News*. Top stage performers in leading roles, with support by New York radio people: Mason Adams, Lawson Zerbe, Edgar Stehli, Karl Weber, Joseph Julian, Joe DeSantis, Luis Van Rooten, Roger DeKoven, Wendell Holmes, etc. **ANNOUNCERS:** Robert Denton, Fred Collins. **SUPERVISOR:** William Welch. **DIRECTORS:** Edward King, Fred Weihe. **WRITERS-ADAPTERS:** Ernest Kinoy, George Lefferts, Claris A. Ross.

Best Plays was based on the theatrical yearbook begun by Burns Mantle in 1919. As a survey of the Broadway stage, it was ideal for radio. The well was deep, providing drama and comedy that had not been overworked on other shows. It was transcribed in New York, "where the American stage begins."

Host John Chapman was also the anthology's editor after Mantle died in 1947. Among the plays were *A Bell for Adano* with Arthur Kennedy, *Night Must Fall* with Alfred Drake, and *Arsenic and Old Lace* with Boris Karloff.

THE BETTER HALF, quiz.

BROADCAST HISTORY: March 22, 1942–Jan. 19, 1950, Mutual. 30m A quagmire of schedule moves; two dozen changes of time. **HOST:** Tom Slater until 1944, then Tiny Ruffner.

The Better Half was created by WOR soundman Jack Byrne and his interest in the work women were doing in munitions factories, aircraft plants, and elsewhere on the home front. Byrne was so impressed with their performance in jobs that had always been filled by men that he wondered how they would do against men in a radio quiz. This wasn't an original idea—Frank Crumit and Julia Sanderson had been doing the same thing on *Battle of the Sexes* as early as 1938—but it was entertaining, and it resulted in scores so close that neither side could claim a clear victory.

Four married couples were brought onstage

and were subjected to various stunts involving traditional concepts of "manhood" and "womanhood" and built around old prejudices: Do women take longer to dress? Is a woman's place in the home? In one stunt, a husband was blindfolded and kissed by his wife, a French poodle, and a sound effects man. While he struggled to guess which had been which, the audience roared.

BETTY AND BOB, soap opera.

BROADCAST HISTORY: Oct. 10, 1932–May 29, 1936, Blue Network. 15m, daily at 3, later at 4. General Mills.

June 1, 1936–May 27, 1938, CBS. 15m, weekdays at 10 A.M., then at 1 (1937–38). General Mills.

May 30, 1938–March 15, 1940, NBC. 15m, weekdays, mostly at 2. General Mills for Wheaties and Bisquick.

Ca. 1940, transcribed syndication.

CAST: Elizabeth Reller and Don Ameche as Betty and Bob Drake, young marrieds caught in a conflict-of-two-cultures theme. Also as Betty: Beatrice Churchill, Alice Hill, Mercedes McCambridge, Arlene Francis. Also as Bob: Les Tremayne, Vinton Hayworth, Onslow Stevens, Spencer Bentley, Carl Frank, J. Anthony Hughes, Van Heflin. Edith Davis as May Drake, Bob's mother. Edith Davis also as the Negro servant Gardenia ("Sho is good tuh have you back, Mistah Bob"). Herbert Nelson and Eleanor Dowling as Carl and Ethel Grainger, friends of the Drakes. Ethel Kuhn as Pamela Talmadge. Bill Bouchey as Harvey Drew. Frankie Pacelli as little Bobby Drake, son of Betty and Bob.

PRODUCERS: Frank and Anne Hummert.

THEME: *Salut d' Amour.*

Betty and Bob was the first true network soap opera of the air, using melodrama at its core. In that first year, only *Clara, Lu, and Em, Judy and Jane,* and *Vic and Sade* were its companions in the world of daytime continuations for women. All were decidedly lighter fare, and *Vic and Sade* was already emerging as classic radio comedy.

Betty and Bob was the first daytime serial of Frank and Anne Hummert, father and mother of all soap opera (the Hummerts had premiered *Just Plain Bill* a month earlier, but that hardy perennial was then in the nighttime schedule). Here the themes were set—love, hate, jealousy, misunderstanding; and their by-products, divorce, murder, betrayal, collusion, insanity—that would fill serial dramas for the next 30 years.

Betty was a girl of humble origins, a simple-but-lovely secretary who worked for Bob Drake, dashing heir to a vast fortune. When Bob fell in love with her, his inheritance was compromised: he was forced into Betty's workaday world and the frightening prospect of making a living. They had a son, Bobby, whose presence did little but slow the pace of the show.

The pre-Bobby shows exploited what would later be regarded as the standard Hummert themes: Bob's dashing demeanor, irresistible to the Depression-era vamps and countesses ever lurking in the wings; Betty's jealousy; Bob's jealousy; and assorted schemes against their happiness by intriguing strangers of both sexes. This was a new kind of daytime fare, and early ratings were spectacular. But interest dropped off after the leads married, and plummeted after the birth of their son. Raymond William Stedman speculates that listeners refused to accept bickering and jealousy when a child was involved. By then the novelty had worn off: the number of serials on the air had soared from three to more than 50, but within the industry the perception lingered that little Bobby had been the chief reason for the *Betty and Bob* decline. Seldom again would children be allowed to influence Hummert storylines. When even that most embattled of heroines, Mary Noble, gave birth to little Larry Jr. on *Backstage Wife,* the child was only occasionally acknowledged, and the Nobles continued their lives filled with murder, amnesia, insanity, and jealousy.

Betty and Bob was reorganized: little Bobby was killed off by pneumonia just as the protagonists were going through a painful divorce. Bob had broken away from the evil Countess Velvaine only to be swept up by the lovely socialite Pamela Talmadge. Betty, forsaken in her hour of need, had opened a dress shop with the help of Harvey Drew, an elderly man secretly in love with her. Bobby's death brought the Drakes together again, but the audience had vanished. Throughout the run, Bob hovered on the verge of mental and physical breakdowns. He was frequently "recuperating at the country home" near the little town of Walton. At one point, late in the run, Betty and Bob ran the *Trumpet,* a crusading newspaper in the midsized city (250,000 population) of Monroe.

Still another reason for the serial's fade may have been the departure of Don Ameche from the lead when he left Chicago in the mid-1930s for a film career. Ameche was one of radio's original heartthrobs, his voice difficult to replace. The final *Betty and Bob* serial was transcribed in 1940. The leads were Arlene Francis and Carl Frank, supported by such notables as Everett Sloane, Ray Collins, Agnes Moorehead, and Edmond O'Brien.

BETTY CROCKER, cooking advice.

BROADCAST HISTORY: 1924, local broadcasts.
1926–36, NBC. 15m, twice a week, usually between 10:30 and 11 A.M. General Mills.
1936–37, CBS. 15m, twice a week at 1:15.
1937–41, NBC. 15m, twice a week at 10:45 A.M.
1941, CBS. 15m, twice a week at 9:45 A.M.
1942–47, NBC. 15m, often Fridays at 2:45; sometimes twice a week.
1947–53, ABC. 15m, five a week at 10:30 A.M.
CAST: Betty Crocker, who was impersonated by various actresses, telling listeners "how to buy, what to buy, how to make the best with what is available."

BETWEEN THE BOOKENDS, poetry and talk.

BROADCAST HISTORY: 1929, KMBC, Kansas City.
July 26, 1934–Sept. 9, 1938, CBS. 15m, many timeslots. Hinds Cream, 1936–37.
Sept. 12, 1938–June 3, 1955, Blue Network into ABC. Many 15m weekday timeslots. Off the air for a year, 1944–45, while the host, Ted Malone, went to Italy and Iceland as a war correspondent. Weekday broadcasts resumed on ABC at 11:45 A.M., later at 11:30 A.M., for Westinghouse, 1945–49, with Ernest Chappell, announcer. Heard weekdays, 1949–55, mostly at 1:15, with co-op advertising.

NOTABLE SPINOFFS: Oct. 15, 1939–May 26, 1940, Blue Network. 30m, Sundays at 1. *Pilgrimage of Poetry.*
Oct. 13, 1940–May 11, 1941, Blue Network. 30m, Sundays at 2, *American Pilgrimage.*

Ted Malone and Tony Wons were the two major poetry readers of network radio. Malone, an unlikely candidate for sex symbol status, was chubby and balding, but when he spoke on the air, women listened. "Malone is Shelley, Prince Charming, Don Juan, and Galahad in one," *Time* noted in 1939, when *Between the Bookends* was at its peak. "One woman has been wiring him daily and hopefully for six months, seeking a rendezvous. From Missouri, a once-misunderstood wife confessed to curling up in her nightie in front of the radio, listening to *Indian Love Lyrics,* being then and there cured forever of the 'coldness' of which her husband had complained." In a busy month, Malone would receive 20,000 letters from his largely feminine audience.

In real life he was Alden Russell, whose story was echoed many times in radio's unpredictable early days. An act failed to appear one day at KMBC, Kansas City, and Russell found himself pushed to the microphone with nothing but a poetry book for moral support. As the clock ticked down, he protested, then warned announcer Hugh Studebaker not to use his name on such a "sissy" broadcast. He ad-libbed his own closing announcement: "Ladies and gentlemen, you have been visiting between the bookends with— Ted Malone."

Under that name, his *Between the Bookends* would run more than 25 years. As Ted Malone, Russell was the nation's top caterer of "poems that are famous and poems that are unknown."

Like Arthur Godfrey, he spoke to the audience as a single being. He never said "Ladies and gentlemen": it was always, "Hello there." "Sometimes I play games with them," he told *Newsweek,* speaking of his female audience in 1935. "Sometimes I make love. If I blow softly across the microphone, their eardrums will vibrate just as though I'd blown in their ears." He was compared with Cupid because of his cherubic appearance and because his shows brought couples together in real life. By 1941 he had accumulated a vast library of verse, and confessed to a reporter that he had come to love it.

Each show had a theme, chosen by Malone a week before the broadcast. He sat at a studio table with the lights dimmed and read to organ accompaniment. Bob Mitchell and Rosa Rio were among the organists. His theme was *Auld Lang Syne.*

His *Pilgrimage of Poetry,* 1939–40, was designed to bring the lives of the poets closer to American audiences. A survey of 700 colleges and universities had produced a list of the greatest American poets. Malone narrowed it to 32 names and took his audience to the places where they had done their work. Listeners heard Malone roll up the shades in Longfellow's home, write a line with Poe's pen, and yell down Whittier's well. Among others, the show visited the homes of Joyce Kilmer, Stephen Crane, and Eugene Field. This series was followed by *American Pilgrimage*, 1940–41, visiting the homes of such literary figures as Mark Twain, Herman Melville, Harriet Beecher Stowe, and Booker T. Washington. In his later years, Malone also became enamored of prose. His postwar shows for Westinghouse were often straight talks on such topics as the Constitution. He was now billed as "that well-known author, war correspondent, and friend of millions." His *Between the Bookends* anthologies went through many editions and are still easily found in used-book stores.

THE BEULAH SHOW, situation comedy.

BROADCAST HISTORY: July 2, 1945–March 17, 1946, CBS. 30m, Mondays at 9 until Aug. 20, then Sundays at 8. *The Marlin Hurt and Beulah Show*. Tums. **CAST:** Marlin Hurt, a white man, in the role of Beulah, a Negro maid who worked for Fibber McGee on Tuesday nights. Hurt also as Beulah's shiftless boyfriend, Bill Jackson, and as himself. **ANNOUNCER:** Ken Niles. **VOCALIST:** Carol Stewart, who also played "the girl down the street from Beulah's house." **MUSIC:** Albert Sack. **PRODUCER:** Helen Mack. **WRITER:** Phil Leslie. The series ended suddenly when Hurt died, a heart attack victim, but it would return three times.

Feb. 24–Aug. 20, 1947, ABC. 30m, Mondays at 9 until April, then Wednesdays at 9:30 until June, then Wednesdays at 9. **CAST:** Bob Corley, another white man, as Beulah.

Nov. 24, 1947–April 10, 1953, CBS. 15m strip show, weekdays at 7. Procter & Gamble for Dreft. **CAST:** Hattie McDaniel as Beulah until early 1952, when she became ill; Lillian or Amanda Randolph thereafter. Hugh Studebaker and Mary Jane Croft as Harry and Alice Henderson, who employed Beulah as maid and cook. Henry Blair as the Hendersons' 10-year-old son Donnie. Ruby Dandridge as Oriole, the housekeeper next door. Ernie "Bubbles" Whitman as Beulah's elusive boyfriend Bill. **ANNOUNCER:** Marvin Miller.

PRODUCER-DIRECTOR: Tom McKnight. **WRITERS:** Sol Saks, Herb Finn, Bill Freedman, Sherwood Schwartz, Arthur Julian, Hal Kanter, Howard Leeds.

Sept. 28, 1953–May 28, 1954, CBS. 15m, five a week at 7:15. General Foods, General Motors, Murine. **CAST:** Amanda Randolph as Beulah. Studebaker, Croft, Dandridge, and Whitman again as the Hendersons, Oriole, and Bill. Sammy Ogg as Donnie Henderson. **ANNOUNCER:** Johnny Jacobs. **PRODUCER-DIRECTOR:** Steve Hatos. **WRITERS:** Same as 1950 staff. Supporting cast over the years included Butterfly McQueen, Nicodemus Stewart, Roy Glenn, Lois Corbet, Jess Kirkpatrick, John Brown, Louise Beavers, and Vivian and Dorothy Dandridge.

Marlin Hurt was a master of what was perceived by the radio audience to be black dialect. Had Freeman Gosden and Charles Correll discovered him, he'd have been a natural for *Amos 'n' Andy*.

But Hurt was discovered by Don Quinn, the man who wrote *Fibber McGee and Molly*. When the war took away some of Quinn's best performers (Bill Thompson alone was doing four characters on the *McGee* show), Quinn remembered Hurt, whose act had impressed him on the Maxwell House *Show Boat* more than four years before.

At that time, Hurt had been "Dick" of *Show Boat*'s singing trio Tom, Dick, and Harry. But Hurt could also do comedy. With his voice he could achieve the character of a woman, a good-natured falsetto that he combined with the "colored people" influences of his youth to produce Beulah.

Hurt's major influence was a black woman named Mary, who cooked for the Hurt family and scolded the children in her heavy accent. For many years Hurt experimented with the voice, thinking that he might use it in show business. His chance came in radio.

For 13 years he worked with Bud and Gordon Vandover on their Tom, Dick, and Harry stage-and-radio act. Occasionally, as on the 1940 *Show Boat*, Hurt used his dialect on the air. When Bud Vandover died in 1943, Hurt became a solo act. He did a radio show, playing saxophone and doing dialects. In Hollywood, he got a job on *The Fred Brady Show*. When Don Quinn heard the broadcast, he remembered Hurt from *Show Boat*.

Hurt's appearance on *Fibber McGee and Molly* was sensational. He would stand with his back to the microphone; then, when McGee yelled for Beulah, he would whirl suddenly and shout, "Somebody bawl fo' Beulah?" The effect on the audience was tremendous: it never failed to bring down the house. The line became famous, carried to every corner of the country. In a widely reported incident, a 5-year-old girl shouted out, "Somebody bawl fo' Beulah?" during her small-town church service. It brought down the house there too.

Best of all from Quinn's viewpoint, Hurt was then 39 years old and beyond the reach of the draft. Quinn added another memorable line: when McGee was most ridiculous, Beulah would say, "Loooove dat man!" This too was widely mimicked. These catchphrases were temporarily left behind when *The Marlin Hurt and Beulah Show* opened as a spinoff series in 1945: created by Quinn, the lines were owned by the *McGee* sponsor, Johnson's Wax. But Phil Leslie, Quinn's cowriter, would do the scripting, assuring the series quality and continuity. It began well and was nearing the end of its first full season when Hurt suffered a heart attack and died.

As envisioned by Hurt, Beulah was in her 30s, "is man-crazy, weighs about 140 pounds, has good teeth, wears her hair in bangs and a page-boy bob. She adores short skirts and extremely high heels. Beulah isn't lazy. She says, 'All work and no play makes jack.' " She was a novelty character, created and sustained by the startling concept of a white man doing a black woman's voice. This was still in evidence a year after Hurt's death, when the character was revived by another white man, Bob Corley. It was not until Hattie McDaniel took the part in a nightly CBS serial format that Beulah outgrew her novelty status and emerged as a character of some staying power.

McDaniel played the role for four full seasons. When she became ill, Amanda Randolph was offered the lead, but a clause in Randolph's *Amos 'n' Andy* contract prevented her from immediately taking it. Her sister Lillian Randolph finished the 1951–52 season. By 1953 Amanda Randolph had signed a new contract with *Amos 'n' Andy*, had struck out the prohibitive clause, and was able to assume the role.

BEYOND TOMORROW, science fiction drama.

BROADCAST HISTORY: April 5–13, 1950, CBS. 30m. **CAST:** Everett Sloane, Bret Morrison, Frank Lovejoy. **CONSULTANT-HOST:** John Campbell Jr., noted SF editor. **MUSIC:** Henry Sylvern, with futuristic effects. **PRODUCER-DIRECTORS:** Mitchell Grayson, William N. Robson.

The significance of *Beyond Tomorrow* is that it almost became radio's first science fiction series for adults. An audition show, *The Outer Limit*, was prepared Feb. 23, 1950, under the title *Beyond This World*. This was later broadcast under the new title, but by then NBC had opened its significant *Dimension X* series, and *Beyond Tomorrow* was canceled after only three episodes.

THE BICKERSONS, situation comedy.

BROADCAST HISTORY: Sept. 8, 1946–June 1, 1947, NBC. 30m, Sundays at 10. *Drene Time*. Drene Shampoo. **CAST:** Don Ameche and Frances Langford as John and Blanche Bickerson, a married couple who fought constantly. Danny Thomas as Brother Amos. **WRITER:** Phil Rapp.

Sept. 24, 1947–June 25, 1948, CBS. 30m, Wednesdays, then Fridays at 9. *The Old Gold Show*, also known as *The Don Ameche Show*. Old Gold Cigarettes. **CAST:** Ameche, Langford, and comic Frank Morgan.

June 5–Aug. 28, 1951, CBS. 30m, Tuesdays at 9:30. First series titled *The Bickersons*. Philip Morris. **CAST:** Lew Parker and Frances Langford as the Bickersons.

The Bickersons attained a fame that far outstripped its importance on radio. Its long-range effect is still being felt on television.

Initially it was a skit on Don Ameche's *Drene Time*, a half-hour comedy-variety show that had an unheralded NBC run in 1946. As John and Blanche Bickerson, Ameche and Frances Langford turned domestic bliss into high-grade warfare. As Brother Amos, young comic Danny Thomas had a role, but the verbal fireworks were handled by the leads.

The bickering usually began because Blanche couldn't sleep. Annoyed by the snoring of her husband, she woke him constantly to tell him off. The skits on *Drene Time* were subtitled *The Honeymoon Is Over*; on *The Old Gold Hour*, Ameche's encore year, the subtitles were *The Bickersons* or *Mr. and Mrs. Bickerson*. Neither

Ameche nor Langford had done this kind of combative comedy before.

Bickersons skits surfaced for three months on *The Charlie McCarthy Show* (NBC, October–December 1948) with Marsha Hunt opposite Ameche. But it wasn't until June 1951 that *The Bickersons* became a fully realized series. Lew Parker played opposite Langford in a short-lived run that generated little excitement ("appalling," said *Radio Life*). But *The Bickersons* was recorded by Ameche and Langford for Columbia Records, and its confrontational style could be seen in such TV shows as Jackie Gleason's *Honeymooners* and, years later, Norman Lear's *All in the Family*.

THE BIG GUY, detective drama.

BROADCAST HISTORY: May 7–Oct. 29, 1950, NBC. 30m, Sundays at 5. CAST: Henry Calvin as Joshua Sharp, "giant among giants," a detective with the bulk and demeanor of Santa Claus. David Anderson and Denise Alexander as his adventurous preteen children Josh Jr. and Debbie; Joan Lazer also as Debbie. Supporting players: Joseph Bell, Anita Anton, Burford Hampden, Bill Zuckert, Lyle Sudrow, Linda Watkins, and Peggy Laughton. Sandy Strauss as Risky Skinner. ANNOUNCERS: Fred Collins, Peter Roberts. MUSIC: George Wright, Jack Ward. DIRECTOR: Thomas Mattigan. WRITER: Peter Barry.

BIG JON AND SPARKIE, children's variety.

BROADCAST HISTORY: 1950–54, ABC. 30m, five a week at 5; 15m beginning in 1951. Co-op advertising. First broadcast as *Big Jon and Sparkie* Feb. 1, 1950.

1950–58, ABC. Saturdays at 9 A.M., 120m until 1951, then 90m. Co-op advertising. The weekend edition titled *No School Today*, first heard Feb. 18, 1950.

CREATOR-PRODUCER-STAR: Jon Arthur (Jonathan Arthur Goerss).

Both the daily *Big Jon and Sparkie* and the Saturday *No School Today* featured a "normal" adult, Big Jon, and a cast of fantasy characters, also played by Jon Arthur. Star of the shows was Sparkie, "the little elf from the land of make-believe, who wants more than anything else in the world to be a real boy." Billing was "for the younger generation and the young at heart":

the fare consisted of stories, songs, and an unforgettable theme, *The Teddy Bears' Picnic*.

Arthur, son of a Pennsylvania minister, took a course in radio announcing as a young man and broke in with a West Virginia station in 1939. When an act failed to arrive, he went on the air with his version of *The Three Little Pigs*, playing directly to two children in the studio observation booth. He created Sparkie and *No School Today* around 1947 at a Cincinnati station and expanded both concepts when the show arrived on ABC.

For the first two years, Sparkie was an invisible voice. But so many fans wondered what he looked like that Arthur asked Leon Jason, a comic book artist, to create a composite from letters sent in by listeners. In only two appeals for "what you think Sparkie looks like," he got 25,000 pieces of mail. Arthur achieved the voice of Sparkie by trick recordings. By 1956 it was estimated that he had played 200 roles on the show, among them Ukey Betcha the comic cab driver and Mayor Plumpfront of Cincinnati. Arthur's 3-year-old daughter Debbie played "the little girl next door." He pretended to have a set of "magic spyglasses," with which he could see into listeners' homes and check up on their hygiene. The show had a continuing "movietime serial" and offered adaptations of such classics as *Treasure Island*. In one memorable skit, Arthur told of two rabbits, black and white, and related a clever parable on race relations. He said that everything on *Big Jon and Sparkie* was taken from life, based on experiences of either his children or the listeners who wrote him. His show was heard on shortwave for years after its network demise. It remained, for those who heard it, one of the most important and poignant pieces of childhood.

THE BIG SHOW, spectacular variety with many top-name stars.

BROADCAST HISTORY: Nov. 5, 1950–April 20, 1952, NBC. 90m, Sundays at 6. Multiple sponsorship. CAST: Tallulah Bankhead, "mistress of ceremonies." Fred Allen in regular support, with Jimmy Durante, Ethel Merman, Frankie Laine, Jose Ferrer, Paul Lukas, Danny Thomas, Groucho Marx, Jane Powell, Fanny Brice, Ezio Pinza, Bob Hope, Eddie Cantor, Rudy Vallee, Danny Kaye, Judy Garland, Judy Holliday, Ed Wynn, etc. ANNOUNCERS: Jimmy Wallington, Ed Herlihy.

ORCHESTRA AND CHORUS: Meredith Willson. PRODUCER-DIRECTOR: Dee Engelbach. WRITERS: Goodman Ace, Selma Diamond, George Foster, Frank Wilson.

The Big Show was mounted on a scale unprecedented in radio. NBC literally threw money into its Sunday night colossus: $300 a minute by one estimate, which, if anything, was low. Some shows cost $100,000—"real television money," as *Newsweek* termed it—a vast budget spent on a dying medium in a timeslot that NBC had owned for years. But CBS had stolen Jack Benny and the cream of NBC's old Sunday lineup, and *The Big Show* was the older network's answer. At the end of the two-year run, a question posed by one of the fan magazines lingered—do big names mean good radio?

The show had a piece of everything: "dahhhling" hostess Tallulah Bankhead; Durante at his word-twisting best; Ethel Merman belting out songs like old times on Broadway. Scenes from top New York plays were dramatized, with the original stars. The press was ecstatic: reviews were generally glowing, though occasionally that lingering question would crop up. *The Big Show*, despite its stated intention not to sound like a star-swamped benefit broadcast, often sounded precisely like that. Worse, it made almost no dent in the ratings of *The Jack Benny Program* and *The Charlie McCarthy Show*, both recently "stolen" by CBS.

Even with deep problems (a horrendous budget and the inability to attract enough sponsors to make it pay), *The Big Show* returned for its second season. It was launched with one of the most lavish publicity stunts ever devised. The entire cast flew off to Europe, to play in London and Paris. The British press was not thrilled; The *Daily Express* found it "90 minutes of bad jokes, tuneless songs, witless dialogue, soapy compliments, and onion-under-the-nose emotion." Perhaps the best line to come out of the trip was Fred Allen's quip that French money was "the thinnest paper you'll ever see in public." By the end of the second season, NBC had reportedly lost $1 million on the show.

For Dee Engelbach, it was a test of endurance. His work on the next installment began each Sunday at 7:30, as soon as the show went off the air. Sunday nights he conferred with writers: the search for a premise could take several hours.

The writers sought unifying lines of action, integrating themes that would keep *The Big Show* from being simply a string of pearls. On Monday Engelbach met with support people. Everyone threw in ideas. By then the writers had come up with rough sketches, which were discussed with the director, and Meredith Willson was consulted about the musical segments. Guest stars arrived on Wednesday and Thursday to go over their routines. The first rehearsal was Friday. Willson rehearsed the orchestra and chorus with the musical guests. This could take three hours. Then came the dialogue rehearsal, the cutting, the revision, additional rehearsal—another five-hour job. On Sunday came the integrated rehearsal, which ran all day. That night the show went on, and the routine began again for the following week.

Was it worth it? *The Big Show* had its moments, but *The Jack Benny Program* rolled along on CBS, as consistently brilliant and funny as ever. The moral, perhaps, is that brilliance and genius cannot be bought, that a buckshot approach never works, and that most good things come finally from a single inspired source.

BIG SISTER, soap opera.

BROADCAST HISTORY: Sept. 14, 1936–Dec. 26, 1952, CBS. 15m, weekdays at 11:30 A.M. until 1941, then at 12:15 until 1946, then at 1. Lever Brothers for Rinso until 1946, then Procter & Gamble. CAST: Alice Frost as Ruth Evans, a heroine who put aside her own happiness for the sake of her younger, orphaned siblings; Nancy Marshall as Ruth by 1942; Marjorie Anderson and Mercedes McCambridge as Ruth, mid-1940s; Grace Matthews as Ruth from 1946. Martin Gabel as Dr. John Wayne, the hero who befriended Ruth Evans and later married her; Paul McGrath and Staats Cotsworth as Dr. John Wayne in later years. Haila Stoddard, Dorothy McGuire, Peggy Conklin, and Fran Carden over the years as Sue Evans Miller, Ruth's little sister. Michael O'Day as little Neddie Evans, Ruth's crippled brother. Ned Wever as Jerry Miller, the newspaperman who married little sister Sue. Ann Shepherd as Neddie's wife Hope; also played by Teri Keane. Santos Ortega as Dr. Duncan Carvell, at City Hospital where both John and Ruth Wayne worked. Berry Kroeger, Ian Martin, Arnold Moss, and David Gothard variously as Dr. Reed Bannister, John Wayne's best friend. Richard Kollmar and Joe Julian as Michael West. **ANNOUNCERS:** Fred Uttal, Jim Ameche, Hugh Conover. **MUSIC:** Richard Leibert on organ. **CREATOR-WRITER:** Lillian Lauferty. **DIRECTORS:** Mitchell Grayson, Wilson Tuttle, Theodore Huston, Thomas F. Vietor. **WRITERS:** Julian Funt, Carl Bixby, Bob Newman, Bill Sweets. **SOUND EFFECTS:** Bill Brown, Lavern Owens, Walt McDonough. **THEME:** *Valse Bluette.*

Ruth Evans always centered her life on her sister Sue and their crippled brother Neddie. Indeed, she tried valiantly to be both mother and father. When Sue married reporter Jerry Miller, Ruth was able to give her full attention to the care of little Ned. But soon she found herself falling in love with Neddie's new doctor, John Wayne.

Loved in return by John, Ruth shelved her own happiness to continue caring for Ned. But John Wayne was not to be denied: he performed a medical miracle and Neddie was cured, suddenly able to walk and lead a regular life. Neddie met Hope Melton, married her, and at last left Ruth free to "follow her heart."

On Oct. 19, 1939, Ruth and John were married. John worked at City Hospital, assisting Dr. Duncan Carvell, and Ruth "looked forward to the birth of their baby" (characters weren't ever pregnant on radio: they had a blessed event, looked forward to the day, or had a little visitor). Their son Richard was born just as John prepared to enter the war. Then John's best friend, Dr. Reed Bannister, arrived in town to carry on John's work in his absence. Ruth went to work in Carvell's office, acting as secretary to both doctors, and Bannister fell in love with her.

John returned from the war with symptoms of shell-shock, having suffered terribly in a Japanese prison camp. At last he decided he must leave and "find himself," insisting that Ruth divorce him and marry Reed for her own happiness. This she resisted. But the long weeks passed, and "the close friendship between Ruth and Dr. Bannister gradually developed into romance." When at last Reed persuaded her that John was not coming back, "a new John Wayne" arrived at the eleventh hour, "determined to fight to regain his wife's love."

New characters came in. Neddie met Valerie Hale, but she fell in love with Reed, who self-lessly married her though he still loved Ruth. Reed knew that Ruth had "mistaken gratitude for love," so he left her free to "follow her heart," back to her husband and son.

Over the years there were scores of subplots. There were bouts of amnesia, a malady that in real life is almost nonexistent; there was always John's eye for a pretty leg, which at one point manifested in an affair with Neddie's wife Hope; there were endless troubles with John's first wife, Norma, who early in the story had a neurotic passion for revenge. At one point Norma was nearly killed in an auto accident. If she lived, she would ruin John's career, naming Ruth as the woman who had wrecked her marriage. In a remote farmhouse, with Ruth shakily holding a flickering lamp, John operated and saved Norma's life. But the operation left Norma's mind impaired, causing John to face disciplinary action from the hospital review board. "Allowed to resign," John signed on as a crewman with a freighter and shipped out at midnight. The freighter was lost at sea with all hands reportedly drowned. Eventually, though, Ruth learned that John was alive and traced him to a remote island (the one place he might go), where she learned that he was blinded in the explosion at sea. And John, mistaking her true devotion for pity, sent her away in anger.

The action for *Big Sister* was based in the fictitious town of Glens Falls. The opening signature was low-key for a serial: four bells from the town hall clock. The serial was perennially popular, spawning a spinoff, *Bright Horizon*, on CBS in 1941. The character of Michael West was lifted out of *Big Sister* and placed in a new environment. To give the new serial a boost, Alice Frost appeared for a short time in her *Big Sister* role of Ruth Evans Wayne.

THE BIG STORY, true crime, heavily dramatized, from newspaper stories.

BROADCAST HISTORY: April 2, 1947–March 23, 1955, NBC. 30m, Wednesdays at 10 until 1951, then at 9:30. Pall Mall Cigarettes until 1954, then Lucky Strike. **CAST:** Bob Sloane, narrator, the only continuing character. Also: Robert Dryden, Bill Quinn, Bernard Grant, Betty Garde, Alice Frost. **ANNOUNCER:** Ernest Chappell. **PRODUCER:** Bernard J. Prockter. **DIRECTOR:** Tom Vietor, Harry Ingram. **WRITERS:** Gail Ingram,

Arnold Perl, Max Ehrlich. SOUND EFFECTS: Al Scott.

The Big Story grew out of a real crime case. Bernard J. Prockter, independent producer of radio shows, read a *Newsweek* account of how two *Chicago Times* reporters had worked for months on a 14-year-old murder case, writing more than 30 stories before uncovering evidence that led to a pardon for a man wrongly convicted. He wondered if a series built around reporters and their "big stories" would work on the air.

It did better than that. In its first year, *The Big Story* leaped into a nip-and-tuck battle with Bing Crosby's *Philco Radio Time*, topping it in several ratings periods before Crosby moved to a timeslot 30 minutes earlier.

In Prockter's eyes, crime thrillers were the stuff of radio drama. Supposedly devised to honor reporters overlooked by Pulitzer committees, it concentrated on old murder cases or other violent crimes against society. A 1949 network press release described the changing hero as "a reporter who has solved a crime, exposed a corrupt political administration, smashed a racket, or performed some other notable public service." Murder was the staple. Andy Tigelietta of the *Long Island Star* uncovered new facts in the mysterious death of silent film star Thelma Todd: the show was rich with stories like that. The names of all characters were fictionalized, except the name of the reporter and the newspaper for which he worked. At the end of each drama, the real reporter was brought before the microphone and given a $500 reward in the name of the sponsor, Pall Mall Cigarettes.

Many reporters who won the *Big Story* award looked back at the show with a mixture of affection and amusement. Their stories were highly dramatized, often to the extent that the subjects had trouble recognizing themselves on the air. But Prockter and his staff did try to match actors with their real-life counterparts, and the stories always involved cases long closed, to avoid the dangers of pretrial publicity.

The *Big Story* signatures were highly charged, with announcer Ernest Chappell booming out the title, and a thrilling, fiery theme, taken from Richard Strauss's *Ein Heldenleben*, opening the show.

BIG TOWN, crime drama with a newspaper background.

BROADCAST HISTORY: Oct. 19, 1937–July 2, 1942, CBS. 30m, Tuesdays at 8 until Oct. 1940, then Wednesdays at 8 until Jan. 1942, then Thursdays at 9:30.

Oct. 5, 1943–June 22, 1948, CBS. 30m, Tuesdays at 8 with a new cast. Ironized Yeast; Bayer Aspirin, 1945.

Sept. 14, 1948–Dec. 25, 1951, NBC. 30m, Tuesdays at 10. Lifebuoy Soap.

Dec. 12, 1951–June 25, 1952, CBS. 30m, Wednesdays at 8. Lifebuoy Soap.

1937–42. CAST: Edward G. Robinson as Steve Wilson, managing editor of the crusading *Illustrated Press*. Claire Trevor as Lorelei Kilbourne, society editor and sidekick in Wilson's racket-busting adventures; Ona Munson as Lorelei from ca. 1940. Ed MacDonald as Tommy Hughes, "fearless, imaginative reporter." Gale Gordon as pompous District Attorney Miller. Paula Winslowe as Miss Foster, Steve Wilson's secretary; Helen Brown as Miss Foster by 1939, when Winslowe was being cast in various "emotional roles, such as heartbroken wives whose husbands are the victims of gangsters." Lou Merrill in many gangster roles (and often present as a potential stand-in for Robinson). Cy Kendall as "various political grafters." Jack Smart in comedy roles, such as Toby the drunk on the 1938 Christmas show. Jerry Hausner, "jack of all trades," who played everything "from a street urchin to a racketeer." ANNOUNCER: Carlton KaDell. MUSIC: Leith Stevens. PRODUCER: Clark Andrews. DIRECTOR: William N. Robson. WRITER-DIRECTOR: Jerry McGill. SOUND EFFECTS: John Powers, Ray Erlenborn.

AFTER 1942. CAST: Edward Pawley as Steve Wilson. Walter Greaza as Wilson, ca. 1952. Fran Carlon as Lorelei. Robert Dryden as Harry the Hack, a cab driver whose encyclopedic knowledge of the dark back alleys and little-used streets of Big Town often gave Steve the jump on things; also played by Ross Martin and Mason Adams. Donald MacDonald as Willie the Weep, a waterfront character who talked in a sob. Larry Haines as Mozart, the blind piano-playing owner of a Big Town bistro. Lawson Zerbe as Dusty Miller the photographer; also played by Casey Allen. Also: Ted de Corsia, Dwight Weist, Bill Adams. Bobby Winckler as the newsboy who opened the show with the shrill cry, "Extra, extra, get your Illustrated Press!" Michael O'Day as the newsboy later in the run. ANNOUNCER: Dwight Weist. MUSIC: John Gart on organ. PRODUCER-DIRECTOR: Jerry McGill.

In its 15-year run on radio and another six on early television, *Big Town* was perhaps the most famous series of reporter dramas. Its early cast was top-line Hollywood, the show a vehicle for Edward G. Robinson and Claire Trevor. Robinson gave Steve Wilson his best *Little Caesar* style, barking his orders with the authority of a tommy gun. He wielded the power of the press heavily but (listeners were often told) handled it wisely. Claire Trevor was then a young starlet with her biggest role, in *Stagecoach*, two years away.

Writer Jerry McGill had been a newspaperman himself but took great creative license, slipping into high melodrama. There was much soapboxing on *Big Town*, with shows attacking juvenile delinquency, racism, and drunk driving. McGill's reporters were diligent, sober champions of justice. The show zealously pushed freedom of the press, creating a memorable slogan that was given the full treatment from an echo chamber: *Freedom of the press is a flaming sword! Use it justly . . . hold it high . . . guard it well*.

The show's first major change came in 1940 with the departure of Claire Trevor. Her part had gradually dwindled, she told a reporter many years later, until she was down to two basic lines: "I'll wait for you in the car, Steve" and "How'd it go, Steve?" Ona Munson, the new Lorelei, won the part in a blind audition (in which readings were recorded, given a number, and later heard by agency people who had no idea which actress they were hearing). "We all felt as if we'd like to take her out on a date," said one agency man after hearing Munson's record. *That's* what they were looking for. But *Big Town* remained a star's vehicle: when Robinson left the show two years later, that seemed to end it.

McGill thought otherwise, and the following year he assembled a new cast headed by Broadway veteran Edward Pawley for a nine-year run from New York. *Big Town* continued its crusading ways, lacking only the flavor, style, and star system of the '30s.

THE BILL GOODWIN SHOW, situation comedy; also known as *Leave It to Bill*.

BROADCAST HISTORY: April 26–Dec. 13, 1947, CBS. 30m, Saturdays at 9 until Oct., then at 8:30. CAST: Bill Goodwin as "hotshot insurance salesman" Bill Goodwin. Peggy Knudsen as his girlfriend Phillipa. Jim Backus as his boss Mr. Hendricks. Bill Johnstone as Groggins, president of the Chamber of Commerce. Elvia Allman and Noreen Gammill as the Dinwiddie sisters. Mary Jane Croft as their niece Dolores. Shirley Mitchell as Goodwin's secretary Helen. PRODUCER-DIRECTOR: Larry Burns.

Goodwin was one of radio's best-known second bananas, stooge and announcer to some of the biggest names on the air. In the storyline, the Dinwiddie sisters were rich screwballs who owned most of the insurable property in town, but, as *Radio Life* noted in its review, Goodwin did "almost everything *except* sell insurance."

THE BILLIE BURKE SHOW, situation comedy.

BROADCAST HISTORY: April 3, 1943–Sept. 21, 1946, CBS. 30m, Saturdays at 11:30 A.M. Titled *Fashions in Rations* until fall 1944. Listerine. CAST: Billie Burke as Billie Burke, a scatterbrain with a heart of gold who lived "in the little white house on Sunnyview Drive." Earle Ross as Julius, her crusty brother. Lillian Randolph as Daisy, the housekeeper. Marvin Miller as Colonel Fitts and Banker Guthrie, suitors for Billie's hand. ANNOUNCERS: Marvin Miller, Tom Dickson. PRODUCER-DIRECTORS: Axel Gruenberg, Dave Titus. WRITERS: Paul West, Ruth Brooks. THEMES: *Look for the Silver Lining* to open the show and *A Pretty Girl Is Like a Melody* at the close of the Listerine commercial.

Best known as Glinda, the good witch in *The Wizard of Oz* (and as the wife of Ziegfeld), Billie Burke had a rosy, upbeat series promoting herself as "that bright morning star." She portrayed a woman of uncertain age who would go out of her way to aid a bum in distress or help neighborhood kids get a playground. She constantly mixed metaphors, as in "Let sleeping dogs gather no moss," and was well placed on Saturday mornings.

THE BING CROSBY SHOW, musical variety.

BROADCAST HISTORY: 1930, sang on the air with the Gus Arnheim Orchestra, from the Cocoanut Grove in Los Angeles.

Sept. 2, 1931–Feb. 27, 1932, CBS. 15m, six a week at 7:15. *Fifteen Minutes with Bing Crosby*, sustained until Nov., then *The Cremo Singer* for Cremo Cigars.

March 8–July 20, 1932, CBS, 15m, various days.

Jan. 4–April 15, 1933, CBS, 15m, Wednesdays and Saturdays at 9. *The Music That Satisfies*. Chesterfield. Lennie Hayton's Orchestra.

Oct. 16, 1933–June 11, 1935, CBS. 30m, Mondays at 8:30 until the 1934 summer break, then Tuesdays at 9. Woodbury Soap. VOCAL GROUPS: Mills Brothers, (1933–34); Boswell Sisters (1934–35). ORCHESTRA: Georgie Stoll.

Jan. 2, 1936–May 9, 1946, NBC. Thursdays at 10 until 1940, then at 9. 60m until 1942, then 30m. Joined *The Kraft Music Hall* in progress with the Dec. 1935 departure of Al Jolson. Kraft Foods. CAST: Bing Crosby, star personality, vocalist, and host. Bob Burns, comedic sidekick until 1941. Mary Martin, feminine presence and singer, 1942. Victor Borge, pianist and comic, 1942. Also: Connie Boswell, Jerry Lester, George Murphy, Peggy Lee, the Music Maids and Hal, the Merry Macs (Judd, Ted, and Joe McMichael and Mary Lou Cook). ANNOUNCERS: Don Wilson, Roger Krupp, and Ken Carpenter, who joined *KMH* early in the Crosby era and remained with him through many subsequent changes of format. MUSIC: Jimmy Dorsey, 1936–37; John Scott Trotter beginning July 8, 1937, an association with Crosby that lasted for decades. PRODUCER-DIRECTOR: Cal Kuhl for the J. Walter Thompson agency; also, Bob Brewster, Ezra MacIntosh, Ed Gardner. THEME: *When the Blue of the Night Meets the Gold of the Day*, which became identified with Crosby.

Oct. 16, 1946–June 1, 1949, ABC. 30m, Wednesdays at 10. *Philco Radio Time*. Philco. Prepared on tape in advance, effectively breaking the networks' strict rule against prerecorded entertainment. CAST: Bing Crosby, Ken Carpenter, John Scott Trotter, Skitch Henderson, Latin singer Lina Romay, the Charioteers, Jud Conlon's Rhythmaires (Conlon, director, with Charlie Parlato, Mack McLean, Loulie Jean Norman, Gloria Wood). PRODUCER-DIRECTORS: Bill Morrow and Murdo MacKenzie. MacKenzie also produced Crosby's subsequent shows.

Sept. 21, 1949–June 25, 1952, CBS. 30m, Wednesdays at 9:30. *The Bing Crosby Chesterfield Show*. Chesterfield Cigarettes. CAST: Crosby, Carpenter, Trotter, and guests.

Oct. 9, 1952–May 30, 1954, CBS. 30m, Thursdays at 9:30, 1952–53; Sundays at 8, 1953–54. *The*

General Electric Show. General Electric. CAST: Crosby, Carpenter, Trotter, guests.

Nov. 22, 1954–Dec. 28, 1956, CBS. 15m, weekdays at 9:15, 1954–55, then at 7:30, 1955–56. Small-group musical accompaniment.

Bing Crosby always liked radio. He didn't have to worry about neckties and pressed pants. He didn't need a priest's collar to re-create Father O'Malley for *The Screen Guild Theater*. He could wear his Hawaiian shirt hanging loose at the belt. This was one of the joys of the medium. He held out against television while clinging to his radio show until slipping ratings and a changing world forced him out.

Crosby's career reached the heights. He was a star performer in every field. His films were top box office, his records sold in the millions, but it was radio that made his fame. On the air he developed the smooth conversational style that people everywhere took to their hearts.

He was born Harry Lillis Crosby in Tacoma, Wa. His birthdate, long accepted as May 2, 1904, has recently been questioned, with one biographer asserting May 3, 1903, as correct. He abandoned his study of law to become a singing drummer in late-1920s vaudeville. His autobiography, *Call Me Lucky*, claims that the name Bing derived from a comic strip he liked in childhood, a thing called *Bingville Bugle*. NBC publicity material claimed it came from his habit of shouting "bing" instead of "bang" when he played cowboys and Indians with his childhood companions. In any event, he left Harry Lillis in Spokane, where his family had moved when he was a boy, and became "Bing" forever after. The lighthearted sound of it, combined with boyish good looks, became part of the mystique, that image that lasted until his death.

Occasionally he referred to his real name on the air. He talked of Spokane and of his brother Everett, who had become his business manager. His early days—the days of obscurity in show business—were 1925 to 1931. But with his first network radio hookup, his star rose as quickly as any in the industry. Immediately he was sought by producers in three separate fields of show business.

He came to Los Angeles in 1925 with Al Rinker, a singing pal from Gonzaga University. Rinker's sister Mildred Bailey was singing jazz on the radio and was able to get them a job at the Tent Cafe. Crosby played traps while Rinker worked the piano, and both sang. They played the Boulevard Theater, toured with revues, and were billed in movie houses as Two Boys and a Piano. In 1927 Paul Whiteman saw them at the Metropolitan Theater in Los Angeles and signed them to tour with his band.

In New York, Whiteman signed Harry Barris to accompany them, and they sang as the Rhythm Boys with the Whiteman band until 1930. They joined Gus Arnheim, and in Los Angeles Crosby met Dixie Lee, a starlet who had just completed *The William Fox Movietone Follies* of 1929. Dixie (real name Wilma Winifred Wyatt) considered him a playboy, but they were married after his energetic courtship, highlighted by the recording *I Surrender, Dear*. His brother Everett, meanwhile, sent the record to the networks, both of which summoned him east for auditions.

Crosby signed with CBS. His premiere was scheduled for late August 1931 but was postponed for what was announced as a severe case of laryngitis (though alleged in some quarters to be too much to drink). By Sept. 2 he had recovered, and announcer Harry Von Zell introduced him to the nation.

He signed a film contract with Paramount, starring in *The Big Broadcast* (1932) and becoming in the next decade one of the best-loved stars of all time. He was the "epitome of niceness," film historian David Shipman would write years later: no one had "given so much pleasure to so many people as Bing Crosby." His movie career would include such high spots as *Holiday Inn, Going My Way,* and, for Republic, *The Bells of St. Mary's*. In 1940 Paramount would team him with Bob Hope on a long series of comedy "Road" films (to Morocco, Zanzibar, and Singapore, among other exotic locations).

By 1935 he was a major star. He took over *The Kraft Music Hall*, a two-year-old variety hour, with the first broadcast of 1936 and held the host's chair for a decade. The hour-long format suited his casual style: it featured jokes, relaxed conversation, and music. Bob Burns, "the Arkansas Traveler," joined the cast and established a reputation for telling tall tales of life back home. Burns's "bazooka" became a celebrated musical instrument, consisting of two pieces of two-inch pipe. "One slid into the other the way a trombone works," recalled writer Carroll Carroll in his memoir (*None of Your Business*).

"At one end was a large funnel. At the other end was Burns. It was a very limited bass instrument, one cut above a jug, and Bob played it as bass as it could be played."

Burns was an effective counter to the serious musicians who appeared on *The Kraft Music Hall*. In one memorable number, he and José Iturbi gave a bazooka-piano rendition of a Tchaikovsky piano concerto. Crosby adored it: he loved good comedy and great jazz, and if the two happened to meet at his corner on Thursday night, so much the better. Duke Ellington, Joe Venuti, Frank Trumbauer, and Jack Teagarden were featured on the *Music Hall*. Jimmy Dorsey was replaced as music director only when a reluctant Crosby could be convinced that his style of swing wasn't compatible with the classical artists who were appearing in greater numbers on his show. John Scott Trotter, the new maestro, would stay with Crosby to the end.

The show developed new stars and spotlighted established professionals. Spike Jones and Jerry Colonna came out of Trotter's band, Jones a drummer, Colonna a trombonist. Mary Martin was lured from Broadway for a year's stay in 1942. Also that year came Victor Borge, a concert pianist who had fled his native Denmark when the Nazis invaded, to begin a new life in Hollywood. Borge was booked as a comedian: a "devilish Dane" who might or might not be able to play piano (all doubt vanished when he stopped mugging and played a full piece). As for Bob Burns, he held the second chair for more than five years and contributed the name of his bazooka to the Army's anti-tank rocket gun. The military used the name so extensively that people forgot where it had originated: Burns had "made and named" it in 1905, according to lexicographer Stuart Berg Flexner.

The *Music Hall* had a low-key, distinctive sound. Crosby wanted no applause: this, he felt, slowed the pace, and today, listening to it on tape, one is struck by the silence, the white space, that appreciative, pregnant lull after a brilliant performance. But the most striking ingredient of *The Kraft Music Hall* was Crosby himself. He was pure ease: his casual dress was discussed on the air, and his banter seemed to flow from some endless inner well. "Everybody thought Bing ad-libbed the whole script," wrote Carroll Carroll in his autobiography. In fact, Carroll wrote the show alone until 1938, thereafter acting as a "script carpenter,'' building on dialogue supplied by writers Elon Packard, Leo ''Ukie'' Sherin, Vic McLeod, and Stanley Davidson. There were no on-air script credits, enhancing the notion that all that glib smoothness was Crosby's alone.

Carroll aimed *KMH* ''for the younger country club set,'' he told a reporter: he and Crosby shared a liking for big words, and the young audience appreciated that. Carroll respected the radio audience: its average intelligence was 21 years, compared with the 11-year-old minds that packed movie houses, he said. ''There is no picture writer living who can do what the average radio writer does in the course of a week.'' Carroll worked for J. Walter Thompson, writing the show as part of an agency production team that also included director Cal Kuhl. ''I usually spent Friday, Saturday, and Sunday interviewing guests,'' he wrote in his memoir. The writing began Monday morning: ''Tuesday evening Bing and Bob each received his script. The guests all got sides in which they were to appear. Then I'd get okays from the guests or try to take what suggestions they had that made sense. Early Thursday morning Bing's script, with any changes *he* had, was picked up. All notes and proposed changes were made, coordinated and/or ignored, and a revised script was sent to mimeo to be ready for rehearsal.''

What went on the air, Carroll said, had a ''gracious informality'' that the guests appreciated. ''Instead of using guests to make the star look good, we worked just the other way.'' Top headliners were in constant attendance: Lionel Barrymore, Humphrey Bogart, and a gamut of other film stars. Robert Benchley became a familiar voice on the Crosby show; Frank McHugh and Pat O'Brien came around often. Bob Hope was a major attraction; ratings were always high when he and Crosby were billed together. They had become a team of sorts with their ''Road'' pictures, appearing together a few times a year to keep interest high. With Hope, Crosby's low-key humor was almost straight: Crosby's assets were his charm and his sometimes remarkable use of the language.

The show had a good-natured this-is-fun sound to it. When a labor dispute caused ASCAP to withdraw its music from radio (knocking out Crosby's *When the Blue of the Night*), the show's theme, without vocal, became *Hail KMH*, a symphonic arrangement that ended in

the ringing of the NBC chimes. The chimes were rung manually by announcer Ken Carpenter until an automatic set arrived, sparking a great rivalry among Crosby, Burns, and Carpenter for the honor of pushing the button that rang NBC into its station breaks.

In the decade that Crosby remained with Kraft, he became the best-loved star on the American scene. He was self-deprecating, insisting that his career stood on a foundation of luck. America did not suffer stuffed shirts gladly, and Crosby exuded not an ounce of pomp or conceit. He was candid and easygoing, and loyal to those who worked for him. Ken Carpenter had met Crosby in 1932 when he was announcing at the Cocoanut Grove: his tenure as Crosby's announcer was unbroken after the early Kraft years. John Scott Trotter was a Crosby institution. Trotter took some ribbing about his weight, but this was all in good fun: Crosby's own physical shortcomings, notably his toupee, were occasional subjects for banter as well. Murdo MacKenzie began with Crosby as an engineer and became director of his later shows.

Behind the scenes, however, Crosby could be difficult and moody. Things were done his way or he walked out. He would leave a broadcast in the lurch and go play golf if something annoyed him. Carroll Carroll tells a tale that epitomizes this. It happened just after Pearl Harbor, when radio stations on the West Coast were declared high security areas. Passes were required to gain access to the studios. One day Crosby forgot his pass. The guard, who had watched Crosby come and go for five years, refused to let him in without it. Crosby walked off. Carroll chased him down in the parking lot and caught him departing for the golf course. Carroll coaxed him back to the studio, but again the guard refused to let him pass. Again Crosby walked out. Frantic, Carroll called Niles Trammel, network boss on the West Coast. Crosby was serious, he said: if someone didn't find a way, right now, to get Crosby past that guard, NBC was going to have ''one of the most eloquent hours of silence'' ever heard on a network. Trammel finally got Crosby past the reluctant guard.

This was not an isolated incident. Crosby in private was easygoing but distant. He was easy to write for, seldom fussing or making major changes in the script. But if he got his back up, there was little room in his makeup for compromise. "He has no friends," his brother Bob told jazz historian Leonard Feather years later. He was seen by some as cold, even ruthless in business matters. He could pass through town without bothering to call a brother he hadn't seen in two years. He had "built a sort of cellophane bag around himself," Bob Crosby told Feather. "He lives in this bag and opens it now and then for a little while. You can only get inside for a minute, then he shuts you out."

Crosby got annoyed with NBC, and with his sponsor, in 1945 and ended his long association with both. He had heard of a new method of sound recording. The Germans had developed a recorder using plastic-backed tape in 1935 and had improved the machines and the tape to a standard that could almost be called professional. Suddenly Crosby saw an enormous advantage in prerecording his radio shows. The scheduling could now be done at the star's convenience. He could do four shows a week, if he chose, then take a month off. But the networks and sponsors were adamantly opposed. The public wouldn't stand for "canned" radio, the networks argued. There was something magic for listeners in the fact that what they were hearing was being performed, and heard everywhere, at that precise instant. Some of the best moments in comedy came when a line was blown and the star had to rely on wit to rescue a bad situation. Fred Allen, Jack Benny, Phil Harris, and, yes, Crosby were masters at this, and the networks weren't about to give it up easily.

Crosby insisted on trying it. Across the trenches, NBC and Kraft stuck to their guns, and Crosby walked out. For the beginning of the 1945–46 season, *The Kraft Music Hall* was carried by comic Frank Morgan and pianist Eddy Duchin, with assist from the Charioteers vocal group. Crosby's walkout was seven months long. He declared his contract with Kraft null and void, while Kraft claimed that the 1937 contract allowed the cheesemaker to sponsor Crosby, at its option, until 1950. Crosby refused to budge, and Kraft went to court. The company sued for declaratory judgment, naming Crosby and J. Walter Thompson as plaintiffs and asking for a ruling on the status of its contract. A settlement brought Crosby back to the air for the last 13 weeks of the season. Morgan and Duchin continued on the show after his return.

The settlement left him free to explore the pos-

sibilities of recording, if he could find a network willing to take the risk. The trades were nervous. Tape would mean "the end of network radio as we now know it," *Radio Life* said: the use of it by a star of Crosby's stature would only accelerate radio's march to oblivion. Crosby had no trouble finding a network: the struggling American Broadcasting Company (NBC's castoff Blue Network) was delighted to have him, on just about any terms the old crooner would dictate. Crosby was affable as always: all he wanted to do was record his shows and play golf whenever the urge arose. This agreement and a weekly budget of up to $35,000 ($8,000 to Crosby) put him on the dotted line for ABC. Philco Radios would pick up the tab, although nervously. A clause was inserted stipulating that if the canned format was clearly not working, Crosby would return to a live series: if he fell below a 12 share in the ratings for four consecutive weeks, his love affair with tape would be over.

Philco Radio Time opened strongly. Bob Hope was the guest for the Oct. 16, 1946, premiere, and he and Crosby were in top form. The jokes were funny and crisp, the delivery flawless, and listening to a tape of the broadcast even 50 years later is a pleasure. Lured by the preshow publicity and the novelty of hearing a recorded broadcast on a national network, 24 million people tuned in—enough to make Crosby the fourth-rated radio show of the week. The tune-out was just as dramatic. By Nov. 6, *Newsweek* reported that Crosby had lost half of his opening-day audience. His rating hovered in the low 12s, a few fractions away from the end of his experiment. The Hooper survey conducted a poll, finding that few listeners were put off by the fact that the show was recorded. Some blamed the quality of the recording, but most blamed the shows themselves. Crosby had done his first four in one week, and the guest scheduling had been haphazard. After Hope, the guests had been Spike Jones, Les Paul, Ralph Mendez, and Ezio Pinza: The agency believed the show needed more stars on the order of Jimmy Durante and Judy Garland. This proved true, and *Philco Radio Time* climbed back into the mid-teens in the ratings. But the real tale of the tape, in Philco's eyes, was the result Crosby got them in the market. The radios he touted on the air sold out nationally after each show.

So *Philco Radio Time* was entrenched, running three years, and tape was here to stay. Now backed by such crowd-pleasers as Al Jolson, Maurice Chevalier, and Gary Cooper, Crosby's Philco show charted a reliable 15 to 17 on the Hooper reports. Crosby was his old self: his on-air banter with the "boys" in Trotter's band—notably with guitarist Perry Botkin—was played up in fan magazines and press notices. Everything was just as it had always been, and even the dreaded words "produced and transcribed in Hollywood" in time lost their fearsome aspects.

Crosby's subsequent series were veritable copies of *Philco*: the quality of tape continued to improve, and the broadcasts for Chesterfield and General Electric followed the well-established routine. The opening signature was followed by an opening song, some banter with Ken Carpenter, a commercial, a guest star, more songs, and that was the package. A highlight of these years was the frequent appearance of jazz violinist Joe Venuti, whose entry into the show was always preceded by the gravel-voiced question "Is this the place?" It was, indeed.

Crosby would remain a potent force long after his radio days. In his 60s he slipped into semi-retirement. He died Oct. 14, 1977—appropriately, it was said, on a golf course in Spain. Upon his death, his character was scrutinized far more intimately than it ever was during his life. Donald Shepherd and Robert F. Slatzer wrote a tough biography, *The Hollow Man*, which depicted Crosby as a cold, calculating dictator who abandoned his first family to start a new one, who turned his back on his wife Dixie Lee as she lay dying of cancer in 1952, who left a cruel will for his second wife, Kathryn, manipulating his money from the grave. The book was condemned by Crosby's most ardent fans as a hatchet job, but the charges lingered.

Perhaps the most revealing piece on Crosby was his interview with Barbara Walters, given a second airing on television after his death. At one point Walters asks what Crosby would do if his daughter began openly living with a man against Crosby's wishes. "Why, I'd never speak to her again," Crosby says, and the way he says it makes a viewer believe there wasn't much compromise in his nature. He did things his way, and that's how people around him did them too.

BIOGRAPHY IN SOUND, documentary.

BROADCAST HISTORY: 1954–58, NBC. Initially heard monthly; weekly beginning Feb. 20, 1955. 60m, various days including Sundays and Thursdays, mostly Tuesdays.

Biography in Sound began when NBC newsman Joseph O. Meyers was assigned to produce a documentary on Winston Churchill, to air on Churchill's 80th birthday, Nov. 30, 1954. Meyers thought a vivid biography in sound might be created by blending actualities of the subject's voice with recollections of his friends, associates, and antagonists. A vast resource was available at NBC. In 1949 Meyers had begun building a tape library with a brief segment by Joe Louis, announcing that he was through with boxing. In five years, more than 150,000 historic statements had been transferred to tape and added to the library. These were indexed and easily retrievable, and Meyers's finished product was cheered around the industry. "He had done the impossible," said *Radio Life:* "turned people's attention once more to radio."

In addition to the file clips, Meyers had Bennett Cerf tell Churchill anecdotes serious and amusing. Laurence Olivier and Lynn Fontanne read from British poetry, and sound effects and music were added for drama. The clamor for another show was immediate and loud. A month later, Meyers answered with a piece on Ernest Hemingway, again to great acclaim. A biography of Gertrude Lawrence followed in another month, and in February it was decided to run the series weekly.

Most of the series is preserved and available on tape. The biography of Hemingway remains superb radio, as do the shows on American writers F. Scott Fitzgerald and Sinclair Lewis (though Thomas Wolfe's reliance on and stormy friendship with his editor, Maxwell Perkins, is given perplexing brevity considering its real importance in Wolfe's career). The series has lost almost nothing with the passing of time: the good ones remain fascinating, the others may have been a little dull when aired. Some of the fine ones were *Meet Carl Sandburg* (Feb. 20, 1955), *Leo the Lip* (Durocher: April 17, 1955), *The Serious George Gershwin* (Aug. 30, 1955), *FPA—Franklin P. Adams* (Sept. 17, 1955), *Mr. Baseball—Connie Mack* (April 10, 1956), and *They Knew Rockne* (Sept. 11, 1956).

THE BISHOP AND THE GARGOYLE, crime drama.

BROADCAST HISTORY: Sept. 30, 1936–Feb. 22, 1937, Blue Network. 30m, Wednesdays at 9:30, then Mondays at 9 beginning in Jan.

July 7–Aug. 25, 1940, NBC. 30m, Sundays at 8. Summer series for Edgar Bergen's *Chase and Sanborn Hour.*

Sept. 6, 1940–Jan. 3, 1942, Blue Network. 30m Fridays at 8 until Oct. 1940, then Tuesdays at 9:30 until Jan. 1941, then Saturdays at 8:30.

CAST: Richard Gordon as the Bishop. Milton Herman and Ken Lynch as the Gargoyle. DIRECTOR: Joseph Bell. WRITER: Frank Wilson.

This unusual crime series told of a bishop whose interest in crime led him to accept an appointment to the Sing Sing parole board. There, he met a convict known only as the Gargoyle. They became friends and, after the Gargoyle's release, formed a crime-fighting duo, with the Bishop supplying the spiritual guidance and the Gargoyle the muscle.

THE BLACK CASTLE, mystery-terror.

BROADCAST HISTORY: 1942–44, Mutual. Various 15m slots, sometimes early evening (8) or mid-afternoon (3); heard in five-a-week and two-a-week runs. CAST: Don Douglas in all roles, including announcer.

The opening signature of this little melodrama gave ample notice of content: a church bell tolling in the distance, followed by a creepy voice asking listeners to "Come, follow me, please, for again we visit the wizard who dwells yonder in the great hall." The listener was then led, with full organ and sound-effect accompaniment along the "stone-wall corridor" to where the wizard waited (with his raven Diabolo) to tell the night's story. The closing signature reversed the trip, back through the corridor "to our place of rendezvous, on the hillside overlooking the peaceful valley." Church bells fade, and out.

THE BLACK HOOD, crime melodrama.

BROADCAST HISTORY: July 5, 1943–Jan. 14, 1944, Mutual. 15m, weekdays at 5:15. CAST: Scott Douglas as Kip Burland, rookie cop who— unknown to all but newswoman Barbara Sutton—

was really "the Black Hood," masked fighter of crime. Marjorie Cramer as Barbara.

The mask worn by Kip Burland in this serial was magical, giving him supernatural power. The opening signature was an ominous challenge to lawbreakers, with gongs and wind effects and a filtered voice.

Criminals, beware . . . The Black Hood is everywhere . . .

I—the Black Hood—do solemnly swear—that neither threats—nor bribes—nor bullets—nor death itself—shall keep me from fulfilling my vow—to erase crime—from the face of the earth!

THE BLACK MUSEUM, crime drama.

BROADCAST HISTORY: 1951, produced by the BBC in London. Transcription run in America Jan. 1–Dec. 30, 1952, Mutual. 30m, Tuesdays at 8. HOST-NARRATOR: Orson Welles. PRODUCER: Harry Alan Towers of the BBC.

The Black Museum was Scotland Yard's "mausoleum of murder," a "repository of crime" filled with ordinary objects that had each in some way contributed to a murder or to the undoing of the villain. It might be a straight razor or an old trunk: maybe a hammer, a cigarette lighter, or a sash cord. As narrator, Welles walked through the empty museum, paused, stopped, picked up an object, and told its story.

BLACK NIGHT, horror.

BROADCAST HISTORY: 1937–38, WBAP, Fort Worth. 30m, Fridays late night beginning Nov. 5, 1937; Mondays at 11, Central time, 1938. CAST: Nelson Olmsted in many roles. MUSIC: Gene Baugh. PRODUCER: Ken Douglass. WRITER: Virginia Wiltten. SOUND EFFECTS: A. M. Woodford.

Though it was not heard on a network, *Black Night*, one of radio's earliest and most effective horror shows, was known far and wide. Strategically placed in Fort Worth and broadcast near midnight, it drew mail from at least ten states coast to coast. It was cited by such publications as *Radio News* for its grisly sound effects and creepy music. It opened with *The Tell-Tale Heart*, by Poe, but in the main used original material by scriptwriter Wiltten.

BLACK NIGHT, musical variety.

BROADCAST HISTORY: Aug. 21–Sept. 25, 1951, ABC. 30m Tuesdays at 8:30. CAST: Don Dowd, with a club-hopping tour of Chicago's night life; vocalists Loretta Poynton and Carolyn Gilbert. MUSIC: Rex Maupin.

BLACKSTONE PLANTATION, musical variety.

BROADCAST HISTORY: 1929–30, CBS. 30m, Tuesdays at 8. Blackstone Cigars.

1930–34, NBC, 30m, Tuesdays at 8; also, 1931–32, Blue Network, Thursdays at 9. Blackstone. Final broadcast Jan. 2, 1934.

CAST: Frank Crumit and Julia Sanderson with light patter, cheerful music, and vocal duets.

Crumit and Sanderson formed one of radio's earliest major husband-wife teams. Crumit played ukelele and was well known in the '20s through his phonograph records. They were heard in other shows over the decade, including:

—*The Bond Bread broadcasts,* 1934–36, CBS, 30m, Sundays at 5:30.

—*The Norge Musical Kitchen* and *It's Florida's Treat,* 15m transcriptions, ca. 1936. Norge, Florida Orange Juice.

—*The Battle of the Sexes,* 1938–42, NBC, quiz. 30m, Tuesdays at 9.

—*The Crumit and Sanderson Quiz,* 1942, CBS.

—*Singing Sweethearts,* 1943, CBS West Coast. Weekdays at noon.

Crumit died Sept. 7, 1943, having attained a repertoire of 7,000–10,000 songs. After his death, Sanderson had a Mutual ladies' series, *Let's Be Charming,* 1943–44, 30m, Thursdays at 1:30.

BLACKSTONE, THE MAGIC DETECTIVE, mystery-trick show.

BROADCAST HISTORY: 1948–49, transcribed syndication; heard on WOR-Mutual Oct. 3, 1948–April 3, 1949, 15m, Sundays at 2:45. CAST: Ed Jerome as Harry Blackstone, "the world's greatest living magician." Ted Osborne and Fran Carlon as Blackstone's friends John and Rhoda. ANNOUNCER: Alan Kent. MUSIC: Bill Meeder on organ.

A typical episode opened with Blackstone telling John and Rhoda about one of his celebrated mystery cases. The case was dramatized in flashback, and there was always a magical ending, explained by Blackstone after a commercial pause during which the audience was challenged to figure it out. At the end of each show, Blackstone described a trick (a balancing egg, a walking hatpin, a disappearing coin, etc.), which kids could practice to "mystify" their friends.

BLIND DATE, audience dating game; human interest.

BROADCAST HISTORY: July 8–Aug. 26, 1943, NBC. 30m, Thursdays at 8. Substitute for Frank Morgan–Fanny Brice show. Maxwell House.

Oct. 25, 1943–Aug. 6, 1945, Blue/ABC. 30m, Mondays at 8:30. From New York. Lehn & Fink,

Aug. 17, 1945–Jan. 18, 1946, ABC. 30m, Fridays at 8. From Hollywood. Hinds Cream.

HOSTESS: Arlene Francis. ANNOUNCERS: Tiny Ruffner, Jimmy Wallington. CREATOR-PRODUCER-DIRECTOR: Tom Wallace.

The premiere broadcast of *Blind Date* set the style of this lively show. In the middle of the stage in Radio City's Studio 6A was a partition. To the right were the studio orchestra, hostess Arlene Francis, and six servicemen carefully selected as contestants: to the left, three beautiful women drawn from the ranks of the screen, radio, and modeling professions. The object was to arrange blind dates pairing three of the servicemen and the three women on opposite sides of the partition. The losers would be consoled by a friendly kiss from the hostess, $15 cash, and tickets to a Broadway show. The winners got a night on the town with their dates, dinner at the Stork Club, $5 pocket money, and a chaperoned ride home. Each woman was paid $50 for "working the show."

The servicemen had to sell themselves to their prospective dates on a telephone line that connected the two halves of the stage. Each contestant had a little more than two minutes to explain his best points: each woman then chose the date she found most interesting, and the three winners were escorted through swinging doors in the partition to meet their blind dates.

For the show's immediate success, no small credit was given to Arlene Francis, the "pretty femcee" described by *Newsweek* as "an ad-lib artist and possessor of a voice which at times can only be described as sexy.'' The hostess herself was so charming, the critic said, that the contestants would frequently ask, ''What are you doing tonight, Miss Francis?'' Usually she was busy, helping chaperone the winners.

Francis had an ability, it was said, to put the most nervous young man at ease. She talked of his home life, his hobbies, his war record. Her infectious laugh, good looks, and sexy air presence were always noted by reporters, male and female, who covered the show. Her double entendres at times were near-scandalous. To advise winners to ''go over to that side of the stage and get familiar'' was one thing: but when she tried to draw out a shy young warrior by noting that he had his ''Purple Heart on,'' the show became a censor's nightmare. She didn't understand, she recalled in her autobiography, why the audience reacted with a wave of laughter: she was so innocent in those days that she still didn't get it when the producers told her, after the broadcast, what that had sounded like on the air.

The ''boys'' were scouted personally by director Wallace and an aide. They were taken from service clubs and, when the show moved to Hollywood, were recruited at the Stage Door Canteen, where Wallace bused tables one night a week. The show was unabashedly patriotic: Wallace wanted boys who had solid American backgrounds, spoke well, and preferably had seen some action overseas. And it wasn't always the smooth ones who won. One soldier, asked if he could dance, replied in a hopeful voice, ''No, but I can crack my knuckles.'' Quickness like that, under fire, won him the date.

The dates often lasted till early morning. Chaperones guided the winners home, leaving them only when they went their separate ways and the sponsor's responsibility ended. But Cupid was not denied: at least half a dozen marriages and many ''lively correspondences'' came out of the show. And the idea worked on television as well. *Blind Date* ran on early ABC-TV, again with Francis as hostess, from 1949 through 1952.

BLONDIE, situation comedy, based on the comic strip by Chic Young.

BROADCAST HISTORY: July 3, 1939–June 26, 1944, CBS. 30m, Mondays at 7:30. Camel Ciga-

rettes. Initially a summer replacement for *The Eddie Cantor Show*: when Cantor did not return, the sponsor continued *Blondie* in the same timeslot.

July 21–Sept. 1, 1944, Blue Network. 30m, Fridays at 7. Super Suds.

Aug. 13, 1944–Sept. 26, 1948, CBS. 30m, Sundays at 8 until mid-1945, then at 7:30. Super Suds. Ran concurrently with Blue Network series for first three weeks.

Oct. 6, 1948–June 29, 1949, NBC. 30m, Wednesdays at 8. Super Suds.

Oct. 6, 1949–July 6, 1950, ABC. 30m, Thursdays at 8, then at 8:30 as of May.

CAST: Penny Singleton as Blondie until 1949. Ann Rutherford as Blondie ca. 1949. Also, Alice White and Patricia Van Cleve as Blondie. Arthur Lake as Blondie's husband, Dagwood Bumstead. Leone Ledoux (a specialist in infant roles) in the pretoddler parts of the Bumstead children, Alexander (Baby Dumpling) and Cookie. Tommy Cook as Alexander as of May 1943. Larry Sims (who played the role in films) as Alexander as of midsummer 1946. Bobby Ellis as Alexander in 1947. Jeffrey Silver as Alexander by 1949. Marlene Aames as Cookie by 1946. Norma Jean Nilsson as Cookie in 1947. Joan Rae subsequently as Cookie. Hanley Stafford as J. C. Dithers, Dagwood's boss. Elvia Allman as Mrs. Dithers (Cora). Frank Nelson as Herb Woodley, the Bumsteads' neighbor, a part also played briefly by Harold Peary. Arthur Q. Bryan and Harry Lang as Mr. Fuddle, another neighbor. Dix Davis as Alvin Fuddle. Mary Jane Croft as Blondie's friend Harriet. Veola Vonn and Lurene Tuttle as Dimples Wilson. Regulars (1939): Rosemary DeCamp, Ed MacDonald, Hans Conried. ANNOUNCERS: Bill Goodwin, Howard Petrie, Harlow Wilcox. MUSIC: Harry Lubin, Billy Artz. PRODUCER-WRITER: Ashmead Scott. DIRECTORS: Eddie Pola, Don Bernard, Glenhall Taylor. WRITERS: Johnny Greene (1940), William Moore. SOUND EFFECTS: Ray Erlenborn (CBS), Parker Cornel (NBC).

According to *Radio Mirror*, *Blondie* was a situation comedy about a ''typical couple.'' Superficially, perhaps, the Bumsteads of ''the small house in Shady Lane Avenue'' fit that description. They bowled, they played bridge with their neighbors, and, it was noted, ''they can't wait for other parents to stop bragging about their babies because they want to talk about Dumpling.''

There the similarity with reality ended. For the next 30 minutes, the Bumsteads were as typical as the Aldrich family. The opening signature, one of radio's best-remembered, gave a hint of the dizziness to follow.

Ah-ah-ah-ah! Don't touch that dial! Listen to—

"BLONNNNNNNNNNNNNNNNDIE!"

Ah, yes. Dagwood Bumstead is home.

The situations in *Blondie* were built around the foibles of Dagwood. The "bubble of his self-importance is burst at every turn," wrote *Radio Life* in 1943. "He walks along singing and people think he's crying. He introduces friends, saying happily, 'I know you'll like each other,' only to have them stare stonily at him. He rushes in where angels fear to tread. . . . In fact, he seems a flagrant and shallow personality. His charm is that he's so splendidly weak: he makes us feel less lonely, realizing that human frailty is a universal thing."

Dagwood was always on the defensive. He wasted time, frittered around, and was forever in hot water—if not with his boss J. C. Dithers, then with Blondie, who was apt to catch him sneaking in late after a night with the boys. Dagwood was an architect of sorts with the Dithers Construction Company. He had a computer-like brain and could add the most complicated figures instantly. His boss was a tyrant, ever threatening to run Dagwood's pinkie through the pencil sharpener or loudly demanding his presence, at attention, in the boss's office. Dagwood arrived at the desk to comical music, a trumpet fanfare.

At home his family grew. Because the radio show was so closely tied to the films (the same actors playing the leads) and beyond that to the comic strip, everything flowed from cartoonist Chic Young. Young believed that his strip should follow the "laws of natural life." The children grew up, and in the funnies Blondie developed "a matronly middle, wider hips, and other signs of maturing womanhood." In time there was a second blessed event: Baby Dumpling grew into boyhood and on the show of April 7, 1941, was joined by a sister. They became Alexander and Cookie. The family owned a dog, Daisy, which became as entrenched in the house on Shady Lane Avenue as Asta was in the New York apartment of Nick and Nora Charles.

All the Young touches were here: the Bumstead sandwiches, piled elbow-high with every possible lunch food, were frequent Dagwood snacks at midnight. It was a triple-play success, comics-to-movies-to-radio. Personal appearances were required of the stars, and Penny Singleton—originally a redhead—took root in Hollywood's beauty parlors, keeping her hair blond. Her first starring film role was in *Blondie*, from Columbia in 1938. Intended as B movies, the series often outdrew the main offerings on double-feature bills. Other films followed: *Blondie Meets the Boss*, 1939; *Blondie Goes Latin*, 1941. It was fluff, and the radio show was exactly the same.

Arthur Lake played Dagwood through three changes of female lead (his wife Patricia Van Cleve serving as Blondie in one of the later seasons). Singleton described Lake as "Dagwood to his toes." Once, she told *Radio Life*, he decided to *shave*, of all things, ten minutes before air time. When Lake tested for the first film, the director reportedly yelled, "If it's alive, that's Dagwood!" Like Dagwood, Lake wore a jazzbo tie, fastened with a clip, as he stood at the microphone and read his lines. Born Arthur Silverlake to a circus family in 1905, he died in 1987.

BLUE MONDAY JAMBOREE, known in the West as "the daddy of all variety shows."

BROADCAST HISTORY: 1927, KFRC, San Francisco. 120m, Monday nights. Heard locally for many years; taken ca. 1929–30 into the Don Lee Network, which carried CBS programming to the West Coast before it merged with Mutual. **CAST:** Bill Wright and Hazel Warner. Juliette Dunne, "solo balladist." Meredith Willson. **CREATOR-EMCEE:** Harrison Holliway, station manager of KFRC. **THEME:** *The Jamboree March*, by Meredith Willson.

1935, CBS. 60m, Mondays at midnight. A coast-to-coast summer run. **CAST:** Juliette Dunne. Baritone Ronald Graham. Blues singers Midge Williams, Nora Schiller, and Jean Ellington. Mezzo-soprano Helen Hughes. Comics Murray Bolen and Harris Brown. Vernita Henry as Mrs. Cornelia Yiffniff, a "burlesque of a Boston Back Bay dowager." Bea Benaderet, comic dialectician and later a major character actress of network radio. Edna O'Keefe as a "hill-nelly" character named Sairy Sloat. **EMCEE:** Harrison Holliway. **MUSIC:** Claude Sweeten and his 16-piece orchestra. **WRITER-PRODUCER:** Arnold Maguire, who also performed "as the darky character, Adhesive Pontoon."

BLUE RIBBON TOWN, comedy-variety.

BROADCAST HISTORY: March 27, 1943–Aug. 5, 1944, CBS. 30m, Saturdays at 10:15 until Oct. then at 8. Pabst Beer. **CAST:** Groucho Marx, host and comic-in-residence. Virginia O'Brien, comedienne. Leo Gorcey (of the Dead End Kids) by spring 1944. Fay McKenzie. **ANNOUNCER:** Dick Joy. **VOCALISTS:** Donald Dickson, Bill Days, and Kenny Baker, who took over as host when Marx left in mid-June 1944. **MUSIC:** Robert Armbruster. **DIRECTOR-PRODUCER-WRITER:** Dick Mack.

Groucho Marx still hadn't found his radio legs when *Blue Ribbon Town* opened. He was rooted in the slapstick of his movie days, a visual kind of comedy that seldom worked in radio. His scripts were filled with zany one- and two-line gags reminiscent of a Marx Brothers film. At a health resort, he would say, "I'm here for my stomach—have you seen it anywhere?" The style was at least ten years old. One week he'd play a loony scientist, the next a doctor, "but every week he's nuts," one critic said, welcoming the show.

All the action allegedly took place in Blue Ribbon Town, a mythical, medium-sized American city whose name tied nicely to the sponsor's beer. Virginia O'Brien had costarred in the latest Marx Brothers screen epic, *The Big Store* (1941): she was best known for her deadpan demeanor and for singing torch songs in a flat monotone. There was an impressive parade of guests (Jack Benny, Barbara Stanwyck, Charles Laughton, etc.), but the show never generated much enthusiasm.

BOB AND RAY, comedy and satire.

BROADCAST HISTORY: 1946–51, WHDH, Boston. *Matinee with Bob and Ray.* Various days and times.

July 2, 1951–Oct. 9, 1953, NBC. Many 15m timeslots: daily at 5:45, 1951–52; at 11:30 A.M. for Colgate, 1952–53; at 6:30, also 1952–53. 30m, daily at noon, mid-1953. **DIRECTOR:** Ken MacGregor.

July 7–Sept. 26, 1951, NBC. 60m in prime time but bounced around the schedule in its brief run. Orchestra, guest stars.

Oct. 3, 1955–Sept. 20, 1957, Mutual. 45m weekday disc jockey series.

June 29, 1959–June 24, 1960, CBS. 15m, weekdays.

1983, 1984, 1987, National Public Radio series, produced in stereo, series of 4, 12, and 13 shows heard on various dates in different parts of the country.

CAST: Bob Elliott and Ray Goulding.

The Bob and Ray Show was a happy accident, created by Robert Brackett Elliott and Raymond Walter Goulding, a team of avant-garde comics who each—when on the air—seemed to know the other's mind. They came along late and played the networks sporadically. But at their best, in their 1959–60 daily series for CBS, they were as funny and fresh, as clever and witty, as anyone who ever used the medium.

Using no script, they performed with a single sense of timing, pace, and direction. A single word or phrase might send them veering into new directions, with only instinct and a keen understanding of each other to guide the way.

Fluffs didn't concern them: their show was so offbeat that it sometimes seemed like a continuous chain of fluffs. They did outrageous satire, parodies on everything American, from eating habits to radio shows, including their own.

They worked together for 40 years. Elliott, born in Boston March 26, 1923, had landed a job at WHDH during the war, returning there after his release from the military. He was doing a morning disc jockey show when the station hired Goulding, another New Englander, born March 20, 1922, a few miles away in Lowell. Ray read the news on the hour, then occasionally engaged in impromptu on-air discussions with Bob. This rambling buffoonery expanded when WHDH got the rights to Braves–Red Sox baseball, and Bob and Ray were asked to do 25 minutes before each game. They began to satirize radio serials with spoofing continuations. Their first such serial was *Linda Lovely*; in such later, more polished epics as *Mary Backstayge, Noble Wife*, they used many of the techniques actually in practice on the serials of Frank and Anne Hummert. The exaggeration was minimal, the comedy achieved in the delivery. As on the real *Backstage Wife*, the identifying adjective became a first name; for instance, Wealthy Jacobus Pike was the backer of the play in which Harry

Backstayge was starring. Supplementing the serial was a company of characters, all played by
Bob and Ray, who chatted inanely about everything. Among the earliest were Mary McGoon,
who had a recipe and menu show; Tex Blaisdell,
who did rope tricks, impossible on radio but all
the funnier because of that; Uncle Eugene, a
stuffed shirt said to be "soft as a grape"; and
Wally Ballou, reporter extraordinaire. Radio was
their natural medium. "All you have to do is *say*
you're in Yankee Stadium," Ray told *Newsweek*: "on TV, you'd have to have it painted
on a wall."

With his deep baritone voice, Ray did all the
low, gruff parts and the falsetto females. He had
one female voice—his Mary McGoon was
everywoman on *The Bob and Ray Show*. Bob
handled the adenoids: Wally, Tex, the European
accents, the straight parts, the old men. Ray did
the tough guys and the roars. Most of the flat
dullards, of which there were many, were done
by Bob.

NBC welcomed them in 1951. An agent had
given a *Bob and Ray* audition record to Bud
Barry, a network executive, and now they were
heard nationwide while chatting and playing records for the local audience on WNBC in the
mornings. Within a year they had won a Peabody
and were considered by their peers the up-and-
coming comics to listen to. Among their biggest
fans were Jackie Gleason, Sid Caesar, and Groucho Marx. J. Edgar Hoover was less thrilled, especially with such "premium giveaways" as the
"Little Jim Dandy Burglar Kit."

They would make the full circle of network
radio, broadcasting on NBC, ABC, Mutual,
CBS, NBC's Monitor, and finally NPR. Their
comedy was adaptable to all timeslots, being
heard as live five-minute skits (*Monitor*, NBC,
circa 1955–59) as well as four-hour marathons
between the records and weather reports of local
radio. They did extensive commercial work from
1960–62, returning that year with an all-
afternoon show on WHN. A Broadway show,
Bob and Ray: The Two and Only, opened in
1970. In 1973 they were heard on WOR.

In private life they were ordinary, said their
friends, and some people thought them dull. On
the air, they were something else. Their mid-
1950s director-producer-soundman, Vic Cowan,
sometimes tried to throw them by putting in a
sudden sound effect. It never worked: one or the

other (or both at once) would veer immediately
into this new traffic, incorporating the sound into
their dialogue. Their greatest influences were
each other, though Bob told the *New Yorker* that
he had been influenced as a child listening to
Raymond Knight's *Cuckoo Hour*. Knight wrote
for *Bob and Ray* in the early '50s, when their
network shows were scripted, and when Knight
died Bob married his widow. Ray died March
24, 1990, of kidney failure.

To recap their many high spots is a delight.
Mary McGoon spawned dozens of spinoffs, from
Irma Shacktalloosengaard to Natalie Attired, and
the fact that all these ladies had exactly the same
voice was in itself a funny touch. Mary made
"mock turkey" each Thanksgiving, a feast composed of mashed potatoes molded to look like a
turkey and hot dogs for "drumsticks." She chatted casually and occasionally sang, always terribly. Her 1949 recording of *Mule Train* and *I'd
Like to Be a Cow in Switzerland* quickly sold
out its 3,000-copy pressing and was soon a collector's item. As Natalie Attired, Ray played a
"song-sayer," speaking song lyrics to the
accompaniment of drums. Bob played Wally
Ballou with an air of stony incomprehension: the
bumbling reporter who has no idea how awful
he is. He interrupted guests, talked over their
voices, and often asked questions that had just
been answered. He introduced himself as "radio's highly regarded Wally Ballou, winner of
over seven international diction awards," occasionally as "personable, well-preserved Wally
Ballou." He always had his microphone off for
the first few minutes of his "remote" and was
always cut off at the end, in the middle of a
word. Wally's wife was Hulla Ballou. They had
a son, Little Boy Ballou.

Bob was also Steve Bosco, the often-
inebriated sports reporter who fretted constantly
about being cut off the air and usually ended his
reports with pleas for money. Ray was the other
sportscaster, Biff Burns, whose trademark was
the towering ego matched only by ignorance. At
the height of the Arthur Godfrey craze, they created Arthur Sturdley, redheaded host of a talent
scouts show, who was described as "just a
jerk." Webley Webster conducted the forum,
and Dean Archer Armstead, farm editor, broadcast from the "Lackawanna Field Station" in rural New York. Chester Hasbrouck Frisbie was
listed as the scriptwriter of *Mary Backstayge*,

Noble Wife, and, as the *New Yorker* told it, "discusses coming episodes as if he were talking about Proust or Joyce." Another name that turned up in the serial writing credits was O. Leo Leahy. Barry Campbell was an over-the-hill bandleader who conducted an all-girl orchestra. Charles the Poet read unbearable verse to the faint, sentimental music of a violin and the chirping of birds. But he never made it to the end of a poem without breaking into fits of uncontrollable laughter.

One Feller's Family was a spoof of the eternal Carlton E. Morse serial *One Man's Family*. Bob played Father Butcher, who in the best Father Barbour manner puttered around the garden mumbling to himself. Ray, as Mother Butcher, would shout, "Oh, shut up and stop mumbling, you senile old man!" while Father Butcher kept muttering, "Fanny, Fanny, Fanny." The writer was T. Wilson Messy, and the serial was a "Messy Production."

There was also *Mr. Treat, Chaser of Lost People*, a poke at the prime-time Hummert detective series *Mr. Keen, Tracer of Lost Persons*, which was also heard as *Mr. Trace, Keener Than Most Persons*. There were *Jack Headstrong, the All-American American; Wayside Doctor, Hawaiian Ear, Eye, Nose and Throat Man*; and *Kindly Mother McGee, the Best Cook in the Neighborhood*. Then came *The Gathering Dusk*, "the heartwarming story of a girl who's found unhappiness by leaving no stone unturned in her efforts to locate it," sponsored by the "Whippet Motor Car Company, observing the 45th anniversary of its disappearance." Among the numerous bogus premium giveaways were the burglary kit, the "Bob and Ray Home Surgery Kit," and membership in "Heightwatchers International," which came with "six ample servings of low vitamins and nutrients in artificial colorings."

Their finest series was probably the 1959–60 quarter-hours for CBS. All the old cast was present, Mary, Tex, Wally, and Steve Bosco, still "rounding third and being thrown out at home." Old serials and new held the air. Now there was *Lawrence Fechtenberger, Interstellar Officer Candidate*, sponsored by "chocolate cookies with white stuff in between them," and teaming the hero with an ever-sneering sidekick, Mug Mellish. There was a tree imitator who had more than two dozen trees in his repertoire and gave a sobbing rendition of a weeping willow. On-

stage was the "great *Bob and Ray* bird," a monster that doubled in size by the week, was frequently described as "a dangerous bird," and one day ate the "*Bob and Ray* popcorn ball." The show was coordinated by "Wilbur Conley, young squirt who works for us," and had the usual array of crazy games and stunts. They made fun of TV laugh tracks, had an audience "warmdown," and offered the game show *Ladies, Grab Your Seats*. Finally there was Smelly Dave, the dead whale obtained by Bob and Ray and sent for a weeks-long national tour on an open flatcar. Reporter Arthur Shrank sent back the details, which could be summed up in one gutteral word—*uuuuggghhhh*!

The signatures hinted at the content, from the opening words ("And now, from approximately coast to coast, Bob Elliott and Ray Goulding present the CBS Radio Network") to their traditional closing:

"This is Ray Goulding reminding you to write if you get work . . ."

". . . and Bob Elliott reminding you to hang by your thumbs."

BOB AND VICTORIA, soap opera.

BROADCAST HISTORY: Jan. 27–June 27, 1947, CBS. 15m weekdays. Dutch Mill Cheese, Sunnybank Margarine, Wakefield Coffee. CAST: Unknown. PRODUCER: George Fogle. WRITERS: Lee and Virginia Crosby.

This was billed as "radio's beautiful story of a man who learns that to lose one's heart is to find it." The hero, Bob Reagan, tried to raise an 11-year-old girl, Victoria Clayton, after her father, Bob's best friend, was killed.

THE BOB BECKER PROGRAM, dog talk.

BROADCAST HISTORY: March 6–May 29, 1932, CBS, regional hookup. 15m, Sunday afternoons. *Outdoor Talks*. Atlas Brewing.

Oct. 21, 1934–July 8, 1944, NBC. 15m, Sundays at 5:45 until 1943, then Saturdays at 10:45 A.M. *Dog Talks*. Red Heart.

In his first brief series, Bob Becker utilized his background as outdoor editor of the *Chicago Tribune*. His *Dog Talks* on NBC was a long-running study of dog breeds and training.

THE BOB BURNS SHOW, regional humor.

BROADCAST HISTORY: Sept. 16, 1941–June 9, 1942, CBS. 30m, Tuesdays at 8:30. *The Arkansas Traveler.* Campbell Soups.

Oct. 7–Dec. 30, 1942, CBS. 30m, Wednesdays at 9. Lever Brothers.

Jan. 7, 1943–June 27, 1946, NBC. 30m, Thursdays at 7:30. Lever Brothers.

Sept. 29, 1946–May 25, 1947, NBC. 30m, Sundays at 6:30. American Home Products.

1949, brief daytime series.

CAST: Bob Burns, "the Arkansas Traveler." Ginny Simms, vocalist on the early shows. Edna May Oliver, often playing the eccentric nurse-figure she had popularized in the movies. Mantan Moreland and Ben Carter, black comedians, ca. 1945. Ann Thomas as Sharon O'Shaughnessy, mid-1940s. James Gleason. Una Merkel. Vocalist Shirley Ross, 1944–47. **MUSIC:** Initially Billy Artz; Spike Jones and his novelty band, 1942–44; later Gordon Jenkins, Ray Sinatra. **PRODUCER-DIRECTORS:** Thomas Freebairn-Smith, Joe Thompson, Andrew C. Love.

The Bob Burns Show followed five highly successful years by Burns as hillbilly-in-residence on Bing Crosby's *Kraft Music Hall.* Burns would be billed as "the Arkansas Traveler," a character patterned after Col. Sanford C. Faulkner, who according to legend roamed the antebellum South, fiddling and singing wherever people gathered.

Burns was born in 1890, and his small-town Arkansas background was evident only in his voice. He was college-educated, trained as a civil engineer. "There is nothing slapstick about him," *Radio Life* would write in 1941, when his *Arkansas Traveler* had just opened on CBS. "He dresses conservatively for his broadcasts. There is no strained effort to make funny 'hillbilly' clothes, bare feet, or props do the work of characterizations."

On his farm in the San Fernando Valley, Burns produced beets, pumpkins, alfalfa, corn, and beans. He worked the farm every day, excepting the day of his broadcasts. He collected exotic songbirds, some of which he had trained to sing the national anthem, as well as his theme, *The Arkansas Traveler.* His aviary was frequently cited among the best in the West, and his interests included folklore, photography, shortwave radio, and weaving. He was a carpenter, a fisherman, a maker of toys, a sailor. He raised prize hogs and did a bit of gunsmithing. By 1944 he had taken up astronomy. His farm had grown to 400 acres, and Burns still liked to work: he and two hired men were farming it by themselves.

He had come far from his hometown, Van Buren, Ark. His name back home was Robin. His earliest try at entertaining was playing a mandolin in the Van Buren Queen City Silver Tone Cornet Band. He was about 15 when he invented a new instrument called the bazooka that would one day make his fortune. It was devised of two pieces of gas pipe, slipped together and looking like a cross between a horn and a gun, with a whiskey funnel at the end "where the music came out." It was an instrument that few could play. Even accomplished trombonists gave up in despair when they tackled the bazooka: those who could play it, Burns said, sometimes lost the ability to play the trombone. After performing in Europe in World War I, he returned home and got into vaudeville. He toured in blackface as half of the comedy team Burns and West and did amusing bazooka numbers. But bookings were scarce in the Depression. Burns was advised to try radio.

He auditioned at KNX. He had an idea for a radio show, to be called *Gawkin' Around,* wherein he would play a guitar and talk about most anything. "They heard him do exactly what he does now at $1,000 a week and said, 'We'll let you know if anything turns up,' " said *Radio Mirror* in 1936. Thanks but no thanks. He played Col. Blaine on a *Show Boat* derivative: there was no salary, and the show died, lacking a sponsor. He worked a show called *Fun Factory,* another freebie, and was billed (in blackface) as a character called Soda Pop in the Gilmore Circus (at $20 a week). At KHJ he did a show called *Hi-Jinks:* the pay was $3. Just a year before he became a household name, he was near-broke and out of work. He fed himself with Rotary Club jobs, *Radio Mirror* said, "but a week when he made $75 was a rarity."

He was now in his 40s, with no big break on the horizon. Still, he had faith in his material. The answer, he said, came to him "in a flash." The only reason he hadn't clicked was because he wasn't a big name. It was too easy for people to say no. If he could get on a big national radio show, it could all change overnight. He chose the biggest: Rudy Vallee's *Fleischmann Hour.* He packed his car and struck out for New York.

He called J. Walter Thompson, arranged an audition, and did a monologue for "cold-eyed gentlemen sitting critically behind glass." They listened for about 20 minutes and put him on the Vallee show.

His first national appearance was on *The Fleischmann Hour* in mid-1935. The Thompson people wanted Burns to talk politics in that rustic backwoods manner. They saw him as a possible political pundit in the Will Rogers mold. His likeness to Rogers would not be lost on others: *Newsweek*, in a brief profile later that year, said that "in appearance Burns resembles Gene Tunney," but "he sounds like Will Rogers." On that first Vallee show, Burns did what they told him, his political monologue winning him a return invitation. But on Aug. 15, Rogers and pilot Wiley Post were killed in an Alaskan plane crash. Instantly Rogers was enshrined in show business myth, his name all but canonized. Burns had to fall back on his old act to avoid being washed away as a second-rate imitator.

But the old act worked. That summer and fall he made eight network appearances, with Vallee and with Paul Whiteman, and became the hottest new radio act since Joe Penner. By telegram he was offered a 26-week engagement on *The Kraft Music Hall*, to begin when Bing Crosby took over in January 1936. Burns hopped a train for Hollywood, stopping long enough to get a hero's welcome in his hometown. In Van Buren, he was met by the entire populace, with marching bands, a police escort, and banners (WELCOME HOME, BUBBER, one read) strung everywhere.

His act seldom changed after that. It was country yarnspinning, carried to the extreme. "Pigs or razorback hogs down in Van Buren, Ark., are certainly something," he would say. "Once a pig ate 16 sticks of dynamite. Then he crawled under the barn. A mule came up and kicked the pig and blew up the barn and killed the mule and blew the windows out of the house, and for a couple of days we certainly had a mighty sick pig around." This was the stuff. Burns dispensed it weekly, his contract with Kraft extended until 1941, a five-year run. It only ended then, by one account, because his salary had grown to $5,000 a week, and the Kraft people thought he'd become too expensive.

So Burns was on his own. His *Arkansas Trav-*

eler put a new twist on situation comedy. Burns played a backwoods sage who roamed the land doing good deeds. This comedy-drama was sandwiched in with two Burns monologues, music, and vocals by Ginny Simms. By 1943 he had dropped the *Arkansas Traveler* title, and the motif was gradually refined, with Ann Thomas playing a regular character named Sharon O'Shaughnessy and more contemporary skits featuring character actors James Gleason and Una Merkel. Burns remained the same. He would tell listeners that Merkel had "one of them smiles you could pour on a waffle" and would offer this wry assessment of radio: "Down home we mash up our corn and get corn likker; out here they mash up their corn and get a radio program." Occasionally he talked of retiring. "A feller gets kinda tired workin' 30 minutes every week."

Burns hit his best stride in his 1943–46 series for Lever Brothers and Lifebuoy Soap: his rating peaked in the high teens, and he remained popular through the war years. His bazooka solos could impress, arranged with orchestra accompaniment. When the Army named its armor-piercing gun after Burns's instrument, he gained a small piece of immortality. He did retire after 1949. Though his comedy is dated, he was an important figure in his day, truly reflecting the taste of a growing America. He died Feb. 2, 1956.

THE BOB CROSBY SHOW, musical variety.

BROADCAST HISTORY:
 July 18, 1943–June 25, 1944, NBC. 30m, Sundays at 10:30. Old Gold.
  Jan. 1–July 17, 1946, CBS. 30m, Tuesdays at 10 until March, then Wednesdays at 9:30. Ford Motor Company.
  Oct. 13, 1949–July 16, 1950, NBC. 30m, Sundays at 10:30. *The Pet Milk Show.*
CAST: Bob Crosby, crooner and front man for orchestras with various personnel. **ANNOUNCERS AND CONVERSATION-MAKERS:** John Lund, Les Tremayne.

The Bob Crosby Show, as such, was a product of the 1940s, but it had its roots in the big band era of the previous decade. Crosby had a strange career. He performed in the shadow of an older brother who was the major star of his day. He had no discernible musical genius, yet Crosby fronted what is still remembered as one of the most exciting bands of all time.

It arrived in the summer of 1935. The Ben Pollack band had broken up, but the men wanted to stay together. They needed a front man, and Crosby, formerly a singer with the Anson Weeks band, filled the role. He sang and was listed as leader, and the orchestra went on NBC Oct. 25, 1935, for a Friday quarter-hour at 8:15. This run ended Jan. 17, 1936, but the band remained together. Among others, it boasted Matty Matlock (clarinet), Yank Lawson (trumpet), Bob Zurke and Joe Sullivan (pianists), Nappy Lamare (guitar), Ray Bauduc (drums), Bob Haggart (bass), and saxes Gil Rodin, Eddie Miller and Deane Kincaide. As Bob Crosby and his Bobcats, the band recorded some classic Dixieland numbers and in 1938 hit the popular charts with the Bauduc-Haggart recording *Big Noise from Winnetka*.

In 1939 the band was heard on Mutual in a 30-minute Wednesday slot. On June 27 that year it was signed for the much-traveled *Camel Caravan* program on NBC; this ran Tuesdays at 9:30 and, beginning in January 1940, Saturdays at 10. Crosby's association with Camel ended Jan. 2, 1941, then heard Thursdays at 7:30.

His Old Gold series was again heavy with swing. After the war, he organized a new orchestra and announced that he would shy away from the Dixieland music that had made him famous. His *Bob Crosby Show* was straight variety, highlighting popular songs by Crosby and such guests as Dinah Shore, Kay Starr, and Peggy Lee. But he was scheduled opposite Bob Hope and was buried in the ratings. A shift to Wednesday didn't help, and his subsequent series was short-lived. Crosby turned up as the maestro figure on *The Jack Benny Program* when Phil Harris departed in 1952. As for the men in Crosby's great '30s band, many played together for years. Lawson and Haggart were still performing in the '70s as part of "the World's Greatest Jazzband."

BOB ELSON ON BOARD THE CENTURY, interviews and talk.

BROADCAST HISTORY: March 4, 1946–June 11, 1951, Mutual. 15m, weekdays.

The Century was a high-speed luxury train, used by the rich and famous traveling between Chicago and New York. Sportscaster Bob Elson

set up a microphone in Chicago's LaSalle Street Station and tried to intercept well-knowns for spontaneous interviews. Among the celebrities who appeared were Rita Hayworth and Eleanor Roosevelt, but architect Frank Lloyd Wright brushed briskly past. When Elson said he loved Wright's work, Wright replied, "In that case, young man, I've done enough for you already."

The show was alive with terminal noise, with trains hissing and chugging and tooting. Train buffs complained that the Century was diesel-powered, but the producers thought the old sounds were more romantic, so the sound effects records remained, at least into the late '40s.

THE BOB HAWK SHOW, quiz.

BROADCAST HISTORY: Oct. 31, 1942–June 23, 1944, CBS. 30m, Saturdays at 7:30; Fridays at 10, summer 1943. *Thanks to the Yanks.* Camel Cigarettes.

July 3, 1944–Sept. 29, 1947, CBS. 30m, Mondays at 7:30 until April 1947, then at 10:30. Camel Cigarettes.

Oct. 2, 1947–Sept. 30, 1948, NBC. 30m, Thursdays at 10. Camel Cigarettes.

Oct. 4, 1948–July 27, 1953, CBS. 30m, Mondays at 10:30 until 1951, then at 10. Camel Cigarettes.

QUIZMASTER-HOST: Bob Hawk. **ANNOUNCERS:** Charlie Stark, Art Gentry, Bob LeMond, etc. **MUSIC:** Peter Van Steeden, Hank Sylvern, Irving Miller. **DIRECTOR:** Kenneth W. MacGregor.

Bob Hawk was one of radio's busiest quizmasters. His earliest efforts in the field, with titles like *Foolish Questions* and *Fun Quiz* (1936) remain obscure, but they helped set the pattern of later man-on-the-street interview shows. Hawk worked on *Quixie Doodles* (Mutual circa 1938), *Name Three* (Mutual for Philip Morris, 1939–40), and *Take it or Leave It* (CBS for Eversharp, 1940–41). On Jan. 9, 1942, he opened *How'm I Doin'?*, a CBS (later NBC) quiz for Camel Cigarettes. It paired him with another Camel favorite, singer Vaughn Monroe, and though it was dropped Oct. 1 that year, it was the beginning of a ten-year association for Hawk with Camel, a mix that would lead to one of the most effective sponsor-related quiz gimmicks on radio.

Hawk's new show for Camel was *Thanks to the Yanks*, a direct forerunner of *The Bob Hawk Show*. Hawk stood in a pulpit at the end of a runway jutting out from the stage and asked questions of audience contestants. Four announcers worked the audience with portable microphones: the contestants, answering from their seats, chose 1,000- or 2,000- or 3,000-cigarette questions. If they answered correctly, the free Camels were sent to servicemen of their choice; if they missed, the smokes were thrown into a duffel bag and sent to the most remote camps in the United States. Hawk's skill at choosing provocative questions kept it lively. The questions often begged clear-cut answers, and Hawk's decisions were sometimes hotly argued. But such questions as ''Does a bull really get angry at red, or just the waving of a flag?'' were used only after scientific evidence pointed (in Hawk's opinion) one way or the other.

In 1945 the serviceman angle was dropped, and *Thanks to the Yanks* became *The Bob Hawk Show*. Now Hawk initiated his memorable Lemac quiz. Winners were crowned Lemacs to the enthusiastic singing, ''You're a Lemac now!'' Lemac, of course, spelled backward, was the name of the sponsor's product. The show moved to Hollywood in 1949. Announcers Bob LeMond and Charles Lyon worked the crowd; the show was transcribed at 45 to 60 minutes and edited to a half-hour. Cash was added to the pot: contestants could now win up to $3,000 by answering five questions, each beginning with a designated letter from the word Lemac. Correct answers brought the contestant onstage, where he or she stepped into the Lemac Box and tried for the big cash prizes. Sample question: ''If Romance begins with a capital *R* and ends in *a-n-c-e*, name five words, each beginning with a letter in the word Lemac, that ends in *a-n-c-e*.'' The contestant had 90 seconds to name them all.

THE BOB HOPE SHOW, comedy.

BROADCAST HISTORY: Jan. 4–April 5, 1935, Blue Network. 30m, Fridays at 8:30. *The Intimate Revue*. Emerson Drug Company, Bromo Seltzer. **CAST:** Bob Hope, singers James Melton and Jane Froman, Patricia ''Honey Chile'' Wilder. **MU-SIC:** Al Goodman.

Sept. 14, 1935–Sept. 3, 1936, CBS. 30m, Saturdays at 7; Thursdays at 7 beginning in June. *The Atlantic Family*. Atlantic Oil. **CAST:** Hope, Patricia Wilder, tenor Frank Parker. **MUSIC:** Red Nichols and his Five Pennies.

May 9–Sept. 26, 1937, Blue Network. 30m, Sundays at 9. *The Rippling Rhythm Revue*. Woodbury Soap. **CAST:** Hope, tenor Frank Parker. **MUSIC:** Shep Fields.

Dec. 8, 1937–March 23, 1938, NBC. 60m, Wednesdays at 10. *Your Hollywood Parade*. Lucky Strike. Hope joined in progress on December 29.

Sept. 27, 1938–June 8, 1948, NBC. 30m, Tuesdays at 10. *The Pepsodent Show Starring Bob Hope*, his major radio work. The cast in 1938–39: Bob Hope, madcap Jerry Colonna, announcer Bill Goodwin, and bandleader Skinnay Ennis. Blanche Stewart and Elvia Allman as high-society crazies Brenda and Cobina. Judy Garland, resident songstress, 1939; Frances Langford for many years thereafter. Barbara Jo Allen as Vera Vague by 1943. Stan Kenton as maestro, 1943, when Skinnay Ennis went into the Army; Desi Arnaz Orchestra, 1946; Les Brown beginning in 1947. Singers of the late 1940s: Gloria Jean, Doris Day. Trudy Erwin as the Pepsodent Girl, whose weekly lament, ''Dear Miriam, poor Miriam, neglected using Irium,'' warned women what might happen to teeth without Pepsodent and its super ingredient, Irium. **ANNOUNCERS:** Bill Goodwin, Wendell Niles, Art Baker, Larry Keating, **PRODUCER-DIRECTORS:** Bill Lawrence, Norman Morrell, Bob Stephenson, Al Capstaff, etc. **WRITERS:** Mel Shavelson, Milt Josefsberg, Norman Sullivan, Norman Panama, Jack Rose, Sherwood and Al Schwartz, Melvin Frank, Dave Murray, Larry Marks, Larry Gelbart, Mort Lachman, Marv Fischer, Paul Laven, Jack Douglas, Hal Block, Ted McKay, Samuel Kurtzman, Fred Fox, etc. **THEME:** *Thanks for the Memory*.

Sept. 14, 1948–June 13, 1950, NBC. 30m, Tuesdays at 9. Swan Soap. **CAST:** Most of the old cast gone as of this series. Doris Day a regular. Guest stars. **ANNOUNCER:** Hy Averback.

Oct. 3, 1950–April 21, 1955, NBC. Various 30m timeslots: Tuesdays at 9 for Chesterfield, 1950–52; Wednesdays at 10 for Jell-O, early 1953; Fridays at 8:30 for American Dairy, 1953–54; Thursdays at 8:30 for American Dairy, 1954–55. Also 15m, weekdays, Nov. 10, 1952–July 9, 1954, at 9:30 A.M. (later at 11:45 A.M. and 10:30 A.M.) for General Foods.

Bob Hope became a radio top-liner after a long career on the vaudeville stage. Like Bing Crosby, his sometime sidekick of movie adventures, once he was under way Hope rose swiftly. Like Crosby, he came to radio early and stayed late. He shared with Crosby an ability with words, a glibness, a keen intelligence. They did not share their styles. Crosby on the air was slow and mellow: Hope was a machine gun. If one joke didn't get an audience, two more were on the way. It was once estimated that in four minutes of monologue he fired off 24 jokes.

He was born Leslie Townes Hope in England, May 29, 1903. He was taught to sing by his mother, a concert performer on the Welsh stage. His father, a stonemason, brought the family of eight to the United States in 1907, and soon young Hope adopted Bob as his name, to avoid ribbings by other kids.

His early career was filled with odd jobs: at one point he entered the ring as "Packy East," advancing to the Golden Gloves finals. He teamed up with a young hoofer, George Byrne, and tried vaudeville, the two playing small towns in the Midwest as Two Diamonds in the Rough. In New York, they sang and danced in blackface and got a part on Broadway; in 1928 they decided to try Chicago. Hope, disenchanted with the blackface routine, made his first try at monologue at a stopover in Newcastle, Ind. He got good laughs, broke up the partnership, and went on alone.

In Chicago, the scene was bleak. Vaudeville excursions in the Midwest were followed by another fling at Broadway. He appeared in *Ballyhoo of 1932*, his first major stage role. This was followed by Jerome Kern's *Roberta* (1933, with Hope as a piano-playing fast-talker named Huckleberry Haines) and a pair of standout roles in 1936: Ziegfeld's *Follies*, with Fanny Brice; and Cole Porter's *Red, Hot, and Blue*, with Ethel Merman and Jimmy Durante. It was during this time that he began the first phase of his radio career.

An engagement at New York's Capitol Theater led to his initiation on the air. In 1932 he did a few Sunday morning shows with Maj. Edward Bowes on *The Capitol Family Hour*. This was a serious program of concert music, and Hope provided the comic relief. But when he submitted his scripts in advance, he discovered on broadcast day that Bowes had taken the best lines for himself. The same year he worked *The RKO Theater of the Air*, an NBC Friday night half-hour that featured vaudeville-type variety.

Later he appeared on Rudy Vallee's *Fleischmann Hour*, in those days radio's top showcase for new talent. But the magic didn't work for Hope: the lightning that would charge the careers of Edgar Bergen, Red Skelton, and Bob Burns on the Vallee show completely missed Hope, and it wasn't until January 1935 that he got his first regular radio job.

The Intimate Revue is notable as establishing Hope's practice of always having a stooge on hand who was crazier than himself. His first radio foil was Patricia Wilder, who became known as "Honey Chile." Hope had met her in an agent's office (she "had a thick spoonbread southern accent," he would write in his autobiography), and when she opened her mouth and said, "Ha you, Mistah Hope?" he thought she was a natural for radio. This first series was short-lived: ratings were mediocre, and "our sponsors took so much of their own product [Bromo Seltzer] they finally shucked the whole deal." Honey Chile went with him to his next radio job, *The Atlantic Family*, (later titled *Family on Tour*), which Hope joined in progress Dec. 14, 1935. Hope's 1937 radio show, *The Rippling Rhythm Revue*, took its title from a musical gimmick by maestro Shep Fields, a blowing of bubbles while the orchestra played. During this run Paramount beckoned: *The Big Broadcast of 1938* was to begin filming, and Hope was offered a part. He moved to Hollywood, continuing his monologues on *Rippling Rhythm* by transcontinental wire. This series soon ran its course, but two months later Hope was installed on the Dick Powell variety show, *Your Hollywood Parade* (NBC for Lucky Strike). Again he joined in progress, Dec. 29, 1937. This would be the launching pad into the major phase of his radio career: concurrently with the release of *The Big Broadcast* (in which he sang a heralded duet, *Thanks for the Memory*, with Shirley Ross), it propelled him into his own half-hour comedy series in the fall of 1938.

The Pepsodent Show quickly became a Tuesday giant. It was one of radio's all-time hits, its Hooper rating peaking at 40 points in 1942 and seldom falling out of the 30s thereafter. Immediately preceded by the equally popular *Fibber McGee and Molly*, it gave NBC a lock on Tuesday nights that was formidable. Hope's top sidekick was Jerry Colonna, perhaps the wildest comic presence of 1940s radio. Colonna had been a serious trombonist, playing with Goodman, Shaw, and the Dorseys: now he infused Hope's program with verbal and vocal mayhem. He sported a four-inch walrus moustache and had an attack-voice comedy style that simply blew away any attempt at logic. His specialty, as noted in *Newsweek*, was "tearing up straight songs in a voice that begins in a mousy whisper and reaches a roaring cresendo. He can—and usually does—hold a note longer than most opera singers, an attribute ordinarily found only in hog callers." He was to Hope what the Mad Russian was to Eddie Cantor, wrote Richard Lamparski: "an utterly mad character who might appear at any time, anywhere, with some ridiculous scheme or remark. As soon as he began walking to the microphone, the studio audience would warn listeners of his approach by gales of laughter." Colonna was described as "the singer's answer to Spike Jones" and "the crazy man of our age." On the Hope show, he was known as "Professor." There were two sides to the Professor, Hope would write: "One is the zany, silly moron, and the other is the deep-thinking, serious moron." Colonna's two running lines were "Greetings, Gate!" and "Who's Yehudi?" Either could reduce an audience to fits of laughter. "Greetings, Gate!" was his standard intro; the Yehudi gag grew out of a contest, begun on *The Pepsodent Show*, to help name Bill Goodwin's new baby. Colonna suggested Yehudi in response to the rise of the Russian-American concert violinist Yehudi Menuhin. The name got laughs from people who had never heard of Yehudi Menuhin, and the gag was off and running. The search for Yehudi became a long-running joke, at one point involving Basil Rathbone and Nigel Bruce as Sherlock Holmes and Dr. Watson.

But Hope was the star. No one had ever told jokes quite like Bob Hope. His monologues were rapid-fire blasts of comedy, extremely topical and wildly appreciated by his live audiences. "Hope tells a gag in three lines," *Radio Life* wrote in appreciation. "He'll work for an hour on a one-word change. By the time he goes on the air, he knows his gags by heart." He probably employed more writers during his career than any other comic. Writing for Hope, one gagster lamented, was a test of endurance: the routine was "write and sweat, throw stuff at each other and come up with a half-hour that

sounds so casually easygoing you figure Hope just tossed it off between lunch and dinner." He demanded long rehearsals, including a 60- to 90-minute runthrough before a live audience. During this trial, Hope would stand at the microphone and highlight his scripts where the big laughs came. The writing staff averaged six men but went as high as 12. At one point, Hope had each writer do a complete script and he chose the best. That system was so cumbersome that it was scrapped for a more traditional approach: three two-man teams, each assigned to write the show's three sections. First came the monologue; then a midshow routine with Colonna or another member of the regular cast; finally, a sketch for the guest star. The biggest problem with Hope, said producer Al Capstaff in 1945, was his inevitable tendency to pack the script. It was always 37 minutes long and had to be whittled down joke by joke until only the surefire material remained. The result on the air was a breathless gush, with six laughs a minute guaranteed.

Once his formula was set, Hope seldom tampered with it. *The Pepsodent Show* was highly predictable in form if not in content. The show was also advanced by Hope's highly active film career (two to four films a year, beginning in 1938), and especially by the success of his "Road" films with Bing Crosby and Dorothy Lamour. The radio cast was solid, most remaining with Hope through the *Pepsodent* era. Brenda and Cobina, the high-society nitwits played by Blanche Stewart and Elvia Allman, were said to be "the ugliest girls in the world." The writers were asking for trouble, modeling them after real-life socialites Brenda Frazier and Cobina Wright Jr. without bothering to change the names. Wright filed suit but settled, Hope remembered, when he invited her on the show as a guest. The squeaky, man-crazed old maid Vera Vague always came on with a "Yoo-hoo! . . . oh, Mr. Hope! . . . yoo-hoo!" Barbara Jo Allen created the character in the 1930s, playing it on such series as *Carefree Carnival* and in appearances at California women's clubs. She fit well between the craziness of Colonna and the foolishness of Hope. But the performer most identified with Hope in those years was probably Frances Langford. When she joined Hope's company, Langford could not have known what great adventure lay ahead. No one knew then that this radio show would take them to distant outposts of a world at war, that seldom in the coming years would they broadcast from the same location twice.

Hope did his first remote from March Field on May 6, 1941. Initially reluctant to leave the studio, he found an audience of servicemen so primed and ready to laugh that he was forever hooked. The roar of laughter and applause was so loud, he would recall, that he "got goose pimples" during the broadcast. The following week, back at NBC, he faced a "tough, unreasonable audience" that demanded funny material. The servicemen would laugh at anything. So they went on the road—Hope, Goodwin, Colonna, Langford, and Ennis—and for the next seven years, by his own reckoning, Hope did only two studio shows. The rest came from bases and camps, and after the war from hospitals. The cast was put on alert, ready to go at the drop of a hat. Langford was given 24-hour notice to "hop a bomber" for Alaska in 1943. They hit 100 camps that year, 36 on the Alaskan tour, doing three to five shows a day in addition to the radio show each week. The troupe also made a 20,000-mile trip into the European war. Hope was the first American entertainer to perform in Sicily. He did a show at Messina just after the enemy had fled the town and was still bombarding the area with its artillery. By the end of the war, it was estimated that Hope had appeared at virtually every camp, naval base, and hospital in the country. He had made half a dozen trips overseas, including a tour of the South Pacific in 1944 that was highlighted by a crash landing in Australia. With him then was the same crew that had gone to Italy the year before: Langford, Colonna, dancer Patty Thomas, guitarist Tony Romano, and an old vaudeville pal, Barney Dean. *Newsweek* called it "the biggest entertainment giveaway in history," a pace that no one in show business has ever equaled. "It is impossible to see how he can do so much, can cover so much ground, can work so hard, and can be so effective," novelist John Steinbeck said of Hope. For his service to the country, Hope was given more than 100 awards and citations and two special Oscars. He was voted a place in the Smithsonian's Living Hall of Fame.

Putting on such a globetrotting show was difficult. Producer Capstaff gave *Radio Life* a glimpse of it in 1945. The writers always tailored the scripts to the audience: if Hope was to play at Quantico Marine Base, lots of local Marine gags were worked in. There were jokes about military police, about officers and the mess, and scouts were sent in to survey the area about two weeks before the broadcast. From talks with public relations people, hitchhiking soldiers, and boys in the mess halls, a guide was worked up for the writers. By the time Hope and the cast arrived, they had a good idea of the raw material they'd be working with. There was also the "big headache," Capstaff said: arranging transportation and hotels for an entourage that included more than 40 people. But out of it all came an enormous sense of accomplishment. Langford was named *Radio Life*'s "number one girl of World War II" as she sang her way around the globe and attained the sure timing of a polished comedienne.

In 1947 Hope opened his season to harsh reviews. The shows had a "same old stuff" aroma, the critics carped. Ratings dropped, and Hope responded with a shakeup the following year. Gone were Vera Vague and Jerry Colonna: the show took on more a semblance of situation comedy. But it was radio itself that was fading. Like Crosby and Benny, Hope stayed with it to the end. In 1952 he opened a quarter-hour show on daytime radio. His first guests were Jack Benny, Groucho Marx, and Dennis Day, a good sendoff but futile. Writer Howard Blake built in all the Hope hallmarks, and there was a "lady editor of the week" spotlight for such glamor queens as Arlene Dahl. Hope began to appear on TV. He was asked to do comic commentary for NBC's coverage of the 1952 national political conventions, and did: his association with NBC was solid from 1938 on. In later years he became the network's senior statesman, doing specials and birthday salutes as his 90th birthday came and went. His theme song, *Thanks for the Memory*, was identified with him for half a century, the two becoming thoroughly synonymous in the national consciousness.

His shows on tape do not wear well. Topical humor can be hilarious at the time, but it seldom holds up. The moment is lost, the immediacy gone, and a modern listener is left, perhaps, with a sense of curiosity. The opening of the June 2, 1942, show from Quantico is a good example. There is little doubt that Hope is playing to the best crowds of his life, a cheering section that many another comedian would die for. His theme is all but drowned in the wild cheering, and he sings his way (''. . . aaah, thank you, so much . . .'') into the opening monologue. ''This is Bob Quantico Marine Base Hope, telling you leathernecks to use Pepsodent and you'll never have teeth that'd make a cow hide.'' The Marines find this a scream. Hope continues with local color. He had an easy time finding Quantico: ''I just drove down U.S. 1 and turned left at the first crap game.'' The boys love it. On another show, Hope talks of the coming baseball season. ''This is Bob Baseball Season Hope, telling you if you use Pepsodent on your teeth, you may not be able to pitch like Bob Feller, but at dinnertime you'll be able to pitch in with what's under your smeller.'' This is hardly timeless humor, though it was timely in the extreme. That's the way to listen to Hope today: with a keen sense of history, with an appreciation of what the world found funny in an unfunny time.

BOBBY BENSON'S ADVENTURES, juvenile western adventure.

BROADCAST HISTORY: Oct. 17, 1932–Dec. 11, 1936, CBS. 15m continuation, three a week at 5 until 1933, then five a week at 6 or 6:15. Also under the title *The H-Bar-O Rangers.* Heckers H-O Cereal. **CAST:** Richard Wanamaker (until ca. March 1933) as Bobby Benson, young owner of the H-Bar-O Ranch (named for the sponsor) in the Big Bend country of south Texas. Billy Halop as Bobby Benson, 1933–36. Herb Rice as Buck Mason, foreman of the ranch (name change to Tex Mason, 1933). Unknown actors as Tex Mason, possibly Neil O'Malley. Cowboy film star Tex Ritter credited in some accounts with occasional roles. Craig McDonnell as Harka, the Indian ranch hand. Florence Halop as Polly Armstead. **ANNOUNCERS:** ''Dangerous'' Dan Seymour, ''Two-Gun'' Andre Baruch, Art Millet, etc. **CREATOR-PRODUCER:** Herb Rice. **WRITERS:** Peter Dixon, John Battle.

June 21, 1949–June 17, 1955, Mutual. Many 30m timeslots, often Saturdays or Sundays; occasionally heard weekdays, sometimes two or three times a week. *Bobby Benson and the B-Bar-B Riders.* Mostly sustained; Kraft Foods, 1951. **CAST:** Ivan Cury (1949–50) as Bobby Benson, now owner of the B-Bar-B spread. Clive Rice (professional name Clyde Campbell) as Bobby, 1951–55. Don Knotts as Windy Wales, ranch handyman and teller

of tall tales. Charles Irving as Tex Mason, 1949–51; Bob Haig as Tex, 1952–55. Craig McDonnell as Harka and as Irish. **ANNOUNCER:** ''Cactus'' Carl Warren. **PRODUCER:** Herb Rice. **DIRECTOR:** Bob Novak. **WRITERS:** Jim Shean, Peter Dixon, David Dixon. **ANIMAL SOUNDS:** Frank Milano (cattle, panthers, dogs, and Bobby's horse Amigo).

Herb Rice created *Bobby Benson* for a CBS affiliate in Buffalo, N.Y. The stories employed standard western themes—rustling, bandits, and smuggling along the Mexican border. In the '30s, however, *Benson* followed the globetrotting of such serials as *Jack Armstrong*, journeying to China for an adventure in the Himalayas. A number of characters were used largely for comic relief, notably Windy Wales and Diogenes Dodwaddle, a pair of incorrigible liars.

The later series, using mostly the same characters, found ranch foreman Tex Mason the main adult influence who often put the pieces of mysterious doings together and solved the puzzles. The half-hour series had a thunderous opening signature, with hoofbeats pounding out of the radio and the announcer calling the action.

Here they come! They're riding fast and they're riding hard! It's time for action and adventure in the modern West with BOBBY BENSON AND THE B-BAR-B RIDERS! And out in front, astride his golden palomino Amigo, it's the cowboy kid himself, Bobby Benson!

BEEEE-BAR-BEEEE!

A spinoff, *Songs of the B-Bar-B*, was a western singalong with a campfire flavor. It aired on Mutual, 30m, twice a week at 5, 1952–54. Clive Rice starred as Bobby, with Tex Fletcher as Tex Mason.

BOLD VENTURE, adventure.

BROADCAST HISTORY: 1951–52, transcribed syndication by Frederic W. Ziv Company; 78 30m episodes produced with a release date March 26, 1951. **CAST:** Humphrey Bogart as Slate Shannon, owner of a small ''quasi-respectable'' Cuban hotel ''tenanted by a motley, shifting cast of characters'' (*Newsweek*). Lauren Bacall as his sidekick and ''ward'' Sailor Duval, ''a smart-talking, tenderhearted'' young woman played by Bacall ''with sultry, sexy monotones.'' Jester Hairston as King Moses, the calypso singer. **MUSIC:** David Rose.

PRODUCER: Bogart's Santana Productions. **DI-RECTOR:** Henry Hayward (or Haywood). **WRITERS:** Morton Fine and David Friedkin.

Humphrey Bogart was finally lured to series radio by the new wonder, tape recording. He had always been firm in his refusal to commit himself to a live microphone every week, but he was interested when writers Morton Fine and David Friedkin approached him with a syndication proposition. He could do the show in takes and have music and sound effects added later. Three or four shows a week could be done, a whole season produced in a short time, leaving the Bogarts free for the rest of the year.

They would be paid $4,000 per show. The Ziv Company, which would distribute, would put up $12,000 for each episode, to ensure that the writing and production be top grade. The Bogarts signed and were in Africa for his role in *The African Queen* as *Bold Venture* was released to stations coast to coast. A season was safely in the can, and 423 stations bought it, paying weekly fees to Ziv ranging from $15 for a small-town small-watter to $750 for a big New York outlet.

Bold Venture was designed to fit the stars' screen images. It was set in Havana, although, as *Newsweek* noted, it "could as easily be Casablanca." It was "a pure Bogie-and-Baby script." In addition to owning the hotel, Slate Shannon also owned a boat, the *Bold Venture*, "ever ready to roar to the rescue of a friend or the search of an enemy." The hotel was a perfect setting for all kinds of Caribbean adventures: a crossroads for modern pirates, treasure hunters and revolutionaries. A calypso singer named King Moses provided the musical bridges, incorporating storylines into his songs. It was never adequately explained why Sailor Duval was Shannon's ward: she sounded quite able to take care of herself and spent the series trying to breach that patented Bogart brushoff when she wanted to get romantic.

BOSTON BLACKIE, detective drama.

BROADCAST HISTORY: June 23–Sept. 15, 1944, NBC. 30m, Fridays at 10. Summer replacement for *The Amos 'n' Andy Show*. Rinso. **CAST:** Chester Morris as Boston Blackie, a private detective described as "a modern Robin Hood, a little on the gangster side, wise to all the tricks but always re-

versing to do a lot of good." Richard Lane as Blackie's would-be nemesis, Inspector Faraday of the police. Lesley Woods as Blackie's girlfriend Mary Wesley. **ANNOUNCER:** Harlow Wilcox.

April 11, 1945–Oct. 25, 1950, transcribed syndication by Frederic W. Ziv (dates are New York); various network outlets, mostly Mutual. Many 30m timeslots. **CAST:** Richard Kollmar as Boston Blackie. Maurice Tarplin as Inspector Faraday. Jan Miner as Mary. More than 200 episodes produced.

Boston Blackie was billed as "enemy to those who make him an enemy, friend to those who have no friend." His specialty was making fools of the police, a simple task with Inspector Faraday heading the official investigations. Chester Morris initiated the role on the screen and played in 14 *Blackie* films.

THE BOSWELL SISTERS, singing trio; popular music.

BROADCAST HISTORY: 1931–33, CBS. 15m, three a week at 7:30 for Baker's Chocolate, 1931–32; twice a week at 10, sustained, 1932–33. Premiere: Oct. 16, 1931. **STARS:** The Boswell Sisters: Connie, Martha, and Helvetia (Vet).

The impact of the Boswell Sisters on the music of the '30s was significant. Their sound was unique: "They merged harmony, rhythm, and feeling to produce a musical togetherness that has been imitated but never equaled," wrote Richard Lamparski. They were all capable musicians, able to provide their own backup on piano, cello, or violin. They set the standard for all the singing sisters who followed them.

Their careers began in New Orleans. Connie and Martha had won an amateur radio contest in the early '20s, and by 1927 they were heard regularly on WSMB. They sang on KFWB, Los Angeles, in 1929 and on the NBC series *Pleasure Time* in 1931. In 1932 they were heard on Chesterfield's *Music That Satisfies* (NBC), and they appeared on Bing Crosby's Woodbury show (CBS) following the demise of their own. In 1936 the act dissolved. Vet had married and Martha was about to, and Connie continued as a solo act, changing the spelling of her name to Connee in the 1940s. She appeared as a regular on Crosby's *Kraft Music Hall* of the '30s and '40s. She performed in a wheelchair, having lost the ability to walk as a child. This was widely attributed to polio, but Connie told *Radio Life* she had fallen out of a wagon at 4 and cracked her spine. She died in 1976, preceded in death by Martha (1958) and followed by Vet (1988).

BOX 13, mystery-adventure.

BROADCAST HISTORY: 1948–50s, transcribed syndication by Mayfair Productions; 30m, premiere date WOR, Aug. 22, 1948. CAST: Alan Ladd as Dan Holiday, a writer who advertised for adventure and usually found more than he bargained for. Sylvia Picker as Suzy, a scatterbrain who screened his mail and ran his office. Regular company: Betty Lou Gerson, Lurene Tuttle, Alan Reed, Luis Van Rooten, John Beal. MUSIC: Rudy Schrager. PRODUCER: Richard Sanville. DIRECTOR: Vern Carstensen. WRITER: Russell Hughes.

Mayfair Productions was a joint venture between film star Alan Ladd and Bernie Joslin (who had previously run a chain of Mayfair Restaurants), formed to capitalize on the coming boom in radio syndication. Ladd, no stranger to the microphone, had begun his show business career as a radio actor at KFWB in 1935. He worked as many as 20 shows a week and for a time was heard as "the Richfield Reporter" on the show of that name.

As Dan Holiday, he was a fiction writer retired from the newspaper game. To find material for his books, he ran a provocative ad in the *Star-Times*: *Adventure wanted—will go anywhere, do anything—Box 13*. The ad brought in adventure of all kinds: one week a racketeer's victim, the next a psychotic killer looking for fun. Some of Ladd's support people came from his early career: he had met actress Sylvia Picker at KFWB, and scripter Russell Hughes had been the man who had hired him, at $19 a week, in 1935.

BRAVE NEW WORLD, documentary drama.

BROADCAST HISTORY: Nov. 1, 1937–May 2, 1938, CBS. 30m, Mondays at 10:30. A joint WPA/CBS project. MUSIC: Bernard Herrmann as of Jan. 1938. PRODUCER: William D. Boutwell of the federal radio project. DIRECTORS: Irving Reis and Earle McGill of CBS.

Brave New World was conceived by John W. Studebaker, U.S. commissioner of education, and Undersecretary of State Sumner Welles, to help counter the destructive effects of propaganda. The show was designed to promote international friendship, to "sing the praises" of America's neighbors without pushing American self-interest. CBS contributed $3,000 a week for the series, while the WPA kicked in another $1,000. The series focused on Latin America, proposing to tell its story not with stuffy facts and dreary figures but with living dramatizations of historical and cultural themes. The first play was a "blood and thunder" script (*Time*) that told of three conquistadors searching for gold. It was written by Bernard Schoenfeld and scored by WPA musician Rudolph Schramm. The scripts were checked for accuracy by authorities on Latin America. It focused on 20 nations and the "democratic ideal we share."

BRAVE TOMORROW, soap opera.

BROADCAST HISTORY: Oct. 11, 1943–June 30, 1944, NBC. 15m continuation, weekdays at 11:30 A.M. Ivory Snow. CAST: Jeanette Dowling as Louise Lambert, mother of a typical family. Raymond Edward Johnson as her husband Hal; Roger DeKoven also as Hal. Nancy Douglass and Flora Campbell as Jean, their married daughter. Frank Lovejoy as Jean's husband Brad Forbes. Jone Allison and Andree Wallace as Marty Lambert, Jean's sister. ANNOUNCER: Ed Herlihy. MUSIC: William Meeder on organ. WRITER: Ruth Adams Knight.

Brave Tomorrow was "a story of love and courage," the challenge of the day being the raising of two daughters in wartime by Louise and Hal Lambert. Jean came of age and married: her husband Brad, waiting to get into the war, was shipped from one small-town Army post to another, places like Dustville, Tex. In one sequence, sister Marty ran away to Texas to join Jean and Brad, and Louise came flying, walking, and hitchhiking in pursuit. Louise and Hal differed in philosophy: she was the disciplinarian; he wanted to let the children "turn life's sharp corners alone." Words of wisdom were read over a soaring organ theme: *Love requires courage . . . out of the challenge of today, we build our brave tomorrow!* This was considered profound enough for readings before and after the melodrama.

BREAK THE BANK, quiz.

BROADCAST HISTORY: Oct. 20, 1945–April 13, 1946, Mutual. 30m, Saturdays at 9:30. Vicks.

July 5, 1946–Sept. 23, 1949, ABC. 30m, Fridays at 9. Vitalis.

Oct. 5, 1949–Sept. 13, 1950, NBC. 30m, Wednesdays at 9. Vitalis.

Sept. 25, 1950–Sept. 21, 1951, NBC. 30m, weekdays at 11 A.M. Vitalis.

Sept. 24, 1951–March 27, 1953, ABC. 30m, weekdays at 11:30 A.M. Various sponsors.

Sept. 28, 1953–July 15, 1955, NBC. 15m, weekdays at 10:45 A.M. Overlapping series: Sept. 27, 1954–March 25, 1955, Mutual, 15m, weekdays at noon. Miles Laboratories, both series.

CAST: Initially featured different hosts each week; John Reed King, Johnny Olson, etc. Bert Parks full-time host from ca. 1946. ANNOUNCERS: Clayton "Bud" Collyer, Bob Shepherd. MUSIC: Peter Van Steeden. PRODUCERS: Walt Framer, Ed Wolfe. DIRECTOR: Jack Rubin.

In 1948, when it had been on the air three years, *Break the Bank* was touted by *Radio Mirror* as "the highest-paying quiz program in the world." Its jackpots, for that time, were indeed huge. Contestants routinely walked out with $3,000. One soon took the bank for $9,000, establishing a new record for such giveaways. The show was "designed for intelligent people" who read widely and had good retentive power.

The game was simple. Before each broadcast, 15 couples were chosen to be interviewed. Producer Ed Wolfe then selected an order. Only the first four or five teams would actually get on the air: the others got $5 for their trouble. The couples could be any combination—man and wife, brother and sister, Army buddies; the only requisite was that the contestants had to be together legitimately and not part of the brigade of regulars who always tried to crash big-money quiz shows. Announcer Bud Collyer made the initial selections: he would point out people to men stationed in the audience with portable microphones.

Once onstage, the couples selected categories. These were often fitted to their backgrounds (one couple in their 70s chose "Life Begins at 75" and broke the bank). The questions increased in difficulty, from $10 to $500. A final question after the $500 level was "for the bank." This was always at least $1,000, and whatever amount a losing team left on the table was deposited in the bank for the next round. The bank grew quickly from week to week and generated great excitement among those who were excited by quiz shows.

One mistake was allowed on the "gateway to the bank"; two misses sent a team back to their seats. Cash winnings were counted out right onstage, except in the case of major winnings, when a check was presented immediately. Joseph Nathan Kane, author of *Famous First Facts*, wrote the questions, sealed them in envelopes, and hand-delivered them to the show.

Tickets were required, and people lined up early in hopes of getting advantageous seats. Anything could happen: that was the effect desired by the producers. One of the most celebrated *Break the Bank* stories occurred when a small child wriggled away from his mother, ran up onstage, and was caught just as the show went on the air. Impulsively, Bert Parks invited the mother to join the contestants. She fired off correct answers to the eight questions, broke the bank, and walked off with $9,020.

BREAKFAST AT SARDI'S, audience show; human interest.

BROADCAST HISTORY: Premiered January 13, 1941, on KFWB, Los Angeles. *Breakfast on the Boulevard.*

Aug. 3, 1942–Feb. 26, 1943, Blue Network. 30m, weekdays at 11 A.M. *Breakfast at Sardi's.* Various sponsors.

March 1, 1943–Jan. 13, 1950, ABC. 30m, weekdays at 11 A.M. as *Breakfast with Breneman* until 1948; at 2 as *Breakfast in Hollywood*, 1948–49; and at 2 as *Welcome to Hollywood*, Jan. 16, 1950–July 6, 1951. Many sponsors ca. 1943, including Minute Man Soups, Planters Peanuts, Aunt Jemima Flour, and Alpine Coffee; Kellogg's Cereals a prime sponsor, with Ivory Flakes, 1943–46.

1952–54, NBC. Saturdays at 10. *Breakfast in Hollywood.* Also, ca. 1947–58, Mutual offshoot. *Luncheon at Sardi's:* Various 45m times.

CAST: Tom Breneman, creator and host until his death April 28, 1948. Garry Moore, Cliff Arquette, John Nelson, and Jack McElroy in subsequent short order. Jack McCoy in the NBC revival of 1952–54. Regulars in the Breneman era: hostess Nell Olson; Bobby Batuga (the restaurant's maître d'); Joe the Railway Express boy. **ANNOUNCER:** Carl Pierce, with Frank Hemingway.

Breakfast at Sardi's was one of the liveliest daytime shows on the air: pure human interest, sometimes funny, often corny, occasionally touching. There were "no scripts, no shills, no plants," as *Newsweek* described it in 1942. Host Tom Breneman "wows the ladies despite his 40 years, thinning hair, and widening waistline." The secret of his success was simple: he had "the magic of making women feel young."

Breneman conceived of his show one day in late 1940, while lunching with friends at Sardi's restaurant on Hollywood Boulevard. He was struck by the layout, Sardi's being arranged in tiers with rows of booths surrounding a large open area. It was a natural setting for a radio remote.

There were no singers, no musical interludes, no quizzes or money to be won. It was wall-to-wall Breneman and his ladies: crazy questions and spontaneous, witty, sometimes devilishly clever answers. "What's your favorite morning fruit juice?" Breneman asked a young woman. "Gin rickey," she said, delighting the crowd. "Did you ever milk a cow?" Breneman might ask out of the blue. There was no telling what marvelous anecdote he might pry out of someone with a question like that. "What's your most embarrassing moment?" was a stock icebreaker. "Who gets up for those midnight feedings, you or your husband?" After bandying this question with the younger women, Breneman turned to an old lady, who said, "It certainly wasn't him. We didn't have bottles in those days."

By daytime standards, the show was a great success. At its peak it played on the most stations and got the highest ratings of all breakfast programs. A film version, starring Breneman, was released in 1946.

But in the beginning, Breneman and his partner John Masterson had to send cabs for people to ensure a full house. Ticket requests soon grew into a groundswell until, at one point, there were 100,000 requests backed up.

The ladies were greeted at the door at 7:30 A.M. They were given corsages and a wakeup starter of fruit juice and coffee. Soon Breneman appeared for his warmup. He was a natural, one who simply "had a way with the ladies." He'd

pause and admire a bit of plumage. "Say, that's a pipperoo of a hat you have on," he'd say, and he'd try it on himself with the audience howling in the background. He was considered a heart-throb of middle-aged women everywhere. His mail was carried in by the bag, many letters beginning "Tom, my darling," and going on from there.

Attendance at *Sardi's* included two shows. At 8 A.M. came a live broadcast to the East Coast, playing there at 11. Then breakfast was served and a second show, heard live in the West, began at 9:30. The shows were quite different, as Breneman picked out new people from the same crowd for the West Coast broadcast. Nothing was rehearsed: like a good cook, "we start from scratch every morning," he told an interviewer. Prominent guests sometimes visited—Orson Welles, Lum and Abner, Andy Devine, and Jimmy Durante, to name a few—but the stars were everyday women from all walks of life. The show staged a goofy hat contest, gave away makeup kits, and awarded orchids to "good neighbors of the day." There was a "wishing ring ceremony," when a woman from the audience was given a ring designed by Joseff of Hollywood. The recipient was asked to tell the wish closest to her heart, and the restaurant and air audiences were asked to wish along with her. One woman wished for new tires, a prize in those days of rubber rationing. Another wished to be rid of annoying tenants and got her wish, Breneman learned later, when she got home and was told that the tenants had heard the broadcast.

Joe the Railway Express boy delivered the orchids and often told a riddle or two. Another fountain of riddles was Bobby Batuga, the Filipino maître d' who directed his puzzlers at the enemy. "Why does Mussolini always carry a handkerchief?" *It's the only thing he can put his nose into without having to ask Hitler.* "Why are Allied armies in Egypt like a good vaudeville act?" *They keep laying the Germans in the Nile.* Breneman also had give-and-take sessions with "Uncle Corny," playing that role himself.

The show continued broadcasting from Sardi's but changed its name to *Breakfast in Hollywood* in 1943, to avoid confusion with Sardi's of New York. By 1945 Breneman was so successful that he was able to buy his own restaurant, Tom Breneman's Hollywood, on Vine Street just off Sunset Boulevard. The last show from Sardi's was March 9, 1945. By then it was heard by an estimated ten million women daily. It was a continuing favorite until April 28, 1948, when Breneman collapsed and died about two hours before air time. He was 46.

The show was turned over to Garry Moore, then host of *Take It or Leave It*. Moore decided immediately to stay away from Breneman's style and make the show heavier on comedy, lighter on sentiment. It didn't work, and neither Moore nor a succession of hosts could recapture Breneman's success. By January 1949 the ratings had plunged to less than 2 points, and a year later it was discontinued. Neither of the subsequent revivals was notably successful.

THE BREAKFAST CLUB, morning variety.

BROADCAST HISTORY: June 23, 1933–Dec. 27, 1968, Blue Network/ABC. 60m at 9 A.M.; six a week until 1946, then weekdays. Sustained until 1941, when Swift and Company bought a segment and became longtime sponsors. Kellogg took 15m, 1942–45; Philco Radios, 1945.

CAST: Host Don McNeill. Many regulars, as per this simplified year-by-year breakdown:

1933: Dick Teela, singer. Walter Blaufuss, orchestra (a position he held until illness forced him off in 1942). Bill Krenz, piano. The Originalities, a small group from the band (Jean Cafarelli, Bill Giese, Bill Short, Jack Rose).

1934: Jim and Marian Jordan (soon to be known nationally as Fibber McGee and Molly) as "Toots and Chickie." Jack Owens replaced Dick Teela and was subsequently billed "the Cruising Crooner." The Merry Macs (Cheri McKay and Joe, Judd, and Ted McMichael). The Morin Sisters (Pauline, Evelyn, and Marge). The Ranch Boys (Jack Ross, Hubert "Shorty" Carson, and Joe "Curley" Bradley). The Songfellows. The Three C's. Bill Thompson with the Wallace Wimple voice that became famous a decade later on the *McGee* program.

1935: Edna O'Dell, the first female singer. Gale Page and "Dr." Russell Pratt, frequent guests. Groups included the King's Jesters, the Hollywood Hi-Hatters, the Rangers, the Doring Sisters.

1936: Clark Dennis replaced Jack Owens. Helen Jane Behlke replaced Edna O'Dell. Singer Annette King joined the show.

1937: Fran Allison and Sam Cowling joined the cast and remained for many years. Cowling joined Lou Perkins and Gil Jones as the Three Romeos. Clark Dennis resigned to go with *Fibber McGee and Molly*; replaced by Jack Baker, "the Louisiana Lark." Johnny Johnston became a regular.

1938: No notable cast changes, but McNeill opened the show to a studio audience, changing its style dramatically. The audience would play an increasingly important role.

1939: Annette King left; Evelyn Lynne and Nancy Martin joined as vocalists. The Dinning Sisters (Ginger, Jean, and Lou), the Vass Family (Frank, Weezy, Jitchey, Sally, and Emily), the Cadets (Homer Snodgrass, Ken Morrow, Carl Schiebe, Al Stracke, and Reo Fletcher), the Vagabonds (Robert O'Neal, Norval Taborn, Ray Grant, and John Jordan) and the Escorts and Betty (Ted Claire, Cliff Petersen, Floyd Holm, Douglas Craig, and Betty Olson) were the year's vocal groups.

1940–44: No notable cast changes. Evelyn Lynne left, 1941; Marion Mann joined, sharing singing duties with Nancy Martin. Bandmaster duties shared by Harry Kogen, Joe Gallicchio, and Rex Maupin. After an absence, Fran Allison and Jack Owens returned.

1945: Walter Blaufuss died, and Eddie Ballantine became orchestra leader. Cliff Petersen graduated from singer to producer but would often return to the microphone for songs with his old group.

1946: Ole Olsen substituted briefly for McNeill and initiated as a feature the "Sunshine Shower," which McNeill continued.

1947–48: Marion Mann and Nancy Martin left. Patsy Lee was added. Jack Paar and Allen Prescott hosted during McNeill's second honeymoon vacation, 1948.

1949: Johnny Desmond replaced Jack Owens. Bernie Christianson, age 11, was interviewed by McNeill, sang, and became a regular.

1950s: Singer Peggy Taylor and comics Homer and Jethro, all joining in 1952. Alice Lon, singer, in 1953 (later famous as Lawrence Welk's "Champagne Lady" on TV).

ANNOUNCERS: Bill Kephart, 1933–36; Bob Brown, 1936–41; Louis Roen, 1941; Durward Kirby, 1941–42; Charles Irving, 1943–44; Fred Kasper, 1946–47; Ken Nordine, 1947–48; Franklyn Ferguson, 1948–51. Other announcers: Bob Murphy, Don Dowd, Jack Callaghan, Jay Arlan, and Bob McKee. Often the show used more than one announcer, with different voices promoting different products: Dowd, Brown, and McKee for Swift; Kirby for Cream of Wheat; Irving for Kellogg's; Kasper for Lustre Creme; Nordine for Toni Home Permanents; Ferguson for General Mills; Callaghan for Jell-O.

For a show that couldn't give away a commercial spot in its first six years, *The Breakfast Club* had an unusually long and distinguished life. Its influence on the development of early-morning broadcasting was whopping, as its corn-fed host might have said. Don McNeill took over "an hour that no one wanted" and slowly built one of the most powerful shows in radio, and in the process established the morning as a prime source of network revenue.

It was the first major show of its kind, combining unabashed sentiment, human interest, music, and song. In its wake would come dozens of breakfast shows, from *Arthur Godfrey Time* and *The Fitzgeralds* to *Breakfast at Sardi's*. Its run spanned virtually the entire era of network radio.

For Don McNeill the rise was anything but dramatic. Born Dec. 23, 1907, in Galena, Ill., he abandoned an early ambition toward editorial cartooning to go into radio. He began at WISN, Milwaukee, in 1928, script editing and announcing. In 1929 he joined the *Milwaukee Journal*, working at WTMJ, the paper's radio station. In 1930 he was at the *Louisville Courier-Journal* and its station, WHAS. He met Van Fleming, a singer: they formed a comedy act, Don and Van, the Two Professors, and took the show to San Francisco, playing radio stations in the West. This act dissolved in 1933 and McNeill had an unsuccessful fling at New York. He had returned to Milwaukee when he decided to apply to NBC. This was in June 1933, and the network answered with an invitation to audition in Chicago.

There was an opening on a forsaken little morning variety hour, *The Pepper Pot*. It was a throwaway on the Blue Network, heard at the impossible time of 8 A.M. in Chicago. Of course there were no sponsors. This meant little budget but lots of flexibility. McNeill drove to Chicago and organized the show in his mind. One story has it that he had the format pretty well worked out by the time he reached the city. He had a new title in mind, *The Breakfast Club*, and an idea that the hour could be divided into four equal segments—the four calls to breakfast. McNeill beat out two other announcers, won the

$50-a-week job, and began his transformation of *The Pepper Pot* with the Friday show, June 23.

"*The Breakfast Club of the Air*," he announced: "a get-together time for all of us who smile before breakfast and then can't break the habit all day long—a place to come to when a feller needs a friend." His first script consisted of topical humor from the newspapers, gags from joke anthologies, and bits of regional fluff. He told a bad joke about a chess tournament, deciding that everyone could use a little "chess expansion." There was no studio audience: just McNeill, singer Dick Teela, an announcer, a sound engineer, and the 12-piece orchestra directed by Walter Blaufuss.

For several months McNeill wrote out his scripts by twisting news events into cornball humor. He wore out two jokebooks in the hunt for fresh material. Then the show passed a plateau: about three months into it, the mail picked up. About 100 letters a day were coming in, many with poems, gags, and cheerful American sentiment. It suddenly occurred to McNeill, as he would often recount in later life, that "the folks who listen in could write this show a whole lot better than I could."

He had written his last script. He asked for permission to do the show off the cuff, and the network didn't care: the prospects for the hour as 1934 approached were still nonexistent. Somehow it survived. With little measurable audience and no commercial backing, McNeill and his slowly expanding cast passed the 1,000-show mark in 1936. By 1940 the formula was well-entrenched. The four calls to breakfast was still the framework, each quarter-hour distinguished by a regular feature. In the first quarter, McNeill interviewed people from the studio audience, which was admitted beginning in 1938. He never knew what to expect in this informal chatfest. There was always risk in putting unknown people in front of a live microphone, and one agency man during the sponsored years confessed that "I get twinges in my ulcer everytime I listen to it." But the informality helped build its reputation as "radio's most unrehearsed show." Also during the first quarter, the orchestra offered some brisk "waker-uppers."

In the second call came "Memory Time," a reading of sentimental verse. On Oct. 28, 1944, McNeill initiated "Prayer Time," asking his audience to say a prayer for American servicemen in harm's way overseas. This was nonsectarian and accompanied by a faint hymn on organ. McNeill's introduction to "Prayer Time" was remembered for years: *All over the nation . . . each in his own words . . . each in his own way . . . for a world united in peace . . . bow your heads, let us pray.* In the studio, the lights were dimmed and a silent prayer was offered for 15 seconds. "Prayer Time" was so popular that it was continued after the war. Often in this segment came "Hymn Time," when a religious chestnut was given a workout by the whole crew. In 1948 the "Sunshine Shower" began, urging listeners to drop lines of cheer to people in hospitals, orphanages, and homes for the elderly.

The third call usually began with "March Time," a rousing march around the breakfast table by the cast and some people from the audience. Breakfast was not served. On tours and in public appearances, a breakfast table would often be decked out with tablecloths and china, but there was no eating done. Interviews and more music filled out the quarter, and the fourth call was for "Inspiration Time," a message or poem designed to lift the spirits of the downcast.

McNeill and his crew appealed to a large section of middle America. The *New Yorker* estimated his audience to be "the solid citizens, the churchgoers, the 'squares,' the butcher, the baker, and the candlestick maker," all the "Eds and Ednas" from Maine to California. By 1941 more than 100,000 letters a year came to the network in Chicago for McNeill and his cast. When Swift Meats took a segment of the show, the wall of resistance from sponsors began to crumble: they were followed closely, in 1941, by Acme Paint and Cream of Wheat, though the show still wouldn't be booked solid until 1946. But its power was evident. In 1944, when the sponsor offered *Breakfast Club* membership cards, 850,000 people wrote in. No more than 15,000 were expected, and McNeill had to go on the air and beg out of the promotion. It still cost the sponsor $50,000 to retreat.

There were road trips, bond rallies during the war, and promotion booklets. In 1946 McNeill asked his listeners to "share a meal" with unfortunates in war-torn Europe. Forty tons of food was collected. The show packed houses wherever it played. At Madison Square Garden in 1946, more than 17,000 people mobbed the tour. The *New Yorker* described the road trip as

a "sort of portable Lourdes. Stirred by the prospect of seeing McNeill in person, thousands of his followers rise at dawn and storm the doors of whatever auditorium he is appearing in."

The theme was snappy, almost raucous, the words changing constantly:

Good morning, Breakfast Club-bers,
It's time to sing ya
Another cheery greeting
So may we bring ya
Four—calls—for break-fast!
Kel-logg's—call—to break-fast!
So every Breakfast Club-ber
Young and old
Come and join our hap-py
Carefree fold.
Yes, wake up Breakfast Club-bers
And smile a-while
A day begun with Kellogg's
Makes life worth while!

Aside from McNeill, the most prominent of the long-running cast members were Fran Allison and Sam Cowling, both 1937 inductees. Allison began as a singer and developed her endearing character Aunt Fanny on *The Breakfast Club*, playing the role as a "lovable chatterbox." Cowling came aboard as part of a singing trio, the Three Romeos (with Gil Jones and Louie Perkins): eventually he became a comic, McNeill's prime heckler and perpetrator of an endless stream of one-line gags. In 1943 he initiated his "Fiction and Fact from Sam's Almanac," a series of silly riddles. (Q: What's the difference between a tiger and panther? A: *A tiger is a big cat, but panther what you wear.*) Neither Allison nor Cowling prepared in advance; Allison (later well known as the costar of Burr Tillstrom's puppet show *Kukla, Fran, and Ollie* on early TV) was particularly quick with an ad-lib. As Aunt Fanny, Allison created a raft of characters, notably Bert and Bertie Beerbower, the Smelsers, and Ott Ort, who came to life in the old maid's dialogue. McNeill's real family appeared often—wife Kay, and sons Don Jr., Tom, and Bobbie. Nancy Martin was known as "li'l ole Nancybelle" to the listening audience: not only did she sing, she also danced in the aisles with men from the audience. The Vagabonds were billed as "one of the nation's greatest colored quartets," and Ray "Pappy" Grant became popular in 1939 with his zany recipes and his basso-profundo greeting, "How-do, gals?'' Johnny Desmond was known as ''Johnny-on-the-spot,'' his job when he wasn't singing to come up with whatever was called for. And little Bernie Christianson was the sensation of 1949: he sang *Galway Bay* for his grandparents, and ''at the first note,'' said *Collier's*, ''both the audience and the cast were electrified.'' It took two minutes to quiet the applause, and the child became a regular, singing on the show three times a week.

It was a happy crew, The *New Yorker* said in an overview: there was little public discord, no self-destructive tantrums of the kind that demolished the career of Arthur Godfrey. ''Once they get on *The Breakfast Club*, they settle down to the most secure job in radio.'' But an attempt to televise it was a flop. The cast was expected to eat breakfast for the cameras, a gimmick no one liked, and McNeill just couldn't project that carefree, spontaneous style for TV. It was a show quite unlike any other. It got under way, McNeill said, and just grew each day. ''Sometimes we stink,'' he told *Collier's*, ''but that's the way the show is. We just have to take what comes.'' What came was a run that few in radio, at any time of the day or night, could touch: 35 years of ''corn with the cornflakes.'' Even the venues were of long duration: 15 years and more than 4,000 broadcasts from Chicago's Merchandise Mart, and a long subsequent run in the Terrace Casino of the Morrison Hotel. When the show was retired in 1968, so, for all practical purposes, was McNeill. He was seldom seen thereafter and became difficult to interview. ''You got two chances,'' he told this writer in the mid-1980s: ''slim and none.'' He apologized for the blunt sound of that and went on with his life.

McNeill died May 7, 1996, at 88.

BREAKFAST WITH DOROTHY AND DICK, morning talk.

BROADCAST HISTORY: April 15, 1945–March 21, 1963, WOR, New York. CAST: Dorothy Kilgallen, Broadway columnist for the *New York Journal-American*, and her husband, actor-producer Richard Kollmar.

Although it was a local series, *Breakfast with Dorothy and Dick* was nationally known and widely discussed. The 50,000-watt WOR signal was regularly heard by 20 million people, and the fame of the husband-and-wife breakfast show

had spread across the land. It was a subgenre of early-morning radio, begun by Ed and Pegeen Fitzgerald in 1942. The Fitzgeralds had popularized it, then left WOR for WJZ and a brief run on ABC. WOR, meanwhile, needed a replacement program.

What they found was *Dorothy and Dick*. Dorothy Kilgallen had covered the theater scene for years, and her sources were varied and deep. Her husband Richard Kollmar was a microphone veteran, playing character roles in *Gang Busters*, *Grand Central Station*, and many other New York radio shows. Unlike the Fitzgeralds, the Kollmars were connoisseurs of the high life, and it was felt that their breakfast-table chats would appeal to a broad cross-section of New Yorkers.

It was a daily show, heard at 8:15 in a 45-minute Monday-through-Saturday format and in a recorded version late Sunday mornings. The Kollmar breakfasts were more formal than those conducted by the earthier Fitzgeralds: more civilized, Dorothy would say. They spoke of opening nights in the theater, shared bits of gossip picked up at celebrity parties, and took listeners on vicarious excursions to the Waldorf or the Stork Club. They had two children, Dickie and Jill, who also appeared. Breakfast was served by their butler Julius, and there was a canary, Robin, whose chirping was considered an essential part of the show. Robin had an understudy, in case of sudden illness, and when Dorothy and Dick did their show from Chicago's WGN while there for one of Dick's play openings, a ''guest canary'' was brought in to keep the chirps coming.

Despite her cosmopolitan demeanor, Kilgallen had serious bouts with mike fright. Her ''knees knocked together,'' wrote her biographer Lee Israel, ''and her hands shook so violently that she could hardly draw the coffee cup to her mouth.'' Kilgallen wrote scripts for the first few shows, then settled into a more spontaneous approach. Her jitters quickly vanished, and soon the show was nip-and-tuck with *The Fitzgeralds* and earning the Kollmars around $75,000 a year.

WOR handouts billed them as ''one of America's most charming couples.'' A newspaper ad described Dorothy as ''Dresden-dollish but practical, the kind of girl every young man dreams of installing in the little cottage that the vines embrace.'' This was laughable: Kilgallen would have screamed in such an environment, and the show was actually done in the Kollmars' 16-room apartment at Park Avenue and 66th Street. The products of more than 18 sponsors were worked into their conversation, as writer Philip Hamburger learned when The *New Yorker* sent him for an interview in August 1946. "My, my, this is good orange juice," Kollmar would purr. "It's Juicy Gem," Dorothy supplied helpfully. In one segment ("as God is my judge," Hamburger swore, anticipating disbelief) Kilgallen said, "Van Raalte undies fit so much better and wash so easily."

Their feud with the Fitzgeralds was spirited and real: neither liked the others' shows, and sniping was frequent from both sides. Kilgallen considered the Fitzgeralds vulgar and coarse; the Fitzgeralds called Dorothy and Dick upper-crust dilettantes. The Kollmars were certainly "not the couple next door," wrote Lee Israel; "they were rich, mobile, quintessentially cosmopolitan." As to their performances on the air: "Dick played tired tuba to Dorothy's frivolous flute."

The Kollmars were married April 6, 1940. The marriage endured, though not without its rough spots. Their radio show was the subject of many lampoons, the most famous being Fred Allen's skit, complete with canary and Tallulah Bankhead. In later life, Kilgallen was a panelist on the TV show *What's My Line?* She was hospitalized in 1963, her final radio broadcast March 21. Kollmar continued the show alone, with a variety of guests, but it closed a month later.

Kilgallen died Nov. 8, 1965, officially of a heart attack but under circumstances that Lee Israel found suspicious. She had been investigating the Kennedy assassination and felt that she was on the verge of the biggest story of her career.

BREEN AND DE ROSE, pioneering husband-wife musical team.

BROADCAST HISTORY: 1923, WEAF, New York. 1927–39, Blue Network. Many timeslots including 30m, Tuesdays at 10:30, 1927–28; 30m, Wednesdays at 8, 1928–29: 15m, Fridays at 7:15, 1929–30; 15m, twice a week at 5:45 for Humphreys Remedies and Witch Hazel, 1936–37; 15m, five a week at 10:45 A.M., 1938–39.

1930–36, NBC. 15m daytime broadcasts: four a week at 2:15, 1930–31; various times for Knox Gelatin, 1931–32; six a week at 10 A.M., 1933–34;

three a week at 10:30 for Humphreys Remedies and Witch Hazel, 1934–36.

May Singhi Breen and Peter de Rose sang popular and sentimental songs of the day and often broadcast under the title *Sweethearts of the Air*. Breen played the ukelele, and they harmonized, often to piano accompaniment. Breen created a ukelele craze circa 1927, but her application for membership in the musicians' union was turned down. She fought for her instrument and won her case by appealing to Dr. Walter Damrosch to judge her. De Rose was also a composer: his music for *Deep Purple* became an evergreen, and the melody was often used as their theme.

BRENDA CURTIS, soap opera.

BROADCAST HISTORY: Sept. 11, 1939–Jan. 19, 1940, CBS. 15m, weekdays at 11:15 A.M. Campbell Soups. **CAST:** Vicki Vola as Brenda Curtis, talented actress who gave up her career to marry Jim Curtis, a lawyer. Hugh Marlowe as Jim. **ANNOUNCER:** Ken Roberts.

A lone episode of *Brenda Curtis* offers standard serial strife. Jim's law practice is in financial jeopardy; Brenda receives an offer from Ziggy, her old manager, to return to the stage, but Jim wants his wife at home and refuses to let her consider it. Stacy Gordon, "a friend of Jim's who once loved Brenda," has returned from South America, and Gloria Bennett, "who wants Jim," has decided to "use this fact for her own purposes." It was billed as "a true-to-life story."

BRENTHOUSE, serial drama.

BROADCAST HISTORY: Jan. 21, 1939–June 4, 1940, Blue Network. 30m, Saturdays at 8:30 until Nov., then Tuesdays at 10:30. **CAST:** Georgia Backus as Portia Brent, who tries to raise three children while running her late husband's publishing business; Kathleen Fitz also as Portia; gossip columnist Hedda Hopper as Portia as of February 1939. Florence Baker as Portia's daughter Jane. Lurene Tuttle as daughter Nancy. Ernest Carlson and Larry Nunn as son Peter. Margaret Brayton and Wally Maher as Martha and Lance Dudley. Ben Alexander as Philip West.

BRIDE AND GROOM, interviews with couples at the marriage altar.

BROADCAST HISTORY: Nov. 26, 1945–Sept. 15, 1950, ABC. 30m, weekdays at 2:30 (at 3, summer 1950). Sterling Drugs. **HOST:** John Nelson. **HOSTESS:** Roberta Roberts, who handled backstage detail. **SINGING ANNOUNCER:** Jack McElroy. **DIRECTORS:** John Masterson, John Reddy, John Nelson, Edward Feldman, Wayne Reeves, Marvin Beck.

During its five-year run, *Bride and Groom* told the stories of almost 1,000 new couples. Though the actual ceremony was performed privately in a small chapel adjoining the Chapman Park Hotel, where the broadcast originated in Los Angeles, the couple was introduced before and interviewed immediately afterward. A couple each day was united. They got on the show by telling their stories in letters to producer John Reddy: he made the selections by the human interest he found there. Occasionally a golden wedding anniversary was celebrated.

One blind couple met at a school for seeing eye dogs. A young man and woman met on adjacent drugstore stools. One young lady had just appeared on Tom Breneman's *Breakfast in Hollywood*, winning the show's "wishing ring" and wishing for a *Bride and Groom* wedding (her cause was helped by the fact that John Masterson, who managed Breneman's show, also ran *Bride and Groom*). Gaylord Carter played the wedding themes on organ, and the minister was often the Rev. Alden Hill. Later shows were done at the Hollywood Knickerbocker. Each couple was given wedding rings, appliances, silver, and other gifts and was sent on a "flying honeymoon" to a location of their choice.

BRIGHT HORIZON, soap opera.

BROADCAST HISTORY: Aug. 25, 1941–July 6, 1945, CBS. 15m, weekdays at 11:30 A.M. Lever Brothers and Swan Soap. **CAST:** Richard Kollmar as Michael West, a character from the serial *Big Sister*, who became the central figure in this spinoff role, a lawyer from the town of Riverfield who now returned to the town where he had been ostracized and driven away. Joseph Julian and Robert Griffin also as Michael. Sammie Hill and Joan Alexander as Carol Bates, who married Michael after his return. Renee Terry as Carol's young cousin Barbara West. Lesley Woods as Margaret McCarey. Lon Clark as Keith Richards. Frank Lovejoy as Larry Halliday. Will Geer as Penny. Dick Keith as Charles McCarey. Helen Claire as Edith Browning. Ronny Liss as Bobby. **ANNOUNCERS:** Marjorie Anderson, with John Harper and Roland Winters; later Grace Russell and Paul Luther in a singing format that drew the sponsor into the signature (*Time . . . for Swan Soap . . . the four-in-one soap! Everybody's on boaaaaarrrrrd! They're going for Swan Soap . . . new, white, floating Swan!*). **MUSIC:** John Gart on organ. **DIRECTOR:** Henry Hull, Charles Powers, Day Tuttle, Ralph Butler. **WRITER:** James and Elizabeth Hart, John M. Young, Ted Maxwell, Stuart Hawkins; novelist Kathleen Norris as of April 2, 1945.

On *Big Sister*, Michael West had been a nomadic folksinger; now, moving into his own serial, his background in law was developed. Because he had defended a man deeply hated in his hometown of Riverfield, Michael had lost his practice. He had traveled around the country, playing an accordion and singing in restaurants. Along the way he had met a waif named Bobby and had taken the child into his life. Early in the new series, he had pursued his singing career, but by 1944 he was again entrenched in the business of law.

Two episodes from that year ring familiar daytime themes. Michael, considering a run for governor, is threatened by public scandal. This involves a four-month gap in his life when he was a kidnap victim. Romantically linked in the press at that time with Mrs. Margaret McCarey, Michael is confronted by a devious woman intent on using the information in order to marry Michael's brother Brian. This disrupts Michael's home life, with wife Carol, their son Michael Jefferson West, and their cousin Barbara ("Punkins" to Michael).

To help give the series a good sendoff, Alice Frost appeared in the earliest episodes, in her *Big Sister* role of Ruth Evans Wayne.

BRIGHT STAR, comedy-drama.

BROADCAST HISTORY: 1952–53, 30m, transcribed syndication, Ziv Company. **CAST:** Irene Dunne as Susan Armstrong, editor of the *Hillsdale Morning Star*. Fred MacMurray as George Harvey, her star reporter. **ANNOUNCER:** Harry Von Zell.

Following in the wake of *Box 13, Bold Venture*, and other recorded dramas using top film stars, *Bright Star* explored the old cynic-idealist conflict. Editor Armstrong tried to keep her financially troubled newspaper afloat while keeping her talented but too eager star reporter under control. Occasionally he ran the paper while she dabbled in philanthropy.

THE BRIGHTER DAY, soap opera.

BROADCAST HISTORY: Oct. 11, 1948–July 8, 1949, NBC. 15m, weekdays at 10:45. Dreft.

July 11, 1949–June 29 1956, CBS. 15m, weekdays at 2:45; at 2:15, 1955–56. Dreft, etc.

CAST: Bill Smith as the Reverend Richard Dennis, pastor of a parish in the town of Three Rivers, where he tried to be both mother and father to daughters Elizabeth, Althea, Barbara, and Patsy. Margaret Draper as Elizabeth (Liz), who soon became the dominant character, taking a maternal role in daily family life; Grace Matthews as Liz later in the run. Jay Meredith and Joan Alexander as Althea, the beautiful, selfish daughter consumed by theatrical ambition. Lorna Lynn, Judith Lockser, and Mary Linn Beller as Barbara, a teenager known as "Babby" throughout the run. Pat Hosley and Lois Nettleton as Patsy. Billy Redfield, Bob Pollock, and Hal Holbrook as son Grayling Dennis, a young man in his 20s who worked on the town newspaper. Ann Hillary as Sandra Talbot, Grayling's love interest. John Raby as Dr. Jerry Forrester, love interest of Liz Dennis. **PRODUCERS:** David Lesan, Beverly Smith, Bob Steel. **THEME:** *At Dawning* by Charles Wakefield Cadman. **DIRECTORS:** Ted Corday, Mary Harris, Edwin Wolfe, Art Hanna. **WRITERS:** Irna Phillips; also, Orin Tovrov, Doris Frankel, John Haggart.

The Brighter Day evolved from the serial *Joyce Jordan, MD.* In the fall of 1948, Joyce introduced the character of Liz Dennis into her melodrama, and by early October Liz had taken over, relegating Joyce to the role of hostess. On Oct. 8, *Joyce Jordan* was discontinued and the saga of the Dennis family began. Typical of Irna Phillips soaps, it opened with an epigraph: *Our years are as the falling leaves—we live, we love, we dream, and then we go. But somehow we keep hoping, don't we, that our dreams come true on that brighter day.*

BRING 'EM BACK ALIVE, jungle adventure.

BROADCAST HISTORY: Oct. 30–Dec. 18, 1932, NBC. 15m, Sundays at 5:45. Melodramas with talk. Frank Buck, famed wild animal hunter, promoted his RKO jungle film of the same name, telling his adventures to sponsor A. C. Gilbert, the Erector Set manufacturer. The climactic scene was fully dramatized.

July 16–Nov. 16, 1934, NBC; Blue Network until Sept. 17, then Red. 15m, weekdays at 7:45. Pepsodent.

BRINGING UP FATHER, comedy based on the Maggie and Jiggs comic strip by George McManus.

BROADCAST HISTORY: July 1–Sept. 30, 1941, Blue Network. 30m, Tuesdays at 9. Lever Brothers. **CAST:** Mark Smith as Jiggs, the roly-poly, henpecked husband, who always tried to slip away for a night with the boys and meekly surrendered with a "Yes, m'darrlinn," when cornered by Maggie, his "virago of a wife." Neil O'Malley also as Jiggs. Agnes Moorehead as Maggie. Helen Shields and Joan Banks as their daughter Nora. Craig McDonnell as Dinty Moore.

BROADWAY IS MY BEAT, crime drama.

BROADCAST HISTORY: Feb. 27, 1949–Aug. 1, 1954, CBS. 30m. Many short runs in at least 15 separate timeslots; heard virtually every night in the week at some point. Only two uninterrupted season-long runs: Sept. 1951–May 1952, Saturdays at 9:30; and a full year, beginning in Oct. 1952, Saturdays at 7.

From New York Feb. 27–May 29, 1949: **CAST:** Anthony Ross as Danny Clover, a detective on the Times Square beat of the New York Police Department. **MUSIC:** Robert Stringer. **PRODUCER:** Lester Gottlieb. **DIRECTOR:** John Dietz.

From Hollywood beginning July 7, 1949: **CAST:** Larry Thor as Detective Danny Clover. Charles Calvert as Sergeant Gino Tartaglia. Jack Kruschen as Sergeant Muggavan. Also: Irene Tedrow, Barney Phillips, Lamont Johnson, Charlotte Lawrence, Herb Vigran, Herb Ellis, Hy Averback, Sam Edwards, Tony Barrett, GeGe Pearson, Byron Kane, Edgar Barrier, Sammie Hill, Betty Lou Gerson, Bill Bouchey, Eddie Fields, Mary Shipp, Harry Bartell, Ben Wright, Sheldon Leonard, Martha Wentworth, Lawrence Dobkin, Paula

Winslowe, Eve McVeagh, Anne Whitfield, Truda Marson, Herb Butterfield, Junius Matthews, Mary Jane Croft. ANNOUNCER: Bill Anders. MUSIC: Wilbur Hatch, Alexander Courage. PRODUCER-DIRECTOR: Elliott Lewis. WRITERS: Morton Fine and David Friedkin. SOUND EFFECTS: David Light, Ralph Cummings, Ross Murray. THEME: *(I'll Take) Manhattan.*

Early CBS press material for *Broadway Is My Beat,* when it was still produced in New York, told how, "as a kid, Danny Clover sold papers and shined shoes along the Great White Way, and later pounded the beat as a policeman. He knows everything along Broadway—from panhandler to operatic prima donna—but he's still sentimental about the street, forever a wonderland of glamor to him."

But its run in the East was barely three months long. In Hollywood it fell to Elliott Lewis, a man of many talents (writer, producer, director, and actor in roles ranging from comedy to melodrama) who was getting his first directing opportunity. Lewis was born in Manhattan and knew the city well. "You should hear the city constantly," he said of his new show, and three soundmen were often needed to re-create that New York flavor. The result was a noisy show, exactly what Lewis was after. "Even the people in New York are noisy," he told *Radio Life.*

The show stretched for the poetic metaphor: *The still of August nighttime is beyond crest now, has broken, begun its downsurge, and in the empty avenue there are trailings of phosphorescence and tricklings of stillness . . . time before dawn.* This announcement, spoken over a trumpet theme, blended into the story proper, with Danny Clover narrating his own adventure. "And where I was—vast room draped in darkening silk light . . ." he would say, setting the stage. Then the noises would come up, the sounds of people argumentative or amused. At the end, a blending out in the same way. *Broadway is sleeping now . . . the furious avenues of the night are still . . . only the sleepwalkers are there . . . the seekers, the sodden. . . .* And if the tone was sometimes heavy and wordy, the scenes were gritty, their crimes of the less-than-glamorous variety. The beat was set out in the opening signature: *from Times Square to Columbus Circle—the grandest, the most violent, the lonesomest mile in the world.*

BROADWAY MATINEE, musical variety, first called *Your Home Front Reporter* and *Home Front Matinee.*

BROADCAST HISTORY: May 10, 1943–Nov. 8, 1943, CBS. 25m, weekdays at 4. *Your Home Front Reporter.* Owens-Illinois Glass Company. CAST: Fletcher Wiley, billed as "the oracle of the home," in the title role of Your Home Front Reporter, offering tips on scientific nutrition, creative menus for wartime rationing, and general home economics help. But this was wrapped in a full entertainment package, with soprano Eleanor Steber, tenor Frank Parker, and a 22-piece orchestra directed by David Broekman. Aired from New York until July 16, 1943; moved to Hollywood as of July 19. Parker and Wiley moved west with the show; Steber and the Broekman orchestra were replaced by Diana Gayle, Phil Hanna, and maestro Wilbur Hatch. On Sept. 29, the show returned to New York; Steber and Broekman rejoined; Don Pryor replaced Wiley as the "reporter."

Nov. 15–Dec. 6, 1943, CBS. 25m, weekdays at 4. *Home Front Matinee.* Owens-Illinois Glass Company. The home economics aspect was dropped in favor of straight music, and the show had a prime-time sound. CAST: Alfred Drake, singing emcee, appearing only four days a week because of a Thursday matinee performance of *Oklahoma,* in which he starred. Early guests were Annamary Dickey (Metropolitan Opera star), Ethel Merman, Celeste Holm, Hildegarde, and soprano Dorothy Sarnoff. ANNOUNCER: Santos Ortega. MUSIC: Allen Roth.

Dec. 13, 1943–Aug. 4, 1944, CBS. 25m, weekdays at 4. *Broadway Matinee.* Owens-Illinois Glass Company. CAST: Drake continued as singing male lead until he departed for the West Coast; on June 2, Ronald Graham became the new singing emcee. HOST: Jim Ameche. ANNOUNCER: Red Barber. VOCALIST: Patsy Garrett. MUSIC: Allen Roth. GUESTS: Helen Forrest, Bea Wain, Helen O'Connell, etc., with popular swing; Rose Bampton, Risë Stevens, Eileen Farrell, Dorothy Kirsten, etc., in the concert vein.

BROADWAY SHOWTIME, musical drama.

BROADCAST HISTORY: Dec. 27, 1943–June 26, 1944, CBS. 30m, Mondays at 10:30. Replacing *Three-Ring Time.* P. Ballantine and Sons. STAR: William Gaxton. ORCHESTRA: Jay Blackton.

This series of "streamlined musical stage productions" opened with *A Connecticut Yankee*, in which Gaxton had played the title role onstage in 1927.

BROADWAY VARIETIES, light, popular, and semi-classical music.

BROADCAST HISTORY: Sept. 24, 1933–April 22, 1934, CBS. 30m, Sundays at 2. Initially titled *Broadway Melodies*, with torch singer Helen Morgan and Jerry Freeman's orchestra and chorus. Bisodol.

May 2, 1934–July 30, 1937, CBS. 30m, Wednesdays at 8:30 until Oct. 1935; then Fridays at 8:30 and (1936–37) Fridays at 8. Bisodol. **CAST:** Elizabeth Lennox, contralto, often in duets with singing hosts Guy Robertson (1935) or Oscar Shaw (1936). Soprano Carmela Ponselle added "for fire" (1936–37). **ORCHESTRA:** Victor Arden.

BROWNSTONE THEATER, dramatic anthology.

BROADCAST HISTORY: Feb. 21–Sept. 23, 1945, Mutual. 30m, Wednesdays at 9:30. **CAST:** Jackson Beck and Gertrude Warner, leads. Clayton Hamilton, narrator. **MUSIC:** Sylvan Levin. **DIRECTOR:** Jock MacGregor.

Brownstone Theater was a pleasant, fluffy half-hour, billed as "a theater of memories, your own memories, perhaps," offering "plays that have entertained and thrilled many an audience in many a theater, plays you will still enjoy." The format was faintly reminiscent of the famous *First Nighter Program*, with the listener led to his seat in the Brownstone Theater, and other trappings of curtains and greasepaint adding to the atmosphere. Actually, the show originated at WOR, New York. The fare was laden with such chestnuts as *The Man Without a Country, The Prisoner of Zenda*, and *Cyrano de Bergerac*.

BUCK PRIVATE AND HIS GIRL, soap opera; a light romance of Army camp life in the shadow of war.

BROADCAST HISTORY: May 26–Aug. 22, 1941, NBC. 15m continuation, weekdays at 9:15 A.M. **CAST:** Myron McCormick as Steve Mason, a young car salesman suddenly in the Army. Anne Seymour as his girlfriend Anne.

BUCK ROGERS IN THE 25TH CENTURY, juvenile science fiction serial, based on the comic strip by John F. Dille, Dick Calkins, and Phil Nowlan.

BROADCAST HISTORY: Nov. 7, 1932–May 22, 1936, CBS. 15m continuation, weekdays at 7:15 for Kellogg's, 1932–33; Monday through Thursday at 6 for Cocomalt, 1933–35; three a week at 6 for Cream of Wheat, 1935–36.

April 5–July 31, 1939, Mutual. 15m, three a week.

May 18–July 27, 1940, Mutual. 30m, Saturdays at noon.

Sept. 30, 1946–March 28, 1947, Mutual. 15m, weekday continuation at 4:45. General Foods for Post Cereals.

CAST: Curtis Arnall (1932) as Buck Rogers, a young adventurer who got trapped in suspended animation and woke up "500 years in the future." Matt Crowley as Buck, mid-1930s; Carl Frank also as Buck; John Larkin as Buck, 1946–47. Adele Ronson as Wilma Deering (early serial run), a lieutenant in the space corps and the series heroine; Virginia Vass as Wilma, 1946–47. Edgar Stehli as Buck's friend the master inventor Dr. Huer (1930s, and again 1946–47). Elaine Melchior as Ardala Valmar, the evil adventuress. Bill Shelley and Dan Ocko as Killer Kane, the long-running villain. Jack Roseleigh and Joe Granby as Black Barney, a stupid but friendly Martian. **ANNOUNCERS:** Paul Douglas, Fred Uttal. **WRITER-PRODUCER-DIRECTOR:** Jack Johnstone (1930s). **WRITERS:** Joe Cross, Albert G. Miller Dick Calkins. **SOUND EFFECTS:** Ora D. Nichols (CBS).

The adventures of *Buck Rogers in the 25th Century* were space oriented. Dr. Huer created such marvels as the "gyrocosmic relativator" and the "mechanical mole," and often Buck's adventures took him to the edges of the solar system to recover a Huer invention stolen by Killer Kane and Ardala Valmar. Black Barney was a former space pirate who had come to realize the errors of his ways.

The serial was one of the important early juvenile adventures. As in the strip, Buck had been surveying an abandoned mine in 1919 when a cave-in rendered him unconscious. A mysterious gas seeped into the chamber and held him in a suspended state for 500 years. Awakening in the 25th century, he found that society as he knew it had vanished. The capital was now Niagara.

Writer-director Jack Johnstone utilized the full assortment of fantasy ingredients: death rays, gamma bombs, and warring space fleets. The propriety of Buck's long space flights with Wilma Deering was debated by parents, who were also fretting over what Tarzan and Jane were doing alone in the jungle together. This was solved in the final episode of the last series, when Buck and Killer Kane fought to the finish. The fight scene took up most of the show, but afterward Buck suggested that he and Wilma take a vacation in Niagara. After all, Niagara was the hotspot for honeymooners in the America he had known. . . .

BUGHOUSE RHYTHM, musical satire.

BROADCAST HISTORY: Sept. 4, 1936–April 26, 1937, NBC. 15m, Red Network, Fridays at 5 until Oct. 9, then Blue Network, Mondays at 7:15. **ANNOUNCER:** Archie Presby. **CREATOR:** Ward Byron. **MUSIC:** Jack Meakin.

Bughouse Rhythm was a direct forerunner to the similarly zany *Chamber Music Society of Lower Basin Street.* These were swing broadcasts draped in somber operatic-like announcements, to poke fun at the highbrow.

BULLDOG DRUMMOND, crime drama, based on the novels of H. C. McNeile.

BROADCAST HISTORY: April 13, 1941–Jan. 12, 1949, Mutual. Many 30m timeslots: Sundays at 6:30, 1941–42; Mondays at 8:30, 1942–43; Sundays at 3:30, 1943–44; Mondays at 7:30, 1944–45; Mondays at 8, 1945–46; Fridays at 9:30, 1946–47; Wednesdays at 10, 1947–49.

Jan. 3–March 28, 1954, Mutual. 30m, Sundays at 6. Dodge Motors.

CAST: George Coulouris as Bulldog Drummond, the British police inspector popularized in the Paramount detective films of the 1930s. Santos Ortega and Ned Wever as Drummond after 1942. Cedric Hardwicke as Drummond in the brief revival of 1954. Everett Sloane as Drummond's sidekick Denny, 1941–42; Luis Van Rooten as Denny, mid-1940s. Rod Hendrickson also as Denny. **PRODUCER-DIRECTOR:** Himan Brown. **WRITERS:** Allan E. Sloane, Leonard Leslie. **SOUND EFFECTS:** Adrian Penner, Walt Gustafson, Walt Shaver.

Bulldog Drummond was a B-grade detective, on the screen and on the air. For the first two months, the series was set in Britain; then Drummond crossed the sea and stepped "out of the fog, out of the night, and into his American adventures." The opening signature was accompanied by hollow footsteps, a foghorn and then— two shots!—three sharp blasts of a policeman's whistle!—and another encounter with underworld characters, counterfeiters, and killers. The series had ambience and was remembered for years by people who thought it better than it was.

THE BURL IVES SHOW, musical folklore.

BROADCAST HISTORY: Many brief timeslots (often on both CBS and NBC) including:

June 24, 1940–April 20, 1941, NBC. 15m, initially Mondays at 9:45 A.M., then various days and times.

Sept. 30, 1940–Feb. 28, 1941, CBS. 15m, various days at 10:30. *Back Where I Came From.*

July 5, 1941–Jan. 24, 1942, CBS. 30m, Saturdays at 10 A.M., then at 11 A.M. *The Burl Ives Coffee Club.*

Jan. 31–June 27, 1942, CBS. 15m, Saturdays at 11:15 A.M. *God's Country.*

Oct. 18, 1946–April 9, 1948, Mutual. 15m, Fridays at 8. Philco Radios.

July 24–Sept. 4, 1949, ABC. 15m, Sundays at 9. Summer replacement for Walter Winchell on the Kaiser program.

Asked once when he'd begun singing, Burl Ives replied, "There wasn't any beginning." He "bummed" his way across the country in the '30s, supporting himself with his banjo and his voice. He learned songs from his grandmother, from farmers, from cowboys in Texas and Negroes in the South.

His first broadcast, June 24, 1940, was one to forget: NBC interrupted his first song with bulletins on the fall of France. He broadcast in many slots other than the ones listed above, his music suited to almost any time of day. His *Burl Ives Coffee Club* of 1941–42 featured soprano Genevieve Rowe and a vocal group, the Symphonettes. On May 4, 1944, he opened a CBS quarter-hour highlighting the "fighting songs and folksongs of the United Nations"; it co-starred a quartet called the Clubmen and was heard Tuesdays and Thursdays at 5:45 P.M. He often broadcast under the title *The Wayfaring Stranger*; his theme was frequently *Jimmy Crack Corn.* Later he became a powerful actor, winning an Academy Award and known for portrayals of swaggering patriarchs.

BURNS AND ALLEN, comedy, with George Burns and Gracie Allen.

BROADCAST HISTORY: 1929, BBC, London, first appearance on the air.

Feb. 15, 1932–June 13, 1934, CBS. 30m, Mondays at 10 through May 16, 1932, then Wednesdays at 9 until Jan. 4, 1933, then Wednesdays at 9:30. Initially *The Guy Lombardo Show* for Robert Burns Panatella and, from May 1933, White Owl Cigars. Burns and Allen joined in progress, the Lombardo series for General Cigar having begun in 1929.

Sept. 19, 1934–March 24, 1937, CBS. 30m, Wednesdays at 9:30 until May 29, 1935, then at 10 until Oct. 2, 1935, then at 8:30. *The Adventures of Gracie* through Sept. 23, 1936, then *The Burns and Allen Show*. White Owl Cigars through September 1935, then Campbell Soups. **ANNOUNCER:** Ken Niles. **VOCALISTS:** Milton Watson, 1934–35; Tony Martin, 1936–37. **ORCHESTRAS:** Ferde Grofé, 1934–35; Jacques Renard, 1935–36; Eddy Duchin, July and Aug. 1936; Henry King, Sept. 1936. **THEME:** *Love Nest* from this point on.

April 12, 1937–Aug. 1, 1938, NBC. 30m, Mondays at 8. Grape Nuts. **ANNOUNCERS:** Ronald Drake, John Conte. **VOCALISTS:** Dick Foran, the Singing Cowboy, April–June 1937, then Tony Martin, with Frank Parker briefly in April 1938. **ORCHESTRAS:** Ray Noble through March, then Jan Garber through June, then Glen Gray.

Sept. 30, 1938–June 23, 1939, CBS. 30m, Fridays at 8:30. Chesterfield Cigarettes. **ANNOUNCER:** Paul Douglas. **VOCALIST:** Frank Parker. **ORCHESTRA:** Ray Noble.

Oct. 4, 1939–June 26, 1940, CBS. 30m, Wednesdays at 7:30. Hinds Cream. **ANNOUNCER:** Truman Bradley. **VOCALIST:** Frank Parker. **ORCHESTRA:** Ray Noble.

July 1, 1940–March 24, 1941, NBC. 30m, Mondays at 7:30. Hormel Meats. **ANNOUNCERS:** John Hiestand, Jimmy Wallington. **ORCHESTRA:** Artie Shaw.

Oct. 7, 1941–June 30, 1942, NBC. 30m, Tuesdays at 7:30. Lever Brothers, Swan Soap. **ANNOUNCER:** Bill Goodwin. **VOCALISTS:** Jimmy Cash, Richard Haydn. **ORCHESTRA:** Paul Whiteman.

Oct. 6, 1942–June 25, 1945, CBS. 30m, Tuesdays at 9 through December 1944, then Mondays at 8:30. Swan Soap.

Sept. 20, 1945–June 23, 1949, NBC. 30m, Thursdays at 8, 1945–46, then Thursdays at 8:30. *Maxwell House Coffee Time*. General Foods.

Sept. 21, 1949–May 17, 1950, CBS. 30m, Wednesdays at 10. Block Drugs.

CAST: beginning in 1942 with situation comedy format: Elvia Allman as Gracie's friend Tootsie Sagwell. Mel Blanc as "the Happy Postman," who sobbed his way through the cheeriest news. Margaret Brayton as Mrs. Billingsley. Sara Berner as Muriel. Clarence Nash as Herman the Duck. Elliott Lewis, Mary Lee Robb, Richard Crenna, Joseph Kearns, Eric Snowden, Bea Benaderet, Hal March, Gerald Mohr, Marvin Miller, Wally Maher, Doris Singleton, Dawn Bender, Tommy Bernard, Gale Gordon, Hans Conried. **ANNOUNCERS:** Bill Goodwin, 1942–50. Harry Von Zell at various times. Tobe Reed a second announcer, 1947–49. **VOCALIST:** Jimmy Cash, ca. 1942–45. **ORCHESTRAS:** Paul Whiteman, 1942–43, then Felix Mills, 1943–45, then Meredith Willson, 1945–48, then Harry Lubin, 1948–50. **SOUND EFFECTS:** Virgil Reimer (NBC); David Light and Al Span (CBS).

DIRECTORS (variously over the entire run): Ed Gardner, Ralph Levy, Al Kaye, etc. **WRITERS:** Harry Conn, Carroll Carroll, John P. Medbury (all 1930s); Paul Henning, Harvey Helm, Hal Block, Henry Garson, Keith Fowler, Aaron J. Ruben, Harmon J. Alexander, Helen Gould Harvey.

Gracie Allen wasn't as dumb as she seemed on the air. She proved that in 1939, appearing on the intellectual quiz show *Information, Please*, and holding her own with the experts. It takes a keen intelligence to play a dumb role that long and well, but Gracie had more than that. From the beginning, she had a singular ability to make audiences love her. "The audience found her, I didn't," said George Burns in a *Playboy* interview years after her death. The crowds they played to in the early '20s, when they were "just a lousy small-time act," defined what Gracie Allen was and would be for the next 35 years. The audience wouldn't stand for it if her lines required sarcasm or spite. Burns learned that if he blew a puff of cigar smoke in Gracie's direction, "the audience would hate me." As he told the interviewer: "She was too dainty, too ladylike,'' for malice or mean humor. ''She was a beautiful little girl, like a little doll, a little Irish doll.''

She was born in San Francisco July 26, 1905. Her given name was Grace Ethel Cecile Rosalie Allen. Her father, Edward Allen, toured with a song-and-dance act, and Gracie appeared onstage with him in childhood. At 14, she was ready to quit school and become a performer. She and her sisters toured with the Larry Reilly vaudeville company until 1922, when she quit over a question of billing. She took up stenography while continuing to room with friends on the fringes of vaudeville. One of her friends, Rena Arnold, was appearing on a program in Union Hill, N.J. When Gracie accompanied her to the theater one night, she met George Burns, a young comic with a gravel voice.

Burns and his partner Billy Lorraine had run out of prospects and were dissolving their act. Born Nathan Birnbaum in New York Jan. 20, 1896, Burns had already had a full life in show business. At 7, he sang in taverns and saloons as part of a schoolboys' group, the Peewee Quartet. Later he'd been a trick roller skater, a dance instructor, and finally a vaudeville comic.

He and Gracie formed a new team, giving their first performance at the Hill Street Theater in Newark. In his memoir, Burns recalls that they made $5 per show. He was the comedian, and Gracie threw the straight lines. But Gracie was strangely transformed in front of a live audience: she ''said the line differently on a stage than in a rehearsal,'' he wrote in his book *Gracie: A Love Story*, and the audience found her delivery more amusing than his payoff. Burns switched roles. That night they double-dated with Gracie's friend Mary Kelly and Kelly's new boyfriend Jack Benny. The night was doubly significant: he discovered a formula that would work for Burns and Allen for decades, and in Jack Benny he met a lifelong friend.

Burns and Allen found vaudeville steady work but low pay. The glory was temporary, fading each night with the closing curtain in another small town. They put in ''hundreds of weeks of vaudeville'' on the way up, said their entry in *Current Biography* of 1940. By 1926 they had been traveling together more than three years, with separate rooms and sleeping berths on the road, and Burns was beginning to want something more substantial.

They were married Jan. 27, 1926. The following year they signed a long contract with the Keith circuit, at $750 a week ''very big time,'' Burns would recall. Bigger times were just ahead. Within half a dozen years they would be making a four-figure weekly salary doing a 30-minute radio show, the easiest work in the world, Burns thought—all he had to do was read his lines without rattling his script. By 1940 their income from radio alone would be estimated at $9,000 a week.

It seems strange that George Burns and Gracie Allen would be discovered, as radio properties, by the British. They were doing a vaudeville tour in England, playing to packed houses everywhere. The British just loved Gracie; her routines became so well known during the six-month trip that the audience would sometimes shout out the punchline in unison. They were aided in this by radio, using the infant medium to promote their stage shows, doing short bits from their act on various BBC stations as they traveled. From the beginning, Gracie had severe mike fright. She never really lost her fear of the microphone, Burns would say in interviews and in his books, but she always coped with it. Returning home, they auditioned for NBC and Grape Nuts in 1930. But the agency executive thought Gracie would be ''too squeaky'' on the air, and they lost the job. It was an irony: a few years later, the same product would be carrying their radio show, then one of the most successful in the nation.

Continued vaudeville bookings led them to a Palace Theater date that included, among other top acts, Eddie Cantor. Cantor had been one of the first major vaudeville performers to crack radio. In the fall of 1931, his show was led only by *Amos 'n' Andy* in the ratings service. When Cantor invited Gracie to come on his program, Burns decided to let her go on. Never mind the veiled insult—that the invitation did not include George, that Cantor himself would work with Gracie and feed her her lines. Burns's only stipulation was that he be allowed to write her material.

Make no mistake, wrote Carroll Carroll in his remembrance of Burns and Allen: Burns was ''*numero uno* in thinking up what Gracie would say, *should* say, and could *not* say'' on the air. But throughout their long career, from the beginning of it, Burns was considered the lesser light in the Burns and Allen partnership. Burns himself fostered this notion—shot through his books is a where-would-I-be-without-her tone. Carroll Carroll reversed it: "Gracie without George would have been Irish coffee without the John Jameson. He poured into her all the upside-down humor that in his later years without her has changed him from an uptight straight man into a relaxed comedian." Glenhall Taylor, who produced *The Burns and Allen Show* beginning in October 1941, considered Burns one of the funniest men alive. And though Groucho Marx, for one, was said to believe that Burns had no talent for comedy, Burns could always send Jack Benny into fits of laughter, often without saying a word.

So the Cantor show was an opportunity for Burns and Allen as a team, despite the format. Burns wrote her skit, stood at her side on a radio program in which he would not speak, and watched her steal the show from Eddie Cantor. In those early network days, one sensational performance on a top-rated show could do it. Suddenly Gracie's scatterbrain humor was a hot radio ticket. They were invited to Rudy Vallee's *Fleischmann Hour*, this time as a team, and in February 1932 were installed as comics-in-residence on the Guy Lombardo program for Robert Burns Cigars, their first regular series.

It seemed the whole world loved Gracie: her wacky, innocent way with a quip, her ability to make the most ridiculous comment seem almost logical. She captured the nation's affection in that first season, 1932. By 1933, Burns remembers, she was one of the five most famous women in America. She set the standard for all the crazy females, from Jane Ace to Marie Wilson, that radio would produce. Her humor wasn't strictly malapropian, though at times it was. It utilized her real persona, not just the fiction that Burns created. Others could copy the dumb part, but no one could copy Gracie.

Lombardo took his band to NBC in 1934, and Burns and Allen were offered the entire half-hour, at $2,000 a week. They would title it *The Adventures of Gracie*, and their theme, *Love Nest*, would become one of the strongest identifying melodies of the air. Their earliest writers were Harry Conn, Burns's brother Willy, Carroll Carroll, and a columnist named John P. Medbury, who was paid by Burns to think up and mail in weekly doses of Gracie-type gags. Car-

roll represented J. Walter Thompson, the agency handling the show. He remembered Conn as "a joker" who tried to get him fired and soon left the show himself. An agency in those days had a lot of power: a big one, like Thompson, provided the writers, producers, and directors of a major show like *Burns and Allen*. Carroll remembered those early writing sessions. Burns would use the gags from Medbury as an impetus for brainstorming, but again, it was Burns who made up the final scripts. Burns had "the ability to pick out the good line from the babble of a group of guys pitching gags," wrote Carroll. "When he heard it, he'd silence everyone and dictate to his secretary, Helen Schorr, the way it should be said by Gracie." It was during this time that someone came up with an idea for a publicity stunt that would truly make Burns and Allen household names—Gracie's search for her "lost brother."

Whose idea was it? In *The Big Broadcast*, Frank Buxton and Bill Owen credit Bob Taplinger, head of publicity at CBS. Carroll thought the idea originated with Burns. In one of his books, Burns said it came out of the agency, whose executives wanted to publicize the show's new 9:30 timeslot. All that mattered was this: it was the most sensational thing of its time. It was launched Jan. 4, 1933. Gracie mentioned that her brother was missing, and this became the centerpiece of the broadcast. The following Sunday she appeared without notice on Eddie Cantor's show. She was looking for her brother, she told Cantor and the nation. She popped up suddenly on Jack Benny's program. She appeared on melodramas and soap operas. Even when she did not appear, the search for Gracie Allen's brother was worked into dramatic skits. Burns remembered that a telephone rang on a tense drama set inside a submarine. From the surface, someone asked the captain, "Is Gracie Allen's brother down there with you?" Department stores worked the gag into their newspaper ads, and people everywhere were telling Gracie's-brother jokes. Celebrities as diverse as Frank Buck and Grace Moore joined the hunt.

The stunt crossed networks, a coup of major proportions, made possible by the fact that the powerful J. Walter Thompson agency was backing it up. Thompson "controlled enough shows on both networks to get it started," wrote Carroll, and soon the stars of those shows understood that a sudden appearance by Gracie might boost their audience. "People began to tune all over the dial trying to catch Gracie visiting some show they'd never heard before." And when NBC did try to put a lid on the gag, it backfired and put the network in a bad light. Gracie was to appear unannounced on *The Fleischmann Hour*. Host Rudy Vallee had been ordered not to mention the lost brother gag. But Vallee "accidentally" picked up the wrong script and mentioned it anyway, and a skittish NBC engineer cut the show off the air. The fallout—a controversy in the press over censorship—gave NBC a black eye and helped keep the lost brother routine running.

The Adventures of Gracie catapulted into the top ten. Meanwhile, Gracie's real brother, a publicity-shy San Francisco accountant named George Allen, had to go into hiding when reporters found him and invaded his life.

Like many vaudeville-based comedy shows, *Burns and Allen* had two distinct phases. The '30s phase was a stage act. Never was it mentioned that they were husband and wife: there were no attempts to develop situations beyond the joke state. The show was simply a vehicle for Gracie's crazy patter, often coming out of the blue with no point of reference to what went before. "You know, if Ray Noble got a nice coat of tan and crossed his legs behind his head, he'd look like a pretzel," she would say for no particular reason. She would talk about her budding career as a surrealistic painter, having just completed a piece called *Love Life of an Hors d'Oeuvre*, painted with her father's shaving brush. A guest remarked that she must come to the Boston Art Institute, where "they're hanging one of my paintings." Without missing a beat, Gracie said, "Oh, yes, you must come to Alcatraz, they're hanging one of my brothers."

There was also the inevitable "flirtation theme." Gracie was a scatterbrain who liked the boys. She'd flirt with anyone except George, who remained strictly her foil. She flirted with the maestro and especially with such romantic film stars as Charles Boyer, when they came on the show. In 1936 she flirted with their singing star, Tony Martin; in 1938 with announcer Paul Douglas. In her routines with Burns she would chatter away at full speed. They would dance and talk, and often Gracie would sing. Mostly her songs were typical '30s musical balderdash,

pieces like *When a Prince of a Fella Meets a Cinderella*. These added charm and a period flavor; then it was back to the madcap dialogue. "Did you know Johnny Weismuller was a great opera singer?—yes, I've heard he was a great diva." And George would sigh and say, "I'll bet he goes swimming in Lily Pons." And Gracie would laugh wildly, ending with a flat "I don't get it."

But this vaudeville style was showing its age as the second generation of radio listeners came along, and the ratings began to slip. It was time for another publicity stunt. Roosevelt was running for a third term; the Republicans were nominating Wendell Willkie for the futile job of running against him. What about a Gracie-for-President stunt? She would run as a candidate from the Surprise Party. Again she turned up unannounced on rival programs, appearing for a moment with a lamebrained pitch for votes and a bit of screwball political philosophy. Her lines were funny and widely quoted. "The president of today is merely the postage stamp of tomorrow," she would declare. When asked about her party affiliation, she said, "Same old party—George Burns." Her previous political experience was touted: she had formerly run for governess in the State of Coma. An article titled *America's Next President Should Be a Woman* appeared under her byline in *Liberty* magazine. A little hardbound book, *How to Become President*, was published by "the Gracie Allen Self-Delusion Institute." They went on a barnstorming campaign by train and scheduled a political convention in Omaha, Neb. This all helped temporarily: the ratings slip was briefly reversed, but the campaign lacked the punch of the search for her brother. In January 1941 their rating had slipped to 14.8.

Burns finally realized what was happening. They were still doing a vaudeville routine, and those days were gone forever. It was time for a "new" *Burns and Allen Show*, a reorganization that would present them, for the first time, in situation comedy as man and wife. Burns announced this change in 1942: it was that simple and quick. The show would still turn on Gracie's absurdities, but now there would be storylines. Gracie would still be flirtatious, but within the bounds of a married woman. The stories turned on classic comedy ingredients: vanity, jealousy, misunderstanding. George is mistaken for Gracie's father, leading to an "Am I getting old?" plot. Gracie becomes involved in the Uplift Society plot to marry off Harry Von Zell. Gracie decides that George should go back to college. She decides that George is as good a singer as Bing Crosby and sets out to prove it. To begin this new era, they were announced by Bill Goodwin as "the people who live in the Burns house, George and Gracie." The show was seldom called *The Burns and Allen Show*, though that's how it was known by fans and within the industry. Like many name comics, Burns and Allen took their show titles from the sponsor's product. They were called *Maxwell House Coffee Time* in the '40s; in the 1949 season, *The Ammident Show*, for the toothpaste that paid the bills. At times they were simply announced, without formal title: "Swan Soap presents George Burns and Gracie Allen. . . ."

The sitcom format paid immediate dividends, pushing their rating back to 20 points, and there it remained. Mel Blanc created his happy postman on the Burns and Allen show. Elliott Lewis played a character of similarly conflicting character traits in the late '40s. He was just a fellow encountered by Burns from week to week—sometimes an usher, sometimes a cab driver—whose routine always began in bliss and ended in rage. "I'm *sooo* happy!" Lewis would cry, telling how delighted he was to have the job driving a taxi. But before the show was over, Lewis would work himself into a maniacal fit, reminding himself of all the silly things wrong with the job, and he'd end up destroying his taxicab.

When radio began to fade in 1950, Burns went straight into TV with good success for eight years. Gracie's retirement in 1958 wrote a finish to the Burns and Allen saga. Burns continued in show business, becoming a Las Vegas headliner and a top nightclub comic. His attempt to continue on television without Gracie was not successful: his *George Burns Show* folded in a year, and another try, *Wendy and Me*, with Connie Stevens, met a similar fate. Gracie suffered a heart attack and died Aug. 27, 1964. Burns continued to work, doing a routine with Carol Channing that was short-lived. For a time it seemed that the old sentiment was to be proved true: that Burns without Gracie was a stale act indeed. Then he got a role in a movie, intended for his friend Jack Benny, who became ill and had to decline it. He won an Academy Award as Best

Supporting actor in *The Sunshine Boys*, a 1975 release. His performance in the title role of the 1977 film *Oh, God* put to rest the "no-talent" argument. In his 90s Burns still appeared in shows and TV specials. He published many books playing on his latter-day celebrity status and his age, and he also wrote extensively about his life with Gracie. His *Gracie: A Love Story* is just that, a humorous, sad remembrance of days long past, a testament of love. He died at 100 on March 9, 1996.

More than 100 *Burns and Allen* shows currently exist on tape, and the enjoyment listeners find there depends in large measure on the their ability to forget much of what they've seen and heard since those shows were new. There is a tendency today to dismiss vaudeville comedy as unsophisticated and even simplistic. Burns himself often apologized when he quoted verbatim from old routines: "This doesn't sound like much now" was usually the tone. But those fascinated by the history of show business cannot but be entertained. Gracie's singing in the shows of the '30s adds an element totally missing from the later run. In the sitcom years it all changed: the lines were perhaps funnier, but the comedy was somehow more predictable. It always started from an absurd premise—Gracie chasing off in all directions—and in this it bore a superficial resemblance to *The Life of Riley* and *The Adventures of Ozzie and Harriet*. But some recently discovered shows from the late '40s are still funny, and one, with Howard Duff in character as Sam Spade, can only be called delightful.

THE BUSY MR. BINGLE, situation comedy.

BROADCAST HISTORY: March 18–June 10, 1943, Mutual. 30m, Thursdays at 8:30. **CAST:** John Brown as J. B. Bingle, "head of the Bingle Pin Company," who "keeps busy getting the firm into and out of trouble." Jackson Beck as Whizzer, the firm's master salesman. There was also a secretary, Miss Pepper, and an office boy, Tommy, the actors playing them unknown. **CATCHPHRASE:** "Mr. Bingle, what are you doing?" "Well, I'm not sure, Miss Pepper, but I'm *so* busy!"

BY KATHLEEN NORRIS, serialized dramatic anthology.

BROADCAST HISTORY: Oct. 9, 1939–Sept. 26, 1941, CBS. 15m continuation, weekdays at 5, 1939–40; at 10 A.M., 1940–41. General Mills for

Wheaties. **CAST:** Narrator Ethel Everett. Players included Ed Jerome, Jay Meredith, Arline Blackburn, House Jameson, Santos Ortega, Chester Stratton, Lawson Zerbe, James Meighan, Joan Banks, Betty Garde, Eleanor Audley. **ANNOUNCER:** Dwight Weist. **PRODUCER:** Phillips H. Lord. **DIRECTOR:** Jay Hanna.

Kathleen Norris was a prolific author whose novels formed the basis for these serials. Producer Phillips H. Lord borrowed a leaf from his police drama *Gang Busters* by having Norris narrate "by proxy" each weekly story. Ethel Everett was the proxy stand-in; the stories were light romantic fare.

BY POPULAR DEMAND, book review.

BROADCAST HISTORY: Jan. 15–April 9, 1938, CBS. 15m, Saturdays at 9:30. Discussions of current books, with up to three works discussed in each broadcast. Among them: *Kaltenborn Edits the News*, by H. V. Kaltenborn; *You Have Seen Their Faces*, by Erskine Caldwell, with photographs by his future wife, Margaret Bourke-White; and *Peril at End House*, by Agatha Christie.

BY POPULAR DEMAND, popular music.

BROADCAST HISTORY: June 27–Nov. 14, 1946, Mutual. 30m, Thursdays at 9:30. **HOST:** Bud Collyer. **VOCALISTS:** Mary Small, Harry Babbitt. **MUSIC:** Ray Bloch. **THEME:** *The Way You Look Tonight.*

This was a poor man's hit parade, with "song hits from everywhere, selected by the foremost bandleaders and celebrities from all over the world."

C

CABIN B-13, mystery anthology.

Broadcast history: July 5, 1948–Jan. 2, 1949, CBS. 30m, originally Mondays at 8:30, summer substitute for *Arthur Godfrey's Talent Scouts*; Tuesdays at 10:30 as of Aug. 31; Sundays at 8:30 as of Oct.; at 10:30 beginning Oct. 31. **Cast:** Arnold Moss as Dr. Fabian, a mystery-spinning ship's doctor who lived in Cabin B-13 on the world-cruising luxury liner *Maurevania*. Alan Hewitt as Dr. Fabian for three broadcasts beginning Aug. 31; Moss resumed Oct. 3. **Music:** Merle Kendrick. **Creator-Writer:** John Dickson Carr. **Director:** John Dietz. **Sound effects:** Jerry McCarty.

Cabin B-13 was developed from the title of John Dickson Carr's *Suspense* play of the same name, though (as Carr biographer Douglas G. Greene reveals) the resemblance to the original story was slight. Dr. Fabian, the hero, told of mysteries, and occasionally solved them, on a cruise route from Southampton along the coast of France and through the Mediterranean to the Near East. For years *Cabin B-13* was a "fabled program," Greene notes, its reputation as one of radio's best all-time mystery series resting upon fading memories. Then three taped copies turned up: the entire run of scripts was retrieved from the Library of Congress, and a more objective evaluation was possible.

"The most obvious impression left after reading the scripts is of Carr's fertility of invention," Greene wrote. One sample script he found "unconvincing," the hero resorting to "foolish-ness." Interestingly, Greene found that the broadcast itself overcame these faults. The stories he described as "good to superb," with "imaginative treatments of impossible crimes." The series began to stall in November, as Carr found meeting deadlines ever more difficult. Several old *Suspense* scripts were used in the final six weeks.

CAFE ISTANBUL, foreign intrigue and adventure.

Broadcast history: Jan. 6–Dec. 28, 1952, ABC. 30m, Sundays at 9:15; Thursdays at 8 as of mid-April; Sundays at 8:30 for Buick beginning Oct. 12. **Cast:** Marlene Dietrich as Mlle. Madou, hostess and singer in a Turkish cabaret. Arnold Moss as her old friend Col. Maurice Lesko. Ken Lynch as Christopher Gard, the "roving American who comes and goes in her life"; later as Steve Lacey, another American who really owned the Cafe Istanbul. **Producer:** Leonard Blair. **Sound effects:** Keene Crockett.

Cafe Istanbul was another of the adventure shows peopled by high-profile Hollywood film stars that dotted the network schedules in the medium's last decade. Dietrich offered "the same romantic *Weltschmertz* role" she had been playing since her first notable film, *The Blue Angel*, in 1930 (*Time*). "She talks a lot to an endless stream of appealing, adventurous men," said *Radio Life*, and sang at least one "foreign-flavored ballad" a week: such old favorites as *Je Vous Aime Beaucoup* and *La Vie en Rose*, sometimes in French, sometimes German, sometimes English.

The cafe was at a crossroads of intrigue. Col. Maurice Lesko was the "prefect of the local police," often known as the commissioner. As Mlle. Madou, Dietrich was usually drawn into a police case after initially refusing to be involved. Christopher Gard infused the show with the love interest "that one would expect in a Marlene Dietrich vehicle" (*Radio Life*), but this character ultimately gave way to Steve Lacey, who, though fascinated by Madou, "wouldn't hesitate to sacrifice her to a jail sentence if she got in the way of his operations. Their ambivalent affection finds them madly in love one moment, and fighting the next."

In 1953 Dietrich took the show to CBS, changed the setting, and emerged with a sound-alike series called *Time for Love*.

CALIFORNIA CARAVAN, West Coast documentary-drama.

BROADCAST HISTORY: 1947–52, Mutual–Don Lee. Premiered on the Don Lee Network June 19, 1947, a 15m series for the California Medical Association; 30m as of 1948; heard regionally, often Sunday afternoons. CAST: Virginia Gregg, continuing leading lady in the early run. Bob Purcell, narrator. Irene Winston, Ken Christy, Irene Tedrow, John Dehner, Harry Bartell, Herb Vigran, Paul Frees, Johnny McGovern. ANNOUNCER: Bruce Buell. PRODUCER-DIRECTOR: Lou Holzer. DIRECTOR: Larry Hays. WRITERS: Beth Barnes, Karl Schlichter, Lee Roddy, Richard Hill Wilkerson.

California Caravan was one of the first shows to be sponsored by physicians. Doctors had always been barred from commercial advertising for ethical reasons, but through their medical association they could advertise as a group. Little-known historical dramas provided the prestige the group sought. Early shows told the stories of poet Edwin Markham, of camels brought into the California desert, of the rainmaker who caused a flood, and of the West's "roughest-toughest" stagecoach driver, Charlie Parkhurst, "who only upon his death was discovered to be a woman."

CALL FOR MUSIC, popular music and song.

BROADCAST HISTORY: Feb. 13–April 16, 1948, CBS. 30m, Fridays at 10. Philip Morris.

April 20–June 29, 1948, NBC. 30m, Tuesdays at 8. Philip Morris.

CAST: Dinah Shore, "mistress of ceremonies," with singer Johnny Mercer, maestro Harry James, and the Harry Zimmerman Chorus. ANNOUNCER: Jack Rourke. DIRECTOR: Jack Runyon. WRITERS: Jerry Lawrence and Bob Lee.

CALL THE POLICE, crime drama.

BROADCAST HISTORY: 1947–49, three summer series as replacements for *The Amos 'n' Andy Show*: June 3–Sept. 23, 1947, NBC. 30m, Tuesdays at 9; June 1–Sept. 28, 1948, NBC, Tuesdays at 9:30 (heard in the *Fibber McGee and Molly* timeslot while replacing *Amos 'n' Andy*, and the *McGee* replacement—Fred Waring—moved elsewhere); June 5–Sept. 25, 1949, CBS, Sundays at 7:30. Sponsored in all three runs by Lever Brothers for Rinso and Lifebuoy Soap (whose commercials telling listeners how to fight BEEE-OOHHH were remembered for years). CAST: Joseph Julian as police commissioner Bill Grant of the city of Ashland, 1947. George Petrie as Bill Grant, 1948–49. Joan Tompkins as his girlfriend, criminal psychologist Libby Tyler, 1947. Amzie Strickland as Libby, 1948–49. Robert Dryden as Sergeant Maggio, Bill Grant's "occasionally bumbling but always caustically dry-humored assistant." ANNOUNCERS: Jay Simms, 1947; Hugh James, 1948–49. MUSIC: Ben Ludlow. DIRECTOR: John Cole. WRITER: Peter Barry.

Bill Grant, the hero of *Call the Police*, was a recently returned war veteran and the son of a police sergeant killed in the line of duty. A recent graduate of the FBI academy, he returned home to find his town in the grip of racketeers. Taking over from an aging police commissioner, Grant began his war against the underworld. Many shows ended with a "Lever Brothers Award of Valor" and a $100 check going to a real cop who had acted with courage, with a "Plaque of Honor" going to his department.

CALLING ALL CARS, police drama.

BROADCAST HISTORY: Nov. 29, 1933–Sept. 8, 1939, CBS West Coast. 30m. Rio Grande Oil Company. WRITER-DIRECTOR: William N. Robson.

Calling All Cars was one of the earliest police shows on the air. It dramatized true crime stories introduced by officers of the Los Angeles and other police departments. The show was a crude forerunner of a type that reached its zenith years later on *Dragnet*: the tedious routine of tracking killers and robbers, often with a postshow recap telling how justice was meted out. None of the cast was credited. The one continuing character was the police dispatcher, Sergeant Jesse Rosenquist of the Los Angeles Police Department, whose voice and name were considered so unusual that he was used for the entire run. The show ran only in areas where Rio Grande "cracked" gasoline was sold. The sponsor promoted its "close ties" with police departments in Arizona and Southern California, urging listeners to buy its product for "police car performance" in their own cars.

CALLING ALL DETECTIVES, combination mystery-quiz show.

BROADCAST HISTORY: April 7–Aug. 25, 1945, Mutual. 30m, Saturdays at 9:30. **HOST:** Vincent Pelletier as "Robin," who gave the clues.

Ca. 1947–50, 15m, syndicated from regional Mutual broadcasts. **CAST:** Paul Barnes, "man of a thousand voices," as Detective Jerry Browning.

The 1945 edition of *Calling All Detectives* had an unusual gimmick. Though it aired on a network, local affiliates were made part of the action. Listeners were selected from cards sent in; then, when the mystery reached its climax, local announcers called their listeners and offered prizes to those who could guess the mystery. At the end of the local segment, the network was rejoined and the story concluded.

In the quarter-hour shows, Paul Barnes played all the voices, working only with a sound effects technician. A melodrama of eight or nine minutes was enacted; Barnes as Detective Browning would then call a number at random from the phone book and quiz a listener on aspects of the show. The live series was sponsored by the Sealy Mattress Company ("sleeping on a Sealy is like sleeping on a cloud"). It was transcribed in progress, and the recordings, without the commercials and telephone calls, were later syndicated.

CALLING AMERICA, wartime variety.

BROADCAST HISTORY: June 13–Oct. 3, 1943, CBS. 30m, Sundays at 8. House of Squibb. **CAST:** Newsman Bob Trout, host. Baritone Wal-

ter Cassel of the Metropolitan Opera. Victor Bay with a 30-piece orchestra and an 11-voice chorus. **PRODUCER-DIRECTOR:** Eleanor Larsen. **WRITER:** Jack Lewi.

Bob Trout, just returned from England, told human interest stories of fighting men overseas, making "Joe Smith, American" the "real star of the program." The show was billed as a "personal letter" to the home front about its "boys and girls in the service."

THE CAMEL CARAVAN, comedy-variety in many formats and timeslots, with many diverse acts. A much-traveled title for the sponsor, Camel Cigarettes.

BROADCAST HISTORY: Dec. 7, 1933–June 25, 1936, CBS. 30m, Tuesdays and Thursdays at 10, 1933–34; at 9, 1934–36. Originally a musical forum for Glen Gray and the Casa Loma Orchestra. Deane Janis, vocalist. Walter O'Keefe added for comedy, 1934–36. F. Chase Taylor and Budd Hulick as Col. Stoopnagle and Budd, 1934.

June 30, 1936–June 20, 1939, CBS. 30m, Tuesdays. *Benny Goodman's Swing School.* Popular music with vocalists Martha Tilton and Johnny Mercer. Linked with the comedy show *Jack Oakie's College* Dec. 29, 1936–March 22, 1938, with Camel sponsoring both on Tuesdays at 9:30 and billing the entire hour *The Camel Caravan.* Another Goodman *Caravan* on NBC, Saturdays at 10, July 8–Dec. 30, 1939.

March 28, 1938–June 26, 1939, CBS. 30m, Mondays at 7:30. See THE EDDIE CANTOR SHOW.

June 27, 1939–Jan. 2, 1941, NBC. 30m, Tuesdays at 9:30, then Saturdays at 10. Bob Crosby continuing in Goodman's slot as Camel bandmaster. Thursdays at 7:30 as of September 1940. Bert Parks, emcee, 1939–40.

Jan. 9, 1941–Jan. 1, 1942, NBC. 30m, Thursdays at 7:30. Xavier Cugat Orchestra.

July 10, 1942–March 19, 1943, CBS. 60m, Fridays at 10. Herb Shriner with a Hoosier-soaked brand of comedy; vocalists Connie Haines, Lanny Ross; announcer Ken Niles; Xavier Cugat, later Freddie Rich, orchestra leaders.

March 25–Oct. 28, 1943, NBC. 30m, Thursdays at 10. A hastily assembled pairing of Jimmy Durante and Garry Moore to finish out the season for *The Abbott and Costello Show* when comic Lou Costello fell ill.

March 26–July 2, 1943, CBS. 45m, Fridays at

10. *The Camel Comedy Caravan.* Jack Carson, host; Ken Niles, announcer. Elvia Allman as Mrs. Ken Niles. Mel Blanc in many roles from Irish cops to Pancho the Mexican to the English butler, Jerkins.

Oct. 8, 1943–March 30, 1945, CBS. 30m, Fridays at 10. *The Camel Comedy Caravan*, with Jimmy Durante and Garry Moore.

1945, CBS. 30m Mondays at 7:30. *The Bob Hawk Show*; subtitled *The Camel Caravan* for part of one season only.

July 4, 1946–April 5, 1954, CBS. 30m, Thursdays, later Saturdays, later Mondays. Various timeslots. *The Vaughn Monroe Show*, sometimes billed as *The Camel Caravan.*

THE CAMEL QUARTER-HOUR, early network dance show.

BROADCAST HISTORY: June 1, 1931–May 28, 1932, CBS. 15m, six a week at 7:45. Camel Cigarettes. **CAST:** Morton Downey, tenor, with announcer Tony Wons. **ORCHESTRA:** Jacques Renard. **PRODUCER:** Erik Barnouw. **DIRECTOR:** Charles Gannon.

The Camel Quarter-Hour was the first short broadcast to lure a major national sponsor from the hour-long variety shows. The producers were praised by the *Forum* for their "elaborate signatures" and "sugar-coating sales messages." The critic was less than thrilled with Tony Wons, radio's first shirttail philosopher. "Approximately one minute [and] 45 seconds of advertising, two minutes of rubbish by Wons, and the remaining time divided between Downey and the orchestra" was the verdict. Because of the success of this show, similar programs came along the same year, and the venerable *Lucky Strike Dance Orchestra* underwent radical surgery. These four—*Camel, Lucky Strike*, and the *Chesterfield* and *Prince Albert Quarter-Hours*—were dubbed "Lady Nicotine's Children" in the press. Their success was impressive but brief.

CAMPANA SERENADE, popular music.

BROADCAST HISTORY: Oct. 10, 1942–April 10, 1943, NBC. 15m, Saturdays at 10:15. **CAST:** Dick Powell, the Music Maids and Matty Malneck's orchestra.

Sept. 4, 1943–Feb. 26, 1944, CBS. 30m, Saturdays at 1. **CAST:** Powell, Martha Tilton and the Lud Gluskin Orchestra.

THE CAMPBELL PLAYHOUSE, dramatic anthology.

BROADCAST HISTORY: Dec. 9, 1938–March 31, 1940, CBS. 60m, Fridays at 9, 1938–39; Sundays at 8, 1939–40. An extension of Orson Welles's *Mercury Theater on the Air* after Campbell Soups joined as sponsor. **CAST:** Orson Welles and the Mercury Players: Ray Collins, Agnes Moorehead, George Coulouris, Frank Readick, Georgia Backus, Bea Benaderet, Everett Sloane, Edgar Barrier, etc. **ANNOUNCERS:** Niles Welch, Ernest Chappell. **MUSIC:** Bernard Herrmann. **PRODUCER:** John Houseman. **DIRECTOR:** Orson Welles. **WRITER:** Howard Koch. **SOUND EFFECTS:** Bill Brown, John Cuomo, Harry Essman. **THEME:** *Piano Concerto no. 1 in B-Flat Minor*, by Tchaikovsky.

Nov. 29, 1940–June 13, 1941, CBS. 30m, Fridays at 9:30. Campbell Soups. **CAST:** major stage and film stars (Humphrey Bogart, Fredric March, Mary Astor, Jeanette MacDonald, etc.) in adaptations. **ANNOUNCER:** Del Sharbutt. **ORCHESTRA:** Lyn Murray. **PRODUCER:** John Houseman. **DIRECTOR:** George Zachary. **WRITER:** Wyllis Cooper.

After Orson Welles terrified the nation with his Halloween 1938 *War of the Worlds* broadcast, his name became a household word. The immediate result was sponsorship for his theatrical air company, *The Mercury Theater on the Air.* Campbell Soups had been sponsoring the once-famed but fading variety hour *Hollywood Hotel*, which closed its doors in December 1938. The soup company immediately picked up Welles and his players, and the first *Campbell Playhouse* under that title was Daphne du Maurier's *Rebecca*, introduced by newsman Edwin C. Hill. The intro made full use of the Halloween notoriety from which Welles had been only too anxious to distance himself a month earlier. The goals of the new *Playhouse* were then stated by Welles: to do "all kinds of stories, mostly modern, and all of them chosen for their suitability to this medium."

The fare would include such chestnuts as *The Count of Monte Cristo, The Magnificent Ambersons*, and *A Farewell to Arms. State Fair* presented Freeman Gosden and Charles Correll in character as Amos and Andy, and *June Moon* starred Jack Benny. Lionel Barrymore continued his annual performance of *A Christmas Carol* for Campbell. The immediate effect of sponsorship was a real operating budget, providing top film stars to play opposite Welles but relegating his talented aggregation to supporting roles.

The 1940–41 series, without Welles, was a different show, though his former partner John Houseman continued in the producer's role. The productions were of such seldom-heard radio fare as *The Go-Getter* (with Helen Twelvetrees, Randolph Scott, and Frank Morgan) and *The Nervous Wreck* (with Eddie Cantor). Fred Allen was starred in Norman Corwin's *My Client Curley*, and again Barrymore provided Yuletide tradition in *A Christmas Carol*.

CAN YOU TOP THIS?, joke-swapping panel show.

BROADCAST HISTORY:

Dec. 9, 1940–Sept. 19, 1945, WOR, New York. 30m, Mondays at 9:30 until mid-May 1941, then Tuesdays at 8 through Jan. 1943, then Wednesdays at 7:30, 1943–45, then Wednesdays at 8. Kirkman's Soap.

Oct. 3, 1942–Sept. 25, 1948, NBC (overlap with New York broadcast). 30m, Saturdays at 9:30, 1942–47; Fridays at 8:30, 1947–48; Saturdays at 9:30, July–Sept. 1948. Colgate.

Sept. 29, 1948–May 24, 1950, Mutual. 30m, Wednesdays at 8.

Sept. 23, 1950–June 26, 1951, ABC. 30m, Saturdays at 9:30 through Nov.; returned Jan. 2 Tuesdays at 8 for Mars Candy.

Oct. 5, 1953–March 26, 1954, NBC. 15m, weeknights at 10:15.

April 2–July 9, 1954, NBC. 25m, Fridays at 9:35.

CAST: Panelists "Senator" Ed Ford, Harry Hershfield, and Joe Laurie Jr.; Peter Donald, joke-teller for the audience. **HOST:** Ward Wilson. **ANNOUNCER:** Charles Stark.

The premise of *Can You Top This?* was simple. The listening audience sent in jokes, which were read to a panel of well-known punsters, each of whom in his turn tried to top it. That's all there was to it, except that the man who read the jokes (Peter Donald) and the trio on the panel were all showmen. At least two of them (Donald and Harry Hershfield) were considered masters

of dialect, and all three members of the panel were veterans of vaudeville.

The show grew out of joke-swapping sessions at New York's Lamb's Club. Ed Ford thought that a jokefest might make a good radio show. He became the driving force, producer, and owner of the series.

The panel became known as the Knights of the Clown Table. They used no notes or scripts on the air, relying on their vast combined knowledge of punchline humor. It was estimated that, among them, they knew 15,000 gags, many of which could be modified to fit multiple situations. The rules required jokes by the panel to follow the same general topic introduced by the listener's joke. But Ford, Hershfield, and Laurie were masters at switching elements. A Scotsman became an Irishman, a Chinese was a cowboy: the same joke worked with different window dressing, the only limitation being the quickness of the teller in a live format.

Ford was known as "Senator," a title given him at a Republicans Club dinner in the teens. He was the toughest of the three to make laugh, described by *Tune In* as "dour and sullen offstage as well as on." Hershfield was a noted cartoonist and after-dinner speaker who gave an estimated 200 talks a year. Laurie had worked as a stickman in a gambling hall, as an exercise rider for a racing stable, and at "about 80 jobs" before gravitating into vaudeville and then radio. And Peter Donald was a radio man of long experience, notably the excitable Ajax Cassidy of *The Fred Allen Show*.

The opening signature seldom varied. Announcer Charles Stark introduced the panel: "Senator Ford . . ." "Good evening." "Harry Hershfield . . ." "Howdy." "Joe Laurie Jr. . . ." "Hel-lo." Then he introduced Wilson, who explained the rules. Any listener could send in a joke. If the joke was selected for the air, the listener got $5 ($10 in later shows). If none of the wits topped the joke, the listener got $2 for each miss. A Colgate "laugh meter" was set up onstage in view of the studio audience. The meter was in the shape of a laughing face, with a gauge in its mouth that registered the decibel level, from 0 to 1,000, from the audience microphone. A reading of 600 on a contestant joke was considered good, but toppers were often in the 800s, and many hit the 1,000-mark. All contestants received recordings of Peter Donald telling their jokes on the air.

Few jokes were original. Ford once said that in all his years on the show, there had never been a joke submitted that he hadn't heard before. In the beginning, taboos were religion, politics, and arson. Nationalities were considered fair game, and Donald could "do" the gamut, Jewish to Irish to Italian. The show could expect protests from a group thus lampooned, though *Time* noted that "Scotsmen never protest." Ford's jokes often featured recurring characters—Ditsy Baumwortle, Elmer Smudgegunk, Mr. Snapgirdle, Mrs. Fafoofnick, Dopey Dillock, or Ockie Bopp. Joke-screener Betty North looked through as many as 3,000 submissions a week. To the list of taboos North added a few of her own. She would not send over anything on death, race, deformities, or stuttering. She looked for "fast jokes, talking stories that don't require anything visual to put them across." The age of a joke was no factor. An audience would laugh as freely at something from antiquity as from that morning's newspaper.

THE CANDID MICROPHONE, human interest, forerunner to *Candid Camera*.

BROADCAST HISTORY: June 28, 1947–Sept. 23, 1948, ABC. 30m, Saturday at 7:30, opening show; Sundays at 7 until late Sept. 1947; Mondays at 9, Sept.–Oct.; Thursdays at 8 until May 1948; then Thursdays at 9:30.

June 6–Aug. 29, 1950, CBS. 30m, Tuesdays at 9:30. Philip Morris.

HOST: Allen Funt.

The Candid Microphone was the result of Allen Funt's experience as a radio writer and "gimmick man." He had written for Eleanor Roosevelt on her Sweetheart Soap chat show of 1940–41. He had worked for agencies and developed stunt ideas for *Truth or Consequences*. He left the agencies with 14 ideas and $300, he said; soon he had $14 and 300 ideas. But he had developed one idea into a gimmick show called *Funny Money Man*. It was "the stupidest show in radio," said Funt, but at its peak it was bringing him $1,200 a week. The idea was loosely rooted in the scavenger hunt: Funt wrote scripts, which were sold to individual stations, where local personalities would handle the emcee work.

While stationed in Oklahoma with the Army, he came up with the idea that would make his fortune. He was reading the gripe column in the GI newspaper *Yank*. It might be interesting, he thought, to record something along this line for broadcast. The problem was that "ordinary people" often became rigid and tense before a microphone. But what if he could record them on the sly: hide the microphone and let them know they had been duped only after the interview was preserved on the wire machine?

After his discharge, he rented an office and opened for business. There were no portable recorders then: the smallest was a bulky wire recorder whose two parts weighed more than 100 pounds. He would have to lure people to his office and record them there. He had located on the 15th floor of a building across from Grand Central Station, well outside the radio district so his victims would have no reason to suspect him of stunt-show shenanigans. He had the office wired for sound and filled an adjacent room with sensitive recording equipment.

One of his first subjects was the man who came to paint the sign on his door. His name was Lester Cannon. Funt told Cannon that was the name he wanted on his door, Lester Cannon. The sign man balked, and Funt learned something that he would refine and use for years. If he simply eavesdropped, he'd fill up his spools with a lot of dull talk, but if he asked a conventional man to do something unconventional, anything could happen. Cannon, for example, would only paint his name on Funt's door after Funt agreed to change it to Kannon. Lester Kannon became Funt's working alias in the early days of *The Candid Microphone*.

Funt called a locksmith, who arrived to find the secretary chained to her desk. Funt explained that he had lost the key and it was time to unlock the woman so she could go to lunch. The locksmith was indignant; Funt was bellicose. He explained that the secretary was a clock-watcher who never got anything done unless she was shackled. "You better not get caught doing this," the locksmith said. Funt snapped, "That's my business." He would soon be known as the nerviest man in radio: he'd ask anybody to do anything, in a deadpan way that made the victims believe he was absolutely serious. "His victims have never met such a stupid, exasperating young man,'' wrote reporter Jerome Beatty in an early profile. But ''no one has ever taken a punch at him—thus far, at least.''

In other stories he was described as ''a great actor'' whose ''Joe Blow personality'' could sell almost any ridiculous premise. ''He can make believe that he's a bootblack one day or a dentist the next,'' wrote *Radio Life.* ''He's posed as a genius, a dolt, even a madman, and gotten away with it.''

Soon a truly portable recorder came on the market. It weighed 27 pounds and could be disguised as a travel bag. Its microphone could be passed off as a hearing aid or hidden in a phony arm cast. Funt took it into a candy store and asked the saleswoman to ''squish'' the chocolates so he could tell the soft ones from the nuts. He posed as a shoe salesman and ''lost'' one of the shoes a customer had worn in. He stationed an engineer behind a tree to record his attempts to pick up girls on a park bench. The show was hard work. Sometimes Funt and his assistants worked all night setting up their equipment, then waited all day for just the right victim. He went into many candy stores before finding the clerk who would backtalk him. In the park, he was brushed off by a succession of potential pickups before a witty young woman arrived who was perfect (she turned out to be married and was stringing him along). Imagination and cheek were the key ingredients, with a vast reservoir of patience.

For every show using half a dozen bits, at least 60 were recorded and thrown away. The editing process was painfully tedious, as many as 100 splices made in a piece of wire that yielded a three-minute stunt. Occasionally he snipped for ''decency,'' inserting a soft female voice cooing ''censored-censored-censored'' in that spot.

The victims usually turned out to be good sports. Seldom was Funt denied permission to air his pranks. ''You're on *Candid Microphone*,'' he would say, and most people succumbed to Funt's offer of $15, anonymity, and the thrill of being on the air. But the show had problems: it was simply too real, and people refused to believe it. Wrote Jerome Beatty: ''*Candid Microphone* is in the same fix that caused *Information, Please* and *The Quiz Kids* to fail, at the beginning, to attract all the listeners they deserve.'' People just wouldn't believe the wits were that witty, the kids that smart, or the stunts on *The Candid Mi-*

crophone unstaged. *The Quiz Kids* and *Information, Please* survived to become important pieces of radio heritage, but it would take a camera to bring out the best in Funt's act. It was first seen on ABC-TV Aug. 10, 1948, still titled *Candid Microphone.* As *Candid Camera*, it achieved TV fame, seen on various networks for more than 20 years.

CANDY MATSON, detective drama with a female protagonist.

BROADCAST HISTORY: June 29, 1949–May 20, 1951, NBC West Coast. 30m. CAST: Natalie Masters as Candy Matson, a chic, tough, and beautiful San Francisco private detective. Henry Leff as police detective Ray Mallard. Jack Thomas as Candy's friend Rembrandt Watson. AN- NOUNCER: Dudley Manlove. MUSIC: Eloise Rowan on organ. WRITER-PRODUCER- DIRECTOR: Monte Masters. THEME: *Candy.*

Candy Matson was aptly described in an early opening signature. ''Figure? . . . she takes up where Miss America leaves off. Clothes? . . . she makes a peasant dress look like opening night at the opera. Hair? . . . blond, of course, and eyes— just the right shade of blue to match the hair.'' She began each episode on the telephone (her number YUkon 28209), in her penthouse on Telegraph Hill in San Francisco.

Candy had an intriguing, brassy voice that conveyed good humor and a hard edge. Her friend Rembrandt Watson, described by *Radio Life* as ''a Clifton Webbish sort of character,'' was slightly effeminate, of little use in a fight, good for record checking and legwork, and inserted for comic relief. The male influence was Detective Ray Mallard, who popped the question in the last episode and announced with great authority that it was her final case.

CAPTAIN FLAGG AND SERGEANT QUIRT, situation comedy.

BROADCAST HISTORY: Sept. 28, 1941–Jan. 25, 1942, Blue Network. 30m, Sundays at 7:30. Mennen Toiletries.

Feb. 13–April 3, 1942, NBC. 30m, Fridays at 10. Brown & Williamson Tobacco.

CAST: Victor McLaglen and Edmund Lowe as Capt. Flagg and Sgt. Quirt, a pair of Marines with a talent for bragging and an eye for an ankle. William

Gargan as Sgt. Quirt as of early 1942. Fred Shields as Sgt. Bliss. **PRODUCER:** Mel Williamson. **WRITER:** John P. Medbury.

Captain Flagg and Sergeant Quirt was based on the play *What Price Glory?* by Maxwell Anderson and Laurence Stallings. Flagg and Quirt, pugnacious leathernecks, were usually embroiled in a squabble over some "dish," also known as "a real eyeful." Writer Medbury researched Marine lingo at the San Diego Marine base, but the show's most memorable lines (Quirt's "Sez who?" and Flagg's slower, denser, equally combative "Sez me!") were already well known. It was the show's pugnacity that ran it aground. The Marines objected loudly to the notion of a captain "being chewed out by a sergeant," and the show was hastily reorganized. Quirt was dropped as a character, replaced by Sgt. Bliss. It didn't matter: the series folded six weeks later.

CAPTAIN MIDNIGHT, juvenile aviation adventure serial.

BROADCAST HISTORY: Oct. 17, 1939–March 27, 1940, transcribed at WGN, Chicago, for the Skelly Oil Company and aired in markets where Skelly products were sold, notably on stations in the Midwest and Southwest.

Sept. 30, 1940–July 3, 1942, Mutual. 15m continuation, weekdays at 5:45. Ovaltine.

Sept. 28, 1942–June 22, 1945, Blue Network. 15m, weekdays at 5:45. Ovaltine.

Sept. 24, 1945–June 17, 1949, Mutual. 15m, weekdays at 5:30. Ovaltine.

Sept. 20–Dec. 15, 1949, Mutual. 30m, Tuesdays and Thursdays at 5:30.

CAST: Bill Bouchey as Captain Midnight (1939–40 Skelly transcriptions), ace aviator and commander of the Secret Squadron, with Shirley Bell as Patsy Donovan. Ed Prentiss as Captain Midnight on the network. Paul Barnes also heard as Captain Midnight. Billy Rose, Jack Bivens, and Johnny Coons heard variously as Chuck Ramsey, Captain Midnight's young sidekick. Angeline Orr and Marilou Neumayer as Joyce Ryan, the young female Squadron member. Art Hern and Sherman Marks as Ichabod "Ichy" Mudd, the mechanic who often flew into adventure with the Secret Squadron. Boris Aplon as Ivan Shark, the master criminal and longtime villain. Rene Rodier and Sharon Grainger as Fury Shark, the criminal's daughter. Olan Soulé as Kelly, Captain Midnight's second-in-command

in the Secret Squadron. **ANNOUNCERS:** Don Gordon (1939–40 Skelly transcription), Pierre Andre (network). **CREATORS-WRITERS:** Robert Burtt, Wilfred "Bill" Moore. **PRODUCER-DIRECTORS:** Alan Wallace, Russell Young, Kirby Hawkes. **SOUND EFFECTS:** Harry Bubeck, Michael Eisenmenger, Bob Graham.

Captain Midnight grew out of the flying craze of the 1930s, which had been generated partly by *The Air Adventures of Jimmie Allen*. The *Allen* serial had been running regionally for Skelly Oil since 1933, and in 1938, when Skelly decided to create a new flying hero, writers Burtt and Moore were engaged from *Jimmie Allen* to develop and write it. Both had been flying aces in World War I, and Captain Midnight, their new hero, would come of similar stuff.

By 1939 *Captain Midnight* was on many of the same stations that had carried *Jimmie Allen* five years before. Moving to Mutual in 1940, the serial was Ovaltine's replacement for *Little Orphan Annie*, which had been canceled after a ten-year run.

Captain Midnight was a man of mystery as the serial premiered on Mutual, a hero whose job was so important that not even his superiors knew his identity. Listeners to the Skelly shows knew: he was Capt. Red Albright, flying ace of the Great War, who was given the name Captain Midnight after returning at that fateful hour from a perilous mission. Captain Midnight was engaged to stop the sinister activities of Ivan Shark, master criminal who sought to control the world. Shark was an old enemy, having encountered Albright in the First War. In his Skelly days, Albright was aided by a youthful pair of adventurers, Chuck Ramsey and Patsy Donovan. Their struggles with Shark took them, in two long adventures that exist in a 92-chapter tape run, to Mexico and the far Northwest. The early show has many of the Skelly trademarks that worked so well on *Jimmie Allen*: listener identification through youthful heroes, numerous premium giveaways, and membership in a club, the *Captain Midnight* "Flight Patrol."

By 1940 more than a million kids had joined. They received an "official junior pilot's application card" and a "burnished bronze medal of membership." On the medal were the faces of Midnight, Chuck, and Patsy, along with "the mysterious secret password that only Flight Patrol members themselves can tell the meaning of.'' On the verso was a replica of a three-blade airplane propeller that would ''spin like a top.'' There was a ''Mystic Midnight Clock,'' which revealed a message by the hands of the clock when the blades stopped spinning. ''It helps decide things like who goes to the store for mother or who's captain of the team,'' said Skelly man Don Gordon. ''But most of all, this medal proves you're a member of the new 1940 Flight Patrol.'' Only members could take part in the new adventure ahead: only they would know the codes that would be worked into the storyline. This was one in a long line of decoders, leading serials historian Raymond William Stedman to describe *Captain Midnight* as ''probably the biggest cryptographer in radio.''

When the show moved to Mutual, a reorganization and recap was in order. Much of the informality of the regional series disappeared (Chuck had actually referred to Captain Midnight as ''Red'' in the old days) and the story, in effect, started anew. The opening chapter told something of Midnight's past—not much, just that he had been a captain of Allied armies in the First War and had taken on a mission ''to save France.'' The odds against him were a hundred to one, but he came roaring back at midnight. For 20 years strange stories were whispered about ''a shadowy plane and a mysterious pilot who, whenever trouble started in any part of the world, was certain to come diving furiously from the night sky.'' Ivan Shark was reprised, and Midnight had to face new dangers from Shark's daughter Fury and from a sinister Asian known as ''the Barracuda.'' The Flight Patrol had given way to the Secret Squadron, in which Captain Midnight was code-named SS-1. Kelly, his second-in-command, was SS-11. Chuck Ramsey was SS-2; Joyce Ryan (the Squadron's new girl, replacing Patsy Donovan) was SS-3; Mechanic Ichabod Mudd was SS-4.

As the United States went into World War II, Captain Midnight and his crew did battle with the enemy. The villains were now Nazis and ''Japs,'' at home and abroad. Homefront shows depicting the fight against saboteurs were filled with dark menace and creepy imagery: sinister figures watched from dirt roads as Squadron planes took off on a mission to England. The show was filled with elaborate battle action and credible sound effects: machine-gun fights in

Yugoslavia, with Midnight manning the gun while Chuck and Joyce fed the bullet-belts. The Squadron was sent to destroy an aircraft instrument factory, to wreck a Nazi submarine base, to counter the ''death from the sky.'' The stories now had titles: *Assignment Under the Sea, The Silver Dagger Strikes*, and others of implied peril. It sounded much like the action-filled *Terry and the Pirates* and also bore traces of *Jack Armstrong*. Like *Armstrong*, the action had a strong adult leader, a teenaged protagonist, and a token girl. The dialogue followed *Armstrong* down the ''gosh all fishhooks'' path. ''Golly, it's gettin' to be a general battle!'' Joyce would cry in a masterpiece of understatement. ''Boy-o-boy, isn't that swell,'' she would croon, watching the Nazi rout. ''Loopin' loops'' might be Chuck's contribution to the verbal antics, while Midnight's ejaculations generally ran to ''Great scott!'' But Midnight always provided the ethical overview for his protégés. ''War *is* terrible, Joyce, but if those rats win, then freedom loses.'' Of necessity, the dialogue was descriptive. ''We're moving out of the hangers,'' Joyce would tell no one in particular. ''Oh, look, the planes are in the air!'' Then, at the end of the day's events, announcer Pierre Andre would return for his breathless teaser. ''Saaay, what do you suppose is going to happen?'' he would say in a hushed voice. Then a word about Ovaltine . . . a long word indeed. The Ovaltine commercials must surely have set endurance records for repetition and wordiness. Andre, a holdover from the *Orphan Annie* days, was perhaps the best-remembered voice on the show. His delivery was truly one of a kind. His opening signature came over the midnight tolling of a churchbell and the furious diving of an airplane:

Cappp—taaiinnMidnight!

Broughttoyoueveryday . . . Mondaythrough-Friday. . . .

. . . by the makers of Ovaltine!

A television version of the mid-1950s failed to impress. Richard Webb played the title role, and Captain Midnight flew in a jet.

THE CAREER OF ALICE BLAIR, soap opera.

Broadcast history: 1939–40, transcribed syndication; heard on WJSV, Washington, WOR, New York, and other outlets. **Cast:** Martha Scott as Alice Blair, an actress caught in a conflict between home life and career. Betty Moran also as Alice.

CAREFREE CARNIVAL, vaudeville-style variety.

BROADCAST HISTORY: June 11, 1933–Sept. 14, 1936, NBC: 30m, Red Network, 1933–34, Sundays at 2 for Crazy Water Crystals; Blue Network, 1934–35, Mondays at 8:30 for Crazy Water; Blue Network, 1935–36, various timeslots, for Blue Jay Corn Plasters mid-1935. 1933–34: CAST: Ray Tollinger, master of ceremonies and general stooge. Gene Arnold and the Commodores; comics Tim (Ryan) and Irene (Noblette); Tommy Harris; announcer Nelson Case. 1934–36: CAST: Singer Gogo DeLys; Ben Klassen and Myron Niesley, tenors and comic philosophers; Rita Lane and the Coquettes ("they do an act like the Pickens Sisters," one critic said); Helen Troy, a Gracie Allen–type screwball; Pinky Lee, a lisping sailor on this show, star of juvenile TV for a later generation; Charlie Marshall, "the lute and lyric man," hillbilly and country singer who also performed with the Mavericks (Johnny Toffoli, Johnny O'Brien, and Ace Wright, fiddler from Arkansas); Elmore Vincent as "Senator Frankenstein Fishface," who offered "dramas" and "political monologues" typified by calls for universal nudism, supported, he said, by "the Open Pore Nudist Cult of Bareback Gulch, Pa." MUSIC: Meredith Willson.

THE CARNATION CONTENTED HOUR, traditional mainstream American music for Carnation Milk.

BROADCAST HISTORY: April 26, 1931, NBC West Coast; premiere on regional network.
Jan. 4–Oct. 24, 1932, Blue Network. 30m, Mondays at 8.
Oct. 31, 1932–Sept. 26, 1949, NBC. 30m, Mondays at 10.
Oct. 2, 1949–Dec. 30, 1951, CBS. 30m, Sundays at 10.
1932–41: CAST: stars of opera, notably Gladys Swarthout, in 30m offerings of concert music. ORCHESTRA: Morgan L. Eastman, Dr. Frank Black, Josef A. Pasternack, Marek Weber, Roy Shield. 1942–45: CAST: Josephine Antoine, soprano, and Reinhold Schmidt, bass, were the stars; guest appearances by Dorothy Kirsten, William Miller, etc. ANNOUNCER: Vincent Pelletier.

ORCHESTRA: Percy Faith. PRODUCER: Harry K. Gilman. 1946–48: CAST: Buddy Clark, lead singer as of July 1946; Dinah Shore also heard regularly. ORCHESTRA: Ted Dale. PRODUCER: Charles Cottington. WRITER: Albert Hansen. 1948–51: CAST: Tony Martin and Jo Stafford, lead singers after Buddy Clark's death in a plane crash Oct. 1, 1949. Dick Haymes later starred. ANNOUNCER: Jimmy Wallington. ORCHESTRA: Victor Young. PRODUCER-DIRECTOR: Robert Redd.

The Carnation Contented Hour had a varied musical history, opening in a half-hour 1932 format that featured an orchestra, a quartet, and a group called the Fireside Singers. In 1946 there was an abrupt shift from a concert to a popular emphasis. The title referred to the product's advertising campaigns, which said that Carnation milk came from "contented cows."

CAROLINE'S GOLDEN STORE, serial drama.

BROADCAST HISTORY: June 5–Aug. 31, 1939, NBC. Weekdays at 1:30. General Mills.
Oct. 9, 1939–July 19, 1940, CBS. 15m, weekdays at 5:15. General Mills.
CAST: Caroline Ellis in the title role, owner of a general store in a small town. Joan Kay, Jack Brinkley, Virginia Jones, Frank Behrens, and a cast of more than 60 players. ANNOUNCER: Franklyn MacCormack.

THE CARTERS OF ELM STREET, soap opera.

BROADCAST HISTORY: Feb. 13, 1939–Jan. 19, 1940, NBC. 15m, weekdays at noon. Ovaltine.
Jan. 22–July 19, 1940, Mutual. 15m, weekdays at 12:45.
CAST: Vic Smith as Henry Carter, head of a large family in the town of Galesville. Virginia Payne as Kerry, his wife. Ginger Jones as Mildred Carter Randolph, Henry's daughter now married to Sid Randolph. Herb Nelson as Sid. Billy Rose and Ann Russell as Jess and Bernice, the two Carter children still at home. ANNOUNCER: Pierre Andre. WRITER: Mona Kent. THEME: *My Heart at Thy Sweet Voice*, on the organ.

The Carters was the "story of a second wife and her fight for happiness." It was an attempt to capitalize on the success of such family-oriented soaps as *The O'Neills* and *Pepper Young's Family*, and the vast popularity of *One Man's Family* in the evening was lost on no one. The family home on Elm Street was the center of family life. The Randolphs lived in "a little cottage a few doors down from the Carter home." Play it on a double bill with *Captain Midnight* to learn how the same announcer marketed the same product to vastly different audiences.

THE CASEBOOK OF GREGORY HOOD, mystery drama.

BROADCAST HISTORY: June 3, 1946–Dec. 25, 1949, Mutual. Many 30m timeslots, beginning as a Mondays-at-8:30 replacement for *Sherlock Holmes*; Petri Wine sponsored in this timeslot for a full season when *Holmes* did not return; subsequently, Tuesday, Monday, Saturday, and Sunday timeslots.

Jan. 25–Aug. 31, 1950, ABC. 30m, Wednesdays at 8:30; Tuesdays at 8 beginning in May. Also, two shows, Oct. 3, 10, 1951.

CAST: Gale Gordon as Gregory Hood, a San Francisco importer and amateur detective. George Petrie also as Hood, early in the run. Elliott Lewis as Hood as of March 1, 1948. Jackson Beck as Hood, ca. 1949. Also, Paul McGrath and Martin Gabel as Hood. Bill Johnstone initially as Hood's sidekick Sanderson "Sandy" Taylor. Howard McNear as Sandy as of March 1, 1948. **DIRECTORS:** Ned Tollinger, Frank Cooper, Lee Bolen, etc. **WRITERS:** Anthony Boucher and Denis Green; Ray Buffum. **SOUND EFFECTS:** Art Sorrance.

The Casebook of Gregory Hood was in some ways an extension of *Sherlock Holmes*. Basil Rathbone had left his *Holmes* role, but the *Holmes* scripters, Anthony Boucher and Denis Green, continued their collaboration on *Hood*. It was a long-distance partnership, Green living in Los Angeles and Boucher in San Francisco. Boucher, a Conan Doyle devotee, had worked out the *Holmes* plots, while Green, less enraptured by "the master," had dialogued Boucher's plots from a detached perspective. It was Boucher and Green who suggested *Gregory Hood* as the replacement series when Rathbone left *Holmes* in 1946.

Richard Gump, a real-life San Francisco importer, became the prototype for Gregory Hood,

serving also as a consultant "whenever they get stuck on a bit of importing business." The artifacts found by Hood and his pal Sandy in the stories usually had intriguing histories and were invariably linked to some present-day mystery.

CASEY, CRIME PHOTOGRAPHER, mystery, based on the novels by George Harmon Coxe.

BROADCAST HISTORY: July 7, 1943–Nov. 16, 1950, with a return run Jan. 13, 1954–April 22, 1955, all CBS. Many 30m timeslots; more than a dozen time changes 1943–50, though the series was seldom off the air during this time; heard virtually every day of the week over the years. Also heard under many titles: initially as *Flashgun Casey*, 1943–44; then as *Casey, Press Photographer*, 1944–45; as *Crime Photographer*, 1945–48 and again 1954–55; and as *Casey, Crime Photographer*, 1947–50. Often sustained, with sponsorship by Anchor Hocking Glass, 1946–48; Toni Home Permanents, 1948–49; and Philip Morris, 1949–50. **CAST:** Casey, crime photographer for the fictitious *Morning Express*, played by Matt Crowley initially, by Jim Backus for a few shows, by Staats Cotsworth from late 1943 on. John Gibson as Ethelbert, the sardonic bartender at the Blue Note Cafe, Casey's favorite hangout. Casey's girlfriend, reporter Ann Williams, played by Jone Allison, 1943–44; by Alice Reinheart, 1944–45; by Lesley Woods, 1945–47; by Betty Furness and Jan Miner in later seasons. Jackson Beck as Inspector Logan, the down-in-the-mouth cop; also played by Bernard Lenrow. Supporting players from the New York radio pool: Art Carney, Bryna Raeburn, John Griggs, Robert Dryden, etc. **ANNOUNCERS:** Bob Hite; Tony Marvin during the Anchor Hocking run. **ORCHESTRA:** Archie Bleyer (mid-late 1940s). **DIRECTORS:** John Dietz, Albert Ward, etc. **WRITERS:** Alonzo Deen Cole, Milton J. Kramer, Gail and Harry Ingram. **SOUND EFFECTS:** Jerry McCarty, Art Strand.

Casey, Crime Photographer had more history than substance. It was a B-grade radio detective show, on a par perhaps with *The Falcon*, better than *Mr. Keen*, but lacking the polish and style of *Sam Spade*. Often a picture snapped at a crime scene led Casey to play detective. At the Blue Note Cafe, the crowd was friendly and the music was more than a backdrop. The jazz piano belonged to Herman Chittison; occasionally the music was by Teddy Wilson, noted alumnus of the Benny Goodman trio. *Casey* was also an early TV item, seen live on CBS, 1951–52. Jan Miner and John Gibson made the transition from radio, though Gibson was soon replaced. Richard Carlyle and Darren McGavin played Casey on television.

THE CAVALCADE OF AMERICA, historical dramatic anthology.

BROADCAST HISTORY: Oct. 9, 1935–May 29, 1939, CBS. 30m, Wednesdays at 8, 1935–38; Mondays at 8, 1938–39. The beginning of an 18-year run under sponsorship of the E. I. du Pont de Nemours Company.

Jan. 2, 1940–March 31, 1953, NBC. 30m, Blue Network, Tuesdays at 9, Jan.–June 1940; then Red Network, Wednesdays at 7:30, 1940–41; Mondays at 8, 1941–49; Tuesdays at 8, 1949–53. All Du Pont.

CAST: Originally heard from New York, its roles played by a prestigious rep company (sometimes called "the cream of the crop") including John McIntire, Jeanette Nolan, Agnes Moorehead, Kenny Delmar, Edwin Jerome, Ray Collins, Orson Welles, Karl Swenson, Ted Jewett, Jack Smart, Paul Stewart, Bill Johnstone, Frank Readick, Raymond Edward Johnson, Ted de Corsia, Everett Sloane, Luis Van Rooten. Later shows from Hollywood utilized the star system, with such as Mickey Rooney, Cary Grant, Tyrone Power, and Ronald Reagan filling the lead roles. NARRATOR-HOST: Walter Huston, briefly in 1944. ANNOUNCERS: Frank Singiser, 1935–38; Gabriel Heatter, Dec.–Jan. 1939; Basil Ruysdael, 1939–40; Clayton "Bud" Collyer, 1940–43; Gayne Whitman, 1944–47; Ted Pearson, 1947–48; Bill Hamilton; Ross Martin. ORCHESTRA: Don Voorhees, Robert Armbruster. PRODUCER-DIRECTORS: Homer Fickett for much of the run; Roger Pryor, Jack Zoller, Paul Stewart, Bill Sweets. WRITERS: Arthur Miller, Norman Rosten, Robert Tallman, Peter Lyon, Robert Richards, Stuart Hawkins, Arthur Arent, Edith Sommer, Halsted Welles, Henry Denker, Priscilla Kent, Virginia Radcliffe, Frank Gabrielson, Margaret Lewerth, Morton Wishengrad, George Faulkner, Irve Tunick, etc. SOUND EFFECTS: Bill Brown, CBS; Al Scott, Jerry McGee, NBC.

Cavalcade was a show with a dual purpose. On the surface its job was to sell America by dramatizing the positive aspects of the nation's history. But its real purpose was to stem the tide of criticism directed at its longtime sponsor, the Du Pont Company, in the years after World War I. The du Ponts had been branded "merchants of death" because of the huge profits the company had made with gunpowders in the war. The company had a long tradition in America; its first plant was established near Wilmington, Del. in 1802. It was still family-controlled, and its directors were sensitive to charges of profiteering in wartime.

The advertising firm Batten, Barton, Durstine, and Osborn was charged with creating a positive campaign, and *The Cavalcade of America* was its answer. In the beginning, in its CBS run, *Cavalcade* was a stale and predictable package. Du Pont was obviously gunshy: nothing could be used that even hinted of its wartime activities. Erik Barnouw, who wrote for the show and later authored a three-volume history of radio, summed it up. There could be no war on *Cavalcade*: "Battle scenes were not permitted. . . . The sound of a shot was taboo. . . . Even explosions were for many years forbidden. The atmosphere was pacifist and highly idealistic. The progress of women was frequently celebrated."

A look at the massive log of *Cavalcade* broadcasts confirms this. The show was conceived in vignette form, with two or more separate-but-related stories making up the half-hour. The first show, *No Turning Back*, told in its two segments of the return of the *Mayflower* and of the great grasshopper plague. *The Spirit of Competition*, the third show, told the stories of the Oklahoma land rush and the Mississippi steamer race. So it went, week after week. But this format had one glaring weakness: a lack of continuity due to the brevity of each segment. Before a listener could become interested, a story was finished and a new one begun. This broken-show format was continued for a full season, limping along in low single digits in the ratings. In the summer came a long musical run, *The Development of Band Music in America*, spread across six weeks in July and August 1936. It wasn't until the third show of the second season (*Sentinels of the Deep*, a story of the lighthouse service) that the broken shows were discontinued.

Now came a run of biographical sketches: Charles Goodyear, rubber baron; Morse and his telegraph; Elizabeth Blackwell, the first female doctor. But there were still prejudices and taboos, as Barnouw noted. "For a dozen years no Negro appeared," and the writers avoided any criticisms, explicit or implied, of the rich.

So the history offered by the early *Cavalcade* was sanitized, accurate as far as it went. Accuracy was its badge of honor: the producers pushed that element in almost every interview. By 1940 the show had hired Dr. Frank Monaghan, associate professor of history at Yale, to oversee production. The budget increased. Top stars from Broadway and Hollywood were now the norm, leaving the talented radio people who had become regulars to supporting roles. Alfred Lunt and Lynn Fontanne made their first radio appearances in separate *Cavalcade* productions. The writing was from the best hands in the business, young playwright Arthur Miller becoming (as Barnouw remembers it) a kind of "utility man" who could be tapped for spur-of-the-moment work on the most rigid deadlines. Special projects were put together by Carl Sandburg, Stephen Vincent Benét, Maxwell Anderson, and Robert Sherwood. The company blew its own horn with a show on E. I. du Pont, June 29, 1938, but increasingly as the new decade came the programs were more palatable to mainstream America. Marquis James and Carl Carmer were the new "historical advisers" and sometime writers: James had won two Pulitzers, and Carmer was well known for his historical books. James's biography of Sam Houston, *The Raven*, was done in two broadcasts in 1940. Shows were also done that year on Benedict Arnold, Stephen Foster, Daniel Boone, and Robert E. Lee.

Gunshots were now allowed. The campaign had been a success, and the company was now perceived, truthfully, as something other than a merchant of death. Du Pont dealt in textiles and plastics, in research of all kinds. Its commercial structure on *Cavalcade* was remarkable. There was no midshow commercial: instead, du Pont took a two-minute spot at the end. Delivered by Bud Collyer or Gayne Whitman, the spots were informative and, at their best, fascinating. There was no hard sell: they were straight reports of breakthroughs in the laboratory and in the field. The memorable slogan, "Better things for better living, through chemistry," became part of the American language through constant repetition on *Cavalcade*.

Then came Pearl Harbor, and the producers took a new view of history. History was what happened yesterday on the sands of the African desert, or last week in the North Atlantic. Hints of what was to come were contained in the *Cavalcade* story of Eli Whitney: what might have been a cut-and-dried rehash of Whitney and his cotton gin was linked to the present, making the point that Whitney was actually the father of the modern-day assembly line. When the series tackled freedom of religion, it wasn't simply with another show on Roger Williams: instead it told of Dr. Martin Niemoeller, who defied Hitler's German Christian Church and was imprisoned for his trouble.

With a story called *Between Them Both* (Jan. 4, 1943), *Cavalcade* took a sharp turn and became a giant of the air. This contemporary homefront tale began a long run, broken occasionally by the traditional historical themes, that focused intensely on the war at home and abroad. *Diary on a Pigboat* was the story of a submarine crew; *Soldiers of the Tide* told of Guadalcanal; *Fat Girl* was an account of life on an oiler on the perilous seas in wartime; *Dear Funnyface* a story of the Seabees. Then the war was over and it was back to business as usual. The postwar *Cavalcade* had little to distinguish it from the other big-name Hollywood star shows of its day.

More than 500 *Cavalcades* are available to anyone with a tape deck. The distinct eras are striking in their disparity. It was like a different show during the war, caught up in the frenzied pace and the immediacy of the moment, rivaling such thrill shows as *Suspense* in pure narrative power. The only shows that equaled it for wartime drama were *Words at War* and William N. Robson's *The Man Behind the Gun*. Also among the high spots were *All That Money Can Buy* (based on the Benét story *The Devil and Daniel Webster*) and Marc Connelly's *The Green Pastures*, both 1941. The Connelly tale was a look at Scripture through Negro eyes. Unfortunately, today it is politically incorrect, but in fact it was a superb, brilliantly acted half-hour, with Juano Hernandez as De Lawd.

THE CBS RADIO MYSTERY THEATER, dramatic mystery anthology, initiated many years after the demise of network radio broadcasting in hopes of promoting a resurgence.

BROADCAST HISTORY: Jan. 6, 1974–Dec. 31, 1982, CBS. 60m, seven nights a week. **CAST:** A mix of television stars and oldtime New York radio people, including, from the latter ranks, Leon Janney, Evie Juster, Ralph Bell, Jackson Beck, Teri Keane, Mason Adams, Roger DeKoven, Robert Dryden, Bryna Raeburn, Joseph Julian, Ian Martin, Mary Jane Higby, William Redfield, Mandel Kramer, Paul McGrath, Amzie Strickland, Joan Lorring, Joan Banks, Elspeth Eric, Santos Ortega, Arnold Moss, Grace Matthews, Bret Morrison, Berry Kroeger. Also taped occasionally in Hollywood with Jim Jordan, Les Tremayne, etc. **HOST-NARRATOR:** E. G. Marshall; later Tammy Grimes. **PRODUCER-DIRECTOR:** Himan Brown. **WRITERS:** Sam Dann, George Lowther. **SOUND EFFECTS:** Peter Prescott, Joe Cabbibo.

For years after radio died, oldtime producer-director Himan Brown had been sounding a forlorn lament: that the medium did not deserve such a fate, that radio drama could still be viable and hold its own with the video monster that had killed it. In 1973 CBS agreed, and Brown was given a slot for the most ambitious comeback attempt in radio's over-the-hill history.

He would produce 195 original shows, on tape, which would be fed to the CBS affiliates along the line. There would be 170 repeat broadcasts, but this still amounted to a show from scratch every 1.9 days, an awesome job that Brown tackled with joy. The series premiered to mixed reviews. There was interest from every quarter. Radio as a dramatic medium had been absent from the scene long enough to again be a novelty, and the show was covered by journals ranging from the *New Yorker* to *Newsweek*. Reporters were also interested in the lineup that Brown had announced for starring roles. Such stars as Agnes Moorehead, Zero Mostel, and Richard Widmark had agreed to work for the $100 base pay, and weaned-on-TV talents Joseph Campanella, Lois Nettleton, and their like would also spice up the casts. *Newsweek* said the series would infuse "radio's hallowed horror show format with such topical themes as abortion and unwed motherhood."

The trouble, from the beginning, was the writing. The premiere wasted Agnes Moorehead, *Newsweek* continued, "and the most frightening thing about this Wednesday's show, which features Kim Hunter as a housewife with an animal phobia, is actor Gilbert Mack's uncanny imitation of a howling mongrel." The conclusion: what *Mystery Theater* needed above all else was help from scripters like Paddy Chayefsky and

Reginald Rose. But at $350 for a 52-minute script, Brown wasn't about to go shopping among TV's best playwrights. Staff writers Sam Dann and George Lowther did heroic duty in the trenches, but many of the scripts were written by people who were by nature performers—Ian Martin, Mary Jane Higby, Elspeth Eric, and even oldtime announcer Fielden Farrington. That they were all talents was never questioned: that they all desperately loved radio was self-evident. Whether they were writers was another question, and their efforts were finally doomed.

But the show went beyond its original year and scored some notable successes: a Peabody Award in 1975; a public relations campaign that focused attention on radio drama at a time when transcriptions of old shows were turning up by the hundred. A good mix of classic and original stories was aired. Lowther adapted seven from Poe to begin the second year; a "Mark Twain Week," beginning the third season, revealed that Clemens had written many stories that could legitimately be called mysteries. O. Henry was celebrated in the fourth year. The format followed Brown's *Inner Sanctum*: a creaking door and a host, Marshall, who walked a listener into and through the story. Brown gave it the good fight, slugging it out for eight years and more than 1,500 shows.

But it was still a poor man's version of what radio once was, an echo of its unfulfilled promise. CBS gave the time but precious little money, and the affiliates felt free to tape-delay or drop it from the schedule at will. At KOA in Denver, it was often a casualty of the station's sports docket. A complaining listener was told that, in effect, he was lucky they were carrying it at all. Sports pays, drama doesn't: that was the bottom line in the '70s and continued to be in the '90s. To have any chance of success, radio drama would have to be approached as it is on the BBC in England, where it has never been allowed to die. As radio actress Virginia Gregg once put it, "The British know a good medium when they hear it."

THE CBS RADIO WORKSHOP, experimental dramatic anthology; a revival of the old *Columbia Workshop*.

BROADCAST HISTORY: Jan. 27, 1956–Sept. 22, 1957, CBS. 30m, Fridays at 8:30 until Nov. 1956, then Sundays at 4. **CAST:** Begun in Hollywood, with many of the best West Coast character actors: William Conrad, Parley Baer, Lurene Tuttle, Jack Kruschen, Joseph Kearns, Vic Perrin, Sam Edwards, Gloria Henry, Charlotte Lawrence, etc. Later shared with New York. PRODUCER: William Froug. DIRECTORS: William N. Robson, Jack Johnstone, Dee Engelbach, Elliott Lewis, Antony Ellis, etc.

The Columbia Workshop was the father of experimental radio drama at CBS. *The CBS Radio Workshop* was its final incarnation, at its best equaling (and some believe surpassing) the original role model. The old show had established a high mark in radio history. Even in its failures it was interesting—the people behind it seemed to know that to be good an artist must have the freedom to be bad. Anything was fair game, and *The CBS Radio Workshop* made full use of the audio techniques pioneered by its predecessor and added a few of its own.

The cutting edges were writing, music, and sound effects, a blend that could be anything from traditional to bizarre. As Howard Barnes, CBS vice president, told *Time*: "We'll never get a sponsor anyway, so we might as well try anything."

Catalyst for the revival was William Froug, who had grown up with the old show. Norman Corwin, the most distinguished alumnus of the old *Workshop*, "was my hero," Froug recalled recently. In 1956 Froug was a CBS vice president working directly under Barnes. Radio drama was in its final days, but there was a consistent demand from a small listenership for more truly creative adult drama. Froug proposed to fill that demand with a new *Columbia Workshop*. Barnes okayed the project, changing only the name. In the '30s the network had been known as Columbia, a moniker now seldom used. Barnes suggested the new title, *The CBS Radio Workshop*, and Froug went to work to get it on the air.

He had an idea for the opening show, a two-part adaptation of Aldous Huxley's *Brave New World*. Anne Nelson, head of business affairs at CBS, got rights to the novel and set up a meeting for Froug at Huxley's home. Froug wanted Huxley's voice as well as his name: Huxley as narrator would give the series a grand sendoff. His voice was thin and high-pitched, definitely not radio timbre. But he read like a pro and agreed to the deal. Froug wrote the script and cast about for a powerful voice to announce it.

He hired the strongest, William Conrad, Matt Dillon of *Gunsmoke*. Now Froug wanted a memorable logo, something to stick in the listener's mind. He wrote an opening that would carry through the series: *This is the CBS Radio Workshop . . . dedicated to man's imagination . . . the theater of the mind*. The final four words would become part of radio's lexicon, used even today to describe a time when the medium was more than just news, weather, sports, and records.

On the air, *The CBS Radio Workshop* was a lightning rod for ideas. "Everybody on the second floor of CBS Radio at Columbia Square was excited about the show," Froug recalled. "Every day guys were coming into my office pitching ideas. Bill Conrad had a show idea; so did [composer-conductor] Jerry Goldsmith. I had never seen such excitement in my nine years at CBS." Froug was executive producer: he assigned the scripts, coordinated the show, and hired directors. The enthusiasm spread to New York; Barnes telephoned Froug with reports of annoyance among the East Coast staff that they had no part in it, so a rotating system was devised allowing every other show to originate in New York. Paul Roberts would produce, becoming Froug's East Coast counterpart.

The entire run is preserved in fine quality on tape. Huxley gave an ominous opening, warning that "if I were writing today, I would date my story not 600 years in the future, but at the most 200." Then came the sounds of the brave new world, "of test tube and decanter," where humans were artificially bred and cultivated. The sound was just 30 seconds long, but it had taken three sound effects men and an engineer more than five hours to create. To a ticking metronome was added the beat of a tom-tom (heartbeats), bubbling water, an air hose, the mooing of a cow, a couple of "boings," and three different wine glasses clinking against each other. The sounds were blended and recorded, then played backward on the air with a slight echo effect. Bernard Herrmann composed and conducted a slender musical score, and the series was off and running.

In the next two seasons were many high spots, strong shows that would retain their listenability four decades later. Shakespeare would be "interviewed." The microphone would probe both inner and outer space on journeys into the human body and to the horrifying world of Venus. Stan Freberg would give an analysis of satire. Elliott Lewis would offer one of the strangest shows ever broadcast, about the nightmares of a man in a coma. At least half of the 87 shows can still be termed strong: some are as creative and time-less as anything done by any series in any time. *The Legend of Jimmy Blue Eyes* (March 23, 1956) was a nifty folk ballad, written by Sam Pierce, enacted in music and rhyme, with a near-flawless narration by William Conrad. *A Matter of Logic* (June 1, 1956) was another Conrad tour de force, though the real star was writer-director Antony Ellis, who made a rare appearance on the business side of the microphone to wage an argument with an obstinate Conrad against a ticking clock. *Report on the Weans* (Nov. 11, 1956) was novelist Robert Nathan's wise and whimsical look at what archaeologists of the distant future might deduce, wrongly, about our way of life. And *1489 Words* (Feb. 10, 1957) remains a favorite of many, a powerful Conrad performance proving that one picture is not necessarily worth a thousand words. A lovely way to end a day, a decade, or an era.

CEILING UNLIMITED, patriotic wartime drama; later variety.

BROADCAST HISTORY: Nov. 9, 1942–June 21, 1943, CBS. 15m, Mondays at 7:15. Lockheed Vega Aircraft. **CAST:** Orson Welles, producer-director-writer-narrator until Feb. 1, 1943. Top-name movie stars featured beginning Feb. 8 in stories of wartime heroism. **PRODUCER-DIRECTOR:** (after Feb. 1943) Thomas Freebairn-Smith. **NARRATOR:** Patrick McGeehan. **MUSIC:** Lud Gluskin, Anthony Collins.

June 28–Aug. 9, 1943, CBS. 15m, Mondays at 7:15. Lockheed Vega. Author James Hilton in book reviews and talks.

Aug. 8, 1943–April 30, 1944, CBS. 30m, Sundays at 2. Reorganized as a variety show, now titled *America—Ceiling Unlimited*. Lockheed Vega. **HOST:** Joseph Cotten. **ANNOUNCER:** Patrick McGeehan. **VOCALISTS:** Nan Wynn, Constance Moore. **MUSIC:** Wilbur Hatch.

Ceiling Unlimited began as a series of informative dramas by Orson Welles, who had just returned from a well-publicized air trip to Latin America with film in the can for an ill-fated movie and a yen to be back on radio. He leaped into two CBS series, *Hello, Americans* (extolling the achievements of South American countries) and *Ceiling Unlimited* (describing aviation's role in the war). Welles's tenure was brief: a blowup with an agency man just before air time one night resulted in a Welles walkout. After a hasty reorganization and a summer series with author James Hilton, the show returned as a half-hour Hollywood variety series.

It was aggressively patriotic. Lockheed Vega took no commercial breaks, being content with three one-line mentions within the show (but as *Radio Life* pointed out, Lockheed had only one customer by then, the Allied nations, so commercial interruption was superfluous anyway). Marlene Dietrich told of relentless Allied bombing in her native Berlin. Joe E. Brown described what he had seen in the Pacific. Ronald Colman, Charles Boyer, Edward G. Robinson, Basil Rathbone, Alan Ladd, and Cary Grant appeared. And there were pure radio stories, such as *Going to Run All Night*, the adventure of a marathon runner in the service who had to run 35 miles through enemy lines to fetch help for his buddies. This was a partnership between actor Wally Maher, who read the lines in a breathless stream-of-consciousness style, and soundman Harry Essman, who jogged in place in a gravel box while two microphones picked up his work ("a tall one for the breathing; a short one for the footsteps"). Narrator Pat McGeehan emphasized the weekly theme: *Man has always looked to the heavens for help and inspiration, and from the skies too will come his victory and his future.*

CENTRAL CITY, soap opera.

BROADCAST HISTORY: Nov. 21, 1938–June 30, 1939, NBC. 15m, Blue Network, weekdays at 10:45 A.M. until Jan., then Red Network, weekdays at 10 A.M. Procter & Gamble for Oxydol. **CAST:** Eric Dressler, Myron McCormick, Van Heflin, Arlene Francis, Shirley Booth, Selena Royle, Eleanor Phelps, Everett Sloane, Kent Smith, Elspeth Eric. **PRODUCERS:** Frank and Anne Hummert.

Little is known of the plot at this writing, despite the notable cast. Serials historian Raymond William Stedman described it as "a *Grand Hotel*–type story of intertwined lives," foreshadowing *Peyton Place*.

CHALLENGE OF THE YUKON, juvenile adventure.

BROADCAST HISTORY: Feb. 3, 1938–May 28, 1947, WXYZ, Detroit. 15m, mostly Thursdays.

June 12, 1947–Dec. 30, 1949, ABC. 30m weekly, various timeslots; 1948–49, Mondays-Wednesdays-Fridays at 5. Quaker Oats.

Jan. 2, 1950–June 9, 1955, Mutual. Various late-afternoon or weekend 30m timeslots, occasionally two or three times a week. Became *Sergeant Preston of the Yukon* in Nov. 1951. Quaker Oats.

CAST: Jay Michael as Sgt. William Preston of the Northwest Mounted Police, ca. 1938-mid-1940s. Paul Sutton as Sgt. Preston, ca. mid-1940s–1954. Brace Beemer briefly as Sgt. Preston, 1954–55. John Todd as Inspector Conrad, Preston's superior officer. Frank Russell as the French-Canadian guide who, in the early years, led Preston on long treks into the northern wilds. ANNOUNCERS: Bob Hite, 1938-ca. 1945; Jay Michael; Fred Foy. PRODUCER: George W. Trendle. WRITERS: Tom Dougall initially; Fran Striker, ca. 1942–44; Betty Joyce, 1944; Mildred Merrill; Bob Green; Dan Beattie; Felix Holt; Jim Lawrence; Steve Mc-Carthy. THEME: *The Donna Diana Overture.*

Challenge of the Yukon was the third major juvenile adventure series to come out of George W. Trendle's Detroit radio mill and make the national networks. *The Lone Ranger* had been a western favorite since 1933; *The Green Hornet* had been battling urban corruption since 1938. *Challenge* took its listeners to the wild north and quickly endeared itself to young listeners everywhere.

The show had been running on Trendle's station, WXYZ, for almost ten years when the network run arrived. Trendle was a master of this kind of programming. His shows bore the common trademarks of simple, vigorous adventure plotting, a staunchly bigger-than-life male hero, and lively music cribbed from the classics. The voices and situations were familiar to *Lone Ranger* and *Green Hornet* fans: many of the same actors and writers worked prolifically on all three shows, giving them common threads and similar sounds.

By 1938 Trendle had decided that he wanted a new adventure show, written in the *Lone Ranger* mold but with a dog as hero. WXYZ writer Tom Dougall thought of the northwest motif: he had been raised on Robert Service poems and had had an affinity for the background. "He had already solved the problem of the dog," wrote Dick Osgood in *Wyxie Wonderland*, a memoir of the station. "It couldn't be a dog like Lassie because this, Trendle said, must be an action story. It had to be a working dog. And a working dog in the wild days of the Yukon could be nothing but a Husky."

And who but a Mountie would own such a dog? Thus was the master born of the dog, to become one of the major characters of radio fiction.

The dog was named Yukon King, the hero of the series in a real sense. Sgt. Preston had a horse, Rex, which he often rode in the summer months, but it was Yukon King who usually saved the day. He mauled bushwhackers and crooks, gnawed guns out of hands, hauled down one villain while Preston polished off the other. Dewey Cole "barked and whined and made other appropriate dog sounds as King," said Osgood in *Wyxie Wonderland*. And at the end, Sgt. Preston was always generous in his praise: "Well, King, thanks to you, this case is closed."

There were 484 local adventures aired before *Challenge* went on the network, according to Trendle advocate Terry Salomonson, who has compiled massive broadcast logs of all three Trendle shows. But it was the network run that made it a pop culture classic, its opening signature an unforgettable piece of radio. With howling winds and barking dogs and gunshots emphasizing almost every word, Quaker Puffed Wheat and Quaker Puffed Rice—"the breakfast cereal shot from guns"—took a listener far "across the snow-covered reaches of the wild northwest." The shows would never be taken for great literature, but they gave inspiration of a kind that hasn't been heard much since. Black was black, good was good, and evil never went unpunished. When the Lone Ranger rode again, and Sgt. Preston mushed his way into the frozen north, the vistas were wide and the experience new and wondrous.

THE CHAMBER MUSIC SOCIETY OF LOWER BASIN STREET, musical satire; a swing show that lampooned the classics.

BROADCAST HISTORY: Feb. 11, 1940–Oct. 8, 1944, Blue Network. 30m, Mondays at 9:30, 1940–41; Wednesdays at 9, 1941–42; Mondays at 10:30, Jan. 4–Feb. 8, 1943; sustained. Resumed April 4, 15m, Sundays at 9:15. 30m as of July 18, 1943. Woodbury Soap.

July 8–Sept. 30, 1950, NBC. 30m, Saturdays at 10.

April 12–Aug. 2, 1952, NBC. 30m, Saturdays at 10:30.

CAST: Gene "Dr. Gino" Hamilton, host. Comic Zero Mostel, summer 1942. Jack McCarthy as Dr. Giacomo. **COMMENTATOR:** Ward Byron. **ANNOUNCER:** Milton Cross. **VOCALISTS:** "Mile." Dinah "Diva" Shore, "our own personal one-woman torchlight parade"; Diane Courtney, "the poor man's Flagstad"; Kay Lorraine, "slow-burning blues chanteuse"; all early 1940s. Jane Pickens, 1950. **ORCHESTRA:** Jack Meakin, Paul Lavalle, Henry Levine. **CREATOR-WRITER:** Welbourn Kelley. **DIRECTORS:** Tom Bennett, Dee Engelbach. **WRITERS:** Jack McCarthy, Jay Sommers.

The Chamber Music Society of Lower Basin Street was "one of radio's strangest offspring," said *Radio Life*: "a wacky, strictly hep tongue-in-cheek burlesque of opera and symphony." It grew out of a quarter-hour series, *Bughouse Rhythm*, broadcast by NBC from San Francisco in 1936. The satire was strictly verbal, for the orchestra—once the music began—provided some of the best swing on the air. But the announcements were intentionally stuffy and ridiculous, the deadpan delivery wickedly deceptive. It is probably safe to say that some people tuned into *CMSLBS* without the faintest idea what they were hearing.

Milton Cross, long the announcer on the *Metropolitan Opera* broadcasts, added humor with nothing more than his presence. He piled long-haired grandeur upon the commonest dispensers of rhythm and blues. "Good evening, lovers of fine music," he would say, opening the show. "Welcome to the no-doubt world-famous *Chamber Music Society of Lower Basin Street*, and another concert dedicated to the perpetuation of the three *B*'s—barrelhouse, boogie-woogie, and the blues." Cross would frequently refer to his audience as "music lovers, as they keep telling me down at the office," and spoke of the masters as having left "a great and priceless heritage—

no doubt." Then he would introduce the host, "Dr. Gino" Hamilton. Almost everyone connected with *CMSLBS* was either a "doctor" or a "professor," the distinction a fuzzy line. Hamilton would introduce "Dr." Henry "Hot Lips" Levine, who performed the "Dixieland Little Symphony for Octet" or gave a "Dixieland reading of an early American classic, written as a chamber cantata with a disfigured bass"—in other words, *My Gal Sal*. Paul Lavalle, who took over the baton when original maestro Jack Meakin left, was billed as the show's "woodwind virtuoso." His group, the Windy Ten, consisted of ten "termite-proof virgin pine woodwinds," and Lavalle doubled on clarinet. Everybody doubled, the ten members of the band playing 24 instruments. Charles "Corn Horn" Marlowe was the trumpeter, his group the Barefoot Harmonic.

Dinah Shore used the show as her launch pad to fame: it was said by Cross that "she starts a fire by rubbing two notes together." Zero Mostel was discovered by network executives while performing in a cafe for pocket change and had a successful stay on *CMSLBS*. The musicians were seriously described as "radio's most versatile . . . men who double occasionally in the NBC Symphony." The show was ahead of its time. Its advocates were an active lot whose willingness to protest may have made more of an impact than their actual numbers would suggest. Though the network reportedly received 20,000 letters at the hint that *CMSLBS* might be dropped, the show never made a serious ripple in the ratings.

Guests included Lena Horne, blues singer Huddie "Leadbelly" Ledbetter, the Lionel Hampton Quartet, Jack and Charlie Teagarden, Earl Hines, Harry James, and "Professor" Benny Carter. The theme was a slow rendition of *Basin Street Blues*. And the closings by Hamilton and Cross were as zany as the rest of it. "The haircut's six bits," Cross said, closing one show in 1940. Hamilton reminded listeners that "the closing opus is played in a Haydn *Farewell Symphony* arrangement, with the musicians leaving the stand one by one until the double bass player is finally left alone, dolefully drumming on his doghouse." A final word from Cross: "As Dr. Gino Hamilton has so pointedly put it, at the end of each discussion, on such a matter as the matter just discussed, this is the National Broadcasting Company, RCA Building, Radio City, New York.'' Three chimes and out.

CHANCE OF A LIFETIME, game of chance, with players testing their luck for expensive prizes, everything they had won at stake.

BROADCAST HISTORY: Sept. 4, 1949–Jan. 19, 1952, ABC; 15m and 30m versions, many time-slots. HOST: John Reed King. ANNOUNCER: Ken Roberts.

CHANDU THE MAGICIAN, juvenile adventure.

BROADCAST HISTORY: 1932–35, transcribed syndication, originally heard on KHJ, Los Angeles, Oct. 10, 1932. Soon spread into the Don Lee Network, a California chain that eventually reached the Northwest. A Mutual Network line added, mid-1930s, to St. Louis and points east. White King Soap sponsored in the West; Beech Nut Gum in the East. The records were also marketed independently in areas not served by the networks. Produced at WGN, Chicago, ca. 1935–36, with a new cast.

June 28, 1948–Jan. 28, 1949, Mutual–Don Lee; 15m continuation, weekdays. White King Soap.

Feb. 3–April 28, 1949, Mutual–Don Lee. 30m, each episode complete, Thursdays. White King Soap.

Oct. 15, 1949–Sept. 6, 1950, ABC. 30m, Saturdays at 7:30 through June 10, then Wednesdays at 9:30.

1932–35: CAST: Gayne Whitman as Frank Chandler, American-born mystic who had learned the secrets of the East from a yogi in India and was known far and wide as Chandu. Margaret MacDonald as Chandler's sister Dorothy Regent. Bob Bixby and Betty Webb as Dorothy's children Bob and Betty Regent. MUSIC: Felix Mills, later Raymond Paige. DIRECTOR: Cyril Armbrister. WRITER: Vera Oldham. 1935–36 from Chicago: CAST: Howard Hoffman as Chandu. Cornelia Osgood as Dorothy Regent. Olan Soulé and Audrey McGrath as Bob and Betty Lou. 1948–50: CAST: Tom Collins as Chandu. Irene Tedrow as Dorothy. Lee Millar and Joy Terry as Bob and Betty. Veola Vonn as the Princess Nadji, Chandler's love interest. Luis Van Rooten as Roxor, a master criminal who aspired to rule the world. ANNOUNCER: Howard Culver. MUSIC:

Juan Rolando (who took air credit under his Hindu name, Korla Pandit) on organ.

Chandu the Magician was among the first and last shows of its kind, in two distinct runs separated by 12 years of silence. Partners Raymond R. Morgan and Harry A. Earnshaw were brainstorming in 1931, looking for a new radio idea, when Earnshaw mentioned the public's high interest in magic. They created Frank Chandler, who would fight the world's evil forces with occult powers and a far-reaching crystal ball. Evil was personified in Roxor, a villain who dominated both runs.

The first 68 chapters told of the search for Robert Regent, the husband of Chandler's sister Dorothy. Regent had vanished in a shipwreck ten years before, but through his occult powers Chandler had learned that he might still be alive, held prisoner all these years by Roxor. Off went the story to Egypt, where many subplots unfolded: Chandler's low-key romance with Nadji the Egyptian princess; the ill-fated romance between young Betty Regent and a bedouin beggar; Dorothy's mounting fear. The latter was a vital element, for Chandler's magic was impotent in the face of blind fear, and this was his weakness.

It was a traveling series, whisking those first-generation radio listeners to Monrovia, Algiers, and other exotic locales in the Middle East. There were also many fictitious settings—the gypsy camp in ''Montabania,'' the lost continent of ''Lemuria''—and these, combined with the bouncy Oriental music, kept the serial popular in radio's early days.

The scripts were written by Vera Oldham, an office girl who tried out as a writer and became so essential to the serial's success that the agency handling the account rewarded her one year with an Oriental vacation and a new Studebaker when she returned. With the serial's demise, Oldham continued in radio, writing for the Maxwell House *Show Boat, Those Websters,* and other shows.

Twelve years after the original *Chandu* folded, Morgan and some assistants were again brainstorming in an effort to create a new radio serial. Someone suggested a revival of *Chandu*; then it was suggested that the original production crew be assembled to work on it. Director Cyril Armbrister was in New York, his credits including such juvenile shows as *Land of the Lost* and

Terry and the Pirates. Morgan lured him back to California. Oldham was reactivated for a light rewrite of the original scripts, to give them a modern, faster-moving flavor. When the show came to be sold, the same executive for White King Soap bought it. Even the gong that had introduced the original serial was resurrected. It opened the show, followed by a deep signature: *CHANNNNDOOOO . . . the Magician!*

And the serial began, again with the search for Robert Regent. Thus did *Chandu* became one of the last, as well as one of the first, juvenile adventure shows of its kind.

CHAPLAIN JIM, war drama.

BROADCAST HISTORY: April 20–Sept. 4, 1942, Blue Network. 15m continuation, weekdays at 10: 45 A.M.

Sept. 6, 1942–April 22, 1945, Blue/ABC. 30m, Sundays at 2.

April 29, 1945–June 30, 1946, Mutual. 30m, Sundays at 2 until Dec. 9; returned Feb. 3, Sundays at 10:30 A.M.

CAST: John Lund as Chaplain Jim, a kindly young man of the cloth who served in both theaters of war and occasionally had time, during a home leave, to help out families of the fighting men with personal problems. Don MacLaughlin also as Jim, for much of the run.

Chaplain Jim was a War Department production designed to boost homefront morale. Broadcast from New York, it told of the problems, "spiritual, moral, and emotional, of your men in the Army." *God Bless America* was played as a musical bridge on the organ. Jim often gave some postshow cheer and advice and closed with a prayer.

CHARLIE AND JESSIE, serial drama.

BROADCAST HISTORY: Dec. 16, 1940–Jan. 17, 1941, CBS. 15m, three a week at 11 A.M. Campbell Soups. **CAST:** Donald Cook as Charlie, a salesman. Diane Bourbon and Florence Lake as his wife, Jessie. **WRITER:** Wyllis Cooper.

CHARLIE CHAN, mystery, with the Oriental detective wizard of the Earl Derr Biggers novels and a long run of B-grade films beginning in 1931.

BROADCAST HISTORY: Dec. 2, 1932–May 26, 1933, Blue Network. 30m, Fridays at 7:30; Saturdays near the end: Heard as part of the Esso Oil *Five Star Theater*, which featured a different entertainment each weekday night at 7:30. Three Biggers novels were dramatized in multichapter 30m installments: *The Black Camel* ran until Jan. 6; *The Chinese Parrot* Jan. 13–Feb. 24; *Behind That Curtain* March 3–May 26. **CAST:** Walter Connolly as Chan.

Sept. 17, 1936–April 22, 1938, Mutual. 15m continuation, weekdays at 5:15.

July 6–Sept. 28, 1944, NBC, 30m, Thursdays at 7:30; Summer replacement for *The Bob Burns Show.* Heard hereafter as *The Adventures of Charlie Chan.* Lever Brothers for Lifebuoy Soap. **CAST:** Ed Begley as Charlie Chan. Leon Janney as his Number One Son.

Oct. 5, 1944–April 5, 1945, Blue Network, 30m, Thursdays at 7:30. **CAST:** Ed Begley, Leon Janney.

June 18–Nov. 30, 1945, ABC, 15m continuation, weekdays at 6:45. **CAST:** Ed Begley, Leon Janney.

Aug. 11, 1947–June 21, 1948, Mutual, 30m, Mondays at 8, Pharmaco. **CAST:** Ed Begley and Santos Ortega as Chan. Leon Janney as Number One Son. **DIRECTOR:** John Cole. **WRITER:** Alfred Bester.

Radio Life praised Ed Begley's Charlie Chan as "a good radio match for Sidney Toler's beloved film enactment," citing such Chanisms as "These ancient eyes perceive a cartridge of unusual caliber" as an example of his detecting demeanor.

CHARLIE WILD, PRIVATE DETECTIVE, mystery-detective drama.

BROADCAST HISTORY: Sept. 24–Dec. 17, 1950, NBC, 30m, Sundays at 5:30; Wildroot Cream Oil.

Jan. 7–July 1, 1951, CBS, 30m, Sundays at 6, Sustained.

CAST: George Petrie as Charlie Wild, a New York detective described by *Billboard* as a "hard-guy hero" with plenty of "tough talk and vivid similes." Kevin O'Morrison as Charlie Wild as of the move to CBS, Jan. 7. John McQuade as Wild as of March 25. Since the show was agency-packaged, the same production crew worked both network runs. **ANNOUNCER:** William Rogers. **PRODUCERS:** Lawrence White, Edwin Marshall.

DIRECTOR: Carlo De Angelo. **WRITER:** Peter Barry.

Charlie Wild was a product of the Red Scare, NBC's hurry-up attempt to salvage something when congressional finger-pointing resulted in the loss of sponsorship for radio's most popular detective, *Sam Spade*. Both Howard Duff (who played Spade) and author Dashiell Hammett had been "listed" in *Red Channels*, making *Spade* sponsor Wildroot Cream Oil increasingly unhappy. After weeks of indecision, Wildroot dropped *Spade* and shifted to a new detective hero, hopefully cut from the same cloth. The final Wildroot *Spade* show was Sept. 17, 1950. The following Sunday *Charlie Wild* premiered from the opposite coast (New York). Howard Duff appeared in character on the first broadcast with a vocal telegram, wishing the new hero well. It would be Duff's last radio appearance for six years, according to *Spade* historian John Scheinfeld.

But *Charlie Wild* had little of the old magic. *Billboard*'s lukewarm review took note of the "fantastic descriptions of females," especially one with "green eyes and flame-colored hair" who the critic thought might find work as a traffic signal in her spare time. Charlie's stock in trade, said Scheinfeld, was "getting in a knockdown drag-out brawl every week." Curiously, Charlie stole Sam Spade's secretary as well as his livelihood when, at some point in the run, Effie Perrine moved to New York and became Wild's girl Friday. The actress who played the role is uncertain, as no shows have yet surfaced. Cloris Leachman played it to Kevin O'Morrison's Charlie on a live TV series.

THE CHARLOTTE GREENWOOD SHOW, situation comedy.

BROADCAST HISTORY: June 13–Sept. 5, 1944, NBC, 30m, Tuesdays at 10. Pepsodent; summer substitute for Bob Hope. **CAST:** Charlotte Greenwood with Shirley Mitchell, Arthur Q. Bryan, Matty Malneck's Orchestra, and Three Hits and a Miss. **PRODUCER:** John Guedel. **WRITERS;** Ray Singer, Phil Leslie.

Oct. 15, 1944–Jan. 6, 1946, ABC, 30m, Sundays at 3 until April 1945, then at 5:30. Hallmark Cards. **CAST:** Charlotte Greenwood as Aunt Charlotte, a kind and good woman, quick with a

homily or a word to the wise ("a man who seeks gold for its own sake may succeed in making a lot of money, but he fails to make anything out of himself"). John Brown, Harry Bartell, Eddie Ryan, Will Wright, Ed MacDonald, Veola Vonn. Edward Arnold sometimes costarred as Mr. Reynolds the lawyer. **ANNOUNCER:** Wendell Niles.

In the initial NBC series, Greenwood played a neophyte reporter on a small newspaper, who aspired to Hollywood stardom. In the regular season, she lived in "the little town of Lakeview," where she took over the raising of the three Barton children (little Robert and teenagers Jack and Barbara) and tried to keep the Barton estate solvent. The estate consisted of a heavily mortgaged house, "a lunchroom near the high school that barely pays for itself, and an unproductive farm." A typical sitcom. Edward Arnold often laughed louder than the audience.

THE CHASE, dramatic adventure anthology.

BROADCAST HISTORY: April 27, 1952–June 28, 1953, NBC, 30m, Sundays at 4: transcribed. **CAST:** Many New York radio actors including Karl Swenson, Lucille Wall, Kermit Murdock, Larry Haines, Stefan Schnabel, Luis Van Rooten, Vinton Hayworth, Wendell Holmes, Norman Rose, Edgar Stehli, Joe DeSantis, Mandel Kramer, Amzie Strickland, Donald Buka, Bryna Raeburn, Grant Richards, Ann Thomas, John Gibson, Elaine Rost, Staats Cotsworth, Sarah Burton, Helen Claire, Roger DeKoven, Leon Janney, Nelson Olmsted, Jan Miner, Maurice Tarplin, Ian Martin, Virginia Payne, Arnold Moss, Paul McGrath, Ed Jerome, Ivor Francis, Bill Quinn. **ANNOUNCER:** Fred Collins. **CREATOR-WRITER:** Lawrence Klee. **DIRECTORS:** Walter McGraw, Daniel Sutter, Edward King, Fred Weihe.

The Chase told tales, highly melodramatic and often improbable, of people on the run. The concept of "hunter and hunted" was built into the signatures, with the lone bugle of a fox hunt, the braying of dogs, the sounds of a man running, a gunshot, and the slowing footsteps and eventual fall of the victim.

THE CHASE AND SANBORN HOUR, a long line of various comedy and variety shows sponsored by Chase and Sanborn Coffee in the 8 to 9 P.M. hour, Sundays on NBC: a title usually

applied, occasionally implied but always favored by the sponsor, as *Camel Caravan* was used by Camel Cigarettes.

BROADCAST HISTORY: 1929–31, NBC, 30m Sundays at 8:30; *The Chase and Sanborn Choral Orchestra*, a musical-variety series. Near the end of the run, Maurice Chevalier became the headliner, at $5,000 a week, said to be a record for that time. Beginning in Jan. 1931, violinist Dave Rubinoff (billed as "Rubinoff and His Violin") was a featured regular.

Sept. 13, 1931–Nov. 25, 1934, NBC, 60m, Sundays at 8, *The Chase and Sanborn Hour*, starring Eddie Cantor, covered under THE EDDIE CANTOR SHOW.

Dec. 2, 1934–March 17, 1935, NBC. 60m, Sundays at 8, *The Opera Guild*, a concert broadcast with Deems Taylor, host.

March 24, 1935–Sept. 13, 1936, NBC, 60m, Sundays at 8, *Major Bowes' Original Amateur Hour*, covered under that title.

Jan. 3–May 2, 1937, NBC. 60m, Sundays at 8, *Do You Want to Be an Actor?*, with Haven MacQuarrie. Also heard Dec. 5, 1937–Feb. 20, 1938, 30m, Sundays at 10:30.

May 9, 1937–Dec. 26, 1948, NBC, Sundays at 8; 60m until 1939, then 30m. *The Chase and Sanborn Hour*, with Edgar Bergen and Charlie McCarthy; also titled *The Charlie McCarthy Show*, covered under THE EDGAR BERGEN–CHARLIE MCCARTHY SHOW.

So well remembered was Edgar Bergen in his *Chase and Sanborn* role that the company initiated a yearly remembrance on NBC in the 1960s with Bergen and his dummy Charlie McCarthy as "hosts." Writer Carroll Carroll put the specials together from old transcriptions, with Bergen supplying the narration. *The Chase and Sanborn 100th Anniversary Show* aired Nov. 15, 1964; the *101st Anniversary* (saluting Fred Allen) Nov. 14, 1965; the *102nd* Nov. 13, 1966. Records of these shows have become collectors' items.

CHEERIO, readings, talk, sunny philosophy.

BROADCAST HISTORY: 1925, KGO, San Francisco; first broadcast said to be June 22.

March 14, 1927–June 14, 1937, NBC, 30m, six a week at 8:30 A.M.

Sept. 29–Dec. 29, 1936, NBC. 15m, Tuesdays.

Cheerio's Musical Mosaics. Sonotone Hearing Aid Company.

Sept. 26, 1937–April 14, 1940, Blue Network. 30m, Sundays at 10:30 Sustained.

Cheerio was the name taken on the air by Charles K. Field, a cousin of poet Eugene Field who became one of radio's most optimistic dispensers of good tidings. He began with only a book of poems, given him by his mother, and a cultivated talent as a toastmaster. His wakeup greeting, "Good morning, this is Cheerio," was a well-known salutation in the Bay Area in the mid-1920s. In 1927 he moved to New York, where his half-hour organ-and-talk series was a morning mainstay on NBC. For much of his career he broadcast anonymously, refusing interviews and declining to have his picture taken in the hope that his audience would form their own mental images. He lived on family money, refused to take a fee, and donated most of what was paid him to charity. Four canaries were heard as background in his shows, which also at times included singers and an orchestra. His autobiography, *The Story of Cheerio*, was published by Doubleday in 1936.

CHEERS FROM THE CAMPS, wartime variety.

BROADCAST HISTORY: June 9–Sept. 22, 1942, CBS, 60m, Tuesdays at 9:30, A cooperative effort between sponsor General Motors, the War Department, and the USO to highlight the talents of actors, musicians, writers, singers, and composers in the service. The show moved to different camps each week.

THE CHESTERFIELD QUARTER-HOUR, dance music.

BROADCAST HISTORY: 1931–32, CBS, Five a week at 10:30. ANNOUNCERS: Ken Roberts, Frank Knight. SOLOISTS: Alexander Gray, baritone; Ruth Etting; the Boswell Sisters. ORCHESTRA: Nat Shilkret.

1932–33, CBS. Twice a week at 9. SINGER: Ruth Etting. ORCHESTRA: Lennie Hayton.

"Lady Nicotine's newest baby," as the *Forum* described the arrival of this "quarter-hour dance series." These were popular for a season; then their sponsors again shifted budgets into longer variety shows.

THE CHESTERFIELD SUPPER CLUB, musical variety.

BROADCAST HISTORY: Dec. 11, 1944–Sept. 2, 1949, NBC, 15m, weeknights at 7. **FEATURED SOLOISTS:** Perry Como (Mondays—Wednesdays—Fridays); Jo Stafford (Tuesdays, Thursdays); Peggy Lee (Thursdays beginning in 1948, when Stafford cut back her schedule). Vocal groups: Mary Ashford and the Satisfiers, an aggregation whose name was derived from the much-used slogan of sponsor Chesterfield Cigarettes—"they satisfy." The Fontane Sisters (Geri, Bea, and Marge). **GUEST STARS:** Frankie Laine, Mel Blanc, the King Cole Trio, Arthur Godfrey, etc. **ANNOUNCERS;** Martin Block, Tom Reddy. **ORCHESTRA:** Ted Steele, Sammy Kaye, Lloyd Shaffer, Glenn Miller (led by Tex Beneke); Mitchell Ayres on Como dates of the late 1940s. Stafford's husband Paul Weston for her Tuesday show; Lee's husband Dave Barbour on Thursdays.

Sept. 8, 1949–June 1, 1950, NBC, 30m, Thursdays at 10; **ANNOUNCER:** Tom Reddy. **SOLOIST:** Peggy Lee. **GUESTS:** Buddy Clark, Johnny Mercer, etc. **ORCHESTRA:** Dave Barbour.

The Chesterfield Supper Club was the final successor to Fred Waring's *Chesterfield Time* (NBC, 1939–44) and Johnny Mercer's *Chesterfield Music Shop* (1944). The theme was *Smoke Rings*, a seductive invitation to relax "while a Chesterfield burns."

THE CHICAGO THEATER OF THE AIR, operetta.

BROADCAST HISTORY: 1940; WGN, Chicago; first heard May 9.

Oct. 5, 1940–May 7, 1955, Mutual. 60m, Saturdays at 10(at 9, 1941–44).

CAST: Marion Claire, soprano, resident prima donna ca. 1940–47. Leading men during her reign included James Melton, Morton Bowe, Thomas Hayward, Thomas L. Thomas, Richard Tucker, Conrad Thibault, Jan Peerce, Igor Gorin. **LATER CAST:** Graciela Rivera, Ann Ayars, Jane Lawrence, Selma Kaye, Winifred Heidt, Giorgio Tozzi, Andzia Kuzak, Dorothy Staiger, Attilio Baggiore, Ruth Slater, Bruce Foote, Earl Willkie, Allan Jones, Robert Merrill, etc. **DRAMATIC CAST:** Bret Morrison, Betty Winkler, Marvin Miller, Willard Waterman, Barbara Luddy, Les Tremayne, Betty Lou Gerson, Rita Ascot, many others from the Chicago radio pool. **COMMENTATOR:** "Col." Robert R. McCormick. **ORCHESTRA:** Henry Weber. **CHORAL DIRECTOR:** Robert Trendler. **DIRECTORS:** William A. Bacher, Jack LaFrandre, Joe Ainley, etc.

The Chicago Theater of the Air grew out of a listener survey conducted by WGN in 1940, which revealed that large blocks of its audience appreciated the music of opera and the escapism of drama. The two were combined in a long-running series of popular operettas. The original works were carefully translated into English by George Mead and Thomas P. Martin, and the melodies—already familiar to the mass audience—were backed up by strong storylines. The goal was to create a 60-minute broadcast that lost no essential plot ingredients or any of the important music.

Soloists came from the stages of the Metropolitan Opera, the San Carlo Opera Company, and the Chicago Civic Opera Company. As many as 100 artists assembled for the individual broadcasts—soloists in center stage, the dramatic cast on the left, the 30-voice chorus on the right. The orchestra was taken from the ranks of the Chicago Symphony. Conductor Weber initially gave commentaries at intermission, a job later assumed by Robert R. McCormick, publisher of the *Chicago Tribune*, which owned WGN. McCormick gave a dry history lesson, usually of five-to ten-minute duration. Included among the featured operettas were *The Vagabond King, The Chocolate Soldier, Madame Butterfly, The Merry Widow, Carmen, The Student Prince,* and other such evergreens.

CHICK CARTER, BOY DETECTIVE, juvenile serial adventure.

BROADCAST HISTORY: July 5, 1943–July 6, 1945, Mutual, 15m, weekdays. **CAST:** Bill Lipton as Chick Carter, adopted son of Nick Carter, famous detective hero of fiction and radio. Leon Janney as Chick beginning mid-1944. Jean and Joanne McCoy, sisters, as Chick's friend Sue. Gilbert Mack as Chick's friend Tex. Stefan Schnabel as the Rattler, the series villain. **WRITERS:** Walter Gibson and Ed Gruskin, Nancy Webb, Fritz Blocki.

CHILD'S WORLD, conversation with children.

BROADCAST HISTORY: Oct. 26, 1947–June 27, 1949, ABC, 30m, Sundays at 7 until March 1948, then Thursdays at 10 until March 1949, then Mondays at 9:30. **CREATOR-HOSTESS:** Helen Parkhurst, a noted educator who had worked in the Montessori system and later founded the progressive Dalton School.

Child's World was a free and unrehearsed talk show, designed to "educate parents through the wisdom of their own children." Widely lauded for its insights into the terrors and joys of childhood, it offered a platform to children aged 4 to 15, from all races, nationalities and economic backgrounds. Hostess Parkhurst chose the subjects: beyond that, the children were free to express themselves in their own words and thoughts. Their comments were wire-recorded in Parkhurst's New York apartment and later used on the air. There was no attempt to hide the microphones, though the engineer was hidden away in another room to promote spontaneity. Among the topics were: teachers, playing hookey, God, jealousy, death, babies, and "being Negro."

CHIPS DAVIS, COMMANDO, war adventure.

BROADCAST HISTORY: July 18, 1942–Oct. 9, 1943, CBS. 30m, Saturdays at 8:30 until Oct. 1942, then Sundays at 7 until July 1943, then Saturdays at 5:30. **CAST:** Clayton "Bud" Collyer as Chips Davis, "an American in Britain's famous fighting unit." **MUSIC:** Charles Paul on organ. **PRODUCER:** Bob Shayon. **DIRECTOR:** John Dietz.

A CHRISTMAS CAROL, annual broadcast of Charles Dickens's classic story.

BROADCAST HISTORY: Heard each Christmas, in various lengths and formats, mostly on CBS, beginning Dec. 25, 1934, until Dec. 20, 1953.

A Christmas Carol with Lionel Barrymore was perhaps radio's best-loved single program. For the 1934 premiere, CBS made a party of it, blocking out almost three hours of its Christmas afternoon schedule for the play and other acts. Alexander Woollcott was master of ceremonies, and Beatrice Lillie appeared in support. Barrymore's portrait of the miser Ebenezer Scrooge was coveted thereafter. On Dec. 25, 1935 and 1937, the show was sponsored on CBS by Campbell Soup. Barrymore's wife died in 1936; his brother John played the role that year on the CBS

Hollywood Hotel. Barrymore was absent for the Dec. 23, 1938, *Campbell Playhouse* broadcast; Orson Welles played Scrooge that year, but Barrymore returned to the CBS-*Campbell* microphone Dec. 24, 1939, and again Dec. 20, 1940. He crossed to NBC for the Dickens classic on *The Rudy Vallee Show* for Sealtest in 1941–42, both shows airing Christmas Eve. From 1943–47, the sketch was offered on Barrymore's own show, *Mayor of the Town*, during the Christmas week broadcasts for Noxzema. On Dec. 25, 1948, it was part of a two-hour CBS special, with many surrounding acts and guest stars. In 1949–50, it was heard on Mutual; 1951 by transcribed syndication; on *The Hallmark Playhouse* Dec. 21, 1952, and *The Hallmark Hall of Fame*, Dec. 20, 1953. Until his death, Nov. 15, 1954, Barrymore captured as did none other the essence of "that grasping, clutching, conniving, covetous old sinner, Ebenezer Scrooge."

Edmund Gwenn, Ronald Colman, and Basil Rathbone also tried it at various times. In 1936 Gracie Allen offered her version on the *Burns and Allen* Dec. 23 broadcast. Spoofs were heard on such diverse series as Dick Powell's *Richard Diamond, Private Detective* and the James Stewart western *The Six Shooter*.

CIMARRON TAVERN, juvenile adventure serial.

BROADCAST HISTORY: April 9, 1945–Sept. 27, 1946, CBS. 15m, weekdays at 5:30. **CAST:** Paul Conrad as Star Travis, a Kentucky-born Indian scout (real name Morning Star) who rode a coal-black Thoroughbred stallion, named Raven in honor of Sam Houston. Chester Stratton, Ethel Everett, Stephen Courtleigh, Ronald Liss. **ANNOUNCER:** Bob Hite. **DIRECTOR:** John Dietz. **WRITER:** Felix Holt.

This serial was billed as "the gateway to the Old West." The juvenile hero was Randy Martin, who rode with scout Star Travis on the "trails of adventure." Randy, whose family had been killed by Indians, had come to live at Cimarron Tavern, a watering hole in Oklahoma run by Ma and Pa Buford.

THE CINNAMON BEAR, children's fantasy.

BROADCAST HISTORY: 1937, transcribed syndication, repeated yearly in many markets because of its universal appeal to children. 26 15m chapters, usually beginning just before Thanksgiving and ending just before Christmas. At this writing, the transcriptions are being prepared for new national syndication, with more than 100 stations signed.

CAST: Barbara Jean Wong as Judy Barton; she and her brother Jimmy are the central characters (the actor who played Jimmy is unknown). Verna Felton as Mother Barton. Buddy Duncan as the Cinnamon Bear. Joseph Kearns as the Crazy Quilt Dragon. Hanley Stafford as Snapper Snitch the Crocodile. Howard McNear as Samuel the Seal and as Slim Pickins the Cowboy. Elvia Allman as Penelope the Pelican. Elliott Lewis as Mr. Presto the Magician. Lou Merrill as Santa Claus. Frank Nelson as Captain Tin Top. Cy Kendall as Captain Taffy the Pirate and as the Indian Chief. Gale Gordon as Weary Willie the Stork and as the Ostrich. Ted Osborne as Professor Whiz the Owl. Joe DuVal as Fe Fo the Giant. Martha Wentworth as the Wintergreen Witch. Dorothy Scott as Fraidy Cat. Ed Max as Assistant Blotto Executioner. Rosa Barcelo as Queen Melissa. Lindsay MacHarrie as Wesley the Whale and others. Bud Hiestand, narrator, also played several roles. VOCALS: The Paul Taylor Quartet. ORCHESTRA: Felix Mills. MUSIC: Don Honrath, lyrics by Glanville Heisch. CREATOR-WRITER: Glanville Heisch. DIRECTOR: Lindsay MacHarrie.

The Cinnamon Bear was set in a world of fantasy, where giants, pirates, dragons, and witches lived. The story began in the home of Judy and Jimmy Barton. Searching their attic for the Silver Star, traditional ornament for the top of their Christmas tree, they meet Paddy O'Cinnamon, a stuffed bear come to life. The Cinnamon Bear introduces himself with a lovely fantasy song that becomes the serial's theme:

I'm the Cinnamon Bear with the shoe-button eyes
And I'm looking for someone to take by surprise
I go prowling and growling each night after dark
But the folks say my growl's just a cinnamon bark
Though I growl—grr-rah!
And I growl—grr-rooh!
My victims only say
Oh, who's afraid of you?

From the Cinnamon Bear, Judy and Jimmy learn that the Silver Star has been stolen by the Crazy Quilt Dragon, who has escaped to Maybeland. They learn to "de-grow," shrinking to a height of four inches, and go through a crack in the wall to a world of make-believe. The chase begins in Paddy's airplane, powered by soda pop gasoline. The quest will take them into the Looking Glass Valley and across the Root Beer Ocean to the land of the Inkaboos, where the penalty for trespassing is to be thrown into a large black inkwell. There are melodious and catchy tunes along the way—*Never Say Boo to a Crazy Quilt Dragon*, *The Wailing Whale*, *The Cockleburr Cowboys from Lollypop Hill*, and others—and many magical adventures in such places as the Wishing Woods and Marshmallow Meadows before the Silver Star is returned.

An advocacy group, the Cinnamon Bear Brigade, operates in Portland, Ore., and claims 400 members nationwide. The outstanding cast was identified by Frank Nelson, with additional names supplied by SPERDVAC, the oldtime radio society of Southern California. But the actor who played the male lead, Jimmy Barton, eludes them all. Not even the most ardent *Cinnamon Bear* advocates have been able to supply his name.

THE CIRCLE, provocative talk by Hollywood stars.

BROADCAST HISTORY: Jan. 15–July 9, 1939, NBC. 60m, Sundays at 10. Kellogg's Corn Flakes.
CAST: Ronald Colman, Carole Lombard, Cary Grant, Lawrence Tibbett, and Groucho and Chico Marx in the original "Circle." Basil Rathbone replaced Colman in Feb.; Madeleine Carroll later added. MUSIC: Robert Emmett Dolan, orchestra, and a singing group, the Foursome. CREATOR: George Faulkner of J. Walter Thompson. DIRECTOR: Cal Kuhl. WRITERS: George Faulkner, Carroll Carroll.

The Circle was a talk show elaborate beyond anything ever attempted. The stars were temperamental, difficult to control, and very expensive. Writer Carroll Carroll called it "radio's most expensive failure." *Time* thought it "the most revolutionary idea since Charlie McCarthy." The show would bring together "the elect of the entertainment world" to discuss in a heavily scripted but spontaneous-sounding hour "anything under the radio sun: poetry, music, drama, death, taxes, fur coats''—all the topics that might be expected to ''come up'' naturally at a social gathering of such luminaries. Colman and Grant were obviously cerebral talents; Lombard and the Marx Brothers, though popularly known as madcaps, were keenly respected intelligences among the Hollywood elite. Kellogg's Corn Flakes, the unlikely sponsor, would budget more than $2 million for the first year, with the stars each earning $2,000–$2,500 a week. There would also be at least one major guest on each show, who might be a singer or a musician able to fit into the dialogue as well as perform.

The audience heard Lombard explain why women were more practical than men, thus better suited to run the world. Colman recounted (with digs at a modern country ''which shall be nameless'') the trial and condemnation of Socrates because he dared to criticize his government. Grant explained, ''by chanting the federal radio law with Gregorian solemnity,'' why interruptions for station identification were necessary. Early guests included pianist José Iturbi and playwright Noel Coward, who ''upstaged everybody and gave Carole stage fright'' (*Time*).

Trouble began in the second month. Colman quit on a week when Lombard, Grant, and Tibbett were scheduled off. Basil Rathbone was lured in, becoming a member, and Grant was persuaded to cancel his night off and come in anyway. The show went on, *Time* reported, ''distinguished mainly by the singing of Negro contralto Marian Anderson.'' The problem, said Carroll Carroll in his memoir, was the lack of control. Each star was given carte blanche approval over his or her segment or appearance. ''It might have worked if actors weren't all children,'' Carroll wrote. But ''each week they'd all phone each other and ask, 'Are you going to be on next Sunday? Oh no? Well, then, I don't think I will either.' '' Thus was the concept defeated. ''They all appeared together almost all the time, and the money ran out fast, fast, fast! There was either a feast or a famine, and when the famines came they were deadly.''

THE CISCO KID, juvenile western adventure.

BROADCAST HISTORY: Oct. 2, 1942–Feb. 14, 1945, Mutual. 30m, mostly Fridays at 8:30 until Jan. 1944, then Saturdays at 8:30 until Oct. 1944;

then Wednesdays at 9:30. **CAST:** Jackson Beck as the Cisco Kid, ''O. Henry's beloved badman who rides the romantic trail that leads sometimes to adventure, often to danger, but always to beautiful señoritas.'' Louis Sorin as Pancho, his fat comedic sidekick. Support from prominent New York radio people: Vicki Vola, Bryna Raeburn, etc. **ANNOUNCER:** Michael Rye (Rye Billsbury). **DIRECTOR:** Jock MacGregor.

1946, Mutual–Don Lee, regional. 30m, Mondays, Wednesdays, and Fridays at 7:30 Pacific time. **CAST:** Jack Mather as Cisco. Harry Lang as Pancho. **PRODUCER:** J. C. Lewis. **WRITER:** Larry Hays.

1947–56, 30m, transcribed syndication. **CAST:** Jack Mather, Harry Lang.

The Cisco Kid was a Mexican adventurer, an outlaw who victimized the rich and the greedy. Jackson Beck and Louis Sorin, in the Mutual series, exchanged an Americanized Mexican dialect. ''Oh, Ceesco, perhaps they weel keel heem,'' Pancho would say in despair. Usually, however, Cisco and Pancho themselves were on the run from the law. ''A favorite plot is to have the sheriff and his posse suspect Cisco and Pancho,'' said *Radio Life* in 1947, when the series had moved to California to be recast. ''The two perpetuate the hoax so the real cowboy-crooks will let down their guard.''

The camaraderie of the trail was a constant. To Cisco, Pancho was ''Chico,'' and their allegiances were first and foremost to each other. Though Cisco would often scold his partner for stupidity, no other man was allowed to denigrate his friend. Cisco was a fighter, a formidable foe with fists or guns. The fights, especially in the Jack Mather syndications, were wildly verbal, with Cisco and Pancho jabbering away even in the thick of fisticuffs. *And now, hombre, we shall see if you are as tough as your words!* (Punch-punch-punch) *Ah'll kill you, Cisco!* (Punch-pummel-pound) *Oh, I think not!* (Punch-punch-slug) *Ceesco! Behind you!* (Jab, dance, punch-punch) *I see him, Pancho! And now it is time to show these hombres that the Cisco Kid means exactly what he says!* A furious finish, with more chatter, punches, and broken chairs, and the final sound of a badman taking a fall. These fights today are hilarious, like a B-movie western in which the hero never loses his hat.

The opening was pure radio: a sound of racing hoofbeats, then gunshots, then the urgent cries of the heroes:

Ceesco! The shereef, he ees getting closer!
Thees way, Pancho, vamanos!

And the closings were also done to formula. There was always a señorita, and Cisco always collected his kiss. Said *Radio Life*: "For each dark-eyed conquest he has a string of pearls ('they belonged to my sainted mother') and a kiss before he rides off with Pancho into a blazing desert sunset." Up came the dreamy organ music: the señorita would breathe, "Ooooooh, Cisco!" and Cisco would answer "Ooooooh, señorita!" The action would cut to the trail, with Cisco and Pancho riding away on their horses, Diablo and Loco. There was always a terrible closing pun by Pancho, with Cisco reacting in great disgust.

Oh, PAN-CHO!
Oh, Ceesco!

Whooping laughter, galloping horses, and out.

CITIES SERVICE CONCERTS, music.

BROADCAST HISTORY: 1925–26, trial broadcasts in local New York market.

Feb. 18, 1927–Jan. 16, 1956, NBC. 60m until 1940; then 30m. Fridays at 8, 1927–49; then Mondays at 9:30. This series, one of the longest-running programs in radio history, was heard under several titles: *The Cities Service Orchestra*, 1920s; *The Cities Service Concerts* until 1944; *Highways in Melody*, 1944–48; and *The Cities Service Band of America*, 1948–56. **CAST:** Jessica Dragonette, soprano, 1930–37; Frank Parker; Lucille Manners; Ross Graham; the Cavaliers. **ANNOUNCERS:** Graham McNamee, 1927; Ford Bond for many years. **MUSICAL DIRECTORS:** Edwin Franko Goldman, 1927; Rosario Bourdon, June 1927–Feb. 1938; Frank Black, 1938–44; Paul Lavalle, 1944–56.

The premise behind the *Cities Service Concerts* never changed: that good music, be it *Stardust* or Sibelius, would always attract an audience. Initially it was an hour-long display of brass music by Edwin Franko Goldman, whose cornet-happy group offered lively, if predictable, concerts. With the arrival of Rosario Bourdon in mid-1927, the emphasis shifted from brass to strings: the large aggregation of 30-plus pieces was decidedly more symphonic, and new vocal

acts such as the Cavaliers quartet were inserted. But the show truly came of age in 1930, with the arrival of Jessica Dragonette.

Dragonette was born in Calcutta, India, in 1910. In New York in her youth she studied with Estelle Liebling, who determined that her voice, though lovely and clear, was too thin for the concert career she had planned. Liebling suggested radio: Dragonette auditioned at WEAF and was scheduled to sing Oct. 26, 1926, when, "still a schoolgirl in pigtails" by one account, she gave her first air performance. She was "overwhelmed" by the response—"an armload of letters" from her listeners—and decided at once that radio was her life. "The lack of established tradition appealed to me," she would recall years later in her memoir *Faith Is a Song*. "I would create and help mold the new medium of expression, instead of following the accustomed practices of the theater."

Soon she was broadcasting on NBC. She was fascinated as the radio business changed before her: "The whole picture was a seething mass of increasing cell growth—technical, financial, educational, historical, world-shaking." The "region behind the microphone" became real to her as she corresponded with her public. She began to dress in formal gowns for her broadcasts.

She began to act, taking on the speaking parts as well as singing the roles of light operettas. She played Vivian, the Coke girl, anonymously, in a half-hour serial for Coca-Cola. Letters began comparing Vivian's voice to that of the rising soprano Jessica Dragonette. By 1927 she had a contract with Philco and a five-year pact with NBC. She was inserted into *Philco Theater Memories*, then the pioneering *Philco Hour*. Critics were calling her "the Jenny Lind of the air," and Nora Bayes christened her "the girl with the smile in her voice." By 1929 she was one of radio's true made-at-the-microphone stars.

But *The Philco Hour* was moving to CBS, leaving Dragonette a conflict. Her contract with NBC prevailed, and she was inserted into the Cities Service show as of Jan. 3, 1930. Her repertoire grew to include 500 songs. "We never repeated a number in under six months' time," she would write. "Of the seventeen selections (in a given hour), I was usually involved in eight—solos, duets, features with the quartet, singing operatic arias, classics from the song literature of the world, operetta music, ballads, and the best of the popular songs, concluding with a hit of the week—a precursor to the *Hit Parade*."

During her reign, the show drew ratings in the mid-20s, far beyond the reach of most concert offerings. Her popularity by 1933 was on a plane with *Amos 'n' Andy*, Eddie Cantor, and Rudy Vallee. She was among the first American goodwill ambassadors of song to Latin America and was featured on early experimental television broadcasts of the late '20s. Her tenure with Cities had an aura of permanence.

When it came, the split between Dragonette and the *Cities Service Concerts* was painful and shocking. Behind the scenes her disenchantment had been growing. She was distressed when Frank Parker left the show for *The Jack Benny Program*. Their duets had been sensational, but Cities refused to pay the tenor more than his weekly base salary as a member of the Revelers Quartet. She had argued his cause without success. She was further disturbed when Cities cut its programs off the network's West Coast outlets. Now people in Los Angeles and San Francisco "had to get me by way of Denver, or by shortwave." But the crux of her discontent was the unwillingness of Cities and NBC to build speaking roles into her concerts. She longed to act as well as sing, but nothing came of it.

Cities began auditioning sopranos, another annoyance. In 1936 her sister and business manager, Nadea Dragonette Loftus, noticed that her current contract contained no option clause. Was this an oversight, or had it been left out intentionally? At the same time, Dragonette was being ardently pursued by Palmolive Soap, which had offered to double her weekly salary to $2,500 and give her a major voice in shaping a proposed new series of operettas, soon to be aired.

Dragonette decided to take the Palmolive job when her Cities contract expired early in 1937. Palmolive insisted that it all be kept quiet, and Dragonette signed their contract, unaware, she wrote in her memoir, that *The Palmolive Beauty Box Theater* was being readied for CBS. NBC executives, when they learned of the deal, were first surprised, then furious. They issued a release, usurping the coming Palmolive announcement, claiming that Dragonette had been fired from *Cities Service Concerts* in favor of new talent. Industry scuttlebutt ignited spontaneously:

rumors spread that she had made outrageous contract demands and had begun believing her own press notices. Her release date was Feb. 5, 1937; she was replaced by Lucille Manners, who had been auditioning for the job and had filled in for Dragonette during the 1936 vacation break. A cry of outrage arose from Dragonette partisans. Some boycotted Cities; some threatened to boycott all of radio until she returned. In the ensuing years, opinion was divided over where the blame belonged. The most prevalent theory is that NBC conspired to wreck her career, a charge the network always denied.

The failure of the *Palmolive Beauty Box Theater* prompted her to retire from radio in 1937. She appeared as a guest soloist on select shows thereafter, among them *The Magic Key* and *The Ford Sunday Evening Hour*, but the great years of her radio stardom were finished. Eventually she found her way into another series, the CBS *Saturday Night Serenade*, in 1944. In 1952 she was invited to Carnegie Hall as part of Cities' 25th anniversary celebration; she accepted and sang, apparently putting old resentments to rest. She was never forgotten by her fans. Her popularity, even in her years off the air, was never in doubt. In open-air concerts she drew as many as 150,000 people. Her autobiography would reveal little if any pretension: she recounted her triumphs and her disappointments in the same steady voice. She died in 1980.

As for the remaining two decades of the Cities Service show, it was business as usual. Ford Bond was its longtime voice at announcer. In addition to music, there was frequent talk, a guest interview segment beginning May 19, 1933, with an appearance by Amelia Earhart on the anniversary of her flight across the Atlantic. Louis McHenry Howe often spoke, beginning Dec. 8, 1933, on national affairs. Ford Bond began his baseball commentaries that year, which gave way to Grantland Rice with football talk as summer blended into autumn.

Lucille Manners, Dragonette's replacement, had been a stenographer in a law office in an earlier career. She studied voice at night, broke into radio, and remained with Cities Service for many years. A prominent male soloist was Robert Simmons, who, like Parker and another *Cities* alumnus, James Melton, came out of the Revelers Quartet. By 1939 Ross Graham was the featured baritone; the singing group was called the Cities Service Singers. In 1942 the regulars were Manners, Graham, and maestro Frank Black, who selected all the music and planned the show weeks in advance. In 1944, with the arrival of Paul Lavalle as bandmaster, the show became *Highways in Melody*. Lavalle brought the series full circle, returning to the brass band sound a few seasons later as *The Cities Service Band of America*. By then few listeners knew that they were hearing the last remnant of a true radio pioneer.

THE CITY, impressionistic drama.

BROADCAST HISTORY: Feb. 2–Aug. 3, 1947, CBS Pacific Network. 30m, Sundays at 5, Pacific time. **NARRATOR:** Frank Goss. **PRODUCER:** Sterling Tracy. **WRITERS:** E. Jack Neuman, Stu Novins, Beth Barnes, etc. **MUSIC:** Wilbur Hatch, Lucien Moraweck. **SOUND EFFECTS:** Harry Essman.

The city was personified in this dramatic series, a difficult goal to attain without sacrificing listener interest. In one story, the focus was on a group of office people. The listener soon learned that one of the elevators was faulty and that someone—the janitor, the scientist, the blackmailer, the detective, the stenographer— was about to fall to his death. As the climax approached, the sounds of the city blended in and became one with the action.

CITY DESK, newspaper thriller drama.

BROADCAST HISTORY: Jan. 2–Sept. 27, 1941, CBS. 30m, Thursdays at 8:30 until July, then Saturdays at 8:30. Colgate-Palmolive. **CAST:** James Meighan and Gertrude Warner as Jack Winters and Linda Webster, reporters who "scoop the town, uncovering crimes that inevitably baffle the police." Jimmy McCallion as a character named Caruso. Ethel Owen as Mrs. Cameron. Geoffrey Bryant as editor Dan Tobin. **MUSIC:** Charles Paul on organ. **DIRECTORS:** Kenneth W. MacGregor, Himan Brown. **WRITERS:** Frank Gould, Frank Dahm, Stuart Hawkins.

CLARA, LU, AND EM, serial drama; radio's first soap opera.

BROADCAST HISTORY: 1930, WGN, Chicago; first broadcast June 16.

Jan. 27, 1931–Feb. 12, 1932, Blue Network.

15m continuation, Tuesday through Saturday nights at 10:30. Colgate-Palmolive.

Feb. 15, 1932–March 23, 1934, Blue Network. 15m, weekdays at 10:15 A.M. Colgate-Palmolive, Super Suds.

March 26, 1934–Jan. 10, 1936, NBC. 15m, weekdays at 10:15 A.M. Off the air July–Oct. 1935, returned at 5:45. Super Suds.

June 26–Sept. 4, 1936, Blue Network. 30m, Friday nights at 9:30. Frigidaire.

June 8–Dec. 4, 1942, CBS. 15m, three a week at 11 A.M. Pillsbury.

1945, transcribed syndication.

1930–36: CAST: Louise Starkey as Clara Roach, a family woman who lived in one side of a duplex apartment. Isobel Carothers as Lulu Casey, a widow who lived in an apartment upstairs with her daughter Florabelle. Helen King as Emma Krueger, another family woman who lived on the opposite side of the duplex. **ANNOUNCERS:** Jean Paul King, Gene Hamilton. **MUSIC:** (1936 evening series) Ted Fio Rito.

1942: CAST: Louise Starkey as Clara. Harriet Allyn as Lu. Helen King as Em. **ANNOUNCER:** Bret Morrison.

(1945 SYNDICATION): CAST: Fran Allison as Clara. Dorothy Day as Lu. Harriet Allyn as Em.

Clara, Lu, and Em began as a skit in a sorority house at Northwestern University around 1925. Urged by their classmates to put it on radio, the three creators—Louise Starkey, Isobel Carothers, and Helen King—went to WGN, Chicago, wheedled a timeslot, and did their first broadcasts gratis. By January 1931 they had attracted enough local attention to go on NBC. For a year it was an evening series, moving to the daytime schedule for Super Suds Feb. 15, 1932, and becoming the first soap opera in broadcast history.

The skirts put on by the three young women bore little resemblance to what would quickly become standard soap opera fare. It was a gentle show about three women in a small-town duplex who, once a day, got together to talk about their world and the world at large.

Like other early network serial dramas, it was lightly scripted, heavily improvised, and almost wholly conversational. Other characters came to life almost exclusively through the chatter of the principals, rather than by appearing at the mike. If a script ran short, the actresses improvised, often gossiping their way to the end.

They talked current affairs. An interesting item in the evening newspaper might be brought up on the next day's show. They carped about the melons down at the grocery store; they griped about the prices of meat and tomatoes. They talked of things they wanted to do when they retired. Clara wanted to be a fine cook. Lu wanted to live in a real house and make hooked rugs. Em wanted to travel.

Mostly they talked about their lives. Emma and her husband Ernest were the parents of six children. Em was neglected by Ernest, whose general irresponsibility was one of the show's recurring themes. Ernest was usually out of work, his mattress business having folded. Clara's husband Charley was a mechanic in a garage. They had three sons. As Clara would often say of her Charley, "He'll never set the world afire, but if it was to catch fire he'd be right there with a bucket to help put it out." Lu was often described as puckish, with a playful spirit.

In addition to being the first daytime serial, *Clara, Lu, and Em* is believed to be the first to offer a premium. For a Super Suds boxtop, a listener would be sent a spoon from the 1933 Chicago World's Fair.

The sudden death of Isobel Carothers in 1936 sent the show into limbo. Starkey and King decided not to continue without her. Six years later they attempted a comeback on CBS, with another Northwestern classmate, Harriet Allyn. But the humor had dated: the nature of *Clara, Lu, and Em* was truly a thing of the '30s. The 1945 syndication also failed.

CLAUDIA AND DAVID, drama, based on the *Redbook* magazine stories by Rose Franken and William Brown Meloney.

BROADCAST HISTORY: July 4–Sept. 26, 1941, CBS. 30m, Fridays at 8. Summer substitute for *The Kate Smith Hour.* General Foods for Grape Nuts and Grape Nuts Flakes. **CAST:** Patricia Ryan as Claudia, "charming childlike bride." Richard Kollmar as her husband, David Naughton, an architect. Jane Seymour as Mrs. Brown, Claudia's mother. Irene Hubbard as Mrs. Naughton, David's mother. **ANNOUNCER:** Charles Stark. **MUSIC:** Peter Van Steeden.

Claudia and David began as a skit on *The Kate Smith Hour* June 6, 1941, a month before becoming a full summer series. Claudia was still in her teens when she fell in love with David; much of the conflict derived from the possessiveness of her mother, with the "everyday drama" focusing on counting pennies, balancing checkbooks, and repairing items around the house. The skits on the Smith show developed the romance; the couple actually wed at "City Hall" in the second regular episode, July 11. A syndication attempt, ca. 1948, starred Katharine Bard and Paul Crabtree.

THE CLICQUOT CLUB ESKIMOS, early radio musical act.

BROADCAST HISTORY: 1923–26, WEAF, New York.

1926–1933, NBC. 30m. Thursdays at 10 until 1927; Thursday at 9, 1927–28; Tuesdays at 10, 1928–30; Fridays at 9, 1930–33.

Jan. 23–July 24, 1933, Blue Network. 30m, Mondays at 8.

Dec. 21, 1935–Jan. 4, 1936, CBS. 30m, Saturdays at 8.

Jan. 12–April 12, 1936, NBC. 30m, Sundays at 3.

PERSONNEL: Harry Reser, banjoist and leader. Andy Bossen, trumpet; Matthew Collen, trombone; Joe Davis, clarinet and alto sax; Clarence Doench, tenor sax and clarinet; Paul Rickenbach, piano; Maurice Black, tuba; Tom Stacks, drums; and others. **ANNOUNCERS:** Graham McNamee; Phillips Carlin; John S. Young; comic Raymond Knight, who was heard on the air as Bill Borealis; Merle Johnston; Jimmy Brierly; Everett Clary.

The Clicquot Club Eskimos were of radio's first generation, before commercials were allowed on the air, when bands and small groups had to assume the names of the companies that subsidized them. Their leader, Harry Reser, was a frequent performer on WEAF in the years preceding the rise of the networks. His playing was sometimes described as "sparkling" in newspaper columns, and this led George Podeyn, WEAF production manager, to pitch Reser's band to the Clicquot Club Ginger Ale Company. Clicquot Club was then a leading rival of Canada Dry and eagerly bought the idea of a "sparkling" musical show to promote itself.

In its earliest days, the group operated under strict rules—no products named or described, no prices mentioned, no offers, no free samples. Like *The A&P Gypsies* and others of the day, the *Eskimos* relied on a groundswell of good will. By 1927 radio had gone irrevocably commercial, though the older acts kept their sponsored names. The Eskimos were initially a six-piece banjo ensemble. With the show's growing popularity, a full orchestra was added, though even then, said *Popular Radio* in January 1927, "the banjo is made to predominate because it creates a sensation of the sparkling of the ginger ale." It was said that Reser, who came out of the early Paul Whiteman, Bennie Krueger, and Sam Lanin bands, could play every instrument in his orchestra.

The budget for the show was about $200,000 in its first network year. It was perhaps the pioneer in sound effects use, the opening signature utilizing sleigh bells, Eskimo dogs, and the cracking of a whip. Reser incorporated a theme, *The Clicquot March*, again believed to be radio's first such. The show was broadcast from WEAF and later from the New Amsterdam Roof Studio on West 42nd Street. Annette Hanshaw was a frequent guest; Frank Weston wrote commercials and continuity. The Eskimos also made many phonograph records for Columbia, at least a few numbers released under the name "Paul Clicquot and his Eskimeaux."

CLOAK AND DAGGER, foreign intrigue, based on the true-adventure book of the same name by Corey Ford and Alastair MacBain.

BROADCAST HISTORY: May 7–Oct. 22, 1950, NBC. 30m, Sundays at 4, with some Fridays. **CAST:** New York radio personnel including Raymond Edward Johnson, Joseph Julian, Berry Kroeger, Ross Martin, Bill Quinn, Everett Sloane, Jackson Beck, Inge Adams, Bill Zukert, Leon Janney, Guy Sorel, Virginia Payne, Lou Sorin, Boris Aplon, Grant Richards, Ralph Bell, Stefan Schnabel, Martin Balsam, Larry Haines, Irene Hubbard, Arnold Robertson, Les Tremayne, Jan Miner, Chuck Webster, Jone Allison, Eric Dressler, Maurice Tarplin, Guy Repp, Luise Barclay, Janice Gilbert, Bryna Raeburn, Karl Weber. **ANNOUNCERS:** Robert Warren, Karl Weber. **MUSIC:** John Gart. **PRODUCER:** Louis G. Cowan. **DIRECTOR:** Sherman Marks. **WRITERS:** Winifred Wolfe, Jack Gordon.

Cloak and Dagger was lost in the summertime NBC schedule, lumped into a mystery block with several other shows of far inferior quality.

It never attracted a sponsor and got almost no critical attention, but the recent discovery of the entire run reveals a gripping show with every story an unpredictable departure from formula. It was the story of the wartime activities of the OSS—the Office of Strategic Services—"this country's first all-out effort in black warfare . . . dropping undercover operators behind enemy lines, organizing local partisans to blow bridges and dynamite tunnels, operating the best spy systems of Europe and Asia." It was a tense half-hour of patriots and traitors, of love affairs doomed by war, of triumph, tragedy, and failure. The stories did not always end with the lovers embraced and the mad-dog Germans reeling in defeat: the hero-agent, in accomplishing his mission, sometimes gave up his life. It opened with a question by actor Raymond Edward Johnson: *Are you willing to undertake a dangerous mission for the United States, knowing in advance you may never return alive?* It was transcribed and had a definite "canned" sound, which may also have helped turn listeners away.

THE CLOCK, dramatic suspense anthology.

BROADCAST HISTORY: Nov. 3, 1946–May 23, 1948, ABC. Various 30m timeslots. **1946–47: CAST:** Originally broadcast from New York, with East Coast radio actors in anthology roles. **ANNOUNCER:** Gene Kirby. **MUSIC:** Bernard Green. **CREATOR-WRITER:** Lawrence Klee. **DIRECTOR:** Clark Andrews. **1948: CAST:** Moved to Hollywood, using West Coast acting talent, notably Jeanette Nolan, Cathy and Elliott Lewis. **MUSIC:** Basil Adlam (Bernard Green's themes). **PRODUCERS:** Ed Rosenberg, Larry White. **DIRECTOR:** William Spier.

The opening signature of *The Clock* set forth the theme: *Sunrise and sunset, promise and fulfillment, birth and death . . . the whole drama of life is written in the sands of time.* The stories were narrated by a deep-voiced "Father Time" figure, to a ticking cadence. "In England they call me Ben, and I have a large and extremely showy flat in Westminster Tower . . . but just between the two of us, I feel much more comfortable at the end of a chain. And there's the quiet old lady who keeps a favored place for me in the corner of her room . . . to her, I'm known as Grandfather." It foreshadowed writer Klee's suspense series *The Chase*, aired six years later.

The West Coast run, under William Spier, had a decidedly different sound, but the themes were the same.

CLUB FIFTEEN, popular music.

BROADCAST HISTORY: June 30, 1947–Jan. 16, 1953, CBS. 15m, weeknights at 7:30 through 1951, then three a week. Campbell Soups. CAST: Bob Crosby, singing host. The Andrews Sisters (Mondays-Wednesdays-Fridays) alternating with Margaret Whiting and the Modernaires (Virginia Maxey, Paula Kelly, Hal Dickinson, Johnny Drake, Fran Scott, and Ralph Brewster), who sang Tuesdays and Thursdays. Also: Patti Clayton, Jo Stafford and Gisele MacKenzie, who arrived from Canada and was discovered on *Club Fifteen*. Dick Haymes, singing star, 1949–50. ANNOUNCER: Del Sharbutt. ORCHESTRA: Jerry Gray. PRODUCER: J. Walter Thompson agency. DIRECTOR: Cal Kuhl. WRITERS: Carroll Carroll, David Gregory.

CLUB MATINEE, comedy-variety.

BROADCAST HISTORY: 1937–43, Blue Network. 60m, at times 30m, weekdays at 4 in the East; sometimes six a week; three a week as of 1941. Chicago origination. CAST: Ransom Sherman, host and star. Garry Moore, 1939–42. ANNOUNCER: Durward Kirby. VOCALISTS: The Three Romeos, the Escorts and Betty, Sam Cowling, Evelyn Lynne, Johnny Johnston, etc. ORCHESTRA: Rex Maupin.

Ransom Sherman channeled his comedy for the thinking man. A highlight of *Club Matinee* was its comic arrangement of musical classics, played slightly out of tune. Bill Jones, the bass player, was also featured in comedy routines, his act done in thick Brooklynese. Garry Moore made his network radio debut here, at the time still using his given name, Thomas Garrison Morfit. In 1940 a woman from Pittsburgh won $50 in a rename-the-Morfit contest by cutting the last name, dropping the Thomas, and rearranging Garrison. Moore alternated with Sherman as host and wrote part of the show. In later years, he often referred to Sherman as "the man who taught me all I know."

THE CLYDE BEATTY SHOW, circus adventure.

BROADCAST HISTORY: 1950, transcribed syndication by Commodore Productions, sold to Mutual for Kellogg's sponsorship, Dec. 11, 1950–Jan. 18, 1952, 30m, three a week at 5:30. CAST: Vic Perrin as Clyde Beatty, circus star and tamer of wild animals. Eve McVeagh as Beatty's wife Harriet. PRODUCERS: Shirley Thomas, Walter White Jr. WRITERS: Frank Hart Taussig, R. T. Smith.

Clyde Beatty's exploits as owner of the Clyde Beatty Circus were well known through books and a film serial. Shirley Thomas brought the idea for a radio series to her husband Walter White, whose Commodore Productions had just struck gold with *Hopalong Cassidy*. The fictionalized stories ranged from circus mysteries to treks through the wilderness in search of new animals.

COAST-TO-COAST ON A BUS, children's show, known as *The Children's Hour*, 1927–34; also known as *The White Rabbit Line*.

BROADCAST HISTORY: 1924–27, WJZ, New York, beginning in May 1924.

1927–1948, Blue Network/ABC. 60m until 1940; 30m and 45m seasons subsequently heard. Sundays at 9 A.M. until 1940; then Sundays at 9, 9:15, or 9:30 A.M.

CAST: Child performers Audrey Egan, Jeannie Elkins, Jackie Kelk, Walter Tetley, Billy and Florence Halop, Bill Lipton, Bill Redfield, Michael O'Day, Renee and Joy Terry, Bob Hastings, Jimmy McCallion, Estelle Levy, Susan Robinson, Eddie Wragge, Junius and Renee Stevens, Niels Robinson, Diana Donneworth, Joyce and Jean Walsh, Carmina Cansino, the Linden Trio, Marie Skinner, Dante Sasaceni, Jean Harris, Edwin Bruce, Ronald Liss, Eleanor Glantz, Peggy Zinke, Billy and Bobby Mauch, Pam Prescott, Margaret MacLaren, Mildred Schneider, Nancy Peterson, Mary Oldham, Tommy Hughes, Donald Kelly, Winifred Toomey, Thomas Brady, Mary Baune, Patsy and Dotty Dowd, Anne Heather, Edna Roebling, Dabby Lewis, John Bates, Peter Fernandez, Laddie Seaman, Joan Tetzel, Helen Holt, Walter Scott, Andy, Jimmy and Tommy Donnelly, Mary Small, Wynn Murray, trumpeter Jimmy Burke. Jimmy McCallion as driver of the White Rabbit Bus. Art Scanlon as the Negro bus porter. HOST: Milton Cross. MUSICAL DIRECTOR: Walter Fleischer. CONTINUITY AND MUSIC SELECTION: Ethel Hart, Sylvia Altman, Hilda

Norton. **PRODUCER-DIRECTORS:** Madge Tucker, Tom DeHuff. **WRITER:** Madge Tucker, who also auditioned the children.

Coast-to-Coast on a Bus began at WJZ as *The Children's Hour*. It became a training ground for many young singers and radio actors, some of whom had notable careers. It was said to be "the pride and joy" of its host, Milton Cross, who stood at the helm across a two-decade run.

In its heyday, the show was built around the concept of a bus ride on the White Rabbit Line, which also was a popular nickname for the series. Cross was the "conductor" of the bus, which made many stops during the hour, each stop punctuated by a blowing horn and a shift in the entertainment. The bus horn was also used in the opening signature, blaring away as a child announcer put the show on the air. "*Coast-to-Coast on a Bus*, the White Rabbit Line, jumps anywhere, anytime!" Then the children, ranging in age from 3 to 16, sang the theme: *Oh, we just roll along . . . havin' our ups, havin' our downs . . . havin' our ups and downs . . . all day long!*

The show grew out of a newspaper campaign to help discover talented children. "It has always remained a one-man show," wrote *Radio Mirror* in 1936; "for no matter how many assistants and child performers came and went, Milton Cross was always the guiding force behind them." Cross had arrived at WJZ as an announcer in 1921, hoping to become a singer. But it was his speaking voice that would be famous, first on *The Children's Hour*, later as announcer on the *Metropolitan Opera Broadcasts*. The show was heavily musical, following Cross's deep interest in classical music and opera. There might be an opening hymn, sung by Audrey Egan; then a poem; then a song from one of the youngest children. "And who is standing here with her ticket ready to pay for a ride on the White Rabbit Bus?" Cross would ask; and a small voice would chirp, "It's Jeannie Elkins, Mr. Conductor." Then came another song, and the members of the Peter Pig Club would clamor for a story, which Cross would narrate and the cast act out. Among the notables to emerge from the show were Metropolitan Opera star Risë Stevens and screen actress Ann Blyth. Vivian Smolen, Jackie Kelk, Walter Tetley, and the Halops had distinguished radio careers as adults.

THE COLGATE SPORTS NEWSREEL, sports legends and tall tales.

BROADCAST HISTORY: Dec. 5, 1937–Oct. 5, 1939, Blue Network. 15m, Sundays at 11:45 A.M. until Sept. 1938, then Thursdays at 6:30. *The Bill Stern Sports Review.*

Oct. 8, 1939–Sept. 28, 1941, Blue Network. 15m, Sundays at 9:45. First broadcasts for Colgate Shave Cream as *The Colgate Sports Newsreel.*

Oct. 4, 1941–June 29, 1951, NBC. 15m, Saturdays at 10 until mid-1943, then Fridays at 10:30. Colgate.

Nov. 30, 1951–Aug. 14, 1953, NBC. 15m, Fridays at 6:15 until April 1953, then five a week at 6:15. *Bill Stern Sports.* Although Colgate had now left the series and no longer figured in the title, it was much the same show.

Sept. 14, 1953–June 22, 1956, ABC. 15m, five a week at 6:30 for Budweiser until Dec. 1954, then five a week for Allstate Insurance and other clients. *Sports Today.*

HOST-NARRATOR-STORYTELLER: Bill Stern, one of the most popular sports broadcasters of his time. **ANNOUNCER:** Arthur Gary. **MUSIC:** Murray Ross on organ. **WRITER:** Mac Davis. **SOUND EFFECTS:** Chet Hill.

True to the old newsman's adage, Bill Stern never let the facts get in the way of a good story. On his *Colgate Sports Newsreel*, he was known to tell the same story twice, a year or so apart, using conflicting facts and passing both versions as truth. Stern covered his tracks, reminding listeners that his stories were "some true, some hearsay, but all so interesting we'd like to pass them along to you." It was his manner that suggested gospel. Stern could put more pent-up emotion into his voice than anyone else outside a soap opera. This style helped make his shows some of the most entertaining quarter-hours ever aired.

His interest in grand theater was not a hollow whim. Born July 1, 1907, Stern was captivated by footlights from an early age. He worked in vaudeville and in stock companies. By 1931 he had become assistant stage manager of the Roxy Theater in New York; he worked at Radio City in a similar capacity in the mid-1930s. A tryout with NBC in 1934 changed his career. For four years he broadcast the Friday night fights on NBC Blue for Adam Hats, building his popularity with the common man. In 1938 he began his long association with MGM's *News of the Day* newsreel, which he plugged prolifically on his weekly sports commentaries.

But it was as host of *The Colgate Sports Newsreel* that Stern achieved his greatest fame. Seldom has a quarter-hour show attracted such a vocal following. Stern eulogized the great, the near-great, the obscure. His fantastic tales broke all rules. He could be tough-sounding one moment and near tears the next, his voice quivering as he relayed the strange story of a blind athlete who won a track meet but lost his love. He told of horse races won by dead jockeys, of armless and legless baseball players, of the profound if tenuous effect that sports had had on the lives of great national statesmen.

His shows were done on location wherever he happened to be as he covered the game of the week. Top stars of screen and radio were his guests: Orson Welles, Jack Benny, Ronald Reagan, Frank Sinatra, and Brace (*The Lone Ranger*) Beemer a few who appeared. Each had a personal tale that related in some way, however small, to sports. But it was the ambience, the atmosphere, that listeners found so seductive. Stern made full use of color, drama, sound effects, and music. His narrative style was prone to relentless repetition, long dramatic pauses, and the exaggeration of every word in a sentence (verbs included) in the constant effort to make a story more dramatic. The organ peppered his tales with sudden stings, and a male quartet hummed and sang appropriate melodies throughout.

The quartet was also used on the signature themes, opening to the tune *Mad'moiselle from Armentières*:

> *Bill Stern the Colgate Shave Cream man is on the air!*
> *Bill Stern the Colgate Shave Cream man with stories rare!*
> *Take his advice and you'll look nice,*
> *Your face will feel as cool as ice,*
> *With Colgate shaves you'll be a fan!*

The lyrics varied from week to week, as did the closings:

> *Bill Stern the Colgate Shave Cream man is on his way,*
> *Bill Stern the Colgate Shave Cream man had lots to say:*

> *He told you tales of sports heroes,*
> *The inside dope he really knows,*
> *So listen in next Fri-day night!*
> *C-O-L-G-A-T-E! Colgate presents Bill Stern!*

"That's the three-o mark for tonight," Stern would say, taking his closing jargon from the traditional symbol—30—that reporters had long used to end their stories. He usually told three or four tales in each show, separating them as Reel One, Reel Two, etc. He closed each segment with the words "*Portrait . . . of a hero!*" or some such. Stern's career and fight against drug addiction was candidly told in his autobiography, *A Taste of Ashes*. He died Nov. 19, 1971, but scores of his shows remain as vivid examples of radio hyperbole. Newsman-showman Paul Harvey displays unmistakable Stern influence today in his daily "news" reports, separating his items into Page One, Page Two, and so on. Harvey also borrows heavily from Stern's personal style—the long pause, the repetition, the hyped emphasis—to lift ordinary events out of the ordinary.

THE COLLIER HOUR, the first significant network dramatic anthology; a variety hour in its later run.

BROADCAST HISTORY: 1927–32, Blue Network. 60m, Sundays at 8:15, running across the hour. *Collier's* magazine. CAST: John B. Kennedy as the *Collier's* "editor," who introduced the stories. Jack Arthur, Phil Barrison, and Arthur Hughes also as the editor. MUSIC: Ernest LaPrade, brother of the producer. CREATOR-PRODUCER: Malcolm LaPrade. DIRECTOR: Colonel Davis.

The Collier Hour was created to boost *Collier's* magazine, which for most of its run was locked in a fierce battle for circulation and revenue with the *Saturday Evening Post*. Initially heard Wednesdays before publication, the show soon moved to Sundays to avoid taking the edge off the stories, which were running concurrently in the magazine. Complete stories and serials alike were heard on *The Collier Hour*, the serials often of the thriller genre. The best-known *Collier* serial was *Fu Manchu*, featuring Sax Rohmer's insidious but brilliant Oriental criminal. Three complete 12-chapter *Fu Manchu* serials were heard: Rohmer himself introduced the May 1, 1931, installment of *Yu'an Hee See Laughs*.

In 1929 *The Collier Hour*, while continuing to broadcast dramatic offerings, shifted its focus to include more music, sports, comedy, and news. The variety hour seemed to fit the magazine's general-interest readership. George M. Cohan made his first appearance on the air at the *Collier Hour* microphone in 1929. Other guests were John D. Rockefeller and Helen Keller, who amazed the nation with her triumph over her triple handicaps (being deaf, blind, and mute).

COLUMBIA PRESENTS CORWIN, dramatic anthology; the works of Norman Corwin. See also AN AMERICAN IN ENGLAND; AN AMERICAN IN RUSSIA; THE COLUMBIA WORKSHOP; ONE WORLD FLIGHT; PASSPORT FOR ADAMS; THE PURSUIT OF HAPPINESS; SO THIS IS RADIO; THIS IS WAR!

BROADCAST HISTORY: May 4–Nov. 9, 1941, CBS. 30m, Sundays at 10:30. *Twenty-Six by Corwin*, technically a part of *The Columbia Workshop* but in fact a continuous series written, produced, and directed by Corwin. The direct forerunner of *Columbia Presents Corwin*. **CAST:** Everett Sloane, Ted de Corsia, John Brown, Frank Gallop, Peter Donald, Kenny Delmar, Karl Swenson, Paul Stewart, Adelaide Klein, Hester Sondergaard, Luis Van Rooten, Frank Lovejoy, House Jameson, Jack Smart, Beatrice Kay, John Gibson, Arthur Vinton, Larry Robinson (as Runyon Jones), Bartlett Robinson, Martin Wolfson, Joel O'Brien, Perry Lafferty, etc. **MUSIC:** Alexander Semmler (New York); Bernard Herrmann, Lyn Murray, Lud Gluskin, Lucien Moraweck (Hollywood). **SOUND EFFECTS:** Ray Kremer, Berne Surrey.

March 7–Aug. 15, 1944, CBS. 30m, Tuesdays at 10. *Columbia Presents Corwin*, a 22-week run, in the same format of and with a few repeats from the earlier *Twenty-Six* series. Written, produced, and directed by Corwin. **CAST:** Many from the earlier series, with Kermit Murdock, Joseph Julian, Minerva Pious, Katherine Locke, Carl Frank, Joan Alexander, Arnold Moss, Ralph Bell, etc. Also many top-name stars: Orson Welles, Fredric March, Charles Laughton, etc. **MUSIC:** Bernard Herrmann, etc.

July 3–Aug. 21, 1945, CBS. 30m, Tuesdays at 9. *Columbia Presents Corwin*, summer series, eight weeks, with a few repeats.

Although Norman Corwin's *Columbia* series ran only in part of the 1944 and 1945 seasons,

the title in a real way summarizes the mainstream of Corwin's radio career. He was active on many fronts, in many series, and with many special broadcasts, before and after the two CBS runs that bore his name. His shows were always sustained by his network, carried as crown jewels in that special genre called "prestige," never offered for sale to any product or cause. At CBS, where he toiled for most of his radio career, Corwin was given the treatment and almost unlimited freedom of a major star.

He was born in Boston, May 3, 1910. At 19 he became a journalist, joining the *Springfield Republican* and quickly establishing himself as a good "color man" in the newspaper's columns. He began broadcasting in 1932, when the newspaper formed an alliance with WBZ, Springfield, and WBZA, Boston, and carried his bylined news commentary each evening. In 1935 he was hired as a late-night newscaster at WLW, Cincinnati, but was fired for violating the station's policies against airing news of labor strikes. He became the *Republican*'s radio editor the same year: among his shows of that period were *Rhymes and Cadences* (WBZ), an early experiment with the poetic radio form that would later make him famous, and *Norman Corwin's Journal* (WMAS). He took a job for 20th Century Fox, churning out publicity for mid-1930s Fox movies. By 1938 he was at WQXR, an unaffiliated New York radio station known for innovative broadcasting. There he initiated *Poetic License*, a Wednesday night show that presented some of the leading poets of the day and presaged what would come to be known as "talking verse" or "conversational poetry." He embellished nursery rhymes and began to dramatize. The series was reviewed in *Variety*, and Corwin appeared as a guest on the NBC variety hour *The Magic Key*. *Poetic License* caught the attention of W. B. Lewis, CBS vice president: Corwin was hired by the network in April 1938, and for most of the next decade CBS was his home.

For about a year he worked in anonymity, declining on-air credit because, as his entry in the 1940 *Current Biography* put it, "he didn't feel he was good enough." He was trying to write for *The Columbia Workshop*, the pioneering CBS experimental series. It was a frustrating apprenticeship. "He attempted one *Workshop* script, a satire," his *Biography* entry noted, "but tore it up halfway through." Corwin didn't know it then, but in less than three years the *Workshop* would turn over to him an entire 26-week block of its schedule to use as he saw fit. So swift was his rise, once it began, that he seemed to burst upon the scene a complete, polished, and original talent. Some critics were calling him radio's first home-grown genius.

He was given a Sunday show, titled *Words Without Music* (CBS, Dec. 4, 1938–June 25, 1939). Heard in shifting mid-to late-afternoon timeslots, this was a free-ranging series that utilized poetic narrative as radio had seldom if ever heard it. His *Plot to Overthrow Christmas* was pure delight: first heard Dec. 25, 1938, on *Words Without Music*, it told of a scheme by the demons of Hell to assassinate Santa Claus. "Did you hear about the plot to overthrow Christmas?" the narrator began: "Well, gather ye now from Maine to the Isthmus/ Of Panama, and listen to the story/ Of the utter inglory/ Of some gory goings-on in Hell." In Hell, the listener met as motley a crew of villains as history and literature had yet devised: Ivan the Terrible, Haman, Caligula, Medusa, Simon Legree, and Circe (*Mercy!*). Nero was fiddling, as was his wont, while Borgia thought of the North Pole jaunt: "Just think how it would tickle us/ To liquidate St. Nicholas!" But the plot failed as Nero, sent to do the deed, turned into mush at Santa's feet. House Jameson starred as Santa, with Will Geer as the Devil and Eric Burroughs as Nero.

The day after the broadcast, Corwin was sought out by fellow CBS staffer Edward R. Murrow, who compared *Christmas* to the best of Gilbert and Sullivan. It was the beginning of a long friendship and great mutual admiration. But Corwin moved on from the whimsy of *Christmas* into the horrors of current events. He had been angered by Mussolini's son Vittorio, then on duty with the Italian air force, who described blowing up a group of horsemen during a bombing run as "exceptionally good fun." Corwin's response was a play without rhyme but with all the cadence of dark poetry. *They Fly Through the Air with the Greatest of Ease* was aired Feb. 19, 1939, dedicated to "all aviators who have bombed defenseless civilian populations." It was the beginning of Corwin's anti-fascist phase. Fascism was a tough opponent that would serve as his audio punching bag throughout the war years.

Words Without Music ran 25 weeks and was followed by a brief series, *So This Is Radio*, and a longer one, the acclaimed *Pursuit of Happiness*. Then came *Twenty-Six by Corwin*, appearing suddenly in the middle of the 1941 *Columbia Workshop* season. He opened with whimsy, a lighthearted look at the radio industry titled *Radio Primer*. In music, prose, and verse he thoroughly ribbed his medium with an A-to-Z accounting of its foibles. But no one could predict what would strike his fancy from week to week: his second show, May 11, was *The Log of the R-77*, a retrospective story of a sunken submarine and the crew's final hours. *Appointment* (June 1) was inspired by a single thought— *no man in the history of the world has had more people wish him dead than Adolf Hitler*—but turned into something else, the story of an escaped POW who plots against the commandant of a concentration camp. One of Corwin's best-loved plays was *The Odyssey of Runyon Jones* (June 8), a fable of a small boy's journey to "Curgatory" in search of his dog Pootzy, killed by an automobile. He wrote *Mary and the Fairy* (Aug. 31) especially for Elsa Lanchester and Ruth Gordon, Lanchester playing a young radio listener who writes a jingle and wins five wishes to be granted by a fairy (Gordon). He had Gale Sondergaard in mind for *Anatomy of Sound* (Sept. 7), and she did a "colossal job," he would write later, in a demanding solo performance. The fare varied from serious to fantastic, but the dark images of a world at war were never far away. The series closed with *Psalm for a Dark Year* on Nov. 9, a month before Pearl Harbor. Narrated by its author, it was an observance of Thanksgiving in a troubled world.

Corwin was now considered radio's "poet laureate." When President Roosevelt suggested to Archibald MacLeish that radio be prodded to help celebrate the 150th anniversary of the Bill of Rights, Corwin was given the job. It was an enormous undertaking, a 60-minute broadcast to air on the four national networks simultaneously. But *We Hold These Truths* was to have a special meaning, for the Japanese had attacked Pearl Harbor the week before, and the show arrived on an unprecedented wave of patriotism. It was estimated by Crossley, the national barometer of radio listenership, that 60 million people tuned in that night, Dec. 15, 1941. Corwin had arranged a stellar cast. James Stewart played the lead, "a citizen" who was the sounding board for the cascade of opinions, historical perspectives, and colloquialisms that flooded the hour. Also in the cast were Edward Arnold, Lionel Barrymore, Walter Brennan, Bob Burns, Walter Huston, Marjorie Main, Edward G. Robinson, Rudy Vallee, and Orson Welles. Bernard Herrmann conducted in Hollywood, and there were cutaways to the East, where Leopold Stokowski led the New York Philharmonic. Roosevelt spoke from Washington. The show was "magnificently produced and directed," wrote historian Erik Barnouw: Corwin's first assignment as "unofficial laureate" had been "to dedicate a war."

Next came another unprecedented venture: an entire series to be heard on all four networks simultaneously. *This Is War!* opened Feb. 14, 1942, and closed May 9: Corwin directed the 13 weeks and wrote six. This was followed by one of his finest series, *An American in England*, shortwaved from London in August and September 1942. *Passport for Adams* and *An American in Russia* were brief Corwin shows of 1943. Then came *Columbia Presents Corwin*.

Unlike the *Twenty-Six by Corwin* series of three seasons earlier, *Columbia Presents Corwin* had no existing *Columbia Workshop* run with which to blend. The *Workshop* had been suspended in 1942, and Corwin's 1944 show, though generally considered a kind of revival, was a series unto itself. The March 7 opener struck the same whimsical chord, with *Movie Primer* giving the ABCs of the film world in music and verse. Again there was an immediate shift to the sobering reality of current events as *The Long Name None Could Spell* (March 14) took up the agony of occupied Czechoslovakia. *The Lonesome Train* (March 21) was a folk ballad telling of the journey of Lincoln's corpse from Washington to its resting place in Springfield, Ill. Burl Ives was the singer. There were some repeats from his earlier series, but in the main *Columbia* was filled with new pieces. In *You Can Dream, Inc.*, Corwin imagined a business that sold daydreams; *Dorie Got a Medal* (April 25) took a musical look, in jazz and with an all-Negro cast, at a naval hero's life; and *The Moat Farm Murder* (July 18) examined a true turn-of-the-century murder and confession, with Charles Laughton as the killer and his wife Elsa Lanchester as the victim. Corwin found material everywhere. His *El Capitan and the Corporal*

(July 25) was the story of a man and woman, their meeting on a three-day train ride, and a poignant promise for the future: the memorable mad scramble to "make" the train in Kansas City was the result of a real experience in that same terminal for Corwin and conductor Bernard Herrmann. As on *Twenty-Six*, he closed with an introspective piece: *There Will Be Time Later* (Aug. 15) was a challenge to House Jameson, who carried it virtually alone, cataloguing the trivial events that must be shelved while "liberty, that dog-eared parchment signed by Christ, the angels, and a most impressive list of sponsors big and little, gets dusted off again."

There were two major specials between the closing of *Columbia Presents Corwin* and the summer series of the same name the following year. Corwin's *Democratic National Committee Program*, aired on the four networks Nov. 6, 1944, was a remarkable piece of radio, not the least so for its eleventh-hour election-swaying scheduling and the results it obtained. This was a 60-minute commercial for Roosevelt, but written as a documentary and aired the night before the election. A parade of stars came to the microphone to sing the president's praises, Judy Garland starting it off with a song playing to a rolling train motif (*Now we're on the right track, right track, right track/Now we're on the right track, we're gonna win the war!/Right behind the president, the president, the president,/Right behind the president in 1944!*). Then came Humphrey Bogart: "Personally, I'm voting for Franklin Delano Roosevelt because. . . ." After a few lines of personal conviction, Bogart introduced the first in a parade of unknowns, a man who had lost a son, who himself had been disabled in the war. Now Corwin took off the gloves. "If our president is defeated," the old vet declared, "I will feel as though *I* were defeated. I don't want to risk my third son's life at the hands of a city district attorney." A young soldier then told why, even in his home state of New York, Gov. Thomas E. Dewey faced many skeptics in his bid to prevent Roosevelt's fourth term. So it went: for an hour Roosevelt was deified and Dewey pummeled. Tallulah Bankhead and Lucille Ball gave endorsements, interspersed between the tributes of the "common man." Millions of Americans went to bed with the show ringing in their ears and got up the next morning to vote. The result was a Roosevelt victory, closer than it looked in the electoral college, and a new set of standards for radio. Never again would such a program be allowed. A line had been crossed: radio was the most powerful communications medium yet devised, and turning over the entire broadcast facilities of the nation for a partisan cause to an artist-playwright who was constitutionally unable to write anything in less than his strongest voice was, at best, less than prudent. Roosevelt was simply grateful, amazed that Corwin could pack so much into an hour.

Corwin was soon at work on another hour that would be widely praised as one of his finest. He was readying a show for the end of the war, a celebration of the coming victory. The only question now was when the end would come, and Corwin worked on his play over the months leading up to V-E Day. When the day was declared, May 8, 1945, *On a Note of Triumph* was ready both as a radio show and as a book. Martin Gabel narrated the show, which featured vignettes and voices from every front. The show was widely praised and was repeated May 13. It seemed to put a closing parenthesis around Corwin's career at CBS. There was more to come, but not much more: "He had opened and closed a war," Erik Barnouw would write; he had "dedicated a parliament of nations and provided an ode to lay presidents to rest." *Triumph* contained most of the lavish Corwin production techniques: the score by Bernard Herrmann (conducted by Lud Gluskin) was dramatic and sharp; the Berne Surrey sound effects just about perfect. Gabel's reading of Corwin's rhythmic prose was broken by mini-scenes of Nazi arrogance and the searching questions of American GIs. William L. Shirer had a speaking part, a cutaway to San Francisco. In terms of popular and critical response, *On a Note of Triumph* was Corwin's crowning touch, exceeding even the landslide of kudos that came with *We Hold These Truths* four years earlier.

In July and August 1945 came the second run of *Columbia Presents Corwin*. Three of the eight shows were repeats from the prior run, but the others were typically strong, funny, unpredictable. In *The Undecided Molecule* (July 17), Corwin returned to the spirit and form of *The Plot to Overthrow Christmas* with a comedy in verse about a molecule (X) that refused to be classified, leading to a fantasy trial. The casting was

inspired: Groucho Marx as the judge; Robert Benchley as the prosecutor; Norman Lloyd as the clerk; Sylvia Sidney as Miss Anima, spokeswoman for the animal kingdom; Elliott Lewis as the vice president in charge of physiochemistry; and Keenan Wynn busy with four disparate roles. Carmen Dragon wrote the score, which Lud Gluskin conducted. On Aug. 14, with the dropping of an atomic bomb on Japan, Corwin turned his slot into a quarter-hour statement called *Fourteen August*. Orson Welles gave the words a fiery reading (*God and uranium were on our side . . . the wrath of the atom fell like a commandment, and the very planet quivered with implications*) and pronounced the occasion "the father of great anniversaries." An expanded version, *God and Uranium*, was aired the following Sunday, with Olivia De Havilland joining Welles at the microphone.

Corwin's shows, though sustained, were given the same first-class ticket on CBS as comedy teams bringing in millions a year. CBS chief William S. Paley was quoted to the effect that there was too much sponsor control in radio, leading to a proliferation of Hollywood names on the air rather than quality material. Corwin was the antithesis of all that, Paley suggested, a departure from safe, proven formulas designed to capture the largest markets at the lowest costs. It was the first time, said *Newsweek*, that CBS had deliberately reserved a part of its prime schedule for a sustaining show. Corwin was gratified to be on the cutting edge of the new wave. "Radio should ultimately produce a great heroic race of writers," he told *Tune In*. "Our language today has tremendous vigor, and radio is the perfect medium for transmitting it." He admitted a Shakespearean influence. "He loves the sweep, texture, cadence and rhythms of those [Elizabethan] days, and believes they can be translated into common modern terms." The magazine cited his "acute ear for down-to-earth idiom, an almost wicked sense of the banalities of everyday speech, which he transfers to paper so slyly that few actors could get the nuances without the author's own direction." His style was marked by staccato narrative and colorful, colloquial speech. Among his favorite themes was the magnificence of the common man, the injustices he suffered and the tyrants he overcame. He was a heavy rehearser. He would fret over each script "as if it were his first" (*Radio Life*), and he remained a stickler for detail. "Usually he keeps rehearsing right up to air time, going over the script line by line until he gets the effect he's striving for."

That he was one of radio's giants seems indisputable, though his work was sometimes considered too heavy and extreme. He was "savagely lampooned" by Abe Burrows, according to *Time*, and was seen by some critics as a "poor man's MacLeish." The most brutal criticism was given him by Bernard DeVoto, who demolished *On a Note of Triumph* in *Harper's* magazine. "Overblown oratory," "vulgar travesty," "flip rhetoric," and "dull, windy, opaque, pretentious, and in the end false" were a few of DeVoto's complaints. But *Time*, whose own criticisms could be cutting, noted that DeVoto "rarely likes anything," and DeVoto himself admitted that, in his blast at Corwin, he was standing virtually alone. Corwin's response was to reprint the most scathing of DeVoto's remarks when *Triumph* was anthologized (*Untitled and Other Radio Dramas*). By then his play had received international praise and many awards. One of his prizes was the 1946 Wendell Willkie One World Award, given to the writer in communications who best exemplified Willkie's "one world" concepts. It included a trip around the world, which became the basis for Corwin's 1947 series *One World Flight*.

But his days at CBS were numbered. When he met William Paley on a train after the war, there was no more talk of too much sponsor control. What Corwin would remember of that meeting was Paley's suggestion that future scripts be geared more for a mainstream audience—in other words, be more commercial. The writing was on the wall: when, in his next contract, CBS tried to usurp half his subsidiary rights money, Corwin quit.

He joined United Nations Radio and in 1948 produced one of his most powerful plays. *Document A/777* was his plea for an "International Bill of Human Rights," with the action set during a role call of the U.N. General Assembly. As each country is named, the delegate votes on the bill. But some countries are worth a closer look, and the action freezes while incidents from that country's history are dramatized. Raw, brutal chapters waft up from the nation's dungeons; wicked little despots are stripped and paraded before the microphone. The action was carried

by a great international cast: Richard Basehart, Charles Boyer, Lee J. Cobb, Ronald Colman, Joan Crawford, Maurice Evans, Jose Ferrer, Reginald Gardiner, Van Heflin, Jean Hersholt, Lena Horne, Marsha Hunt, Alexander Knox, Charles Laughton, Laurence Olivier, Vincent Price, Edward G. Robinson, Robert Ryan, Hilda Vaughn, Emlyn Williams, and, as the voice of the roll call, Robert Young. Aaron Copland composed the score, which was played by the Boston Symphony Orchestra.

Also from the U.N. came *Citizen of the World*, starring Lee J. Cobb and given an airing on CBS July 10, 1949. Corwin's wishful play *Could Be*, "a synopsis of what could happen if the nations of the world got together and attacked common problems with the same vigor, determination, and resources with which, from time to time, they have attacked each other," was produced by the U.N. and heard on NBC Sept. 11, 1949. Ben Grauer, Robert Trout, Martin Gabel, and a supporting cast of New York radio actors gave it voice. Alexander Semmler conducted for both shows. Corwin has remained active as a writer. Among his books are *Overkill and Megalove* (1963) *Holes in a Stained Glass Window* (1978), *Greater than the Bomb* (1981), and *Trivializing America* (1983). He lives and writes in California.

THE COLUMBIA WORKSHOP, experimental dramatic anthology.

BROADCAST HISTORY: July 18, 1936–Nov. 8, 1942, CBS. 30m, Saturdays at 8 until Feb. 28, 1937; Sundays at 7 until Dec. 9, 1937; Thursdays at 10:30 until Jan. 8, 1938; Saturdays at 7:30 until Sept. 15, 1938; Thursdays at 10 until Jan. 9, 1939; Mondays at 10:30 until July 6, 1939; Thursdays at 10 (also 10:15 and 10:30) until May 5, 1940; Sundays at 10:30, then at 2:30, until June 12, 1942 (encompassed within this schedule was *Twenty-Six by Corwin*, May 4–Nov. 9, 1941); Fridays at 10:30 through July 3, 1942; Mondays at 10:30, July 13–Oct. 19, 1942; a lone show, Sunday at 8, Nov. 8, 1942.

March 7–Aug. 15, 1944, CBS, 30m, Tuesdays at 10; and July 3–Aug. 21, 1945, Tuesdays at 9. See COLUMBIA PRESENTS CORWIN.

Feb. 2, 1946–Jan. 25, 1947, CBS. 30m, Saturdays at 2:30 until April 21, then Sundays at 4 until Sept. 21, then Saturdays at 6:15. Continued as *Once upon a Tune* until April 26.

Jan. 27, 1956–Sept. 22, 1957, CBS. 30m Fridays at 8:30 until Nov. 1956, then Sundays at 4. See THE CBS RADIO WORKSHOP.

CASTS: Many New York actors in anthology roles: Karl Swenson, Neil O'Malley, Fred Stewart, Minerva Pious, Orson Welles, Burgess Meredith, Carl Frank, Joan Alexander, Arnold Moss, etc. AN-NOUNCERS: John Reed King, Robert Trout, Niles Welsh, Harry Clark, Sandy Becker, Don Baker, David Ross, Bert Parks, John Tillman, Tony Marvin, etc. MUSIC: Bernard Herrmann, Alexander Semmler, Lyn Murray, Mark Warnow, Raymond Scott, Howard Barlow, John Cage, Victor Bay, etc. DIRECTORS: Irving Reis (1936–38), William N. Robson (late 1930s), Brewster Morgan, Earle McGill, Norman Corwin, Marx Loeb, Betzy Tuthill, James Fassett, Albert Ward, Carl Beier, Richard Sanville, Perry Lafferty, Guy della Cioppa, George Zachary, Martin Gosch, Howard Barnes. WRITERS: (original material and adaptations by) Charles R. Jackson, Margaret Lewerth, Irwin Shaw, Val Gielgud, Stephen Fox, Pauline Gibson, Vick Knight, Sheldon Stark, Charles Tazewell, William Merrick, Milton Geiger, Max Wylie, Charles Vanda, Brian J. Byrne, James Frederick, David Redstone, James and Elizabeth Hart, etc. SOUND EFFECTS: Walter Pierson, Henry Gauthier, Charles Fenton, Al Binnie, Charles Range, Jerry McCarty, Bob Mautner, George Lehman, etc., all CBS New York; Ray Erlenborn, Al Span, Dick James, etc., CBS Hollywood.

The importance of *The Columbia Workshop* in the history of radio is underscored by the state of the art in mid-1936. Network radio was just a decade old. For much of that time, what was heard was a crude product by its later standards. Radio spent its earliest years groping with fundamental issues. Would it be commercial or a public entity? What would be allowed in the name of "art"? Was radio by its nature simply another vehicle for pop culture, to be absorbed by the lowest common denominator and immediately forgotten? Among those who had little respect for the new medium was a sizable percentage of the country's writers, actors, and musicians. If radio was to become a serious art form, clearly that direction had to come from within the industry. Radio had to develop its own artists, writers, actors, musicians.

When *The Columbia Workshop* opened, "there was no show on the air without many limitations, taboos, and sacred cows," wrote CBS executive Douglas Coulter in *Columbia Workshop Plays*. "The way was clear for the inauguration of a radio series without precedents, one that would experiment with new ideas, new writers, new techniques; a series that would stand or fall by the impression made on a public of unbiased listeners, with no restriction save the essential and reasonable one of good taste."

Into this breech stepped Irving Reis, "a jittery onetime control engineer who thought the production, not the play, was the thing" (*Time*, July 17, 1939). Reis had been lobbying for such a show for months, but only with the arrival at CBS of William B. Lewis did the idea solidify. Lewis "had little originality, but he quickly recognized it in others, and he set them going," wrote Erik Barnouw in *The Golden Web*. Lewis listened to Reis's pleas for a *Columbia Workshop*, then wrote it into the schedule. It was that simple.

Reis himself had written three plays, *St. Louis Blues, The Half-Pint Flask*, and *Meridian 7–1212*. Lewis, seeing before him a man of many talents, made Reis the director of the new show. With production help from Phil Cohan and Shirley Ward, the *Workshop* was soon on the air. The premiere was less than thrilling. Reis had put two one-act plays, *Comedy of Danger* and *Finger of God*, into the single half-hour, and the effect was ragged and unsatisfying. But the second broadcast, wrote Coulter, "really sounded the keynote of the *Workshop*." The play was *Broadway Evening*, a cascade of audio impressions, "a noisy job, at times incoherent and hard to listen to, but it demonstrated conclusively that, with laboratory experimentation *on the air*, new techniques and ideas could be developed that would raise the standards of all radio programs." Written by Leopold Proser, *Broadway Evening* was simply a stroll up the famous street between 42nd Street and Central Park, and the discovery in sound of what the walking couple found there—"milling crowds, the roar of the subways, the pitchmen on the curbs, the barkers in front of the movie palaces, the sirens of the fire engines and ambulances, bits of conversation overheard at juice stands, the inevitable street brawl." The third show, *Cartwheel*, was an experiment in compression—nine actors performed 34 characterizations, eating up 22 scenes in 30 minutes. Perhaps a medium other than radio could do such a thing, but that has yet to be demonstrated.

The rather glib assessment that *Time* would offer ("the production, not the play, is the thing") was already proving—three years before it was written—to be shallow and a little false. The most effective *Columbia Workshops* would respect technique and the play on an equal footing. And there were limitations. "A microphone cannot create the whole picture of life," wrote CBS director Earle McGill. "Wondrous and magical gifts pour from the loudspeaker. It can give back the sound of a voice that is far away, but in this year of grace can offer no substitute for the twinkle in a maiden's eye. The moment you try to push its boundaries beyond their natural limits you are committed to folly." The interpretation of lines, McGill asserted, should not be lost in the rush by soundmen and directors to infuse a play with noise. Sometimes an effect could be achieved with music, as Bernard Herrmann did for the *Workshop* production *The Devil and Daniel Webster* (Aug. 6, 1938). Webster's race by carriage to Jabez's farm to argue the farmer's case before "Old Scratch" the devil is accomplished in a scene of just under a minute. Herrmann's "ride music," coupled with the horses' hoofbeats and the crack of a whip, was all that was needed. The perfect harmony was achieved when music and sound combined with a lively, imaginative script in the hands of a director who knew how to do it.

McGill, Brewster Morgan, and William N. Robson were three such directors. There were many others at CBS in the '30s, and most were exhilarated at a chance to serve on *The Columbia Workshop*. It had become apparent that what Reis had begun could not be continued by one man. "Reis was not merely the director," wrote Coulter; he also "looked over all the manuscripts submitted, answered fan mail, took care of music and sound effects, edited and cast all the productions, and ran the publicity." Already the *Workshop* was known as a "writer's theater"; the pay was only $100 per script, but "manuscripts were pouring in at an unforeseen rate, sound and music became more and more specialized, and more extensive promotion was needed to acquaint the public with the experiments being made."

Soon the network was getting 7,000 plays a year: the result was that, in the course of time, almost every director at CBS would have a hand in *The Columbia Workshop*. They "sweated with oscillators, electric filters, and echo chambers to produce some of the most exciting sounds ever put on the air" (*Time*); they worked with new parabolic microphones, picking voices out of crowds "as a spotlight picks out faces" (*Newsweek*). Walter Pierson, head of the CBS sound department, was challenged to come up with "the footsteps of the gods" for one play and "the sounds of fog" for another. Many of the effects were already in the soundman's library: it was a matter of new and creative applications, of embellishments. Indeed, a look at the library of recorded effects at CBS in those days is impressive. As given by McGill in his book *Radio Directing*, it fills 13 pages of very small type, with four additional pages of manual effects and devices. The recordings are detailed and specific, noting the differences between various kinds of birds, dogs, and lions. There are categories for voices and applause, automobiles and motorcycles, airplanes, trains, weather, rivers, trees (crashing and chopping), fires, traffic, boats, machinery, construction, war, whistles, bells, clocks, carnivals, miscellaneous sounds, and radio itself.

In 1937, for the *Workshop*'s most famous play (*The Fall of the City*, by Archibald MacLeish), McGill would discover that recordings of a crowd, played under the sounds of a real crowd performing live on the air, gave an effect "of having a much greater mob of people than was actually appearing in the broadcast." This made the show all the more chilling.

But the greatest thing about the series, those who worked it generally agree, was the sense of freedom it offered. There was no pressure to hit a home run every week. The show was sustained, its timeslot earmarked "withheld from sale," so there were no sponsors or agency men to satisfy. As with any form of experiment, some of the shows were unexciting, poorly conceived, or just plain dull. But many, as Coulter put it, "were milestones on the path of creative thinking and writing in radio."

There were straight demonstrations of sound (Oct. 10, 1936), radio music (Nov. 7, 1936), and a look at the control booth mixer on a radio show ((Jan. 9 and 16, 1937). There were adaptations: *The Happy Prince*, by Oscar Wilde (Dec. 26,

1936), and *The Signalman*, by Charles Dickens (Jan. 23, 1937). In *A Voyage to Brobdingnag* (Sept. 12) and *A Voyage to Lilliput* (Jan. 9), new voice filters enabled engineers to play with the speech of giants and pygmies, interpreting Jonathan Swift in ways that could not have been done before. Orson Welles, 21 years old and unknown, offered Shakespeare: *Hamlet* (Sept. 19 and Nov. 14, 1936) and *Macbeth* (Feb. 28, 1937). On Oct. 3, 1936, Reis directed his own play *St. Louis Blues*, one of the earliest "radio looks at itself" pieces ever done: the story concerns a radio jazz show, with cutaways at intervals to see how the music affects listeners in half a dozen different settings. The *Workshop* may have been the first major show to fully utilize the slice-of-life technique—a little piece of action that illuminates the whole range of the protagonist's existence in 29 minutes and 30 seconds. Like a good short story, the radio drama was a prism through which that life was seen, the action merely a cutting edge, a moment of truth when the character is revealed in all his dimensions. The present hinted at the past, and the climax offered a roadmap—clear and certain, unstated but inescapable—to what the future held. A good radio play was so much like a short story that, when one declined in the 1950s, the concurrent decline of the other should have come as no great surprise.

From beginning to end, it was a director's showcase. No fewer than four directors worked on *The Fall of the City*, the trailblazing broadcast of April 11, 1937. That a playwright with the stature of Archibald MacLeish would write it for radio assured keen attention from the press. It was an allegory in verse, dark and chilling in a time when the Nazi war machine was on the rise. The action took place in the square of a city, which managed while remaining unnamed to suggest both antiquity and a hereafter. The city seemed eternal: its imminent fall was, through the understated technique, rendered all the more powerful from the opening lines.

As the play begins, a thoroughly frightened populace awaits the arrival of a conqueror. Fear mounts throughout. A harbinger (a voice from the dead) warns that "the city of masterless men will take a master," while the narrator (Orson Welles) describes the movements of the people in the manner of an unfolding newscast. The crowds mill about, buzzing with nervous excitement, listening to speeches, fretting, anticipating. The writing is filled with bitter irony (*The city is doomed! . . . Let the conqueror have it! . . . He's one man, we are but thousands! . . . Who can defend us from one man?*), and the one terrible constant is the noise of the crowd.

It was a technical challenge. Too often, as McGill would note, recorded mob effects sounded exactly like what they were—recorded mob effects. Reis suggested moving the broadcast out of the studio and into an environment more acoustically suitable—the Seventh Regiment Armory in New York—and doing the show with a real mob, 200 students from the City College. William N. Robson directed the crowd, Brewster Morgan the cast, and McGill the sound effects, while Reis synchronized and gave it overall direction. An isolation booth was constructed for Orson Welles, giving his voice a strange kind of detached intimacy. A crisis arose when tennis players arrived on the afternoon of the broadcast, claiming they had booked the Armory for a game. Another cropped up that night when, just before air time, the National Guard came in for its regular Sunday maneuvers. But promptly at 7 P.M. the show went on, an unrated, unheralded, sustained half-hour on which the actors, from Orson Welles to Burgess Meredith (the pacifist) to Edgar Stehli (the high priest), collected their union-mandated minimum paychecks: $18.50.

But *The Fall of the City* was not just another radio show. "It seemed to go to the terror of its time," Barnouw would write; and it opened the way for radio as a new and accepted art form. There was now an understanding, said *Newsweek*, "that radio drama, in both the writing and presentation, was something radically different from drama of the stage and screen." Suddenly established writers were taking note. Pare Lorentz, Alfred Kreymborg, Stephen Vincent Benét, Dorothy Parker, and William Saroyan were appearing in credits on *The Columbia Workshop*. MacLeish wrote an encore—*Air Raid* (Oct. 27, 1938)—and this strong, technically intricate antiwar statement in verse was acclaimed as loudly as his first. Norman Corwin, still struggling to find his voice, was soon to emerge as radio's most creative product. His play *My Client Curley* (March 7, 1940), though adapted from an unpublished Lucille Fletcher fantasy, served notice of Corwin's arrival as a *Workshop* force.

With the departure of Irving Reis for Paramount Pictures, William N. Robson became the *Workshop*'s main director. One of the interesting spinoffs of the late '30s was *The Ghost of Benjamin Sweet* (Jan. 8, 1938, with a sequel on March 5), a spook show with a ghost-as-hero twist. This became its own series, running on CBS later that year. In 1939, celebrating its third anniversary, the *Workshop* offered a "summer festival" from July 6 through Sept. 28: four new plays by such as Benét, Saroyan, and Lord Dunsany were mixed with *Workshop* classics, ending with a *Fall of the City* rebroadcast. The show remained alive and well until 1942, when CBS—recalling the panic caused by the Orson Welles *War of the Worlds* broadcast on the 1938 *Mercury Theater*, and citing the *Workshop*'s own *Air Raid* as a disturbingly similar simulation of life—classified the series as "too frolicsome for wartime consumption" and canceled it.

It resumed after the war. Corwin opened it Feb. 2, 1946, with *Homecoming*, a bittersweet slice of life about a GI who comes home to the farm. The show continued as if there had been no gap: *Slim* (March 3), a story of a young hobo riding the rails with a ghostly companion, was followed two weeks later by a straight T. S. Eliot reading of his *Four Quartets*. The second run was unfortunately brief, the finale Jan. 25, 1947, with a thing called *The Natural History of Nonsense*. Then, for three months, the *Workshop* was given over to a musical series, *Once upon a Tune*, which had begun on January 5 and broadcast three installments as its own entity before being merged with *The Columbia Workshop* on February 1. Thirteen episodes of *Once upon a Tune* were then heard as an announced part of the *Workshop*, closing April 26, 1947.

A third series, *The CBS Radio Workshop*, is covered under that title in this book.

More than 225 of the 1930s *Columbia Workshop* and its 1946–47 revival are available on tape. That this was not a show for the masses is especially true today. Some of these shows, on first listening, seem to move at a glacial pace; some seem quite old and dated. The techniques they pioneered have become so routine, their high-tech counterparts bombarding people in radio commercials around the clock, that a listener seldom gives a thought to a time when they didn't exist. Reis, Robson, McGill, and the others put a modern listener on notice: you may come to the picnic, but you must bring something to it. The listener is offered nothing less than a full partnership.

COMEDY OF ERRORS, quiz; contestants from the studio audience tried to spot the mistake in a skit, for a prize of $5 per round.

BROADCAST HISTORY: Dec. 24, 1949–Feb. 2, 1952, Mutual. 30m, Saturdays at 7:30. **HOST:** Jack Bailey. **ANNOUNCER:** Fort Pearson. **MUSIC:** Eddie Dunstedter on organ.

COMEDY THEATER, comedy variety-drama.

BROADCAST HISTORY: Oct. 29, 1944–June 10, 1945, NBC. 30m, Sundays at 10:30. Old Gold Cigarettes.

STAR/FORMAT: Harold Lloyd, silent film star whose antics on building ledges and swinging from giant clock hands thrilled an earlier generation, introduced condensations of movie comedies (such as *True to Life*, with Victor Moore). Though he attempted to preside "in the manner of Cecil B. DeMille," said the *New York Times*, he was too often burdened by "dreadful gags," and his voice had a "flat, high quality" not conducive to radio. As a consequence, said the critic, his timing and inflection suffered.

THE COMEDY WRITERS SHOW, a "comedy-writing session on the air, starring the writers for America's greatest comedians."

BROADCAST HISTORY: June 6–Sept. 5, 1948, ABC. 30m, Sundays at 10. **HOST:** Ben Brady. **CREATOR-PRODUCER:** Sy Fischer.

Working from a rough outline sent in by a Hollywood celebrity, teams of professional radio writers attempted to fashion an acceptable script in 30 minutes. In one show, Loretta Young asked for "a Fred Allen–type program." The writers included Sherman Burns (then working for Groucho Marx), Roger Price (Bob Hope), Leonard Stern (Abbott and Costello), and Sidney Fields (Eddie Cantor). The writers worked through an opening skit in which Allen would discuss vacations with Portland Hoffa, an "Allen's Alley" routine, and a celebrity skit with Allen and guest Jack Haley looking for gold in the Yukon. Each writer also told some behind-the-scenes story about the famous comedian who employed him. The show was transcribed at 45 minutes and edited for a 30-minute timeslot. A purist might consider that fudging, but not much. Comedy writers might reasonably expect two full days to rough out a script for a 1940s radio show.

COMMAND PERFORMANCE, spectacular wartime variety.

BROADCAST HISTORY: March 1, 1942–Dec. 20, 1949, Special Services Division of the War Department; Armed Forces Radio Service from 1943.

Oct. 7, 1945–April 21, 1946, CBS. 30m, Sundays at 9. Spinoff series; *Request Performance.* Campbell Soups.

CAST: Major personalities in performances requested by servicemen. ANNOUNCERS: Paul Douglas, Ken Carpenter. CREATOR: Louis G. Cowan. PRODUCERS: Vick Knight, Maury Holland, Cal Kuhl. DIRECTOR: Glenn Wheaton. WRITERS: Melvin Frank, Norman Panama.

Command Performance was lauded by *Time* as "the best wartime program in America," though few Americans at home ever got to hear it. The show was produced by the War Department for direct shortwave transmission to troops fighting overseas. It was estimated that $75,000 a week would be needed to produce such an extravagant hour, yet *Command Performance* had no budget and paid no money to anyone. All talent was donated, including the production staff. Both CBS and NBC gave free use of network studios for production. Such stars as Bing Crosby, Bob Hope, the Andrews Sisters, Red Skelton, Edgar Bergen, Ethel Waters, Spike Jones, Dinah Shore, Kay Kyser, and Charles Laughton could be heard on a single show. The radio acts of Lum and Abner and Fibber McGee and Molly were sandwiched between Vincent Price, Bob Burns, Judy Garland, Frank Sinatra, Jimmy Durante, and George Burns and Gracie Allen.

The show arose when the War Department asked Lou Cowan of its Radio Division to think up a format for entertaining troops overseas. The troops were desperate for American radio, and Cowan decided to let them choose their own fare. It would be a "command performance"— the GI "who was trained to obey commands could now command anything he wanted from

the radio world," wrote Edward M. Kirby and Jack W. Harris in *Star-Spangled Radio.* Once the premise was settled, the show was literally written from the battle fronts.

The initial shows were put together from verbal requests, but soon the mail poured in. For producers Wheaton and Knight, every mailbag was an adventure. One soldier wanted only to hear actress Carole Landis sigh. Another requested that Charles Laughton instruct Donald Duck in the finer points of elocution. The bizarre fed upon itself, and engineers were sent to record the sounds of birds chirping in one soldier's Indiana hometown and, for another, the sounds of a nickel slot machine paying off a jackpot. The show was described by Bob Burns as "so important and expensive that only Uncle Sam is big enough to sponsor it."

After its first year, the series was transferred to the new Armed Forces Radio Service and moved from New York to California so the flood of requests involving Hollywood screen stars could be more easily filled. Ken Carpenter took over as announcer from Paul Douglas and assorted hosts. The move created havoc for Vick Knight, who finally resigned a $1,000-a-week job producing Fred Allen's New York-based comedy show and moved west to work gratis on *Command Performance.*

Among the show's highlights were these: a special Christmas Eve broadcast in 1942, heard domestically for the first time and carried on all four networks; an all-jive show with the orchestras of Tommy Dorsey, Lionel Hampton, Count Basie, and Spike Jones; a "fiddle fight" between Jascha Heifetz and Jack Benny; and the six-girl harmony that became the traditional closing number at Christmas (the first year the singers were Judy Garland, Dinah Shore, Ginny Simms, Frances Langford, Connie Boswell, and Shirley Ross). On Feb. 5, 1945, an all-star cast spoofed America's most popular comic strip in an hour-long play, *Dick Tracy in B-Flat; or, For Goodness Sake, Isn't He Ever Going to Marry Tess Trueheart?* The stars were Bing Crosby as Dick Tracy; Dinah Shore as Tess Trueheart; Harry Von Zell as Old Judge Hooper; Jerry Colonna as the Chief of Police; Bob Hope as Flat Top; Frank Morgan as Vitamin Flintheart; Jimmy Durante as the Mole; Judy Garland as Snowflake; the Andrews Sisters as the Summer Sisters; Frank Sinatra as Shaky; and Cass Daley as Gravel Gertie.

Though the main reason for the show's existence ended with the war, *Command Performance* continued through the '40s, shortwaving specials to American servicemen all over the world. There were more than 400 shows, from half-hours to two-hour specials. A spinoff series, *Request Performance* (see entry under that title), lacked the urgency and punch of the the original and lasted only one season.

COMMUNITY SING, comedy-variety.

BROADCAST HISTORY: Sept. 6, 1936–Aug. 29, 1937, CBS. Sundays at 10. 45m until April 1937 then 30m. Also titled *The Gillette Original Community Sing*, for the sponsor, the Gillette Razor Company. CAST: Wendell Hall, "the Red-Headed Music Maker"; Billy Jones and Ernie Hare, singing duo; Eileen Barton; Betty Garde; comedians Tommy Mack, Milton Berle, and Bert Gordon (as Mischa Moody). ORCHESTRA: Andy Sannella. PRODUCER: Myron Kirk. WRITER: Irving Brecher.

Community Sing is notable as one of the earliest radio efforts of comedian Milton Berle. Though the show was obviously heavy on comedy, the title derived from the group-singing of the studio audience. Wendell Hall, aided by Billy Jones and Ernie Hare (best known as the Happiness Boys), led the songfests, while the audience was aided by slide projections of the lyrics. *Radio Mirror* found Berle's "machine-gun comedy" well rehearsed—no fault "if he can keep it up." In his autobiography, Berle recalled that the show's theme was *Let's All Sing Like the Birdies Sing*, to which the audience would sing out, "Tweet, tweet, tweet, tweet, tweet!

CONCERT BROADCASTS, "serious music" as opposed to band remotes, usually done in-studio by large symphony orchestras under the batons of celebrated maestros.

Despite the handicaps of oppressive costs and the initial reluctance of renowned soloists to "stoop to the masses," the concert music schedule on all four national chains was varied and rich. CBS had been formed by Arthur Judson, who, in alliance with the Columbia Phonograph Company, sought mainly to put a symphony orchestra on the air with classical music. Its opening program, Sept. 18, 1927, was auspicious but indicative of the problem: the group went broke,

and the network passed to William S. Paley. But the first decade of national broadcasting saw a rise in musical consciousness that only radio could have achieved. Both NBC and CBS had in-house symphony orchestras of long standing. By the mid-1930s, the music columns of *Radio Guide* had bulged to two pages. People in Wisconsin and rural Kansas could now hear the symphony orchestras of Rochester, Cleveland, or Indianapolis on a weekly basis, and the names of Toscanini, Walter, Ormandy, and others— long famous in their fields—became known in the heartland. Soon the great soloists came along as well: Jascha Heifetz, for one, changed his early opinion that his music was for the elite and realized that, through radio, millions of people might be added to the thousands who might come to a concert hall.

What follows is a checklist of the season-spanning concert series. Certain commercial programs (e.g. *The Voice of Firestone, The Telephone Hour, Cities Service Concerts*) are discussed under their own main entries.

AMERICA PREFERRED, Alfred Wallenstein, conductor; Deems Taylor, commentator. July 13, 1941– May 30, 1942, Mutual, 45m, Sundays at noon, then, Saturday evenings.

AMERICAN MUSIC HALL, Paul Whiteman, maestro; Glenn Osser last five months. Aug. 17, 1952–Dec. 13, 1954, ABC, 60m, Sundays at 8.

ANDRE KOSTELANETZ, heard largely in concert formats, though with much crossover into commercial work and popular appeal. Kostelanetz was well known, his career spanning 20 years on CBS. Born in Russia in 1901, he arrived in the United States in the early 1920s, well schooled in the classics. His first radio appearance was on *The Atwater-Kent Hour* in 1924. He joined CBS in 1929, conducting on many shows with titles like *Snowdrift Melodies* and *Threads of Happiness*. All series listed are CBS.

Feb. 8–Nov. 5, 1931, 15m, Sundays at 5:30; Tuesdays and Fridays beginning in May. Mary Eastman, featured soloist. Manhattan Soap.

1931–34, many series of short duration. Heard Wednesdays at 10:15 in a 15m format for American Chain and Cable, Nov. 1931–Feb. 1932. Concurrently Thursdays at 9 for Southern Cotton Oil, Dec. 1931–Feb. 1932. Tuesdays at 9:15, 15m for Spool Cotton, Sept. 1932–June 1933. On Dec. 28,

1932, he opened a run for General Motors: heard for Pontiac Wednesdays, then Thursdays at 9:30 in 1932–33, and Saturdays at 9:15 in 1933–34; for Buick Thursdays at 9:15 Dec. 1933–Feb. 1934, with comic Robert Benchley.

April 2, 1934–June 22, 1938, the Chesterfield broadcasts for Liggett & Myers Tobacco. Also heard as *The Chesterfield Show* and *Chesterfield Presents*. Various 30m timeslots, usually Wednesdays at 9 (1934–38) but often supplemented by Monday, Friday, or Saturday shows. The orchestra had now grown to 65 pieces and a 16-voice chorus. It featured soloists Rosa Ponselle and Grete Stueckgold (1934), Lily Pons and Nino Martini (1935–36), Kay Thompson and Ray Heatherton (1936–37), and Lawrence Tibbett (1937–38).

Jan. 12, 1939–June 24, 1940, Thursdays at 10 in a 45m format until June 1939, then Mondays at 8. *Tune-Up Time.* Ethyl Gasoline. With Walter O'Keefe, Kay Thompson, Tony Martin.

Dec. 1, 1940–Dec. 10, 1944, 30m, Sundays, various times, often 4:30, *The Pause That Refreshes on the Air.* Coca-Cola.

Sept. 6, 1945–May 30, 1946, 30m, Thursdays at 9. Chrysler.

THE ARMCO IRON MASTER, a brass band directed by Frank Simon, heard on NBC (mostly Blue) for American Rolling Mills for six seasons beginning Nov. 10, 1933. Timeslots: 1933–34, Fridays at 10; 1934–35, Red Network, Sundays at 6:30; 1935–36, Mondays, later Wednesdays at 8:30; 1936–37, Tuesdays at 10. Also Jan. 15–April 9, 1939, Sundays at 3. All 30m.

THE BOSTON SYMPHONY ORCHESTRA, whose major series of broadcasts spanned the entire era of network radio. Russian-born conductor Serge Koussevitzky was said to be able to look at photographs of himself conducting and name the pieces being played. The Boston Symphony was first heard on the Blue Network in 1926, in a two-hour Saturday night timeslot starting at 8:15. Also: 1932–33, Blue Network, 120m, Saturdays at 8:15; 1933–34, NBC, 105m, Saturdays at 8:15; 1935–36, Blue, 60m, Saturdays at 8:15; 1942–43, Blue, 60m, Saturdays at 8:15; 1943–46, Blue/ABC, 60m, Saturdays at 8:30 for Allis Chalmers; 1947, ABC, 60m, Tuesdays at 8:30 for John Hancock; 1947–48, ABC, 60m, Tuesdays at 9:30; 1948–49, beginning a 30m daytime series, NBC, Mondays at 12:30; 1949–50, NBC, 30m, Mondays at 1; 1950–51,

NBC, 30m, Saturdays at 9:30 A.M.; 1954–55, NBC, 60m, Saturdays at 8:30; 1955–56, NBC, 45m, Mondays at 8:15. The *BSO* slots were sometimes taken in the summer months by Arthur Fiedler and his Boston Pops Orchestra (noted on the Blue in the 1936–38 seasons), which specialized in familiar semi-classics and light masterworks not usually heard in the regular season.

THE CADILLAC SYMPHONY ORCHESTRA, Bruno Walter, conductor. Dec. 24, 1933–May 5, 1935, Blue Network, 60m, Sundays at 8 Cadillac Motor Car Co.

THE CARBORUNDUM HOUR, Edward d'Anna, director; Francis Bowman, host. 1929–38, CBS, various timeslots for Carborundum Abrasives: 1929–30, 60m, Tuesdays at 7; 1930–35, 30m, Saturdays at 9; 1935–38, 30m, Saturdays at 7:30.

CARNEGIE HALL broadcasts, ABC, 30m, Sundays at 7:30, 1948–49; Tuesdays at 8, 1949–50. American Oil.

THE CASTORIA PROGRAM, Donald Voorhees, conductor. 1933–34, CBS, 30m, Wednesdays at 8:30. Violinist Albert Spalding and singer Conrad Thibault.

THE CHICAGO A CAPELLA CHOIR, Noble Cain, director. NBC, four seasons beginning in 1932: 1932–33, Blue Network, Sundays at 4; 1933–34, Red Network, Sundays at 2:30 for Hoover Vacuums; 1934–35, Blue Network, Tuesdays at 4:30; 1936–37, Blue Network, Thursdays at 5. All 30m.

THE CHICAGO CIVIC OPERA, the first regular opera company of the air, heard on KYW, the Westinghouse outlet in Chicago in Nov. 1921. *Chicago Opera* became a force over the next ten years with the refusal of the Metropolitan Opera to allow its programs to be aired. It was part of the first-year NBC schedule, 1926–27, heard on 22 outlets in a 45m Friday night timeslot at 10:30. In 1927 it moved to the Blue Network, where it ran on the following schedules: 1927–28, Tuesdays at 10; 1928–29, Wednesdays at 10; 1929–30, Saturdays at 10, all 60m sponsored by Baulkite. Also, 1931–32, 30m, Saturdays at 9. The company failed in 1932, and subsequent companies were formed in later years. See METROPOLITAN OPERA.

THE CHICAGO CIVIC ORCHESTRA, NBC: 1930–31, Blue Network, 60m, Saturdays at 10; 1931–32,

Red Network, 30m, Saturdays at 8. Also, *The Chicago Symphony Orchestra*, 1938, Blue Network, Saturdays at 9:15, Frederick Stock, conductor. Also, *The Chicago Women's Symphony Orchestra*, 1940–41, CBS, 30m, Sundays at 5.

THE CINCINNATI CONSERVATORY SYMPHONY, Alexander von Kreisler, conductor, for most of the run, all CBS: 1935–36, 60m, Saturdays at 11 A.M.; 1936–37, 90m, Fridays at 3; 1937–38, 30m, Fridays at 3 and 60m, Saturdays at 11 A.M.; 1938–41, 60m, Saturdays at 11 A.M. Also, brief runs 1941, 1946.

THE CLEVELAND SYMPHONY ORCHESTRA, Artur Rodzinski, conductor ca. 1932–43; Erich Leinsdorf thereafter. 1932–33, NBC, 60m, Sundays at 1:30; 1933–34, CBS, 120m, Saturdays at 2:30; 1935–36, NBC, 30m, Sundays at 4:30; 1936–38, Blue Network 60m, Wednesdays at 9; 1941–43, CBS, 60m, Saturdays at 5; 1943–47, Mutual, 60m, Sundays at 9 (1943–44), Saturdays at 6 (1945–47).

THE COLUMBIA SYMPHONY ORCHESTRA, Howard Barlow, conductor; Bernard Herrmann occasionally. Barlow arrived at CBS in 1927 and quickly enlarged the house band of 16 pieces to symphonic size, believing that symphony music could be scheduled as popular entertainment. 1929–30, 30m, Mondays at 10:30; otherwise heard irregularly. See also CONCERT BROADCASTS—EVERYBODY'S MUSIC.

THE CURTIS INSTITUTE MUSICALE, Fritz Reiner, director of a 90-piece orchestra. 1933–34, CBS, 45m, Thursdays at 3:45; 1934–38, CBS, 45m, Wednesdays at 4 or 4:15; 1938–40, CBS, 60m, Mondays at 3 or 4; 1940–41, NBC, 30m, Saturdays at 5:30; 1941–42, CBS, 30m, three a week at 4.

THE DETROIT SYMPHONY ORCHESTRA, Fritz Reiner and John Barbirolli, frequent conductors. 1944–45, Mutual, 60m, Saturdays at 8:30 for Reichold Chemicals; 1947, ABC, 60m, Sundays at 4 for Reichold; 1947–48, ABC, 60m, Sundays at 8 for *Music Digest*; 1948–49, ABC, 45m, Tuesdays at 9:45. See also THE FORD SUNDAY EVENING HOUR.

THE EASTMAN SCHOOL OF MUSIC SYMPHONY, conducted by Dr. Howard Hanson, director of the Eastman School at the University of Rochester. In the main, afternoon concerts emphasizing American works. 1932–42, NBC, Blue Network until 1938, Red thereafter: 1932–33, 45m, Thursdays at 4; 1933–35, 45m, Thursdays at 3:15; 1937–38, 30m, Thursdays at 9; 1938–39, 30m, Saturdays at 11:30 A.M.; 1940–42, 30m, Saturdays at noon.

THE EDWIN FRANKO GOLDMAN BAND, a large brass band that offered free summer concerts in New York's Central Park and other sites, many of these broadcast on network radio. Goldman, aided by a Guggenheim grant, never missed a performance from 1918 until 1955, and the band continued after his death under the direction of his son. Praised by critics for its musicianship, Goldman's band was said to be a "symphony orchestra in brass," and Goldman was considered the musical successor to John Philip Sousa. His summer concerts were aired by WEAF in 1925. The band was on hand for NBC's Nov. 15, 1926, inaugural broadcast and over the next 15 years was carried in the summer on all networks at one time or another.

EVERYBODY'S MUSIC, a series of 60m concerts by Howard Barlow and the Columbia Symphony Orchestra; not a broadcast of popular music, but a serious offering of classics. May 3, 1936–Oct. 17, 1937, CBS, Sundays at 2: also, May 15–Oct. 23, 1938, 60m, Sundays at 3.

THE GENERAL ELECTRIC CONCERT, with tenor Richard Crooks and orchestra. NBC, 1931–32, 30m, Sundays at 5:30; 1932–33, 30m, Sundays at 9. General Electric.

GENERAL MOTORS CONCERTS, heard in several formats on the two NBC networks between 1929 and 1937. 1929–31, Red, 30m, Mondays at 9:30, Frank Black, conductor. 1935–37, Red, 60m, Sundays at 10, with maestro Erno Rapee and such soloists as tenor Lauritz Melchior, violinists Erica Morini and Yehudi Menuhin, and sopranos Florence Easton, Lotte Lehmann, and Kirsten Flagstad. In April 1937 this series moved abruptly to the Blue Network, becoming *The General Motors Promenade Concerts*: it ran 60m, Sundays at 8 until June 1937, featuring male and female leads in shows with themes (such as a broadcast of Victor Herbert music with Rose Bampton and Jan Peerce). For the fall, GM announced a sensational new series, radio's first concert stock company, comprised of the biggest names of the day: Grace Moore, Helen Jepson, Maria Jeritza, Erna Sack, Richard Tauber,

Donald Dickson, Jussi Bjoerling, and Joseph Schmidt, with two, three, or more slated for each broadcast. Erno Rapee returned as maestro; John B. Kennedy told dramatic stories of science, and Milton Cross announced. Critics predicted backstage feuds and shivered at the expense while applauding GM for its courage. Whatever the reason, this imposing *General Motors Concert* ran only its initial 13 weeks, Oct. 3–Dec. 26, 1937, Blue Network, 60m, Sundays at 8, and the company was dissolved.

GREAT MOMENTS IN MUSIC, George Sebastian, conductor. A symphony orchestra with vocal soloists (Jan Peerce, Jean Tennyson, etc.). 1941–46, CBS, 30m, Wednesdays at 10.

THE HELEN TRAUBEL PROGRAM, early 1937, Blue Network, 30m, Sundays at 7.

THE HOOVER SENTINELS, 1933–35, NBC, 30m, Sundays at 5. Hoover Vacuums. Mme. Ernestine Schumann-Heink, vocalist.

THE INDIANAPOLIS SYMPHONY ORCHESTRA, Fabien Sevitzky, director. One of the newest groups in the nation (est. 1930), moving quickly to national prominence because of Sevitzky's ability to secure network radio contracts. Sevitzky (shortened from Koussevitzky to avoid confusion with his uncle, Serge Koussevitzky of the Boston Symphony) was a champion of American composers, and his programs reflected this. 1937–38, Mutual, 90m, Sundays at 9:30. Then on CBS: 1938–39, 60m, Wednesdays at 3; 1939–40, 30m, Wednesdays at 10:30; early 1941, 30m, Sundays at 10:30 A.M.; 1942–43, 30m, Thursdays at 3:30.

JACK FROST MELODY MOMENTS, a 30m symphonic series named for the sponsor. 1929–31, NBC, Thursdays at 9:30; Eugene Ormandy, conductor. 1931–34, Blue Network, Wednesdays at 8:30 (1931), Mondays at 9:30 (1932–34); Josef Pasternack, conductor.

THE LONGINES SYMPHONETTE, a series of time-honored classics, sponsored by "the world's most honored watch." Prerecorded, it played on many Mutual stations in nightly quarter-hours, ca. 1943–49. Also, 1949–57, CBS, 30m, Sundays at 2. Macklin Marrow, initial conductor; Mishel Piastro for most of the run. Frank Knight, announcer. *The Longines Choraliers* was a popular offshoot, heard

on CBS in various 30m timeslots, March 13, 1949–April 22, 1955.

THE LOS ANGELES SYMPHONY ORCHESTRA: 1946–47, Mutual, 30m, Saturdays at 4.

THE MAXWELL HOUSE HOUR, early Blue Network concert series, initially with tenor Richard Crooks; later with soprano Frieda Hempel. 1926–28, 60m, Thursdays at 9; 1928–32, 30m, Thursdays at 9:30, with maestro Donald Voorhees.

THE MINNEAPOLIS SYMPHONY ORCHESTRA, Eugene Ormandy, conductor. NBC, 1933–34, 30m, Sundays at 10:30; 1935–36, 30m, Thursdays at 11:30.

MOBILOIL CONCERT, Erno Rapee, conductor; James Melton, tenor, on the early shows. 1929–32, NBC, 30m, Wednesdays at 8 until 1930, at 8:30 until 1931, then at 9:30.

MUSIC AMERICA LOVES BEST, 1944–45, NBC, 30m, Saturdays, then Sundays, for RCA. This title was also used as a descriptive phrase on *The RCA Victor Show*, heard in various 30m Sunday slots on NBC, 1945–49, with baritone Robert Merrill.

THE NATIONAL SYMPHONY ORCHESTRA, early 60m series with Walter Damrosch, conductor. 1926–27, NBC, Saturdays at 9; 1927–28, Blue Network, Saturdays at 8; 1928–29, NBC, Saturdays at 8.

THE NBC STRING SYMPHONY, a 30-piece group organized by Dr. Frank Black in 1933 and heard in summer concert runs most years until 1939–40, its first full season; 30m, Sundays at 2 through 1940–41.

THE NBC SYMPHONY ORCHESTRA, Arturo Toscanini, conductor, Nov. 13, 1937–April 4, 1954. Toscanini's personal appearances were usually limited to fewer than 20 concerts per season, beginning Christmas Day 1937. Artur Rodzinski, coconductor, 1938; Leopold Stokowski, coconductor, 1941–44. Among others who led during Toscanini's overall directorship were Pierre Monteux, Adrian Boult, Bernardino Molinari, George Szell, Fritz Reiner, Dimitri Mitropoulos, and Guido Cantelli.

Timeslots: 1937–38, Red Network, 90m, Saturdays at 10. 1938–40, Blue Network, 90m, then 60m, Saturdays at 10; 1940–41, Blue, 85m, Sundays at 9:35; 1941–42, Blue, 90m, Saturdays at 9, also 60m, Tuesdays at 9:30; 1942–43, 60m, Sundays at 5 on Blue and 45m, Saturdays at 2 on Red. With the breakup of NBC, the Symphony remained with the main NBC Network, as the Blue became ABC. 1943–46, 60m, Sundays at 5 for General Motors. 1946–47, 60m, Sundays at 5, sustained. 1947–53, Saturdays at 6:30 with timeslots varying from 60m to 90m, E. R. Squibb sponsoring 1950–52. Also, 60m, Mondays at 10, 1950–51. 1953–54, 60m, Sundays at 6:30 for Socony Oil. *Announcers*: Howard Claney; Ben Grauer for most of the run.

The NBC Symphony Orchestra was unique. As Thomas A. DeLong noted, "never before or since has a radio network or corporate entity created an orchestra of this calibre or size." That it was a tribute to one man made it all the more remarkable.

It was created for Toscanini in a successful attempt by NBC's David Sarnoff to draw the world-famed maestro out of retirement in his native Italy. Toscanini had left his post as head of the New York Philharmonic in 1936. Sarnoff's emissary concluded a deal that paid Toscanini $40,000 (tax-free, as NBC agreed to pick up the tax bill as well) for ten broadcasts with a world-class orchestra of the maestro's own choosing, no limit on expenses. Maestro Artur Rodzinski of the Cleveland Symphony Orchestra was engaged to select and train the musicians and to serve as conductor for half of the season.

The news of Toscanini's return created a sensation in radio circles. He was widely believed to be the world's greatest living musician, one whose interpretations of the old masters (Brahms, Beethoven, Mozart, Verdi, and Wagner) were described by critics in such superlatives as "the purest and noblest of all time." From that first broadcast, the press covered the *NBC Symphony* as a musical event rather than a radio broadcast. The networks's large studio, 8-H, seated 1,200 people, and there were reports of ticket bootlegging for as much as $100.

This became Toscanini's orchestra: here he remained for 17 seasons, still conducting in his 87th year. He permitted no clocks in his studio, and his performance often ran over the allotted time. Noted *Radio Guide*: "Toscanini and President Roosevelt are the two people who can run long or short without being cut off by the networks."

A disagreement with NBC in 1941 almost led to his resignation. He withheld his services, and Leo-pold Stokowski took his place. But Sarnoff suggested that Toscanini lead the orchestra in a series of concerts to benefit the war bond drive, and by the beginning of the 1942–43 season he had returned as director. He and Stokowski split the season, but further disagreements resulted in Stokowski's departure in 1944. Toscanini remained at the helm thereafter, retiring in April 1954, three years before his death.

NEW FRIENDS OF MUSIC, 1938–41, Blue Network, 60m, Sundays at 6. Initially a showcase for small groups; later, a 40-piece orchestra under the direction of Fritz Stiedry.

THE NEW YORK PHILHARMONIC ORCHESTRA, the main CBS counter to the strong NBC concert schedule: Arturo Toscanini, conductor in the early radio years, sharing the schedule at one point with Willem Mengelberg; John Barbirolli, conductor upon Toscanini's retirement in 1936; Artur Rodzinski, conductor ca. 1942–47. Guest conductors: Bruno Walter (1932–35), Otto Klemperer (1935–36).

Timeslots: (all CBS): 1927–29, 120m, Thursdays at 8:30; 1930–50, 120m, later 90m, Sundays at 3, sponsored by U.S. Rubber 1943–47, Socony Oil 1948–49; 1950–51, 90m, Sundays at 1; 1951–63, 90m, Sundays at 2:30, sponsored by Willys Motors 1952–53.

Under Toscanini in the early 1930s, the New York Philharmonic achieved a distinct sound, drawing praise from critics and the maestro's peers. Stokowski called him the "supreme master of all conductors." Britain's John Barbirolli infused the orchestra with his personality and style upon assuming the baton in 1936. Noted soloists included violinist Efrem Zimbalist, soprano Kirsten Flagstad, and pianists Jose Iturbi, Josef Hoffman, and Artur Rubinstein. Deems Taylor was commentator on many shows.

The Philharmonic also aired a long-running series of *Children's Concerts*, Saturdays at 11 A.M., ca. 1931–37. Ernest Schelling conducted until 1935; Rudolph Ganz thereafter.

THE OKLAHOMA CITY SYMPHONY ORCHESTRA, 1949–56, Mutual, various times.

THE OLD COMPANY PROGRAM, 1928–29, NBC, 30m, Sundays at 7, starring Reinald Werrenrath for Old Company Coal. Also, 1931–32, NBC, 15m, Sundays at 1:45 with conductor William Wirges.

OPERA CONCERT, 1949–52, Mutual, 30m, 45m, and 60m, Sundays at 9; in-house maestro Sylvan Levin.

OPERA GUILD BROADCASTS, 1934–35, NBC, 60m, Sundays at 8, with commentary by Deems Taylor; Chase and Sanborn, sponsors.

THE PHILADELPHIA SYMPHONY ORCHESTRA, Leopold Stokowski, conductor, 1931–35; Eugene Ormandy, 1935–36; Stokowski and Ormandy in a shared program, 1937–38; Ormandy made permanent director in 1938.

Timeslots: 1931, CBS, 15m, Sundays; 1932–33, CBS, 30m, Tuesdays at 10; 1933–34, CBS, 15m, six nights a week at 9 for Chesterfield; also 1933–34, CBS, 90m, Fridays at 2:30; 1936–37, CBS, 30m, Fridays at 10 for American Banks; 1937–38, Blue Network, 60m, Mondays at 9 for American Banks; 1939–40, CBS, 60m, Saturdays at 11 A.M., *PSO Children's Concerts*; 1945–48, CBS, 60m, Saturdays at 5; 1953–57, CBS, Saturdays, various lengths and timeslots.

Also prominent were the orchestra's seasonal *Robin Hood Dell Concerts*, heard on Mutual in the summer of 1938 and on the Blue Network in 1939. The broadcasts originated from a wooded amphitheater in Fairmount Park on the Schuylkill River, where the natural surroundings were said to be acoustically superb.

RADIO CITY MUSIC HALL OF THE AIR, Erno Rapee, conductor. 1932–42, Blue Network, 60m, Sundays, usually at noon, 12:15, or 12:30. At various times the series featured tenor Jan Peerce, baritone Robert Weede, and a Stradivarius string quartet. The fare was rich, sometimes daring: Rapee's seven-symphony Sibelius cycle in 1937 was described as a "marathonic undertaking never attempted previously in radio."

RCA RADIOTRONS, 1926–27, Blue Network, 60m, Wednesdays at 9; an early forum for singer John Charles Thomas.

THE RCA VICTOR HOUR, 1927–28, Blue Network, 60m, Fridays at 10, with tenor John McCormack. Also 1930–31, NBC, 30m, Sundays at 7:30.

THE ROCHESTER CIVIC ORCHESTRA, Guy Fraser Harrison, director. A Blue Network mainstay for ten seasons: 1929–31, 30m, Mondays at 10; 1933–40, many afternoon and evening timeslots, some concurrent; 1941–42, 30m, Mondays at 7:30.

THE ROCHESTER PHILHARMONIC ORCHESTRA, scattered seasons, Blue Network: 1929–30, 60m, Fridays at 3:15; 1935–37, 30m, then 60m, Thursdays at 8:30; 1939–41, 30m, Thursdays at 9; 1941–42, 30m, Wednesdays at 10, with singers Conrad Thibault and Vivian Della Chiesa. Jose Iturbi became the director in 1936.

ROXY SYMPHONIC CONCERT, 1928–31, Blue Network, 60m, Sundays at 2 (1928–30), then at 11 (1930–31); 1931–32, CBS, 30m, Sundays at 9 with the Fred Waring Orchestra.

THE ST. LOUIS SYMPHONY ORCHESTRA, 1931–32, CBS, 30m, Sundays at midnight; 1934–35, NBC, 60m, Mondays at 11:30.

SINFONIETTA, Alfred Wallenstein, conductor of a small symphony orchestra, originally 16 and later 30 pieces. According to *Radio Guide*, Wallenstein "discovered an immense literature for small ensembles" and held the Mutual air with this series for a decade, 1935–45; various evenings, mostly 30m timeslots.

THE SONORA HOUR, 1928, CBS, 60m, Thursdays at 9; 1929, 30m, Thursdays at 9:30. Sonora Radios.

THE SQUIBB GOLDEN TREASURY OF SONG, 1940–41, CBS, 15m, five a week at 3:15, with tenor Jan Peerce. 1941–42, 15m, five a week at 6:30, with Frank Parker. E. R. Squibb, sponsor.

STEEL HORIZONS, 1944–45, Mutual, 30m, Sundays at 9. Allegheny Steel.

THE STRADIVARI ORCHESTRA, 1943–45, NBC, 30m, Sundays at 12:30, with Paul Lavalle. Also: March–May 1946, ABC; Oct.–Dec. 1946, CBS.

SYMPHONIC STRINGS, 1937–43, Mutual, various evening timeslots, Alfred Wallenstein, conductor.

TREASURE HOUR OF SONG, 1942–47, Mutual, various evening timeslots. Josephine Tuminia, coloratura soprano, featured with the Alfred Antonini Orchestra, 1942; also, Licia Albanese. Solid timeslot, 30m, Thursdays at 9:30, 1944–47, sponsored by Conti.

UNITED STATES MILITARY BANDS: United States Army Band heard in brief runs from the earliest days of the networks; noted on CBS in 1938, conducted by Capt. Thomas d'Arcy. Full seasons beginning 1940, Blue Network, through 1943;

Mutual, 1942–43; NBC, 1952–53; ABC, 1953–55; also, NBC, 1953–54; Mutual, 1955–56; ABC, 1955–56. Often heard under the titles *Musical Express* or *Front and Center*.

United States Marine Bands: Blue Network, 1940–41; CBS and NBC, 1941–42; Blue, 1942–43; NBC, 1943–44; NBC, 1950–51; ABC, 1951–56; also NBC, 1952–54; Mutual, 1954–56.

United States Navy Bands: Blue and Mutual Networks, 1940–41; Mutual, 1941–42; NBC, 1943–44; ABC, 1949–56.

THE VINCE PROGRAM, another early sponsor-named series, begun on the Blue Network Oct. 11, 1933, as a forum for singer John McCormack, 30m, Wednesdays at 9:30, with William Daly's Orchestra. For the 1935–36 season John Charles Thomas was added; 30m, heard Wednesdays at 9, later at 10; it became known as *Our Home on the Range*, then as *John Charles Thomas and His Neighbors*. Frank Tours led the orchestra. Final broadcast: April 15, 1936.

CONFESSION, crime drama anthology.

BROADCAST HISTORY: July 5–Sept. 13, 1953, NBC. 30m, Sundays at 9:30. **CAST:** Hollywood radio character actors including Paul Frees, Virginia Christine, Herb Butterfield, Jonathan Hole, Don Diamond, Jack Moyles, Peter Leeds, Parley Baer, Barney Phillips, etc. **ANNOUNCER:** John Wald. **INTERMISSION COMMENTATOR:** Richard McGee, director of the California Department of Corrections. **PRODUCERS:** Warren Lewis, Homer Canfield. **DIRECTOR:** Homer Canfield.

Confession had a texture and sound not unlike *Dragnet*: indeed, the *Dragnet* influence was evident throughout. These were true stories of crime and punishment, the most obvious difference that *Dragnet* began with the crime while *Confession* unfolded in reverse order, from the end. *Confession* was less noisy: its theme was played on a single piano, but there was still the deadpan dialogue, the thief or killer giving his confession with an air of resignation and defeat. The criminal thus became a stream-of-consciousness narrator, with the action frequently cutting away into drama. Names were changed "to protect the legal rights of the subject," and a capsule summary at the end told the results of the trial, "in the Superior Court, State of California, in and for the Country of Los Angeles."

CONSTANCE BENNETT CALLS ON YOU, talk, Hollywood news, interviews.

BROADCAST HISTORY: May 21, 1945–March 15, 1946, ABC. 15m, weekdays at 1:15.

Film star Constance Bennett and announcer Bob Latting talked about "families, friends, world events, books, home, new hats, funny little things that happen to her and you." There was a "woman of the week" segment: in one show a New York dealer in pearls. Latting spent some time discussing Bennett's wardrobe, and Fridays were given to answering mail.

THE CONTINENTAL CELEBRITY CLUB, variety.

BROADCAST HISTORY: Dec. 8, 1945–June 29, 1946, CBS. 30m, Saturdays at 10:15. Continental Can Company. **CAST:** John Daly, host, Jackie Kelk, comic. Margaret Whiting, vocalist. Ray Bloch, orchestra. **DIRECTOR:** Marx Loeb.

Jackie Kelk, long known as Homer Brown on *The Aldrich Family*, delivered his lines in much the same voice here. His opening routines with host Daly (a well-known CBS Radio newsman) were cascades of one-liners. There were a couple of songs, an orchestra number, and a short drama built around such guests as Carole Landis and Bonita Granville.

CORRECTION, PLEASE, quiz show based on misinformation.

BROADCAST HISTORY: Sept. 25, 1943–Dec. 2, 1944, CBS. 30m, Saturdays at 8, then at 10:15. Tums.

June 15–Sept. 14, 1945, NBC. 30m, Fridays at 10. Ipana. **HOSTS:** Jim McWilliams, 1943–44; Jay C. Flippen, 1945.

Contestants from the studio audience were given $10 each, bid against each other to see who could spot mistakes in a series of questions, then bid again for a chance to correct the mistakes. Wrong answers were penalized; correct ones could increase bankrolls tenfold.

THE COTY PLAYGIRL, music and song.

BROADCAST HISTORY: March 8–May 31, 1931, CBS. 15m, Sundays at 9. Coty Cosmetics. **STAR:**

Irene Bordoni as the Coty Playgirl. **ORCHESTRA**: Eugene Ormandy.

Irene Bordoni had a brief air career, its nostalgic value greater than its importance. Her primary career was on the musical stage, where she starred in saucy revues from the mid-teens through the '30s. Born in France in 1895, she hit her pinnacle in the stage show *Paris*, which was, according to theater historian Gerald Bordman, "as succinct, sophisticated, and naughty as its title and star could make it."

On the air, she sang a few songs and spoke in broken English that the audience found charming. She frequently referred to a small notebook for the English translations of song lyrics, but on one occasion she lost her place and thumbed the book for 18 frustrating seconds while the music droned on. Her on-air reaction—"Zis ees terrible!"—was simply more endearing to her fans, who remembered her for years after her short radio series ended. She died in 1953.

THE COUNT OF MONTE CRISTO, adventure drama, based on the novel by Alexandre Dumas.

BROADCAST HISTORY: 1944–45, Don Lee Network, West Coast only. Tuesday nights.

Dec. 19, 1946–June 26, 1947, Mutual. 30m, Thursdays at 8:30.

1947–48, Mutual. Summers only.

June 12, 1949–Jan. 1, 1952, Mutual. 30m, Sundays at 9 until mid-Sept. 1949, then various timeslots.

1944 WEST COAST RUN: CAST: Carleton Young as Edmond Dantes, the enigmatic and swashbuckling Count of Monte Cristo. Anne Stone as the Count's friend and conspirator, the lovely Marie Duchene. Ferdinand Munier as Rene, the Count's faithful manservant and ardent admirer. Supporting players: Joseph Kearns, Barbara Lee, Vic Rodman, Paul Marion, etc. **ANNOUNCER:** Rod O'Connor. **DIRECTOR:** Thomas Freebairn-Smith.

MUTUAL RUN: CAST: Young as Dantes. Parley Baer as Rene. Support from William Conrad, Jay Novello, Virginia Gregg, Howard McNear, John Dehner, etc. **DIRECTOR:** Jaime del Valle.

The weekly stories followed Edmond Dantes, who escaped from an infamous French prison in the early post-Napoleonic era and rose to become one of literature's great crusaders for justice. Originally imprisoned on a false charge of treason, Dantes became established as the count of the island of Monte Cristo, and from this home base he poured reprisals upon the heads of his evil and hated enemies.

COUNTERSPY, espionage adventure drama.

BROADCAST HISTORY: May 18, 1942–Aug. 31, 1950, Blue Network/ABC. Many 30m timeslots including Mondays at 9 for Mail Pouch Tobacco, 1942–44; Wednesdays at 8:30 for Mail Pouch, early 1945; Wednesdays at 10 for Pharmacraft, 1945; Sundays at 5:30 for Schutter Candy, 1946–48; Tuesdays and Thursdays at 7:30 for Pepsi Cola, 1949–50.

Oct. 13, 1950–Sept. 24, 1953, NBC. 30m, Fridays at 9:30, then Sundays at 5, 1950–51; Thursdays at 9:30, 1951–52; Sundays at 5:30, 1952–53; Thursdays at 9, mid-1953. Gulf Oil, 1951–53.

Oct. 5, 1953–Nov. 29, 1957, Mutual. 30m, Mondays at 8:30, 1953; Sundays at 4, early 1954; Fridays at 8, 1954–57. Multiple sponsorships.

CAST: Don MacLaughlin as David Harding, chief of "United States Counterspies," who were "especially appointed to investigate and combat the enemies of our country, both at home and abroad." Mandel Kramer as Peters, his assistant. Supporting roles by New York radio actors. **ANNOUNCERS:** Roger Krupp, Bob Shepherd, etc. **CREATOR-PRODUCER:** Phillips H. Lord. **DIRECTORS:** Bill Sweets, Marx Loeb, Leonard Bass, Robert Steen, Victor Seydel. **WRITERS:** Milton J. Kramer, Stanley Niss, Emile C. Tepperman, etc. **SOUND EFFECTS:** Joe Cabbibo, Walt Gustafson, Harry Nelson.

The plots on *Counterspy* were exactly what the title implies. In the beginning, this meant counterespionage against Germany's Gestapo and Japan's Black Dragon. The approach was slightly above the juvenile. Perhaps one reason for its durability was its reputation for upstaging the news. *The Case of the Missing Soldier* (Oct. 24, 1945) related the cruel rackets feeding on the families of dead war heroes just two days before a sensational arrest in a real such case. The series also beat by two days the arrest of "the unchallenged Mata Hari of World War II," a woman whose photographic memory was used for espionage.

After the war, the activities of agent David

Harding and his counterspies were expanded, with the focus more generic: it became much the same kind of show as *This Is Your FBI* and *The FBI in Peace and War*. For years the opening remained basically the same: *Washington calling David Harding, counterspy!... Washington calling David Harding, counterspy!* Then, after a frantic burst of teletype activity: *Harding, counterspy, calling Washington!* and the theme up full.

COUNTY FAIR, audience game show.

BROADCAST HISTORY: July 10–Nov. 27, 1945, Blue Network. 30m, Tuesdays at 7:30. Borden's Milk.

Dec. 8, 1945–April 1, 1950, CBS. Various 30m timeslots, notably Saturdays at 1:30, Borden's Milk.

HOST: Jack Bailey; later Win Elliot. **HOST ASSISTANTS:** Larry Keating, Lois January. **ANNOUNCER:** Lee Vines. **PRODUCER:** Bill Gannett.

The motif of *County Fair* was a stroll down a fair midway, where players would find everything from a dart game to apple-ducking and a wheel of fortune. A "rollicking calliope" provided the background, and games were staged between celebrity guests and the audience.

COUNTY SEAT, serial drama.

BROADCAST HISTORY: Oct. 27, 1938–Aug. 26, 1939, CBS. 15m, five a week at 7 until April then 30m, Saturdays at 7:30. **CAST:** Ray Collins as Doc Will Hackett, a town philosopher with feet of clay who owned a drugstore in the little hamlet of Northbury. Cliff Carpenter as Jerry Whipple, his wisecracking nephew, a high school student often in love. Charme Allen as Sarah Whipple, Jerry's mother, Will's sister and a widow. Elaine Kent as Lois Johnson, Jerry's would-be girlfriend, who kept Jerry running while flirting with his fresh and sassy rival Billy Moorehead. Jackie Jordan as Billy. Lucille Meredith as Laura Paige, a young widow and town councilwoman. Guy Repp as Dr. Abernathy. Luis Van Rooten as George Priestly, the high school chemistry teacher with the mysterious past. **DIRECTOR:** Norman Corwin. **WRITER:** Milton Geiger.

County Seat was notable for the early Norman Corwin appearance as director. The serial was set in a town of 5,000 people that might be anywhere. It had a Main Street, library, school, and college, "just around the bend of the river." It was 60 miles from "the big city." The hero, Doc Hackett, had a sharp wit "whetted in banter."

THE COUPLE NEXT DOOR, serialized comedy-drama.

BROADCAST HISTORY: 1935–37, WGN, Chicago, for the Holland Furnace Company. Also: Mutual Network run, April 12–Sept. 16, 1937, 15m weekday continuation; Procter & Gamble for Oxydol. **CAST:** Olan Soulé and Elinor Harriot as Tom and Dorothy Wright. **ANNOUNCERS:** Jack Brinkley (1936), Pierre Andre, 1937. **THEME:** *Love Nest*.

Dec. 30, 1957–Nov. 25, 1960, CBS. 15m, weekdays. **CAST:** Peg Lynch and Alan Bunce as the unnamed married leads. Margaret Hamilton as Aunt Effie. **WRITER:** Peg Lynch.

The revival of *The Couple Next Door* in 1957 had Peg Lynch and Alan Bunce playing the same characters they had created on *Ethel and Albert*. But the characters referred to each other only as "dear" and were never named.

THE COURT OF HUMAN RELATIONS, dramatized human interest.

BROADCAST HISTORY: Jan. 1–April 22, 1934, NBC. 45m, Mondays at 7, then Sundays at 7.

May 4, 1934–Aug. 30, 1935, CBS. 30m, Fridays at 8:30

Sept. 6, 1935–May 26, 1938, NBC. 30m, Fridays at 9:30.

Oct. 9, 1938–Jan. 1, 1939, Mutual. 30m, Sundays at 4:30.

CAST: Percy Hemus as "the Judge." Character roles enacted by top New York radio actors including Lucille Wall (usually cast as a wronged wife or deserted sweetheart), Helene Dumas (heartbreaker roles), Florence Baker (expert screamer), Rita Vale, Hanley Stafford, Wilmer Walter, Vera Allen, Alice Reinheart, Ned Wever, Betty Worth, etc. **ANNOUNCERS:** Charles O'Connor, Paul Douglas (ca. 1935). **MUSIC:** Arnold Johnson. **WRITER-PRODUCER-DIRECTOR:** William Sweets.

The Court of Human Relations, sponsored by *True Story* magazine, presented real-life legal dramas, with the audience challenged to render verdicts. The stories came from current issues of the magazine.

THE COURT OF MISSING HEIRS, true human interest drama; also known as *The Board of Missing Heirs* and *Are You a Missing Heir?*

BROADCAST HISTORY: Oct. 11, 1937–July 10, 1938, CBS regional. Heard Mondays in the Midwest for Skelly Oil. Originally from Chicago.

Dec. 19, 1939–Sept. 29, 1942, CBS. 30m, Tuesdays at 8:30 until mid-1940, then Tuesdays at 8. Ironized Yeast.

March 31–June 9, 1946, ABC. 30m, Sundays at 5, then at 4. Also, Jan. 26–April 6, 1947, Sundays at 6, then at 7.

CAST: Anthology roles by New York radio actors including Jeanette Nolan, Everett Sloane, Kenny Delmar, Carl Frank, etc. James Marshall, narrator, 1947. MUSIC: Rosa Rio, organ. CREATOR: James Waters. PRODUCER: Alfred Shebel. DIRECTOR: John Loveton, Charles Harrell, 1947. WRITER: Ira Marion, 1947.

The Court of Missing Heirs was created as a book manuscript by young lawyer James Waters. When no publisher would take it, Waters brought it to radio.

Waters had long found the stories of probate cases more interesting than the law involved in settling them. His cases were heavily dramatized, the stories unfolding almost in a *March of Time* style. In reviewing it, *Time* magazine pegged its target audience as that "which succumbs to bank night and sweepstakes tickets and dreams of unforeseen inheritances." People everywhere imagined themselves as missing heirs.

Two cases were dramatized each week. By the beginning of his third show, Waters had found his first heir, the nephew of a recluse who had died leaving $18,000 in the bank. The show took off from there. Using an urgent-sounding hook in the opening signature (*Are you the heir to $10,000?*), Waters soon found a sizable audience. Skelly, always quick with premium tie-ins (see THE AIR ADVENTURES OF JIMMIE ALLEN), published a *Court of Missing Heirs* bulletin, giving details of open cases: less than two months into the show, *Time* reported that a print order of 500,000 copies had been exhausted in one day.

During the run, Waters and his partner Alfred

Shebel found more than 150 heirs worth more than $800,000. Most had no idea they were anyone's heir; many were destitute; some were found just as deadlines were about to expire for filing their claims. The show employed five investigators who combed through probate records of more than 3,000 county courts. Waters and company took no fees for finding the heirs, profiting only by what the show earned on the air. Fifty years after its premiere, the basic idea was being used as part of the TV show *Unsolved Mysteries.*

COUSIN WILLIE, situation comedy.

BROADCAST HISTORY: July 7–Sept. 29, 1953, NBC. 30m, Tuesdays at 9:30. CAST: Bill Idelson as Willard O. Knotts, "Cousin Willie" to the Sample family, who came from Milwaukee to "visit" his California relatives and showed little inclination to leave. Marvin Miller as Marvin Sample. Patricia Dunlap as Fran Sample. Dawn Bender and Stuffy Singer as Susie and Sandy Sample. Bob Sweeney, Frank Nelson, Les Tremayne, and others from Hollywood's Radio Row. ANNOUNCER: Jimmy Wallington. ORCHESTRA: Robert Armbruster. PRODUCERS-DIRECTOR: Homer Canfield. WRITERS: Doris and Frank Hursley.

CREEPS BY NIGHT, horror melodrama.

BROADCAST HISTORY: Feb. 15–Aug. 15, 1944, Blue Network. 30m, Tuesdays at 10:30. Heard from California until May 23, then from New York. CAST: Boris Karloff, host, narrator, and star from Hollywood, with Peter Lorre occasional star. Unnamed host, known only as "Dr. X," from New York. New York radio personnel: Jackson Beck, Ed Begley, Mary Patton, Juano Hernandez, Everett Sloane, Abby Lewis, etc. MUSIC: Albert Sack, Joseph Stopak, etc. PRODUCER: Robert Maxwell. DIRECTOR: Dave Drummond.

THE CRESTA BLANCA CARNIVAL OF MUSIC, also known as *The Carnival of Musical Contrasts* because of the mix of classical, popular, and jazz music it offered.

BROADCAST HISTORY: Oct. 14, 1942–April 7, 1943, Mutual. 45m, Wednesdays at 9:15. CAST: Comedian Jack Pearl, straight man Cliff Hall. ORCHESTRA: Morton Gould.

April 14, 1943–May 30, 1944, CBS. 30m, Wednesdays at 10:30 until May 1944, then Tuesdays at 9:30. Cresta Blanca Wines. HOST: Frank Gallop. MUSICAL COMMENTATOR: Eric Hatch. ORCHESTRA: Morton Gould.

The memorable commercials on *Cresta Blanca Carnival* began with a cascade of music, indicating a verbal pouring of wine. Then, in a catchy jingle out of an echo chamber, with each letter punctuated by a plunking violin: *C-R-E-S-T-A B-L-A-N-C-A . . . Cresta Blanca!*

THE CRESTA BLANCA HOLLYWOOD PLAYERS, dramatic Hollywood fare, with a company of film stars in rotating roles.

BROADCAST HISTORY: Sept. 3, 1946–Feb. 26, 1947, CBS. 30m, Tuesdays at 9:30 until Dec., then Wednesdays at 10. Cresta Blanca Wines. CAST: Claudette Colbert, Joseph Cotten, Bette Davis, Joan Fontaine, John Garfield, Paulette Goddard, Gene Kelly, and Gregory Peck in a standing rep company. MUSIC: Bernard Katz.

"Each week a great star, each week a great story" was the calling card of *Hollywood Players.* It offered such plays as *Golden Boy,* by Clifford Odets, starring John Garfield; *Elizabeth the Queen,* with Bette Davis; and *Fifth Avenue Girl,* with Paulette Goddard. For Christmas 1946 the sponsor pulled out the stops and used up four male leads (Garfield, Kelly, Cotten, and Peck) in support of starlet Janet Leigh, who was making her radio debut. The series might have had a longer run but for the glut of similar Hollywood shows then on the networks.

CRIME AND PETER CHAMBERS, detective drama, based on the novels of Henry Kane.

BROADCAST HISTORY: April 6–Sept. 7, 1954, NBC. 30m, Tuesdays at 9:30. CAST: Dane Clark as Peter Chambers, "a private investigator, duly licensed and duly sworn." Bill Zuckert as Lt. Parker. Transcribed in New York with support by Evelyn Varden, Patricia Wheel, Roger DeKoven, Bryna Raeburn, William Griffis, Elaine Rost, Leon Janney, Fran Carlon, Everett Sloane, Lesley Woods, Edgar Stehli, Lawson Zerbe, etc. CREATOR-PRODUCER-WRITER: Henry Kane. DIRECTOR: Fred Weihe.

Peter Chambers was an undistinguished half-hour, filled with glib dialogue that played into Dane Clark's image as a screen tough guy.

THE CRIME CASES OF WARDEN LAWES, prison melodrama.

BROADCAST HISTORY: Oct. 20, 1946–Sept. 23, 1947, Mutual. 15m, Sundays at 1, then at 2; Tuesdays at 8 beginning in April 1947. Triamount, Clipper Craft Clothes. ANNOUNCER: Cy Harrice. PRODUCER: Bernard J. Prockter. DIRECTOR: Arnold Michaelis. WRITER: Max Ehrlich.

Crime Cases dramatized stories from the files of Lewis E. Lawes, former warden at Sing Sing Prison. It followed and was a shadow of Lawes's trailblazing *Twenty Thousand Years in Sing Sing,* a radio show that spanned almost the entire '30s, and a book of the same name.

CRIME CLASSICS, historical crime drama with witty undertone.

BROADCAST HISTORY: Audition disc, Dec. 3, 1952.

June 15, 1953–June 30, 1954, CBS. 30m, Monday at 8 until Sept., then Wednesday at 9:30. CAST: Lou Merrill as the narrator, Thomas Hyland, "connoisseur of crime, student of violence, and teller of murders." Hollywood radio regulars in anthology roles: Mary Jane Croft, Herb Butterfield, Bill Johnstone, Ben Wright, Paula Winslowe, Jeanette Nolan, Betty Harford, Jack Kruschen, Irene Tedrow, John Dehner, Sam Edwards, Lillian Buyeff, Barney Phillips, Norma Varden, Alec Harford, etc. ANNOUNCERS: Bob LeMond, Roy Rowan. MUSIC: Bernard Herrmann. CREATOR-PRODUCER-DIRECTOR: Elliott Lewis. WRITERS: Morton Fine, David Friedkin.

Crime Classics grew out of a long-standing and deep interest of actor-director Elliott Lewis in history's great murder cases. Lewis had compiled an extensive library of true crime cases, often primary source material dating from the 17th century. He decided to re-create not only the facts of the crimes but also the times in which they had occurred. This would encompass the sounds of an Edinburgh street in the 1830s as well as the dialects, the attitudes, and the way people thought in that distant time.

Writers Morton Fine and David Friedkin

would dramatize lightly: their routine (as described to *Radio Life*) was more a matter of discussion than writing. With Lewis, they would comb through the original periodicals, seldom rewriting but making "verbal revisions" as they went. Once they got an outline down, the scripting was easy. They took little literary license, staying with the facts while creating a humorous edge to the narratives. It wasn't enough to make light of murder, said *Radio Life*: "just enough to let a breath of fresh air enter their tale-of-horror scripts."

In fact, the humor was extraordinary. The narrator, Thomas Hyland, was played absolutely deadpan by Lou Merrill. Over the sound of rainfall came his droll voice. "That's the way it sounded when it rained, because the room was just below gutter level, and the rainwater rushed by the room's only window, and many lodgers caught cold in this room. *They* were lucky. Many other lodgers wound up on dissecting tables. *They* were murdered, by Mr. Burke, who smothered, and by Mr. Hare, who held. So tonight, my report to you, *If a Body Needs a Body, Just Call Burke and Hare*." Other stories had similar titles: *John Hayes, His Head, and How They Were Parted; The Younger Brothers—Why Some of Them Grew No Older*; and *Good Evening, My Name Is Jack the Ripper*.

The music also contributed greatly to the show's period flavor. Bernard Herrmann caught precisely the right mood, usually employing only one or two instruments in a given play. The stories spanned the ages, going back as far as A.D. 62 for *Your Loving Son, Nero*, and the many amusing attempts by the Roman emperor to murder his mother. The series at one point ran back-to-back with another exceptional Lewis anthology, *On Stage*. On Dec. 9, 1953, Lewis gave in to the inevitable urge to link them by offering *The Assassination of Abraham Lincoln* on *Crime Classics* and the play that Lincoln was watching at Ford's Theater, *Our American Cousin*, on *On Stage*. This was a mistake, Lewis admitted years later: *Our American Cousin* was dull beyond salvation, and it earned him the only rebuke he ever received from CBS chief William Paley. The next morning there was a note on his desk. It said: "Interesting idea. Don't do it again."

CRIME CLUB, murder-mystery anthology, based on and featuring some of the stories in the Doubleday Crime Club novel imprint.

BROADCAST HISTORY: Dec. 2, 1946–Oct. 16, 1947, Mutual. 30m, Mondays at 8 through Dec., then Thursdays at 10; also heard Wednesdays and Sundays. **CAST:** Barry Thomson as the "librarian" of the Crime Club, host of the series. **PRODUCER-DIRECTOR:** Roger Bower.

Sample opening: "Yes, this is the *Crime Club* . . . I'm the librarian. *Silent Witness*? Yes, we have that *Crime Club* story for you. Come right over." Then the "reader" (listener) would arrive, and the "librarian" would put him in "the easy chair by the window." The book was opened, and the story began.

An earlier series, *The Eno Crime Club*, was also composed in part from Crime Club novels.

CRIME DOCTOR, crime drama.

BROADCAST HISTORY: Aug. 4, 1940–Oct. 19, 1947, CBS. 30m, Sundays at 8:30. Philip Morris. **CAST:** Ray Collins as Dr. Benjamin Ordway, criminal psychologist; House Jameson, John McIntire, Hugh Marlowe, Brian Donlevy and Everett Sloane also as Ordway. Walter Greaza as Inspector Ross. Jeanette Nolan, Edith Arnold, Elspeth Eric, etc: many radio regulars of both New York and Hollywood. **ANNOUNCER:** Ken Roberts. **PRODUCER-WRITER:** Max Marcin. **DIRECTORS:** Paul Monroe, Jack Johnstone, etc. **SOUND EFFECTS:** Al Binnie, Jimmy Dwan, Al Hogan, Jerry McCarty, Charles Range, etc.

Dr. Benjamin Ordway, the hero of *Crime Doctor*, was one of radio's classic amnesia cases. Originally a criminal himself, he lost his memory after a blow on the head. With the help of a kind doctor, he built a new life and a new identity, studying medicine and eventually going into psychiatry. When Dr. Ordway regained his memory, his new life was complete: he decided to specialize in criminal psychology because of his understanding of the criminal mind.

Early in the series, Ordway was appointed to the parole board, listening to the pleas of convicts who appeared before him. Each show explored a different case, and the fate of the prisoner was decided by a "jury" assembled from the studio audience. The jury was evenly divided between men and women: the prisoners were granted release on a two-to-one margin, it was said, because women jurors tended to vote in their favor.

By the mid-1940s the format had changed: Ordway had retired from public service and operated out of his home, called in by police for special cases. By 1945 his appearance was often delayed until the second act, when he appeared to trap a murderer whose motive and crime had been dramatized in the first half. The killer was known to listeners throughout: the challenge was trying to guess how he would trap himself. The announcement at the end became a catchphrase: "Ladies and gentlemen, in exactly 57 seconds, Dr. Ordway will be back to tell you the piece of evidence overlooked by the suspect." The evidence was usually guilty knowledge, a trick of semantics, or some other old-hat device.

Ray Collins, John McIntire (through early 1942), and Hugh Marlowe (beginning in June 1942) were the leads from New York. Brian Donlevy took the role with the first West Coast broadcast, Nov. 8, 1942. Everett Sloane became Ordway Jan. 31, 1943. Edith Arnold played gun moll roles throughout the '40s: by one estimate, she had "bumped off more than 200 guys" on the air. Producer Max Marcin got unusual pre-title billing when, in 1945, the show was titled *Max Marcin's Crime Doctor*. In 1943 the radio show was the basis for a film, with Warner Baxter as Ordway. This became an inevitable series, with ten films produced in the '40s.

CRIME DOES NOT PAY, crime drama, based on the Metro Goldwyn Mayer short film series of the same name.

BROADCAST HISTORY: Transcribed at WMGM, the Metro Goldwyn Mayer station in New York, and originally aired there Oct. 10, 1949–Oct. 10, 1951 (including repeats).

Jan. 7–Dec. 22, 1952, Mutual. 30m, Mondays at 8:30.

CAST: Anthology roles by Donald Buka, John Loder, Joan Lorring, Everett Sloane, Lionel Stander, Ed Begley, etc.; even Bela Lugosi took one role. **MUSIC:** John Gart, composer-conductor. **DIRECTOR:** Marx B. Loeb. **WRITER:** Ira Marion.

This series had all the trademarks of transcribed drama, the "canned" sound that proponents of live radio found so objectionable. The stories were message pieces, in keeping with the title; the stars usually returned after the play for talks with the audience.

CRIME FIGHTERS, crime drama.

BROADCAST HISTORY: Nov. 7, 1949–Aug. 2, 1956, Mutual. Various 30m timeslots, with frequent schedule gaps. **CAST:** New York radio personnel including Raymond Edward Johnson, Abby Lewis, Allan Stevenson, Ian Martin, etc. **DIRECTOR:** Wynn Wright. **SOUND EFFECTS:** Joe Keating.

This was the story of policemen on all fronts: "master manhunters to match master criminals, shrewd experts in a thousand rackets, or simple men who study human nature—the city dicks who work in teams, county sheriffs covering lonely regions—federal men with a nation to police or scientists whose weapon is the laboratory."

CRIME FILES OF FLAMOND, psychological crime drama.

BROADCAST HISTORY: 1946–48, transcribed syndication.

Jan. 7–July 1, 1953, Mutual. 30m, Wednesdays at 8. General Mills, Lever Brothers, etc.

April 4, 1956–Feb. 27, 1957, Mutual. 30m, Sundays at 8:30, then at 8.

CAST: Arthur Wyatt as Flamond, "the most unusual detective in criminal history . . . famous psychologist and character analyst . . . who looks beyond laughter and tears, jealousy and greed, in order to discover the reason why." Myron "Mike" Wallace as Flamond, ca. 1948. Everett Clarke as Flamond, 1950s. Patricia Dunlap as his secretary, Sandra Lake (Wallace version). Muriel Bremner as the secretary in the 1950s.

The cases of *Flamond* were dramatized as "Card Files," with the psychologist-detective explaining the definitive clue in the last scene.

THE CROUPIER, tales of fate, sometimes with supernatural themes.

BROADCAST HISTORY: Sept. 21–Nov. 16, 1949, ABC. 30m, Wednesdays at 9:30. **CAST:** Hollywood character actors, Dan O'Herlihy, Howard Culver, Margaret Brayton, Paul Frees, etc, sometimes with such film star leads as Vincent Price. **MUSIC:** Rex Koury on organ. **DIRECTOR-WRITER:** Milton Geiger.

Radio's *Croupier* played strongly upon Webster's definition of the word—an attendant who collects and pays money at a gaming table. The host was omniscient, offering wry commentary on the movements of the characters. *I am the Croupier. . . . I spin the wheel of life. . . . Madame et monsieur, place your bets!* The wheel stops, the ball drops, and a long feminine sigh is heard. *Thirteen black!* . . . and the wondrous voice of the male player: *I've won!* It was billed as "man's eternal conflict with fate," moments of truth when life itself is sometimes at risk.

THE CUCKOO HOUR, comedy-variety; groundbreaking pioneer of satire.

BROADCAST HISTORY: Jan. 1, 1930–April 30, 1932, Blue Network. 30m, Wednesdays at 9:30 until fall 1930; Tuesdays at 10:30 until Feb. 1931; 15m, Saturdays at 10:15 thereafter.

March 21–Sept. 8, 1934, NBC. Blue Network, 30m, Wednesdays at 9 until June 13. Returned Red Network July 7, 15m, Saturdays at 10. AC Spark Plugs.

May 6, 1935–March 9, 1936, Blue Network. 30m and 60m versions, Mondays at 10.

CAST: Raymond Knight as himself, master of ceremonies at "Station KUKU." Knight also as Ambrose J. Weems, who ran the mythical radio station. Adelina Thomason as Mrs. George T. Pennyfeather, who offered absurd hints for the home with her "Personal Service for Perturbed People." Mary Hopple, Ward Wilson, Sallie Belle Cox, Carl Matthews, and singers Mary McCoy and Jack Arthur. Supporting players, 1934: James Stanley, Wilfred Pelletier. **MUSIC:** Robert Armbruster. **PRODUCER:** Joe Rines.

Raymond Knight was a radio original. He came to the medium with no prior experience in vaudeville or burlesque. Born in Salem, Mass., Knight studied law at Boston University and passed the bar in his home state. But drama had a greater appeal than law, and he returned to school to study acting and writing at Harvard's renowned 47 Workshop. Later he studied at Yale.

He thought of radio as a career while confined to a sickbed in 1928. A job at NBC followed, a time of writing continuity and commercials, and in late 1929 he was asked by NBC programmer Bertha Brainard if he could come up with a comedy show to fill a gap in the Blue Network schedule. She suggested "something cuckoo" and got *The Cuckoo Hour.*

Knight wrote the show, enacted the two main roles, and played "a lot of other disreputable characters" as well. His standard self-intro was as "the voice of the diaphragm, e-nun-ciating." He referred to his listeners as "fellow pixies," and his show mixed satire and the lampoon quite effectively for its day, paving the way for *Stoopnagle and Budd* a year later. Knight kidded almost everything that could be printed in a daily newspaper. He was dubbed radio's top wit in a 1932 newspaper poll.

Knight believed his lack of vaudeville experience to be one of the main reasons for his success: his comedy avoided most of the ancient gags that clogged the air in network radio's first decade. His rapid rise on *The Cuckoo Hour* led to new shows on NBC. *Making the Movies* (Blue Network, March 20–June 12, 1932, Sundays at 9:45 for Kelly-Springfield Tires) offered Knight's backstage view of such early film series as *Kelly Komedies, The Hazards of Helen,* and the *Kelly News Reels.* Then there were two quarter-hour sketch shows for Wheatena on NBC: *Wheatenaville Sketches* (Sept. 11, 1932–May 4, 1933, Sundays through Thursdays at 7:15) and *Billy Bachelor Sketches* (Sept. 25, 1933–April 20, 1934, weekdays at 7:15, with a second season Aug. 27, 1934–March 22, 1935, weekdays at 6:45). As Billy Bachelor, he played the editor of a small-town newspaper.

Knight tried his hand at playwrighting after his series left the air. He returned to radio as a director in the 1940s and died Feb. 12, 1953. His comedy was a major influence on Bob Elliott of *Bob and Ray* fame.

CURTAIN TIME, romantic drama.

BROADCAST HISTORY: July 22, 1938–March 31, 1939, Mutual. 30m, Fridays at 10. Kix Cereal.

July 4, 1945–June 27, 1946, ABC. 30m, Wednesdays at 9 until Oct. 1945, then Thursdays at 10. Mars Candy.

July 13, 1946–March 29, 1950, NBC. 30m, Saturdays at 7:30 until Oct. 1948, then Wednesdays at 10:30. Mars Candy. **1938–39: CAST:** Olan Soulé as the featured male lead in anthology roles, with various Chicago actresses (Betty Lou Gerson, Louise Fitch, etc.) as costars. **ANNOUNCERS:** Don Gordon, etc. **MUSIC:** Henry Weber. **DIRECTOR:** Blair Walliser. **1945–48: CAST:** Harry Elders and Nannette Sargent in anthology roles for much of the series. Chicago personnel including Betty Winkler, George Cisar, Beryl Vaughn, Sunda Love, Sidney Ellstrom, Maurice Copeland, and Michael Romano in support. **HOST:** Patrick Allen, ca. 1948. **ANNOUNCER:** Myron "Mike" Wallace. **MUSIC:** Bert Farber. **DIRECTOR:** Harry Holcomb.

In both runs, *Curtain Time* attempted to play to the same sizable audience that had made *The First Nighter Program* a radio powerhouse. It had a theater setting, announcements that the curtain was "about to go up," and the same fare, generally bubbly boy-girl romances. There was an usher in the later run, who called out "Tickets, please, thank you, sir," and escorted "theatergoers" to their imaginary seats in "seventh row center, seats seven and eight." The announcer, Myron Wallace, became famous decades later as the tough TV reporter on *60 Minutes*.

D

THE DAMON RUNYON THEATER, dramatic anthology: the stories of Damon Runyon.

BROADCAST HISTORY: 1948, transcribed syndication, Mayfair Productions; 30m, 52 shows produced on records. Premiere dates: Jan. 11, 1949, on KFI, Los Angeles; June 22, 1950, WOR, New York; sold well into the mid-1950s.

CAST: John Brown as Broadway, narrator, in Brooklynese, of Runyon's "guys and dolls" tales of old Manhattan. Anne Whitfield as Little Miss Marker. Gerald Mohr as Sorrowful Jones. William Conrad as Dave the Dude. Alan Reed as Little Mitzi. Herb Vigran as Harry the Horse. Also: Frank Lovejoy, Sheldon Leonard, Eddie Marr, Luis Van Rooten, Joe DuVal, Willard Waterman, Ed Begley, Jeff Chandler, Sam Edwards, Hans Conried, Parley Baer, and other Hollywood radio talents. **PRODUCER:** Vern Carstensen. **DIRECTOR:** Richard Sanville. **WRITER:** Russell Hughes.

In an era when radio emphasis was on Hollywood stars in film adaptations, *The Damon Runyon Theater* was like a cool breeze. The series had charm: the guys were guys, the dolls were dolls, and a gun was a roscoe. "Runyon mobsters are naive, easily hurt, and endowed with hearts of gold and the childlike whimsies of Margaret O'Brien," wrote *Radio Life*. The range was broad, from comedy to tragedy.

Here were some of Runyon's best-known tales: *Butch Minds the Baby; Hold 'Em, Yale; Baseball Hattie; All Horseplayers Die Broke.* The central character, known only as Broadway, led his listeners in a thick present-tense vernacular through a world of thugs and touts, dames and palookas. Broadway's New York had a crisis each week, though the streets had a rose-tinged aura. The sad shows then were all the sadder: plays like *For a Pal* had a special poignance. The bulk of Runyon's work had been untapped by radio, and the well was deep.

DAN HARDING'S WIFE, soap opera.

BROADCAST HISTORY: Jan. 20, 1936–Feb. 10, 1939, NBC. 15m, weekdays at 1:30, 1936–37; at 9:45 A.M., 1937–38; and finally at noon. Nabisco, Jan. 3–Sept. 30, 1938.

CAST: Isabel Randolph as Rhoda Harding, a widow who tries to find a new life and her own identity after her husband's death. Merrill Fugit and Loretta Poynton as the teenage twins Dean and Donna Harding. Carl Hanson as Arnie Topper. Cliff Soubier in several roles. Also: Templeton Fox, Herb Butterfield, Herb Nelson, Willard Farnum. **AN-NOUNCERS:** Les Griffith, Norman Barry. **DI-RECTOR:** J. Clinton Stanley. **WRITER:** Ken Robinson.

DANGER, DR. DANFIELD, detective melodrama.

BROADCAST HISTORY: Aug. 18, 1946–April 13, 1947, ABC. 30m, Sundays at 3, later at 2; syndicated into the 1950s.

CAST: Michael Dunne (heard on other shows as Steve Dunne) as Dr. Dan Danfield, criminal psychologist. JoAnne Johnson as Danfield's pert and sassy secretary Rusty Fairfax, who usually had too much to say and said it badly. **PRODUCER:** Wally Ramsey. **WRITER:** Ralph Wilkinson.

DANGEROUS ASSIGNMENT, globetrotting adventure and generic espionage.

BROADCAST HISTORY: July 9–Aug. 20, 1949, NBC. 30m, summer series, Saturdays at 9:30.

Feb. 6, 1950–Feb. 13, 1953, NBC. Many 30m timeslots. Largely sustained; Ford Motors on a few early shows; General Mills, mid-1950.

Feb. 18–July 1, 1953, NBC. 25m, Wednesdays at 10:35.

1954, transcribed syndication; produced in Australia.

CAST: Brian Donlevy as Steve Mitchell, world-traveling troubleshooter for some Big Brother–type government agency. Herb Butterfield as the Commissioner, Mitchell's boss. Betty Moran as the Commissioner's secretary. A top cast of Hollywood supporting players including Betty Lou Gerson, Dan O'Herlihy, Paul Frees, GeGe Pearson, and Ken Peters. **PRODUCER:** Don Sharpe. **WRITER:** Bob Ryf.

There was a week-to-week sameness about *Dangerous Assignment.* "Yeah, danger is my assignment, I get sent to a lot of places I can't even pronounce, they all spell the same thing, though, trouble," agent Steve Mitchell said each week in a gush. First he'd be summoned to the office of his boss, a nameless administrator who'd heard about trouble about to erupt in some vital hotspot around the globe. Mitchell's job: crack into the bed of discontent, rout the perpetrators, and get it all under control again. One week he'd be sent to Egypt; the next week, Saigon. It never mattered much, the results were the same. Star Brian Donlevy narrated in first-person present tense, giving it more immediacy than it might have had but never quite overcoming the absolute predictability of the stories.

The 1954 syndications came packaged to a memorable signature. An opening musical sting was followed by the announcement: *Bagdad! Martinique! Singapore! And all the places of the world where danger and intrigue walk hand in hand—there you will find Steve Mitchell, on another dangerous assignment!* Lloyd Burrell played Mitchell on the transcriptions.

DANGEROUS PARADISE, romantic adventure serial.

BROADCAST HISTORY: Oct. 25, 1933–April 2, 1934, and Oct. 1, 1934–Dec. 31, 1935, Blue Network. 15m continuation, Wednesdays and Fridays at 8:30, 1933–34; Mondays, Wednesdays, and Fridays at 7:45, 1934–35. Woodbury Soap.

CAST: Elsie Hitz as Gail Brewster and Nick Dawson as Dan Gentry, castaways on a desert island; the setting moved to the wild north in 1934–35, with Dawson playing a Canadian mountie.

Hitz and Dawson were perhaps radio's first romantic adventure duo. At its peak, *Dangerous Paradise* drew 1,000 letters a week, many for Elsie Hitz, who was described by radio columnists as having the most beautiful speaking voice on the air. Dawson and Hitz were also paired in similar serials, *The Magic Voice* and *Follow the Moon,* described under those titles.

THE DANNY KAYE SHOW, comedy-variety.

BROADCAST HISTORY: Jan. 6, 1945–May 31, 1946, CBS. 30m, Saturdays at 8 until April 1945; Fridays at 10:30 until March 1946; then Fridays at 10. Pabst Blue Ribbon Beer.

CAST: Danny Kaye, Eve Arden, Lionel Stander. Frank Nelson as Mr. Pabst, the sponsor. The show was aired from Hollywood and later from New York, with a good mix of East Coast (Kenny Delmar, Everett Sloane, etc.) and West Coast talents (singer Joan Edwards, dialect comedienne Butterfly McQueen, etc.). **ANNOUNCERS:** Ken Niles in Hollywood; Dick Joy in New York. **MUSIC:** Harry James, Lyn Murray, David Terry, Harry Sosnik. **DIRECTOR:** Dick Mack. **WRITERS:** Sylvia Fine, Goodman Ace, Abe Burrows.

Danny Kaye was an energetic comedian with a nimble tongue, a master of tongue-twisters, of double-and sometimes triple-talk. It was said that he was at home with almost any dialect. "He loves the sound and rhythm of foreign languages," wrote *Radio Life* soon after his radio premiere. "He can double-talk them perfectly, although he doesn't understand a word. He has given some of his best performances on the spur of the moment for his family and intimate friends."

One of his famous routines, first heard in his breakthrough musical, *Lady in the Dark,* and performed on his opening broadcast, was a song that merely rattled off the names of Russian composers—50 of them delivered in 30 seconds. He scat-sang his way into and out of his radio shows: asked by *Radio Life* where the words came from, he said, "I just start singing and out they come." With some variation, they came out "Get-gat gittle de-de reep fasan, get-gat gittle de-de reep fasan, gat-gat gittle de-de BEEP!"

He was born David Daniel Kaminski, Jan. 18, 1913. His first appearances on the air were on WBBC, Brooklyn, in the early '30s. In 1939 he met writer-composer Sylvia Fine during a summer engagement in Pennsylvania: they were married Jan. 3, 1940, and she took charge of his career. She was "his personal director, coach, critic, and occasionally his accompanist," said his entry in the 1952 *Current Biography*. His radio show followed his first major film, *Up in Arms* (1944). Eddie Cantor was his first guest. The series consisted of unrelated skits, separated by Harry James swing numbers, or by music from one of the other bands heard on the run. Eve Arden was largely wasted. Lionel Stander gave a gravelly performance in a Brooklyn dialect and was referred to by Arden as the show's "Sandpaper Sinatra." The commercials were often integrated, as in one skit when announcer Ken Niles picked up the entire troupe in a Pabst Beer truck loaded with 33 barrels and thus playing on the company's slogan, "33 fine brews, blended into one great beer."

Kaye was quick to credit his wife for his success, once quipping that "Sylvia has a fine head on my shoulders." Others were not so generous. Goodman Ace had a strained relationship with Sylvia Fine, departed, and later described the show as a "bomb." It drew lukewarm ratings, in the 12s. Kaye died March 3, 1987, leaving at least a score of shows on tape, packed with such semantical high spots as his "Oh, really"–"O'Reilly" skit and his comedic treatment of the vocal chestnut *Dinah* (*Dena* [his daughter's name], *is there anyone feenah . . .*).

DARK VENTURE, psychological thriller drama.

BROADCAST HISTORY: May 30, 1945–Feb. 10, 1947, ABC, West Coast regional until Feb. 19, 1946, then full network. 30m, various evening times. Brief sponsorship by Wildroot; otherwise sustained.

CAST: Betty Moran, Dwight Hauser, etc.; anthology roles. **NARRATOR:** John Lake. **MUSIC:** Dean Fossler. **PRODUCER:** J. Donald Wilson. **DIRECTOR:** Leonard Reeg.

This series grew out of a deep interest in psychology on the part of producer Wilson. It explored the moment when a character stood at the brink of a crime, stepped over the brink, and was brought to account.

DARTS FOR DOUGH, quiz-participation hybrid.

BROADCAST HISTORY: 1943, WFAA, Dallas.
    Aug. 6, 1944–Dec. 25, 1947, Blue Network/ABC. 30m, Sundays at 4, 1944–46; Sundays at 5, 1946–47; Thursdays at 9:30 from Oct. 1947. Dr. Pepper.
HOST: Orval Anderson. **DARTMASTER:** Stewart Dean. **PAYMASTER:** Bert Mitchell (his wife Jill, while he was in the Army). **ANNOUNCERS:** Frank Graham, Ted Meyers. **CONTESTANT ESCORT:** Poni Adams. **CREATORS:** Orval Anderson and Bert Mitchell. **GAG WRITER:** Eddy McKean.

Darts for Dough began on local Texas radio and became so popular that it soon won the summertime network slot replacing Al Pearce. When Pearce did not return, his sponsor, Dr. Pepper, carried *Darts* on into the regular schedule.

Contestants were selected from the studio audience. By answering an initial question, a contestant won three darts, which he threw at the "Dr. Pepper dartboard." The board was ten feet high and contained circles with values ranging from $2 to $16. Three darts in the $16 circle netted a contestant the top preliminary prize, $48. If a contestant missed his question, he was given the chance to win his darts anyway, through a variety of forfeit stunts. In one such, a woman had to keep her composure and try to hit the dartboard while sitting on the lap of a stranger, a soldier from the audience. In a finale, the contestants were assembled, given numbered darts, and allowed to compete in a one-shot-only toss at the bull's eye for a $100 grand prize.

A DATE WITH JUDY, teenage situation comedy.

BROADCAST HISTORY: June 24–Sept. 16, 1941, and June 23–Sept. 15, 1942, NBC. 30m, Tuesdays at 10. Summer replacement for *The Bob Hope Show*. Pepsodent. Also: June 30–Sept. 22, 1943, NBC. 30m, Wednesdays at 9. Summer replacement for *The Eddie Cantor Show*. Bristol Myers.

Jan. 18, 1944–Jan. 4, 1949, NBC. 30m, Tuesdays at 8:30. Tums.

Oct. 13, 1949–May 25, 1950, ABC. 30m, Thursdays at 8:30. Revere Cameras and Ford Motors.

CAST: **1941:** Ann Gillis as Judy Foster, "lovable teenage girl who's close to all our hearts." Paul McGrath as Melvin Foster, Judy's father. Margaret Brayton as Dora Foster, Judy's mother. Tommy Bond as Randolph, Judy's kid brother. Lurene Tuttle as Gloria, Judy's "friend in mischief." CAST: **1942:** Dellie Ellis as Judy. Stanley Farrar as Mr. Foster. Louise Erickson as Mitzi, Judy's new co-conspirator. CAST: **1943–50:** Louise Erickson as Judy. Joseph Kearns as Mr. Foster, 1943; John Brown as Mr. Foster from 1944. Bea Benaderet as Mrs. Foster, 1943; Georgia Backus and Lois Corbet as Mrs. Foster, 1944; Myra Marsh as Mrs. Foster from 1945. Dix Davis as Randolph. Harry Harvey as Oogie Pringle, Judy's boyfriend; Richard Crenna as Oogie from ca. 1946. Sandra Gould as Judy's friend Mitzi. ANNOUNCERS: Ken Niles, Marvin Miller. CREATOR-WRITER: Aleen Leslie. PRODUCER-DIRECTORS: Tom McAvity; Helen Mack from ca. 1943. SOUND EFFECTS: Robert Holmes, Clara Groves.

A Date with Judy and its CBS counterpart, *Meet Corliss Archer*, were the female answers to *The Aldrich Family* and *Archie Andrews*: typical '40s teenage craziness. The show took shape when Pepsodent began looking for a summer show to replace Bob Hope. While filming at Paramount, Hope had met 14-year-old Ann Gillis: he introduced her to his radio sponsors; she auditioned and won the title role in an adolescent comedy being prepared by writer Aleen Leslie.

Leslie had come up through the Hollywood ranks the hard way: she had worked for (and been fired from) the shorts department at Columbia Pictures; she had written lines for Deanna Durbin, Mickey Rooney, and *Henry Aldrich* films and was well versed in the patter. She had written the lead with her friend Helen Mack in mind for the role. But Mack was soon to have a child and had to decline. In three summertime runs, two for Hope and one for Eddie Cantor, Judy was played by three different actresses.

Louise Erickson, whose voice was heard on numerous sitcoms of the day, was best known in the role, outgrowing the summer status and playing it for seven years. After the birth of her child, Mack came in as producer-director, relieving her husband Tom McAvity, who was already producing and directing *Meet Corliss Archer* and the Joan Davis show. In the mid-1940s, Mack was radio's only female director.

In the storyline, Judy's father Melvyn owned the Foster Can Company. Her mother was a typical radio housewife. Her brother Randolph had a large vocabulary and a "supreme distaste for girls" (*Radio Life*). Oogie Pringle, Judy's boyfriend, was a paragon of radio adolescents. Her friends were named Gloria, Mitzi, Eleanor, Stinky Edwards, and Jo-Jo Duran. The plots were almost interchangeable with others involving teenagers of either sex: less zany, certainly, than *The Aldrich Family*, about on a par with *Corliss Archer*, and perhaps more palatable than *Archie Andrews*.

Many of the shows revolved around Judy's life on the telephone, arranging, discussing, and lamenting the lack of dates. "Her idea of the end of everything is the night the phone doesn't ring by 6:30 (signoff time in the West) to announce the arrival of a super date," wrote *Radio Life* in the summer of 1943. To "not rate a date," for three nights in a row was for Judy her "absolute low." The characterization combined an infectious giggle and a good dose of teenage slang ("oh, how dreeeaaamy!" . . . "that's just sensash!") with the usual teenage breathlessness. More than 30 shows are available on tape. They are high spots to those who grew up with them, but like most of their kind, they sound old today.

THE DAVE GARROWAY SHOW, talk with music.

BROADCAST HISTORY: Ca. 1946, WMAQ, Chicago. *The 11:60 Club*.

Circa 1947–48, WMAQ-NBC, Chicago. *The Dave Garroway Show*. HOST: Dave Garroway. ANNOUNCER: Charles Chan. MUSIC: Art Van Damme Quintet. PRODUCER: Parker Gibbs.

Nov. 21, 1949–Dec. 11, 1950, NBC. 30m, Mondays at 10:30; at 11:30 beginning Feb. 1950.

Dec. 21, 1949–Oct. 30, 1953, NBC. 15m, weekdays at 11:15 A.M., 1949–50; at 12:15, 1950–51; at 11:45 A.M., 1951–52; at 2, 1952–53. *Reserved for*

Garroway. Title changed to *Dial Dave Garroway* with sponsorship by Armour Meats, 1950–53. HOST: Garroway VOCALISTS: Connie Russell, Jack Haskell. MUSIC: by the Art Van Damme Quintet (jazz).

April 18, 1954–June 17, 1955, NBC. 120m, Sundays at 8; later 90m, Fridays at 8:30 as *Fridays with Dave Garroway*.

Even in his earliest days, as a local radio personality, Dave Garroway could be heard in many states via WMAQ's 50,000-watt signal.

DAVID HARUM, soap opera.

BROADCAST HISTORY: Jan. 27, 1936–Jan. 10, 1947, NBC. 15m continuation, weekdays at 11 A.M. until Oct. 1940, then at 11:45 A.M. Babbitt Corporation for Bab-O Scouring Powder.

Feb. 2, 1942–May 14, 1943, CBS. Concurrent 15m broadcast weekdays at 3.

Jan. 13, 1947–Jan. 6, 1950, CBS. 15m continuation, weekdays at 10:45 A.M. (3 P.M. in 1948). Bab-O.

Jan. 9, 1950–Jan. 5, 1951, NBC. 15m continuation, weekdays at 11:45 A.M. Bab-O.

CAST: Wilmer Walter as David Harum, banker in the small town of Homeville; a town-philosopher figure typical of afternoon serials. Craig McDonnell and Cameron Prud'Homme also as David Harum. Peggy Allenby as Susan Price Wells, his friend; Gertrude Warner and Joan Tompkins also as Susan. Philip Reed, Donald Briggs, and Ken Williams as Brian Wells. Charme Allen and Eva Condon as Aunt Polly. Ethel Everett as Elsie Anderson. Junius Matthews as Grandpa Eph. Richard McKay as Henry Longacre. Roy Fant as Deacon Perkins. Joseph Curtin as John Lennox. William Shelley as Lish Harem. Florence Lake as Tess Terwilliger. Ray Bramley as Silas Finke. Marjorie Davies and Claudia Morgan as Clarissa Oakley. Arthur Maitland as villain Zeke Sweeney, ca. late 1930s to mid-1940s. ANNOUNCER: Ford Bond. PRODUCERS: Frank and Anne Hummert. DIRECTORS: Ed King, Martha Atwell, Art Hanna, etc. THEME: *Sunbonnet Sue*, hummed and played on guitar by Stanley Davis.

Typical of many Hummert serial creations, David Harum always had a shoulder for a friend to cry on and a pointed opinion that could reach deep into another person's business. He spoke with a slight twang and had a good measure of spunk. As he told John Lennox one winter day in 1940: "If you do one thing to hurt Susan, I'm gonna beat the livin' tar outta ya ... and when I get through, you'll be such a sight that no woman would want to have anything a-tall to do with ya."

His friends were Susan Price, Aunt Polly, Deacon Perkins, Henry Longacre, Grandpa Eph, Clarissa Oakley (Clarissy to David), and, yes, despite the ominous warning, John Lennox. These characters and others formed the little community of Homeville.

The serial was based on the 1934 Will Rogers film, and the character went beyond that to an 1898 novel. David Harum made his living as a banker, but his passion was horse trading. His office in the bank was open to all. Many of the shows began there, fading in upon David as he sang a little song. A survey of four 1940 episodes reveals the typical Hummert trappings: John Lennox is not sure that he still wants to marry Susan Price; Silas Finke has absconded with $5,000 from the poorhouse and David is being charged with the theft, leading easygoing Henry Longacre to observe that his friend is looking more and more like a quitter. David has also taken up photography, and a listener just knows that the tiny candid camera he obtained from young Gene Evans will figure prominently in the plot. Sure enough, Bab-O offers one as a premium: a real camera can be yours for just 25 cents and one green Bab-O label. The serial was a great premium-giver: according to Raymond William Stedman, 400,000 responses arrived for the show's first contest, to rename David's horse. For a time, Stedman said, the sponsor gave away a horse a week, and at last David's steed was named Table Talk.

A DAY IN THE LIFE OF DENNIS DAY, situation comedy.

BROADCAST HISTORY: Oct. 3, 1946–June 30, 1951, NBC. 30m, Thursdays at 7:30 until Jan. 1947; Wednesdays at 8 until Aug. 1948; Saturdays at 10 until June 1949; then Saturdays at 9:30. Colgate for Lustre Creme Shampoo.

CAST: Dennis Day in the same naive addlebrained role he'd been playing since 1939 on *The Jack Benny Program*. Sharon Douglas as Mildred Anderson, his girlfriend; Barbara Eiler and Betty Miles also as Mildred. Francis "Dink" Trout as

Mr. Anderson, Mildred's henpecked father. Bea Benaderet as Mrs. Anderson, Mildred's mother. John Brown as Mr. Willoughby, owner of a store where Dennis worked. ANNOUNCERS: Verne Smith, Jimmy Wallington, Frank Barton. MUSIC: Charles Bud Dant, Robert Armbruster. PRODUCER-DIRECTOR: Frank O'Connor. WRITERS: Arthur Alsberg, Frank Galen, Bill Davenport, Frank Fox.

A Day in the Life of Dennis Day, also known as *The Dennis Day Show*, had several formats in its five-year run. Day was a man of great vocal and comedic talent, an accomplished tenor, and Irish to his toes. In his earliest series, he was a singing soda jerk in the town of Weaverville. His name was Dennis Day, but not, he emphasized, the same Dennis Day as that bright young man on the air with Jack Benny. He could sing as well (some said better), and his ability with dialect humor kept the soda fountain lively.

His problems revolved around his girlfriend, Mildred Anderson, his efforts to impress her unimpressible parents, his lowly status in the world, and the fact that he was usually broke. The parents were more inclined to favor Mildred's other suitor, the heel Victor Miller. Later, Dennis was found working in Willoughby's store. In yet another era, ca. 1950, the show took on a variety format, with Day as master of ceremonies. Throughout, he played the wisecracking innocent. Day continued his role on *The Jack Benny Program* all through his own show and beyond. It became a running gag with Benny, that Day and Phil Harris each had two shows while he, Benny, rated only one.

Ken Carson sang the memorable Lustre Creme commercial:

Dream girl, dream girl,
Beautiful Lustre Creme girl;
You owe your crowning glory to
A Lustre Creme shampoo . . .

DEADLINE DRAMAS, improvisational drama.

BROADCAST HISTORY: Dec. 29, 1940–July 20, 1941, NBC. 30m, Sundays at 10:30. CAST: Bob White, Ireene Wicker, William Fadiman.

Dec. 26, 1943–Sept. 24, 1944, Blue Network. 30m, Sundays at midnight. CAST: Bob White, Joan Banks, Elsie Gordon ("the girl with 100 voices"); later Ireene Wicker.

CREATOR: Bob White.

Bob White was quick to point out that he had cribbed the idea for *Deadline Dramas* from a medieval court game. In the 15th century, Italian jesters would improvise short plays from plots offered by noblemen. In the 1930s, when White was working in Chicago radio, he and his wife often staged the game for friends who dropped in—mostly radio people who could think on their feet. Eventually it occurred to White that his game might in itself make an interesting radio show.

Listeners submitted plot situations of no more than 20 words. White and his cast of two would retire to a soundproof control room where they had just two minutes to work out a fully developed plot. While they frantically picked at story threads, a soundman listened in via earphones, improvising his effects and devising cues for organist Rosa Rio. When the three players emerged, they delivered a polished seven-minute playlet, to the amazement of those listening at home.

While most of the skits sounded quite professional on the air, "the studio audience is aware of the tension and strain as they watch the taut bodies and nervous fingers of the three players," said *Tune In* in July 1944. Three playlets were developed on each broadcast, with prizes of $25 war bonds given for ideas. The plays were praised by trade magazines, some calling them worthy of Poe. White, the plotmaster, had by his account written more than 1,000 radio scripts and habitually thought in terms of situations and characters. At the time of his 1944 series, he was directing *Dick Tracy* and writing another serial, *The Sea Hound*. Ireene Wicker, who appeared on both runs, was well versed in the game, having played it as a guest in White's home.

DEADLINE MYSTERY, crime drama with a newspaper background.

BROADCAST HISTORY: April 20–Aug. 31, 1947, ABC. 30m, Sundays at 2. Knox (pharmaceutical) Company.

CAST: (Michael) Stephen Dunne as Lucky Larson, fast-talking columnist syndicated in more than 250 newspapers around the world. Hollywood regulars in support: June Whitley, Sam Edwards, Jack Kruschen, etc. DIRECTOR: Dave Titus.

DEATH VALLEY DAYS, western adventure anthology.

BROADCAST HISTORY: Sept. 30, 1930–Aug. 11, 1931, NBC Red. 30m, Tuesdays at 9:30. Pacific Borax Company and its products, 20 Mule Team Borax and Boraxo.

Aug. 17, 1931–June 3, 1938, Blue Network. 30m, Mondays at 8 through Sept. 1932, then Thursdays at 9 until Sept. 1936, then Fridays at 8:30. Borax.

June 10, 1938–June 27, 1941, NBC. 30m, Fridays at 9:30 until Oct. 1939, then Saturdays at 9:30 through April 1940, then Fridays at 8:30. Borax.

July 3, 1941–Aug. 3, 1944, CBS. 30m, Thursdays at 8 until July 1942, then at 8:30. Borax.

Aug. 10, 1944–June 21, 1945, CBS. 30m, Thursdays at 8:30. *Death Valley Sheriff.* Borax.

June 29, 1945–Sept. 14, 1951, ABC. 30m, Fridays at 9:30. *The Sheriff.* Borax through March 23, 1951, then Procter & Gamble and American Chicle.

CAST: Jack MacBryde as the Old Ranger (1931–40s), narrator and teller of Old West tales; Tim Daniel Frawley, George Rand, and Harry Humphrey also as the Old Ranger. Harvey Hays as the Old Prospector. John White as the Lonesome Cowboy. Jean King, who mastered several western dialects for various female roles, joined the company ca. 1932. Also: Edwin Bruce, Frank Butler, Geoffrey Bryant, Milton Herman, Paul Nugent, Rosemarie Broncato, Helen Claire. **ANNOUNCERS:** George Hicks, Dresser Dahlstead; also, John Reed King. **MUSIC:** Joseph Bonime. **PRODUCER:** Dorothy McCann. **CREATOR-WRITER:** Ruth Cornwall Woodman. **WRITER:** Ruth Adams Knight.

SOUND EFFECTS: Bob Prescott, Keene Crockett. **BUGLE CALL:** Harry Glantz.

CAST: Post–1944 (when the series became *Death Valley Sheriff*): Robert Haag as Sheriff Mark Chase of Canyon County, Calif.; Bob Warren and Donald Briggs also as Chase. Olyn Landick (a male actor) as Cousin Cassie (Cassandra) Drinkwater, a character used for comic relief. **DIRECTORS:** Walter Scanlan, Florence Ortman, etc.

Ruth Cornwall Woodman was an advertising copywriter in the summer of 1930, when the Pacific Borax Company decided to sponsor a rugged series about the Old West. Asked to create the format and write the scripts, Woodman first encountered the problem of geography. She was living in New York, a Vassar graduate with little knowledge of the desert or its people. Travel in the western states was still an adventure, with many of the roads through Utah, Nevada, Arizona, and California, where the series was to be set, little more than trails.

A banker's wife with two children, Woodman undertook the story-gathering pilgrimage and was soon writing one of the most respected dramas of early radio. One of the sponsor's employees in California, a self-styled "desert rat" named W. W. "Wash" Cahill, was lined up as her guide. Her trips into the desert became annual events, and soon she was well versed in the ways of prospectors, outlaws, and saloon girls. She spent up to two months a year prowling through ghost towns, interviewing oldtimers, sifting through museums, and poring over yellowing newsprint. She packed into the back country, scaled the mountains west of Death Valley, talked with small-town newspaper editors, old men who ran gas stations, lonely wives on the fringes of nowhere, and—when she could get into the saloons—bartenders. Then she returned to New York to write the stories she had gathered, and the next year she did it all again.

The show immediately established its ties to the sponsor. The product, 20 Mule Team Borax, got a boost as early as the seventh show, *The 20-Mule Team Makes Its First Trip.* Other "Mule Team" themes were worked in liberally. But most of the shows were of pioneer life, of the gold rush, of the horrors of a sandstorm, the joys of Easter and Christmas in the camps. There were multipart stories based on historical personages (Lola Montez, Billy the kid, etc.). To tell the tales, Woodman created the Old Ranger, a composite character who ostensibly had known by name the lawmen, bushwhackers, and desperadoes of whom he spoke. The format was memorable, underplayed, suggestive of loneliness. In the early days, the signature was interspersed with the singing of western balladeer John White, "the lonesome cowboy." Later this gave way to a fading, forlorn bugle call, heralding announcer Dresser Dahlstead's simple announcement: "As the early-morning bugle-call of covered wagon trains fades away among the echoes, another true *Death Valley Days* story is presented for your entertainment by the Pacific

Coast Borax Company, producers of that famous family of products—20 Mule Team Borax, 20 Mule Team Borax Soap Chips, and Boraxo. Well, Old Ranger, what's your story about tonight?''

Through many changes of format, it remained a hardy perennial, eventually becoming a filmed TV series with Ronald Reagan as host.

DECEMBER BRIDE, situation comedy.

BROADCAST HISTORY: June 8, 1952–Sept. 6, 1953, CBS. 30m, Sundays at 7 (summer show in the Jack Benny slot) until Sept. 1952; Sundays at 6 until mid-Feb.; Wednesdays at 10 through May; then Sundays at 9.

CAST: Spring Byington as Lily Ruskin, the kind mother-in-law who lived with her daughter's family. Doris Singleton as Ruth Henshaw, the daughter. Hal March as Matt Henshaw, Ruth's husband. Hans Conried as Pete Porter, their dour and sullen neighbor. Also: John Brown, Alan Reed. **CREATOR-WRITER-DIRECTOR:** Parke Levy.

Lily Ruskin, the pivotal character of *December Bride*, was the precise opposite of the stereotypical mother-in-law. A widow, Lily was a dear lady in every aspect. Creator Parke Levy took inspiration for the character from his own mother-in-law, who came to visit and was suddenly besieged by would-be suitors. Many of the plots turned on efforts by the Henshaws to find a suitable man for Lily because they thought she needed companionship in her December years. The comedy of errors that grew out of this passing parade fueled the show.

On a smaller scale, *December Bride* did for mothers-in-law what Eve Arden did for schoolteachers in *Our Miss Brooks*: made them human. Spring Byington also played Lily on television, supported by Frances Rafferty, Dean Miller, Verna Felton, and Harry Morgan. Hal March vaulted to fame a few years later as host of the scandal-plagued *$64,000 Question* on TV.

DEFENSE ATTORNEY, crime drama.

BROADCAST HISTORY: Aug. 31, 1951–Dec. 30, 1952, ABC. 30m, Fridays at 8 until Sept. 1951; Thursdays at 8 through Oct. 1952; Tuesdays at 8, then at 8:30, thereafter. Clorets (1951–52); Kix Cereal and Goodyear (1952).

CAST: Mercedes McCambridge as Martha Ellis Bryant, idealistic defense lawyer. Howard Culver as her friend and fellow sleuth, newspaper reporter Jud Barnes. Also: Tony Barrett, Irene Tedrow, Harry Bartell, etc. **MUSIC:** Rex Koury. **DIRECTOR:** Dwight Hauser. **WRITER:** Joel Murcott, etc.

The defense attorney of the title was as often in the field, investigating, as in the courtroom, filing briefs. McCambridge, who had a couldn't-miss-it-in-a-crowd voice, opened the show from an echo chamber, reciting her pledge: *Ladies and gentlemen, to depend upon your judgment and to fulfill mine own obligation, I submit the facts . . . fully aware of my responsibility to my client and to you, as defense attorney.*

DESTINATION FREEDOM, Negro civil rights dramatic anthology.

BROADCAST HISTORY: June 27, 1948–Aug. 13, 1950, WMAQ, Chicago. 30m, Sunday mornings. Sponsored briefly in the first 13 weeks by the *Chicago Defender*, a black newspaper with a long history. Also: Oct. 15, 1950–Nov. 19, 1951, WMAQ, a new *DF* series in name only: an abrupt turn away from the civil rights themes of the early show.

CAST: Fred Pinkard, Oscar Brown Jr., Wezlyn Tilden, and Janice Kingslow, heading a Chicago rep company of regular performers. Also: Tony Parrish, Jack Gibson, Harris Gaines, Louise Pruitt. Arthur Peterson, Norma Ransom, Forrest Lewis, Studs Terkel, Hope Summers, Boris Aplon, Jess Pugh, Ted Liss, Don Gallagher, Harry Elders, Everett Clarke, Jack Lester, Art Hern, Les Spears, Dean Olmquist, Russ Reed. **ANNOUNCERS:** Hugh Downs, etc. **MUSIC:** Emil Soderstrom, Jose Bethancourt. **CREATOR-WRITER:** Richard Durham. **DIRECTORS:** Homer Heck, Dick Loughran.

Destination Freedom, though it never appeared on a national network, was one of the most powerful and important shows of its day. It was a striking achievement, a voice whose passion and courage overcame every budgetary shortcoming to become perhaps the strongest plea for Negro rights ever heard on American radio.

Its original purpose was to dramatize and reveal little-known lives from black Americana. But even in such early shows as *Railway to Freedom* (the story of Harriet Tubman and her underground railroad) and *Dark Explorers* (the story of blacks who came over on the earliest ships from Europe), the singular voice of its author could not be missed. As time went on, the voice would grow stronger.

Richard Durham was a black writer whose credits in radio would run a gamut from Irna Phillips serials to prestige plays for such as *The CBS Radio Workshop*. But in *Destination Freedom* Durham wrote from the heart. Anger simmers at the foundation of these shows, rising occasionally to a wail of agony and torment. On no other show was the term "Jim Crow" used as an adjective, if at all: nowhere else could be heard the actual voices of black actors giving life to a real black environment. There were no buffoons or toadies in Durham's plays: there were heroes and villains, girlfriends and lovers, mothers, fathers, brutes; there were kids named Joe Louis and Jackie Robinson, who bucked the tide and became kings in places named Madison Square Garden and Ebbets Field. The early historical dramas soon gave way to a more contemporary theme: the black man's struggle in a modern racist society. Shows on Denmark Vesey, Frederick Douglass, and George Washington Carver gave way to Richard Wright's *Black Boy* and the lives of Louis Armstrong, Fats Waller, and Nat King Cole. *The Tiger Hunt* was a war story, of a black tank battalion; *Last Letter Home* told of black pilots in World War II. The stories pulled no punches in their execution of the common theme, making *Destination Freedom* not only the most powerful but the only show of its kind.

It was all the more remarkable because the rep company that worked it was headed by black performers, with whites carrying the supporting roles. Radio in the '40s was a white actor's playground. "There were no blacks in [serious] dramatic radio at that time," recalled Arthur Peterson, a white character actor who could "do" black dialect and who worked with the small black company on *Destination Freedom*. His wife Norma Ransom also worked the show, as did Forrest Lewis (who, the Petersons remembered, could "play a great old black man") and Studs Terkel, who went on to greater fame as a social historian and Chicago talk show host. Before *Destination Freedom*, these and other dialecticians were called whenever a black voice was demanded. "Arthur played some, I did, we

all did," said Norma Ransom, who couldn't think of a "single black actor" who had made any significant inroads in white radio. The Petersons recalled one other series of black heritage that had aired locally in Chicago: it was called *It Can Be Done*, but again the roles were all played by whites.

Now came *Destination Freedom*, and the blacks were the stars. Fred Pinkard played most of the male leads in the first year. Oscar Brown Jr. alternated between bit parts and leads, sharing top billing with Pinkard as the show went on. The female leads were Wezlyn Tilden and Janice Kingslow: among them these four could stretch the perimeters of age, culture, economic background. Homer Heck, the white director, had spent five years directing *Vic and Sade*, as far removed from *Destination Freedom* as two shows can be yet sharing the essential ingredients, uniqueness, strength, and the vision of a single talented writer.

Durham produced his plays as a freelancer; he was never part of the WMAQ staff during his show's run. "I had spent a lot of time studying Dickens," he said in a 1983 interview, a few years before he died. "I had discovered that a Dickens character made you love him or hate him almost at once, and I used that same approach, of setting the characters as quickly as possible, as sharply as possible." Homer Heck "had a sense of what characters could bring about," Durham said: Heck understood both the power and limitations of short dramatic formats, and Durham found as the series went on that he was free to produce ever-stronger scripts without much fear of censorship or rebuke.

The show was initially approved and scheduled by Judith Waller, WMAQ program director, who, ironically, had been involved in bringing *Amos 'n' Andy* to WMAQ almost two decades earlier. "She was quite enthusiastic about the new characterizations that we were presenting, so I look back upon Miss Judith Waller now as quite an innovative promoter in the business of radio," Durham recalled. The brief period of sponsorship by the *Chicago Defender* expired, but the show continued, sustained by the station. Durham knew at the time that he was breaking new ground: he had been impressed by a special broadcast years earlier, when director William N. Robson had probed the causes of race riots in Detroit, but on a week-by-week basis no one had attempted what *Destination Freedom* was now doing routinely. There were all-out attacks on the Ku Klux Klan, on southern bias, on the attitudes of rednecks and the mentality of the mob. The show soon drew the wrath of white supremacists, "15 or 20 of them," from the White Knights of Columbus, Durham recalled. "They stayed there three or four weeks . . . marching across the door, denouncing the show." But Durham's writing continued as strong as ever.

He followed a routine. "I had to submit the name and a short description of the character that I wanted to depict. These would generally be accepted; now and then there would be a question." But Durham could not remember ever being pressured to soften the rhetoric. What had begun as an experiment "for a few weeks" lasted more than two years: "then I left for other writing ventures." He finally succumbed to the lure of money, Durham said: he got a job writing a "Don Ameche vehicle," and "there was such a big gap in money between a network show and a sustained [local] program that I began to gravitate toward Ameche." He wasn't burned out: "we hadn't scratched the surface on the theme." But his departure brought a radical change. With the show *Paul Revere Speaks* (Dec. 15, 1950), *Destination Freedom* became a white show. It was now straight history, without a hint of the black spirit that had ignited and guided it since 1948. It was a poor man's *Cavalcade of America*.

The black series was long one of radio's great forgotten stories. Then, around 1980, a good run of transcriptions was found and its voices heard again. There was Tony Parrish, personifying the slums. *You've seen me around. Slums are the cemeteries of the living, HE says. Jim Crow is the undertaker, HE says. He's the one I want to tell you about, this AME reverend, this Windy City alderman who's trying to run slums outta town.* There were the stories of Ralph Bunche, Satchel Paige, Sugar Ray Robinson, Roscoe Dungee, and Lena Horne, who encountered bigotry in a "Jim Crow cafe" between flights. A listener with any sense of history knows immediately that, in the '40s, on American radio, this was strong medicine.

DETECT AND COLLECT, comedy-quiz.

BROADCAST HISTORY: June 13–Sept. 5, 1945, CBS. 30m, Wednesdays at 9:30. Old Gold.

Oct. 4, 1945–Sept. 28, 1946, ABC. 30m, Thursdays at 9:30 until Aug. 1946, then Saturdays at 8:30. Goodrich Tires.

QUIZMASTERS: Fred Uttal and Wendy Barrie (1945); also, Lew Lehr. **PRODUCER:** Mildred Fenton. **DIRECTOR:** Herb Polesie, Walter Tibbals.

Detect and Collect had a simple premise. Contestants were each given $25 and up to six chances to identify a mystery prize. If the contestant guessed the prize on the first try, he won the $25 and the prize: for each clue he needed, the cash was diminished by $5. Often the prizes were novelty gifts, barber chairs and the like.

DETECTIVES BLACK AND BLUE, early comedy-mystery serial.

BROADCAST HISTORY: 1932–35, transcribed syndication, 15m daily; 333 episodes produced and syndicated.

This serial followed the careers of two unlikely adventurers named Black and Blue. They were shipping clerks in a Duluth market, but a yearning for adventure led them to a correspondence course in criminology. Using the motto "Detec-a-tives Black and Blue, good men tried and true," they opened an agency and promptly set the art of detection back 40 years. The shows were primitive, with virtually no sound effects, the "action" carried in dialogue. The cast is unknown.

THE DICK HAYMES SHOW, musical variety.

BROADCAST HISTORY: June 20, 1944–Oct. 9, 1945, NBC. 30m, Tuesdays at 7:30. Initially heard as *Everything for the Boys*, taking over the Arch Oboler–Ronald Colman series of that name. Autolite.

Oct. 13, 1945–July 1, 1948, CBS. Saturdays at 8 until mid-1946, then Thursdays at 9. Autolite.

CAST: singer Dick Haymes, with Helen Forrest (1944–46), Martha Tilton, Lina Romay (1947–48). Cliff Arquette as Mrs. Wilson, owner of a flower stand, who never knew the time of day (1947–48). **ORCHESTRA:** Gordon Jenkins.

For a time Dick Haymes was considered a serious rival to Bing Crosby and Frank Sinatra at the top of the male vocal field. Haymes had first starred on radio in *Here's to Romance* (Blue Network, CBS, 1943–44) with vocalist Helen Forrest. Both had worked in the Harry James band, and Forrest went on with Haymes into his own series.

Haymes was also starred in *Club Fifteen* and *The Carnation Contented Hour* in 1949–50.

DICK TRACY, juvenile police serial, based on the comic strip by Chester Gould.

BROADCAST HISTORY: 1934, NBC New England stations. 15m, weekdays.

Feb. 4–July 11, 1935, CBS. 15m, four a week at 5:45. Sterling Products.

Sept. 30, 1935–March 24, 1937, Mutual. 15m, four or five a week, usually at 5:45.

Jan. 3, 1938–April 28, 1939, NBC. 15m, five a week at 5. Quaker Oats.

April 29–Sept. 30, 1939, NBC. 30m, weekly, mostly Saturdays at 7; also Mondays at 8 in Aug. Quaker Oats.

March 15, 1943–July 16, 1948, Blue Network/ABC. 15m strip show, initially three a week at 5:15, five a week at 5:15, 1943–45; at 5:45, 1945–46; at 4:45, 1946–47; at 5, 1947–48. Tootsie Rolls, 1943–46. Also: Oct. 6, 1945–June 1, 1946, ABC, concurrent with the serial run. 30m, Saturdays at 7:30. Tootsie Rolls.

CAST: Bob Burlen as the first radio Dick Tracy (1934 New England). Barry Thomson, Ned Wever, and Matt Crowley heard variously as Dick Tracy, "protector of law and order." Walter Kinsella and others as Pat Patton, Tracy's ever-present partner. Jackie Kelk and Andy Donnelly as Junior Tracy. Helen Lewis as Tess Trueheart. **ANNOUNCERS:** Dan Seymour, Ed Herlihy, etc. **DIRECTORS:** Mitchell Grayson, Charles Powers, Bob White, etc. **SOUND EFFECTS:** Bill McClintock (Mutual); Al Finelli and Walt McDonough (ABC); Keene Crockett (NBC).

Dick Tracy proved almost as durable on the air as he was in the comics. The serial came with the full gallery of Chester Gould strip characters: sidekick Pat Patton, Tracy's adopted son Junior; his girlfriend Tess Trueheart; Vitamin Flintheart and the villain, Flattop. The opening signature of the '40s would be fondly remembered by those who heard it as children: a furious burst of radio codes and Tracy's terse, voice-filtered commands (via wrist radio, of course). There was always a summary, by Tracy, along with the

story titles: *This is Dick Tracy, leading a search party on a hunt for Junior and Moccasin Joe, in "The Case of the Hooting Owl."* The Saturday half-hours were developed to the unlikely theme *Toot Toot Tootsie*, a tip of the hat to the sponsor.

DIMENSION X, science fiction dramatic anthology. See also X-MINUS ONE.

BROADCAST HISTORY: April 8, 1950–Sept. 29, 1951, NBC. Scheduled irregularly: initially 30m, Saturdays at 8; later, Fridays, Sundays, then Saturdays again. General Mills for Wheaties, two months beginning July 7, 1950; otherwise sustained.

CAST: New York radio personnel including Joseph Julian, Bill Griffis, Joe DeSantis, Peter Capell, Luis Van Rooten, Santos Ortega, Wendell Holmes, John McGovern, Alexander Scourby, Bryna Raeburn, Bill Quinn, Ed Jerome, Lawson Zerbe, Karl Weber, Arnold Moss, Joan Alexander, Rita Lynn, Jackie Grimes, Matt Crowley, Roger DeKoven, John Larkin, Jan Miner, Berry Kroeger, Bill Zuckert, Bill Lipton, Raymond Edward Johnson, Denise Alexander, Les Damon, Leon Janney, Donald Buka, Inge Adams, Joseph Curtin, Arthur Maitland, John Gibson, etc. **NARRATOR:** Norman Rose. **ANNOUNCERS:** Robert Warren, occasionally Fred Collins; Frank Martin for Wheaties. **MUSIC:** Albert Berman. **PRODUCERS:** Van Woodward, William Welch. **DIRECTORS:** Edward King, Jack Kuney, Fred Weihe. **WRITERS-ADAPTERS:** Ernest Kinoy, George Lefferts. **STORIES BY:** Ray Bradbury, Isaac Asimov, Robert Heinlein, Clifford Simak, Robert Bloch, Jack Williamson, Kurt Vonnegut, Graham Doar, Murray Leinster, Donald Wollheim, etc. **ENGINEER:** Bill Chambers. **SOUND EFFECTS:** Agnew Horine, Sam Monroe, etc.

Dimension X was radio's premier series of adult science fiction tales, preceded briefly by the little-known and soon-forgotten *Two Thousand Plus*. The vast and fertile S-F field had been curiously neglected for the entire 25-year history of the medium. Fantasy had been relegated to such kiddie epics as *Flash Gordon* and *Buck Rogers*, with such occasional hybrids as NBC's *Latitude Zero* (1941). Occasionally an S-F story might appear on the mainstream series *Escape* or *Suspense*, and in July 1950 CBS and Wrigley's Gum carried three episodes of a Chicago-produced fantasy series, *Cloud Nine*, which contained the work of Jack Finney and others. But until *Dimension X* arrived, radio left the deeper reaches of the universe unexplored.

The appearance of *Destination Moon* in movie houses helped make 1950 the year of S-F on radio. *Dimension X* rose to the task, proving that radio and science fiction were ideally compatible. The series demonstrated (though it would take the perfection of television to prove it) that adding a picture to a story of vision, illusion, or myth does not automatically enhance things. The tube is too small, the props too artificial (no matter how ingenious or technologically advanced) to compete with the landscape of the mind. For its time, *Dimension X* was a wonder. Two and sometimes three sound effects men worked each show. NBC engineer Bill Chambers described the process in a letter to *D-X* advocate Bill Sabis, excerpted in the massive log that Sabis compiled on *Dimension X* and its offspring series, *X-Minus One*. The shows were done in a huge studio, "two stories high with a tour observation booth," Chambers said. This enabled the crew to obtain "tremendous echo effects," so deep in fact that they could not be truly recorded by the equipment of the time. Blended with the sound effects were futuristic musical scores, composed by Albert Berman and played on the organ. Host-narrator Norman Rose was the perfect voice, combining an authoritative resonance with a touch of dark irony. Rose opened the show cold:

Adventures in time and space . . . told in future tense!

DIMENSION X . . . X . . . x . . . x . . . x . . . x . . .

Up came the organ, a crescendo sting, mingled on later shows with tympanic rolls and symbals. Also used liberally was the Theremin, an exotic electronic musical instrument that set the stories in a haunting framework. But as impressive as the sound was, the show's success began, as success always does, with the writing. The point of origin for many of these tales was *Astounding Science Fiction Magazine*, a market used by the best writers in the field. The opening show, *The Outer Limit*, was an unfortunate choice: it had been done to death on *Suspense, Escape,* and other anthology series, and its premise depended too much on a gimmicky ending. With all the great S-F material at its disposal, it was up to staff writer George Lefferts to produce a true radio classic: *No Contact* was a chilling, original

tale of ships lost to a mysterious "galactic barrier," and of one ship that tried again. The premise of Fredric Brown's *Knock* was simply stated: "The last man on earth sat alone in his room . . . and then there was a knock on the door." Heinlein's *Green Hills of Earth* was a lovely piece about a blind spacefarer and folksinger. Bradbury was well represented: he ended the world twice in a single show, by atomic war in *There Will Come Soft Rains* and by invasion in *Zero Hour*. His *Mars Is Heaven* got a creative assist from adapter Ernest Kinoy, and *The Martian Chronicles* was a Bradbury mix blended into a smooth, riveting half-hour, again by Kinoy. *Universe* was a fantastic Heinlein tale about a giant spaceship, in transit for so long that the distant descendants of the original inhabitants lost touch with the purpose of their endless trip (nice ironies here on the dangers of religious zealotry). And Kinoy's original story of *The Martian Death March* was one of the best in the entire series: the heartbreaking premise taken from American history, of all places, and the death march of the Cherokee Indians in 1838.

The show was produced live for the first 13 weeks and recorded on tape thereafter. It was bumped around the NBC schedule, heard Fridays, Sundays, Saturdays, dropped from the lineup for weeks at a time, and in one period (almost all of the first half of 1951) it was missing for 19 weeks. Like *Escape*, the CBS series of high adventure, *Dimension X* overcame its poorboy scheduling to offer some of the best radio drama of its season. Fifty shows were produced, including repeats: the run is happily complete on tape in uniformly excellent sound.

THE DINAH SHORE SHOW, musical variety.

BROADCAST HISTORY: Aug. 6, 1939–Jan. 14, 1940, Blue Network. 15m, Sundays at 7. Paul Lavalle, maestro.

June 14–Sept. 27, 1940, Blue Network. 15m, Fridays at 10:15. Irving Miller, maestro.

Nov. 2, 1941–April 26, 1942, Blue Network. 15m, Sundays at 9:45. *Songs by Dinah Shore.* Bristol Myers. From New York with maestro Paul Lavalle and announcer-stooge Harry Von Zell.

May 1, 1942–April 23, 1943, Blue Network. 15m, Fridays at 9:30. *In Person, Dinah Shore.* Bristol Myers. From Hollywood, with maestro

Gordon Jenkins and announcer Truman Bradley.

Sept. 30, 1943–June 29, 1944, CBS. 30m, Thursdays at 9:30. *The Birdseye Open House.* Birdseye Foods. Robert Emmett Dolan, maestro; Harry Von Zell, announcer; guest stars including Groucho Marx, Peter Lorre, and Ozzie and Harriet Nelson. Glenhall Taylor, producer.

Oct. 5, 1944–May 30, 1946, NBC. 30m, Thursdays at 8:30. *The Birdseye Open House.* Birdseye Foods.

Sept. 18, 1946–June 11, 1947, NBC. 30m, Wednesdays at 9:30. *The Ford Show.* Ford Motor Company. Robert Emmett Dolan, maestro; Peter Lind Hayes, comic foil; guests.

Feb. 13–April 16, 1948, CBS. 30m, Fridays at 10. *Call for Music.* Philip Morris Cigarettes. A triple-star half-hour with singer Johnny Mercer and maestro Harry James. John Holbrook, announcer.

April 20–June 29, 1948, NBC. 30m, Tuesdays at 8. Pabst Beer.

April 20, 1950–Dec. 26, 1952, CBS. 15m, weeknights at 7:15. *The Jack Smith Show,* with Dinah Shore. Oxydol.

March 23, 1953–July 1, 1955, NBC. 15m daily, then twice a week. Simulcast, with the TV audio heard as a radio show. Chevrolet.

The radio career of singer Dinah Shore began in her native Tennessee when, around 1937, she appeared on WSM, Nashville. In 1938 she went to New York, where she was heard on Martin Block's WNEW show. She sang with Ben Bernie, and the national exposure on Bernie's CBS show in the spring of 1939 led to her own Blue Network quarter-hour series.

Her star rose quickly. When NBC scheduled its strange and wonderful *Chamber Music Society of Lower Basin Street* in February 1940, Shore was its first diva. That fall Eddie Cantor hired her as his regular singer. Her rendition of *Yes, My Darling Daughter* on the Cantor show was a national sensation, followed by the equally appreciated *Blues in the Night.* She was now selling records in the hundred-thousands and was such a hot commodity by 1941 that a skirmish broke out between Cantor and Edgar Bergen for her services. When Cantor neglected to promptly exercise his option, Bergen offered her a raise to $750 a week. It went to arbitration, Cantor won, and she got a raise anyway.

Meanwhile, her quarter-hour Blue Network series was ending, but Bristol Myers was in the wings. Cantor was on hand to give her new show, *Songs by Dinah Shore,* a sendoff. By mid-1942 *Radio Life* was calling Dinah Shore the most popular singing star since the rise of Kate Smith in the early '30s. Movies beckoned: she moved to Hollywood, taking her radio show with her and continuing with the Cantor show, which was also moving west. Until then she had been a brunette: at the suggestion of Warner cosmeticians she became a "honey blonde" and remained one evermore.

Her revamped radio career missed less than a beat: within a week of her exit from New York, she was on the air from Hollywood. It was basically the same show, a straight songfest—none of her quarter-hours were much more than that. Her new announcer, Truman Bradley, was described in the trades as "the last word for products appealing to feminine listeners." But Shore was perturbed: she didn't think plugging a laxitive, Sal Hepatica, was at all feminine, Truman Bradley or no, and she was all the more annoyed when Bristol Myers worked Mum deodorant into the mix. Bradley did what he could with it (Mum, he intoned, "is your word for charm," that final word to "banish undaintiness"), but Shore still didn't like it. She did remain with Bristol Myers almost 18 months. Her theme, *Dinah,* was hummed wistfully against a restrained Gordon Jenkins orchestra.

A summer job arose, singing on the Paul Whiteman NBC Sunday-nighter from June 6 to Aug. 29, 1943. By fall she was again installed in her own series, this time a full half-hour for Birdseye Foods. Again, a format was quickly established, the full timeslot allowing for chatter with guests in addition to the usual Shore vocals. The same continued into her series for Ford Motors and Philip Morris, the latter notable for its three-star billing and its opening collage of four themes (*Dinah,* hummed by herself; *Ciribiribin,* played by Harry James on open trumpet; *Accent-tchu-ate the Positive,* sung by Johnny Mercer, and Ferde Grofé's *Grand Canyon Suite,* which, in a masterpiece of advertising strategy, had been absorbed by and become synonymous with Philip Morris Cigarettes). And if the opening wasn't busy enough, there was Johnny, the Philip Morris bellhop, chanting "Callll for Philip Morraiss!" over and over.

Shore did another short series, on NBC for Pabst Beer. She rejoined Cantor Oct. 1, 1948, appearing on his Pabst show until June 24, 1949. The quarter-hours resumed. Radio died, but Shore continued to be a potent personality in television.

DOC BARCLAY'S DAUGHTERS, soap opera.

BROADCAST HISTORY: Jan. 23, 1939–Jan. 19, 1940, CBS. 15m continuation, daily at 2. Personal Finance.

CAST: Bennett Kilpack as Doc Barclay, druggist in the small town of Brookdale, trying valiantly to raise three temperamental daughters alone. Elizabeth Reller as Connie Barclay, former socialite and woman of the world, who has left her husband, a millionaire playboy, to return to her hometown as Doc Barclay's daughter. Mildred Robin as Mimi Barclay, the second daughter, self-centered and flirtatious, married to Tom Clark. Vivian Smolen as the third daughter, Marge, single and pretty, who keeps house for her father. Albert Hayes as Tom Clark, clerk in the Jenkins Hardware Store, who is too weak to stand up to his tempestuous wife Mimi. ANNOUNCER: Tom Shirley. ORGANIST: Ann Leaf.

DR. CHRISTIAN, light drama.

BROADCAST HISTORY: Nov. 7, 1937–Jan. 6, 1954, CBS. 30m, Sundays at 2:30 until April 1938; Tuesdays at 10, 1938–39; Wednesdays at 10 until Jan. 1940; Wednesdays at 8:30, 1940–54. Chesebrough Manufacturing Company for Vaseline.

CAST: Jean Hersholt as Dr. Paul Christian, a kindly doctor-philosopher in the little town of River's End. Rosemary DeCamp as Nurse Judy Price (1937, and again 1943–54); Lurene Tuttle as Judy (1937–43); Kathleen Fitz occasionally as Judy; Helen Claire as Judy when the show aired from New York. ANNOUNCERS: Art Gilmore (1942–54, after a brief stint the first year), Andre Baruch (1938), Perry King (1938–41). MUSIC: Ivan Ditmars, Lew White, or Milton Charles on organ. PRODUCER: Dorothy McCann. DIRECTORS: Neil Reagan, John Wilkinson, Florence Ortman. SOUND EFFECTS: Ray Erlenborn, Gus Bayz, Bill Brown, Clark Casey. THEME: *Rainbow on the River*.

Dr. Christian may have been the best-known light drama on the air. It was created especially for Jean Hersholt on the strength of his role in the 1936 film *The Country Doctor*. In that film, Hersholt had portrayed Dr. Allan Roy Dafoe, the physician who had become an instant celebrity when he delivered the Dionne quintuplets. Hersholt liked the character but couldn't get the rights to use Dafoe's name on the air. So he created his own doctor-name. He had always loved the work of Hans Christian Andersen. Christian was a strong name: it had obvious biblical strengths and a long heritage in Hersholt's native Denmark. It would work well with Hersholt's Scandinavian accent and would have strong appeal in middle America, where Dr. Paul Christian's practice in the town of River's End would be set.

It was billed as *The Vaseline Program*, also known as *Dr. Christian's Office* because of the pretitle dialogue in which Nurse Judy Price answered the phone that way. It started slowly and doubled its listenership in each of its first three years, holding an audience estimated at 15-20 million thereafter. The show was viewed as slightly hayseed in the Hollywood radio center: Radio Row insiders saw that rating coming largely from the midwestern Bible belt, from people who appreciated Dr. Christian's Golden Rule approach to life. Dr. Christian was a philosopher, but radio had plenty of those. He was also a philanthropist and an unabashed Cupid. Many of his stories concerned romance gone awry, true love that needed only a guiding hand from a wise and gentle friend. Other stories were of misguided youth, kids who finally listened to reason when it looked them straight in the face through the good doctor's spectacles.

Listeners knew the town as well as the hero. River's End was the typical whistle stop, half a dozen square blocks carved out of the corn country in some universal part of America. There were two surrounding thoroughfares, River Road and Black Mountain Road. The main drag through town was State Street. There were stores, a bank, post office, church, school, hospital, and a block where the "best people" lived. On the fringes were the farms, a dairy, a lumber yard, and an awning works. Dr. Christian lived in a white house surrounded by lawns and gardens at the corner of River Road and State Street. The side door went directly into the waiting room.

In the beginning, the show was written by various scripters, among them Ruth Adams Knight. In 1942 the producers tried a new approach: a contest in which listeners could submit scripts and be eligible for large cash prizes at season's end. This may have been the most important single factor in the show's long run. Suddenly everyone in the country was a scriptwriter. Weekly awards ranged from $150 to $500, good money in 1942, and the grand prize script won its author $2,000. Now it became *The Vaseline Program—the only show in radio where the audience writes the script. Newsweek* reported that 7,697 scripts were received in 1947; sometimes the number went as high as 10,000. Many were called but few were chosen. The scripts that made it to air continued the appeal to traditional values, showing Dr. Christian as the symbol of all that. The subject matter could include anything, even fantasy. One show was about a mermaid; on another, a humanlike jalopy named Betsy fell in love with a black Packard owned by a woman chief of police. The 1947 prize play concerned Dr. Christian's effort to convince an unborn child that earth wasn't so bad after all. Only when murder was the theme did listeners complain: they liked the show when it was mellow, *Radio Life* said; that's what Dr. Christian was about.

So closely did Jean Hersholt become identified with his role that listeners wrote for medical advice. Hersholt straddled a clever line, referring them to real physicians without ever saying what should have been obvious—that he was just an actor and anyone with a measurable brain should have known it. He shattered no illusions, on air or off. Eventually he began refusing acting jobs that would take him outside his character. It didn't matter: Dr. Christian would move from radio to the screen, and in private life Hersholt was kept busy with honorary, volunteer, and philanthropic duties. He founded the Motion Picture Relief Fund to aid movie people who had fallen on hard times; he served as president of the Academy of Motion Picture Arts and Sciences, finally having a special Oscar (the Jean Hersholt Humanitarian Award) named in his honor. Neither he nor his show took summer vacations. In the mid-1940s it was reported that he had never missed a *Dr. Christian* broadcast. Even from a hospital bed his voice was heard.

When he went to Denmark in 1945, Claude Rains took over as Dr. Webb in his absence, but Dr. Christian was still heard via transatlantic shortwave.

THE DOCTOR FIGHTS, dramatic war anthology.

BROADCAST HISTORY: June 6–Aug. 29, 1944, CBS. 30m, Tuesdays at 9:30. Schenley Laboratories. CAST: Raymond Massey in a new portrait each week of a doctor on some far-flung battlefield. ANNOUNCER: Frank Gallop. MUSIC: Vladimir Selinsky. PRODUCER-DIRECTOR: Devere (Dee) Engelbach. WRITERS: Norman Rosten, Milton Geiger, Joseph Liss, etc.

June 5–Sept. 11, 1945, CBS. 30m, Tuesdays at 9: 30. Schenley Laboratories. CAST: Guest stars in anthology roles of doctors at war: Gene Lockhart, Ronald Colman, Robert Young, Robert Montgomery, Vincent Price, Robert Cummings, Van Heflin, etc. ANNOUNCER: Jimmy Wallington. MUSIC: Leith Stevens. PRODUCER-DIRECTOR: Devere (Dee) Engelbach. WRITERS: Lou Pelletier, Jacques Finke, Milton Geiger. SOUND EFFECTS: Al Schaffer.

The purpose of *The Doctor Fights* was twofold: to honor the nation's 180,000 doctors, 60,000 of whom were in the theaters of battle, and to acquaint the public with the new miracle drug, penicillin. The sponsor, Schenley Laboratories, was one of 22 companies charged with making penicillin, and often the stories described wondrous cures effected with its use by doctors in distant and primitive outposts. Many listeners at that time had never heard of the drug.

It was a solid series, the only major difference in its two seasons the weekly appearance by Massey in the 1944 starring roles. Among 1945 stories, Franchot Tone played a doctor who, with two companions, took a frightening jeep trip into the wildest parts of China to rescue an American officer stricken with infantile paralysis. Gregory Peck starred as a medical officer on a destroyer who was faced with the grim prospect of using his small stock of penicillin to treat German prisoners rather than saving it for possible use on his own men. Cary Grant was a doctor in a Japanese stockade whose "live to fight another day" philosophy paid off, allowing him to move to a more civilized prison ("a better place than this is, Gunga Din," he said, a nice little touch), where his treatments could be more effective. Often the real doctors whose experiences were dramatized were interviewed from remote locations, relating asides that had not been used in the stories.

Director Dee Engelbach had risen to that post just six years after beginning at NBC as a page boy. Engelbach had transcriptions made of the dress rehearsals for the purpose of a final critique and cut. Many of these survive and are on tape. Often they are indistinguishable from the on-air broadcasts, but occasionally the casts indulge in extraneous dialogue and clowning. On the Gregory Peck rehearsal, announcer Jimmy Wallington promos the next week's broadcast as "George Brent in a thrilling true story, *His Brother Uses a Bagel.*" This breaks up the crew, including Wallington, who can barely get through his remaining credits.

DR. I. Q., THE MENTAL BANKER, quiz.

BROADCAST HISTORY: April 10–July 3, 1939, Blue Network. 30m, Mondays at 10:30. Mars Candy.

July 10, 1939–Oct. 28, 1949, NBC. 30m, Mondays at 9, 1939–42; at 9:30, 1942–44; at 10:30, 1944–47; at 9:30, 1947–49. Mars Candy, 1939–42, and again 1944–49; Vick Chemical Company, 1942–44.

Jan. 4–Nov. 29, 1950, ABC. 30m, Wednesdays at 8. Embassy Cigarettes.

CAST: Lew Valentine as quizmaster Dr. I. Q., 1939–42 and 1946–50; Jimmy McClain as Dr. I. Q., 1942–46; Stanley Vainrib as Dr. I. Q. briefly in 1947. ANNOUNCER: Allen C. Anthony. ANNOUNCER-ASSISTANTS: Frank Barton, Ralph Rogers, Jim Doyle, Hank Weaver, Ed Shaughnessy, Johnny Frazer, many others. CREATOR: Lee Segall. DIRECTORS: Paul Dumont, Harry Holcomb.

Dr. I. Q. was the first great quiz show of the air. None before it possessed the style, pace, or longevity of this brisk item. The "doctor" offered a new lightning-fast quiz, with listeners in almost every major city eventually eligible to play. The show traveled across the country, broadcasting from the stages of movie houses from Boston to Los Angeles, spending a month or six weeks in

each locale and using nine microphones to achieve its effects. Two of the mikes were for the audience, to pick up laughter and applause. Six were for roving assistants, announcers who were stationed throughout the theater looking for contestants. The ninth microphone was for the man himself, "Dr. I. Q."

Standing at center stage, Dr. I. Q. showered silver dollars upon the lucky and smart contestants who were chosen and could answer under fire. The show had a quicksilver velocity, with the quizmaster asking an average of 35 to 40 questions per half-hour. "I have a gentleman in the balcony, doctor," an announcer would offer. Immediately Dr. I. Q. would bark, "*Six* silver dollars to that gentleman if he can answer this question!" The questions were tough, even the cheap ones. "Why are a cat's whiskers the same length as the width of his body?" *They act as "tactile" instruments, preventing the cat from entering dark passages that might be too narrow.* "Give a proverb that uses a term in dressmaking." *A stitch in time saves nine.* They were tough but not too tough: the contestants answered correctly around 52 percent of the time, the ten-second time limit and the live format sometimes cited as pressure factors.

Mars Candy budgeted $700 a week in silver-dollar prize money, and by the end of its run *Dr. I. Q.* had become a modestly big-money quiz show. One contestant in Denver won $3,100 for identifying Lincoln's Gettysburg Address as the source of a "Famous Quotation" segment. In the "Right or Wrong" part of the show, Dr. I. Q. read six rapid-fire statements, giving a contestant a chance at $1,000 for right-or-wrong answers to all six. Other well-remembered features were the "Biographical Sketch" and the "Thought Twister." In the "sketch," six clues were given to the identity of a famous person; these puzzlers were submitted by listeners whose prizes increased as the contestant missed each clue and watched *his* prize decrease. The Thought Twister was read "one time and one time only," and the contestant had to repeat it verbatim. A typical twister: "Boxes can be opened when they're closed; boxes when they're opened can be closed."

The main attraction was the pace. "There may be more sophisticated quiz shows," said *Radio Guide* in 1939, "but for sheer showmanship and variety, none can beat *Dr. I. Q.*" A contestant got one quick shot at the money and the microphone moved on: the roving announcers picked people at their discretion, and the phrase "I have a lady in the balcony, doctor" was bandied nationally, with a slight hint of impropriety. When the contestant lost, Dr. I. Q. always offered sincere condolences—"I'm *soooooo* sorry, but a box of Dr. I. Q. Candy to that lady!"—and moved on to the gentleman in the third row before that lady or the audience could catch a breath.

Lew Valentine, who started in radio as a singer-announcer at WOAI, San Antonio, left the show in 1942 for a three-year hitch in the Army. His replacement, Jimmy McClain, was a theology student preparing for an Episcopalian ministry. On May 27, 1946, when Valentine returned, there were two "doctors" on stage, as he and McClain double-teamed it. Then McClain dropped out of radio to devote his time to church work. He did return for a short stint as Dr. I. Q. on television, in 1954. Valentine continued on radio to the end, dropping out for a brief ten-week period (beginning Dec. 8, 1947) to prepare for the new *Dr. I. Q. Jr.* show. During his absence, Stanley Vainrib played the part. Allen C. Anthony, the Mars announcer, was well known for his ability to make the candy as appealing as the money.

DR. I. Q. JR., juvenile quiz.

BROADCAST HISTORY: May 11–Aug. 24, 1941, NBC. 30m, Sundays at 6:30. Mars Candy.

March 6, 1948–April 2, 1949, NBC. 30m, Saturdays at 5, then at 5:30. Mars Candy.

CAST: Jimmy McClain as Dr. I. Q., 1941; Lew Valentine as Dr. I. Q., 1948. Allen C. Anthony, announcer, as Bugs Beagle.

Dr. I. Q. Jr. was a veritable copy of the famed adult quiz show, wrapped in a juvenile format. The silver-dollar prizes were replaced by silver dimes, the questions were slightly easier, but the pace was the same. The children had five seconds to answer such tricky questions as these: "There are twelve children in a class. All but eight are boys. How many are girls?" (No, the answer is not four.) "Betty got to school ten minutes after Jane did. Mary got to school five minutes before Betty did. Who got to school first?" Features included the "Tongue Twister"

(a variation of the parent show's "Thought Twister") and "History in Headlines," in which great historical events were retold in newspaper language, with a 100-dime award to the contestant who pegged it.

Quizmaster Jimmy McClain used the early version to prep for his later appearance as Dr. I. Q. on the main show. As Bugs Beagle, announcer Allen C. Anthony told stories that contained three factual errors. Prizes were given to the kids who pointed out the mistakes.

DR. KILDARE, medical drama, also known as *The Story of Dr. Kildare,* based on the Metro Goldwyn Mayer films.

BROADCAST HISTORY: 1949, transcribed syndication, produced on the West Coast but launched at WMGM, New York, Feb. 1, 1950. Opened a run of one season on WOR Jan. 1, 1952, 30m, Tuesdays at 8:30.

CAST: Lew Ayres as Dr. James Kildare, a young and idealistic physician at Blair General Hospital. Lionel Barrymore as Dr. Leonard Gillespie, the crusty, lovable diagnostician. Jane Webb as Mary Lamont. Ted Osborne as Dr. Carough, chief of administration. Virginia Gregg as the chattering Nurse Parker. Also: Paul Dubov, Stacy Harris, Isabel Jewell, Jay Novello, Georgia Ellis, Paul Frees, Raymond Burr. **ANNOUNCER:** Dick Joy.

Dr. Kildare brought to the microphone the stars of the popular MGM film series in a wave of recorded dramatic fare of the late '40s. Doctors Kildare and Gillespie helped make Blair General Hospital "one of the great citadels of American medicine," listeners were told: the facility was described as "a clump of gray-white buildings planted deep in the heart of New York, where life begins, where life ends, where life goes on." The opening signature faded in on Kildare's medical oath: ". . . whatsoever house I enter, there will I go for the benefit of the sick, and whatsoever things I see or hear concerning the life of men I will keep silence thereon, counting such things to be held as sacred trusts."

Dr. Kildare was about battles with silly hospital administrators, conflicts with ignorant patients, medical dilemmas building to personal crises. Sometimes it seemed that Blair was peopled with eccentrics. Dr. Gillespie, played to the hilt by Barrymore, was eccentric in his own right; the petty bureaucrat Dr. Carough was their chief antagonist, and Nurse Parker was an unbelievable fussy old maid.

DR. SIXGUN, western drama.

BROADCAST HISTORY: Sept. 2, 1954–Oct. 13, 1955, NBC. 30m, Thursdays at 8:30 through Sept. 1954, then Sundays at 8 until April 21; off the air until Aug. 18, then Thursdays at 8.

CAST: Karl Weber as Dr. Ray Matson, "the gun-toting frontier doctor who roamed the length and breadth of the old Indian territory, friend and physician to white man and Indian alike, the symbol of justice and mercy in the lawless west of the 1870s. This legendary figure was known to all as *Dr. Sixgun*." Bill Griffis as Pablo, the doctor's gypsy sidekick, who told the stories. **ANNOUNCER:** Fred Collins. **DIRECTOR:** Harry Frazee. **WRITERS:** Ernest Kinoy, George Lefferts.

DOCTORS AT WAR, docudrama.

BROADCAST HISTORY: Dec. 26, 1942–June 26, 1943, and Jan. 15–June 24, 1944, NBC. 30m, Saturdays at 5, 1942–43; at 4:30, 1944.

NARRATOR: Dr. W. W. Bauer, director of health education for the American Medical Association. **WRITER:** William Murphy.

Doctors at War was a joint project of NBC, the American Medical Association, and the Armed Forces. Its purpose was to give the public an idea of what the nation's physicians were contributing to the war effort. Topics covered included combat training programs, dealing with plasma under desert wartime conditions, the mortality rate for the wounded, and the work of Navy doctors and Army nurses.

The series had long periods of prehistory and posthistory. It grew out of an AMA educational format, begun on NBC in 1935, wherein Dr. W. W. Bauer delivered straight health talks. These were heard on the Red and Blue Networks, becoming dramatized by 1938. On Nov. 13, 1940, it became *Doctors at Work*, heard on the Blue Network, Wednesdays at 10:30 (1940–41), and on the Red Network, Saturdays at 5 (1941–42). This was followed by *Doctors at War*, which in turn became *Doctors Look Ahead* (Jan.–June 1945), *Doctors at Home* (Dec. 1945–June 1946), *Doctors Then and Now* (Dec. 1946–

June 1947), and *Doctors Today* (Dec. 1947–June 1948), all NBC, Saturdays at 4.

DOLLAR A MINUTE, audience show.

BROADCAST HISTORY: Oct. 4, 1950–May 20, 1951, CBS. 30m, various times.

HOST: Bill Goodwin. **CREATOR-PRODUCER:** Jess Oppenheimer. **DIRECTOR:** Al Span.

Dollar a Minute was not, as the title implied, a giveaway show: in fact, it was probably radio's first notable *takeaway* show, offering participants a national platform to use as they wished, at a dollar a minute. "Any student of a radio advertising rate card will say it is the greatest bargain of the generation," proclaimed *Radio Life*. For the privilege of addressing six million people, the magazine asked, "would you pay a dollar a minute?" Creator Oppenheimer got the idea while watching an audition for a new giveaway show. He noticed that most of the contestants seemed to have stories that never got told because the hosts kept interrupting and turning the conversation back to the game. What if talk, not the game, was the whole point? Among the people presented were a convict with an appeal for an anti-delinquency program, a Nebraska housewife fed up with her husband's constant boasting about Texas, and an ant colony enthusiast espousing the "therapeutic value" of having ants in the living room—"under glass, of course."

DON WINSLOW OF THE NAVY, juvenile adventure serial, based on the comic strip by Frank Martinek.

BROADCAST HISTORY: 1937, WMAQ, Chicago.
Oct. 19, 1937–May 26, 1939, Blue Network (briefly on the Red, May–Aug. 1938). 15m, weekdays at 5:15, 1937–38; at 7, 1938–39; at 5:30, March–May 1939. Kellogg Cereals, 1938–39; Ipana Toothpaste, March–May 1939.
Oct. 5, 1942–Jan. 1, 1943, Blue Network. 15m, weekdays at 6:15.

CAST: Bob Guilbert as Don Winslow, a young Navy commander assigned to Intelligence. Raymond Edward Johnson as Don Winslow, 1942. Edward Davison as Don's friend Lt. Red Pennington; John Gibson as Pennington, 1942. Betty Lou Gerson as Mercedes Colby, Don's best girl; Lenore Kingston also as Mercedes. **ANNOUNCERS:** Paul Luther, etc. **WRITERS:** Al Barker, Albert Aley. **SOUND**

EFFECTS: Michael Eisenmenger, Ray Kremer, Bob Graham.

In the original *Don Winslow* serial, Winslow and his pal Red Pennington were assigned to counter "the Scorpion," his daughter Tasmia, and their worldwide organization of evil. In the 1942 revival, the enemies were "the Japs and Nazis," Pennington announced. Almost at once, the boys were in the thick of battle: a fight with a submarine, then an explosion that wrecked the plane's tail controls and sent it plummeting to earth, too low to parachute. Tune in tomorrow!

DOORWAY TO LIFE, dramatized case histories; childhood psychology.

BROADCAST HISTORY: July 2, 1947–June 20, 1948, CBS. 30m, Wednesdays at 10:30, then Sundays at 1:30, then at 1.
CAST: Anthology roles by top Hollywood juvenile talent: Marlene Aames, Norma Jean Nilsson, Anne Whitfield, Henry Blair, Johnny McGovern, etc. **CREATOR-PRODUCER-DIRECTOR:** William N. Robson. **WRITERS:** Virginia Mullen, Bill Alland.

The goal of *Doorway to Life* was to offer palatable "message" drama that illustrated common mistakes made by parents and the likely effects on their kids. Subjects included adoption, school, and dating, but hassles with parents were at its heart. It's probably safe to say that no other show offered a drama on the consequences of poor toilet training.

THE DORIS DAY SHOW, transcribed song series.

BROADCAST HISTORY: March 28, 1952–May 26, 1953, CBS. 30m, various times.
CAST: Singer Doris Day with such guests as Danny Thomas, Kirk Douglas, Jack Smith, and Jack Kirkwood. **ANNOUNCER:** Roy Rowan, Johnny Jacobs, Don Wilson. **DIRECTOR-EDITOR:** Sam Pierce. **THEME:** *It's Magic.*

DOROTHY GORDON, children's series: songs, folk tales, classics. Also known as *The Children's Corner.*

BROADCAST HISTORY: May 4, 1936–Jan. 14, 1938, CBS. 15m, Mondays-Wednesdays-Fridays at 5:15.

Dec. 16, 1938–March 17, 1939, Mutual. 15m, three a week at 5:45. Wheatena.

Dorothy Gordon had a long career in children's programming, beginning on WEAF as early as 1924. She was musical director of the CBS *American School of the Air* from 1931 to 1938. She viewed her own series as alternatives to the thrillers that had come to dominate the 5 to 6 P.M. hour. She read such classics as *Peter Pan* and *Alice in Wonderland:* she could tell her tales in eight languages and frequently told obscure legends that she had collected in her travels around the world. Gordon managed to persuade her sponsor, Wheatena, to limit the shrill superlatives in its advertising and to refrain completely from the premium offers then so prolific in children's radio.

THE DOROTHY LAMOUR SHOW, musical variety. See SEALTEST VARIETY THEATRE.

BROADCAST HISTORY: Dec. 30, 1935–Feb. 26, 1936, Blue Network. 10m, three a week at 11:05.

DOUBLE OR NOTHING, quiz.

BROADCAST HISTORY: Sept. 29, 1940–June 15, 1947, Mutual. 30m, Sundays at 6 into May 1941; Fridays at 8, May–Sept. 1941; Sundays at 6, Sept.–May 1942; Fridays at 9:30, 1942–45; Sundays at 9:30, 1945–47. Feenamint.
June 30, 1947–June 25, 1948, CBS. 30m, five a week at 3. Campbell Soups.
May 31, 1948–June 19, 1953, NBC. 30m, five a week at 2 until Dec. 21, 1951. Also heard at 10:30 A.M. (two daily broadcasts on the same network for the same sponsor) beginning April 24, 1950. After Dec. 1951, only the morning show remained. Campbell Soups.
June 22, 1953–Jan. 15, 1954, ABC. 30m, weekdays at 11:30. Campbell Soups.
HOSTS: Walter Compton, ca. 1940–43; John Reed King, 1943–45; Todd Russell, 1945–47; Walter O'Keefe, 1947–54. **ANNOUNCERS:** Alois Havrilla, Fred Cole, Murray Wagner. **MUSIC:** Elliott Jacoby, early 1940s (Frank Forest, tenor, added an unusual ingredient to a quiz show); Nat Brusiloff, maestro, ca. 1943; Irv Orton, musical director after 1947. **PRODUCERS:** Ken Fickett, Lou Crosby, Diana Bourbon. **DIRECTORS:** Harry Spears, Thomas Vietor, John Wellington. **WRITERS:**

Carroll Carroll, Gerald Rice, Harry Bailey. **THEME:** *Three Little Words*.

The format of *Double or Nothing*, one of radio's hardiest quizzes, changed somewhat over the years. In 1940 host Walter Compton would begin by asking a question for $5. The contestant then had to speak off the cuff about the subject of his question, while a clock ticked off 60 seconds. For each fact that the contestant brought out in his speech, Compton would award more cash, in increments of $2 to $4 depending on the importance or amusement value of the fact. Then the contestant faced another question. If he answered correctly, he doubled the pot he had accumulated in his talk; if he muffed it, he lost all but the original $5 he had won with his first question.

The tenure of John Reed King was distinguished by the host's glib tongue and ability to fast-talk with contestants. The show continued in its prime-time run through the two years with Todd Russell as quizmaster. The shift to CBS in 1947 brought *Double or Nothing* to the daytime schedule. By then the quiz had become, in the words of writer Carroll Carroll, a "bargain basement" version of the *$64 Question*. Host Walter O'Keefe asked an easy question for $2, then a harder one for $4, and so on up a ladder until a $10 plateau was reached. At that point, a contestant could keep his money or take on one more question for "double or nothing." Later a "grand slam" element was added, in which a player could earn as much as $80. Higher prizes were awarded in the *Double or Nothing* "Sweepstakes," but the cash remained small by comparison with other such shows, and the suspense was certainly bearable.

Double or Nothing endured because of the nimble ad-libbing of its hosts and because, over the years, the show gained a reputation for double entendres and unexpected embarrassment. By far the most sensational of these came to be known as the "waitress episode," which was so shocking to audiences of that innocent late 1940s era that its content could not even be hinted in the press (reporter Shirley Gordon mentioned it in *Radio Life* years later without ever telling her readers what she was talking about). While interviewing a waitress, O'Keefe asked if she'd had any experiences she could share on the ra-

dio. Yes, she said, she once had a friend, male, who had had some psychological problems. She didn't know what she could do for him, but a mutual friend had suggested that he "get a good-looking girl like you and take her home and just have a big screwing party." O'Keefe hustled her through the quiz fast, but the damage was done: the show had been carried live to the East Coast, and CBS was inundated with angry calls. The network ordered all its West Coast affiliates (which had transcribed the show for broadcast in a later timeslot) to cancel it and destroy the transcriptions. Obviously, at least one was saved: the show exists on tape, a nice curiosity piece.

DRAGNET, police drama; a pioneering series of unprecedented realism.

BROADCAST HISTORY: June 3, 1949–Feb. 26, 1957, NBC. 30m, various times in the first four months; 1949–50, Thursdays at 10:30, Fatima Cigarettes; 1950–52, Thursdays at 9, Fatima, 1950–51, then Chesterfield; 1952–53, Sundays at 9:30, Chesterfield; 1953–55, Tuesdays at 9, later 8:30, Chesterfield; 1955–57, Tuesdays at 8:30, repeat broadcasts, multiple sponsorship.

CAST: Jack Webb as Detective Sergeant Joe Friday of the Los Angeles Police Department. Barton Yarborough as Sergeant Ben Romero, Friday's first partner. Barney Phillips as partner Ed Jacobs, a new role created upon Yarborough's sudden death on Dec. 19, 1951. Ben Alexander as Officer Frank Smith, Friday's partner beginning in the fall of 1952. Peggy Webber as Ma Friday, the detective's mother, with whom he lived. Raymond Burr as Ed Backstrand, chief of detectives. Herb Butterfield as Lt. Lee Jones of the crime lab. Also: Sam Edwards, Parley Baer, Vic Perrin, Stacy Harris, Georgia Ellis, Virginia Gregg, and many other Hollywood radio people. **ANNOUNCERS:** Hal Gibney and George Fenneman, alternating lines. **MUSIC:** Walter Schumann. **CREATOR-DIRECTOR:** Jack Webb. **DIRECTOR:** Bill Rousseau (early episodes). **WRITER:** James E. Moser; also, Jack Robinson. **SOUND EFFECTS:** Wayne Kenworthy, Jack Robinson, Bud Tollefson, etc. **THEME:** *Dragnet March,* by Walter Schumann.

Jack Webb had been active in radio for several years before *Dragnet* propelled him to national prominence. He had arrived at KGO, the ABC outlet in San Francisco, an unknown novice in 1945. Soon he was working as a staff announcer and disc jockey. His morning show, *The Coffee Club*, revealed his lifelong interest in jazz music, and in 1946 he was featured on a limited ABC-West network in the quarter-hour docudrama *One out of Seven*. His *Jack Webb Show*, also 1946, was a bizarre comedy series unlike anything else he ever attempted. His major break arrived with *Pat Novak*: for 26 weeks Webb played a waterfront detective in a series so hard-boiled it became high camp. He moved to Hollywood, abandoning *Novak* just as that series was hitting its peak. Mutual immediately slipped him into a *Novak* sound-alike, *Johnny Modero: Pier 23*, for the summer of 1947. He played leads and bit parts on such series as *Escape*, *The Whistler*, and *This Is Your FBI*. He began a film career: in *He Walked by Night* (1948), Webb played a crime lab cop. The film's technical adviser was Sergeant Marty Wynn of the Los Angeles police. Webb and Wynn shared a belief that pure investigative procedure was dramatic enough without the melodrama of the private eye. The seeds of *Dragnet* were sown on a movie set.

Webb was born April 2, 1920, in Santa Monica. His interest in radio developed early: he moonlighted on various Los Angeles stations as a young man while supporting his mother with a string of menial day jobs. He later wrote, directed, hosted, and performed in variety programs for the Army Air Forces, and his arrival at KGO in 1945 was followed by a rapid rise through the ranks of Radio Row to front-rank stardom.

But *Dragnet* evolved slowly. Webb pondered the idea he had received from Marty Wynn and developed it for more than a year. Realism should be the show's hallmark: the stories should be authentic to the last sound effect. He began hanging out at police headquarters, riding with detective teams on house calls. He attended classes at the police academy, becoming fluent in police terminology and technique. But when he prepared his series proposal, NBC was unimpressed. It sounded like just another cop show, without the contrived thrill trappings. Webb was told to prepare an audition record: he had one week to pull it together.

With his audition disc in hand, his next job was to obtain the cooperation of the police. This was essential, for the series Webb envisioned could not be done without it. He wanted to get his stories from official files, to show the step-by-step procedure used by real officers in tracking down a real criminal. Accompanied by writer James E. Moser, Webb took the record to C. B. Horrall, chief of police in Los Angeles. Horrall listened to ten minutes, then got up and left the room. A deputy chief working at a nearby desk looked up and grunted occasionally but offered no encouragement. Horrall never returned. It was an inauspicious beginning.

Surprisingly, the police approved the show. The conditions were clear: the police wanted control over sponsorship; they wanted Webb's agreement that his access to the files would not compromise confidentiality; and they wanted assurance that the department would not be "scripted into any unflattering entanglements."

They needn't have worried: Webb was, and remained, a staunch police advocate. He was a sympathetic ear, a true believer in the difficulty and often impossibility of the jobs they do. "We try to make cops human beings," he would say years later. "We try to combine the best qualities of the men I've seen downtown, incorporate their way of speaking, make a composite." But the show began in unspectacular fashion. There was still no theme music: the soon-to-be-famous *Dragnet March* was in place within the month, but the second show (the earliest episode yet heard) reveals a strange *Dragnet* indeed. Webb was engaged in an on-air laboratory, as real as *The Columbia Workshop* set up a dozen years earlier on another network. Week by week the show was refined, the dialogue pared, the delivery made ever more deadpan. In the trade this was called underplaying, a term Webb disputed. "Underplaying is still acting," he told *Time* in 1950. "We try to make it as real as a guy pouring a cup of coffee."

When the cops walked up the steps at headquarters, listeners heard *exactly* the number of steps between floors in the real police building. When Webb picked up a crime report and read off the description of a suspect, the listener heard him turn a page first, because descriptions were always on the second page of real reports. The cops became fans as well as technical advisers. Marty Wynn, who had helped start it all, served in that capacity, as did Sgt. Vance Brasher. Chief Horrall got on-air credit in the earliest shows; he was succeeded by William H. Parker, and it was Parker whose name was most associated with the technical excellence of *Dragnet*.

Webb's portrayal of Joe Friday would become classic. Friday was a cop's cop, tough but not hard, conservative but caring. It was through Friday's eyes that *Dragnet* unfolded each week. The show opened with a startling burst of music—four stinging notes that became immediately celebrated, indelibly linked through the decades with Webb, *Dragnet*, and composer Schumann. Schoolboys hummed it in back lots when bullies were pummelled: that DUM-DE-DUM-DUM an unstated symbol of justice and retribution that extended beyond the reaches of the show itself. Then, as the theme faded, announcer Hal Gibney came up full: *Ladies and gentlemen . . . the story you are about to hear is true. Only the names have been changed to protect the innocent.* Now came another innovation—two announcers, Gibney and George Fenneman, whose voices bounced back and forth, complementing even as they contrasted, giving the opening greater authority than either, alone, could have done.

Friday's first partner, Ben Romero, was also a sergeant. Friday and Romero had a solid working friendship, as police partners must, and Webb had the same kind of friendship with Barton Yarborough, who played the role. When plans were made to put *Dragnet* on television, Webb ignored the wisdom of the time and prepared to use radio people, including Yarborough, in key roles. The question of the day, whenever radio people were considered for TV roles, was often cruelly blunt—will he *look* right? Webb answered it bluntly for *Radio Life*: "I'll take the actor and he'll look right." One *Dragnet* TV show was shot with Yarborough as Romero, a preseries special, aired on NBC's *Chesterfield Sound-Off Time* Dec. 16, 1951. Then Yarborough died suddenly, leaving a void on both *Dragnets* that was impossible to fill. Webb plugged in Barney Phillips, a frequent *Dragnet* heavy, as Ed Jacobs, but the search for a new partner continued. The solution was not found in the easygoing characterization of Ben Romero but in a new character who would come in whole, his own man, and add the element of humor.

Like Yarborough, Ben Alexander had had a long radio career. His forte had been comedy roles and stints as quizmaster: he had never considered himself *Dragnet* material until another comedy actor, Cliff Arquette, worked a *Dragnet* TV show and recommended him to Webb. By October 1952, Alexander had been fitted into the series as the second lead, a paunchy police detective named Frank Smith. Frank had the necessary police requisites—he was dependable and courageous under fire—but he was also a perpetual worrywart. He fretted over his disputes with his wife Fay; he fussed over his pills and was always concocting some exotic recipe. Frank became such a vital part of the show that when he was wounded in a two-part story and his life hung in the balance, fans reacted with thousands of letters.

Friday remained a bachelor who lived alone with his mother. Peggy Webber, who played the mom, was a young woman who could "do" an old woman perfectly on the air. "Jack never let me rehearse with the rest of them," she said 30 years later. "He always believed I gave a better performance when I read my lines cold." However Webb achieved his results, the show's realism and originality were startling. Even such austere journals as *The Commonweal* were impressed. On *Dragnet*, the reporter promised, a listener would find "no stereotyped hoodlums with congenital inability to voice the tongue-point dental fricative; no dem's and dose's. If intelligence can be measured as the number of shades visible between black and white, *Dragnet* is an intelligent program. Character is not subordinated to the arbitrary requirements of an action-packed script."

The listener was hooked by situation (*a woman is missing and her husband suspects foul play*) and propelled by the investigation (*your job . . . find her*): often he was touched by the climax and solution. Not all *Dragnets* ended happily. "We don't even try to prove that crime doesn't pay," Webb said in a 1950 *Time* profile. "Sometimes it does." But the *Dragnet* technique of putting "you on the side of the law," letting the listener discover the case step by step with the cops, was unique in its time.

It was Tuesday, June 17th. It was warm in Los Angeles. We were working the day watch out of burglary. My partner's Ben Romero, the boss is Ed Backstrand, chief of detectives. My name's

Friday. I was on my way to work that morning and it was 7:53 A.M. when I got to Room 45. Burglary Detail . . .

Dragnet was one of the first radio shows to break the taboo against dramatizing sex crimes. Children were killed, another taboo. The heartbreaking holiday show known as *A Gun for Christmas* was a brash counterpoint to the commercialized fluff and synthetic joy offered everywhere else. "What's it all prove, Joe?" Romero would ask, feeling hopeless in the face of tragedy. And Friday, in that dry, lovely way, would put it to rest. "You don't give a kid a gun for Christmas." And the famed four-note theme would burst over the statement, louder than the shot that had just killed little Stevie Morheim. When mail flooded in protesting this show, Webb passed it along to Chief Parker. The cops promised such groups as the National Rifle Association "ten more shows illustrating the folly of giving rifles to children." On graphically brutal stories, Fenneman would make a preshow announcement—"this story is for you, not your children"—and the world of *Dragnet* began anew.

It was a world of sound, as many as 300 effects on each show, keeping five soundmen busy for 30 minutes. The music was best described by Tim Brooks and Earle Marsh in their *Complete Directory to Prime-Time Network TV Shows*: the opening theme was "possibly the most famous four-note introduction since Beethoven's *Fifth Symphony*," and the bridge music was "laced throughout every episode, dark and tension-filled, then erupting in a loud 'stinger' after an especially significant revelation." Marsh and Brooks were writing of TV, but they perfectly describe the music on *Dragnet* radio.

Finally there was the lingo of the squad room. Dispatcher terminology was terse and correct, with no exposition to help a listener understand it. The faithful came to know that an APB was an all-points bulletin, and running a car through DMV meant checking with the Department of Motor Vehicles. When officers were sent on a 211, a 484, a 459, a 390, a 415, or a 311, that meant robbery, theft, burglary, a drunk, disturbing the peace, or lewd conduct, the numbers corresponding to the real sections of the penal code. R&I meant Record and Identification; a suspect's physical characteristics were recorded on his I-sheet. MO was method of operation. And so it

went, the terms washing over a listener in a way that was strangely enhanced by not being explained and completely understood.

Dragnet was the peak of Webb's professional career. His *Pete Kelly's Blues* (NBC, 1951) was also powerful, but it was as Joe Friday that he was known for the rest of his days. He died Dec. 23, 1982, a heart attack victim. Upon his death, the Los Angeles Police Department flew its flags at half-staff.

DRAMAS OF YOUTH, dramatic anthology.

BROADCAST HISTORY: 1933–ca. 1941, Mutual, regional West Coast network.
CAST: Louise Erickson, Rolland Morris, Peter Rankin, Barbara Eiler, Helen Thomas, Geraldine Nolan, Jean Lang, Don Chapman, Charles West, etc.
DIRECTOR: Marion Ward.

Dramas of Youth was a workshop of developing juvenile talent. It offered stories about famous people when they were young, and later turned to classic dramatizations. Marion Ward developed it and directed until her death in 1940.

THE DREFT STAR PLAYHOUSE, Hollywood drama in serial form.

BROADCAST HISTORY: June 28, 1943–March 30, 1945, NBC. 15m continuation, weekdays at 11:30 A.M. Dreft.
CAST: Hollywood film stars in adaptations of popular movies: *Bachelor Mother*, with Jane Wyman; *Hold Back the Dawn*, with Maureen O'Sullivan; *Take a Letter, Darling*, with Mary Astor, etc. West Coast radio people in support: Les Tremayne, Cathy Lewis, George Couloris, Rosemary DeCamp, etc. **ANNOUNCERS:** Marvin Miller, Terry O'Sullivan. **MUSIC:** Richard Aurandt. **DIRECTORS:** Les Mitchel, Axel Gruenberg.

The Dreft Star Playhouse was a noble experiment, devised to see if daytime radio would support a show of purported nighttime quality. It was initially titled *The Hollywood Theater of the Air* but underwent the name change to avoid confusion with other shows using the "Hollywood" angle. It was ambitious, with Procter & Gamble budgeting $3,000 a week for name talent. The fare was largely romantic: *Dark Victory*, with Gail Patrick, ran two months in daily quarter-hour doses, but the series never generated more than average soap opera ratings.

DUFFY'S TAVERN, situation comedy.

BROADCAST HISTORY: July 29, 1940, CBS. 30m. First appeared on the audition series *Forecast.*

March 1, 1941–June 30, 1942, CBS. 30m, Saturdays at 8:30, Schick Razors, March–June 1941; Thursdays at 8:30, Schick, 1941–42; Tuesdays at 9, Sanka, March–June 1942.

Oct. 6, 1942–June 27, 1944, Blue Network. 30m, Tuesdays at 8:30. Bristol Myers and Ipana.

Sept. 15, 1944–Jan. 18, 1952, NBC. 30m, Fridays at 8:30, Bristol Myers, 1944–46; Wednesdays at 9, Bristol Myers, 1946–49; Thursdays at 9:30, Blatz Beer, 1949–50; Fridays at 9:30, multiple sponsorship, 1950–52.

CAST: Ed Gardner as Archie, the manager of Duffy's Tavern, "eyesore of the East Side" where "the elite meet to eat." Shirley Booth as Miss Duffy, daughter of the never-present proprietor; Florence Halop as Miss Duffy, 1943–44 and again 1948–49; Sandra Gould as Miss Duffy, 1944–48; others to play Miss Duffy were Helen Lynd, Doris Singleton, Sara Berner, Connie Manning, Florence Robinson, Helen Eley, Margie Liszt, Gloria Erlanger, Pauline Drake, and Hazel Shermet. Charlie Cantor as Clifton Finnegan, a dimwit who frequented the tavern. Eddie Green as Eddie the wisecracking waiter. Alan Reed as Clancy the cop, who dropped in from time to time. F. Chase Taylor as Colonel Stoopnagle. Dickie Van Patten as Finnegan's kid brother Wilfred. **ANNOUNCERS:** John Reed King, Jimmy Wallington, Marvin Miller, Perry Ward, Rod O'Connor, etc. **MUSIC:** John Kirby, ca. 1941; orchestra by Peter Van Steeden; later, groups led by Joe Venuti, Reet Veet Reeves, Matty Malneck. **VOCALISTS:** Johnny Johnston, Benay Venuta, Tito Guizar, Helen Ward, Bob Graham. **DIRECTORS:** Rupert Lucas, Jack Roche, Tony Sanford, Mitchell Benson. **WRITERS:** gags and lines by Abe Burrows, Larry Marks, Larry Gelbart, Ed Reynolds, Norman Paul, Lew Meltzer, Dick Martin, Vincent Bogert, Manny Sachs, Alan Kent, Bill Manhoff, Raymond Ellis, Bob Schiller, Larry Rhine, etc.; final scripts by Ed Gardner. **SOUND EFFECTS:** Virgil Reimer (NBC). **THEME:** *When Irish Eyes Are Smiling,* blending in on piano to a ringing telephone (inevitably Duffy calling).

Duffy's Tavern was a state of mind. Allegedly located in downtown Manhattan on Third Avenue at 23rd Street, Duffy's catered to the Irish working class. Its bill o' fare included corned beef, cabbage, and pickled pigs' feet. The food was bad but the service was lousy. The proprietor, Duffy, never put in an appearance, but his disagreeable nature was constantly evident in his frequent telephone calls to Archie, his manager.

A listener heard only Archie's side of the talk, but it was enough. Archie described the guests who were expected to drop in, then weathered Duffy's displeasure for the remainder of the show. Duffy disdained everything, it seemed, but Irish tenors.

At Duffy's, said Archie, they caught the "after-Bingo crowd." But the most famous people in show business were apt to turn up in a given half-hour, to be insulted by Archie and his gang. The gang included Duffy's daughter, "a gabby, gum-chewing, featherbrained Brooklyn miss who exposes her blissful ignorance every time she opens her mouth" (*Radio Life*); Clifton Finnegan, a customer so dumb he couldn't say "duhhh" without thinking it over; a beat-walking cop named Clancy; and a streetwise Negro waiter, Eddie, whose cunning dialogue contained some of the show's funniest lines.

But it was Archie, the creation of an eccentric radio writer-director named Ed Gardner, who refined the insult and made it an art form. When the tavern was visited by noted critic Clifton Fadiman (the similarity of whose name to Clifton Finnegan needed no elaboration), Archie greeted him with "Whaddaya know, besides everything?" Dancer Vera Zorina was introduced as "da terpsicorpse from da ballet." To heavyweight party-giver Elsa Maxwell, Archie quipped, "Speakin' of th' Four Hundred, how're you and the other 398?" About highbrow music critic Deems Taylor, Archie informed Duffy: "He's got no talent of his own, he just talks about the other guys at the Philharmonica."

Gardner was born Eddie Poggenburg in Astoria, Long Island, June 29, 1905. His accent was pure New York—not Brooklyn, as he was always quick to point out. "There is as much difference between New Yorkese and Kings (Borough) English as there is between Oxford and Choctaw," he wrote in a 1941 bylined *Radio Life* article. "A New Yorker, for instance, would say, 'Laertes poizinned the point uv his foil.' In Brooklyn they say, 'Lay-oytees purzined the pernt of his ferl.' " He believed that both forms of speech were learned in grammar school. While he was attending New York's Public

School #4, his future wife and first Miss Duffy, Shirley Booth, was becoming the voice of Brooklyn in that borough's Public School #152. They met at a party and were married Nov. 23, 1929.

But while Booth became well established in theater, Gardner toiled in anonymity. He was a theatrical hustler and promoter, working for small stock companies in every imaginable capacity from director to script typist to "the guy who paints the scenery." In agency work, he said, "I was the guy who gave radio actors the brushoff." He admitted that he did not handle his wife's success well. At J. Walter Thompson, he became a radio director, working Ripley's *Believe It or Not*, *Good News*, *Burns and Allen*, and *The Rudy Vallee Hour*, among others. He was directing *This Is New York*, a short-lived CBS series of 1939, when a difficult character role gave him the idea that would make his fortune.

The show needed an actor who could talk New Yorkese, Gardner remembered, but "all we could get was voices that sounded like Dodger fans in the left field bleachers." Gardner stepped onto the soundstage to demonstrate how the lines should read, and there in the flesh was Archie. It was his own voice he had been seeking, and more than that, it became the inspiration for a new radio show.

Duffy's Tavern was hailed by critics as the most original new comedy show of 1941. The telephone rang as the faint barroom piano strains faded away, and there was Archie in full regalia. Gardner was often photographed in costume: porkpie hat and white apron, signed by all the visiting celebrities at Duffy's Tavern. "Hello, Duffy's Tavern, where the elite meet to eat, Archie the manager speakin', Duffy ain't here . . . oh, hello, Duffy . . . no, no Duffy, it isn't Orson Welles tonight," he said when his "guest" was Raffles the mynah bird: "*this* bird you can shut up."

Gardner and Booth divorced in 1942, but she finished the season as Miss Duffy, and in guest appearances on *The Fred Allen Show* and other programs used her Miss Duffy voice under the name Dottie Mahoney. Her departure in 1943 was a serious loss. Gardner conducted a nationwide search for her replacement: the network staged a contest, but no one could satisfy Gardner's ear. He kept falling back to his premise: "Where they went to grade school, that's what

counts in the way you do the lingo." An actress could fake a southern drawl, "but that Brooklyn twist just about has to be real." As the fall season approached, he resorted to mass auditions by telephone and transcription. The actress he finally selected was Florence Halop, 20, who auditioned by record. Gardner's new wife, Simone, listened and thought she was hearing Shirley Booth. That settled it, but surprise!—Halop had grown up not in Brooklyn but on Long Island, attending the private Professional Children's School in Manhattan. She was Miss Duffy's opposite in almost every way (fluent in French, loved classical music) and had been in radio since an appearance, at age 5, on the Milton Cross *Children's Hour*. Her debut came on the show of Oct. 5, 1943.

As for Duffy, *Tune In* gave the opinion that "only in radio could such a strong personality be nonexistent. Gardner has so completely established the character of Duffy that most listeners can almost hear his voice when he calls in." The reporter also discovered that Gardner, after years of playing Archie, had buried his own personality (though some would dispute that such a separate identity had ever existed) deep inside that of his character.

The show was done live until 1949, then Gardner moved it to Puerto Rico to avoid the oppressive tax structure then in effect in the States. The shows were recorded; the entire cast lived and worked on the island. The illusion remained intact: Duffy's was still in high gear on Third Avenue, and no one could tell eight million listeners otherwise. The show was a famous part of its decade. Convicts at San Quentin voted it their favorite radio program: a premium, *Duffy's First Reader*, was published in 1943, and the *New York World-Telegram* noted that "it drips with grammatical gore." When the sponsor tried to drop the word "tavern" from the title in 1943 (someone at Bristol Myers found the "saloon" connection unsavory), fans went on calling it *Duffy's Tavern* as before. With characters like Two-Top Gruskin (a two-headed character who, like Duffy, was never heard but often discussed and who had once gone to a masquerade party disguised as a pair of bookends propping up the Howard Spring bestseller *My Son, My Son*), *Duffy's* wasn't about to go highbrow. Culture was okay in its place, said Gardner: "I imagine if I knew what it was, I'd probably think it was a very fine thing, if I didn't overdo it. I always wondered where it began and ended.''

Gardner died Aug. 17, 1963.

DUNNINGER, THE MENTALIST, audience show; mind-reading demonstrations.

BROADCAST HISTORY: Sept. 12, 1943–Dec. 27, 1944, Blue Network. 30m, Sundays at 6:30 until Jan.; then Wednesdays at 9. Sherwin-Williams Paints.

June 8–Sept. 28, 1945, NBC. 30m, Fridays at 10; also June 4–June 25, 1946, NBC. 30m, Tuesdays at 9. Summer replacements for *Amos 'n' Andy*. Rinso.

CAST: Joseph Dunninger, magician, hypnotist, and—it was claimed—reader of minds. Also: Marilyn Day, Bill Slater, Andy Love. ANNOUNCERS: Roger Krupp, Don Lowe. MUSIC: Mitchell Ayres.

The radio debut of Dunninger, "the Master Mentalist," created a minor sensation, but by the time his first series left the air in 1944, critics were calling it repetitious. His shows would begin with random readings from the studio audience—birthdays, names, addresses—and progressed to more elaborate tricks as the half-hour went on. He usually dismissed his subjects quickly with an "I thank you very much" after "reading" a brief bit of thought. He emphasized that he was right "only 90 per cent of the time," but speculation persisted on the possibilities of chicanery. To counter this, Dunninger surrounded himself with "unimpeachable" judges—entertainers, politicians, editors, and in one case a New York Supreme Court justice—who participated in the mind-reading stunts and swore to their authenticity.

But Evelyn Bigsby of *Radio Life* remained unimpressed. She questioned Dunninger's practice of having subjects write down the messages that the mentalist claimed to "read" by telepathy. Dunninger replied with some irritation that this helped drive the subject to a deeper level of thought. Not so, said Bigsby: it was all part of a simple magic trick, not telepathy; bandleader Richard Himber, who also dabbled in magic, could do the same thing and would put up $1,000 to prove it before a national radio audience. Dunninger did not respond to this challenge, though he continued his own offer: a $10,000 award to anyone who could prove that he used an accomplice.

EARL WILSON'S BROADWAY COLUMN, gossip and talk; also called *It Happened Last Night*.

BROADCAST HISTORY: Jan. 7–July 1, 1945, Mutual. 15m, Sundays at 10. General Cigar.

CAST: Broadway columnist Earl Wilson, with such guests as Fred Allen and Tallulah Bankhead. **ANNOUNCER:** Paul Douglas.

This series was a mix of gossip and straight news about the rich and famous. Wilson swapped a few insults with Paul Douglas, told a few gags, and often referred to his "silent partner," known as "BW" ("Beau-tiful Wife"). *Radio Life* liked it well enough: while labeling Wilson a "negligee nighthawk" with a "poisonous personality," the reporter noted that he could pack as much variety into a quarter-hour "as he gets into a whole week of columns."

EARPLAY, dramatic anthology.

BROADCAST HISTORY: 1972–1990s, National Public Radio, 26 hour-long plays a year, in stereo.

CAST: A mix of top-name film, TV, and old radio stars: Meryl Streep, Vincent Gardenia, Laurence Luckinbill, Brock Peters, Lurene Tuttle, Leon Ames, etc. **PRODUCER:** Karl Schmidt. **ASSOCIATE PRODUCER:** Howard Gelman. **DIRECTORS:** Daniel Freudenberger, etc. **WRITERS:** Donald Barthelme, John Gardner, David Mamet, etc.

Earplay was another revival of radio drama, launched by Karl Schmidt at NPR station WHA in Madison, Wis., with a $150,000 grant. Schmidt's initial idea was to compete with Top 40 radio by offering playlets of five to ten minutes. Gradually the scope broadened until full hour-long dramas by top novelists and playwrights were presented. *Earplay* thus became the most serious of the revival shows, departing notably from nostalgia to demonstrate the modern viability of radio drama.

The breakthrough came in 1975, when Edward Albee offered his play *Listening*. Other big names followed. A David Mamet play, written for the air, later went to Broadway. The Arthur Kopit *Earplay* production *Wings* went on to be staged in New York and London. The stories were as contemporary as their authors cared to make them: Brock Peters starred in a tale of interracial love in South Africa. But the budgets were small ($100 a day to the actors), and the people involved did it either for love of the medium or the pleasure of a new experience. Many of the performers had never done radio drama. The series won the Prix Italia, the pinnacle of international radio awards, and Schmidt remained optimistic into the 1980s that the long-awaited radio renaissance was at hand. In an interview with Joel Makower of *Mainliner* magazine, he pointed to the situation in England, where 1,500 plays a year are produced for radio, making the medium a vibrant training ground for young Harold Pinters. "If we had the opportunity to really do it intelligently, we could run all the remnants of 1930s radio right off the air and make them hide their heads in shame," he said, a rather obvious jab at such revival shows as *The CBS Radio Mystery Theater*.

THE EASY ACES, situation comedy, comedy-drama, skits.

BROADCAST HISTORY: 1930–31, KMBC, Kansas City.

1931, CBS, 13-week tryout from Chicago, beginning in Oct.

March 1, 1932–May 30, 1933, CBS. 15m, three a week (sometimes Tuesday-Thursday-Saturday, sometimes Monday-Wednesday-Friday) at 10:15. Lavoris.

Oct. 10, 1933–Jan. 31, 1935, CBS. 15m, sometimes three or four times a week at 1:30; at 3:45 beginning 1934, Jad Salts.

Feb. 4, 1935–Oct. 22, 1942, NBC: Red Network at 7:30 until June 1935; then Blue Network at 7. 15m, three a week throughout. Anacin.

Oct. 28, 1942–Nov. 26, 1943, CBS. 15m, three a week at 7:30. Anacin.

Dec. 1, 1943–Jan. 17, 1945, CBS. 30m, Wednesdays at 7:30. Anacin.

1945–47, transcribed syndication, Frederick Ziv Company; old shows recycled.

Feb. 14–Dec. 31, 1948, CBS. 30m, Saturdays at 7 through May, then Fridays at 8, then 8:30. Sitcom, *mr. ace & JANE*. U.S. Army, General Foods.

1930–45: CAST: Goodman and Jane Ace as the Aces. Mary Hunter as Jane's friend Marge; Peggy Allenby as Mrs. Benton; both from early 1930s. Ethel Blume as Betty; Alfred Ryder as Carl; Martin Gabel as Neil Williams; all as of 1939. Helene Dumas as Laura the maid. Ann Thomas as Miss Thomas. **ANNOUNCER:** Ford Bond. **THEME:** *Manhattan Serenade*.

1948: (*mr. ace & JANE*): **CAST:** Goodman and Jane Ace, John Griggs, Evelyn Varden, Pert Kelton, Eric Dressler and Cliff Hall. **ANNOUNCER:** Ken Roberts.

The Easy Aces was billed as "radio's laugh novelty," and Jane Ace was Mrs. Malaprop of the air. Jane had a twangy midwestern voice, slightly softer in natural conversation, that reminded a listener of Bernardine Flynn's Sade Gook (*Vic and Sade*). She was one of radio's enduring female screwballs, Gracie Allen and Marie Wilson being the others. Under the guidance of her husband and writer, Goodman Ace, she defined the term "malapropism" to a generation that had never heard of it or its creator.

Mrs. Malaprop was a character in an 18th century play by Richard Brinsley Sheridan. Her sentences were filled with wrong words that vaguely resembled proper speech and had a great comedic effect on audiences of that time. In the early 1930s, the Aces were effectively combining malapropisms with general "dumb blonde" humor.

A problem to Jane became "the fly in the oatmeal." Her "time wounds all heels" and "Congress is still in season" transcended radio and became general slang. When Jane had a hard day, she would tell Ace that she'd been "working my head to the bone." Her bridge partner, Marge, was her "insufferable friend." When Ace fretted over her bidding, she'd say, "Don't finesse, it makes me nervous." She always led with the first card on the right side of her hand, explaining that it was easiest that way. Of a man whose wife was his main means of support, she'd say, "He lives by the sweat of his frau." One of her most-quoted witticisms was "familiarity breeds attempts." She kept her house "spic and spat"; New Years' resolutions were made to "go in one year and out the other." Whenever Ace made a particularly astute observation, she'd say, "You hit the nail right on the thumb that time." She hated to "monotonize the conversation" but usually managed to. She didn't smoke or drink, being a "totalitarian," and had relatives "too humorous to mention." When people said hello to her, her response was often, "Just fine." In interviews, Ace was always in character, witty and a bit on the gruff side. Asked what Jane was really like, he'd usually respond, "Well, she's kinda stupid. She's all right, if you like Jane."

Their show, though never a ratings success, was always a favorite of Radio Row insiders. Like Fred Allen and Henry Morgan, Ace was considered an intelligent man's wit. His show limped along with Crossley numbers in the mediocre 5-to-7 range. But it lasted across several formats for more than 15 years and was one of radio's fondest memories.

Both Aces were born in Kansas City, Mo.: Ace on Jan. 15, 1899; Jane (Sherwood) on Jan. 12, 1905. They met at a dancing school and were married in 1928. Ace was a reviewer of movies and plays, employed by the *Kansas City Post*. His wit surfaced early: once, reviewing a vaudeville act, he noted that the performer could not be heard beyond the third row and advised patrons to request seats at least four rows back. His radio show on KMBC, the Kansas City CBS outlet, paid a mere $10 per appearance, but it supplemented his $75 newspaper salary and required little of his time. On Aug. 1, 1930, he began a series of film reviews on the air under the billing *The Movie Man*. This led directly to *The Easy Aces* when a subsequent act failed to show up. He was signing off one day when he received through the glass a signal to keep talking. He had to improvise. He saw his wife waiting for him in the studio; he motioned her in and, between programs, they worked out the basics of a talk skit.

They would talk about the bridge game they had played the night before with two friends. The main topic of conversation had been a Kansas City murder in which a woman had killed her husband over a hand of bridge. "You be dumb," Ace told Jane (as he reconstructed it years later for Jerome Beatty of *American Magazine*): "I'll try to explain the finer points of bridge, and why murder is sometimes justified." The station got good mail response, and the Aces got two regular slots a week at $30. The early plots continued to play out at the bridge table. Ace was not wild about Jane's game, on the air or off, and he kept picking at her until she lost her temper and threatened to quit. The show settled into a new niche, a more universally based domestic comedy revolving around Jane's improbable situations and her impossible turns of phrase.

An advertising man caught their act in Kansas City and lured them to Chicago in 1931 for a tryout with CBS. Ace was in typical form: he demanded $500 a week and, to his surprise, got it. Ace did the writing and directing and continued playing the male lead. They were heard three times a week, sometimes more, on various networks with no summer vacations for a decade. The broadcasts were informal, the principals sitting around an old card table with a built-in concealed microphone. This gave the illusion of old friends sitting down for a casual chat. To keep his small cast fresh, Ace permitted only one reading before the broadcast.

He never used his first name on air: he was simply known as "Ace." The story element was a continuation of sorts, but the situations most often existed to serve the lines. Ace always tried to dovetail the malapropisms into one punchy closing line, to which he'd react with great disgust—"Isn't that awful?" In the serial days, the stories involved the Aces and two supporting players: Jane's "insufferable" friend Marge and a Mrs. Benton, who some reviewers noted really was insufferable. Mary Hunter, who played Marge, was working a receptionist's desk at WGN when Ace walked through the studio, heard her giggle, and hired her for *The Easy Aces*.

Ace was an original: a fiercely independent writer who seemed proud to have made it in radio without pandering to lowest common denominators or playing for belly laughs. Every year he placed an ad in the trade press, making fun of his own low ratings: the ratings, he pointed out, were conducted by telephone poll, and his audience never answered the phone while the show was on. He would rattle off lists of "never-haves:" he had never changed announcers, never been asked for an autograph, never won a radio popularity poll, never had a script returned for changes. His scripts dealt with the minutiae of life: Jane getting called to jury duty; Jane getting into Ace's real estate business. That they were simple did not mean they were always easy. He smoked while he wrote: the fewer cigars, the better the script.

For years he avoided personal contact with his sponsors, the makers of Anacin, worrying that personalities would ruin a good thing. In this he was a prophet: he first heard from the company in 1944, when a spokesman criticized a musical bridge he was using. Ace replied in kind: he didn't care much for the packaging of Anacin either, he wrote—the company's practice of using cardboard boxes instead of tin was a gyp. Anacin was not amused: after 14 years, the show was canceled.

Ace didn't languish. At $3,500 a week, he became one of radio's highest-paid writers, working on *The Danny Kaye Show* until that series left New York for the West Coast. Also that year, he sold some 1,300 transcriptions of his old show to Ziv for syndication: it was estimated that 100 stations signed up, earning Ace another $75,000 a year. In syndication, *The Easy Aces* played to a larger audience than it ever had as a live show. In August 1946 Ace was coaxed back to CBS as "supervisor of comedy and variety," heading a team of writers that became a kind of troubleshooting task force. "I tell them how to do things and they say yes and don't do them'' was his description of his job. He worked on the Robert Q. Lewis *Little Show* and voiced disgust when the producers took the ''tight little 15-minute job'' he had suggested and turned it into just another splashy half-hour, with orchestra and trimmings. He conceived and helped create one of the most unusual shows of its time, *CBS Is There*, which later became *You Are There* and consisted of great historical events reenacted as a modern radio news team might report them.

He went back on microphone in 1948 with *mr. ace & JANE*: the exotic lower-and-upper-case usage was his, and the show was an expanded version of *The Easy Aces*. Again, Jane was the none-too-bright housewife; again, her bouts with the language were emphasized. But it was a prime-time sitcom with an orchestra, a slick supporting cast, and a sponsor, albeit a strange one. The U.S. Army and Air Force Recruiting Service carried the show, which became a problem when Ace wrote several skits that had Jane appear in court before eccentric judges. When a congressman, who might have found more important business on his desk, complained that the Army Air Forces were promoting disrespect for the judicial system, Ace had to begin self-censoring his scripts. By fall he had a more conventional sponsor, General Foods.

In *mr. ace*, he played an advertising man whose neighbor was a radio announcer in ''the typical little eastern town known as New York.'' He lampooned both industries with great enthusiasm. The fourth show of the series was titled ''Chapter Four: Jane Discovers Hidden Talent In A Newsboy And Mr. Ace Has A Client Interested In Putting On A Radio Program So Jane Puts Two And Two Together And Gets A Hooper Of 4.6 And Before Mr. Ace Can Stop Her Jane Has Her Discovery On The Air, or, As Mr. Ace Puts It, To Err Is Human, To Forgive Is Divine.'' Among the prominent continuing characters were Ace's boss (who had ''a child for every occasion'') and Jane's brother Paul (who hadn't worked in twelve years ''because he's waiting for the dollar to settle down''). The theme, as always, was *Manhattan Serenade*. The Aces, with more than a little justification, were billed as ''radio's original comedy couple.''

Ace was known as ''Goody'' to his friends. In appearance he was lanky and professorial. Jane looked nothing like her radio self. Pretty,

perhaps striking in her youth, she had cream-colored blond hair and an ever-present, infectious smile. She died Nov. 11, 1974. Ace died March 25, 1982.

THE ED SULLIVAN SHOW, gossip, talk, music.

BROADCAST HISTORY: Jan. 12–Aug. 18, 1932, CBS. 15m, Tuesdays at 8:45, then at 8:30. La Gerardine.

April 27–Sept. 28, 1941, CBS. 30m, Sundays at 6. International Silver.

Sept. 13, 1943–June 5, 1944, CBS. 15m, Mondays at 7:15. *Ed Sullivan Entertains*. Mennen.

April 2–Sept. 30, 1946, Blue Network. 15m, Tuesdays at 9, then Mondays at 8:15. *Ed Sullivan's Pipelines*.

It was on Sullivan's 1932 series that listeners first heard the voices of Jack Benny, Jack Pearl, Irving Berlin, Florenz Ziegfeld, and George M. Cohan. Sullivan's radio fame was enhanced by his newspaper column, ''Little Old New York,'' in the *New York Daily News*. His *Toast of the Town* (CBS, June 20, 1948–June 6, 1971) was the biggest variety hour of early television.

ED WYNN, THE FIRE CHIEF, comedy-variety; vaudeville-style slapstick.

BROADCAST HISTORY: April 26, 1932–June 4, 1935, NBC. 30m, Tuesdays at 9:30. also known as *The Texaco Fire Chief*. Texaco. **CAST:** Ed Wynn as the Fire Chief. Graham McNamee as his straight man. **ANNOUNCER:** Louis Witten. **ORCHESTRA:** Don Voorhees (1932–34), Eddy Duchin (1934–35).

Feb. 13–May 7, 1936, CBS. 30m, Thursdays at 9:30. *Gulliver*. Plymouth.

May 12–Aug. 4, 1936, NBC 30m, Tuesdays at 9:30. *Ed Wynn's Grab Bag*. Plymouth. **MUSIC:** Lennie Hayton.

Nov. 14, 1936–May 8, 1937, Blue Network. 30m, Saturdays at 8. *The Perfect Fool*, based on Wynn's best-known characterization. Twenty Grand Cigarettes.

Sept. 8, 1944–Feb. 26, 1945, Blue Network/ABC. 30m, Fridays at 7, then Mondays at 9. *Happy Island*. Borden's Milk. **CAST:** Ed Wynn as King Bubbles. Winfield Hoeny as the villain, King Nasty of Castor Isle. Evelyn Knight and Jerry Wayne as the lovers, Princess Elaine and Prince

Richard. Rolfe Sedan as Blotto, adviser to the King. In the Borden commercials: Hope Emerson as Elsie the cow; Lorna Lynn as Beulah the calf; Craig McDonnell as Elmer the bull. **MUSIC:** Mark Warnow. **WRITER:** Raymond Knight.

Ed Wynn was never a comedian. His son Keenan made that point years later in a taped interview. Wynn was a clown, a vastly different breed of entertainer. A comedian made you laugh: a clown could make you cry. In a way, Keenan Wynn regretted that his father had ever tried his hand on radio. "Suddenly he was locked in to coming up with 55 jokes every week. Basically he was visual, a very gentle man who was put under great stress by everyone. He did the best he could. He was a sad man."

By most accounts, Wynn never wanted to be in radio. He was a vaudeville headliner who rose to the lure of money. Asked by an adman what it would take to get him on the air, Wynn threw out the absurd price of $5,000 a week. He was astonished when the gentleman handed him a contract and a pen.

He was born Isaiah Edwin Leopold, Nov. 9, 1886, in Philadelphia. His stage name was a simple separation and derivative of "Edwin," and the Ziegfeld Follies of 1914 was the crowning touch of his stage career. In 1919 he was embroiled in a labor dispute: his support of rank-and-file actors and his walkout from a $1,700-a-week starring role drew the wrath of the Shuberts and other powerful producers. He was blacklisted and, unable to find work, created his own musical shows. *Ed Wynn's Carnival* (1920) was followed by *The Perfect Fool*, his best-loved characterization, and others. He was the first performer to bring an entire comedy show to the microphone. The date: Feb. 19, 1922. The place: WJZ, Newark. The production was a two-and-a-half-hour radio version of *The Perfect Fool*. He appeared on the air in costume and is said to have created the first studio audience: at WJZ, when no laughter greeted his *Perfect Fool* gags, he hurriedly assembled an audience of studio hands to react to the performance.

For his *Texaco Fire Chief* series, he also performed in costume. He told a *Radio Stars* reporter that the clown clothes "made me feel funny, and if I felt funny I hoped I would sound

funny." He wore funny hats and bell-bottom coats: occasionally a raccoon coat, often a fireman's garb, complete with helmet. He had severe mike fright. The reminder by Graham McNamee just before his first broadcast that 29 million people were listening didn't help, and when he began his routine, his voice leaped out in a wild giggle of hysteria. The audience loved it, and Wynn used it ever after on the air. The insane whoop, the *whoo-whoo-hoowhee* that accompanied every other punchline, sounds primitive today. Most likely it was Wynn's security blanket, a cover for the fact that he was out of his element. He was forever bound to footlights and greasepaint: his appeal was to an earlier audience of simple and innocent tastes, a crowd that was already fading fast in 1932. But his show began with an enormous following. McNamee's estimate was probably on the low side, but it lost ground year by year. Wynn's last radio show, in 1945, registered less than 5 on the Crossley charts.

The Fire Chief opened and closed with the sirens of a fire truck. Announcer Louis Witten then introduced the orchestra, then Graham McNamee, and finally, in a burst of noise, Wynn. He came on with the clanging of bells and the tooting of horns and the ever-present hysterical laugh. His opening line, delivered in a cracking falsetto, was often "Tonight the program's gonna be different, Graham." His trademark was a long "Sooooo-ooo-ooo," which he could stretch to five syllables and make sound like a Swiss yodel. It became, for a short time, a national catchphrase. McNamee was his costar, not announcer: the two of them threw the jokes back and forth. "I hear there was an explosion on the farm," McNamee would say. "Well," said Wynn, "my pet hen ate some popping corn and sat on a stove, y'know." It was vaudeville on the air. A few minutes of this would be followed by music, then more jokes, more music, and that was the format.

The departure of *The Fire Chief* in 1935 was, for all practical purposes, the end of Wynn's radio career. Three more shows of the '30s were marked by brief runs and diminishing ratings. He retired in 1937: business losses and a divorce sent him into a severe depression, which his son Keenan helped him battle for two years. He returned to the stage in 1940 and to radio in 1944. But his *Happy Island* airshow was not successful: his time had passed. He was still the clown, dressing for the air, going to elaborate lengths to set up effects that the radio audience would never know. *Happy Island* was a fully decorated show, with flashy sets and lighting effects and the entire cast in full dress. Wynn played King Bubbles, ruler of the mythical Happy Island, where good humor and joy were the orders of the day. The king wandered through the Worry Park, helping people solve their woes, but he never really got a handle on his own. Wynn was often described as a "sweet man" given to dark spells and worry. But he had dramatic success on TV's *Playhouse 90*, giving a powerful performance in Rod Serling's *Requiem for a Heavyweight*, and this led to other significant movie and television work. He was nominated for an Academy Award in 1959, for *The Diary of Anne Frank*. He died June 19, 1966.

THE EDDIE BRACKEN SHOW, situation comedy.

BROADCAST HISTORY: Jan. 28–May 27, 1945, NBC. 30m, Sundays at 8:30. Standard Brands.

Sept. 29, 1946–March 23, 1947, CBS. 30m, Sundays at 9:30. Texaco.

CAST: Eddie Bracken as himself, the same sad bumpkin of his hit films, the eternal helper who always managed to leave a situation more muddled than he found it. Ann Rutherford as his girlfriend Connie Monahan. William Demarest as Connie's crusty father. Janet Waldo as another Bracken girlfriend. Jim Bannon, narrator. Also: Cathy Lewis, Wally Maher, Edwin Cooper, Irene Ryan, Jack Morton, Alan Bridge, Ruth Perrott, and sportscaster Clem McCarthy. **ANNOUNCERS:** John Wald (1945), Jimmy Wallington (1946). **MUSIC:** Leigh Harline; Paul J. Smith. **DIRECTOR:** Nat Wolff. **WRITERS:** Robert Riley Crutcher (1945), George Hope (1946). **SOUND EFFECTS:** Bill Gould (CBS).

On the air, Eddie Bracken extended the basic situations and characterizations developed with William Demarest in the films *The Miracle of Morgan's Creek* and *Hail the Conquering Hero*. Though the 1946–47 storyline was continuous, each show could be heard as a complete entity.

THE EDDIE CANTOR SHOW, comedy-variety.

BROADCAST HISTORY: Sept. 13, 1931–Nov. 25, 1934, NBC. 60m, Sundays at 8. *The Chase and Sanborn Hour*. Chase and Sanborn.

Feb. 3, 1935–May 10, 1936, CBS. 30m, Sundays at 8 until Jan., then at 7. Pebeco Toothpaste.

Sept. 20, 1936–March 23, 1938, CBS. 30m, Sundays at 8:30, 1936–37; then Wednesdays at 8:30. Texaco.

March 28, 1938–June 26, 1939, CBS. 30m, Mondays at 7:30. *Camel Caravan*. Camel Cigarettes.

Oct. 2, 1940–June 19, 1946, NBC. 30m, Wednesdays at 9. *Time to Smile*. Bristol Myers and Sal Hepatica.

Sept. 26, 1946–June 24, 1949, NBC. 30m, Thursdays at 10:30, 1946–48; Fridays at 9, 1948–49. Pabst Beer.

Oct. 14, 1951–July 1, 1954, NBC. Mainly disc jockey format. 30m, Sundays at 9:30 until Jan. 1952, then Tuesdays at 10 until the summer break, then Thursdays at 9:30. Philip Morris, 1951–52; Coleman Company, Sept.–Oct. 1953.

1931–34: CAST: Eddie Cantor, singer and comedian; violinist Dave Rubinoff; guests. Harry Einstein as Nick Parkyakakas (or Parkyakarkas) as of 1934. **ANNOUNCER:** Jimmy Wallington. **DIRECTOR:** Abbott K. Spencer. **WRITERS:** Carroll Carroll, David Freedman, Bob Colwell, Phil Rapp.

1935–39: CAST: Cantor, Einstein, and, beginning ca. 1935, Bert Gordon as "the Mad Russian"; guests; juvenile performers Bobby Breen and Deanna Durbin; vocals by Kay St. Germain (1938). **ANNOUNCERS:** Walter King; Bert Parks (1938–39). **MUSIC:** Louis Gress, 1935–36; Jacques Renard, 1936–38; Edgar "Cookie" Fairchild thereafter.

1940–46: CAST: Cantor, Gordon, and guests. Vocalist Dinah Shore (1940–41). Ventriloquist Shirley Dinsdale (1942–43). Hattie McDaniel, 1942. **ANNOUNCER:** Harry Von Zell. **MUSIC:** Bob Sherwood, Leonard Sues, Cookie Fairchild. **DIRECTOR:** Vick Knight. **WRITERS:** Joe Quillan, Charles Marion, Carl Foreman, Stanley Joseloff, Izzy Elinson.

1946–49: CAST: Cantor, Gordon, announcer and straight man Von Zell, guests. Also: Gerald Mohr, Sara Berner, Veola Vonn, Frank Nelson, Elvia Allman, Herb Vigran. **MUSIC:** Cookie Fairchild. **DIRECTOR:** Vick Knight. **WRITERS:** Jay Sommers, Jess Goldstein.

AT VARIOUS TIMES: DIRECTOR: Manning Ostroff. **MUSIC:** George Stoll. **VOCALS:** Margaret

Whiting; the Sportsmen Quartet. **WRITERS:** Barbara Hotchkiss, Matt Brooks, Eddie Davis, Ed Beloin, Sam Moore, Everett Freeman, Bob O'Brien, etc. **SOUND EFFECTS:** Virgil Reimer (NBC), Cliff Thorsness (CBS). **THEME:** *One Hour with You*, modified to fit the night of the week that the show was heard.

He was the first of the top stars of vaudeville and burlesque to also reach the top in radio. Almost a full year ahead of Al Jolson, Ed Wynn, Fred Allen, and Jack Benny, three years ahead of Bing Crosby, seven years before Bob Hope: Eddie Cantor trailed only Rudy Vallee, but Vallee was cut from a different log. There were half-joking reminders of Cantor being a Vallee "discovery," but by the time he appeared on Vallee's *Fleischmann Hour* (Feb. 5, 1931), Cantor was a national figure. He was variously dubbed "the king of clowns," the "apostle of pep," and other high-octane titles: he was a bundle of boundless energy who in 1931 galloped across a stage and back, thrilling audiences with songs and gags. He made full use of almost every comedic device. His bulging eyes were show business trademarks, so well promoted by the affectionate nickname "Banjo Eyes" that listeners didn't need a picture to see them. "The keynote of his capers is impudence," *Radio Stars* advised in 1933: "a flip defiance of powers or persons more powerful than himself." Listeners could identify with that. When Cantor encountered a bone-crunching osteopath in one of his early shows, the audience pulled for Eddie. People loved the defiant "pfurrt" sound he made when confronted with authority.

Cantor was born to a family of Russian immigrants, Jan. 31, 1892, in New York's Lower East Side. His mother died soon after his birth; his father died of pneumonia a year later. His given name was either Isadore Itzkowitz or Edward Israel Iskowitz (he claimed both during his life). He was raised by a grandmother who was 60 when he was born. In his autobiography he describes a childhood filled with tenement-life hardship, "poverty, misery, and disease." At 6, when he entered public school, his Grandma Esther enrolled him under her name, Kantrowitz, which the registrar wrote down as "Kanter." When he was older, he changed it to "Cantor." He began calling himself "Eddie" because his girlfriend Ida Tobias, the "belle of Henry

Street," liked the way it sounded on him. In his own words, he was "truant from school, pilferer of pushcarts, hooligan, street fighter, liar." He slept on rooftops and sang for change on street corners. For years he remembered wearing shoes "pulpy with wet cardboard" and clothes that held the damp of snow all day long.

He discovered the power of performing in school. "The sound of applause was heat and food, mother and father, pink champagne," he wrote. He played a clown in camp and decided to go into show business. With a pal, he played weddings, socials, amateur nights. At Miner's Bowery Theater he played to the toughest audience of the day, pushed onstage to a cascade of Bronx cheers and a bombardment of spoiled fruit. He earned a dollar even if he "got the hook," and the prize for winning the night was a $5 pot.

Cantor got a job as a singing waiter at Coney Island. There he met and became friends with Jimmy Durante, the piano player. He worked in a Gus Edwards play, appearing in blackface as a butler. His early years were packed with vaudeville and burlesque dates, the blackface characterization following him through the teens and '20s. He was with Ziegfeld in the famed *Follies* of 1917, '18, and '19, a stormy relationship that had a successful reunion in 1923, when Cantor played a rascally but lovable golf caddy in Ziegfeld's *Kid Boots*. A rewritten version of *Boots*, with Clara Bow as his costar, became his first film, a silent of 1926. Again Cantor and Ziegfeld reconciled, this time in 1928 for the record-breaking *Whoopie*, in which Cantor played a hypochondriac. He was now a major star of stage and screen, and in 1931 he added radio to his list of accomplishments, as his *Chase and Sanborn Hour* made ratings history.

Cantor had done a few isolated broadcasts in the '20s, but his air career really began with that February 1931 appearance on the Vallee show. It led to a four-week tryout with Chase and Sanborn, whose ad people were looking for a replacement for French showman Maurice Chevalier (soon to return to Paris). Instinctively Cantor must have realized what radio could do for him, but only much later did he do the arithmetic. "Say you played in a Ziegfeld show at the New Amsterdam Theater, which seats 1,600. In a week you play to 13,000. Play that Ziegfeld show for 50 weeks, you would play to 650,000.

If you played it for ten years, you'd play to 6½ million. In 20 years it would be 13 million. And if you played it for *40* years, to packed houses, standing room only, you'd play to less people in 40 years than you played to in *one night* on *The Chase and Sanborn Hour*.''

He studied everything on the air, ''listened to radio until it was coming out of my ears, getting the feel of it.'' This was a brand new ball game: ''it wouldn't do any good to roll your eyes or clap your hands'' to capture an audience. He decided to rope in the studio audience and let them laugh—on microphone—at his gags. This was unknown territory: before Cantor, studio audiences were sternly warned to make no noise of any kind while the shows were on the air. No laughter was permitted: even a muffled cough would bring an usher with a finger to his lips. This policy changed forever when Cantor and announcer Jimmy Wallington went down into the audience, snatched the hats off their wives' heads, and chased each other around the stage while the audience shrieked hysterically. After the broadcast, John Reber of J. Walter Thompson called with the excited news that Cantor had ''just invented audience participation.''

Cantor's 60-minute *C&S* shows were largely carried by himself, Wallington, and violinist Dave Rubinoff, with occasional guests. Rubinoff supposedly led the orchestra. It was typical early '30s variety: Cantor singing and mugging, situation skits, orchestra numbers, violin solos. Rubinoff's segments were billed as ''Rubinoff and His Violin,'' and his radio-fed fame in those days was greater than that of most noted concert violinists. He ''was a good violinist rather than a great violinist,'' Cantor wrote years later: but Rubinoff was ''a showman who gave the impression of being all the great violinists put together.'' His Russian accent was so formidable that he did not speak on the air. In the early days, Cantor did Rubinoff's lines: he would ask a question in his natural voice and answer it with a Russian accent. Cantor played every conceivable dialect, from ''an Irish policeman to a Swedish cook.'' Later he hired people for his skits: Teddy Bergman (Alan Reed) and Lionel Stander played dialects, including the Rubinoff role.

The show was quick to catch on. At the end of his four weeks, Cantor was signed for a year. Then the ratings simply exploded. The industry

was rated by Crossley (CAB), which soon showed Cantor leapfrogging over Rudy Vallee and even *Amos 'n' Andy* to claim the top spot going away. His second-year peak of 58.6 was the highest ever recorded. At times 15 points, a healthy rating in itself, separated Cantor from the second-place show in the nation. This led to widespread disbelief within the industry and the eventual collapse of Crossley as a viable audience barometer. While it lasted, Cantor rode the crest, on top of the radio world, and there was little doubt—as writer Carroll Carroll later noted—that Cantor did indeed have ''a remarkable listenership.''

Cantor began a practice, long associated with Vallee, of introducing new talent via radio. Gracie Allen made her first radio appearance with Cantor: Burns and Allen would occasionally be mentioned, only half-jokingly, as a Cantor ''discovery,'' but George Burns had his own grim version of that affair (see BURNS AND ALLEN). A more legitimate discovery was Harry Einstein. Cantor was in Boston in 1934 when he happened to hear, on a local radio station, a man doing a funny Greek dialect. Einstein was then the advertising director of Boston's Kane Furniture Company. He had been dabbling radio for years and had created a character named Nick Parkyakakas, a comedy candidate for mayor who could be heard on WNAC Mondays and Fridays at 10:30. Cantor thought it the funniest Greek impersonation he had ever heard: by wire, he offered Einstein a slot on NBC, and the following Sunday Parkyakakas played to the nation for the first time. He was a smash and became a regular. Also during this time Cantor initiated a ''Night Court of the Air'' skit, playing a judge in a series of mock trials. The skits were notable for their changes of pace: Cantor would ''try'' three or four madcap ''cases,'' then he'd bring on a serious story that illustrated some pressing problem of the day—juvenile delinquency, drunk driving, suicide. This fed into Cantor's ''tears along with the smiles'' approach to comedy, humanizing the show, making it real to people beyond the microphone who experienced those tragedies on a daily basis. He began using a similar technique in his closing talks: he would ''go serious'' for a moment and tell his listeners exactly why they should use Chase and Sanborn Coffee. In one candid talk, Cantor admitted that he himself was not a coffee-drinker. If he did drink coffee, he was sure it would be Chase and Sanborn because his wife drank it, his daughters drank it, friends drank it, and they all assured him that it was very good. This was unheard of: the kind of reverse advertising that made sponsors quake. But it brought Cantor kudos for honesty and helped boost C&S sales.

His theme might well have been *Ida*: it was a number he sang often in tribute to his wife. The theme might also have been the lively and often-requested *Tomatoes are cheaper, potatoes are cheaper/now's the time to fall in loooove!* But the song most associated with Cantor during that time was his closing bit, crooned in a way that wooed the audience.

I love to spend
Each Sunday with you
As friend to friend
I'm sorry it's through
I'm telling you
Just how I feel
I hope that you
Feel that way too . . .

In a 1932 stunt, Cantor announced his candidacy for president. His campaign—highlighted by the weekly chant *We want Cantor! We want Cantor!*—actually netted him some write-in votes. He was the hottest act on the air, even after his rating settled down to a mere 50 points. One of the indelible images of Cantor, his show, and the times was given by Carroll Carroll in his memoir: of a road engagement and Cantor taking his percentage of the gate in cash, of the ride home with Eddie Cantor and a big bag full of money.

Cantor left Chase and Sanborn in late 1934. Goldwyn had a movie job for him on the West Coast, and his power in radio was such that he could return at his own pleasure, for any of a dozen sponsors. His film was followed by a vacation in Europe, where he met and was impressed by Mussolini. But he refused to go to Germany: "Why should I make people laugh who make my people cry?" he said. His return to radio in the fall of 1935 was in many respects a start from scratch. His new sponsor was Pebeco Toothpaste. There was a new rating system—Hooper: gone were the days of 50-plus audience shares. Cantor began in the teens, well back in the middle of the pack. His show was now in a 30-minute timeslot, aired from Hollywood. Rubinoff had remained in the East: the

new orchestra was directed by Louis Gress, but Harry Einstein had rejoined him. Einstein's Greek character was now being spelled Parkyakarkus in radio guides, an easier visual link to the comic undertones of the name. In 1935 Cantor hired another dialect comic, Barney Gorodetsky, who as Bert Gordon was about to create one of the memorable second bananas of the air. This was "the Mad Russian."

The Russian was a harebrained character with a thick Slavic accent who burst upon the scene at odd moments, often when Cantor was interviewing some dignified guest. The more distinguished the guest, the better the routine. Gordon would enter with his popular catchphrase "How do you doooo," which never failed to register with the audience. It was highbrow-lowbrow stuff, Gordon's low comedy playing against such show business icons as Tallulah Bankhead and Lawrence Tibbett. Gordon was to enjoy a long career with Cantor, filling the role that Jerry Colonna would assume, a few years later, with Bob Hope: a lunatic so addled that his presence immediately converted the boss into a straight man.

Also that year, 1935, Cantor intensified his search for young talent. He was looking for a child singer for his Christmas show and found one: Bobby Breen, whose rendition of *Santa Bring My Mommie Back to Me* wrung tears from the studio audience. Cantor was becoming known, like Rudy Vallee, as a top radio talent scout. Breen would remain with Cantor for three seasons. He had an electrifying voice, riveting to the mass audience, which always loves even the hint of a prodigy. But Breen lost his job when his brother Mickey, acting as his agent, made rigid demands on Cantor near the end of the third year. Miffed, Cantor dropped him, and he was seldom heard again.

The 1935 season saw Cantor initiate his audience preview, a dress rehearsal before a live audience a day or two before each show. The crowd reaction told him which gags were winners and which ones got the hook. By autumn 1936 he had a new sponsor, Texaco. His Hooper had risen steadily until he was again on top with almost 30 points. But it was a peak he would not see again. Soon he was topped by Jack Benny, then by a wave of new radio big-timers: Bob Hope, Fibber McGee, and Edgar Bergen, who had taken his place on *The Chase and Sanborn Hour*. The show continued to spotlight talented youth. A casting director at Universal introduced Cantor to a lovely 13-year-old girl named Deanna Durbin. Cantor was captivated by her talent: it was, he would write, "a thrill to present her." Skits were developed, romantic duets with Durbin and Breen, and these were great crowd-pleasers. By 1938 both were gone, Breen into obscurity, Durbin back to the studio and a brief but brilliant career in films. Cantor, meanwhile, had "discovered" Bert Parks, who became his new announcer–singer–straight man and was teamed with singer Kay St. Germain in a more mature version of the Durbin-Breen romantic fluff of an earlier season. In the midst of this, Cantor was ostensibly trying to marry Parks to one of his daughters. It became a running gag, making Cantor's wife Ida and their daughters (Marjorie, Natalie, Edna, Marilyn, and Janet) better-known offstage than many front-line comics who had their own shows. The show had settled in, ratings-wise, at about 17 points—half the share commanded by Bergen on *The Chase and Sanborn Hour*, but still respectable. However, Cantor was about to learn a hard lesson: that respectable is not good enough when trouble arrives, and the power he had enjoyed seven seasons earlier had shifted to others.

In a speech at the 1939 New York World's Fair, he attacked by name some of the nation's most prominent advocates of right-wing politics. He was most vocal about Father Charles Coughlin, the "radio priest" whose pulpit of the air was seen by some as a major dispenser of racial disharmony and anti-Semitism. Cantor also denounced George Sylvester Viereck, a German-American poet, frequent contributor to Coughlin's *Social Justice* magazine, and admitted admirer of Hitler and Mussolini. The speech made national headlines, and overnight Cantor was a controversial figure. His sponsor, Camel Cigarettes, dropped him immediately. Worse, no other client would touch him. He was out of radio for a year, until Jack Benny intervened on his behalf. Benny pressured an executive with Young and Rubicam, a leading agency in the radio business, to help get Cantor back on the air, and Bristol Myers was persuaded to pay for it. The new show sounded much like the old show: the title was *Time to Smile*, a double-edged reminder that the sponsor had Ipana for the "smile of beauty" and Sal Hepatica for "the

smile of health." Harry Von Zell was the new announcer and stooge, but Bert Gordon was back, and Dinah Shore quickly became Cantor's newest "discovery." With Shore's departure, Cantor featured Thelma Carpenter, one of the first Negro singers to be given a regular spot on a major variety show. Another black regular was Hattie McDaniel.

The 1942 season also saw the appearance of Shirley Dinsdale, a 16-year-old ventriloquist, and her dummy Judy Splinters. Dinsdale first appeared Nov. 11, 1942: she created a mild sensation and for a time was bandied in the press as "Bergen's rival." Bergen was generous, citing Dinsdale as "the best natural ventriloquist I ever saw." She was one of the few whose puppet could truly sing, not just in falsetto. Judy Splinters was a rich soprano but in the end was no match for Charlie McCarthy.

Cantor's Pabst shows (1946–48) hoed familiar soil. There was another "run for president," with more *We want Cantor* chants and a running gag with Gerald "Baby Face" Mohr as a Cantor kidnapper. The closing theme was now *I Love to Spend Each Thursday with You*, and the whole package had a common and familiar ring. He tried a new formula in 1949: master of ceremonies on the NBC-Eversharp quizzer *Take It or Leave It*. It was, he told *Radio Life*, "more fun than I've had in ten or twelve years." But the radio era was just about over. In September 1950 he went into television, becoming one of several rotating hosts on NBC's Sunday night *Colgate Comedy Hour*. He did a new radio series, for Philip Morris, in 1951–52, but was little more than a glorified disc jockey. In September 1952, just after completing a *Colgate* TV show, he suffered a heart attack. He returned to *Colgate* in 1953 and did another disc jockey NBC radio show, sustained now. Between records, he reminisced about the old days and his beginnings in show business.

Cantor's reputation for philanthropy was widespread and appreciated. He was frequently cited, during his lifetime and after, as one of America's best-loved stars, though there were those who found him difficult and egocentric. He helped start the March of Dimes, did numerous benefits, worked for Jewish refugees in World War II, and established a $5,000 college scholarship fund for young essayists and orators. The fund, begun during the Texaco shows of the 1930s, was tainted when the first winner was discovered to have plagiarized his piece word for word. But Cantor stayed with it for a decade, putting a dozen youths through school.

Cantor died Oct. 10, 1964. Like most comics who came to radio from vaudeville, he was rooted in one-liners, and his humor perished quickly. There are some laughs in the Pabst shows, but the historically interesting Depression-era shows have yet to surface.

EDDIE CONDON'S JAZZ CONCERTS, Dixieland swing shows with prominent players.

BROADCAST HISTORY: May 20, 1944–April 7, 1945, Blue Network/ABC. 30m, Saturdays at 1:30, then at 1.

PLAYERS: Eddie Condon, guitarist and host. Gene Schroeder and Jess Stacy, piano. Bob Haggart, bass. Ernie Caceres, clarinet and saxophone. Pee Wee Russell and Hank D'Amico, clarinet. Benny Morton, trombone. Bobby Hackett, trumpet. Muggsy Spanier, cornet. George Wettling and Gene Krupa, drums. **NOTABLE GUESTS:** Woody Herman, clarinet; Willie "the Lion" Smith and James P. Johnson, piano; Sidney Bechet, soprano sax. **ANNOUNCER:** Fred Robbins. **VOCALIST:** Lee Wiley.

The Condon *Jazz Concerts* were aired from New York's Town Hall, 30 minutes of no-frills jazz. Standard free-for-all numbers (*Indiana, Everybody Loves My Baby*, etc.) were alternated with slower mood pieces featuring individual artists and special guests. Singer Lee Wiley had a husky, torchy, erotic voice that still earns praise from critics of classic jazz. Many of the Condon shows are available on commercial LP recordings, but they have been badly edited, and often the sound quality is suspect. Producers of these modern packages don't put much value in the talk, in the historic wholeness of a radio show, and transcriptions don't often survive being sanitized and transferred to modern LPs with their full fidelity intact.

EDGAR A. GUEST, drama, homespun philosophy, rustic poetry, and variety.

BROADCAST HISTORY: Oct. 4, 1932–March 29, 1938, Blue Network. 30m, Tuesdays at 9 until 1934; at 7:30, 1934–35; then at 8:30. Household Finance. A widely varied series heard under several titles and in several formats, with Guest, the host, the bridging element between them. Heard as *Musical Memories*, 1932–35, with Guest's rustic reading as its centerpiece. A continuing feature, while still running as *Musical Memories*, was a dramatic sketch, *Welcome Valley*, about the Ferguson family: this became its full focus and title in the spring of 1935. **CAST:** Cliff Arquette as Sheriff Luke Ferguson. Isabel Randolph as Grace Ferguson. Judith Lowry and Betty Winkler as Emmy and Esther Ferguson. Art Van Harvey and Bernardine Flynn as Jeffrey and Mathilda Barker. Harold Peary as Dr. Haines. Joan Blaine as Dolores Dumont. Raymond Edward Johnson as Bill Sutter. Also many Chicago radio regulars: Sidney Ellstrom, Don Briggs, Ted Maxwell, etc. **MUSIC:** Joseph Gallicchio's orchestra. **DIRECTOR:** Ted Sherdeman. Abruptly, in April 1937, while still on the Blue Network, the *Welcome Valley* format was scrapped and the show retitled *It Can Be Done*.

April 6, 1938–June 28, 1939, CBS. 30m, Wednesdays, alternating between 10 and 10:30. *It Can Be Done*. Household Finance. **MUSIC:** Frankie Masters. **DIRECTOR:** Henry Klein.

Jan. 15–May 30, 1941, partial Blue Network. 15m, Wednesdays through Fridays at 4:45. With songs by Eddy Howard.

Edgar A. Guest was one of the most popular verse writers in America (critics and highbrows refused to call him a poet, and in this he humbly agreed). Born in England, Guest was a naturalized citizen who spoke on the air with an accent cultivated from the heartland of America. He was unpretentious and "down home," and Americans rewarded him with a commercial success that the "true poets" could only envy.

Musical Memories, his earliest series, was 30 minutes of music, readings, and drama. *Welcome Valley* was straight drama: the noted cast included many who were already or would become stars of the medium. The switch to *It Can Be Done* was sudden and sweeping: Guest, the timeslot, and the sponsor remained, but almost everything else about the show was changed. It was kind of an inspirational passing parade, with Guest reading his work and interviewing people who had triumphed in their chosen fields despite hardship and adversity. One of the featured stories was of Mrs. William Walrath, manager of the adoption agency that had provided babies for the Jack Bennys, the Al Jolsons, and the George Burnses.

THE EDGAR BERGEN/CHARLIE MC-CARTHY SHOW, comedy-variety.

BROADCAST HISTORY: Dec. 17, 1936, first appearance on the air: Rudy Vallee's *Royal Gelatin Hour*, NBC.

May 9, 1937–Dec. 26, 1948, NBC. 60m until fall 1939, then 30m, Sundays at 8. *The Chase and Sanborn Hour* for Standard Brands until 1939; thereafter, under continued Standard Brands sponsorship, *The Edgar Bergen/Charlie McCarthy Show* or, through most of the 1940s, *The Charlie McCarthy Show*. Chase and Sanborn Coffee, Royal Puddings.

Oct. 2, 1949–July 1, 1956, CBS. 30m, Sundays at 8, 1949–53; at 9:30, 1953–54; 60m at 9, 1954–55; 55m at 7, 1955–56. Coca-Cola, 1949–52; Hudnut, 1952–53; Kraft Foods, 1954–55; otherwise multiple sponsorship.

STAR: Edgar Bergen, comic ventriloquist, with his primary dummy, the brash and wisecracking "little boy," Charlie McCarthy. Other dummies: Mortimer Snerd, dopey and slow-talking, introduced in 1939; Effie Klinker, gossipy old maid, introduced in 1944; Podine Puffington, "the belle of the air," and Lars Lindquist, Swedish fisherman, used later and sparingly. SUPPORTING CAST: 1937–39: W. C. Fields (part of 1937–38 season); Don Ameche and Dorothy Lamour; singer Nelson Eddy. The Stroud Twins (Clarence and Claude) until Sept. 25, 1938, then the Canovas (Judy, Zeke, and Annie) until mid-1939. 1939 ON: Bud Abbott and Lou Costello (ca. 1941). Don Ameche and Frances Langford, occasionally as the Bickersons; Marsha Hunt also as Blanche Bickerson. Pat Patrick as Ercil Twing, a creampuff character who appeared at odd moments. Richard Haydn as Professor Lemuel Carp, who could talk like a fish underwater. Barbara Jo Allen as Vera Vague. Norman Field as Charlie's school principal. ANNOUNCERS: Wendell Niles (1937–39), Buddy Twiss (1939 into 1940s), Ken Carpenter (mid-late 1940s), Bill Baldwin (early 1950s). MUSIC: *1937–39:* Werner Janssen, Robert Armbruster. *1939 on:* Ray Noble's orchestra (Noble was also worked into the comedy). VOCALISTS: Donald Dickson (1939), Dale Evans, Anita Ellis, Anita Gordon. DIRECTOR: Earl Ebi. WRITERS: Carroll Carroll, Dick Mack, Shirley

Ward, Stanley Quinn, Joe Bigelow, Joe Connelly, Bob Mosher, Alan Smith, Zeno Klinker, Royal Foster, Roland MacLane, etc. SOUND EFFECTS: John Glennon, etc. (NBC), Cliff Thorsness, (CBS).

The question of the hour was, what was a ventriloquist doing on the radio? John Reber of J. Walter Thompson (the agency handling the Rudy Vallee show) summed it up: the guy had *better* be funny if he hoped to overcome the limitations of the medium. Edgar Bergen, the man in question, was certainly aware that a single appearance on *The Rudy Vallee Hour* had been the making of other entertainers. Vallee had caught his act at an Elsa Maxwell party and had invited him on the air. Now, with the show imminent, both he and Bergen were having second thoughts.

Vallee's introduction was hesitant, almost apologetic. "Why—people have been asking me for the last two days—why put a ventriloquist on the air? The answer is, why not? True, our ventriloquist, Edgar Bergen, is an unusual one—a sort of Noel Coward or perhaps Fred Allen among ventriloquists, a dexterous fellow who depends more upon the cleverness and wit of his material than upon the believe-it-or-not nature of his delivery. Mr. Bergen works with a dummy—several of them, in fact—but this one is a typical ventriloquist's dummy except that it is arrayed with top hat and tails. Just imagine a dummy and take my word for it that both voices you will hear are owned and operated by just one man—Edgar Bergen.''

Well, they were on. Bergen and his dummy, who at that moment had no name to the vast radio audience, broke in with a few shaggy-dog jokes about how the dummy had come to be thus decked out, in formal evening dress and monocle. The dummy, who said his name was Bemby, spoke in an upper-crust British accent. The audience warmed slowly. Bergen asked about the dummy's parentage, getting a good laugh with the question "Is your mother living yet?" . . . and the rapid "Not yet" reply. Bergen expressed disbelief of everything the dummy had been saying, including his name. Finally he got a reluctant admission that the name was, "Uh, Charlie McCarthy."

The icebreaker came a moment later. Bergen, offering to give Charlie a reading in his crystal ball, spoke of the swirling center of the ball as resembling a whirlpool. The resulting exchange got a huge laugh from the studio audience and set in motion the Bergen technique—rapid questions and short answers, constant voice changes and repetition. *You have never seen a whirlpool?* "Uh, no." *I see.* "Awfully sorry." *Oh, that's all right.* "I never have, you know, actually." *I see.* "Awfully sorry." *That's all right.* "I, uh, will say this, though: not long ago I fell in a pool." *But it wasn't a whirlpool?* "Uh, no . . . awfully sorry." *Oh, that's all right.* "It was a cesspool." *A cesspool!* "I was sorry for that, too." *I imagine . . . but, my good man, that is neither here nor there.* "No, that was up in Connecticut."

In this short opening routine, Bergen also established the character he would play throughout—the moralistic father figure, stern and lecturing in the face of Charlie's mischievous nonchalance. The talk turned to drinking, and Bergen's baritone voice became sanctimonious and preachy. *Don't you know, young man, that alcohol is slow poison?* "Is what?" *It's slow poison.* "Is that so?" *Yes.* "Slow poison?" *That's what it is.* "Slow poison, eh?" *Yes.* "Well, I'm in no hurry."

He was a smash hit, so successful that Vallee signed him for 13 weeks. After almost 15 years in vaudeville and nightclubs, Bergen was an overnight success.

He was born in Chicago on Feb. 16, 1903. His parents were Swedish immigrants named Berggren, who settled in the American Midwest and took up dairy farming. Bergen's interest in magic and ventriloquism began at age 11, when he sent away for a book called *The Wizard's Manual*. In his own voice he discovered a priceless commodity: the ability to "belly talk," to force the voice up from the abdomen and through the larynx in such a way that the voice would sound distant or "thrown" from another place. He began doing trick voices: he would knock on his chair and call from "outside," sending his parents to the door when no one was there. When the noted ventriloquist Harry Lester played Chicago, Bergen went to see him. Lester was impressed with Bergen's ability and gave him some tips, free of charge.

Bergen decided to create a dummy to complete his act. The face would be modeled after a neighborhood kid named Charlie who sold newspapers. The carver was a bartender-carpenter named Theodore Mack, who charged Bergen $35 for the service. The face was carved in a block of white pine, and the finished dummy was named Charlie McCarthy, after the newsboy and the carver, with an ancient Celtic suffix tacked on for good measure.

In high school, Bergen learned that he could say things through his dummy that might have embarrassed him before. His wry commentaries on teachers and administrators, and on school life in general, were widely admired: one history teacher was so thrilled with his talent that she tutored him in her subject, which he was in danger of failing. He began working amateur nights in Chicago. He was billed as "Edgar Bergen, the Voice Illusionist." He attended Northwestern as a pre-med student, earning his way by playing parties and socials, but he never graduated. The lure of vaudeville was too great: he and Charlie struck out on the "sawdust trail."

He traveled across America, working his way up to a performance at New York's Palace Theater in 1930. He toured Europe and South America, returning home to find vaudeville vanquished by sound movies and radio. He refined his act for nightclubs: one of his most successful routines was called "The Operation," with Bergen playing a doctor, Charlie the patient, and a nurse rounding out the cast. By then he had outfitted his accomplice well: the top hat, tails, and monocle seemed to provide a counterpoint to the depression that was settling in around the world. Bergen, too, dressed for his acts: tie and tails, elegance all the way. His voices were complementary yet different: he could change in midsentence from the stern father to the high-pitched brat. And sometimes it seemed that Charlie had a mind of his own. He berated Bergen, mocked his receding hairline, and frequently reminded the master that "you'd be nothing without me." He chided mercilessly whenever Bergen fluffed a line or allowed his lips to move. One of the oddities of the Bergen-McCarthy act was that, while Bergen often fluffed, Charlie never seemed to.

His season with Vallee was followed by his own show for Chase and Sanborn. He was surrounded on *The Chase and Sanborn Hour* with as powerful an aggregation of talent as radio had yet seen. Don Ameche was then at the height of his fame as a dashing leading man (he was also, Bergen would remember, one of the cleverest comic ad-libbers in radio); Dorothy Lamour was an up-and-coming glamour girl who had reinvented the sarong; W. C. Fields had long been a vaudeville and movie comic of front-rank billing. The show soon turned into a verbal battlefield between McCarthy and Fields. Of all the great "feuds" in radio—Jack Benny/Fred Allen; Ben Bernie/Walter Winchell; Bing Crosby/Bob Hope—none was more memorable or potent than this, and it ran just over five months. When Fields came on, usually in the second half-hour, the insults often departed from the script. Fields is generally acknowledged to have been the better comedian, but in Charlie's voice Bergen certainly held his own. "Why, you long-nosed anteater," Charlie would say, "I'll put a wick in your mouth and use you for an alcohol lamp." "Why, you little blockhead," Fields would counter, "I'll whittle you down to a coathanger; I'll sick a beaver on ya." The insults came without regard to continuity, though occasionally the segue was perfect. "Is it true your father was a gateleg table?" Fields asked on one broadcast. "If it is," answered McCarthy, "your father was under it."

A typical show (June 13, 1937) has Ameche playing announcer, straight man, and Mr. Ramshackle, the truant officer. Bergen lectures his ward on the virtues of education. The guest spot features Richard Rodgers and Lorenz Hart and a medley of their music. Then comes a dramatic sketch, with Ameche and guest Joan Blondell as a young couple meeting on a park bench. Bergen returns with Dorothy Lamour, who sings with Werner Janssen's orchestra. After the station break Fields arrives. The writing plays heavily on Fields's image as a guzzler of gin and hater of every popular sentiment, notably Christmas, children, and dogs. The Fields segment has Joan Blondell introducing her nephew Rollo, a monster in short pants. "Ah, he's a cute little fellow, isn't he?" Fields says. "What a lovable little nipper. Sit down here and play with some broken glass." Blondell: "He'd be very good-looking if his teeth were straight." Fields: "I may be able to straighten 'em for him." This gets a tremendous laugh, which Fields plays masterfully, continuing as it fades: ". . . or even remove some of 'em, if he doesn't keep quiet. Does his nose bleed easily? . . . We'll find out a little later."

Then Charlie arrives and the argument heats up. Charlie: "Come on, Rollo, let's gang up on

'im. You clip him and I'll mow him down." Rollo: "Yeah, come on, let's get him!" Fields: "You keep outta this or I'll pull off one of Charlie's legs and beatcha brains out. Go away, McCarthy, I'll prune every twig off your body." Blondell: "Don't you really like children, Bill?" Fields: "Sure, I like 'em, if they're properly cooked—browned on one side." Blondell: "Aw, don't cry, Rollo, Uncle Willie will bring you a nice little bunny rabbit." Fields: "And an open-face razor, too."

The Chase and Sanborn Hour spent most of its first 30 months as the top show in the nation, and it was still in the top five a decade later. Charlie had captured the public's fancy. He was variously described as "saucy, lethally precocious, and irreverent," a "magnificent splinter," and a "fugitive from a picket fence." The *New York Times* thought him a "little vulgarian," and what W. C. Fields called him on the air might have paled by comparison to what was said later. Some people close to the show claimed that Fields developed a hatred of the dummy that went beyond the hyperbole of fan magazines. Charlie matched and often topped Fields on the air. When Fields drew laughs by threatening to carve Charlie into a venetian blind, Charlie got a bigger laugh with "That makes me shudder." When Fields insulted McCarthy's "pine-cone ancestry" or spoke of "the woodpecker's snack bar," Charlie took aim at Fields's nose or his reputation as a drinker. "Is that a flamethrower I see or is that your nose?" he would ask. One of Charlie's classic lines was "Pink elephants take aspirin to get rid of W. C. Fields."

With the departure of Fields, Charlie aimed his lance at guests. He insulted the men and cuddled verbally with the women. The dialogues between Bergen and McCarthy often concerned growing up: Charlie's problems with teachers, with school, with girls; his adventures with his pal Skinny Dugan. But somehow it seemed that Charlie was so much wiser in the ways of the world than was his preachy master. Don Ameche joined others in the notion that Charlie was "definitely a living personality."

On Dec. 12, 1937, the show was embroiled in controversy because of the notorious Mae West "Adam and Eve" skit. Arch Oboler had written a silly playlet, based on the conflict of the original sin and designed especially for Mae West. The skit was routinely passed by the NBC censor, who had not considered how West might deliver her lines or how they might sound on the air. West seemed unable to say hello without being sexually provocative. Her dialogue with the snake in the Garden of Eden was packed with suggestive imagery. When the snake got stuck trying to slither through the slats of the fence that protected the apple tree, West cheered him on. "Oh, shake your hips! Yeah, you're doin' all right. Get me a big one, I feel like doin' a big apple. Nice goin', swivel-hips." Adam, she said, would eat the forbidden fruit "like women are gonna feed men for the rest of time—applesauce!"

The phone bank at NBC erupted with protests. Within days, 1,000 letters had arrived, attacking the show's "immoral," "obscene," and "filthy" parable. Ministers railed. Chase and Sanborn customers threatened to boycott the product. The *Chicago Tribune* pronounced the show "vomitous," and of course congressmen hemmed and hawed. The result, according to *Time*, was that a "thoroughly alarmed" NBC and J. Walter Thompson apologized publicly and "announced that they would never do it again." Mae West became an instant persona non grata in radio: at NBC it was forbidden to utter her name on the air, an unwritten ban that was still in effect 12 years later. The Federal Communications Commission got involved. A transcription of the show was demanded and supplied; the FCC also demanded a copy of the network's contract with the sponsor and the call letters of all stations that had carried the show. The threat was implicit.

In January 1938 FCC chairman Frank McNinch wrote NBC, outlining his findings in the Mae West affair. The Commission was offended on behalf of all "right-thinking people," he said: radio must demonstrate that it could police itself. Included was the chilling promise that, "upon application for renewal of the licenses of the stations carrying this broadcast, the Commission will take under consideration this incident along with all other evidence tending to show whether or not a particular licensee has conducted his station in the public interest." In other words, despite the fact that affiliates had no control over NBC content, nor had they any idea what was coming until it was on the air, the FCC strategy was to bully the little guys. *Time* reacted with comparisons of press and radio responsibility,

pointing out the dangers to freedom of expression when "right-thinking people" or any other group blessed with FCC approval controlled the air.

By the beginning of the 1940 season, the producers decided that Bergen was in fact what he had been all along: the star attraction, strong enough to carry the program alone. Ameche and Lamour departed, and the show was condensed to 30 minutes. It was cozy: time enough for a band number by Ray Noble, a guest spot, and some witty routines between Bergen and his dummies. Bergen had a new dummy now, the dopey Mortimer Snerd. Mortimer had a lot in common with the Disney character Goofy: they spoke in similar drawls; physically, they shared the characteristics of the buck teeth and the sleepy, jowly countenance. Mortimer was introduced to lazy music and always entered with a stupid guffaw. "Parlez vous français?" Bergen asked on one show, when Mortimer was introduced as Pierre la Snerd, famous French cook. Mortimer's reply: "Wuh-huh-huh, there yuh go— you're always clownin', you and your Swedish accent." Bergen asked, "What's the nicest dish you serve?" Mortimer again: "Well, there're several: the other day a tall blonde in a bathing suit. . . ."

Running gags were an integral part of the '40s package. In 1942, to help promote enlistments in the Armed Forces, Charlie joined the Army Air Corps as a master sergeant. The following week he tried to obtain a second commission by joining the Marines. This culminated in a highly publicized court-martial, done on location at the Army base near Stockton, Calif. Lt. James Stewart was imported to defend Charlie, who was finally found as guilty as he was.

Ameche returned in guest appearances. Bandleader Ray Noble became a personality, wisecracking with Bergen and McCarthy in his dry British accent. In 1944 Bergen added a third dummy, Effie Klinker. She was modified from a character he had used in nightclubs and in audience warmups for his radio shows. Her original name was Ophelia, and she consisted of a little greasepaint and a bandana draped over Bergen's closed fist, with his thumb and index finger forming a mouth. As Effie, the old-maid aspects were heightened, and her predominant trait, said *Radio Life*, was that she "whispers, gossips, and repeats herself." But Charlie remained the major character, in Bergen's heart and in the affections of the public. In 1938 the dummy received an honorary degree from Northwestern: he was a "master of innuendo and the snappy comeback." The original McCarthy head was insured for $5,000, later $10,000. Bergen made provisions for the dummy in his will.

Bergen married Frances Westerman in 1945. Their daughter, Candice, who would be an important film and TV star of her generation, was born May 8, 1946. "Candy" first appeared on radio with her father when she was 6 years old: she became a frequent visitor to *The Edgar Bergen Hour* of the '50s, a transcribed series that also featured Jack Kirkwood, Gary Crosby, Carol Richards, Ray Noble, the Mellow Men, and announcer John (Bud) Hiestand. Much has been written of the negative effects of growing up as "Charlie McCarthy's sister"—the dummy, after all, had its own room in Bergen's house, complete with wardrobe and, at one time, a private bath. Writing in 1948 of her daughter's relationship with Charlie and Mortimer, Frances Bergen said, "We are not quite sure whether she thinks they're humans or dolls, but we are sure we'll have some explaining to do when she gets older." This was an understatement, though for different reasons than Mrs. Bergen might have imagined then. The final word was her daughter's, in a frank and touching memoir, *Knock Wood*. Yes, there were disagreements; there were plenty of generation-gap misunderstandings. At the bottom of it was a girl who desperately needed the approval of a father who felt stripped when he had to speak as himself, with no dummy on his lap to make light of things. The book is a love story on both sides: in the end Candice Bergen has placed Charlie McCarthy in an open, healthy spotlight, as a vital piece of her personal history.

Bergen did little in television. He was a radio man, even though his art was primarily visual. With Charlie and Mortimer, he emceed the 1956 CBS audience show *Do You Trust Your Wife?*, and he made numerous guest appearances on TV variety shows of the '50s. He grew old and gray. Charlie, of course, was eternally young. In September 1978 Bergen announced his retirement: he would do a few more shows, then give his dummy to the Smithsonian. Charlie had been his companion for 56 years. A week later he appeared with Andy Williams at Caesar's Palace in Las Vegas. He died in his sleep after this performance, Oct. 1, 1978.

A generous sprinkling of Bergen shows is available from beginning to end. Most interesting, historically, is the Rudy Vallee *Royal Gelatin Hour* that launched his career. The Fields-McCarthy battles are still quite funny, and the Mae West fiasco will interest students of the human comedy who want to confirm again how silly people can be. The "Adam and Eve" skit does not stand up as modern entertainment, its lone saving grace the listener's knowledge that all the "right-thinking people" were about to erupt. Bergen is unusual in one respect: his comedy seemed to arrive on radio in a state of wholeness. It didn't change much from 1936 until he left the air 20 years later. Perhaps this was why he was such a phenomenon. He arrived fully formed, ahead of his time. The others simply caught up, in the wartime growth spurt that infused radio comedy about six years later.

ELEANOR ROOSEVELT, talk, Washington color, public affairs.

BROADCAST HISTORY: Dec. 9, 1932–March 3, 1933, NBC. 30m, Fridays at 9:30. Pond's Cream. Nine-minute talks by Mrs. Roosevelt, with music by Leo Reisman and vocals by Lee Wiley and William Sholtz.

1933–34, various outlets, isolated broadcasts: one six-week run on CBS, 15m, Sundays, Nov. 11–Dec. 16, 1934.

Feb. 15–April 19, 1935, CBS. 15m, Fridays at 7. *It's a Woman's World.* Selby's Arch-Preserver Shoes.

April 21–July 14, 1937, Blue Network. 15m, Wednesdays at 7:15. Pond's Cream.

April 30–July 25, 1940, NBC. 15m, Tuesdays and Thursdays at 1:15. Sweetheart Soap. ANNOUNCER: Ben Grauer.

Sept. 28, 1941–April 12, 1942, Blue Network. 15m, Sundays at 6:45. *Over Our Coffee Cups.* Pan American Coffee.

Nov. 8, 1948–Sept. 2, 1949, ABC. 15m, three a week at 10:45 A.M. *Eleanor and Anna Roosevelt,* with her daughter, Anna Boettiger.

Oct. 11, 1950—Sept. 7, 1951, NBC. 45m, weekdays at 12:30.

First Lady Eleanor Roosevelt was heard often on radio beginning soon after her husband's inauguration in 1932. To stem inevitable criticism, all fees from her commercial broadcasts were donated to charity. Her shows were often behind-scenes color pieces: on one 1937 Blue Network Pond's Cream broadcast, her topic was "White Housekeeping," a discussion of life in the White House, with recipes. Her early talks were given in a hesitant, nervous voice, leading to widespread mimicry and even cruel ridicule. "Eleanor" jokes became common at parties and in the workplace.

Perhaps her best radio series came after her husband's death, when she had attained a kind of senior stateswoman status. She was in Paris for the opening programs of *Eleanor and Anna Roosevelt*, and her voice was heard by transcription while her daughter, Anna Boettiger, handled the rest of the show live from California. It made instant news: Mrs. Roosevelt blasted the "Dixiecrat" wing of the Democratic Party and called upon party bosses to throw the boll weevils out. While Washington buzzed, *Variety* raved about her courage and cited her as one of the "standout commentators of the air." The *Eleanor and Anna* show was created and produced by John Masterson, with John Reddy and John Nelson.

THE ELECTRIC HOUR, popular music.

BROADCAST HISTORY: Sept. 20, 1944–June 9, 1946, CBS. 30m, Wednesdays at 10:30 until Dec. 1944, then Sundays at 4:30. Sponsored by the nation's "170 business-managed electric companies."
CAST: Nelson Eddy, baritone, with guests. **ORCHESTRA:** Robert Armbruster. **ANNOUNCER:** Frank Graham. **PRODUCER:** Charles Herbert.
   Also: *The Electric Hour Summer Series*, CBS, 30m, Sundays at 4:30. July 8–Sept. 9, 1945, with Francia White and Felix Knight; June 9–Sept. 22, 1946, with soprano Anne Jamison, baritone Bob Shanley, and the Sportsmen Quartet; July 13–Aug. 31, 1947, with Woody Herman, Peggy Lee, and Dave Barbour's orchestra.

In the regular-season *Electric Hour* run, Nelson Eddy offered folk songs, film melodies, and ballads from many lands. The shows were aired from the soundstage of the Walt Disney Studios. The closing "talks about the electric business" allowed local co-ops to cut away for messages of their own. Eddy closed each show with this wish: "May happiness light your home, and more power to you."

THE ELECTRIC THEATER, dramatic anthology.

BROADCAST HISTORY: Oct. 3, 1948–May 29, 1949, CBS. 30m, Sundays at 9. The Electric Companies of America.
CAST: Helen Hayes in adaptations of film and other stories, with Hollywood radio performers in support. **ORCHESTRA:** Vladimir Selinsky. **PRODUCER:** Joseph Stauffer. **DIRECTOR:** Lester O'Keefe. **WRITER/ADAPTER:** Robert Cenedella.

Helen Hayes was in London, finishing her stage run of *The Glass Menagerie*, when her new radio series opened. Henry Fonda, Basil Rathbone, and Margaret Sullavan handled the leads in her absence.

ELSA MAXWELL'S PARTY LINE, gossip and talk.

BROADCAST HISTORY: Jan. 2–June 26, 1942, Blue Network. 15m, Fridays at 10. Ry-Krisp.
CAST: Elsa Maxwell, with announcer Graham McNamee.

Elsa Maxwell was a celebrated party-giver and champion of the overweight set. She told stories about the great and near-great people she had known and conducted an on-air war against obesity. Using a scale especially built by the network and operated by announcer McNamee, she gave weekly reports of her progress (starting at 190 pounds). Her sponsor, Ry-Krisp, was promoted as a great aid in fighting fat.

Maxwell was also heard on Mutual, ca. 1943–47, in a similar format, quarter-hours weekdays, broadcast from her apartment in the Bel-Air Hotel. Tony LaFrano produced; Marvin Best announced.

ENCORE, musical variety.

BROADCAST HISTORY: Dec. 8, 1952–March 16, 1953, NBC. 30m, Mondays at 10.
ANNOUNCER: Kenneth Banghart. **VOCALISTS:** Marguerite Piazza and Robert Merrill, with encores of great operatic moments, musical stage highlights, etc. **ORCHESTRA:** Meredith Willson.

THE ENO CRIME CLUB, mystery drama, based initially on the Crime Club novels.

BROADCAST HISTORY: Feb. 9, 1931–Dec. 21, 1932, CBS. Various timeslots: initially a daily 15m thrill show at 6:45; moved several times in 1931; beginning in Jan. 1932, 30m, Tuesdays and Thursdays at 9:30, with each story complete in two parts; then from Nov. 9, Wednesdays only at 9:30. Eno "Effervescent" Salts.

Jan. 3, 1933–June 30, 1936, Blue Network. 30m, Tuesdays and Wednesdays at 8; Tuesdays only beginning September 1934. *Eno Crime Clues.* Eno Salts.

CAST: Edward Reese and Clyde North as Spencer Dean, Manhunter. Walter Glass and later Jack MacBryde as his partner Danny Cassidy. Helen Choate as Jane Elliott. New York supporting personnel including Ray Collins, Adele Ronson, Georgia Backus, etc. WRITER: Stewart Sterling. DIRECTOR: Jay Hanna (ca. 1933).

The Eno Crime Club was a detective series, early and primitive, one of the first shows of its kind. Its novel adaptations unfolded in the classic tradition, with locked-room mysteries and many clues throughout. The later series, *Crime Clues,* was not based on the Crime Club mystery novels; the listener was challenged to "match wits with the manhunter."

ERSKINE JOHNSON'S HOLLYWOOD, film talk and gossip.

BROADCAST HISTORY: 1942, Blue Network and KECA. Weeknights at 9:30, West Coast. *Hollywood Spotlight.* Two-year run.

1945, CBS. 15m, Fridays at 8:15, West Coast. *Tonight in Hollywood.* Jergens Lotion.

1946–50, Mutual. Various times, weekdays. *Erskine Johnson's Hollywood.* Sponsored by Ry-Krisp 5m, three times a week, 1949–50.

A popular feature of *Erskine Johnson's Hollywood* was "Hollywood Confessions," in which celebrities revealed aspects of their private lives. Examples: Jack Benny telling how Mary Livingstone heckled him from the audience before they were married; Roy Rogers confessing his hatred for lemon pies; Dan Duryea confessing that, contrary to his tough-guy screen image, he really enjoyed rooting around in his flowerbeds.

ESCAPE, dramatic adventure anthology.

BROADCAST HISTORY: July 7, 1947–Sept. 25, 1954, CBS. 30m. Scheduled erratically; heard at some time in its run every night of the week. Mostly sustained; Richfield Oil Company, April–Aug. 1950.

CAST: William Conrad and Paul Frees, heard alternately as the "voice" of *Escape*; Lou Krugman also as the opening "voice." Conrad and Frees also heard in leading and support roles, with Krugman and other top names of West Coast radio: Elliott Lewis, Jack Webb, Peggy Webber, Eric Snowden, Herbert Rawlinson, Harry Bartell, Jack Edwards, Frank Lovejoy, Ramsey Hill, Joseph Kearns, B. J. Thompson, Joan Banks, Hans Conried, Barton Yarborough, Luis Van Rooten, Nestor Paiva, Jack Kruschen, Jeanette Nolan, Morgan Farley, Raymond Lawrence, Berry Kroeger, Don Diamond, Sarah Selby, Jeff Corey, Alec Harford, Jay Novello, Lou Merrill, Byron Kane, Lillian Buyeff, Frank Gerstle, Wilms Herbert, Bill Bouchey, John Dehner, Charlotte Lawrence, Lawrence Dobkin, Ben Wright, Gloria Blondell, Eleanor Audley, Constance Cavendish, Lois Corbet, Sam Edwards, Vivi Janiss, Parley Baer, Laurette Fillbrandt, Edgar Barrier, Herb Butterfield, Ann Morrison, Ed Begley, Joy Terry, Barney Phillips, Junius Matthews, Jeanne Bates, Tudor Owen, Paul Dubov, Georgia Ellis, Vic Perrin, Michael Ann Barrett, Stanley Waxman, Jack Moyles, Virginia Gregg, Charlie Lung, Peter Leeds, Herb Ellis, Eleanore Tanin, Lynn Allen, Paula Winslowe. ANNOUNCERS: Frank Goss, Roy Rowan, etc. MUSIC: Cy Feuer, Leith Stevens, Wilbur Hatch with full orchestras; Ivan Ditmars, Del Castillo, Eddie Dunstedter on organ. PRODUCER-DIRECTORS: William N. Robson, 1947–48; Norman Macdonnell, 1948–49, again late 1950–52, again early 1954; Richard Sanville, Morton Fine, David Friedkin, Antony Ellis, etc. WRITERS-ADAPTERS: Les Crutchfield, John Dunkel, Walter Newman, Irving Ravetch, Gil Doud, David Ellis, John and Gwen Bagni, E. Jack Neuman, Kathleen Hite, William Froug, John Meston, etc. SOUND EFFECTS: David Light, Carl Schaele, etc; later Bill Gould, Cliff Thorsness, etc. THEME: *Night on Bald Mountain,* by Mussorgsky.

Escape is today widely considered radio's greatest series of high adventure. Ironically, it was never a major part of the broadcast schedule at its home network, CBS. Seldom allowed to develop a faithful audience, it was shifted to at least 18 different timeslots in its seven-year run: it was used as summer replacements, dropped from the schedule for weeks only to turn up in different timeslots much later. The audition episode was produced March 21, 1947, the series beginning four months later. There was never a period of serious commercial backing; hence, a modest operating budget. It should have run that summer of 1947 and disappeared, if the track records of other such programs are indicative. It came late in radio's history, a fact that may have contributed in a strange way to its artistic success. The people who remained in Hollywood radio were its most serious and talented artists, and in *Escape* they saw something special.

It was so good that *Radio Life*, for one, found the title misleading. This was not garden-variety escapism. "These stories all possess many times the reality that most radio writing conveys," *RL* wrote in August 1947. *Escape* had opened with dramatized short story classics: Kipling's *The Man Who Would Be King*, F. Scott Fitzgerald's *The Diamond as Big as the Ritz*, and Joseph Conrad's *Typhoon*. These tales were naturally compatible with radio. They gave the series a fresh appeal at a time when the air was full of Hollywood film adaptions, repeated in endless monotony.

The opening signature was classic, remembered for years by those who heard it. In the beginning it utilized a second-person hook, putting "you" the listener into the shoes of some embattled hero. *You are alone and unarmed in the green hell of the Caribbean jungle, you are being trailed by a pack of fiercely hungry dogs and a mad hunter armed for the kill. . . .* "Escape with us now to ancient Egypt," the announcer would invite: escape to a raft, and a group of men marooned in the vast South Pacific; escape with us now to occupied France. *You are alone*: this was a recurring *Escape* theme—the strong protagonist, facing the impossible alone, rising to conquer or be conquered.

A full orchestra gave *Night on Bald Mountain* a fiery treatment, as thrilling as any theme for any radio show in any time. In the late '40s, the listener was tantalized by three questions: "Wor-

ried about the United Nations? . . . Anxious about those bills piling up? . . . Want to get away from it all? We offer you . . . *ESCAPE!*" For a time this three-pronged opening was varied weekly, the questions often tied to current events or seasonal ambience. "Did you lose an election bet yesterday? . . . Feel a bad cold coming on? . . . Want to get away from it all?" was the opening Nov. 5, 1947, the day after an off-year election. The key phrase was "Want to get away from it all?"—this was the bridge to the evening's premise. Eventually, in the '50s, the opening became consistent, with Paul Frees or William Conrad using mostly the same words:

Tired of the everyday grind?

Ever dream of a life of . . . romantic adventure?

Want to get away from it all?

We offer you . . . ESCAPE!

Many of the *Escape* stories also became radio classics, later repeated on its well-to-do sister series, *Suspense*. *Suspense* was everything *Escape* was not: it had sponsors, fame, tradition, and timeslots that were consistent, at least for seasons at a time. But week in and out, *Escape* held its own, the main difference being the emphasis. *Suspense* concentrated largely on mystery and crime: on *Escape*, if mystery was used, it was often an exclamation point to the life-or-death situation that accompanied it. *Escape* used more stories of the supernatural, of man against the jungle, of war and the Old West. Never on radio was the action formula more effectively utilized.

Among the best shows were these, some of which have attained cult followings: *The Most Dangerous Game* (Oct. 1, 1947), a showcase for two actors, Paul Frees and Hans Conried, as hunted and hunter on a remote island; *Evening Primrose* (Nov. 5, 1947), John Collier's too-chilling-to-be-humorous account of a misfit who finds sanctuary (and something else that he hadn't counted on) when he decides to live in a giant department store after hours; *Confession* (Dec. 31, 1947), surely one of the greatest pure-radio items ever done in any theater—Algernon Blackwood's creepy sleight-of-hand that keeps a listener guessing until the last line; *Leiningen vs. the Ants* (Jan. 17, 1948) and *Three Skeleton Key* (Nov. 15, 1949), interesting as much for technical achievement as for story or character development (soundmen Gould and Thorsness utilized ten turntables and various animal noises in their creation of *Three Skeleton Key*'s swarming pack of rats); *Poison* (July 28, 1950), a riveting commentary on intolerance wrapped in a tense struggle to save a man from the deadliest snake in the world—Jack Webb stars in the Roald Dahl tale, but William Conrad steals the show; and *Earth Abides* (a two-parter, Nov. 5 and 12, 1950), George Stewart's story of a plague gone wild, still packing its full punch in the era of AIDS. Of the more than 240 shows aired, almost all survive in at least decent quality. On some titles, two distinct versions are preserved: those with the full orchestra are thought to be East Coast broadcasts; those with organ music are West Coast, generally repeats by the same casts a few days later.

THE ETERNAL LIGHT, religious drama.

BROADCAST HISTORY: Oct. 8, 1944–1981, NBC. 30m, Sundays. Joint project of NBC and the Jewish Theological Seminary.

CAST: New York radio personnel, with some major name stars in the 1940s: Jeff Chandler, Edward G. Robinson, Robert Preston, Mel Ferrer, etc. **DIRECTORS:** Frank Papp, Anton M. Leader, Andrew C. Love, etc. **SUPERVISOR AND ASSISTANT PRODUCER:** Barbara Gair. **RESEARCH:** Dr. Moshe Davis of the Jewish Theological Seminary. **SEMINARY PRODUCER:** Milton E. Krents. **CANTORS:** Robert E. Seigal, David Patterman. **ORIGINAL SCORES:** Morris Mamorsky. **ORCHESTRA:** Milton Katims, later Robert Armbruster. **WRITERS:** Morton Wishengrad, etc.

The Eternal Light dramatized incidents from the ancient Judaic past, interspersed with such contemporary works as *The Diary of Anne Frank*. The show's central theme was "brotherly love."

ETHEL AND ALBERT, comedy; also titled *The Private Lives of Ethel and Albert*.

BROADCAST HISTORY: Early 1940s, local radio, KATE, Albert Lea, Minn.

May 29, 1944–June 24, 1949, Blue Network/ABC. 15m, weekdays at 4 until mid-1944, then at 6:15.

Jan. 16, 1949–Aug. 28, 1950, ABC. 30m, Mondays at 8.

CAST: Peg Lynch and Alan Bunce as Ethel and Albert Arbuckle, who find humor in the common things of life. Richard Widmark as Albert, mid–1944 only. Madeleine Pierce as Baby Suzy, their daughter. **ANNOUNCERS:** George Ansbro, Glenn Riggs, etc. **MUSIC:** Rosa Rio, etc., on organ. **CREATOR-WRITER:** Peg Lynch. **DIRECTORS:** Robert Cotton (quarter-hours), William D. Hamilton (1949–50). **THEMES:** *Love Nest; Side by Side; There's No Place Like Home*.

Ethel and Albert was the story of a young married couple living in the little town of Sandy Harbor. Entire episodes could be consumed with the principles standing at the kitchen sink, talking and doing the dinner dishes. Albert was the manager of an office in town, but the focus of the comedy was on minuscule domestic logjams. He fretted over a cigarette case he had bought his brother-in-law for Christmas, then exchanged it, and learned that his brother-in-law had quit smoking. Ethel made a $5 bet with a neighboring housewife on a heavyweight championship fight, hoping to cancel out Albert's bet with her friend's husband. "The big events in one's life occur only now and then, but there are smaller events that are familiar to every family," said the announcer, opening the show. "it's these daily incidents that make up the private lives of Ethel and Albert."

Lynch created the show at a station in Minnesota, where she first worked in radio in 1938. "At first Ethel was as dumb as a doornail," she told *Newsweek*, kicking off the TV version in 1953. "She'd buy a grand piano and then go and buy one or two more." She was made considerably wiser for the network run. As Paul Rhymer did with *Vic and Sade*, Lynch peopled Sandy Harbor simply by having her two protagonists talk about their friends. When their daughter Suzy was born in the show's third year, hers became only the third voice heard on the series.

Alan Bunce, who got the male lead when Richard Widmark left six months into the run, had never heard of *Ethel and Albert* when he auditioned for the part. He arrived at the audition late and was generally considered, by those who heard him read, the weakest of the candidates. But Lynch thought he just might "be" Albert:

he needed some time to work himself out of his recent, long-running role as radio's *Young Dr. Malone*. Bunce would play the role for nine years, including a TV run, seen on three networks over three seasons, 1953–56. "All Peg needs is a word and she can write a script," Bunce told *Newsweek*. "She can write about nothing and do it entertainingly."

An *Ethel and Albert* derivative returned to CBS ca. 1957–60, as *The Couple Next Door*.

THE ETHEL BARRYMORE THEATER, dramatic anthology.

BROADCAST HISTORY: Sept. 30, 1936–April 7, 1937, Blue Network. 30m, Wednesdays at 8:30. Bayer Aspirin.

CAST: Ethel Barrymore with a company known as the Famous Actor's Guild, in a series of such chestnuts as *Trelawny of the Wells* and *Alice-Sit-by-the-Fire*. No episodes have been heard; little is known of the supporting players or crew.

THE ETHEL MERMAN SHOW, musical variety/situation comedy.

BROADCAST HISTORY: May 5–Sept. 22, 1935, CBS. 30m, Sundays at 8. *Rhythm at Eight*. Lysol. Music and song with Al Goodman's orchestra.

July 31–Nov. 14, 1949, NBC. 30m, Sundays at 9:30 through mid-Sept., then Mondays at 10:30. Sustained. Situation comedy. **CAST:** Ethel Merman as herself, star of a revue in need of a backer. Arthur Q. Bryan as Homer Tubbs, a crusty Syracuse mop tycoon who was sometimes inclined to back a show. Also: Leon Janney, Allen Drake, Santos Ortega, Charles Webster. **WRITERS:** Will Glickman, Joe Stein.

Ethel Merman proved that vast success onstage was no guarantee of even a modest triumph on the air. Her 1935 song show, *Rhythm at Eight*, was wrapped in a simple format: each show offered a thin storyline based on one of Merman's hit songs. Her forte was the gusty musical show-stopper. The problem was the timeslot, directly opposite the year's top show, *Major Bowes' Original Amateur Hour*.

Her 1949 sitcom fared little better. The storyline concerned her friendships with pianist-arranger Eddie McCoy and with Homer Tubbs, the hoped-for backer of her show. Reviews were luckwarm, praising Merman's voice, timing, and "starch" while panning the "feeble," "ungainly," and "unnecessarily corny" gags.

AN EVENING WITH ROMBERG, music.

BROADCAST HISTORY: June 12, 1945–Aug. 31, 1948. NBC. Summers only, 30m, mostly Tuesdays at 10:30. Replacement series for Hildegarde's *Raleigh Room* (1945) and *The Red Skelton Show* (1946–48). Raleigh Cigarettes.

CAST: Sigmund Romberg with orchestra; vocalists Anne Jamison, Reinhold Schmidt, Robert Merrill. **HOST-ANNOUNCER:** Frank Gallop.

THE EVEREADY HOUR, pioneering variety.

BROADCAST HISTORY: Dec. 4, 1923, premiere on WEAF, New York. In 1924, WEAF linked up with WRG, Buffalo, and WJAR, Providence, to carry *The Eveready Hour* to what were then considered far-flung audiences. National Carbon Company for Eveready Batteries.

Nov. 16, 1926–Dec. 16, 1930, NBC. 30m, Tuesdays at 9. Eveready.

CAST: Top headliners of the Broadway stage in guest appearances. Also: Wendell Hall, "the Red-Headed Music Maker;" Moran and Mack; John Drew; Eddie Cantor; Ignaz Friedman; Lionel Atwill; George Palmer Putnam; Beatrice Herford; Francis Wilson; Richard Dix; Laurette Taylor; Belle Baker; "Bugs" Baer; Pablo Casales; the Flonzaley String Quartet; Irvin S. Cobb; Walter C. Kelly, "The Virginia Judge;" and the singing-dancing-comedy team of Gus Van and Joe Schenck. **ORCHESTRA:** Nathaniel Shilkret. **DIRECTORS:** Paul Stacey (until 1927), Douglas Coulter.

The Eveready Hour was the first major variety show of the air. It was "the most ambitious project of its day," wrote William Peck Banning in his comprehensive history of WEAF: "a full hour of entertainment and information that was a radical departure from the ordinary 'sponsorship' of a dance orchestra. It was a venture that, considering current conditions, was extremely imaginative and courageous."

It was glamor, drama, news, and comedy in a single package. On its air, a farmer in distant Pennsylvania could experience what had, until then, been the exclusive province of cosmopolites. He could hear Will Rogers talk political humor and D. W. Griffith tell about making epic films. He could hear grand opera and Shakespeare, jazz and minstrels, poetry, adventure, and George Gershwin himself at the piano. Immediately after its premiere on WEAF, wrote media critic Ben Gross, it became "the most important program in broadcasting."

It was created by George Furness of National Carbon Company. Furness got the idea in mid-1923, while listening to a dramatic reading of Ida Tarbell's *He Knew Lincoln* on WJZ. Edgar White Burrill was the star, and his delivery excited Furness about the potential of radio. The future of commerce in the industry was far from settled, but Furness envisioned an Eveready program of greater scope than had yet been done. Furness was the guiding hand of *The Eveready Hour*: its parent, nursemaid, producer, supervisor.

At first the show was heard irregularly, sometimes once a week, occasionally three times. "But even through this irregular stretch they presented imposing programs," wrote Julia Shawell in the May 1928 *Radio News*. Eveready showcased Cissie Loftus, May Irwin, and Yap's Hawaiian Ensemble. Julia Marlowe offered Shakespeare excerpts. Ernest Thompson Seton talked about nature. Emma Dunn appeared in *The Governor's Lady*. Edwin Markham read his poetry. The concept of continuity was developed: shows were now subjected to the never-before practice of rehearsal, and the featured acts and announcements alike were scripted. As new stations were added to the WEAF network, the sponsor began sending its stars on cross-country tours, much as publishers of a later day would do with their bestselling authors. The stars would appear on local radio stations not served by the network; there they would do their routines and promote Eveready products. Wendell Hall, the Red-Headed Music Maker, toured widely for the sponsor in the show's pre-NBC days, plunking his banjo and singing his hit, *It Ain't Gonna Rain No Mo'*, becoming an ambassador of goodwill for Eveready wherever he appeared. He was married on *The Eveready Hour* in 1924.

One of the most sensational early features was developed from a William Beebe book on the Galapagos Islands. Reading it, Furness was in-

terested in Beebe's chance encounter with New York cab driver Martin "Red" Christianson, who had once been shipwrecked. Christianson came on *The Eveready Hour* and held the audience virtually breathless. "His was the art of the Arabian Nights storyteller, magnified via the loudspeaker," remembered Ben Gross: his tale was so popular that it was repeated four times, always to great acclaim. "Different cities begged for a visual staging of it," wrote Julia Shawell.

The budget soared (from $3,850 in 1923–24 to $400,000 in 1927–28), but so did Eveready sales. Will Rogers was paid $1,000 for a single performance, an unprecedented fee for its time. With the advent of NBC and the constant addition of new stations, the show was soon being heard on more than 30 outlets.

Its duration was brief, its impact and influence enormous. The stars became national figures. Rosaline Greene was known as "the girl with the most beautiful speaking voice on the air": she appeared in the radio adaptation of *Joan of Arc*. Edgar White Burrill, the man who had started it all, was invited by Furness to perform his Tarbell Lincoln sketch each year near Lincoln's birthday. Arthur H. Young described his bow-and-arrow hunting adventures in Africa and Alaska. Singers Elsie Janis and Annette Hanshaw were popular offerings: so were the comedy routines of Joe Weber and Lew Fields, whose old-fashioned standup numbers were laced with slapstick and simple gags from the Victorian era. George Moran and Charlie Mack (in private life George Searchy and Charles Emmett Sellers) appeared as *the Two Black Crows*, a forerunner to *Amos 'n' Andy*: Moran, glib of tongue, played straight man; Mack fretted and fumed and often punchlined "Why bring that up?" It was typical blackface, funny in its day.

The entire lifespan of *The Eveready Hour* was played out in radio's infancy, yet from it unfolded the whole concept of variety entertainment.

EVERYMAN'S THEATER, dramatic anthology.

BROADCAST HISTORY: Oct. 4, 1940–March 28, 1941, NBC. 30m, Fridays at 9:30. Oxydol.

CAST: Major film stars: Norma Shearer, Marlene Dietrich, Franchot Tone, etc., with Hollywood radio players in support. **ORCHESTRA:** Gordon Jenkins. **WRITER-DIRECTOR:** Arch Oboler.

Everyman's Theater was a mix of Arch Oboler dramas, originals and adaptations. It displayed the same Oboler techniques (offbeat plotting, realistic sound effects, and stream-of-consciousness narration) that had captured national attention in *Lights Out* and *Arch Oboler's Plays*. In fact, Oboler recycled several stories from these shows.

He opened with *This Lonely Heart*, the Tchaikovsky drama that had first been offered on *Plays* in 1939: Russian actress Alla Nazimova reprised her role of Tchaikovsky's patron, Mme. von Meck. The third broadcast, *Cat Wife*, had been one of his most famous *Lights Out* horror stories. Oboler admitted that the new title ''was pulled out of a very old hat.'' But again, prominent guests flocked to his side, and the 26 weeks were dotted with glamorous names. Charles Laughton and Elsa Lanchester were heard in *The Flying Yorkshireman,* Eric Knight's fable about a man who believes he can fly; Joan Crawford was heard in *The Word*; Bette Davis in *Of Human Bondage*. Many of these stars had admired Oboler's work and sought out opportunities to appear in his plays. Maestro Gordon Jenkins praised Oboler's style, which, he said, was conducive to creative radio scores. But the series was tainted at the start, Oboler wrote, by a ''venomous'' review in *Variety*, which made his sponsors ''doubt their own ears'' and hear the show with ''suspicion'' thereafter.

EVERYTHING FOR THE BOYS, dramatic anthology/musical variety.

BROADCAST HISTORY: Jan. 18–June 13, 1944, NBC. 30m, Tuesdays at 7:30. Autolite. Dramatic anthology with Ronald Colman in Arch Oboler adaptations and plays.

June 20, 1944–June 25, 1945, NBC. 30m, Tuesdays at 7:30. Autolite. Musical variety with Dick Haymes and Helen Forrest.

ANNOUNCER: Frank Martin. **ORCHESTRA:** Gordon Jenkins. **PRODUCER-WRITER-DIRECTOR:** Arch Oboler. **ASSOCIATE PRODUCER:** Barbara Smitten (Merlin). **WRITERS:** Jerome Lawrence, Milton Merlin.

Everything for the Boys threw actor Ronald Colman and writer-director Arch Oboler together for a stormy 21-week collaboration. It was Colman's first regular dramatic vehicle (discard *The Circle*, a 1939 talk show). It was not an auspicious beginning.

The idea originated with George Armstrong, owner of the Electric Autolite Company. Pairing Colman, the epitome of screen savoir faire, with one of radio's most talked-about writers seemed a natural. Colman would be heard in a variety of mini-plays, ranging from classics to film adaptations to Oboler originals. After the plays, servicemen in far-flung theaters of war would be connected, via shortwave, with wives and family. The sponsor, Autolite, would be seen as a friend of the ''boys'' overseas. A good idea, if only it had worked.

From the beginning, hostilities between Colman and Oboler created an atmosphere of anger, which finally became untenable. The press knew little of this: even a *Radio Life* reporter, who attended a rehearsal in March, mistook a sharp Oboler dig (''What's the matter, Ronnie, is it too early in the morning to turn on your charm?'') for good-natured camaraderie. It was suggested that the series was a partnership, growing out of a mutual admiration. In fact, Oboler revealed to writer Sam Frank, ''we hated each other's guts.'' Their differences existed on almost every front, personal and professional.

It began, according to Juliet Benita Colman's biography of her father, with Oboler's wardrobe. He worked in ''dirty dungarees, no socks, thong sandals, and a hat with a grease-stained band— you can imagine Ronnie's reaction!'' Colman's idea of casual dress was an immaculate sweater and well-pressed tweeds. Associate producer Barbara Merlin told Juliet Colman of an incident that illustrated the entire feud. ''I wish you'd tell Mr. Colman that is not the way to read a line,'' Oboler suggested to his assistant director. Colman snapped back: ''I wish you'd tell Mr. Oboler to get his pants pressed.'' Radio insiders' annoyance with Oboler was heightened by the suspicion that his was a ''cultivated eccentricity,'' put on for effect. He would scream and rant and often produce his script at the last moment, giving the impression that he had just dashed it off between more urgent business.

The Colman-Oboler feud extended to the show itself. Oboler wanted to do more original plays; Colman liked adaptations of classics and films. Oboler felt doing *Of Human Bondage* in 20 minutes was ridiculous on the face of it; Colman felt more at home in those parts. Colman, who had the clout, usually won out, though Oboler did use a few originals. The first show, *The Petrified Forest*, starred Ginger Rogers opposite Colman: other highlights were *Berkeley Square* with Greer Garson, *Death Takes a Holiday* with Ingrid Bergman, and *Blythe Spirit* with Loretta Young. Oboler always had an alternate script ready, in case the shortwave portion failed. The talks with servicemen were done in four-to six-minute segments, from Australia, New Guinea, Algiers, and other remote locations.

The show was preempted on D-Day. It returned for one final airing under the old format; then, on June 27, it was reorganized as a musical variety series with Dick Haymes and Helen Forrest. For a time it continued as *Everything for the Boys*, but eventually it became *The Dick Haymes Show*.

EXPLORING THE UNKNOWN, science documentary.

BROADCAST HISTORY: Dec. 2, 1945–Aug. 31, 1947, Mutual. 30m, Sundays at 9. Revere Copper and Brass Company.
   Sept. 2, 1947–March 14, 1948, ABC. 30m, Sundays at 7:30. Sustained.
CAST: Major stars with Hollywood backup: Orson Welles, Miriam Hopkins, Cedric Hardwicke, Pat O'Brien, Veronica Lake, Paul Lukas, etc. **NARRATOR:** Charles Irving. **ANNOUNCER:** Andre Baruch **ORCHESTRA:** Don Bryan. **MUSICAL SCORES:** Ardan Cornwall. **PRODUCER-DIRECTOR:** Sherman H. Dryer.

Exploring the Unknown took the science theme to its broadest aspects, from entomology to sociology to psychology. It told of man's battles with disease one week, the fight against race hatred the next.

EXPLORING TOMORROW, science fiction dramatic anthology.

BROADCAST HISTORY: Dec. 4, 1957–June 13, 1958, Mutual. 25m, Wednesdays at 8:05.
CAST: New York radio personnel: Mandel Kramer, Bryna Raeburn, Lawson Zerbe, Lon Clark, etc. **HOST:** John Campbell Jr., editor of *Analog* magazine. **PRODUCER-DIRECTOR:** Sanford Marshall. **THEME:** *As Time Goes By*.

EYES ALOFT, documentary drama.

BROADCAST HISTORY: 1942–43 (first broadcast Aug. 24, 1942), NBC West Coast. 30m, Mondays at 6, Pacific time.
CAST: Hollywood radio personnel, with occasional guest stars (Henry Fonda, etc.). **HOST:** Gayne Whitman. **ANNOUNCER:** Ben Alexander. **ORCHESTRA:** Gordon Jenkins. **DIRECTOR-WRITER:** Robert L. Redd.

Eyes Aloft was the result of an appeal by the Army to help bolster the Aircraft Warning System on the West Coast, where fear of a Japanese attack was widespread in the months following Pearl Harbor. But the initial heat of the Japanese attack had begun to subside, and reports of enemy submarine sightings off the West Coast had diminished; the numbers of volunteers had accordingly dropped. *Eyes Aloft* told of lonely skywatchers in mountain outposts and sentinels watching the sea from coastal pillboxes. Writer Redd, author of the successful comedy series *Point Sublime*, prepared by traveling 25,000 miles along coastline roads.

THE FABULOUS DR. TWEEDY, situation comedy.

BROADCAST HISTORY: June 2, 1946–March 26, 1947, NBC. 30m, Sundays at 7 for Lucky Strike, substituting for *The Jack Benny Program* through the show of Sept. 22; Wednesdays at 10 for Pall Mall thereafter.

CAST: Frank Morgan as Thaddeus Q. Tweedy, dean of men at Potts College. Nana Bryant as Miss Tilsey, head of the school. Barbara Eiler as one of the students. Harry Von Zell as Welby. Also: Eddie Green, John (Bud) Hiestand. **ORCHESTRA:** Eliot Daniel. **WRITER:** Robert Riley Crutcher.

The Fabulous Dr. Tweedy came after the breakup of the *Maxwell House Coffee Time* series when its stars, Frank Morgan and Fanny Brice, went into separate sitcoms. In *Tweedy*, Morgan played an absent-minded professor who lived with his adopted son Sidney and an ex-hobo manservant named Welby.

THE FALCON, mystery-detective drama.

BROADCAST HISTORY: April 10–Dec. 29, 1943, Blue Network. 30m, Saturdays at 7 through Aug., then Wednesdays at 7.

July 3, 1945–April 30, 1950, Mutual. 30m, Tuesdays at 8:30, 1945–47; Mondays at 8, 1948; Sundays at 7, 1949–50. Gem Razors and Blades, 1945–47; Anahist, Jan.–March 1950.

May 7, 1950–Sept. 14, 1952, NBC. 30m, usually Sundays at 4 but occasionally used in other timeslots (Wednesdays at 8:30 for *The Great Gildersleeve*, summer 1951). Kraft Foods 1950–51.

Jan. 5, 1953–Nov. 27, 1954, Mutual. 30m, Mondays at 8. General Mills, Jan.–July 1953.

CAST: Berry Kroeger (1943) as Michael Waring, the freelance detective, also known as "the Falcon," who was "always ready with a hand for oppressed men and an eye for repressed women." Also as Michael Waring: James Meighan (1945–47), Les Tremayne (late 1940s), Les Damon (early 1950s), and George Petrie. Supporting players from New York radio ranks: Joan Banks, Robert Dryden, Mandel Kramer, etc. **ANNOUNCERS:** Ed Herlihy, Jack Costello. **PRODUCER:** Bernard L. Schubert. **DIRECTORS:** Carlo De Angelo, Richard Lewis, Stuart Buchanan, etc. **WRITERS:** Gene Wang, Bernard Dougall, Jay Bennett. **SOUND EFFECTS:** Adrian Penner (Mutual).

The character of the Falcon was created by Michael Arlen in a 1940 story, *Gay Falcon*, which, almost immediately, became an RKO film and, subsequently, a movie series. The early *Falcon* films followed the Arlen story to this extent: the hero, played by George Sanders, was then named Gay Lawrence, using his Falcon identity in his dealings with the underworld. Sanders tired of the film role and, in *The Falcon's Brother* (RKO, 1942), the character was killed onscreen, leaving the Falcon's brother, thereafter played by Sanders's brother, Tom Conway, to carry on.

On radio, the character's name was Michael Waring. Each show began with a telephone ringing. It was always a woman calling. Waring, whose smooth voice was laced with a hint of the British, usually addressed her as "angel," or some other endearment; inevitably he had to beg out of a date, using such excuses as "I've got to teach some gangsters that you can't get away with murder, especially since the murder they want to get away with is mine." This preceded the opening signature.

Waring's methods crossed somewhere between *Ellery Queen* and *Richard Diamond*: he had a certain eye for detail but was frequently on the outs with the cops. The police were usually portrayed as stumblebums, and Waring was quick to point that out in snappy, sarcastic dialogue.

During the Les Damon run, Waring worked for Army Intelligence, solving espionage crimes overseas.

Among the most memorable commercials of the time were those for Gem Razor Blades, circa 1945. In a whispering voice, the announcer spoke against the ticking and tolling of a clock, dropping each word between the chimes:

Avoid . . .
> *. . . five . . .*
>> *. . . o'clock . . .*
>>> *. . . shadow!*

Use Gem Blades!
Use Gem Blades!
Use Gem Blades!

FAMILY SKELETON, serial drama

BROADCAST HISTORY: June 8, 1953–March 5, 1954, CBS. 15m continuation, weekdays at 7. Multiple sponsorship.

CAST: Mercedes McCambridge as Sara Ann Spence. Also: Russell Thorson, Bill Idelson, Herb Vigran. **ANNOUNCER:** Charles Lyon. **CREATOR-PRODUCER-WRITER:** Carlton E. Morse.

Family Skeleton was loosely fashioned after the long-running Morse serial *One Man's Family*, being written in "episodes" and "phases" rather than "chapters" and "books." Episode 20, Phase 2, is titled *Sarah, Have You Come Home to Cry Over Spilled Milk?* The heroine, pregnant and worried, creates a scandal when she arrives home unable to prove her marital status

(her marriage license was obliterated by bloodstains). She thus became the "family skeleton," the family consisting of her father, Judge Rodger Lincoln Spence; the mother, Grace Addison Spence, and the siblings, Lincoln, Kiplinger, and Marie.

FAMILY THEATER, dramatic anthology.

BROADCAST HISTORY: Feb. 13, 1947–July 4, 1956, Mutual. Many 30m timeslots (still heard on some Mutual stations in reruns in the 1960s).

CAST: Top Hollywood movie stars. **ANNOUNCER:** Tony La Frano. **CREATOR-PRODUCER-HOST:** Father Patrick Peyton. **PRODUCER:** Bob Longenecker. **DIRECTORS:** Richard Sanville, Mel Williamson, Fred MacKaye, Jaime del Valle, Joseph Mansfield, Robert O'Sullivan, John Kelley, Dave Young, etc. **WRITERS:** True Boardman, etc.

Family Theater was created by Father Patrick Peyton of the Holy Cross Fathers in an effort to promote family unity and prayer. Initially it was seen as a forum to broadcast the Rosary: when the networks refused to allow such a narrow one-denominational appeal, Peyton broadened the scope, made it a weekly drama, added the glamor of Hollywood, and saved the "message" for the slots normally reserved for commercials. Throughout the ten-year run, only one commercial was heard: the continuous appeal for family prayer in America. Al Scalpone created the slogans that were used on each broadcast: *A world at prayer is a world at peace* and, most memorably, *The family that prays together stays together*. A line from Tennyson was used to open each broadcast: *More things are wrought by prayer than this world dreams of.*

Father Peyton first became aware of radio's power in 1942, when Station WABY, Albany, offered a 15-minute forum in which a family might stand and say the Rosary. The show drew unexpected and strong response. Subsequently, Peyton was astonished when Msgr. Fulton J. Sheen offered, on his Sunday radio broadcast, a rosary and pamphlet prepared by Holy Cross seminarians, and 50,000 requests poured in. Peyton talked his way into Mutual, where he was offered a special Mother's Day slot May 13, 1945. The show would be cinched, the network people said, if a major star could be enticed to participate. Bing Crosby's name was mentioned, and Peyton got on the telephone. He tracked Crosby to the set of *The Bells of St. Mary's*, where Crosby was working on the role, ironically, of a priest. On the spur of the moment, Crosby agreed to do the show. Francis Cardinal Spellman also appeared, and the Mother's Day broadcast was such a success that Peyton pushed ahead with plans for a regular series.

Mutual donated the time, under four conditions: that the show be of top quality; that it be strictly nonsectarian; that a major film star be involved each week; and that Peyton pay production costs himself. He met Loretta Young, who advised him how to approach the stars and became the "first lady" of *Family Theater* (Young appeared on the first show and on more than 30 subsequent broadcasts). In other "cold" phone calls, Peyton lined up Irene Dunne, Charles Boyer, Ethel Barrymore, and Maureen O'Sullivan. Actors of equal stature were tapped for introductions. James Stewart introduced Loretta Young and Don Ameche on opening night. In another early broadcast, Edward G. Robinson introduced Pat O'Brien. It can safely be said that no series offered more Hollywood personalities in the same span of time: Gary Cooper, Gregory Peck, Shirley Temple, Jack Benny, Robert Mitchum—the list, after a while, becomes meaningless. The stories reveal little or no religious dogma: they are virtually indistinguishable from other high-quality anthologies on the air. There were 482 dramas broadcast. Father Peyton himself released almost the entire run to collectors. In 1967 he published his autobiography, *All for Her*, which includes several chapters on his radio work.

FAMOUS JURY TRIALS, dramatic anthology: "legal thrillers disinterred from judicial archives."

BROADCAST HISTORY: Jan. 5, 1936–Dec. 20, 1937, Mutual. Initially Sundays, then Mondays at 10 in an unusual 45m timeslot. Mennen.

Nov. 2, 1938–March 8, 1939, Mutual. 30m, Wednesdays at 10. Goodrich.

Nov. 11, 1940–June 25, 1949, Blue Network/ABC. Many 30m timeslots, notably Tuesdays at 9, 1941–44; Fridays at 8:30 or 9, 1944–46; Saturdays at 8:30, 1946–49. Oh Henry Candy, 1940–46; General Mills, 1947–48.

CAST: Maurice Franklin as the judge. Roger De-

Koven, DeWitt McBride, and others in the role of reporter-narrators. New York radio personnel in support: Raymond Edward Johnson, Frank Readick, Mandel Kramer, etc. **PRODUCER-WRITER:** Don Becker (ca. 1936). **DIRECTORS:** Clark Andrews, Carl Eastman, etc. **WRITERS:** Milton J. Kramer, Jerry McGill, Stedman Coles, etc. **SOUND EFFECTS:** Don Foster (Mutual).

Famous Jury Trials was billed as "the dramatic story of our courts, where rich and poor alike, guilty and innocent, stand before the bar of justice." That said, the listener was taken into the courtroom, where a judge was instructing a jury: *Be just and fear not, for the true administration of justice is the foundation of good government.*

The stories were delivered flat, without music, giving the testimony added reality and weight. The shows were taken from actual case histories; they were heavily fictionalized, though "not enough to fool you," *Radio Mirror* noted, if the case was recent and celebrated. Among the then-novel techniques developed on *Famous Jury Trials* (a good 15 years before *You Are There* adopted it as a general format) was that of transporting a radio announcer back in history, to report old trials as they allegedly happened. The later shows were developed entirely through dialogue, the reporter's cut-ins the only side narrative. The testimony was limited to the most explosive parts of the case, the reporter bridging the rest. The crowd was a constant part of the ambience, the hollow tone suggestive of chambers in large old-fashioned courthouses. The verdict was given at the end, often surprising the radio audience.

THE FAT MAN, detective drama, based on a character created by Dashiell Hammett.

BROADCAST HISTORY: Jan. 21, 1946–Sept. 26, 1951, ABC. 30m, Mondays at 8:30 until Jan. 1947; Fridays at 8 until Jan. 1951; then Wednesdays at 8:30. Pepto Bismol, 1947–50; American Chicle, 1951.

CAST: J. Scott (Jack) Smart as Brad Runyon, an overweight but powerful detective hero. Ed Begley as Sergeant O'Hara. Mary Patton as Lila North, Runyon's secretary. Amzie Strickland as Cathy Evans, Runyon's friend. Also: Betty Garde, Linda Watkins, Paul Stewart, Alice Frost, Vicki Vola, Robert Dryden, Jimmy McCallion, Sarah Burton,

etc. **ANNOUNCER:** Charles Irving for most of the run; Don Lowe, Gene Kirby. **MUSIC:** Bernard Green; in his absence, Joseph Stopak or Mark Winston. **PRODUCER:** Ed Rosenberg. **DIRECTORS:** Charles Powers, Robert Sloane, Clark Andrews, etc. **WRITERS:** Richard Ellington and Lawrence Klee; later, Robert Sloane, Dan Shuffman and Harold Swanton. **SOUND EFFECTS:** Ed Blainey.

The Fat Man made good use of author Dashiell Hammett's name, though the crime novelist had little to do with it. Radio producer Ed Rosenberg felt that a viable detective feature could be spun out of Hammett's character Gutman in *The Maltese Falcon*. Chapter 11 of that modern classic was titled *The Fat Man*, though Gutman's resemblance to the character who emerged on the air began and ended with the title. Gutman was sinister and brooding; radio's *Fat Man* was a charmer, a witty ladykiller named Brad Runyon.

He was hard-boiled but soft-hearted: his voice conveyed a rough edge, a thick beefy countenance. The image was set in an immortal opening signature, packed with contrasts. It began with the sweet trill of a harp (the woman who played it got a 20-second workout each week), which blended into the pretitle teaser for Pepto Bismol.

When your stomach's upset . . .
Don't add to the upset . . .
Take soooooooothing Pepto Bismol,
And feel—gooood again!

Up came the harp again, a soaring "feel-good" sound. Then the hero walked into the drugstore.

WOMAN: There he goes, into that drugstore . . . he's stepping on the scale.
SOUND EFFECT (A penny tumbling into a scale).
WOMAN: Weight? . . . two hundred thirty-seven pounds.
SOUND EFFECT (The click of a fortune card popping out of a scale).
WOMAN: Fortune—danger!
MUSIC STING.
WOMAN: Whooooo is it?
RUNYON: *The Fat Mannnnnnn . . .*

Now came the music, a marvelously fat theme, eight notes created especially for the series and blown plumply out of a bass horn. The stories were typical of 1940s detective radio: the em-

phasis was on action and adventure, with logic the frequent loser. Runyon was a bachelor. He had a good friend named Cathy, whose appearance early in the series was said to "curb wolfish women." Despite Runyon's popularity with the opposite sex, the end of the first episode found him mournfully telling Cathy that "nobody loves a fat man." He slurred his words, drawing out *San Quen-n-tinn* and the oft-used word *murrr-derrr*. He was strong, his iron grip and no-nonsense voice putting the skids to many a roughneck. J. Scott Smart, who played the role, was typecast. He tipped the scales at 270 pounds in real life and had a long career in radio. He was born in Philadelphia in 1902 and started acting with a Buffalo stock company in 1925. He was an artist, a musician, and a dancer (he is sometimes seen in period photographs, heavy of girth but light on his feet, jitterbugging with Hedda Hopper or Julie London). But *Radio Life* found him "a recluse, an extremely shy and even lonely man."

As Jack Smart, he was much in demand in '30s radio: he was a utility man on *The March of Time* and played character roles on *Theatre Guild* and comic roles with Jack Benny, Bob Hope, Fred Allen, and others. He lived in a fisherman's shack on the Maine coast, painting seascapes during the week and flying to New York long enough to do his airshow and, in one instance, win a Charleston dance contest. He brought *The Fat Man* to the screen in 1951, with support from Rock Hudson, Julie London, and Emmett Kelly. Smart died Jan. 15, 1960.

As for *The Fat Man*, it vanished along with the other Hammett shows when Hammett was listed in *Red Channels* and his name was no longer an asset.

FATHER COUGHLIN, the "radio priest"; commentary.

BROADCAST HISTORY: 1926, WJR, Detroit.
1926–30, WMAQ, Chicago; WLW, Cincinnati.
Oct. 5, 1930–April 5, 1931, CBS. 60m, Sundays at 7.
1931–42, private network; heard Sundays throughout the land on many independent stations.

Father Charles Coughlin used radio as few have ever done to build and support a powerful political machine. He was born in Hamilton, Ontario, Oct. 25, 1891. He was ordained a Catholic priest in 1916, and in 1926 he became pastor of the Shrine of the Little Flower in Royal Oak, Mich.

His initial airtalk on WJR, Detroit, drew five letters from listeners—a far cry from the million a week he got a few years later, when his influence was at its peak. Coughlin's early talks were said to be lacking in confidence. If so, it was a failing he soon overcame. He rose to power quickly after his 1930 CBS debut, and his voice—just in time for the 1932 presidential election—became one of the most potent in the land. Coughlin bitterly attacked President Herbert Hoover, then turned his wrath upon bankers, socialists, and the uneven distribution of wealth.

He established an early rapport with Franklin D. Roosevelt, strongly supporting his candidacy. When Roosevelt was elected, rumors spread that Coughlin was in line for a high administrative post and would quit the church to enter government service. But this failed to materialize, and Coughlin became disenchanted with Roosevelt as well. His first public break with Roosevelt came in 1934, when he urged payment of a soldiers' bonus and the president publicly threatened to veto it. By 1935 Coughlin's break with Roosevelt was complete; by 1937 his attacks on the president had become so violent that they led, ultimately, to a rebuke from the pope. Roosevelt, whose own radio persona was highly developed, found Coughlin a formidable adversary. The priest had a staff of confidential investigators in Washington, headed by a former Hearst journalist, and his advisers in financial matters consisted of bankers and brokers in New York.

His themes centered more and more on money. His constant charge was that Roosevelt had betrayed the people by failing to "drive the moneychangers from the temple," and that Congress had all but delegated its lawmaking powers to the president.

He formed his own radio chain. He had been dropped by CBS in 1931 when the network attempted to censor a speech and Coughlin used his hour to loudly berate CBS on its own air. He tried to move to NBC, but that network was having none of it, hiding behind a policy of not accepting "commercial religious broadcasting." Using WOR, New York, and WJR, Detroit, as his flagship outlets, Coughlin gradually increased his scope, buying time on individual stations until he could be heard virtually anywhere in the nation. He paid for the time with voluntary contributions estimated at $500,000 a year. Coughlin often said that he never asked his listeners for money, but his broadcasts always closed with the gentle reminder by his announcer that "this hour has been made possible by the outstanding financial support of the radio audience."

This may have been the only gentle thing about him. Coughlin could work himself into a rage on the air. He could be heard pounding his pulpit in anger, denouncing the "black bread" of Roosevelt's programs. His magazine, *Social Justice*, amplified his political views, and by 1939 he was buying his time in 60-minute blocks. Coughlin's attacks now included Jews; he came to be seen as one of the most virulent promoters of anti-Semitism in his time. He was seen by prominent Jews as a hate-monger, and by 1940 his influence had begun to decline. In 1942 his magazine was banned from the mails by the Espionage Act. It soon folded, and leaders of the Catholic Church (some of whom had long considered him an embarrassment) began a move to have his voice silenced as well. Coughlin yielded to the pressure and dropped abruptly from the political scene in 1942.

He retired as pastor of the Shrine of the Little Flower in 1966 and died Oct. 27, 1979.

FATHER KNOWS BEST, situation comedy.

BROADCAST HISTORY: Aug. 25, 1949–Nov. 19, 1953, NBC. 30m, Thursdays, mostly at 8:30 (at 8, 1951–52). General Foods.

CAST: Robert Young as Jim Anderson, an insurance man and head of radio's most typical family. June Whitley as his wife Margaret; Jean Vander Pyl later as Margaret. Rhoda Williams as the Andersons' daughter Betty. Ted Donaldson as their son Bud. Norma Jean Nilsson as the youngest Anderson child, Kathy. Eleanor Audley, Herb Vigran, and Sam Edwards as the neighboring family, Elizabeth and Hector Smith, and their son Billy. **ANNOUNCERS:** Marvin Miller, Bill Forman, etc. **CREATOR-WRITER:** Ed James. **WRITERS:** Paul West, Roz Rogers. **DIRECTORS:** Fran Van Hartesveldt, Murray Bolen, Ken Burton.

Father Knows Best grew up on television. The characters matured significantly from their radio days, and the show became a milestone of wholesome situation comedy, cited with *Leave It to Beaver* and *The Adventures of Ozzie and*

Harriet as the best of the sweetness-and-light school, where misunderstanding is life's most serious problem and everything works out fine in the end.

An audition disc, produced by writer Ed James Dec. 20, 1948 (eight months before the show got on the air), gives a good look at the series in its embryonic state. The family was named Henderson then, and the father hadn't yet begun to develop the wisdom-in-depth that would be his on TV. Jim Henderson is something of a dunderhead, a typical male malady in radio sitcoms: he suffers through degrees of the Nelson-Riley syndrome, an illness found most often in the homes of Ozzie Nelson and Chester A. Riley. He has constant foot-in-mouth trouble; he is a scatterbrain; his wife Margaret is a trifle too sweet, and the kids act like refugees from an *Aldrich Family* reject. A listener gets the feeling, hearing Robert Young and company in their first adventure together, that writer James was playing the title for laughs.

But all this would pass. By 1953, its last full year on radio, *Father Knows Best* had combined the basic ingredients for what would become one of the most successful television shows of its day.

Jim Anderson was an agent for General Insurance in Springfield, an average town in the average Midwest at an average time in American history. He and Margaret raised three children: in order, Betty, Bud, and Kathy. Each night he arrived home with a cheery greeting that became a series catchphrase—"Margaret! I'm home!"—and the fun would start. The stories often revolved around the teenage problems of Betty or Bud: broken dates, the generation gap, and coming-of-age faux pas that got blown out of any realistic magnitude were all grist for the mill. It's Betty's night to go to the library with her boyfriend Ralph, but Jim has arranged a blind date for her with a client's son. Furious, Betty refuses to go; Jim must then call the client and cancel, but then Ralph cancels out on Betty, Jim must revive the original date, Ralph has second thoughts, and Betty ends up with two dates. By the end of the half-hour, what started out as an unhappy twosome is a fairly contented quintet, three girls going out with two boys. While all this is building, Bud interrupts constantly, asking for help with his "My Embarrassing Moment" essay, and Kathy wants Father to help her pull

the taffy. Bud's exasperation with life usually manifested in the catchphrase "Ho-ly cow!" Jim's pet names for his daughters were Princess (Betty) and Kitten (Kathy).

The show sometimes opened with a little pretitle commercial hype, such as this, which finds Kathy and Margaret in the kitchen:

Mother, are 40 percent Bran Flakes really the best-tasting cereal of them all?

Well, your father says so, and father knows best.

Robert Young, who became the epitome of warm-hearted fatherhood, was the only member of the radio cast to survive the move to television. Jane Wyatt was the TV Margaret; Elinor Donahue played Betty; Billy Gray was Bud; and Lauren Chapin played Kathy. The series premiered on CBS-TV Oct. 3, 1954, and was seen on various networks until April 5, 1963.

FAVORITE STORY, transcribed dramatic anthology, classics.

BROADCAST HISTORY: 1946–49, 30m, Ziv syndication. Heard on KFI, Los Angeles, June 25, 1946–April 19, 1949.

CAST: Ronald Colman, host (beginning ca. 1947) and frequent star. Hollywood radio actors in support: Hans Conried, Herb Butterfield, Lurene Tuttle, Byron Kane, William Conrad, Janet Waldo, Joseph Kearns, Jimmy Lydon, Eric Snowden, Norman Field, Gloria Gordon, Raymond Burr, Jeff Corey, John Beal, Helen Craig, Berry Kroeger, Edmund MacDonald, etc.

ORCHESTRA: Claude Sweeten. **PRODUCER-WRITERS:** Jerome Lawrence and Robert E. Lee. **SOUND EFFECTS:** Jack Hayes.

Favorite Story was a nationally syndicated outgrowth of a local dramatic offering, developed and continued on KFI, Los Angeles. The fare was classic literature, both the novel and short story, with such evergreens as *Vanity Fair*, *Pride and Prejudice*, *The Three Musketeers*, and *The Moonstone* filling the bill. In 1947 writers Lawrence and Lee approached frequent star Ronald Colman and asked him to host it. The format—that of having the "favorite stories" of prominent personalities—was continued. Production stopped in late 1949, after 118 episodes, but the shows were heard in various local markets for years.

THE FBI IN PEACE AND WAR, crime drama.

BROADCAST HISTORY: Nov. 25, 1944–Sept. 28, 1958, CBS. 30m, Saturdays at 8:30, 1944–45; Thursdays at 8:30, 1945–47; Fridays at 9:30, late 1947; Thursdays at 8, 1947–52; Wednesdays at 8, 1952–55; Wednesdays at 8:30, 1955–56; Sundays at 6:05, 1956–57; then at 5:30, 1957–58. Lava Soap, 1944–50; Wildroot Cream Oil, 1951–52; Lucky Strike, 1952; Nescafe, 1953; Wrigley's Gum, 1954–55.

CAST: Martin Blaine as Field Agent Sheppard of the Federal Bureau of Investigation. Donald Briggs as Mr. Andrews. New York radio personnal in support: Jackson Beck, Walter Greaza, Ralph Bell, Ed Begley, Elspeth Eric, Frank Readick, Rosemary Rice, Harold Huber, Edith Arnold, Robert Dryden, Charita Bauer, Grant Richards, etc. ANNOUNCERS: Warren Sweeney, Len Sterling, Andre Baruch (for Lucky Strike). ORCHESTRA: Vladimir Selinsky. PRODUCER-DIRECTORS: Max Marcin, 1940s; Betty Mandeville, beginning circa 1949. WRITERS: Louis Pelletier, Jack Finke. SOUND EFFECTS: Ed Blainey, Al Hogan, Byron Wingett. THEME: March from *Love for Three Oranges*, by Sergei Prokofiev.

The FBI in Peace and War was one of two durable crime-busting series (the other being *This Is Your FBI*) dedicated to the power and glory of the Bureau. Comparing the two in 1947, *Radio Life* found little to choose between them. Both honed "the same high standards of playing down the attractions of criminal life and playing up the infalibility of the Bureau." Both were sold as completely "authentic"; both original authors visited the FBI academy; both shows were packaged to rousing march music. On *Peace and War*, the theme was lifted from Prokofiev's classical *Love for Three Oranges* and given a sassy treatment by a full orchestra; it became one of radio's best-loved signatures. Combined with extraordinary commercials for the first sponsor (a deep male voice, accompanied by a bass drum, rhythmically booming L-A-V-A! L-A-V-A! out of an echo chamber), this created a framework that usually exceeded the rather predictable, run-of-the-mill story content.

Each episode was billed as "another great story based on Frederick L. Collins's copyrighted book, *The FBI in Peace and War*— Drama! Thrills! Action!" *Peace and War* was not blessed with Bureau approval: Jerry Devine of *This Is Your FBI*, on the other hand, was sanctioned. Both FBI shows remained popular, with the unauthorized version, *Peace and War*, usually a few ratings points ahead. The Bureau was never presented in anything but the most favorable light on either series. *Peace and War* was virtually an anthology, bound only by acts of crime and by the sometimes-thin FBI involvement. The main characters were usually the criminals, the stories unfolding from their viewpoints. Occasionally the scene shifted to the pursuing FBI, with the busy clatter of teletype machines a near-constant. The FBI was personified as Field Agent Sheppard; his boss was the enigmatic Mr. Andrews. Rackets and swindles were the staples.

FIBBER McGEE AND MOLLY, comedy.

BROADCAST HISTORY: April 16–July 2, 1935, Blue Network. 30m, Tuesdays at 10. Johnson's Wax. Aired from New York until May 7, then from Chicago.

July 8, 1935–March 7, 1938, NBC; Blue Network until June 1936, then Red. 30m, Mondays at 8, 1935–37; Mondays at 9, 1937–38. Johnson's Wax. Broadcast from Chicago.

March 15, 1938–June 30, 1953, NBC. 30m, Tuesdays at 9:30. Johnson's Wax, 1935–50; Pet Milk, 1950–52; Reynolds Aluminum, 1952–53. Broadcast from Chicago until 1939, then from Hollywood.

Oct. 5, 1953–March 23, 1956, NBC. 15m, five a week, various days and times. Various sponsors.

June 1, 1957–Sept. 6, 1959, NBC. Five vignettes of about 4m, each Saturday and Sunday on *Monitor*.

CAST: Jim Jordan as Fibber McGee of 79 Wistful Vista, teller of tall tales, incurable windbag. Marian Jordan as Molly McGee, his long-suffering wife. Marian Jordan as Teeny, the little girl who dropped in frequently to pester McGee. Isabel Randolph in miscellaneous "snooty" parts, beginning Jan. 13, 1936, and culminating in her long-running role as the highbrow Mrs. Abigail Uppington. Bill Thompson as Greek restaurateur Nick Depopoulous, first heard Jan. 27, 1936. Bill Thompson in various con man roles, first named Widdicomb Blotto and later Horatio K. Boomer, mimicking W. C. Fields from the show of March 9, 1936. Bill Thompson as the Old Timer, beginning May 31, 1937. Bill Thompson as Wallace Wimple, henpecked husband and bird fancier, introduced April 15, 1941. Cliff Arquette as Wallingford Tuttle Gildersleeve, the original Gildersleeve impersonation, first heard April 13, 1936. Harold Peary as Throckmorton P. Gildersleeve, McGee's windy neighbor, beginning Sept. 26, 1939, after a long string of miscellaneous Gildersleeve characters, 1938–39. Gale Gordon as Mayor LaTrivia, beginning Oct. 14, 1941. Gale Gordon, much later, as Foggy Williams the weatherman. Arthur Q. Bryan as Doc Gamble, first heard April 6, 1943. Shirley Mitchell as Alice Darling, a "Rosie the Riveter" character who worked in a war plant and rented the McGees' spare bedroom beginning Oct. 5, 1943. Marlin Hurt as Beulah, the McGees' Negro cook, first heard Jan. 25, 1944. Bea Benaderet as Mrs. Millicent Carstairs. Hugh Studebaker as McGee's friend Silly Watson. Ransom Sherman, briefly, as Molly's drunken Uncle Dennis, a character that, in the main, was silent. Gene Carroll as Lena, the maid, 1947. **AN-NOUNCERS:** Harlow Wilcox, (1935–53). John Wald (1953–56). **VOCALISTS:** Kathleen Wells, Ronnie and Van, Gale Page, the Three Kings, the Bennett Sisters and Lynn Martin (all mid-1930s); Clark Dennis (1936–38); Perry Como (with the Ted Weems band, 1936–37); Donald Novis (1938–39); Jimmy Shields (1939–40); Martha Tilton (1941). **VOCAL QUARTET:** The King's Men (Bud Linn, Jon Dodson, Rad Robinson, and arranger Ken Darby), 13 years beginning Feb. 6, 1940. **ORCHESTRA:** Rico Marcelli (1935–36), Ted Weems (1936–38), Jimmy Grier (1937), Billy Mills (Jan. 17, 1938–June 30, 1953). **PRO-DUCER-DIRECTORS:** Cecil Underwood, Frank Pittman (1940s), Max Hutto (1950s). **WRITERS:** Don Quinn; later Phil Leslie. Also: Keith Fowler, Ralph Goodman, Tom Koch, Joel Kane, Leonard L. Levinson. **SOUND EFFECTS:** Monty Fraser, Virgil Reimer, Warren Allen, Parker Cornel, Jack Wormser, Cliff Thorsness, Bud Tollefson, Frank Pittman (early 1940s, prior to becoming director). **THEME:** *Save Your Sorrow for Tomorrow*, with secondary musical bridge *Ridin' Around in the Rain* (1935–40); *Wing to Wing*, composed by Billy Mills (post-1940).

The story of Jim and Marian Jordan has probably been told and retold more than any other tale of the microphone: how two ordinary people from the heartland, through tenacity and hard work, climbed to the heights and showed the Hollywood insiders how radio should be done.

In the mountain of publicity, fact, and hype, a Jordan advocate named Tom Price undertook a herculean task: to pin down every conceivable fact about the Jordans, their times, and the heartwarming radio show they did for more than 20 years. Price, a California teacher, produced a document that can only be called formidable. Self-issued in a severely limited edition (100 copies), his *Fibber McGee's Closet* is a 1,193-page statistical abstract on the show, its people, its gags, the music, sound effects, writers, sponsors, spinoffs, influences, competitors. "If Jim Jordan belched, Tom Price was there to record it," one collector of radio material said recently. Price befriended Jordan in the last ten years of his life. He was given access to voluminous scrapbooks and script files; he was given many interviews, and also interviewed most of the people still living who had worked the show. His book has an index of closet jokes: how many were done, who opened the closet door (Fibber did, 83 of 128 times), and what he was seeking there (everything from Mayor LaTrivia's hat on the show of Jan. 20, 1946, back to the first time the gag was used, March 5, 1940, when Molly went looking in the closet for a dictionary). Price's work stands as a monument to one of the most important shows of the radio era, yet today it is largely unavailable even to comedic radio's most vocal proponents. The oversized two-volume edition sold out, leaving a still-substantial abridgment in print from the author. Most of the dates on the obscure Jordan radio shows of the 1920s and early 1930s come from Price, taken firsthand from Jim Jordan's bound scripts. Dates on first character appearances, on developing gags, and on many obscure specifics likewise come from Price. An article on *Fibber McGee and Molly* in a book such as this could not be done as effectively or as accurately without Price's massive work.

The Jordans had, to say the least, a long and hard hill to climb. By the time they arrived at the top of the radio heap, Jim and Marian Jordan—he the amiable braggart and she the salt of the earth, patient and sweet—were middle-aged veterans of the vaudeville wars. They had done literally thousands of radio shows in Chicago and on the fledgling networks. They never played the Palace, but as Robert M. Yoder noted years later in the *Saturday Evening Post*, the Jordans could "match their vaudeville bruises" with anyone. "They played the tank towns."

Jim Jordan was born on a farm near Peoria, Ill. Nov. 16, 1896. He met Marian Driscoll, a coal miner's daughter, at choir practice at St. John's Church in Peoria. Marian was born in Peoria April 15, 1898. She shared Jordan's dream of a life in the theater, though her parents discouraged it. Her parents were also unenthused when she took up with the farmer's boy who was full of the same silly ideas.

Jordan's family sold the farm and moved into town. He studied voice; Marian gave lessons on the piano. On a referral from his vocal teacher, Jordan went off to Chicago alone, getting work in a traveling revue titled *A Night with the Poets*. But he tired of the solitary, nomadic way of life: the one-night stands, the poor hotels, the bad hash-house food—these things were tolerable, but the homesickness made it hard. He quit after 39 weeks and returned to Peoria. He found work as a mailman, and on Aug. 31, 1918, he and Marian overcame the continued reluctance of her parents and were married.

The next seven years were full of show business attempts and failures. Jordan was drafted five days after his wedding, arriving in France in time for the Armistice. He joined a troupe and toured postwar France, giving shows. Returning to Peoria, he found his wife still teaching music, and found himself a succession of menial jobs. The lure of the theater remained, enticing them both, and at last Marian suggested that they try it as a team.

They traveled, off and on, for four years, playing in small-town movie houses, on opera stages, and in lodge halls throughout the Midwest. Marian returned home to give birth to their first child, Kathryn; then, leaving the child with Jordan's parents, went out on the road again. Their son, Jim Jr., was born at the end of another vaudeville tour. Jordan tried a solo act, leaving his wife with the children. He had, wrote Yoder, a miserable time. "Singers were a dime a dozen, and what they were paid wouldn't cover room rent." Marian rejoined him, dragging the children out on the road. It was a thankless and sometimes cruel existence. They went broke in Lincoln, Ill. in 1923, and their parents wired them money to come come.

Jordan went to work in a department store,

selling toys he couldn't afford to buy for his children. Again they succumbed to vaudeville. But "a cheerless odyssey of midwestern mediocrity confronted them, and they had little hope of breaking into the big time," summarized *Current Biography* almost 20 years later. Jordan went to Chicago: he joined Egbert Van Alstine and Clem Dancy in a traveling musical show, and did his first broadcast on a small station while traveling through Minneapolis with the Van Alstine revue.

He was performing in Chicago in 1924 when his real air career began. Marian had come over for a visit: they were at the home of Jordan's brother, Byron, and were listening to a singing act on the radio. "We can do better than that," Jordan said (or words to that effect, for this story has been told so many times that something like this must have occurred). Byron bet him $10 he couldn't, and they rushed to the station, where an obliging programmer let them sing *Can't You Hear Me Callin', Caroline*? and *Knee-Deep in the Daisies*, a performance that Price says lasted about six minutes. When it was over, they were given their first radio contract, a nighttime slot, once a week for Oh Henry Candy, which would pay them $10 a show for six months.

Price gives general or specific dates for almost a score of radio series that followed, leading finally to *Fibber McGee and Molly*. Under that first contract, they were heard on WIBO, Chicago, as *The O'Henry Twins* for 26 weeks. From 1925 until 1927, they played over Chicago's WENR, a series called *Marian and Jim in Songs*, making a "gradual transition to comedy patter." On the same station they were heard in *The Air Scouts* (Oct. 3, 1927–Dec. 31, 1929), a children's show on which Marian created her little-girl voice, used to such advantage as Teeny on later broadcasts. "Dozens of voices" were developed on this series, says Price, and on the shows that followed and surrounded it. He estimates that in this Chicago training period, the Jordans developed so many voice variants that they were able to do 145 different parts for *Smackout*, their early-1930s forerunner to *Fibber McGee and Molly*. *The Air Scouts* was sponsored by the Commonwealth Edison Company; concurrently, they were heard on *Marian and Jim's Grab Bag* and as *Luke and Mirandy* (both WENR, 1928–31). On *Luke and Mirandy*, Jordan played a character named Uncle Luke, a fibber of sorts, and Marian was Aunt Mirandy, his wife. They began a series of "Uncle Luke and Aunt Mirandy of Persimmon Holler" skits on *The National Farm and Home Hour* (WMAQ, Chicago, and NBC Blue, 1928–35). They were also featured players in *The Smith Family* (June 9, 1929– April 3, 1932, WENR, WMAQ), a local soap opera that Price believes was the first show of its kind. In a strange bit of casting, Marian played Mrs. Nora Smith, mother of the woman whom Joe Fitzgerald, a prizefighter played by Jordan, courts and marries. If this wasn't enough, says Price, "they would move on to the theater [in the evenings] to perform their vaudeville acts."

But there were still more radio shows. In 1929 the Jordans began working the noonday barnyard circuit on a WENR series, *The Farmer Rusk Hour*. This was notable, for here they met their future writer and partner, Don Quinn, an aspiring cartoonist who, of necessity, turned to radio when the Depression deflated the comic market.

Quinn frequented WENR in the evenings: the hostesses and receptionists sometimes stayed around to dance to the music of the nighttime shows. One night the Jordans came in; an acquaintance became friendship, and Quinn began writing gags for their use on the air. This was all highly informal. Quinn picked up an occasional $10 for his contributions, which were funnier by far than the material ground out by the station's continuity man.

It was, wrote Robert Yoder, "like the gin meeting the vermouth in the story of the martini." Quinn was the *x* factor in the Jordan formula, his wit like a core of plutonium in an explosive device that couldn't yet be imagined. There were no set schedules: the Jordans would swing past Quinn's place on their way to the station; if Quinn had nothing for them, they ad-libbed their lines and sang. Early that year (1931), the telling ingredient slipped into place. Jordan was doing a farm broadcast, and from the "proprietor," E. W. Rusk, he heard a true story about an old man from Missouri who owned a store that was always "smack out of everything." In fact, the store was "stocked full," the story went, but the old man would never sell any of his merchandise—he would simply claim to be "smack out" of that item, and order it from St. Louis, to be delivered the next day. The stu-

dents of nearby Columbia had begun hanging out in the store, calling it "Smackout" and being enthralled by the tall tales the old man could spin at the drop of a hat.

This was grist for the radio mill. With Quinn's help, the Jordans created a new scenario. They reworked their fibber-man, Uncle Luke, named him Uncle Luke Gray, and moved him into a store that would be called *Smackout*, at the junction known as *The Crossroads of the Air*. The series opened under that title March 2, 1931. Broadcast from WMAQ to a national CBS audience, *Smackout* was the direct forerunner of *Fibber McGee and Molly*: many of the characterizations were developed in its four-year run. The show moved to NBC with the sale of WMAQ to that network in late 1931; it ran on the Blue Network, weekdays at noon in the east. Jordan continued to play Uncle Luke; and he and Marian also played themselves, in their natural voices. In the storyline, the Jordans were Luke's nephew and niece, who came to the store, "away down in the country, to visit him and make life cheerier with their songs." Jordan delivered the bread, and sang old favorites in a rich tenor; Marian played piano and organ, accompanied him on vocals, and, as Price puts it, was "blonde, sweet, and optimistic." Marian also gave life to a fully realized Teeny, the little girl who lived across the road with her aunt. Teeny would drop in from time to time to pester Luke and ask for goods that weren't in stock. If Teeny wanted a baseball, Luke was smack out of baseballs. By 1932 *Smackout* had taken on characteristics of a serial. One storyline, that summer, took up more than three months. In a 22-chapter story, culminating just before Christmas 1932, Teeny's aunt died and Luke adopted the little girl and became her legal guardian.

Marian played a dizzying assortment of character roles: a glance through Price shows that she did 69 separate characters ranging from an unnamed female customer to a young boy. She played a flapper, a Kentucky matron, a Scandinavian, an old lady, a "middle-aged country gal," and a snob. Among her continuing characterizations was Bertha Boop, a film star come to Smackout Crossroads to escape her tinsel life in Hollywood. She was Mrs. Bedelia Thomas, who hoped to get her hooks into Luke, and the widow Cornelia Wheedledeck, who came to the store to ask the prices of merchandise but never bought anything. She played Geraldine, a "giddy, gabby, gurgling, giggling girl from the hill," who talked about her husband Gerald and otherwise rambled on about nothing. And she was Mrs. J. Highhat Upson, a pretentious society woman whose character would return (though played by another actress) when the series made the jump to *Fibber McGee and Molly* a few seasons later.

Jordan, in addition to playing himself and Luke, was heard in 71 separate character roles. He played delivery boys, customers, and odd bits. He was August Carl Pigmeyer, a farmer of German extraction who owned the farm where the fishing pond was located. He played Mort Toops, Luke's friend and rival at horseshoes. And his was the voice of Squire Lovejoy, described by Price as "a wealthy old chiseler and investor from Petersville." There were also 120 "silent characters," who were characterized simply by being talked about. There were names like Lump Murphy and Sam Tappit, Jorp Cankle (champion horseshoe-pitcher) and Snipe McFee, who could stand 8,000 feet away and sharpen a pencil with the bullets from his gun (all references from Price).

As for Quinn, he was quickly becoming a master of the absurd. He and the Jordans were known to listen to *Vic and Sade* and *Lum and Abner*, landmark comedies that were getting under way at about the same time. Quinn wrote about woodpeckers who could tap messages in Morse code, and hybrid tomatoes that came up square, so their slices fit perfectly in bacon-tomato sandwiches. This is precisely the kind of humor Paul Rhymer was writing on *Vic and Sade*, and there was probably a fair amount of cross-listening among these writers and artists in 1931–35.

Smackout ran on NBC until Aug. 3, 1935. The Jordans remained highly active on other Chicago radio fronts all through its run. Among their shows were these: *Marquette, the Little French Girl* (a quarter-hour musical drama, WMAQ, July 22, 1931–June 1, 1932); another *Marian and Jim in Songs* (WMAQ, August 1931, again in 1932–33, and still again in 1934); *Mr. Twister, Mind Trickster* (WMAQ, June 24, 1932–Nov. 10, 1933, a quiz show without Marian, with Jordan as quizmaster); *Kaltenmeyer's Kindergarten*

(WMAQ and NBC, 1932–36); *The Breakfast Club* (as "Toots and Chickie," WMAQ and NBC Blue, 1933–36); and *Saturday Night Jamboree* (WMAQ, mid-1930s).

When it finally arrived on the air, *Fibber McGee and Molly* was hardly earthshaking. Two shows that survive from the beginning of the run reveal an act still mired in vaudeville. The situations were simplistic, the characters little more than cartoon-like props. But something was happening: Don Quinn bloomed in radio. So did the Jordans, who, as Robert Yoder described it, developed "unexpected skill as comedians" until no one on the air surpassed them in timing or delivery.

The show began to take shape in 1934. Johnson's Wax of Racine, Wis., was looking for a new show to sponsor. The company had been carrying the broadcasts of Tony Wons, popular heartthrob and dispenser of tired poetry, but Johnson executives were interested in the idea of taking on unknown people and letting the show come of age on the air. John J. Lewis, Chicago adman, was referred by his wife to *Smackout*, which she had recently heard on a car radio.

Quinn wrote a script. He took the character Luke Gray out of the store and, in an inspired moment, renamed him Fibber McGee. He called his script *Fibber McGee and Molly*, but for some reason the agency people handling the Johnson account didn't like it. They wanted to call it *Free Air*. It was, after all, about a middle-aged pair of married vagabonds who travel down America's highways, stopping occasionally for gasoline and some engaging talk about Johnson's Car Wax. But there was a problem with this title: Sinclair Lewis had used it on a short story and, as Yoder was told, wanted $50,000 for its release. So *Fibber* it was—perhaps the luckiest bad break in all radio. An audition record was made, and Johnson's Wax bought the show. It would premiere on Monday night, April 16, 1935, with *Smackout* still running on the same (Blue) network, as a six-a-week quarter-hour feature at 10 A.M.

The Jordans handled both shows until August, when *Smackout* left the air. For 20 weeks, the *Fibber McGee* show rolled along in this basic format: in each broadcast there were two "traveling" segments, short skits following them down U.S. Route 42 in their dilapidated jalopy.

The sketches were interspersed with music and song. Bandleader Rico Marcelli offered typical Depression-era melodies, novelty numbers augmented by a singing trio. Announcer Harlow Wilcox always turned up in the endless string of gas stations where the McGees stopped en route. Wilcox pumped the gas (18½ cents a gallon for red gas; 17 cents for blue; 15 for white) and always found a way to turn the talk to Johnson's Car Wax. McGee was introduced on the first broadcast as "that ambulating Ananias, that humbug of the highways"; Molly as "his constant companion and severest critic." Jordan played his role in a countrified burlesque, his voice hitting the upper registers almost in a whine. Marian lived up to her "severe" billing: her complaining Irish brogue offered little but comeuppance to McGee, who was usually trying to stretch a point or bluff his way out of a jam.

The difficult and well-remembered Jordan tongue-twisters—when in one long breath Fibber would expostulate some argument or embellish a truth with a gush of sound-alike words beginning with the same letter—started on the opening show. The first one was a rambling bit of nonsense in traffic court about whether a "red light was a dead light if the light ain't lit." These would improve dramatically: Jordan's ability to mix words at high speed dazzled and delighted his audiences. "Pretty Please McGee, I was known as in those days," he would say in a more polished time. Molly would groan as McGee prepared to tell about his former prowess as a prosecuting attorney. "Pretty Please McGee, proclaimed by the press and public the peerless prosecutor of pilfering pickpockets, political parasites, and persons performing petty peccadilloes, putting prison pajamas on poker players preyin' on poor punks with peculiar pasteboards, pleadin' with passion and pathos for poor people in pretty pickles—a peppy personality with a capital *P!*" Jordan seldom fluffed one of these, no matter how convoluted. When he did, Marian's hearty and genuine guffaw led the studio audience in laughter.

But there wasn't any laughter for Molly McGee in the beginning. Throughout the early weeks (the "vagabond stage," as Price calls it) she remained a tough old Irish crone whose stern rebuke—"*McGee!*"—yanked Fibber instantly back to earth and riddled his inflated ego. Wilcox and the McGees were the main components. The integrated commercial was established in the first broadcast: this meant that the product could be mentioned at almost any time, giving Johnson's Wax a lot of play for its money. Fibber called Wilcox "Harpo" or "Carwax," a practice that would continue, with modifications, for years. The vagabond period lasted 19 weeks: then the McGees arrived in a little town called Wistful Vista, somewhere in America. Fibber bought a raffle ticket and won the prize, a house, whose address at 79 Wistful Vista was soon to become the best-known habitat on the air. The McGees moved in Sept. 2, 1935.

Now the shows revolved around the McGees at home: a pleasant half-hour could be devised around the simple prospect of avoiding work, or doing work badly. Scrubbing the back porch, hanging wallpaper, trying to light the furnace: Fibber could always be counted on to botch such jobs thoroughly. Occupation themes were introduced: McGee running the public library, or the post office, or an antique store, all with predictable results. Income tax trouble was an evergreen, usable almost every year. The show began taking on a semblance of its real nature. Molly's rough edges vanished: her character mellowed, assuming more of Marian's personality as she became one of America's best-loved comediennes. She was totally without glamor, real to a growing audience that suddenly numbered in the double-digit millions. Marian had turned the show away from its outlandish beginnings. What couldn't happen back home in Peoria, she insisted, shouldn't happen on *Fibber McGee and Molly*.

The burlesqued voices disappeared. Jordan's high-pitched speaking voice was perfect for the new McGee; Marian was the soul of understanding and tolerance as the new Molly. Running gags abounded. Fibber's tall tales were used on almost every show in the late '30s. A company of solid Chicago regulars was established in support: Isabel Randolph, Bill Thompson, and Harold Peary. Jordan would need all this support and more: the show was still building in 1937, when Marian suddenly dropped out of it.

She was gone for 18 months, from Nov. 15, 1937, until April 18, 1939. Her absence was explained to the press as fatigue. In some quarters it was believed that she had suffered a nervous breakdown. In fact, she was engaged in a long and difficult battle with alcohol, a problem that was kept under wraps for 30 years after her death. It was hoped, most ardently by Jordan himself, that her recovery would be quick. But as the weeks passed and the opposite became more apparent, the show was revamped as *Fibber McGee and Company*. New players were added, notably Betty Winkler, who played most of the female and juvenile roles.

Marian returned to a warm welcome, and the show continued to climb. The closet gag was established. The cascade of rubbish that came tumbling down, usually on Fibber's head, was the soundman's challenge, and potentially his worst nightmare. The closet gag was intricately staged on a makeshift set of stairs, and the soundmen fretted throughout the run that it might come down before its time. So important did the sound effects become that Ken Darby immortalized the craft in a musical selection, *The Sound Effects Man*, which was heard periodically.

Suddenly it was a ratings giant. By January 1940 it was packing a powerful 30.8 Hooper: it was the top-rated show in the nation in 1943, and for the rest of the decade ran nip-and-tuck for that honor with Bob Hope, Jack Benny, and Edgar Bergen. Its supporting characters came and went: some returned, some did not, it didn't seem to matter. The writing remained razor-sharp throughout the '40s, the lines often clever plays on words. Some lines became national catchphrases. "That's pretty good, Johnny, but that ain't the way I heerd it!" was Bill Thompson's approach to a dusty and irrelevant joke as the Old Timer. "You're a haaaard man, McGee" was Harold Peary's inevitable retort as Gildersleeve. McGee and Gildersleeve lambasted each other throughout Marian's long absence, the Gildersleeve character coming to full prominence during that time. They snarled and bickered, borrowed tools and forgot who owned them, fought it out with hoses while watering their lawns. In August 1941 *The Great Gildersleeve* became the first major series to spin out of another program; Peary and Gildersleeve left Wistful Vista for the town of Summerfield, where Gildersleeve would become the water commissioner and raise his niece and nephew.

The ever-reliable Bill Thompson filled the gap with a new character, Wallace Wimple. Wallace gave new meaning to the word "wimp," for this was the nickname pinned on him by Fibber McGee. Wimple was terrified of his "big old

wife," the ferocious, often-discussed but never-present "Sweetie Face." Also in 1941 came Gale Gordon as Mayor LaTrivia, who would arrive at the McGee house, start an argument, and become so tongue-tied that he'd blow his top. A year later, all these characters disappeared: Gordon went into the Coast Guard, and when Thompson joined the Navy, four characters went with him. With LaTrivia, Boomer, Depopoulous, Wimple, the Old Timer, and Gildersleeve all on the "recently departed" list, Fibber found a new devil's advocate in the town doctor. Arthur Q. Bryan, who had played the voice of Elmer Fudd in the Warner Brothers cartoons, became Doc Gamble, continuing the verbal brickbats begun by Gildersleeve. Their squabbles could begin over a disputed doctor bill—McGee always disputed doctor bills—or erupt out of nowhere about anything at all. They usually parted amicably. "So long, you dear old man," Fibber would say in his tenderest voice. "Yes, ours is a very warm friendship," Gamble said once. "On a hot day you can smell it for 50 miles."

Another transition character, in for the war's duration, was the charming, scatterbrained war worker Alice Darling (Shirley Mitchell). Marlin Hurt's Beulah gave the show a lift in 1944. The audience never failed to respond when Hurt, a white man, gave sudden voice to a bubbly, cheerful black woman in a low falsetto catchphrase, "Somebody bawl fo' Beulah?" Beulah laughed heartily at McGee's corniest jokes, the laugh ending in a second catchphrase, "Looove dat man!" Marian, of course, played her little girl, Teeny, throughout the run, her best-remembered line "Whatcha doin', huh mister, whatcha?" And there were dozens of characters never or seldom heard but much discussed: Molly's drunken Uncle Dennis (personified briefly by Ransom Sherman but silent through most of the run); Fred Nitny, Fibber's pal from vaudeville days; Willie Toops; and Myrt the telephone operator, whose whole existence was manifested in Fibber's one-sided phone conversations. "Oh, is that you, Myrt? . . . How's every little thing, Myrt? . . . Your uncle? . . . Smashed his face and broke one of his hands?" To this, Molly would usually say, "Oh, dear!" in obvious distress. On this particular night, however, she was allowed to guess the punchline: "What's the matter, McGee, did he drop his watch?"

Quinn was a full partner in the show. By 1941 he and the Jordans were splitting a $6,000 weekly paycheck three ways. His contributions to the canon of radio comedy are today considered of first-rank importance. His playful dialogue will delight people forever. Seldom did a character say as common an oath as "I'll be darned" in Quinn's dialogue. "Well, I'll be an old Hemingway expression," Fibber would say instead. The subtleties grew from show to show. One of the funniest understatements, Quinn thought, was his constant use of the intersection at 14th and Oak. Price lists more than 120 entities there, including the Bon Ton Department Store, Doc Gamble's office, the Searsmont & Warbuck Store, the county courthouse, the museum, the library, the Wistful Vista Gazette, the power and light company and a turkish bath. While Quinn continued to pile new offices into the cross-streets, hardly anyone noticed.

With the exception of *The Bob Hope Show*, *Fibber McGee and Molly* was the most patriotic show on the air. Whole runs of shows illustrated homefront themes. Fibber bought black market beef, which of course was spoiled. At the end, he and Molly signed off with personal messages and pleas for war bonds, volunteers, and scrap drives. Then the war was over: Bill Thompson and Gale Gordon returned with their old characters, and the show was touted by the press as the smoothest, most polished comedy on the air. "Nothing ever goes wrong," Yoder wrote. He had just watched a sound effects man arrange a closet gag consisting of golf clubs, roller skates, trays, a guitar, shoes, a briefcase, a pith helmet, a sword, a speargun, a suitcase, several packages, and a broken clock. As always, it teetered precariously throughout the live half-hour, then came down right on cue, the tiny tinkle of the customary bell capping it off. The show always began with a burst of laughter. "Eleven seconds before air time, Pittman points a finger at Bill Thompson," wrote Yoder. "Thompson hands Fibber a glass of water . . . Fibber takes a lunge at the clock, gulps the water, and then, in apparent nervousness, tosses the glass over his shoulder. Instead of breaking, it bounces—it's plastic. And on a roar from the audience, they take to the air."

The closings were always simple: Molly's "Goodnight, all" was as much a catchphrase as her celebrated "T'aint funny, McGee" and "heavenly days!" The themes were lively, the music a vital part of the show. Billy Mills, who joined the company in Chicago, moved with it to the coast in 1939, along with Hal Peary, Isabel Randolph, and Bill Thompson. Mills had a happy-sounding aggregation, with such notable swing masters as Red Nichols often sitting in. The series has been widely syndicated in recent years, but the syndicator unfortunately deemed the music and other topical material to be "dated," thus expendable. But collectors rejoice in the fact that long runs were saved by both NBC and Johnson's Wax, and more than 700 episodes exist, in their entirety, on tape.

All the principals are dead now. Arthur Q. Bryan died Nov. 30, 1959. Harlow Wilcox died Sept. 24, 1960. Marian Jordan died April 7, 1961. Bill Thompson died July 15, 1971. Billy Mills died Oct. 20, 1971. Don Quinn died Jan. 11, 1973. Harold Peary died March 30, 1985. Jim Jordan married Gretchen Stewart after Marian's death and lived in semi-retirement for almost 30 years. He died April 1, 1988, at 91.

After Jordan's death, his widow and children donated the bound volumes of *Smackout* and *Fibber* scripts to the Museum of Broadcast Communications in Chicago, where they may be read by students of comedy. The museum also has a *Fibber* closet exhibit.

THE FIRST NIGHTER PROGRAM, dramatic anthology; light, romantic fare with a theater motif.

BROADCAST HISTORY: Nov. 27, 1930–Sept. 29, 1933, Blue Network. 30m, Thursdays at 8:30; Wednesdays at 8 from May 1931; Saturdays at 9:30 from mid-Sept. 1931; Fridays at 9 from mid-Aug. 1932; Fridays at 10 from mid-Aug. 1933. Campana Balm.

Oct. 6, 1933–Feb. 12, 1937, NBC. 30m, Fridays at 10. Campana.

Feb. 19–Dec. 21, 1937, CBS. 30m, Fridays at 9:30. Campana.

Jan. 7–Aug. 26, 1938, NBC. 30m, Fridays at 9:30. Campana.

Sept. 2, 1938–May 29, 1942, CBS. 30m, Fridays at 8 until July 1939; Fridays at 9:30 until the summer break in May 1940; Tuesdays at 8:30, 1940–41; Fridays at 9:30, 1941–42. Campana.

Oct. 4, 1942–Oct. 25, 1944, Mutual. 30m, Sundays at 6 until April 1944, then Wednesdays at 9:30. Campana.

Oct. 20, 1945–April 13, 1946, CBS. 30m, Saturdays at 7:30. Campana.

Oct. 4, 1947–Oct. 20, 1949, CBS. 30m, Saturdays at 8 until mid-Dec. 1947; Thursdays at 10:30, 1947–49; Thursdays at 10 beginning June 1949. Campana.

April 27, 1952–Sept. 27, 1953, NBC. 30m, Sundays at 7; then Tuesdays at 10:35; then Sundays at 7 as of Sept. 13, 1953. Miller Beer. Repeat broadcasts.

CAST: Charles P. Hughes as "Mr. First Nighter," the genial host who walked listeners through an elaborate opening and introduced the play; Macdonald Carey, Bret Morrison, Marvin Miller, Don Briggs, and Rye Billsbury also heard as the First Nighter. Teams of romantic leading players including Don Ameche and June Meredith (1930–36), Ameche and Betty Lou Gerson (1935–36); Les Tremayne and Barbara Luddy (1936–43), Olan Soulé and Barbara Luddy thereafter. Cliff Soubier a regular, early to mid-1930s. AN-NOUNCER: Vincent Pelletier. ORCHESTRA: Eric Sagerquist (1930–44), Frank Worth. PRO-DUCER-DIRECTOR: Joseph T. Ainley. SOUND EFFECTS: Robert Opper, Virgil Reimer, (NBC); Urban Johnson, Ed Vojtal (CBS). THEME: *Neapolitan Nights*, slowly, with heavy violin emphasis.

An elaborate format and a deep American fascination for the theater world are undoubtedly responsible for much of the early success of *The First Nighter Program*. The illusion was that anyone might be transported to "the little theater off Times Square" to witness an "opening night performance" of a fine romantic comedy. The opening signature was one of the greatest ever devised, ranking with the *Inner Sanctum* door and *The Shadow*'s electric laugh. It took 135 seconds to deliver in 1944. During that time the audience was introduced to the host, "Mr. First Nighter," walked with him along Broadway to the theater (couldn't get a cab in those hectic wartime nights), and arrived just in time for the first-act curtain.

The listener was absorbed by the sounds of Broadway: the car horns, police whistles, the people milling about. Up Broadway to 42nd

Street, where an attendant shouted, "Have your tickets ready, please! have your tickets ready, please! . . . Good evening, Mr. First Nighter, the usher will show you to your box." Then, in the "fourth-row center" seats, the First Nighter gave a quick reading of the program—title, cast, author—and the "famous First Nighter orchestra" played a few bars of music. An usher came down the aisle, shouting "Curtain! Curtain!" Buzzers sounded. Ushers reminded people that smoking was permitted in the lobby only. Then, listeners were told, the lights were dimmed and the play began. Afterward, the effect was reversed, with Mr. First Nighter weaving his way through the still-humming crowd and melting away into the street.

It was elaborate, all right, and it was all audio balderdash. In fact, *The First Nighter Program* never got within 1,000 miles of New York. Originated in Chicago, then the hub of broadcasting for the nation, the show played from the Merchandise Mart until 1946, when star Barbara Luddy left for Hollywood and the series followed her west.

In typical theater fashion, the plays were staged in three acts, with commercials for Campana Balm between the curtains. The format was unique and enjoyed a huge ratings success (28.0 in 1933–34). Inevitably, it was copied, with such shows as *Knickerbocker Playhouse* and *Curtain Time* doing poor-man's retreads. The fare was light romance, with occasional dips into melodrama. The stories were original, written for the series by freelance scripters (Arch Oboler among them). Don Ameche in the weekly lead became radio's first sex symbol, his popularity so great after a few seasons that he left for a film career. His replacement, Les Tremayne, was 24 years old, with a voice not unlike Ameche's and a bright future as a leading man. In 1937 Barbara Luddy arrived to become the longest-running regular, playing the female leads until the show expired 16 years later.

The job of the First Nighter was a simple one, recalled Macdonald Carey, who played it in 1937. In his autobiography, he recalled his job as "to introduce the play and serve as a surrogate host to the studio audience." He worked in a tux and warmed up his crowd with a little speech just before air time.

The series was usually upbeat and nonviolent;

it was said to be a great favorite in the mid-western "Bible belt." A memorable offering was *The Little Town of Bethlehem*, which became the annual Christmas play after its first broadcast in 1936.

THE FITCH BANDWAGON, initially a bandstand series of popular music; then musical variety with Cass Daley; finally, situation comedy with Phil Harris and Alice Faye.

BROADCAST HISTORY: Sept. 4, 1938–May 23, 1948, NBC. 30m, Sundays at 7:30 (timeslot consistent through all format changes). F. W. Fitch Shampoo Company.

Sept. 4, 1938–June 17, 1945. A true forum for band music, with such orchestras as Freddy Martin, Jan Savitt, Harry James, Tommy Dorsey, Harry Sosnik, and Jimmy Grier offering popular tunes of the day. **HOST:** Dick Powell (ca. 1944) with top guests (Eddie Cantor, Andy Devine, etc.). **ANNOUNCERS:** Dresser Dahlstead (ca. 1939), Wendell Niles. **PRODUCERS:** Ward Byron (early shows), Bill Lawrence (ca. 1944).

Sept. 23, 1945–June 16, 1946. **CAST:** Cass Daley, headliner. Francis "Dink" Trout as a wimpy character named Horace. Also: Henry Russell. **ANNOUNCER:** Larry Keating. **MUSIC:** Visiting bands.

Sept. 29, 1946–May 23, 1948. A shift into situation comedy, a well-developed forerunner of *The Phil Harris/Alice Faye Show*. **CAST:** Phil Harris and Alice Faye as themselves. Elliott Lewis as Frankie Remley, the wisecracking guitar player in the Harris orchestra. Robert North as Alice's brother Willie. Jeanine Roose and Anne Whitfield as Little Alice and Phyllis, the Harris children. Walter Tetley as Julius Abbruzio, the sarcastic delivery boy from the grocery store. **ANNOUNCER:** Bill Forman. **MUSIC:** Walter Scharf. **DIRECTOR:** Paul Phillips. **WRITERS:** Joe Connelly and Bob Mosher; later Ray Singer and Dick Chevillat.

The Fitch Bandwagon was initially what its title implies: a weekly showcase for the nation's big bands. The bands played hit music, and at the end the maestro's musical biography was offered. By 1944 the shift away from straight music had begun, with some comedy skits and standup routines. In 1945, with the arrival of Cass Daley, the shift was more pronounced: Daley, who had become popular through guest

appearances on *The Kraft Music Hall*, was featured in connecting comedy skits. The "bandstand" angle was kept alive by having name orchestras appear with three or four selections spaced around Daley's skits. "Well, this week Cass is working as a salesgirl in a music shop," Larry Keating would announce. Daley, after creating chaos in the music store, would suggest listening to a record by, say, Glen Gray. Gray, of course, was on hand with his Casa Loma Orchestra to give a live rendition.

The final format, with Phil Harris and Alice Faye, was virtually identical to and is covered under THE PHIL HARRIS/ALICE FAYE SHOW. The theme throughout the various format changes was zestily sung to the melody *Smile for Me*:

> *Laugh a-while,*
> *Let a song be your style,*
> *Use Fitch Sham-poo!*
> *Don't despair,*
> *Use your head, save your hair,*
> *Use Fitch Sham-poo!*

THE FITZGERALDS, husband-wife breakfast talk.

BROADCAST HISTORY: 1940–1945, WOR, New York.

1945–1947, WJZ, New York/ABC Network.

Ca. 1948–1982, WOR, New York.

The Fitzgeralds was the first major husband-wife at-home breakfast program. It grew out of a series of broadcasts done on WOR in the 1930s by newsman-turned-broadcaster Ed Fitzgerald and his wife Pegeen. For most of their run they were heard locally, but they were so well parodied on a national level that their fame reached beyond the limits of their signal.

Ed Fitzgerald had been a print journalist, working for newspapers in Seattle, Los Angeles, and San Francisco. He met Margaret Worrall in 1929; they married in June 1930. Fitzgerald went to work at KFRC in 1933, hosting a series called *Feminine Fancies* for three years and developing a good air presence. He was hired at WOR around 1936: there he initiated his literary series, *Book Talk, Back Talk, and Small Talk*. When the 1939 New York World's Fair opened, Fitzgerald became the station's town crier. His wife had also broken into radio. Using an Irish derivative of her real name, she too broadcast from the World's Fair, a show called *Here's Looking at*

You. She began a morning series called *Pegeen Prefers*, and during this time she developed the idea from which the entire husband-wife breakfast formula of the '40s would spring.

They would do a show from home, talking about life in New York, their neighbors, the mail, the newspapers: just about anything that might come up over breakfast. Neither Fitzgerald nor WOR could work up much enthusiasm: only after Pegeen became ill and was forced to broadcast from home did the idea take root. The fan mail was good enough that WOR reconsidered. *Breakfast with the Fitzgeralds* opened in 1940, later becoming simply *The Fitzgeralds*. It was completely spontaneous, and Fitzgerald was probably the most unpredictable of all the morning husbands. Once, after Pegeen had gone through his pockets and taken a dollar, he exploded on the air, branding her a pickpocket in front of all New York.

But much of the time they were suspiciously lovey-dovey. "Good morning, little Peggy, Mrs. Fitz-G, honey," he would coo. Such dialogue (none of it scripted) was ripe for lampooning by such national comics as Fred Allen. But Fitzgerald could also complain, on the air, of a morning hangover, and once he stalked back to bed in a huff when his wife needled him for boorish behavior at a party the night before. It was, wrote Vance Packard in the *American Magazine*, a slice of life. "When their phone rings during the broadcast, they answer it, even if it is a listener calling to furiously contradict them, or the landlord demanding his rent. The dog barks whenever anyone comes near the door, and the show is regularly thrown into pandemonium when one of the many cats creeping about the place starts batting bric-a-brac off the china cabinet."

The show was broadcast from the Fitzgerald apartment on East 36th Street, though they also rented a duplex, a hideaway overlooking the East River that they nicknamed "Shangri-oo-la-la" and frequently discussed on the air. But the real listener appeal came from his unpredictable nature. "Lambie-puss, you look like an old hophead this morning," he might say, noting in passing that she was getting thick around the middle. Their disagreements on the air often turned heated. By 1945, when they moved to WJZ and an ABC microphone, they were big radio business, with 17 commercial accounts hand-picked by themselves. They were soon doing a daily 40-minute show, a 30-minute Sunday broadcast, and three evening *Dinner with the Fitzgeralds* programs each week. Though their tenure on the network was brief, the form they initiated prospered. Their departure from WOR in 1945 prompted the station to hire Dorothy Kilgallen and Richard Kollmar for another enduring husband-wife chat show, *Breakfast with Dorothy and Dick*. A third nationally known couple, Tex McCrary and Jinx Falkenburg, rose to prominence in the mid-1940s. Competition, especially between the Fitzgeralds and Kollmars, was fierce. *The Fitzgeralds* could still be heard, having returned to WOR, into the 1980s. Fitzgerald died in 1982; Pegeen in 1989, having broadcast on WNYC as a solo act ca. 1984–88.

THE FIVE MYSTERIES PROGRAM, panel-mystery.

BROADCAST HISTORY: Aug. 10, 1947–March 27, 1950, Mutual. Various 30m times; Sundays at 2, 1947–48.

Five mini-mysteries were enacted, fully dramatized with music and sound effects. A panel, assembled from cards sent in by listeners, tried to guess the solutions. The panel was asked to guess how the criminal had slipped up, for the culprit's identity was revealed within the sketch. It was simplistic, often turning on guilty knowledge or the had-I-but-known situation. Neither the host nor the panel members were identified on the lone available show.

FIVE-STAR JONES, serial drama.

BROADCAST HISTORY: Feb. 4, 1935–June 26, 1936, CBS. 15m, weekdays at 12:45. Mohawk Rugs.
July 6, 1936–Feb. 5, 1937, Blue. 15m, weekdays at 10:15 A.M. Oxydol.
CAST: John Kane as Tom "Five-Star" Jones, ace reporter. Elizabeth Day as Sally Jones. Bill Johnstone as Jones's editor at the *Register*. PRODUCERS: Blackett-Sample-Hummert.

FLASH GORDON, juvenile science fiction serial.

BROADCAST HISTORY: Ca. April–Oct. 1935, 15m, transcribed for Hearst newspapers and running weekly on various stations in the West, to coincide with comic strip publication. CAST:

Gale Gordon as Flash Gordon, interplanetary traveler who battled the evil Emperor Ming on the planet Mongo. Maurice Franklin as the scientist Dr. Zarkov, Flash's friend. Unknown actress as Dale Arden, Flash's companion and love interest. Bruno Wick as Ming. **PRODUCER:** Himan Brown.

Ca. Sept. 1935–Feb. 1936, 15m, heard weekdays in the East (across networks and on nonnetwork stations alike: WMCA and WOR, New York; WJR, Detroit; etc.). A different production with new cast and new musical effects. **CAST** and production crew unknown; James Meighan credited as Flash Gordon in some sources.

Flash Gordon, though made famous in comics and in the film serials of Larry (Buster) Crabbe, had a limited run on radio. The weekly Hearst serial ended after 26 weeks with Flash and his companions crashing in the jungle and getting rescued by Jungle Jim. Thus *Jungle Jim* became the new Hearst serial; it continued for years.

FLOW GENTLY, SWEET RHYTHM, jazz; also known as *The John Kirby Show*.

BROADCAST HISTORY: April 7, 1940–Jan. 12, 1941, CBS. 30m Sundays at 5:30 until September, then at 2:30.
NARRATOR: Canada Lee. **THEME:** *Pastel Blue*.

Flow Gently, Sweet Rhythm was one of the first network forums for an all-black band. John Kirby, a bass player, had "the biggest little band in the land," a sextet comprised of Charlie Shavers, Russ Procope, Buster Bailey, Billy Kyle, O'Neill Spencer, and himself. The vocalists were his wife Maxine Sullivan and, occasionally, Ella Fitzgerald. Paul Phillips wrote continuity, praised by Max Wylie in *Best Broadcasts* for its understanding of "ear music" and its realistic use of "Negro talk."

THE FLYING RED HORSE TAVERN, musical variety.

BROADCAST HISTORY: Oct. 4, 1935–Sept. 25, 1936, CBS. 30m, Fridays at 8. Socony Oil.
CAST: 1935–36: Osgood Perkins, host. Eleanor Powell, singing tap dancer. The "Tavern Singers" and the Freddie Rich Orchestra. *From Feb. 7, 1936*: Walter Woolf King, host. Beatrice Lillie, comedienne; replaced by Joan Marsh in summer 1936. Lennie Hayton Orchestra.

FLYING TIME, juvenile aviation adventure serial.

BROADCAST HISTORY: July 1, 1935–Dec. 4, 1936, NBC. 15m, weekdays at 6.
CAST: Willard Farnum as Harry Blake. Sidney Ellstrom as Hal Falvey and as Halvorsen. Betty Lou Gerson as Sue. Philip Lord as Sprague. Ted Maxwell as Captain Ross. Loretta Poynton as Ruth Morrow. Billy Lee as Beasley. Harold Peary as Major Fellowes and as "Tony the Wop."

FOLIES DE PARIS, musical variety.

BROADCAST HISTORY: April 15, 1936–July 28, 1937, Blue Network. 30m, Wednesdays at 8. Sterling Products for Dr. Lyons Tooth Powder.
CAST: Willie and Eugene Howard, comics, mimicking popular singers and songs, and such operas as *Rigoletto*; Fifi D'Orsay; Victor Arden's orchestra. *As of Sept. 30, 1936*: *Revue de Paree*. Fanny Brice, vocalist-comedienne; Victor Arden's orchestra. *As of Jan. 6, 1937*: *Broadway Merry-Go-Round*. Beatrice Lillie, vocalist-comedienne; Al Rickey's orchestra.

FOLLOW THE MOON, action-mystery serial.

BROADCAST HISTORY: Jan. 4–July 2, 1937, NBC. 15m, weekdays at 4:30. Jergens Lotion.
Oct. 4, 1937–April 1, 1938, CBS. 15m, weekdays at 5. Pebeco Toothpaste.
CAST: Nick Dawson and Elsie Hitz, radio's best-known romantic serial adventure duo, as Clay Bannister and Judith Page.

FOR YOUR APPROVAL, variety.

BROADCAST HISTORY: Nov. 30, 1946–June 28, 1947, Mutual. 30m, Saturdays at 5.
HOST-DIRECTOR: Jock MacGregor.

For Your Approval recycled an idea tried on CBS seven years earlier (see FORECAST): both shows enlisted the listening audience as critics, the premise being that a groundswell of positive opinion might put a show into the regular network schedule. By and large it was a parade of the unknown, the occasionally talented, the often-forlorn dog-and-pony shows. One limp sitcom that made it briefly into the regular schedule from *For Your Approval* was *The Mighty Casey*. By far the most significant contribution of this audition series, however, was *This Is Jazz*, which premiered on *FYA* Jan. 18, 1947, made the regular lineup within three weeks, and graced the Mutual air much of that year.

THE FORD FESTIVAL OF AMERICAN MUSIC, musical variety.

BROADCAST HISTORY: June 30–Sept. 22, 1946, ABC. 60m, Sundays at 8. Ford Motor Company. CAST: Alfred Drake, "singing emcee." ORCHESTRA: Leigh Harline. PRODUCER: George Zachary.

The *Festival of American Music*, sponsored by Ford immediately after the demise of its long-running *Ford Sunday Evening Hour*, covered the full range of music particularly American—classical, folk, swing, film and stage songs, and the tunes of Tin Pan Alley.

THE FORD SUNDAY EVENING HOUR, concert music.

BROADCAST HISTORY: Oct. 7, 1934–March 1, 1942, CBS. 60m, Sundays at 9. Ford Motor Company.

Sept. 30, 1945–June 23, 1946, ABC. 60m, Sundays at 8. Ford Motor Company.

PRODUCER: William Reddick (from ca. 1936).

The Ford Sunday Evening Hour was defined by producer Reddick as catering "to the human weakness of wanting to feel cultured without really being so." It offered classical music, opera, popular ballads, and hymns, but always the overtures or the best-known arias, the melodies that a broad cross-section of Americans could appreciate. As it evolved, *Ford* featured different soloists and conductors each week. John Barbirolli and Fritz Reiner were among the conductors; Gladys Swarthout and Helen Jepson were frequent singers. John Charles Thomas was a regular in 1936–37; Lawrence Tibbett was also often heard. It was a good platform for young artists.

Henry Ford took personal interest in the program, hiring most of the Detroit Symphony as his orchestra-in-residence and himself selecting the theme, *The Children's Prayer* from *Hansel and Gretel*. The aim was to please the public, though the tone was decidedly prestigious. Commercials were kept to a few brief mentions. Each week W. J. Cameron gave a talk of several minutes' duration at intermission. Sometimes Ford was mentioned prominently; other times, not at all. The talks ranged from business and recovery to baseball or the Constitution. It was heard as *The Ford Summer Hour* during vacations, these broadcasts featuring, among others, Jane Pickens, James Melton, Francia White, and maestros Donald Voorhees and Meredith Willson. A 1942 casualty of the slashed Ford wartime ad budget, it bounced back in 1945, with the same basic format.

THE FORD THEATER, dramatic anthology.

BROADCAST HISTORY: Oct. 5, 1947–June 27, 1948, NBC. 60m, Sundays at 5. Ford Motor Company. CAST: New York radio performers in well-known plays and adaptations: Eric Dressler, Anne Seymour, Gary Merrill, Arnold Moss, Paul Douglas, Everett Sloane, Ed Begley, John Larkin, Virginia Gilmore, Shirley Booth, Wendell Holmes, Les Damon, Vicki Vola, Claudia Morgan, Santos Ortega, Les Tremayne, Ted de Corsia, Muriel Kirkland, Evelyn Varden, Lauren Gilbert, etc. HOST: Howard Lindsay, co-author of *Life with Father*. MUSICAL SCORE: Lyn Murray. PRODUCER-DIRECTOR: George Zachary. WRITERS-ADAPTERS: Lillian Schoen, Will Glickman, Charles Gussman, Stanley Evans, etc.

Oct. 8, 1948–July 1, 1949, CBS. 60m, Fridays at 9. Ford Motor Company. CAST: Top Hollywood stars including Claude Rains, Marlene Dietrich, Burt Lancaster, Joan Bennett, Lucille Ball, Ray Milland, Ronald Colman, Jean Arthur, Jack Benny, Bob Hope, Bing Crosby, etc. ANNOUNCER: Nelson Case. MUSIC: Cy Feuer. PRODUCER-DIRECTOR: Fletcher Markle. SCRIPT EDITOR: Vincent McConnor. WRITERS-ADAPTERS: Brainerd Duffield, Hugh Kemp.

The Ford Theater came along in the wake of *The Ford Sunday Evening Hour*, a change from music to drama while attempting to retain the same general approach. Ford wanted to appeal to mainstream America with plays that had tradition: the best of literature, film, stage, and musical comedy. No expense would be spared: it was billed in preseason network press releases as the highest-budgeted program of its kind. But it began modestly, and continued that way through its first year. Instead of chasing *The Lux Radio Theater* down the yellow brick road of Hollywood, Ford used the less expensive (though usually superior, mikewise) talents of radio actors. The fare included such chestnuts as *Cimarron, The Front Page, The Informer*, and *My Sister Eileen*. It drew good reviews, and a few raves, but the ratings were flaccid. The midseason Hooper was a mere 5.7, and the show limped off the air six months later.

Ford didn't give up. The show was completely reorganized, moved from NBC to CBS, and rescheduled for fall. Broadcast at times from Hollywood and on other dates from New York, this version had glitter and big names galore. Fletcher Markle, a young Canadian who had impressed radio critics with his direction of *Studio One*, took over the helm. With stars like Bette Davis, Montgomery Clift, and Edward G. Robinson appearing weekly, it was soon clear that Markle had taken *The Ford Theater* down the yellow brick road after all. He was not always thrilled with this: in interviews, he frequently expressed the desire to break out of the tried-and-true and do new things on the air. The fare still had a familiar ring, with plays like *Double Indemnity, Of Human Bondage*, and *Wuthering Heights* dotting the schedule. The Hollywood formula doubled the rating, but it still wasn't good enough.

The failure of *The Ford Theater* perhaps proves that what works in music will not necessarily work in drama. People were always ready for another spirited playing of *The Washington Post March* or *Pomp and Circumstance*, but one can only hear *A Star Is Born* so many times before boredom sets in. *Theatre Guild, Lux*, and a gamut of half-hour shows were all working the same properties, and even when *The Ford Theater* offered relatively untouched pieces (*Carmen Jones, The Man Who Played God*, and *The Palm Beach Story*, to name a few), the presentations still had the same kind of sound. By the time Markle arrived, the Hollywood formula had paled from overuse. The *Ford Theaters* on tape reveal a solid, polished program, as good as any, but probably doomed on the drawing board.

FORECAST, variety.

BROADCAST HISTORY: July 15–Sept. 2, 1940, and July 14–Sept. 1, 1941, CBS. 30m, some 60m, Mondays at 9.

Forecast was an on-air audition of potential CBS series programs, with the public solicited to voice support. The fare was necessarily varied, ranging from the folk cantata to the horror show. The series had two notable successes. *Duffy's Tavern* made its bow July 29, 1940: Ed Gardner's comedy about life in a New York bar got a good sendoff, with support by F. Chase Taylor (Colonel Stoopnagle), Larry Adler, Gertrude Niesen, the John Kirby jazz band, and announcer Mel Allen. *Suspense*, the remarkable long-running CBS crime anthology, was first heard on *Forecast* July 22, 1940, but the show was merely a forum for film director Alfred Hitchcock, who had nothing to do with the series that resulted from it. Among the shows of the 1941 summer was the first radio adaptation of *Hopalong Cassidy* (no cast information known), but almost a decade would pass before William Boyd brought the character to series status.

FOREIGN ASSIGNMENT, foreign intrigue-adventure drama.

BROADCAST HISTORY: July 24, 1943–Jan. 8, 1944, Mutual. 30m, Saturdays at 8:30.

CAST: Jay Jostyn as Brian Barry, foreign correspondent for the *American Press*. Vicki Vola as Carol Manning, his lovely assistant. Also: Bartlett Robinson, Maurice Wells, Joseph Julian, Guy Repp, etc. **MUSIC:** Henry Sylvern. **DIRECTOR:** Chick Vincent. **WRITER:** Frank H. Phares.

Produced in New York, *Foreign Assignment* reteamed the male and female leads from *Mr. District Attorney*. The hero was involved in wartime espionage, often battling the Gestapo in occupied France.

FOREVER ERNEST, situation comedy.

BROADCAST HISTORY: April 29–July 22, 1946, CBS. 30m, Mondays at 8. Bromo Seltzer.

CAST: Jackie Coogan as Ernest Botch, lovable, bumbling soda jerk. Lurene Tuttle as his girlfriend Candy Lane. Arthur Q. Bryan as his friend Duke. **ANNOUNCER:** Dick Joy. **ORCHESTRA:** Billy May. **PRODUCER:** John Guedel. **DIRECTOR:** Harry Kronman. **WRITER:** Rupert Pray.

FORT LARAMIE, western drama.

BROADCAST HISTORY: Jan. 22–Oct. 28, 1956, CBS. 30m, Sundays at 5:30.

CAST: Raymond Burr as Lee Quince, captain of cavalry at Fort Laramie, on the Wyoming frontier. Vic Perrin as Sgt. Gorce. Harry Bartell as Lt. Seiberts. Jack Moyles as Maj. Daggett. ANNOUNCER: Dan Cubberly. MUSIC: Amerigo Marino. PRODUCER-DIRECTOR: Norman Macdonnell. WRITERS: John Meston, John Dunkel, Les Crutchfield. SOUND EFFECTS: Bill James, Ray Kemper, Tom Hanley.

Producer Norman Macdonnell saw *Fort Laramie* as "a monument to ordinary men who lived in extraordinary times": their enemies were "the rugged, uncharted country, the heat, the cold, disease, boredom, and, perhaps last of all, hostile Indians." Men died at Fort Laramie: some died of drowning, some of freezing, some of typhoid and smallpox. "But it's a matter of record," Macdonnell said on the opening, "that in all the years the cavalry was stationed at Fort Laramie, only four troopers died of gunshot wounds."

The series was less intense, and far less known, than Macdonnell's major western, *Gunsmoke*: the stories focused as much on atmosphere and mood as on violence and action. The run of 40 shows is complete on tape in excellent quality. The star, Raymond Burr, went from obscurity to national prominence a year later, taking on the title role in TV's *Perry Mason*.

THE FORTY MILLION, educational drama.

BROADCAST HISTORY: Nov. 8–Dec. 28, 1952, NBC. 30m, Saturdays at 7:30, then Sundays at 1:30.
NARRATOR: Peter Roberts. PRODUCER: Wade Arnold. DIRECTOR: Harry Frazee.

The Forty Million dramatized the health and safety problems of America's children. It opened to increasing numbers of children chanting, *We are the 40 million . . . we are the 40 million*, and was sponsored by the Health Information Foundation. The fare included stories on child mortality before the development of vaccines, child surgery techniques, and how physical illness affects mental health.

FOUR CORNERS THEATER, rustic drama.

BROADCAST HISTORY: July 19–Sept. 13, 1938, CBS. 30m, Tuesdays at 8.
　Oct. 8, 1938–March 25, 1939, CBS. 30m, Saturdays at 10:30 A.M.

CAST: Unknown. MUSIC: Bernard Herrmann. DIRECTOR: Earle McGill.

Four Corners Theater (not to be confused with the *Four Corners USA* spinoff of *Snow Village Sketches*) was an anthology of perennially popular plays from the hinterlands of America. They were "crossroads dramas," said *Newsweek*, "replete with villainy and virtue, foiled dastards and triumphant maidens, foreclosed mortgages and brave widows." Some of them had been running in country theaters for more than half a century. The opening broadcast was *Aaron Slick from Punkin Crick*.

FOUR-STAR PLAYHOUSE, Hollywood star dramatic anthology.

BROADCAST HISTORY: July 3–Sept. 11, 1949, NBC. 30m, Sundays at 8.
CAST: Four famous film stars, Fred MacMurray, Loretta Young, Rosalind Russell, and Robert Cummings, in rotating leads. Support: Janet Waldo, Jeanne Bates, Joe DuVal, Willard Waterman, Jack Edwards, Mary Jane Croft, Frank Nelson, Charles Seel. Herb Butterfield, Ira Grossel (Jeff Chandler), Shep Menken, Dan O'Herlihy, Ken Christy, etc. CONDUCTOR-COMPOSER: Albert Harris. PRODUCER: Don Sharpe. DIRECTOR: Warren Lewis. WRITER-ADAPTER: Milton Geiger.

The Four-Star Playhouse was developed for NBC, partly to help counter the CBS talent raid that had lured Jack Benny, *Amos 'n' Andy*, and Edgar Bergen away from the older network. The NBC response was predictable: a barrage of new shows with big-name Hollywood talent. It didn't work: by then there were so many similar shows on the air that the public didn't care, and most of the new NBC shows soon vanished.

The idea of *Four-Star* was to have each star play one role a month. The plays ranged from comedy to melodrama, and each was built around one strong central character. The stories were adapted from *Cosmopolitan* magazine.

THE FRANK MORGAN SHOW, comedy-variety.

BROADCAST HISTORY: Aug. 31, 1944–May 31, 1945, NBC. 30m, Thursdays at 8. Maxwell House Coffee.
CAST: Frank Morgan, star comedian and teller of

tall tales. Cass Daley, comedienne. Robert Young, host. **ANNOUNCER:** Harlow Wilcox. **MUSIC:** Albert Sack.

The Frank Morgan Show was what remained after Fanny Brice left the dual format she shared with Morgan on *Maxwell House Coffee Time*. Morgan's tall tales still formed the backbone of the program. On one show he told of a victory garden with vegetables as large as auto tires grown overnight: these were harvested by pilots in Lockheed P-38s, who swooped down and cut them with propeller blades, leaving the giant tomatoes and melons ready to be rolled downhill to the barn. Morgan's character was brash; on a later series he was described by *Radio Life* as "just short of offensive" when he asked Frances Langford if he could carry her bundles and "Frances didn't have any bundles to carry."

Morgan was prominent on many series, including *Good News, The Kraft Music Hall, The Don Ameche Show*, and *The Fabulous Dr. Tweedy*. He came from a prominent acting family: his brother was actor Ralph Morgan, and his niece radio actress Claudia Morgan. He was best known as the Wizard of Oz in the 1939 Judy Garland film. He died in 1949.

THE FRANK SINATRA SHOW, musical variety.

BROADCAST HISTORY: Oct. 27, 1942–Dec. 26, 1943, CBS. 15m, various times. *Songs by Sinatra.*

Jan. 5, 1944–May 16, 1945, CBS. 30m, mostly Wednesdays at 9. Lever Brothers until Jan. 1945, then Max Factor. **CAST:** Guest stars; regular comic Bert Wheeler. **ANNOUNCER:** Truman Bradley. **DIRECTOR:** Bob Brewster. **WRITER:** Carroll Carroll.

Sept. 12, 1945–June 4, 1947, CBS. 30m, Wednesdays at 9. *Songs by Sinatra.* Old Gold Cigarettes. **ANNOUNCER:** Marvin Miller. **VOCAL GROUP:** The Pied Pipers. **DIRECTOR:** Mann Holiner. **WRITER:** Frank Wilson.

Sept. 5, 1949–June 2, 1950, NBC. 15m, weekdays at 7. *Light-Up Time.* Lucky Strike. **CO-STAR:** Metropolitan Opera star Dorothy Kirsten.

Oct. 29, 1950–July 22, 1951, CBS. 45m and 60m formats, Sundays at 5. *Meet Frank Sinatra.* Songs, records, and talk.

Nov. 10, 1953–July 15, 1955, NBC. 15m, twice a week, various days at 8:15.

The career of Frank Sinatra was radio-made. Inspired by the success and style of Bing Crosby, Sinatra decided on a singer's career early in life. Born Dec. 12, 1917, in Hoboken, N.J., he was still in his teens when he got his first break on a national network. In 1935 Sinatra and three pals won a Major Bowes amateur show on NBC: billing themselves as "the Hoboken Four," they became part of Bowes's traveling stage shows. Sinatra quit on the road and returned to New Jersey, singing, often gratis, on local radio stations. By 1939, it was estimated, he was appearing on 18 regular radio shows for stations in the greater New York–New Jersey area.

He became a waiter and master of ceremonies at the Rustic Cabin, a hotbed of big band activity in the '30s, with lots of radio exposure. Harry James, then playing trumpet with Benny Goodman, caught his act. James was planning his own band, which formed in mid-1939, with Sinatra its featured singer at $75 a week. Six months later, Tommy Dorsey stole Sinatra away from James, and Sinatra's stardom was assured.

Dorsey had one of the best-known bands in America, and Sinatra was spotlighted in such dance halls as Frank Dailey's Meadowbrook, served by radio wires for late-night jitterbugs from coast to coast. Sinatra left Dorsey as he had left James, breaking his contract in 1942, striking out on his own at a time when the bands were foundering in a labor dispute and singers were the coming rage. He set attendance records at the Paramount in New York. Suddenly he was a teenage heartthrob on the scale of Rudolph Valentino, Rudy Vallee, Bing Crosby, and few others. Girls stood in line for ten hours at the CBS Vine Street Theater in Hollywood to see him perform for 30 minutes. By 3 P.M., they swarmed around the building, long rows of sweaters and skirts and white socks rolled down over brown-and-white shoes, ready to scream and fill his shows with noise.

On Feb. 13, 1943, he became a regular on *Your Hit Parade* (CBS, Saturday nights), a stint that lasted almost two years. For his own radio shows, Sinatra hired arranger Axel Stordahl away from Dorsey: Stordahl had been with Dorsey seven years, and Dorsey did not suffer quietly the news that he was quitting to work for Frank Sinatra. Stordahl would work with Sinatra throughout his radio career, giving his shows a certain texture and style. The Lever Brothers show promoted a vitamin supplement called Vimms, a subtle amusement because Sinatra barely topped 135 pounds and was often the butt of ''skinny'' jokes by the comics of the day. The show was highlighted by frequent ''serious'' talks by Sinatra, usually on some patriotic or worthwhile cause; it was written by Carroll Carroll of J. Walter Thompson.

During his three and a half years in the CBS Wednesday-at-9 stand, Sinatra staged a midroad musical variety series. The big-name guest list included Gene Kelly, Jane Powell, Lawrence Tibbett, and Fred Allen: even Tommy Dorsey appeared, putting aside the rumors of an ugly rift between them. On Sept. 6, 1947, Sinatra returned to *Your Hit Parade*, remaining there until May 28, 1949. His departure from that show was sudden, leading to new rumors of strife with the sponsor, Lucky Strike. But Luckies picked up his autumn quarter-hour, squelching that talk, teaming Sinatra in the unlikely company of Met Opera soprano Dorothy Kirsten.

Sinatra's final radio days were filled with minor quarter-hours and one full-length series in which he was relegated to the role of a disc jockey. By 1950 people were writing his professional obituary. His public image had taken a beating, his personal life a succession of wives, scrapes, and alleged friendships with gangsters. It would take a 1953 film, *From Here to Eternity*, and a subsequent acting career to save him.

THE FRED ALLEN SHOW, comedy.

BROADCAST HISTORY: Oct. 23, 1932–April 16, 1933, CBS. 30m, Sundays at 9. *The Linit Bath Club Revue*. Linit Bath Soap.

Aug. 4–Dec. 1, 1933, NBC. 30m, Fridays at 9. *The Salad Bowl Revue*. Hellmann's Mayonnaise.

Jan. 3, 1934–June 26, 1940, NBC. Initially 30m, Wednesdays at 9:30 as *The Sal Hepatica Revue*. Expanded to the full hour at 9 under the title *Hour of Smiles* as of March 21, 1934. Retitled *Town Hall Tonight* as of July 11, 1934. Retitled *The Fred Allen Show* as of Oct. 4, 1939. Bristol Myers, promoting Ipana Toothpaste and Sal Hepatica.

Oct. 2, 1940–June 25, 1944, CBS. 60m, Wednesdays at 9 until March 8, 1942; Sundays at 9 through June 28; 30m, Sundays at 9:30 from Oct. 4, 1942. *The Texaco Star Theater*. Texaco.

Oct. 7, 1945–Dec. 28, 1947, NCB. 30m, Sundays at 8:30. Tenderleaf Tea.

Jan. 4, 1948–June 26, 1949, NBC. 30m, Sundays at 8:30 until Jan. 1949, then at 8. Ford Motors.

CAST: Fred Allen, resident comic and wit. His wife, foil, and stooge, Portland Hoffa.

1932–33, *Linit*: Torch singer Helen Morgan. Impersonator Sheila Barrett. Double-talk artist Roy Atwell. Tenor Charlie Carlisle. Character actor Jack Smart. **ANNOUNCER:** Ken Roberts. **MUSIC:** Louis Katzman. **ORGANIST:** Ann Leaf. **PRODUCER:** Roger White.

1933, *Salad Bowl*: Allen, Hoffa, Atwell, Smart. Also, Minerva Pious, ethnic character actress. **ANNOUNCER:** Edmund ''Tiny'' Ruffner. **ORCHESTRA:** Ferde Grofé.

1934, *Sal Hepatica*; *Hour of Smiles*: Allen, Hoffa, Pious, Smart, Ruffner, Grofe. Lionel Stander and Eileen Douglas replacing Roy Atwell. *The Ipana Troubadors* added. **THEME:** *Smiles*.

1934–39, *Town Hall Tonight*: Allen, Hoffa, Pious, Smart, etc. Also, the Town Hall Quartet (Scrappy Lambert, Bob Moody, Randolph Weyant, Leonard Stokes), circa mid-1930s; Hi, Lo, Jack, and the Dame, late 1930s; the Merry Macs (Helen Carroll and the McMichael boys—Joe, Ted, and Judd), late 1930s. **ANNOUNCERS:** Tiny Ruffner, 1934–35; Harry Von Zell thereafter. **ORCHESTRA:** Lennie Hayton, 1934–35; Peter Van Steeden thereafter. **PRODUCERS:** Sylvester ''Pat'' Weaver, mid-1930s; Vick Knight, beginning late 1930s. **THEME:** *Smile, Darn Ya, Smile*.

1939–44, *Fred Allen Show; Texaco Star Theater*: Allen, Hoffa, Pious, Smart, Alan Reed, John Brown, Charlie Cantor, etc. Allen's Alley format beginning Dec. 6, 1942. Minerva Pious as Mrs. Pansy Nussbaum. Alan Reed as Falstaff Openshaw. Jack Smart as Senator Bloat. Pat C. Flick as Pablo Itthepitches. Charlie Cantor as Socrates Mulligan. John Brown as John Doe. **ANNOUNCERS:** Harry Von Zell, Arthur Godfrey (six weeks beginning in Oct. 1942); Jimmy Wallington (for Texaco). **VOCALIST:** Kenny Baker, ca. 1940–42. **ORCHESTRA:** Peter Van Steeden; Al Goodman (beginning in the fall of 1940). **PRODUCERS:** Vick Knight, Howard Reilly.

1945–49: Allen, Hoffa, and the Allen's Alley cast: Minerva Pious as Mrs. Nussbaum. Peter Donald as Ajax Cassidy. Parker Fennelly as Titus Moody. Kenny Delmar as Senator Beauregard Claghorn. **ANNOUNCER:** Kenny Delmar. **VOCAL GROUP:** The De Marco Sisters (Ann, Gene,

Gloria, Marie, and Arlene). **ORCHESTRA:** Al Goodman.

Also: Writers Harry Tugend (1934–38); Arnold Auerbach and Herman Wouk (1936–41), Roland Kibbee, Nat Hiken, Albert G. Miller, Herb Lewis, Larry Marks, Aaron Ruben, etc.

Fred Allen was perhaps the most admired of radio comics. His fans included the president of the United States, critically acclaimed writers, and the intelligentsia of his peers. William Faulkner was said to have liked Allen's work; John Steinbeck, who became his friend and later wrote the foreword for Allen's autobiography, called him "unquestionably the best humorist of our time." As early as 1933, when he had been on the air less than six months, he got a heartening letter of support from Groucho Marx. To Jack Benny he was "the best wit, the best extemporaneous comedian I know." Edgar Bergen, who normally shied away from gushy superlatives, told a *Time* reporter that Allen was the "greatest living comedian, a wise materialist who exposes and ridicules the pretensions of his times." His work, *Time* continued, had "an angry big-city clank, a splashy neon idiom, and a sort of 16-cylinder poetry."

His formats changed but his style did not. His earliest broadcasts reveal the same dry wit that was last heard on a weekly series in 1949. Like Don Quinn of *Fibber McGee and Molly*, he was word-oriented. But where Quinn dealt in timeless situation comedy, Allen's humor was rigidly topical and, like the news of the day, perishable. His shows were wry commentaries on the day's events—not necessarily on the headlines; more often on the little fillers that got bumped to the back pages. He read nine daily newspapers: even when he was in Hollywood, working on films, he had to have his *New York Times* flown to the coast. He ripped and tore his way through the news, stuffing his pockets with cuttings and tearsheets. "When he sits down to write a script," said J. Bryan in a 1940 *Saturday Evening Post* profile, "he will have a hundred or more notes and clippings." Perhaps six would survive the winnowing process. These Allen would dramatize and adorn with gags. He employed writers, but they served largely as a sounding board. Allen wrote his final scripts himself. He put in 80-hour weeks, 12- and 14-hour days, toiling away in his Manhattan apartment on the coming

week's show. "The callboy's warning always finds him in a frenzy of editing," wrote Bryan.

He had five names at different times in his life. Four times he changed his name for professional reasons, and finally, as Fred Allen, he became known to the nation. He was born John Florence Sullivan in Cambridge, Mass., May 31, 1894. His mother died when he was not quite three, his father eleven years later. Shortly before his death, the elder Sullivan got his son a job, paying 20 cents an hour, in the Boston Public Library, where he had long worked as a bookbinder. The Sullivan boys, John and his brother Bob, lived with their aunt after their father's death. Money was tight: most of what John earned in the library was turned over to his aunt, but he was allowed to keep out a small amount so that he might attend the theatricals and amateur nights that had caught his interest.

In the library, he read a book on juggling, and he began to practice. In 1912 he began working with promoter Sam Cohen on the New England amateur nights circuit. "His era of apprenticeship had begun," wrote his biographer, Robert Taylor. "Over the next two years, Johnny would perform in virtually every small-time theater from Nova Scotia to Connecticut." His first professional engagement came in south Boston. He performed as "Paul Huckle, European Entertainer," then as "Fred St. James," plucking his surname from the St. James Hotel in Bowdoin Square. He was subsequently billed as "Freddy James, the World's Worst Juggler." He was becoming disenchanted with the juggler's art and had begun emphasizing comedy in his act. But the life was one of extreme poverty, he recalled to Bryan years later. He ate in hash houses where "liver and bacon, coffee and doughnuts cost a dime." Gradually his bookings picked up: he began getting jobs outside New England—in Ohio, Michigan, and, finally, in Chicago, where he was seen by the visiting owner of a vaudeville circuit in Australia. This led to an Australian tour, described by his biographer as "rife with boredom and loneliness." He bought a ventriloquist's dummy, named it Jake, and set about learning ventriloquism. The dummy was added to his act in the latter stages of the Australian trip, which lasted most of a year, including trips to tiny outposts as well as engagements in Sydney and Brisbane.

Returning home in 1916, he played theaters

around San Francisco, then worked his way east through a long string of bookings in the United States and Canada. Back in New York, his agent was enthused at the remarkable growth he had achieved as a comic. He was still too well known as Freddy James, second-rater, to command more than a second-rate salary, so yet another name change was in order. It came about by mistake: through a mixup with an old agent named Edgar Allen, he arrived for a booking to learn that he had been inserted in the program as Fred Allen.

His appearance in *The Passing Show of 1922* was a milestone. Here he met Portland Hoffa, a chorus girl named for the Oregon city of her birth. They appeared together in *The Greenwich Village Follies* of 1925–26 and were married in the spring of 1927. She would become his air-headed second banana when Allen took his act to radio five years later.

For his first radio show, *The Linit Bath Club Revue*, he was paid $1,000 a week. From this he was expected to pay all costs. He was expected to write his own material or pay to have it written by others. He decided to write his own, a task that soon became impossible. Radio was voracious: it consumed material at a rate that vaudevillians found frightening. He hired his first writer, Harry Tugend, who would remain with him for four years. His shows followed a formula from the beginning. The earliest series was built around occupational themes. From week to week, Allen played a judge, a newspaper reporter, a banker, and so on. His jokes were a cut apart from what other comics of vaudeville were bringing to the air. There was no slapstick on the Linit program: compared with Cantor, Jolson, and Ed Wynn, Allen was positively cerebral. Though he would later criticize his earliest scripts as reading like "museum fun today," there was a difference between Allen and the others. Cantor "wore funny costumes, pummeled his announcer with his fists, and frequently kicked his guest star to obtain results," Allen wrote in his first memoir, *Treadmill to Oblivion*. The desired result was laughter in the studio, which was discovered in the early 1930s to be infectious, spreading to listeners and boosting ratings. Ed Wynn whooped and hollered and wore silly hats. Allen did none of this. His humor from the beginning was rooted in satire. When told that organist Ann Leaf would solo in

each broadcast because the sponsor's wife liked organ music, he found this similar to "planting a pickle in the center of a chocolate russe."

The Linit show ended its six-month run, and Allen was summoned to rescue a failing radio show that Hellmann's Mayonnaise was offering on NBC. The mayonnaise show became a fairly transparent copy of Allen's Linit broadcasts, with several original cast members reassembled. Spoonerist Roy Atwell returned, along with Jack Smart, but now joining the cast was Minerva Pious, who would remain with Allen for 16 years. Portland, as always, played herself, a naive and simple asker-of-questions whose presence was an obvious springboard for Allen's wit. This was like stepping from treadmill to treadmill, to use Allen's own analogy: the Hellmann show was the Linit show, with a few slight variables. There was a skit, there were a few guest stars (the pay, now $4,000 a week, offered a bit more latitude in booking guests); there was a Fred-and-Portland routine, a bit of double-talk from Atwell, and some music. Allen began an etiquette department, soliciting questions from the audience and answering them with nonsense. This was done simply to draw mail. The etiquette department gave way to a question box, allowing Allen to advise listeners on any question he could "get by the censor." Often the etiquette questions involved table manners, allowing Allen to plug his mayonnaise at the same time. He started a "newsreel," forerunner to his satiric commentary on current events that would be one of his strongest trademarks in the last half of the decade. His ratings began to climb: he was still not as popular as the shouters and the robbers of Joe Miller, but his numbers had climbed into double digits.

But mayonnaise was a summer product, requiring lettuce and other salad fixings that did not grow in the cold, so *The Salad Bowl Revue* closed Dec. 1, 1933. Allen had already auditioned for Sal Hepatica, a Bristol Myers laxative. His new show, *The Sal Hepatica Revue*, was again an extension of the others, with few personnel changes: when it opened in January 1934, the rating was almost in the 20s, highly respectable in any category. Fine-tuning continued into the spring. Bristol Myers had bought the entire hour from 9 to 10 P.M. on NBC Wednesdays. In the 9 o'clock half-hour was the venerable *Ipana Troubadors*; Allen followed at 9:30. The problem, from Bristol Myers's viewpoint, was that the *Troubadors* had been on NBC for Ipana Toothpaste since 1926 and had managed to stir up no measurable Crossley numbers in all those years, while Allen had gained millions of listeners in just a year. It was decided that the entire hour be turned over to Allen and his company, the benefits to be evenly split between Ipana and Sal Hepatica. It would be called *The Hour of Smiles*: Ipana for "the smile of beauty;" Sal Hepatica for "the smile of health." Again, much of the previous flavor was maintained, with Allen, Pious, and the cast cutting their teeth on dialect and ethnic comedy roles. *The Ipana Troubadors* were incorporated into the show, at least in name: the orchestra was suddenly known by that name and would carry it for several seasons. But Allen was unhappy with the *Hour of Smiles* title. He wanted something that smacked of small-town entertainment, believing that a show that played well in the heartland would also score on the ratings charts. The title should suggest an overall theme—something like *Show Boat*, which had pushed a riverboat motif high onto the popularity polls. By the end of the 1934 season, he had it: *Town Hall Tonight*.

Ferde Grofé departed as maestro: the new orchestra was known as Lennie Hayton and his Ipana Troubadors. The theme, keeping some tie to the product, was *Smiles*. But the sponsor continued to tamper: at its "suggestion," half the show was now given over each week to a talent scout format. After the halftime network break, Allen would introduce up to half a dozen amateur performers, who would compete for a $100 prize. These contestants he interviewed off the cuff, meeting none of them before Wednesday night. At least this part of the show required no writing: Allen and Tugend had their plates quite full trying to write and produce a 60-minute show each week as it was. The amateurs did their acts, and the voting was done by mail, by the listening audience rather than the studio. Winners were sent to distant cities as part of *Town Hall Tonight* road shows. The show was thus a forerunner of the hugely successful *Original Amateur Hour* of Major Edward Bowes, which premiered nationally less than four months later. Allen's biographer, Taylor, believes that the success of these *Town Hall* amateur shows accelerated the development of the Bowes program. He names actress Ann Sheridan, comedian Garry

Moore, and singer Frank Sinatra as prominent *Town Hall* discoveries. Sinatra was also discovered by Bowes the following year.

The schedule was hectic, with Allen working almost around the clock on broadcast day. In the mornings and afternoons he was busy with rehearsals; in the evenings with last-minute changes brought on by censorship or time constraints; at night with the show itself. *Town Hall Tonight* went live to the East at 9 P.M. A second show was broadcast live to the West at midnight. Including the inevitable postmortems and planning for the following week, Allen seldom got to bed before 4 or 5 A.M. Thursday.

The show roared into living rooms. Typical was the season premiere, Oct. 23, 1935: the theme, *Smiles*, was positively sedate compared with the rousing, marching signature that followed. The scene was a train depot, where—as Tiny Ruffner told the listening audience—the whole town had turned out to welcome Fred and Portland back to the air. The band, now Peter Van Steeden and his Ipana Troubadors, shifted into a high-octane rendition of *Hot Time in the Old Town Tonight*, with the crowd cheering wildly. It was loud and raucous, a circus atmosphere that Allen would use throughout the decade. The band moved on: into the thrilling *Stars and Stripes Forever*, with the opening signature still unfolding. Allen himself was the town hall barker. "Inside" the town hall, the orchestra kicked off yet another melody, the current hit *Pocketful of Sunshine*. Then Allen gave his "Town Hall Bulletin," a rustic bit of nonsense about his friend, Hodge White, and the problems he was having with tobacco-chewing musicians using his French horn for a cuspidor at the GAR-hall band practice Friday nights. Thus did Allen integrate one of his old friends from Massachusetts. White never appeared on the show but became a national celebrity of sorts as he sat in his Dorchester grocery store and listened to Allen build his character week by week.

Next came the "Town Hall News." These "news of the day" routines would extend throughout Allen's career, the Allen's Alley gags of a later time being just another form of them. *THE TOWN HALL NEWS! SEES NOTHING! SHOWS ALL!* The sound of a movie projector was heard, suggesting a newsreel flickering on a screen. The "news" again was pure nonsense, the real news items lost in the comic opinions of the *Town Hall* surveys. Minerva Pious was often featured as a Jewish mother, setting up her role as Mrs. Nussbaum in Allen's Alley years later. Van Steeden and the Troubadors returned with more music. There was a routine with Portland, who came on crowing "Mis-ter Allen! . . . Mister Allen!" in a high-pitched squeal. It must have been mike fright, Allen sometimes said, that first made her use that squeak on the air. Her speaking voice was soft and gentle, but the chirp took hold and became one of the prime echoes of old-time radio.

The *Town Hall* quartet was then heard singing *Isle of Capri*. Finally came the "drama"—Allen, Pious, and the "Mighty Allen Art Players" in a hillbilly skit. After the break came the amateur show featuring, among others, an opera aspirant from Brooklyn and a "musical chef," who played kitchen utensils—spoons against glasses and cups that had been found to have perfect pitch—and managed to sound like a poor man's Lionel Hampton on a vibraphone.

By the week of Jan. 22, 1936, Harry Von Zell had replaced Tiny Ruffner as announcer and there was a new theme. The drowsy *Smiles* had vanished, replaced by the lively *Smile, Darn Ya, Smile*, which fit far more easily into the booming *Town Hall* format. The amateur contest was still stubbornly entrenched, though Allen would soon drop it and leave the talent scouting in Bowes's paunchy lap. The show was a hit: the ratings would never be in the powerhouse class, but numbers in the high teens and low 20s would keep Allen on the air for almost 18 years.

In 1936, the show got a boost when Allen's famous feud with Jack Benny was initiated. Allen started it one night after Benny had been regaling his Sunday audiences with his questionable prowess on the violin. Benny had promised a playing of *The Bee* on a future show, and on Wednesday Allen replied. "Ladies and gentlemen, on Sunday last an itinerant vendor of desserts who has a sideline called by some a radio program announced to an apprehensive world that he would murder a bee. This dire news has seeped into every nook and cranny of the country, and I understand citizens are fleeting these shores by the thousands rather than submit to such torture." Allen then introduced Master Stuart Canin, "violinist extraordinary," who was 10 years old and who proceeded to give Jack Benny verbal instructions of the most elementary

kind, beginning with how to hold the bow and instrument. Young Canin then played *The Bee*, and Allen's chiding continued. "That was *The Bee*, Mr. Benny, played by a 10-year-old boy. Why, Mr. Benny, at 10 you couldn't even play on the linoleum." Allen ad-libbed his way through this part of the script, adding lines to the effect that Benny should pluck the horsehairs out of his bow and give them back to the horse.

Benny was listening in the West. By Taylor's account, he "burst out laughing" and immediately set up a retort. Allen had no idea at that point whether Benny would respond at all. "*The Jack Benny Program* was the highest-rated show in radio at that time," he recalled in *Treadmill*. "With our smaller audience it would take an Academy Award display of intestinal fortitude to ask Jack to participate in a feud with me." But the following Sunday Benny returned the insult, and radio's most successful running gag was under way. Benny was born anemic, Allen charged: "When he was born, people thought *he* was delivering the *stork*." When Portland cautioned that Benny was apt to get mad, Allen retorted, "Why, I'll pull those three hairs he's got down over that peachstone fob he has hanging out of his vest and play *The Bee* on them." Benny's arms, said Allen, "look like buggy whips with fingers . . . I've got veins in my nose bigger than Benny's arms." With his snarling, nasal voice, he delivered Benny insults weekly. "Benny was doing a monologue with a pig on stage. The pig was there to eat up the stuff that the audience threw at Benny. Some weeks he had to use two pigs."

Benny's initial response was on *The Jell-O Program*, Jan. 3, 1937. Allen and *The Bee* haunted him every week. On Jan. 24, he continued to practice; on Jan. 31, he had a Fred Allen nightmare. He promised to play *The Bee* on his show Feb. 7, but his violin was stolen and the performance delayed yet again. At last he played, Feb. 28, 1937. The retorts continued from opposite coasts. Benny brought his show east. Young Stuart Canin was Benny's guest, in New York, on March 7. It was decided that Benny and Allen would meet in the "fight of the century" the following week. NBC coped with an avalanche of ticket requests—the entire country, it seemed, had been caught up in the foolishness, and the network had no studio large enough to hold the crowd. The show was moved to the grand ballroom of the Hotel Pierre, where the battle was to take place. Predictably, it was completely verbal. At last the two stepped outside to have it out. But when they returned to the ballroom they were backslapping and remembering old days in vaudeville.

From then on, cracks about Benny were surefire. The feud transcended everything of its kind on radio. It continued through changes of format, across networks, and to the end of radio as a viable network medium. Once or twice a year they exchanged visits, and these became the seasonal high spots. If in the end Allen was conceded to have been the greater natural wit, Benny was surely his equal in showmanship, comedic instinct, and timing. Some of their best moments came off the cuff. "You couldn't ad-lib a belch at a Hungarian dinner" was an Allen classic. Benny's answer has been duly noted in all the radio histories: "You wouldn't dare talk to me that way if my writers were here." Once, when Benny broke into a sudden laugh in the middle of a give-and-take, Allen went immediately off the script. "Laughing at your next Sunday's show already, eh?" This got a huge laugh, but Benny, missing only a heartbeat, said, "I'd give a thousand dollars if I could think of an answer." Which was a pretty good answer in itself.

Town Hall Tonight passed into history. The sponsor changed agencies, and the agency people (always part of a lower life form in Allen's book) thought the town hall idea had run its course. It became *The Fred Allen Show* in the fall of 1939, though Allen was less than thrilled at being elevated to title billing. "We became just another group of actors gathered around a microphone in a radio studio," he recalled in *Treadmill*. "The colorful illusion had been completely stripped from the program." But to the listener's ear, the show went on as before. The "Town Hall News" was replaced by the "March of Trivia," and Allen's wry commentary on the piddling and bucolic elements of modern life was unabated. Harry Tugend had abandoned radio to write films; Allen's writers were now Arnold Auerbach and Herman Wouk (later famous as the author of *The Caine Mutiny* and other bestselling novels). Wouk and Auerbach may have been the most rewritten team in radio, for Allen continued to do the script's final drafts. Shades of the future were occasionally

heard, as when Minerva Pious played a Mrs. Messbaum with a Jewish accent, but *The Fred Allen Show* of 1939–42 still bore far more resemblance to the '30s-era variety hour than to the streamlined half-hour yet to come. Now there was a "People You Don't Expect to Meet" routine, and a parody of *The University of Chicago Round Table* called "Mr. and Mrs. Average Man's Round Table." Allen continued offering detective spoofs, starring his self-played Oriental sleuth, One Long Pan.

The most sensational show of the year was the "eagle broadcast" of March 20, 1940. Allen had invited falconer Charles Knight in for a "People You Don't Expect to Meet" interview. Knight arrived with a full-grown golden eagle perched on his arm. When the eagle, "Mr. Ramshaw," flew to the top of the studio and Knight could not retrieve it, the audience went into ripples of periodic laughter that went on for more than half an hour. The script was forgotten. "All we need," Allen ad-libbed, "is for Mr. Ramshaw to, uh, make his own station break, and we. . . ." The audience got the point, and the conclusion was lost to thunderous, prolonged laughter. Ultimately Mr. Ramshaw obliged, depositing what Allen later called a "ghost's beret" squarely onstage. Harry Von Zell incorporated the eagle into the Sal Hepatica commercial, while Knight continued to lure the bird with raw meat and chicken heads. "Tapes of the broadcast don't capture the rampant backstage chaos," wrote Taylor. The show was now hopelessly off schedule. Some attempt was made to get back to the script, but in a "Question of the Week" skit the eagle flew again. After the show, Allen got a testy letter from NBC, whose executives had not been amused. This was neither the first time nor the last that he would run afoul of network bureaucrats.

There were a few cosmetic changes when Texaco came on as sponsor in the fall of 1940. Now it was called *The Texaco Star Theater*; the Mighty Allen Art Players became the Texaco Workshop Players, and the show opened in the traditional Texaco manner, with a siren and a bell. The opening was toned down after Dec. 7, 1941, because of growing public tension and the use of sirens to warn of air raids. Still more changes came with the trim to 30 minutes in 1942. Arthur Godfrey was the new announcer, though briefly. Godfrey was one of the most talked-about new stars on the radio scene, and the press was ecstatic. But the promise of radio's two greatest ad-libbers on one show was never realized: Godfrey and Allen never quite hit it off, and Godfrey was gone in six weeks. More important, from Allen's viewpoint, was the coming of what would be his primary format for the 1940s. On that first broadcast of 1942–43, Alan Reed played a fully realized Falstaff Openshaw, who would become the poet laureate of Allen's Alley when that noble thoroughfare opened two months later.

Falstaff, as always, had a poem. It was typical of the times, flavored by war and spiced with a cadence that was pure Allen.

My little niece is saving grease
To help to beat the Japs.
To help to beat the Nazis
She's collecting bacon scraps.
The drippings from each mutton roast
She knows make ammunition;
The doughnut fat my niece collects
May bomb a Jap position.
You too should save your fatty wastes,
Your butter, lard, and suet.
If my niece can save her grease,
Surely you can do it.
When the Axis time at last has come,
And the world's restored to peace;
The day that Hitler's goose is cooked,
My little niece will save the grease.

Allen's Alley would borrow a leaf from newspaper columnist O. O. McIntyre, who had once written an occasional feature called *Thoughts While Strolling*. "O. O. never left his hotel room, but he would describe the sights he saw and the people he met strolling through the shabby streets of Chinatown and the Bowery," Allen recalled (*Treadmill*). The same thing could be done in radio: the locale would be specific rather than general, and the characters would be continuing. Taylor pinpoints the first Allen's Alley broadcast as Dec. 6, 1942. This may have been a dry run, as Allen felt the Alley was "officially opened" Dec. 13. The Alley would present all of Allen's "news of the day" nonsense in a compact and punchy package. Portland's role was emphasized: she would be the impetus for those weekly strolls, her question "Shall we go?" becoming radio's best-known traveling line. The trip wasn't far: a short musical bridge did the trick, and Allen stepped into a collage of American neighborhoods. Eventually he would find, living side by side, a Jewish tenement dweller, an Irish resident of Shantytown, a New England farmer, and a Dixie senator. The earliest continuing residents were Minerva Pious as Mrs. Pansy Nussbaum and Alan Reed as Falstaff Openshaw. John Brown played a character named John Doe, but this was much too generic: Allen was looking for colorful, contrasting character types whose ethnic and environmental origins would add a layer of burlesque to the topical comedy. John Doe was dropped: the Alley went through a period of transition in the search for the third and fourth regulars. Taylor reports that residents in this early period included "Samson Souse, a drunk; the indistinct Miss Tallulah Traub; and Miss Prawn, an uncomely lady on the order of a Gilbert and Sullivan contralto."

By mid-1943, Jack Smart was playing the puffy politico, Senator Bloat. Pat C. Flick opened the fourth door as Pablo Itthepitches, and for a time Charlie Cantor played a dimwit named Socrates Mulligan. Pablo disappeared, but Bloat became a regular, residing in the Alley for two seasons while describing his efforts to get his "Bloat bill" through Congress. The format was solidifying. The traveling theme was *East Side, West Side*, but Allen's Alley went much further than all around the town.

Hypertension forced him off the air after the 1944 season, but he returned in October 1945 with an Allen's Alley that mixed old and new. Jack Smart had left New York for Hollywood, and Allen Reed's character, Falstaff Openshaw, was dropped. Peter Donald was added as Ajax Cassidy, the ranting Irishman with whom Allen hoped to reach "the Irish who had a sense of humor" (there were some who didn't, he wrote later, in *Treadmill*). Pious returned as Mrs. Nussbaum, who was always relating the problem of the week to the doings of her husband Pierre. Pierre was described as "just a schnook"; Pious, on the other hand, was lauded by Allen as "the most accomplished woman dialectician ever to appear in radio." There was no nationality that she could not do in all the inflections and subtleties. Parker Fennelly became Titus Moody, and again Allen felt blessed: "the finest simulator of New England types we have in radio, the theater, in Hollywood or even in New England" was his *Treadmill* assessment. Allen wrote particularly well for Moody, the rustic farmer who delivered his lines in a deadpan monotone (Titus was so anemic that, when he cut a finger, it didn't bleed—it just puckered and hissed). His catchphrase was his greeting, the dry "Howdy, bub."

The crowning touch came with the addition of Kenny Delmar as Senator Beauregard Claghorn. It was Minerva Pious who heard him do an impression of a southern blowhard and brought him to Allen's attention. The Texas windbag had been lifted from life when, 17 years earlier, Delmar had been hitchhiking and had been picked up by the living personification of that never-say-die Dixie zealot. "Everything he said he bellowed, and everything he bellowed he repeated," Delmar told a journalist later. "Ah own 500 acres—500 acres, that is!"

Allen knew at once that this was the final link. Delmar made his bow as Senator Claghorn Oct. 5, 1945, and was an immediate sensation. His door opened with a bang. "Somebody, ah say, somebody knocked?... Claghorn's the name, Senator Claghorn! I'm from the South!" What followed was a gush of southern superlatives, during which Allen struggled to get his question of the week asked and answered. Claghorn drank only from Dixie Cups; he never went to the Yankee Stadium, danced only at the Cotton Club, and ate only the part of the turkey that was facing south. By the end of his first month on the air (a total of perhaps five minutes of air time) people across the country were mimicking his voice. Commercial firms turned out Claghorn shirts and compasses (the needles always pointed south, son); Delmar cut two Claghorn records, *I Love You, That Is* and *That's a Joke, Son*, and Warner Brothers pirated the concept for use in a series of cartoons. The strutting cartoon rooster, Foghorn J. Leghorn, was an obvious steal from Delmar: the cutting irony, he said years later, was that the cartoons were copyrighted, so that, from then on, "in order to do Claghorn, I had to ask permission from Warner Brothers."

The new Allen's Alley was a smash. The show opened with the harmonizing De Marco Sisters, who came crooning after an orchestrial fanfare, "Mister Allen!... Mister Aaaallen!" Allen's rating, for the first time in his career, climbed to the top. In 1948, he posted a 28.7 Hooper, leading perpetual front-runners Jack Benny, Edgar Bergen, and *Fibber McGee and Molly*. But his reign was brief: he led the pack for two weeks, then began to fall. During his prime seasons, 1945–49, he produced the comedy that people would remember for years. His musical parodies were as timeless as the originals that inspired them. He ribbed Gilbert and Sullivan, inviting Brooklyn Dodgers manager Leo Durocher to *sing* (if that can be believed) in a skit called "The Brooklyn Pinafore." He joshed Rodgers and Hammerstein with Beatrice Lillie in "Picadilly," a good-hearted spoof of *Oklahoma*. He brought the Jack Benny feud to its riotous conclusion in a show titled *King for a Day*, wherein Benny literally loses his pants and the studio laughter is so long and loud that Kenny Delmar gets cut off in midsentence as he tries to get in that final word for Tenderleaf Tea. Allen was probably cut off the air more than any other comedian. He packed his shows, then ran long because of ad-libbing and was cut off rudely by the NBC chimes. In the '40s, he was cut off for other reasons, notably for his on-air criticisms of network vice presidents (they were "molehill men," he said: they came to work every morning at 9 o'clock and found a lot of molehills on their desks; then they had until 5 o'clock to make mountains out of them).

This became a serious feud within his own network. He had written a Gilbert and Sullivan skit, "The Radio Mikado," containing references to "the hucksters of radio," the "vice presidents and clerks" who were, confidentially, a bunch of "jerks." The network censored him viciously. Gone were jokes about "Button, Burton, Bitten, and Muchinfuss," the ad agency, and its boss, Philmore Updyke Muchinfuss (old P-U for short). The fight spilled out into the press. Allen blasted the censors. "They are a bit of executive fungus that forms on a desk that has been exposed to conference. Their conferences are meetings of men who can do nothing but collectively agree that nothing can be done." The thin-skinned network reacted again, cutting Allen off in the middle of a barb.

Now other comics joined the fray. That week Red Skelton said on his show that he'd have to be careful not to ad-lib something that might wound the dignity of some NBC vice president. "Did you hear they cut Fred Allen off on Sunday?" That's as far as he got—the network cut him off. But Skelton went right on talking, for the studio audience. "You know what NBC means, don't you? Nothing but cuts. Nothing but confusion. Nobody certain.'' When the network put him back on the air, Skelton said, ''Well, we have now joined the parade of stars.'' Bob Hope, on his program, was cut off the air for this joke: ''Vegas is the only town in the world where you can get tanned and faded at the same time. Of course, Fred Allen can be faded anytime.'' Allen told the press that NBC had a vice president who was in charge of ''program ends.'' When a show ran overtime, this individual wrote down the time he had saved by cutting it off: eventually he amassed enough time for a two-week vacation. Dennis Day took the last shot. ''I'm listening to the radio,'' he said to his girlfriend Mildred on his Wednesday night NBC sitcom. ''I don't hear anything,'' said Mildred. ''I know,'' said Dennis: ''Fred Allen's on.'' On that note, the network gave up the fight, announcing that its comedians were free to say whatever they wanted. It didn't matter, said *Radio Life*: ''They all were anyway.''

Allen took a major ratings dive in 1948. Some claimed he was a victim of *Stop the Music*, a big-money giveaway show that ABC had inserted into the 8 o'clock Sunday timeslot. But other critics suggested that the old formulas that Allen had been using for 18 years had simply worn themselves out. He dropped from the top to 38th on the charts in one year. His sponsor offered to move him, but he refused to take a more advantageous schedule. He was a regular on *The Big Show*, but his life after weekly radio was confined to guest spots and to a few TV appearances (as a regular on *The Colgate Comedy Hour* and others).

In 1952, he was to begin a TV series when he suffered his first heart attack. He returned on CBS TV as a panelist for the game show *What's My Line?* He died on the night of March 17, 1956, collapsing just outside the West 75th Street home of a friend.

His reputation rests on his standing as the wit of his day, though his shows are seldom cited as the funniest in radio. His humor has paled, and today he plays to a tougher audience than he ever faced in life. This is a crowd reared on comedy that censors nothing. It has no hook, but it is harsh, impatient, and unforgiving. In some quarters he is found lacking, but others see him as a humorist in the truest sense. ''Fred will last,'' predicted comic Steve Allen, no relation. Listening to an old *Town Hall Tonight*, a modern lis-

tener might wonder, where is the humor? Some of these sound as dusty as the museum pieces that he himself found them to be in later life: as dead as yesterday's newspaper. Perhaps this is the answer. When Allen went into topical humor, at the beginning of his career, he may have forfeited his only opportunity to be the Mark Twain of his century. He had flashes of undeniable brilliance. But the main body of his work deals with the day-to-day fodder of another time, and sons have seldom been amused by the embarrassments or tragedies of their fathers.

Throughout his life, he was the opposite of all show business clichés. His marriage endured: by all accounts, he dearly loved his wife. Words most often used by those who knew him were ''decent,'' ''genial,'' ''gentle,'' and ''generous.'' He was a constant target of panhandlers and always had a roll of money in his pockets for handouts. He was not, apparently, a chummy man. His few real intimates, old friends like Doc Rockwell and Uncle Jim Harkins, had been with him in vaudeville and appeared occasionally on his show. He and Portland avoided crowds, lived simply in a New York apartment, and never owned a car. ''I don't want to own anything,'' he once told a reporter, ''that won't fit in my coffin.''

THE FRED BRADY SHOW, comedy-variety.

BROADCAST HISTORY: Brief summer run in 1941, CBS.

July 8–Sept. 30, 1943, NBC. 30m, Thursdays at 7:30. Summer substitute for *The Bob Burns Show*. **CAST:** Fred Brady as himself. Also: Shirley Mitchell, Charlie ''Buzz'' Kemper, Joe De Rita, Marlin Hurt, Lou Lubin. **ORCHESTRA:** Gordon Jenkins. **PRODUCER:** Nate Tufts.

The 1943 *Fred Brady Show* is notable for prefacing acts that later became well known. Marlin Hurt gave an early version of Beulah, the Negro maid soon to rise to stardom on *Fibber McGee and Molly*; Lou Lubin, who later became the stuttering Shorty the Barber on *Amos 'n' Andy* had a dry run here as a character who couldn't get a line out straight.

THE FRED WARING SHOW, musical variety.

BROADCAST HISTORY: Ca. 1923, WWJ, Detroit: first radio broadcast.

Feb. 8, 1933–Jan. 31, 1934, CBS. 30m, Wednesdays at 10. Old Gold.

Feb. 4, 1934–Dec. 29, 1936, CBS. Various 30m and 60m timeslots. Ford Motor Company.

Jan. 17–Dec. 25, 1936, Blue Network. 30m, Fridays at 9:30 until June, then at 9. Ford Motor Company.

Oct. 8, 1938–March 4, 1939, NBC. 30m, Saturdays at 8:30. Bromo Quinine.

June 19, 1939–June 9, 1944, NBC. 15m, weekdays at 7. Chesterfield. Also titled *Chesterfield Time*; occasionally *Pleasure Time*.

Sept. 7, 1944–May 31, 1945, Blue Network. 30m, Thursdays at 7 until Jan., then at 10.

June 4, 1945–July 8, 1949, NBC. 30m daily at 11 A.M., later other mid-late morning slots. Various sponsors including the American Meat Company and Florida Citrus Growers.

June 18–Sept. 24, 1946, NBC. 30m, Tuesdays at 9:30 for *Fibber McGee and Molly* and Johnson's Wax. Also heard as *McGee* substitutes June 24–Sept. 30, 1947, Tuesdays at 9:30; and again June 7–Sept. 29, 1948, the latter outside the *McGee* timeslot, Mondays and Wednesdays at 11 A.M., all for Johnson's Wax.

Oct. 6, 1947–Sept. 29, 1949, NBC. 30m, Mondays at 10:30, 1947–48; then Thursdays at 10:30. General Electric.

July 16, 1949–July 22, 1950, NBC. 30m, Saturdays at 10 A.M. Minnesota Canning Company.

Oct. 1, 1956–March 15, 1957, ABC. 30m, five a week at 2.

April 9–Oct. 4, 1957, ABC. 30m, five a week/three a week at 9:30/10:30.

CONDUCTOR: Fred Waring, leader of a large orchestra and chorus, sometimes billed as "more than half a hundred Pennsylvanians." **ASSISTANT CONDUCTOR:** Fred Culley. **CHORAL LEADER:** Robert Shaw. **SINGERS AND SOLOISTS:** Rosemary and Priscilla Lane (Rosemary often teamed in romantic duets with Waring's brother Tom); Stella and the Fellas (Stella Friend, Paul Gibbons, Roy Ringwald, Craig Leitch); Kay Thompson; Babs and Her Brothers (Blanche Redwine with brothers Charlie and Little Ryan, also known as the Smoothies); comic Roy Atwell with a simplistic stuttering routine; Poley McClintock, comedic singer. Also: Jane Wilson, Joanne Wheatley, Gordon Goodman, Gordon Berger, Jimmy Atkins, Don Craig, Daisy Bernier, Donna Dae, Ruth

Cottingham, Stuart Churchill, Honey and the Bees (Diane Courtney, Hal Kanner, and Murray Kane); Three Girl Friends (Stella Friend, June Taylor, and Ida Pierce); Mac Perrin; comic singers Lumpy Brannum (bass and violin) and Johnny "Scat" Davis (trumpet); Ferne Buckner (violin); the McFarland Twins (Arthur and George); and the piano duo Livingston Gearhart and Virginia Morley. **ANNOUNCERS:** David Ross; Bob Considine; Paul Douglas for Chesterfield; Bill Bivens, 1940s. **PRODUCERS:** Tom Bennett, etc.

Fred Waring rose to fame with one of the largest musical aggregations in modern show business. He was born June 9, 1900, in Tyrone, Pa. His original band, formed in 1917, included Waring, his brother Tom, Freddy Buck, and drummer Poley McClintock. As students at Penn State, they played many local dates in the early '20s, evolving from the small but energetic "banjazztra" into a national musical force.

It was constantly growing and changing. The 1920s group was collegiate-related. The original four had been joined by Nelson Keller (trumpet), Art Horn and Park Lytell (saxes), Jim Gilliland (trombone), and Bill Borscher (bass). "The Waring act usually was fast-paced, curtain-to-curtain nonstop with no talk and no encores," wrote Peter T. Kiefer for an RCA historical release years later. This "left the audiences breathless and applauding." The band hit the record charts with its mid-1920s recordings *Sleep* and *Collegiate*. By then, Waring had seen the power of radio, having promoted the group on WWJ, Detroit, into a number of dates in local theaters and dance clubs.

By 1929, the band numbered about 20 pieces. The following year, Waring took a Roxy Theater booking that called for 50 instruments. It was a demanding date, but he was held over and stayed six months. During this time, his interest shifted away from pure instrumental music and into the harmonies of the human voice. On the program with Waring at the Roxy was the Hall Johnson Choir. When Johnson took ill on opening night, Waring led the group. He was thrilled at the sound achieved by those blended voices and decided to create a glee club for his own band.

By some accounts, Waring turned down two dozen radio offers because the producers were disinterested in his glee club concepts. His first major radio show, on CBS for Old Gold in 1933, allowed him to develop the vocal arrangements, but the sponsor grew dissatisfied, and the show ran just one season. Waring was still tinkering with new vocal-instrumental concepts the following year, when he broadcast for Ford: long musical passages blended several well-known melodies into a general theme, but he was also still playing spirited jazz arrangements and college songs. The theme was his big hit from the '20s, *Sleep*. By 1939, when he began a five-year association with Chesterfield, his themes were well established: *I Hear Music* opened the show; *Sleep* closed it. Another well-remembered theme, working the sponsor into the formula, was *A Cigarette, Sweet Music, and You*. He now fronted an 81-piece orchestra and glee club, the size alone making his show one of the most expensive propositions on the air.

On June 4, 1945, Waring became part of an NBC experiment to bring nighttime quality to daytime radio. At $18,000 a week just for orchestra costs, it was believed to be the most expensive daytime show ever. He was busy on radio throughout the decade and beyond. His music had a distinct sound: it appealed to listeners in the same way that Guy Lombardo's did, using familiar melodies in arrangements that sounded unique. The enormous glee club gave his show a body and spirit, whether singing on its own or used to "frame" the soloists and small groups. Robert Shaw was its leader and coach, but Waring was its taskmaster. He was often described as genial and affable away from the bandstand and a tireless perfectionist at work. His people talked of constant rehearsals, sometimes eight hours a day. Often he prepared twice as much material as he needed, then chose numbers that still seemed fresh despite the strenuous hours of rehearsal. He would also arrange a single tune three different ways, rehearsing it in straight time, as a waltz, and in jive. "He does not tell the gang which of the numbers they rehearse during the afternoon will go on the air that night," said *Radio Life*. Theoretically, this kept the group alert, ready to play anything.

"Waring had one of the best-staged shows I've ever seen, with the dancing dominoes and things like that," said singer Charlie Ryan. "He got a real soft, beautiful sound from that glee club, just like a campus group sitting around singing pretty harmonies." His drive took his success across more than five decades, keeping him active long after most bands of his era had disappeared. He died July 29, 1984.

THE FREE COMPANY, documentary drama.

BROADCAST HISTORY: Feb. 23–May 11, 1941, CBS. 30m, Sundays at 2.

CAST: Burgess Meredith, host. Major film stars in anthology roles: Paul Muni, John Garfield, Franchot Tone, Orson Welles, etc. ORCHESTRA: Leith Stevens, Bernard Herrmann, etc. CREATOR: James Boyd. COMPANY OF CONTRIBUTORS: Robert Sherwood, Sherwood Anderson, George M. Cohan, Orson Welles, Ernest Hemingway, Stephen Vincent Benét, Archibald MacLeish, Maxwell Anderson, Marc Connelly, Paul Green, William Saroyan, Norman Corwin, Elmer Rice. PRODUCER: Charles Vanda. DIRECTOR: Irving Reis.

The Free Company was an attempt by 14 major American writers to counter what was seen as a tide of foreign propaganda infiltrating the American press and radio. James Boyd, author of the novel *Drums* and a "dollar-a-year man" at the U.S. Department of Justice, was asked by Solicitor General Francis Biddle to create a radio company that could shed light on the greatness of America and its Bill of Rights. Host Burgess Meredith announced the company's goal, to prove that the American way, "in the spring of 1941, with all our flaws and all our problems, is still the best way of life on earth."

Boyd promised that the group would be "unpaid, unsponsored, and uncontrolled—just a group of Americans saying what they think about this country and about freedom." But less than two months after its opening, *The Free Company* was accused of promoting the same subversive propaganda that it was created to blunt. The accuser: William Randolph Hearst. The target: Orson Welles. It was widely speculated that Welles had rudely dissected Hearst in his upcoming film, *Citizen Kane*, and that Hearst had mounted a Herculean effort to block the film's release, buy up the prints, and destroy it. Failing in that, he opened fire on Welles and *The Free Company*, with front-page condemnation in Hearst newspapers from coast to coast.

The blast came a day after Welles had produced, directed, and narrated a self-written *Free Company* piece titled *His Honor, the Mayor* (April 6). The story was of a small-town mayor who pushes his belief in the Bill of Rights to its ultimate test, by allowing a group of fascists known as the "White Crusaders" to freely assemble and brew their campaigns of hate. The message was clear: freedom isn't real, unless it's for everyone. Hearst saw it differently: his news stories were based on accusations from the American Legion and the California Sons of the American Revolution, whose officials had found the Welles broadcast "suspiciously communistic." Welles immediately denied being a Communist, but the attacks continued. The American Legion condemned Marc Connelly's play *The Mole on Lincoln's Cheek*, which was a plea for truth in textbooks. *Time* magazine put the complaints in perspective: the Legion was really upset because Connelly's characters included "a few witch-hunting operatives of a 'Veteran's League,'" and Hearst's problem with Welles was still tied to *Citizen Kane*, which "looked too much like an unflattering portrait of Citizen Hearst."

But *The Free Company* had successfully been put on the defensive. For its April 20 show, Meredith read a lengthy justification of the group's mandate, goals, and overall patriotism. He read this twice, making the tone almost imploring in its eagerness to convince. He talked of the unimpeachable reputations of the writers, the prizes they had won, their military as well as literary service to America. Fifty years later, Meredith remembered the atmosphere of oppression that had fallen over the show. Welles was told, "For God's sake, don't ad-lib anything," Meredith remembered.

High spots in the short run were Benét's antislavery drama, *Freedom Is a Hard-Bought Thing*, Paul Green's *A Start in Life* (a tough look at the hardships of contemporary black life), and Maxwell Anderson's *Miracle of the Danube*, based on the premise that even a Nazi might hold Christian values. The actors for the Welles broadcast were mostly *Mercury Theater* personnel: Agnes Moorehead, Ray Collins, Paul Stewart, Everett Sloane, and Erskine Sanford. Sherwood Anderson died during the run: one of his works was presented posthumously. Hemingway and Cohan, among others, never really participated beyond lending their names.

A fascinating series with some good episodes on tape. Even a modern listener will hear the tensions in a company broadcasting in the shadow of war and under the threat of the pointed finger. The McCarthy era was just around the corner.

FREE WORLD THEATER, philosophical dramatic anthology.

BROADCAST HISTORY: Feb. 21–June 27, 1943, Blue Network. 25m–30m, Sundays at 6:05 until April 18, then at 6:30.
CAST: Major Hollywood stars: Fred MacMurray, Dinah Shore, Beulah Bondi, John Garfield, etc. MUSIC: Gordon Jenkins. DIRECTOR-WRITER: Arch Oboler.

The *Free World Theater* was conceived by Arch Oboler in conversation with William Lewis of the Office of War Information. Oboler had given up a $3,000-a-week income in commercial radio to work for the war cause free of charge. The idea behind *Free World* was to obtain brief statements from world leaders, "some piece of information that they would like to have expressed to the American people," then dramatize those thoughts for radio. Among those solicited were Thomas Mann, Aldous Huxley, Winston Churchill, Franklin D. Roosevelt, George Bernard Shaw, Josef Stalin, and Chiang Kai-shek. Oboler wrote the first play, based on an idea by Henry Wallace: two vignettes of Europe and the Pacific that starred Alla Nazimova, Conrad Veidt, and Walter Brennan. He assigned Budd Schulberg and Jerome Lawrence the wish by Thomas Mann that "people begin planning for this world that is to come after the war." The writers forged a play about a young soldier returning home to find his family bickering as if there were no war being fought. The turning point came when the soldier told his family what a buddy had said just before he died: "Join hands around the world and don't let go—that's the only way to get peace and keep it."

Working in a government show, Oboler had the top writers and actors in Hollywood at his disposal. The world leaders responded well enough, Oboler said, "but some of these gentlemen don't understand what a drama is. We got some important statements, but some very dull ones." Only George Bernard Shaw refused to cooperate, pronouncing the whole idea a ridiculous waste of time. Oboler said he'd even use that, in a drama about the "negative approach" to the war.

FREEDOM USA, political melodrama.

BROADCAST HISTORY: 1952, 30m transcribed syndication, Ziv Company.
CAST: Tyrone Power as Senator Dean Edwards. NARRATOR: Edwin C. Hill. ANNOUNCER: Jimmy Wallington.

Freedom USA proposed to take listeners "into the Senate chambers, the cloakrooms, the private offices" of "political Washington."

FRIENDLY FIVE FOOTNOTES, musical variety and aviation news.

BROADCAST HISTORY: 1930–31, Blue Network. 15m, Thursdays at 7:45. Friendly Five Shoes.
1931–32, CBS. 15m, Fridays at 9:45. *Aviation News.* Friendly Five Shoes.

Friendly Five Footnotes captured its era in music, song, and tidbits from the fledgling world of aviation. The host was a character identified only as "Friendly Fred," who tapdanced to the theme, *I've Got Five Dollars.* The orchestra, in reality the Freddie Rich band, was billed as The Friendly Five Orchestra. Aviation news was given by Casey Jones, vice president of the Curtis-Wright Corporation. As a premium, local Friendly Five outlets offered a booklet, *It's Easy to Learn to Fly.* Wonderfully evocative of the early Depression.

THE FRONT PAGE, lighthearted crime drama, based loosely on the play by Ben Hecht and Charles MacArthur.

BROADCAST HISTORY: May 6–Sept. 16, 1948, ABC. 30m, Thursdays at 8.
CAST: Dick Powell as reporter Hildy Johnson. William Conrad as his nemesis, managing editor Walter Burns. Hollywood radio players in support. DIRECTOR: Bill Rousseau. WRITERS: Morton Fine and David Friedkin.

The Front Page drew scathing reviews for the liberties it took with the original play. "It retains neither the Chicago setting nor the late twenties era," noted *Radio Life* while nonetheless coming to its defense. The dialogue departed from the "snappy and clever" only in Dick Powell's "sardonic musings about Life," and though William Conrad's Walter Burns role was "comedyized a bit . . . no great harm has been done to

it and Conrad shades the lines well, giving them character they may not actually have."

FRONT PAGE FARRELL, soap opera.

BROADCAST HISTORY: June 23, 1941–March 13, 1942, Mutual. 15m, weekdays at 1:30. Anacin.
Sept. 14, 1942–March 26, 1954, NBC. 15m, weekdays at 5:45 through 1951, then at 5:15. Anacin initially, then the Whitehall Pharmaco Company for Kolynos Toothpaste, etc.
CAST: Richard Widmark (ca. 1941–42) as David Farrell, ace reporter for the *Brooklyn Eagle*; Carleton Young also as David; Staats Cotsworth as David through most of the later run. Florence Williams and Virginia Dwyer as Sally Farrell, David's wife. Frank Chase as George Walker, the newspaper's managing editor. Robert Donley as Lieutenant Carpenter of the New York police. Also: Evelyn Varden, Vivian Smolen, Elspeth Eric, Betty Garde, etc. PRODUCERS: Frank and Anne Hummert. DIRECTORS: Blair Walliser, Art Hanna, Richard Leonard, etc. THEME: *You and I Know,* played by Rosa Rio on organ.

Though *Front Page Farrell* was couched as a crime serial and slated in the late afternoon to take advantage of potential male listeners just home from work, there was little doubt of its sudsy content. In its earliest days it was billed as "the unforgettable story of marriage and a newspaper office—the story of a handsome, dashing young star reporter on one of New York's greatest newspapers, and the girl he marries on impulse, to save her from throwing herself away on a rich man twice her age."

Farrell's job was the catalyst for adventure, and Sally always went along for the ride. Mayhem and murder alike, it mattered little: she went on the house calls, questioned the suspects, and often solved the cases. During the war, the Farrells looked into homefront problems: the themes were fed to the producers by the Office of War Information. Postwar topics included the usual: a blackmail scheme, a beautiful but suspicious heiress, and murder. The stories, which were usually wrapped up in about two weeks, had colorful titles: *The Case of the Fatal Smile; The Lady and the Cheetah; The Man Who Knew All the Angels.*

FRONTIER GENTLEMAN, western adventure drama.

BROADCAST HISTORY: Feb. 2–Nov. 16, 1958, CBS. 30m, Sundays at 2:30 through March, then at 7.

CAST: John Dehner as J. B. Kendall, reporter for the *London Times* who roamed the territories of the western United States in search of stories. Support from Hollywood radio personnel: Jack Kruschen, Virginia Gregg, Barney Phillips, Stacy Harris, Harry Bartell, Joseph Kearns, Vic Perrin, Jack Moyles, Lawrence Dobkin, Jeanette Nolan, etc. **ANNOUNCERS:** Johnny Jacobs, John Wald, Dan Cubberly, Bud Sewell. **MUSIC:** Wilbur Hatch; Jerry Goldsmith. Original trumpet theme by Jerry Goldsmith. **CREATOR-WRITER-DIRECTOR:** Antony Ellis.

The opening signature of *Frontier Gentleman* defined it: *Herewith, an Englishman's account of life and death in the West. As a reporter for the* London Times, *he writes his colorful and unusual accounts. But as a man with a gun, he lives and becomes a part of the violent years in the new territories.* What the signature didn't say was that *Frontier Gentleman* was a solid cut above most westerns on radio or television in a western-filled decade.

It came in radio's final years, successfully combining wry insights, humor, suspense, and human interest. As J. B. Kendall roamed the West, his adventures came in all guises and forms. He met nameless drifters, outlaws, and real people from history. Writer-director Antony Ellis asked his listeners to believe that one of the men in Wild Bill Hickok's last poker game was J. B. Kendall. Kendall met Calamity Jane, Jesse James, and the "richest man in the West." He won a slave girl, Gentle Virtue, in a card game and became friends with a gambling queen. He defended an unpopular man against a murder charge and almost accompanied George Armstrong Custer in a certain outing against the Sioux. He was usually strapped for cash: often he was found waiting for his remittance from the *Times*, which always seemed to be a town or a territory behind him. He wandered by stage and riverboat, to outposts with names like Bear Claw and South Sunday, and one night, on the wild Kansas prairie, he even had a brush with the supernatural.

The series was produced on tape, and the whole run is available in superb sound. A listener cannot help thinking, what talented people these were! An actress like Virginia Gregg could be a Chinese slave one week, a prim schoolmarm the next, a romantic lead the third. Jeanette Nolan had a range that amazed even her peers, but she was never better than in stories that called for a Calamity Jane–type battleaxe. Dehner himself was a versatile actor, at one point taking a second role, the wheezing sheriff of Shoshone. Jerry Goldsmith's lovely trumpet theme adds greatly to the lonely western ambience, but it was Antony Ellis's show. A lovely piece of radio.

FU MANCHU, serial melodrama, based on the stories by Sax Rohmer.

BROADCAST HISTORY: 1929–31, Blue Network. First heard as part of the 60m *Collier Hour*, a series of 12-chapter serials, following the stories then being serialized in *Collier's Magazine*. **CAST:** Arthur Hughes as Dr. Fu Manchu, Oriental prince of darkness, master scientist, and evil genius.

Sept. 26, 1932–April 24, 1933, CBS. 30m, Mondays at 8:45. Campana Balm. Weekly continuations from Chicago. **CAST:** John Daly (no relation to the CBS newsman) as the evil Dr. Fu; Harold Huber also as Fu Manchu. Charles Warburton and Bob White as the heroes, Nayland Smith and Dr. James Petrie. Sunda Love as the beautiful Karamaneh, slave to the evil scientist's powers; Charlotte Manson also as Karamaneh. **DIRECTOR:** Fred Ibbett.

May 8–Nov. 1, 1939; rebroadcast March 18–Sept. 11, 1940, New York dates of 15m transcribed syndication. *The Shadow of Fu Manchu*. **CAST:** Hanley Stafford as Nayland Smith. Gale Gordon as Dr. James Petire.

A long run of the 1939 *Shadow of Fu Manchu* syndication survived and was taped from scratchy discs, giving some idea of the moody atmosphere of this serialized thriller. The show captured admirably the creeping yellow fog of London at midnight and the sense of evil that were such a part of Rohmer's books. Fu Manchu might have revolutionized science but chose the path of evil instead. His arsenal of weapons included a snake in a cane handle and a green mist, delivered in letters, which fills a room and kills instantly. In one episode, police are attacked and killed by a fungus growing in Fu Manchu's basement. The heroes, Smith and Petrie, are drugged, threatened, and tortured. They encounter a paralyzing "flower of silence," a "coughing death," a "fiery hand," a sacred white peacock, and poisoned claws. Such imaginative elements made *Fu Manchu* an effective early thriller.

FURLOUGH FUN, musical comedy.

BROADCAST HISTORY: Nov. 2, 1942–June 23, 1944, NBC West Coast.

CAST: Beryl Wallace, hostess. Spike Jones and the City Slickers, comedy music. George Riley, comedian. **ANNOUNCERS:** Verne Smith, Larry Keating. **PRODUCER:** Bradford Brown.

This early version of the Spike Jones show featured the usual crazy music, as well as interviews by Beryl Wallace with servicemen from camps, flying fields, and redistribution centers. The interviews were of the "most thrilling moment in the war" type. The show continued, with different personnel, after Jones left in June 1944.

G

THE GALLANT HEART, serial drama.

BROADCAST HISTORY: 1944, NBC West Coast. 15m, weekdays at 9 A.M. Pacific time.

CAST: Janet Logan as Grace Kingsley. Howard Culver as Stephen Biggs. Martha Wentworth as Ma Daniels. Ken Christy as Ed Prentiss (a character named, apparently, for a radio actor). Irene Tedrow as Capt. Julia Porter. Howard McNear as Chaplain William Duncan. Truda Marson as Alice Marley. Janet Waldo as Jennifer Lake. Tom Collins as Capt. John Blanding. Ge Ge Pearson as Daisy Mulligan. Herb Lytton as Sgt. Bill Johnson. Ruby Dandridge as Mammy Brown. Bob Frazer as Dr. Fletcher. Gwen Delano as Mrs. Nellie Kingsley. Bob Bruce as Operator 63. Also: Pat McGeehan, Forrest Lewis, Hans Conried, Sharon Douglas, etc. **ANNOUNCER:** John Saar. **WRITER:** Virginia Cooke.

The Gallant Heart was NBC's attempt to launch Hollywood into the world of the daytime serial. In the spring of 1944, 39 serials were on the network air between 8 A.M. and 4 P.M., all originating in New York or Chicago. NBC executives in Los Angeles, seeking an inroad, invested $15,000 seed money and assembled a large cast of prime-time Hollywood radio actors for their cause. It was described by *Radio Life* as the story of "today's young people, who grew to adulthood after World War I and had just achieved a fine adjustment to life when they were catapulted into the chaos of another universal conflict."

GAMBLING'S MUSICAL CLOCK, music, talk, calisthentics.

BROADCAST HISTORY: Ca. 1925–59, WOR, New York.

Although it was not heard on a network, *Gambling's Musical Clock* was one of the pioneering shows of the air. Because of its centralized location and a 50,000-watt WOR signal, it was eventually heard by a daily audience of one million people from Maine to Virginia and as far west as the Central time zone.

John B. Gambling began his radio career as an engineer and became, in almost 30 years before the microphone, one of the best-known personalities in the East. He was hired at WOR in March 1925 and a few months later was asked to fill in for Bernarr MacFadden, who had a calisthentics program. Gambling's smooth baritone voice contrasted well with MacFadden's gravelly, authoritarian approach, and he got the job permanently when MacFadden left the station a few months later. The original show was 90 minutes long, beginning at 6:30 A.M. Colgate Toothpaste became a sponsor soon after Gambling took over, and in 1927 he interspersed some husband-wife chatter. He missed being the first such breakfast show only by the fact that he was not married to the actress who played his opposite. The skits were scripted, thus fictitious.

In the late 1920s he was joined by Vincent Sorey's three-piece band. Later his permanent musicians were Sorey on violin, Michael Rosco ("Rudolph" on the air) on piano, Pietra "Froz"

Frosini on accordion, and Louis Biamonte on saxophone and other instruments. The physical fitness craze ended in the mid-1930s; Gambling then concentrated on talk. He was known as "the human alarm clock" as the show settled into a 7:15–8 A.M. niche and became the day's starting point for hundreds of thousands.

In 1939 Gambling began his school-closing reports. To the ringing of a bell, he attempted to give bad-weather schedules of up to 600 New York–New Jersey schools. A second show, *Rambling with Gambling*, began in 1942. Initially an afternoon program, it moved into the 6 A.M. slot, becoming a lead-in for the *Musical Clock*. Among Gambling's many sponsors were Broadcast Brand Corn Beef Hash and Hartz Mountain Birdseed. His show was augmented by the chirping of canaries, whose cages were kept directly behind the band.

Gambling retired in 1959 and died in 1974. He left his show to his son, John A. Gambling, who had first appeared on Gambling's 1934 Christmas Eve broadcast. John A. retired in 1990, leaving the show to his son, John R. Gambling. It was cited as the longest-running radio show in the *Guinness Book of World Records*.

GANG BUSTERS, dramatic crime anthology.

BROADCAST HISTORY: July 20–Oct. 12, 1935, NBC. 30m, Saturdays at 9. Initially heard as *G-Men*. Chevrolet.

Jan. 15, 1936–June 15, 1940, CBS. 30m, Wednesdays at 10, 1936–38; Wednesdays at 8, 1938–39; Saturdays at 8, 1939–40. Colgate-Palmolive, 1936–38; *Cue* magazine, 1939–40.

Oct. 11, 1940–Dec. 25, 1948, Blue Network/ABC. 30m, Fridays at 9, 1940–45; Saturdays at 9, 1945–48. Sloan's Liniment, 1940–45; Waterman Pens, 1945–48; Tide Detergent, 1948.

Jan. 8, 1949–June 25, 1955, CBS. 30m, Saturdays at 9, 1949–54; Mondays at 9:30, 1954–55. Grape Nuts, 1949–54; Wrigley's Gum 1954–55.

Oct. 5, 1955–Nov. 27, 1957, Mutual. 30m, Wednesdays at 8.

CAST: New York radio actors including Alice Reinheart, Santos Ortega, Bryna Raeburn, Don MacLaughlin, Elspeth Eric, Frank Lovejoy, Leon Janney, Larry Haines, Grant Richards, Roger DeKoven, Julie Stevens, Art Carney, Richard Widmark, Raymond Edward Johnson, Louise Fitch, Joan Banks, Robert Dryden. **INTERVIEWER-**

NARRATOR: Phillips H. Lord; Col. H. Norman Schwarzkopf (from Jan. 1938); Commissioner Lewis J. Valentine (from ca. 1945). **ANNOUNCERS:** Charles Stark, Frank Gallop, Roger Forster, Don Gardiner, Gilbert Martin, etc. **CREATOR-PRODUCER-DIRECTOR:** Phillips H. Lord. **DIRECTORS:** Jay Hanna, George Zachary, Leonard Bass, Bill Sweets, Paul Munroe, Harry Frazee. **WRITERS:** John Mole, Stanley Niss, Brice Disque, etc. **SOUND EFFECTS:** Ed Blainey, James Flynn, Harry Nelson (Blue Network/ABC); Jerry McCarty, James Rogan, Orval White, Byron Wingett (CBS); Bob Prescott (several networks); Harry Bubeck, Ray Kremer.

Gang Busters was the noisiest show on the air. The sharp blast of a policeman's whistle. Shuffling feet. Gunshots. A broken window. The stark metallic voice of a burglar alarm, and the forlorn answer of a police siren. Machine guns spraying bullets like Flit. Tires screeching, more glass breaking.

And this was only the opening signature.

This best-remembered of all police shows was produced "in cooperation with police and federal law enforcement departments throughout the United States." It was billed as "the only national program that brings you authentic police case histories." It was so loud that it created its own term in slang: to "come on like gangbusters," meaning "to enter, arrive, begin, participate, or perform in a sensational, loud, active, or striking manner" (Wentworth and Flexner, *Dictionary of American Slang*).

It began in 1935 when Phillips H. Lord, radio's venerable "Seth Parker," was looking for a new radio idea. The popularity of *Seth Parker* had been severely compromised when Lord had been accused of a publicity stunt in a South Pacific shipwreck, and he needed a fresh approach for a radio comeback. The era of gangsterism in movies was at its peak: films like *Little Caesar* and *The Public Enemy* had had good box office. What was missing, Lord decided, was the authoritative approach. Even *Scarface*, which had purported to be about Al Capone, had avoided mentioning the Chicago racketeer by name. Lord envisioned a hard-hitting series in which all names would be used, with everything verified from official files.

At his first case, he would dramatize the story of John Dillinger, killed by G-men the summer before as he exited the Biograph Theater in Chicago. Lord sold the idea to Chevrolet, then flew to Washington with the automaker's admen to persuade J. Edgar Hoover, director of the Division of Investigation (soon to be FBI), to cooperate. Hoover was less than thrilled, but his reluctance was countered by the approval of the attorney general. Hoover stipulated that only closed cases could be used, and Lord wrote his opening show in a small office on the fifth floor of the Department of Justice Building in Washington.

Adding another authoritative element was Lewis J. Valentine, crime-busting commissioner of New York police, who gave advice and delivered a short talk on the opening broadcast. It premiered as *G-Men* in mid-1935. For his second show, Lord dramatized the violent career of Lester Gillis, better known as George "Baby Face" Nelson, another killer who had died in a shootout with G-men. For a time he concentrated on nationally notorious criminals: George R. "Machine Gun" Kelly; Bonnie Parker and Clyde Barrow; Charles Arthur "Pretty Boy" Floyd; and Arthur Flegenheimer, also known as Dutch Schultz. But Hoover was not happy, and what little help Lord was getting from the FBI continued to diminish. As the initial *G-Men* ran its course, the concept was revised as *Gang Busters*. This series would cut a broad swath through radio crime drama with no help whatever from the FBI.

The scope broadened to include lesser-known though perhaps more interesting stories. The sound effects continued to be elaborate and aggressive. Cutting into the opening was a filtered voice, giving descriptions of wanted men in a "calling all cars" manner. "More to follow on *Gang Busters* Clues!" the announcer would promise, and the sirens and submachine guns would come up full as the story began.

The "clues" became one of the most successful gimmicks in radio. At the end of each story, a national alert was aired for actual criminals wanted by the police or the FBI. The fine details of a criminal's appearance, with special attention to scars, moles, or other distinguishing marks, helped capture 110 wanted men in the first three years. By 1943 more than 1,500 clues had been broadcast, sometimes as many as six per show. The tally that year was 286 "armed and extremely dangerous" men who had been brought to justice by *Gang Busters*.

The show utilized an interview format. It began with Lord interviewing, "by proxy," a local lawman or federal agent who had figured prominently in the story. Later, Col. H. Norman Schwarzkopf (whose son would become a hero half a century later in the Persian Gulf War) was brought in as interviewer. Schwarzkopf had been superintendent of the New Jersey State Police during the investigation of Bruno Richard Hauptmann for the kidnapping of the Lindbergh baby and had battled Hoover for jurisdiction of the case. Having Schwarzkopf on the show would be a double bonus for Lord: it would continue the authoritative air begun with Valentine, and it would annoy Hoover.

Meanwhile, Valentine continued his association with the show for years, though often by name only. "Now picture our setting as a special office, turned over to *Gang Busters* by Commissioner Lewis J. Valentine of the New York City police," the announcer would say. Lord, and later Schwarzkopf, would chat informally in this fictional office, reviewing the case in chronological order. Then the voices of Lord/Schwarzkopf and their proxy policemen would fade, and the cases were handled as straight drama.

In the fall of 1945, Valentine stepped down as police chief and became the regular *Gang Busters* narrator. In 1946 he left the show at the request of Gen. Douglas MacArthur, who wanted him to reorganize the police departments in defeated Japan.

Gang Busters was among several old radio shows rebroadcast by syndication in the 1960s. It was not well received, considered too pro-police for that time, but was still on the air in some markets in the 1990s. Another of the show's ingredients was still quite potent in the '90s: the TV show *Unsolved Mysteries* regularly telecast clues to the identity of con men, robbers, and killers, roping in lawbreakers who had eluded capture, sometimes for years.

THE GARRY MOORE SHOW, variety.

BROADCAST HISTORY: July 1–July 29, 1942, Blue Network. 30m, Wednesdays at 10.

Aug. 17, 1942–Nov. 20, 1943, NBC. 30m, Mondays through Saturdays at 9 A.M. Initially called *The Show Without a Name*; changed to *Everything Goes* ca. March 1943, when a listener won a $500 contest to name it.

Sept. 12, 1949–Aug. 25, 1950, CBS. 60m,

weekdays at 3:30, then at 4; then 30m at 7 in summer 1950.

Sept. 28, 1959–Sept. 21, 1961, CBS. 10m weekdays at 11:30 A.M.

HOST: Garry Moore. ANNOUNCERS: Howard Petrie (1942–43, 1949–50); Durward Kirby (1950 evening show; 1959–61). VOCALISTS: Brad Reynolds, Marie Green (1942–43); Ken Carson, Ilene Woods (1949–50); Denise Lor (1950 evening show). VOCAL GROUP: The Merry Men Quartet (1942–43). ORCHESTRA: Irving Miller (1942–43, 1949–50); Billy Wardell (1949–50).

Garry Moore had a busy radio career, in series that bore his name and in others that did not. For the latter, see BEAT THE BAND, BREAKFAST IN HOLLYWOOD, THE CAMEL CARAVAN, CLUB MATINEE, THE JIMMY DURANTE SHOW, and TAKE IT OR LEAVE IT.

Moore came out of local radio in Baltimore, St. Louis, and Chicago. It was on Ransom Sherman's *Club Matinee* that he changed his name, his original being Thomas Garrison Morfit. A lively, effervescent personality, Moore was seen by NBC as a possible alternative to Don McNeill's *Breakfast Club* when he took the helm of a six-a-week early-morning series in 1942. Though it was never properly christened *The Garry Moore Show*, it was in many ways a direct forerunner to the 1949 CBS series, including some of the same personnel. Announcer Howard Petrie mugged with Moore in 1943, chiding him about the differences in their height; Petrie then worked with Moore on *The Camel Caravan*, and again when *The Garry Moore Show* opened on CBS in 1949.

Moore worked well in daytime or evening programs. When CBS put him on in the evenings in 1950, he initiated free-roving question-and-answer sessions with the studio audience, which were highly popular. These were simulcast on early TV; though the radio half was discontinued, the TV show went on through 1951. Moore thus got his big push into television, eventually hosting the highly rated game show *I've Got a Secret*.

GASOLINE ALLEY, comedy serial, based on the comic strip by Frank King.

BROADCAST HISTORY: Feb. 17–April 11, 1941, NBC. 15m, weekdays at 6:45. Returned April 28–May 9, 1941, Blue Network. 15m, weekdays at 5:45.

CAST: Jimmy McCallion as Skeezix, a young man just coming of age. Janice Gilbert as his girlfriend Nina Clock. Cliff Soubier as Wumple, Skeezix's boss. Junius Matthews as Ling Wee, a philosophical waiter in a Chinese restaurant. *Other cast, unknown times and tenure*: Bill Idelson as Skeezix, perhaps in a regional (Chicago) series, as early as 1931. Jean Gillespie as Nina at some point. DIRECTOR: Charles Schenck. WRITER: Kane Campbell.

1948–49, 15m, weekly transcriptions with slots for local Autolite dealer commercials. New York origination with Bill Lipton, Mason Adams, Robert Dryden, etc. Heard on WOR July 16, 1948–Jan. 7, 1949, Fridays.

Gasoline Alley was an unusually literal transfer from the comics, when it appeared on NBC in early 1941. Listeners got the same storyline that had appeared in the comic pages that morning. The strip was also unusual in that Skeezix, the hero, was allowed to age from infancy to young adulthood. When it began in newspapers in 1921, Skeezix was found in a basket on a doorstep. By 1941 *Radio Life* found him "a strapping 20-year-old with a pert sweetheart, a host of friends, and a few enemies." In the opening chapter, *Variety* found Skeezix annoyed with Nina Clock because she failed to notice his new mustache. Ling Wee, the waiter, had "a sub rosa master's degree" and gave sage advice to the hero.

In the 1948 transcription, Skeezix Wallet and Wilmer Bobble were partners in the Wallet and Bobble Garage.

GATEWAY TO HOLLYWOOD, talent show.

BROADCAST HISTORY: Jan. 8–Dec. 31, 1939, CBS. 30m, Sundays at 6:30. Wrigley's Gum.

HOST: Film producer Jesse L. Lasky. ANNOUNCER: Ken Niles. MUSIC: Wilbur Hatch; also Carl Hohengarten. DIRECTOR: Charles Vanda.

Gateway to Hollywood was a series of on-air screen tests, culminating each 13 weeks in a 30-minute drama that determined male and female winners from six finalists. Two glamorous-sounding screen names were concocted for each contest. The winners, said movie mogul Jesse L. Lasky, would "receive their new names" at the end of each competition: they would then "own" these names, which had been publicized on the air each week and were thus estimated to be worth "thousands of dollars." The winners would also receive Screen Actors Guild membership cards and would instantly become part of the motion picture industry. Five judges from RKO would make the selections, basing their decisions on photographic potential, personality, and dramatic ability.

In the first competition, concluding April 2, Rowena Cook and Ralph Bowman received the names Alice Eden and John Archer (Archer later played the Shadow for a time). On July 1, Dorothy Howe and Kirby Grant won the names Virginia Vale and Robert Stanton. The final winners were Josephine Cottle, a 17-year-old high school student from Houston, Tex., and Lee Bonnell. Cottle became Gale Storm and went on to a lukewarm film career and stardom on early TV, notably as the good-natured daughter in *My Little Margie*. Bonnell's career as Terry Belmont was less distinguished, but he did, in real life, marry Gale Storm.

THE GAY MRS. FEATHERSTONE, situation comedy.

BROADCAST HISTORY: April 18–Oct. 10, 1945, NBC. 30m, Wednesdays at 8:30. Raleigh Cigarettes.

CAST: Billie Burke as Mrs. Featherstone, a woman who tinkered rather than meddled in the lives of her daughter and son-in law, with whom she lived. Also: John Brown, Florence Lake. ANNOUNCER: Marvin Miller.

THE GAY NINETIES REVUE, musical variety.

BROADCAST HISTORY: July 2, 1939–Nov. 13, 1944, CBS. 30m, Saturdays, various times, 1939–41; Mondays at 8:30 for Model Tobacco, 1941–44. CAST: Joe Howard, host. Beatrice Kay, lead singer, 1939–43; Lillian Leonard thereafter. Genevieve Rowe, soprano. Billy Greene, comedian; Danny Donovan, comedian, 1943–44. Frank Lovejoy as a color character named Broadway Harry. Harmony by the Elm City Four, a barbershop quartet (Philip Reep, Claude Reese, Darrel Woodyard, and Hubie Hendry), and by the Floradora Girls (Elizabeth Newberger, Marjorie Bullard, and Ann Seaton). ANNOUNCER: John Reed King. ORCHESTRA: Ray Bloch. PRODUCER: Al Rinker.

Nov. 11, 1944–April 28, 1945, NBC. 30m, Saturdays at 8. Spinoff series: *Gaslight Gayeties*. Procter & Gamble. CAST: Beatrice Kay, Gay Nineties songstress. Sally Sweetland, soprano. Michael O'Shea, singing host. The Rockaway Four (Bill Days, Art Davies, Frank Holliday, and Harry Stanton). The Daisy Belles (personnel unknown). ORCHESTRA: Charles "Bud" Dant.

Aug. 14–Sept. 4, 1946, Mutual. 30m, Wednesdays at 10. Spinoff series: *The Beatrice Kay Show*. STAR: Beatrice Kay, first lady of "Mrs. Patch's School of the Theater." VOCAL GROUP: The Elm City Four. ORCHESTRA: Sylvan Levin. DIRECTOR: Herb Polesie. WRITERS: Howard Merrill and Coleman Jacoby. THEMES: *Row Row Away* (opening); *The Strawberry Blonde* (closing).

The Gay Nineties Revue (and the two spinoffs that followed it) was the nostalgia of the '40s, taking a look at what America was singing, saying, and dancing to in the days of gaslights and horse-drawn carriages. Joe Howard, master of ceremonies for the original show, was 73, said to be the oldest man ever to host a major network radio series. Howard had written more than 500 songs, including the all-time barbershop favorite, *I Wonder Who's Kissing Her Now*.

But it was Beatrice Kay, playful songstress, who gave Howard's music airs of burlesque and melodrama, and stole the show. The themes, said *Radio Life*, were "broken hearts, trusts betrayed, weeping women under weeping willows, and faded floral wreaths on forgotten graves," and Kay delivered them with a "raspy" voice that was well suited to the material. The cast dressed in period costumes for the broadcasts.

Gaslight Gayeties was a veritable continuation of the original show, the staples such favorites as *After the Ball, Tell Me Pretty Maiden*, and *On Moonlight Bay*. The short-lived *Beatrice Kay Show* attempted to set the old tunes into a thin storyline.

GENE AND GLENN, comedy duo.

BROADCAST HISTORY: Sept. 29, 1930–Dec. 31, 1932, NBC. 15m, six a week at 8 A.M. *The Quaker Early Birds Program*. Quaker Oats.

April 23–Nov. 30, 1934, NBC. 15m, weeknights at 7:15. Gillette.

Sept. 26, 1938–Aug. 31, 1941, NBC. 15m, mostly six a week at 8:15 or 8:30 A.M.

CAST: Gene Carroll and Glenn Rowell as themselves. Gene Carroll also in the voices of "Jake and Lena," handyman and owner of a boarding house where Gene and Glenn allegedly lived.

Comedian Gene Carroll first experimented with voices on a Tony Wons broadcast at WLS, Chicago in the late 1920s. Wons had a feature called *Woodside Theater*, in which he told stories and played all voices himself, but on a dramatization of *Rip Van Winkle*, Wons couldn't get his voice "up" for Rip's wife. Carroll was called in to play the part. An announcer proclaimed his performance "just like Jake" and invited him to return sometime and bring his "girl Lena" with him.

Later, Carroll found himself on a *National Barn Dance* program with the same announcer. "Lena" was demanded and performed, and Carroll found in himself the ability to do quick voice changes. With practice, he could switch from his normal voice to Jake and Lena so casually that listeners argued over how many people were actually on the air.

When he teamed up with Glenn Rowell, the distinction became even more difficult. Often they recorded themselves in dialogue, then played the record on the air and augmented it with live dialogue, making it seem that the studio was full of actors. A controversy arose briefly over Lena's morality when a church group figured out that Lena was living in a boarding house without benefit of matrimony. But it came to little, and the pair remained popular, both nationally and locally, for more than a decade. Aside from their *Quaker Early Birds* broadcasts, they worked in Cleveland radio, sponsored for years by Spang Bakery. They dissolved their team in 1943, Rowell settling in Hartford, Conn., Carroll returning to Cleveland to broadcast again for Spang Bakery. Carroll again hit the network in 1947, joining *Fibber McGee and Molly* as Lena, the McGees' maid.

GENE AUTRY'S MELODY RANCH, western musical variety; adventure drama.

BROADCAST HISTORY: Jan. 7, 1940–Aug. 1, 1943, CBS. 30m, Sundays at 6:30. Wrigley's Gum.

Sept. 23, 1945–May 13, 1956, CBS. 15m until June 16, 1946, then 30m. Sundays at 7, 1946–48; Saturdays at 8, 1948–51; Sundays at 6, 1953–56. Wrigley's Gum.

CAST: Gene Autry, Republic Pictures cowboy star. Pat Buttram, his sidekick. Johnny Bond, who joined the show in 1941, doubling in music and comedy. Carl Cotner, steel guitar player. Vocal groups including the King Sisters, the Pinafores, Cotner's Melody Ranch Six, the Gene Autry Blue Jeans, and, notably, the Cass County Boys (Bert Dobson, Fred Martin, and Jerry Scroggins). Sara Berner in various dramatic roles, often Mexican señoritas. Also: Frankie Marvin, Alvino Rey, Eddie Dean, Jimmy Wakely, Harry Lang, Jack Mather, Horace Murphy, Jerry Hausner. **ANNOUNCERS:** Tom Hanlon, Lou Crosby, Charlie Lyon. **PRODUCER:** Bill Burch. **SOUND EFFECTS:** Jerry McCarty, Gene Twombly, Ray Erlenborn, David Light, Gus Bayz. **THEME:** *Back in the Saddle Again.*

Melody Ranch enjoyed one of the longest, steadiest runs on the air. The only break in a 16-year radio stint came when the star, Gene Autry, joined the Army Air Corps. Autry took his oath on the air in July 1942; his show departed the following season. Otherwise, he enjoyed an unfettered run on the same network for the same sponsor, "healthful, refreshing Doublemint Gum."

Autry was born Sept. 29, 1907, in Tioga, Tex. He had many jobs as a young man, losing several because of his frequent singing, to a self-taught guitar. He worked on ranches in Texas and Oklahoma; in later life he enjoyed telling how Will Rogers had come into a telegraph office where he was working, heard him sing, and encouraged him to pursue it. His voice led inevitably to radio. He sang on KVOO, Tulsa, in 1930, billed as "Oklahoma's Yodeling Cowboy" and telling tales of the trail. In 1931 he sang on WLS, Chicago, for $35 a week. He was also heard on *The National Barn Dance* and *The National Farm and Home Hour*.

Autry's screen career began in 1934, when he joined Republic as a star of B-grade westerns. Oddly, he became one of the top stars in America via the Saturday matinee route. By the mid to late 1930s, he was making guest appearances on such major variety shows as Rudy Vallee's *Fleischmann Hour* and *The Eddie Cantor Show*.

He was on the set of *Shooting High*, his 39th film, when Danny Danker of J. Walter Thompson called. Autry told longtime sidekicks Frankie Marvin and Carl Cotner to pack their fiddles:

they were going to audition for the Wrigley people at CBS.

The show changed little over the years. Longtime announcer Lou Crosby opened it with the phrase "Where the pavement ends and the West begins." The setting purported to be Autry's home, the real Melody Ranch in the San Fernando hills. His regular cast consisted of many sidekicks from his pictures, a few of whom had been with him since his stage show days of the early 1930s. Frankie Marvin, who had known Autry since 1927, appeared on the first broadcast. Carl Cotner was in Autry's company some 40 years. Pat Buttram was Autry's best-known sidekick, his routines audio slapstick. "Mister Artery," he would croak, and the banter between them was sure to end with Autry's exasperated groan. "Patrick, how can you be so stupid?" Autry would ask. The reply was obvious. "Well, it ain't easy when you ain't got no brains."

Autry's dramas were fully realized 10- to 15-minute stories about rustlers and owlhoots, with Autry of course the two-fisted hero. Announcer Charlie Lyon was well remembered for his opening signature of the late 1940s: "Now here's the boss man himself, America's favorite cowboy, Gene Autry!"

THE GEORGE JESSEL SHOW, comedy-variety.

BROADCAST HISTORY: Jan. 2–Aug. 26, 1934, CBS. 30m, Tuesdays at 9:30; then Saturdays at 8:30. Singers Mildred Bailey and Vera Van, with the Freddie Rich Orchestra, ca. Jan.–May. Heard as *George Jessel Variety Hour* beginning June 17, 60m, Sundays at 8.

Oct. 10, 1937–July 3, 1938, Mutual. 30m, Sundays at 6. *Thirty Minutes in Hollywood.* CAST: Singer Amy Arnell. Josephine Starr (the "wonder child"). Dorothy McNulty as Jessel's secretary. Frequent costar: film actress Norma Talmadge, Jessel's wife. ORCHESTRA: Tommy Tucker. DIRECTOR: Ward Byron. WRITER: Sam Carlton. THEME: *California, Here I Come.* SECONDARY THEME: *Give My Regards to Broadway*, as Jessel was introduced.

March 21, 1939–March 28, 1940, NBC. Jessell joined, as emcee, the series *For Men Only*, in progress since Jan. 10, 1938; the cast then included Fred Uttal, Peg La Centra, the Merry Macs, and Peter Van Steeden's Orchestra; various days and times. Became *George Jessel's Celebrity Program*, with the Merry Macs and Van Steeden's Orchestra, ca. autumn 1939; various 30m timeslots; Vitalis.

Oct. 15, 1953–Jan. 28, 1954, ABC. 30m, Thursdays at 9. *George Jessel Salutes.* CAST: Little Jack Little, Shirley Harmer.

George Jessel may have been one of the best-known American entertainers, but he never made any headway in radio. Vaudeville star, renowned toastmaster—none of it mattered: Jessel's radio shows were plagued by little excitement, no appreciable ratings strength, and no encore seasons.

His 1937–38 series for Mutual failed even with Norma Talmadge as his costar. Guests included oldtime comics Joe Weber and Lew Fields, Hildegarde, the Our Gang Kids, Gus Edwards, Larry "Buster" Crabbe, and Sigmund Romberg. Mutual tried but was unable to sell it: it was heard under the auspices of such local sponsors as the Southern California Association of Fresh Fish Dealers. Jessel's lack of success in radio was explained as (1) he was uncomfortable with the precise timing required by the medium, (2) he felt restrained by the scripts, and (3) his material was of primary relevance to New Yorkers and was lost on listeners in the "outer regions."

G. I. LAFFS, variety gagfest, with gags sent in by GIs.

BROADCAST HISTORY: June 28–Aug. 22, 1945, CBS. 30m, Thursdays, then Wednesdays. CAST: William Gargan, host. Martha Mears, singer. MUSIC: Ivan Ditmars. PRODUCER: Charles Vanda. DIRECTOR: Arthur Q. Bryan.

THE GIBSON FAMILY, musical comedy.

BROADCAST HISTORY: Sept. 15, 1934–June 23, 1935, NBC. 60m, Saturdays at 9:30 until March 31, then Sundays at 8. Procter & Gable. Continued June 30–Sept. 8, 1935, as *Uncle Charlie's Tent Show.*

CAST: *Speaking roles*: Adele Ronson as Sally Gibson. Jack Clemens as her brother, Bobby Gibson. Warren Hull as Jack Hamilton, the robust hero in pursuit of Sally. Loretta Clemens as Dotty Marsh. Jack Roseleigh and Anne Elstner as Pa and Ma Gibson. Ernie "Bubbles" Whitman, "popular colored comedian," as Awful, the butler. *Singing roles*: Lois Bennett as Sally Gibson. Conrad Thibault as Jack Hamilton. Jack and Loretta Clemens sang their own roles. **ANNOUNCER:** Jimmy Wallington. **ORCHESTRA:** Don Voorhees, directing 30 pieces. **DIRECTOR:** Carlo De Angelo. **WRITERS (MUSIC AND LYRICS):** Howard Dietz and Arthur Schwartz. **WRITERS (BOOK):** Courtney Ryley Cooper; Owen Davis.

The Gibson Family was the major flop of the 1934–35 season, gulping half a million Procter & Gamble dollars in a spectacular attempt to create a musical comedy especially for the air. The notion looked good on paper: engage a top music-and-lyrics team from Broadway and have them write a show, with bright new musical numbers, just for radio; get a novelist to write the "book"; and hire the best singing voices for the leading roles.

This was not a new idea. Others had considered it and shelved it as too expensive, difficult and risky. But P&G and its agency men were intrigued, enough to launch it wholeheartedly. In Dietz and Schwartz, they obtained one of the country's top songwriting teams, authors of *The Bandwagon, Three's a Crowd,* and *Flying Colors.* Courtney Ryley Cooper, certainly a successful novelist, did the scripting. But after months of collaboration, this triad emerged with an ordinary continuation of "an average family in an average American community, somewhere in the United States." The parents, Ma and Pa Gibson, were a bit rustic, but their children, Bobby and Sally, were singers of no small ability. The plot turned on simple romance, with Sally wooed by the hero, Jack Hamilton.

It took to the air, said *Radio Guide,* "amid terrific fanfare and hullabaloo. Writers and critics everywhere hailed *The Gibson Family* as something new and worthwhile." The Dietz-Schwartz songs were termed excellent, and the Cooper script was said to be at least adequate. But some "vital spark" was missing. The audience left early, its numbers fading with each week. A new writer, Owen Davis, was brought in to replace Cooper, to no avail. The timeslot was changed, but nothing helped. A meeting between the sponsors and producers resulted in radical surgery. Director De Angelo suggested what was embraced as a brilliant idea—to bring in Charles Winninger, erstwhile Captain Henry of the Maxwell House *Show Boat,* to top the cast.

The format, too, would be revised, to suit Winninger's image and personality. He would play "Uncle Charlie," head of a group of tent show performers. The cast of *The Gibson Family* would blend into this environment, and the show would usurp (it was hoped) much of the huge *Show Boat* audience of years gone by. Winninger was aboard by June 16, 1935, though the show was still called *The Gibson Family.* By June 30 it had become *Uncle Charlie's Tent Show,* with Winninger barking, "Hurry-hurry-hurry, just-a warmin' up, folks," and describing an array of "freaks, midgets, and snake-charmers" parading before his tent. Lois Bennett continued the singing role of Sally Gibson; Anne Teeman now performed the spoken lines. Suitor Jack Hamilton was dropped from the show, but Conrad Thibault continued singing romantic ballads. Jack and Loretta Clemens were retained in their *Gibson* characters, and Ernie "Bubbles" Whitman was joined by Negro comic Eddie Green (they played characters named Sam and Jerry and were billed as "the only colored comics" in network radio). Voorhees continued as maestro, and vocal numbers were by the Ivory City Four (Bob Moody, Lou Stokes, Scrappy Lambert, and Randolph Weyant), under the direction of Ken Christie. The new writers were Tom McKnight (story) and Mort Lewis (comedy). But despite Winninger's great national popularity, the new format failed to generate much listener response, and Procter & Gamble finally cut its losses nine weeks later.

THE GINNY SIMMS SHOW, musical variety.

BROADCAST HISTORY: Sept. 19, 1941–May 29, 1942, CBS. 5m, Fridays at 9:55.

Sept. 8, 1942–Sept. 4, 1945, NBC. 30m, Tuesdays at 8. Philip Morris. Originally *Johnny Presents,* a sponsor-related title (see THE PHILIP MORRIS PLAYHOUSE); later *The Purple Heart Show,* with emphasis on wounded servicemen; still later (summer 1945) *Talent Theater,* with Simms interviewing returning service personnel who had been in show business before the war. **ANNOUNCER:** Frank Graham. **ORCHESTRA:** David Rose (1942), Edgar "Cookie" Fairchild (1943–45).

Sept. 28, 1945–June 13, 1947, CBS. 30m, Fridays at 7:30, 1945–46; at 9, 1946–47. Borden's Milk. **COMEDIAN:** Donald O'Connor (1947). **ANNOUNCER:** Don Wilson (ca. 1945). **MUSIC:** Frank De Vol.

Sept. 17, 1950–March 18, 1951, ABC. 15m, Sundays at 10. *The Botany Song Shop*. Botany Mills. **Music:** The Buddy Cole Trio.

Ginny Simms was a popular singer with Kay Kyser's orchestra and on *The Bob Burns Show*.

GIRL ALONE, soap opera.

Broadcast history: July 8, 1935–April 25, 1941, NBC. Aired from Chicago. 15m, weekdays at 4:30, 1935–36; at noon, 1936–38; at 4:45, 1938–39; at 5, 1939–41. Kellogg, 1936–38; Quaker Oats, 1938–41.

Cast: Betty Winkler as Patricia Rogers, who inherited a fortune and fell in love with John Knight, trustee of her estate. Karl Weber as John Knight; Les Damon, Macdonald Carey, Bob Bailey, and Syd Simons also as John. Don Briggs as Scoop Curtis, the Phoenix newspaper reporter with whom Patricia began a love affair after she and John Knight parted and she left Chicago; Pat Murphy and Arthur Jacobson also as Scoop Curtis. Laurette Fillbrandt and Joan Winters as Patricia's friends, Virginia Hardesty and Alice Ames. June Travis as Stormy Wilson, member of a traveling daredevil troupe, who married Scoop Curtis after he, paralyzed in an auto accident, rejected Patricia in the belief that her concern was motivated by pity. **Announcers:** Bob Brown (1936); Charles Lyon (ca. 1938). **Directors:** Gordon Hughes; Axel Gruenberg. **Writer:** Fayette Krum.

GIVE AND TAKE, quiz.

Broadcast history: Aug. 25, 1945–Dec. 26, 1953, CBS. Various 30m timeslots; usually Saturdays, occasionally weekdays. Chef Boyardee, 1945–46; Toni, 1946–51; Cannon Mills, 1951–53.

John Reed King was host for this simple quiz format. Contestants were shown a prize-laden table, picked prizes, and answered questions.

GLAMOUR MANOR, situation comedy, musical variety, audience interview.

Broadcast history: July 3, 1944–June 27, 1947, Blue Network/ABC. 30m, weekdays at noon; Procter & Gamble. A show with a convoluted history, several format changes, various personnel changes.

1944: From Hollywood. **Cast:** Cliff Arquette as the manager of the Glamour Manor Hotel; also as Captain Billy, and as Mrs. Wilson, an elderly female impersonation he used for years. Tyler McVey as Tyler the desk clerk. Lurene Tuttle as Gloria Kenyon, Tyler's girlfriend. John McIntire as Hamlet Mantel. Bea Benaderet as Wanda Werewolf. Will Wright as Maloney. **Announcers:** Jack Bailey and Terry O'Sullivan for Crisco and Ivory Snow respectively (Bob Bruce the Crisco man after Bailey left for *Queen for a Day*). **Vocalist:** Ernie Newton. **Music:** Charles "Bud" Dant. **Theme:** *There's a Small Hotel*.

Jan. 1945: Move to New York. **Cast:** Arquette and McVey continued their roles from the East. Jan Miner briefly as Gloria; Virginia Vass later in the New York run as Gloria. **Vocalist:** Jack Smith. **Orchestra:** Harry Lubin.

Fall 1945: Return to Hollywood. **Cast:** Arquette, McVey, Vass, and maestro Lubin moved with the show. Ernie Newton rejoined as vocalist. Michael Raffetto as Chief Quigley, the hotel cook, whose role was just a front to extoll the virtues of Crisco. **Announcer:** Rod O'Connor.

June 1946: Arquette resigned to work in nighttime radio. **Cast:** Kenny Baker as the new singing proprietor of Glamour Manor, a slightly addled emcee. Barbara Eiler as Baker's girlfriend, the hotel bookkeeper, Barbara Dilley. Don Wilson as the star boarder, generous with bad advice. Sam Hearn as Schlepperman, a village idiot who usually managed to deepen whatever trouble Wilson had initiated. Elvia Allman as Mrs. Biddle, a socialite. **Announcer:** Don Wilson. **Orchestra:** Harry Lubin. **Director:** Ken Burton.

Glamour Manor was part of an NBC effort to bring a nighttime sound to daytime radio. It was unusual in that, twice a week, it departed from the sitcom and became an audience interview show. The misadventures of the hotel people were dramatized on Mondays, Wednesdays, and Fridays, while on Tuesdays and Thursdays Cliff Arquette and Lurene Tuttle conducted lively talks in the audience. These interview segments continued after the cast change in 1946.

THE GOLD DUST TWINS, early musical variety.

Broadcast history: 1923–26, WEAF, New York.

The Gold Dust Twins were Harvey Hindermeyer and Earl Tuckerman. Their joint career was played out mainly in radio's earliest days, before the rise of national networks. They were heard on WEAF and later on an eight-city hookup that took them to Providence, Buffalo, as far west as Pittsburgh and Cleveland, and south to Philadelphia. They broadcast anonymously, taking as their air names "Goldy" and "Dusty," on behalf of their sponsor, Gold Dust (scouring) Powder. There were no overt commercials, so the promotion of the product through the names was Gold Dust's main benefit. They sang light novelty numbers, often in Negro dialect. *Hear Dem Bells* was a favorite. In publicity stills, they posed in burnt cork and kinked hair. Their catchphrase, opening and closing, was an invitation to let them "brighten the corner where you live."

THE GOLDBERGS, serialized comedy-drama.

BROADCAST HISTORY: Nov. 20, 1929–May 23, 1931, Blue Network. 15m, Wednesdays at 7:15, 1929–30; Saturdays at 7:30, 1930–31. *The Rise of the Goldbergs.*

July 13, 1931–July 6, 1934, NBC. 15m, six a week at 7:45 until 1932, then five a week. Pepsodent.

Jan. 13–July 10, 1936, CBS. 15m, weekdays at 5:45 until May, then at 11 A.M.

Sept. 13–Dec. 31, 1937, NBC. 15m, weekdays at 12:15. Oxydol.

Jan. 3, 1938–March 30, 1945, CBS. 15m, weekdays, various times. Oxydol. Also heard on WOR, ca. 1938–40, weekdays at 8:45 A.M.; also on NBC, briefly, beginning June 1941.

Sept. 2, 1949–June 24, 1950, CBS. 30m weekly sitcom, Fridays at 8 until Feb. 1950, then Saturdays at 8:30. General Foods. (This run closely followed the TV series, which had premiered on CBS, Jan. 10, 1949).

CAST: Gertrude Berg as Molly Goldberg. James R. Waters as Jake Goldberg, her husband. Alfred Ryder and Roslyn Silber as Sammy and Rosalie, their children. Everett Sloane as Sammy, late 1930s. Menasha Skulnik as Uncle David. Anne Teeman as Joyce. Helene Dumas as Edna. Sidney Slon as Solly. Joan Tetzel as Jane. Arnold Stang as Seymour Fingerhood. Zina Provendie as Sylvia. Bruno Wick as Mr. Fowler, the handyman. Artie Auerbach as Mr. Schneider. Joan Vitez as Esther. Howard Merrill as Mickey Bloom. Carrie Weller as Martha Wilberforce. Jeanette Chinley as Libby. Tito Vuolo as Uncle Carlo. THEME: *Toselli's Serenade*, on organ.

CAST: 1949–50, identical with TV show: Gertrude Berg as Molly. Philip Loeb as Jake. Larry Robinson as Sammy. Arlene McQuade as Rosalie. Eli Mintz as Uncle David.

Gertrude Berg created an image of herself on paper, then found it nationally accepted as a true reflection of an entire ethnic group. Her Molly Goldberg possessed to millions the breath of the Jewish ghetto. It was a world Berg knew well, though she never lived there.

She was born Gertrude Edelstein in Harlem, Oct. 3, 1899. At 19 she married Lewis Berg, spending the next decade as a housewife and mother. During this time she wrote out her first skits, telling of a middle-aged Jewish woman whose husband was "a no-good." The husband, she explained in her memoir, "wasn't bad by intention, just by circumstance, and could he help it if women happened to fall in love with him?"

Her character changed as she did. "I gave her a new husband, one who wasn't such trouble and who was a little more helpful. I gave her two children, a boy and a girl more than a little like my two." Her name became Molly. She chose the surname Goldberg "because it sounded right and that was the only reason." Her husband became Jake, named for her father. The children were Sammy and Rosalie.

Now came the matter of getting it on the air. She was given an audition, and a job reading a commercial in Yiddish on WMCA. She wrote a new skit, called *Effie and Laura*, and took it cold, "trembling, in fact," to CBS. The show was scheduled but canceled after one performance. That fall, she finished another script based on her Goldberg family: it was called *The Rise of the Goldbergs*, and it followed Jake, "a cloak-and-suit operator," as he struggled to raise his family in the tenements.

She took this script to NBC, whose executives mulled it over for two weeks. They offered her a one-month contract at $75 a week, and she was expected to pay the cast. The original family members, Berg, James Waters, Alfred Ryder, and Roslyn Silber, played the roles for more than 15 years.

The stories revolved around Molly's relation-

ship with her vigorous and sometimes fiery husband ("Now I want it understood that I'm the
head of this house and I will not stand for any
more of this shilly-shallying!"), the children, or
Molly's Uncle David on her father's side. The
Goldbergs lived at the mythical address 1038
East Tremont Avenue, which Berg later identified as an intersection in the Bronx. It may have
been the least tense of all daytime dramas.
Shows were done on concepts as basic as a visitor coming to supper, Sammy bringing home a
report card, Rosalie's graduation, or Sammy's
bar mitzvah. Molly was a kindly homespun philosopher who "yoo-hooed" her way through
life; Jake was a poor tailor; and Uncle David was
added to the family after the show was under
way.

After a short trial as a weekly show, the serial
leaped to a 1932 rating of 25 points, becoming
one of the all-time favorites of the air. Berg journeyed into the Lower East Side for her research,
browsing among the rat-infested tenements, vegetable stands, and pushcarts. She went incognito,
to avoid inhibiting the people with her celebrity.
She did take a *Radio Mirror* reporter on a tour
through narrow Orchard Street in 1936, showing
him the wellspring of *The Goldbergs*. Another
reporter, Ben Gross of the *New York Daily News*,
found her browsing among peddlers in Allen
Street. She was keeping in touch, she said: if she
stayed away from the well too long, she lost her
ability to render it truly on air.

It was the first Jewish comedy, an innovation
when Phillips Carlin, then chief of sustaining
shows at the Blue Network, decided to schedule
it in 1929. It was Berg's show, beginning to end.
As sole owner, she was a benevolent dictator,
insisting on control over even the sound effects.
Everything was authentic: when a scene was set
in the Goldberg kitchen, Berg broke real eggs
into a real frying pan, and each member of the
cast rattled his own china. Once she gave Roslyn
Silber an on-air shampoo, when the script called
for Molly to wash Rosalie's hair. Her ear for the
dialect was critically tuned for each reading. Said
William Birnie in *American Magazine*, "I've
watched her make Waters, who has played Jake
for ten years, repeat a simple line like 'Sammy,
you're breaking your father's heart,' 17 or 18
times, until she feels it will register with the unseen audience."

By then the characters were so familiar that
Berg could write a script in half an hour. "Once
when an important character failed to show up
at the last moment, she turned out an entirely
new script in eight minutes flat," Birnie wrote.
Molly must have "yoo-hooed" a lot in that one,
a radio actress said in obvious disbelief, hearing
the tale years later. But when *The Goldbergs* was
at its peak, Berg was writing and starring in two
shows a day and turning out a soap opera, *Kate
Hopkins*, at the same time.

There was something "cosmic and compelling
in the humanity of the Goldbergs," wrote Birnie.
Time put it another way: Berg played Molly
"with a full complement of shrugs, flutters, malapropisms, and a passionate capacity for making
something dramatic of the commonplace." It
bore a fundamental rather than superficial resemblance to *One Man's Family*: the kids grew up,
changed, got married; the parents got plump, old,
and fretful. Through it all Molly was the wise
mother figure whose best pearls of wisdom
("better a crust of bread and enjoy it than a cake
that gives you indigestion") were often
ad-libbed. Her one-way conversations up the
dumbwaiter with the unheard Mrs. Bloom
("Yoooooo-hooooo, Mrs. Bloooo-oooom!"),
her worries about the premature loves of Sammy
and Rosalie, her efforts to keep Jake's blood
pressure out of the stratosphere, all contributed
to one of radio's most unusual success stories.

A Goldbergs play was staged on Broadway.
The show became one of the smash hits of early
television, seen on various networks for four
years. A feature-length film, *Molly*, was released
in 1951. The character seemed eternal until Gertrude Berg died, Sept. 14, 1966. But the original
concept died with the demise of those quarter-
hour vignettes in 1945. Seldom thereafter would
Berg venture into the ghetto. "It's hard, darling," she told a *Newsweek* reporter with the advent of the television show in 1949. "Everybody
now is getting to know what I look like."

GOOD NEWS OF 1938, musical variety.

BROADCAST HISTORY: Nov. 4, 1937–July 25,
1940, NBC. 60m, Thursdays at 9 until March
1940, then 30m; Thursdays at 8 from July 1940.
Titled by year, *Good News of 1939, 1940* became
Maxwell House Coffee Time to begin the 1940–41

season, though the *Good News* title was still used for a few broadcasts. Maxwell House Coffee.

CAST: Hosts: James Stewart, 1937; Robert Taylor, early to mid-1938; Robert Young, beginning in fall 1938; various hosts, 1939–40; Dick Powell, ca. 1940. Frank Morgan, resident comic. Fanny Brice as Baby Snooks beginning Dec. 23, 1937. Hanley Stafford as Daddy. Also many MGM film stars including Judy Garland, Joan Crawford, Mickey Rooney, Alice Faye, Spencer Tracy, Lionel Barrymore, Clark Gable, etc. ANNOUNCERS: Ted Pearson, Warren Hull. MUSICAL DIRECTOR: Meredith Willson. DIRECTORS: Ed Gardner, etc. THEME: *Always and Always.*

Good News of 1938 was announced as the most spectacular radio show ever launched, though the finished product fell somewhat short of preshow hyperbole. It did, as *Newsweek* pointed out, mark the "first major collaboration of a movie studio and a broadcasting system in behalf of a commercial sponsor." The result cost Maxwell House $25,000 a week for a series that drew lukewarm critical response.

The idea was, simply put, to "dazzle 'em with glitter." Metro Goldwyn Mayer would produce it, making every star in its fold ("except Garbo") available for the air. It would be big-time variety, with stories and songs, musical comedy, and intimate glimpses of Hollywood with its hair down. Each week a new MGM film would be previewed in fully dramatized capsule versions, with the original stars in the radio roles. One of the features, "Backstage at the Movies," would let listeners in on executive conferences at MGM; listeners would get audio tours of favored stars' dressing rooms. It was seen as a splashy successor to the Maxwell House *Show Boat*, which had had five successful seasons in the Thursday-at-9 hour and was now being dropped.

The signatures were done to the famed MGM trademark, the roar of Leo the Lion. The concept created a mild sensation in Hollywood, where Paramount and Warner Brothers immediately began laying plans to follow suit. But by the time the show was a month old, critics were complaining that something was lacking. "Listeners couldn't decide," said *Newsweek*, "whether Metro Goldwyn Mayer was trying to sell Maxwell House, or if the coffeemakers were putting

out Metro Goldwyn Mayer in airtight containers." There was too much control by the studio. MGM's primary interest seemed to be self-promotion, and that didn't play well on radio.

After eight weeks on the air, Fanny Brice was added, effectively launching her Baby Snooks broadcasting career. Mary Martin was a regular vocalist in 1940, near the end of the *Good News* format. The music was lush, with Meredith Willson offering both popular music and original works in the classical mode—pieces written by such as Peter de Rose, Morton Gould, Dana Suesse, and himself.

THE GOODRICH SILVERTOWN ORCHESTRA, musical variety for B. F. Goodrich.

BROADCAST HISTORY: Feb. 12, 1925–July 11, 1928, WEAF, New York, joining with NBC as of Nov. 18, 1926. 60m, Thursdays at 10 through Nov. 11, 1926, then at 9 (1926–27), then Wednesdays at 9:30 (1927–28). Various titles: *Silvertown Orchestra; The Goodrich Zippers; The Silvertown Zippers; The Silvertown Cord Orchestra; Silvertown Quartet.*

Ca. 1935–36, 15m transcribed syndication. B. A. Rolfe, maestro.

March 8–Aug. 2, 1935, NBC. See THE JOE COOK SHOW, aka CIRCUS NIGHT IN SILVERTOWN.

The Goodrich show of 1925 brought radio its first singing heartthrob, Joe White, "the Silver-Masked Tenor." White had been singing on WEAF since 1923, but the addition of the silver mask and the well-guarded secret of his identity brought him vast popularity. He received bags of mail from lovesick women, and when the orchestra joined the Keith vaudeville circuit, White had to be escorted into theaters by police.

But his popularity was brief. Most of the fun, it seemed, was in the guessing (many guessed him to be tenor John McCormack), and when his identity was finally revealed, his career went into a decline. He was still a formidable personality in 1926, performing on NBC periodically through the 1930s. But he had few regular network slots (one noted on the Blue Network, Wednesdays at 3, 1934–35), and by 1940 he was considered a topic of nostalgia.

With the advent of NBC in November 1926, Goodrich began emphasizing its small banjo ensemble, the Zippers, which held the spotlight for two seasons.

GOODWILL COURT, human interest; legal advice.

BROADCAST HISTORY: 1935–36, WMCA, New York (premiere date March 31, 1935).

Sept. 20–Dec. 20, 1936, NBC. 60m, Sundays at 8. Chase and Sanborn.

HOST: A. L. Alexander.

Goodwill Court offered legal help to the poor, long before such terms as "legal aid" became common. The subjects were simply required to come before an NBC microphone and tell their stories to the nation. Their identities were protected, and they were ever under the eye of mediator A. L. Alexander, lest profanity or the name of an actual person slip out over the the air. The people told of marital trouble, of garnished wages and loan sharks, of all the little tragedies common to the average listener. It made compelling radio for its day.

It was created by Alexander while he was working as a staff announcer at WMCA, New York. Alexander had been a police reporter and had seen some of the inequities of the legal system. With his radio show, he proposed to do something about them. His initial shows were too general and drew little response, so Alexander keyed in on specific problems. He went into courtrooms and asked defendants if they would discuss their cases on the air. He then created a legal panel to hear the cases and offer advice. Jonah J. Goldstein and Pelham St. George Bissell, a pair of New York judges, agreed to sit.

The show was an immediate sensation. Alexander offered as many as 15 cases per session. His staff answered all mail, giving advice even to those who were not chosen to appear. More than 40 judges were heard over the short run of *Goodwill Court.*

The show had an equally brilliant success on the network, rocketing into the top ten almost immediately. But its sudden national prominence brought it under fire from the legal establishment. The New York County Lawyers' Association rose up against it, and less than three months after its national premiere, *Goodwill Court* was squashed. The New York Supreme Court barred judges and lawyers from appearing,

Chase and Sanborn dropped it, and the show was dead in the water. But during its tenure, its staff answered 6,000 questions from people who could not afford attorneys.

In 1943 Alexander returned with a similar series, *A. L. Alexander's Mediation Board,* which offered a panel of sociologists and educators. But the novelty was gone, and it never approached the wildfire success of *Goodwill Court.*

THE GOODWILL HOUR, human interest; advice.

BROADCAST HISTORY: 1937, WMCA, New York.

Aug. 1, 1937–April 14, 1940. Mutual. 30m until Jan. 1938, then 60m, Sundays at 10. McFadden Publications, 1937; Ironized Yeast, 1938–40.

April 21, 1940–Oct. 10, 1943, Blue Network. 60m, Sundays at 10. Ironized Yeast.

Dec. 5, 1943–Nov. 26, 1944, Mutual. 45m, Sundays at 10:15. Clark Gum.

March 19, 1945–Dec. 27, 1946, Mutual. 15m, five a week at 1:45. *The John J. Anthony Program.* Carter Products. Also heard 1947, 1949.

Dec. 9, 1951–Jan. 4, 1953, Mutual. 30m, Sundays at 9:30. *The John J. Anthony Program.* Sterling Drugs.

HOST: John J. Anthony. **ANNOUNCER:** Roland Winters.

The Goodwill Hour was a long reach from *Goodwill Court,* though the concepts were similar and there were connecting links. When *Goodwill Court* was knocked off the air by a 1936 court ruling, a Bronx hustler named Lester Kroll created a format that would capitalize on its popularity while avoiding its legal problems. Instead of using lawyers for his panel of experts, *he* would be the lone voice of authority. He would focus on financial and marital problems and set himself up as an expert in all areas of human relationships. He took for his air name John J. Anthony, complied a resumé that included his alleged establishment of a "Marital Relations Institute" in 1927, and took to the air.

He promptly persuaded WMCA, originator of *Goodwill Court,* to give him a timeslot. By midsummer 1937, the Anthony program was on a national network. Throughout its run, the show was under constant attack by judges, social organizations, and radio critics, many of whom considered Anthony a rogue. As Earl Wilson described him in the *Saturday Evening Post*, there were two John J. Anthonys—"the real one, who struggled upward through the tough, competitive life of New York, and the invented one, sculptured from pure imagination, who supposedly studied under Freud and then was summoned, as a matter of course, to conduct *The Goodwill Hour*." Anthony claimed to have three university degrees: in fact, said Wilson, he had "found American high schools confining and never bothered to finish." Anthony was so thorough in his character self-revision that he decided to make the *J* in his name stand for Jason.

On the air he was a mix of P. T. Barnum and the stern taskmaster. His answers were simple and brief, even to the most difficult of questions; his advice built around fidelity and the Golden Rule. If a person confessed infidelity, which often happened, Anthony unleashed a stern scolding on the air. *Variety* considered the show "revolting drivel," laced with "unintentional pathetic comedy." At times, in the rush of being heard by millions, subjects would reveal startling facts. One woman confessed to murder: another guest revealed plans to kill his girlfriend's new love interest. This did wonders for ratings even as it increased professional suspicion that Anthony was a charlatan.

Anthony draped his show in dignity. He referred to it, simply, as *The Hour*. Announcer Roland Winters opened with the simple statement, "You have a friend and adviser in John J. Anthony, and thousands are happier and more successful today because of John J. Anthony." Then Anthony would hear his first guest, opening with "What is your problem, madam?" (The majority of the guests were women, bringing, in the main, troubles with men.) Only initials were used; even those were fictitious. Frequently he reminded people to use "no names, please." During his heyday, Anthony was widely parodied, the object of many "Ask Mr. Anthony" jokes by Eddie Cantor, Bob Hope, and other comics.

THE GRACIE FIELDS SHOW, musical variety.

BROADCAST HISTORY: Oct. 12, 1942–July 9, 1943, Blue Network. 5m, weeknights at 9:55 until Jan., then 15m, at 10:15. Pall Mall Cigarettes.

Oct. 11, 1943–Jan. 14, 1944, Mutual. 15m, weeknights at 9:15. *The Gracie Fields Victory Show*. American Cigars.

June 11–Aug. 27, 1944, NBC. 30m, Sundays at 8. Substitution for Edgar Bergen. Chase and Sanborn.

Nov. 14, 1944–Feb. 6, 1945, ABC. 30m, Tuesdays at 9. Bristol Myers.

Jan. 11, 1952–Jan. 2, 1953, Mutual. 30m, Fridays at 8:30.

The Gracie Fields Show began in an unusual five-minute format. So enchanted was America with the saucy lady from England that American Tobacco was willing to pay her $2,500 a week. She sang one song and told a humorous story in her thick Manchester brogue. Her voice, in the opinion of one critic, "rivals that of many grand opera stars" and could be used in serious, sentimental, or comedic songs. Favorites were *Ave Maria*, *The White Cliffs of Dover*, and the raucous *Walter, Walter, Lead Me to the Altar*. In her half-hour shows, she was often backed by maestro Lou Bring. Her 1952–53 series was transcribed, featuring the Keynotes (British vocal group), Bernard Braden, and music by Bill Ternent.

GRAMPS, situation comedy.

BROADCAST HISTORY: July 2–Aug. 20, 1947, NBC. 30m, Wednesdays at 8.

CAST: Edgar Stehli as an aging geezer who comes to visit and disrupt the lives of the younger generation. Also: Craig McDonnell, Anne Seymour, Edwin Bruce, Joan Lazer. **PRODUCER:** Daniel Sutter. **DIRECTOR:** Welbourn Kelley.

GRANBY'S GREEN ACRES, situation comedy.

BROADCAST HISTORY: July 3–Aug. 21, 1950, CBS. 30m, Mondays at 9:30.

CAST: Gale Gordon and Bea Benaderet as John and Martha Granby, ex–bank teller and wife who moved to the country to become farmers. Louise Erickson as Janice, their daughter. Parley Baer as Eb, the hired hand. **ANNOUNCER:** Bob LeMond **MUSIC:** Opie Cates. **WRITER-PRODUCER-DIRECTOR:** Jay Sommers.

Granby's Green Acres grew out of characters played by Gale Gordon and Bea Benaderet on the Lucille Ball series *My Favorite Husband*. The names were changed, but the basic characters remained the same.

GRAND CENTRAL STATION, light dramatic anthology.

BROADCAST HISTORY: Oct. 8, 1937–April 15, 1938, Blue Network. 30m, Fridays at 8. Listerine.

April 24, 1938–Oct. 18, 1940, CBS. 30m, various times. Listerine.

Nov. 12, 1940–July, 1, 1941, Blue Network. 30m, Tuesdays at 9. Rinso.

July 9–Oct. 1, 1941, CBS. 30m. Wednesdays at 8. Rinso.

Oct. 10, 1941–July 3, 1942, NBC. 30m, Fridays at 7:30. Rinso.

March 4, 1944–Sept. 5, 1953, CBS. 30m, Saturdays in various timeslots from 11 A.M.–1 P.M. Pillsbury, 1944–51; Toni, 1951–52; Cream of Wheat, 1952–53.

Jan. 18–April 2, 1954, ABC. 25m, weekdays at 11 A.M. Campbell Soups.

CAST: Jack Arthur, longtime narrator. Stuart Metz, Alexander Scourby, narrators. Actors in anthology roles: Helen Claire, Frances Reed, Hume Cronyn, Arnold Moss, Roger DeKoven, Sydney Smith, Nancy Coleman, Martin Ashe, Jim Ameche, etc. ANNOUNCERS: Tom Shirley, Ken Roberts, George Baxter, etc. PRODUCERS: Martin Horrell, Himan Brown, etc. DIRECTORS: Bill Rousseau, Ira Ashley, etc. SOUND EFFECTS: Ed Blainey (NBC), James Rogan and Frank Mellow (CBS), Harold Johnson Jr. (ABC).

Grand Central Station is remembered far more for its opening signature than for its stories. During its heyday, the Pillsbury commercials were worked in from an echo chamber, giving the illusion of an announcer in a giant train terminal: *All aboard for better baking, finer cakes . . . you're on the right track with Pillsbury Sno-Sheen Cake Flour!* Then, in a cascade of words and sound effects, one of the most famous openings in radio:

As a bullet seeks its target, shining rails in every part of our great country are aimed at Grand Central Station, heart of the nation's greatest city. Drawn by the magnetic force of the fantastic metropolis, day and night great trains rush toward the Hudson River, sweep down its eastern bank for 140 miles, flash briefly by the long red row of tenement houses south of 125th Street, dive with a roar into the two-and-one-half-mile tunnel which burrows beneath the glitter and swank of

Park Avenue, and then . . . (*Train sound*: EEEEEEESSSSSSHHHHHHsssss *Grand Central Station!* Crossroads of a million private lives! Gigantic stage on which are played a thousand dramas daily!

The passengers got off the train, and listeners went with one each week. There was no binding theme beyond that: once the Grand Central element was done, it was straight drama thereafter. The stories were generally light comedies and fluffy romance. *Miracle for Christmas*, telling of a bitter man's return to faith, became the standard Yule show.

GRAND HOTEL, light dramatic anthology.

BROADCAST HISTORY: 1930–33; local Chicago radio (premiere Oct. 1, 1930).

Oct. 1, 1933–March 28, 1938, NBC, Blue Network except 1936–37, when aired on Red Network. 30m, various timeslots: Sundays, early evenings, 1933–37; Mondays at 8:30, 1937–38. Campana.

Jan. 7–March 31, 1940, CBS. 25m, Sundays at 1:35. Campana.

Nov. 4, 1944–Oct. 27, 1945, NBC. 30m, Saturdays at 5. Campana.

CAST: Male-female pairings in romantic anthology roles: Don Ameche and Anne Seymour in the early days; later Jim Ameche and Betty Lou Gerson. Most of the Chicago radio contingent worked the show: Les Tremayne, Barbara Luddy, Olan Soulé, Raymond Edward Johnson, etc. DIRECTOR: Joe Ainley, etc.

Like many of these romantic anthologies, the *Grand Hotel* format was mere window dressing to general romance. The opening had a switchboard operator (Betty Winkler) connecting calls to rooms. The people in those rooms became the story of the week. Arch Oboler wrote some early shows.

GRAND MARQUEE, light dramatic anthology.

BROADCAST HISTORY: July 9, 1946–Sept. 25, 1947, NBC. 30m, various times; Thursdays at 7:30 beginning in Dec. Rayve Shampoo, ca. 1947.

CAST: Jim Ameche and Beryl Vaughn in male-female romantic comedies. Olan Soulé later as male lead. Chicago radio personnel in support. PRODUCER-DIRECTOR: Norman Felton. At the opening of each episode, the announcer, as if reading from a theater billboard, promised "another exciting evening in the world of make-believe."

GRAND OLE OPRY, country variety.

BROADCAST HISTORY: 1925–90s, WSM; local Nashville radio. First heard on WSM Nov. 28, 1925. Saturdays, up to four hours.

Oct. 14, 1939–Dec. 28, 1957, NBC. 30m, Saturdays at 10:30 until late 1951, then at 9:30. Prince Albert Tobacco.

CAST: George Dewey Hay, known on the air as "the solemn ole judge." Uncle Jimmy Thompson, fiddler, from 1925. Uncle Dave Macon, banjoist. Harmonicist DeFord Bailey. Other early acts: Humphrey Bate's Possum Hunters; Arthur Smith and his Dixie Liners; Uncle Ed Poplin and his Old-Timers; the Binkley Brothers and their Dixie Clod-hoppers; Paul Warmack and his Gully-Jumpers; Kitty Cora Kline (zither); Kirk and Sam McGee; fiddler Sid Harkreader; George Wilkerson and the Fruit Jar Drinkers, who were said to pass around a jar of moonshine between numbers; Robert Lunn, the "talking blues boy," who for more than ten years sang an endless song in bits and pieces; the Vagabonds (Herald Goodman, Dean Upson, and Curt Poulton); Asher and Little Jimmy Sizemore, father-and-son guitar-and-vocal team; Jam-up and Honey (blackface comics Bunny Biggs and Lee Davis Wilds); Jack Shook and the Missouri Mountaineers; Curly Fox and "Texas" Ruby Owens; Sarie and Sallie (comics Edna Wilson and Margaret Waters); Zeke Clements, the Dixie Yo-deler.

CAST CA. 1930: (from a double-page photograph in *Nashville's Grand Ole Opry*, by Jack Hurst) Buster Bate, Claude Lampley, H. J. Ragsdale, Tom Lefew, George Wilkerson, Charlie Arrington, Tom Andrews, Gayle and Amos Binkley, Oscar Stone, Oscar Albright, Dr. Humphrey Bate, Walter Liggett, Dorris Macon, Uncle Dave Macon, Paul Warmack, Roy Hardison, Burt Hutcherson, Herman and Lewis Crook, Sam and Kirk McGee, Robert Lunn, Bill Etter, Staley Walton, Blythe Poteet, Alton and Rabon Delmore, Dee Simmons, Nap Bastian, George D. Hay, DeFord Bailey (the only black face in the crowd, for a time called the cast "mascot," but a "wizard" on the harmonica, according to Hay). ANNOUNCER: David Stone.

CAST OTHER ERAS: Roy Acuff and his Smoky Mountain Boys; "Cousin" Minnie Pearl (standup comedienne who told of the simple life in Grinders Switch, Tenn.); the Willis Brothers; Bill Monroe; Pee Wee King; Kay Carlisle; Ernest Tubb; Eddy Arnold; Tommy Jackson; Jimmy Selph; George Morgan; Carl Smith; the Carter Sisters; Rod Brasfield; Rachel Veach; Hank Williams; etc.

NETWORK SEGMENT: HOST: Whitey Ford, "the Duke of Paducah." ANNOUNCER: Louie Buck. DIRECTORS: Jack Stapp, Ott Devine, Kenneth W. MacGregor, etc. STAGE MANAGER: Vito Pellettieri.

Grand Ole Opry, king of all hillbilly shows, began almost spontaneously and kept growing until, by the 1990s, it was a national country music institution, far from its hillbilly origins. The catalyst was George Dewey Hay, "the solemn ole judge," who discovered an affinity for simple mountain life on a mule expedition into the Ozarks in his youth. There he found a people unchanged since Valley Forge, and he became an advocate of the primitive (but sometimes startlingly polished) mountain music performed at country dances and socials.

Hay was at WLS, Chicago, in 1924, helping to formulate that other rustic Saturday-nighter, *The National Barn Dance*. He was hired to direct programming at WSM, Nashville, and arrived in 1925 to find a program of country music already in place. Dr. Humphrey Bate and his Possum Hunters had been playing on the station for about a month. Hay believed that such "tuneful melodies" should become a fixed part of the schedule. He heard about an old fiddler named "Uncle" Jimmy Thompson, then 83, who had fought in the Civil War and in a lifetime of fiddling competitions had never been defeated. Hay invited the old man to perform: he scheduled the first broadcast in November 1925, and Thompson—accompanied on the piano by his niece— let rip with some of the hundreds of melodies he had stored in his head.

There were a few complaints, but Hay stayed with it. Soon mountain men and farmers began swarming into the studio on Saturday nights, bringing ancient stringed instruments and unwritten songs handed down through generations. They came on foot, on mules, in wagons, and by truck. Their earthy ballads were of unknown age and origin, with titles like *Greenback Dollar, Brown's Ferry Blues*, and *Rabbit in a Flea Patch*. None could read music. They scraped and sawed away by ear, producing the closest thing to pure musical Americana ever heard on the air.

The show got its name in 1927. It had been scheduled to immediately follow an NBC network feed from New York, the highbrow *Music Appreciation Hour* with Dr. Walter Damrosch. On this night, Damrosch closed with a musical railroad theme, and by one account ended with these words: "While we do not believe there is a place in the classics for realism, this work so depicts the onrush of the locomotive that I have decided to include it in this program of grand opera." Hay reportedly replied, as his show went on, "From here on out, folks, it will be nothing but realism of the realest kind. You've been up in the clouds with grand opera: now get down to earth with us in a shindig of grand ole opry!"

The show soon outgrew both its 60-minute timeslot as well as its studio. Both "uncles," Jimmy Thompson and banjoist Dave Macon, thought that an hour wasn't a good warmup time, so Hay extended it until it spanned the block between 8 P.M. and midnight. The fiddling and stomping continued for the live audience long after the show was off the air. In 1930 Hay suffered a nervous attack and was replaced as station manager by Harry Stone. Hay continued to host the show, while Stone became more involved in its commercial possibilities. By 1934 it had outgrown the 500-seat studio that WSM had constructed for the broadcasts. It was moved to the Hillsboro Theater, outgrew that, and in 1936 went to the Dixie Tabernacle, described by *Opry* historian Jack Hurst as having "a couple of thousand crude, splintery bench seats." The crowds continued to grow: WSM boasted the "world's largest radio tower," and with 50,000 watts in those days of uncluttered radio bands, it could sometimes be heard for a thousand miles. Even in its earliest days, *Opry* could reach into 30 states.

In 1939 the show was moved into Nashville's War Memorial Auditorium, which seated 2,000 people. Also that year, NBC took note. R. J. Reynolds had taken on a 30-minute segment for Prince Albert Tobacco, and in October this half-hour was made available to scattered NBC stations around the country. There was still resistance at big-city affiliates to the hillbilly,

country, folk, or "clodhopping" musical arts, and for four years the show's network coverage remained spotty. In early 1943, Ralston Purina began carrying another *Opry* segment to NBC stations in the south and southwest. Nine months later, in October, NBC decided to carry the show on its full network. Prince Albert became sole sponsor. Whitey "Duke of Paducah" Ford hosted the 30-minute network package. He was, said Hurst, a veteran of "big-time entertainment" and a former player on the WLS *National Barn Dance*. The network required a script, but it was always followed loosely.

This drastically changed its open-doors policy. What had begun as a "come on down and let's play some music" free-for-all was now all but closed to newcomers. Players traveled hundreds of miles only to be politely told that the show was "all filled up." Even Roy Acuff, who would become one of its brightest stars, tried for three years before getting on the show in 1939.

By 1941 *Opry* had outgrown the War Memorial Auditorium. It moved that year into the Ryman Auditorium, a facility with 3,600 seats that would be its home for more than three decades. In 1974, with most of the old guard gone and a new generation of performers swathed in glitter and gold, *Grand Ole Opry* moved into its "permanent" new home, "Opryland," a $15 million building with 4,400 seats.

GRAND SLAM, quiz.

BROADCAST HISTORY: Sept. 30, 1946–Aug. 14, 1953, CBS. 15m, weekdays at 11:30. Continental Baking. Outgrowth of *Irene Beasley Songs*, 1943–45, CBS. 15m, weekdays at 3:15. Wesson Oil.

CREATOR–SINGING HOSTESS: Irene Beasley. ANNOUNCER: Dwight Weist. PIANIST: Bob Downey. ORGANIST: Abe Goldman. DIRECTORS: Victor Sack, Kirby Ayers. WRITERS: Irene Beasley, Lillian Schoen.

Grand Slam was set up as an audio bridge game, a spirited competition between listeners and the studio audience. Listeners submitted five-part questions, to be sung by the hostess. Each part of the question was called a "trick." If the studio contestant won a trick, he won a prize; if not, the listener won the prize. Five tricks won by either side was a "grand slam," netting the winner a $100 savings bond.

GRAPEVINE RANCHO, comedy variety.

BROADCAST HISTORY: March 4–May 27, 1943, CBS. 30m, Thursdays at 8. Roma Wines.

HOST: Ransom Sherman, with guest stars and a company of regulars. Sherman as a rancher with Leo Carrillo as Pedro, his Mexican hand. Lionel Stander as Hoolihan, ranch foreman. Anne O'Neal as Cynthia Veryberry, a paying guest. **ANNOUNCER:** Fred Shields. **VOCALIST:** Carlos Ramirez, South American baritone. **ORCHESTRA:** Lud Gluskin.

THE GREAT GILDERSLEEVE, situation comedy.

BROADCAST HISTORY: Aug. 31, 1941–March 21, 1957, NBC. 30m, Sundays at 6:30, 1941–46; Wednesdays at 8:30, 1946–54; weeknights in 15m strip-show format at 10:15, 1954–55; then 25m, Thursdays at 8, 1955–57. Kraft Foods, 1941–54; multiple sponsorship thereafter.

CAST: Harold Peary (Aug. 31, 1941–June 14, 1950) as Throckmorton P. Gildersleeve, water commissioner in the town of Summerfield, USA. Willard Waterman as Gildersleeve (Sept. 6, 1950–March 21, 1957). Walter Tetley as Leroy Forrester, Gildersleeve's wisecracking nephew. Lurene Tuttle (1941–44) as Marjorie Forrester, Gildersleeve's niece. Louise Erickson as Marjorie, mid-1940s; Mary Lee Robb as Marjorie thereafter. Earle Ross as Judge Horace Hooker, Gildersleeve's friendly nemesis, rival, and fellow lodge member. Lillian Randolph as Birdie Lee Coggins, the Gildersleeve maid and cook extraordinaire. Richard LeGrand as Mr. Peavey, the druggist with the twang. Forrest Lewis as Peavey, late in the run. Arthur Q. Bryan as Floyd Munson the barber, another member of Gildersleeve's lodge, the Jolly Boys, and a nonstop talker when wielding the scissors. Ken Christy as Police Chief Gates, another Jolly Boys member, who added deep harmony to their frequent songfests. Gildersleeve girlfriends: Shirley Mitchell as Leila Ransom, conniving southern-belle widow; Una Merkel as Adeline Fairchild, Leila's cousin; Bea Benaderet as Eve Goodwin, the school principal (1944); Cathy Lewis as Nurse Kathryn Milford, a Gildersleeve heartthrob of the 1950s, sweet and unattainable. Ben Alexander (mid-1940s) as Bashful Ben, one of Marjorie's early suitors. Richard Crenna as Bronco Thompson, the man Marjorie finally married. Gale Gordon as Rumson Bullard, the rich, obnoxious neighbor who lived across the street from Gildersleeve. Jim Backus as Bullard, ca. 1952. Tommy Bernard as Bullard's son Craig, a chip off the old block. Pauline Drake as Bessie, Gildersleeve's well-baked secretary at the water department. Gloria Holliday also as Bessie. **ANNOUNCERS:** Jim Bannon (1941–42), Ken Carpenter (1942–45), John Laing (1945–47), John Wald (1947–49), Jay Stewart and Jim Doyle (1949–50), John Hiestand. **ORCHESTRA:** William Randolph (1941), Billy Mills (1941–42), Claude Sweeten (into mid-1940s); Jack Meakin (later 1940s), Robert Armbruster (1950s). **PRODUCER-DIRECTORS:** Cecil Underwood, Frank Pittman, Fran Van Hartesveldt, Virgil Reimer, Karl Gruener. **WRITERS:** Leonard L. Levinson (1941–42), John Whedon and Sam Moore, Jack Robinson and Gene Stone, John Elliotte and Andy White. Also: Paul West, Virginia Safford Lynne. **SOUND EFFECTS:** Floyd Caton, Virgil Reimer, Monty Fraser.

The Great Gildersleeve began with a departure, when a portly man of 42 years stepped onto a train in a mythical town and started a trend known as the series spinoff. Throckmorton P. Gildersleeve, owner of the Gildersleeve Girdle Works, was taking a business trip from his hometown, Wistful Vista, to Summerfield, a small town at the end of the line. But except for occasional visits, Wistful Vista would not see Gildersleeve again. He would give up his old occupation—making "Gildersleeve's Girlish Girdles"—but would never give up his reputation as a windbag, a most eligible bachelor, or a bumbling-but-enthusiastic ladies' man.

The character emerged from *Fibber McGee and Molly* as a strong comedic entity. Actor Harold Peary had joined the *McGee* cast in 1937, playing scores of bit parts, often two or more in a single show. His range was vast: he could switch into almost any Americanized foreign dialect, from British to Chinese to a Portuguese piccolo player. He could play thugs, Jews, and Indians, a talent honed by long experience.

Peary was born in 1908, son of a Portuguese immigrant, and christened Harrold José de Faria. He once pinpointed his first radio job as Jan. 21, 1923, at KZM, Oakland. In the late 1920s he worked at NBC in San Francisco. *The Spanish Serenader*, a series vintage 1928, gave him a chance to use his singing voice as well as acting talent. Landing in Chicago in 1937, he soon became one of radio's insiders, gaining a reputation as a top utility man. For a year he played various characters named Gildersleeve on the *McGee* program: then he approached writer Don Quinn with an idea of a meatier role for himself—a pompous windbag, perfect foil for McGee, who himself ran the biggest bluff in Wistful Vista.

For Quinn it was simply a matter of creating a single Gildersleeve, moving him to 83 Wistful Vista, and letting the fur fly. Peary's first show as Throckmorton P. Gildersleeve, neighbor, was Sept. 26, 1939: he was seldom absent from then until his final regular appearance, June 24, 1941. Gildersleeve and McGee argued constantly. Peary's classic line, repeated in almost every show, was "You're a haaaarrd man, McGee!" His "dirty laugh," perfected during the *McGee* run, was certain to ring out whenever one of McGee's schemes backfired. Quinn knew at once the value of sarcasm in comedy: never again would McGee fail to have a rival in the long battle of words. Nor was this principle lost on Leonard L. Levinson, the first *Gildersleeve* writer. Gildersleeve's long-running feud with crusty old Judge Horace Hooker began on that first broadcast, during the ride from Wistful Vista to Summerfield. Hooker and Gildersleeve, opening their acrimony over a lower berth, would find hundreds of things to argue about over the years. But they would also become brothers in the Jolly Boys Club and, when the chips were down, birds of a feather.

In Summerfield, Gildersleeve was the guardian of his orphaned niece and nephew, Marjorie and Leroy Forrester. Marjorie was a teenager who seldom gave any trouble. Leroy, age 12, was a wiseguy. The town was a pleasant slice of rural Americana. Most of the action took place in an eight-block area. There was a city park with an old-fashioned bandstand. There was a large reservoir that—in a promotional map released by NBC—looks impossibly close to the downtown area. It would soon come to play a major role, as on Oct. 18, 1942, Gildersleeve would be appointed water commissioner, beginning an illustrious career that might be described as doing nothing at all.

Gildersleeve lived with Marjorie and Leroy on Lakeside Avenue, where their Negro housekeeper, Birdie Lee Coggins, also had a room. He soon became friends with Mr. Peavey, whose drugstore stood at Lakeside and State streets. Directly across State from Peavey's pharmacy was the rambling old house where Judge Hooker lived. A little further along was Floyd Munson's barber shop, where the five chief members of the Jolly Boys Club (Gildy, Peavey, Floyd, Hooker, and Police Chief Gates) frequently gathered for conversation and harmony. Peary, using his singing talent, often performed solo, but there were many group numbers introduced to the Jolly Boys' theme:

Oh, it's always fair weather,
When good fellas get together . . .

And if in the end the meeting deteriorated into bickering, Chief Gates would valiantly try to rescue it: "Fel-las! Fel-las! Let's all be Jolly Boys!"

Just down the street from Gildersleeve, in the next block, lived the widow Leila Ransom. In the second full year she became a pivotal character who on June 27, 1943, got Gildersleeve to the altar and to the last line of the wedding ceremony. The show had much of the appeal of a serial, a 30-minute sitcom whose episodes were connected—sometimes into storylines that ran for months—but were also complete in themselves. Gildersleeve's romances were often at the crux of it: he was sued for breach of promise, got fired from his job, and ran for mayor—situations that each took up many shows. In a memorable sequence beginning Sept. 8, 1948, a baby was left in Gildersleeve's car. This played out through the entire fall season, the baby becoming such a part of the family that Kraft ran a contest offering major prizes to the listener who could coin the child's name. But in a teary finale, Dec. 22, the real father turned up and took the baby away.

The show was blessed with a stellar supporting cast. At 18, Walter Tetley was a radio veteran, having worked *The Children's Hour, The Fred Allen Show, Raising Junior,* and many other dramas and serials. As Leroy, he was a perfect deflater of Gildy's tender ego. "Are you kiddin'?" he would snarl, bringing out the inevitable Gildersleeve retort—"Leee-eee-roy!" To Leroy, Gildy was simply "Unk," a guy who tried hard, whose performance was usually outstripped by his intentions. "What a character!" Leroy would bleat as he caught his uncle in the fib of the week. Tetley, who would go on to play the ultimate wiseguy kid on *The Phil Harris/Alice Faye Show*, could still be heard in little-boy roles into his 30s.

Two of the three actresses who played Marjorie, Lurene Tuttle, and Louise Erickson, had vast radio experience between them. The third, Mary Lee Robb, got the role (and played it longest) through her friendship with Erickson, attending rehearsals and reading Marjorie's lines when Erickson was busy elsewhere.

The druggist, Peavey, was the sounding board for all of Gildy's triumphs and troubles. "Well, now, I wouldn't say that, Mr. Gildersleeve," was Peavey's inevitable reaction to almost any Gildersleeve assertion. Delivered in a mellow midwestern twang, it became the best-remembered catchphrase on the show. Richard LeGrand, who played the role, had been in show business since 1901: he had come up through vaudeville, had been heard in his own series, *Ole and the Girls*, and had worked for Carlton E. Morse on *One Man's Family* and *I Love a Mystery*.

Lillian Randolph, who had also played a maid on *The Billie Burke Show* and eventually took the lead on *Beulah*, was at her peak as Birdie, playing the role all the way. Birdie was perhaps the most endearing in radio's long parade of Negro maids, cooks, and housekeepers. She had genuine warmth, an infectious laugh, and a heart as big as the great man's midsection. She also had a feisty side, being fully capable of deflating Gildersleeve's ego. She spoke her mind, did it respectfully while making certain that her voice was heard, and remained a sympathetic character to both races in mid-1940s America.

Earle Ross played Judge Hooker with a billygoat laugh. Ross was often heard in Hooker-type roles on other comedy shows and for several seasons was part of the *Lux Radio Theater* dramatic troupe. Shirley Mitchell brought a dripping dose of honeysuckle to the Widow Ransom. "Throck-mahhhtin," she would coo, becoming such a strongly negative character to female listeners that at one point members of a California women's club picketed NBC, urging Gildersleeve with their signs not to marry her. Mitchell, who had come to Hollywood from Toledo, Ohio, in the early 1940s, had been on the verge of giving up radio when her luck turned and, almost overnight, she became a major supporting player. She was also heard as Alice Darling on *Fibber McGee and Molly*, a naive, slightly addled voice that bore no resemblance to the drawling belle she became on *The Great Gildersleeve*. Una Merkel gave an equally convincing southern performance as her cousin, Adeline Fairchild, and for a time in 1948 a spirited rivalry was waged for the great one's affections. This had a predictable outcome, with Gildersleeve engaged to both women at the same time.

The show was one of radio's most consistent until 1950, when Harold Peary announced that he was quitting his starring role. Rumor had it that Peary had held out for more money. His series was still carrying a rating in the mid-teens—certainly no disgrace at any time, and highly respectable in radio's final years, when the once-lofty Hope, Bergen, Benny, and *Fibber* powerhouses were doing little better themselves. Peary admitted he was bored: he had slowly tired of the role and was frustrated that his once-remarkable versatility had been eclipsed under a blanket of *Gildersleeve* typecasting. People forgot that he had been a singer, he said, and that he had been one of the best of the old Chicago dialect men in the days before he moved with *Fibber McGee and Molly* to Hollywood. This might have killed most shows, but NBC and Kraft had on tap one Willard Waterman, who had once been denied acting jobs on *McGee* because his voice sounded so much like Peary's.

Waterman and Peary had traveled similar routes on their climb through radio. Waterman had arrived in Chicago around 1936 and had played many of the same bit parts that Peary would do the following year. While Peary was establishing himself on *McGee*, Waterman was working *The First Nighter Program*, *Ma Perkins*, and *The Story of Mary Marlin*. Like Peary, Waterman was a prolific and versatile talent, doing up to 40 parts in a week.

In the fall of 1950, Waterman became the new Gildersleeve. Peary, meanwhile, jumped to CBS with a new sitcom, *Honest Harold*. In a dual review (*Gildy vs. Gildy*, Sept. 29, 1950), *Radio Life* summed up the general reaction. Waterman was a "splendid" replacement in a tough situation "about which actors have nightmares. The Gildy chortle and other mannerisms closely associated with the role were left out, and Waterman was to build his own interpretation. On his opener, he won over the studio audience almost to the point of receiving an ovation at the broadcast's close. Cast members rooted for him wholeheartedly, Frank Pittman gave deftness to direction, and Waterman's own intrinsic thespian integrity contributed to an initial performance that was greeted with enthusiasm.''

The same review panned *Honest Harold* as derivative, unexciting, and, in the end, ''just another show.'' It would fail in its lone season to develop any appreciative audience, while *Gildersleeve* under Waterman did a slow, inevitable fade and expired in 1957, at the advanced age of 16. Though Peary played the role in its best years, he and Waterman shared about equally in real time as Gildy at the NBC microphone. After *Gildersleeve*, Peary shaved his mustache, lost 50 pounds, and, in 1954, turned up as a disc jockey on KABC. He died March 30, 1985; Waterman died Feb. 1, 1995.

Like *McGee*, the series is abundant and easily available to collectors and listeners. The long run begins with the first show, Gildersleeve's arrival in Summerfield in 1941. There was a certain '30s silliness to cast off: a growth spurt that seemed to come to all timeless radio comedy around 1942–44. Suddenly *Gildersleeve* was a polished, smooth entity, a joy to hear. Well represented in this run is Gildy's romance with Leila Ransom. The listener can hear the children grow up, be present at Marjorie's wedding, share the birth of her twins. Leroy remains the same throughout: so do the wonderful Birdie and the equally fine Judge Hooker. It has the sound of a happy show before and after Peary's departure. Listeners can judge that for themselves as well, as the series is solid on tape during the transition period. This listener's opinion is that the show didn't lose much. Waterman didn't sing the solos, and the laugh certainly wasn't the same (more a chuckle, Waterman later said, a deliberate attempt on his part to stay away from a characteristic that ''belonged'' to Peary). In all other aspects, the resemblance was remarkable.

GREAT PLAYS, legitimate drama.

BROADCAST HISTORY: Feb. 26, 1938–Aug. 23, 1942, Blue Network. 60m, Sundays, usually early to mid-afternoon.
DIRECTORS: Blevins Davis (from ca. 1938). Also: Charles Warburton.

The great plays of the stage, from Aristophanes to Shakespeare, Richard Brinsley Sheridan to James M. Barrie and George Bernard Shaw.

GREAT SCENES FROM GREAT PLAYS, dramatic anthology.

BROADCAST HISTORY: Oct. 1, 1948–Feb. 25, 1949, Mutual. 30m, Fridays at 8. National Council of the Protestant Episcopal Church.
HOST: Walter Hampden. **CAST:** Films stars in anthology roles: Boris Karloff in *On Borrowed Time*; Joan Caulfield in *Little Women*; etc. **ORCHESTRA:** Nathan Kroll.

The purpose of this series was to encourage church attendance of any denomination. It followed Father Patrick Peyton's *Family Theater* in keeping the message subtle, the plays free of moralizing, the pitch confined to postshow discussion.

THE GREAT TALENT HUNT, musical oddity.

BROADCAST HISTORY: 1948, Mutual. Summer run, 30m, Thursdays at 8:30.
HOST: Jim Backus. **ANNOUNCER:** Ted Brown.

The Great Talent Hunt was a dip into musical idiocy, a takeoff on talent shows that highlighted the absurd. There were players of stringed toilet seats, players of inner tubes and spatulas; there was a man who could open his mouth and whack himself on the head with vibraphone hammers, playing a recognizable rendition of *Nola*. Spike Jones it wasn't.

THE GREATEST OF THESE, drama.

BROADCAST HISTORY: Ca. late 1940s; 30m, transcribed syndication.
CAST: Tom Collins as philanthropist Harvey Desmond, a young attorney who moved into ''the very poorest section of the city'' in order to help the destitute. Mary Lansing as Betty Crane, his fiancee, a ''young heiress who shares his ideals.'' Using a $1 million legacy, they establish a trust for this purpose, known as the Helping Hand. **ANNOUNCER:** Gayne Whitman.

THE GREATEST STORY EVER TOLD, religious drama.

BROADCAST HISTORY: Jan. 26, 1947–Dec. 30, 1956, ABC. 30m, Sundays at 6:30 until Sept. 1949, then at 5:30. Goodyear Tires.

CAST: Warren Parker as Christ, the only continuing role. **ANNOUNCER:** Norman Rose. **ORCHESTRA:** William Stoess, composer and conductor; later orchestras led by Jacques Belasco and Willard Young, who also directed the chorus. **PRODUCER:** Wadill Catchings. **DIRECTOR:** Marx Loeb. **ASSISTANT DIRECTOR:** Leonard Blair. **WRITER:** Henry Denker. **WRITER-CONSULTANT:** Fulton Oursler (based on his book of the same name). **SOUND EFFECTS:** Terry Ross.

The Greatest Story Ever Told was an ambitious show, with a full orchestra and a 16-voice chorus, dramatizing the life and times of Jesus Christ. It was billed as "the greatest story ever told, from the greatest life ever lived." It was the first radio series to simulate the voice of Christ as a continuing character. This was done with a slight echo effect, giving perhaps the same effect as a halo in a work of art.

The producers were uneasy about being the first to characterize Christ on the air. Many scholars were consulted, and no dialogue was concocted, all words spoken by Christ being directly attributed in the Bible. There were no cast credits: Warren Parker played the role in anonymity. No pictures were taken of the performers at work, and there was no studio audience. There were no commercials: just a simple tag reminding listeners (in accordance with FCC requirements) that "this program was brought to you by the Goodyear Tire and Rubber Company." The stories effectively captured the essence of Fulton Oursler's book, a simple, popular dramatization of Christ's life as set down in the four Gospels. Oursler and writer Henry Denker approached the show in terms of modern problems, then found a corollary in the life of Christ and emerged with a theme.

The show was guided by an interdenominational advisory board, yet the end result was simple and lean. The sound effects were praised as being faithful to the time, with sandals prolifically simulated and animal noises recorded at the Bronx Zoo. In some areas, the show was an integrated part of school and church work.

THE GREEN HORNET, juvenile crime drama.

BROADCAST HISTORY: Jan. 31, 1936–April 7, 1938, WXYZ, Detroit. Originally Fridays, then Tuesdays and Thursdays. United Shirt Shops; Detroit Creamery.

April 12, 1938–Nov. 9, 1939, Mutual. Various 30m timeslots.

Nov. 16, 1939–Dec. 5, 1952, Blue Network/ABC. Many 30m timeslots, usually late afternoon or early evening, 4:30–8:30; various days, sometimes twice a week. Heard on some Mutual stations as well as Blue Network, 1940–41. On the air with few gaps from Nov. 16, 1939–Sept. 8, 1950; returned Sept. 10–Dec. 5, 1952. Mostly sustained; General Mills, Jan.–Aug. 1948; Orange Crush, Sept.–Dec. 1952.

CAST: Al Hodge (1936–43) as Britt Reid, masked crimefighter known as the Green Hornet. Also as Reid: Donovan Faust (1943), after Hodge went into the service; Bob Hall (1944–51); Jack McCarthy (1951–52). Tokutaro Hayashi (renamed Raymond Toyo by director James Jewell for professional reasons) as Kato, Britt Reid's "faithful Filipino valet." Rollon Parker and Michael Tolan later as Kato. Leonore Allman as Lenore "Casey" Case, Reid's secretary. Jim Irwin as Michael Axford, reporter. Gilly Shea as Michael Axford upon Irwin's death in 1938. Jack Petruzzi as ace reporter Ed Lowry of Britt Reid's crusading newspaper, the *Daily Sentinel*. John Todd as Dan Reid from *The Lone Ranger*, infrequent appearances. Rollon Parker as the newsboy who closed each broadcast, shouting the inevitable headlines telling of the Green Hornet's latest triumph. **ANNOUNCERS:** Fielden Farrington, Charles Wood, Mike Wallace, Hal Neal, Bob Hite. **PRODUCER:** George W. Trendle. **DIRECTORS:** James Jewell, Charles Livingstone. **WRITERS:** Fran Striker, Dan Beattie, Leo Boulette, Steve McCarthy, Tom Dougall, Lee Randon, Jim Lawrence. **SOUND EFFECTS:** Tony Caminito, Dewey Cole, Jimmy Fletcher, Fred Flowerday, Fred Fry, Bill Hengsterbeck, Ken Robertson (all WXYZ). **THEME:** *Flight of the Bumblebee*, by Nicolai Rimsky-Korsakov.

The Green Hornet was one of radio's best-known and most distinctive juvenile adventure shows. With its companion shows, *The Lone Ranger* and *Challenge of the Yukon*, it was fed to the network by its originating station, WXYZ, and was distinguished by its use of classical music for themes and bridges between dramatic acts.

It was not by chance that Britt Reid, the hero, had all the earmarks of a modern-day *Lone Ranger*. Faithful listeners would remember that the Ranger's family name had been Reid: that the lone Texas Ranger who survived the ambush of the treacherous Butch Cavendish gang, long ago in the West, was in reality John Reid, who would don his mask and ride the plains astride his great white horse, Silver, and accompanied by his faithful Indian friend, Tonto, punishing rustlers and restoring the reputations, freedom, ranches, and livelihoods of the God-fearing, the oppressed and the wrongly accused.

The Lone Ranger had put WXYZ on the broadcasting map. It was fairly sophisticated radio fare for a local station to attempt, but WXYZ was no ordinary station. A remarkable aggregation of creative talent worked there, a pool of acting, writing, musical, and sound artists that could produce programs worthy of any network.

The head man was George W. Trendle, who by 1935 had *The Lone Ranger* well established and was looking for a *Ranger* derivative. This would not be a spinoff as such, except for the fact that the character who would appear as a very young boy on *The Lone Ranger* would be an old man on *The Green Hornet*. Thus did Dan Reid, nephew of John Reid, become father to Britt Reid: the Lone Ranger was the Green Hornet's great-uncle.

The show still, at that time, had no name. Writer Fran Striker was summoned and told to think about it. Trendle did not rush the idea onto the air: he conferred with Striker and with *Ranger* director James Jewell, and gradually the character and setting evolved. Trendle wanted a modern-day hero, recalled writer Dick Osgood, who worked at the station for 36 years and in *Wyxie Wonderland* wrote its "unofficial diary." Trendle wanted to show that a political system could be riddled with corruption and that one man could successfully combat this white-collar lawlessness. He was entranced with the sound of a bee and wanted to incorporate that into the show. Osgood relates many experiments that soundmen were put through, trying to re-create the buzzing that Trendle remembered, of a bee trapped in a hotel room where he had once stayed.

They played with names. Trendle liked *The Hornet*, but that had been used and posed potential rights problems. Colors were added: blue and even pink were considered before Britt Reid became the Green Hornet.

The parallels to *The Lone Ranger* continued. The Green Hornet would ride in a sleek modern automobile, the '30s equivalent of "the great horse Silver." Like the Ranger, the Hornet would fight for the law but operate outside it and usually be mistaken by police for one of the criminals. And there would be a faithful sidekick: as the Lone Ranger had his Tonto (brave and stoic, man of a different race, with a simple name of two syllables, ending in *o*), Britt Reid's Filipino valet, Kato, would be "the only living man to know him as the Green Hornet." Kato was a master chemist who created the gas guns and smokescreens that became part of the Green Hornet's arsenal. He was an expert in the secrets of Oriental combat, and he was blessed with keen intelligence. A college graduate, he could cook, care for a house, and drive with the skills of a racecar professional. The car too had a name: Black Beauty. It whirred distinctively as Reid and Kato went into action in the abandoned-looking building that was reached "through a secret panel in Britt Reid's bedroom . . . along a narrow passage built within the wall itself . . . down narrow, creaking steps that led around a corner" to the structure "on a little-used dead-end side street."

A rumor persists that Kato was Japanese until the events of Dec. 7, 1941, when abruptly he became Filipino. This seems to be false, as Kato was described as a Filipino of Japanese descent at least two years earlier. As for Britt Reid, he was seen in the early days as a playboy, a clever disguise for his true personality. He was the worry of his father's life. So concerned was old Dan Reid that his son would be a frivolous man that Britt was installed as publisher of the Reid family business, a newspaper called the *Daily Sentinel*. With the job came a bodyguard and overseer, one Michael Axford, former cop and dumbest of all dumb Irishmen. Axford was plucked whole cloth from another Trendle melodrama, *Warner Lester, Manhunter*, which Trendle was discontinuing. Later, Axford would become a *Sentinel* reporter, though he remained throughout the series a voice without a brain. Axford's goal in life was to "captuure the Haarnet," but in truth he had trouble catching a streetcar.

Rounding out the cast of regulars were Ed

Lowry, top *Sentinel* reporter, and secretary Lenore Case. Lowry dug up the stories that Reid eventually exposed, his role as an active participant effectively canceled by Reid. Lenore Case ("Casey" to Axford but ever "Miss Case" to Reid) was the show's muted love interest. Casey worked late, tried hard, and eventually moved up to writing for the society page. But romance on a Trendle show was virtually nil: though Casey occasionally got to cover a good story, she never got to cover Britt.

They all came roaring out of the radio to a fully orchestrated *Flight of the Bumblebee*, with heavy violin emphasis. Trendle finally got his bee effect right: the buzz of the Hornet, a little-used musical instrument called the Theremin, was one of the show's most striking features.

He hunts the biggest of all game! Public enemies that even the G-men cannot reach! This 1939 signature was reportedly revamped after top G-man J. Edgar Hoover complained. For many years thereafter it was *He hunts the biggest of all game! Public enemies who try to destroy our America!*

With his faithful valet, Kato, Britt Reid, daring young publisher, matches wits with the underworld, risking his life that criminals and racketeers within the law may feel its weight by the sting of the Green Hornet! And at the end, the inevitable newsboy, hawking his wares: "Special extry! Paper! Police smash smuggling racket! Foreign diplomat involved! Read all about it! Green Hornet still at large!"

THE GREEN LAMA, adventure drama, based on novels by Richard Foster.

BROADCAST HISTORY: June 5–Aug. 20, 1949, CBS. 30m, Sundays at 5:30 until July 9, then at 7:30.

CAST: Paul Frees as Jethro Dumont, "wealthy young American who, after ten years in Tibet, returned as the Green Lama, to amaze the world with his curious and secret powers, in his singlehanded fight against injustice and crime." Ben Wright as Tulku, his faithful Tibetan servant. Jack Kruschen in many roles. Also, from the Hollywood radio ranks, Georgia Ellis, William Conrad, Gloria Blondell, Lillian Buyeff, Lawrence Dobkin, etc. **ANNOUNCER:** Larry Thor. **MUSIC:** Richard Aurandt. **PRODUCER-DIRECTORS:** Norman

Macdonnell, James Burton. **WRITERS:** Richard Foster, William Froug.

In this scenario, Jethro Dumont was made a lama because of his amazing powers of concentration. He chose the color green because it was one of the "six sacred colors of Tibet," symbolizing justice. His chant, opening and closing each show, was *Om manipadme hum!*

GREEN VALLEY, USA, patriotic wartime drama.

BROADCAST HISTORY: July 5–Oct. 21, 1942, CBS. 30m, Sundays, later Wednesdays. Also heard 15m, weekdays, CBS, early 1943.

Feb. 27–Aug. 20, 1944, Mutual. 30m Sundays at 5. Emerson Radio.

CAST: Santos Ortega, narrator (1944). New York radio personnel: Ed Begley, Richard Widmark, Elspeth Eric, Ann Shepherd, etc. **PRODUCER-DIRECTOR:** Himan Brown.

THE GROUCH CLUB, talk.

BROADCAST HISTORY: Oct. 17, 1938–April 25, 1939, CBS West Coast. Mondays, later Tuesdays.

April 16, 1939–Jan. 21, 1940, NBC. 30m, Sundays at 6:30. Corn Kix Cereal.

CREATOR-HOST: Jack Lescoulie, "grouchmaster." **CAST:** "Grouches" Jack Albertson, Don Brody, Mary Milford, Arthur Q. Bryan, Ned Sparks, Phil Kramer, Eric Burtis, Emory Parnell. Beth Wilson, singer. **ANNOUNCERS:** Neil Reagan, Jim Barry. **MUSIC:** Leon Leonardi. **PRODUCER:** Owen Crump. **SOUND EFFECTS:** Allan Bode.

The Grouch Club was a forum for people who wanted to complain. The complaint could be about anything—personal, professional, or civil—from street potholes to wasted taxes to the early-morning temperament of the better half. Host Lescoulie often engaged his cheerful announcer, Neil Reagan, in on-air arguments, so people wouldn't lose the spirit of the show.

THE GUIDING LIGHT, soap opera.

BROADCAST HISTORY: Jan. 25, 1937–Dec. 26, 1941, NBC. 15m, weekdays at 3:45, then at 11:45 A.M. White Naphtha Soap.

March 17, 1942–Nov. 29, 1946, NBC. 15m, weekdays, mostly at 2. General Mills. (In 1944, a block of soaps by writer Irna Phillips made up a *General Mills Hour*, 2 to 3 P.M. daily: characters from *Today's Children*, *The Woman in White*, and *The Guiding Light* crossed over and interchanged in respective storylines.)

June 2, 1947–June 29, 1956, CBS. 15m weekdays at 1:45. Procter & Gamble's Duz Detergent.

CAST: **1937 to mid-1940s:** Arthur Peterson as the Rev. John Ruthledge of Five Points, the serial's first protagonist. Mercedes McCambridge as Mary Ruthledge, his daughter; Sarajane Wells later as Mary. Ed Prentiss as Ned Holden, who was abandoned by his mother as a child and taken in by the Ruthledges; Ned LeFevre and John Hodiak also as Ned. Ruth Bailey as Rose Kransky; Charlotte Manson also as Rose. Mignon Schrieber as Mrs. Kransky. Seymour Young as Jacob Kransky, Rose's brother. Sam Wanamaker as Ellis Smith, the enigmatic "Nobody from Nowhere"; Phil Dakin and Raymond Edward Johnson also as Ellis. Henrietta Tedro as Ellen, the housekeeper. Margaret Fuller and Muriel Bremner as Fredrika Lang. Gladys Heen as Torchy Reynolds. Bill Bouchey as Charles Cunningham. Lesley Woods and Carolyn McKay as Celeste, his wife. Laurette Fillbrandt as Nancy Stewart. Frank Behrens as the Rev. Tom Bannion, Ruthledge's assistant. The Greenman family, early characters: Eloise Kummer as Norma; Reese Taylor and Ken Griffin as Ed; Norma Jean Ross as Ronnie, their daughter. **Transition from clergy to medical background, mid-1940s:** John Barclay as Dr. Richard Gaylord. Jane Webb as Peggy Gaylord. Hugh Studebaker as Dr. Charles Matthews. Willard Waterman as Roger Barton (alias Ray Brandon). Betty Lou Gerson as Charlotte Wilson. Ned LeFevre as Ned Holden. Tom Holland as Eddie Bingham. Mary Lansing as Julie Collins. **1950s:** Jone Allison as Meta Bauer. Lyle Sudrow as Bill Bauer. Charita Bauer as Bert, Bill's wife, a role she would carry into television and play for three decades. Laurette Fillbrandt as Trudy Bauer. Glenn Walken as little Michael. Theo Goetz as Papa Bauer. James Lipton as Dr. Dick Grant. Lynn Rogers as Marie Wallace, the artist. ANNOUNCERS: Fort Pearson, Clayton "Bud" Collyer, Herb Allen. PRODUCER: Carl Wester, long associated with Phillips on this and other serials. DIRECTORS: Joe Ainley, Gordon Hughes, etc. CREATOR-WRITER: Irna Phillips. ORGANIST: Bernice Yanocek. THEME: Thundering rendition of *Aphrodite*, by Goetzel.

The Guiding Light is the longest-running serial in broadcast history. Still seen on CBS television, its roots go back almost 60 years, to radio's pioneering soaps. Though its original characters have been swallowed and eclipsed by time, it still has faint ties to the show that was first simulcast July 20, 1952, and in time replaced its radio counterpart with a daily one-hour TV show.

Its creator, Irna Phillips, was often called "the queen of soaps." She was so influential in the field that she was compared with Frank and Anne Hummert, though the comparison was weak. While the Hummerts employed a huge stable of writers and turned out dozens of serials, Phillips wrote her own—two million words of it each year. Using a large month-by-month work chart, Phillips plotted up to half a dozen serials at once, dictating the action to a secretary. Mentally juggling the fates of scores of characters, she churned out quarter-hour slices of life in sessions filled with high drama, acting the parts and changing her voice for the various speaking roles, while secretaries scribbled the dialogue that flowed from her lips.

She gave up teaching early in life to enter radio as an actress at Chicago's WGN. She was 25 that year, 1930. In 1932 she began to write. She discovered that cliffhanger endings were surefire for bringing those early audiences back to their sets each day, but that slow and skillful character development was what kept the audience for years. She decided that the organ was the ideal musical instrument for those little shows and that the instrument should be played with pomp and power, with all the authority of a religious service in a great European cathedral. The music gave weight to the dialogue, which was usually focused and intense.

A Phillips serial (in contrast to the jerky, obvious, and corny melodramas of the Hummerts) usually contained just one main scene in each installment, peopled by only two characters. Her scenes were sparse, the settings lean, the people clear without the endless repetition of names that filled a Hummert soap. Phillips was the first serial writer to effectively blend her soaps. Her popular *Today's Children* was phased out of its first run in 1938 by having its characters sit around the radio and listen to *The Woman in White*, which replaced it. When three of her soaps were scheduled consecutively and sponsored by General Mills in 1944, Phillips expanded this idea of integrated storylines. The major characters of the resurrected *Today's Children* drifted through *The Guiding Light*, and mutual visits with *The Woman in White* were also common. Ed Prentiss, who was then playing Ned Holden of *The Guiding Light*, was used as a "master of ceremonies" for the hour, a guide through the intricate framework of the three soaps. The fourth quarter-hour was filled with nondenominational religious music, *Hymns of All Churches*. At one time during this period, Phillips was considering breaking the traditional lengths, running stories of ten to 20 minutes each rather than the precise quarter-hours. After a season of this experimenting, the block was dismantled, and *The Guiding Light* went into its postwar phase.

In the earliest phase, it followed the Ruthledge family. The Rev. John Ruthledge had come to Five Points two decades before, establishing himself and his church as the driving force in the community. This had not been easy. Five Points was a "melting pot of humanity," as Phillips described it, with Poles, Slavs, Swedes, Germans, Irish, and Jews living in uneasy proximity. As one character described it, it was a neighborhood of "poverty, gossipy neighbors, sordid surroundings," with "no chance to get ahead." Ruthledge had run into stiff neighborhood opposition, but now he was accepted and even beloved. His Little Church of Five Points had become popularly known as the Church of the Good Samaritan: Ruthledge himself was the guiding light, the good samaritan. He had a daughter, Mary, who grew up without a mother. Helping him raise the child was a kindly housekeeper, Ellen. Then there was Ned Holden, abandoned by his mother, who just turned up one night; being about Mary's age, he forged a friendship with the little girl that inevitably, as they grew up, turned to love. They were to marry, but just before the wedding Ned learned that his mother was convicted murderess Fredrika Lang. What was worse, Ruthledge had known this and had not told him. Feeling betrayed, Ned disappeared. He would finally return, crushing Mary with the news that he now had a wife, the vibrant actress Torchy Reynolds.

Also prominent in the early shows was the Kransky family. Abe Kransky was an orthodox Jew who owned a pawnshop. Much of the action centered on his daughter Rose and her struggle to rise above the squalor of Five Points. Rose had a scandalous affair with publishing magnate Charles Cunningham (whose company would bring out Ned Holden's first book when Ned took a fling at authorship), only to discover that Cunningham was merely cheating on his wife, Celeste. In her grief, Rose turned to Ellis Smith, the eccentric young artist who had come to Five Points as "Mr. Nobody from Nowhere." Smith (also not his real name) took Rose in to "give her a name." The Kransky link with the Ruthledges came about in the friendship of the girls, Rose and Mary. In 1939, in one of her celebrated experiments, Phillips shifted the Kranskys into a new serial, *The Right to Happiness*.

The Ruthledge-Kransky era began to fade in 1944, when actor Arthur Peterson went into the service. Rather than recast, Phillips sent Ruthledge away as well, to the Army as a chaplain. By the time Peterson-Ruthledge returned, two years later, the focus had moved. For a time the strong male figure was Dr. Richard Gaylord. By 1947 a character named Dr. Charles Matthews had taken over. Though still a preacher, and still holding forth at Good Samaritan, Ruthledge had moved out of center stage. The main characters were Charlotte Wilson, "whose strange past is darkly troubled" (*Radio Life*), and Ray Brandon, a bitter ex-con on parole. By the early 1950s, the Bauer family had become the serial's center: Bill and Bertha (Bert), their 11-year-old son, Michael, and Meta Bauer, Bill's sister. Three decades later, the TV serial was still focused on the Bauer brothers and their careers in law and medicine. The Ruthledges and the Kranskys were fading memories, and the "guiding light" of the title was little more than symbolic.

In its heyday, it was one of Phillips's prime showpieces. She produced it independently, sold it to sponsors, and offered it to the network as a complete package. Phillips paid her own casts, announcers, production crews, and advisers (two doctors and a lawyer on retainer) and still earned $5,000 a week. She dared to depart from formula, even to the extent of occasionally turning over whole shows to Ruthledge sermons. Her organist, Bernice Yanocek, worked her other shows as well, and the music was sometimes incorporated into the storylines, as being played by Mary Ruthledge in her father's church.

A few episodes exist from the prime years. Of equal interest is an R-rated cast record, produced for Phillips when the show was moving to New York and the story was changing direction. It's typical racy backstage stuff, full of lines like "When your bowels are in a bind, try new Duz with the hair-trigger formula." It shows what uninhibited fun these radio people had together.

THE GUMPS, situation comedy, based on the comic strip by Sidney Smith.

BROADCAST HISTORY: 1931, WGN, Chicago.
Nov. 5, 1934–Nov. 1, 1935, CBS. 15m, weekdays at 12:15. Korn Products, Karo Syrup. Returned Oct. 5, 1936–July 2, 1937, CBS. 15m, weekdays at noon. Pebeco Toothpaste.
CAST: *Early shows*: Jack Boyle as Andy Gump. Dorothy Denvir as Min, his wife. Charles Flynn as Chester, their son. Bess Flynn as Tilda the maid. *Network, ca. 1935*: Wilmer Walter as Andy. Agnes Moorehead as Min. Lester Jay and Jackie Kelk as Chester. **PRODUCER-DIRECTOR:** Himan Brown. **WRITER:** Irwin Shaw.

Andy and Min Gump were "a cranky couple, the Archie and Edith Bunker of their day," wrote Irwin Shaw's biographer, Michael Shnayerson. Producer Himan Brown had had some success adapting comics to the air: Shaw was then writing *Dick Tracy*, and Brown asked him if he thought he could write comedy. "He was sensational," Brown told Shnayerson. *The Gumps* is also notable for giving Agnes Moorehead her first radio role.

GUNSMOKE, western drama.

BROADCAST HISTORY: April 26, 1952–June 18, 1961, CBS. 30m Saturdays until 1955, then Sundays; brief Monday schedule, summer 1954. Various timeslots; two broadcasts heard weekly in 1955, both Saturdays, at 12:30 and 8; then from 1955–61, Sundays at 6:30 with repeats Saturdays at 12:30. Post Toasties, Oct. 3–Dec. 26, 1953; Liggett & Myers Tobacco, July 5, 1954–April 7, 1957, first for Chesterfield and then L&M Cigarettes; multiple sponsorship, 1957–61.
CAST: William Conrad as Matt Dillon, U.S. marshal, of Dodge City, Kan. Parley Baer as Chester Wesley Proudfoot, his deputy. Georgia Ellis as Kitty Russell, the saloon girl. Howard McNear as Dr. Charles Adams. Also: Harry Bartell, Lawrence Dobkin, Sam Edwards, Don Diamond, Lou Krugman, Barney Phillips, Jack Kruschen, Vivi Janiss, Lillian Buyeff, Ben Wright, John Dehner, Paul Dubov, Jim Nusser, Frank Gerstle, Mary Lansing, Michael Ann Barrett, Virginia Gregg, Junius Matthews, Joseph Kearns, Sammie Hill, Jeanette Nolan, John McIntire, Ralph Moody, Joe DuVal, Jeanne Bates, Charlotte Lawrence, Johnny McGovern, Peter Leeds, Byron Kane, Helen Kleeb, Edgar Barrier, Joyce McCluskey, Virginia Christine, Clayton Post, Eleanore Tanin, Joe Cranston, Richard Beals, Jack Moyles, Lynn Allen, Frank Cady, Vic Perrin, and others from Hollywood's Radio Row. **ANNOUNCERS:** Roy Rowan, George Walsh; George Fenneman for Chesterfield. **MUSIC:** Rex Koury. **PRODUCER-DIRECTOR:** Norman Macdonnell. **WRITER:** John Meston. **OTHER WRITERS:** Herb Purdum, Les Crutchfield, Antony Ellis, Kathleen Hite, John Dunkel, Marian Clark, etc. **SOUND EFFECTS:** Tom Hanley, Ray Kemper, Bill James.

Gunsmoke was slowly developed by producer-director Norman Macdonnell and writer John Meston over a two-year period beginning in mid-1950. Macdonnell had been working as assistant director to William N. Robson on *Escape*; Meston had become story editor at CBS. Both men were interested in the concept of a western series for adults. Radio had relegated the western, like science fiction, to the children's hour, with such series as *The Lone Ranger, The Cisco Kid*, and *Red Ryder* its most prominent offerings. In 1946–48 Robson had produced and directed *Hawk Larabee*, which he himself would describe years later as "a pictureless B-grade western— the same kind of plot and character development that you'd find in a Roy Rogers movie." Even the venerable *Death Valley Days* had never contained the kind of gritty realism that Macdonnell and Meston envisioned.

The framework for such a series was already in place. Harry Ackerman, director of programming for CBS West, had coined a title—*Gunsmoke*—and had recorded two audition shows. The first had starred Rye Billsbury as lawman "Mark Dillon" and had been produced on June 11, 1949. This was redone July 15, with Howard Culver playing the lead. The records were never aired, and when the Ackerman project fell by the wayside, Macdonnell and Meston continued their discussions of adult western concepts. They began working these into existing programs. Robson had left *Escape*: Macdonnell had become its director, and on Dec. 22, 1950, he aired a Meston story of the West titled *Wild Jack Rhett*. This was followed by *Pagosa*, written by Meston and produced by Macdonnell on *Romance*, Aug. 6, 1951. Again Macdonnell approached CBS about a western series. His timing was right: the network was canceling Robson's spy series, *Operation Underground* (June 26, 1951–April 19, 1952), and Macdonnell was told he had one week to get his show together.

"In that week we had to find a writer, we had to find a star, we had to have a theme composed," Macdonnell told John Hickman on a five-hour *Gunsmoke* radio documentary in 1967. "We got Walter Brown Newman to come in—one of the better writers in town—we gave him an acetate recording of *Pagosa* and, I believe, *Wild Jack Rhett*, and said, this is the style, this is the color, this is the feel. We laid out no other guidelines, except we told him how Matt Dillon should be written, and the kind of character he was."

In *Rhett* and *Pagosa*, they had experimented with "exaggerated sound patterns." The shows had an uncluttered sound. "There was lots of dead air," said Macdonnell on Hickman's show; "you could hear all the sound effects." There was little or no narration, the action being carried largely in dialogue. When a man walked across the street, a listener heard every step. This style would continue in *Gunsmoke*. The music was assigned to Rex Koury, who had never done a western. Macdonnell wanted a theme with a "big, wide-open sound to it, something that suggested the wide-open spaces." The show was being set in Dodge City, Kan. in the 1870s: a cow town and a brawling outpost on the frontier. So wild was Dodge that writer Lucius Beebe had termed it a "suburb of hell." It was a plains town, and Koury's music should reflect that, and perhaps suggest something of the man Matt Dillon, who had come to tame it.

Koury always wrote his interior music first: then, after satisfying himself with the sound and feel of the bridges, he would develop a theme that pulled it together. The night before the broadcast, he decided to go to bed early, get up early, and write his theme in the morning. "I

knew pretty well what I wanted," he said. But he overslept and didn't remember the unwritten theme until he was shaving. "I gathered a magazine and a piece of manuscript and a pencil, and I sat down in the most convenient spot, and that is where the *Gunsmoke* theme was composed." It took ten minutes to write and became one of radio's all-time best-known pieces of music.

The casting had been more difficult. Macdonnell and Meston both wanted William Conrad for the lead, but CBS objected. Conrad was known as a heavy from his movie roles (*Body and Soul; Sorry, Wrong Number; The Killers*). He was also a busy radio actor (*Escape, Suspense, The Adventures of Sam Spade*, many others) with a distinctive air presence. As Conrad told Hickman: "I think when they started casting for it, somebody said, 'Good Christ, let's not get Bill Conrad, we're up to you-know-where with Bill Conrad.' So they auditioned everybody, and as a last resort they called me. And I went in and read about two lines . . . and the next day they called me and said, 'Okay, you have the job.' "

Newman's initial script was a one-man show, a lynch-mob story building to the less-than-original conclusion that the little boy so enthralled by Dillon's gunfighting prowess was none other than William Bonney, soon to be known as Billy the Kid. But the power of the script was in a two-minute standoff between Dillon and the mob, a scene delivered by Conrad with raging fire. Only once had anything like it been heard, a Conrad performance of equal intensity on the *Escape* show *Poison*. The series was launched. Buried in the background on that first broadcast were two characters who would become regulars: Chester, the deputy, and the ghoulish Doc.

Newman's script had given Chester no name. His designation as TOWNSMAN in the script had left Conrad cold. "Bill Conrad named Chester," said Parley Baer, who would play the role from beginning to end. " 'Call him Chester or something,' Bill said." Later in the series he would be fully named, when Baer ad-libbed, "Well, as sure as my name is Chester Wesley Proudfoot. . . ." By then Baer had a clear idea who Chester was. He would disagree with a critic's view that Chester was a "dimwitted town loafer," preferring his own description, "a dependable nonthinker." As Baer told Hickman: "Dillon trusted Chester and Doc as much as he dared trust anyone. He knew that if he needed someone to stand at his back, Chester would be there, but he wasn't sure that Chester would function at all times. I think he had the same feeling about Doc: Doc was dependable, but every now and then he'd get soused up, and maybe at the moment of removing the appendix Doc could've been a little snockered. Chester was dishonest with many people, but he had to be completely honest with Dillon, and there was Dillon's strength! *Everyone* had to be honest with Dillon, because Dillon was the one who was *most* completely honest, in his dealings with lawbreakers, in his dealings with the town, in his dealings with his everyday associates.''

Doc was truly a vulturous character in the opening episode, so delighted over the carnage strewn by Dillon's blazing guns that at one point Dillon threatened to knock him down. Conrad again suggested a name: why not borrow from cartoonist Charles Addams, whose vampire panels were then popular, and name the *Gunsmoke* doctor Dr. Charles Adams? Howard McNear played the role all the way. Also in the cast that opening day was Georgia Ellis, who played the widow of the murdered man. Within weeks Ellis would join as the fourth regular, the saloon girl, Kitty Russell. ''She was a generous, loving human being,'' Ellis said of Kitty. Macdonnell, in a 1953 *Time* interview, put it bluntly: ''Kitty is just someone Matt has to visit every once in a while. We never say it, but Kitty is a prostitute, plain and simple.''

''Nobody was sure whether we had a hit or a miss,'' Macdonnell said of the first broadcast. Conrad was not yet playing Dillon with a great amount of warmth—an understatement, as a review of the tape reveals. But soon the characters underwent a strange metamorphosis, a process that always happens as props become flesh and blood. Chester became more humorous, Dillon more understanding, Doc less bloodthirsty, and Kitty emerged as the quietly understood love interest. She and Dillon had their understanding: ''There was no forgiveness to be given,'' said Ellis, ''because I don't think Kitty was available to anybody but Matt.'' The relationship between Chester and Dillon moved from tolerance to open affection. Chester drove him crazy: Dillon cringed when Chester put sugar in his rye whiskey, and he always wondered what Chester was looking for, rummaging through the desk drawers. But as the show matured, a special bond grew between them. Once, after he'd saved Dillon's life, Chester refused to let the marshal discuss it in town: it would only be embarrassing to them both.

Dillon was a ''lonely, sad, tragic man,'' said Macdonnell. He played his hand and often lost. He arrived too late to prevent a lynching. He amputated a dying man's leg and lost the patient anyway. He saved a young girl from brutal rapists, then found himself unable to offer her what she needed to stop her from moving into town and a fairly obvious life as a prostitute. Meston rejoiced in such freedom. In a letter to the *New York Tribune*, he welcomed the opportunity to destroy a character he had always loathed, the western guitar-thumping hero, singing his synthetic, nasal ballad. ''I spit in his milk, and you'll have to go elsewhere to find somebody to pour out the lead for his golden bullets.'' In Meston's view, Dillon was almost as scarred as the homicidal psychopaths who drifted into Dodge from every direction. ''Life and his enemies have left him looking a little beat-up. There'd have to be something wrong with him or he wouldn't have hired on as a United States marshal in the heyday of Dodge City, Kansas.''

The opening signature left little doubt that Dillon was the law.

Around Dodge City, and into territory on west, there's just one way to handle the killers and the spoilers: that's with a U.S. Marshal, and the smell of gunsmoke!

Gunsmoke!... starring William Conrad... the story of the violence that moved west with young America, and the story of a man who moved with it.

I'm that man... Matt Dillon. United States marshal... the first man they look for, and the last man they want to meet... it's a chancy job, and it makes a man watchful... and a little lonely.

The show drew critical acclaim for unprecedented realism. It was compared—though the two sounded nothing alike—to Jack Webb's *Dragnet.* When Dillon and Chester rode the plains, the listener heard the faraway prairie wind and the dry squeak of Matt's pants against saddle leather. When Dillon opened the jail door, the listener heard every key drop on the ring. Dillon's spurs rang out with a dull clink-clink, missing occasionally, and the hollow boardwalk echoed dully as the nails creaked in the worn wood around them. Buckboards passed, and the listener heard extraneous dialogue in the background, just above the muted shouts of kids playing in an alley. He heard noises from the next block, too, where the inevitable dog was barking.

In the second year, Meston left his job as CBS story editor to freelance the writing of *Gunsmoke*. For the next three years, he was virtually the author of *Gunsmoke*, turning out about 40 scripts a years. His writing was described by Macdonnell as "understated and simple." Conrad found it "seasoned and highlighted by red streaks of magnificent violence," yet filled with "a final total compassion with whatever the problem was." The violence often went beyond that of radio's fabled horror shows: there were mutilated bodies left by Indians to rot on the plains, men killed by axes or knives, families burned out or slaughtered. "This is the way I work," said Meston in 1955. "I decide that it's time for an Indian story, or an Army story, or maybe a Civil War vet returning home. Then I think of the people I knew as a kid in Colorado. And I think of what I've read about the west of 1870, and I put a character together. Let's say I decide on a man who can't take the land, it's too rough for him and he wants to get back east. Then I have my character and can build a story."

The company formed close personal friendships. Parley Baer wept on Hickman's show, remembering his days with Howard McNear. "The dearest man, there was just nobody who didn't like him." Conrad considered McNear "the life of our cast. . . . Howard and Parley are two people that everybody should know in their lives." The recording sessions rippled with camaraderie and became known as "dirty Saturdays," filled with laughter and ribald jokes. Vic Perrin, who with John Dehner, Harry Bartell, and Lawrence Dobkin was among the show's steadiest character actors, once said that doing *Gunsmoke* was more fun than attending the Academy Awards.

As early as 1953 there was talk of television. Perhaps Macdonnell saw the writing on the wall when he told the press that "our show is perfect for radio," that *Gunsmoke* confined by a picture couldn't possibly be as authentic or attentive to detail. Behind the scenes, he was intrigued. If the cast could be left intact (a major problem, for the once-slender Bill Conrad had ballooned in recent years, giving him an appearance far different from what a listener saw in the mind) and if the spirit and integrity of the radio show could be maintained . . . well, it might be interesting.

In the end, CBS simply took it away from him. The radio cast was given a token audition (and this only because of a persistent newspaper columnist), and with the radio show going strong, a new regime moved in for television. Charles Marquis Warren would direct, Macdonnell would be allowed to produce, and Meston—wisely, for he would become its greatest asset—would continue as writer (the early shows used Meston's radio scripts). James Arness would star as a very different Dillon; Amanda Blake would play Kitty; Milburn Stone would be a good Doc Adams; and Dennis Weaver would be given a wooden leg and a greater drawl as Chester. Two things amused Parley Baer in later life: that the new people would find it necessary to change Chester's surname (from the Baer-coined Proudfoot to Goode) and that Dennis Weaver eventually came to hate the role. Isn't it interesting, Baer was asked in 1984, that what was the highlight of his professional life became for Weaver a limiting, confining trap, like the picture tube itself? "That *is* interesting," Baer said, as if such a thought had never occurred to him.

For Bill Conrad, the television show was a bitter loss. He became unavailable to interviewers, especially when they wanted to talk about his radio career. He became Cannon on TV, and a generation came of age never knowing that the declining Matt Dillon (age overtook even James Arness) they watched on Monday nights owed his existence to the fat detective who waddled across their screens on Tuesday. The acrimony was probably unavoidable: certainly it was understandable. There would always be champions of radio vs. TV, and among radio people *Gunsmoke* is routinely placed among the best shows of any kind and any time. That radio fans considered the TV show a sham, and its players impostors, should surprise no one. That the TV show was not a sham was due in no small part to the continued strength of Meston's scripts.

Gunsmoke is another story with a happy ending. Virtually every episode from the first four years exists on tape, and the shows are widely circulated. A new listener can begin with *Billy the Kid* in 1952 and go straight through. A fringe benefit can be found in some of the dress rehearsal material that was saved and put on tape. There are hilarious excerpts: Conrad struggling to say "sod hut" and blowing it every time, with the cast rolling in laughter. Notable is the rehearsal of *New Hotel*, recorded in late 1955 and aired in its polished version Feb. 19, 1956. Rex Koury's musicians break into a fire scene suddenly with *I Don't Want to Set the World on Fire*, and the show falls apart. A digestive indiscretion occurs at the microphone. "That goddamn shrimp curry does it every time," one of the actors says, and Bill Conrad is reduced to helpless laughter. A listener must wonder how after such hilarity they managed to get the actual broadcast recorded. The broadcast version of the same show testifies that they were all professionals, and when they played for the money, they played it straight. Suddenly the listener is back in Dodge, with its dusty streets and its Long Branch Saloon, its Texas Trail and shoe-leather buffalo steaks. The marshal is steely-eyed and a little lonely, and the deputy cradles the shotgun and covers his back. So strong a show was bound to gather advocates, and did, when SuzAnne and Gabor Barabas published *Gunsmoke: A Complete History* (McFarland, 1990). This 836-page book covers the show in every conceivable aspect—radio and television—with reminiscences of both casts, a huge section of photographs, and show-by-show descriptions with titles, dates, story synopses, and players for every episode.

_H_

THE HALL OF FANTASY, horror-supernatural dramatic anthology.

BROADCAST HISTORY: Aug. 22, 1952–Sept. 28, 1953, Mutual. 30m, Fridays at 9:30 until Sept. 26, 1952; returned Jan. 5, 1953, Mondays at 8:30.

CAST: Chicago radio performers including Harry Elders, Eloise Kummer, Carl Grayson, and Maurice Copeland. **WRITER-CREATOR-PRODUCER-DIRECTOR:** Richard Thorne, who also played many of the character roles. **DIRECTOR:** Leroy Olliger; also, Glenn Ransom. **MUSIC:** Harold Turner.

In this series of dark fantasy, man struggled against the unknown and often lost. The supernatural was portrayed as a force that could be dangerous, awesome, sometimes devastating, and always frightening. Situations ranged from a killer fog to the walking dead. There were often shock endings, with the vampire's teeth sinking into the hero's throat, etc.

THE HALLMARK HALL OF FAME and **HALLMARK PLAYHOUSE,** dramatic anthologies.

BROADCAST HISTORY: June 10, 1948–Feb. 1, 1953, CBS. 30m, Thursdays at 10, 1948–50; at 9:30, 1950–51; at 8:30, 1951–52; Sundays at 9, 1952–53. _Hallmark Playhouse._ The Hallmark Greeting Card Company. **CAST:** James Hilton, host. Well-known stories from literature with top Hollywood actors: _Cimarron_, by Edna Ferber, starring Irene Dunne; _Elmer the Great_, by Ring Lardner, starring Bob Hope; _The Prairie Years_, by Carl Sandburg, starring Gregory Peck; etc. **ANNOUNCER:** Frank Goss. **MUSIC:** Lyn Murray; later, David Rose. **DIRECTOR:** Dee Engelbach; later, William Gay. **ADAPTATIONS (SCRIPTS):** Jean Holloway, with Jack Rubin; also, Milton Geiger; later, Jerome Lawrence and Robert Lee.

Feb. 8, 1953–March 27, 1955, CBS. 30m, Sundays at 9, 1953–54; at 6:30, 1954–55. _The Hallmark Hall of Fame._ **CAST:** Lionel Barrymore, host. Top stars in true stories of Americana. **ANNOUNCER:** Frank Goss. **DIRECTORS:** William Gay, William Froug.

The Hallmark Playhouse was an abrupt change for sponsor Hallmark cards: away from its _Radio Reader's Digest_ and into a literary mode. Bestselling British novelist James Hilton would host and select the books that would be adapted for the air. Hilton announced plans to "ransack the past" and search out never-before-broadcast tales from the 2,000-year history of written literature. This was easier said than done: _The Columbia Workshop_ had beaten Hilton to the punch with his opener, _The Devil and Daniel Webster_, by more than a decade. A second announced plan, to stay away from the high-profile glitz so prevalent on other shows, fell almost immediately. But the series did manage to produce many seldom-heard works (_O'Halloran's Luck_, by Stephen Vincent Benét; _Free Land_, by

Rose Wilder Lane; etc.), as well as familiar tales from Hilton's own bibliography (*Lost Horizon; Random Harvest; Goodbye, Mr. Chips*).

The shift to the *Hall of Fame* format was another abrupt about-face, suddenly offering stories of Madame Curie, Mary Todd Lincoln, and Robert Livingston, who helped orchestrate the Louisiana Purchase. Host Lionel Barrymore bellowed "Gooood eeeevening, laydies and gentlemen!" as if he really meant it. In its seldom-seen TV version, *The Hallmark Hall of Fame* has become the grandfather of all prestige shows, a dignified though increasingly expensive promotion for the slogan that was a standard even in 1948: *Remember—a Hallmark Card, when you care enough to send the very best.*

THE HALLS OF IVY, situation comedy.

BROADCAST HISTORY: Jan. 6, 1950–June 25, 1952, NBC. 30m, Fridays at 8 until May 1950, then Wednesdays at 8. Joseph Schlitz Brewing Company.

CAST: Ronald Colman as William Todhunter Hall, president of Ivy College in "Ivy, USA," somewhere in middle America. Benita (Colman) Hume as Vicky, his wife, the former Victoria Cromwell of the English theater. Herb Butterfield as Clarence Wellman, the most difficult member of Ivy's rigid board of governors. Willard Waterman as John Merriweather, Hall's lone voice of support on the Ivy board. Elizabeth Patterson and Gloria Gordon as the Hall's maid. Support from Hollywood radio actors: Jerry Hausner, Paula Winslowe, Raymond Lawrence, Sheldon Leonard, Herb Vigran, Ken Christy, Jean Vander Pyl, Jeffrey Silver, Johnny McGovern, Charles Seel, Bob Sweeney, Virginia Gregg, Rolfe Sedan, etc. **ANNOUNCER:** Ken Carpenter. **MUSIC:** Henry Russell. **CREATOR-WRITER:** Don Quinn. **PRODUCER-DIRECTOR:** Nat Wolff. **WRITERS:** Jerome Lawrence and Robert Lee; later, Milton and Barbara Merlin. **THEME:** *The Halls of Ivy,* sung in hallowed Ivy League fashion, by soft male voices in an echo chamber.

The Halls of Ivy was a warm, literate comedy, created by Don Quinn of *Fibber McGee and Molly.* Quinn had been thinking about such a show for several years. Though his partnership with Jim and Marian Jordan on the *McGee* program had been a happy one, he wanted to try something new. Producer Nat Wolff encouraged

him to write it, nagging it into tangible shape in the form of an audition disc. This initial proposal starred Edna Best, Wolff's wife, with Gale Gordon as the college president. It proved ill-timed: the stars had prior commitments, and the proposal failed to generate much interest.

Then Wolff thought of Ronald Colman. He had long been Colman's friend and agent, and he knew that Colman was a natural. But Colman had shown little interest in weekly series radio: only in recent years, with semi-regular appearances on *The Jack Benny Program,* had Colman shown himself to be a master of dry comedy. His Benny shows, usually in company with his wife, Benita, were critically acclaimed as high spots of the Benny seasons.

Colman would play the erudite but charming William Todhunter Hall. Benita would play Vicky, who in earlier days had starred in such musical plays as *Lulu's Mad Moment* ("I spent the whole second act on a ladder singing *'ool 'old out a 'elpin' 'and'*"), but had given it all up to become a scholar's wife. Who could resist such a suitor (referenced ever after as "Toddy-dear"), so persistent that he would happily sit through one of her plays 25 times?

"I wanted an excuse for a literate type of comedy," said Quinn, explaining the college setting. His problem was that he couldn't handle the writing. "Quinn was a terrific joke writer, but he couldn't have handled a plot or an overall design," writer Milton Merlin told Juliet Benita Colman for the biography she wrote on her father. Quinn contributed ideas, situations, endless cheer in the studio, an occasional full script, and, usually, Toddy's closing line. The scripts were constructed week to week by Lawrence and Lee or by the Merlins.

The stories concerned critical turning points in the lives of students, teachers, or friends of the Halls—occasionally a crisis for Ivy itself. Toddy always took a personal hand in these matters, often bucking the school's board of governors in the process. Typical *Ivy* situations involved a student who had to choose between careers as an architect and a prizefighter, the alumnus who wanted to build a new gym for the school but attached impossible strings to the gift, and a touching account of a professor losing his eyesight. At the critical moment, Toddy would often find some corollary in his past, when he and Victoria were courting, that would show him the way. And though he soloed on relatively few scripts, Quinn's influence is all over the series. The shows are highly conversational, reflecting the same love of words that made *McGee* such a classic. Quinn especially liked to reverse clichés: Wellman "is a snob with a capital dollar-sign, if I may phrase a coin" and spring "is the time of year when the man rises in a sap's veins." Both are obvious Quinn lines. A good sampling of *Ivy* is available on tape. It's a pleasant half-hour that holds its charm even after four decades.

HANNIBAL COBB, detective drama.

BROADCAST HISTORY: Jan. 9, 1950–May 11, 1951, ABC. Unusual daytime format, 30m and 15m timeslots, weekdays at 3:30. Sustained from New York. Santos Ortega as Cobb, whose adventures were cross-promoted in "the photocrime pages of *Look* magazine."

HAP HAZARD, comedy-variety.

BROADCAST HISTORY: July 1–Sept. 23, 1941, NBC. 30m, Tuesdays at 9:30. Summer replacement for *Fibber McGee and Molly*. Johnson's Wax.
CAST: Ransom Sherman as Hap Hazard, harried proprietor of the Crestfallen Manor, a ramshackle hotel in the "Stop-and-Flop" chain. **ANNOUNCER:** Harlow Wilcox. **VOCALIST:** Edna O'Dell. **ORCHESTRA:** Billy Mills. **WRITER:** Ransom Sherman.

Hap Hazard spent most of his time on this series rescuing guests from the hazards of the hotel. Its floors creaked, the doors wouldn't shut, the water taps dripped, and when the president of the chain came and wanted to look at the books, Hap could only ask, "Fiction or nonfiction?"

THE HAPPINESS BOYS, songs and patter: the best-known radio name (though there were many others) for the early comedy-and-song duo Billy Jones and Ernie Hare.

BROADCAST HISTORY: Oct. 18, 1921, first broadcast, WJZ, Newark.
   Aug. 22, 1923, WEAF, New York. Happiness Candy.
   1926–29, NBC. 30m, Fridays at 8, 1926–27; at 7:30, 1927–29. *The Happiness Boys*. Happiness Candy.

1929–31, Blue Network, 30m, Fridays at 9. *The Interwoven Pair*. Interwoven Socks.
   1931–38, NBC, variously on both networks, Red and Blue. 15m, three a week. Heard as *The Flit Soldiers* for Standard Oil; as *The Best Foods Boys* for Hellman's Mayonnaise (1932); and under several names (*The Tastyeast Jesters, The Tasty Loafers, The Tasty Breadwinners*) for Tastyeast Bakers (ca. 1931–38).
   1939–40, WMCA, New York.

Billy Jones and Ernie Hare were radio pioneers. They claimed the distinction of being the first paid performers of the air and stayed in the business long enough to do an estimated 2,000 broadcasts. Jones (born March 15, 1889) met Hare (March 16, 1881) in a recording studio in 1920. Bandleader Gus Haenschen asked them to sing a vocal accompaniment to a record he was making, and they were launched as a team.

On their first broadcast, in 1921, they held the WJZ air for 90 minutes, talking, singing, and cracking jokes. There was much favorable mail, and soon they were in demand. Their Happiness Candy show began on WEAF in the era when no direct advertising was permitted: thus began their long practice of taking their names from whatever product was their current patron. In all their formats the act was much the same: high-hearted novelty numbers (such as *Henry Made a Lady out of Lizzie*) mixed with standup vaudeville jokes. They came on singing, their theme a reminder of the product:

We two boys without a care
Entertain you folks out there
That's our hap-hap-hap-pi-ness!

They were said to be remarkably alike: same height, same weight, birthdays just a day apart; even their mothers shared a maiden name. Their best-known theme song could be modified to fit almost any sponsor:

How do ya do, everybody, how do ya do?
Gee, it's great to say hello to all of you!
I'm Billy Jones!
I'm Ernie Hare!
And we're the Interwoven Pair!
How do ya doodle-doodle-doodle-doodle-do?

Their comeback attempt on WMCA was cut short by Hare's death March 9, 1939. Jones continued for a time with Hare's teenage daughter, Marilyn, but he died the following year, Nov. 23, 1940.

THE HARDY FAMILY, situation comedy, based on the MGM film series.

BROADCAST HISTORY: 1949–50, MGM transcribed syndication.

Jan. 3, 1952–Jan. 1, 1953, Mutual. 30m, Thursdays at 8:30.

CAST: Mickey Rooney as Andy Hardy, quintessential 1930s teenager of Centerville, USA. Lewis Stone as his father, Judge James Hardy. Fay Holden as his mother, Emily. **MUSIC:** Jerry Fielding. **DIRECTOR:** Thomas McAvity. **WRITER:** Jack Rubin.

In this series, Andy Hardy had graduated from his teen years and become a young businessman. But as *Radio Life* noted, Mickey Rooney played the part just as when Andy was in high school: with pandemonium and chaos.

THE HARRY RICHMAN SHOW, musical variety.

BROADCAST HISTORY: April 18, 1934–March 6, 1935, Blue Network. 30m, Wednesdays at 10:30. Conoco. **ORCHESTRA:** Jack Denny.

Richman was a showman, a crooner of '30s-style ballads and novelties. He was also syndicated on behalf of "your local Dodge dealer" (ca. 1936–37) and by the state of Florida for its orange and grapefruit growers (1937–38). The latter show, *It's Florida's Treat*, featured the music of Freddie Rich and such guests as Cliff Edwards and Lee Wiley. The theme was *I Love a Parade*.

HARV AND ESTHER, comedy-variety.

BROADCAST HISTORY: Sept. 12, 1935–March 5, 1936, CBS. 30m, Thursdays at 8. Harvester Cigars.
CAST: Teddy Bergman and Audrey Marsh in the title roles, names obviously concocted for the sponsor's benefit. **VOCALIST:** Jack Arthur. **ORCHESTRA:** Vic Arden.

THE HARVEST OF STARS, concert music.

BROADCAST HISTORY: Oct. 7, 1945–March 28, 1948, NBC. 30m, Sundays at 2, 1945–46; at 2:30, 1946–48. International Harvester. **CAST:** Raymond Massey, host, with Howard Barlow's orchestra (1945–46); James Melton, "singing host," with orchestra directed by Dr. Frank Black

(1946–48). **PRODUCER:** Glan Heisch.

April 7, 1948–March 30, 1949, CBS. 30m, Wednesdays at 9:30. International Harvester. **CAST:** James Melton with orchestra led by Bernard Herrmann. **ANNOUNCER:** Don Hancock. **PRODUCER:** Glan Heisch.

April 3, 1949–Sept. 17, 1950, NBC. 30m, Sundays at 5:30. International Harvester. **CAST:** James Melton with Dr. Frank Black.

Harvest of Stars was an agency show, developed for Harvester by Russ Johnston of McCann-Erickson, featuring a broad cross-section of traditional melodies. There was much music on the order of *Night and Day, Through the Years, April in Paris*, and the always-appreciated tunes from *Carmen* and *The Student Prince*. If newer pieces were used, they tended to be from mainstream Broadway hits: *Carousel, Oklahoma!*, and *Annie Get Your Gun*.

On NBC, Dr. Frank Black mapped out his broadcasts a month at a time. It was regularly broadcast from NBC's Studio 8-H in New York but was frequently on tour. Musicians, choral groups, and actors would be lined up on location, often weeks ahead. Black and choral director Harry Simeone would arrive a few days before and "front" their respective groups. There was also a five-minute dramatic skit, the stories selected by producer Glan Heisch. In 1948 *Harvest of Stars* hit its peak, with a rating of almost 12 points. On tour, the show was always sold out, turning away 1,000 people at the 3,000-seat San Francisco War Memorial Opera House.

HASHKNIFE HARTLEY, western melodrama, based on the novels of Wilbur C. Tuttle.

BROADCAST HISTORY: July 2, 1950–Dec. 30, 1951, Mutual. 30m, Sundays at 3:30, then at 2:30.
CAST: Frank Martin as Hashknife Hartley, a wandering cowboy. Barton Yarborough as Sleepy Stevens, his Texas-reared sidekick. **NARRATOR:** Wilbur C. Tuttle. **MUSIC:** Harry Zimmerman. **PRODUCER-DIRECTOR:** Tom Hargis. **WRITER:** Fred Luke.

THE HAUNTING HOUR, mystery-horror anthology.

BROADCAST HISTORY: 1944–46, 30m transcribed syndication. There were no credits, so casts and production crews are unknown. But the series is prolific, with 40-odd shows on tape. Typical mystery ambience: tolling churchbells, echoing footsteps, high melodrama.

HAVE GUN, WILL TRAVEL, western adventure.

BROADCAST HISTORY: (Originated on TV: Sept. 14, 1957–Sept. 21, 1963, CBS.) *Radio*: Nov. 23, 1958–Nov. 27, 1960, CBS. 30m, Sundays at 6. Multiple sponsorship.
CAST: John Dehner as Paladin, soldier of fortune, western knight errant, gunfighter. Ben Wright as Heyboy, the Oriental who worked at the Carlton Hotel in San Francisco, where Paladin lived. Virginia Gregg as Missy Wong, Heyboy's girlfriend. Virginia Gregg also in many leading dramatic roles. Supporting players from Hollywood's Radio Row, most of the same personnel listed for *Gunsmoke*. **ANNOUNCER:** Hugh Douglas. **PRODUCER-DIRECTOR:** Frank Paris. **CREATORS-WRITERS:** Herb Meadow and Sam Rolfe. **WRITERS:** Gene Roddenberry, John Dawson, Marian Clark, etc. **SOUND EFFECTS:** Ray Kemper, Tom Hanley.

Have Gun, Will Travel was an oddity: the only significant radio show that originated on television. Beginning as a TV series for Richard Boone, *Have Gun* leaped immediately into the top ten and gained such an enthusiastic following that CBS decided to add it to the fading radio chain. Boone had established the premise well: as the gunfighter Paladin, he did the sometimes-dangerous work that others would not or could not do for themselves. That he did these jobs for a hefty price did not diminish the fact that he was a man with a conscience.

Paladin had studied at West Point and emerged from the Civil War to settle in San Francisco. He wined and dined beautiful women, announcing his services with a simple card, containing the words *Have Gun, Will Travel/Wire Paladin/San Francisco* and the symbol of a white chess knight—a Paladin. On television, Boone wore black and conveyed the image of a man not to be trifled with.

John Dehner approached the radio role as if Boone had never existed. "I don't imitate," he said in an interview years later. His was a streamlined version, perhaps slighter of build but just as deadly. The radio scripts closely followed the TV format, using the same staccato musical theme and opening with a small piece of Paladin dialogue. This was often a threat, delivered to some as-yet-unknown badman. "If the girl who's being held prisoner has been harmed in any way, I'll flip a coin to see which one of you I gun down first," he said to open one show.

He was a loner, man of no friends. His relationship with the bellhop Heyboy was cordial but cool: Paladin was always "Meestah Paladin," and Heyboy was always Heyboy. At the end of the radio run, Paladin left San Francisco to claim an inheritance. On TV, it remained a strong show.

HAWAII CALLS, Hawaiian music.

BROADCAST HISTORY: 1935–90s, mostly Mutual regional networks; first heard July 5, 1935, on the West Coast Mutual–Don Lee hookup. National run 1945–56: 30m, Saturdays at 7, 1945–51; at 9, 1951–52; Sundays at 8, 1952–56. Regional, 1956–75, and from October 1992.
PERFORMERS: Al Kealoha Perry, Harry Owens, Haleloke (who went on to fame with Arthur Godfrey), Hilo Hattie, Alfred Apaka. **CREATOR-PRODUCER-DIRECTOR:** Webley Edwards; Danny Kaleikin, 1972–75; Bill Bigelow, 1990s. **ASSISTANT DIRECTOR:** Jim Wahl.

Webley Edwards thought up his *Hawaii Calls* series while listening to a "terrible" Hawaiian broadcast at KFRC, San Francisco, in 1934. He decided he could do better, and did. Each week his program of islander music was beamed from the shores of Waikiki Beach to the United States. Hawaii's best singers and musicians were featured, backed by the swish of wahine skirts and the roar of the Pacific (a soundman was stationed at the oceanfront with a microphone). The musicians used only drums, ukeleles, and steel guitars. They performed ten songs per week: three were pure Hawaiian, the rest in English.

The shows were performed live before an audience that eventually grew to more than 2,000 people. Edwards made great use of the campfire atmosphere, emphasizing that his show was produced "right under the banyan trees," with the famous Diamond Head in the background. The shortwave transmission had a pulsing quality, which added to the waves and enhanced the exotic flavor. Edwards died in 1972.

HAWK LARABEE, western adventure.

BROADCAST HISTORY: July 5, 1946–Feb. 7, 1948, CBS. Various 30m timeslots. Initially heard as *Hawk Durango* (six weeks).

CAST: **1946:** Elliott Lewis as Hawk Durango. Barton Yarborough as his sidekick. **1946–47:** Barton Yarborough as Hawk. Barney Phillips as his sidekick, Somber Jones, whose gloomy demeanor was characterized by his name. **As of late 1947:** Elliott Lewis as Hawk. Barton Yarborough as his sidekick, Brazos John. MUSICAL BRIDGES: The Texas Rangers, vocal quartet (Rod May, Fran Mahoney, Bob Crawford, and Tookie Cronenbold); later, Andy Parker and the Plainsmen. PRODUCER-DIRECTOR: William N. Robson. ASSISTANT DIRECTOR: Richard Sanville (as of mid-1947). WRITERS: Dean Owen, Kenneth Perkins, Arthur E. Orlock.

Hawk Larabee was radio's first half-hearted attempt at an adult western drama, a concept that was not fully realized until the arrival of *Gunsmoke* five years later. The series underwent several changes in its brief history, with actors Elliott Lewis and Barton Yarborough switching roles between the lead and the sidekick in a convoluted succession of cast changes.

Hawk, evolving from the brief *Hawk Durango*, told of Texas in the 1840s, a world seen through the eyes of a cattleman. Hawk's spread was near the town of Sundown Wells: his tales, self-narrated and understated, were billed as "stories of the men and women, famous and infamous, who loved and hated, lived and died, in the colorful drama of the American West."

Yarborough brought to the role a genuine Texas accent. He played Hawk as a good-natured cowboy, a Samaritan who'd always rather talk his way out of a situation than fight. By late 1947, Lewis (the original Hawk) had returned to the lead, and Yarborough slipped easily into the sidekick's role, with the same voice he'd been using as the hero. Lewis gave Larabee a more heroic portrayal, with no accent whatever. The ranch was now located on Black Mesa, and the show opened to "the hawk's whistle," the sound of hoofbeats, and the announcement that "the hawk is on the wing." The vocal bridges by the Texas Rangers, and later by Andy Parker's Plainsmen, provided all the music, giving it a distinct sound.

HAWTHORNE HOUSE, serial drama.

BROADCAST HISTORY: Ca. 1935 to mid-1940s, NBC West Coast (premiere from San Francisco, Oct. 28, 1935). 30m, weekly.

CAST: Pearl King Tanner as Mother Sherwood, a widow, who struggled through the depression by turning her mansion into a rooming house for paying guests. Her three children, Mel, Marietta, and the adopted Billy were thus portrayed: Monty Mohn originally as Mel, the part also played for many years by Jack Moyles; Bobbe Deane and Florida Edwards as Marietta (1930s), with Natalie Park as Marietta (1940s) in the later storyline; Eddie Firestone, Sam Edwards, and Gordon Connell as Billy. Boarders: Natalie Park as Lois Liston Tremaine. Donald Dudley and John Pickard as Jerry Tremaine. Ruth Peterson as Linda Carroll, a singer who was married to Chick Morgan. Ted Maxwell as Chick Morgan. Ruth Sprague as Alice James, Billy's girlfriend. Billy Byers as Miriam Bracefield, Mel's flame and later his wife. Betty Lou Head as Lolly Martin, Mel's confidential secretary. Bert Horton as Duke Calloway. Jack Kirkwood as Uncle Jim. Dixie Marsh, "famed colored impersonator and singer of darky songs" (*Radio Life*), as Martha the cook. PRODUCER-WRITER: Ray Buffum. WRITERS: David Drummond, Cameron Prud'Homme.

Hawthorne House followed the pattern set by *One Man's Family*, a weekly half-hour continuation of family life in the West. But while *One Man's Family* became a national force, *Hawthorne House* was confined to the regional West Coast NBC network, where it originally aired at 9:30 Monday nights.

The serial took a page from the life of Pearl Tanner King, the actress who played Mother Sherwood. The stock market crash of 1929 had changed her life: her husband had died, and their affluent life had disappeared. To support her children, Tanner had turned her mansion into a rooming house. The success of this venture was the basis of the serial.

In the storyline, Mother Sherwood and her children met, lived with, and sometimes came to love their boarders. Their home was a catch-all of trouble, strife, and joy. The first guest, Lois Liston, was a lovely young woman seeking shelter for herself and her grandmother.

Son Mel Sherwood fell in love, but Lois loved Jerry Tremaine, a penniless writer who had come to live at Hawthorne House. Over the years, Jerry became successful: he and Lois married, and Mel had a long affair with Miriam Bracefield, which also ended in marriage after many difficulties.

HEAR IT NOW, documentary

BROADCAST HISTORY: Dec. 15, 1950–June 15, 1951, CBS. 60m, Fridays at 9.
COMMENTATOR: Edward R. Murrow. **SPORTS COMMENTATOR:** Red Barber. **ENTERTAINMENT COMMENTATOR:** Abe Burrows. **COMMENTATOR ON THE PRESS:** Don Hollenbeck. **MUSICAL SCORE:** Virgil Thomson, composer. **WRITER-PRODUCER:** Fred Friendly.

Hear It Now was an outgrowth of a Columbia Records series, *I Can Hear It Now*, produced by Fred Friendly and Edward R. Murrow. The success of the records spurred new interest in audio documentary, and CBS was seeking a vehicle for Murrow, soon to return from Korea. Friendly was intrigued by the possibilities of TV documentary. Murrow, according to biographer Joseph E. Persico, "distrusted a medium that depended more on pictures than words." So it began on radio.

It was a magazine of sorts, covering the news events of the previous six days in the voices of the newsmakers themselves, by transcription and with hot live microphones. It won a Peabody and was described by one critic as "the biggest adventure in news gathering ever attempted." The subjects ranged from "postelection job seekers" to Sugar Ray Robinson to MacArthur's return to the States.

But the radio show, said Persico, "was rather like building the best gas lamp at the turn of the century, when most people were wiring their homes for electricity." Murrow relented and took it to TV, premiering *See It Now* on CBS Nov. 18, 1951. This would become classic video news documentary, highlighted by Murrow's battle with Sen. Joseph McCarthy over the tactics of congressional Communist-hunters. It was seen until July 5, 1955.

HEART'S DESIRE, human interest giveaway show.

BROADCAST HISTORY: Sept. 9, 1946–Jan. 30, 1948, Mutual. 30m, weekdays at 3, 1946–47; at 11:30 A.M., 1947–48.
HOST: Ben Alexander. **ANNOUNCER:** Cliff Johnson. **CREATORS:** Charlie Morin and Roy Maypole. **PRODUCER:** Bud Ernst. **DIRECTOR:** Dave Grant.

The premise of *Heart's Desire* was simple: people wrote in asking for things; the better the cause, the better their chances of getting it. Up to 50,000 letters a week came in, to be read and judged by staff. The goal was, first of all, entertainment: letters that would make good air copy. This usually meant a tug at the heartstrings, a hearty laugh, or something bizarre (one woman wanted a washing machine so she wouldn't have to wash her husband's pants in the creek—he had refused to speak to her since finding a frog in his pocket).

The letters judged best were then turned over to the studio audience before the broadcast: the audience selected the best of these, to be read by audience participants on the air. The author of the letter was given her heart's desire, and her studio sponsor was given a prize as well. At the end of each broadcast came a secret jackpot, an item placed inside a cabinet onstage, with the audience challenged to guess its identity. About 20 rapid guesses were allowed: if no one guessed correctly, the item was removed and placed on top of the cabinet, and a new item was hidden inside for the next show. The eventual winner got the entire jackpot.

THE HEDDA HOPPER SHOW, gossip, talk.

BROADCAST HISTORY: Nov. 6, 1939–Oct. 30, 1942, CBS. 15m, three a week at 6:15. Sunkist Fruits.
Oct. 2, 1944–Sept. 3, 1945, CBS. 15m, Mondays at 7:15. Armour.
Sept. 10, 1945–June 3, 1946, ABC. 15m, Mondays at 8:15. Armour.
Oct. 5, 1946–June 28, 1947, CBS. 15m, Saturdays at 10:15, then at 10. *This Is Hollywood*. Procter & Gamble.
Oct. 14, 1950–May 20, 1951, NBC. 30m variety series, Saturdays at 8:30 until Nov. 19, then Sundays at 8.

Hedda Hopper had had several careers before moving into radio and becoming one of the two major outlets for Hollywood gossip. She was born Elda Furry, June 2, 1890. She was a chorus girl, a silent-screen actress, and a real estate saleswoman. She had married comedian De Wolf Hopper and changed her name to Hedda, though she was occasionally confused with Edna Wallace Hopper, who gave beauty tips on the networks ca. 1930–32.

In 1936 she decided to break into radio. Louella Parsons was then the country's top purveyor of gossip, and Hopper—with her 25-year background in Hollywood—thought she could do as well. She hired a manager, Dema Harshbarger, a heavy-set, powerful Hollywood insider who in later years liked to recall that Hopper "told me more about Hollywood in two hours than I'd learned in ten years." But Hopper was not easy to place. She appeared on Rudy Vallee's variety hour and did a brief radio series for Maro-Oil Shampoo. She joined NBC as a fashion commentator, doing her shows from Santa Anita Park and other remote locations. In February 1939 she took the lead in the short-lived Blue Network soap opera *Brenthouse*.

But her quarter-hour gossip shows for Sunkist made her a celebrity. Her radio success led to a newspaper column, to syndication, and to near-equal status with the hated Parsons. In 1943 she was the femcee of *Hollywood Showcase*, a CBS Friday night West Coast variety series: she personally selected the four young performers to be showcased each week, and she reviewed the hot new movies and told backstage stories of the film capital. In 1944 she returned to quarter-hour gossip. But the gossip era was ending: people weren't sinning as much, she said, and she wanted something new. Her *Hedda Hopper Show* of 1950 was a good change of pace, featuring music, chatter, and dramatized film excerpts (Broderick Crawford did a scene from *All the King's Men* on one show). It also had a decidedly pro-American flavor. Hopper was a staunch political conservative who drew praise from J. Edgar Hoover for her commentaries.

Her power in the film city was significant. She seemed to take herself less seriously than did Parsons, though she was considered more accurate and more willing to personally check out her tips. "On the radio, Miss Hopper cheerfully admits her errors by giving herself the bird with a gold-plated mechanical canary," wrote *Current Biography* in 1942. Her feud with Parsons was

real, and in most popularity contests she came out the winner, pronounced by *Life* "infinitely more liked by the movie colony than her ruthless rival." Her personal demeanor was highlighted by a colorful vocabulary and outrageous hats. She died Feb. 1, 1966.

THE HEINZ MAGAZINE OF THE AIR, musical variety with soap opera.

BROADCAST HISTORY: Sept. 2, 1936–April 10, 1938, CBS. Initially 30m, Mondays, Wednesdays, and Fridays at 11 A.M. Heinz Foods. An unusual and expensive "magazine" format: chatter, interviews, music, and guests, with a soap opera, *Trouble House*, sandwiched into the mix. As of Aug. 31, 1937, *Trouble House* was replaced by a new serial, *Carol Kennedy's Romance*, which was both integrated with the *Magazine* format (on Wednesdays and Fridays) and an independent serial on days when the *Magazine* did not run (Mondays, Tuesdays, and Thursdays at 11:15). The original *Magazine* ended Nov. 26, 1937; *Carol Kennedy* continued as an independent serial until March 18, 1938. Meanwhile, a new weekly *Heinz Magazine* was initiated for a four-month run, Dec. 2, 1937–April 10, 1938; 30m, Thursdays at 3:30 until Dec. 30, then Sundays at 5.

1936–37: CAST: Delmar Edmondson, "editor," with guests Theodore Dreiser, Christopher Morley, Albert Payson Terhune and others from the book tour circuit; Amelia Earhart was a notable guest, just before her ill-fated flight. Frank Crumit and Julia Sanderson, regulars after mid-1937. **ANNOUNCERS:** Bill Adams, John Reed King. **VOCALIST:** Reed Kennedy. **CHOIR:** Lyn Murray. **ORCHESTRA:** Leith Stevens (1936), then B. A. Rolfe.

1937–38: CAST: Channing Pollock, "editor," who often lectured on the various forms of happiness. **VOCALIST:** Morton Bowe, tenor. **ORCHESTRA:** Mark Warnow.

Trouble House: **CAST:** Anne Elstner as Martha Booth, heroine, whose trouble began when her destitute brother John descended upon her with his family. Ray Collins as John. Joan Madison as Ann Lowry. Ted Reid as Ted Booth. Carleton Young as the amorous Bill Mears. Ed Jerome as "wandering Roger Byron, whom Martha has loved since childhood." Jerry Macy and Elsie Mae Gordon as Harvey and Phoebe, devoted servants. Gene Leonard as Dr. Clem Allison, who loved Martha. **WRITER:** Elaine Carrington.

Carol Kennedy's Romance: **CAST:** Gretchen Davidson as Carol Kennedy, an orphan who broke away from her restricted life to seek adventure. Carleton Young as Dr. Owen Craig, prominent surgeon. Mitzi Gould as Kathy Prentice, Carol's cousin and Dr. Craig's fiancee. Gene Morgan as dapper-dan Gary Crandall. Joan Madison as Isobel Bronson, Carol's friend.

THE HELEN HAYES THEATER, dramatic anthology.

BROADCAST HISTORY: Oct. 1, 1935–March 24, 1936, Blue Network. 30m, Tuesdays at 9:30. Sanka Coffee. Serialized love story, *The New Penny*, with Hayes as a small-town rebel. **OR-CHESTRA:** Mark Warnow. **WRITER:** Edith Meiser.

Sept. 28, 1936–March 22, 1937, Blue Network. 30m, Mondays at 8. Sanka. Another season-long serial, *Bambi*; James Meighan, leading man. **OR-CHESTRA:** Mark Warnow.

Sept. 29, 1940–Feb. 1, 1942, CBS. 30m, Sundays at 8. Lipton Tea. Popular stories and bestselling novel adaptations: *Let the Hurricane Roar*, by Rose Wilder Lane; *Kitty Foyle*, by Christopher Morley; etc. Leading men from New York radio. **ANNOUNCER:** George Bryan. **ORCHESTRA:** Mark Warnow.

Feb. 25–July 1, 1945, Mutual. 15m, Sundays at 10:15. Textron.

Sept. 8, 1945–March 23, 1946, CBS. 30m, Saturdays at 7 *The Textron Theater*, promoting the recruitment of nurses for the armed forces. Textron: **ANNOUNCER:** Frank Gallop.

Oct. 3, 1948–May 29, 1949, CBS. *The Electric Theater*, covered under that title.

The Helen Hayes Theater was considered prestige drama, but it was heard sporadically and never built the reputation or the audiences of the great theaters of the air. Appearances with Orson Welles's *Mercury* troupe in 1939 confirmed her belief that, "next to the stage, radio is the best medium for drama." Her Lipton Tea series, beginning the following year, was her best and longest forum. She supervised the entire production, playing the leads, helping with casting and sound effects, and even participating in the tea commercials. But it became the first casualty of World War II when, three weeks after Pearl Harbor, Lipton announced its cancellation in anticipation of tea shortages from India.

HELEN HOLDEN, GOVERNMENT GIRL, romantic crime serial.

BROADCAST HISTORY: March 3, 1941–March 20, 1942, Mutual. 15m, weekdays at 1:15.
CAST: Nancy Ordway as Helen Holden, young, single G-woman in Washington, D.C. Nell Fleming as Mary Holden, her aunt. Robert Pollard as David, her boyfriend.

HELLO AMERICANS, documentary drama.

BROADCAST HISTORY: Nov. 15, 1942–Jan. 31, 1943, CBS. 30m, Sundays at 8.
HOST-STAR: Orson Welles.

Hello Americans was the result of Orson Welles's trip to South America in 1942. His purpose: to make a film, the ill-fated and never-released *It's All True*. He was jointly funded by RKO, which planned to distribute the film, and by Nelson Rockefeller's Interurban Affairs Committee. Though the film ran over budget and was taken away from him by the studio, Welles did emerge with a radio show.

It was "a cook's tour of Brazil," as described by *Time*, a half-hour that was "lively though bumpy in spots." Carmen Miranda was co-starred: the opening show was built around the samba, and Welles "amazed everyone," said *Radio Life*, by singing it himself. Subsequent shows told the stories of Bolívar and Montezuma and of the culture of other countries.

HELPMATE, soap opera.

BROADCAST HISTORY: Sept. 22, 1941–June 30, 1944, NBC. 15m, weekdays at 10:30 A.M. Old Dutch Cleanser.
CAST: Arlene Francis and Fern Persons as Linda Harper. Myron McCormick and John Larkin as Steve Harper, her husband. Judith Evelyn and Karl Weber as their friends Grace and Clyde Marshall. Beryl Vaughn and Sidney Ellstrom as their friends George and Holly Emerson. **PRODUCERS:** Frank and Anne Hummert. **WRITER:** Margaret Lewerth.

THE HENRY MORGAN SHOW, comedy.

BROADCAST HISTORY: 1940, WOR, New York. 15m. Initially heard Saturday mornings as *Meet Mr. Morgan*; later in the summer, three a week; by Sept. five a week at 6:45.

Oct. 28, 1940–Jan. 25, 1943, Mutual. 15m, weeknights at 6:45. *Here's Morgan*. Various sponsors, including Life Savers and the Adler Elevator Shoe Company.

Oct. 8, 1945–July 16, 1946, WJZ, New York, ABC affiliate. 15m, six a week.

Sept. 3, 1946–June 24, 1948, ABC. 30m, Initially Tuesdays at 8:30; Wednesdays at 10:30, 1946–47; returned Jan. 29, 1948, Thursdays at 7:30. Eversharp for Schick Razors until Dec. 24, 1947; Rayve Shampoo, 1948.

March 13, 1949–June 16, 1950, NBC. 30m, various times with some breaks. Bristol Myers, from ca. July 1949.

Feb. 6–June 23, 1950, NBC. 15m, weekdays at 6:30.

1940–48: CAST: Henry Morgan, comedian, solo in early 15m shows, 1940–46. Arnold Stang, beginning in his 30m shows for Eversharp, 1946, as a skinny New Yorker named Gerard. Also, ca. 1946–47: Art Carney, Florence Halop, Madeline Lee. **ANNOUNCERS:** Ted Husing, Charles Irving, Art Ballinger, Dan Seymour, David Ross, Ed Herlihy. **ORCHESTRA:** Bernie Green. **DIRECTOR:** Charles Powers. **WRITERS:** Joe Stein, Aaron Ruben, Carroll Moore Jr.

CA. 1949–50: CAST: Arnold Stang, Kenny Delmar, vocalist Lisa Kirk. **ANNOUNCER-STRAIGHT MAN:** Ben Grauer. **ORCHESTRA:** Milton Katims. **DIRECTOR:** Kenneth MacGregor. **THEME:** *For He's a Jolly Good Fellow.*

Three radio comedians became celebrities by heckling the establishment. Fred Allen and Arthur Godfrey needled their victims. Henry Morgan battered his with a club. His most vulnerable victims were often his sponsors.

Morgan clobbered his clients with such unprecedented candor that some of them fired him and one threatened to sue. This was delightful to listeners who scorned the radio commercial as an odious interruption of an otherwise enjoyable half-hour. It made Morgan the darling of his generation's rebels and thinkers, the grand guru of a hard core of intellectuals who considered the jousts of Godfrey and Allen soft.

While Godfrey kidded his sponsors by inference and innuendo, Morgan accused his of fraud. He charged Life Savers with cheating the public by drilling holes in its candy, and he offered to peddle the holes as "Morgan's Mint Middles."

His version of the "six delicious flavors" began with "cement, asphalt, and asbestos." The candy company was not amused: sponsorship was canceled the next day. This was an old story to Morgan, hardly the first time he had been in trouble with clients or station executives. But a Morgan cult had cropped up: as *Liberty* put it, "an astonishing collection ranging from professional humorists and show people to clergymen, children, taxi drivers, and an admiring clique in an insane asylum."

Morgan professed to care nothing for prestige, though he admitted to the *Saturday Evening Post* that he hated to be on the receiving end of the ridicule that he regularly dispensed. In a way, it was a replay of the Godfrey story: Morgan got away with things that others wouldn't even try. By the time the powers finally caught on, he was too popular and out of their control.

He was born March 31, 1915, christened Henry Lerner von Ost Jr. He dropped the trappings and became Henry Morgan in the early 1930s. In 1931 he started as a page boy at WMCA, New York. By 1933 he was being called "the youngest announcer in radio." Over the next seven years, he held jobs at WABC, New York; WCAU, Philadelphia; WNAC, Boston; and WOR, New York. During these years he became fluent in the dialects of Germany, England, France, and Russia and adept at creating madcap characters on the spur of the moment. At WOR, he ran afoul of station bosses for impromptu remarks, drifting away from carefully prepared copy for cutting asides. Once he was sent to do a remote from a tavern that wanted to promote its alleged proximity to New York. "Only 15 minutes from the city as the crow flies," he was supposed to say, and did, adding: "if the crow happens to be driving a supercharged motorcycle."

WOR didn't want to fire Morgan, but something had to be done. Morgan's suggestion seemed prudent: give him a quarter-hour of his own and allow him to "let off steam." The station put him as far out of the way as possible, in an early-morning Saturday slot. He proved too bizarre for that timeslot and was moved into the early evening, three times a week at 6:45. He was alternating with *Superman*, a juvenile serial carried by WOR Tuesdays and Thursdays in the same timeslot. Here Morgan became a cult hero:

his brash style caught on with the Manhattan intelligentsia, and his cause was championed by Robert Benchley, Fanny Brice, James Thurber, and Clifford Goldsmith. Soon *Superman* was moved to another time, Morgan was given five spots a week, and he quickly brought the art of negative advertising to a new peak.

Among his early sponsors were Shell Oil, Ironized Yeast, and Adler Elevator Shoes. The shoe company with its mushy slogan ("Now you can be taller than she is") was most vulnerable to Morgan's wit. "I wouldn't wear them to a dogfight," he said on one broadcast. When company president Jesse Adler called for an apology, Morgan told listeners he had reconsidered: he *would* wear the Adlers to a dogfight after all. Adler became known to the radio audience as "old man Adler," occasionally appearing at the WOR microphone to give Morgan a dressing-down. When Adler claimed his shoes could add two inches to a man's height, Morgan wondered what would happen to the man's pants if that should occur. Three times Adler withdrew his sponsorship, said *Radio Life*, "but Morgan was in their blood—they always came back." When Morgan was called on the carpet, his listeners were sure to hear about it the next day. Once he auctioned off the station and threw in a vice president just "to air the place out." Said *Current Biography*: he loved to "send parents away from the radio so he could incite their children to insurrection," and if his jokes fell flat, he invited listeners to see if they could get a better show from Lowell Thomas on the other dial.

His opening signature—to the novelty theme *For He's a Jolly Good Fellow*, which would be identified with him through most of his career—was the self-delivered salutation "Hello, anybody, here's Morgan." He closed similarly: "Morgan'll be on this same corner in front of the cigar stand next week at this same time." Occasionally he signed off with comedy weather reports: "High winds, followed by high skirts, followed by men," or "Muggy tomorrow, followed by Tuegy, Wedgy, Thurgy, and Frigy." The bogus weather was disdained by the U.S. Navy, which protested and tried to stop it. His quarter-hours were largely ad-libbed, with a few notes thrown together an hour or two before air time. Often he utilized his collection of records, strange music and exaggerated opera: he would

play a few bars, then tear the needle roughly across the grooves. Whatever he did was spontaneous, with no rehearsal and no studio audience.

His postwar shows were cut from different cloth. His Eversharp show for Schick Razors and Blades was a prime-time half-hour, with guests, a cast, an orchestra, and a studio audience. The announcer opened as if in disbelief: "*The Henry Morgan Show??!*" He was still, he said, in front of the same cigar store, but it was felt that his comedy had suffered in the transition. He was criticized in some quarters for soft-pedaling his sponsor. Eventually the Schick Razor commercials proved too tempting, the slogan "push-pull, click-click" becoming, in Morgan's hands, "push-pull, nick-nick." When Eversharp dropped him in 1947, citing flabby material, low ratings, and declining sales, Morgan responded typically, on the air: "It's not my show, it's their razor." He was picked up by Rayve Shampoo, which he drubbed mercilessly, even to the extent of negatively cross-promoting his new product in a guest appearance on *The Fred Allen Show*. His most prominent cast member of the 1946–50 era was Arnold Stang. By 1948 Stang had become so important that *Radio Life* was complaining that it should be called "The Arnold Stang Show."

In the end, Morgan's negative approach withered and died. He couldn't sell like Godfrey and was never considered in the same class, comedically, as Fred Allen. On television, he became known to a new generation as the dour-faced panelist on the Garry Moore game show *I've Got a Secret*.

Morgan died May 19, 1994.

HER HONOR, NANCY JAMES, soap opera.

BROADCAST HISTORY: Oct. 3, 1938–July 28, 1939, CBS. 15m, weekdays at 12:15. Kleenex.

CAST: Barbara Weeks as Nancy James, though still in her 20s, a woman judge in the "Special Court of Common Problems" in Metropolis City. Joseph Curtin as Mayor Richard Wharton, who appointed her; he had loved her since both were law students, but in marriage chose a wealthy and selfish socialite. Kay Strozzi as Evelyn Wharton, the mayor's wife. Ned Wever as Anthony Hale, dashing district attorney, who forged an ever-growing "friendship" with the pretty young jurist. Alice Reinheart as Carrie Dean, ace reporter on the *Metropolis Daily Star*, and Nancy's greatest ally. Janice Gilbert as Madge Keller, "flower of the slums," ever trying to better her lot in a neighborhood beset by poverty and the Cranston mob. Chester Stratton as Stan Adamic, racketeer-turned-good. Joan Banks as Ellen Clark, Nancy's secretary. Maurice Franklin as George Novack, caretaker of the Settlement Center, a place for the poor on the South Side. **ANNOUNCER:** Frank Gallop. **DIRECTOR:** Basil Loughrane, who also closed each show as the "voice of the wise man."

HERB SHRINER TIME, comedy-variety.

BROADCAST HISTORY: Sept. 27, 1948–June 10, 1949, CBS. 15m, weekdays at 5:45, then at 6:30. Alka-Seltzer.

This simple series spotlighted Hoosier comic Herb Shriner, his prowess on the harmonica, and music by the Raymond Scott Quintet. Shriner's Indiana boyhood richly colored his show business routine, giving him a strong regional style faintly reminiscent of Will Rogers. He was linked by *Time* to other young comics (Danny Thomas, Jack Paar, Henry Morgan, and Danny Kaye) who had tried without notable success to "buck radio's old guard" (Jack Benny, Fred Allen, *Amos 'n' Andy*). His show was well reviewed but poorly scheduled, fading after a year. As for *Time*'s failed young comics, all found success in television as the old guard fell away. But Shriner was killed, along with his wife, in an auto accident, April 23, 1970.

HERCULE POIROT, mystery drama, based on the novels by Agatha Christie.

BROADCAST HISTORY: Feb. 22–Oct. 14, 1945, Mutual. 30m, Thursdays at 8 until Oct. 7; then Sundays at 9.
April 1, 1946–Nov. 21, 1947, CBS. 15m, weekdays, various evening timeslots. *Mystery of the Week*. Continuations told in five-chapter stories, concluded each Friday. Procter & Gamble.
CAST: Harold Huber as Poirot, the supposedly ingenious but decidedly immodest Belgian detective. **DIRECTOR:** Carl Eastman.

HERE'S TO ROMANCE, musical variety.

BROADCAST HISTORY: April 18–Oct. 10, 1943, Blue Network. 25m, Sundays at 6:05.
Oct. 14, 1943–April 5, 1945, CBS. 30m, Thursdays at 10:30. Bourjois and its Evening in Paris Powder.
CAST: Buddy Clark, original singing star, April–July 1943. Dick Haymes, 1943–44, with Helen Forrest briefly in 1943. Martha Tilton and Larry Douglas, 1944–45. **ANNOUNCER:** Jim Ameche. **ORCHESTRA:** David Broekman, 1943; Ray Bloch, 1943–45.

Though primarily a musical series, *Here's to Romance* also offered light dramatic skits. Robert Ripley appeared with *Believe It Or Not* tales. After the original format had run its course, Bourjois continued its Thursday-at-10:30 half-hour on CBS with *Romance, Rhythm, and Ripley* (April 12–Oct. 4, 1945) and then with *The Powder Box Theater* (Oct. 11, 1945–April 11, 1946), with Evelyn Knight, Danny O'Neil, and the Bloch band.

HERITAGE, documentary.

BROADCAST HISTORY: Dec. 11, 1952–Oct. 8, 1953, ABC. 30m, Thursdays at 8:30.
NARRATOR: Charles Irving. **MUSIC:** Ralph Norman. **PRODUCER-DIRECTOR:** Sherman H. Dryer.

Based on *Life* magazine's *Picture History of Western Man* series, *Heritage* presented "dramatic adventures from ten centuries of Western civilization," with stories on *The Adventures of Marco Polo, Benjamin Franklin, The Languages of Man*, etc.

THE HERMIT'S CAVE, horror anthology.

BROADCAST HISTORY: Ca. 1935–mid 40s, WJR, Detroit, and syndicated widely on disc in this version, mostly 30m with some 15m stories in the first year. Olga Coal, sponsor, from ca. 1937. **CAST:** John Kent as the Hermit, the cackling narrator who told horror stories in his cave, amidst howling wind. Charles Penman, Toby Grimmer, and Klock Ryder also as the Hermit. Featured roles by "the Mummers," a Detroit radio acting group that included Lillian Popkin, Margery Richmond, Jack Kessler, Ted Johnstone, Jan Koste, and Bill Saunders. Many actors, such as Paul Hughes and Rollon

Parker, were familiar to listeners of *The Lone Ranger*. **PRODUCERS-WRITERS:** Eric Howlett, Geraldine Elliott. **SOUND EFFECTS:** Sidney Brechner, John Foster.

Ca. 1940–44, KMPC, Los Angeles, 30m. **CAST:** Mel Johnson as the Hermit. John Dehner as the Hermit after 1942. Character roles by Elliott Lewis, Tyler McVey, William Hall, Shirley Crowell, etc. **MUSIC:** Rex Koury. **ACTOR-PRODUCER:** William Conrad. **PRODUCER:** Bill Forman. **WRITERS:** Lou Huston, Herbert R. Connor. **SOUND EFFECTS:** Dwight Hauser.

The Hermit's Cave became nationally known, spreading from its local origin through the syndication of its Detroit version to many large markets. "The Mummers" co-titled their show "The Little Theater of the Air," a rather literary moniker for such a blood-and-thunder spook show. The framework is memorable almost sixty years later: howling winds and the rusty-as-nails voice of the Hermit. *Ghhhhhooooooossssssttttttt shories! . . . Weeeeeiiiiirrrrrrddddd stories! . . . and murders, too! The Hermit knows of them all! Turn out your lights! TURN THEM OUT! . . .*

The show had a reputation for network quality and grisly sound effects. G. A. Richards, who owned WJR, later initiated the separate broadcast at his West Coast facility, KMPC. This was a training ground of sorts for young actors with network aspirations (William Conrad was 22; John Dehner 28): Mel Johnson, who was playing the ancient Hermit when the show was at its peak in 1942, was only 24 years old.

HIGH ADVENTURE, dramatic adventure anthology.

BROADCAST HISTORY: March 8, 1947–Jan. 22, 1949, Mutual. 30m, many timeslots; constant shifting with some breaks.

Jan. 29–Oct. 8, 1950, NBC. 30m, Sundays at 4:30.

Jan. 13, 1953–Sept. 21, 1954, Mutual. 30m, Tuesdays at 8:30. **HOST:** Film star George Sanders. **WRITER-DIRECTOR:** Robert Monroe, Elliott Drake. **ANNOUNCERS:** George Hogan, Carl Caruso. **MUSIC:** Sylvan Levin.

High Adventure followed the *Escape* formula, with a deep-voiced narrator sketching in the evening's story in a few sentences. The 1947–49 series was set at a "High Adventure Society," where people told tales of "hard action, hard men, and smooth women."

HILDEGARDE'S RALEIGH ROOM, musical variety.

BROADCAST HISTORY: June 13, 1944–July 24, 1946, NBC. 30m, Tuesdays at 10:30 until Dec. 1945, then Wednesdays at 8:30. *The Raleigh Room*. Raleigh Cigarettes.

Oct. 6, 1946–March 30, 1947, CBS. 30m, Sundays at 9. *The Campbell Room*. Campbell Soups.
STAR: "The Incomparable Hildegarde," with guests. **ORCHESTRA:** Harry Sosnik (1944–46), Paul Baron (1946–47).

Hildegarde was a singer of uncertain nationality, the product of an intense publicity campaign to give her a deliberate international flavor. As her *Current Biography* entry noted, she was known as "the little Hollander" in France, was written about as "the Viennese star" in a Dutch newspaper, and had left the British press wondering whether she was "an American with a French accent or French with an American accent."

In fact, she was Hildegarde Loretta Sell of Milwaukee, Wisc. Her persona was almost total fiction, concocted with the aid of her friend and agent, Anna Sosenko. Sosenko was relentless in promoting her, creating stories of her escapades and feeding them to a hungry American press. She had learned to sing in French, Russian, Italian, and German, as well as in English: she developed "a precise diction which made every word clearly audible and which reduced her accent to an unidentifiable exotic flavoring of speech."

She had already appeared on American radio (the Ed Wynn show, *Believe It Or Not*, and the 1939 NBC series *Ninety-Nine Men and a Girl*) and had substituted for Red Skelton on a revamped *Beat the Band* in 1943. She was so popular in the summer Skelton slot that she was brought in as his full-time replacement when Skelton went into the service in 1944. Her *Raleigh Room* immediately drew ratings in the upper teens, ten points less than Skelton had been carrying but quite acceptable for a fill-in. On the air, she exhibited such bubbly energy and good humor that her act was infectious. She reached for a nightclub atmosphere, setting the studio with tables where special guests (Deems Taylor, Bert Lahr, and Georgie Price on one broadcast) might be found sitting. She worked her audience well, snatching people at random and thrusting them before the microphone. She was still doing well when Skelton returned, so Raleigh continued both shows, shifting Hildegarde to Wednesdays in 1946. But her rating dropped, so Raleigh dropped her. Campbell Soups picked her up for a final season. Again she displayed her courageous good nature by allowing guest Jackie Kelk to sing her theme, *Darling Je Vous Aime Beaucoup*, on her air. Kelk, according to *Radio Life*, gave a riotous impersonation of the chanteuse.

HILLTOP HOUSE, soap opera.

BROADCAST HISTORY: Nov. 1, 1937–March 28, 1941; CBS. 15m, weekdays at 5:45, 1937–38 (also carried on Mutual at 11:30 A.M., first season only); CBS at 10:30 A.M., 1938–40; at 4:30, 1940–41. Palmolive Soap.

May 17, 1948–July 1, 1955, CBS. 15m, weekdays at 3:15 until 1951, then at 3. Miles Laboratories for Alka-Seltzer.

Sept. 3, 1956–July 30, 1957, NBC. 15m, weekdays, mostly at 3:30.

1937–41: CAST: Bess Johnson, appearing in her own name, as Bess Johnson, dedicated caseworker at Hilltop House, an orphanage in the small town of Glendale. Carleton Young and Spencer Bentley as Dr. Robby Clark, friend of Bess and the town physician. Alfred Swenson and Jack Roseleigh as Paul Hutchinson, town banker and another good friend to Bess. Irene Hubbard as Thelma Gidley, Bess's backbiting assistant. Jimmy Donnelly and Janice Gilbert as Jerry and Jean Adair, orphans. John Moore as David Barton. David Gothard as Captain John Barry. **DIRECTORS:** Carlo De Angelo, Jack Rubin. **WRITERS:** Addy Richton and Lynn Stone, under the pseudonym Adelaide Marstone. **THEME:** Brahms' *Lullabye*.

FROM CA. 1948: CAST: Jan Miner and Grace Matthews as Julie Erickson. Robert Haag as Dr. Jeff Browning. Phil Sterling as Reed Nixon.

Hilltop House was Palmolive's initial entry into daytime radio drama. Chicago radio actress Bess Johnson enjoyed a popularity that had transcended her fictitious role: it was widely known that she had played Lady Esther on the commercials for Wayne King's band broadcasts for

six years, and the producers took the unusual step of creating a heroine in her name. The serial was still popular in 1941, when Palmolive tried to cut its budget. Producer Ed Wolfe yanked it off the air instead, and the following Monday Johnson crossed networks to begin a new serial, playing the same character, herself. As *The Story of Bess Johnson*, it was heard March 31, 1941–Sept. 25, 1942, NBC, weekdays at 10 A.M. for Kleenex; a concurrent broadcast remained on CBS March 31–June 27, 1941, weekdays at 4. In this scenario, she had left Hilltop House to begin a new life as superintendent of a boarding school.

The later run of *Hilltop House* was aired from New York, with a new heroine, orphanage supervisor Julie Erickson.

HIS HONOR, THE BARBER, situation comedy-drama.

BROADCAST HISTORY: Oct. 16, 1945–April 9, 1946, NBC. 30m, Tuesdays at 7:30. Ballantine Ale.

CAST: Barry Fitzgerald as Judge Bernard Fitz of the Vincent County District Court. Bill Green as Sheriff McGrath, "Vincent County's own little Hitler," a frequent antagonist of the kindhearted judge. Barbara Fuller as Susan, the judge's lovely young niece. Leo Cleary as the bailiff. Dawn Bender as little Mary Margaret McAllister. **WRITER-PRODUCER-DIRECTOR:** Carlton E. Morse. **ANNOUNCER:** Frank Martin. **ORCHESTRA:** Opie Cates.

This show bore many of the trademarks that writer Carlton E. Morse had established on *One Man's Family*: stories containing the breath of life, realistic conflicts, and a character who, as *Time* put it, was "surefire for cornfed philosophizing." Before his election to the bench, Judge Fitz had been the barber of a small (pop. 3,543) community in the county. At times, when his legal career tried his patience, he longed again for that simpler life. He was staunchly Irish (what else, with Barry Fitzgerald in the lead?) and could be painfully sentimental. One reviewer noted that "he criticizes the law as much as he enforces it, and slyly finds a loophole when he thinks a culprit needs a helping of simple kindness." The sheriff, on the other hand, had a "lock 'em up and throw away the key" mentality.

HIT THE JACKPOT, quiz.

BROADCAST HISTORY: May 9–June 13, 1948, CBS. 30m, Sundays at 9. *Catch Me if You Can.*

June 29, 1948–Dec. 27, 1949, CBS. 30m, Tuesdays at 9:30, then at 10. Chrysler (after June 13, 1949).

May 28–Sept. 3, 1950, CBS. 30m, Sundays at 7:30. Summer replacement for *Amos 'n' Andy* Rinso.

QUIZMASTER: Bill Cullen. **ANNOUNCER:** George Bryan. **ORCHESTRA:** Al Goodman, Ben Ludlow. **PRODUCERS:** Mark Goodson and Bill Todman.

As *Catch Me if You Can*, this series pitted contestants on a chase "up a ladder" on which correct answers advanced them rung by rung. At the top was a "golden door," where the correct answer to a mystery phrase won a huge jackpot. After the show of June 13, 1949, it acquired a sponsor (Chrysler's DeSoto automobile) and modified its format under the title *Hit the Jackpot.* Cards were solicited from listeners: these people were called at random and given a chance to guess the mystery phrase. Winners got free trips, furniture, and a new car from the sponsor. Values of jackpots were often more than $25,000.

THE HOAGY CARMICHAEL SHOW, jazz; musical variety.

BROADCAST HISTORY: 1944–45, Mutual. 30m, Sundays at 8:30, Pacific time. *Tonight at Hoagy's.* **HOST:** Hoagy Carmichael, who also sang. **SINGERS:** Loulie Jean Norman, Dave Marshall, the Thrasher Sisters (DeeDee, Mary, and Betty). **CAST:** Ruby Dandridge, Negro comedienne, as Ella Rose. Harry Evans, "permanent houseguest." **ANNOUNCER:** Larry Keating. **MUSICIANS:** Pee Wee Hunt, Opie Cates, Jimmy Briggs, Joe Venuti, etc. **PRODUCER:** Walter Snow.

1945–46, NBC. 30m, Mondays at 6, Pacific time. *Something New.* **HOST:** Hoagy Carmichael. **FEATURED JAZZ BAND:** The Teenagers, composed entirely of players 16 to 19 years old: Jimmy Higson, leader; sax-clarinetists Wayne Marsh, Harold Kuhn, Bob Drasnin, and Gordon Reeder; trumpets Ralph Clark, Ollie Mitchell, and Don Davies; Chick Parnell, string bass; Norman Barker, trombone; Hal Terry, guitar; Bob Jacobs, piano; Phil Rammacher, drums. **VOCALISTS:** Carol Stewart Gale Robbins. Comedians: Pinky

Lee; comic duo Bob Sweeney and Hal March.

Oct. 26, 1946–June 26, 1948, CBS. 15m, Sundays at 5:30. Luden Cough Drops until June 1947; returned sustained in November, Saturdays at 7:45.

Hoagy Carmichael claimed to have no vocal talent. His friend Hollywood columnist Harry Evans used this argument to coax him onto the air: what Carmichael had was style; the same kind of rough-cut singing voice that Jack Teagarden had, and a flawless sense of delivery. He also had a reputation, being one of America's best-known composers, writer of many popular classics including *Star Dust. Tonight at Hoagy's* brought in jazz notables, re-creating the jam sessions that frequently took place at Carmichael's home. The specialty of *Something New* was twofold: discovering new talent and rediscovering talent that had been neglected. Only his final series, on CBS, ran under his name: a pleasant quarter-hour of songs.

HOBBY LOBBY, human interest.

BROADCAST HISTORY: Oct. 6, 1937–March 30, 1938, CBS. 30m, Wednesdays at 7:15. Hudson Motor Car Company.

July 3–Sept. 25, 1938, NBC. 30m, Sundays at 7. Substitute for *The Jack Benny Program.* Jell-O.

Oct. 5, 1938–Sept. 27, 1939, Blue Network. 30m, Wednesdays at 8:30. Fels Naphtha Soap Chips.

Oct. 8, 1939–March 31, 1940, CBS. 30m, Sundays at 5. Fels Naphtha.

Oct. 4, 1941–Aug. 28, 1943, CBS. 30m, Saturdays at 8:30. Colgate.

Aug. 30, 1945–Aug. 1, 1946, CBS. 30m, Thursdays at 9:30. Anchor Hocking Glass.

Jan. 15–March 5, 1949, Mutual. 30m, Saturdays at 4.

1950, NBC, summer series, 30m, Thursdays.

CREATOR-HOST: Dave Elman; Bob Dixon, host, 1945–46. **MUSIC:** Harry Salter, Harry Sosnik, etc.

Hobby Lobby spotlighted people with unusual hobbies: the hobbies ranged from merely colossal to truly outlandish, thus offering entertaining insight into the human comedy. One woman collected facts about Friday the 13th. A secretary made lifelike sculptures from burnt toast. An insurance clerk collected baby elephant hairs. Another hobbyist headed the "Society for the

Prevention of Propagation of Disparaging Remarks About Brooklyn.'' To qualify for the show, the hobby had to be a true pastime, not something the subject did for a living.

Host Dave Elman was known as "the man of 100,000 hobbies.'' Elman's hobby was hobbies, and collecting unusual information about them. His show doubled its audience each year for three seasons and at its peak received 3,000 letters a week from people wanting to appear. It didn't always work out well: a beekeeper arrived with a swarm of bees that escaped into the studio, but such unexpected moments kept interest high and the show among radio's most frequently revived. One of Elman's most celebrated stunts came in 1942, when he advertised for a talking dog ("must have a vocabulary of ten words of more, preferably no accent''). He turned up several people whose dogs could produce a fair imitation of English. One barked "I love mamma,'' when bribed with hamburger; another growled "Hooray for Roosevelt!'' In a turnaround, Elman then presented a man whose hobby was talking to dogs. Occasionally a celebrity appeared to "lobby his hobby.'' Roland Young, for instance, discussed his collection of poetry and of fine canes.

HOLLYWOOD BARN DANCE, country-western musical variety.

BROADCAST HISTORY: 1943–48, CBS West Coast (premiere Dec. 4, 1943).
CREATOR-HOST: Cottonseed Clark; singer-guitarist Merle Travis, host as of a ca. 1947. **REGULARS:** *ca. mid-1940s*: Charlie Linvalle, Kentucky state champion fiddler; yodeler Carolina Cotton; singer Kirby Grant; comic Johnny Bond; the Riders of the Purple Sage (Foy Willing, Kenny Driver, Al Sloey). *ca. 1947*: Maureen O'Connor; Clem Smith; singing cowboy Ken Curtis; Andy Parker and the Plainsmen. **FREQUENT NAME GUESTS:** Bob Hope, Roy Rogers, etc.

HOLLYWOOD BYLINE, film talk; panel discussion.

BROADCAST HISTORY: Dec. 31, 1949–Sept. 17, 1950, ABC. 30m, mostly Saturdays at 8:30; finale Sunday at 7.
CREATOR: Frank Latourette. **PANELISTS:** Bob Thomas of Associated Press; Darr Smith of the *Daily News*; Virginia MacPherson of UPI; Lloyd Sloan of the *Hollywood Citizen-News*. Guests: Top

film stars including Ida Lupino, Ronald Reagan, Jimmy Durante, Gloria Swanson, Charles Laughton, Kirk Douglas, etc. **ANNOUNCER:** Bill Spargrove. **DIRECTOR:** William Johnson.

Hollywood Byline was an unusual press conference, unusual in that the reporters asked only half the questions: then the stars were allowed to question the reporters. Questions were submitted in advance, so no one was too surprised at the outcome.

HOLLYWOOD CALLING, big-money giveaway show, with Hollywood glamor.

BROADCAST HISTORY: July 3, 1949–Jan. 15, 1950, NBC. 60m, Sundays at 7; then 30m Jan. 15 only. Gruen Watches.
HOST: George Murphy. **CREATOR:** Louis G. Cowan. **PRODUCER:** Max Hutto. **DIRECTOR:** Vick Knight.

Hollywood Calling was NBC's ill-considered answer to the CBS "talent raids'' of 1949. CBS had "stolen'' *The Jack Benny Program*, *The Amos 'n' Andy Show*, and most of NBC's Sunday night listeners with sweet deals involving huge capital gains tax benefits to the stars of those shows. At the same time, ABC had made deep cuts into the ratings of the few remaining NBC stalwarts, sending Fred Allen plunging into the Hooper gutters with an upstart giveaway show, *Stop the Music*. NBC, which had long "owned'' Sunday nights, vowed to take the high road. In a policy paper issued that year, NBC promised that it would not get into the morally questionable capital gains business, that it would not schedule tacky giveaway shows or offer gory crime drama in the children's hour. The paper particularly condemned giveaways as an abdication of entertainment and a flagrant attempt to buy an audience. But in this lofty statement of ideals, NBC had failed to reckon with the full impact of its loss.

The first principle to fall was the stand against giveaways. It was decided to create a super giveaway, book it into Jack Benny's Sunday-at-7 timeslot, and let it build an audience in Benny's summertime absence. Hopefully, when Benny returned to his Sunday stand, now on CBS, the new show would do to him what *Stop the Music* had done to Fred Allen.

To create the show, NBC hired Louis G. Cowan, architect of the *Stop the Music* debacle.

Cowan's formula combined gold with glamor, bringing in two film stars of undoubted stature each week to place random calls to people across the land. Just for answering the telephone a contestant would receive a 17-jewel Gruen watch, plus a unique gift from Hollywood (such as the scarf worn by Jennifer Jones in *Portrait of Jenny*). The contestant would also enjoy the thrill of talking to major celebrities. For answering a preliminary question on the movies, the listener won a prize worth several hundred dollars. Along with that went a chance at the $31,000 "Film of Fortune" jackpot.

It was pretentiously gaudy, utilizing 21 microphones, 12 singers, 6 arrangers, 15 actors, 6 writers, 6 researchers, 10 telephone operators, and a 35-piece orchestra. June Allyson and Walter Pidgeon kicked it off; Van Johnson and Deborah Kerr were on the second program. None of it mattered, because by virtually every account the result was a wretched show. It "failed to excite the approval of a single major radio critic," said *Newsweek*. *Time* was equally blunt, finding it "more intent on revenge than entertainment." The questions were embarrassingly easy in the frantic effort to give away money. Even more embarrassing, many of the contestants couldn't answer them. The result was never in doubt: Jack Benny returned in the fall and leaped to his customary perch atop the ratings while *Hollywood Calling* failed to register an appreciable digit. What Cowan and NBC had failed to realize was that the giveaway trend had peaked. The boon of 1948 was the boondoggle of 1949, and even as *Hollywood Calling* was being readied for the air the audience was abandoning similar shows in vast numbers. By the opening of the 1949 season, even *Stop the Music* had lost half its listeners.

A listen to tapes only confirms the judgment of contemporary critics. This was truly a bad show, a creaking monstrosity, an ill wind whose time had inexplicably come. Who *cared* if the contestant won the refrigerator? Refrigerators were boring.

HOLLYWOOD HOTEL, musical variety, with drama and talk.

BROADCAST HISTORY: Oct. 5, 1934–Dec. 2, 1938, CBS. 60m, Fridays at 9:30, 1934–35; then at 9. Campbell Soups.
HOSTESS: Louella Parsons. MC: Dick Powell,

1934–37; Fred MacMurray, 1937; Jerry Cooper, Ken Murray, 1937–38; Frank Parker, 1938; William Powell as host (replacing Parsons) and star beginning Oct. 2, 1938; Herbert Marshall, occasionally in fall 1938. ANNOUNCER: Ken Niles. TELEPHONE OPERATOR: Duane Thompson, the young woman who opened the show each week, "Hello, Hollywood Hotel." VOCALISTS: Rowene (Jane) Williams, 1934–35; Frances Langford, 1934–38; Anne Jamison, Lois Ravel, Shirley Ross, Loretta Lee. ORCHESTRA: Ted Fio Rito; Raymond Paige; Victor Young. DIRECTORS: George MacGarrett, from ca. 1934; William A. Bacher, ca. 1937; F. G. Ibbett, 1937–38; Brewster Morgan, 1938. WRITERS: Wyllis Cooper, 1934–38; John McClain, 1938. SOUND EFFECTS: Al Span. THEME: *Blue Moon*.

Hollywood Hotel was the first major network show to broadcast from the West Coast. The film capital was rich in nationally known talent untapped by radio. It had remained untapped because of a telephone company policy that cost the networks up to $1,000 to reverse radio circuits: everything then was geared to broadcast from east to west, and it was sometimes said that a producer could bring a film star east for a five-day train trip for less money than it cost him to air a radio show from California. In 1934 the radio centers were Chicago and New York.

This all changed with *Hollywood Hotel*. Hostess Louella Parsons immediately offset the technical tariff by persuading the elite of the film world to appear on the show without pay. Parsons was then the most feared and powerful newspaper columnist in Hollywood: her column, which appeared across the nation in Hearst newspapers, was widely seen as a maker or breaker of films and careers. She lined up stars who otherwise might be paid $1,000 for a single radio appearance, and scheduled as many as half a dozen each week. The result was the most glamorous show of its time—and a source of festering resentment in the film community.

Parsons was known for ruthlessness and a long memory. The biggest celebrities in America came when "invited," with Ginger Rogers, Katharine Hepburn, and Greta Garbo among the few to ignore Parsons's call. In truth, those who worked *Hollywood Hotel* usually prospered. Their films became box office hits, their personal fame was enhanced, and all for an hour's work. But many found it demeaning. Even the radio players who took the bit parts got paid (a $20 union-mandated scale fee), while the million-dollar movie star took home Parsons's blessing and a case of Campbell Soup.

The show's format was built around the illusion of a glamorous hotel. Later this was downplayed somewhat in favor of an "insider" Hollywood flavor. There was a lot of talk and film babble, as the stars supposedly made their way in and out of the theater. "Hello, Tyrone," Parsons would gush, allegedly surprised at spying Tyrone Power. "I haven't seen you since— well, since last week!" Then: "Jimmy Stewart, as I live and breathe!" After these walk-ons, she would banter with announcer Ken Niles and perhaps indulge in more stargazing. In her memoir, radio actress Mary Jane Higby recalls working the show. The "underpaid radio actors" soon took to calling themselves "the Gay Ad-Libbers." They "would circle the microphone, trying to simulate people having a marvelous time. 'What *fun* to be here!' they would cry. 'My, doesn't Myrna Loy look gorgeous! Whoops, there's Bette Davis!' "

Then there was music by the Fio Rito band, then a song by Powell, some music by a guest artist, and an interview segment by Parsons. After the station break, a new movie was dramatized in a 20-minute sketch. Parsons selected the films to be featured, making her hand ever more powerful. In 1935 the telephone company dropped the prohibitive fee structure, but the exploitation of the stars continued. Eventually more than $2 million worth of movie talent appeared gratis on the show. The radio people likewise were expected to work free if they wanted billing. When Barbara Luddy refused to forgo her paycheck, her name was stricken from the credits.

In 1938 the Radio Guild took a stand against free broadcasting, bringing the Parsons era to an end. The new host, William Powell, continued to focus on popular films, playing the leads in *Of Human Bondage*, with Margaret Sullavan, and *Death Takes a Holiday*, with Gale Page. Powell helped Ken Niles sell the soup, and such stars as Miriam Hopkins and Carole Lombard were now well paid. If she had done nothing else, Parsons had opened the West to radio. Within a year, *The Lux Radio Theater* was in California; Bing Crosby brought *The Kraft Music Hall* west, and Al Jolson opened in *Shell*

Chateau. Advertising agencies with heavy radio budgets opened overnight, and the networks poured money into their West Coast facilities. By the 1940s, Chicago was history and even New York was playing second fiddle.

HOLLYWOOD JACKPOT, quiz.

BROADCAST HISTORY: Sept. 30, 1946–March 28, 1947, CBS. 30m, three a week at 4:30. Whitehall Drug.

HOST: Kenny Delmar. ANNOUNCER: Bill Cullen. PRODUCER: Louis G. Cowan.

Contestants tried to recall famous lines of dialogue from the movies to win merchandise jackpots.

HOLLYWOOD MYSTERY TIME, detective melodrama; aka *Hollywood Mystery Theater*.

BROADCAST HISTORY: July 20–Oct. 13, 1944, CBS. 30m, Thursdays, then Fridays.
Oct. 15, 1944–Dec. 16, 1945, ABC. 30m, Sundays at 9:15. Woodbury Soap.

CAST: Carleton Young as Jim Laughton, independent producer of mystery movies who was an amateur detective on the side. Gloria Blondell as Gloria Dean, his assistant both in films and in murder. Dennis O'Keefe and Constance Moore starred as of mid-1945.

HOLLYWOOD PLAYHOUSE, dramatic anthology.

BROADCAST HISTORY: Oct. 3, 1937–Dec. 25, 1940, NBC. Blue Network, 30m, Sundays at 9 until Sept. 1939; then Red Network, 30m, Wednesdays at 8. Woodbury Soap, Jergens Lotion.

CAST: Tyrone Power, Charles Boyer, and Herbert Marshall starred at various times. Leading ladies changed weekly: Margaret Sullavan, Joan Blondell, etc. Jim Ameche and Gale Page, frequent leads. MUSIC: Harry Sosnik.

Hollywood Playhouse was created as a starring vehicle for young film sensation Tyrone Power. The fare came from Broadway and top short stories. Power was considered such a hot film property that Fox mogul Darryl F. Zanuck made a rare radio appearance to send him off. But by the second season, Charles Boyer had arrived as a fill-in. Power returned by January, but Boyer took over again that spring. Gale Page and Jim Ameche starred in the summer, and in October Herbert Marshall was the new headliner. Page and Ameche were heard in November–December 1939, and Power was not heard again. Boyer, meanwhile, had gone to France to make a film. War broke out; Boyer went into the French army and was mustered out, it was said, because France had deemed his film work more important than military service. Boyer replaced Ameche on *Hollywood Playhouse* Jan. 3, 1940. If the series wasn't confusing enough, Ameche and Page were recycled yet again, heading a *Hollywood Playhouse* continuation, *Promoting Priscilla*, from July to October 1940.

HOLLYWOOD PREMIERE, dramatic anthology; movie adaptations.

BROADCAST HISTORY: March 28–Nov. 28, 1941, CBS. 30m, Fridays at 10. Lifebuoy Soap.
HOSTESS: Louella Parsons. **ANNOUNCER:** Harlow Wilcox. **ORCHESTRA:** Felix Mills. **PRODUCER:** Charles Vanda.

Hollywood Premiere was an attempt by gossip columnist Louella Parsons to restore a segment of her *Hollywood Hotel* glory, with gratis performances by major film stars in return for lavish plugs of their newest films. Whatever problem Parsons had with the idea of paying people for their work, this time it backfired. Even before it reached the air, *Hollywood Premiere* was under attack by the Screen Actors Guild, which was joined by the American Federation of Radio Artists in condemning the show's policies. Parsons soon announced that the policy would be discontinued after the first 13 weeks. *Premiere* was like a reduced *Hollywood Hotel* without the music and song. A film was dramatized in 20 minutes, followed by a "question time," when Parsons interviewed the stars with questions submitted by the audience. Among the films dramatized were *Blood and Sand*, with Tyrone Power, and *Rise and Shine*, with Linda Darnell and Jack Oakie.

HOLLYWOOD SHOWCASE, variety show with talent competition.

BROADCAST HISTORY: July 24, 1937–Sept. 21, 1942, CBS, mostly West Coast (summer substitute for *Hollywood Hotel*, 1938). 30m, many timeslots;

moved frequently with some gaps in continuity. Hudnut, 1941.
HOSTESS: Mary Astor (1941). **CAST:** Hollywood stars (Betty Grable, Edward G. Robinson, Larry "Buster" Crabbe, etc.) along with promising unknowns, performing in the newest music, song, and drama of the film world. Also: such varied vocalists as Tito Guizar and Maxine Sullivan. Actor Edmund MacDonald a regular in 1938; vocals by the Ray Scott Quintet. **ANNOUNCER:** Bill Goodwin (1938). **ORCHESTRA:** Lud Gluskin. **PRODUCER:** Charles Vanda. **DIRECTOR:** Bill Lawrence.

Hollywood Showcase had a long and varied career, with many personalities moving in and out over the years. Its purpose was always to showcase new talent. Its offbeat method of choosing its "best performers" was described in 1941: a dozen ping-pong balls were thrown into the studio audience, and the people who caught them were allowed to vote.

The title and the "showcase" format were revived six years later in a coast-to-coast series for Mickey Rooney (series covered below).

HOLLYWOOD SHOWCASE, talent show.

BROADCAST HISTORY: July 4–Sept. 12, 1948, CBS. 30m, Sundays at 10.
CAST: Mickey Rooney, host, with various musical, vocal, and dramatic talent, in a spirited competion before a three-chair panel of Hollywood judges. **ANNOUNCER:** Bob LeMond. **ORCHESTRA:** Lud Gluskin. **PRODUCER:** Larry Berns. **WRITERS:** Jean Holloway, Bill Manhoff.

Hollywood Showcase in its later incarnation was an attempt by CBS to harness Mickey Rooney's obvious energy and talent in a different way, after Rooney's newspaper drama, *Shorty Bell*, folded in June 1948. The show highlighted little-known talents in several disciplines: in the opener, Rooney sang a duet with vocalist Julie Wilson, accompanied pianist Buddy Cole on drums, and played opposite actress Barbara Fuller in a segment from a Maxwell Anderson play.

HOLLYWOOD SOUNDSTAGE, dramatic anthology; Hollywood film fare.

BROADCAST HISTORY: Dec. 13, 1951–April 3, 1952, CBS. 30m, Thursdays at 10. Broadcast (with a similar series of the time, *Stars in the Air*) under the aegis of *The Screen Guild Theater*, offering almost identical fare, and assuming the *Screen Guild* title as well as the format in the last month of the series. Hugh Douglas announced a slick, impressive package, but by then the air was so saturated with similar shows that impact was nil. **MUSIC:** Alexander Courage. **WRITER-DIRECTOR:** Harry Kronman.

HOLLYWOOD STAR PLAYHOUSE, dramatic anthology.

BROADCAST HISTORY: April 24, 1950–July 16, 1951, CBS. 30m, Mondays at 8. Bromo Seltzer.
   July 26, 1951–Jan. 17, 1952, ABC. 30m, Thursdays at 8:30.
   Feb. 24, 1952–Feb. 15, 1953, NBC. 30m, Sundays at 5. American Bakers.
HOST-NARRATOR: Herbert Rawlinson; later, Orval Anderson. **CASTS:** Top film stars in suspense tales written for the series: James Stewart, Deborah Kerr, Victor Mature, etc. Supported by radio regulars: William Conrad, Betty Lou Gerson, Harry Bartell, etc. **ANNOUNCERS:** Norman Brokenshire (CBS), Wendell Niles (NBC). **MUSIC:** Jeff Alexander, Basil Adlam. **DIRECTOR:** Jack Johnstone. **WRITERS:** Milton Geiger, Frank Burt, Robert Libbott, etc.

On the face of it, *Hollywood Star Playhouse* seemed to be just another dramatic series milking the tired Hollywood film formula. The difference here was in the stories: tense, original suspense plays well suited for the half-hour. The initial run, on CBS, was particularly well staged, with a stirring musical score by Jeff Alexander and even the Bromo Seltzer "talking train" commercials adding to the flavor. Marilyn Monroe made her dramatic radio debut on *Hollywood Star Playhouse* in September 1952. Another high spot of 1952 was *The Six Shooter*, with James Stewart, which later became an NBC series.

HOLLYWOOD STAR PREVIEW, dramatic anthology; talent showcase.

BROADCAST HISTORY: Sept. 28, 1947–April 1, 1950, NBC. 30m, Sundays at 6:30, 1947–48; Saturdays at 8, 1948–50, title change to *Hollywood Star Theater*.
CAST: Hollywood film stars introducing newcomers: Ronald Colman introducing Shelley Winters; Sydney Greenstreet introducing Richard Basehart;

Jack Carson introducing Patricia Neal; John Payne introducing Jayne Meadows; etc. **ANNOUNCER:** Ken Peters. **MUSIC:** Bernard Katz. **PRODUCER:** Joe Thompson. **DIRECTORS:** Nat Wolff, Jack Van Nostrand.

The established star introduced the newcomer, who then performed in a 20-odd-minute drama especially written for the series. At the conclusion, the newcomer and the old pro were reunited onstage to tell how they had met and how the old star had been impressed by the newcomer's talent, with plugs for the films of all concerned.

HOLLYWOOD STARTIME, interviews and talk.

BROADCAST HISTORY: May 29–Nov. 24, 1944, Blue Network. 15m, weekdays at 3:15. Talks with stars (Cary Grant, Eddie Cantor, etc.) in the RKO commissary. *Hosts*: Larry Keating, Gary Breckner.

HOLLYWOOD STARTIME, dramatic anthology; Hollywood film fare.

BROADCAST HISTORY: Jan. 6, 1946–March 27, 1947, CBS. 30m, Sundays at 2:30 until June, then Saturdays at 8 until the final broadcast, Thursday at 10:30. Frigidaire.
CAST: Major film stars in well-known screen stories, with glamorous score and lavish framework: Lee J. Cobb, Vincent Price, and Vanessa Brown in *The Song of Bernadette*; Cary Grant, Herbert Marshall, and Marguerite Chapman in *Talk of the Town*; etc. Herbert Marshall, permanent star-host as of second season. **ANNOUNCER:** Wendell Niles. **COMPOSER-CONDUCTOR:** Alfred Newman. **DIRECTORS:** Robert L. Redd; Jack Johnstone.

Hollywood Startime had a lush, big-time sound, making an immediate bid as prestige drama in the *Lux Radio Theater* mold. But it was surrounded by such similar shows as *Academy Award*: the public was gorged with Hollywood stardom, this was old hat, and it never broke out of the single-digit ratings doldrums.

HOME OF THE BRAVE, serial drama.

BROADCAST HISTORY: Jan. 6–Sept. 19, 1941, CBS. 15m, weekdays at 2:45; as of April 28, NBC,

15m, weekdays at 5. Calumet Baking Powder and Swansdown Flour.

CAST: Tom Tully as Joe Meade, a telephone lineman in Colorado, a rugged individualist who loved America as she headed into one of her darkest hours. Ed Latimer also as Joe Meade. Jeanette Nolan and Sammie Hill as Casino, Joe's unrequited love interest. Richard Widmark and Vincent Donehue as Neil Davison. Joan Banks and Jone Allison as Lois Farmer, Neil's flame, and later his wife.

HONEST ABE, historical drama based on the life of Abraham Lincoln.

BROADCAST HISTORY: July 13, 1940–June 28, 1941, CBS. 30m, Saturdays at 9:30 A.M. until April 5, then at 11 A.M..

CAST: Ray Middleton as Lincoln. Henry Hull also as Lincoln. Muriel Kirkland as Mary Todd. DIRECTOR: Sidney Harmon. WRITER: E. P. Conkle.

HONEST HAROLD, situation comedy.

BROADCAST HISTORY: Sept. 17, 1950–June 13, 1951, CBS. 30m, Sundays at 7:30 for two weeks, then Wednesdays at 9.

CAST: Harold Peary as "Honest" Harold Hemp, "popular radio entertainer of Melrose Springs." Kathryn Card as his mother. Jane Morgan later in the run as Mother Hemp. Parley Baer as Pete the marshal, Harold's friend. Joseph Kearns as Old Doc "Yak-Yak" Yancy. Gloria Holliday (Peary's wife) as Harold's best girl, Gloria, who worked as the PBX operator at the radio station. Mary Jane Croft as Evelina, another of Harold's girlfriends. Sammy Ogg as Marvin, Harold's nephew. ANNOUNCER: Bob LeMond. MUSIC: Jack Meakin. DIRECTOR: Norman Macdonnell. WRITERS: Harold Peary, Gene Stone, Bill Danch, Jack Robinson.

Honest Harold was created by Harold Peary after his departure from *The Great Gildersleeve* in mid-1950. The show failed to gain any measure of an audience in its lone season. Its failure was much discussed at the time and was attributed to several factors. Willard Waterman was considered excellent as the new Gildersleeve, and in *Honest Harold* Peary seemed to be hanging onto too many *Gildersleeve* elements. Peary had professed boredom with the role but had

emerged on the rival network with a strong sound-alike, complete with the famous "dirty laugh."

As Honest Harold Hemp, he lived with his mother and nephew and did a homemaker's program on the air. Among his friends was Doc "Yak-Yak" Yancy, a strange cross between the crustiness of Judge Hooker and the nasal whine of Mr. Peavey, both notable *Gildersleeve* characters. Peary sang frequently; the show opened with the dirty laugh and closed with Peary giving background dialogue over credits, all *Gildersleeve* throwbacks. Despite the lack of ratings power and the general negative attitude of the critics, *Harold* was the near-equal of *Gildersleeve* in several respects. Shows on tape reveal funny writing and well-drawn characters, and the supporting cast and production crew were first-rate.

HONOLULU BOUND, comedy variety.

BROADCAST HISTORY: Jan. 14–Oct. 4, 1939, CBS. 30m, Saturdays at 9, then Wednesdays at 8. Hawaiian Pineapple.

CAST: Phil Baker, comedian-accordionist, with Mary Kelly, the Andrews Sisters, and Harry McNaughton. ANNOUNCER: Harry Von Zell. MUSICAL DIRECTOR: Eddie DeLange, Lyn Murray, Harry Salter.

This was simply an extension of the old *Phil Baker Show*, wrapped in an islander format that complemented the sponsor. McNaughton played Bottle the butler, and Baker played the accordion between comedy skits.

HOOFBEATS, western serial melodrama.

BROADCAST HISTORY: 1937, 15m continuation, transcribed and syndicated for Grape Nuts Flakes, with commercials and premium offers intact (cowboy hat, western chaps, and club membership badge, each for a dime and a red boxtop): 39 episodes were said to have been produced, running in one market June 25, 1937–March 18, 1938. The openings and closings were chronologically general, so they might play daily, weekly, or several times a week. The stories, narrated by a western hand known only as "the Old Wrangler," told the adventures of cowboy film star Buck Jones (Charles Frederick Gebhart) and his horse Silver (named in the Jones films before the advent of *The Lone Ranger*).

HOP HARRIGAN, juvenile aviation adventure serial.

BROADCAST HISTORY: Aug. 31, 1942–Aug. 2, 1946, Blue/ABC. 15m, weekdays at 5:15; at 5 (1943–44); at 4:45 (1944–46). Grape Nuts Flakes, 1944–46.

Oct. 2, 1946–Feb. 6, 1948, Mutual. 15m, mostly weekdays at 5.

CAST: Chester Stratton as Hop Harrigan, young aviator known as "America's ace of the airways." Ken Lynch and Jackson Beck as Tank Tinker, his pal and fellow adventurer. Mitzi Gould as Gail Nolan, Hop's girlfriend. **ANNOUNCER:** Glenn Riggs. **WRITERS:** Albert Aley; Bob Burtt and Wilfred Moore. **SOUND EFFECTS:** Ed Blainey (Blue Network).

The young hero of the air, Hop Harrigan, was first seen in All-American Comics. Hop was a daredevil with more than a coincidental similarity to the crew of Captain Midnight's Secret Squadron. Contributing writers Bob Burtt and Wilfred Moore were the *Midnight* creators, and both serials were most active in the late-afternoon battle of juvenile heroes against the evils of the Axis.

With his pal Tank Tinker, Hop was ever away to distant missions in dangerous territory behind enemy lines. They dove out of the skies in life-and-death dogfights, went underground in war-torn Berlin, saw heavy service in the Pacific during the battle for Okinawa.

The opening was pure radio, with the drone of a plane and Hop's voice asking for clearance to land:

CX-4 calling control tower. CX-4 calling control tower . . .
Control tower back to CX-4 . . . wind southeast, ceiling twelve hun-dred . . . all clear!
OKAAAY, this is Hop Harrigannn, coming in!

And there was announcer Glenn Riggs with another fascinating public service aviation announcement. Riggs told of men and planes in real-life missions overseas, ending each spot with the urgent message: "America needs fliers!" Then his voice would drop to a near-whisper. "And now to our story . . . Hop and Tank are in Berlin . . ." At the end he reminded his listeners to save waste paper, tin, and rubber,

and turn in these resources to salvage depots. The clatter of Hop's engine blended in, as the young heroes departed for another night:

CX-4 to control tower. CX-4 to control tower . . . standing by . . .
Control tower to CX-4 . . . all clear . . .
OKAYYY . . . this is HOP HARRIGANNN, taking off! . . . see ya tomorrow, same time same station!

Sporadic chapters, beginning in 1942, have survived and been transferred to tape. A long run of postwar stories, covering most of the Mutual era (175-plus shows, eight near-complete stories ending with the final broadcast) is also available in near-fine sound quality.

HOPALONG CASSIDY, western adventure drama.

BROADCAST HISTORY: 1948–50, transcribed syndication, Commodore Productions.

Jan. 1–Sept. 24, 1950, Mutual. 30m, Sundays at 4. General Foods.

Sept. 30, 1950–March 15, 1952, CBS, 30m, Saturdays at 8:30. General Foods. Rebroadcast April 26–Dec. 27, 1952, CBS mountain states regional. 30m, Saturdays at 9:30. Cella Vineyards.

CAST: William Boyd as Hopalong Cassidy, foreman of the Bar-20 Ranch and an ace western detective hero. Andy Clyde as California Carlson, his sidekick. **PRODUCERS:** Walter and Shirley White. **DIRECTOR:** Ted Bliss. **WRITERS:** Howard Swart, Dean Owen, Harold Swanton, etc.

Hopalong Cassidy was the success story of 1950, a commercial juggernaut that defied all reason to become the radio and TV triumph of its day. On radio, it was the making of Commodore Productions, the shoestring syndicate founded by Walter and Shirley White. It was the Whites who first became convinced that a radio show built around the Hopalong Cassidy character, as played by William Boyd in the 1930s B-western films, would be a solid winner. Boyd had a unique voice, radiating power and authority. There was simply no other cowboy hero quite like him.

It was far from an instant success. The first transcription discs were produced on borrowed money in mid-1948, the Whites pounding the pavement along with their few salespeople to try and place it. Concurrently, Boyd had been buying up his old films, securing his rights to the

Cassidy character for the coming of television. He too had borrowed money, $350,000, in an all-or-nothing gamble on the notion that Cassidy offered a striking alternative to Roy Rogers, Gene Autry, and the other heroes of juvenile western radio.

Cassidy had been created by Clarence Mulford, writer of formula western novels and pulpy short stories. In the stories, Cassidy was a snorting, drinking, chewing relic of the Old West. Harry Sherman changed all that when he bought the character for the movies. Sherman hired Boyd, a veteran of the silent screen whose star had faded, to play a badman in the original film. But Boyd seemed more heroic, and Sherman switched the parts before the filming began. As Cassidy, Boyd became a knight of the range, a man of morals who helped ladies cross the street but never stooped to kiss the heroine. He was literally black and white, his silver hair a vivid contrast to his black getup. He did not smoke, believed absolutely in justice, honor, and fair play, and refused to touch liquor.

Boyd's personal life was not so noble. Born in Ohio in 1898, he had arrived in Hollywood for the first golden age, working with Cecil B. DeMille in a succession of early silents. By the mid-1920s he was a major star. Wine, women, and money were his: he drank and gambled, owned estates, married five times. But it all ended when another actor named William Boyd was arrested for possession of whiskey and gambling equipment. Newspapers ran the wrong mugshots, and it was the self-fulfilling prophecy: the studios, believing his name had been damaged, canceled his contracts. Only four years later did Hopalong Cassidy ride up and save him.

Boyd made more than 50 *Cassidy* films with Sherman, and another dozen on his own between 1943 and 1946. His acquisition of the *Cassidy* film library was complete by 1948, when he joined the Whites in the radio venture. They made their first sales to independent stations with only a few shows "in the can" and were paying production costs for new episodes as money came in from initial clients. Suddenly it caught on: their station in Atlanta reported a rating of 17 points, a feat that was soon being duplicated all along the East Coast. Edited versions of the old films appeared on New York television in late 1948. These "electrified the junior television slave," as *Time* put it: the radio shows sold in

the West, and new films were shot to supplement the edited movies. With the syndicated show playing in more than 80 radio markets, *Hopalong Cassidy* premiered on NBC-TV June 24, 1949.

One medium fed on the other, and by 1950 Boyd was at the center of a national phenomenon. For two years he was as big a media hero as the nation had seen. In personal appearances he was mobbed: 85,000 people came through a Brooklyn department store during his appearance there. His endorsement for any product meant instant sales in the millions. It meant overnight shortages, frantic shopping sprees, and millions of dollars for Boyd. There were Hopalong Cassidy bicycles, rollerskates (complete with spurs), Hoppy pajamas, Hopalong beds. The demand for Hoppy shirts and pants was so great that a shortage of black dye resulted. His investment in Hopalong Cassidy paid off to an estimated $70 million.

Why a man of 52 years appealed to so many children remains a mystery. Possibly some of it had to do with the novelty of television: just as *Amos 'n' Andy* had capitalized on the newness of radio a generation earlier, a TV sensation was bound to occur. And the hero had a no-nonsense demeanor: he was steely-eyed and quick on the draw, and he meted out justice without the endless warbling and sugar-coated romance that came with the others. As for Boyd, he became Cassidy in a real sense. His personal habits changed; he gave up drinking and carousing and lived with his fifth wife until his death in 1972.

The radio series differed from TV in a few cosmetic aspects. On TV, Boyd was flanked by sidekick Red Connors, played by Edgar Buchanan; on radio, it was Andy Clyde as grizzled old California Carlson ("the same California you've laughed at a million times"). Hoppy clanked down the boardwalk to the announcer's signature: *The ring of the silver spurs heralds the most amazin' man ever to ride the prairies of the early West.* Often the stories were of trouble shrouded in mystery, and the listener was not privy to the culprit's identity till the end, making it a true cowboy detective show. Hoppy's white horse Topper furthered the black-and-white image, even on radio: the Hoppy belly laugh was true-grade Bill Boyd. A fine assortment of Commodore transcriptions has been transferred to tape: the capital from their initial syndication enabled the Whites to branch into new Commodore productions—*The Clyde Beatty Show* and *Tarzan, Lord of the Jungle*.

THE HORACE HEIDT SHOW, music, sometimes in quiz formats.

BROADCAST HISTORY: Many formats, networks, and timeslots, including:

1932, Blue Network. Two brief series: *Ship of Joy*, for Shell Oil; and *Answers by the Dancers*, early dance-interview show.

Feb. 26, 1935–Dec. 20, 1937, CBS. Various 15m and 30m times. *Captain Dobbsie's Ship of Joy* until April 23, 1935; also heard as *Horace Heidt's Alemite Brigadeers*. Alemite.

1937–39, NBC, Blue and Red. 30m, various times. Alemite.

Sept. 26, 1939–June 5, 1941. *Pot o' Gold*, covered under that title.

June 11, 1940–Jan. 11, 1944, NBC. 30m, Tuesdays at 8:30. *Tums Treasure Chest*. Tums.

1943–44, Blue Network. 60m, Saturday afternoons, various times.

Jan. 24, 1944–Jan. 15, 1945, Blue. 30m, Mondays at 7. Hires Root Beer.

Dec. 7, 1947–Aug. 28, 1949, NBC. 30m, Sundays, various times. *The Youth Opportunity Program*. Philip Morris.

Sept. 4, 1949–Dec. 16, 1951, CBS. 30m, Sundays at 9:30. *The Youth Opportunity Program*. Philip Morris.

Jan. 1–Dec. 24, 1953, CBS. 30m, Thursdays at 10. *The American Way*. Lucky Strike.

Horace Heidt was one of the most popular bandleaders of two decades. He had what serious critics of swing called a "schmaltz band," containing as much gimmickry as musicianship, though George Simon says that at times Heidt hired fine people and let them play. Among his gimmicks on radio were big-money giveaways and the playing of a toy piano. His groups were variously known as Horace Heidt and his Musical Knights and as the Horace Heidt Brigadeers. His series *Anniversary Night with Horace Heidt* was inaugurated on NBC in February 1935, giving married couples quizzes for prizes. In the mid-1930s, his personnel included the King Sisters (Louise, Maxine, Donna, Alyce, Yvonne, and Anita, the only sister sextet in radio) and Alvino Rey (with his "singing guitar"). His sound was said to have Waring influence: he

had a glee club around this time and was also playing lush mainstream numbers.

His big-money giveaway, *Pot o' Gold*, had great national success in 1939, but its popularity was short-lived. Heidt's 1940–43 series, *The Tums Treasure Chest*, emphasized music, not money, and his Monday night gig for Hires Root Beer (1944–45) had the human interest element, with war veterans telling their stories and asking for jobs while a teletype was set up onstage to tick off the offers as they came in. But perhaps Heidt's best-remembered series was his *Youth Opportunity Program*, first heard Dec. 7, 1947. It bore strong resemblance to Major Bowes's amateur show, with Heidt's troupe going from town to town auditioning local accordionists, piano players, and abusers of the harmonica and holding talent contests each Sunday night. His first national winner, accordionist Dick Contino, won $5,000 and rode a brief crest of popularity into his own show.

HORATIO HORNBLOWER, adventure drama, based on the novels by C. S. Forester.

BROADCAST HISTORY: Transcribed in England for the BBC; aired on CBS, July 7–Dec. 12, 1952, in various 30m timeslots; on ABC, Jan. 22–March 26, 1954, 30m Fridays at 9:30; and on Mutual, March 6–May 22, 1957, 30m Wednesdays at 8:30.

CAST: Michael Redgrave as Horatio Hornblower, in a swashbuckling series with broadsides to starboard, drumrolls, slashing swords. MUSICAL SCORE: Composed and conducted by Sidney Torch. PRODUCER-DIRECTOR: Harry Alan Towers. WRITER: Philo Higley.

THE HORMEL GIRLS' BAND AND CHORUS, music.

BROADCAST HISTORY: Dec. 18, 1949–July 2, 1950 ABC. 30m Sundays at 6:30.

Dec. 10, 1950–Dec. 2, 1951, NBC. 30m Sundays at 3.

May 20, 1950–Feb. 13, 1954, CBS. 30m Saturdays at 2; then at 1:30, 1953–54.

ANNOUNCER: Marilyn Wilson. MUSICAL DIRECTOR: Al Woodbury. PRODUCER: Bill Conner.

The Hormel band was an all-female group that followed the more famous *Hour of Charm*. It was formed in 1947, with 12 women from military service comprising a promotional group for Hormel Foods. The unit gradually grew into a 60-piece orchestra.

THE HORN AND HARDART CHILDREN'S HOUR, juvenile variety, usually logged as *The Children's Hour*.

BROADCAST HISTORY: April 26, 1931–May 28, 1939, WABC, New York. 60m until 1939, then 30m. Sundays at 11 A.M. until 1936, then at 10:30 A.M. Horn and Hardart Automats.

June 4, 1939–Oct. 6, 1957, WEAF, New York (which became WNBC in 1947 and WRCA in 1954). 60m, Sundays at 10:30 A.M. Horn and Hardart Automats.

HOSTS: Paul Douglas, Ralph Edwards, Ed Herlihy. CAST: About 20 juvenile performers each Sunday, including some who had subsequent radio careers: Arnold Stang, Carol Bruce, Bobby Hookey, Eddie Fisher, Bea Wain, Connie Francis, etc. PIANIST: W. M. James. WRITER-DIRECTOR: Alice Clements. THEME: *Less Work for Mother*.

Horn and Hardart was a local offering, but because of its big-station scheduling and its run spanning three decades, its *Children's Hour* was widely known and heard in the East. It was also occasionally confused with the Blue Network's *Children's Hour*, which developed into *The White Rabbit Line*, or, *Coast to Coast on a Bus*.

The show is said to have originated on WCAU, Philadelphia, the sponsor's home city, in 1927. Its arrival in New York in 1931 kicked off an unusual commercial identity—a children's song-dance-and-story hour sponsored by one of the strongest symbols of New York city life, the automat (where nickel coffee and a piece of pie was a Broadway tradition). With its first New York broadcast, Horn and Hardart admitted it had nothing to sell to kids but reasoned that a strong appeal to children would reach adults as well.

A sample of its fare was the show of Dec. 7, 1941, a few hours before Pearl Harbor. The entire hour was a tribute to ailing George M. Cohan, with the kids singing such favorites as *Give My Regards to Broadway*, *Yankee Doodle Dandy*, and *Harrigan*.

HOT COPY, mystery drama.

BROADCAST HISTORY: Oct. 4, 1941–Sept. 26, 1942, NBC. Various 30m evening timeslots.

July 18, 1943–Nov. 19, 1944, Blue Network. 30m, Sundays at 3:30, then at 5:30. O Cedar Polish.

CAST: Eloise Kummer, Fern Persons, and Hugh Rowlands. The fictitious murder-solving career of Anne Rogers, newspaper columnist.

THE HOUR OF CHARM, music: radio's most celebrated "all-girl orchestra."

BROADCAST HISTORY: May 18–Sept. 26, 1934, CBS. 15m, Fridays at 10:30 until June 6, then Wednesdays at 8. Cheramy.

Jan. 3–June 25, 1935, CBS. 30m, Thursdays at 8; later at 9:30. Linit Bath Oil.

Feb. 23–June 21, 1936, CBS. 30m, Sundays at 6:30. Zotos Machineless Permanent Wave.

Nov. 2, 1936–Sept. 1, 1946, NBC. 30m, Various times. General Electric.

Sept. 29, 1946–May 2, 1948, CBS. 30m, Sunday afternoons. Combined electric co-ops.

LEADER: Phil Spitalny. FEATURED PLAYER: Evelyn Kaye Klein, billed as "Evelyn and Her Magic Violin." VOCALISTS: Vivien, soprano; Maxine, contralto; later, "the distinctive voices of Jeannie and Francine" (the "girls" used only first names on the air. Also: Three Little Words, vocal trio; Frances, Connie, and Fern. MUSICIANS: Rochelle and Lola, piano duo; Velma, trombone; Grace, guitar; Helen Blue, trombone; Jan Baker, tuba, etc.; Viola Smith, drums. MISTRESS OF CEREMONIES: Rosaline Greene (ca. mid-1930s; later, Arlene Francis. ANNOUNCERS: Ken Roberts (from 1935); Ron Rawson, Richard Stark (1940s). DIRECTOR: Joseph Ripley.

The Hour of Charm was a novelty in 1935, the notion of an "all-girl orchestra" dismissed out of hand by many in the music business. It was believed that women lacked the discipline and concentration necessary to become top musicians. Maestro Phil Spitalny thought otherwise.

He had witnessed a concert in 1932 containing an electrifying performance by a brilliant female violinist. If an entire orchestra of equally talented women could be formed, Spitalny thought, it would be a "natural" for radio.

He dissolved the all-male orchestra he was then leading, in order to hunt for exceptional female talent. His family questioned his judgment.

The Spitalnys had a deep musical heritage. Immigrants from Russia, they had settled in Cleveland, where Spitalny and his brother Leopold played in local bands. By the time he was 30, Spitalny had directed a 50-piece symphony orchestra in Boston, had led bands in theaters, on radio, and in recording sessions, and had just completed a successful world tour.

He auditioned women in New York, Chicago, Pittsburgh, Detroit, and Cleveland. The quest was not encouraging. Pittsburgh, he claimed, did not have a single female musician capable of playing in the kind of orchestra he wanted to build. But at New York's Juilliard School of Music, he met Evelyn Kaye Klein, who became his first violinist and concertmistress. They now searched together, broadening the hunt into the smaller communities where, common sense told them, girls might have been required to practice their music. They listened to more than 1,000 violins, trumpets, and saxophones. At the end of a year, Spitalny had spent more than $20,000 in the search, but he had his first 22-piece all-girl orchestra.

But bookings were elusive, the old prejudice cropping up the moment the prospect of an all-girl band was broached. When Spitalny auditioned for Linit, it was a "blind" test, with the music piped in from a remote location so the "girls" couldn't be seen. Linit bought the show despite some misgivings, extending the initial 13-week contract to six months, and the following season Spitalny began a ten-year run for General Electric.

The orchestra specialized in familiar music, played in a style described by Spitalny as a cross between popular and symphonic. All of the girls sang in chorus, some solo, and all were proficient on more than one instrument. Jan Baker could play a dozen instruments: she took on the tuba and mastered it when Spitalny could find no woman to play it even after a nationwide search. Spitalny's hiring practices were influenced by voice and good looks, but musicianship was always his first consideration. "No performer is hired who can't give a finished rendition of two sonatas and two concerti, who hasn't the individual gifts of rhythm and melodic perception, who can't read music fluently, and who hasn't had a good deal of experience," said his 1940 *Current Biography* entry.

He was also looking for "sweetness and charm," and it is doubtful that any other orchestra has ever been so stringently governed. The girls were not allowed to marry: they signed contracts to that effect, agreeing to stay single for two years. They wore uniform attire, with the exception of the three principals, Evelyn, Vivien, and Maxine. They wore evening gowns, with no jewelry, their hair styled in "long, soft bobs." No one would weigh more than 122 pounds. Curbs were enforced on personal behavior, with Evelyn in charge of backstage disputes and Spitalny handling such professional matters as musical arrangements, themes, and dress. "Associations in the all-girl orchestra are much like sorority life," wrote Evelyn in a 1942 *Radio Life* article. A committee of five was formed to pass judgment on all offstage matters, including dating. "Whenever a girl wants to go out, she goes to the committee and says, 'I want a date with Mr. So-and-So.' They ask her who the man is, what he does, and for references. If he passes muster, she gets her date. But if the committee feels that it would hurt the orchestra for a member to be seen with that man, the engagement doesn't materialize."

As "Evelyn," she became one of the major musical figures of the air. Her "magic violin" was a 1756 Bergonzi. Spitalny staunchly defended the musicianship of all his girls, and he once bet bandleader Abe Lyman $1,000 that they could outplay Lyman's all-male group. The women had professional pride, said Spitalny: they didn't have problems with alcohol, and, when the war broke out, his was the only band in the land that didn't have trouble with the draft. He continued lecturing newcomers about the need to be good: they had to be better than their male counterparts to be taken seriously. If a man muffed a note, nobody cared; if a woman did, the attitude was "well, what can you expect?"

The show opened and closed with hymns, especially during the war. The opening theme was *The American Hymn of Liberty*; the closer, often a favored hymn of someone in the service. This gave the show a serious, almost solemn air. The closing signature blended out of the theme and into the song *We Must Be Vigilant*, sung by the orchestra to the tune of *American Patrol*.

Spitalny married Evelyn in June 1946. They lived in Miami, where Spitalny died in 1970.

THE HOUR OF MYSTERY, dramatic suspense anthology.

BROADCAST HISTORY: June 9–Sept. 1, 1946, ABC. 60m, Sundays at 10. Substitute for *Theatre Guild on the Air*. United States Steel.

CAST: Well-known mystery stories with well-known stage and film stars: *Journey into Fear*, with Laurence Olivier; *Turn On the Heat*, with Frank Sinatra; *Murder, My Sweet*, with William Holden; etc.

A HOUSE IN THE COUNTRY, serial drama.

BROADCAST HISTORY: Oct. 6, 1941–Oct. 28, 1942, Blue Network. 15m, weekdays at 10:30 A.M.

CAST: Joan Banks, Frances Chaney, and Patsy Campbell variously as Joan. John Raby and Lyle Sudrow as Bruce. Also: Ed Latimer, Parker Fennelly. CREATOR-WRITER: Raymond Knight (who also played the role of a shopkeeper).

A House in the Country had Joan and Bruce, a young couple from the city, trying to cope with country living. In the early 1930s, Knight, one of radio's earliest innovators in comedy, created the groundbreaking series *The Cuckoo Hour*.

HOUSE OF GLASS, serial drama.

BROADCAST HISTORY: April 17–Dec. 25, 1935, Blue Network. 30m, Wednesdays at 8:30. Palmolive.

Oct. 23, 1953–March 12, 1954, NBC. 25m, Fridays at 9:35.

CAST: Gertrude Berg as Bessie Glass, operator of a hotel in the Catskill Mountains. Joseph Greenwald (1935) as Barney Glass, her husband. Josef Buloff as Barney, 1953–54. WRITER: Gertrude Berg.

House of Glass was quickly created by Gertrude Berg after the initial cancellation of her popular serial, *The Goldbergs*. She took the setting and characters from her own life: her father had run such a place in the teens, giving her experiences with waiters, bellboys, cooks, and guests from all walks of life. The character of Barney Glass was an almost literal lift from her father. The stories she wrote were the stories she remembered, and "where there were unhappy endings I added happy ones. . . . The radio hotel always solved its problems with a laugh." But it couldn't beat *Burns and Allen*, its competition on CBS, and it faded after eight months.

THE HOUSE OF MYSTERY, dramatic mystery anthology.

BROADCAST HISTORY: Jan. 15–May 11, 1945, Mutual. 15m, weekdays.

Sept. 15, 1945–June 1, 1946, Mutual. 30m, Saturdays at noon. General Foods.

Oct. 6, 1946–Dec. 25, 1949, Mutual. 30m, Sundays at 4. General Foods.

CAST: John Griggs as Roger Elliott, "the mystery man," who hosted and narrated. DIRECTOR: Olga Druce.

The format of *The House of Mystery* was almost identical in its serial and weekly versions. Roger Elliott, the fictitious host, was billed as a ghost chaser, a scientist of the supernatural who tried to prove that "ghosts and phantoms exist only in the imagination." It was set up as an old-fashioned storytelling soiree, with Elliott relating his tales to the ooohing and aaahing of children, who were allowed to question him at the conclusion. The tales were filled with mysterious lights, footprints that vanished before the eyes, and things that went bump in the night. It opened to creepy organ music and the salutation *Thisssss is the Houssssse . . . of Mysssssstery!*

HOUSE PARTY, audience show.

BROADCAST HISTORY: Jan. 15, 1945–Jan. 10, 1947, CBS. 25m, weekdays at 4; three a week, 1946–47. General Electric.

Dec. 1, 1947–Dec. 31, 1948, CBS. 25m, Weekdays at 3:30. General Electric.

Jan. 3–July 1, 1949 ABC. 30m, weekdays at 3:30. General Electric.

Sept. 19–Dec. 30, 1949, ABC. 25m, weekdays at noon. Sustained.

Jan. 2, 1950–Oct. 13, 1967, CBS. 30m, weekdays, various times: 10:30, then 11:30 a.m., 1950–52; otherwise mostly within the 3–4 timeslot. Pillsbury, 1950–52; Lever Brothers, 1952–56; multi, 1956–57.

HOST: Art Linkletter. PRODUCER: John Guedel. WRITER-DIRECTOR: Marty Hill.

House Party was a spontaneous show that relied heavily on the ad-libbing skills of host Art Linkletter. Linkletter may have been the smoothest man in radio: he was called the medium's best ad-libber by Eddie Cantor and others. Like his first major show, *People Are Funny, House*

Party grew out of his association with producer John Guedel.

Guedel had set out to be a writer but had been frustrated by rejections. He had worked for Hal Roach on some of the Laurel and Hardy and Little Rascals film shorts, and had gravitated into radio. Linkletter, born in Canada July 17, 1912, had been raised by adoptive parents after being given up by his birth family, whose name was Kelley. He kept the name of his new family, Linkletter, throughout his professional life. When the Linkletters moved to California, the father became an evangelist, and Linkletter's first exposure to crowds and audiences came in those religious gatherings. In college, his ability to talk was his greatest asset: it was said that he could discuss any topic at any length. Before his graduation he found work in radio, landing at KGB, San Diego, in 1933. By 1941, the year he met Guedel, he estimated that he had appeared on 9,000 radio shows.

Two years later, Linkletter became the host of Guedel's stunt show, *People Are Funny*. In 1945, Guedel heard that an ad agency was looking for a new daytime audience show. He got on the phone and began to sell, certain only that he could produce Linkletter as host. Invited to submit an outline, Guedel and Linkletter brainstormed the program and came up with a potpourri of human interest that would give Linkletter maximum unrehearsed exposure to the audience.

There would be hints for the ladies: how to cook, how to look, how to dress, how to solve problems at home. There would be gags, with Linkletter's prying limited only by the boundaries of good taste. He was a master of the double entendre, able to turn an innocent remark into a near-ribald flirtation, without ever running afoul of the censor.

House Party dabbled in everything. There were hunts for missing heirs; over the years the show found heirs whose estates totaled more than $1 million. There were contests, one of Linkletter's favorites being "What's in the House?," a guessing game with progressive clues and a grand prize. There were searches for colorful personalities. Who's the youngest grandmother in the audience, Linkletter would ask . . . who's the youngest father? . . . What woman has the longest hair? In 1945 he conducted weekly searches for the woman in the audience most recently married. This led to a series of nosy and embarrassing questions: How many children would she have? What was more popular nowadays, double beds or single beds? But far and away the most popular feature was Linkletter's talks with children.

Each day five or six kids, chosen by their principals for intelligence and personality, were brought to CBS by special limousine from Los Angeles grammar schools. Linkletter knew the questions that were sure to provoke laughter. "What does your mommy do?" might bring the response "Nothing, she's too busy having babies" or "Sits around all day reading the racing form." One little boy answered Linkletter's "if you had one wish" question by wishing for his "daddy back from heaven." Linkletter interviewed an estimated 23,000 children; the best lines turned into a book, *Kids Say the Darndest Things*.

The ideas for *House Party* were created by Guedel and his father, Walter, but Linkletter never rehearsed or used scripts. Throughout his career, he remained one of daytime's most popular personalities. Three-quarters of his listeners were said to be housewives, for whom Jack Slattery's cheerful greeting, "Come on in, it's Art Linkletter's *House Party*," was a radio catchphrase. On TV, the series also had a long CBS run: Sept. 1, 1952–Sept. 5, 1969.

HOWIE WING, juvenile aviation adventure serial.

BROADCAST HISTORY: Oct. 3, 1938–June 30, 1939, CBS. 15m weekdays at 6:15. Kellogg Cereals.

CAST: William Janney as Howie Wing, 21-year-old "junior pilot." Mary Parker as Donna Cavendish, Howie's girlfriend. Neil O'Malley as Captain Harvey, ace pilot of the World War and Howie's mentor. John Griggs as Zero Smith, one of the best tough-weather pilots but disagreeable and devious, suspected of working for the enemy. Raymond Bramley as Burton York, the villain, who posed as an insurance agent in order to sabotage the clipper and discredit Captain Harvey. **WRITER:** Wilfred G. Moore. **SOUND EFFECTS:** Al Binnie.

HOW'M I DOIN'?, quiz.

BROADCAST HISTORY: Jan. 9–July 3, 1942, CBS. 30m, Fridays at 7:30, later at 10:30. Camel.

July 9–Oct. 1, 1942, NBC. 30m, Thursdays at 7:30. Camel.

QUIZMASTER: Bob Hawk. **ANNOUNCER:** Bert Parks. **VOCALS:** Vaughn Monroe.

Players were given $30 and asked questions, each of which added to or subtracted from their bankrolls by $10.

THE HUMAN ADVENTURE, documentary drama.

BROADCAST HISTORY: July 25, 1939–Sept. 28, 1940, CBS. Various times; broken runs. Aired from New York in 60m and 30m formats. **PRODUCER:** Sherman Dryer. **DIRECTOR:** Brewster Morgan. **SOUND EFFECTS:** Bill Brown.

1943–46, Mutual. Many brief runs, various times. Broadcast from Chicago. **MUSIC:** Kenneth Churchill, composer; Henry Weber and Robert Trendler, conductors. **DIRECTOR:** Morrison Wood.

The Human Adventure was produced by the University of Chicago in an effort to "open up the closed books of man's past and future." Among the subjects covered in the CBS run were the Black Plagues, the Arthurian legends, termites, the dime novel, Einstein, Babylonian business practices, hobo jungles, and the role of the abnormal person in politics.

The Mutual series included an attempt to explain Einstein's theory of relativity in 30 minutes, using a name cast and an imaginative script. F. Chase Taylor (Colonel Stoopnagle)

played a "know-nothing layman"; Clifton Fadiman was the "omniscient explainer." *Time* felt both were typecast. "Whenever Fadiman got too hot to handle, Stoopnagle was to order the orchestra to play. There was a good bit of music in the half-hour."

HUSBANDS AND WIVES, spirited marital discussions.

BROADCAST HISTORY: July 5–Oct. 4, 1936, Blue Network. 30m, Sundays at 7:30. *The Baker's Broadcast.* Summer substitute for *Believe It or Not.* Fleischmann.

Oct. 6, 1936–Dec. 28, 1937, Blue Network. 30m, Tuesdays at 9:30 until April, then at 8. Ponds Cream.

HOST/HOSTESS: Sedley Brown and Allie Lowe Miles.

Husbands and Wives grew out of a home economics show done on WOR, New York, by Allie Lowe Miles in 1935. An acquaintance, Sedley Brown, thought the marital chatter of the guests might be interesting in prime time. In the 1935–36 season, Miles held a 30-minute Mutual slot, giving advice to the lovelorn twice a week at 3:30. *Husbands and Wives* was a turnaround: each week half a dozen husbands and half a dozen wives were brought to the microphone to complain about marriage. Brown coached the men; Miles, the women. Tales of woe flowed freely: it was described by *Radio Mirror* as "a three-ring circus of domestic scraps."

7

I DEAL IN CRIME, detective drama.

BROADCAST HISTORY: Jan. 21, 1946–Oct. 18, 1947, ABC. 30m, Mondays at 9 until Oct. 1946; Saturdays at 8:30 until May 1947, then at 8.

CAST: William Gargan as Ross Dolan, a veteran private investigator before serving a hitch in "Uncle Sugar's Navy"; returned now to his old haunts at 404 Melrose Building to again "deal in crime." **ANNOUNCER:** Dresser Dahlstead. **MUSIC:** Skitch Henderson. **DIRECTOR:** Leonard Reeg. **WRITER:** Ted Hediger.

I FLY ANYTHING, adventure drama.

BROADCAST HISTORY: Nov. 29, 1950–July 19, 1951, ABC. 30m, various times.

CAST: Dick Haymes as Dockery Crane, "fast-moving, hard-hitting, romantic air cargo pilot." George Fenneman as Buzz, his co-pilot and sidekick. Georgia Ellis as June, their office manager. Support from Hollywood radio regulars: Lurene Tuttle, Eddie Marr, etc. **ANNOUNCERS:** Lou Cook, Jay Arlen. **MUSIC:** Basil Adlam, Rex Maupin. **DIRECTOR:** Dwight Hauser. **WRITERS:** Arnold Perl and Abe Ginniss, with Les Crutchfield, etc.

The pairing of Dick Haymes (who had made his name as a popular singer) and George Fenneman (one of radio's smoothest announcers) as actors in an adventure series was unusual. As Crane, Haymes played a pilot whose seat-of-the-pants operation included one old DC-4, appropriately named "the Flying Eight-Ball." The opening signature gave ample evidence of content:

Flight 743 calling La Guardia Field . . .

Is that you, Crane? What're you bringing in, tea, teak, or teepee poles?

I got a tradewind tan, a tall tale about a tribal treasure, a tropical tramp, and a torrid Tahitian tomato. You know me—I fly anything!

I LOVE A MYSTERY, adventure-mystery serial drama.

BROADCAST HISTORY: Jan. 16–Sept. 29, 1939, NBC West Coast network. 15m, weekdays at 3:15, Pacific time. Standard Brands for Fleischmann's Yeast.

Oct. 2, 1939–March 29, 1940, NBC full network. 15m, weeknights at 7:15. Fleischmann's Yeast.

April 4–June 27, 1940, NBC. 30m weekly continuation, Thursdays at 8:30. Fleischmann's Yeast.

Sept. 30, 1940–June 29, 1942, Blue Network. 30m continuation, Mondays and Wednesdays at 8. Fleischmann's Yeast (discontinued because of wartime shortages by the sponsor).

March 22, 1943–Dec. 29, 1944, CBS. 15m, weeknights at 7. Procter & Gamble for Oxydol and Ivory Soap.

Oct. 3, 1949–Dec. 26, 1952, Mutual. 15m, weeknights at 7:45, 1949–50; at 10:15, 1950–52. Produced from the original scripts; transcribed in New York.

CAST: *From Hollywood, 1939–44*: Michael Raffetto as Jack Packard, head of the A-1 Detective Agency in Hollywood, and leader of a trio of soldiers of fortune. John McIntire and Jay Novello, briefly, as Jack Packard during the CBS run. Barton Yarborough as Doc Long, his Texas-born sidekick—lover of women, picker of locks, willing fighter in tight spots. Walter Paterson as Reggie Yorke, the trio's third member, a Britisher whose surface propriety was balanced by an equally willing-and-able talent for roughhouse. (The character of Reggie was written out of the serial in 1942, with the suicide of Walter Paterson: he was replaced in the stories by Jerry Booker, the beautiful and curvaceous secretary at the A-1 agency, and for a time the show was billed as "the adventures of Jack, Doc, and Jerry.") Gloria Blondell as Jerry. Mercedes McCambridge in many character roles, often a fiery hellcat, sometimes a victim, occasionally a femme fatale. Barbara Jean Wong in Chinese roles (as P. Y. Ling, Lee Taw Ming, etc.). Also: Cathy and Elliott Lewis, Jack Edwards, Lal Chand Mehra, Ben Alexander, Edgar Norton, Richard LeGrand, Cliff Arquette, Naomi Stevens, etc. *From New York, 1949–52*: Russell Thorson as Jack Packard. Robert Dryden as Jack Packard late in run. Jim Boles as Doc Long. Tony Randall as Reggie Yorke. Mercedes McCambridge (then in New York pursuing a stage career) in many of the same roles she had played in Hollywood. Robert Dryden as crusty oldtimers. Luis Van Rooten in many character roles. **ANNOUNCERS:** Dresser Dahlstead, etc. **CREATOR-WRITER-PRODUCER-DIRECTOR:** Carlton E. Morse. **ASSISTANT PRODUCER:** Buddy Twiss. **SOUND EFFECTS:** Ralph Amati (NBC); Al Span (CBS); George Cooney, Barney Beck. (Mutual). **THEME:** *Valse Triste*, by Sibelius.

It should be admitted at the outset: even today, *I Love a Mystery* weaves a spell over its fans that is all but inexplicable to an outsider. It is simply the most-sought of all radio shows, the one most fraught with rumors. For years collectors have believed that discs to both Hollywood and New York runs have been hoarded by a California miser, who refuses to release them. The thrills and pleasures of the serial were first trumpeted by writer Jim Harmon more than two decades ago. Harmon flatly described it as the greatest radio show of all time.

It told of three adventurers who traveled the world in search of action, thrills, and mystery. From the ghost towns of wind-swept Nevada to the jungles of vampire-infested Nicaragua, these three pillars of strength righted wrongs, rescued women in distress, did battles with evils of natural and supernatural origin, and explored the most unlikely terrain ever conjured up by the brain of man.

Jack Packard was a deadpan hero who exuded quiet strength and a man's courage. A former medical student, Jack tended to shrug off superstition and unnatural manifestations, believing—even while under attack by werewolves—that everything has a logical answer. Jack was a master detective and strategist, a cool head in any emergency, the voice of reason and decisive action. He was unaffected by women. Both Harmon and serials historian Raymond William Stedman maintain that the reason for this was explicitly spelled out at some point: Jack had once gotten a girl in trouble, an almost inconceivable bit of business for the censor to allow, even as innuendo, in the curiously asexual world of oldtime radio. Be that as it may, Jack never gave the ladies a tumble.

Doc Long was a different breed of cat. A red-headed alley fighter from Texas who defied the laws of chance to fill inside straights, Doc loved women beautiful and otherwise. To Doc, few were otherwise. He liked them tall or short, sweet, sassy or shy. Sass and backtalk made his heart beat faster, and a challenge in a skirt was almost as irresistible as an unsolved murder. Doc spoke in a deep Panhandle drawl, finding voice in the catchphrase "Honest to my grandma. . . ."

Reggie Yorke was a distinctive third voice, as clear a departure from the generic ruggedness of Jack and the country naiveté of Doc as was likely to be found. Reggie was from England, and his voice reflected that: physically, he was the strongest of the three.

Together they were the three musketeers of the airwaves: all for one, one for all. They had met during China's war with Japan, when all three had enlisted in the Chinese cause. After the war they returned to California to form the A-1 Detective Agency. Their office was just off Hollywood Boulevard, one flight up, but they were seldom found there. Their cases took them to exotic locales, the titles themselves (*The Fear That Creeps Like a Cat*; *Temple of Vampires*; *The Snake with the Diamond Eyes*; etc.) dripping dangerous adventure. This was not standard juvenile fare. Children certainly listened, but often covertly, under blankets with the volume low. The fact that Mutual scheduled it at 10:15 p.m. says much about the content of *I Love a Mystery*.

As many as three characters were murdered in a single quarter-hour *ILAM* episode. People were killed in ghoulish, imaginative, and sometimes mystifying ways. Throats were ripped out by wolves; there were garrotings and poisonings and mysterious slashings. In the story *Monster in the Mansion*, a headless black cat was found in a lady's bed, and a man had his arm amputated while he slept; in *The Thing That Cries in the Night*, a slasher was at work in an old mansion, and murder was done to the cry of a baby, while everyone insisted that there had been no baby in the house for twenty years. *Temple of Vampires* was considered so vivid in its Hollywood heyday that the Nicaraguan government lodged a protest. The show was framed with unforgettable signatures: the wail of a train, the sting of an organ, and the haunting *Valse Triste*, a shimmering theme suggesting death. The chime of a clock brought listeners back to the hour when last they left their heroes. The theme played under the ominous recap:

Twelve midnight, high on the ledge above the floor of the Temple of Vampires, somewhere in the jungles of Central America. Jack and Doc Long are facing one of the strangest, most hair-raising moments in their experience. They're out in the center of the temple, each clinging to separate ropes 50 feet in the air. There is only one chance for Jack and Doc . . . .

But with Jack and Doc, one chance was enough.

Perhaps the most extraordinary thing about *ILAM* was its creator. Carlton E. Morse was already nationally known for another powerful serial, but *One Man's Family* was as far removed from blood and thunder as he could be. Writing *ILAM*, Morse once said, made "the family" go better: they played off each other in a way that stimulated rather than drained his imagination. In 1943, with both shows running on different networks, Morse would write *OMF* on Mondays and Tuesdays and spend the rest of his week on *ILAM*. He worked with a globe close at hand, not knowing himself where his three comrades might be sent next. He had a collection of reference books, including histories of pagan symbols and heathen gods. Jack, Doc, and Reggie

were often sent where ancient rites were a way of life.

Morse broke into radio in the 1920s. At KGO, San Francisco, he produced mystery dramas and serials, among them a series titled *Split Second Tales*, a forerunner of the *Adventures by Morse* stories that he would syndicate some 15 years later. He was already acquainted with, and using, some of the actors who would play the pivotal roles in the famed serials to come. Michael Raffetto, who played Capt. Carter Post on *Split Second*, would emerge the following year as Paul Barbour of *One Man's Family*, and eight years later would step easily into the role of Jack Packard. Barton Yarborough had played a "Sergeant Long" in one of the early epics; a native of Texas with all the trimmings, Yarborough was natural for Doc Long. Morse wrote *ILAM* off the cuff: he never worked out the killer's identity in advance, preferring to learn through his own process of discovery who had done it. He fleshed out his tales with many suspects, giving everyone the motive and opportunity, and sometimes a puzzling alibi. Jack, Doc, and Reggie may have been radio's first true anti-heroes. They were neither fearless nor overly principled nor entirely without blame for their own predicaments. They respected the law in a grudging kind of way but were known to hide evidence. They would never be unjustly arrested without a fight, unless it suited Jack's greater purpose. The stories were fast-paced and quickly concluded: most in the 15-minute days were wrapped up within three weeks, with the weekly half-hour stories running eight to thirteen weeks.

Perhaps the story best remembered and most coveted by *ILAM* advocates is *Stairway to the Sun* (June–July 1943), a fantastic setting reached by going through "the great gloomy cavern behind the mile-high waterfall, at the foot of the lost plateau, somewhere in the tropical jungle vastness of Venezuela." Jack and Doc have led an expedition far up the Orinoco River, 700 miles from civilization. Attacked by prehistoric flying reptiles and forced down into the jungle, they now face the prospect of a perilous journey overland. But they are momentarily awed by the wonders of the plateau. It is 9,000 feet high and contains 400 square miles, an incomparable setting where, in the words of one character, "the birds are not quite birds and the animals are not quite animals and even some of the trees look as if they are wearing human skin instead of bark.'' It is an ''island in the sky,'' still in primitive stages of evolution. The waterfall is so huge that it generates a kind of incandescent power: the cavern behind it is reached along a treacherous rocky path, charged with ethereal light, and as they approach it the effect becomes almost supernatural. Is that a celeste playing in the waterfall, or are their minds being warped? And those sounds they hear . . . could they be voices, calling them from the tons of cascading water?

In his script, Morse tried to help the soundman achieve some semblance of what he envisioned. The waterfall, he wrote, ''must be a tremendous sound . . . perhaps you have a waterfall record . . . maybe supplement this with thunder-sheet and rushing river records . . . anyway, the biggest sound you can conceive.'' Then, as the comrades enter the mind-warping environment, it ''should not be a dead roar but a roar with lights and shades in it . . . piercing sounds . . . crashing sounds.'' He suggested a ''wild cat whistle, a tree crashing to ground, a ricocheting rifle shot, cannon fire . . . all this interspersed with crash and roll of thunder from time to time.'' And then the music: ''on cue, bring in celeste, in hall with echo chamber''; then, the multitude of voices as the group passes under the water, and one of the most eerie sound effects in radio is achieved. As each person passes under the waterfall, he hears a chorus of voices calling his name, in his own voice: *Jaaaaaaack Paaaaaaaaackard!* . . . *Jaaaaaaackkkk!* . . . and the roar diminishes, then suddenly stops in the singing of a mockingbird.

They have passed through the cavern and come into a canyon a mile deep. Across the canyon they see a set of stairs cut into the side of the cliff—stairs that go up through the clouds, apparently to infinity—''a dad-blamed stairway to the sun,'' as Doc Long puts it. Up they go on a stairway just six feet wide, ''with sheer walls on the inner side and sheer fall on the outside.'' It is Morse's greatest technical achievement. In a series that bowed to none where atmosphere and imagery were concerned, these chapters of *Stairway to the Sun* were knockouts.

Fifty years later the question remains: was this, as Jim Harmon asserted, the greatest radio show ever staged? Probably not, but it certainly was one of a kind. Nothing on the air quite compared with *ILAM*; nothing in the vast archive still being amassed by historians and hobbyists packs

quite the same wallop, for those who like it. Not everyone does—that should be noted, now that the flush of rediscovery has paled somewhat. There are those who find this corny and contrived. These are generally people who never experienced it as a child, huddled in a dark room, when those terrifying strains of *Valse Triste* could raise gooseflesh before the first word was spoken. Most of the available *ILAM* material comes from the New York run: three full stories—*The Thing That Cries in the Night*; *Bury Your Dead, Arizona*; and *The Richards Curse* (lacking one chapter)—along with enough of *Temple of Vampires* and a few other stories that the action can be followed. The best available piece of the Hollywood run, at this writing, are two half-hour chapters and surrounding fragments from *The Pirate Loot of the Island of Skulls*. Again the listener can hear Doc Long climb to the roof of the Temple of Jaguars and battle the high priest Holy Joe to the death. These shows have all been in circulation more than 20 years. Since then: almost nothing. Connoisseurs of the Hollywood run generally disdain the New York shows as inferior product. But as William Faulkner once said, ''Given a choice between Scotch and nothing, I'll take Scotch.''

I LOVE ADVENTURE, thriller drama.

BROADCAST HISTORY: April 25–July 18, 1948, ABC. 30m, Sundays at 7.

CAST: Michael Raffetto as Jack Packard, head of the A-1 Detective Agency in Hollywood, whose adventures were formerly heard on *I Love a Mystery*. Tom Collins as Reggie Yorke, his British companion. Barton Yarborough as Doc Long, the third of their adventurous trio. Support from Hollywood radio performers: Russell Thorson (before he departed for the East to star as Jack Packard in the revived *ILAM* run), Lillian Buyeff, Earl Lee, Harry Lang, Janet Logan, John McIntire, Jeanette Nolan, Rolfe Sedan, Donald Morrison, Luis Van Rooten, Lal Chand Mehra, Alma Lawton, Barbara Jean Wong, Henry Blair, Betty Lou Gerson, Dix Davis, Peggy Webber, Lou Krugman, Frank Richards, etc. Jeanne Bates as Mary Kay Jones, ''the cutest secretary in Hollywood.'' Everett Glass as the spokesman for ''the Twenty-One Old Men of Ten Grammercy Park.'' **ANNOUNCER:** Dresser Dahlstead. **MUSIC:** Rex Koury on organ. **PRODUCER-DIRECTOR:** Carlton E. Morse. **WRIT-**

ERS: Carlton E. Morse, John Paul Schofield. THEME: *Valse Triste.*

I Love Adventure was the bridge between the West and East Coast versions of *I Love a Mystery.* But it lacked the dramatic tension and cohesion of either.

Jack, Doc, and Reggie had split up during the war and had lost touch. Jack went into American intelligence; Doc became a fighter pilot after a stint with the Flying Tigers in China; Reggie returned to his native England to join the RAF. Now Jack was summoned to London, to work for a top-secret organization, "the Twenty-One Old Men of Ten Grammercy Park," dedicated to fighting the enemies of international peace. The "Old Men" convened in an enormous room behind a wall-sized two-way mirror where Jack could hear but never see them. Jack's first assignment took him to Indo-China. In the second installment, he was reunited with Reggie, who again became his partner in adventure. Reporting weekly to Ten Grammercy Park, they were sent to a lost city to rescue a Burmese princess, to Italy to rescue kidnapped schoolgirls, and so on.

Abruptly, in the seventh show, the "Old Men" angle was dropped, and again Jack and Reggie were operating their detective agency in California. Just as abruptly, in episode, 9, Reggie dropped from the series and Doc Long appeared, giving no explanation where he'd been or how he happened to turn up. It was as if author Carlton E. Morse couldn't decide from week to week what to do with the show. The result is a jerky mishmash, preserved in its entirety on tape, though from discs that were often marred by scratch.

I LOVE LUCY, situation comedy.

BROADCAST HISTORY: A landmark TV series with an audition episode produced for radio, Feb. 27, 1952, but never broadcast. Prepared for CBS, with ads for Philip Morris, the extant show is an edited TV soundtrack with narrative bridgework by Desi Arnaz, one of the principals. A noble experiment: good fun nonetheless.

CAST: Lucille Ball, Arnaz, Vivian Vance, William Frawley.

I WAS A COMMUNIST FOR THE FBI, espionage-thriller drama.

BROADCAST HISTORY: 1952–54, 30m, transcribed syndication; Frederick Ziv.

CAST: Dana Andrews as Matt Cvetic. DIRECTOR: Henry Hayward.

This series capitalized on the new Red scare of the early 1950s: 78 episodes were recorded, without any assistance from the FBI, which refused to cooperate. It didn't matter: anti-Communist hysteria was at a peak, and by the end of 1952 *I Was a Communist* was scheduled on more than 600 stations—far more than if it had been on any network.

The show was based on the book (and subsequent movie) by Matt Cvetic and purportedly told of his adventures as an undercover operative who joined the Communist Party to spy from within. Many of the stories contained double-edged conflicts: Cvetic constantly jockeyed for information, walking a tightrope among suspicious Party officials while unable to reveal his true mission even to his family, who shunned him. Communists were stereotyped, much as Hitler's Nazis had been a few years before: they were seen as cold and humorless, with their single goal to enslave the world. Cvetic could never be sure who might be a Party spy. Dana Andrews gave it an air of Hollywood glamor, always closing with these words: "I was a Communist for the FBI. I walk alone."

I WAS THERE, true adventure accounts.

BROADCAST HISTORY: 1935–45, CBS West Coast. Mobil.

NARRATORS: Knox Manning, Chet Huntley, etc. MUSIC: Lud Gluskin, etc. PRODUCERS: Robert Hafter, Russ Johnston. RESEARCHER-WRITER: Tommy Tomlinson. WRITERS: La Verne Burton, Ernest Martin, Norman Rose, John Dunkel.

These were dramatic first-person accounts of true human adventures, including such varied fare as René Belbenoît's escape from Devil's Island, the lone survivor of Custer's last stand, witnesses to the assassinations of presidents, and the Russian girl who had become a deadly wartime sniper.

IDA BAILEY ALLEN, cookery.

BROADCAST HISTORY: 1926, WMCA, New York.

1928–35, CBS. Various 15m to 60m timeslots. 1935–36, NBC. 15m, twice a week.

Ida Bailey Allen was known as "the nation's homemaker." Her CBS series was also known as *The Radio Homemakers Club*.

I'M AN AMERICAN, interviews with naturalized Americans.

BROADCAST HISTORY: May 11, 1940–March 1, 1942, NBC. 15m, Saturday afternoons, on the Red Network until Oct. 1940 then Sundays on the Blue.

Most of the subjects on *I'm an American* had attained some degree of fame in their new land: actresses Elissa Landi, Vera Zorina, Alla Nazimova, and others praised America and told why they had become citizens.

INDICTMENT, true crime stories dramatized.

BROADCAST HISTORY: Jan. 29, 1956–Jan. 4, 1959, CBS. 25m, Sundays at 5:05.
CAST: Nat Polen as Edward McCormick, assistant district attorney. Jack Arthur as Tom Russo, his assistant. **PRODUCER:** Nathan Kroll. **DIRECTORS:** Ira Ashley, Paul Roberts. **WRITERS:** Robert Corcoran, Allan Sloane.

Indictment, based on the files of former assistant DA Eleazer Lipsky of New York, presented the step-by-step and tedious checking that went into a case before an indictment could be obtained.

INFORMATION, PLEASE, the great radio quiz program of the intellectual set.

BROADCAST HISTORY: May 17, 1938–Nov. 5, 1940, Blue Network. 30m, Tuesdays at 8:30. Sustained until Nov. 15, 1938, then Canada Dry Ginger Ale.
Nov. 15, 1940–June 24, 1946, NBC. 30m, Fridays at 8:30 for Lucky Strike until Feb. 5, 1943; Mondays (at 10:30, 1943–44; at 9:30, 1944–45) for Heinz Foods until Feb. 5, 1945; then Mondays at 9:30 for Mobil Oil.
Oct. 2, 1946–June 25, 1947, CBS. 30m, Wednesdays at 10:30. Parker Pens.
Sept. 26, 1947–June 25, 1948, Mutual. 30m, Fridays at 9:30.
1950–51, transcribed repeats, syndicated on various stations.
MODERATOR: Clifton Fadiman. **REGULAR PANELISTS:** Franklin P. Adams and John Kieran; Oscar Levant twice a month. Guests for the all-important fourth chair from the worlds of Broadway, politics, literature, cinema, music, radio, etc. **ANNOUNCERS:** Howard Claney, Milton Cross, Ed Herlihy, Ben Grauer. **PIANIST:** Joe Kahn. **CREATOR-PRODUCER-DIRECTOR:** Dan Golenpaul.

The idea behind *Information, Please* was almost incidental to its long-running success. What made it an immortal piece of radio was the mix of personalities who fit the idea so perfectly. The quiz, in fact, was the least important part of the formula. The questions were an intellectual exercise, something to get the talk rolling and the humor bubbling from within. "An uproarious error or a brilliant bit of irreverence was rated far above any dull delivery of truth," wrote John Kieran, one of its four major personalities, in his memoir. Kieran had no qualm in naming *Information, Please* "the most literate popular entertainment program ever to go out over the air on radio or television."

It was created, owned, and run by Dan Golenpaul, a controversial personality who knew what he wanted, was relentless in his pursuit of it, and then, having attained it, did battle with everyone, from an equally feisty sponsor to the president of a network, to maintain its integrity and prestige. He was "extremely jealous of his prerogative in choosing guests," said the *Saturday Evening Post*: there would be "no interference from his sponsor, the network, or anybody else." He was said to be arrogant and aloof. Once, when the show traveled west and the editor of *Radio Life* asked for an interview, Golenpaul told her he cared nothing about her publication or the 60,000 people who read it, and she was left to piece together a story as best she could.

He had never liked quiz shows: they had always struck him as inane and ultimately embarrassing. He had dabbled in radio since the early 1930s, producing a few shows that were intellectually based and predictably short-lived. He was listening to *Professor Quiz*, an early and typical show of its type, when the idea came to him. The problem with most quiz formats was inherent: they appealed to a lowest common denominator by putting some ignorant contestant onstage and spotlighting his ignorance. Golenpaul proposed to reverse the formula: let an intelligent, educated public ask the questions and put the alleged authorities on the spot. The networks were skeptical, fearing that such a show would be stuffy, pretentious, and far over the heads of its listeners. Even the men Golenpaul would choose as his experts would share that concern, in the beginning.

At 34, Clifton Fadiman had already enjoyed a solid career in letters. Born in Brooklyn in 1904, Fadiman had been an editor at Simon and Schuster and was now, in 1938, book critic for the *New Yorker*. He was a prodigious reader. But nothing in Fadiman's career remotely suggested that he was about to become one of radio's truly singular talents. He had done a book review series in 1934, and that was it. With an almost uncanny eye for what the show could become, Golenpaul asked him to moderate. Fadiman was not convinced that the show could work, but he agreed to do the audition, figuring he had little to lose.

Franklin P. Adams was a longtime newspaper columnist and a well-known literary light. He was as celebrated under his initials, FPA, as with his full name. Born in Chicago in 1881, Adams came to New York in 1913 to begin his column, "The Conning Tower," in the *New York Tribune*. Adams was also a wit: a member of the Algonquin Round Table, that remarkable group of lunch partners that included Dorothy Parker, Robert Benchley, George S. Kaufman, Heywood Broun, and Alexander Woollcott. But Adams had fallen on hard times. Unemployed, he nevertheless rejected Golenpaul's initial overture. But he was persuaded to give it a try when Golenpaul—never an easy man to dissuade—personally ran him through a few paces.

The audition record was cut, with Fadiman moderating a panel that included Adams, Columbia University economics teacher Louis M. Hacker, Marcus Duffield of the *New York Herald-Tribune*, and science writer Bernard Jaffe. Golenpaul had decided that there should be four "experts" on each panel and that two of these chairs should be permanent—filled by people of broad interests and knowledge who also had the prime requisite, the quick and slicing wit. He wanted a Shakespearean expert, and probably someone who knew the natural sciences. In Adams he had one such renaissance man: Adams knew poetry, was a student of Gilbert and Sullivan, and had more than a passing acquaintance with Shakespeare. He knew a few things about

baseball, and sports was another field that, for popular interest alone, should be well covered. As Sally Ashley put it in her biography of Adams, "the permanent panelists would afford the stability on which to drape the rest of the show"; the visiting chairs could then be filled by people in other colorful pursuits, giving the show a constantly fresh sound.

Bill Karlin, chief of programming at NBC Blue, heard the record in April 1938 and gave Golenpaul a summer slot.

Ashley describes the preparation that went into that first broadcast. As yet there was no listening audience, so questions had to be concocted whole cloth. This was done by Golenpaul, his wife, Ann, and Gordon Kahn, a high school teacher selected by Golenpaul as the "editor-in-chief" of his board of editors. Working in Kahn's back yard, they wrote the questions and then persuaded their friends to come to the live broadcast as "ringers." Friends, wives, and Golenpaul's secretary were among the fictitiously named participants on the first broadcast. It contained almost the same panel as the audition record, with Hacker replaced by Dr. Harry Overstreet, professor of philosophy at the College of the City of New York. Fadiman was announced by Howard Claney as an "intellectual Simon Legree, the Toscanini of quiz," and they were off. "You, the very much quizzed public, will quiz the professors," Claney said. "Yes, the worm turns, and now the experts will have to know the answers to your questions, or else you win five dollars." This, admittedly, wasn't much of a prize. But Golenpaul had been given only $400 a week by the network to stage his show. This had to be split seven ways, so there wasn't much left for the listener.

The first broadcast set the tone and was lauded as a charmer. The dialogue was snappy and brisk. "Why would it never be necessary for the man in the moon, if married to a chatterbox, to tell her to shut up?" Jaffe answered immediately: there was no atmosphere on the moon, and sound waves require air to be transmitted. Fadiman pursued it: a real chatterbox might have enough of her own hot air to make herself heard. "That's rather weak science there, Mr. Fadiman," Jaffe said. On another question, Adams knew half the answer, and Duffield, too late, professed to know the rest. "Now, Mr. Duffield," scolded Fadiman, "if you'd only had the good sense to whisper what you knew to Mr. Adams, and if he had whispered what he knew to you, perhaps we might have saved that five dollars.'' Adams, his voice laced with disdain, said, ''I *scorn* such methods,'' and the audience laughed heartily. The cleverest question of the evening was ''What sextet sang their way to fame recently?'' Jaffe guessed it: the Seven Dwarfs from *Snow White*, a sextet by the fact that one of the Dwarfs, Dopey, was mute.

Jaffe and Duffield did regular service while Golenpaul continued to mull the problem of the second regular chair. He had met John Kieran at a Dutch Treat Club luncheon and had been impressed with the depth and scope of Kieran's knowledge. Kieran was a sports columnist for the *New York Times* whose writings had earned him the title ''sports philosopher.'' He was fluent in Latin and a scholar of Shakespeare, knew music, poetry, ornithology and the other branches of natural history, and had a strong base of general knowledge. This was wrapped up in a Tenth Avenue New York accent, a streak of what one writer termed ''pugnacity concealed by modesty.'' But like Adams and Fadiman before him, Kieran was initially disinterested. This disinterest was again defeated by Golenpaul, through determination and tenacity, and Kieran appeared on the fourth broadcast, June 7, 1938. He surprised himself by having ''a lot of fun.'' It was so much fun that he stayed the full ten years.

Later that summer came the fourth cog in this quiz-wheel, the redoubtable Oscar Levant. Levant was a pianist and composer, friend of the Gershwins and an all-around ''wag of Broadway.'' He was the youngest of the regulars, born in Pittsburgh in 1906 and dubbed the show's *enfant terrible*. Kieran would remember him as a bundle of nervous energy—constantly whistling, shuffling, drumming his fingers, and humming under his breath. Like Kieran, he wrapped a formidable intellect into a common man's front. He was a ''remarkable musical talent,'' Kieran would write: Levant had ''a positive genius for making offhand cutting remarks that couldn't have been sharper if he'd honed them a week in his mind. Oscar was always good for a bright response edged with acid.'' Listeners were astounded when Levant unscrambled musical omelets and identified several pieces that had been jumbled into one by staff pianist Joe Kahn. They shouldn't be so amazed, said Levant: any

competent musician could have done the same thing. His basic problem: ''I'm a concert pianist, and nobody'll believe me.''

By December 1938, Levant had become the third regular. Golenpaul would use him every other week, an ideal formula that still left him with six chairs a month to fill with guests. Questions could now be geared to the guests' talents and interests, as well as those of the regulars. Everything possible was done to make the guests look good and still keep the questions difficult and challenging. Gone were the phony interrogator-plants in the studio audience: having listeners mail in the questions gave Golenpaul the advantage of time to double-check the answers. At its peak, the board of editors would screen as many as 75,000 questions a week, throwing out anything on current politics, race, or religion: ''anything smacking of trouble,'' as *Time* put it.

By the end of its first summer, the show had attracted the attention of most major press outlets. *Time* wrote a cute piece recapping some of the best ad-libs. When guest John Gunther identified Reza Pahlavi as the Shah of Iran, Fadiman asked, ''Are you shah?''—to which Gunther instantly replied, ''Sultanly.'' When the panel was asked to name four prominent women with the names Marina, Elzire, Hepzibah, and Farida, Duffield thought the name Elzire was familiar: ''As a matter of fact, I used to play Indians with her.'' Fadiman's comeback brought down the house. ''Well, you must have had a lot of fun. Elzire is Mrs. Dionne,'' mother of the celebrated quintuplets.

Kieran was particularly alert when Fadiman asked what political leader was a bastard's son. Levant thought it might be Adolf Hitler, né Schicklgrüber, an answer challenged by a woman in the audience who thought Hitler himself was the bastard. ''He is, if he wasn't,'' said Kieran to thundering laughter. When Kieran's son sent in a Shakespeare question that stumped them all, Kieran quipped, ''How sharper than a thankless tooth it is to have a serpent child.'' Adams and guest Groucho Marx once burst into song, a lively rendition of Gilbert and Sullivan. Alfred Hitchcock answered a question on a real murder case in such detail that Fadiman asked if he knew how the tide was running at the time. Especially appreciated were questions that stumped the experts on the trivia of their own lives. Adams could not name a passage from one of his poems. Novelist Rex Stout failed to identify a recipe for Lobster Newburg, forgetting that his detective Nero Wolfe had used it in the book *Too Many Cooks*. Elliott Roosevelt had no idea that certain quotations had appeared in his mother's newspaper column the week before.

And then there were the know-it-alls. Gracie Allen was a charming guest, proving that her radio persona, the airhead, was pure fiction. Orson Welles answered almost everything thrown at him, prompting Fadiman to comment dryly, "This is your last appearance on this program, Mr. Welles."

Being a guest, wrote Kieran, "became a badge of distinction." For many it was a tense experience. As air time approached, even such seasoned players in the public arena as New York mayor Fiorello La Guardia grew nervous. Golenpaul's practice was to meet the guests in his office, share a small Scotch, and walk over to the studio. His chief problem was keeping his sponsors out of the selection process. Because many of his guests were in government or in some way involved in political activity, their appearance on the show suggested a bias to a sponsor perhaps not free of his own. In this Golenpaul was resolute: he alone would make the selections, and his determination paid off with a range of personalities, viewpoints, and intellects the like of which was heard nowhere else. Among the guests who appeared on *Information, Please* were Ben Hecht, George S. Kaufman, Basil Rathbone, Dorothy Thompson, Lillian Gish, Alexander Woollcott, H. V. Kaltenborn, Alice Roosevelt Longworth, Carl Sandburg, Albert Spalding, Boris Karloff, Marc Connelly, Dorothy Parker, Beatrice Lillie, and Postmaster General James Farley. Prizefighter Gene Tunney surprised the nation with his knowledge of Shakespeare. Moe Berg, Boston Red Sox catcher, had a quick mind and a vast store of general knowledge (and later became a spy, searching out atomic secrets for the OSS in Europe). Harpo Marx appeared without speaking, whistling his way riotously through the program. Fred Allen took over the show, relegating Fadiman to a panelist's chair. Wendell Willkie did the same. Deems Taylor was a regular fill-in, appearing no less than 30 times. Playwright Russel Crouse lived near the studio and could usually be rounded up in an emergency. Chris-

topher Morley was on at least 18 times. The most frequently heard female voices were those of Cornelia Otis Skinner and British novelist Jan Struther, author of *Mrs. Miniver*. Struther was a strong guest, with keen intelligence and a quick wit and an enchanting English accent laced with Americanisms. But she was dropped abruptly after innocently answering an Agatha Christie question by using the English title, *Ten Little Niggers*.

The arrival of Canada Dry as sponsor in November 1938 brought a sweeping change of fortune. Now Golenpaul was shepherding $10,000 a week, and Kieran soon found his radio salary equal to what he was earning at the *New York Times*. Eventually the regulars were raised to $1,500 a week. The prize money also went up, and in October 1939 the *Encyclopedia Britannica* became part of the package, giving away sets of its junior encyclopedia to those whose questions were used and the main encyclopedia to those who "stumped the experts." For the cost of an occasional set of books, *Britannica* forged a stronger identity with the show than did sponsors who footed the entire bill. By 1943 listeners who stumped the experts received both encyclopedias and $57 in war bonds and stamps a clever plug for the sponsor, Heinz, and its "57 varieties" of foods. In September 1944, Golenpaul began paying a $500 war bond, with encyclopedia, to anyone who could stump the experts on all parts of a multiple-part question. The payouts were made to the sound of a cash register. Later, with the vast influx of questions by mail, Golenpaul built a question file, saving even the best for exactly the right occasion. This meant that if Helen Traubel appeared as a guest, the editors had at their disposal a deep well of questions on opera. Some questions were years old, and as the jackpots grew, so did the difficulty of finding people who had now moved elsewhere. Some winners never were found.

The show had a distinct sound. There were no musical themes: it simply opened to the crowing of a rooster and a cheery greeting from announcer Milton Cross (or others): "Wake up, America, it's time to stump the experts!" By 1939 Cross was announcing to a growing audience of ten million. The show was cited for excellence that year by such disparate publications as the *Saturday Review* and *Hobo News*. Also in

1939, the show became the first to break NBC's firm rule against prerecorded entertainment. Being spontaneous, it was impossible to repeat, so the choice for Blue Network outlets in the Pacific zone was bleak: either carry it at 5:30 or record it for playback later. Reluctantly, NBC chose the latter, and for the first time listeners heard the phrase "This show has been transcribed from an earlier network presentation, for release at this more convenient time." *Time* couldn't help wondering if this might be the beginning of an odious trend, a suggestion NBC laughed off in the flippant comment of a network spokesman: "Would you rather kiss a girl or her picture?" Little did he know. Tradition had been broken, and soon this practice would be common on every network.

Sponsor-producer relations took a serious downturn with the arrival of American Tobacco and its strong-willed president, George Washington Hill, in November 1940. Hill assumed that, as sponsor, he would be the boss, and he sent Golenpaul a list of people he wanted kept off the show. Golenpaul quickly staked out his territory, telling Hill he would never allow such interference from anyone, and for most of the 26 months that Lucky Strike sponsored the show it was an uneasy standoff between them. The disagreement became critical with the broadcast of Nov. 6, 1942, when Hill initiated a new campaign to announce a change in the cigarette packaging. He had received data indicating that women, who were smoking in increasing numbers, responded better to the white packaging of archrival Chesterfield than to the dark green long associated with Luckies. The green had to go. It was decided to structure an ad campaign hinting that the green had disappeared because of dye shortages, thus casting a purely commercial decision in a patriotic light. The slogan "Lucky Strike green has gone to war" was the perfect kind of hard sell that Hill favored. Basil Ruysdael, with his deep, commanding, and unique voice, was the Luckies pitchman. *Lucky Strike green has gone to war! Lucky Strike green has gone to war!* The phrase popped up incessantly, barked by announcers between questions, whenever a spot of dead air occurred, with no regard whatever for traditional commercial breaks.

Golenpaul erupted. By one account, he accosted Hill and shouted, "You're lousing up my program and I won't stand for it!" Hill reminded Golenpaul that it was *his* show, *he* was paying the bills, and there was nothing Golenpaul could do about it. Golenpaul filed suit, and the story spilled onto front pages everywhere. The suit was ultimately dismissed, but Golenpaul had won a public relations battle. He was seen as a man fighting for quality and integrity, while American Tobacco was viewed as mercenary and crass. In the tide of negative publicity, Hill released Golenpaul from his contract in February 1943.

A far more serious loss that year was Oscar Levant, who left as Maurice Zolotow reported, "when a series of arguments with Golenpaul culminated in a fistfight." Heinz Foods, the new sponsor, also proved difficult for Golenpaul to tolerate. Heinz objected strongly to the appearance of certain New Dealers, wrote Sally Ashley, and the sponsor that followed, Socony Oil, was "even more rigid and conservative." After a season pushing Mobil Oil, NBC decided to cancel the show. Campbell Soups wanted it, according to Ashley, but NBC did not, and the soup company would not carry it on another network. Golenpaul moved it to CBS, where another battle awaited at the top level of network management. When William S. Paley objected to the scheduling of controversial Georgia governor Ellis Arnall, Golenpaul again stood his ground. Paley threatened to cut him off the air: Golenpaul counterthreatened to fight it in the press if Paley should dare censor his show. The Arnall show went on, though the days of *Information, Please* were numbered: Golenpaul was now widely known as a troublemaker, and when his Parker Pen contract expired, no further sponsor could be found. It aired on Mutual in 1948, a seldom-heard sustainer.

But it left deep footprints in the industry. As Ashley put it, "the ghosts of Golenpaul, Kahn, Fadiman (the only principal still living in 1996), Adams, Kieran, and Levant sit behind people like Johnny Carson and David Letterman, simultaneously encouraging lunacy and demanding respect for the audience." When the show ended, Golenpaul continued to publish his yearly *Information Please Almanac*. An attempt to bring it to TV failed: it ran one summer on CBS, June 29–Sept. 21, 1952. Adams, then in the early stages of Alzheimer's disease, could only appear in the premiere program. He died in 1960; Levant in 1972; Golenpaul in 1974; Kieran in 1981. Fadiman became chairman of the Book-of-the-Month Club board of judges and went on with his literary career.

More than 200 *Information, Please* shows are on tape for posterity, a marvelous run beginning with the first broadcast and continuing into the mid-1940s. It is simply superb entertainment for any time, wherever people care about history, humor, and the delightful, unexpected, slicing turn of phrase from first-rate minds. Golenpaul must be forgiven every alleged personal shortcoming: his genius and judgment where *Information, Please* was concerned is amply demonstrated. His first decision—hiring Fadiman as moderator—was his most important. Fadiman was the spark plug: on those rare occasions when he was absent, the difference was immediately apparent. In the words of *Current Biography*, Fadiman was ''the perfect mixture of bright interest and delicate malice that spurs the experts to do their desperate best. No one can so well snub an irrepressible Levant, point up Kieran's uncanny accuracy, wring the last drop of wry erudition out of FPA, or encourage a stage-struck guest.'' The truth of this is immediately evident by sampling just about any program.

INNER SANCTUM MYSTERIES, horror anthology.

BROADCAST HISTORY: Jan. 7, 1941–Aug. 29, 1943, Blue Network. 25m, Tuesdays at 9:35 until March 16, 1941; then 30m, Sundays at 8:30. Carter's Pills.

Sept. 4, 1943–April 17, 1950, CBS. 30m, Saturdays at 8:30 until Nov. 22, 1944; Wednesdays at 9 until Jan. 2, 1945; Tuesdays at 9 until June 18, 1946; then Mondays at 8. Colgate through Dec. 27, 1944; Lipton Tea, Jan. 2, 1945–June 18, 1946; Bromo Seltzer, July 29, 1946–April 17, 1950.

Sept. 4, 1950–June 18, 1951, ABC. 30m, Mondays at 8. Mars Candy.

June 22–Oct. 5, 1952, CBS. 30m, Sundays at 8. Pearson Pharmaceutical.

HOSTS: Raymond Edward Johnson until May 22, 1945; Paul McGrath beginning Sept. 28, 1945. Also: House Jameson. **CAST:** Film stars known for the macabre—Boris Karloff, Peter Lorre, etc.—in lead roles, ca. 1941–42. New York radio performers in subsequent leads and in support: Richard Widmark, Larry Haines, Everett Sloane, Lesley Woods, Anne Seymour, Stefan Schnabel, Arnold Moss, etc. **ANNOUNCERS:** Ed Herlihy for Carter's Pills; Dwight Weist for Bromo Seltzer; Allen C. Anthony for Mars Candy. **CREATOR-PRODUCER-DIRECTOR:** Himan Brown. **WRITERS:** Milton Lewis, John Roeburt, Robert Sloane, Robert Newman, Harry and Gail Ingram, Sigmund Miller, etc. **SOUND EFFECTS:** Keene Crockett, Harold Johnson Jr. (ABC); Jack Amrhein, Bobby Prescott (CBS).

Himan Brown would tell the story years later: in a studio where he once worked, the door to the basement gave off an ungodly creak whenever anyone opened it. One day it occurred to him—he would make that door a star.

It was a classic moment in radio broadcasting, for the show that grew out of it would be remembered decades after radio itself ceased to be dramatically viable. The campy horrors of *Inner Sanctum Mysteries* began and ended with that creaking door. It may have been the greatest opening signature device ever achieved. It pushed its listeners into that dank inner chamber of the mind, where each week for a decade were staged some of the most farfetched, unbelievable, and downright impossible murder tales ever devised in a medium not known for restraint.

Though the show was a strange combination of horror and humor, the stories were played strictly for chills. No matter how strained the conclusion or how deeply into his bag of improbables a writer had to reach to knit it all together, there was never a hint that this dark world was anything but real. At the same time, the stories were introduced by a host who trotted out every conceivable ghoulish pun in his effort to liven things up.

It opened to grim organ music, a deep generic creepiness that set the stage. Someone was about to die, and horribly at that. The organ became one of the star players: peppered by sharp stings and cascading cresendos, it trickled through the show, brooding, ever-present, worrying, fretting, a macabre bed for the narrator's voice or a sudden revelation for the villain. This was the epitome of radio melodrama.

The opening music was a study in contrasts: three bars in the lowest register, then a sting, and the announcement—*Inner Sanctum Mysteries!* A doorknob turned. The door swung in slowly, the creaking agonized and broken. Then came Raymond, the host, with gruesome jokes about losing one's head or hanging around after the show, or perhaps beating the high cost of dying. Ectoplasm with two lumps of cheer. *And now, if your scalpels are sharpened and ready, we'll proceed with the business of the evening...* Raymond's story was about to begin.

The early days of *Inner Sanctum* gave a generous mix of classics and original stories. Boris Karloff was a regular, appearing in, among others, the Poe classics *The Telltale Heart* and *The Fall of the House of Usher*. Peter Lorre was heard in *The Horla*, by Maupassant, and George Coulouris, Paul Lukas, and Claude Rains were also starred performers. But Karloff propelled it: fueled by his film portrayals of Frankenstein's monster, he appeared more than 15 times in 1941–42. While the network was under pressure from parents' groups to curtail graphic violence, Karloff wanted even more gore. His public expected it, he argued.

But Karloff was gone as a regular by 1943, to return only in infrequent guest roles. The series settled into its own niche, the roles enacted by the unsung radio professionals of New York. The stories turned on the wildest happenstance. Only on *Inner Sanctum* could a man be haunted for 40 years by the wailing of his dead wife, then learn that the sound was the wind rushing through a hole in the wall where he had sealed her body. Only here would a man be sentenced to life imprisonment after committing murder to obtain a scientific formula that made him immortal. Clichéd literary devices were shamelessly used to fool listeners, the most common of these employing the first-person killer viewpoint, the narrator who was insane but seemed normal. Self-loathing had buried his crimes beyond conscious recall, giving the writers the freedom to conjure up all kinds of ghostly manifestations. Dead men were seen in crowds; ghosts fluttered in the window at midnight; voices wafted on the wind. Without benefit of the guilty knowledge, the listener was recruited as the killer's sidekick. The listener then saw that ghost, heard that wail, got that chilling call from a long-dead spouse, and the fear of the killer-narrator became the listener's lullabye.

At the end, the host returned for the body count.

Everybody dead but the cat, and we only over-looked him because we couldn't find him... heh-heh-heh...

And now it's time to close that squeaking door...

Good niiii-iiight...

Pleasant dreeeeeaaaaammmmmsssss...

And the agonized squeak reversed, and the door slammed shut.

Raymond Edward Johnson used his first name as host; Paul McGrath, who followed in 1945, had a lighter, brighter demeanor, losing a bit of Johnson's underlying menace. Though the series took its name from, and promoted, Simon and Schuster's Inner Sanctum line of mystery novels, the radio stories were mostly originals. More than 100 shows are available, valued today as high camp.

INSIDE STORY, documentary drama; interviews.

BROADCAST HISTORY: March 14–Oct. 3, 1939, Blue Network. 30m, Tuesdays at 8. Ralston.
HOST: Fred Sullivan. **MUSIC DIRECTOR:** Glenn Welty. **ORCHESTRA:** Roy Shield.

Inside Story re-created news events, using eyewitness accounts and dramatization. Among the guests were Texas Rangers, other lawmen, and a "professional ribber" (a man planted in the audience at crooked auctions to drive up the bidding). The show made national news in June by yanking off the air at the last minute a story detailing the 1937 escape from Alcatraz of convicts Ralph Roe and Theodore Cole. The FBI had always maintained that Roe and Cole drowned, a point hotly disputed by ex-inmate Pat Reed, the story's main source. NBC pulled the show at the FBI's request, leaving Reed crying coverup.

INSPECTOR THORNE, crime drama.

BROADCAST HISTORY: July 20–Sept. 27, 1951, NBC, 30m, Fridays at 9; Thursdays at 9 in Sept.
CASTS: Karl Weber as Thorne. Staats Cotsworth as Thorne. Sept. 27, Dan Ocko as Sergeant Muggin.

INTO THE LIGHT, soap opera.

BROADCAST HISTORY: Aug. 18, 1941–March 20, 1942, Blue Network. 15m, weekdays at 2:30.
CAST: Film star Margo as Tanya, the girl loved by warring brothers. Peter Donald and Martin Wolfson as the brothers. Charme Allen as Ma Owen.

Morris Carnovsky as Mr. Kriss. Mitzi Gould as Emily. **DIRECTOR:** Ted Corday. **WRITER:** Larry Bearson.

INTRIGUE, thriller drama: "tales of espionage, manhunts, high adventure."

BROADCAST HISTORY: July 24–Sept. 11, 1946, CBS. 30m, Wednesdays at 9:30.

CAST: Well-known Hollywood character actors (Virginia Bruce, Vincent Price, etc.); Joseph Schildkraut, featured actor and narrator. **MUSIC:** Lud Gluskin, Lucien Moraweck. **PRODUCER-DIRECTOR:** Charles Vanda. **WRITER:** Robert Tallman.

INVITATION TO LEARNING, great books discussion.

BROADCAST HISTORY: May 26, 1940–Dec. 28, 1964, CBS. 30m, Sundays at 4:30 Tuesdays at 10:30, 1940–41, then Sundays, various timeslots.

HOST: Lyman Bryson. **ROUNDTABLE PARTIC-IPANTS:** Huntington Cairns, Allen Tate, Quincy Howe, Mason Gross, Mark Van Doren, etc.

Based on a class at St. John's College, Annapolis, *Invitation* was developed for radio at the suggestion of Stringfellow Barr, school president, who also served on the CBS Adult Education board.

THE IPANA TROUBADORS, musical variety.

BROADCAST HISTORY: 1923, WEAF, New York. 1926–34, NBC. 30m, Red Network, Wednesdays at 9, 1926–28; Blue Network, Mondays at 8:30, 1929–31; Red Network, Wednesdays at 9, 1933–34. Bristol Myers for Ipana Toothpaste. Merged into Fred Allen's *Hour of Smiles* in 1934.

MUSICIANS: *Mid-1920s:* Sam Lanin, Red Nichols, Joe Tarto, Harry Horlick, Arthur Schutt, Tony Colucci, Vic Berton, Dick Johnson, Alfie Evans, Hymie Faberman, Chuck Campbell, Leo McConville, etc. Vocalists Billy Jones, Irving Kaufman, Scrappy Lambert and the Singing Sophomores (Lambert, Franklyn Baur, Ed Smalle, Wilfred Glenn, Lewis James, Elliott Shaw). *Ca. 1928–29:* Tommy Dorsey, Frank Teschmacher, Phil Napoleon, Harold Peppie, Jimmy Mullen, Benny Goodman, Manny Klein, Jimmy Dorsey, Pete Pumiglio, Babe Russin, Stan King, etc. Vocalists Smith Ballew, Willard Robison, etc. *1930s:* Jack Teagarden, Joe Lindwurm, Henry Levine, Tony Gianelli, Eddie Lang, Joe Venuti, Al Duffy, Lou Raderman,

Murray Kellner, Miff Mole, etc. Vocalists Chick Bullock, Dick Robertson, etc.

The Ipana Troubadors was the commercial name of a remarkable group of early radio and recording artists, performing in the interests of Ipana Toothpaste. No commercial mentions were allowed in the prenetwork days at WEAF, perhaps the most rigid station of that day on rules keeping the medium free of hard sell. Almost without exception, the acts took on the names of the sponsors. As the personnel would indicate, the fare was a mix of novelty tunes and hot swing.

IRENE BEASLEY, THE OLD DUTCH GIRL, music and song.

BROADCAST HISTORY: 1930–39, many 15m timeslots, frequently moved, various networks: 1930–32, CBS, three a week, at 8:30 A.M. (8:45 A.M., 1931–32); for Old Dutch Cleanser; Blue Network, Wednesdays at 6:30, 1933–34; NBC, 15m, various times, 1933–34; and as part of *The Dupont Zerone Jesters*, 1936–37; CBS, 15m, five a week at 2, sustained, 1938–39, as *R.F.D. No. 1.*

Irene Beasley was known as the "long, tall gal from Dixie." Born in Tennessee and raised in various parts of the South, she arrived on the networks with her own songs as specialties, as well as distinctive arrangements of the day's popular melodies.

IRENE RICH DRAMAS, dramatic anthology in serial form.

BROADCAST HISTORY: Oct. 4, 1933–May 31, 1942, Blue Network. 15m, weekly. Longest runs: Fridays at 8, 1934–37; Sundays at 9:45, 1937–39; at 9:30, 1939–42. Welch's Grape Juice.

June 5, 1942–May 28, 1944, CBS. 15m, Sundays at 6:15, 1942–43; at 5:45, 1943–44. Welch's Grape Juice.

Heard under many titles, depending on format:

Talk with Irene Rich, ca. 1933, also known as *Hollywood with Irene Rich* and *Behind the Screen.* Chatter with NBC announcer Norman Ross on Hollywood news, received by telegraph just before the broadcast.

Jewels of Enchantment, beginning May 23, 1934, and running through the year. Rich in a serial continuation about a titled Englishwoman seeking her lost fiancé in the South Seas.

Various 15m dramas complete in each episode beginning Jan. 4, 1935. Gale Gordon, frequent male lead.

The Lady Counsellor, 15m weekly continuation beginning April 24, 1936. Rich as Irene Davis, female attorney; Carleton Young as a criminal lawyer who was both rival and suitor.

Mid-late 1930s: more one-shot dramas. Ned Wever, leading man.

Glorious One, the story of Judith Bradley, confined to a sanitarium for five years, returning home cured to learn that an old friend had been romantically pursuing her husband, Jake. Rich as Bradley. John Lake as Jake. Larry Nunn and Florence Baker as their children, Don, 8, and Susan, 16. Pauline Hopkins, writer. Jan. 7–Sept. 8, 1940.

Dear John, the story of the Chandler family. Rich as Faith Chandler. Ray Montgomery as Noel Chandler. Betty Moran and Lois Collier as Carol. Norman Field as Josh. Also: Howard Duff, Tom Collins, Gerald Mohr. Melville Ruick, announcer. Sept. 15, 1940–Jan. 9, 1944.

Woman from Nowhere. Rich as an enigmatic woman. Bill Johnstone, Gerald Mohr, Herb Allen, and Anne Sloane in support. Marvin Miller, announcer. Jan. 16–May 28, 1944. Sponsored by Ry-Krisp.

Irene Rich had been a notable star of the silent screen in the 1920s, playing opposite Will Rogers, Dustin Farnum, and Wallace Beery. But a disagreement with Warner Brothers sent her into a new career—*radio*! By her own account, it was an inspiration: at "three o'clock in the morning I took a plane for New York, and the next day I presented myself at the National Broadcasting studios." *Irene Rich Dramas*, which ran for more than a decade in various forms, was the result.

ISABEL MANNING HEWSON, home economist; also known as *Market Basket*.

BROADCAST HISTORY: 1939–42, NBC. 15m, three, later five, times a week at 9 A.M., then at 9:30 A.M.

1942–43, Blue Network. 15m, six a week at 10 A.M.

1943–44, CBS. 15m, six a week at 9:45 A.M.

ISLAND VENTURE, adventure drama.

BROADCAST HISTORY: Nov. 8, 1945–June 20, 1946, CBS. 30m, Thursdays at 10. Wrigley's Gum.

CAST: Jerry Walter as Gil Perry, ex-Navy pilot who returns to the South Pacific to set up an air-freight line.

IT HAPPENED IN 1955, dramatized stories illustrating man's achievements to come.

BROADCAST HISTORY: April 24–July 17, 1945, Mutual. 15m, Tuesdays at 10:15. New York Stock Exchange and U.S. Treasury. *Host*: Del Sharbutt, "guide to the future."

IT PAYS TO BE IGNORANT, quiz show spoof.

BROADCAST HISTORY: June 25, 1942–Feb. 28, 1944, Mutual. 30m, Thursdays at 8 until Nov. 1942; returned March 29, 1943, Mondays at 7:30.

Feb. 25, 1944–Sept. 27, 1950, CBS. 30m, various times with some notable schedule gaps. Fridays at 9, 1944–46; Fridays at 10, 1946–48; Saturdays at various times, 1948; Sundays at 10:30 beginning Jan. 1949. Ended Sept. 13, 1949, but returned for summer series, July 5–Sept. 27, 1950, Wednesdays at 9. Philip Morris, 1944–48; Chrysler, summer of 1950.

July 4–Sept. 26, 1951, NBC. 30m, Wednesdays at 9. Substitute for *You Bet Your Life*. DeSoto.

HOST-QUIZMASTER: Tom Howard. PANELISTS: George Shelton, Harry McNaughton, Lulu McConnell. ANNOUNCERS: Ken Roberts, Dick Stark. MUSIC: Tom Howard, the host's son (Mutual run). ORCHESTRA: Harry Salter, with vocals by the Esquires Quartet and Al Madru (CBS run). CREATORS-WRITERS: Bob and Ruth Howell. DIRECTOR: Herb Polesie.

It Pays to Be Ignorant was radio's lamebrained answer to such intellectual quizzes as *Information, Please* and *The Quiz Kids*. It was a feast of the absurd in which questions were asked but seldom answered. The three nitwits who made up the "board of experts" spent most of the time trying to figure out what the questions were, between rambling monologues, irrelevancies, and rude interruptions.

The questions were as moronic as the panel. What beverage do we get from tea leaves? From what kind of mines do we get gold ore? Who came first, Henry the Eighth or Henry the First?

The basic format was created by Bob Howell,

program director at WELI, New Haven, Connecticut. In 1941 Howell found himself working with Ruth Howard, daughter of oldtime vaudevillian Tom Howard and herself an aspiring scriptwriter. Howell, who had long believed that the quiz show of intellect was ripe for lampooning, had produced an outline built around "a board of experts who are dumber than you are and can prove it." Ruth Howard confiscated his outline and worked it into a script.

She called it *Crazy Quiz*, submitting it to a promoter with her father billed as star. Tom Howard had been in vaudeville since early in the century, his credits including a stint with Ziegfeld. The first job in staging the show was to assemble a suitable group of fools for the panel. George Shelton had teamed with Howard in vaudeville. Harry McNaughton was a Britisher who had reached his greatest fame as Phil Baker's butler, Bottle, on the Baker radio show. Initially the third chair was filled by Ann Thomas, but soon Lulu McConnell gave the show its final crazy ingredient. McConnell had a sawblade voice and an abrasive on-air persona. She too had come up from the vaudeville ranks.

Together they made a shambles of the halfhour, interrupting with incessant nonsense, with insults and terrible poems and puns. "What president was the city of Washington, D.C., named after?" Howard might ask. He was then bombed with a barrage of foolery. The D.C. bit was stumping them, one of the panelists remarked. It stood for District of Columbia, said Howard, which led into a long discussion about Christopher Columbus and the resentful revelation that he, Columbus, had never been elected president because he was a Republican, no doubt. "What insect weaves a spider web?" asked Howard. Shelton didn't know, but it reminded him of his Uncle Webfoot. McConnell, as always at the mention of a man, shrieked, "Is he *single*? . . . Where's he at?" And so it went.

Howard had a gravel voice that almost rivaled McConnell's. McConnell was usually introduced by Howard in terms quite hideous—"the woman whose face looks as if she'd been on a sightseeing tour through a meat grinder," or some such. Whenever a male guest from the audience drew a question from the "dunce cap," McConnell would croak, "Hey, honey, are you married?" McNaughton, in the introduction, would inevitably say, "I have a poem, Mr. Howard." This

would be predictably simplistic, as, *I eat my peas with honey/I've done it all my life/It makes the peas taste funny/But it keeps them on my knife.* Shelton's stock line was "I used to work in that town." Howard's introduction might describe him as "a man whose father was an electrician, and he was his first shock." The pregnant silence following such stumpers as "Of what material is a silk dress made?" suggested deep thought, the furrowed brow, vast intellect wrestling with a toughie. "No help from the audience, please," Howard would warn. In a rare moment of quiet, he might summarize the entire series by saying, "If you're waiting for the program to improve, you don't know us."

The show was almost universally panned upon its initial appearance on Mutual. Even critics who admitted to a grudging laugh gave it no hope for success. It was far too corny, too filled with "irrelevancies and chaos." It fooled everyone, running more than nine years. Ruth Howard and Bob Howell married and co-wrote it until his death in 1944, a job she continued thereafter. Tom Howard edited the scripts to keep the gags flowing nonstop. For a time in 1944, it was also heard as a skit on *The Kate Smith Hour.* During the CBS run, Al Madru sang the theme:

It payyys to be ignorant,
To be dumb, to be dense, to be ignorant . . .
It payyys to be ignorant,
Just like me!

And Howard would close with his weekly catchphrase: "Good night, and good nonsense."

IT'S A CRIME, MR. COLLINS, detective drama.

BROADCAST HISTORY: Aug. 9, 1956–Feb. 28, 1957, Mutual. 30m, Thursdays at 8:30, transcribed in New York.

CAST: Mandel Kramer as Greg Collins, "infamous private eye" of San Francisco.

The stories were told by Collins's wife, Gail, who struggled with jealousy when female clients appeared.

IT'S A GREAT LIFE, comedy.

BROADCAST HISTORY: 1948, CBS West Coast. 30m Saturdays at 8. Summer series.

CAST: Steve Allen, June Foray, Hans Conried, Parley Baer, Frank Nelson, and vocalist Nancy Norman. **ANNOUNCER:** Jack McCoy. **ORCHESTRA:** Wilbur Hatch. **PRODUCER-DIRECTOR:** Milton Stark. **WRITERS:** Bob Carroll Jr., Madelyn Pugh.

Steve Allen was far better known as Ed Sullivan's archrival on TV than he was as a radio comic. *It's a Great Life*, his first network series, opened in June 1948 and was carried all along the West Coast and into the Southwest.

Allen came to radio as an announcer, at KOY, Phoenix, in 1942. In 1944 he joined Mutual, where his most notable contribution was a quarter-hour weekday series called *Smile Time*, heard on West Coast outlets in 1946–47. He moved to CBS in 1947: assigned to KNX, he was heard in a local disc jockey show, *Breaking All Records*, which ran six nights a week at midnight in a 55-minute timeslot. Allen's ad-lib talents were obvious, and he gradually phased out the records and phased in impromptu comic routines. He played a good comic piano and specialized in composing songs off the cuff. Soon up to 1,000 people were attending his early-morning broadcasts. He gained further notoriety by winning a $1,000 bet with singer Frankie Laine that he, Allen, could write 50 songs a day for a week. CBS broadened his base with *It's a Great Life*.

The series offered a variety of light skits. Many situations were contributed by the audience and improvised—the hapless fellow who sold his car to a dealer and then wanted to buy it back; the couple who tried to build their home from a prefab kit—and there were "Steve and Dot" routines of domestic bliss. There were occupational sketches, often featuring Frank Nelson in the kinds of caustic parts (the mailman,

the cop, etc.) that had become his trademark on *The Jack Benny Program*.

But Allen's day had not yet arrived. On radio he was limited to brief runs, often as summer fill-in. His tenure at CBS included summer shows in 1950 and 1952 and appearances on both Saturday and Sunday nights in the October–January period of 1952–53.

IT'S ALWAYS ALBERT, situation comedy.

BROADCAST HISTORY: July 2–23, 1948, CBS. 30m, Fridays at 8:30.

CAST: Arnold Stang as Albert, would-be composer who can't find work. Jan Murray as his brother. Pert Kelton as his girlfriend. **ANNOUNCER:** George Bryan. **ORCHESTRA:** Jack Miller. **PRODUCER:** Irving Mansfield. **WRITERS:** Jacqueline Susann, Beatrice Cole.

IT'S HIGGINS, SIR, situation comedy.

BROADCAST HISTORY: July 3–Sept. 25, 1951, NBC. 30m, Tuesdays at 9.

CAST: Harry McNaughton as Higgins, a British butler bequeathed to an average American family. Also: Vinton Hayworth, Peggy Allenby, Charles Nevil, Pat Hosley, Denise Alexander. **WRITER-DIRECTOR:** Paul Harrison.

IT'S MURDER, crime drama.

BROADCAST HISTORY: June 8–July 6, 1944, Blue Network. 15m, Thursdays at 11:15. National Safety Council.

CAST: Edgar Stehli as Rex A. Starr, amateur criminologist. Support from New York radio actors: Joan Alexander, Parker Fennelly, etc.

𝒥

JACK AND LORETTA CLEMENS, brother-sister piano-patter-and-song duo.

BROADCAST HISTORY: Throughout 1930s, various networks and 15m timeslots, including NBC, 1933–34, four a week at 4:30; NBC, 1934–35, Sundays at 11:45 A.M.; CBS, 1937, five a week at 9:15 A.M. for Kirkman Soap; Blue Network, 1937–38, three a week at 1:45; Blue, 1938–39, six a week at 8:45 A.M.

JACK ARMSTRONG, THE ALL-AMERICAN BOY, juvenile adventure serial.

BROADCAST HISTORY: July 31, 1933–April 24, 1936, CBS. 15m continuation, Mondays through Saturdays at 5:30 until Nov. 5, 1934, then Mondays through Fridays. General Mills for Wheaties.

Aug. 31, 1936–Sept. 26, 1941, NBC. 15m continuation, weekdays at 5:30 (5:45 beginning June 1941); heard seasonally, Sept. to April, 1936–39; year-round beginning Sept. 1939. Wheaties.

Sept. 29, 1941–July 3, 1942, Mutual. 15m continuation, weekdays at 5:30. Wheaties.

Aug. 31, 1942–Aug. 29, 1947, Blue Network/ABC. 15m continuation, weekdays at 5:30. Wheaties.

Sept. 1, 1947–June 1, 1950, ABC. 30m, complete episodes, staggered with *Sky King*, heard Monday-Wednesday-Friday one week, Tuesday-Thursday the next, at 5:30. Again heard seasonally ca. Sept.–June beginning 1947. Wheaties.

Sept. 5, 1950–June 28, 1951, ABC. 30m twice a week at 7:30. *Armstrong of the SBI*. General Mills.

CAST: Jim Ameche (ca. 1933–38) as Jack Armstrong, hero of Hudson High School, who with his friends, Billy and Betty Fairfield, and their uncle, Jim Fairfield, had a continuous run of adventures around the world. Stanley Harris as Jack Armstrong, 1938. Frank Behrens as Jack Armstrong, ca. 1939. Charles Flynn as Jack Armstrong, 1939–43, and again 1944–51. Rye Billsbury (Michael Rye) as Jack Armstrong while Charles Flynn was away in the Army, 1943–44. St. John Terrell is also noted as having played the lead, though sources are contradictory as to when and for how long. John Gannon (a circuit court judge in later life) as Billy Fairfield, 1933–43, and again briefly after the war. Roland Butterfield as Billy during Gannon's wartime absence. Murray McLean and Milton Guion also heard briefly as Billy. Dick York as Billy in postwar years. Shaindel Kalish as Betty Fairfield, 1933, departing after a few months for a New York stage engagement. Sarajane Wells (then playing a character named Gwendolyn Duval, presumably related in some capacity to Jack Armstrong's early archrival, Monte Duval) as Betty from 1933–41. Loretta Poynton as Betty beginning in Oct. 1941. Naomi May as Betty as of 1943. Patricia Dunlap as Betty, postwar. Jim Goss as Uncle Jim Fairfield throughout. Don Ameche as Captain Hughes, friend of Jack Armstrong. Frank Dane and Jack Doty also as Captain Hughes. Herb Butterfield as Weissoul, the master spy known as "the man with 100 faces." Butterfield also as the criminal Lorenzo. Ed Davison, Arthur Van Slyke, and Olan Soulé, as Coach Hardy. Ken Christy as Talia-San and as Sullivan Lodge. Frank Behrens as Babu. Michael Romano as Lal Singh. Robert Barron as Blackbeard Flint. ANNOUNCERS: David Owen, Truman Bradley, Tom Shirley, Paul Douglas, 1930s; Franklyn MacCormack, early 1940s (probably the announcer best identified with the show); Norman Kraft and Bob McKee, both postwar. VOCAL GROUP: The Norsemen (Ed Lindstrom, Ted Kline, Kenneth Schon, Al Revere, James Peterson). DIRECTORS: David Owen (who also produced and announced ca. early to mid-1930s), Pat Murphy, James Jewell, Ed Morse, Ted MacMurray, WRITERS: Robert Hardy Andrews (ca. early 1930s), James Jewell, Lee Knopf; also, ca. 1936–40, Talbot Mundy, popular pulp novelist and author of *King of the Khyber Rifles*; also, ca. early 1940s, Irving Crump, managing editor of *Boys' Life*; also, Col. Paschal Strong. SOUND EFFECTS: Harry Bubeck, Ed Joyce, Curt Mitchell, Bob Graham, etc. THEME: *Wave the Flag for Hudson High, Boys.*

CAST: 30m transition and into *Armstrong of the SBI*: Charles Flynn, Dick York, and Patricia Dunlap as Jack, Billy, and Betty. Ken Griffin as Vic Hardy, a crimefighter who replaced Uncle Jim as the adult influence. Carlton KaDell also as Vic Hardy. ANNOUNCERS: Ken Nordine, Ed Prentiss. PRODUCER-DIRECTOR-WRITER: James Jewell. WRITERS: Alan Fishburn, Donald Gallagher, Kermit Slobb, Paul Fairman, Jack Lawrence, Thomas Elvidge.

Jack Armstrong was a pinnacle of juvenile American radio serials, heard for the same sponsor across a two-decade run that touched all four networks. Conceived in the shadow of Frank Merriwell, Jack went Merriwell one better: in addition to his fabled athletic prowess, Jack employed inventions and mechanical devices that were unknown in Merriwell's day. With his friends, Billy and Betty Fairfield, and their Uncle Jim, Jack Armstrong flew to distant regions of the globe and plunged headlong into the most thrilling adventures (and some of the most far-fetched) ever to grace the 5-to-6-P.M. children's thriller hour.

A glance at the program log compiled by *Armstrong* advocate Fred L. King confirms Jack's place as radio's champion teenage globe-trotter. The series opened at the 1933 Chicago World's Fair, but Jack and his friends were soon off to Canada for a wild chase through the ice floes. Then it was a cattle-rustling story in Arizona and, by 1935, a return to the Arctic and the "city of White Eskimos." In 1936 they winged away on a China clipper, catching a boat in Manila for a rendezvous with Uncle Jim in Shanghai. In 1937 it was Africa and an elephant hunt (with cameras, of course), and a year later they were in Zanzibar, chasing and being chased by pirates in their quest of a ship sunk in the Indian Ocean. This was followed by a trek through South American jungles, to rescue Betty from captivity in an underground city. Tibet was the scene in 1938, as Jack retrieved a precious lost manuscript for the grand lama. A jaunt to Easter Island in 1940 was followed by an adventure in the Philippines, looking for a missing scientist and his stash of U-235 (listeners might not know what U-235 would come to signify just five years later, but the missing Professor Loring had it, and there were badmen afoot who would stop at nothing to get it). From the Philippines it was into the Andes, then into the war, to Morocco, and a tale of Nazi espionage.

These were the golden years of *Jack Armstrong*, when the four companions would fly away in Uncle Jim's wonderful hydraplane, the *Silver Albatross*; would sail after the unscrupulous adventurer Dr. Shupato in the schooner *Spindrift*; would glide silently over sinister terrain in the dirigible *Golden Secret*. Whether they were fighting side-by-side with Spanish guerrillas off Casablanca or trekking into Africa in search of the legendary elephants' graveyard, their listeners went with them—generations of boys and girls passing through the wonder years between 8 and 15.

The serial came out of the Blackett-Sample-Hummert agency, whose head, Frank Hummert, was just beginning to build his empire of soap operas. The agency was handling the account of General Mills, a five-year-old company then sponsoring *Skippy*, a continuation based on the comic strip by Percy Crosby. GM wanted a show for slightly older children; Hummert gave the assignment to his chief writer, Robert Hardy Andrews. What happened next depends on which story is believed. By one account, Andrews went home and created the character whole cloth: he got the hero's name while staring at a box of Arm-and-Hammer baking soda in his kitchen and realizing that the strong-arm trademark on the box symbolized the kind of all-American hero he wanted. Voila! ... *Jack Armstrong, the*

All-American Boy! But there is also a story that Andrews used the name of a General Mills employee. By all accounts, the serial was off the drawing board by the summer of 1933.

Jack Armstrong would be a high school student at Hudson High, in the fictitious town of Hudson, USA, population around 40,000. Again in the Merriwell mold, he was a super athlete whose last-of-the-ninth antics glorified team athletics. The show had a rah-rah high school framework. In the first year, still without a theme, it was announced to the cheers of a school crowd. The only music in those days was the Wheaties song, performed by a quintet and sung without instrumental accompaniment:

> *Have you tried Wheaties?*
> *They're whole wheat with all of the bran!*
> *Won't you try Wheaties?*
> *For wheat is the best food of man!*
> *They're crispy, they're crunchy*
> *The whole year through,*
> *Jack Armstrong never tires of them*
> *And neither will you!*
> *So just buy Wheaties,*
> *The best breakfast food in the land!*

Soon a theme was developed, again sung in harmony and still playing on the high school background. No matter how far Jack Armstrong would travel from Hudson, this was the reminder of his All-American roots. *Wave the Flag for Hudson High, Boys* would become one of the great themes of the air. It featured the singers, without instruments, to the gridiron fight melody of Chicago University—*Wave the Flag for Old Chicago*:

> *Wave the flag for Hudson High, boys!*
> *Show them how we stand!*
> *Ever shall our team be champions,*
> *Known throughout the land!*

Jack's daily adventures would follow the same storyline for months without resolution. Villains were recycled into subsequent adventures, often on opposite sides of the globe. Skillful use of peaks—of mini-crises that worked hard but accomplished little—gave the series an air of hustle while in fact the pace was glacial. Sometimes the comrades were sidetracked for days on a colorful, dangerous side-journey, only to emerge no closer to their true goal than before. Then, as the season ended, obstacles were swept away and the story raced to conclusion.

The characters were clearly drawn, the voices easy to define. Uncle Jim was the owner of an aircraft factory and a former teacher at West Point. His decisions were firm and his was the final word. In his absence, Jack became the man-figure. He too projected a firm image, higher of voice than Uncle Jim. Billy was higher-pitched yet, probably about the age of the kids listening at home, and Betty was just a girl, often waiting in agony for something to happen or there to be rescued. Typical of Hummert originations, the characters were identified to a fault. Every spoken sentence was directed at someone by name. Billy also had his catchphrases, with every exciting thought set off by "Gosh-all-hemlock!" or "Gosh-all-fishhooks, Jack!"

The show played strongly to the demands of parents. As early as 1935, there were complaints about its "blood-and-thunder" and about the fact that the young heroes never seemed to be in school. On a jaunt to South America that year, they took a tutor, who presumably kept them minding their p's and q's while they sliced through jungles in search of a lost city. But if Jack Armstrong ever cracked a schoolbook on his global adventures, the episode describing it has yet to be discovered for posterity. In charge of keeping things wholesome was Dr. Martin L. Reymert, child psychologist and director of the Mooseheart Laboratory for Child Research. Reymert combed each script, analyzing each scientific feat for feasibility and difficulty, deleting epithets that carried even a hint of profanity, and, in the words of one trade journal, "vacuuming out all possible deleteriousness," such as torture, brutal murder, or kidnapping.

Jack's ties to the sponsor were extraordinary: he was a champion at moving product, selling Wheaties by the trainload and singlehandedly turning General Mills into a major advertiser of the air. Legend has it that the first premium offer so swamped GM with orders that the supply of Wheaties was demolished nationwide for months. Later offers were so well planned that the company had trainloads of cereal stationed at strategic points to replenish grocers' shelves. The goodness of the cereal was secondary: what the kids wanted was the boxtop, which could be used to obtain a Jack Armstrong ring, medallion, bombsight, or pedometer. King's *Armstrong* log contains a remarkable history of premium offers. The earliest known premium was a shooting plane, offered in 1933 for two boxtops and drawing 424,441 orders. Almost any tangible object mentioned in a storyline could be expected to turn up as a premium. Pedometers were big deals: Jack and his friends were always on the march, and compasses and pedometers were the standard tools. The Hike-o-Meter of 1937–38 drew astonishing response: more than 70,000 orders a day poured in, with highs peaking in the 150,000–200,000 range. A similar pedometer was offered for the 1940–41 adventure in the Philippines, touted on the air as "just like the one Jack Armstrong used" to plot the location of a hidden cache of rifles. For another boxtop and a dime, a sister could get a luminous bracelet "just like the one Betty wears."

Among the premiums lovingly described by King are these: an Oriental stamp offer, 1936, one boxtop and a nickel; a Secret Egyptian Whistling Ring, 1938–40, a boxtop and a dime; an explorer telescope, 1938, two Wheaties packages (almost six million orders); a "Dragon's Eye Ring" that glowed in the dark, 1940, one champ seal and ten cents. There was also a wartime "Write-a-Fighter Corps," whose members pledged to send at least one letter a month to fighting servicemen. The Corps collected scraps of paper, rubber, and tin, sold war bonds, and planted victory gardens. On each broadcast, members received urgent-sounding instructions, making them feel an integrated part of the war effort.

In the final years of the daily serial, a new adult came into the story as Jack clashed with a gangland figure known only as the Silencer. Finally unmasked, the Silencer was found to be Victor Hardy, a great scientist and inventor who had had a respectable life before amnesia had led him down a ten-year path of crime. After a sensational trial, Hardy's memory was restored, leaving him completely dedicated to justice and honor. "Because he understands the criminal mind," explained announcer Norman Kraft, "he has dedicated the remainder of his life to the readjustment of criminals and the prevention and correction of crime. In this way, he intends to repay society for those ten years in which he lived outside the law." Gradually Hardy assumed the main adult lead, and Uncle Jim was relegated to recapping each episode. Eventually Jim disappeared. The grand age of exploration was over: the last remote regions of earth were becoming civilized; technology was the coming

thing. The beginning of the end came in 1947, when ABC vice president Ed Boroff canceled the quarter-hour format. Boroff had been critical of juvenile cliffhangers for some time, and one particular *Armstrong* episode contained all the elements he had long disdained. Jack had bailed out of an airplane wearing a suit of armor and a parachute. The chute didn't open, but wait!— there was a backup chute! When the second chute failed, there was Jack, encased in steel, plummeting to earth late one Friday afternoon, leaving his fans in the lurch until Monday.

It was too much, Boroff decided: the serial had to go. Two weeks later, *Jack Armstrong* became a watered-down half-hour. It was never the same after that. Gone was the breathless pace, the sense of wonder. The show struggled for two seasons; then, in one bold stroke, Jack grew up, moved into prime time, and made his last stand in a series called *Armstrong of the SBI*, the SBI being the Scientific Bureau of Investigation. Here he was just another faceless agent in the *Counterspy* ilk, one among many. Predictably, it disappeared after a single season. But Jack Armstrong really disappeared that day in 1947, dropping through the clouds into eternity. Questions of violence will continue forever: the same charges aimed at radio in the '30s are here for television to answer in the '90s. The difference, then, was the certainty that right would prevail and the hero would survive on Monday. Jack had a third chute tucked up under all that armor. If Boroff had been among the faithful, he'd surely have known that.

THE JACK BENNY PROGRAM, comedy.

BROADCAST HISTORY: May 2–Oct. 26, 1932, Blue Network. 30m, Mondays and Wednesdays at 9:30. *The Canada Dry Program*. Canada Dry Ginger Ale. CAST: Jack Benny, with announcer George Hicks, maestro George Olsen, and singer-comedienne Ethel Shutta. Benny's wife, Sadye Marks, as Mary Livingstone beginning Aug. 3. WRITER: Harry Conn.

Oct. 30, 1932–Jan. 26, 1933, CBS. 30m, twice a week (Sundays at 10; Thursdays at 8:15, then beginning in Jan., at 8). A continuation of *The Canada Dry Program* on a new network. CAST: Benny, Mary Livingstone, maestro Ted Weems, and other various bandleaders.

March 17, 1933–April 1, 1934, NBC. 30m, Fridays at 10 until the summer break, June 23; returned Oct. 1, Sundays at 10. *The Chevrolet Program*. General Motors. CAST: Benny, Mary Livingstone. Tenors James Melton (1933) and Frank Parker (1933–34). Announcers Howard Claney (1933) and Alois Havrilla (1933–34). Maestro Frank Black.

April 6–Sept. 28, 1934, NBC. 30m, Fridays at 10. *The General Tire Show*. CAST: Benny, Mary Livingstone, Frank Parker. Announcer Don Wilson. Maestro Don Bestor from New York; Jimmy Grier when the cast visited the West Coast.

Oct. 14, 1934–May 31, 1942, NBC. Blue Network until Oct. 4, 1936, then Red. 30m, Sundays at 7 throughout. *The Jell-O Program*. CAST: Benny, Mary Livingstone, Don Wilson, maestro Johnny Green, and temporary singer Michael Bartlett. Kenny Baker the new singer and comedic stooge as of Nov. 3, 1935. Phil Harris as the wisecracking maestro-figure beginning Oct. 4, 1936. Eddie Anderson intermittently, beginning as a Pullman porter March 28, 1937; becoming Benny's gravel-voiced Negro valet, Rochester Van Jones, with the show of June 20, 1937. Dennis Day, tenor, replacing Kenny Baker as singer and resident scatterbrain with the show of Oct. 8, 1939. SUPPORTING PLAYERS: Sam Hearn as Schlepperman from ca. 1935. Andy Devine in periodic "Buck Benny" western spoof skits. Mel Blanc in many roles, notably as Carmichael, the polar bear in Benny's basement, and as Benny's sputtering, coughing antique automobile, a Maxwell. Frank Nelson in nameless sarcastic roles. Final New York broadcast: April 7, 1935; Hollywood thereafter. WRITERS: Harry Conn until early 1936; Al Boasberg, Howard Snyder, Hugh Wedlock Jr., on a transitional basis; then Bill Morrow and Ed Beloin.

Oct. 4, 1942–June 4, 1944, NBC. 30m, Sundays at 7. *The Grape Nuts and Grape Nuts Flakes Program*. CAST: Benny, Mary Livingstone, Phil Harris, Dennis Day, Rochester (Eddie Anderson), and Don Wilson. SUPPORTING PLAYERS: Mel Blanc, Frank Nelson, Joe Besser, etc. WRITERS: Bill Morrow and Ed Beloin until 1943, then a longtime staff of four: Sam Perrin, Milt Josefsberg, George Balzer, and John Tackaberry.

Oct. 1, 1944–Dec. 26, 1948, NBC. 30m, Sundays at 7. *The Lucky Strike Program*. CAST: Benny, Mary Livingstone, Phil Harris, Dennis Day, Rochester, and Don Wilson. SUPPORTING PLAYERS: Mel Blanc as the Maxwell. Blanc also

as the announcer at the train station, first heard Jan. 7, 1945. Blanc also as Benny's violin teacher, Professor LeBlanc, beginning April 29, 1945. Blanc also as Benny's parrot, Polly, beginning Oct. 14, 1945. Blanc also as Sy, the little Mexican, and in many other roles. Frank Nelson in many abrasive roles ("the guy whose whole purpose in life was to annoy the hell out of Jack Benny," he would recall years later). Artie Auerbach as Mr. Kitzel the hot dog man. Larry Stevens substituting as singer for Dennis Day, late 1944 until March 1946, while Day was in the service. Sara Berner in many roles calling for Brooklyn accents, and as Benny's girlfriend, Gladys Zybysko. Sara Berner and Bea Benaderet as Mabel Flapsaddle and Gertrude Gearshift, telephone operators who talked about Benny between connections. Jane Morgan and Gloria Gordon as Martha and Emily, a pair of old ladies who found Benny irresistible. Joe Besser and Benny Rubin as crazy men encountered periodically by Benny. Sheldon Leonard as the racetrack tout, often encountered by Benny at the train station. Joseph Kearns as Ed, the guard who'd been protecting Benny's vault since the Revolutionary War. Ronald and Benita Colman as special guests, several times a year. VOCAL QUARTET: The Sportsmen (formed in the 1930s, consisting of Bill Days, Max Smith, John Rarig, and Gurney Bell; later members included Jay Mayer, Marty Sperzel and Thurl Ravenscroft). ORCHESTRA: Mahlon Merrick. THEMES: *Yankee Doodle Boy*, blending into *Love in Bloom* (Benny's personal theme); *Hooray for Hollywood* (closing theme).

Jan. 2, 1949–May 22, 1955, CBS. 30m, Sundays at 7. *The Lucky Strike Program*, a direct continuation of the NBC show, lured to CBS in the controversial "talent raids," without missing a week. CAST: Continued with few changes. Bob Crosby replaced Phil Harris as the token bandleader as of Sept. 14, 1952.

Oct. 28, 1956–June 22, 1958, CBS. 30m, Sundays at 7. *The Best of Benny*, repeat broadcasts. Home Insurance Company, 1957–58.

AT VARIOUS TIMES: Announcers Bob Gregor, Sid Silvers, and Paul Douglas. Actors Dix Davis, Elliott Lewis, Eddie Marr and Blanche Stewart. Veola Vonn with baby cries and French accents, ca. 1940s. Frank Fontaine as John L. C. Sivoney, a slow-talking nitwit who won the sweepstakes. PRODUCERS: Hilliard Marks, Irving Fein. SOUND EFFECTS: Ed Ludes, Virgil Reimer, Jack Wormser, Monty Fraser (NBC); James Murphy, Gene Twombly, Cliff Thorsness (CBS).

The Jack Benny Program evolved slowly from its vaudeville roots to become the quintessential American radio comedy show. Today, four decades after his last original broadcast, Benny's reputation is alive and well, and the show he created is consistently ranked among the most timeless classics ever produced. The secret of his success was deceptively simple: he was a man of great heart. Who else could play for four decades the part of a vain, miserly, argumentative skinflint, and emerge a national treasure? Others could try—a Milton Berle might play the vain role, giving his audience a few laughs and a faint suspicion that he had been typecast. Few people had that reaction to Jack Benny. Occasionally he'd get a letter like the one in 1947 from the silly attorney in Ohio, chastising him for his parsimonious treatment of his Negro valet, Rochester, and threatening to sue on Rochester's behalf. But as Cleveland Amory pointed out in the *Saturday Evening Post*, the real Rochester wasn't complaining: he "has never been anybody's valet, has a block-large estate and three servants of his own, drives an expensive car and a big station wagon, and, when not working—which he does two days a week for some $700 per air-time minute—spends his leisure hours either yachting or supervising his well-stocked racing stable."

Not only that: Rochester got some of the biggest laughs on the show. Benny was generous that way, too: he became the butt of his own best gags and gave away the good lines to his stooges. Benny became the braggart, always ripe for the needle. He was the show-off, relentlessly pushing his own cause at Academy Awards time. He was smug and opinionated, always ready to engage the cast—especially announcer Don Wilson—in a tiff over some obscure historical fact or point of grammatical usage. He was always wrong. His pride took every conceivable form. He boasted about his blue eyes and his prowess on the violin, and tenaciously stopped aging at age 39. He was jealous and insensitive and often cowardly. And if all this wasn't enough, Benny was the stingiest man in all radio, eclipsing even Lionel Barrymore's Scrooge in his love of gold. His "vault gag," in which his money was hidden in an underground chamber surrounded by a moat and protected by chains, locks, sirens, and an old guard who hadn't seen daylight since the Revolutionary War, was pure radio genius.

Benny was remarkable in many ways, but in none more than this: he built a character of every sour ingredient in life, but somehow his real personality trickled through and made it wonderful. Would a *real* miser act that way before 30 million people each week? The Benny of the air was a fraud, a myth, a creation. It should have surprised no one to learn—after years of toupee jokes that played so well into the vanity theme— that Benny never wore one. He overtipped in restaurants, gave away his time in countless benefit performances, and was lavish in his praise of almost everyone else. "Where would I be today without my writers, without Rochester, Dennis Day, Mary Livingstone, Phil Harris, and Don Wilson?" he asked a *Newsweek* profiler in 1947. The reporter supplied his own answer, since Benny wasn't about to. "That he himself has hand-picked the writers and the cast is something Benny never admits. He dismisses lightly the fact that he directs his own rehearsals, down to the last fine reading of a line. Nor will he ever say that part of his success stems from his own sense of timing and showmanship."

He was born on Valentine's Day, Feb. 14, 1894, in Chicago. His father, Meyer, had come to the United States from Lithuania in 1889, settling in the Chicago suburb of Waukegan, Ill., where he bought and managed a saloon. The family was Jewish: Jack's name at birth was Benjamin Kubelsky, and his journey into show business began at age 6, when his father gave him a violin. In later life he mused that he might have gained enough proficiency to play in some symphony orchestra. But he was never going to be the great artist his parents had hoped, and in 1917 he took a fling at vaudeville.

He had met a woman named Cora Salisbury, who played piano at the Barrison Theater in Waukegan. Salisbury worked up an act consisting of musical selections arranged for piano and violin. Benny toured with her for two years, traveling through Illinois and Wisconsin under the billing "Salisbury and Kubelsky: From Grand Opera to Ragtime." When Salisbury retired, Benny continued the act with pianist Lyman Woods. For six years he played his violin and never spoke or told a joke. He enlisted in the Navy for the First World War and found himself in a maritime revue at the Great Lakes Naval Station. Here he told his first jokes, and by the end of the war he had begun to think of himself as a monologuist.

He changed his name several times. For a

while he was Ben K. Benny, but people confused him with another showman and so-called violinist, Ben Bernie. Jack Benny would be his professional name. His rise through the vaudeville ranks of the 1920s paralleled that of other comics who found their metier in radio a decade later—a long succession of stage engagements culminating at New York's Palace Theater.

Meanwhile, on Jan. 14, 1927, Benny had married Sadye Marks, a teenage clerk at the hosiery counter of the Los Angeles May Company. She joined him on the road, playing a character named Marie Marsh in his stage shows. By 1932 he was a vaudeville headliner. He was on Broadway as part of Earl Carroll's *Vanities* when newspaper columnist Ed Sullivan invited him to appear on a radio interview and gossip show. At the time he had no great interest in the new medium, but he went on Sullivan's quarter-hour show March 19, 1932, as a favor. His first words on the air were these: "Ladies and gentlemen, this is Jack Benny talking. There will be a slight pause while you say, 'Who cares?' I am here tonight as a scenario writer. There is quite a lot of money in writing scenarios for the pictures. Well, there would be if I could sell one. That seems to be my only trouble right now, but I'm going back to pictures in about ten weeks. I'm going to be in a new film with Greta Garbo. They sent me the story last week. When the picture opens, I'm found dead in the bathroom. . . ."

This led to an offer for his own regular airshow, and suddenly Benny saw radio as the coming thing. Canada Dry was interested, and his first show went on the Blue Network May 2. It had a strong '20s flavor: maestro George Olsen had made a reputation with such rousing novelty numbers as *Doin' the Raccoon* and *The Varsity Drag*. Olsen's wife, Ethel Shutta, specialized in such bouncy and clever vocals as *Listen to the German Band*, and Benny's comedy was sandwiched into a half-hour that was largely musical. Olsen played seven musical selections, including the popular hits *I Found a Million-Dollar Baby in a Five-and-Ten-Cent Store* and *I Beg Your Pardon, Mademoiselle*. Benny was a humorous master of ceremonies, and this was his first radio format.

He was working with Harry Conn, his first writer, who helped him establish the beginnings of the cheap character. Benny and Conn also cre-

ated the Mary Livingstone character, to compensate for a short timing on a rehearsal. She would become a young Benny fan from Plainfield, N.J. Eventually she would read humorous poetry and letters from her mother, and much later she would become one of the main deflators of Benny's ego. Benny asked his wife to play the part, and Sadye Marks became Mary Livingstone. She discovered mike fright, a malady that never really left her. She had never been unusually nervous in vaudeville, but now, performing for the nation, her jitters were acute. The infectious laugh that squeaked out of her was the result of nerves, but it stuck and became part of her character.

During this time Benny began the practice of ribbing his sponsor in a gentle, good-natured way. The people at Canada Dry were less than thrilled, and he was canceled in January 1933, amidst largely positive press notices and clear indications that he was a young comic on the rise. Chevrolet, which had just lost Al Jolson, was waiting in the wings. The new show, with maestro Frank Black, was still music-heavy: a glance at the comprehensive Benny log compiled by Gary A. Dunn and John and Larry Gassman reveals that up to six numbers were used on each broadcast. The emphasis was different: Black was more rooted in folklore and concert arrangements, though there was still a generous sampling of such popular numbers as *Shuffle Off to Buffalo* and *I Love a Parade*. A few hallmarks of the later Benny era began to emerge with the 1933–34 season. Benny argued with his cast: on Nov. 5, 1933, he and announcer Alois Havrilla squabbled about Havrilla's introduction; the following week, Benny quarreled with Frank Black. The music began to give way to fully developed comedy skits, with titles like "My Life as a Floorwalker" and "Duel in the Graveyard." Skits played into the vanity theme, and the ratings soared. In midseason of his second year on the air, Benny clocked a 25 on the CAB survey.

Chevrolet rewarded him with a pink slip: one of the executives in the company didn't like the shift into comedy, and Benny was replaced by an all-music series featuring the Victor Young orchestra. General Tire signed immediately, and the show continued without a break. Maestro Don Bestor gave it a new dance band sound, a clear contrast to Frank Black's studio crew. On April 6, 1934, Don Wilson became the new announcer. Wilson would remain with Benny to the end of the TV show in 1965. His deep, rich voice was one of the show's trademarks, and the role he played—a roly-poly Gargantua—was yet another stretch of Benny's imagination. In reality, Wilson stood a little over six feet and weighed in the mid-220s: hardly the behemoth that Benny would chide with endless fat jokes in the years to come. Wilson also brought to the show a deep belly laugh that could often be heard above the studio audience. Benny liked laughter from his cast and orchestra and assistants: he was "extremely dependent on a favorable studio audience," Amory would write years later, and laughter was a contagious business.

Three of the six major Benny players (Wilson, Livingstone, and Benny himself) were now in place. Tenor Frank Parker was playing a fourth character type, the singer with a penchant for saying the ridiculous. Parker was also a romantic counter to Benny's emerging notion of himself as a ladies' man and sex symbol. The run for General Tire was brief, and in the fall of 1934 Jell-O became the new client. This was a highly successful eight-year run, during which the remainder of the classic Benny format was solidified and cast. Hollywood was opening up as a center of broadcasting, and Benny moved west just ahead of the tide. Parker elected to stay in the East: his eventual replacement, Kenny Baker, brought another dimension of comedy to the singer's role, the addled young man with the voice of gold. His tenure was solid, four full seasons. He was almost, but not quite, the answer in the singer's role.

In early 1936, Benny lost his writer. Harry Conn, convinced that he was the chief reason for the show's success, made contract demands that Benny found unreasonable, and they parted in acrimony. Conn later sued Benny for $65,000, disputing who had created what in a format that Benny continued to use and embellish. This was settled out of court.

Far more important was the arrival of Phil Harris on the first show of the new year, Oct. 4, 1936. Harris was the fourth cog in the Benny formula, a swaggering blowhard whose demeanor might have been, in real life, as offensive as Benny's, but on the air was touched with the Benny magic, making him one of the show's most popular personalities. Harris drubbed Benny about being vain and cheap, but he shared the vanity and added a layer of riotous stupidity. He butchered English: he couldn't spell the simplest words; he didn't know Mongolia from Minneapolis. In reality, Harris was a comic genius whose sense of timing and showmanship was as fine-tuned as Benny's. His greeting, "Hiya, Jackson," brought the audience to ripples of laughter before the first jokes were said. Ostensibly he was the new bandleader, but he was actually a supercharged front man (Mahlon Merrick, who came aboard about the same time, arranged the music and conducted throughout the later era). On the Benny show, Harris became a master of insult humor, an incomparable vulgarian. His character was a self-centered dapper-dan playboy with curly hair, flashy clothes, an orchestra full of reprobates, and a fondness for liquor in any form.

There were now two writers, Bill Morrow and Ed Beloin. The long-running feud with Fred Allen began. On April 5, 1936, Benny satirized Allen's show with a skit called "Clown Hall Tonight"; the following year, when Allen criticized his violin prowess, Benny rose to the bait, and a 15-year battle of wits ensued. Highlight of the spring of 1937 was the appearance of Eddie Anderson as a train porter. Anderson had a saw-blade voice that Benny considered a natural for radio. He was used intermittently until June, when Rochester Van Jones was first mentioned, beginning his long-running role as Benny's valet. His part was usually confined to scenes at home—preparing the frugal courses for Benny's dinner parties, deciding which of Benny's moth-eaten suits was suitable for dinner at the Colmans—and to driving Benny's automobile, that model of dilapidation known as the Maxwell. This gave Rochester some marvelous gags at Benny's expense, which he delivered with good-natured and well-timed excellence. In one respect, his role was the most difficult of the six. He was a black man in the white world of network radio. White rednecks would take offense if his character became too brash, while black firebrands would fume when, to them, his part smacked of toadyism. To Rochester, Benny was always "Boss" or "Mr. Benny"; others in the cast were "Miz Livingstone," "Mr. Harris," etc. Somehow the scripts managed to suggest that this subservience was due to economic status rather than race.

On June 18, 1939, Kenny Baker defected to

The Fred Allen Show. Though his sudden departure took Benny by surprise, this would turn into a blessing when it brought forth the last of Benny's major characters and set up the show's immortal run through the 1940s. The part would go to young Eugene Patrick McNulty, a fresh new talent discovered by Mary when she saw his photograph in a file at the office of Benny's agents, then heard a transcription of his singing voice. McNulty was summoned for an audition and arrived in a state of nervous tension. When Benny called him over an intercom, his response was a shaky "Yes, please." Mary thought he should get the job on the strength of that classic reply. Benny recognized his talent, but he was very green. McNulty was given a tentative contract: he would have only two weeks to make his mark.

On the air, McNulty was Dennis Day. The writers kept his speaking lines brief in the opening weeks, concentrating more on Benny's abusive relationship with Day's "mother," a battleaxe role aptly handled by Verna Felton. Day was then signed for 13 weeks, then another 13, and his character settled in. He was a sweet Irish kid with a head full of air. The writing for Dennis sharpened, his character becoming a contrast to all the others. Dennis used logical irrelevancies in a way that drove Benny crazy. His most ridiculous lines often paid off later in the script, and the funniest were recycled for weeks. But in the beginning, as writer Milt Josefsberg noted in his history of the Benny show, "nobody knew that Dennis had uncanny timing for the feed and punch lines of jokes, nor did anyone know that he was one of the best mimics extant."

This was the show that Benny took into the 1940s. In 1943 the writing staff was increased to four: Sam Perrin (who had done Benny a great favor during the Harry Conn crisis of 1936, churning out a funny script on an emergency basis when Conn refused to write it) headed a team that included Josefsberg, George Balzer, and John Tackaberry. There was an immediate growth spurt: the comedy became ever more polished and timeless, a factor that George Balzer, many years later, was inclined to attribute to the war. Suddenly everything moved faster: old vaudeville standards and routines disappeared, and the Benny show was the slickest and most consistently funny comedy on the air. Its effects were never achieved by ad-lib or chance: they were pondered, calculated, and meticulously weighted for effect. Each Sunday, immediately after the show, the writers would meet in the star's dressing room to discuss the theme of next week's script. The show was divided into two segments, the opening banter among the cast and the dramatic spoof. The writers would split these chores, one team doing the cast segment while the other team handled the drama, then trading off the following week. Much was said about Benny's lack of spontaneity (Fred Allen once remarked that Benny couldn't "ad-lib a belch at a Hungarian dinner"), but no one questioned his judgment. Benny would go into spasms of laughter at the lines his writers created when, on Thursday, he would review and edit the rough script. Hilliard Marks, Mary's brother and longtime Benny producer, then got his script and began lining up supporting talent, which might include Mel Blanc, Frank Nelson, Artie Auerbach, Veola Vonn, Sheldon Leonard, or Elliott Lewis. On Saturday there was a cast reading. Benny was wary of overrehearsing, so there was just a loose reading on Sunday. At 7 p.m. the show emerged live in the East, one of the brightest pieces of radio in radio's best decade.

The supporting players were almost as memorable as the regular cast. Mel Blanc joined the show Feb. 19, 1939. Benny was adding a new touch to the miser theme: a polar bear, who would live in his basement and help protect his money. Blanc gave an audition, showing off some of the voices he was then using in Warner Brothers cartoons. Benny asked if he could do a polar bear, and Blanc (as he recalled it in his memoir) let out with "a roar so savage, I nearly frightened myself." Benny "went into convulsions" and put him into the show. The bear was christened Carmichael, and in 1941, according to Rochester, he ate the gas man. Blanc also assumed the role of Benny's automobile, whose starting gyrations made it a character in every sense. Doors fell off in transit, the car clanked and clattered, and Benny bought gasoline a gallon at a time. Even the name was archaic, the Maxwell having seen its last production in 1925. Blanc went on to speaking parts, playing a wide variety of sardonic and hysterical characters. He played caustic delivery men and punchdrunk fight trainers. As Benny's beleaguered French violin teacher, he suffered through Benny's scrapings and then had to plead for his money. Inevitably, Benny had no small change—he was a dime off, and this called for a trip to his vault. At last, liberated, Professor LeBlanc would scream, "I'm free! I'm free!" and storm out joyously, singing the *Marseillaise*.

The night of Jan. 7, 1945, was especially creative: the writers came up with several memorable gimmicks that became long-running gags. The vault was used for the first time, with Ed, Benny's guard from antiquity, perched there beyond the moat. Also debuting was the racetrack tout, another of the crazy characters who turned up periodically with no purpose other than to annoy Jack Benny. "Hey, bud . . . c'mere," he would call: then he'd try to tout Benny into changing destinations, candy brands, newspapers—whatever Benny had purposely gone to do, the tout would be there with contradictory advice. Benny Rubin originated the role, but it soon went to Sheldon Leonard, a perfect prototype of the humorous Hollywood gangster. Jan. 7 was also the night when Mel Blanc was first heard as the train announcer, solemnly calling, *Train now leaving on track five for Anaheim, Azusa and Cuc . . . amonga*. Many variations on the train gag were used over the years: the spacing between *Cuc* and *amonga* lengthened and grew funnier, finally sandwiching most of the show between the syllables.

There were more memorable Blanc creations: a croaking role as Benny's parrot, Polly, and a character known as the Little Mexican. Usually encountered by Benny in the train depot, the Mexican rarely spoke more than a single word at a time. A typical routine went like this: "Are you waiting for the train?" *Sí*. "Are you meeting someone?" *Sí*. "A relative?" *Sí*. "What's your name?" *Sy*. "Sy?" *Sí*. "This relative you're waiting for—is it a woman?" *Sí*. "What's her name?" *Sue*. "Sue?" *Sí*. "Does she work?" *Sí*. "What does she do?" *Sew*. "Sew?" *Sí*. And each year, beginning in the mid-1940s, Blanc played a high-strung clerk in a department store at Christmas, driven berserk when Benny kept returning gifts he'd bought for the cast (did Don Wilson prefer shoelaces with plastic tips or metal tips?).

One of Benny's busiest utility actors was Frank Nelson, who first appeared June 1, 1934. But the character Nelson created in the 1930s was not fully realized until the mid-1940s, when he became one of the funniest voices on the air. One week he'd be a psychiatrist, the next week a floorwalker; he was a doorman at a posh hotel, a lawyer, a ticket clerk at the train depot. No matter what he was, Nelson's voice and manner were always the same. "There's the floorwalker," Benny would say in a department store skit: "Oh, mister! . . . Mister!" On this cue, Nelson would whirl into the microphone and scream, "*Yeeeeessss?*" For the next few minutes, Benny was abused, insulted, and berated for even the simplest requests. "You really do hate me, don't you?" Benny would ask, and Nelson's reply—a screaming, "Ooooooooooh, *do* I!"—never failed to draw huge laughs from the audience.

Perhaps the best Frank Nelson story involved a fluff. Such accidents occurred often, usually with hilarious results. Two notorious fluffs by Mary—"I'll have a chiss swease sandwich" (Oct. 27, 1946) and "Run my car up on the grass reek" (Dec. 3, 1950)—became running gags for weeks. Benny, despite his reputation for being no great shakes as an ad-lib man, was usually quick on his feet when this occurred. Once, when Rochester bobbled a line, Benny shouted, "Just one rehearsal a week, that's all I ask!" and the crowd roared. On Jan. 8, 1950, Nelson was to appear as a doorman in a restaurant. Early in the show, Don Wilson bobbled a line referring to Drew Pearson, the famous columnist, making it "Drear Pooson," and Benny joined the audience in helpless laughter. Immediately the writers summoned Nelson into the booth and, without Benny's knowledge or permission, changed his coming lines. Nelson was leery ("Nobody adlibbed with Jack," he recalled years later) but agreed to do it if the writers would take responsibility. The scene arrived. "Oh, mister! Mister!" Benny called. "Are you the doorman?" At his absolute surliest, Nelson snarled, "Well, who do you think I am in this uniform, *Dreeeeeaaaarrr* Pooooosssson?" Benny was instantly convulsed. "He began to laugh," Nelson recalled; "he slid down the mike to the floor, pounded on the floor, got up, staggered clear across the stage to the far wall, turned around into the curtains, slid down the curtains, pounded the floor some more, got up, staggered back to the mike, and we're on live and laughter is going on through this whole thing." Nelson thought this laugh exceeded even that of Benny's most famous gag, when a robber demanded, "Your money or your life!" and the hilarity kept building while Benny thought it over.

In 1946 Artie Auerbach came into the show as Mr. Kitzel, the hot dog man, who, in a heavy Jewish accent, popularized the phrase "peekle in the meedle with the mustard on top." Joe Besser played another zany character, who exaggerated words ("Not so *faaaast!* . . . oh, you *craaaazee*, you!") to great effect. Benny Rubin had one memorable line: "I dunno," he would say to almost any question. He was often found behind the information desk at the train depot or in some other "helpful" occupation. The most successful additions of the mid-1940s came when the show had begun to lag in the ratings for the first time in its history. In late 1945 the writers came up with the "I Can't Stand Jack Benny Because" contest, with $10,000 in Victory Bonds as prizes and the grand winner picking up $2,500. This instantly revitalized the show: more than 300,000 letters flooded NBC. The judges included Goodman Ace, Peter Lorre, and Fred Allen, who quipped, "I am the greatest living authority on Jack Benny. I have seen him reach for his pocketbook. No other living American can make that statement."

At the same time, Ronald and Benita Colman began their frequent visits to the show. Their first appearance was Dec. 9, 1945: both proved immediately to be first-rate comics. The Colmans were Benny's nearby neighbors in Beverly Hills, but for the purposes of radio they were moved next door, where Benny harassed them for years. He borrowed incessantly and never returned anything. He crashed their parties and made a colossal nuisance of himself. It was Colman who read the winning entry in the "I Can't Stand Jack Benny" contest, Feb. 3, 1946. Submitted by Carroll P. Craig Sr., it proved—as Colman said—that "the things we find fault with in others are the same things we tolerate in ourselves."

I Can't Stand Jack Benny Because—

He fills the air with boasts and brags
And obsolete obnoxious gags.
The way he plays the violin
Is music's most obnoxious sin.
His cowardice alone, indeed
Is matched by his obnoxious greed.
And all the things that he portrays
Show up my own obnoxious ways.

Finally came the Sportsmen Quartet, a highly polished comic song team, first heard on the Benny show Sept. 29, 1946. Benny made ingenious use of the quartet in the middle commercial, which he controlled and integrated into the storyline. Usually Don Wilson would arrive at an inopportune time and insist that Benny hear their number without delay. This produced numerous blowups and a long string of running gags in which Benny tried to fire the quartet. The songs they sang were hit tunes or traditional chestnuts rewritten with lyrics extolling the virtues of Luckies. Charged with the difficult task of writing for the group was musical director Mahlon Merrick. The ideas he found difficult; the verses usually came quickly. The payoff was great both in comedy and in sales. Benny was one of the few men in radio who had no trouble with George Washington Hill, the feisty president of the American Tobacco Company, who died two years into the Lucky Strike run, Sept. 13, 1946.

The show coasted to its end. Phil Harris departed in 1952, a move described by Milt Josefsberg as a matter of economics. In 1954 Mary began recording her lines at home: script girl Jeanette Eymann played the Mary role for the audience, and the real Mary was dubbed in for the broadcast tape. Radio was just about finished. By then Benny was on CBS, lured there by William S. Paley in 1949, in a bold masterpiece of tax jockeying. An accountant had discovered a loophole in the tax code, which would ultimately mean millions in savings for artists in Benny's bracket. Under the old code, performers were assessed 77 percent of all personal earnings over $70,000. But by incorporating himself as a business and selling his show to the network, Benny would pay only 25 percent under capital gains regulations. NBC executives David Sarnoff and Niles Trammel, unsure of the legality, hesitated. Paley took the big gamble and won, sweeping *Amos 'n' Andy*, Bing Crosby, Red Skelton, and others into his camp and setting up CBS as the network to beat in the pioneering days of television. The biggest prize of all was Jack Benny. He had been at the top of his profession for so long that he was a true statesman, respected everywhere. There is little doubt that the advantage CBS enjoyed in early TV was due to Paley's decisive and, some said, ruthless action. First seen Oct. 28, 1950, Benny's show would eventually fade on TV as well, knocked off by *Gomer Pyle* in 1965. But his presence helped CBS moved irrevocably out of the shadow of the older network and become the communications force of the 1950s.

Benny died at 80 on Dec. 26, 1974. He was followed in death by the others: Eddie "Rochester" Anderson, Feb. 28, 1977; Don Wilson, April 25, 1982; Mary Livingstone, June 30, 1983; Dennis Day, June 28, 1988; and Phil Harris, Aug. 11, 1995.

More than 600 Benny shows are available on tape, a major treasure. These have been meticulously logged by Gary Dunn and the Gassman brothers, whose work has been invaluable in pinpointing specific dates in the Benny chronology. Listeners can follow the building feud with Fred Allen, the development of the cast, the gradual refining of personalities. Benny's mannerisms and audio gestures would become better known to the masses than the best jokes of many another. "Now cut that out!" he would scream to a silly Dennis Day. "Hmmmm," he would ponder, wondering if the insult was intentional. The growth spurt comes with the arrival of Perrin, Josefsberg, Balzer, and Tackaberry as writers: the humor is as fresh as the day it was written. The timing of the crew is a marvel of the medium. Benny was a total delight. His legacy is vast.

THE JACK BERCH SHOW, variety and talk; also known as *Jack Berch and His Boys.*

BROADCAST HISTORY: 1935–54, many 15m timeslots on various networks, including 1935–36, Blue, Fridays at 10:15 A.M.; 1937, CBS, twice a week at 1 for Fels Naphtha Soap and Mutual, three a week at 9:45 A.M.; 1939–40, NBC, twice a week at 7:45 Sweetheart Soap; 1939–40, Blue, three a week for Sweetheart; 1939–40, Mutual, twice a week at 12:15; 1943–44, Mutual, weekdays at 1:15 for Kellogg; 1944–46, ABC, weekdays at 11:45 A.M., later at 4, for Prudential Insurance; 1946–51, NBC, weekdays, mostly at 11:30 A.M., for Prudential; 1951–54, ABC, various times, Prudential.

Jack Berch had been a coffee and tea salesman before radio, and he structured his series along the same lines of salesmanship that he had been using door to door. He chatted and sang and was said to have "the friendliest show in radio." His "heart-to-heart hookup" was a regular feature: during the war it helped reunite a soldier erroneously reported killed, with his mother, who had moved and left no forwarding address.

THE JACK CARSON SHOW, comedy-variety.

BROADCAST HISTORY: June 2, 1943–June 25, 1947, CBS. 30m, Wednesdays at 9:30, 1943–44; at 8, 1944–47. Campbell Soups.

Sept. 11, 1947–July 8, 1948, NBC. Thursdays at 9:30. *The Sealtest Village Store*, covered under that title.

Oct. 8, 1948–July 1, 1949, CBS. 30m, Fridays at 8. Sealtest.

Oct. 3, 1955–Dec. 20, 1956, CBS. 25m, weeknights at 9:05.

CAST: *1943–47*: Jack Carson, film star, in a characterization of himself as generally bumbling and dumb. Dave Willock as his nephew, Tugwell, who regularly punched holes in Carson's ego. Arthur Treacher as Carson's butler. Eddie Marr as Carson's press agent, who could sell anything to Carson, including the gun for his suicide. Agnes Moorehead as the fierce Mrs. Freddy Martin. Also: Mel Blanc, Elizabeth Patterson, Irene Ryan, Jane Morgan, Norma Jean Nilsson. ANNOUNCERS: Del Sharbutt, Carlton KaDell, Howard Petrie. VOCALISTS: Anita Ellis (1943), Dale Evans (ca. 1944). ORCHESTRA: Johnny Richards (1943), Freddy Martin (1944), Charles Bud Dant. PRODUCER-DIRECTORS: Vick Knight, Sam Fuller, Larry Berns. WRITERS: Leonard Levinson and Lou Fulton (1943).

Jack Carson began his career in vaudeville in the early 1930s. His stage partner, Dave Willock, was also his constant supporting player on the air. An appearance on Bing Crosby's *Kraft Music Hall* in 1938 led Carson and Willock into radio. Crosby's announcer, Ken Carpenter, recommended him for the host's job on the NBC West Coast series *Signal Carnival*, and this led to Carson's nationwide series on CBS.

Carson was well known for his doorbell routine, a creative way of introducing guests. It was said to "combine the features of a carnival wheel, an alarm clock, a fire alarm, and a factory whistle."

THE JACK HALEY SHOW, musical variety.

BROADCAST HISTORY: Oct. 9, 1937–April 2, 1938, NBC. 30m, Saturdays at 8:30. *The Log Cabin Jamboree.* Log Cabin Syrup. CAST: Haley, with Virginia Verrill, Warren Hull, Joe Oakie, Wendy Barrie. ORCHESTRA: Ted Fio Rito.

Oct. 14, 1938–April 7, 1939, CBS. 30m, Fridays at 7:30. Wonder Bread. HOST: Warren Hull. CAST: Haley, Virginia Verrill, Wendy Barrie. ORCHESTRA: Ted Fio Rito.

July 8, 1943–June 26, 1947, NBC. 30m, Thursdays at 9:30. *The Sealtest Village Store,* covered under that title.

Haley, a nimble comic, was best known as the Tin Man in *The Wizard of Oz.*

THE JACK KIRKWOOD SHOW, comedy.

BROADCAST HISTORY: Ca. 1938, KFRC, San Francisco.

May 17, 1943–Feb. 12, 1945, NBC. 15m, weekdays at 12:30 until Dec. 1943, then at 9 A.M. *Mirth and Madness.* CAST: Kirkwood and his wife, Lillian Leigh, Bill Grey, Tom Harris, Herb Sheldon, Lee Brodie, Mike McTooch, and Ransom Sherman, who continued the show with Kirkwood's departure. VOCALISTS: Don Reid, Jean McKeon. ORCHESTRA: Irving Miller and his "Dripsyland Twelve." THEME: *Hi, Neighbor.*

Jan. 1, 1945–March 29, 1946, CBS. 15m, weekdays at 7. Procter & Gamble. CAST: Many of the same players. ANNOUNCER: Jimmy Wallington. VOCALISTS: Don Reid, Jean McKeon. ORCHESTRA: Irving Miller. PRODUCER: Jack Hill.

July 1–Aug. 19, 1946, CBS. Mondays at 9:30. 30m as partial summer replacement for *The Lux Radio Theater.* Supporting Cast: Lillian Leigh, Gene Lavalle. ORCHESTRA: Lud Gluskin. PRODUCER: Paul Franklin.

1948–50, ABC regional. *At Home with the Kirkwoods,* followed by *The Kirkwood Corner Store.*

Aug. 25, 1950–Feb. 20, 1953, Mutual–Don Lee. 30m, weekdays at various times. *Mirth and Madness,* at times heard only on the West Coast Don Lee Network, other times as a full Mutual offering. CAST: Kirkwood, Leigh, Wally Brown, Steve Dunne, Lee Albert. PRODUCER: J. C. Lewis.

The essential ingredients of *The Jack Kirkwood Show,* by whatever name and in whatever format, were always the same. Kirkwood was extremely witty, with a delivery straight from vaudeville. He wrote his own material, acted many of the roles, and put in ten- and twelve-hour days on his creations. He was a "comic's comic," appreciated as much by his peers as by his public. His humor was decidedly madcap. He satirized westerns and detective shows in a style that was frenzied and packed with hilarious irrelevancies. Kirkwood might be doing a western skit about pioneers "trudging wearily on packmule and oxcart," then turn suddenly to his accomplices and say, "You remember Packmule and Oxcart, those two Dutch comics on the Butterfield Circuit." And on it went.

In his western spoofs, Kirkwood was inevitably shot and spent the last few minutes dying, muttering, "He got me, Lil . . . I'm dyin' . . . I'm goin', Lil." He gained notoriety with frequent appearances on *The Bob Hope Show:* his memorable line from that series—"you gotta put something in the pot, boy"—was picked up and aped all over the nation. Among his continuing characters were "Dr. Heartburn," "Phineas Front Deadline," "Sloppy Sue," "Sadie Black, lonely girl riveter," and "Maw and Paw Jenkins." The shows are still funny today, packed with biting wit and highlighted by that striking vaudeville style.

JACK OAKIE'S COLLEGE, musical comedy.

BROADCAST HISTORY: Dec. 29, 1936–March 22, 1938, CBS. 60m (1936–37): 30m (1937–38), Tuesdays at 9:30. Also heard as *The Camel Caravan,* and linked in 1937–38 with *Benny Goodman's Swing School* under the *Caravan* banner, forming "radio's first double-feature program—two great shows within a single hour." Camel Cigarettes.

CAST: Jack Oakie, former vaudevillian and movie character actor, as the "prez" of a mythical university bearing his name. British character actor William Austin as the professor of the English Department. Comic Raymond Hatton as the football coach. Also: Stuart Erwin, Helen Lynd, and such guests as Judy Garland, Frank Fay and Dorothy Lamour. ANNOUNCER: Bill Goodwin. VOCAL GROUP: The Camel Chorus. VOCALISTS: Harry Barris, Katherine "Sugar" Kane. ORCHESTRA: Benny Goodman, 1936–37; George Stoll, intermittently, and beginning regularly on

Sept. 28, 1937, when the Goodman orchestra was separated for the second half-hour.

The "college" setting of the Jack Oakie show was integrated throughout, with the entire package framed as a pep rally and such guests as "Professor Josephus" (Joe) Penner doing their routines as class lectures. When Benny Goodman went east, Camel began the "double feature" approach, Oakie broadcasting from Hollywood at 9:30, Goodman following (usually from New York's Hotel Pennsylvania) at 10, and the whole hour billed as *The Camel Caravan*.

THE JACK PAAR SHOW, situation comedy.

BROADCAST HISTORY: June 1–Sept. 28, 1947, NBC. 30m, Sundays at 7. Summer replacement for *The Jack Benny Program*. Lucky Strike.

Oct. 1–Dec. 24, 1947, ABC. 30m, Wednesdays at 9:30.

CAST: Jack Paar as himself, with Elvia Allman, Lionel Stander, and other Hollywood players. ANNOUNCER: Hy Averback. ORCHESTRA: Jerry Fielding. VOCALIST: Trudy Erwin. VOCAL GROUP: The Page Cavanaugh Trio. PRODUCER: Bob Nye. WRITERS: Larry Marks, Larry Gelbart, Artie Stander, Seaman Jacobs.

Jack Paar was discovered by Jack Benny when Benny was entertaining troops in the Pacific. They met on Guadalcanal in 1945: two years later, Paar found himself in the enviable position of inheriting the biggest audience in America for a summer run on NBC. Benny had taken such an interest in Paar's career that he wanted to produce the show himself. According to Benny writer Milt Josefsberg, each of Benny's four writers served the series on a rotating advisory capacity. Paar was given every advantage, including a sendoff on Benny's final show of the season (with guest Fred Allen, ensuring the best possible audience), May 25, 1947.

The Paar show drew good notices: the comedy was reminiscent of Benny's, and *Time* joined others in praising it. When Benny returned in the fall, American Tobacco decided to continue Paar's show on ABC. This was short-lived. According to Paar, a consultant insisted that he devise a gimmick that would play from week to week. This resulted in an unfortunate incident in which Paar was quoted as saying he wanted to get away from that kind of old-hat comedy, the

kind being practiced by Jack Benny and Fred Allen. Luckies canceled, and Paar might have faded away if not for television. In the interim was another radio show, a disc jockey effort on ABC (July 2, 1956–March 29, 1957, 15m, weekdays at 11 or 11: 15 A.M.) that Parr himself described as "so modest we did it from the basement rumpus room of our house in Bronxville." In the cast with Paar were Jose Melis, his wife Miriam, daughter Randy, and dog Schnaaps. Then he went on to great success as host of *The Tonight Show* on TV, though the "spoiled kid" image pursued him.

THE JACK PEARL SHOW, comedy-variety.

BROADCAST HISTORY: Sept. 8, 1932–Dec. 23, 1933, NBC. 60m, Thursdays at 10 until the summer break, June 29; resumed Oct. 7, 30m, Saturdays at 9. Lucky Strike. CAST: Jack Pearl as Baron von Munchhausen, teller of tall tales in a heavy German dialect. Cliff Hall, stooge and straight man, known as "Sharlie" by "the baron." Musical and comic talents as guests. ORCHESTRA: Abe Lyman, George Olsen, etc. WRITER-CREATOR: Billy Wells.

Jan. 3–Sept. 26, 1934, NBC. 30m, Wednesdays at 8. Royal Gelatin. CAST: Pearl, Hall, etc. ORCHESTRA: George Olsen.

Feb. 13–May 22, 1935, CBS. 30m, Wednesdays at 10. *Peter Pfeiffer*, covered under that title. Frigidaire.

Nov. 9, 1936–June 25, 1937, Blue Network. 30m, Mondays at 9:30 until mid-March, then Fridays at 10. Continued by Tommy Dorsey after Pearl's departure until Sept. 20, 1939. *The Raleigh-Kool Program*. Brown and Williamson Tobacco. CAST: Jack Pearl, Cliff Hall and guests. Tenor Morton Bowe. Stooges Suzy, Algy and Boris. ORCHESTRA: Tommy Dorsey. VOCALIST: Edythe Wright, Jack Leonard. VOCAL GROUP: The Three Esquires. ANNOUNCER: Paul Stewart.

June 9–Sept. 15, 1948, NBC. 30m, Wednesdays at 8:30. *Jack and Cliff*. U.S. Treasury.

June 19–Sept. 25, 1951, NBC. 30m, Tuesdays at 9:30. Summer substitute for *Fibber McGee and Molly*. Pet Milk. SINGING COSTAR: Mimi Benzell.

The Jack Pearl Show, commonly known as *Baron Munchhausen*, streaked across the horizon of early radio and faded just as fast. It was a sensation in 1932 (leaping to a CAB-rated 47.2, and second only to Eddie Cantor in the January 1933 charts) but began its unprecedented plunge even before its first season was finished. Pearl was tagged early in his career as being one-dimensional. His meteoric fade was a heart-breaker, and decades later he was still somewhat resentful of what he saw as a fickle public.

Pearl was one of radio's earliest and best dialecticians. He was born Oct. 29, 1895, a product of the Lower East Side ghetto that had served up Al Jolson, Eddie Cantor, Fanny Brice, and other top talents. Pearl joined Gus Edwards's *School Days* company around 1910, worked in vaudeville and burlesque, graduated to Shubert revues, and finally became a Ziegfeld headliner. His first major radio exposure came on *The Ziegfeld Follies of the Air* (CBS, April 3–June 26, 1932). He was on vacation in England that summer when he received a cable from comedy writer Billy Wells: Lucky Strike was looking for a new act for its 60-minute Thursday-night variety hour. The show had been running through the summer with the two Walters, O'Keefe and Winchell, as stars: Winchell was leaving, and Wells thought a dialect act built around tall tales might fill the bill. He had talked it over with an adman who happened to be reading the exploits of Baron von Münchhausen, an officer in the 18th-century German cavalry: in his later years, von Münchhausen had taken up writing, recording some of the wildest adventures (purportedly based on his own experiences in Russia) ever set to paper.

Wells knew of Pearl's ability with dialect, and he summoned Pearl home quickly. It was decided to do the act in vaudeville style, with a straight man feeding setup lines and Pearl punching them with witty comebacks. Cliff Hall, who had worked with Pearl in vaudeville, was brought in as stooge. But Wells never could remember Hall's name, so he called him Charlie. This led to one of the great catchphrases of the day, "Vass you dere, Sharlie?"

It was a simple brand of comedy. The Baron might be discussing a friend. Hall would ask, "Is he still at Penn State?" Munchhausen would reply, "No, now he iss in der state pen and he's going to die." There would be news from Uncle Hugo ("Hoogo" to the Baron). Hall might express doubt when Munchhausen said he'd once known a man whose wooden leg pained him: the Baron would reply, "His vife hit him on der

headt mit it.'' The Baron would relate his adventures in Africa—"Und dere in frundt of me vuz a green elephundt.'' Hall would be skeptical. "Now wait a minute, Baron—do you mean to tell me you actually saw a green elephant?'' Such doubt brought a verbal explosion from the Baron, who inevitably asked, "Vass you dere, Sharlie?''

Pearl's accent was lauded for accuracy: his timing, honed onstage, was keener than that of many who outlasted him. He took over the Lucky Strike Hour in September, and by January he was a major radio star, soon pulling down $8,000 a week. But his 1934 show for Royal Gelatin played to less than half of his peak audience a year before. Thereafter, his career was a string of comeback attempts, none of them successful. The 1948 summer show, *Jack and Cliff*, dusted off the Munchhausen accent and character, though Pearl played it in his own name. His final try was a quiz show, *The Baron and the Bee* (NBC, July 21–Sept. 8, 1953, Tuesdays at 9).

Cliff Hall was with him, beginning to end. Pearl died Dec. 25, 1982.

THE JACK SMITH SHOW, popular music.

BROADCAST HISTORY: Aug. 21, 1945–Dec. 26, 1952, CBS. Many 15m timeslots, notably 1945–51, at 7:15 for Procter & Gamble. Smith popularized a happy singing style, running counter to the crooner trend. **COSTARS:** Dinah Shore and Margaret Whiting, both 1950–51. **ORCHESTRA:** Frank DeVol. **ARRANGER-CONDUCTOR:** Earle Sheldon. **PRODUCER:** Bill Brennan.

THE JACK WEBB SHOW, madcap comedy-variety.

BROADCAST HISTORY: Spring 1946, ABC West Coast, from KGO, San Francisco. 30m, Wednesdays at 9:30 Pacific time, premiering March 20.

This insane bit of fluff was one of Jack Webb's earliest efforts, so out of character for the man who created *Dragnet* and airing three years before that landmark police show. The routines were packed with absurd one-liners and nonstop silliness. Webb's love of traditional jazz is reflected in a roaring Dixieland backup by Phil Bovero and "eight retards known as the Raggedaires.'' As for the rest of the cast, Webb's ripping closing signature says it best. ''Tonight's egg was laid on the vocal side by Clancy Hayes and Nora McNamara. John Galbraith blew the lines and Dick Breen glued the joints together'' (translation: Breen wrote the script, as he would for Webb's 1947 detective show, *Pat Novak*).

THE JACKIE GLEASON–LES TREMAYNE SHOW, comedy-variety.

BROADCAST HISTORY: Aug. 13–Oct. 22, 1944, NBC. 30m, Sundays at 10:30. Heard as *Double Feature*, with Alfred Drake, July 2–Aug. 6.
CAST: Jackie Gleason, comic. Les Tremayne, straight man. ORCHESTRA: Toots Camarata. VOCALISTS: Andy Russell, Patsy Garrett.

THE JAMES AND PAMELA MASON SHOW, dramatic anthology: action drama with strong male-female roles; initially titled *Illusion*, with the subtitle *Run, Man, Run*.

BROADCAST HISTORY: July 14–Sept. 1, 1949, NBC. 30m, Thursdays at 9:30.
CAST: British film star James Mason in leading male roles. His wife, Pamela Kellino, as his opposite. Lurene Tuttle and others from Hollywood's Radio Row in support. ANNOUNCER: Frank Barton. WRITER-DIRECTOR: Arch Oboler (first three episodes). DIRECTOR: William Spier (last five episodes).

The Masons had charmed radio audiences with appearances on *The Fred Allen Show*, and their own dramatic series seemed triply blessed when noted radio man Arch Oboler was engaged to write and direct. Oboler had just returned from Africa, laden with new material: his opening script, *The African Story*, followed an Englishman on the trail of the man responsible for his wife's death. But trouble soon developed between Oboler and the Masons, and Oboler left after only three stories had been transcribed. As aired, however, Oboler's shows opened and closed the series.

THE JAMES MELTON SHOW, concert programs, also known as *Texaco Star Theater*.

BROADCAST HISTORY: July 4, 1943–Sept. 22, 1946, CBS. 30m, Sundays at 9:30. Texaco. Heard as the summer replacement for *The Fred Allen Show* July 4–Dec. 5, 1943, and again beginning July 2, 1944, continuing on for Texaco when Allen failed to return for the 1944–45 season. CAST: Metropolitan Opera tenor James Melton with the Al Goodman Orchestra.

JANE ARDEN, soap opera, based on the comic strip by Monte Barrett.

BROADCAST HISTORY: Developed locally and heard on WJZ, New York beginning in June 1938.
Sept. 26, 1938–June 23, 1939, Blue Network. 15m, weekdays at 10:15 A.M. Ward Baking.
CAST: Ruth Yorke as Jane Arden, ''fearless girl reporter, the most beautiful woman in the newspaper world.'' Helene Dumas as unscrupulous reporter Louise West. Maurice Franklin as E. J. Walker, publisher of the *Globe*, the newspaper that had fallen on hard times and merged with the *Comet*, its archrival. Frank Provo as *Comet-Globe* photographer Bob Brandon, object of an additional Jane-Louise rivalry. Bill Baar as *Comet* staffer Jack Fraser, who sided with Louise. Henry Wadsworth as Alabama Randall, the publisher's stepson, who sided with Jane and, predictably, was in love with her. Howard Smith as city editor Jack Galloway, Jane's friend, who survived the merger but found much of his authority undermined by Louise West. ANNOUNCER: Alan Kent. DIRECTOR: Lawrence Holcomb. SOUND EFFECTS: Manny Siegel.

JANE FROMAN, musical variety.

BROADCAST HISTORY: 1930, WLW, Cincinnati. 1931, WENR, Chicago. ''Discovered'' by Paul Whiteman while singing at WENR, and then heard on Whiteman's *Pontiac Hour* (Blue, Fridays at 10, 1931–32), leading to her own series.
1932–33, NBC. 15m, three a week at 7. Sustained. Also 15m, Sundays at 4. Iodent.
Sept. 30, 1934–March 24, 1935, NBC. 30m, Sundays at 10. *The Pontiac Parade*. ORCHESTRA: Frank Black. VOCAL GROUP: The ''Modern Choir.''
July 4–Sept. 26, 1937, NBC. 30m, Sundays at 7. Substitute for *The Jack Benny Program*, with her husband, Don Ross. Jell-O.
June 11–Sept. 17, 1939, CBS. 30m, Sundays at 7:30. *The Gulf Musical Playhouse*. Substitute for *The Screen Guild Theater*. Gulf Oil. COSTAR: Tenor Jan Peerce. MUSIC: Erno Rapee.
July 5–Sept. 27, 1942, CBS. 30m, Sundays at 9:30. Substitute for *The Fred Allen Show*. Texaco.

THE JANE PICKENS SHOW, music and song.

BROADCAST HISTORY: June 29, 1948–Aug. 22, 1949, NBC. 30m. Tuesdays at 8:30 for Tums, Summer 1948. Then, Oct. 24, 1948–March 20, 1949, Sundays at 5, sustained; returned July 4–Aug. 22, 1949, Mondays at 9:30.

Feb. 5, 1951–June 12, 1955, NBC. Various 15m and 30m formats.

Dec. 3, 1955–April 13, 1957, NBC. 15m, Saturdays at 6:45. *Pickens Party*.

CAST: Jane Pickens, soprano, the lone member of the famed Pickens Sisters who continued in show business beyond the 1930s. Also: Jack Kilty (1948), Bob Houston (1949). ANNOUNCER: Robert Warren (1948). ORCHESTRA: Norman Cloutier (1948–49). DIRECTOR: Edwin L. Dunham.

JASON AND THE GOLDEN FLEECE, adventure drama.

BROADCAST HISTORY: Oct. 29, 1952–July 19, 1953, NBC. 30m, Wednesdays at 10 until Jan., then Sundays at 4:30.

CAST: Macdonald Carey as Jason, owner of a cafebar in the French Quarter section of New Orleans, who also owned the *Golden Fleece*, a boat frequently chartered by adventurers and people on the lam. William Conrad as his sidekick and bartender, Louis Dumont. MUSIC: Frank Worth. WRITERS: Herb Ellis, Cleve Herman.

JEFF REGAN, INVESTIGATOR, detective drama.

BROADCAST HISTORY: July 10–Dec. 18, 1948, CBS West. 30m, Saturdays at 9:30 Pacific Time.

CAST: Jack Webb as Jeff Regan, a tough private eye in a detective bureau run by Anthony J. Lyon (''I get ten a day and expenses . . . they call me the Lion's Eye.'') Wilms Herbert as Lyon. MUSIC: Richard Aurandt. PRODUCER: Sterling Tracy. WRITER: E. Jack Neuman.

Oct. 5, 1949–Aug. 27, 1950, CBS West. 30m, Wednesdays, then Sundays. CAST: Frank Graham as Regan. Paul Dubov also as Regan. Frank Nelson as Lyon. MUSIC: Richard Aurandt. WRITERS: William Froug, William Fifield.

Jeff Regan was a response to a groundswell of demand for Jack Webb's services in the wake of his hilarious hard boiled performances in *Pat*

Novak: For Hire. Webb had built almost a cult following, and *Regan* was the transition show away from *Novak* and into *Dragnet*. It was, momentarily, a step back: it lacked the originality and flavor of *Novak*, and it certainly lacked the humor. Webb played the role well into 1949, but by January he had confided to a *Radio Life* reporter that his next character ''might be called Joe Friday.'' A reorganization of *Regan*, titled *The Lion's Eye*, followed Webb's inevitable departure.

THE JIMMY DURANTE SHOW, musical comedy.

BROADCAST HISTORY: Sept. 10–Nov. 12, 1933, and again from April 22–Sept. 30, 1934, NBC. 60m, Sundays at 8. *The Chase and Sanborn Hour*, substituting for Eddie Cantor. ANNOUNCER: Jimmy Wallington. ORCHESTRA: Dave Rubinoff.

Oct. 29, 1935–Feb. 25, 1936, NBC. 30m, Tuesdays at 9:30. *The Jumbo Fire Chief Program*, covered under that title. Texaco.

March 25–Oct. 28, 1943, NBC. 30m, Thursdays at 10. *The Durante-Moore Show*, with costar Garry Moore, also heard as *The Camel Caravan* (replaced *The Abbott and Costello Show* and finished the season when Lou Costello had to retire temporarily because of illness). Camel Cigarettes. ORCHESTRA: Xavier Cugat. PRODUCER: Phil Cohan.

Oct. 8, 1943–March 30, 1945, CBS. 30m, Fridays at 10. *The Durante-Moore Show*, with costar Garry Moore. Camel. CAST: Elvia Allman as the secretary. Also: Hope Emerson. ANNOUNCER: Howard Petrie. VOCALIST: Georgia Gibbs. ORCHESTRA: Roy Bargy. PRODUCER: Phil Cohan. WRITER: Syd Resnick.

April 6, 1945–June 27, 1947, CBS. 30m, Fridays mostly at 10 until mid-1946, then at 9:30. A continuation of *The Durante-Moore Show*. Rexall.

Oct. 1, 1947–June 23, 1948, NBC. 30m, Wednesday at 10:30. *The Jimmy Durante Show*. Rexall. CAST: Durante with singer Peggy Lee, Candy Candido, maestro Roy Bargy, and announcer Howard Petrie. Florence Halop as Hotlips Houlihan. Arthur Treacher and Victor Moore (''the Lothario of the lumbago set''), regulars. PRODUCER: Phil Cohan. THEMES: *You Gotta Start Off Each Day with a Song*; *Inka Dinka Doo*.

Oct. 8, 1948–June 30, 1950, NBC. 30m, Fridays at 8:30, 1948–49; at 9:30m, 1949–50. Camel.

CAST: Durante with costar Alan Young until April 1949, then with Don Ameche.

Radio gave Jimmy Durante new life as an entertainer. After a solid career onstage throughout the Prohibition era, Durante's star had cooled: though he remained highly visible on Broadway (*Jumbo* and *Red, Hot, and Blue*), radio reignited Hollywood's interest and helped keep him a household word in the 1940s.

Durante was a unique personality. His props were the battered hat and the piano; his trademark an oversized nose, at which he poked good-natured fun throughout his professional life. His act consisted of half-sung songs interrupted by one-liners, delivered in a growly but cheerful voice, highlighted by a sometimes amazing ability to butcher English in a way that almost made sense. His appeal was deep in a simpler America: he was the guy of humble origin, the common man.

He was born Feb. 10, 1893, in New York's Lower East Side. At 17 he learned to play the piano, beginning his musical career in the beer gardens of old Coney Island, picking out tunes for $25 a week. In Terry Walsh's club he played while a waiter named Eddie Cantor sang. By 1916 he had assembled a small Dixieland combo for the Club Alamo in Harlem. There he met Eddie Jackson, who was to become his partner. In 1923 he and Jackson opened the Club Durant and acquired a third partner, Lou Clayton.

The club thrived, but the partners ran afoul of the law, and the business was closed by Prohibition agents. But Clayton, Jackson, and Durante arrived on Broadway in 1928. Their formal partnership dissolved in the 1930s, but Jackson and Clayton remained Durante's pals for life, following him to Hollywood and serving as his business managers in his later career. Durante was already a national figure when Eddie Cantor left his *Chase and Sanborn Hour* in 1934. Durante was tapped for the lead. He inherited the Cantor show virtually intact, with a full 60-minute format, an audience share in the 40s, and the music of "Rubinoff and His Violin." The Cantor audience increased his celebrity, but he could not hold it: the subsequent erosion may have been inevitable with or without Cantor. In 1935 Durante was installed into the Texaco *Fire Chief* slot then held by Ed Wynn, whose own huge rating had begun to dissolve. Durante's *Jumbo*

Fire Chief (covered in this book under its own heading) was extravagant beyond anything radio had yet attempted, but it was not a success. The skid that had begun with Wynn continued with Durante, and in January 1936 the show registered only 4.1 in the ratings charts. This was followed by a string of second-rate films that sent Durante into a decline, broken only when he resurfaced on radio in 1943.

Durante's wife Jeanne had died in February that year. He was financially strapped and at loose ends, but two bookings were to change his life and revitalize his career. He had appeared on NBC's *Camel Caravan* and would soon open at the Copacabana in New York. The *Caravan* date was to have long-range significance. Intended as a single guest appearance, it propelled Durante again into the national spotlight. Producer Phil Cohan was struck by the contrast between Durante and a young comic on the same bill named Garry Moore. Moore was a crewcut with a breathless delivery; Durante was the grand old man of vaudeville and burlesque. Durante and Moore had never met before that night. Moore was being readied by Camel to take over the Abbott and Costello timeslot in the summer. Cohan asked if they might be willing to try a team approach, perhaps for the following fall.

Then illness forced Lou Costello off the air, and a replacement show was needed immediately. Moore was the obvious choice, but the agency was concerned about his youth and lack of name recognition. Cohan suggested the Durante-Moore cobilling. Everybody knew Jimmy Durante, and Cohan was convinced that the contrast was viable.

The first show was rushed into production in two weeks. It was a ragged job, and reviewers said so. But soon *Durante-Moore* found its niche, and Durante had new life as an entertainer. His booking at the Copacabana was a smash, and the *Durante-Moore* ratings climbed into the mid-teens. Durante's trademarks were now known to new millions who had never seen him in person. His nose was berated constantly; his reputation as "the Schnozz" or "Schnozzola" (a term coined by Clayton years before) grew into radio folklore. Durante talked of his mythical character Umbriago, telling his audiences of their exploits together. His act opened musically, with *Inka Dinka Doo*, a song that became his musical calling card. The age gap between Durante and Moore was emphasized, Durante speaking of Moore as "Junior" and chanting "Dat's my boy dat said dat" so often that many listeners believed they were father and son.

Moore wrote his own material, while Durante ad-libbed his way profusely through the half-hour. Scripts were prepared by a team of writers, who tossed in as many multi-syllabled brain-twisters as Durante could handle in 30 minutes. But writer Jackie Barnett told Durante biographer Gene Fowler that Durante's way of mangling words was wholly natural. If scripts were prepared with words distorted, Durante would straighten them out in his delivery. So the writers wrote "catastrophe" and Durante said "catastrostroke"; they wrote "corpuscles" and he said "corpsuckles." In one 1944 interview, Durante said he "mangled da big woids just ta hear 'em scream."

Moore was master of ceremonies. He told a few glib jokes, then brought Durante on for some dual banter. Then the singing star, "her nibbs," Miss Georgia Gibbs, sang a song. Durante and Moore returned with a comedy sketch, often based on some occupational enterprise, such as running a circus, becoming scientists, or working on an oil pipeline. There was a "Garry Moore Radio Workshop," which featured "problem" scenarios (the servant problem, the meat shortage, censorship in wartime, etc.) and played on such Moore characters as Murgatroyd Croomsboogle, Toodles Bongschmook, and Comastalk Pilderdrentch. Drummer Jack Roth, who had been with Durante for 25 years, became part of the show; old partners Clayton and Jackson were added to the business end, and producer Phil Cohan was a full partner.

Moore departed in 1947, an "honest separation" (as Fowler reported it) fuelled by Moore's need to "keep his own identity as a comic." Durante continued on the air for three more years, with Cohan continuing as his producer-director. Now it was simply *The Jimmy Durante Show*: he was billed as "Rexall's prescription for a pleasant evening," opening each week with *Inka Dink*, but seldom getting beyond a line or two. Either someone came barging onstage or Durante himself would bellow, "Stop da music! Stop da music! There's somethin' wrong wit da orchestrial harmonics!" His catchphrases were "Ev-ry-body wants ta git into da act!" or, after

applause, "I got a million of 'em!" His songs were old favorites in the style of *I Know Darn Well I Can Do Wit'out Broadway, but Can Broadway Do Wit'out Me*? He was berated by "butler" Arthur Treacher and abetted by Victor Moore. His stooges were Hotlips Houlihan and Candy Candido. Hotlips was a sultry femme fatale whose lines were delivered in Mae West style by Florence Halop. Candido had a miracle voice that could go mighty high or mighty low. On the low end, he played Tyrone Touchbottom. A heavy schedule of top guests included Bing Crosby, Boris Karloff, and Charles Boyer. Tommy Harmon, former football star, gave gridiron picks in midseason. Durante wrapped it up each week with another enduring closing line—"Goodnight, Mrs. Calabash, wherever you are!" This was sometimes said to refer to his first wife, but Durante would never tell. After his death (Jan. 28, 1980), the second Mrs. Durante revealed that it was just another show business prop, created for radio.

JIMMY FIDLER, gossip reporter.

BROADCAST HISTORY: Sept. 16, 1934–May 28, 1950, many 15m series on various networks, including:

Sept. 16–Oct. 14, 1934, NBC. Sundays at 3:30. Maybelline.

Jan. 16, 1935–Jan. 15, 1936, Blue. Wednesdays at 10 until May 15, 1935; returned Oct. 30, Wednesdays at 10:30. Tangee Lipstick.

Jan. 21, 1936–June 30, 1939, NBC. Tuesdays at 10:30 until Nov. 8, 1938. Concurrent broadcasts, Fridays at 10:30 beginning May 21, 1937; Fridays at 7:15 as of Aug. 26, 1938. George W. Luft for Tangee Lipstick until April 21, 1936; Ludens Cough Drops, 1936–37; Procter & Gamble beginning March 16, 1937.

Nov. 15, 1938–April 23, 1940, CBS. Tuesdays at 7:15. Procter & Gamble for Drene.

July 11–Aug. 15, 1941, CBS West, Fridays at 8:30 Pacific time. Also, Aug. 22–Nov. 28, 1941, Don Lee Network. Fridays at 6:15 Pacific time. Tayton Company, both shows.

Nov. 1941, Mutual. Three weeks only.

March 2, 1942–May 28, 1950, Blue Network/ABC. Mondays at 7 until June 1942, then Sundays, various times. Concurrent broadcasts: March 2–Oct. 5, 1943, Mutual. Tuesdays at 10:30 A.M. Sept.

7, 1947–June 26, 1949, Mutual. Sundays at 8:30. Carter Products and Arrid Deodorant.

During his two decades in radio as a network Hollywood gossip reporter, Jimmy Fidler was one of the medium's most controversial figures. He came to Hollywood as an aspiring actor in 1919 and, after a career as a movie star press agent, turned to radio, tattling on the stars, chronicling their foibles, tantrums, and divorces. He is generally thought to have operated in the shadows of Hedda Hopper and Louella Parsons, but he was more feared by some studios and stars than either. His reviews of movies were caustic and blunt. He condemned those he considered "stinkers" with entertaining invective, and sometimes used the same adjectives for the people who had made them.

His trademarks included a film rating service (four bells for a top-notcher; one bell for a stinkeroo), a scathing series of "open letters" to the stars, his "notes from the little black book," and a celebrated and often-mimicked signoff— "Good night to you, and I *do* mean *you!*" Many studios tried to blacklist Fidler from talking to their people. He was denied access to back lots, but this did nothing to stem the tide of his infuriating stories.

He quit CBS in 1941, charging that the network was pandering to the studios by insisting that he give good notices to "big" pictures. His long association with the Blue Network was soon tested, when actress Gene Tierney threatened to sue over a Fidler story that she had begun smoking cigars in an effort to acclimatize herself to her husband's smoke. An example of the kind of innocuous item that kept Fidler in constant Dutch was this "open letter" to Constance Bennett for the new year: "Resolved that the only splinters you get on the ladder of fame are those you get sliding down."

Fidler's appeal was based on a reputation for fearlessness (he always claimed to be just a guy trying to tell the truth) and a rapid-fire air delivery that reminded some of Walter Winchell. He packed his shows with material, often getting 3,000 words into the quarter-hour. His 1945 Hooper rating was 13.4, twice that of Hedda Hopper. By 1948 he was also writing a syndicated newspaper column, appearing in 175 papers and on more than 400 radio stations. He himself often varied the spelling of his name,

signing publicity photos "Jimmie" in the 1930s and "Jimmy" in later life. He continued syndicating his show into the 1970s.

JOAN AND KERMIT, serial love story, though usually complete in each episode.

BROADCAST HISTORY: April 24–July 10, 1938, CBS. 30m, Sundays at 7. From WBBM, Chicago. CAST: Olan Soulé as Dr. Kermit Hubbard. Frances (Fran) Carlon as Joan Martell. Also: Butler Mandeville, David Gothard. ANNOUNCER: Franklyn MacCormack. WRITER: Milton Geiger.

JOAN DAVIS TIME, comedy, variety, and situation comedy.

BROADCAST HISTORY: 1941–43, appearances on *The Rudy Vallee Show,* sponsored by Sealtest, led comedienne Joan Davis to assume the starring role when Vallee went into the Coast Guard. Retitled *The Sealtest Village Store,* it ran with Davis as lead July 8, 1943–June 28, 1945, and is covered under that title.

Sept. 3, 1945–June 23, 1947, CBS. 30m, Mondays at 8:30. *Joanie's Tea Room.* Lever Brothers and Swan Soap. SUPPORTING CAST: Verna Felton, Sharon Douglas, Shirley Mitchell, Wally Brown. ANNOUNCERS: Harry Von Zell, Bob LeMond. ORCHESTRA: Paul Weston; also, Lud Gluskin. DIRECTOR: Dave Titus. WRITERS: Jack Harvey, Jay Sommers, David Victor, Herb Little.

Oct. 11, 1947–July 3, 1948, CBS. 30m, Saturdays at 9. *Joan Davis Time.* Co-op advertising. SUPPORTING CAST: Hollywood regulars including Mary Jane Croft, Hans Conried, etc. Lionel Stander as the gravel-voiced manager of the tea shop. ANNOUNCER: Ben Gage. MUSIC: John Rarig. VOCAL GROUP: The Choraliers quintet. THEME: *Nobody's Sweetheart.*

July 4–Aug. 22, 1949, CBS. Mondays at 9. Replaced the first 30m of *The Lux Radio Theater* as *Leave It to Joan.* Lever Brothers.

Sept. 9, 1949–March 3, 1950, CBS. 30m, Fridays at 9. *Leave It to Joan.* American Tobacco. CAST: Shirley Mitchell, Willard Waterman.

July 3–Aug. 28, 1950, CBS. 30m, Mondays at 10. Fill-in for *My Friend Irma.* PRODUCER-DIRECTOR: Dick Mack, spanning several series. WRITERS: Si Wills (the star's husband until 1944).

Joan Davis and her husband, Si Wills, caught the final days of vaudeville in the 1930s and arrived on radio in 1941. An appearance on the *Rudy Vallee Show* Aug. 28, 1941, led to a regular role with Vallee beginning in November. She played a crazy and man-crazed female whose aim in life was to capture Vallee's heart. This, coupled with her voice—a squeaky trill of sharply rising inflections—set her apart and drew much favorable notice. When Vallee left the show in 1943, she was promoted to the top despite concern in the agency that a female lead could not successfully follow him. But the show rocketed into the top ten. It was clear that Davis was the reason for its success, despite the hasty recruitment of Jack Haley as her costar.

In her subsequent shows, she played the same basic character: for *Joanie's Tea Room* she was removed from the village store and placed in a tea shop in the town of Smallville. *Joan Davis Time* perpetuated the tea-room motif under a new title. *Leave It to Joan* continued the same characterization. Davis's daughter, Beverly Wills (then 12 years old), was occasionally featured on the air as her sister. Davis was also a star of early TV, in the NBC sitcom *I Married Joan* (1952–55).

JOE AND ETHEL TURP, daytime comedy serial, based on the stories of Damon Runyon.

BROADCAST HISTORY: Jan. 4–Sept. 24, 1943, CBS. 15m, various times, three to five times a week.

CAST: Jackson Beck as Joe. Patsy Campbell as Ethel. Art Carney as Billy Oldham. Jack Smart as Ethel's Uncle Ben.

JOE AND MABEL, comedy.

BROADCAST HISTORY: Feb. 13, 1941–Sept. 27, 1942, NBC. 30m, intermittent run, Thursdays, then Sundays.

CAST: Ted de Corsia as Joe, a cab driver. Ann Thomas as Mabel, his girlfriend. Walter Kinsella as Mike, Joe's best friend and fellow cabbie. Jackie Grimes as "Shoiman," Mabel's brother. Betty Garde as Mabel's mother. **ANNOUNCER:** George Putnam. **DIRECTOR:** Howard Nussbaum. **WRITER:** Irving Gaynor Nieman.

THE JOE COOK SHOW, the popular name for two brief variety series.

BROADCAST HISTORY: June 18–Nov. 12, 1934, NBC. 30m, Mondays at 9:30. Colgate. Cook took over an existing series and left in midrun (*House Party*, aka *The Colgate House Party*, March 3, 1934–Feb. 25, 1935). **ORIGINAL CAST:** singers Frances Langford and Donald Novis; comic Arthur Boran; maestro Don Voorhees. **LATER CAST:** singer Conrad Thibault, maestro Al Goodman.

March 8–Aug. 2, 1935, NBC; Blue Network until May, then Red. 30m, Fridays at 10: *Circus Night in Silvertown*, Goodrich Tires. **CAST:** Joe Cook as the show's "barker." Tim Ryan and Irene Noblette. **ORCHESTRA:** B. A. Rolfe.

Cook was a popular vaudevillian who came to national attention with an appearance on *The Rudy Vallee Hour* and was subsequently invited to appear on *House Party*. His guest performance was so successful that he took over the show the following month. His comedy was described as cerebral rather than madcap. He was sometimes compared with Fred Allen.

THE JOE DIMAGGIO SHOW, baseball drama and trivia.

BROADCAST HISTORY: Sept. 17, 1949–March 11, 1950, CBS. 30m, Saturdays at 10 A.M., later at 10:30 A.M. M&M Candy. Transcribed in New York, with the former "Yankee Clipper" conducting a sports quiz, answering questions sent in by mail, and offering a dramatized "favorite story" of a well-known sportswriter. **SUPPORTING PLAYERS:** Charlotte Manson, Mandel Kramer, Jackson Beck, Charles Irving, etc. **HOST:** Jack Barry. **DIRECTOR:** Dan Enright. **THEME:** *Joltin' Joe DiMaggio*.

April 15–Aug. 19, 1950, NBC. 30m, Saturdays at 7:30. Continuation of earlier series, same general format and personnel.

THE JOE E. BROWN SHOW, comedy-variety.

BROADCAST HISTORY: Oct. 8, 1938–Sept. 28, 1939, CBS. 30m, Saturdays at 7:30 until April, then Thursdays at 7:30. General Foods.

CAST: Joe E. Brown, wide-mouthed comic of stage and screen, as a frustrated talent agent. Gale Gordon as his boss, the apoplectic Mr. Bullhammer. Paula Winslowe as Jill, Joe's sweetheart. Comics Bill Demling and Frank Gill. **ANNOUNCER:** Don

Wilson. **VOCALIST:** Margaret McCrae. **ORCHESTRA:** Harry Sosnik.

JOE PALOOKA, comedy-thriller; based on the comic strip by Ham Fisher.

BROADCAST HISTORY: April 12–Aug. 16, 1932, CBS. 15m, Tuesdays and Thursdays. Heinz Rice Flakes.
CAST: Teddy Bergman as Joe, "amiable, dim-witted champion of the ring, the store clerk who fights his way to the heavyweight championship of the world." Also: Karl Swenson, Norman Gottschalk. Elmira Roessler, Elsie Hitz, and Mary Jane Higby as Joe's girlfriend, Ann Howe. Frank Readick and Hal Lansing as Palooka's friend and manager, Knobby Walsh.

THE JOE PENNER SHOW, comedy-variety.

BROADCAST HISTORY: Oct. 8, 1933–June 30, 1935. *The Baker's Broadcast*, covered under that title.
Oct. 4, 1936–June 26, 1938, CBS. 30m, Sundays at 6. Cocomalt. **CAST:** Joe Penner in situational episodes as "the black sheep" of the "Park Avenue Penners." Martha Wentworth as his mother. Gay Seabrook as Joe's girlfriend, Susabella. Margaret Brayton as Gertrude. **ANNOUNCER:** Bill Goodwin. **VOCALISTS:** Joy Hodges, Gene Austin, Paula Gayle. **ORCHESTRA:** Jimmy Grier. **WRITER:** Harry Conn.
Oct. 6, 1938–March 30, 1939, CBS. 30m, Thursdays at 7:30. Huskies.
Oct. 5, 1939–April 25, 1940, Blue Network. 30m, Thursdays at 8:30. *The Tip Top Show*. Ward Baking. **CAST:** Gay Seabrook continues as Susabella. Also: Russ Brown. **ANNOUNCER:** Jim Bannon. **VOCALIST:** Kenny Stevens. **ORCHESTRA:** Jacques Renard.

Joe Penner had been the sensation of *The Baker's Broadcast* but had walked out of that show at the height of its popularity. Now, after a year's absence, he returned with hopes of capturing the magic that had made Jack Benny a top radio comic. He hired away Benny's writer, Harry Conn; Conn did to Benny what Penner had done to Fleischmann (his *Baker's* sponsor), and their "Park Avenue Penners" skits struggled for two years in the long inevitable slide.
Penner simply lacked the imagination to be a

Jack Benny, and Conn had oversold his own importance as Benny's writer. Penner had one dimension, a standup style rooted in vaudeville and built around one silly line—"Wanna buy a duck?" When the public tired of the duck gag, he had little left. His post-Cocomalt shows, for Huskies and later Tip Top Bread, drew dreary ratings, about a quarter of the audience that Penner had regaled in his Fleischmann days. On Jan. 10, 1941, Penner died of a heart attack. He was 36.

JOHN CHARLES THOMAS, concert music by "America's beloved baritone."

BROADCAST HISTORY: Jan. 10, 1943–June 30, 1946, NBC. 30m, Sundays at 2:30. Also known as *The Westinghouse Program*. Westinghouse.
CAST: Met Opera star John Charles Thomas performing popular songs, ballads, and light classical pieces. Lee Sweetland was his summer replacement in 1944. **SIDE FEATURE:** *The Passing Parade*, narratives by storyteller John Nesbitt. **ORCHESTRA:** Mark Warnow, replaced by Victor Young in March 1943. **CHORUS:** Lyn Murray, replaced by Ken Darby in March 1943. **PRODUCER:** Clarence Olmstead. **THEME:** *Home on the Range*, sung robustly by Thomas.

JOHN STEELE, ADVENTURER, thriller drama.

BROADCAST HISTORY: April 26, 1949–July 16, 1956, Mutual. Various 30m timeslots; frequently moved.
CAST: Don Douglas as John Steele, who narrated stories of "suspense and hard, fast action." New York radio actors in support: John Larkin, Bryna Raeburn, Jack Edwards, etc. **MUSIC:** Sylvan Levin; later, Doc Whipple. **PRODUCER-WRITER:** Robert Monroe.

Though it never made much impact, *John Steele* had a gritty sound and offered highly competent adventure entertainment. The music added much to the stark background, which ranged from jungles to deserts.

JOHNNY FLETCHER, comedy-detective drama.

BROADCAST HISTORY: May 30–Nov. 27, 1948, ABC. 30m, Sundays at 7:30 until mid-Sept., then Saturdays at 8.

CAST: Bill Goodwin as Johnny Fletcher, the opposite of most detective heroes—a clumsy, inept drunk, who played his role for laughs. Sheldon Leonard as his pal Sam.

JOHNNY LUJACK OF NOTRE DAME, juvenile adventure drama.

BROADCAST HISTORY: June 6–Sept. 2, 1949, ABC. 30m at 5:30, Tuesday-Thursday one week, Monday-Wednesday-Friday the next.
CAST: Lujack, Notre Dame football hero, as himself. Ed Prentiss in support.

JOHNNY MERCER'S MUSIC SHOP, popular songs.

BROADCAST HISTORY: June 22–Sept. 14, 1943, NBC. 30m, Tuesdays at 10. Summer substitute for Bob Hope. Pepsodent. CAST: Singer-songwriter Johnny Mercer with Jo Stafford and the Pied Pipers, Ella Mae Morse, and guests. ORCHESTRA: Paul Weston.
June 12–Dec. 8, 1944, NBC. 15m, weekdays at 7. *The Chesterfield Music Shop.* Chesterfield Cigarettes. CAST: Same as 1943. ANNOUNCER: Wendell Niles. WRITER: Bob Mosher.
June 8–Sept. 25, 1953, CBS. 15m, weekdays at 7:30. *The Johnny Mercer Show.*
Oct. 10, 1953–May 22, 1954, CBS. 60m, Saturdays at 7. ANNOUNCER: Johnny Jacobs. DIRECTOR: Bill Brennan. WRITER: Glenn Wheaton.

JOHNNY MODERO: PIER 23, detective adventure.

BROADCAST HISTORY: April 24–Sept. 4, 1947, Mutual. 30m, Thursdays at 8.
CAST: Jack Webb as Johnny Modero, a San Francisco waterfront troubleshooter, who rented boats and did "anything else you can blame on the environment." Gale Gordon as Father Leahy, the waterfront priest. William Conrad as the menacing policeman, Warchek. ANNOUNCER: Tony LaFrano. MUSIC: Harry Zimmerman. DIRECTOR: Nat Wolff. WRITERS: Richard Breen; Herb Margolis and Lou Markheim.

Johnny Modero came to the air after Jack Webb left San Francisco for Hollywood in 1947. Webb had been playing the title role in *Pat Novak*, perhaps the most caustic detective of the air. Writer Richard Breen created the character with a bile-dipped pen; the result was a hilarious show and the emergence of Webb as a national radio personality.

In Hollywood, Webb and Breen reunited and decided to continue their Novakian adventures. But *Novak* was unavailable: it was still in production in San Francisco, with a new actor (Ben Morris) and a new writer (Gil Doud) producing a far different sound. Webb and Breen thus created *their* Novak under another name, Johnny Modero. It was Webb's first coast-to-coast excursion into staccato metaphor. Modero had the same chip on his shoulder, the same snappy comeback. The stories were almost devoid of sensible plots: they existed to serve the one-liners. Each week, Modero consulted Father Leahy, who was a bit devious for a man of the cloth. With a bit of double-dealing, the pair managed to stay ahead of Warchek the cop while chasing down the real culprits.

JOHNNY PRESENTS, a title used generically by Philip Morris Cigarettes to announce shows of many kinds under its sponsorship, much as Camel had done with its *Camel Caravan.*

The "Johnny" of the title referred to the sponsor's unforgettable bellhop, Johnny Roventini (see *The Philip Morris Playhouse*), whose high-pitched cry, "Callll forrrr Philip Morrraaaiiisss," was one of the great commercial gimmicks of the air. Though the bellhop was used on virtually all PM-sponsored shows, the *Johnny Presents* title can be tracked through a twelve-year run on two networks, a series of variety shows well-mixed with drama, big bands, and popular vocalists.

BROADCAST HISTORY: 1934–37, NBC. 30m, Tuesdays at 8. Began with Leo Reisman's Orchestra Jan. 2, 1934. "Johnny" given billing, though the point at which it became *Johnny Presents* is uncertain. A mix of music and drama, with vocalists Phil Duey, Sally Singer, and the Three Sweethearts; Loretta Clemens, the Giersdorf Sisters, and the Rhythm Rogues as of 1936. Earliest dramatic segments directed by Phillips H. Lord, who also presented guest speakers. Charles Martin, dramatic director ca. 1936.
Feb. 13, 1937–March 14, 1941, CBS. 30m, Saturdays at 8:30, 1937–38; at 8, 1938–39; Fridays at 9, 1939–41. Russ Morgan, maestro, with singers Frances Adair and Genevieve Rowe, tenors Glenn

Cross and Floyd Sherman. Also: Johnny Green's Orchestra; Ray Bloch's Swing Fourteen; the Marsh Sisters (Beverly and Audrey). Jack Johnstone, dramatic director.

Nov. 4, 1941–Jan. 15, 1946, NBC. 30m, Tuesdays at 8. Timeslot consistent through several format changes, all with Ray Bloch's Swing Fourteen Orchestra. Starring Una Merkel, 1941–42; Tallulah Bankhead as of March 1942; *Johnny Presents Ginny Simms* (see THE GINNY SIMMS SHOW), 1942–45; Barry Wood, 1945–46.

JOHN'S OTHER WIFE, soap opera.

BROADCAST HISTORY: Sept. 14, 1936–March 20, 1942, NBC; Red Network until March 1940, then Blue. 15m continuation, weekdays at 10:15 A.M.; at 3:30 as of 1940. Bisodol, Freezone, Kolynos Toothpaste, Old English Wax, etc.

CAST: Hanley Stafford as John Perry, owner of a department store. Matt Crowley, Luis Van Rooten, William Post Jr., Joseph Curtin, and Richard Kollmar also as John Perry. Adele Ronson and Erin O'Brien-Moore as John's wife, Elizabeth. Franc Hale as Annette Rogers, John's secretary. Phyllis Welch and Rita Johnson as Martha Curtis, John's beautiful assistant. New York regulars in other character roles: Alice Reinheart, Joan Banks, Mary Jane Higby, etc. PRODUCERS: Frank and Anne Hummert. THEME: *The Sweetest Story Ever Told*, sung by Stanley Davis to his own guitar accompaniment.

John's Other Wife was such a perfect title for a soap opera that it was lampooned by Fred Allen (as *Duncan's Other Fife*, etc.) and other comics for years. The main point of contention was the romantic triangle—store owner John Perry, his wife Elizabeth, and John's secretary, Annette, who became fixed in Elizabeth's mind as "John's other wife." While Elizabeth wrung her hands and fretted, John was trying to survive the furious competition from Sullivan's luxurious department store across the street. At one point in the serial, John's assistant, Martha, came in for the brunt of Elizabeth's "other wife" jealousies.

THE JOHNSON FAMILY, dialect comedy.

BROADCAST HISTORY: 1934–36, local formats on WTAR, Norfolk; WBAL, Baltimore; and WLW, Cincinnati.

1937–50, Mutual. 15m continuation, late afternoons, most often at 4:15.

CAST: Jimmy Scribner in a one-man show, portraying an entire village of Negro characters. PRODUCER: J.C. Lewis. ANNOUNCER: Don McCall. CO-WRITER: Floyd Christy. SOUND EFFECTS: Tom Hanley, Art Sorrence. THEMES: *Listen to The Mockingbird; The Whistler and His Dog*.

The Johnson Family told of life in a mythical hamlet of southern blacks, the town of "Chickazola." Jimmy Scribner, who created all the voices and wrote the scripts, was described as "multi-voxed." He began his serial with eight characters. By 1944 he was using 22 voices and had practiced as many as 67 distinct characterizations.

The main characters were Mama and Papa Johnson, their daughter Lucy, Lucy's boyfriend Peewee, Peewee's stuttering friend Stumpy, Grandpa, Lawyer Philpotts, and Deacon Crumpet. The characters were all based on people Scribner had known in his youth. Mama Johnson was "created in the image of a lovable old Negro mammy who lived with us. Peewee is an exact copy of a little colored boy named Shine who lived with my aunt, and Peewee's expressions—such as 'great day in the mornin' '—are those Shine always used."

In the beginning, Scribner wrote all his material, did his own sound effects, and provided music on the banjo. Arguments between his characters were most challenging, calling for quick voice changes and proper spacings of microphones to achieve the desired effect. "Scribner guides his characters in and out of rapid conversations in almost unbelievable fashion," wrote *Radio Life* in 1947. The show was especially popular in the South and among rural blacks. It was a poor-man's *Amos 'n' Andy*, linked by the similarity of a white performer mimicking blacks. Like Freeman Gosden and Charles Correll, Scribner frequently expressed great affection for the black race and gave many shows to all-black audiences.

JOLLY BILL AND JANE, early-morning music and song for children.

BROADCAST HISTORY: 1928–38, NBC, Red and Blue Networks at various times. Many timeslots, often 15m, sometimes 25m, frequently in the 7-to-8 A.M. hour. Cream of Wheat, 1928–ca. 1931.

CAST: Bill Steinke (lauded in the trade press for his

"hearty laugh and cheerful nonsense at the un-godly hour of 7:15"), with Muriel Harbater in the child's role of Jane. Peggy Zinke as Jane, ca. 1935.

JONATHAN TRIMBLE, ESQUIRE, drama.

BROADCAST HISTORY: May 4–Sept. 7, 1946, Mutual. 30m, Saturdays at 9:30.

CAST: Donald Crisp as Jonathan Trimble, a news-paperman at the turn of the century: "a pompous gentleman, a tyrant in his own household," but beneath it all "a kindly, likable soul." Gale Gordon also as Trimble. Irene Tedrow as Alice Trimble. Jean Gillespie as Mildred. Earle Ross as Mayor Turner. ANNOUNCER: Art Gilmore.

JOYCE JORDAN, M.D., soap opera; early shows as *Joyce Jordan, Girl Interne*.

BROADCAST HISTORY: May 30, 1938–March 23, 1945, CBS. 15m continuation, weekdays at 10:30 A.M., 1938; at noon, later at 3, 1939; at 2:15, 1940–44; at 2, 1945. Calox Tooth Powder, 1938–39; General Foods, 1939–45.

April 2, 1945–Oct. 8, 1948, NBC. 15m, week-days at 10:45 A.M., 1945–46; at 10:30 A.M., 1946–47; at 10:45 A.M., 1947–48. Procter & Gamble for Dreft.

Dec. 10, 1951–April 11, 1952, ABC. 15m, weekdays at 3:30. Lever Brothers.

Jan. 3–July 1, 1955, NBC. 15m, weekdays at 10:15 A.M.

CAST: Elspeth Eric as Joyce Jordan (1938–40), in-tern at Heights Hospital, where she struggled to find happiness in a man's world. Helen Claire as Joyce ca. 1940. Ann Shepherd as Joyce, 1940–41. Betty Winkler as Joyce beginning in March 1942. Also as Joyce: Rita Johnson, Gertrude Warner, Fran Carlon. Clayton Bud Collyer as Dr. Henry Powell, one of many Joyce-suitors. Erik Rolf as Dr. Hans Simons. Bill Johnstone as Dr. Hunt. Theodore Newton as Dr. Christopher Parker. Rich-ard Widmark as Dr. Alan Webster. George Cou-louris as Neil Reynolds, a wealthy man who courted Joyce. Myron McCormick as Paul Sher-wood, the not-so-understanding newspaperman Joyce married, setting up a marriage-vs.-career theme. Lesley Woods as Paul's sister, Margot. Ste-fan Schnabel as Herbert Yost. Ethel Owen as Dr. Molly Hedgerow. Patricia Ryan as Myra Wilder. Also: Agnes Moorehead, Charlotte Holland, Do-rothy McGuire, Claudia Morgan, Mary Jane

Higby, Michael Fitzmaurice, etc. Voice mimic Do-lores Gillen in child roles. ANNOUNCERS: Ken Roberts, Len Sterling, etc. PRODUCER: Himan Brown. WRITERS: Julian Funt, etc.

Joyce Jordan progressed slowly from *Girl In-terne* to *M.D.*, the change becoming complete around 1942. But the theme of a woman's dif-ficulty in a man's world remained. In the earliest days it was a progression of suitors. Then Joyce faced the "necessity of choosing between a bril-liant career as a physician or becoming the wife of a wealthy man," hospital trustee Neil Reyn-olds. At last, married to foreign correspondent Paul Sherwood, Joyce found happiness threat-ened by Paul's bitter and neurotic sister, Margot. Eventually Paul was written out of the script, and Joyce practiced medicine in the little town of Preston, becoming a surgeon at Hotchkiss Me-morial Hospital.

The show dissolved in October 1948, with the introduction of Liz Dennis as a major character. Dennis would be the lead on the new serial, *The Brighter Day*, which took over the *Joyce Jordan* timeslot as of Oct. 10, 1948. *Jordan*, meanwhile, was revived in the 1950s.

JUBILEE, black-oriented swing, jazz, bop, and variety.

BROADCAST HISTORY: Oct. 9, 1942–Aug. 14, 1953, transcribed by the Special Services Division of the War Department until ca. 1943, then by the Armed Forces Radio Service.

CAST: Black jazz and swing bands (Fletcher Hen-derson, Duke Ellington, Count Basie, Cootie Wil-liams, the King Cole Trio, etc.) and other black entertainers (Lena Horne, Ethel Waters, the Ink Spots, Eddie "Rochester" Anderson, Ella Fitzger-ald, trumper-vocalist Valaida Snow, etc.), ca. 1942–45. Postwar, a more racially mixed series of playbills, with music by an AFRS orchestra led by Michael Perriere. HOST: Ernie Whitman (1943–45). ANNOUNCERS: Verne Smith, Bob Moon. PRODUCERS: Charles Vanda, Mann Holiner, Jimmy Lyon.

Jubilee filled an important gap in the musical history of radio, though it was transcribed for distribution to service personnel and was not heard at home. Conceived (at least in part) as a morale-building service for Negro troops overseas, it presented bands and entertainers that had been given short shrift by the networks. The wartime host, Ernie "Bubbles" Whitman, was a jive-talking bundle of energy.

Most of the shows were recorded before live audiences in Los Angeles: either at network studios or in the facilities of such syndicators as C. P. MacGregor and Universal Recorders. The series has emerged as an important piece of black heritage: its War Department status exempted the performing artists from the union-mandated recording bans of 1942–43 and 1947–48, and many of the discs contain unique performances. A massive two-volume history and discography of the series was compiled by Rainer E. Lotz and Ulrich Neuert in 1985.

JUDY AND JANE, soap opera.

BROADCAST HISTORY: Feb. 8–June 17, 1932, CBS; also, Oct. 10, 1932–April 26, 1935, NBC. 15m. Heard on network regional lines in the Midwest only, for Folger's Coffee.

CAST: Margie Calvert as Judy. Donna Reade and Betty Ruth Smith as her wisecracking friend, Jane Lee. Also: Ireene Wicker and Margaret Evans as Jane; Joan Kay as Judy. **ANNOUNCER:** Jack Brinkley. **PRODUCERS:** Frank and Anne Hummert. **WRITER:** Robert Hardy Andrews.

Judy and Jane was one of radio's first soap operas, becoming a great favorite in the Central time zone where the sponsor's coffee was sold. Long after its network run, it was distributed by transcription. It was still heard for its original sponsor as late as 1947.

THE JUDY CANOVA SHOW, comedy-variety.

BROADCAST HISTORY: July 6, 1943–June 27, 1944, CBS. 30m, Tuesdays at 8:30. Colgate.

Jan. 13, 1945–June 30, 1951, NBC. 30m, Saturdays at 10, 1945–47; at 9:30, 1947–49; at 10, 1949–51. Colgate.

Dec. 29, 1951–May 28, 1953, NBC. 30m, Saturdays at 9 until July, sustained; returned in Oct. Thursdays at 10, multiple sponsorship, including Emerson Drug, Smith Brothers, and General Motors.

CAST: Judy Canova as herself, a pigtails-and-calico bumpkin, who had come to Hollywood from "Rancho Canova" in "Cactus Junction." Verna Felton as her Aunt Aggie, with whom she lived. Ruth Perrott also as Aunt Aggie. Ruby Dandridge as Geranium, the fat Negro maid who also lived there. Mel Blanc as Pedro, the Mexican gardener-chauffeur. Hans Conried as Mr. Hemingway, the house guest who complained about everything. Sheldon Leonard as Joe Crunchmiller, Judy's boyfriend, who drove a cab. Gerald Mohr as the muscular Humphrey Cooper. Joe Kearns as the nonsensical Benchley Botsford. Also: Gale Gordon, George Niese, Elvia Allman, Sharon Douglas. **ANNOUNCERS:** Ken Niles (early to mid-1940s); Verne Smith (mid-1940s), Howard Petrie (later period). **MUSIC:** Opie Cates, Charles Bud Dant, Gordon Jenkins. **VOCAL GROUP:** the Sportsmen Quartet. **PRODUCER-DIRECTOR:** Joe Rines. **WRITERS:** Fred Fox, Henry Hoople.

Judy Canova was a Jacksonville native who aspired to a serious career in music. But early in her career she was typed as a hillbilly, hog-caller, and hayseed, a female answer to Bob Burns, and she never shook it off. In the early 1930s she was billed with her sister Annie and her brother Zeke as the Three Canovas. Rudy Vallee caught the act, and in 1933 she appeared on his *Fleischmann Hour*. She was a regular on Paul Whiteman's *Musical Varieties* of 1936–37 and on Edgar Bergen's *Chase and Sanborn Hour* in the fall of 1938.

Her own show, accompanied by a barrage of publicity stills depicting her with shotgun and wolf traps, created a pigtails-and-calico fad on college campuses everywhere in the fall of 1943. Her shows opened with a monologue and novelty song, which were followed by the comedy skit and a more serious vocal. Canova told tall tales about her pig, Loverboy, or about Cousin Ureenus, who loved chopped-liver ice cream. A notable catchphrase was that of Mel Blanc in his character of Pedro, the Mexican gardener: "Pardon me for talking in your face, senorita—thirty days hacienda, April, June, and sombrero."

During the war, Canova's closing theme was *Goodnight, Soldier* ("wherever you may be . . . my heart's lonely . . . without you"). Later she closed to a memorable nursery song:

Go to sleep-y, little ba-by,
Go to sleep-y, little ba-by,
When you wake

You'll patty-patty cake
And ride a shiny little po-ny.

THE JUMBO FIRE CHIEF PROGRAM,
spectacular musical variety.

BROADCAST HISTORY: Oct. 29, 1935–Feb. 25, 1936, NBC. 30m, Tuesdays at 9:30. Texaco.
CAST: Jimmy Durante as Claudius "Brainy" Bowers, comical press agent of the troubled Considine Wonder Circus. Arthur Sinclair as John A. Considine, owner of the circus. W. J. McCarthy as Matthew Mulligan, Considine's archrival, owner of the more prosperous Mulligan circus. Gloria Grafton as Mickey Considine, daughter of the down-and-out circus owner. Donald Novis as aerialist Matt Mulligan, Mickey's beau and son of her father's rival. **ANNOUNCER:** Louis Witten. **CREATED AND STAGED BY:** Billy Rose. **ORCHESTRA:** Adolph Deutsch. **WRITERS:** book by Charles MacArthur and Ben Hecht; score by Richard Rodgers and Lorenz Hart.

Jumbo was the most extravagant radio show of its day, eclipsing even *The Gibson Family* in hyperbolic glitter. It was produced in conjunction with the stage show of the same name, both mounted "from the sawdust ring" of New York's Hippodrome, playing to audiences of 4,500 people. The radio show opened two weeks ahead of its stage counterpart, taking over the Texaco *Fire Chief* half-hour being vacated by Ed Wynn.

It was a circus story and a veritable circus in itself, with animal acts, aerialists, a 35-piece orchestra, a 32-voice male choir, and a $15,000 weekly budget. Paul Whiteman was musical director for the stage show but could not appear on air because of contractual conflicts. Producer Billy Rose spared no cost in making it lavish, hiring some of the best-known theatrical talent in America. The story, continuing from week to week, was an old one: Considine, about to lose his circus because of hard luck, hard drink, and back taxes, has his life complicated by the love affair between his daughter Mickey and young Matt Mulligan, the son of his bitter rival. Considine struggles to save his show with the aid of Jumbo, "the best-loved elephant from here to the High Sierras." Durante as "Brainy" Bowers eventually saves the day, though his methods are slightly devious. Among the Rodgers and Hart melodies written into the score was *My Ro-*

mance, introduced by Gloria Grafton and Donald Novis on the premiere broadcast.

But the show drew only mediocre ratings and ran one short season. The stage show was likewise troubled, with huge expenses that were never offset by attendance. It closed in mid-1936, in a sea of red ink.

JUNGLE JIM, juvenile adventure serial, based on the comic by Alex Raymond.

BROADCAST HISTORY: Ca. Nov. 2, 1935–Aug. 1, 1954, transcribed for the Hearst comic weekly, dramatizing the same stories running in the Sunday comics. 15m weekly; scheduling varied from market to market.
CAST: Matt Crowley as Jungle Jim Bradley. Gerald Mohr as Jungle Jim, ca. 1938. Juano Hernandez as Kolu. Franc Hale as Shanghai Lil. **ANNOUNCERS:** Glenn Riggs, Roger Krupp, etc. **PRODUCERS:** Jay Clark. **WRITER:** Gene Stafford.

JUNIOR MISS, situation comedy, from the novel by Sally Benson.

BROADCAST HISTORY: March 4–Aug. 26, 1942, CBS. 30m, Wednesdays at 9. Procter & Gamble. **CAST:** Shirley Temple as Judy Graves, typical radio teenager. Elliott Lewis as her father, Harry Graves. Mary Lansing as her mother, Grace. Barbara Eiler as her elder sister, Lois. Priscilla Lyon as Judy's pal, Fuffy Adams, "the odd child from the apartment downstairs." Patsy Moran as Hilda the housekeeper. **WRITERS:** Doris Gilbert, Sally Benson.

April 3, 1948–Dec. 30, 1950, CBS. 30m, Saturdays at 11:30 A.M. Lever Brothers. **CAST:** Barbara Whiting as Judy. Gale Gordon as Harry. Sarah Selby as Grace. Peggy Knudsen as Lois. Beverly Wills as Fuffy. Myra Marsh as Hilda. **MUSIC:** Composed and conducted by Walter Schumann. **PRODUCER:** Fran Van Hartesveldt. **DIRECTOR-WRITER:** Henry Garson. **WRITER:** Robert Soderberg.

Oct. 2, 1952–July 1, 1954, CBS. Various times and formats, 30m weekly with some stretches of 15m strip shows. Virtually the entire 1948–50 cast was restored.

JUST PLAIN BILL, soap opera.

BROADCAST HISTORY: Sept. 19, 1932, CBS regional. First broadcast as an evening show from Chicago.

Jan. 16, 1933–June 12, 1936, CBS from New York, coast to coast. 15m, weekdays at 6:45 until June 30, the summer break; returned Sept. 25, 1933, at 7:15; heard concurrently at 2, 1933–34, and at 1, late 1934; then at 7:15, 1934–35; at 11:45 A.M., 1935–36; at 11:30 A.M., Jan.–June 1936. Whitehall Pharmacal Company for Kolynos Toothpaste.

Sept. 14, 1936–March 25, 1954, NBC. 15m, weekdays, Red Network at 10:30 A.M. until March 22, 1940; Blue Network, 3:45, until March 20, 1942; Red Network thereafter, at 11:45 A.M. briefly in 1942; at 5:30, 1942–51; at 5, 1951–54. Whitehall Pharmacal Company for Anacin, Kolynos, Bisodol, etc.

Sept. 27, 1954–Sept. 30, 1955, NBC. 15m, weekdays at 5; at 3:45 at end of run. Miles Laboratories for Alka-Seltzer.

CAST: Arthur Hughes as Bill Davidson, "barber of Hartville . . . a man who might be your next-door neighbor" in "a story of people just like people we all know." Ruth Russell as Nancy Donovan, his daughter. James Meighan as Kerry Donovan, Nancy's husband. Madeleine Pierce and Sarah Fussell, actresses who specialized in little-boy roles, as the Donovans' son, Wiki. Actors from New York's Radio Row in supporting roles: Bill Lytell, Macdonald Carey, Clayton "Bud" Collyer, Teri Keane, Anne Elstner, Charles Egleston, Ann Shepherd, Charlotte Lawrence, Bill Quinn, Ray Collins, etc. ANNOUNCERS: Andre Baruch, Tom Shirley, Ed Herlihy, Fielden Farrington, Roger Krupp, etc. PRODUCERS: Frank and Anne Hummert. DIRECTORS: Martha Atwell, Art Hanna, Blair Walliser, Norman Sweetser, Ed King, Gene Eubank, etc. WRITERS: Robert Hardy Andrews, from circa 1932–33; also, John Kelsey, Barbara Bates, Evelyn Hart, etc. THEMES: *Polly Wolly Doodle* to open, played vigorously on the harmonica by Hal Brown; to close, *My Darling Nellie Gray*, in a few stark chords from Brown's guitar.

Just Plain Bill was one of the biggest (and first) successes of daytime radio, enjoying a run of more than two decades. It exploited a favored theme of producers Frank and Anne Hummert: life in a small town. The precise location of Hartville was not revealed, but it was always thought to be somewhere in the Midwest. The serial was unusual in at least two aspects: the protagonist was male, and the musical bridges were played on guitar and harmonica, giving it a sound quite unlike the organ-drenched serials around it.

Bill Davidson was one of the first great philosophers of serial drama. He was the male counterpart of Ma Perkins, predating that staunch old mother of the air by almost a year. He ran a barbershop, but what Bill did best was meddle in the lives of his friends, all for their own good. He got involved under protest, arguing in that marvelously caring voice that "this is really none of my affair" while the announcer returned to put it in perspective: *How can Bill, drawn into the middle of this romantic triangle, straighten out the lives of his friends?*

But trouble in Hartville often ran deeper than that. As early as 1933, the serial was engulfed in dark melodrama, as "the murderous madman, Old Man Willis," stalked the town with a gun, trying desperately to "get past the guards that patrol Hartville and strike at Bill." During this tense manhunt, Nancy, Bill's beloved daughter, lay in critical condition, hovering between life and death. Much of the action in *Just Plain Bill* centered on Nancy and on Kerry Donovan, her husband, a highbrow who was described as "sometimes jealous, often moody." Donovan dabbled in politics, and often hard feelings against him paid off in vengeance plots against Nancy or Bill.

Bill was a gentle soul but had more than his share of murders to solve. The serial bore all the Hummert trademarks: devious, treacherous villains, cunning and conniving women, and the simplistic overidentification of characters through heavy-handed narration and dialogue. Through it all Bill remained a pillar of integrity, "the salt of the earth," as described by Arthur Hughes, the actor who played the role all the way. "He looked for integrity in others and generally found it, and he believed in the golden rule." He was a widower, often remembering his much-loved wife, finding strength as he remembered the days of their youth.

When the serial finally died in 1955, its passing was noted in such unlikely literary quarters as the *Saturday Review*. Many people could not remember a time when *Just Plain Bill* had not been part of their lives.

JUVENILE JURY, children's question-and-answer panel show.

BROADCAST HISTORY: May 11, 1946, WOR, New York: Five-week trial series.

June 15, 1946–April 1, 1951, Mutual. 30m, Saturdays at 8:30 in 1946; then Sundays, mostly at 1:30 (1947–48), 3:30 (1948–50), and 7:30 (1950–51). Gaines Dog Food, General Foods.

Sept. 28, 1952–Feb. 15, 1953, NBC. 30m, Sundays at 6:30.

MODERATOR: Jack Barry. **EARLY PANELISTS:** Maryann Maskey, Buddy Robinson, Ginger Henkel, Glenn Mark Arthurs, Art Stone, Marilyn Kandler, Francey Aransohn. **LATER PANELISTS:** Elizabeth Watson, Peggy Bruder, Dickie Orlan, Patsy Walker, Johnny McBride, Laura Mangels, Billy Knight, Charlie Hankinson, Jerry Weissbard, Robin Morgan, etc. **ANNOUNCER:** John Scott. **PRODUCER:** Dan Enright (Ehrenreich).

Juvenile Jury might be described as the common child's answer to *The Quiz Kids*. There were no prodigies or genius toddlers on its panel: just five normal but articulate kids, aged 5 to 12, who aired their views on the problems of their peers.

The idea originated with Jack Barry, who became its host. While working at WOR as a staff announcer, Barry produced his audition record with five children who had come to the studio to watch an *Uncle Don* broadcast. Using most of the same children, Barry and his partner, Dan Ehrenreich, got the series booked on WOR, then on Mutual. The show was completely unrehearsed and employed no writers. Barry and Ehrenreich selected the questions from the 5,000 weekly submissions from children, teachers, and parents. The kids fenced over the sticky problems of allowances, makeup, spankings, school dress, study habits, and even kissing. The "jury" was never a rubber stamp for the juvenile's case: the kids displayed a strong sense of fairness and often sided with the parent.

KALTENMEYER'S KINDERGARTEN, madcap comedy-variety.

BROADCAST HISTORY: Oct. 14, 1932, WMAQ, Chicago, origination.

Dec. 16, 1933–Sept. 14, 1940, NBC. 30m, mostly Saturdays at 5:30 or 6, with occasional forays into other evenings to replace vacationing programs. Quaker Oats, 1935–37.

CAST: Bruce Kamman as Prof. August Kaltenmeyer, who conducted his lessons in "a frantic jumble of English and German" in the "nonsense school of the air." Jim Jordan as Mickey Donovan, a dimwitted but mischievous pupil; also as Cy Wintergreen. Marian Jordan as Gertie Glump; also as Mrs. Van Schuyler. Johnny Wolf as Izzy Finklestein, a student said by *Radio Guide* to be "always trying to sell the famous Finklestein two-pants suit in class." Bruce Kamman as Elmer Spivens, hard-of-hearing trustee; also as Mickey Donovan's father. Isabel Randolph as Mrs. Donovan. Harold Peary, in Italian accent, as the father of one of the students. Thor Ericson as Yonny Yohnson, who excelled in "smart-aleck Swedish dialect." Cecil Roy as Daisy Dean, "the little girl with the perpetual giggle." Merrill Fugit as the pusillanimous Percy Van Schuyler. Billy White as Cornelius Callahan. Sidney Ellstrom as Chauncey, the bum. CREATOR: Bruce Kamman. ORCHESTRA: Harry Kogen. DIRECTOR: J. Clinton Stanley. WRITERS: Bruce Kamman, Harry Lawrence.

Kaltenmeyer's Kindergarten, said *Radio Guide*, "never existed in a schoolboy's wildest dreams." The only order was disorder: students were awarded top grades in deportment for throwing paper wads and engaging in other similar absurd situations. Adult comedians took the roles of students ("poopuls," as Kaltenmeyer called them), and the roles were filled by many of the principals who later worked *Fibber McGee and Molly*.

The character of Kaltenmeyer was created by Bruce Kamman from memories of an old schoolteacher he had met in France in World War I. In the beginning, there were only four performers: Kamman, Jim and Marian Jordan, and Johnny Wolf. The Jordans departed in 1936, with Harold Peary and Isabel Randolph following them into the *McGee* program. In 1940, with hostilities against Germany appearing ever more inevitable, the show was abruptly changed to *Kindergarten Kapers*, and the headmaster's name became Professor Ulysses S. Applegate.

KATE HOPKINS ANGEL OF MERCY, soap opera.

BROADCAST HISTORY: Oct. 7, 1940–April 3, 1942, CBS. 15m, weekdays at 4:45; at 2:45 the second year. "The exciting story of a visiting nurse."

CAST: Margaret MacDonald as Kate. Clayton Collyer as Tom Hopkins. Raymond Edward Johnson and Constance Collier as Robert and Jesse Atwood. WRITERS: Gertrude Berg, Chester McCracken.

THE KATE SMITH HOUR, musical variety.

BROADCAST HISTORY: March 17–April 23, 1931, NBC. 15m, twice a week at 11:30. *Kate Smith Sings.*

April 26–Sept. 12, 1931, CBS. 15m, Sundays at 7:45 for the opening show; then four a week at 7:45; later six a week at 7. *Kate Smith Sings.*

Sept. 14, 1931–Oct. 31, 1933, CBS. 15m, various times, usually several times a week. *Kate Smith and Her Swanee Music.* La Palina Cigars. Jack Miller, pianist.

July 16–Sept. 7, 1934, CBS. 15m, three a week at 8. A brief series announcing her return to radio after a long cross-country vaudeville tour in 1933: a prep of sorts for the more ambitious fall season to come.

Sept. 12, 1934–May 22, 1935, CBS. 60m, Wednesdays at 3. Network-sponsored (rather than sustained, as Smith was paid at a star's level and given full celebrity status, and the series was not offered for sale). *The Kate Smith Matinee.*

Sept. 13, 1934–May 27, 1935, CBS, concurrent with *Matinee.* 30m, Thursdays at 8; Fridays at 10:30 beginning in Oct.; Mondays at 8:30 for the Hudson Motor Car Company beginning in Dec. *The Kate Smith New Star Revue,* starring Kate Smith, "the Songbird of the South," with Jack Miller's Orchestra, the Three Ambassadors, and guests (baseball pitcher Dizzy Dean, etc.). Continued through the summer, May 30–Aug. 15, 60m, Thursdays at 8.

Oct. 1, 1935–Sept. 10, 1936, CBS. 15m, three a week at 7:30. Jack Miller's Orchestra. Great Atlantic & Pacific Tea Company.

Sept. 17, 1936–June 10, 1945, CBS. 60m, Thursdays at 8 through mid-1939; Fridays at 8 through mid-1944; then Sundays at 7. *The Kate Smith Hour (The Kate Smith A&P Bandwagon,* 1936–37). Great Atlantic & Pacific Tea Company, 1936–37; General Foods thereafter, for Calumet Baking Soda and Swans Down Flour (1937–39), Grapenuts (1939–42), Jell-O (1942–43), and Sanka Coffee (1943–45). **CAST:** Kate Smith, with master of ceremonies Ted Collins, maestro Jack Miller, the Ted Straeter Chorus, comedian Henny Youngman, and many top guests from Broadway and Hollywood. Also: The Three Ambassadors; the La Brun Sisters, 1936–37. A "Hero of the Month" feature as part of the series' "Command Appearance," 1937–38. Jim Crowley (original Notre Dame "horseman") in "Football Forum"

(1937–38). Comedians Bud Abbott and Lou Costello (1938–40). *The Aldrich Family* skits, with Ezra Stone (1938–39). *Snow Village Sketches* skits (1939–40). Nan Rae and Maude Davis, comics (1940–41). Charlie Cantor and Minerva Pious, comedy duo (1940–41). Newscast (5m) with Elmer Davis (1940–41); with Cecil Brown, Bill Henry, etc. (1942–44). **ANNOUNCER:** Andre Baruch. **THEME:** *When the Moon Comes over the Mountain.*

Sept. 14, 1945–June 29, 1947, CBS. 30m, Fridays at 8:30, 1945–46; then Sundays at 6:30. *The Kate Smith Show.* General Foods for Postum and Sanka.

April 4–June 22, 1938, three a week at 3:30. Also, Jan. 10–June 6, 1939, Tuesdays at noon; Diamond Salt. All CBS, 15m. Talk shows titled *Kate Smith's Column* and *Speaking Her Mind.*

Oct. 9, 1939–June 20, 1947, CBS. 15m, weekdays at noon. *Kate Smith Speaks.* General Foods.

Mar. 22–July 26, 1947, Mutual. 15m, Saturdays at 10:15 A.M. *Kate Smith's Serenade.*

June 23, 1947–June 15, 1951, Mutual. 15m, weekdays at noon. *Kate Smith Speaks.* Cooperative advertising.

July 7, 1947–Sept. 9, 1949, WOR/Mutual. 15m, weekdays at 12:15 or 12:45. WOR, New York, 1947–48; Mutual, 1948–49. Phillip Morris, 1948–49. *Kate Smith Sings.*

Aug. 8, 1949–Jan. 30, 1950, ABC. 60m, Mondays at 9. *Kate Smith Calls.*

April 1–Sept. 14, 1951, Mutual. 15m, weekdays at 12:15. *Kate Smith Sings.*

Sept. 17, 1951–Sept. 12, 1952, NBC. 40m, weekdays at noon.

Jan. 6–Aug. 1, 1958, Mutual. 15m, weekdays at 2:15. Reader's Digest.

Kate Smith was one of radio's busiest major stars. Her career compares with that of Arthur Godfrey a decade later: both were prolific performers in many formats and under many titles.

Smith was born May 1, 1907 (her biographer and advocate, Richard K. Hayes, corrects a long-held 1909 date, and provides many of the dates in the Smith broadcast log), in Washington, D.C. She worked in vaudeville in the '20s, playing numerous "fat" roles opposite comedians who made sometimes-cruel heavy-handed ad-libs at her expense. But Smith had a voice, a genuine contralto that could rattle the timbers of an auditorium. Her rendition of *Hallelujah* in *Hit the Deck* was a high spot, but these bright moments were offset by humiliation over her weight. In the George White revue *Flying High*, she was savaged each night by Bert Lahr, whose choicest lines came at Smith's expense. Lahr refused to let up on the ad-libs even when her family came up from Washington for the show. When White refused to let her off to visit her dying father's bedside, she decided to quit the stage.

Chance had intervened in 1930, when a talent scout for Columbia Records named Ted Collins caught her act in *Flying High*. Collins had missed a train and had time to kill. What he saw was a fairly forgettable play. What he heard was something else. Smith virtually stopped the show with the power of her voice.

Collins came to her dressing room and briefly introduced himself. She would remember him years later as "a young man of about middle height with black hair and a round, pugnacious face." Collins persuaded her to come to Columbia for a recording session. They became friends, and her records began to sell. Soon Collins offered to become her manager. He would fight the battles on the business front: mold her career, help select her songs, make all the decisions about where she should go. All she had to do was sing. Profits would be split 50-50, and they would share the real work on a half-and-half basis. She shook his hand, entering one of the most remarkable partnerships in radio history. They never had a written contract, yet Collins was to guide her for the rest of his life, more than 30 years, and fulfilled many times over his promise to make millionaires of them both.

Collins introduced her to a new world, radio, where she could do her best and never again play the stooge. After a brief late-night 1931 NBC series, heard by almost nobody, Collins arranged for CBS chief William S. Paley to hear her. Her first CBS timeslot was a tough one: she was booked opposite *Amos 'n' Andy*, yet still made an impressive showing. Her CAB rating soon leaped into double digits, and later that fall La Palina Cigars arrived as a sponsor. Suddenly she had a budget—$1,500 a week—and was elevated to star status. But Collins was careful to keep simplicity as her trademark. He seldom took a chance on anything that compromised her integrity or prestige.

Her personal theme had long been settled: *When the Moon Comes over the Mountain*, a song that would identify her ever after. It was decided that she would avoid a heavy verbal buildup: she would simply walk on and introduce herself, and would exit the same way. "Hello, everybody, this is Kate Smith" was her standard opening for years; "Thanks for listenin' and good night, folks" was her closing. Collins quit his job at Columbia and devoted the rest of his life to her career. By 1935, even Smith was able to laugh at her weight for a *Newsweek* reporter. "I'm big and I'm fat, but I have a voice, and when I sing, boy, I sing all over."

Jack Miller, the pianist of her earliest shows, became musical director in September 1933. Her shows for La Palina had been simple affairs, song sessions with piano, and Collins was in no rush to push her into another. She was a headliner by 1933: Collins had never been comfortable with sponsorship by a cigar firm, and at the end of it he had Smith thank the sponsor without personally embracing the product. At this point, Collins decided to go on the road, a vaudeville tour designed to put her in touch with her fans. Expected to last six weeks, it stretched into eight months. She returned to New York with her popularity actually enhanced in her absence. Camel Cigarettes wanted to take her on, as did the Vick Chemical Company. Collins turned both down, believing neither cigarettes nor drugs to be the proper client. When Paley suggested that Smith launch an afternoon show, with CBS paying the bills, it seemed a perfect reentry. At the same time, Smith began an evening show, soon picked up by Hudson Motors at $30,000 a week. This was a talent scout series, discontinued after its one season because of expenses and the difficulty of finding top unsung talent.

Then came *The A&P Bandwagon* and, in 1937, her major radio work, *The Kate Smith Hour*, for General Foods. Typical of its time, this 60-minute variety series offered a broad mix of music, drama, comedy, and human interest. Smith opened with songs, then offered a dramatic sketch, with major personalities in their starring roles from stage and film work. Bud Abbott and Lou Costello were launched as radio and film stars in a two-year run on the Smith show; *The Aldrich Family* went on to become the powerhouse radio comedy of 1940, after being heard as a series of skits with Kate Smith. One of the regular departments, begun in 1936, was called "Command Appearance," awarding up to $1,000 to people who had done "unselfish deeds that had saved the lives of others.'' For Armistice Day in 1938, she introduced Irving Berlin's *God Bless America*, which she sang into immortality during the time that Berlin granted her the exclusive right to use it. By 1940, she had won a trunkful of awards, citations, and keys to American cities. She was consistently listed among the nation's most outstanding women, and *Time* had dubbed her ''the first lady of radio.'' She and Jack Benny had the only contracts in radio that could not be canceled: technically, only war could force them off the air. And when war did come, Smith was one of the champions of the Allied cause, stumping the country to drum up $600 million in war bond sales.

Her *Kate Smith Speaks*, heard to the announcement that ''it's high noon in New York,'' was also considered an important morale booster for women on the home front. She was seen on television in three series. Collins died May 27, 1964. Smith was last seen July 30, 1976, in a special TV show commemorating the Bicentennial. Appropriately, she sang *God Bless America*. Her health deteriorated after 1982, and she died June 17, 1986.

KAY KYSER'S KOLLEGE OF MUSICAL KNOWLEDGE, musical quiz.

Broadcast history: Ca. 1937, WGN, Chicago. Then eight-week trial on Mutual beginning Feb. 1, 1938.

March 30, 1938–June 26, 1948, NBC. 60m until Sept. 1946, then 30m. Wednesdays at 10, 1938–46; at 10:30, 1946–47; Saturdays at 10, 1947–48. Lucky Strike, 1938–44; Colgate, 1944–48.

Nov. 4, 1948–July 29, 1949, ABC. 30m, weekdays at 11 A.M. until Jan., then at 4. Pillsbury.

Cast: Bandleader Kay Kyser as ''the old professor,'' quizmaster. **Announcers:** Ken Niles, Bud Hiestand, Verne Smith, Bill Forman (billed as ''Dean Forman, 39 throats behind a single collarbutton''); Jack McCoy, ABC daytime. **Vocalists:** (billed on air as ''faculty''): Ginny Simms, followed by Trudy Erwin, Julie Conway, Gloria Wood, Lucy Ann Polk, and Georgia Carroll. Also: Harry Babbitt, tenor, whose long duration was interrupted only for a hitch in the Navy; Mike Douglas, Sully Mason, and the King Sisters (Louise, Donna, Alyce, and Yvonne). Merwyn A. Bogue as Ish Kabibble. **Organist:** Rex Koury, ABC daytime. **Producer:** Frank O'Connor.

Directors: Ed Cashman, John Cleary, William Warwick, Harry Saz. **Theme:** *Thinking of You.*

The *Kollege of Musical Knowledge* grew out of an idea initiated by maestro Kay Kyser during a long mid-1930s engagement at Chicago's Blackhawk Restaurant. It started as a combination community sing and amateur night, and demanded a brand of quick-on-the-feet personal patter at which Kyser would prove a master. Its subjects were Blackhawk patrons, not professionals, and it offered a new and zany kind of musical quiz.

After a short trial on Mutual, American Tobacco moved the show to New York and NBC. It was an instant hit, with ratings in the 20s; in the early war years, Kyser was clocking numbers between 25 and 30 on the CAB survey, just off the pace set by Jack Benny and the other national leaders. The 60-minute show was a blend of corn, musical antics, and contests, with up to $400 cash for contestants who could answer the ''kollege brainbuster question.'' Kyser was a cheery host, with a generous nature that seldom allowed a contestant to leave empty-handed. Often in the quiz, Kyser required his true-false answers backward, contestants giving ''false'' answers to ''true'' statements. When they did, Kyser would shout, ''That's right, you're wrong!'' Invariably, when a contestant missed a question, Kyser turned to the audience and shouted, ''Students!'' The crowd then boomed the answer.

The aggregation always appeared in costume: Kyser himself wore a long black robe and a mortarboard hat; the band often wore beanies and lettered sweaters, the letters spelling out the sponsor's name when the musicians lined up in proper proximity. Probably the most popular Kyser personality was Merwyn A. Bogue, who as Ish Kabibble developed a comic haircut with bangs and specialized in novelty songs, which Kyser featured in great numbers. The show helped make famous such Kyser evergreens as *Three Little Fishes* and *Praise the Lord and Pass the Ammunition.*

Kyser's warm southern drawl (''Evenin', folks, how y'all?'') was a genuine trademark. He was born in Rocky Mount, N.C., June 18, 1906. He formed his first band in 1926 while attending the University of North Carolina: his early trademarks—singing song titles and announcing numbers with four bars of the melody—earned him a reputation for "hokum" music among swing and jazz musicians and critics. He was successful where it counted, at the box office and record stores. He was one of the most ardent bond salesmen on the air during the war years, making an estimated 1,000 appearances at camps, hospitals, and other bond-raising functions.

Kyser married one of his singers, Georgia Carroll, in 1944. A TV version of his *Kollege* ran on NBC in 1949–50, and another in 1954: neither approached the success of the radio show. He disbanded soon thereafter, retiring to North Carolina with his family. There he lived a private life, gave no interviews, and refused to discuss the old days even with friends. He became manager of the film and broadcasting department of the Christian Science Church, to which he gave much of his time in later life. He died June 23, 1985.

KEEP 'EM ROLLING, war-related variety; a homefront morale-booster.

BROADCAST HISTORY: Nov. 9, 1941–May 17, 1942, Mutual. 30m, Sundays at 10:30. Office of Emergency Management.
HOST: Clifton Fadiman. ORCHESTRA: Morton Gould. PRODUCER: Arthur Kurlan. THEME: *The Flame of Freedom Is Burning*, written for the series by Richard Rodgers and Lorenz Hart.

Like most patriotic programs of the war years, *Keep 'Em Rolling* had its pick of top screen and stage talent, free of charge. The opening show had Maurice Evans in a short dramatic version of *Valley Forge*, by Maxwell Anderson. Ethel Merman also appeared. Subsequent plays were by such writers as Paul Gallico, Pearl Buck, Lillian Hellman, and Arch Oboler.

KEEPING UP WITH ROSEMARY, drama.

BROADCAST HISTORY: July 4–Sept. 5, 1942, NBC. 30m, Saturdays at 8.
CAST: Fay Wray as Rosemary, reporter for a magazine. Ben Lockwood, Sydney Smith, Ruth McDevitt, Henry M. Neely, Joseph Julian, Raymond Ives.

KEEPSAKES, musical variety.

BROADCAST HISTORY: Sept. 5, 1943–Sept. 24, 1944, Blue Network. 30m, Sundays at 8:30 for Carter Products.

CAST: Metropolitan Opera stars Dorothy Kirsten, soprano, and Mack Harrell, baritone, in programs of "evergreens"—songs with enduring appeal. MUSIC: Harry Sosnik.

THE KEN MURRAY PROGRAM, comedy-variety.

BROADCAST HISTORY: Jan. 4–March 8, 1933, NBC. 30m, Wednesdays at 8. *The Royal Vagabond*. Standard Brands and Royal Gelatin.
March 24–Dec. 15, 1936, CBS. 30m, Tuesdays at 8:30. *Laugh with Ken*. Lifebuoy Soap and Rinso. CAST: Murray; Phil Regan, tenor; Eve Arden, comedienne. ORCHESTRA: Russ Morgan.
March 31–Sept. 22, 1937, CBS. 30m, Wednesdays at 8:30. Campbell Soups. CAST: Murray with vocalist Shirley Ross, Marlyn Stuart, Eve Arden, and Tony Labriola as Oswald, a stooge whose catchphrases—"Oh-h-h yeah-h-h" and "Oh-h-h no-o-o" and "Can't think of it right now"—became brief national favorites. ORCHESTRA: Lud Gluskin.

THE KING'S MEN, vocal quartet.

BROADCAST HISTORY: June 7–Sept. 6, 1949, NBC. 30m, Tuesdays at 9:30. Substitute for *Fibber McGee and Molly*. Johnson's Wax.
CAST: The King's Men (Ken Darby, Rad Robinson, Jon Dodson, Bud Linn), with guests (Dan Dailey, Hoagy Carmichael, etc.). ANNOUNCERS: Harlow Wilcox, Ken Niles. ORCHESTRA: Eliot Daniel. WRITERS: Phil Leslie, Arthur Jones.

KING'S ROW, soap opera, based on the novel by Henry Bellamann.

BROADCAST HISTORY: Feb. 26–Oct. 12, 1951, CBS. 15m, weekdays.
Oct. 15, 1951–Feb. 29, 1952, NBC. 15m, weekdays at 11:30 A.M. Colgate.
CAST: Francis DeSales as Parris Mitchell, chief of psychiatry at State Hospital. Charlotte Manson as Randy Monahan, the young widowed realtor. Susan Douglas as Elise Sandow, Mitchell's frail new wife. Charlotte Holland later as Elise. Chuck Webster and Jim Boles as Fulmer Green, ambitious, ruthless attorney. WRITER: Welbourn Kelley.

KITTY FOYLE, soap opera.

BROADCAST HISTORY: Began as part of a serialized anthology, *Stories America Loves* (CBS,

Oct. 6, 1941–Oct. 2, 1942), which offered modern classics of romance by such authors as Edna Ferber and Christopher Morley. Most popular was Morley's *Kitty Foyle*, the story of a common girl wooed by a son of Philadelphia society, and her trouble adapting to her new life. *Kitty Foyle* began in June 1942, and by Oct. had taken over the *Stories* timeslot (10:15 A.M.), title, and sponsor.

Oct. 5, 1942–June 9, 1944, CBS. 15m continuation, weekdays at 10:15. General Mills. CAST: Julie Stevens as Kitty. Clayton "Bud" Collyer as the indecisive Wyn Strafford. Mark Smith as Pop Foyle.

KITTY KEENE, INCORPORATED, soap opera.

BROADCAST HISTORY: Sept. 13, 1937–April 25, 1941, heard on some NBC, CBS, and Mutual Network stations, 15m, at various times. Procter & Gamble.

CAST: Beverly Younger as Kitty Keene, owner of a detective agency bearing her name. Gail Henshaw and Fran Carlon also as Kitty, who developed as a woman of mystery (she had once been a *Follies* showgirl, and beyond that, listeners and even Kitty's daughter, Jill, knew little). Dorothy Gregory and Janet Logan as Jill. Bob Bailey and Dick Wells as Bob Jones, Kitty's husband. CREATOR-WRITER: Wally Norman. PRODUCERS: George Fogle, Alan Wallace. WRITERS: Day Keene, Lester Huntley. THEME: *None But the Lonely Heart.*

KNICKERBOCKER PLAYHOUSE, dramatic anthology.

BROADCAST HISTORY: May 21–Aug. 9, 1939, CBS. 30m, Sundays at 10 through July 9, then Wednesdays at 9. Procter & Gamble. CAST: Elliott Lewis with guest stars: a big-name Hollywood series, with Walter Huston, Orson Welles, and Franchot Tone in such plays as *Abe Lincoln in Illinois* and *Seventh Heaven.*

Sept. 21, 1940–Jan. 17, 1942, NBC. 30m, Saturdays at 8. Procter & Gamble for Drene Shampoo. A notable departure from the first series, this was a virtual copy of *The First Nighter Program*, with lighthearted romance fare and most of the "theater" trappings—an authoritative host named "Mr. Knickerbocker," a stagehand bustling about warning that the play was about to begin, a buzzer with the announcement "Curtain going up!" that had made the older show a success. Bob Bailey, Barbara Luddy, and other notable radio performers enacted the stories. On Jan. 24, 1942, *Abie's Irish Rose* became the continuing story, and *Knickerbocker Playhouse* was discontinued.

THE KRAFT MUSIC HALL, a major NBC variety show covered under THE BING CROSBY SHOW and THE AL JOLSON SHOW.

BROADCAST HISTORY: June 26, 1933–Sept. 22, 1949, NBC. Mondays for six weeks, then a long-running Thursday night series. Kraft Foods.

The Kraft Music Hall was created to help launch the new salad dressing, Miracle Whip, and soon made it the leading product of its type. The earliest series (June 26, 1933–Dec. 26, 1935) starred Paul Whiteman, with support from singing pianist Ramona, soprano Helen Jepson, tenor Jack Fulton, Roy Bargy, and wisecracking music critic Deems Taylor. Al Jolson was the singing star into and beyond the Whiteman era (Aug. 3, 1933–Aug. 16, 1934), though his tenure was erratic. Bing Crosby occupied the main *KMH* years, Jan. 2, 1936–May 9, 1946. A period of transition, 1945–47, was handled by Edward Everett Horton, Eddie Foy, and Frank Morgan. Al Jolson was again the singing star from Oct. 2, 1947, until May 26, 1949. Nelson Eddy was starred in *Kraft* summer shows in 1947, 1948, and 1949, with Dorothy Kirsten as his costar the last two years.

LADIES BE SEATED, weekday audience show.

BROADCAST HISTORY: June 4, 1943–June 23, 1944, Blue Network. 30m, weekdays at 2:30. *Ed East and Polly.*

June 26, 1944–July 21, 1950, ABC. 30m, weekdays at 2:30, 1944–45; late afternoon, at 3 or 3:30, 1945–49; at noon as of Jan. 1950. Quaker Oats, 1945–47; Philip Morris, 1949–50.

CAST: Ed East and his wife Polly, 1943–44, with Murray Grabhorn and singer Lee Sullivan. Johnny Olson and his wife Penny, ca. 1945–49; Tom Moore, summer host, 1949; Olson again, 1949–50.

Ladies Be Seated had its roots planted in the 1930 series *Sisters of the Skillet*, in which Ed East and Ralph Dumke lampooned the household hints programs. East and his wife reorganized the idea in 1943, with blindfold husband-and-wife gags, spaghetti-eating contests, and other forms of audio slapstick. Interim host Tom Moore dovetailed into a similar series, *Ladies Fair* (Mutual, Jan. 23, 1950–Jan. 1, 1954). In the latter, Moore was assisted by Holland Engle and Don Gordon. Johnny Olson, meanwhile, continued the ABC noon slot as *Johnny Olson's Luncheon Club* (ABC, July 24, 1950–July 20, 1951).

LADY BE BEAUTIFUL, audience show.

BROADCAST HISTORY: Mid-1946, Mutual. 30m, weekdays at 3:30.

HOST: Ben Alexander. **CREATOR-WRITER:** Helen Morgan (not the torch singer).

A hapless victim was plucked from the studio audience to have her appearance criticized by a panel of beauty experts. She was then "made over" before the very ears of the radio audience, while host Alexander commented wryly on the progress ostensibly being made.

THE LAMPLIGHTER, talk show.

BROADCAST HISTORY: Jan. 3, 1936–April 13, 1941, Mutual. 15m, various times, with some gaps in continuity. Host: Jacob Tarshish. Continued into 1942 on the West Coast with Ted Yerxa.

THE LAND OF THE LOST, children's fantasy.

BROADCAST HISTORY: Oct. 9, 1943–Sept. 22, 1945, Blue Network/ABC. 30m, Saturdays at 11:30 A.M.

July 4–Oct. 3, 1944, ABC. 30m, Tuesdays at 7.

Oct. 14, 1945–July 6, 1946, Mutual. 30m, Sundays at 3:30 until mid-Jan., then Saturdays at 11:30 A.M.

Oct. 11, 1947–July 3, 1948, ABC. 30m, Saturdays at 11:30 A.M. Bosco chocolate-flavored milk syrup.

CAST: Isabel Manning Hewson as narrator of a series of undersea fantasy adventures, purportedly her adventures as a child. Betty Jane Tyler as Isabel in childhood. Ray Ives as her brother, Billy, who shared her adventures "in that wonderful kingdom at the bottom of the sea, where all lost things find their way, and where the world is bathed in a shimmering green light." Junius Matthews as Red Lantern, "the wisest fish in the ocean." William Keene and Art Carney also as Red Lantern. ANNOUNCER: Michael Fitzmaurice. CREATOR-WRITER-PRODUCER: Isabel Manning Hewson. DIRECTOR: Cyril Armbrister. VOCAL ARRANGEMENTS: (singing mermaids and such): Peggy Marshall. LYRICS: Barbara Miller. SOUND EFFECTS: Maurice C. Brachhausen, with a realistic underwater ambience.

The Land of the Lost was an enchanted kingdom at the bottom of the sea, a place of white sands and pearly palaces, all ruled by an invisible monarch named King Find-All. Here came everything that was lost on earth—hats, rings, umbrellas, toys—to form the kingdom's streets and avenues and begin their lives anew. There was the Street of Lost Shoes, the Hall of Lost Lamps, the Treasury of Lost Coins, and Lead, Pencilvania, where all lost pencils went. Here lived strange and mysterious sea creatures— Mike Pike with his "fin-feriority complex," Kid Squid the boxing octopus, and Ralph Royster the singing oyster. There was a Lost Game Preserve, where all the lost backgammon and Parcheesi games were kept on file.

Isabel and Billy reached this kingdom with the aid of Red Lantern, the talking fish, who glowed underwater and helped the children find their way past the magic seaweed to the Land of the Lost. The seaweed enabled them to breathe underwater, giving the show a vivid and long-remembered atmosphere. In her narration, Isabel Hewson addressed her listeners as "pollywogs" and reminded them of her motto: "Never say lost."

THE LANDT TRIO, vocal harmony.

BROADCAST HISTORY: 1928–38, NBC, various 15m timeslots, both networks; 1941–46, CBS, various.

The Landt Trio (Dan, Karl, and Jack) came from Scranton, Pa., and became one of early radio's busiest singing groups. They had learned harmony while singing at home for the entertainment of their parents. Their professional act materialized when they began singing with Howard White, a local banker who happened to be a

pianist, also self-taught. Their first air appearances were with White on Stations WGBI and WQAM, Scranton. Encouraged by the response, the four went to New York and successfully auditioned at NBC. They subsequently took part in many prime-time broadcasts and held their own morning series on various networks for more than a dozen years.

Their shows were often billed as *The Landt Trio and White* until 1937, when White died. Curly Mahr filled the accompanist's role, and they were then known as *The Landt Trio and Mahr*.

THE LANNY ROSS SHOW, music and song.

BROADCAST HISTORY: 1929–52, many 15m series sandwiched between the star tenor's appearances on major prime-time variety series.

1929–31, NBC. 15m, Saturdays at 11, 1929–30; Sundays at 11, 1930–31.

June 1–Sept. 16, 1931, NBC. 15m, five a week at noon. *The Hellmann Mayonnaise Troubador.*

Oct. 29, 1931–March 10, 1932, NBC. 30m, Thursdays at 9:30. Maxwell House. Also: Midsummer 1932, 15m, three a week at 7:30. Maxwell House. (These series were stepping stones to *Show Boat*, the biggest variety hour of its day, which premiered on NBC for Maxwell House Oct. 6, 1932, and made Ross a household name.)

1932–33, NBC. 15m, Fridays at 10:45.

Sept. 8, 1934–April 17, 1935, NBC. 30m, Wednesdays at 8:30. Log Cabin Syrup. Harry Salter, band.

July 21–Sept. 22, 1935, Blue Network. 30m, Sundays at 7. Substitute for Jack Benny. *Lanny Ross State Fair Concert*, with Howard Barlow's Concert Orchestra.

Sept. 7, 1937–March 1, 1938, NBC. 60m, Tuesdays at 9:30. *Mardi Gras*. Packard Motors. See THE PACKARD HOUR.

Oct. 9, 1939–May 1, 1942, CBS. 15m, various schedules. Franco-American.

April 1–June 28, 1946, CBS. 15m, weekdays at 7. Evelyn Knight, costar.

1948–52, Mutual. 15m, weekdays at various times, generally late morning or around noon.

Ross was also heard on *Your Hit Parade* (Nov. 1938–Oct. 1939, CBS) and on *The Camel Caravan* (CBS, one season beginning July 1942). He died April 25, 1988.

LASSIE, juvenile adventure.

BROADCAST HISTORY: June 8, 1947–May 30, 1948, ABC. 15m, Sundays at 3. Morrell Packing for Red Heart Dog Food.

June 5, 1948–May 27, 1950, NBC. 15m, Saturdays at 5, 1948–49; at 11 A.M., 1949–50. Morrell.

STAR: Lassie, the wonder dog of the MGM films. DOG TRAINER: Rudd Weatherwax. ANNOUNCER: Charlie Lyon. ORGANIST: John Duffy. PRODUCER: Frank Ferrin. DIRECTOR: Harry Stewart. WRITER: Hobart Donovan.

Lassie was an unusual series in that the canine star did its own acting, with owner-trainer Rudd Weatherwax giving cues and providing on-air narration. The original Lassie (a male named Pal) took "about 15 whining and barking cues a week. He also pants with exquisite nuance, but cannot be depended upon to growl or snarl on cue" (*Time*) Animal imitator Earl Keen was thus on hand to fill in where Lassie failed to speak, and to play the roles of other dogs.

The stories were lighthearted and simple, carried by narration and thin dialogue. But Lassie knew how to please a sponsor. Weatherwax would ask the collie's favorite color and get stony silence to the questions "Is it blue? . . . pink?" . . . then a frenzy of joyous barking as he announced, "It's Red Heart!"

LATITUDE ZERO, science fiction adventure.

BROADCAST HISTORY: Feb. 11–Sept. 27, 1941, NBC, West Coast until June 7, then full network. 30m continuation, Saturdays at 8.

CAST: Lou Merrill as Capt. Craig McKenzie, skipper of a mysterious submarine. SUPPORTING PLAYERS: Bruce Payne, Jack Zoller, Ed Max, Charlie Lung, etc. WRITER: Ted Sherdeman.

Latitude Zero was the first serious attempt to break the science fiction story out of the category of juvenile entertainment. It was remarkable in many ways, deserving of a better run than its one partial season. Almost everything known about the show comes from one surviving disc, the premiere episode.

It opened with three down-on-their-luck adventurers—Brock Spencer, Burt Collins, and Tibbs Canard—battling through a storm in the Bering Sea. The imagery was extraordinary for a sustained adventure series at that time. There

was a huge wind effect, emphasizing the puniness of their boat's engine.

Soon they discover a beached submarine, amazed to find it one smooth shell, with no rivets in sight. Tapping on the shell, they hear an answering tap, an SOS. By code they are directed to open the hatch by an outside combination lock. Inside, they meet Capt. Craig McKenzie and his guard Simba, an enormous black man who cannot be harmed by gunshots. Simba has a fatal-looking chest wound, which heals before their astonished eyes. McKenzie tells them only that he himself built the craft and that his home port is "Latitude Zero." Later, the men see a date engraved on the hull—"launched July 11, 1805." This would mean that McKenzie is at least 150 to 200 years old.

It's a marvelous opening, guaranteed to leave a listener wishing for more. The serial has the gritty feel of an *I Love a Mystery*: unusually realistic for its day. It was billed as "a story of five men against the world—heroic men with ideals and the courage to fight for their Latitude Zero!"

LAVENDER AND NEW LACE, music.

BROADCAST HISTORY: Feb. 16, 1941–Jan. 4, 1942, NBC. 15m, Sundays at 4. Harpsichordist: Sylvia Marlowe. Vocalists: Kay Lorraine, Joan Brooks, Felix Knight.

LAVENDER AND OLD LACE, music.

BROADCAST HISTORY: June 19, 1934–Sept. 23, 1936, CBS. 30m, Tuesdays at 8 until April 14, 1936, then Blue Network, 30m, Wednesdays at 8:30. Bayer Aspirin.

SINGERS: Frank Munn, Lucy Monroe, Fritzi Scheff, etc. ORCHESTRA: Abe Lyman. PRODUCERS: Frank and Anne Hummert.

Lavender followed the Hummert formula established on *Waltz Time* and *American Album of Familiar Music*. Many of the same singers were starred and, like all Hummert shows, it appealed to tradition. It was laden with waltzes and ballads, the lyrical emphasis always on clarity.

LAWYER Q, quiz show with drama.

BROADCAST HISTORY: April 3–June 29, 1947, Mutual. 30m, Thursdays at 8; Sundays at 3 beginning April 27.

HOST: Dennis James. DRAMATIC CAST: Karl Swenson, Joseph Julian, Eleanor Audley, Neil O'Malley, etc.

A jury of twelve was assembled from the audience to hear dramatizations of real court cases, which were enacted. A jackpot, starting at $60, was split among the jury if it guessed the true verdict. The premise was that "common sense is always good law, but good law is not always common sense."

LAWYER TUCKER, comedy-drama.

BROADCAST HISTORY: June 12–Sept. 4, 1947, CBS. 30m, Thursdays at 9. Substitute for Dick Haymes. Autolite.

CAST: Parker Fennelly as Dan Tucker, a lawyer with a rustic respect for the legal system. Maurice Wells as Warren Biggers, Tucker's law partner. Mae Shults as Sarah Tucker, sister and housekeeper. Arthur Anderson as Mark Davis, office boy and "reform school graduate." ANNOUNCER: Don Hancock ORCHESTRA: John Gart. PRODUCER-DIRECTOR: Knowles Entrikin. WRITERS: David Howard, Howard Breslin.

LAZY DAN, THE MINSTREL MAN, song and patter.

BROADCAST HISTORY: March 12, 1933–June 23, 1936, CBS. 15m-30m, various times. Old English Wax.

CAST: Irving Kaufman, tenor, as Lazy Dan.

LEAVE IT TO MIKE, situation comedy; also heard as *Paging Mike McNally*.

BROADCAST HISTORY: June 7, 1945–Feb. 12, 1946, Mutual. 30m, various times.

CAST: Walter Kinsella as Mike. Joan Alexander as his girlfriend, Dinny. Jerry Macy and Hope Emerson as the Berkeleys (Mike's boss and Mrs. Boss).

LEAVE IT TO THE GIRLS, panel show with female panelists.

BROADCAST HISTORY: Oct. 6, 1945–Jan. 21, 1949, Mutual. 30m, Saturdays at 9, 1945–46; Saturdays at 9:30, 1946–47; then Fridays at 8:30.

MODERATOR: Paula Stone. HOST: Ted Malone. PANELISTS: Robin Chandler, Eloise McElhone, Florence Pritchett, Jinx Falkenburg, Ilka Chase, Madge Evans, Dorothy Kilgallen, Lucille Ball, Constance Bennett, Edith Gwynn, Binnie Barnes, Sylvia Sidney, etc. CREATOR-PRODUCER: Martha Rountree. DIRECTORS: Joan Sinclaire, Jean Wright.

Leave It to the Girls was a discussion show in the *Information, Please* mold, described by *Radio Life* as an affair of "bright spontaneity and bristling female wit." Producer Martha Rountree (who also created *Meet the Press*) initially wanted a serious panel discussion by four career women on problems sent in by listeners. But the show became far more comical than serious, focusing on the hazards and joys of male-female relationships. The requisites for the panel were obvious intelligence and a razor-sharp, spontaneous wit. The panel was never allowed to see the questions before the broadcasts, forcing its members to react off the cuff.

Usually there was one slick-talking male on hand (George Jessel, Henry Morgan, etc.) to "defend the men of America." The men were equipped with a whistle that brought the viewpoint to their side, and they were allowed to look at questions in advance (the panel being a four-to-one stacked deck). The series began in New York and moved to Hollywood in 1948. George Brent moderated in the West.

LEE WILEY, singer.

BROADCAST HISTORY: June 10–Sept. 2, 1936, CBS. 15m, Wednesdays at 7.

Lee Wiley was a distinctive singer of popular music and blues, who rose to fame in the summer of 1934 on the Paul Whiteman Kraft show. She was also heard on CBS with Willard Robison's orchestra and then arrived in this unadorned summer series. "I just sing songs," she said. She went on to a long career in jazz, earning great respect from critics and then historians for her husky one-in-a-million voice, which, on such numbers as *You've Got Me Crying Again*, was instantly recognizable to the unseen audience.

LEONIDAS WITHERALL, detective drama.

BROADCAST HISTORY: June 4, 1944–May 6, 1945, Mutual. 30m, Sundays, various evening timeslots.

CAST: Walter Hampden as Leonidas Witherall, amateur sleuth created in the novels of Phoebe Atwood Taylor (writing as Alice Tilton). Ethel Remey as Mrs. Mollet, his housekeeper. **PRODUCER:** Roger Bower. **WRITER:** Howard Merrill.

Leonidas Witherall led a busy life. First, he owned and taught at Meredith, "an exemplary school for boys in a present New England town." On the sly, he was the creator of "Lieutenant Hazeltine," a radio detective who was a "master of every situation." Finally, he was ever stumbling into his own cases of intrigue and murder, where he found himself competing with his creation, the fabulous Hazeltine. There was one other thing about Leonidas: his beard made him a ringer for William Shakespeare. Some people called him Shakespeare: others called him just plain Bill.

LES MISERABLES, the first dramatic effort by Orson Welles and his then-forming *Mercury Theater* group.

BROADCAST HISTORY: July 23–Sept. 3, 1937, WOR-Mutual. 30m continuation, Fridays at 10.
CAST: Orson Welles as Jean Valjean, the thief persecuted for years by the relentless detective, Javert. Martin Gabel as Inspector Javert. Estelle Levy as Cosette, the little girl adopted by Jean Valjean, who becomes the love of his life. Virginia Welles as the older Cosette. Also: Ray Collins, Alice Frost, Agnes Moorehead, Everett Sloane, Bill Johnstone, Peggy Allenby, Hiram Sherman, Betty Garde, Adelaide Klein, Frank Readick. **PRODUCER-DIRECTOR:** Orson Welles.

This classic Victor Hugo story of injustice and persecution hit the air a full year ahead of Orson Welles's famous *Mercury* series. The sprawling novel was scoped into seven half-hour high points, beginning with Jean Valjean's theft of the bishop's silver. All chapters survive in good sound, giving listeners perspective from the beginning of the most talked-about rep company in theater and on radio.

THE LESLIE HOWARD THEATER, drama.

BROADCAST HISTORY: Oct. 6, 1935–March 29, 1936, CBS. 30m, Sundays at 8:30 until Jan., then at 2. Hinds Honey and Almond Cream.
CAST: Leslie Howard, film star, in the title role of *The Amateur Gentleman.* Elizabeth Love, leading

lady. Little else is known, as no shows are available at this writing. Howard's daughter, Leslie Ruth, appeared occasionally.

LET GEORGE DO IT, detective drama

BROADCAST HISTORY: Oct. 18, 1946–Sept. 27, 1954, Mutual–Don Lee, West Coast. 30m, Fridays, then Mondays. Standard Oil.
CAST: Bob Bailey as George Valentine, freelance detective. Olan Soulé as George, ca. 1954. Frances Robinson as his secretary, Claire Brooks ("Brooksie"). Virginia Gregg as Brooksie in later shows. Lillian Buyeff as Brooksie, 1954. Eddie Firestone Jr. as Sonny the office boy, Brooksie's kid brother. Joseph Kearns as Caleb the elevator man. Wally Maher as Lt. Riley. **ANNOUNCER:** John Hiestand. **MUSIC:** Eddie Dunstedter on organ. **PRODUCERS:** Owen and Pauline Vinson. **DIRECTOR:** Don Clark. **WRITERS:** David Victor, Jackson Gillis.

George Valentine obtained his cases with a newspaper ad, which usually got pretitle emphasis: *Personal Notice—Danger's my stock-in-trade. If the job's too tough for you to handle, you've got a job for me, George Valentine.* Despite this, the early George was cerebral in nature, downplaying brawn and playing up his knowledge of science to catch wrongdoers. The show was also heard briefly in New York, Jan. 20, 1954–Jan. 12, 1955, Wednesdays at 9:30, by transcription.

LET'S PRETEND, "radio's outstanding children's theater."

BROADCAST HISTORY: Sept. 7, 1929–March 17, 1934, CBS. 30m, Saturdays at noon or in late-morning timeslots. *The Adventures of Helen and Mary,* forerunner of *Let's Pretend.* **WRITER:** Yolanda Langworthy.
    March 24, 1934–Oct. 23, 1954, CBS. 30m, Saturdays except Jan. 1938–April 1939, when heard twice a week in early evening. Saturday timeslots usually late morning, noon, or early afternoon. Cream of Wheat, 1943–52. **HOST:** "Uncle" Bill Adams. **CAST:** Estelle Levy and Patricia Ryan as Helen and Mary in the pre-*Pretend* era; both continued well into *Let's Pretend,* Levy taking the name Gwen Davies. Many child actors developed especially for this series: Miriam Wolfe, Sybil Trent, the Mauch Twins (Billy and Bobby), Arthur

Anderson, Billy Halop, Nancy Kelly, Roslyn Silber, Dick Van Patten, Anne Francis, Lamont Johnson, Patricia Peardon, Albert Aley, Michael O'Day, Skippy Homeier, Marilyn Erskine, Jack Grimes, Kingsley Colton, Bobby Readick, Vivian Block, Gerrianne Raphael, Patsy O'Shea, Lorna Lynn, Jack Ayers, Alec Englander, Larry Robinson, Robert Lee, Mary Ellen Glass, Barbara Adams, Bill Lipton, Betty Jane Tyler, Judith Lockser, Joan Lazer, Jackie Kelk, Joan Tetzel, Jimmy Lydon, Michael Dreyfuss, Donald Buka, Hope Miller, Evelyn Juster, Lillian Collins, Daisy Aldan, Roger Sullivan, Rita Lloyd, Donald Madden, Lynn Thatcher, Stanley Martin, Diana Hale, Walter Tetley, Jack Jordan, Robert Morea, Jimsey Somers, Julian Altman, Donald Hughes, Florence Halop, Lester Jay, Eddie Ryan, Denise Alexander, Ivan Cury, Anne-Marie Gayer, Dick Etlinger, Elaine Engler, Sidney Lumet, Butch Cavell, Alan Shay. ANNOUNCERS: George Bryan, Jackson Wheeler. ORCHESTRA: Maurice Brown. CREATOR-WRITER-DIRECTOR: Nila Mack. SOUND EFFECTS: Arthur Strand, George O'Donnell, Bill Brown, Jimmy Dwan. TECHNICIAN: Fred Hendrickson (1940s). AFTER MACK'S DEATH IN 1953: Jean Hight, director; Johanna Johnston, writer; Warren Sweeney, announcer.

Perhaps *Newsweek* best summarized its charm in 1943, when *Let's Pretend* was at the peak of its success. It made no attempt to compete with cliffhanger serials: "*Let's Pretend* is filled with kings and queens who ride talking horses through enchanted forests. It has beauteous maidens who must be rescued from witches, dragons, gnomes, dwarfs, and other mythical fauna. Its characters travel in golden coaches, wear purple robes, pass through emerald halls to jade rooms, and drink from golden goblets." By the story's end, the princess had been rescued, the dragon slain, and everyone lived happily ever after.

Let's Pretend was the major life work of Nila Mack, a Kansas woman who had been an actress on Broadway and in vaudeville. She arrived at CBS in 1928, and in August 1930 assumed directorship of the children's show *The Adventures of Helen and Mary*, which had been running on Saturdays for almost a year. Mack felt that the best way to tell a children's story was to let the children tell it: to develop a com-

pany of juvenile talent whose members would be so versatile that they could shift from week to week from leads to character roles, and even into the parts of old people. She favored fairy tales: *The Arabian Nights*, Andrew Lang, Hans Christian Andersen, and the brothers Grimm had regaled her as a child, and she began her work convinced that other children would be similarly enchanted.

The show became a radio laboratory for budding child stars. Mack "trained and directed two generations of child actors," said her *Current Biography*: many of them went on to solid careers on stage, screen, or radio. On *Helen and Mary* she found two talented players immediately: Estelle Levy and Patricia Ryan, who played the title roles. As early as 1930, Levy was able to "age" her voice and play the role of a queen mother. The company was built through a long process of auditions, rehearsals, and tryouts. Mack soon became director of children's programming at CBS. She and her NBC counterpart, Madge Tucker, had open-door policies, allowing any child from any walk of life to be tested. "When a child applies for an audience, it can be told at once if he has the makings," wrote James Street in *Radio Guide*. "If he's got it, he's given a small part on a program. He must first play a child his own age, and when he's mastered that he is given a character part—maybe the role of an old man. His errors are not chalked against him if he can recover his composure. If he makes a mistake and can cover it up by ad-libbing, it's a score in his favor. The ability to think fast on his feet is what counts. He's always given small parts at first to keep him from getting cocky." Thus could Miriam Wolfe, at age 12, vividly portray an 80-year-old witch, developing a specialty she would use for years.

The plays, adapted by Mack, emphasized the virtues of human nature. She modified freely, changing even the classics if the changes suited her notions of "honor, service in a good cause, courtesy, and kindness." She favored enduring tales: *Little Red Riding Hood*, *Cinderella*, *Goldilocks*, and their like were repeated many times. Mack's *House of the World* was the annual Christmas show, promoting the themes of brotherhood and tolerance. In the early years, the children got $3.50 per show—less than half the going rate for sustaining programs—but few complained. Being a regular on *Let's Pretend* had many fringe benefits. The children learned radio acting by doing it, and even among the youngest there was a sense that they were doing something serious.

Among the notables was Sybil Trent, discovered by Mack at a community sing and brought into the company in 1935, at age 9. She remained with the show for years. Arthur Anderson joined the show in 1936 and stayed till the end, 18 years. Bobby and Billy Mauch went on to Hollywood, working in *The Prince and the Pauper* in 1937 and a number of films based on Booth Tarkington's *Penrod*. Roslyn Silber graduated into the long-running role of Rosalie in Gertrude Berg's serial, *The Goldbergs*. Nancy Kelly became a film star; Patricia Peardon went to Broadway and the title role of *Junior Miss*. Maurice Brown was longtime maestro. Mack wanted "carefree" music, "juvenile in spirit while performing the necessary function of establishing the mood and characters of the fantasy." There were lots of violins, and the *Let's Pretend* theme was one of the hallmarks of juvenile radio. In 1943, this was adapted by the "Pretenders" with words to fit the show's only sponsor.

> *Cream of Wheat is so good to eat*
> *Yes, we have it every day.*
> *We sing this song, it will make us strong*
> *And it makes us shout HOORAY!*
> *It's good for growing babies*
> *And grown-ups too to eat.*
> *For all the family's breakfast*
> *You can't beat Cream of Wheat!*

Longtime host for the half-hour, beginning with the Cream of Wheat sponsorship, was "Uncle" Bill Adams, who opened each session with "Hel-looo, Pretenders!" The studio audience would roar its answer: "Helloooo, Uncle Bill!" Bill would then ask, "How do we travel to Let's Pretend?" and one of the kids would answer. "Why don't we go on a railroad train?" might be the suggestion, and up would come the sound effects to take listeners to the land of *Rumpelstiltskin, Beauty and the Beast,* or *The Brave Little Tailor.*

Nila Mack suffered a heart attack and died Jan. 20, 1953. She was lauded as "the fairy godmother of radio," and in the show's final two years the Nila Mack Award was given to the players who gave the best performances.

LET'S TALK HOLLYWOOD, panel discussion and quiz.

BROADCAST HISTORY: July 4–Sept. 26, 1948, NBC. 30m, Sundays at 7. Summer substitute for *The Jack Benny Program.* Lucky Strike.

HOST: George Murphy. PANELISTS: Eddie Bracken weekly; film columnists Edith Gwynn and Erskine Johnson alternating from week to week; the remaining chairs filled by movie stars, technicians, and others close to the film scene.

Let's Talk Hollywood was a flagrant attempt to copy the *Information, Please* formula. Listeners sent in questions about Hollywood films and stars, and the panel, with many humorous asides, tried to answer them, prizes going to those who stumped the experts. For each question used, the listener got a subscription to *Photoplay* magazine; for stumping the panel, he got a gold pass for free admission to his favorite theater all year long. The problem with this show was obvious: George Murphy was not Clifton Fadiman, and the panelists were not John Kieran, Franklin P. Adams, and Oscar Levant.

THE LIBERTY BROADCASTING SYSTEM, a bold venture built around reconstructions of baseball games in progress, and eventually a powerful network of more than 400 stations.

BROADCAST HISTORY: March 1948–May 1952. Began at KLIF, Dallas. *Liberty* was created by Gordon McLendon, a broadcaster who was also its main announcer. Using recorded sound effects (from the crack of a base hit to the cries of vendors in the stands), McLendon was able to recreate with great accuracy the sounds of a live game. The minute-by-minute accounts came into the studio on ticker tape and were turned into action broadcasts with the aid of several assistants and four turntables. McLendon, known on the air as "the Old Scotsman," saw his network grow into a national force before organized baseball rose up to defeat it. Restrictions and outright bans resulted in an antitrust lawsuit by McLendon against baseball, finally settled for $200,000 as *Liberty* disappeared from the scene. The network also offered game shows, news, disc jockeys, and reconstructions of historic games. Other announcers were Wes Wise, Al Turner, Lindsey Nelson, and Jerry Doggett.

THE LIFE AND LOVE OF DR. SUSAN, soap opera.

BROADCAST HISTORY: Feb. 13–Dec. 29, 1939, CBS. 15m, weekdays at 2:15. Lux Flakes.

CAST: Eleanor Phelps as Dr. Susan Chandler, who returns to Valleydale to help her father-in-law practice medicine, after her husband disappears on a South American jungle expedition. Fred Barron as Dr. Howard Chandler, her in-law. Mary Cecil as Miranda Chandler, Susan's mother-in-law. Gloria Mann and Tommy Hughes as Susan's twins, Marilyn and Dickie. ANNOUNCER: Frank Luther. DIRECTOR: Ed Rice. WRITER: Edith Meiser.

LIFE BEGINS, soap opera.

BROADCAST HISTORY: Jan. 22, 1940–July 18, 1941, CBS. 15m, weekdays at 11:15 A.M. Title change to *Martha Webster,* mid-July 1940. Campbell Soups.

CAST: Bess Flynn as Martha Webster, housekeeper with the Craig family. Ray Collins as Alvin Craig, the father. Jimmy Donnelly and Carleton Young as the Craig boys, Dick and Winfield. Betty Philson as Lucy Craig. Toni Gilman as Virginia Craig. Donald Cook as Lloyd Crawford, Virginia Craig's love interest. Ralph Dumke as Wilbur. Jeanette Nolan as Kay Smith. DIRECTOR: Diana Bourbon. WRITER: Bess Flynn.

As this serial began, heroine Martha Webster, a woman in her 40s, found herself penniless in the big city. The storyline followed her efforts to find work and survive.

LIFE BEGINS AT 80, panel show.

BROADCAST HISTORY: July 4, 1948–Sept. 24, 1949, Mutual. 30m, Sundays at 3:30 until Sept. 1948, then Saturdays at 9.

Oct. 1, 1952–May 6, 1953, ABC. 30m, Wednesdays at 8:30. Belltone Hearing Aids.

HOST: Jack Barry. REGULAR PANELISTS (MUTUAL RUN): Fred Stein, 81; Eugenia Woillard, 83; Joseph Rosenthal, 84; Georgiana P. Carhart, 83. Also: Rose Baran, 89; Ella Pomeroy, "81-plus"; Pop Gordon, 92; and Capt. Edwin Lane, 81, a former sea captain with a long white beard. CREATOR: Jack Barry. PRODUCER: Dan Enright (Ehrenreich).

Life Begins at 80 was patterned in reverse after Jack Barry's successful *Juvenile Jury.* On *Jury,*

Barry assembled a panel of children, ages 5 to 12, to discuss the problems of their peers. On *80,* the panelists were octogenarians at least, and they offered uninhibited talk about almost anything. The panelists were so frank that Barry had to tape it and censor the indelicate slips of tongue for the air. On the earliest panels, Rosenthal was said to be the deep thinker, and Carhart was a shameless flirt. Barry closed the show each week with a piece of dubious philosophy from Julia Ward Howe, who wrote of old age, at 90, that "all the sugar is at the bottom of the cup."

LIFE CAN BE BEAUTIFUL, soap opera.

BROADCAST HISTORY: Sept. 5–Nov. 4, 1938, NBC. 15m, weekdays at 4:30. Procter & Gamble.

Nov. 7, 1938–June 21, 1946, CBS. 15m, weekdays at 1:15 until 1940, then at 1. Procter & Gamble for Ivory Soap, etc. Concurrent broadcasts: July 3, 1939–April 25, 1941, NBC. 15m, weekdays at 9:45 A.M., 1939–40; then at 5:45, 1940–41. Ivory Soap.

June 24, 1946–June 25, 1954, NBC. 15m, weekdays at 3, Procter & Gamble for Ivory Soap and Spic and Span.

CAST: Alice Reinheart as Carol Conrad, waif from the streets who became known as "Chichi," fiery and impetuous. Teri Keane also as Chichi. Ralph Locke as Papa David Solomon, owner of the Slightly Read Bookshop, who took in Chichi and gave her a home. John Holbrook as Stephen Hamilton, a hopeless cripple, also taken in by Papa David. Earl Larrimore also as Stephen Hamilton. Carl Eastman as Toby Nelson, Chichi's "chum from the streets." Waldemar Kappel and Paul Stewart as Gyp Mendoza, bully of the neighborhood. Richard Kollmar and Dick Nelson as Barry Markham, another of Chichi's boyfriends. Charles Webster and Peggy Allenby as Dr. and Mrs. Markham. Ruth Weston as Maude Kellogg. Adelaide Klein as Mrs. S. Kent Wadsworth. Roger DeKoven as Dr. Myron Henderson. ANNOUNCERS: Ralph Edwards, Ed Herlihy, Don Hancock, Ron Rawson, Bob Dixon. PRODUCER-DIRECTORS: Don Becker, Oliver Barbour, Chick Vincent, etc. WRITERS: Don Becker and Carl Bixby.

Life Can Be Beautiful was one of the strongest soaps of radio. To radio insiders, it was soon known by its initials and was widely referred to as "Elsie Beebe." It was the story of Carol Conrad, child of the ghetto, who—still in her teens—ran into a used-book store seeking shelter and a hiding place from Gyp Mendoza, the town racketeer.

The kindly old book dealer, Papa David Solomon, was soon to become one of the great philosophers of daytime radio. Carol became "Chichi" and was installed on a pallet in the back room as the old man's ward. Fifteen years later, she was still there: *Time*, in a rare look at daytime radio, found her romances with two men (a "levelheaded lawyer" and a "headstrong young doctor") then at the heart of the serial. Which one did Chichi really love? The answer *Time* believed less important than the serial's general outlook. "Actually Elsie Beebe ranges less frequently over the tearstained world of suffering women than many of its kind, prides itself on its philosophic asides."

In fact, *LCBB* had its share of tears and trouble. It wasn't philosophy that booted it into the daytime top ten soon after its premiere and kept it there (including a period of unusual double-network status, 1939–41) for most of its 16-year run. Chichi had fallen in love with crippled law student Stephen Hamilton, whose disability was offset by a keen intellect. Chichi, impressed by Stephen's mind, was amazed that she could be loved by such a man. Their romance was interminable, on again and off for seven years as one thing after another disrupted their lives. The disruptions were standard serial fare—Stephen's self-pity, jealousy, spite, and the ever-present fickle nature of soap opera males. In 1943, Stephen ran off to California with Maude Kellogg. At another point, he was partly cured of his paralysis in an amazing operation, but lost his legs again in an accident.

Enough was enough. In the sixth year, listeners began clamoring for a marriage, and writers Don Becker and Carl Bixby (identified as "Beckby" in *Time*, with no distinction as to who was speaking) yielded to the crowd. Chichi and Stephen were married, and almost immediately Beckby realized this was a mistake. Alone, Chichi had been the most exciting of daytime heroines. Saddled now with a whiny husband and then a child, she was hamstrung. Beckby did the obvious: "We had the baby die of pneumonia after Stephen had taken him out in the rain, and then we killed *him* off with a heart attack. For two weeks afterward we kept Chichi off the air

in the interests of good taste, and that was that." Stephen was never mentioned again.

The true constant in her life was Papa David, who had become a father in every sense. Her other reliable man was Toby Nelson, her "chum from the streets," who loved her passionately but without hope. To Chichi he was "just a pal," a shoulder to cry on, someone who never paid much attention to her, she thought. Toby disappeared in Korea near the end of the run.

The show was billed as "an inspiring message of faith drawn from life." Beckby began each show with some heavy piece of philosophical profundity. Often it was, "John Ruskin wrote this—*Whenever money is the principal object of life, it is both got ill and spent ill, and does harm both in getting and spending; when getting and spending happiness is our aim, life can be beautiful.*" Also much-used was "Longfellow expressed the opinion that the Sabbath is the golden clasp that binds together the volume of the week—by the way, how long has it been since you've been to church, where you'll find new assurances that life can be beautiful."

A LIFE IN YOUR HANDS, murder melodrama and courtroom procedural.

BROADCAST HISTORY: 1949–52, NBC/ABC, summer status only. Breakdown as follows:

June 7–Sept. 13, 1949, and again June 27–Sept. 12, 1950, NBC. 30m, Tuesdays at 10:30. Substitute for *People Are Funny*. Raleigh Cigarettes.

June 29–Sept. 21, 1951, ABC. 30m, Fridays at 9. Substitute for *The Adventures of Ozzie and Harriet*. Heinz Foods.

July 10–Aug. 21, 1952, NBC. 30m, Thursdays at 8. Substitute for *Father Knows Best*. Sustained.

CAST: Ned LeFevre (1949) as Jonathan Kegg, "amicus curiae," or "friend of the court." Carleton KaDell as Jonathan Kegg, 1950 and again in 1952. Lee Bowman as Jonathan Kegg, 1951. ANNOUNCER: Myron (Mike) Wallace, ca. 1949; also, Ken Nordine. MUSIC: Adele Scott, Bernard "Whitey" Berquist. CREATOR: Erle Stanley Gardner. PRODUCER-DIRECTORS: Jack Simpson, Patrick Murphy, John Cowan, Homer Heck. WRITER: Bob McKee. Doug Johnson, etc.

Jonathan Kegg, the fictitious hero of *A Life in Your Hands*, represented neither the prosecution nor the defense in these murder stories, but was allowed to examine witnesses on both sides in order to learn the truth. Erle Stanley Gardner contributed only his name.

THE LIFE OF MARY SOTHERN, soap opera.

BROADCAST HISTORY: 1934–36, WLW, Cincinnati.

Nov. 4, 1935–April 30, 1937, Mutual. 15m, weekdays at 4:15. Hinds Honey and Almond Cream.

Oct. 4, 1937–April 22, 1938, CBS. 15m, weekdays at 5:15. Hinds.

1939–43, transcribed release to independents.

CAST: Minabelle Abbott as Mary Sothern in "the fast-paced story of a young mother who finds it difficult to keep her well-meaning husband's two feet on the ground." Fran Carlon and Betty Caine also as Mary. Jack Zoller, Joseph Julian, and Leon Janney as Danny Stratford. Florence Golden as Danny's wife Phyllis. Jay Jostyn as "impulsive" Max Tilley, who vied with Dr. John Benson in a good-natured battle for Mary's hand, and emerged victorious. Jerry Lesser as John Benson. Frank Lovejoy as Chaney. ANNOUNCER: Ken Roberts. DIRECTOR: Chick Vincent. WRITER: Don Becker. THEME: *Just a Little Love, a Little Kiss.*

THE LIFE OF RILEY, situation comedy.

BROADCAST HISTORY: April 12–Sept. 6, 1941, CBS. 30m, Saturdays at 10 A.M. until July, then at 11 A.M. This early *Life of Riley* bore scant resemblance to the far better known William Bendix series that followed. CAST: Lionel Stander as J. Riley Farnsworth, a rough-cut gadabout with a heart of gold. Grace Coppin as Maude, an old maid. Jackie Grimes as Davie, her nephew. Peggy Conklin as Peggy, daughter of the richest man in town and Riley's love object. ANNOUNCERS: Jackson Wheeler, George Bryan, etc. DIRECTORS: Leonard Bercovici, Marx Loeb. WRITERS: Bercovici, Sidney Harmon.

Jan. 16, 1944–July 8, 1945, Blue Network/ABC. 30m, Sundays at 3 through June 1944, then Sundays at 10. American Meat Institute.

Sept. 8, 1945–June 29, 1951, NBC. 30m, Saturdays at 8 until the mid-1948 summer break; Fridays at 10, 1948–49; Fridays at 9, late 1949; Fridays at 10 beginning Jan. 1950. Procter & Gamble for Teel, Prell, etc., 1945–49; Pabst Beer, 1949–51.

1944–51: CAST: William Bendix as Chester A. Riley, radio's resident hard-hat, riveter in a California aircraft plant. Paula Winslowe as Riley's long-suffering wife Peg. Conrad Binyon and Sharon Douglas initially as the Riley children, Junior and Babs. Scotty Beckett, Jack Grimes, Bobby Ellis, and Tommy Cook later as Junior. Barbara Eiler as Babs as of January 1947. Hans Conried as Uncle Baxter, a permanent nonpaying guest who never let Riley forget that he had once loaned him a pint of blood. John Brown as Riley's coworker and pal, Gillis. John Brown also as Digby O'Dell, "the friendly undertaker." Francis "Dink" Trout as Waldo Binny. Charlie Cantor as Uncle Buckley. Shirley Mitchell as Honeybee Gillis. ANNOUNCERS: Ken Niles (ca. 1944); Ken Carpenter for P&G; Jimmy Wallington for Pabst. ORCHESTRA: Lou Kosloff. CREATOR-PRODUCER: Irving Brecher. DIRECTORS: Al Kaye, Don Bernard. WRITERS: Alan Lipscott and Reuben Ship, with Ashmead Scott, Robert Sloane. and Dick Powell (not the actor of the same name). SOUND EFFECTS: Monty Fraser, etc.

The Life of Riley in its best-known version evolved from a prospective Groucho Marx vehicle called *The Flotsam Family.* The Marx series failed at audition when the would-be sponsor wouldn't accept Groucho in what was, for him, a straight role—as head of a family. Then producer Irving Brecher saw a film, *The McGuerins of Brooklyn*, with a rugged-looking and typically American blue-collar man, William Bendix, in one of the leading roles. There, on the screen, was his character. A new audition was recorded, with Bendix as star and the character renamed Chester A. Riley. It became a solid midlevel hit.

Riley was a true no-brainer. He was easily exasperated but difficult to defeat. The difficulty increased by degrees with the flimsiness of Riley's cause, his character best revealed on thin ice. A leaking roof, trouble at the aircraft plant where he worked, or the manifestations of his kids' growing problems were enough to send Riley scurrying off into pandemonium. Wife Peg tried to remain the loving spouse, but even she had limits. The children, Junior and Babs, were awed and often dismayed by the bullheaded determination their father could muster. And as he blundered through the half-hour, Riley was given questionable advice by his coworker Gillis and by Digby (Digger) O'Dell, the "friendly undertaker''—two widely dissimilar characters played by one talent, John Brown.

Gillis played a role not unlike Ozzie Nelson's neighbor Thorny, but with more sarcasm. Digger O'Dell was good for one walk-on per show, a tête-à-tête that always led to a funny series of black humor and undertaker jokes. "The grass is always greener on the other fellow," Digger would say in that clammy baritone. Brecher approached the undertaker character carefully, knowing that death was seldom a suitable subject for radio comedy. But Digger soared in popularity, and was most popular with those in the undertaker's profession. He always arrived with the stock phrase "You're looking fine, Riley—*very* natural" and departed with "Cheerio—I'd better be . . . shoveling off."

Bendix came out of the New Jersey Federal Theater project, a latecomer to the profession, beginning at 30 when the grocery store he was running was closed by the Depression. His film career began in 1942, in a string of similar roles, the beefy tough guy with the heart of gold. Riley was his best-remembered character. The constantly heard grumble "What a revoltin' development this is" became a national catchphrase.

A TV version opened on NBC Oct. 4, 1949. Bendix was contractually unavailable, and Jackie Gleason became the first Riley on television. Rosemary DeCamp, Lanny Rees, and Gloria Winters were the supporting players, with Sid Tomack as Jim Gillis. John Brown as Digger O'Dell was the only member of the radio cast who made the transition. But with the Bendix series still airing on radio, Gleason was an unacceptable Riley, and the show expired March 28, 1950. A Bendix filmed TV version was seen on NBC Jan. 2, 1953–Aug. 22, 1958. Marjorie Reynolds was Peg, Wesley Morgan was Junior, Lugene Sanders played Babs, and Tom D'Andrea was Gillis. Digger O'Dell did not appear in this run.

Bendix died Dec. 8, 1964, at age 58. It was said that he had always looked 58.

LIFE WITH LUIGI, situation comedy.

BROADCAST HISTORY: Sept. 21, 1948–March 3, 1953, CBS. 30m, Tuesdays at 9 for most of the run; heard Sundays Jan.–Sept. 1949. Wrigley's Gum, 1950–53. Also noted in a 15m strip-show format, ca. 1954.

CAST: J. Carrol Naish as Luigi Basco, Italian immigrant who grew up on the outskirts of Rome and became the center of a "clash of cultures" comedy theme when he came to live and open an antique store in Chicago. Alan Reed as Pasquale, Luigi's sponsor in America, owner of Pasquale's Spaghetti Palace in the Little Italy section of Chicago. Jody Gilbert as Rosa, Pasquale's fat daughter. Gil Stratton as Jimmy, Luigi's young partner in the antique business. Mary Shipp as Miss Spaulding, teacher at the night school class where Luigi studied citizenship and government so as to be a credit to his new country. Hans Conried as Schultz, a crusty German also enrolled in night school. Joe Forte and Ken Peters, respectively, as Luigi's other classmates, Horowitz and Olsen. ANNOUNCERS: Bob LeMond, 1948; later, Bob Stevenson. ORCHESTRA: Wilbur Hatch, 1948; Lyn Murray by mid-1949; Lud Gluskin, later. CREATOR-PRODUCER: Cy Howard. DIRECTORS: William N. Robson, 1948; then Mac Benoff. WRITERS: Hy Kraft and Arthur Stander, ca. 1948; later, Mac Benoff and Lou Derman. SOUND EFFECTS: Jack Dick, Ray Kemper, James Murphy, etc. THEME: *Chicago* by the full orchestra, blending into an Italian-sounding *Oh, Marie*, on accordion.

Life with Luigi, conceived as *The Little Immigrant*, was announced by that title and changed just before the first broadcast. Its creator, Cy Howard, gave up a salesman's job to become one of the big success stories of radio's dwindling days. By some accounts, Howard was a shy introvert when he decided to change his ways and turn his life around. He created *My Friend Irma*, and soon, with *Luigi*, he had two of radio's most popular shows. *Luigi* had the tougher schedule, opposite Bob Hope, but within a year the sitcom had pulled even with Hope and in some surveys had topped him.

The show had a remarkable cast, so skilled in the uses of ethnic dialogue that listeners completely bought the Italian scenario (though the title role was played by an Irishman). Luigi Basco was by nature a shy man with a sweet and loving disposition, consumed with the hope of someday becoming an American citizen. In his night school class, he met other newcomers from Germany and Scandinavia. The funniest of these was Schultz, whose rheumatism was always killing him.

Soon after his arrival in Chicago, Luigi rented a building adjacent to Pasquale's Spaghetti Palace and opened his antique store. But it didn't take long for *Luigi* to settle into one long storyline—Pasquale's ruthless campaign to persuade, bribe, or coerce Luigi to marry his daughter, Rosa. Luigi was awed by Rosa: her 300-pound frame, the squeaky voice, the giggles, and the stinging belly laugh were prime staples of the program. Pasquale was a lying, conniving plotter, a heartless saboteur of Luigi's love life. At the end, he always had Rosa on hand to help pick up the pieces of Luigi's broken heart. "Just so happen I'm-a bring-a my little baby with-a me. I'm-a gonna call-er over . . . Oh, Roooosssa! . . . Roooosssa! . . . *ROSA!!*" And Rosa would shriek, "You call me, Papa?" And Pasquale would purr, "Say allo to Luigi." And Rosa would erupt with the loudest fat-girl laugh in all radio, ending with a squeaky "Hello, Luigi."

The situations were framed by the accordion, with *Oh, Marie* playing softly in the background. The premise was that each episode was a letter by Luigi to his Mamma Basco in Italy. "Dear-a Mamma-mia," he would begin. At the end the accordion came up for the closing theme. "So long-a, Mamma-mia. Your lovin-a son-a, Luigi Basco, the li'l immigrant."

THE LIGHT OF THE WORLD, serial drama based on the Bible.

BROADCAST HISTORY: March 18, 1940–June 2, 1950. 15m, continuations, various weekday timeslots. NBC until June 5, 1944; CBS from June 1944–Aug. 1946; resumed on NBC Dec. 2, 1946, to the end of the run. Softasilk, 1940; General Mills, 1941–50.

CAST: Bret Morrison as "the Speaker," the deity-like narrator who spoke his lines from an echo chamber. David Gothard and Arnold Moss also as the Speaker. New York radio players in continuing biblical roles. Albert Hayes and Eleanor Phelps as Adam and Eve. Philip Clarke as Adam, ca. mid-1940s. Mandel Kramer and Chester Stratton as Cain and Abel, 1944. Bernard Lenrow as Nebucadnezzar. Richard Coogan as Jonathan. Barbara Fuller as Jehosheba. Ogden Miles as Jehoida. Mitzi Gould as the evil queen Athaliah. Sanford Bickart as Aram. Humphrey Davis as Shallum. William Hollenback as Daniel. Inge Adams as Elona. Louise Fitch and John Thomas as Astra the slave girl and Caleb, fictitious characters. *CBS run:* Louise Fitch as Deborah, daughter of the freed slave Astra. John Griggs as Mattan. Charles Webster as Jehoida. Alexander Scourby as Jonathan. **ANNOUNCERS:** James Fleming, Stuart Metz, Ted Campbell, etc. **MUSIC:** Clark Whipple on organ. **PRODUCER:** Don Becker **DIRECTOR:** Basil Loughrane (both networks). **WRITERS:** Katharine and Adele Seymour. **SOUND EFFECTS:** Jack Anderson. **ADVISORY BOARD:** Rabbi Abraham Burstein, Dr. Everett Clinchy, Rev. John LaFarge, and Dr. James Moffatt of the Union Theological Seminary.

Though it purported to be "the story of the Bible, an eternal beacon lighting man's way through the darkness of time," *Light of the World* bore much resemblance to the soap operas that surrounded it in the daytime schedule. The daily installments often ended with what *Time* described as a "regulation cliff-hang." *Will Adam tell Cain and Abel why their parents were kicked out of the Garden of Eden? And if he does, what will the unmanageable Cain do?*

There was great apprehension when *Light of the World* was announced with the intent of modernizing Scripture. Dialogue would be created, and scenes that were only suggested in ancient texts would be fully developed and fleshed out. The public would not stand for this, critics predicted.

The critics were wrong. The serial leaped into high single digits, most respectable for daytime, and the feedback from biblical scholars was largely positive. A real attempt was made to be historically accurate—no slang would be allowed, and there would be no false sound effects, with only an occasional swish of robes or the rustle of opening parchment breaking the silence. But certain liberties were taken: fictitious characters were inserted to help move the action. "It has sometimes been necessary to invent women who must have existed though they were not mentioned," said *Tune In* in 1944. "Because of the comparative unimportant social position of women in Old Testament days, many wives and mothers were never identified" and had to be written into the script.

In 1946, General Mills dropped the show in the midst of a flour shortage. The outcry was great, and the serial resumed, beginning anew with the story of Adam and Eve.

LIGHTS OUT, horror drama.

BROADCAST HISTORY: Jan. 1, 1934–April 10, 1935, WENR, Chicago. 15m weekly until April 1934, then 30m weekly; Mondays, then Wednesdays; usually heard around midnight. **CREATOR-WRITER:** Wyllis Cooper.

April 17, 1935–Aug. 16, 1939, NBC. 30m Wednesdays at 11:30 (sometimes after midnight). Aired from Chicago. **CAST:** Film stars, notably Boris Karloff, in lead roles, with Chicago radio regulars in other leads and in support: Harold Peary, Betty Winkler, Mercedes McCambridge, Willard Waterman, Arthur Peterson, Betty Caine, Ed Carey, Sidney Ellstrom, Murray Forbes, Robert Griffin, Robert Guilbert, Rupert LaBelle, Philip Lord, Raymond Edward Johnson, etc. **WRITER-PRODUCER-DIRECTOR:** Wyllis Cooper until ca. May 1936, then Arch Oboler. **SOUND EFFECTS:** Bob Graham, Ed Joyce, Ed Bailey.

Oct. 6, 1942–Sept. 28, 1943, CBS. 30m, Tuesdays at 8. Ironized Yeast. Broadcast from New York; later from Hollywood. **CAST:** Arch Oboler, host, with regular players Irene Tedrow, Lou Merrill, Gloria Blondell, Wally Maher, Ted Maxwell, Earle Ross, Tom Lewis, Theodore von Eltz and Templeton Fox (an actress who had also worked the show in Chicago). **WRITER-PRODUCER-DIRECTOR:** Arch Oboler. **SOUND EFFECTS:** Bill Brown, Jerry McCarty.

July 14–Sept. 1, 1945, NBC. 30m, Saturdays at 8:30 from New York. *Fantasies from Lights Out*, new versions of old Wyllis Cooper scripts. **CAST:** Will Geer, Mason Adams, Lon Clark, Edgar Stehli, Betty Winkler, Alexander Scourby, Vinton Hayworth, Bill Griffis, etc.

July 6–Aug. 24, 1946, NBC. 30m, Saturdays at 10 from New York. A mix of Cooper stories and adaptations from Dickens. **NARRATOR:** Boris Aplon. **DIRECTOR:** Albert Crews.

July 16–Aug. 6, 1947, ABC. 30m, Wednesdays at 10:30 from Hollywood. Schick. **MUSIC:** Leith Stevens. **WRITER:** Wyllis Cooper, with Paul Pierce. **DIRECTOR:** Bill Lawrence.

1970–73: transcribed syndication of original broadcasts from ca. 1942–43, under the title *The Devil and Mr. O.* **HOST:** Arch Oboler.

With its premiere on the nationwide NBC hookup in 1935, *Lights Out* was billed "the ultimate in horror." Never had such sounds been heard on the air. Heads rolled, bones were crushed, people fell from great heights and splat-tered wetly on pavement. There were garrotings, chokings, heads split by cleavers, and, to a critic at *Radio Guide*, "the most monstrous of all sounds, human flesh being eaten." Few shows had ever combined the talents of actors and imaginative writers so well with the graphic art of the sound technician. In April 1935, *Newsweek* reported that one listener fainted from excitement and another called police to her home after listening to the show. "I was frightened out of my wits," she said.

Wyllis Cooper, who created, wrote, and produced it, was then a 36-year-old staffer in Chicago's NBC studios. Cooper, *Newsweek* continued, created his horror "by raiding the larder." For the purposes of *Lights Out* sound effects, people were what they ate. The sound of a butcher knife rending a piece of uncooked pork was, when accompanied by shrieks and screams, the essence of murder to a listener alone at midnight. Real bones were broken—spareribs snapped with a pipe wrench. Bacon in a frypan gave a vivid impression of a body just electrocuted. And that cannibalism effect was actually a zealous actor, gurgling and smacking his lips as he slurped up a bowl of spaghetti. Cabbages sounded like human heads when chopped open with a cleaver, and carrots had the pleasant resonance of fingers being lopped off. Arch Oboler's celebrated tale of a man turned inside-out by a demonic fog was accomplished by soaking a rubber glove in water and stripping it off at the microphone while a berry basket was crushed at the same instant. The listener saw none of this. The listener saw carnage and death.

Cooper left the show in 1936 for a minor Hollywood screenwriting career (*Son of Frankenstein* and some of the Mr. Moto movies were his work), and Oboler was given the job. Oboler lost no time establishing himself as the new master of the macabre. Between May 1936 and July 1938, he wrote and directed more than 100 *Lights Out* plays. "It was here that he developed his much-copied stream-of-consciousness technique," wrote historian Ray Stanich in 1974. Stanich, who also compiled the detailed log giving many of the precise *Lights Out* dates and players, remembered other well-known Oboler techniques learned in those early *Lights Out* plays: his unusual use of sound effects, the sharp, terse dialogue, the mastery of precise timing.

"His first play, *Burial Services*, concerned the

burial of a paralyzed girl who was still alive. It caused such a furor (more than 50,000 letters were written to NBC) that Oboler would never again write a story with such a personal theme that could adversely affect a vast audience.'' Oboler remembered it this way: "I had taken a believable situation and underwritten it so completely that each listener filled the silences with the terrors of his own soul. When the coffin lid closed inexorably on the conscious yet cataleptically paralyzed young girl in my play, the reality of the moment, to thousands of listeners who had buried someone close, was the horrifying thought that perhaps sister, or brother, or mother, had also been buried . . . alive.''

To follow Cooper was a challenge: he was "the unsung pioneer of radio dramatic techniques," Oboler acknowledged, but Oboler had passed the test with his first play. His own name soon became synonymous with murder and gore, though horror as a genre had always left him cold. Oboler aspired to more serious writing. "He tried to write two camouflaged 'message' plays for every straight horror drama,'' said Stanich. An example of such was the story of three travelers who crash their car and are thrown back into prehistoric times. They encounter a Neanderthal man who doesn't respond to reason and must be shot. "This is Oboler's oblique approach to alerting the public that tyranny could only be dealt with by force of arms, not appeasement.''

As his fame grew, Oboler found himself in the enviable though frightening position of competing with himself. Each week he strove to top his last performance, an exhausting and ultimately impossible goal. But the pursuit produced seasonal high spots that kept his name on radio front burners. Hollywood stars listened, and some made the trip to Chicago to appear on *Lights Out*. Boris Karloff arrived in April 1938, for four consecutive Oboler shows capped by the famous and long-remembered *Cat Wife*. This tale of a man whose wife turns into a human-sized cat was joined on the list of notables by *Revolt of the Worms* and *Chicken Heart*. Both latter shows used the theme of sudden growth, of the commonplace transforming into the bizarre and terrifying. In *Worms*, a scientist's formula tossed into a yard makes earthworms grow larger than houses, a vivid play climaxed by the suffocation of the principal characters in a slithering wall of wet flesh. *Chicken Heart* took it to even greater effect: that tiny organ kept growing until—with a dull thump-THUMP, thump-THUMP, thump-THUMP—it consumed the world.

Like the plays, the signatures made good use of sinister imagery. Churchbells and a gong were the usual effects. The 1930s show opened with twelve somber chimes. In subsequent versions, announcers played with the notion of midnight as a force frightening unto itself. *This is the witching hour! . . . it is the hour when dogs howl, and evil is let loose on the sleeping world. Want to hear about it? Then turn out your lights!*

By July 1938, Oboler had had enough of it. In Hitler he had seen the real dark man, and he decided to move on to the capitals of serious radio, New York and Hollywood, and fight the Nazi menace with more direct and powerful mainstream plays. *Lights Out* continued from Chicago for another year, written and directed by other NBC staffers. In 1942, Oboler resurrected the series from New York. He was still busy with patriotic broadcasts, so he recycled some of his scripts from the Chicago run. Oboler was his own host, Bob LeMond was the announcer, and the series again utilized the familiar signatures of the gongs. The gong took on the tempo of a metronome, and with each chime Oboler spoke a single word: "It . . . is . . . later . . . than . . . you . . . think.'' Among the classics heard by many for the first time were *Revolt of the Worms, Cat Wife, Chicken Heart*, and *Valse Triste*. Aired for the first time at a viable hour, this became the best-remembered year of the sporadic run.

Thereafter, it was relegated to summer status. Oboler had taken his leave once and for all, returning to *Lights Out* material only in syndication almost three decades later. The summer shows of 1945–47 consisted largely of old Cooper scripts. As far as radio was concerned, it ended there. A TV version ran on NBC ca. 1949–52, but the legend of *Lights Out* is firmly rooted in the radio days.

Oboler's shows are well represented on tape, many in their full 1942–43 network versions, many more as syndicated in the *Devil and Mr. O.* offerings of 1970–73. That Oboler was an innovator is beyond doubt: love him or hate him, almost everyone in radio will give him that. If his horror plays do not often stand the test of time, it may simply be that freedoms of the modern age have allowed so much more graphic horror to be seen as well as heard. What frightened so deeply 50 years ago can seem dated and even preposterous today.

Still to be unearthed at this writing are the bulk of the Cooper shows. Cooper's reputation today, among connoisseurs of radio horror, is probably higher than Oboler's, though Oboler is far better known to the rank and file. Cooper's standing rests largely upon his eerie show *Quiet, Please* (1947–49). In a handful of collectible shows, that series produced two horror masterpieces, giving Cooper a modern-day cult following that ensures avid interest in his *Lights Out* plays, should they exist and someday be discovered.

LI'L ABNER, comedy serial, based on the comic strip by Al Capp.

BROADCAST HISTORY: Nov. 20, 1939–Dec. 6, 1940, NBC. 15m, weekdays at 6:45.
CAST: John Hodiak as Li'l Abner, hillbilly of the mythical village Dogpatch. Laurette Fillbrandt as Daisy Mae, Abner's curvy girlfriend. Hazel Dopheide and Clarence Hartzell as Mammy and Pappy Yokum. **ANNOUNCER:** Durward Kirby.

Film star of the future John Hodiak began his career with this role, beating out 170 actors by being able to distinguish traditional southern speech from the "mountain kentry" dialect required. As Abner, he loved his "po'k chops."

LINCOLN HIGHWAY, dramatic anthology.

BROADCAST HISTORY: March 16, 1940–June 6, 1942, NBC. 30m, Saturdays at 10 A.M., 1940–41; at 11 A.M., 1941–42. Shinola Shoe Polish.
CAST: Top stars of Broadway and Hollywood, including Ethel Barrymore, Joe E. Brown, Harry Carey, Claude Rains, Victor Moore, Gladys George, Luise Rainer, Ruth Gordon, etc. **HOST-ANNOUNCER:** John McIntire. **DIRECTORS:** Don Cope, Theodora Yates, Maurice Lowell. **WRITERS:** Jack Hasty, Brian Byrne, Ed Sherry.

Lincoln Highway offered the kind of dramatic stories usually reserved for prime time, and thus began a trend toward quality programming on Saturday mornings. The stories were of people scattered along the 3,000-mile length of U.S. Route 30, which stretched from Philadelphia to Portland and was popularly known as the Lincoln Highway. Most surprising, even to radio insiders, was the long line of top performers willing to appear at that time of day. Listeners could rise on days off and hear Burgess Meredith portraying a young man who flees the city for farm life, or Raymond Massey as the owner of a trailer camp somewhere in middle America.

LINDA'S FIRST LOVE, soap opera.

BROADCAST HISTORY: 1939—ca. 1950, transcribed 15m continuation.
CAST: Arline Blackburn as Linda, "a girl in love with the world around us, and in love with wealthy young Kenneth Woodruff."

This violin-filled soap opera told of the romance between a shop girl and a society man. Listeners were actually solicited to contribute plot complications, the lowest common denominator factor in action.

THE LINEUP, police drama.

BROADCAST HISTORY: July 6, 1950–Feb. 20, 1953, CBS. 30m, many timeslots and schedule changes. Mostly sustained; Wrigley's Gum and Plymouth, briefly in 1952.
CAST: Bill Johnstone as Lt. Ben Guthrie, police officer in a great American city. Joseph Kearns as Sgt. Matt Grebb. Wally Maher as Grebb from ca. 1951. Support from Hollywood regulars: John McIntire, Raymond Burr, Jeanette Nolan, Sheldon Leonard, Howard McNear, etc. **MUSIC:** Eddie Dunstedter. **PRODUCER-DIRECTOR:** Elliott Lewis, 1950; then Jaime del Valle. **WRITERS:** Morton Fine and David Friedkin, 1950; Blake Edwards later.

The Lineup took its listeners behind the scenes of a police headquarters "where under the cold, glaring lights pass the innocent, the vagrant, the thief, the murderer." The police lineup opened and closed each broadcast: Sgt. Grebb would be heard instructing the prisoners and thus setting up how the case was investigated and solved. *Dragnet* was the trendsetter in police drama, and realism was what each new show was striving for. Grebb was quick-tempered and often bored: Lt. Guthrie was soft-spoken and calm. There were few heroics, said *Newsweek*: "Everything they do is just a job." Director del Valle and scripter Edwards cruised with police and watched many lineups. Del Valle also read about a dozen newspapers a day and freely adapted truth to fiction.

THE LISTENER'S PLAYHOUSE, dramatic anthology.

BROADCAST HISTORY: June 29, 1940–Jan. 18, 1942, NBC, sometimes Red Network, sometimes Blue. 30m, many timeslots.

Though *Listener's Playhouse* was occasionally reminiscent of *The Columbia Workshop*, it was not nearly as well showcased. It was never left in one place long enough to find an audience. One of its shows, *And Six Came Back*, was selected for *Best Broadcasts, 1940–41*. It was a harrowing account of the 1883 Greely expedition to the Arctic, adapted by Ranald R. MacDougall from a survivor's diary. Music was by Tom Bennett.

LISTENING POST, serial drama; stories from the *Saturday Evening Post*.

BROADCAST HISTORY: Feb. 8, 1944–Oct. 29, 1948, ABC. 15m continuation, four a week at 10:45 A.M.; three a week, 1947–48. **HOST:** Bret Morrison; also Clayton "Bud" Collyer.
CAST: New York radio actors including Mary Jane Higby, Myron McCormick and Everett Sloane.

LITTLE HERMAN, comedy-mystery.

BROADCAST HISTORY: Jan. 1–July 12, 1949, ABC. 30m, Saturdays at 9 until May, then Tuesdays at 8. Vaseline.
CAST: Bill Quinn as Little Herman, paroled convict gone straight, who now, operating out of a candy store, helps police solve crimes. Edwin Bruce as Joey, the motherless waif taken in by the hero. Cameron Prud'homme as Governor Bradley, who helped Herman get his parole from Sing-Sing. Barry Thomas as Gordon, the cop on the beat, still unconvinced of Herman's sincerity. William Podmore as Potter, the butler.

LITTLE JACK LITTLE, singer-pianist.

BROADCAST HISTORY: 1930–35, Blue Network (1930–31), then CBS. 15m, various times. Wonder Bread, CBS, 1934; Pinex (cough medicine), 1935.
April 17–Aug. 4, 1944, Blue Network. 15m weekdays at 1:45.

LITTLE OL' HOLLYWOOD, variety.

BROADCAST HISTORY: Nov. 21, 1939–Feb. 7, 1942, Blue Network. 30m, various slots with some gaps. **HOST:** Ben Alexander. **VOCALIST:** Gogo DeLys. **ORCHESTRA:** Gordon Jenkins.

This was a mix of music, comedy skits, episodic segments from current movies, and trade talk from the film capital.

LITTLE ORPHAN ANNIE, juvenile serial adventure, based on the comic strip by Harold Gray; the first late-afternoon children's serial.

BROADCAST HISTORY: 1930, WGN, Chicago.
April 6, 1931–Oct. 30, 1936, Blue Network. 15m, six a week at 5:45; weekdays beginning 1934. Ovaltine.
Nov. 2, 1936–Jan. 19, 1940, NBC. 15m, weekdays at 5:45. Ovaltine. Concurrent broadcast: 1937–38, Mutual. 15m, weekdays at 5:30. Ovaltine.
Jan. 22, 1940–April 26, 1942, Mutual. 15m, weekdays at 5:45, then at 5. Sponsored in part by Quaker Puffed Wheat Sparkies.
CAST: Shirley Bell as Annie, the waif taken in by Mr. and Mrs. Silo, a kindly farm couple who lived near the rural junction of Simmons Corners. Floy Hughes as Annie in a separate production, broadcast from San Francisco to the Pacific Coast for the first two years, then discontinued with the completion of the Blue Network lines to the West. Bobbe Deane briefly as Annie, ca. 1934–35, during a contract dispute involving Shirley Bell. Janice Gilbert as Annie, 1940–42. Jerry O'Mera and Henrietta Tedro as Mr. and Mrs. (Byron and Mary) Silo. Allan Baruck as Annie's friend Joe Corntassel, who lived nearby and accompanied her on many outings. Mel Tormé also as Joe Corntassel. Henry Saxe, Boris Aplon, and Stanley Andrews heard variously as Oliver "Daddy" Warbucks, master capitalist and ruthless dispenser of justice. Unknown actor as Punjab, Warbucks's sidekick. Brad Barker, animal imitator, as Annie's dog, Sandy. **ANNOUNCER:** Pierre Andre. **DIRECTOR:** Alan Wallace, etc. **WRITERS:** Frank Dahm, Roland Martini, Wally Norman, Ferrin Fraser, Day Keene.

Little Orphan Annie was the genesis of juvenile radio serial drama. Nothing like it could have been imagined by earlier generations, and it took children of 1931 by storm, setting the pattern for all that came after. It was breathless action, heavily descriptive, carried mainly by dialogue and peopled by heroes who themselves were only 10 years old. The reactions of youthful listeners were sometimes frightening to their parents: children were unable to sleep; some were inconsolable when Annie was taken by kidnappers. The scripts, though they would seem mild to the point of disbelief half a century later, got a quick reputation for daring and saltiness, and a flood of complaints soon forced the writer, Frank Dahm, to tone it down.

By 1935 it was entrenched. *Radio Guide* discovered that children who had been forbidden to listen were often right back at the radio the next afternoon, with parents at their sides. "Adults eat it up."

Dahm had a free hand in the writing: he could follow lines opened by Harold Gray in the comic strip, or stay with his own imagination. Annie's adventuring branched out from her home in Simmons Corners to include exotic locales. She and her pal Joe Corntassel chased gangsters, criminals and pirates. Often lurking in the background was Daddy Warbucks, a war profiteer who took a distant though fatherly interest in Annie's welfare. Annie's great furry dog, Sandy, "arfed" through the run.

The show opened to one of the catchiest and best-remembered themes of the air.

Who's that little chatter box?
The one with pretty auburn locks?
Whom do you see?
It's Little Orphan Annie!

She and Sandy make a pair,
They never seem to have a care!
Cute little she,
It's Little Orphan Annie!

Bright eyes, cheeks a rosy glow,
There's a store of healthiness handy.
Mite-size, always on the go,
If you want to know—"Arf," goes Sandy!

Always wears a sunny smile,
Now, wouldn't it be worth the while,
If you could be
Like Little Orphan Annie?

Dahm's challenge was to make the serial thrilling but not too chilling. The Silos were rustic people (she was Maw; he was Paw) who often learned a thing or two from their little ward.

It was almost always Annie who came up with the ideas that forced the storylines to their climaxes and satisfactory conclusions. Her catchphrase, "Leapin' Lizards," was a lift from the strip.

Pierre Andre read the interminable commercials for Ovaltine, at times droning on for as much as three minutes. Annie was one of the early premium-givers, dispensing decoders and shake-up mugs for ten cents and accompanying aluminum strip seals from the insides of Ovaltine cans. "It's a two-in-one gift," Andre would coax: "When you put the top on, it makes a keen shaker for mixing your chocolate-flavored Ovaltine shake-up. Then, when you take the bright red top off, presto!... the shaker turns into a swell big drinking mug!" Late in the run, the serial was titled *Adventure Time with Orphan Annie*: the theme was played on the organ, and the opening effects included an airplane, a train whistle, and a steamer's horn.

In 1940, Ovaltine shifted its budget into the new aviation thriller, *Captain Midnight*. Shirley Bell, who had grown up playing Annie, was still playing the lead at age 20; ironically, she was also playing Captain Midnight's young friend Patsy in the prenetwork regional developmental days of that serial. *Annie*, meanwhile, was resurrected a year later with a new cast. In the storyline, she had suddenly become the sidekick of a flyer named Captain Sparks, a plug for her new sponsor, Quaker Puffed Wheat Sparkies.

LITTLE WOMEN, serial, based on the novel by Louisa May Alcott.

BROADCAST HISTORY: Feb. 9–Feb. 27, 1942, Mutual. 15m, weekdays at 4:15.
CAST: Elaine Kent, Patricia Ryan, Joyce Howard, and Sammie Hill as Jo, Amy, Meg, and Beth. Irene Hubbard as Mrs. March.

Mutual's experimental airing of classics in the adventure hour ran as a whole from September 1941 to February 1942, with each novel running about a month. *Jane Eyre* was heard in November–December.

LIVE LIKE A MILLIONAIRE, amateur show.

BROADCAST HISTORY: June 5, 1950–Sept. 12, 1952, NBC. 30m, weekdays at 2:30. General Mills. Nov. 3, 1952–Aug. 28, 1953, ABC. 30m, weekdays at 11 A.M.
HOST: Jack McCoy. **ANNOUNCER:** John Nelson.

Children promoted the talents of their parents: the parents then engaged in spirited talent competitions for prizes and a chance to "live like a millionaire" for a week.

LIVING 1948, documentary and drama (also *Living 1949–51*).

BROADCAST HISTORY: Feb. 29, 1948–Sept. 29, 1951, NBC. 30m, various times with notable breaks April–June 1949, Jan.–Oct. 1950, and Jan.–June, 1951.
HOST: Ben Grauer. **DRAMATIC CASTS:** from New York radio—Grace Keddy, Barry Thomson, Marilyn Erskine, Charles Penman, Alexander Scourby, etc. Impersonators such as Art Carney as retired Gen. Dwight D. Eisenhower. **ANNOUNCER:** Robert Warren. **ORCHESTRA:** Milton Katims. **DIRECTOR:** James Harvey.

Living 1948 was conceived as a "radio mirror" of contemporary American life. The shows ranged from straight statistical surveys (with George Gallup providing the facts on at least one show) to dramatic histories (the story of the Red Cross) to commentary (by Fred Allen) on the state of American humor. On some occasions, presidential candidates (Earl Warren, Robert Taft, Norman Thomas) were given the entire timeslot to expound their views. This series apparently became *The People Act* on the rival CBS network, as production methods were virtually identical.

LONE JOURNEY, soap opera.

BROADCAST HISTORY: May 27, 1940–June 25, 1943, NBC. 15m, weekdays at 5:15; at 11:30 A.M., 1941–42; at 10:45 A.M., 1942–43. Dreft.
April 1, 1946–Sept. 26, 1947, 15m, weekdays. NBC at 10 A.M. until Sept. 30, 1946, then CBS at 2:30. Carnation, both networks.
July 2, 1951–June 27, 1952, ABC. 15m, weekdays at various times between 11 A.M. and noon. Lever Brothers.
CAST: Les Damon as Wolfe Bennett, an architect who lived with his wife Nita on the Spear-T Ranch in the mining district near Lewistown, Mont.

Staats Cotsworth as Wolfe Bennett, 1946–47, and again 1951–52. Henry Hunter and Reese Taylor also as Wolfe Bennett. Warren Mills as Wolfe in childhood, during periodic flashbacks. Claudia Morgan, Betty Ruth Smith, Eloise Kummer, and Betty Winkler as Nita. Wylie Adams and DeWitt McBride as Mel Tanner, ranch foreman. Cameron Andrews and Bob Jellison as Enor, top hand on the ranch. Nancy Osgood as Wolfe's mother. Charlotte Holland and Laurette Fillbrandt as Wolfe Bennett's friend Sydney Sherwood. John Larkin as Sydney's husband Lance McKenzie. **ANNOUNCERS:** Durward Kirby, Nelson Case, Richard Stark, Charles Woods. **CREATOR-WRITER:** Sandra Michael.

Lone Journey was at times billed as "the distinguished American radio novel," with *America the Beautiful* as a theme. Sandra Michael, who wrote it in collaboration with her brother, Peter, steered away from artificial cliffhanging and aimed at quality drama. Michael, who had won a Peabody Award for her serial *Against the Storm*, filled her scripts with leisurely conversations, understated situations, and deep moods. The Montana setting was a place she had lived: the show was based on real people and incidents.

THE LONE RANGER, the pinnacle of juvenile western thriller dramas.

BROADCAST HISTORY: Jan. 31, 1933, first broadcast on WXYZ, Detroit, and seven other stations of the newly formed Michigan Radio Network; 30m, three a week at 9. Silvercup Bread, sponsor as of Nov. 29, 1933. Additional stations added in January 1934: WGN, Chicago; WOR, New York; WLW, Cincinnati. This alliance became the Mutual Broadcasting System, launched with *The Lone Ranger* as its cornerstone program. Three a week at 7:30, ca. 1934. To the West Coast in January 1937, with the addition of the Don Lee Network; then, three months later, to the far Northeast via the Colonial and Yankee networks. Its sponsors were generally regional bakeries—Gingham Bread in the West, Merita Bread in the South, and Silvercup for most of the country through Feb. 10, 1939.
Feb. 13, 1939–May 1, 1942, Mutual. 30m, three a week at 7:30. Bond Bread until Aug. 9, 1940; General Mills for Cheerios as of May 1941.
May 4, 1942–Sept. 3, 1954, Blue Network (ABC beginning in 1944). 30m, three a week at

7:30. General Mills for Cheerios (Merita Bread continuing sponsorship in the South). Repeats by transcription, still sponsored by General Mills, until May 25, 1956.

CAST: George Stenius as the Lone Ranger, Jan. 31–May 9, 1933 (Stenius was later well known as a film director under the name George Seaton). Transition period, Lone Ranger role played briefly by a man known only as "Jack Deeds," and by director James Jewell, one performance each. Earle Graser as the Lone Ranger, May 16, 1933–April 7, 1941. Brace Beemer as the Lone Ranger, April 18, 1941–Sept. 3, 1954. John Todd as Tonto, the hero's faithful Indian companion. Paul Hughes in dozens of roles, from badmen to pompous Army colonels. Paul Hughes also as the Ranger's friend Thunder Martin. Ernie Winstanley as Dan Reid, the Ranger's nephew. Dick Beals and James Lipton also as Dan Reid. Jay Michael as Butch Cavendish, the Lone Ranger's arch enemy. Also: John Hodiak (who specialized in villains), Rollon Parker, Bob Maxwell, Frank Russell, Ted Johnstone, Jack Petruzzi, Herschel Mayall, Elaine Alpert, Mel Palmer, Fred Rito, Bertha Forman, Ruth Dean Rickaby, Malcolm McCoy, Jack McCarthy, Bill Saunders, Beatrice Leiblee. ANNOUNCERS: Harold True, Brace Beemer, Harry Golder, Charles Wood, Bob Hite, and Fred Foy (the last and best-remembered of all *LR* announcers). CREATOR-OWNER: George W. Trendle. DIRECTOR: James Jewell until ca. 1938, then Charles D. Livingstone. WRITER: Fran Striker. Also: Felix Holt, Dan Beattie, Leo Boulette, Bob Green, Tom Dougall, Gibson Fox, Betty Joyce, Steve McCarthy, Ralph Goll, etc. SOUND EFFECTS: Bert Djerkiss, Fred Flowerday, Ted Robertson, Ernie Winstanley, Jim Fletcher, Dewey Cole, Fred Fry. THEME: *The William Tell Overture*, by Rossini. Internal themes and bridges: *Les Preludes*, by Liszt; *The 1812 Overture*, by Tchaikovsky; *Polovtsian Dances*, from the opera *Prince Igor*, by Borodin; incidental music from the *Rosamunde Suite*, by Schubert, and various passages from Mendelssohn, Wagner, Strauss and many other classical composers.

He was a knight of the range, a western hero who quickly became part of popular American folklore. His beliefs and personal habits were sketched as a guideline to those who wrote his adventures. "The Lone Ranger believes that our sacred American heritage provides every individual the right to worship God as he desires. The Lone Ranger never makes love on radio, television, in movies, or in cartoons. He is a man who can fight great odds, yet take the time to treat a bird with a broken wing. The Lone Ranger never smokes, never uses profanity, and never uses intoxicating beverages. The Lone Ranger at all times uses precise speech, without slang or dialect. His grammar must be pure: he *must* make proper use of 'who' and 'whom,' 'shall' and 'will,' 'I' and me.' The Lone Ranger never shoots to kill: when he has to use his guns, he aims to maim as painlessly as possible. Play down gambling and drinking scenes as far as possible, and keep the Lone Ranger out of saloons. When this cannot be avoided, try to make the saloon a cafe, and deal with waiters and food rather than bartenders and liquor."

If a cynic should doubt that all this purity could possibly be accepted by a large listening public for more than 20 years, he should perhaps be excused as a product of a different and less noble time. The Lone Ranger endured, prospered, thrived, and his name is as famous today as ever it was. He is simply the best-known hero of the West ever created. On name recognition alone, he would chalk up more votes than Matt Dillon, Zorro, Red Ryder, and all the heroes of Zane Grey and Louis L'Amour combined. And in virtually every survey, at least half his listeners were adults. In 1940, it wasn't surprising when an elderly couple was arrested for speeding through the Broadway tunnel in San Francisco and used this as their defense: it was time for *The Lone Ranger*, and they couldn't get radio reception inside the tunnel. The judge may have been a fan as well: he dismissed the case.

The story of *The Lone Ranger* is actually two stories. First there is the fictional account, of how a lone Texas Ranger survived ambush by a gang of outlaws, and lived to become the most feared instrument of justice in the early western United States. Then there is the real story—how a radio program, established without sponsorship on a failing station in Detroit, saved the station in the worst depression the nation has known, grew in stature beyond anything anyone could have imagined, and became the prime selling point in the creation of a fourth national network.

The fictional account did not, in actual chronology, begin with the first radio show. Over the years there were conflicting versions (including a show, in 1941, that had a woman saving the life of that Texas Ranger). The best-remembered explanation was concocted and broadcast for the 20th anniversary program in 1953. It told how six Rangers chased the ruthless Butch Cavendish gang through the badlands to a final showdown at a place called Bryant's Gap. The Rangers were headed by Capt. Dan Reid, and among those in his command was his younger brother, John. The Reid brothers had been partners in a rich silver mine strike before duty called, and were planning to return to the mine when their service with the Rangers was finished.

But their scout, Collins, betrayed them, and they were ambushed from above. Pinned down on the smooth rocky floor, Capt. Dan Reid asked one last promise of his younger brother. "My wife and son Danny are coming out here soon. If you get through this, work our silver mine and see that they get my share."

Then both men were hit, and at last the floor of the canyon was quiet. From the rim, Butch Cavendish watched, and left Bryant's Gap littered with the dead.

That night an Indian examined the bodies by moonlight and found that one man lived. He carried the survivor to a cave and dressed the wounds. Then he buried the five Texas Rangers. Realizing that the outlaws might return, he made a sixth grave and left it empty.

For four days he cared for the lone surviving Ranger. When Reid's eyes finally fluttered open, he recognized the Indian as a childhood friend whose life he had saved long ago.

"Your name is . . . Tonto."

"You remember," said the Indian with satisfaction.

"Years ago you called me kemo sabe."

"That right, and you still kemo sabe. It mean 'faithful friend.' "

Reid asked about his companions.

"You only Ranger left," said Tonto. "You lone Ranger."

Then and there John Reid decided to dedicate the remainder of his life to the fight for justice. He created the mask that would become his trademark, and he and Tonto made a pact. "As long as you live, as long as I live, I will ride with you."

The silver mine became his source of income, the fountainhead of the silver bullets that filled his matched set of silver six-guns. He found a wild white stallion, named it Silver, and made silver shoes for the horse's feet. He hired an old Texas Ranger named Jim Blaine to work the mine. Then he set out to find his nephew, Dan Reid, and to bring the Cavendish gang to justice.

That was fiction. The real story of *The Lone Ranger* is less romantic and more complicated. Who contributed what, how much, and when, to the show's creation and subsequent success was a matter of contention for 50 years. Fortunately, two detailed books were written on the subject, each containing firsthand accounts by some of the principals. In *Who Was That Masked Man?*, David Rothel gives verbatim, often conflicting, interviews with people in key positions at the time of *The Lone Ranger*'s creation. And Dick Osgood, who worked 36 years at the Ranger's birthplace, combines his experience with the accounts of his coworkers in *Wyxie Wonderland: An Unauthorized 50-Year Diary of WXYZ, Detroit.* As important though perhaps less accessible is the work of Terry Salomonson, a *Ranger* advocate whose ongoing research, begun in 1978, resulted in a massive show-by-show log of *The Lone Ranger*, and smaller logs of its companion programs, *The Green Hornet* and *Challenge of the Yukon.* Salomonson, whose collection includes unique memoranda and first-year correspondence among the owner, writer, and director of the series, is today considered the authority on questions of personnel, plotlines, and dates (and has supplied Jan. 31, 1933 as the true premiere date).

This much is certain. In April 1930, Radio Station WGHP in Detroit was purchased by John King and George W. Trendle, partners who had just liquidated a chain of movie theaters. They planned to make the station "the last word in radio," and soon changed the call letters to WXYZ, to reflect this motto. King was simply an investor: Trendle would become the managing partner, building a hub of creativity that rivaled—and in some aspects, it was said, surpassed—network capability in New York.

Already in place was a radio repertory company, directed by James Jewell and titled "the Jewell Players." The sound effects department was highly competent, with innovative technicians backed by a solid library of recorded effects. The music library was also well stocked, with serious and classical selections from all major labels. The staff was capable of staging dramatic offerings of far higher quality than what was usually heard on local stations.

But the country was economically depressed, and Trendle was losing hundreds of dollars a week. He thought he could reverse his fortunes through locally produced programming, but where was he to put it? The station was a CBS affiliate: the network controlled the prime-time schedule and allowed no tampering. In 1932, Trendle decided to go it alone. The contract with CBS was not renewed, and WXYZ began its precarious life as an independent.

Precarious it was. Without network shows, Trendle faced a deepening well of red ink. He needed something big: the station's survival depended on it. A western, he thought, would do well. If you wanted to play to packed houses in the movie business, you ran a western. Sometime in December 1932, Trendle called together his key personnel to brainstorm the idea. The makeup of the meeting is uncertain, but Ted Robertson, a sound effects man who later became one of the directors, offered an educated guess to Rothel. In addition to Trendle and Jewell, it would have included station manager Harold True, attorney Raymond Meuer, and salesman H. Allen Campbell, who was quickly becoming the station's "financial brain." Seen in hindsight, this is important, for in later years many people would claim to have created *The Lone Ranger*—many more, noted Osgood, than could possibly have been there.

The legal substance of it was simple. Trendle was the catalyst: he was the owner, and all the others were working for him. But he had little more than a general idea what he wanted: a western hero, as writer J. Bryan III described it in a 1939 *Saturday Evening Post* article, "who goes around righting wrongs against tremendous odds and then disappearing immediately." Trendle is given the salient quote. "I see him as a sort of lone operator. He could even be a former Texas Ranger." At this point, according to Bryan, one of the XYZ staffers cried, "There's his name! The Lone Ranger! It's got everything!" This was Harold True, embittered in later years over the fact that Trendle profited so enormously while the others were essentially shut out.

Also parting in acrimony years later was James Jewell, whose early contributions were acknowledged by everyone. "There was nothing Jim Jewell couldn't do," Robertson told Rothel. The show became Jewell's "baby," as one of the actors told Osgood. Trendle got the ball rolling, and Jewell was charged with implementing, improvising, adding to the mix. So *The Lone Ranger* was created by committee. As far as Trendle was concerned, Osgood summed it up best: "It began in his mind and ended with his approval." But it ignited the station, touching off "the greatest burst of creativity WXYZ has ever known."

Perhaps the man most responsible for the show's success was unaware of those early meetings. Fran Striker was a writer living in Buffalo, New York. He had been selling scripts to WXYZ for some time; working through Jewell, he was writing three series then running on the station: *Warner Lester, Manhunter*; *Dr. Fang*; and *Thrills of the Secret Service*. Salomonson and others believe that most of the developmental work was done by Striker in Buffalo. Striker's first western scripts were rehashes from a series, *Covered Wagon Days*, that he had written for a Buffalo station. Trendle nixed these because the hero was a laughing, happy-go-lucky type. He wanted a man of sterner stuff, "the embodiment of granted prayer," as he later told Bryan. Soon all trace of humor vanished: "The Ranger never smiled again," Bryan wrote. There may have been a few late-night on-air shakedown shows prior to the official Jan. 31, 1933 premiere date. Lacking concrete evidence, Salomonson is inclined to doubt it. "There was nothing in any of the Detroit papers to indicate this, but that in itself doesn't mean much. The papers didn't even list the show in their radio logs at first."

It was Striker, most agree, who came up with the ideas of the silver bullets and the silver shoes for the great stallion. It was Striker who at least pointed the way toward the Ranger's famous call, "Hi-Yo, Silver!" The early scripts had the hero shouting "Hi-Yi," a cry that didn't impress Jewell or True, who would announce it. They worked on it right up to air time, according to Osgood, settling on "Hi-Yo, Silver!" with less than a minute to go. Jewell scrambled into the booth as the theme rolled into the air. They had chosen Rossini's *William Tell Overture*, wanting something from the classics suggestive of a gallop. Little did they know, nor would they have believed, how completely *The Lone Ranger* would consume Rossini's melody in the minds of common men.

Striker continued to improvise. He created Tonto for the simple reason that the Lone Ranger needed someone to talk to. Salomonson's log reveals that Tonto's first appearance was on the 12th show, Feb. 25, 1933. It was sometimes said that Tonto belonged to the Potawatomi tribe of northern Michigan, though the origins of the term "kemo sabe" puzzled scholars for years. One academic made a lighthearted attempt to trace it through various Indian dialects and finally gave up. In later years, Jewell admitted that he had coined it: his father-in-law had once run a camp called Ke-Mo-Sah-Bee in upper Michigan.

Striker was a writing machine—"the greatest hack writer who ever lived," as Jewell asserted to Rothel. In 1939, Bryan estimated that Striker was writing 60,000 words a week, "the equivalent of the Bible every three months." He produced 156 *Lone Ranger* scripts a year, 104 *Green Hornets*, 52 episodes of *Ned Jordan, Secret Agent*; he had written 12 *Lone Ranger* novels, 355 *Lone Ranger* comic strips, and a couple of scripts for *Lone Ranger* movie serials. He had created 10,000 characters and had "shattered four typewriters." For this he was paid $10,000 a year, roughly one-third of a cent per word. In 1934, Striker and Jewell were pressured by Trendle into signing releases to whatever rights of authorship they might own. Striker—always described as a humble, honest man—looked askance at the document but signed it. Jewell was more cautious, but finally he too signed. One of the few men close to the action who never claimed any part in the creation was H. Allen Campbell. But it was Campbell who sold the show. It was Campbell who talked it into the big-watt stations in New York, Cincinnati, and Chicago. It was Campbell who, using *The Lone Ranger* as bait, linked these stations together and formed the Mutual Broadcasting System.

Like most of its kind, the show was rich with premiums. A popgun was offered on the broadcast of May 16, 1933. The station prepared for as many as 1,000 requests. When almost 25,000 flooded in, the Lone Ranger himself had to ask

for relief on the air. Later that year he made his first public appearance: 70,000 young fans stormed police lines and created a hazard to the public safety. Trendle was spooked: he wanted no accidents involved with any *Lone Ranger* activity. A Lone Ranger Safety Club, begun in 1935, had more than two million members four years later. The Ranger remained credible though he never killed. In a career that saw him bring more than 2,000 owlhoots to justice, only one man comes to mind as having died at the hands of the Lone Ranger. This was his deadly enemy, Butch Cavendish, who broke out of the federal prison and finally faced the masked man in a death struggle at Bryant's Gap, on the cliffs high above the original massacre site.

The stories, hacked out on the most rigid deadlines, were simple and often trite. Injustice would spontaneously ignite, and in much the same way the masked rider of the plains would appear with his trusted Indian companion to combat and inevitably defeat it. Sometimes he worked unmasked, in disguise, often posing as an old prospector in order to get close to the action without tipping his hand. Then he was gone, vanished as suddenly as he had come. He wanted and accepted no thanks. Nor did he expect apologies from the chagrined lawmen who naturally mistook him for an outlaw. At the end, the contrite sheriff would turn and say, "Why, if it hadn't been for the masked man here . . . look, he's gone! . . . say, who was that masked man?" And then came the eternal closing: "Why, sheriff, don't you know? . . . he's the Lone Ranger!" Up came the theme, and far away, in the hills, the faint cry, "Hi-Yo, Silver, away!"

It had long been rumored that the role was first played by a man named Jack Deeds, but Salomonson, Osgood, and Rothel all pinpoint George Stenius as the first. "Jack Deeds" played the lead for one performance, May 11, 1933. Salomonson believes that Deeds was a businessman named Lee Trent, who did not do well, was intimidated by the experience, and seldom spoke of it thereafter. The show was still in transition on May 13, so director Jewell stepped in and played the Ranger for that night only. By May 16, the role had been filled by Earle Graser, a slender young man who had joined the station in the summer of 1931. Graser's voice soon became as well known as the president's, though his name remained unknown. Trendle wanted the actor to remain anonymous, to further the idea of the "man of mystery" he was portraying. Even Graser's neighbors had no idea what he did for a living until the morning of April 8, 1941, when he fell asleep at the wheel of his car and was killed instantly in the resulting wreck.

The show went on the following night. Salomonson describes a transition series, five shows from April 9 to April 18 with a connecting storyline that had the Lone Ranger critically ill and unable to speak above a whisper. The action was carried by Tonto while, behind the scenes, intense discussions were in progress regarding Graser's successor. The man chosen was Brace Beemer, who had been announcing the show and had been with the station off and on for several years. Beemer had been discovered by H. Allen Campbell, reading poetry on a station in Indianapolis. His voice was deeper and, if anything, more distinctive than Graser's. He would be the Ranger till the end, another 13 years.

Tonto was always played by John Todd, a middle-aged bald-headed man who looked nothing like the image he created on the air. Todd was the stage name of Fred McCarthy, an old performer in vaudeville and in Broadway musical comedies.

Most of the dramatic staff at XYZ worked the show, giving it a rotating cast of up to 50 voices. Paul Hughes, with a slurring kind of delivery, became the third-most-familiar voice on the show. Ernie Winstanley played nephew Dan Reid until his voice began to change: thereafter, he played older roles and did sound effects. The sound department was so good, said Osgood, that in 1936 NBC tried to "lure it to New York in toto," but the six men decided to remain in Detroit. They created a distinct sound for the Lone Ranger's six-guns, unlike any other gunshot on the air. They perfected the sounds of running horses, using bathroom plungers in a trough filled with sand. For trivia buffs, Tonto's horse was named Scout (an early Tonto steed was named White Feller); Dan Reid's horse was Victor.

And finally there was an immortal opening signature. "A fiery horse with the speed of light" was partly in place from the beginning, modified through the years as the announcers changed. The announcement by Fred Foy is to-

day considered a true radio classic. It came to a rousing orchestral rendition of *William Tell*, with gunshots and hoofbeats and shouts of "Hi-Yo Silver!" throughout.

A fiery horse with the speed of light, a cloud of dust and a hearty Hi-Yo, Silver! The Lone Ranger!

With his faithful Indian companion, Tonto, the daring and resourceful masked rider of the plains led the fight for law and order, in the early western United States. Nowhere in the pages of history can one find a greater champion of justice. Return with us now to those thrilling days of yesteryear. From out of the past come the thundering hoofbeats of the great horse Silver! The Lone Ranger rides again!

Hundreds of episodes are available on tape. The show has been widely syndicated in the last 20 years, and many of the circulating copies are airchecks from contemporary rebroadcasts. Purists, of course, will avoid these, preferring originals with original commercials to the sanitized offerings with arbitrary, intrusive breaks for the 1982 Buick. The vast majority of *Lone Ranger* broadcasts were preserved on transcriptions, and ultimately 2,000 or more may be transferred to tape. Listeners should be warned that most of the shows were copyrighted in script form, Trendle being ever diligent in such matters that most others took for granted. Trendle sold the show and all its assets in 1957, and the property has been resold since. Since millions changed hands, it should be assumed that copyrights will continue to be aggressively protected. Private collectors will seldom be bothered, but the syndicators have been known to threaten stations over unlicensed broadcasting, and in one or two instances commercial dealers have been sued.

The show today retains its eternal airs: the virtues of purity were never better utilized. It matters little that each episode was a duplicate of all the others, that they were mass-produced by an overworked writer (leading, allegedly, to such wonderful boners as "I hear a white horse coming"). They contained the essence of harmless fun, where good always triumphed and evil was justly punished.

THE LONE WOLF, detective drama, based on the books by Louis Joseph Vance.

BROADCAST HISTORY: June 29, 1948–Jan. 1, 1949, Mutual. 30m, Tuesdays at 9:30 until Aug. 24; returned Dec. 4, Saturdays, at 2.

CAST: Gerald Mohr as Michael Lanyard, a roguish gumshoe also known as the Lone Wolf. Walter Coy also as Michael Lanyard. Jay Novello as Lanyard's butler, Jameson. **ANNOUNCER:** Dick Winn. **MUSIC:** Rex Koury on organ. **PRODUCER:** Frank Danzig. **WRITER:** Louis Vittes.

The Lone Wolf probably derived more from the string of B movies than it did from the novels. Michael Lanyard could usually be found in his favorite haunt, the Silver Seashell Bar and Grill, sipping highballs.

LONELY WOMEN, soap opera.

BROADCAST HISTORY: June 29, 1942–Dec. 10, 1943, NBC. 15m, weekdays at 2:15. General Mills.

CAST: Betty Lou Gerson as Marilyn Larimore, a Fifth Avenue model. Barbara Luddy as Judith Clark, a lovesick secretary. Patricia Dunlap as Bertha Schultz, Marilyn's sister. Eileen Palmer as Jean Evans, "bewildered young girl." Nannette Sargent as Nora, the fluttery housekeeper. Harriette Widmer as Peggy the elevator operator. Virginia Payne as Mrs. Schultz. Murray Forbes as Mr. Schultz. Reese Taylor as George Bartlett. Karl Weber and Les Tremayne as Jack Crandall. **ANNOUNCER:** Marvin Miller. **ORGANIST:** Bernice Yanocek. **WRITER-DIRECTOR:** Irna Phillips.

This Chicago origination explored the problems of women separated by war from their men. The action was centered at the Towers, a hotel for women. Critics doubted that even Irna Phillips could long maintain a sexless soap, and apparently she agreed: into the drama stepped George Bartlett and Jack Crandall. The serial blended into a revival of *Today's Children*, with that transition complete as of Dec. 13, 1943.

LONESOME GAL, disc jockey syndication.

BROADCAST HISTORY: Oct. 13, 1947, first broadcast on WING, Dayton, Ohio. Broadcast locally for two years, then, beginning in Dec. 1949, syndicated nationally by transcription. Heard through the mid-1950s. **DJ:** Jean King as Lonesome Gal.

Lonesome Gal was one of radio's best rags-to-riches sagas. Jean King, a 30-ish Dallas native, had arrived in Dayton, Ohio, after a lukewarm career in Hollywood. She had first appeared on radio playing a Texan on *I Love a Mystery* in 1943, but the film city had otherwise not been kind to her. She arrived in Dayton broke and out of work, just at a time when WING had dissolved its network affiliation and needed talent. King proposed a show in which she'd wear a kitten-like mask, bill herself as *The Lonesome Gal*, play romantic records, and talk to all the lonesome guys about loneliness. This to King was real life. "I was damned lonely in Dayton," she would recall a few years later.

She took to the air with a haunting voice and a "come hither" style, referring to her listeners as "muffin" and "baby." The show was a local sensation, its commercial power immediate. One of her first clients was a restaurant with 1,000 seats, most of them empty: at the end of 39 weeks of *Lonesome Gal* sponsorship, the place was jumping and the owners had $60,000 in the bank.

King returned to California in 1949. But stations on the coast were unimpressed with her Dayton history until she met Bill Rousseau and Bob Reichenbach, two radio men who helped her sell it. Rousseau, then producer of *Dragnet*, married King in August 1949, though this was not revealed for four years. The *Lonesome Gal* syndication was localized for each market, a difficult accomplishment achieved by intense communication with Chambers of Commerce in cities where the show was running. She was thus able to give it a "gal across the street" flavor unequaled in radio syndication. Production was a mammoth job: during the salad days, she had to do as many as 300 recordings in a week. It required many all-night stints in her studio, recording and writing commercials, which were also personalized. She started with four stations and a gross weekly income of $185; by 1951, she had more than 50 stations and an annual payoff of $200,000. Philip Morris took on sponsorship in seven major markets. King built a studio in her home, with a microphone so sensitive that, as *Time* put it, it could "pick up each wisp of her breath and every sugary nuance of her voice." She wore the mask to all public appearances and purred, "Hiii, bayyybeee," ever in character. Her true identity was revealed in 1953.

LORA LAWTON, soap opera.

BROADCAST HISTORY: May 31, 1943–Jan. 6, 1950, NBC. 15m, weekdays at 10 A.M.; at 10:15 A.M., 1945–47; at 11:45 A.M. thereafter. Bab-O.

CAST: Joan Tompkins as Lora Lawton, housekeeper to important, dynamic shipbuilder Peter Carver, later his wife. Jan Miner as Lora Lawton from ca. 1944. James Meighan and Ned Wever as Peter Carver. Ethel Wilson as May Case, Lora's beloved friend, confidante, and secretary. James Van Dyk as Clyde Houston, feature editor at the magazine where Lora went to work. Elaine Kent as Houston's wife Iris. Marilyn Erskine and Charita Bauer as Gail Carver MacDonald, Lora's nasty little sister-in-law, ever causing trouble. William Hare as Angus MacDonald. Ann Shepherd as Hilary Strange. Lawson Zerbe as Lora's brother-in-law Rex. **PRODUCERS:** Frank and Anne Hummert. **DIRECTORS:** Martha Atwell, Art Hanna, etc.

Lora Lawton was billed as "what it means to be the wife of one of the richest, most attractive men in all America—the story of the conflict between love and riches in a world so many dream of, but where so few dreams come true."

Divorced by Harley Lawton, Lora had gone on to become a brilliant photographer for a prominent magazine, as well as wife of the head of Washington-based Carver Shipbuilding Company. Her ex-husband was often afoot, causing trouble; her sister-in-law Gail, who had been pampered and spoiled, blamed Lora when Peter Carver insisted that she live on the income generated by her young husband, Angus MacDonald. There were the usual Hummert themes, with Peter infatuated by a phony princess, Erica Van Kuyper, and by the "strange girl" Ilsa Bourg. There were many premiums: in 1947, listeners were offered Christmas cards "just like the ones that brought Lora and Peter together again." The theme was first sung, later played on organ: *Just a little love, a little kiss / I would give you all my love for this . . .*

LORENZO JONES, comedy soap opera.

BROADCAST HISTORY: April 26, 1937–Sept. 30, 1955, NBC. 15m weekday continuation at 4, 1937–38; at 11:15 a.m., 1938–39; at 4:30, 1939–51; at 5:30, 1951–54; at 5:15, 1954–55. Sterling Drugs for Phillips Milk of Magnesia and Bayer Aspirin, 1937–49; Procter & Gamble, 1949–55.

CAST: Karl Swenson as Lorenzo Jones, inventor of strange gadgets. Betty Garde as Belle, his wife. Lucille Wall also as Belle. Joseph Julian as Lorenzo's friend Sandy Matson. John Brown as Jim Barker, owner of the garage where Lorenzo worked as an auto mechanic. Frank Behrens also as Jim Barker. Mary Wickes, Grace Keddy, and Nancy Sheridan as Irma, Jim Barker's wife. **ANNOUNCERS:** Don Lowe, George Putnam. **ORGANISTS:** Rosa Rio, Ann Leaf. **PRODUCERS:** Frank and Anne Hummert. **DIRECTORS:** Ernest Ricca, Stephen Gross, etc. **WRITERS:** Theodore and Mathilde Ferro. **THEME:** *Funiculi, Funicula.*

Lorenzo Jones was a successful departure for Frank and Anne Hummert—a comedy serial that enjoyed fine ratings from beginning to end with comparatively few touches of misery. It was aptly described by its opening signature: "We all know couples like lovable, impractical Lorenzo Jones and his devoted wife, Belle. Lorenzo's inventions have made him a character to the town, but not to Belle, who loves him. Their struggle for security is anybody's story, but somehow, with Lorenzo, it has more smiles than tears." For many years, the show opened with the cheery invitation, "And now let's smile awhile with Lorenzo Jones and his wife, Belle."

Lorenzo's problem was that he never could keep his mind on his work at Jim Barker's garage. He'd begin staring off into space, dreaming of some invention that would make him a million. But his inventions were more eccentric than practical: outdoor vacuums; teapots with three spouts (for strong, medium, and weak); etc. An automatic foot-warmer did net him $2,500 cash, a fortune in 1949 to people like Lorenzo and Belle. At last they were able to buy the house they had rented so long.

Belle was the salt of the earth, the sweetest woman of the daytime until a change late in the run made the plots more Hummert-like and gave Belle a silly personality. She would sit and watch, interested and encouraging, while Lorenzo turned their living room into a circus of junk with his newest brainstorm. When the show changed directions, it became just another Hummert washboard weeper. Lorenzo, kidnapped by jewel thieves, was wounded and awoke in a strange hospital with (what else?) amnesia. This most common of all soap saws consumed *Lorenzo Jones* for more than a year. While Belle searched frantically, Lorenzo drifted about, supporting himself with day labor and odd jobs. On one occasion he was nearly led to the altar. The Hummert formula had truly settled in.

LOUELLA PARSONS, gossip. See also HOL-LYWOOD HOTEL; HOLLYWOOD PREMIERE.

BROADCAST HISTORY: Feb.–June 1931, CBS. Wednesdays. Sunkist Oranges. **INTERVIEWEES:** Top stars: Wallace Beery, Mary Pickford, Bebe Daniels, Norma Shearer, etc. **ORCHESTRA:** Raymond Paige. Also: Ca. late 1931, more of the same show for the Charis Corset Company.

Feb. 28–May 23, 1934, CBS. 15m, Wednesdays at 12:15.

Dec. 3, 1944–Dec. 23, 1951, ABC. 15m, Sundays at 9:15. Jergens Lotion.

April 1, 1952–June 22, 1954, CBS. 15m, Tuesdays at 9:30, later at 10. Jergens.

Louella Parsons was considered the queen of Hollywood gossip writers and broadcasters. She was one of the most feared (and many said hated) figures on the Hollywood scene during her peak years of power, 1935–50. Parsons wrote for the Hearst chain, appearing in 400 newspapers worldwide, and what she wrote as "fact" could have adverse consequences for those she wrote about.

Her first attempt at radio came in 1928. Nothing is known of that show but that it failed: Parsons had a nasally voice that sounded slightly whiny on the air, but in 1931 she had a quarter-hour interview show than ran through much of the year. She fought with maestro Raymond Paige over whose show it was: Paige wanted more music, Parsons more talk. Once, when she decided to extend an interview with actress Constance Bennett, Paige and his musicians stalked off, went to an adjacent studio, had the line switched over, and played merrily on while Parsons and Bennett concluded their interview to dead microphones. Despite this, Paige remained with the show when Charis Corsets picked up the option. The highlight of this series was the commercial, a humorous affair in which the word "corset" could not be used (listeners were told in couched terms how to "avoid abdominal bulge"). She also began using film stars in adaptations of forthcoming films. The sponsor did not approve of this, and it was used sparingly, but it foreshadowed her work on *Hollywood Hotel*, which made her voice nationally known.

Parsons's best-remembered series was her six-year Sunday night run for Jergens Lotion (1944–51): this reinstalled her in the radio gossip fray in which she had lost the edge to her archrival, Hedda Hopper. It was a companion piece to Walter Winchell's *Jergens Journal*, with Winchell broadcasting at 9 P.M. from New York and Parsons immediately following at 9:15 from Hollywood. This unholy alliance began chummily, but hostility soon set in. Parsons was jealous and protective of her West Coast turf, and she would sit tensely through Winchell's show, fretting that he might beat her on some Hollywood item. This he did often enough to keep their relationship chilly. When it turned out that Winchell was raiding her own column for material, "her hatchet was unsheathed," said Parsons biographer George Eels. Parsons timed her choicest items for simultaneous newspaper release with her radio show, holding back the best material for weekend final editions. But in the East the paper was delivered to Winchell just before his air time.

LUKE SLAUGHTER OF TOMBSTONE, western drama.

BROADCAST HISTORY: Feb. 23–June 15, 1958, CBS. 25m, Sundays at 2:05.

CAST: Sam Buffington as Luke Slaughter, Civil War cavalryman turned Arizona cattleman. ("Slaughter's my name, Luke Slaughter; cattle's my business. It's a tough business; it's big business. And there's no man west of the Rio Grande big enough to take it from me!") Junius Matthews as Wichita, Slaughter's sidekick. **ORCHESTRA:** Wilbur Hatch. **DIRECTOR:** William N. Robson. **WRITER:** Fran Van Hartesveldt, etc.

LUM AND ABNER, dialect comedy; country humor.

BROADCAST HISTORY: (Closing dates 1931–33 uncertain; listed here as currently accepted by the Lum and Abner Society)

April 26–July 5, 1931, KTHS, Hot Springs, Ark. Sundays.

July 27, 1931–ca. April 1, 1932, NBC regional, mostly from Chicago. 15m, weekdays, sometimes six a week, at 8 A.M. Quaker Oats.

April 4, 1932–ca. May 19, 1933, NBC. 15m, mostly weekdays. Sustained.

May 22, 1933–March 30, 1934, NBC, from

WTAM, Cleveland. 15m, Mondays through Thursdays at 7:30, Fridays at 10:45. Ford Motors.

April 2, 1934–Aug. 30, 1935, Mutual. 15m, various days at 6:15. Horlick's Malted Milk.

Sept. 2, 1935–Feb. 25, 1938, Blue Network. 15m, weekdays at 7:30 through Nov. 1937; then Mondays-Wednesdays-Fridays. Horlick's.

Feb. 28, 1938–March 29, 1940, CBS. 15m, Mondays-Wednesdays-Fridays at 6:45 until Sept. 1938, then at 7:15. Postum.

May 26–Sept. 19, 1941, NBC Pacific Network. 15m, Mondays-Tuesdays-Thursdays-Fridays at 7:15 Pacific time. Alka-Seltzer.

Sept. 29, 1941–Oct. 2, 1947, Blue Network/ABC. 15m, Mondays-Tuesdays-Thursdays-Fridays at 6:30, 1941–42, then Mondays through Thursdays at 8:15, 1942–45; at 8, 1945–47. Miles Laboratories and Alka-Seltzer.

Oct. 6, 1947–Sept. 24, 1948, CBS. 15m, weekdays at 5:45. Alka-Seltzer.

Oct. 3, 1948–June 26, 1949, CBS. 30m, Sundays at 10. Frigidaire. Switch to comedy-variety series, with orchestra and guest stars.

Nov. 2, 1949–April 26, 1950, CBS. 30m, Wednesdays at 10:30. Sustained until Jan., then Ford Motors.

Feb. 16–May 15, 1953, ABC. 15m, weekdays.

Nov. 9, 1953–May 7, 1954. Syndicated with "Abner" doing recorded commercials for local sponsors.

1931–48: CAST: Chester Lauck and Norris Goff as Columbus "Lum" Edwards and Abner Peabody, owners of the Jot 'Em Down Store in Pine Ridge, Ark. Other residents of this backwoods community also played by Lauck and Goff. Chester Lauck as Cedric Weehunt, the blacksmith's son; as Snake Hogan, the town tough; and as Grandpappy Spears, whose passion was beating Abner at checkers. Norris Goff as Dick Huddleston, the postmaster; as weak-kneed Mousy Gray; as Doc Miller in the annual Christmas show; and as Squire Skimp, the show's villain, a loan shark, insurance hustler, and con man. Also (from ca. 1937): Jerry Hausner in many roles. Frank Graham as Diogenes Smith, B.J. Webster, and in other parts. Lurene Tuttle as Ellie Conners (the orphan girl adopted by Lum and Abner) and in many female roles. Francis X. Bushman with pompous, stuffed-shirt characters. Clarence Hartzel as Ben Withers from 1946. Elmore Vincent as Abner's father, Phinus Peabody. **ANNOUNCERS:** Charles Lyon, Del Sharbutt, Gene Hamilton, and Carlton

Brickert, all chronologically 1931–38; Lou Crosby, 1938–44; Gene Baker, 1944–45; Forrest Owen, 1945–48. **ORGANISTS:** Sybil Chism Bock, etc.; Ralph Emerson; Elsie Mae Emerson. **WRITERS:** Roz Rogers, Betty Boyle (1940s). **THEMES:** *Eleanor*, by Jessie L. Deppen, ca. 1931–41; *Evalena*, by Sybil Bock, 1941–46; *Down on the Old Party Line*, by Ralph and Elsie Mae Emerson, 1946–53.

1948–50: CAST: Chester Lauck and Norris Goff as Lum and Abner, etc. Clarence Hartzell as Dr. Benjamin Franklin Withers, an addle-brained character who boarded with Lum, 1948–49. Also, 1949–50, Zasu Pitts, Andy Devine, Cliff Arquette, Francis "Dink" Trout, Opie Cates. **ANNOUNCERS:** Wendell Niles, 1948–50; Bill Ewing, 1953–54. **ORCHESTRA:** Felix Mills, 1948–49; Opie Cates, 1949–50. **PRODUCER:** Larry Berns. **WRITERS:** Roz Rogers, Betty Boyle, Jay Sommers, Hugh Wedlock, Howard Snyder, etc. **SOUND EFFECTS** (over the years): Betty Boyle, Monty Fraser, etc. (NBC); Harry Essman, David Light, etc. (CBS).

And now, let's see what's going on down in Pine Ridge.

Those simple words, said without frills or fanfare, made up the daily opening of *Lum and Abner*, a gentle and humorous continuation set in a mythical Arkansas hamlet on the fringes of the Ouachita Mountains. The most imposing building in Pine Ridge belonged to Dick Huddleston, who ran the general store and post office. Directly across the road was the blacksmith shop, run by Caleb Weehunt. Next door to that was the barbershop where Mose Moots trimmed beards and caught up on town gossip. Above the barbershop (the only building in town with a second story) was the lodge hall, where the town council met and the Pine Ridge Silver Cornet Band practiced. Next to the tonsorial emporium was Luke Spears's Lunch Room (Luke was always fresh out of everything on the eatin' card). A short distance down the road from Luke's place was the Jot 'Em Down Store, Lum Edwards and Abner Peabody, props.

In real life, as Chester Lauck and Norris Goff, they were hill people who never took kindly to the term "hillbilly," believing that it mocked Arkansans unfairly. They leaped into radio in the early days of the networks, following the *Amos 'n' Andy* success formula (two parts comedy to one part soap opera) without ever giving offense to anyone. "We try to make our program amusing through the situations we build up rather than through the ignorance or obtuseness of any character," Lauck told *Radio Guide* in 1937. They operated on one strong premise: "that the simple philosophy of the Arkansas hills, genuine and unadorned, is very interesting."

Lauck and Goff were born and raised in the country of which they wrote and spoke. Lauck was born Feb. 9, 1902, in Alleene, Ark.; Goff May 30, 1906, in Cove, a few miles away. Both moved "up the road" to Mena (pop. 4,000), with their families as children, and there they met in grade school. Goff was at a four-year disadvantage at 10, but he soon developed a reputation of being able to handle himself with older boys, earning the nickname "Tuffy." He and Lauck became great friends and soon began to mimic the voices around them. During these days the nucleus of *Lum and Abner* was formed.

Contrary to their radio images, both were college educated. They studied at the University of Arkansas, but Goff switched to Oklahoma and Lauck went away to the Academy of Fine Arts in Chicago. Neither graduated: both returned to Mena, married, and settled down in steady jobs. In their spare time, they experimented with comedy. They considered themselves solid blackface comics, appearing in burnt cork. Their popularity grew steadily at home. It might have come to no more than that but for a natural disaster, a flood, and the relief efforts on Station KTHS in Hot Springs. Lauck and Goff were asked to perform. They arrived with a sketch in Negro dialect, but *Amos 'n' Andy* was then at its peak and the station was inundated with blackface imitators. At once they shifted their focus, dragged out their "fellers from the hills," and logged their skit as *Lum and Abner*.

Lauck was Lum. It was a strange name with a backwoodsy sound, and he had never known anyone who had been called that. Goff chose Abner, a solid country name. The town of Pine Ridge was taken from Waters, a sleepy little place in the road with no electricity, 200 people, and an old-world way of doing things. The Jot 'Em Down Store, which Lum and Abner operated in partnership, might have been any number of such stores in the backwoods hill towns. With these ingredients, *Lum and Abner* was on the air. The station brought them back eight times, to

increasingly favorable mail response, and in July 1931 they decided to try Chicago.

They auditioned at NBC in the Merchandise Mart and were offered a slot at $150 a week. Lauck figured they had one clear shot at the big time, and they held out for $350. This was a gamble, as he told *Radio Guide*. "We knew if we didn't put it across with the original idea, we were sunk. What we had to have was a long enough engagement to show listeners what we were trying to do." They were also advised by experienced radio people to hire women for their skits. Nothing succeeded on radio without at least a hint of the "sex angle." But neither was good at female mimicry, and the actresses who tried out for them never could capture the essence of that hill country dialect. So *Lum and Abner* would make it or break it in its earliest forms without a female voice being heard.

They also knew that, if they were to make any money in radio, they had to find a sponsor. Goff knew the salesman for Quaker Oats. It happened that Quaker was then sponsoring *Gene and Glenn*, a series going off for the summer, and the company was looking for a replacement. Lauck and Goff were invited to audition then and there, on the spot. But they were afraid their act would be spoiled by a visual impression (they were in their 20s, playing oldtimers), so they asked the Quaker people to sit facing a wall and just listen. They played to a broomstick held up between them, representing a microphone, and got the job.

The characters took shape and came to life. Abner loved checkers and horse-trading; Abner loved trading of any kind. Lum was the store's self-appointed executive, while Abner usually got "the short end of the dog's leg." Their checker games were epic and serious: Abner, it was said in a vivid episode remembered for years, once set up a game against a fictitious guy named Abner and, when he lost, wouldn't speak to himself for days. They also enjoyed talking on the party line. "I-grannies, Abner, I believe that's our ring," Lum would say. "I-doggies, Lum, I believe you're right," came Abner's answer.

Lum was careful about money and legal wheeling-dealing, though both were vulnerable to con men. The problem of females was solved in much the same way that Freeman Gosden and Charles Correll had done it on *Amos 'n' Andy*:

those characters were all developed offstage, discussed in such detail that they became real to listeners. Abner often spoke of his wife Lizzabeth; there was much talk of Sister Simpson, of Lum's heartthrob, Evalena, and of Aunt Charity Spears, who did hemstitching and quiltmaking. Lurene Tuttle added female voices beginning in 1937. The partners did their own writing until 1941, a script usually being completed in two hours or less. The storyline ranged from single-show incidents to plots that continued for weeks. When a mysterious stranger left some valuables in the store safe and one of his bags turned out to be filled with diamonds, this was good for a two-week story. When Lum became interested in the new town schoolteacher, this led to the formation of the Jot 'Em Down Store and Library: combined with the adventure of an escaped lion, it ran three weeks. A classic sequence took place in 1942, when a woman asked Lum to watch her baby for a moment and then disappeared. This story ran across 40 chapters and culminated in a full-page *Radio Guide* ad, offering listeners a chance to win $750 in war bonds for naming the baby.

The store was seldom described but had a life of its own. A *Lum and Abner* listener could see the potbellied stove and the maze of treasures and junk, from buggywhips to washtubs, lye soap to garden tools. It seemed real because it was rooted in truth: there were many stories in the hill country like the ones told on *Lum and Abner*. Long after Lauck and Goff had become stars and moved to Hollywood in January 1937, they made frequent trips home to Mena, to go hunting, swap yarns, and pick up tales for future shows. The program was treasured in Arkansas. Dick Huddleston had a sign made up for his store, telling the world that, yes, he was *the* Dick Huddleston of *Lum and Abner*. Asked if they sometimes exaggerated a character for effect, Lauck said, "We have to underdraw them. If we pictured them true to life in every instance, folks would think we were kidding them. Even the Pine Ridgers wouldn't recognize their own antics."

It was a quiet show, compared with those around it. There were few sound effects, the most notable being the screen door that creaked open whenever someone came into the store. The show's power was consistently underestimated, even by its stars. In 1936, when Lum cam-

paigned for president and offered a campaign button to anyone who wanted to write in, they thought they might have to send out 5,000 buttons. They were off by almost 250,000. Perhaps the show's finest tribute came that same year, when Waters went through an act of Congress and officially changed its name to Pine Ridge.

In 1948, the serial was replaced by a typical sitcom, with an orchestra and, for the first time, a studio audience. It was funny but lacked the eternal flow of the old show. It was enhanced by the continued appearance of Clarence Hartzell (who had joined in 1946 for the end of the serial run) as Ben Withers, a veritable copy of the Uncle Fletcher role he had been playing on *Vic and Sade* for years. This half-hour series was a smooth Hollywood production: there were more belly laughs, but it had lost the charm of the original.

Goff died June 7, 1978; Lauck, Feb. 21, 1980. The preservation of *Lum and Abner* in huge blocks is one of radio's brightest stories, with entire sequences available in multiple chapters from 1935 on. Much of the 1941–45 run was cut up for syndication, and these have recently been retaped in lovely sound with original commercials intact. As many as 1,500 near-consecutive episodes can be heard, and the best is available to radio stations from the National Lum and Abner Society in Dora, Ala. There are, sadly but not surprisingly, pitifully few takers as this is written in 1996. These quarter-hours bristle with wit, so unlike the cookie-cutter, throwaway radio of today. They are ideal for drive-time listening, but remain unknown to the vast majority of program directors, who prefer to crank out noise and appeal to the lowest common denominators.

LUNCHEON AT THE WALDORF, musical variety–interview show.

BROADCAST HISTORY: Feb. 24, 1940–May 17, 1941, Blue Network. 30m, Saturdays at 1:30. Camel Cigarettes.
HOSTESS: Ilka Chase, interviewing "women of fashion, women in the headlines, women who make the wheels go round," including Ireene Wicker, Florence Lake, Lotte Lehmann. From the Empire Room at the Waldorf Astoria Hotel in New York. **MUSIC:** Paul Baron. **VOCALIST:** Frank Luther. **WRITER:** Edith Meiser.

THE LUX RADIO THEATER, drama based on popular films.

BROADCAST HISTORY: Oct. 14, 1934–June 30, 1935, Blue Network. 60m, Sundays at 2:30 from New York. Lever Brothers for Lux Soap.

July 29, 1935–June 28, 1954, CBS. 60m, Mondays at 9 from New York through May 25, 1936; from Hollywood beginning June 1. Lux Soap.

Sept. 14, 1954–June 7, 1955, NBC. 60m, Tuesdays at 9 from Hollywood. Lux Soap.

HOSTS: John Anthony, fictionalized as "Douglass Garrick," 1934–35; Cecil B. DeMille, June 1, 1936–Jan. 22, 1945; transition hosts including Lionel Barrymore, Walter Huston, William Keighley, Mark Hellinger, Brian Aherne, and Irving Pichel, most of 1945; William Keighley, 1945–52; Irving Cummings, 1952–55. **CAST:** Major motion picture stars, sometimes as many as four in a single broadcast: Clark Gable, Gary Cooper, Spencer Tracy, Bette Davis; virtually every headliner in Hollywood. Radio performers in supporting roles: Frank Nelson, Earle Ross, Lou Merrill, Margaret Brayton, Florence Lake, Bill Johnstone, Jeff Chandler, etc. **ANNOUNCERS:** Melville Ruick beginning with the first broadcast from Hollywood; John Milton Kennedy beginning in the early 1940s and for most of that decade; Ken Carpenter in later years. **ORCHESTRA:** Robert Armbruster, 1936; Louis Silvers until ca. 1951; then Rudy Schrager. **DIRECTORS:** Tony Stanford, mid-1930s; Frank Woodruff until ca. 1943; Fred MacKaye through ca. 1951; then Earl Ebi. **WRITERS:** George Wells, Sanford Barnett, etc. **SOUND EFFECTS:** Max Uhlig, David Light, Walter Pierson, Charlie Forsyth.

The Lux Radio Theater was the most important dramatic show in radio. It had the biggest stars, the highest budgets, the most acclaim. It had a full hour and, during its heyday, Hollywood's most prominent film director as host. It had an austere sound, almost solemn. As *Tune In* noted in 1943: when Cecil B. DeMille opened the broadcast with his weekly "Greetings from Hollywood, ladies and gentlemen," it almost sounded like "This is God, speaking from heaven."

The show had arrived in Hollywood in 1936, luring Marlene Dietrich and Clark Gable to its microphones and drawing an audience that was estimated as high as 40 million people. It had arrived just ahead of the mass migration of stars and shows from New York and Chicago, staked its ground, and stood off all challengers to the throne. *Lux* was power on a scale that even movie people found intimidating. This was not a show to be indulged, perhaps, when shooting schedules permitted: when *The Lux Radio Theater* called, shooting schedules were abandoned. Entire movie companies stood idle while stars rushed off for radio rehearsals. A top star could collect $5,000 for a 60-minute appearance, but the power was far deeper than that. Producers knew that when a film was dramatized on Monday night, it automatically translated into big box office.

It had begun modestly, as a lukewarm anthology of the Broadway stage, heard on Sunday afternoons. The first broadcast was *Seventh Heaven*, with Miriam Hopkins. Though the New York run occasionally used similar plays from Hollywood, the main focus was on such dramas as *What Every Woman Knows* (Helen Hayes) and *Mrs. Dane's Defense* (Ethel Barrymore). The initial guiding principle was simple: "Buy the rights to a fine play, hire the biggest names available, and hope the public will listen." But competition for big names was fierce in New York. When film stars came east—usually on a train between movies, en route to Europe—they were mobbed by agents seeking their appearances on the big variety shows. An appearance on *The Rudy Vallee Hour* or *Shell Chateau* paid more and was less demanding—a bit of fluff between musical selections, which an actor could learn in a single rehearsal. The demand for top stars was so desperate that *Lux* scouts created devious ways of snaring them. One "bright young fellow," as described by *Radio Guide*, simply grabbed up Leslie Howard's suitcases and led him through a gauntlet of competing agents to a waiting cab. Only when they were settled in the car did it occur to Howard to ask who he was. "I'm from *The Lux Radio Theater*, and you're going to act for us tomorrow night," said the brash young fellow. He had caught (and subsequently booked) a hot young star by knowing that "a man will always follow his suitcases."

But the talent well in New York was drying up. By 1935, the rating had dropped four points and the show faced certain extinction. Given the job of revamping it was Danny Danker, an executive with J. Walter Thompson, the agency handling the Lever Brothers account. Danker knew that the future of radio was in the West. *Hollywood Hotel* had broken the ice, becoming the first big California glamor show. Danker recommended a super-extravagant production, with major stars in highly commercial film adaptations, broadcast from Hollywood. The show moved west in June 1936, when New York was still the center of things. In little more than a year, *Radio Guide* was reporting that 90 percent of the "big-time personality programs" were based in Hollywood.

Lux struck gold at once. The first West Coast show was the initial outing for Cecil B. DeMille, hired at $2,000 a week to host the series. DeMille was synonymous with bigness. He had parlayed a "damn the cost" attitude into Hollywood immortality, going through as many as 10,000 extras and covering studio lots with costly sets to achieve a single effect for *The Ten Commandments*. Accounts vary as to how much DeMille had to do with *The Lux Radio Theater* beyond his job of announcing the plays. He was billed as producer and sometimes referred to as director, though he certainly never directed and was probably limited to consulting on prospective plays. In one magazine account, he was shown in the booth, allegedly giving orders from on high. The accompanying copy suggested that *Lux* was his show, that he was the Boss, as much in command here as on a movie set. But most people who worked the show agree that DeMille had little to do with it beyond hosting, interviewing the stars after the play, and signing off with a memorable flourish: "This is Cecil B. DeMille saying goodnight from Holly—*wood*!" But he was a showman: J. Walter Thompson writer Carroll Carroll would remember him arriving straight from a movie set, wearing "director-type puttees spattered with mud and other stable litter." In another incident of show-must-go-onsmanship, DeMille was transported to the theater in an ambulance. He was recovering from surgery, and was said to be performing against doctor's orders. He spoke his lines from a stretcher, photographed, of course, by the press.

The move to Hollywood was a transfusion, its effect immediate. Show after memorable show wafted from the Music Box Theater, where *Lux* set up shop on Hollywood Boulevard just off Vine Street. The house had more than 1,000 seats, which filled to capacity each week. The audience played a subdued though vital part of each broadcast, applauding thunderously during all three signatures (there was a network break, usually between the second and third acts, about 40 minutes in) or laughing subtly at the proper moments in a comedy. There were some close calls, but the show always went on. *The Plainsman* almost didn't make it on May 31, 1937, when stars Gary Cooper and Jean Arthur came down with a last-minute flu. Arthur played her role, weak and feverish, while Fredric March, brought in to replace Cooper, sat up all night before the broadcast working on a western dialect that he had never done before. Another near-catastrophe had occurred in 1936, when frenzied fans of Robert Taylor and Jean Harlow had stormed a fire door, invading the theater, shutting out legitimate ticket-holders, and bringing the crowd to the brink of a riot. Even in this the show led a charmed existence: the main disruption came at a point in the play that called for a mob scene.

At least 50 people were required for each broadcast. Louis Silvers's orchestra alone numbered 25. There were often 20 or more speaking parts, and when technicians were added, the crew overflowed the stage. Each play was a five-day commitment, the first rehearsal coming on Thursday with a table-reading of the script. The serious rehearsals began on Friday, with a two-hour session at noon, an hour-long lunch break at 2 P.M., and more readings in the afternoon. On Saturday there were readings with sound effects. On Sunday the orchestra was integrated. Two dress rehearsals were held on Monday, the first at 10 A.M., recorded on transcription so that the director could hear the show as it would play to the listening audience. The final dress came at 7:30, to work out any remaining rough spots. The broadcast went on live at 9 P.M.

Lux directors had two major problems, working with stars of such importance. Temperament was always a danger, and fear was a constant factor. Tony Stanford, transition director between the New York and Hollywood eras, had little trouble with temper tantrums in those early days. Movie stars were a little timid in radio, he told a news magazine: "It makes them humble, and they take every bit of direction I give them." His successor, Frank Woodruff, had a different experience with temperament, and the stars' fears of the microphone, if anything, intensified.

The fright was attributed to factors they had never encountered. All through rehearsals there was a growing awareness of timing: every word was scheduled to an exact second. Then there was the specter of the vast invisible audience. The sudden sensation of being heard by 30 million people brought some to the edge of hysteria. Finally there was the microphone itself: the dreaded symbol of everything that could go wrong when the red light flashed and the announcer cried, "*Lux* presents Hollywood!" Ruby Keeler confessed to terrors before her first broadcast. Lupe Velez tried to run to "the little girls' room" even as the show was going on: Stanford whirled her around and said, "Sorry, Lupe, you're on the air"—the little girls' room would have to wait. Joan Crawford seemed fine all through the preliminary rehearsals for *Chained*; then, on Sunday, her hands began to shake so violently she couldn't hold the script. Harlow too was badly frightened. Lily Pons became so distraught that Woodruff had her fiancé, maestro Andre Kostelanetz, flown in from New York, allowing Kostelanetz to take over the baton for the final dress and broadcast. Another Met Opera prima donna, Grace Moore, arrived amidst expectations of temperament, but all she wanted was a stick of gum to calm her jitters: her knees, she said, were "knocking together like castanets."

As to temper, Woodruff tolerated little of it. In 1937, *Radio Mirror* described him as "a miracle worker with headstrong stars," a director who "cracks the whip over filmdom's pets and makes them like it." But there were some celebrated blowups, which critics occasionally blamed on Woodruff's youth. Stars resented a director that young telling them what to do. Marlene Dietrich breezed in and, "after snubbing the entire cast," announced that there would be no dress rehearsal because she was "not in the mood." Woodruff told her calmly that "we haven't got time to wait for moods here," and the rehearsal went on. Claudette Colbert insisted on cutting a line that Woodruff felt was essential to the story: Colbert had gotten the line out of the film, but it stayed in the radio show. Ginger Rogers hated every word of the script she was given, but Woodruff coaxed her through it. Maybe the script wasn't a world-beater, he admitted, but there it was, waiting to be done, and it did offer some good lines to a comedienne

who wanted to be known as something other than Fred Astaire's dancing partner.

Then there was a major disruption with Errol Flynn, who arrived at rehearsal in the midst of a heated argument with his wife Lili Damita. The couple kept bickering through the reading until Woodruff erupted. "It was magnificent," said Flynn's costar, Olivia De Havilland, in *Radio Mirror*. "Never in all my life have I seen such wrath. I stood before my mirror night after night, trying to register anger like that."

The first Hollywood show cost a reported $17,000, roughly $300 a minute. Almost half the cost went to the two leads: $5,000 to Dietrich; $3,500 to Gable. But the show was launched into radio's top ten, where it remained for most of its run. DeMille loved it: "I wouldn't take a million dollars for the experience I've had in radio," he said in 1938. At the end of each play, he would chat briefly with the stars, asking about current projects, with plugs all around. The ladies gushed over Lux, how soft it left their complexions, and there were a few words about next week's show. The audience usually reacted with an audible "aaaah" when DeMille announced the spectacular lineup.

But DeMille's tenure came to an abrupt end in January 1945, in a political dispute with the American Federation of Radio Artists, the actors' union. At issue was Proposition 12, a ballot proposal popularly known as the "right to work" law. This would allow anyone to work in radio without union membership. AFRA decided to build a war chest to fight it, levying a one-dollar fee against each union member for this purpose. DeMille refused to pay it, or to allow it to be paid on his behalf. He claimed to sympathize with union ideals, but in fact he distrusted AFRA power. It was an issue of freedom, he insisted, and on that there could be no compromise. The argument dragged through late 1944, with AFRA setting and then extending several arbitrary deadlines. DeMille refused to budge, and on Jan. 22 the man who "wouldn't take a million" for his *Lux* job gave it up over a dollar, hosted his final show, and never returned. In the fall, William Keighley was given the job on a permanent basis.

Near the end of the run it was estimated that *Lux* had gone through 52,000 pages of script, 496 stars, 1,467 supporting players, 18,667 music cues, and 22,667 sound effects. Longtime soundman Charlie Forsyth was equipped with a *Lux* soundmobile, containing sophisticated recording equipment for capturing authentic sounds as he traveled during summer breaks. Forsyth developed some innovative manual effects as well—among others, being able to make the closing of a briefcase latch sound exactly like a car door clicking shut. Fred MacMurray and Loretta Young headed the "most numerous appearances" list of stars, with 26 and 25 roles respectively. Others often heard were Claudette Colbert (24), Barbara Stanwyck (23), Cary Grant (22), Don Ameche (21), and Brian Aherne, Ray Milland, and George Brent (20 each). Director Fred MacKaye, following Woodruff, brought an actor's viewpoint to the job, having appeared in many *Lux* supporting roles prior to 1943, when he assumed directorship. Host William Keighley was lavish in his praise of the radio regulars ("those AFRA people are just great"), expressing amazement at their versatility. A prime example occurred on May 24, 1948, when Burt Lancaster forgot the time and arrived late for the broadcast, *I Walk Alone*. At air time, MacKaye summoned bit player Ira Grossel (later himself a star under the name Jeff Chandler) and said, "You do Burt's part, I'll do yours." Few listeners knew the difference, even when Lancaster arrived and took over in the middle of an act.

The *Lux* library is long and rich, with several hundred shows on tape in various sound quality. The earliest show heard by this writer is *Dulcey*, with Zasu Pitts and Gene Lockhart, from Oct. 28, 1935, when the show was still in New York.

It was dreary by later standards. Many from the DeMille era are easily available: *It Happened One Night* (Gable and Colbert, March 20, 1939) retains much of its period charm, and *Dark Victory* (Bette Davis, Spencer Tracy, Jan. 8, 1940) holds up quite well. Also circulating are many dress rehearsals, near-duplicates of the actual broadcasts, but without the studio audience. Occasionally on the rehearsals there is backstage dialogue: the action is stopped and the situation discussed between the stars at the mike and the men in the booth. On the rehearsal of *It Happened One Night*, the men take over the female lines in the commercial, mugging about "Luxing dainty underthings" and the like. As with most long-running series, *Lux* matured and offered more timeless drama as it aged. *National Velvet* (Elizabeth Taylor and Mickey Rooney, Feb. 3, 1947), *King Solomon's Mines* (Stewart Granger and Deborah Kerr, Dec. 1, 1952), and *The African Queen* (Humphrey Bogart, with Greer Garson in the Katharine Hepburn role, Dec. 15, 1952) are quite representative of the films that inspired them. *All About Eve* (Bette Davis, Anne Baxter, Gary Merrill, Oct. 1, 1951) and *No Highway in the Sky* (James Stewart, Marlene Dietrich, April 28, 1952) stand with just about any drama done on radio in this commercially fading but creative era. Two of the best westerns ever heard were done in the waning years of *Lux*: *Broken Arrow* (Burt Lancaster, Jeff Chandler, and Debra Paget, Jan. 22, 1951) and *Shane* (Alan Ladd, Van Heflin, and Ruth Hussey, Feb. 22, 1955).

M

MA AND PA, rustic conversational character study.

BROADCAST HISTORY: June 28–Oct. 25, 1936, CBS. 30m, Sundays at 6, later at 4. Sustained.

Dec. 29, 1936–June 25, 1937, CBS. 15m, three a week at 7:15; weeknights beginning in March. Atlantic Refining.

CAST: Parker Fennelly and Margaret Burlen as Pa and Ma, an elderly Cape Cod couple who own an antique shop and eating place. Margaret Dee as Ma as of 1937 run. Harry Humphrey and Ruth Russell as Horace and Penelope. Effie Palmer as Ella Mae. Roy Fant as Elmer. **ANNOUNCER:** Del Sharbutt. **DIRECTORS:** Earle McGill, 1936; Robert Burlen, 1937.

MA PERKINS, soap opera.

BROADCAST HISTORY: Aug. 14–Dec. 1, 1933, WLW, Cincinnati. 15m, weekdays.

Dec. 4, 1933–July 8, 1949, NBC. 15m, weekdays at 3, 1933–34, then at 3:15. Oxydol.

Sept. 28, 1942–Nov. 25, 1960, CBS; double-network status 1942–49. 15m, weekdays at 1:15. Oxydol until 1956, then various.

Concurrent broadcasts: 1935–36, Mutual, 11:30 A.M.; Jan.-May, 38, CBS, 10:45 A.M.; Blue Network, 10:15 A.M., Feb.–Dec. 1937, and 10:45 A.M., June–Nov. 1938.

CAST: Virginia Payne as Ma Perkins, homespun philosopher and owner of a lumber yard in the small town of Rushville Center. Charles Egelston as Shuffle Shober, her best friend and partner, ca. 1933–58. Edwin Wolfe (who also directed for much of the run) as Shuffle, ca. 1958–60. Dora Johnson as Ma's oldest daughter, Evey. Laurette Fillbrandt also as Evey. Kay Campbell as Evey, ca. 1945–60. Rita Ascot as Ma's younger daughter, Fay. Laurette Fillbrandt, Cheer Brentson, Marjorie Hannan, and Margaret Draper also as Fay. Gilbert Faust as Ma's son, John Perkins. Murray Forbes as Willy Fitz, who married daughter Evey. Cecil Roy, Bobby Ellis, and Arthur Young as Junior Fitz, son of Evey and Willy. Nannette Sargent and Judith Lockser as Fay's daughter, Paulette. Maurice Copeland as Augustus Pendleton, town banker and most prominent citizen. Beverly Younger as Pendleton's wife, Mathilda, leader of high society, head of the Jolly Seventeen, and a major antagonist to Evey Perkins Fitz. Patricia Dunlap and Helen Lewis as Gladys Pendleton, their daughter. Jonathan Hole as Fay's ill-fated husband, Paul Henderson. McKay Morris as Gregory Ivanoff. Rye Billsbury as Gary Curtis. Ray Suber as Charley Brown. John Larkin and Casey Allen as Tom Wells. **ANNOUNCERS:** Bob Brown from 1933; also Jack Brinkley, Dick Wells, Marvin Miller as "Charlie Warren," Dan Donaldson, etc. **PRODUCERS:** Frank and Anne Hummert. **DIRECTORS:** Roy Winsor, George Fogle, Philip Bowman, Edwin Wolfe, etc. **WRITERS:** Robert Hardy Andrews, Lee Gebhart, Orin Tovrov (20 years), etc. **THEME:** Original music by Larry Larsen and Don Marcotte, often mistaken for *My Old Kentucky Home* because of similar composition.

Ma Perkins, "America's mother of the air," was an audio milestone that spanned almost the entire lifetime of network radio drama. Typical of Hummert serials, Ma had tears, maniacs, and melodrama in her arsenal of cliffhangers. But she overcame this with long quiet spells, with deep conversations about the meaning of life against an unfolding panorama of family and personality conflicts.

She was an ageless widow, probably in her 60s, who owned and managed a lumber yard in Rushville Center (pop. about 4,000). She was described by *Time* just before her 25th anniversary as "a shrewd combination of *Dr. Christian, David Harum,* and *Tugboat Annie*"; the woman's answer to *Just Plain Bill.* Ma was the salt of the earth, a sage whose life was never too busy for the problems of others. She lived staunchly by the Golden Rule, but didn't hesitate to go to war if she saw the forces of evil thriving unopposed. She was the town's conscience, its best-loved sounding board, its guide in matters of the head and the heart.

Supporting players came and went, but the main cast remained consistent. The characters were Ma, her partner Shuffle Shober, her three children, their children, and the people who married into her family. In chronological order, Ma's three children were Evey, John, and Fay. All were grown as the serial got under way in 1933. The earliest known episode, the eighth broadcast (Dec. 13, 1933), reveals Ma as a combative old hen, determined to persuade daughter Evey to leave her naive husband, Willy Fitz. In this very early show, Ma was in a primitive stage of development, and it took all the common sense of John and Fay to convince her of her mistakes.

Evey was a superficial character, a social climber whose greatest ambition was to become president of Rushville Center's little bastion of society, the Jolly Seventeen. She was sometimes shrewish and was often irritated at life's financial burdens. Her husband, Willy, was less than a flaming success; their son, Junior, was described as the town's version of "a refined 'Dead-End Kid.' " Evey filled her spare time with bridge games among the socially elite. She was known to be a heartache to Ma, who cared little for posturing or appearances. But Evey had one saving grace: she was "warm and kind" in spite of her flaws. Willy Fitz, at 38 three years her senior, was a "good Joe" (*Radio Life*) who "likes flashy clothes and cigars, has interminable schemes to make himself a million dollars," but "is devoid of a sense of humor."

Young John Perkins was a steadying influence. But he was killed in World War II, buried "somewhere in Germany in an unmarked grave." Fay, the youngest, was said to be "in her late 20s" in 1948, but the timeless flow might well have allowed her to be about the same age a decade earlier. She was Ma's darling, a smaller version of the heroine herself. Fay went through many love affairs during the long run and was said to be "thoroughly at the mercy of her emotions." Her husband, Paul Henderson, was killed in 1940, less than a year after their marriage. Over the years, Fay came to the brink of matrimony with such diverse characters as Gary Curtis (John's embittered pal from the war), playboy Dr. Andrew White, millionaire Carl Michaels, and the self-satisfied Spencer Grayson.

Shuffle Shober, co-owner of the lumber yard, was in many ways like Ma Perkins—tough honesty combined with an understanding of the human spirit. Though not as rustically articulate as Ma, Shuffle sometimes saw through deceit faster. Ma's guiding principle was that all people deserved trust until they proved otherwise, while Shuffle often believed the reverse of this. Many a night they sat together on Ma's front porch, talking sentimentally about their loved ones and the world around them. On those warm wartime evenings they would watch the lights up and down the block go out; then, with their troubles still unresolved but somehow easier to bear, Shuffle would shuffle off, leaving Ma contented with the blessings in life.

Others in town were August Pendleton the banker, Charley Brown the grocer, and Fred Sweeney the stationmaster, who ran the telegraph office and waited for trains that were seldom on time. The main street was intersected by streets bearing the names of trees. There was a "moving picture house" and, of course, a church, though the scripts took care never to refer to Ma's denomination of preference.

The serial had its share of dark melodrama: two isolated chapters from 1938 have Ma sheltering a political escapee from Russia. The man's wife, Sonya, is shot by agents through the window of Ma's house and dies in his arms. Fay's beau Gary Curtis was a negative force, settling in the Perkins home after his Navy discharge and causing no end of trouble. People were divorced, killed, and disgraced, and in one memorable story Ma Perkins exposed a baby black market.

But the show had a river-like movement, unusual in soap operas, that took it through no more than two or three major complications a year. Entire programs were devoted to celebrations of major American holidays.

In an incredible performance, Virginia Payne played Ma Perkins without missing a show in 27 years. Payne, just 23 when the show premiered, gave a convincing portrayal of a middle-aged battleaxe despite her youth. It was Payne who softened the character by degrees until the real Ma Perkins emerged. Unlike her fictitious counterpart, Payne had a college education and finally a master's degree: at $50,000 a year, she earned more than any other actress in the soaps. Because of her youth, her identity was kept secret; later she made personal appearances in a wig, "frumpy" clothes, and spectacles, though *Time* revealed that the getup made her feel "like an impostor." Through 7,065 performances, Payne respected her character: "I've never played her short," she said. Payne died Feb. 10, 1977.

By daytime standards, *Ma Perkins* was a ratings champion, peaking at 11-plus in 1939. When it went to two networks, the combined rating was usually over 13, and one year it was over 16. It aired from Chicago until 1947, when it moved to New York. So strong was the sponsor identification that it was billed as "Oxydol's own Ma Perkins." In 1956, Procter & Gamble leased the show to Lever Brothers, to promote Spry, but would not sell it outright. At the height of its fame, *Ma Perkins* was heard in Hawaii, Canada, and throughout Europe on Radio Luxembourg.

THE MAD MASTERS, situation comedy.

BROADCAST HISTORY: July 12–Aug. 31, 1947, NBC. 30m, Saturdays at 8:30. **CAST:** Monte and Natalie Masters as themselves: he a shoe salesman; she an addled housewife. **WRITER:** Monte Masters. They also collaborated on *Candy Matson*, the female detective series, which was longer running and better received.

MAGIC ISLAND, fantasy juvenile serial.

BROADCAST HISTORY: 1936, transcribed syndication, 15m continuation: the fictionalized search by Mrs. Patricia Gregory for her young daughter Joan, shipwrecked in the South Seas and missing for 14 years. **CAST:** Rosa Barcelo as Joan Greg-

ory. Sally Creighton as Mrs. Patricia Gregory. Tommy Carr as Jerry Hall. Will H. Reynolds as Capt. Tex Bradford. **AUTHOR-PRODUCER-ANNOUNCER:** Perry Crandall. This serial survives in its entirety, 130 chapters.

THE MAGIC KEY, musical variety.

BROADCAST HISTORY: Sept. 29, 1935–Sept. 18, 1939, Blue Network. 60m, Sundays at 2 until June 1939; Mondays at 8:30 until Aug. 1939, then at 9. RCA.

HOST: Milton Cross. Many diverse acts from around the globe, with emphasis on, but by no means confined to, concert music. **COMMENTATOR:** John B. Kennedy. **ANNOUNCER:** Ben Grauer. **ORCHESTRA:** Frank Black and the NBC Symphony. **PRODUCERS:** Bertha Brainard of NBC, with Tom McAvity and Gregory Williamson of the Lord and Thomas ad agency.

The Magic Key of RCA mixed symphony musicians and opera stars with purveyors of swing, radio stars from *Stoopnagle and Budd, Amos 'n' Andy* and *Lum and Abner*, and occasionally such popular bands as Paul Whiteman's or Rudy Vallee's Connecticut Yankees. The show's sole purpose, as described by *Radio Guide*, was "to sell radio itself." Anything that showed off the miracle of radio was grist for the mill: it was a "jigsaw puzzle of the air," employing remotes from far-flung arenas, the more distant the better.

A listener might hear a short drama, a male chorus from Stockholm, jazz from Chicago, an account of Mussolini's campaign in Africa, and a conversation with the crew of a submerged submarine. "It was a stunt program," said *Radio Guide:* the stunt was radio's ability to shrink the world. A renowned violinist such as Efrem Zimbalist might in any circumstance be exciting to hear, but on *The Magic Key* the excitement lay in the technical difficulties of shortwaving him in from Amsterdam.

The show was put together in small bites, but could also provide a 60-minute concert by Polish pianist Ignace Jan Paderewski. On May 8, 1938, reporter Linton Wells began a 30,000-mile tour of South America, shortwaving his stories live each Sunday. Also that year, Eleanor Roosevelt spoke on "This Troubled World." The diversity was the broadest of its time. A St. Patrick's Day broadcast in 1936 contained a remote from Blarney Castle in Ireland, the Vienna Boys' Choir in

New York, Benny Goodman's orchestra from Chicago, mimic Sheila Barrett with impersonations in New York, a classical composition by the NBC Symphony; a dialogue between commentator John B. Kennedy in New York and a colleague sitting at the BBC in London, and a song by Gladys Swarthout. Others who appeared: the orchestras of Ray Noble, Guy Lombardo, and Richard Himber in a single act; Eugene Ormandy and the Minneapolis Symphony; Lauritz Melchior, Fred MacMurray, Walt Disney, Ruth Etting, and the Pickens Sisters. Milton Cross opened the show with a straight weekly announcement: *"The Magic Key of RCA* turns to present . . ."* whatever the day's bill o' fare happened to be. The show was closed by both announcers, tossing their taglines back and forth:

"This is Ben Grauer . . ."
"And Milton Cross . . ."
"Speaking for one member of RCA . . ."
"The National Broadcasting Company."

THE MAGIC OF SPEECH, talk; speech improvement.

BROADCAST HISTORY: 1929–37, NBC. Red Network, 1929–36; Blue Network, 1936–37. Various 30m times and formats. **WRITER-DIRECTOR:** Vida R. Sutton.

THE MAGIC VOICE, romantic adventure serial.

BROADCAST HISTORY: Nov. 15, 1932–June 27, 1933, CBS. 15m, twice a week at 8:15. Ex Lax.
March 30–Aug. 28, 1936, Blue Network. 15m, weekdays at 4:45. Chipso.
CAST: Nick Dawson and Elsie Hitz, famous romantic pair. Content unknown.

THE MAGNIFICENT MONTAGUE, situation comedy.

BROADCAST HISTORY: Nov. 10, 1950–Nov. 10, 1951, NBC. 30m, Fridays at 9 until May 1951; then Saturdays at 8:30; final month at 8. Anacin, Chesterfield, RCA.
CAST: Monty Woolley as Edwin (the Magnificent) Montague, former Shakespearean actor forced to make his living in (*ugh!*) radio. Anne Seymour as Lily, his wife. Art Carney as Montague's father. Pert Kelton as Agnes, the Brooklynese maid, who

lives in the Montagues' New York apartment and delights in verbal jousting with her boss. John Gibson as Montague's agent. **MUSIC:** Jack Ward on organ. **PRODUCER-WRITER:** Nat Hiken.

Monty Woolley had first appeared on radio as an acid-tongued foil for Al Jolson. As Montague, he had fallen on hard times. At the height of his Shakespearean glory, 25 years ago, he had married his leading lady, Lily Boheme. Now he must play Uncle Goodheart on the radio while maintaining his membership in the exclusive Proscenium Club and trying desperately to keep his acting friends from learning of his double life.

THE MAIN LINE, documentary drama.

BROADCAST HISTORY: Ca. 1944–46, Don Lee Network, West Coast, Wednesdays (exact tenure unknown, but known to be on in these years). **NARRATOR:** Wally Maher, 1944; Ted von Eltz, 1946. **CREATOR-WRITER:** Lew Lansworth.

The Main Line was a railroad documentary about the Southern Pacific Line. Producer Lew Lansworth spent months in preparation—walking the yards and roundhouses, eating with crews, talking with hands all along the line. It was highly authentic, backed by a vast library of railroad sound effects, transcribed by soundman Art Fulton in a mobile sound unit. Researcher Pat Barba (Barbagelata) was later written into the scripts and portrayed by actress Betty Lou Head.

MAISIE, situation comedy, based on the MGM film series.

BROADCAST HISTORY: July 5, 1945–March 28, 1947, CBS. 30m, Thursdays at 8:30 until mid-Aug.; Wednesdays at 9:30, 1945–46; Fridays at 10:30, 1946–47. Eversharp. **CAST:** Ann Sothern as Maisie Revere, secretary to an unsuccessful attorney. **ORCHESTRA:** Albert Sack. **DIRECTOR:** Tony Sanford. **WRITER:** Samuel Taylor, etc.
1949–53, transcribed syndication from MGM, offered for distribution beginning Nov. 24, 1949. Also: Jan. 11–Dec. 26, 1952, Mutual. 30m, Fridays at 8. **CAST:** Ann Sothern as Maisie Revere, a Brooklyn beauty and Jane-of-all-trades who usually ended up broke in some remote dive. Support from Hollywood's Radio Row: Hans Conried, Sheldon Leonard, Ben Wright, Lurene Tuttle, Marvin Miller, Joan Banks, Bea Benaderet, Frank Nel-

son, etc. **ANNOUNCER**: Jack McCoy. **MUSIC**: Harry Zimmerman. **WRITER**: Arthur Phillips.

The ten *Maisie* films (1939–47) were strictly B-fare, and the radio series was more of the same. Maisie was a sassy commoner who fell in love often but, as in the films, gave up the hero and went her own way in the end. The catch-phrase, Maisie's answer to everything, was "Likewise, I'm sure." The show was also titled *The Adventures of Maisie*.

THE MAJESTIC THEATER OF THE AIR, variety, also known as *The Majestic Theater Hour*.

BROADCAST HISTORY: 1928–30, CBS. 60m, Sundays at 9. Grigsby-Grunow Company, makers of Majestic Radios. **CAST**: George Moran and Charlie Mack (real names George Searchy and Charles Emmett Sellers) as "the Two Black Crows." Also: Ruth Etting, Helen Morgan, George Gershwin, Dolores Del Rio, Fanny Brice, Edgar A. Guest, etc. **MASTER OF CEREMONIES**: Wendell Hall, "The Red-Headed Music-Maker." **PRODUCER-DIRECTOR**: Wendell Hall.

The Majestic Hour was remembered by CBS president William S. Paley as "a lifesaver" for his network, the client his first big sponsor. Grigsby-Grunow had been in radio since 1924, broadening its base from a parts manufacturer to a maker of full sets. But Grigsby had encountered stiff competition from RCA, which claimed to hold patents on radio tubes essential to the manufacture of modern radio equipment. Grigsby thus had to pay royalties to its staunchest competitor. Grigsby "loved CBS," Paley recalled in his memoir, "because they hated RCA," and RCA was the parent company of NBC.

The Majestic Hour was typical late-1920s variety, spotlighting "the Two Black Crows" and enlisting the support of top vocalists and personalities of the day. Moran and Mack were crude forerunners of *Amos 'n' Andy*, a blackface team that milked the brash-vs.-ignorance theme and never really broke out of the vaudeville patter that had launched them. Moran was the straight man: his questions were often laced with sarcasm. Mack's stock answer to embarrassing

questions was "Why bring that up?" Wendell Hall sang novelty numbers to his own banjo accompaniment.

MAJOR BOWES' CAPITOL FAMILY, concert music and variety.

BROADCAST HISTORY: July 26, 1925–Aug. 30, 1936, WEAF, New York, until ca. Nov. 1926, then NBC. Sundays at 7:30 on the Blue Network, 1926–27, then Red Network. Timeslots ranging up to 120m; 1929–30, 60m, Sundays at 7:30; 1930–31, 30m, Sundays at 8. March-Dec. 1931, 45m, Fridays at 8. Moved into a long-running slot, 60m, Sundays at 11:30 A.M. Dec. 21, 1931. Also known as *Capitol Theater Concerts*, in earliest days.

Sept. 6, 1936–May 25, 1941, CBS. Mostly 60m, occasionally 45m, Sundays at 11:30 A.M.

CAST: "Major" Edward Bowes, with long-standing concert and variety talents including Helen Alexander, soprano; Tom McLaughlin and Edward Matthews, baritones; Nicholas Cosentino, tenor; Roy Campbell's Royalists; the Dalton Boys (Kelly, Jack, and Pete); the Sizzlers; accordionist Charles Magnante; and xylophonist Sam Herman. Also: Joey Nash, tenor, one season; Bob Hope, comedian, 1932; Beverly Sills (Belle Silverman), singer for three seasons. **MASTER OF CEREMONIES**: Robert Reed. **ORCHESTRA LEADER/VIOLINIST**: Waldo Mayo. **THEME**: *Clair de Lune*.

The Capitol Family grew out of an earlier show, *Roxy and His Gang*: both were remotes from the stage of the Capitol Theater, at Broadway and 50th Street in New York. The *Roxy* broadcasts were of radio's earliest days, 1922–25, on WEAF.

The Capitol opened in 1919, one of the largest movie theaters in the world, with a partnership comprised of S. L. Rothafel, "Major" Edward Bowes, and others. Rothafel, known as Roxy, was initially more interested in broadcasting, but Bowes quickly became fascinated with the new medium. When Roxy left the Capitol in 1925, Bowes took over the show.

Though it remained largely a "serious" music show, enough comedy and talk was mixed in to classify it as variety. Bowes often waxed philosophical and indulged a weakness for sentimental verse. According to Bob Hope, who worked the show in 1932, he also had a bad habit of stealing his guests' material. Hope was required to submit his routines in advance, and arrived for the broadcast to find his material reworked and the best gags given to the major.

It was a family of the air, an aggregation that stayed together across several seasons. Young Beverly Sills sang regularly after winning one of Bowes's *Amateur Hour* contests in 1936, when she was seven years old. The series ended in 1941, when Bowes was asked to take a 30-minute time cut and refused. By then he was well established as host of *The Original Amateur Hour*.

MAJOR BOWES' ORIGINAL AMATEUR HOUR, talent contest.

BROADCAST HISTORY: 1934, WHN, New York. *The Amateur Hour.*

March 24, 1935–Sept. 13, 1936, NBC. 60m, Sundays at 8. *The Original Amateur Hour.* Chase and Sanborn.

Sept. 17, 1936–July 19, 1945, CBS. 60m, Thursdays at 9 until Jan. 22, 1942, then 30m. Chrysler.

Sept. 29, 1948–Sept. 18, 1952, ABC. 60m, Wednesdays at 8 until July 28, 1949, then 45m, Thursdays at 9. Revived by Ted Mack, an associate of the late "Major" Edward Bowes, and sometimes heard as *Ted Mack's Original Amateur Hour.* Old Gold Cigarettes.

HOST: "Major" Edward Bowes, 1934–45; Ted Mack, 1948–52. ANNOUNCERS: Graham McNamee from ca. 1935; Phillips Carlin, Jimmy Wallington, Norman Brokenshire, Dan Seymour, Ralph Edwards, Tony Marvin, Don Hancock, Warren Sweeney; Dennis James among announcers, ca. 1948–52. DIRECTORS: Robert Reed, Lloyd Marx. PRODUCER: Lou Goldberg.

The rise of Major Edward Bowes in the summer and fall of 1934 led to a national rage of frantic and sometimes tragic proportions. Amateur fever it was, and by 1935 America was on fire with it. For anyone with busfare and a harmonica, *The Original Amateur Hour* was a grab at the brass ring. Some came without busfare, hitching rides across the country. Poor blacks came up from the South; cowboys from the West. Freak acts came from everywhere. Many had sung in choirs back home. Some had played tank towns in the corn belt, with three-piece combos held together by long strings of one-night stands. They were supposed to be "simon pures," strictly amateur, but who was to know? The common denominator was desperation. The Depression hung over the nation like a shroud. If a man with a smooth baritone singing voice was told by enough friends that he sounded better than Bing Crosby, he began to believe it. Major Bowes gave him a chance to prove it.

Many sold their homes, put their instruments on their backs, and headed east. Two blind boys, one carrying a 75-pound accordion, hitchhiked to New York from South Bend, Ind. They were turned away at the CBS door. The major did not want blind performers on his show, it was explained. When this made the press, Bowes denied it; the boys were turned away, he said, because they had run away from home and he was not in the business of encouraging runaways. Still they came by the thousand, most without ever considering the odds they were bucking. *The Original Amateur Hour* was getting 10,000 applications a week: the producers could only hear 500 to 700 amateurs in weekly auditions; only 20 were selected for the broadcast, and the rest were sent back into the streets. Broke and alone, they soon ended up on the city's already bulging relief rolls.

In one month of 1935 alone, *Newsweek* reported, 1,200 amateurs had applied for emergency food and shelter. Among them was Jewell Duncan, a singer who had come from Oklahoma to find himself in a long line of people to be auditioned. Most of the hopefuls, he said, were "colored boys from the South." There were players of washboards and jugs, tap dancers, piano players, and mimics. There were tellers of old jokes, unaware that *The Amateur Hour* would turn them away without a hearing. There were trios of hopeful blacks, all trying in vain to sound like the Mills Brothers. There were yodelers and harpists, chime-ringers and harmonicats. The harmonica may have its virtues, but they were seldom heard on *The Original Amateur Hour.*

Jewell Duncan stood among them with a good voice, he thought, and a bushel of hope. At last he was admitted to the studio and asked to sing. Major Bowes was nowhere to be seen: instead there were some men in the control room, taking notes. He thought his number went fine. The men said he'd be hearing from them if they thought they could use him. "That was a couple of months ago," he told *Newsweek*. He waited and went on relief with thousands of others, and thought of Oklahoma and going home.

While all this was happening, one man grew rich. Major Edward Bowes, at 61 and with only his easygoing and friendly demeanor to sell on the air, grew very rich. Bowes was radio's first $2 million-a-year man. He was making twice the take-home pay of such stars as Al Jolson, Eddie Cantor, and Jack Benny. Edward Bowes was radio's unlikeliest star, and in 1935 its biggest.

Bowes was born June 14, 1874. Long before radio, he was a businessman, involved in real estate and theatrical development. His Capitol Theater, built in partnership with Messmore Kendall in 1919, was New York's premier movie-and-stage showplace. The Capitol had its own concert orchestra, widely emulated in other large movie palaces. It also had a 14-room suite where Major Bowes lived for much of his later life. Seldom was any amateur or network official allowed to look into this private world. One who did described dark rooms filled with antiques, rare paintings, and silver.

In 1925, Bowes took over *Roxy and His Gang*, a pioneering variety show, and turned it into the *Major Bowes Capitol Family Hour*. By 1934 he had become, in addition to his other enterprises, the manager of WHN, a radio station in New York. Abruptly his fortunes took a dramatic turn for the better. At WHN were two producers, Perry Charles and Fred Raphael, who had been experimenting with amateur hour concepts since the mid-1920s. Charles had shows featuring amateurs in 1925 and 1930; neither had amounted to much, but in 1934 the pair hit on a formula that would revolutionize the field. They suddenly saw the amateur hour in terms of a prizefight. The amateurs were the combatants. The more the audience knew about the fighters' personalities, the higher the levels of interest would climb. The bell between the rounds might also be utilized— a gong of sorts, to dismiss an amateur who wasn't making it. The gong was like sudden death, like the hook in the rough-and-tumble days of amateur nights in vaudeville. It was rude and crude, but its presence would add another element of suspense. The station's original *Amateur Hour* ran Tuesdays at 8 P.M. for 90

minutes. It was one of radio's most sensational success stories: in some published reports, it was said to hold 90 percent of New York's radio listeners, an almost unbelievable feat for any station, let alone a small independent of small wattage bucking major network affiliates. When Bowes saw what was happening, he stepped in and took the show over.

"From the beginning, he turned the amateur hour into a parade of human interest stories," said *Radio Guide* after a lengthy investigation of the show and its proprietor. WHN had about one-fiftieth the power of a network station, but it caught the amateur craze building to a crest. It was the talk of the town and soon of the entire industry. There was no question that it would soon be tapped for a network—the only real questions were when, where, how, and who would own it. Did it belong to WHN, to Charles and Raphael, or to Bowes? The problem became acute when a competing show, *National Amateur Night* with Ray Perkins, was launched on CBS in December 1934. Time was fleeting.

Bowes fished for a sponsor. He trolled among national advertisers, asking $3,500 a week (some reports said $5,000), and was quickly rewarded with a Chase and Sanborn contract and a choice timeslot on NBC. *Radio Guide* reported that WHN was so incensed that there was talk of an injunction prohibiting Bowes from opening. The station considered serving its papers just before air time. But word of this reached Bowes, and he "had a magistrate and a bondsman standing by to meet it." Bowes took to the NBC air without a hitch: WHN folded its cards and gave up without a fight, continuing its local amateur night with Jay C. Flippen as host. From that moment, *The Amateur Hour* belonged to Bowes.

He was launched, a national figure overnight, and the flood of humanity began. It was a tide to rival the great migration of workers from Oklahoma to California in the Dust Bowl years. Bowes promised them nothing, and still they came. A *Radio Stars* reporter arrived to find in the waiting crowd a "fingerless pianist" and "a colored lad who went into a tapdance that included such acrobatics as somersaulting without using his hands." There were mothers with babies in their arms: many had traveled the breadth of the land without a thought of the odds against them—70,000 to one against getting on the show, by one estimate. When news stories described the deepening despair of relief agencies, Bowes established a rule: no one was eligible who did not live in greater New York City. But as *Newsweek* reported, this formality was easily defeated; new transients arrived hourly, establishing residence "if only at a relief station."

The show came under fire even as it rose to the top of the ratings polls. By January 1936, it had posted a phenomenal 45.2 in the Hooper poll, a full 20 points over most other top ten programs. But soon charges of exploitation were on the rise. In addition to the radio show, Bowes had also established a company of traveling performers, made up of winners and finalists from the air. These troupes played cities and towns along the network line, their stage shows eagerly anticipated by audiences primed by the radio program. Bowes paid them little, usually around $50 a week, and out of this they were expected to cover their own food and shelter, with Bowes paying for the travel. He had as many as 18 groups on the road at any given time, bringing him a gross weekly income of $15,000—this in addition to his fee for the radio show, which had now ballooned to another $15,000 to $20,000 a week. There was also an *Amateur Hour* game, a series of RKO short films, a magazine, and a "Major Bowes Alarm Clock." At the beginning of his second year on the national air, the charge of exploitation arose, with *Radio Guide* in the vanguard.

The magazine sent Bowes a list of questions, which the major chose to ignore. *Guide* then launched an intense investigation of Bowes and his program, and the results appeared in a series of lengthy articles in 1936. Specifically, *Guide* wanted the answers to these questions. How did Bowes conduct himself in the auditions, which were cloaked in secrecy? (so secret that a network vice president was once ejected by a Bowes bodyguard). Were the on-air interview segments truly unrehearsed, as Bowes always claimed, or were the amateurs given scripts and forced to learn speaking roles before being allowed on the show? Were even the "gong" segments so well planned that Bowes knew in advance who would get "gonged-off" cruelly in mid-act? Were professional ·"ringers" allowed in from the lower ranks of vaudeville, passing themselves off as amateurs and violating the show's fundamental purpose? Perhaps most troubling was the suggestion that the show might be rigged, that the voting for winners was so loose that it might easily be compromised.

The magazine sent a reporter, Orville Edwards, under cover to find out. Edwards had been trained in voice: he was an amateur, though hardly an unpolished one. He went through the audition process and defied the odds, appearing on the broadcast of Feb. 23, 1936. His first contact was with Robert Reed, longtime Bowes assistant: Reed heard him sing and gave him a second audition at the Capitol Theater two days later. Bowes did not attend either session, but it was later revealed that he often eavesdropped by loudspeaker on various auditions from his office in the Capitol. Edwards was scheduled for a third audition, at NBC, this time with Bowes present. Bowes questioned Edwards about his life and had a stenographer take down the answers.

On Saturday, the day before the broadcast, there was an audition at the microphone. Bowes watched from a desk in the studio. Edwards was given a script and told by a secretary, "These are the questions the major will ask and the answers you are to give." He would have to know his lines perfectly, she said, or he couldn't be on the program. Then another Bowes associate, Bessie Mack, gave him a legal release to sign. Bowes was taking a one-year option on Edwards's services. Edwards, on the other hand, could not refer to Bowes or his appearance on the show in his future attempts to secure bookings. But if he did get work as a result of the *Amateur Hour*, he agreed to pay Bowes 15 percent of whatever money he earned. Edwards signed the paper and became a contestant.

On Sunday afternoon there was a rehearsal, with Reed directing from the booth. Bessie Mack ran Edwards through his speaking part, herself taking Bowes's role. At five o'clock, Edwards was brought before the major. The script was read and lines were changed. The script called for Bowes to ask what song he sang the very best, and for Edwards to answer, "*When the Stars Were Brightly Shining*, from Puccini's opera *Tosca*." Bowes changed the line so that Edwards would give only the title and he, Bowes, would then say, "from Puccini's opera *Tosca*," implying that the major was indeed a man of culture.

Then the amateurs were fed. It was widely known that Bowes gave contestants $10 each and "all they could eat" for appearing on the show. They were given meal cards for Bickford's cafeteria across the street. There, Edwards said, "a big meal could be had for about fifty cents."

With their man on the show, *Radio Guide* stationed its staff at telephones, in an attempt to rig the voting. Many of the staffers claimed to represent groups, with all their members voting for Edwards. Some of these votes were accepted, some rejected, some taken in part: if the caller claimed to be part of a formal club or service organization, all the votes claimed by that person were allowed. The magazine drummed its singer into a fourth-place finish, proving to its own satisfaction at least that *The Original Amateur Hour* was highly riggable.

An article the following week charged that one amateur had been cruelly set up for national ridicule. Barely had his song begun when Bowes gave him the gong. The audience roared with laughter: the major smiled, not unkindly. But when the defeated amateur was ushered backstage, he stole a peek at the program log. He had been scheduled for one minute only, confirming his sudden realization that he'd been made a goat. "I knew I couldn't do my song in just one minute." The article also repeated the charge that vaudeville professionals were sneaking in, people "willing to work for the major's ten dollars in order to keep from starving." Bowes continued to insist that every effort was made to keep professionals out.

The voting system for *The Original Amateur Hour* was well established and widely known. Each week a town along the network was selected as the show's "honor city." That edition of the *Amateur Hour* was dedicated to the honor city, and its citizens were allowed to join New York in voting for the winners. Phone banks were set up: a city the size of Nashville, Tenn., might cast as many as 18,000 votes during its designation. Votes were also taken by mail, and the network took thousands of votes—30,000 for the week wasn't unusual. The winners were announced on the following show. Often they were invited for encore performances, and three-time winners became finalists for the year's championship. Anyone from the radio show might be asked to join a road unit: this de-

pended on the need of individual units rather than an amateur's standing in the voting. The road companies were comprised of 20 to 25 amateurs, and were warmly received in the cities where they played. They were honored and fed at local Rotary or Kiwanis clubs, a much-needed fringe benefit, and were given more attention than most had ever known. Some roomed together to help make ends meet. It was fun and adventure despite the hardships, for many the time of their lives. One bus was lost in a North Dakota snowstorm, finally limping into a village, where the company was snowed in for days. Strong feelings of camaraderie and friendship grew on the road, and there were squabbles and inevitable love affairs. It was, wrote one young woman, "like one big happy family. I'm getting $50 a week, which is more than I ever made in my life, I'm in with the swellest bunch of fellows and girls I've ever known, just like my old high school crowd."

Bowes was a paunchy man, once termed "as expert a showman as the world has seen since Phineas Barnum." Throughout his years on the air he remained a little-known, private figure. His rating, though it began spectacularly, simmered to 23.2 the second year. It dropped steadily, though the show remained a top ten force through most of the late 1930s. Bowes collected many honorary titles in his life: his real title, "major," was often suspected of being a trumped-up, but it was genuine enough—he had held that rank in the U.S. Army Reserve during World War I. In retrospect, the show produced few stars of the first magnitude (Beverly Sills, Frank Sinatra, and Robert Merrill were the best-known *Amateur Hour* winners). "To be sure, minor talents have been discovered," *Radio Guide* conceded. "But even the best half-dozen performers who have moved up in the entertainment world through the *Amateur Hour* still are not averaging more than $100 a week. Compare this figure with Major Bowes' own income of something like $40,000 a week, and compare that with the $40–60 earned by players in his units. It's something to think about."

Bowes would reply that it was, after all, an amateur show. On the face of it, amateurs had not yet (and most never would) develop the disciplines or skills of a professional. Many were painful to watch, they were so bad, and the charm of *The Original Amateur Hour* was in presenting a performer in his rugged embryonic state, warts and all. Once, asked to name the "lousiest amateur" he had ever seen, Bowes replied, "If you were hit by a buzz saw, could you tell which tooth hurt you most?" His big fear was that a defeated amateur might become violent on live radio. You could never predict what a man might do when he'd traveled 2,000 miles, slept in boxcars, fought his way through the audition process, and found himself gonged off after singing less than 30 seconds (one hapless contestant got the gong before opening his mouth—he missed his cue). So Bowes had a bodyguard, "a good strongarm," he told the *New Yorker*, "who hustles them up to the microphone and down again. I always signal him before letting the bell go, and he is always ready to grab the poor boob before he can say anything vile."

The show opened with a "wheel of fortune," which Bowes had used in the WHN days. "A-spinning goes our weekly wheel of fortune," he would say at the top of the show: "Around and around and around she goes, and where she stops, nobody knows." Amateurs were now big business. *National Amateur Night* was still on CBS; another show, *NTG and His Girls*, was running an amateur game on NBC, and even Fred Allen had given half his *Town Hall Tonight* hour to the search for unknown talent. But the fever waned as the '40s dawned: Bowes's show was trimmed to half an hour, and by 1945 the rating was a puny 7.2. Bowes dropped out of radio, old and sick and rich. He died the following year, June 13, 1946.

Two years after his death, the show was revived by Ted Mack, who had been a master of ceremonies on some of Bowes's road units. He launched the new *Original Amateur Hour* in the spirit of the old, reviving the wheel of fortune, the telephone voting banks, and the traveling stage units. Dennis James was his announcer. Mack also revived *The Capitol Family Hour*, now titled *The Ted Mack Family Hour*. This ran on ABC TV, January-November 1951, in an hour-long format with the final 30 minutes simulcast.

MAJOR HOOPLE, situation comedy, based on the comic strip *Our Boarding House*, by Gene Ahern.

BROADCAST HISTORY: June 22, 1942–April 26, 1943, Blue Network. 30m, Mondays at 7. CAST: Arthur Q. Bryan as "Major" Amos Hoople, a windbag who claimed a former association with every military fighting unit ever assembled. Patsy Moran as Martha, his "patient but none-too-trusting wife." Conrad Binyon as Alvin, Hoople's "precocious little nephew." Franklin Bresee also as Alvin. Mel Blanc as Tiffany Twiggs, the Hooples' star boarder and number one complainer. PRODUCERS: Arnold Maguire; later Louis Quinn. WRITERS: Jerry Cady, Phil Leslie.

Major Hoople and his wife Martha ran the Hoople Boarding House in this scenario. Hoople spun endless tales of how he'd captured San Juan Hill and won the Boer War single-handedly, or how his great-great-grandfather Phineas Hoople forged the shoes for Paul Revere's horse. The hero claimed lineage from a line of English barons, one of whom had served in every prominent historical skirmish.

MAKE-BELIEVE BALLROOM, disc jockey show.

BROADCAST HISTORY: Feb. 3, 1935–Jan. 1, 1954, WNEW, New York. Various lengths to 210m.

Although *Make-Believe Ballroom* was a local series, its fame was national. Creator-host Martin Block borrowed a page (and the title) from a West Coast disc jockey named Al Jarvis, who had done a platter show called *Make-Believe Ballroom* in the early '30s and was still active in the '40s. Initially a filler between developments in the trial of Bruno Richard Hauptmann for the Lindbergh baby kidnapping, Block's show expanded and employed clever illusion. As the *New Yorker* put it, he made listeners believe "that the country's foremost dance bands are playing on four large stands in a glittering crystal-chandeliered ballroom." In reality, wrote David T. MacFarland in *American Broadcasting*, "the show came from an unglittering studio that contained a microphone flanked by two phonograph turntables."

Block was later heard on ABC (*The Martin Block Show*, 1954–61, weekdays, in midafternoon slots of up to 90 minutes), and still later at WOR, where he worked until 1967.

MAKE-BELIEVE TOWN, HOLLYWOOD, light romantic drama.

BROADCAST HISTORY: Aug. 1, 1949–Dec. 31, 1950, CBS. 30m, weekdays at 3:30 until Oct. 1950, then Sundays at 3:30.

July 21–Sept. 8, 1951, CBS. 30m, Saturdays at 11:30 A.M.

HOSTESS: Virginia Bruce with boy-girl tales of the film city. Hollywood radio stars in anthology roles: Lurene Tuttle, Howard Culver, Mary Shipp, Terry O'Sullivan, etc. ANNOUNCER: John Jacobs. MUSIC: Ivan Ditmars on organ. PRODUCER-DIRECTOR: Ralph Rose.

MALCOLM CLAIRE, storyteller; children's stories.

BROADCAST HISTORY: 1931–40, NBC. 15m, various times.

Malcolm Claire was a one-man storyteller, portraying a cast of regular characters who helped illustrate his tales. Often he borrowed from the brothers Grimm or from Joel Chandler Harris. His "cast" included several blackface types with such names as "Whitewash, the dandy of darktown," and "Spareribs," described by *Radio Guide* as "a shabby, serene-spirited darky whose greatest pleasure is drawling his old yarns to the spellbound youngsters." He also played "the Old Witch," who told the fairy tales, and "Uncle Mal," who was known as "the old man." He was often heard in early morning, including a six-a-week series at 8 A.M., 1936–38.

MAN ABOUT HOLLYWOOD, interviews and variety.

BROADCAST HISTORY: July 17–Sept. 4, 1939, CBS. Mondays at 9 in 30m of the *Lux Radio Theater* summer slot, designed for "Hollywood" continuity. Lux Soap.

July 12–Sept. 27, 1940, CBS. 30m, Fridays at 8 for vacationing Kate Smith. Grape Nuts.

HOST: George McCall, chatting with radio people, film technicians, Hollywood restaurateurs and nightclub entertainers, a motion picture censor, etc. ORCHESTRA: Wilbur Hatch.

THE MAN BEHIND THE GUN, war drama.

BROADCAST HISTORY: Oct. 7, 1942–March 4, 1944, CBS. 30m, Wednesdays at 10:30 until March 1943; Sundays at 10:30 until July 1943; then Saturdays at 7. Elgin Watches, 1943. NARRATORS: Everett Sloane, Jackson Beck. Casts from New York's Radio Row: Myron McCormick, Bill Quinn, Larry Haines, Paul Luther, etc. MUSIC: Bernard Herrmann, Nathan Van Cleave. DIRECTOR: William N. Robson. WRITERS: Ranald MacDougall, Allan Sloane, Arthur Laurents, Forrest Barnes, Robert Lewis Shayon. SOUND EFFECTS: Ralph Curtiss, Paul Mowry, James Rogan.

The Man Behind the Gun was a major series, highly respected within the industry and by the modest but enthusiastic audience that heard it. It was a three-time winner of *Billboard*'s "top documentary program" citation and in 1943 won a Peabody Award as radio's outstanding dramatic program.

It was "dedicated to the fighting men of the United States and the United Nations," presented "for the purpose of telling you how your boys and their comrades-in-arms are waging our war against Axis aggression." The stories were "based on fact," but the names and characterizations were "wholly fictitious," giving the writers and director maximum freedom to develop composite representations of fighting-man types. One week the "man behind the gun" might be a spitfire pilot in the Royal Air Force; another week the skipper of a torpedo boat; later in the run, a submarine man somewhere in the Pacific. The stories were told by a steel-voiced narrator, always in the present tense from a second-person viewpoint. This action narrative put "you" the listener into the shoes of the hero, and made the series (with *Words at War* and *Cavalcade of America*) one of the three most vivid and historically significant dramas of its time.

The idea was developed by Ranald MacDougall. It was assigned to CBS staff director William N. Robson, who saw its powerful potential at once. For Robson, this was a full-time job. "You didn't do other shows when you had one like that," he recalled 45 years later. "Randy and I used to be on the road half the time. You couldn't do it sitting in New York. When the *Boise* limped into the Philadelphia Navy Yard all shot up from the Battle of the

Coral Sea, we were down there to interview the crew and examine the ship. We were down in Texas, flying with pursuit planes. We were down in Kentucky, at Fort Knox with the tank corps.''

Then, returning to New York, Robson and MacDougall selected their viewpoint for the week's story and created a character to embody it. They were sometimes closer to truth than the government wanted radio to be. Anticipating an invasion of Sicily, Robson sent writer Allan Sloane to Massachusetts, where engineers were being trained in the art of beachhead landings. ''I knew they were gonna go in someplace,'' he said, ''and there had to be beachfront landings. So we knew ahead of time all the techniques that were being taught, and we just dramatized a textbook landing.'' The news bulletins came on a Friday evening, Robson remembered. ''I called Allan and asked how the script was going. He said he was nearly finished. I said, 'You'd better be finished, because we're goin' with it on Sunday.' ''

Robson was an authoritative director. ''You did it my way or else,'' he said. The show came first: his dedication to it was fierce, and actors who couldn't give it the same commitment went their separate way. Early in the run, Robson crossed swords with narrator Everett Sloane and composer-conductor Bernard Herrmann. Sloane was the show's ''voice,'' the all-important thread that would pull a story together through the music and sound effects. Timing was everything: in the battle scenes, the actors, narrator, music, and sound had to be coordinated and cued ''literally on a split-second.'' Each broadcast took two days to rehearse, and Sloane—then one of radio's busiest actors—felt he couldn't spare the time. He was a pro, he argued: ''I just don't need that much rehearsal.'' Robson replied, ''Everett, I know you don't, but I do.'' Jackson Beck became the voice of the series for its duration.

Herrmann, long known as one of radio's most tempestuous musicians, disagreed loudly with Robson's decision to use a robust theme. ''He screamed at me in the first rehearsal,'' Robson said—''*You wanna win the war with music, get Wagner's music! Don't get my music! I can't win the war with my music!*'' Herrmann departed, and Nathan Van Cleave gave Robson the gusty sound he wanted.

There was high creativity, constant improvisation. ''I had two 18-inch speakers brought into the studio and placed on the dead sides of the cast mikes,'' Robson said. ''We were using dynamic microphones, with two live sides and two dead sides.'' This instantly increased the intensity of the readings. ''Now when the guns went off, the actors had to yell to hear themselves. When the planes went off with four motors going, they had to yell to be heard above it, and the actuality was magnificent!'' It was like directing a symphony, Robson said. A New York magazine editor who witnessed a broadcast agreed, describing Robson's two-handed direction as he called up voices, music, sound, diving airplanes, and barrages of artillery. She could only liken it to Toscanini leading the NBC Symphony. ''I know it sounds arrogant,'' Robson said, ''but I felt that way. Everything came off my fingers . . . everything.''

The show was not generous with acting credits: the unmistakable voice of Frank Lovejoy can sometimes be heard among the East Coast actors who worked the series. Unfortunately, there are few shows available at this writing, but the half-dozen on tape pack plenty of punch and offer high listener involvement 50 years after they aired.

THE MAN CALLED X, espionage melodrama.

BROADCAST HISTORY: July 10–Aug. 28, 1944, CBS. 30m, Mondays at 9:30. Lockheed Aircraft.

Sept. 9, 1944–March 3, 1945, Blue Network. 30m, Saturdays at 10:30. Lockheed.

June 12–Sept. 4, 1945, and again June 18–Sept. 17, 1946, NBC. 30m, Tuesdays at 10. Substitute for Bob Hope. Pepsodent.

April 3, 1947–Sept. 26, 1948, CBS. 30m, Thursdays at 10 until Nov., then Sundays at 8:30. General Motors for Frigidaire.

Oct. 13, 1950–May 20, 1952, NBC. Many 30m timeslots, often Friday or Saturday nights but moved frequently. Ford Motors, late 1950; RCA, Whitehall Pharmacal, and/or Liggett and Myers Tobacco, 1950–51.

CAST: Herbert Marshall as Ken Thurston, ''the man called X,'' an international troubleshooter, sent wherever intrigue lurked and danger was the byword. Leon Belasco as Pegon Zeldschmidt, Thurston's friendly nemesis. Hollywood radio actors in support: Joan Banks, Will Wright, Peter Leeds, Harry Lang, Carleton Young, Barbara Fuller, William Conrad, Lou Merrill, Stanley Waxman, B. J.

Thompson, George Niese, etc. **ANNOUNCERS:** John McIntire, 1944; Wendell Niles, 1947–48. **ORCHESTRA:** Gordon Jenkins, CBS, 1944; Claude Sweeten and Felix Mills, 1944–45; Johnny Green, 1947–48. **DIRECTORS:** William N. Robson, CBS, 1944; Jack Johnstone for much of the run; Dee Engelbach in the late run. **WRITERS:** Milton Merlin, Sidney Marshall, etc.

The Man Called X was conceived and initially produced as an FBI adventure series. But soon hero Ken Thurston became a nation-hopping agent described by announcer John McIntire as "the man who crosses the ocean as readily as you and I cross town. He is the man who travels today as you and I will travel tomorrow. He is the man who fights today's war in his unique fashion, so that tomorrow's peace will make the world a neighborhood for all of us." Again, this was quickly modified, becoming the epigram best remembered: "Wherever there is mystery, intrigue, romance, in all the strange and dangerous places of the world, there you will find *The Man Called X.*" This descriptive motif was lifted, almost literally, for the later series *Dangerous Assignment.*

Thurston, played suavely by British actor Herbert Marshall, traveled to India, Monte Carlo, and other exotic locales. His cases often involved mysterious women with shady pasts. Thurston's dubious ally, Pegon Zeldschmidt, had a streak of larceny in his soul but somehow managed to stay right with the law. He would help if the price was right.

THE MAN FROM G-2, espionage thriller, based on stories by F. Van Wyck Mason; also known as *Major North, Army Intelligence.*

BROADCAST HISTORY: April 12, 1945–Feb. 2, 1946, ABC. 30m, various times. **CAST:** Staats Cotsworth as Major Hugh North. Also, Joan Alexander.

THE MAN FROM HOMICIDE, police drama.

BROADCAST HISTORY: June 25–Oct. 1, 1951, ABC. 30m, Mondays at 8:30. From Hollywood. **CAST:** Dan Duryea as tough cop Lou Dana ("I don't like killers"). Bill Bouchey as Inspector Sherman. Lawrence Dobkin as Dave the sergeant. Also: Herb Butterfield, Tony Barrett, Jo Gilbert, Barney Phillips, etc. **ANNOUNCER:** Orval An-

derson. **PRODUCER-DIRECTOR:** Dwight Hauser. **WRITER:** Dick Powell. (An audition show was recorded in 1950, starring Charles McGraw as Dana, with Joan Banks, Arthur Q. Bryan, Tom Tully, Lawrence Dobkin, and Jim Backus, with direction by Helen Mack.)

THE MAN I MARRIED, soap opera.

BROADCAST HISTORY: July 3, 1939–May 2, 1941, NBC. 15m, weekdays at 10 A.M. Oxydol.
July 21, 1941–April 3, 1942, CBS. 15m, weekdays at 11:15 A.M. Campbell Soups.
CAST: Van Heflin as Adam Waring. Clayton "Bud" Collyer also as Adam Waring. Vicki Vola, Gertrude Warner, Betty Winkler, Dorothy Lowell, and Barbara Lee as Evelyn Waring. **WRITERS:** Carl Bixby and Don Becker.

Little is known of the plot, beyond Raymond William Stedman's description: "the story of a disinherited son of a millionaire, trying to make a new start in a small town."

A MAN NAMED JORDAN, adventure serial, forerunner of the series ROCKY JORDAN.

BROADCAST HISTORY: Jan. 8–June 29, 1945, CBS West Coast. 15m, weeknights.
July 2, 1945–ca. 1947, CBS West. 30m, weekly, various times.
CAST: Jack Moyles as Rocky Jordan, proprietor of the Cafe Tambourine, a small restaurant "in a narrow street off Istanbul's Grand Bazaar," permeated by the smoke of Oriental tobacco, alive with the babble of many tongues, and packed with intrigue. Also: Paul Frees, Dorothy Lovett, and Jay Novello. **WRITER-DIRECTOR:** Ray Buffum.

Rocky Jordan, in his serial days, was a hero in the *I Love a Mystery* mold: rough-cut, formidable, with a code of ethics rooted in practicalities rather than sentiment. He was strongly motivated by profit potential, and his search for fortune was often wrapped up in dangerous enterprise. His sidekicks at the Tambourine were a native "man Friday" named Ali, a girlfriend named Toni Sherwood, and his pal Duke O'Brien.

MANDRAKE, THE MAGICIAN, adventure serial, based on the King Features comic strip by Lee Falk.

BROADCAST HISTORY: Nov. 11, 1940–Feb. 6, 1942, Mutual. 15m, three a week at 5:30 until 1941, then weekdays at 5:15. **CAST:** Raymond Edward Johnson as Mandrake, a mystic educated in Tibet by a master of magic. Juano Hernandez as Mandrake's servant, Lothar, a giant who could "rip a crocodile's jaws apart or break the back of an anthropoid ape." Francesca Lenni as the Princess Narda. **DIRECTOR:** Carlo De Angelo.

In this scenario, Mandrake and his servant Lothar lived in a "house of mystery and many secrets." The magician's chant, *invoco legem magicarum*, invoked the laws of magic and set into play his bag of tricks.

MANHATTAN AT MIDNIGHT, romantic drama.

BROADCAST HISTORY: July 24, 1940–Sept. 1, 1943, Blue Network. 30m, Wednesdays at 8:30. Energine, Sterling Drugs. **CAST:** Jeanette Nolan, Teddy Bergman, Ted de Corsia, etc.

MANHATTAN MERRY-GO-ROUND, popular music.

BROADCAST HISTORY: Nov. 6, 1932–April 17, 1949, NBC. 30m, Blue Network, Sundays at 3:30 until April 9, 1933, then Red Network, Sundays at 9. Dr. Lyons Tooth Powder. **VOCALISTS:** Thomas L. Thomas, Marian McManus, Dick O'Connor, Dennis Ryan, Barry Roberts, Glenn Cross, Rodney McClennan. **VOCAL GROUPS:** "The Men About Town"; the Jerry Mann Voices. **ORCHESTRA:** Andy Sannella; Victor Arden and "the Boys and Girls of Manhattan." **ANNOUNCERS:** Ford Bond, Roger Krupp. **PRODUCERS:** Frank and Anne Hummert. **DIRECTOR:** Paul Dumont.

The Manhattan Merry-Go-Round was the Hummert version of *Your Hit Parade*, but filled with much the same musical sound as the Hummerts' other prime-time musicales, *The American Album of Familiar Music* and *Waltz Time*. By 1933, Frank Hummert had bought a 60-minute block of NBC's Sunday night schedule, slotting *Merry-Go-Round* and *American Album* as back-to-back complementary programs. *Album* stayed with traditional melodies; *Merry-Go-Round* offered current hits and was kept as up-to-date as possible. The show was based largely on sales of sheet music and records.

It was built around the concept of a wining-dining whirl through New York nightclubs, where the top tunes of the week were "sung so clearly you can understand every word and sing them yourself." The show plugged such nightspots as the Diamond Horseshoe and the Stork Club, and such mention was good for heavy out-of-town trade. In fact, the cast never went out of the broadcast studio, but listeners were given such full ambience that they often asked to see cast members when they came to New York and visited the actual clubs. *Newsweek* noted an attempt to achieve a continental flavor in the '30s by featuring Rachel Carlay "and her French ditties," her partners a series of young men all of whom "adopted the nom-de-mike of Pierre Le Kruen (pronounced Croon)."

The format was Hummert-tested and seldom varied, calculated to appeal to the vast cross-section of middle America. There was some experimentation with variety in the '30s, when comics Bert Lahr, Beatrice Lillie, and Jimmy Durante appeared, but the format was a steady eight songs a week. Thomas L. Thomas was billed as "beloved star of stage and radio." The theme was catchy, remembered for years.

Jump on the Manhattan Merry-Go-Round,
We're touring alluring old New York town.
Broadway to Harlem a musical show,
The orchids that you rest at your radio.
We're serving music, songs and laughter,
Your happy heart will follow after.
And we'd like to have you all with us
On the Manhattan Merry-Go-Round!

MANHATTAN MOTHER, soap opera.

BROADCAST HISTORY: 1938, WBBM, Chicago; later also WABC, New York. Then, March 6, 1939–April 5, 1940, CBS, various 15m weekday slots (between 9 and 10 A.M.) from Chicago; moved to New York Jan. 1, 1940, 15m, weekdays at 4:30. Procter & Gamble for Chipso. **CAST:** Kaye Brinker (Chicago and New York) as Patricia Locke, who gave up a career to raise her daughter, Dale, in New York. Louise Fitch as Dale Locke (Chicago); Vicki Vola as Dale (New York). Ned Wever as Patricia's new husband, Lawrence Locke (Chicago); John Davenport Seymour as Lawrence Locke (New York). **ANNOUNCERS:** Ed Roberts,

John Fleming, George Watson. **DIRECTORS:**
Bobby Brown, Basil Loughrane. **WRITER:** Orin
Tovrov.

MANHUNT, crime drama.

BROADCAST HISTORY: 1945–46, 15m transcribed syndication (Ziv), with crime stories complete in each episode. **CAST:** Larry Haines as
Drew Stevens. New York players in support.

MARCH OF GAMES, juvenile game and quiz
show.

BROADCAST HISTORY: April 25, 1938–July 13,
1941, CBS. 15m, twice a week at various times,
generally between 5 and 6 until Oct. 1939; 30m,
Sundays at 10:30 A.M. through June 23, 1940, then
at 1:30. **CAST:** Arthur Ross, age 14 (1938), the
"youngest master of ceremonies in radio." Sybil
Trent, the show's "drum-major" who "moves the
game along" by introducing quizzes in rhyme.
Also, many from the cast of *Let's Pretend*: Jack
Grimes, Estelle Levy, Kingsley Colton, Florence
Halop, Arthur Anderson, etc. **MUSIC:** Louise
Wilcher on organ. **PRODUCER-DIRECTOR:**
Nila Mack.

All the contestants were children, tackling
questions and answers, tongue-twisters, and puzzles, for prizes of $5 and *March of Games* books.
The listening audience contributed the questions,
with sets of *Junior Encyclopedia* given for the
best.

THE MARCH OF TIME, news documentary
and dramatization.

BROADCAST HISTORY: March 6, 1931–April 26,
1935, CBS. 30m, Fridays at 10:30 through June
1931; at 8:30, 1931–33; at 8, 1933–34; at 9, 1934–
35. *Time* magazine; also, Remington-Rand,
beginning Oct. 13, 1933.

Aug. 26, 1935–Sept. 25, 1936, CBS. 15m,
weeknights at 10:30. Remington-Rand until March
30, then Wrigley's Gum.

Oct. 15, 1936–Oct. 7, 1937, CBS. 30m, Thursdays at 10:30. Electrolux Refrigerators.

Oct. 14, 1937–April 28, 1939, Blue Network.
30m, Thursdays at 8:30 until Jan. 1938; at 8 until
July 1938; then Fridays at 9:30. Electrolux Refrigerators, 1937–38; *Time* magazine.

Oct. 9, 1941–June 5, 1942, Blue Network. 30m,

Thursdays at 8 until Feb. 1942, then Fridays at
9:30, later at 9. *Time*.

July 9, 1942–Oct. 26, 1944, NBC. 30m, Thursdays at 10:30. *Time*.

Nov. 2, 1944–July 26, 1945, ABC. 30m, Thursdays at 10:30. *Time*.

CAST: Ted Husing, Westbrook Van Voorhis, and
Harry Von Zell, variously, as narrators known as
"the Voice of *Time*" or "the Voice of Fate."
Also, many skilled imitators of world newsmakers.
Bill Adams as Franklin Delano Roosevelt. Bill
Johnstone, Staats Cotsworth, and Art Carney also
as Roosevelt. Bill Johnstone also as King Edward
VIII and as New Dealer Cordell Hull. Frank Read-
ick as Cordell Hull, as former New York mayor
Jimmy Walker, as Charles Lindbergh, and as Jo-
seph Zangara, killer of Chicago mayor Anton
"Tony" Cermak. Jack Smart as Louisiana Sen.
Huey Long. Ted de Corsia as Huey Long, and as
Herbert Hoover, Benito Mussolini, Gen. Hugh
Johnson, Pierre Laval, and in many gangster roles.
John Battle, specializing in southerners, as Huey
Long and as Vice President John Nance Garner.
Marion Hopkinson as Frances Perkins, first female
cabinet member, and as Eleanor Roosevelt. Agnes
Moorehead, Nancy Kelly, and Jeanette Nolan as
Eleanor Roosevelt, and in other roles. Dwight
Weist as Bruno Richard Hauptmann for almost
two years. Dwight Weist also as Adolf Hitler, as
Joseph Goebbels, John L. Lewis, William Ran-
dolph Hearst, George Arliss, Father Charles
Coughlin, Mayor Fiorello La Guardia, George Ber-
nard Shaw, and as Fred Allen. Dwight Weist also
(according to *Radio Guide*) as "all three Barry-
mores, including Ethel." Edwin Jerome as Josef
Stalin, Haile Selassie, and King Alfonso of Spain.
Maurice Tarplin as Winston Churchill. Peter Don-
ald as Neville Chamberlain. Also: Ted Jewett, Ev-
erett Sloane, Orson Welles, Paul Stewart, Juano
Hernandez, Arlene Francis, John McIntire, Harry
Browne, Charles Slattery, Herschel Mayall, Arnold
Moss, Pedro de Cordoba, Ray Collins, Gary Mer-
rill, Porter Hall, Kenny Delmar, Georgia Backus,
Claire Niesen, Lotte Staviski, Myron McCormick,
Karl Swenson, Elliott Reid, Martin Gabel, Ade-
laide Klein, etc. **ORCHESTRA:** Howard Barlow
(CBS); Don Voorhees (NBC). **PRODUCER-
DIRECTOR:** Arthur Pryor Jr., of Batten, Barton,
Durstine and Osborne. Also: Donald Stouffer,
Thomas Harrington. **SUBSEQUENT DIREC-
TORS:** William Spier and Homer Fickett, alter-
nating weeks in the mid-1930s; Lester Vail,

WRITERS: Fred Smith, Dwight Cook, Ann Barley, Bob Tallman, Jimmy Shute, John Martin, Bob Richards, Ruth Barth, Paul Milton, Richard Dana, Carl Carmer, Garrett Porter and Brice Disque. SOUND EFFECTS: Initially Ora D. Nichols and her assistants at CBS, George O'Donnell and Henry Gauthier; also, Al Van Brackels, Walter Pierson, James Rinaldi, Roland Fitzgerald and Edward Fenton (CBS); Keene Crockett (NBC); also, Bob Prescott, Edwin K. Cohan, etc.

The March of Time was the first radio newsreel: dramatized news events, elaborately staged with sound effects and music, but put together like a newspaper—often on deadline, with impact and accuracy its twin goals. Its roots are found in a series of ten-minute newscasts heard on WLW, Cincinnati, in 1928.

It was conceived in part by Fred Smith, WLW station manager, to help counter radio's lack of news-gathering ability. The wire services then confined their clientele to print outlets, which were uneasy at the prospect of radio entering the news business. Radio stations could only clip the papers, make some cursory attempt to rewrite, and broadcast the news in bulletin form. Smith thought an arrangement with *Time* might benefit both radio and the magazine. The station would get a news show, which could be offered in script form to other stations around the country. *Time* would get stronger name identification and perhaps new advertising accounts in areas where the show ran.

Smith approached Roy Larsen, director of circulation for *Time*, whose offices were in Cleveland. Larsen obtained permission, and on Sept. 3, 1928, *Time* began syndicating the scripts to other stations. In September 1929, the operation expanded into active syndication, with full shows transcribed and sent to subscribers. Soon more than 100 stations were carrying it. Imitators sprang up, and Smith pushed the idea into a new mode that would, perhaps, make imitation more difficult. He wanted to dramatize the news: as *Radioland* summarized, "to create for the listener the illusion of being right there on the spot" when news was made. Larsen had qualms about the legality of impersonating living people in a nonsatiric format, in what would undoubtedly be taken by many as a serious news broadcast. Smith countered with this argument: it *would* be a serious news show; there would be absolutely no fiction,

no words taken out of context, no doctoring of the actual statements of the subjects. How could the newsmakers object, unless they objected to what they themselves had said?

A closed-circuit audition program was prepared and, on Feb. 6, 1931, was given a private performance for CBS executives and editors of *Time*. The show was broadcast directly to Larsen's home, where (according to Raymond Fielding in his book, *The March of Time*) CBS chief William S. Paley and *Time* publisher Henry R. Luce were conspicuously present. Few in the assembled party liked the show, but plans continued for its premiere, which took place on a partial CBS hookup a month later. Luce remained uneasy over the show's bellicose nature: it sounded like a midway event, with barkers and hustlers hawking the news. It seemed to fly in the face of journalistic integrity, causing many *Time* editors to remain skeptical even when it quickly caught on with critics and the public. *The March of Time* was a success whether Luce liked it or not.

It was nothing if not an attention-grabber. Its sound was like an authentic Movietone newsreel, with shouting mobs, riveting sound effects, and music that conveyed the merciless, relentless pace of time. Through this vivid audio potpourri, listeners would "see" the rise of Hitler, the trial of Bruno Richard Hauptmann, the abdication of Edward VIII, the controversy over the New Deal, the Italian conquest of Ethiopia, and the tragedy of the Spanish Civil War. Many listeners were convinced that they were hearing the voices of real newsmakers on the scene, and some wondered aloud how it was done.

It was done by a company of New York actors who became known as the cream of the crop. "Nine men and one woman work at a fixed salary of $150 a week," wrote *Radio Guide* in 1936, as the show opened its sixth season. "They are *Time*'s regular acting staff. But if they sound like actors, they are fired. *Time* actors must forget themselves completely; must *be* the persons they impersonate. There is more to perfect mimicry than voice and accent. There must be a feeling of sympathy, even for those people whose lives they abhor." The regular cast, wrote *Radio News* in 1938, was supplemented by an "available list" of 700 names with specific talents. "Here may be found the voices of Swedes or Abyssinians, gnomes or elves—even the piping, squeaky voice that was once needed to represent a supposedly talking and singing mongoose found on the Isle of Man. To get on *The March of Time* is the ambition of many a radio voice, for this program has become to radio actors what the old-time Palace Theater was to vaudeville troupers. It is the open sesame to any radio director's sanctum. Out of 1,200 voices auditioned during 1937, only 18 were suitable.''

And like any good newspaper, the show had severe critics. It was damned left and right. Real newsmen condemned it for hamming up the news. Communists called it fascistic. William Randolph Hearst labeled it Communist propaganda and forbade mention of it in the pages of his newspapers. It was banned in Germany. It even ran afoul of Roosevelt, who asked and later demanded that it stop impersonating him, because the actors were so good they were diminishing the impact of his Fireside Chats. It was accused of being pompous, pretentious, melodramatic, and bombastic. But it was never dull. In the mid-1930s, *Time* had Hooper numbers in the 25-point range.

It was produced by Batten, Barton, Durstine and Osborne, the agency handling the *Time* account. Arthur Pryor, head of the agency's radio department, ran the show while delegating the director's job to Donald Stouffer and Thomas Harrington. From the beginning it was known that *The March of Time* would face the stiffest production challenges that radio had yet known. It would be a balancing act between the disciplines of drama and the pressures of news that sometimes continued to break right up to air time. The focal point would be the magazine, which was constantly receiving dispatches from all over the world. When a big story broke at the last minute, a polished ready-to-air show was reorganized: the entire menu was shifted as events demanded. Newspapers are accustomed to this: a top reporter can write a new lead or a new story with only minutes to spare. Drama was developed at a more leisurely pace. But in radio, a new breed of actor had come to the fore, players who could deliver superb performances from scripts they had never seen before going live on the air. Sight reading, they called it: reading always two lines ahead and acting the lines they had already read.

Actors, sound artists, and musicians worked feverishly to accommodate the bulletins from *Time*'s reporters in the field. Managing editor William Geer was *Time*'s man in the slot for the radio show: his was the final word on last-minute changes and cuts, all rewritten to the style of the magazine. If a subject died minutes before air time, a new top was put on the show, and newspapers were scooped, to their disbelief, by a drama.

In 1937, the airship *Hindenburg* exploded at Lakehurst, N.J., just two hours before *The March of Time* went on the air. Only bulletins were available at air time, but it was enough: the segment focused on the history of dirigible travel and ended with a news flash on the Lakehurst tragedy. The orchestra and sound effects produced an unprecedented sense of reality, said *Radio News*: ''of storm, explosion, frenzied cries, crackling flames, and crumpling girders.'' These early effects were created by the pioneer sound artist at CBS, Ora D. Nichols, and her assistants. ''The scripts may call for anything from staccato noises of a busy office to a storm at sea,'' reported *Radioland* in January 1934. ''The two hardest jobs they ever had to reproduce were an oil well burning and the sound of a locomotive being hit by a tornado.''

Time saw itself as the show's producer, though the magazine was usually the sponsor as well. Luce was most contented, however, when other products picked up the tab. When Remington-Rand took on sponsorship in October 1933, *Time* boasted in its pages that this was the first time an advertiser had been persuaded to put on another advertiser's program. The magazine had its hands full with the hectic production schedule, a Sunday-to-Friday grind. Seven or eight sketches, running in length from 90 seconds to four minutes, could be used on the show. More were prepared, giving directors finished scripts in case an unexciting story suddenly ''got hot.'' Scripts were prepared from Sunday to Wednesday. On Wednesday director Pryor met with maestro Howard Barlow and soundwoman Nichols: the music was set and the sound cued in. Casting also began on Wednesday and concluded on Thursday. On Friday it aired, ''a clockwork machine,'' as *Radio Guide* saw it, ''run by the power of human excitement.''

It opened to the tramp-tramp-tramp of shuffling feet, indicating ''the relentless, impersonal progress of events.'' The central speaking part was that of the narrator, ''the Voice of *Time*.''

A second announcer was called "the Voice of Fate," heard on stories of catastrophic proportions or when some notable person died. "As it must to all men, death came today to . . . ," Fate would proclaim, closing the book on another life. Ted Husing was the first Voice of *Time*, with Westbrook Van Voorhis as Fate. By the fall of 1931, Harry Von Zell had become *Time*. He could exude nothing in this role: "I have to sound as impersonal, as imperturbable, as time itself," he said. In October 1933, Westbrook Van Voorhis moved up to the lead role, becoming synonymous with the program. His staccato readings were perfectly accentuated by Barlow's musical stings and bouncy newsreel music. Often he ended the show with the terse announcement "Time . . . MARCHES ON!"

The actors bonded in strange ways to their real-life counterparts. Edwin Jerome impersonated King Alfonso of Spain so realistically that the king's son thought his father was in the studio. Dwight Weist lived the life and death of Bruno Richard Hauptmann. Weist studied everything about Hauptmann from his childhood to the bone structure of his head—bone, he told *Radio Guide*, affects voice. He attended the trial and, while loathing the accused killer of the Lindbergh baby, made himself feel what Hauptmann must be feeling until he could play the role with empathy. When the night came for the reenactment of the execution, Weist felt frightened, sick, as if a part of himself had died in the electric chair. "I can't explain it, but we all have it," he said, "when something happens to the people we impersonate. Ted de Corsia had it too, when Huey Long was murdered. He'd been Huey for a long time."

In 1943, *Radio Life* highlighted a decade of *Time* broadcasts. The first story done on the series was the renomination of "Big Bill" Thompson as mayor of Chicago. Adolf Hitler appeared only once in 1931. Most of the action focused on domestic issues, with Americans worried about the Depression. Herbert Hoover, Mahatma Gandhi, King Alfonso of Spain, Huey Long, and Al Capone (in that order) were the people most impersonated. Hoover remained the dominant figure in 1932; Franklin D. Roosevelt from 1933 to 1937. At the end of the 1930s, people began looking outward, at the rise of Hitler, at Italy's invasion of Ethiopia, at the war in Spain. In 1938, Hitler was the most-mimicked figure on the show; Roosevelt slipped to third, behind Japan's Saburo Karusu and Russia's Josef Stalin, a few years later. Rubber and steel shortages were the top stories at home as the United States entered the war. People wanted to know how other people were coping, and when Jack Benny donated his Maxwell to the scrap drive, he did it on *The March of Time*.

The emphasis shifted. In 1942, *Time* became more a straight news show, with only one or two events dramatized each week. *Time* reporters were rushed onto the air from distant locations with live shortwaved reports. Amid the clatter of teletypes, the show was compiled from London, Singapore, and China. Among the many newsmen who contributed were Harry Zinder from Cairo, Robert Sherrod and George Strock from Australia, William Fisher and Theodore White from New Delhi, and Walter Graebner from Moscow.

MARIE, THE LITTLE FRENCH PRINCESS, soap opera.

BROADCAST HISTORY: March 7, 1933–Oct. 18, 1935, CBS. 15m continuation, four times a week at 1 until April 27, 1934; returned Oct. 15, weekdays at 2. Louis Phillipe. **CAST:** Ruth Yorke as Marie, a young woman of wealth and nobility who gave it all up to live as a common girl in America. James Meighan as Richard Collins. **PRODUCER-DIRECTOR:** Himan Brown.

This was the first daytime soap opera on CBS.

THE MARIO LANZA SHOW, musical variety.

BROADCAST HISTORY: June 10–Sept. 30, 1951, CBS. 30m, Sundays at 8. Substitute for *The Edgar Bergen Show*. Coca-Cola.
   Oct. 8, 1951–Sept. 26, 1952, NBC. 30m, Mondays at 10 until Jan. 25, then Fridays at 9. Coca-Cola.
CAST: Singing star Mario Lanza, with popular vocalist Gisele MacKenzie. **ANNOUNCER:** Bill Baldwin. **ORCHESTRA:** Ray Sinatra.

Tenor Mario Lanza arrived on the air at the crest of his popularity, having just finished his starring role in the film *The Great Caruso*. Though popularly believed to be Caruso's equal, Lanza was not without critics in the world of music. His discipline was lax, he grew fat, had troubles with alcohol, fell from the peak as quickly as he had attained it, and died of a heart attack in 1959, at age 38.

MARION TALLEY, soprano.

BROADCAST HISTORY: April 3, 1936–Sept. 18, 1938, NBC. 15m, Fridays at 10:30 ca. summer 1936, then 30m, Sundays at 5. Ry-Krisp. **ORCHESTRA:** Josef Koestner.

Talley was a Metropolitan Opera star of the late 1920s. She left the Met after four seasons, refusing to answer persistent questions of "did she jump or was she pushed?" She was highly popular on the air, offering "homey" and down-to-earth songs.

MARK TRAIL, juvenile adventure drama, based on the comic strip by Ed Dodd.

BROADCAST HISTORY: Jan. 30, 1950–June 8, 1951, Mutual. 30m, three a week at 5. Kellogg's.
   Sept. 10, 1951–June 27, 1952, ABC. 15m continuation, three a week until Jan., then weekdays at 5:15.
CAST: Matt Crowley as Mark Trail, a forest ranger whose enemies were spoilers and criminals who came into the wilderness. John Larkin and Staats Cotsworth also as Mark Trail. Ben Cooper and Ronald Liss as Scotty, Mark's young friend. Amy Sidell and Joyce Gordon as Cherry, the girls' interest. **ANNOUNCERS:** Jackson Beck, Glenn Riggs. **DIRECTOR:** Drex Hines.

The opening signature of *Mark Trail* gave good evidence of its juvenile-comic-strip content:
   Battling the raging elements!
   Fighting the savage wilderness!
   Striking at the enemies of man and nature!
   One man's name resounds from the snow-capped mountains down across the sun-baked plains!
   (Voice from echo chamber): *MAAAAAR-RRRRKKKKK TRAIL!*

THE MARRIAGE, drama.

BROADCAST HISTORY: Oct. 4, 1953–March 28, 1954, NBC. 30m, Sundays at 7:30. **CAST:** Hume Cronyn and Jessica Tandy as Ben and Liz Marriott. Denise Alexander as Emily, their daughter. Also: Bill Griffis, Ralph Bell, Adelaide Klein, Burford Hampden, William Lipton, Edgar Stehli, Roger DeKoven, Louis Sorin, Edwin Bruce, Alexander Scourby, Pat Hosley, etc. **DIRECTOR:** Edward King. **WRITER:** Ernest Kinoy.

The Marriage was a light affair, distinguished mainly as a vehicle for stage notables Hume Cronyn and Jessica Tandy. Cronyn's character, Ben Marriott, was a New York lawyer. His wife, Liz, had formerly been a buyer in a New York department store. Often plots revolved around her attempt to adjust to life as "just a housewife," or focused on problems with their children, Pete and Emily. The Marriotts were urbane sophisticates, interested in theater, art, literature, and philosophy. They alternated viewpoints, Cronyn narrating one week, Tandy the next.

THE MARTIN AND LEWIS SHOW, comedy-variety.

BROADCAST HISTORY: April 3, 1949–Jan. 30, 1950, NBC. 30m, Sundays at 6:30 until June; returned in Oct., Fridays at 8:30; Mondays at 10 beginning in Nov. 1949.
   Oct. 5, 1951–July 14, 1953, NBC. 30m, Fridays at 8:30 until April 25, 1952; returned Sept. 16, Tuesdays at 9 for Chesterfield and Anacin.
CAST: Dean Martin and Jerry Lewis, comics, with guest stars. Regulars, ca. 1949–50: Ben Alexander, Sheldon Leonard. **ORCHESTRA:** Dick Stabile. **DIRECTORS:** Robert L. Redd, 1949; later, Dick Mack. **WRITERS:** Ed Simmons, Norman Lear.

The Martin and Lewis Show was developed by NBC in the wake of the stinging CBS talent raids that lured Jack Benny and others to the younger network. NBC announced a talent hunt: the network was searching for rising young performers for radio and television. Soon thereafter a network executive caught the nightclub act of Dean Martin and Jerry Lewis, who had been performing together for several years and had developed some name recognition within the industry while remaining largely unknown to the general public.

NBC offered a contract, the pair moved to Hollywood, and their show was concocted over the next three months. Expectations were high for the April premiere. The budget was huge, reportedly $10,000 a week, and this enabled the producers to hire top guests (Lucille Ball for the first broadcast). But the show was unexciting, and the critics said so: the nightclub act, which had drawn raves from every quarter, did not transfer well to the air. Like Milton Berle, Jerry Lewis was a visual comic, dependent on mugging. It was standard variety fare: an opening song by Martin, some verbal slapstick, a guest spot, more Lewis antics, and a closing number by Martin.

Despite the lack of success, NBC wanted it back after a short season, upping the fall ante to a reported $12,000 a week. Maestro Dick Stabile became one of Lewis's main foils, but Lewis was screechy and shrill, and the show closed at the end of the season. Martin and Lewis went into movies, but returned to NBC in the fall of 1951. Martin was billed as "master of ceremonies." Lewis inevitably arrived "late," turning up at the end of Martin's song, which he (Lewis) continued to sing in that terrible screech. But it was more of the same, a short season and an uninspired encore.

On TV they were more effective, appearing on Ed Sullivan's *Toast of the Town* and seen numerous times on *The Colgate Comedy Hour*.

MARTIN KANE, PRIVATE EYE, detective drama.

BROADCAST HISTORY: Aug. 7, 1949–June 24, 1951, Mutual. 30m, Sundays at 4:30. U.S. Tobacco.

July 1, 1951–Dec. 21, 1952, NBC. 30m, Sundays at 4:30. U.S. Tobacco.

CAST: William Gargan (1949–51) as Martin Kane, a New York private detective. Lloyd Nolan as Martin Kane, 1951 to mid-1952; Lee Tracy as Martin Kane from mid-1952. Walter Kinsella as Hap McMann, proprietor of the tobacco shop where Kane hung out. **DIRECTOR:** Ted Hediger.

Martin Kane was conceived as a TV show— one of the earliest detective series of that young medium—but it ran concurrently on radio. The hero was a quiet, calculating, introspective type who had an unusually good relationship with the police, smoked a pipe, and could usually be found at Happy McMann's Tobacco Shop. This was a natural tie-in for the sponsor, and commercials for U.S. Tobacco were sometimes integrated into the stories.

William Gargan played the lead on both radio and TV, until the TV shows became (as he alleged in his autobiography) "a vehicle for the flesh parade." The actresses were "pretty and emptyheaded," hired more for "cleavage" than acting ability. He threw down the gauntlet—"get decent scripts or get another boy." He was replaced by Lloyd Nolan on both shows. But Gargan sidestepped into a sound-alike series, *Barrie Craig*, on radio alone, where cleavage wasn't a factor.

THE MARX BROTHERS, comedy.

BROADCAST HISTORY: Nov. 28, 1932–May 22, 1933, Blue Network. 30m, Mondays at 7:30. Titled *Beagle, Shyster and Beagle* for the first three shows; *Flywheel, Shyster and Flywheel* thereafter. Standard Oil and Colonial Beacon Oil for Esso Gasoline. **CAST:** Groucho Marx as lawyer Waldorf T. Beagle, later known as Flywheel. Chico Marx as Emmanuel Ravelli, his assistant. **WRITERS:** Nat Perrin, Arthur Sheekman, George Oppenheimer, and Tom McKnight.

March 4–April 15, 1934, CBS. 30m, Sundays at 7. Also titled *The Marx of Time*. American Oil. **CAST:** Groucho Marx as Ulysses H. Drivel, reporter. Chico Marx as Penelli.

The first Marx Brothers series, best known as *Flywheel, Shyster and Flywheel*, was part of the *Five Star Theater* for Esso Oil. This was an unusual umbrella approach to radio advertising, wherein Esso sponsored a different show each weeknight. The shows ran on various networks and were vigorously cross-promoted, with the Marx Brothers kicking it off on Monday nights. Other shows ranged from symphonic broadcasts to opera to melodrama. *Charlie Chan*, the Oriental detective, closed the week.

The shows starred Groucho and Chico Marx (Harpo did not speak in his film characterizations, and thus did not appear) as down-in-the-mouth lawyers. Almost everything that is known about the series comes from Michael Barson, who unearthed 25 of the 26 scripts in the Library of Congress and published them in a book. Fortunately, with near-complete scripts available, the show is easy to imagine.

It was both an extension of and a contributor to the Marx Brothers films. They ran a law office, staffed by a receptionist, Miss Dimple, who answered the phone and shuffled hapless clients in and out. The title change to *Flywheel* came after a real lawyer named Beagle threatened to sue. It was explained by Miss Dimple that the boss had obtained a divorce and changed his name back to Flywheel. The rest of the show was equally inane, the crazy one-liners tossed back and forth in much the style that fans of their early films will readily recall. In an epilogue each week, Groucho and Chico did their bit for Esso.

Barson, who interviewed writer Nat Perrin for his book, reports that the series liberally lifted material from Marx Brothers films, and that no fewer than 15 routines from *Flywheel* were used in *Duck Soup* (the radio writers were given credit on the film for "additional dialogue"). The series began and ended in New York, with the middle episodes broadcast from a RKO Hollywood studio, as NBC had no West Coast facility at that time. It was a moderate success, hitting respectable CAB numbers of 20-plus in January 1933, but was not extended for an encore season.

MARY AND BOB, love drama.

BROADCAST HISTORY: Jan. 6, 1928–June 26, 1931, CBS. 60m, Fridays at 9. Also known as *The True Story Hour* and *Mary and Bob's True Stories*. *True Story* magazine.

June 29, 1931–June 28, 1932, NBC. 45m, Mondays at 10 until Jan. 5, then 30m, Tuesdays at 8:30. *The True Story Hour*. *True Story* magazine.

Oct. 11, 1938–May 16, 1939, Blue Network. 30m, Tuesdays at 9. *True Story* magazine.

CAST: Nora Stirling and William Brenton as Mary and Bob, newlyweds who toured the country in an old car and related their experiences. David Ross and Cecil Secrest also as Bob. For the 1938–39 series, Elizabeth and Eddie Wragge took over as Mary and Bob, now relating tales submitted by people who had faced difficult problems.

Mary and Bob was one of the first romance shows on the network air.

MARY LEE TAYLOR, cooking expert.

BROADCAST HISTORY: Nov. 7, 1933–Oct. 16, 1948, CBS. 15m, twice a week at 11 A.M. until 1943, then 30m, Saturday at 10:30 A.M. Pet Milk.

Oct. 23, 1948–Oct. 9, 1954, NBC. 30m, Saturdays at 10 A.M. until 1949, then at 10:30 A.M. Pet Milk.

MARY MARGARET McBRIDE, interviews and talk.

BROADCAST HISTORY: 1934–40, WOR, as "Martha Deane"; first aired May 3, 1934.

Oct. 4, 1937–Aug. 21, 1941, CBS. 15m, weekdays and sometimes three a week, at noon until 1940, then at 3. Minute Tapioca, 1937–38; Satina and LaFrance, 1938–39; Florida Citrus, 1940–41.

Sept. 2, 1941–Oct. 6, 1950, NBC. Weekdays at 1. 15m, 1941–42; then 45m on WEAF, New York. Many sponsors.

Oct. 9, 1950–May 15, 1954, ABC. Various lengths, weekdays at 1.

She was sometimes called "the female Arthur Godfrey," combining a down-home charm with a keen and astute interviewing style. Her voice was "girlish, hesitant, often bewildered," in the opinion of *Life* magazine. Her stock in trade was innocence: "she preserved the air of a little girl lost in the big city," but managed to draw from the rich and famous revealing anecdotes and warm insights. She interviewed more than 1,200 people, from Sally Rand and Harry Truman to the Grand Lama of Tibet.

Mary Margaret McBride was born in 1899, and she came to radio after a career in letters. She wrote several books in the 1920s and was one of the country's best-paid article writers until the Depression arrived and demolished her markets. She auditioned at WOR and was hired to play a grandmother who filled a half-hour (2:30–3 P.M.) with household hints and chats about her fictitious family. Her character was named Martha Deane, a name owned by the station. McBride would play this role for more than six years, aided by her friend and business manager Stella Karn, and by Janice Devine, who produced, researched, and set up interviews. Other regulars were Hilda Deichler, her secretary; Berta and Elmer Hader; Juliette Nicole (Nikki); Hattie Silverman; Patti Pickens (mother of the Pickens Sisters); Enid Haupt, grower of orchids; food authority Herman Smith; Helen Josephy (McBride's collaborator on travel books); silent film star Olga Petrova; and Frances Gallacher, Myra Washington, or "whoever was my housekeeper at the time." Vincent Connolly became her announcer, remaining with her for many years.

The original Martha Deane idea was soon changed: one day early in the series, McBride simply admitted that she was no grandmother, predicted that she'd be fired for saying it, and told her listeners that if she wasn't back the next day, they'd know the reason why. This began her open chatter. From then on she just talked about anything that came into her mind. "It was about the oddest kind of chatter heard on the air," wrote Ben Gross in his memoir. "Comments on art, literature, politics and human relations, but not a single household hint or recipe in the entire hour. Mary Margaret, furthermore, was not a smooth talker . . . she held forth in a high-pitched nasal twang; at times she stumbled over words; occasionally she giggled and, now and then, she would begin a sentence without taking the trouble to end it." But she was a penetrating reporter. She could read two or three books in a day, interview an author, ask delightful questions, and quote verbatim from his book without looking up the passage she wanted. Clients discovered that a mention on her show was, like Godfrey's, a ticket to better business.

She joined CBS in 1937, heard at noon under her own name while continuing her Martha Deane broadcasts at 2:15 (later 3 P.M.) on WOR. Her network quarter-hour was barely a warmup for a woman who had found her radio legs and loved to talk. She dropped the WOR show in 1940, leaving the Martha Deane moniker to other actresses who did what they could with it. McBride settled into the 1 o'clock timeslot on NBC in 1941. But she yearned for a longer timeslot and got it, dropping back into local radio on WEAF, the NBC outlet in New York. Vincent Connolly's simple intro—"It's one o'clock and here's Mary Margaret McBride"—was a classic piece of understatement. She held no rehearsals and used no script: in fact, as *Radio Life* noted, "she has no act; she is completely natural." Connolly was a "perfect partner for balance; he listens to her experiences and genially reminds her why they are on the air when she lets her enthusiasm forget the clock or their sponsors." She often chided Connolly for his continuing status as a bachelor, but when she asked, "Why don't you get married, Vincent?" his reply was usually, "I don't know, Mary Margaret."

Time thought her "a brilliant interviewer": she "titters through her interview and in the last ten minutes she really goes into her act, mugging through commercials for thirteen sponsors, who pay her about $100,000 a year." Sometimes, in her frantic rush against the clock, her "commer-cials" were little more than one-liners strung together. Often she talked of two or more products in a single sentence. Occasionally she would get lost. "Now where am I?" she would ask. "You were about to speak of Griffin Allwite," Connolly would prompt, drawing an eruption of superlatives for the shoe polish. She accepted no client whose product she hadn't used. Many of her sponsors were rich foods, which she loved—and she had the ample frame to prove it. Often she could be heard enjoying a pudding or a frosted cake on the air.

Her network career ended in 1954. Her long-time friend and partner, Stella Karn, had died, and McBride moved upstate, to Kingston, and retired from the national radio scene. But she was still dabbling in 1976, the year of her death, doing a three-a-week local talkshow on WGHQ.

MARY PICKFORD DRAMAS, light dramatic anthology.

BROADCAST HISTORY: Oct. 3, 1934–March 27, 1935, NBC. 30m, Wednesdays at 8. Royal Gelatin.
CAST: Mary Pickford with supporting players in "wholesomely sentimental if slightly old-fashioned plays" (*Radioland*). Little else is known: no shows have yet been discovered.

MARY SMALL, songs.

BROADCAST HISTORY: Oct. 7–Nov. 12, 1933, Blue Network. 15m, Saturdays.
Feb. 18, 1934–May 12, 1935, NBC. 30m, Sundays at 1:30. *Little Miss Bab-O's Surprise Party*, with guests (Lucille Manners, Ernest Charles, etc.). Bab-O. ORCHESTRA: William Wirges.
Dec. 20, 1935–June 28, 1937, NBC. Red Network, 15m, Fridays at 6:15, 1935–36; Blue Network, 15m, Mondays at 7, 1936–37.
June 2–Nov. 24, 1941, Mutual. 15m, Mondays at 10:15. Imperial Margarine.
June 14–Oct. 9, 1942, CBS. Various 15m formats.
Feb. 27, 1944–March 24, 1946, ABC. 30m, Sundays at 5; at 4:30 from Dec. 2, 1945. *The Mary Small Revue*. Clark Candy. ANNOUNCER: Clayton Bud Collyer. ORCHESTRA: Ray Bloch.

Mary Small was a child who sang like a woman. First heard on *The Rudy Vallee Hour* in 1933, she was 11 years old but possessed of such a fully developed voice that listeners refused to believe her age.

MASQUERADE, soap opera.

BROADCAST HISTORY: April 8–June 28, 1935, NBC. 15m, weekdays at noon. Returned Sept. 10–27, weekdays at 3:30. **CAST:** Gale Page as blues singer Gertrude Lamont. Murray Forbes as Bill, her accompanist and confidant. Ted Maxwell as Fred Nino, her hardboiled mentor.

This brief series was mainly geared to display Gale Page the singer in such blues numbers as *Why Was I Born?* It bore no relationship to the later serial of the same name.

MASQUERADE, soap opera.

BROADCAST HISTORY: Jan. 14, 1946–Aug. 29, 1947, NBC. 15m, weekdays at 2:30. General Mills. **CAST:** Art Seltzer as Bill Summers, editor of the *Clarion*, a newspaper in the small town of Fairview, Iowa. Beryl Vaughn as Alice, his wife. Jack Petruzzi as Dick Bailey, the cynical associate editor. Jack Swineford (Jack Lester) and Carlton KaDell as Tom Field, principal of Fairview High. Mary Marren Rees as Marian, his wife. Geraldine Kay as Barbara Palmer, a schoolteacher new in town. Sondra Gair as Jeannie Rourke. Ned LeFevre as Phil. Aired from Chicago until July 1946; Hollywood thereafter, with only Sondra Gair and Ned LeFevre in original roles. Cast in Hollywood included Herbert Rawlinson, Francis X. Bushman, Nancy Gates, Janet Scott, and Griff Barnett. **MUSIC:** Richard Aurandt. **PRODUCER:** Carl Wester. **DIRECTOR:** Les Mitchel (Hollywood). **WRITER:** Irna Phillips.

This *Masquerade* was part of the interrelated *General Mills Hour*, in which characters from four Irna Phillips soaps spilled over into each other's shows. *Masquerade* was set in the hometown of the heroine of *The Woman in White*. The other serials were *The Guiding Light* and *Today's Children*, giving Phillips the entire block from 2 to 3 P.M.

MATINEE AT MEADOWBROOK, band remotes.

BROADCAST HISTORY: Jan. 18–March 22, 1941, CBS. 60m, Saturdays at 4. **CAST:** Bert Parks, host, with Jim Backus. Guest bands including Bobby Byrne, Tommy Dorsey, Al Donahue, and Gene Krupa.

May 24–Dec. 6, 1941, CBS. 60m, Saturdays at 5. **CAST:** John Tillman, host, with Art Carney, comic. Guest bands, leading off with Vaughn Monroe.

This swing series was produced before live audiences of up to 2,000 people at Frank Dailey's Meadowbrook, a hotbed for jitterbugs, in Cedar Grove, N.J.

MATINEE THEATER, dramatic anthology.

BROADCAST HISTORY: July 2–Oct. 15, 1944 as *Dangerously Yours*, then Oct. 22, 1944–April 8, 1945, as *Matinee Theater*: All CBS, 30m, Sundays at 2. Vick Chemical Company. **CAST:** Victor Jory, regular star, with New York regulars in support: Jackson Beck, Gertrude Warner, Martin Gabel, etc.

MAUDE AND COUSIN BILL, comedy serial.

BROADCAST HISTORY: Sept. 21, 1932–June 16, 1933, Blue Network. 15m, twice a week at 10:30 A.M., later at 6. A&P Foodstores. **CAST:** Vivian Block and Andy Donnelly as Maude and Bill Ricketts. **WRITER:** Novelist Booth Tarkington.

MAUDIE'S DIARY, light comedy, based on stories by Graeme and Sarah Lorimer.

BROADCAST HISTORY: Aug. 14, 1941–Sept. 24, 1942, CBS. 30m, Thursdays at 7:30. Wonder Bread. **CAST:** Mary Mason as Maudie Mason, a girl in her teens. Charita Bauer also as Maudie. Bill Johnstone and Betty Garde as her parents, Wilfred and Kate. Marjorie Davies as Sylvia, Maudie's big sister. Robert Walker as Maudie's friend Davy Dillon. Caryl Smith as Maudie's friend Pauline (Pauly) Howard. **ANNOUNCER:** Art Millet. **ORCHESTRA:** Elliott Jacoby. **WRITER:** Albert G. Miller.

Maudie's Diary was "the personal history of a girl in her teens," seen through her confessions to her "diary dear." The tone was realistic rather than insane (contrast with *Archie Andrews*, *The Aldrich Family*, etc.); the writing effectively captured the sarcastic-affectionate way teens have always talked to each other. "Oh, file it away, Davy," Maudie would say. The show was good enough that one of its scripts was selected for *Best Broadcasts of 1940–41*.

MAYOR OF THE TOWN, comedy-drama.

BROADCAST HISTORY: Sept. 6–Sept. 27, 1942, NBC. 30m, Sundays at 7:30. Rinso.

Oct. 7, 1942–May 31, 1947, CBS. 30m, Wednesdays at 9:30, 1942; at 9, Jan. 6–Dec. 29, 1943. Rinso. Returned March 11, 1944, Saturdays at 7; Mondays at 9, July and Aug. 1944; Saturdays at 7, 1944–45; at 8, mid-1945; at 8:30, 1945–47. Noxzema.

Oct. 8, 1947–June 30, 1948, ABC. 30m, Wednesdays at 8. Noxzema.

Jan. 2–July 3, 1949, Mutual. 30m, Sundays at 7:30. Mutual Benefit Insurance.

CAST: Lionel Barrymore as the mayor of the town of Springdale. Agnes Moorehead as Marilly, his housekeeper. Conrad Binyon as the mayor's ward, Butch. Gloria McMillan as Sharlee Bronson, Butch's best girl. Priscilla Lyon as Holly-Ann, the mayor's granddaughter. Also: Will Wright, Sharon Douglas, Irvin Lee, Marjorie Davies, and other Hollywood actors. **PRODUCER:** Murray Bolen; later Knowles Entrikin. **DIRECTOR:** Jack Van Nostrand. **WRITERS:** Jean Holloway, Leonard St. Clair, Howard Blake, Erna Lazarus, etc.; Howard Breslin and Charles Tazewell wrote alternate weeks, ca. 1945. **ORCHESTRA:** Gordon Jenkins (ca. 1943); Bernard Katz (1945); Frank Worth. **SOUND EFFECTS:** David Light, Mary Ann Gideon.

Mayor of the Town was a perfect vehicle for Lionel Barrymore: rich with warmhearted humor and good-natured grumbling, its "mayor" had a fierce bark but a mushy heart when confronted with the plight of an orphan or a stray dog. The mayor cared little about political advantage: he even found time, once a year, to turn the town of Springdale into a special theater, to give his traditional performance as Ebenezer Scrooge in Charles Dickens's *A Christmas Carol*.

The town, as described by Barrymore in *Radio Life*, was not unlike Dr. Christian's River's End or Gildersleeve's Summerfield. There was a broad Main Street, flanked by secondary streets, First and Spring. The cross-streets bore the names of trees—Cherry, Walnut, Locust, Elm. At the foot of Main Street were Hill and Market streets. At Market and Main were the Idle Hour Theater, Fred Jackson's service station, and the two town newspapers, the *Globe* and the *Clarion*. On Main Street were Grayson's Drug Store, the Bon-Ton Department Store, Veeder's Tobacco Shop, and the Bijou Theater. The big hotel in town was the Grover House, at Main and Third. Next to the hotel was the Greyhound Bus Depot; next to that, a tea room called the Pantry, where the mayor's secretary, Toni McCafferty, took her lunches. The train station was at the foot of Hill Street, and across the tracks was the shabbier part of town, marked by the Avon Hotel, a "parcel of juke joints," and a couple of poolrooms. The town church was at Maple and Spring. Reverend Dinwiddie was a fussy little man "but gives the congregation a good sermon for its money." The sexton, farmer George Meader, "swings a mean call to church."

Other town characters were Police Chief Archie Chamberlain; dog catcher Clem Adams; the town physician, Dr. Case; and Mrs. Bronson, Sunday school teacher. Miss Grew ("Gruesome" to her students) was the teacher at Elmwood School. And Judge Williams was the best checker-player in town—"next to me," said the mayor.

The main characters were the mayor, his housekeeper, Marilly, and his ward, Butch, who was often found hanging on the gate when the mayor came home from City Hall. The mayor's house was at Elm near Main. Butch, whose real name was Roscoe Turner, had come to live with the mayor (after the first season) when his mother died and his dad went to fight with the Seabees. On warm nights he liked to play under streetlamps, chasing fireflies with his friends, Bitsy Morgan, Peewee Taylor, and Sharlee Bronson. Often the stories were coming-of-age pieces, focusing on the mayor's special relationship with Butch. They fished together and swam at the hole near Rock Creek. Marilly entered the stories with complaints about the mayor's tardiness, or repeating the gossip of her friendly enemy, Abby Peters.

McGARRY AND HIS MOUSE, comedy-detective drama.

BROADCAST HISTORY: June 26–Sept. 25, 1946, NBC. 30m, Wednesdays at 9. Summer substitute for Eddie Cantor.

Jan. 6–March 31, 1947, Mutual. 30m, Mondays at 8. General Foods.

CAST: Wendell Corey (1946) as Detective Dan McGarry, a stumblebum hero, whose friend and companion, Kitty Archer, was known as "the Mouse." Roger Pryor and Ted de Corsia also as McGarry. Peggy Conklin as Kitty Archer. Shirley Mitchell and Patsy Campbell also as Kitty. Betty Garde as Kitty's mother. ANNOUNCER: Bert Parks. MUSIC: Peter Van Steeden (NBC).

ME AND JANIE, situation comedy.

BROADCAST HISTORY: July 12–Nov. 1, 1949, NBC. 30m, Tuesdays at 8:30. CAST: Lurene Tuttle and George O'Hanlon as a married couple with a wiseguy for a son. Also: Jeffrey Silver, Hope Emerson, Marvin Miller, Willard Waterman.

MEET CORLISS ARCHER, teenage situation comedy.

BROADCAST HISTORY: Jan. 7, 1943–Sept. 30, 1956, CBS, with two noted exceptions. 30m, many shifts in timeslot; some gaps in continuity. Anchor Hocking Glass, 1944–45; Campbell Soups, 1946, 1947, 1948, in broken runs; electric company co-ops, 1949–52; Toni, late 1954.

June 15–Sept. 7, 1948, NBC. 30m, Tuesdays at 10. Summer replacement for Bob Hope. Pepsodent.

Oct. 3, 1952–June 26, 1953, ABC. 30m, Fridays at 9:30. Electric co-ops.

1943: CAST: Priscilla Lyon as teenager Corliss Archer. Irvin Lee as Dexter Franklin, her hapless boyfriend. Bill Christy, David Hughes, and Burt Boyar also as Dexter. Frank Martin as her father, lawyer Harry Archer. Gloria Holden initially as her mother, Janet Archer, Irene Tedrow as Janet by Feb. Norman Field as Uncle George. Mary Wickes as Louise, the Archer maid. COMPOSER-CONDUCTOR: Wilbur Hatch. WRITER-CREATOR: F. Hugh Herbert.

AFTER 1943: CAST: Janet Waldo as Corliss. Lugene Sanders, briefly, as Corliss. Sam Edwards as Dexter, ca. 1944–56. Fred Shields and Irene Tedrow as Harry and Janet Archer, 1943–56. Tommy Bernard and Kenny Godkin as the brat Raymond Ames. Bebe Young and Barbara Whiting as Corliss's best friend, Mildred. Dolores Crane as Betty Cameron, Corliss's rival in all things vital. DIRECTORS: Bert Prager of J. Walter Thompson during the Campbell sponsorship; Helen Mack, 1950s. WRITERS: F. Hugh Herbert, Jerry Adel-

man, Carroll Carroll (supervised for Thompson in Campbell era).

Meet Corliss Archer was typical teenage fluff. F. Hugh Herbert created the characters in a magazine story, "Private Affair," which was so well received that he wrote a dozen more. Then came a play, *Kiss and Tell*, the radio show, a Shirley Temple film, and finally television.

The growing pains of his own two daughters gave Herbert all the inspiration he needed to write of Corliss (going on 15) and her parents, Harry and Janet Archer. Corliss emerged as the CBS answer to NBC's *A Date with Judy*, which had begun its long run in June 1941. Corliss Archer and Judy Foster were cut from the same log: both were charming and breathless, prone to endless exasperation. But the men in her life set Corliss apart.

First there was Dexter Franklin, the boy next door, as faithful as a sheepdog, wonderfully good-hearted, and, as perfected by Sam Edwards in a lengthy performance, one of the biggest bumblers ever to walk through Radio Row. His personality began with a laugh, a deep nasal bellow that became one of the show's trademarks, and was punctuated with the stock phrase "Holy cow!" All the problems of Dexter's world could be solved with a dollar in his pocket and the presence of Corliss Archer at his side. He botched almost everything he touched.

The other man in Corliss's life was her father. Harry Archer may have practiced law for a living, but what truly inspired him was the eternal war with the female gender. He was cynical, dry, and full of schemes. Usually Dexter was the pawn in his devious plots to prove which sex was the better man. On the face of it, he disdained Dexter mightily, but in a pinch, his good heart shone through. For Corliss and Dexter were sweethearts, and even Dexter's elephantine roar— "COOOOORRRR-LAISS!"—across the hedge at 8 o'clock in the morning couldn't change that.

Herbert's daughters, Diana and Pamela, both wanted to play the lead. Herbert saved himself the agony of choosing, saying he didn't want them becoming professionals at 13. Priscilla Lyon was Corliss in that first short season: "a strange and rather delightful mixture of child, woman, and she-devil," as the character was described on the opening broadcast. "She's very pretty and she knows it, although she doesn't let *you* know she knows it.'' The opener played heavily on a wartime theme, Corliss scheming for the honor of christening a destroyer and in the end giving away the thrill in an act of unselfish patriotism. Irvin Lee played Dexter straight. It wasn't until Janet Waldo and Sam Edwards were solidly in place by 1944 that the characters assumed their eternal flow. Waldo played the role with oh-my-golly wonderment, the perpetual ingenue. Forty years later, her youthful demeanor was alive and well. ''She's still Corliss Archer,'' said Sam Edwards in 1984.

MEET ME AT PARKY'S, comedy.

BROADCAST HISTORY: June 17, 1945–April 6, 1947, NBC. 30m, Sundays at 10:30. Old Gold. CAST: Harry Einstein as Nick Parkyakarkus, owner of a Greek restaurant. Joan Barton as the cashier. Also: Sheldon Leonard, Frank Nelson, Ruth Perrott, Leo Cleary, etc. ANNOUNCER: Art Gilmore. VOCALISTS: Betty Jane Rhodes and David Street; also, Peggy Lee, Patty Bolton. ORCHESTRA: Opie Cates. DIRECTOR: Hal Fimberg.

Oct. 19, 1947–July 11, 1948, Mutual. 30m, Sundays at 9.

Harry Einstein created the Parkyakarkus prototype as a boy, mimicking the Greeks who frequented his father's importing warehouse. He entertained at club functions and in 1932 began appearing regularly on a Boston radio station. Eddie Cantor caught his act in 1934, and Einstein was soon nationally known through his appearances on *The Eddie Cantor Show*. He also appeared with Al Jolson in 1938.

Meet Me at Parky's was largely self-written, featuring Einstein as chief cook and bottle washer of a Greek beanery. At the end of the NBC run, Einstein underwent spinal surgery to relieve chronic back pain. But this left him mostly paralyzed, a condition he struggled for years to overcome. For the opening of his Mutual series, he had to be carried in and propped up at a microphone.

MEET MILLIE, situation comedy.

BROADCAST HISTORY: July 2, 1951–Sept. 23, 1954, CBS. 30m, various times. CAST: Audrey Totter as Millie Bronson, a none-too-bright secretary from Brooklyn. Elena Verdugo as Millie, ca.

1953. Earle Ross as J. R. Boone, her boss. Rye Billsbury as Johnny Boone Jr., the boss's son, with whom Millie had a romance of sorts. Bea Benaderet as Mamma, who lived with daughter Millie in an apartment house. Florence Halop also as Mamma. Bill Tracy as Morton. Bill Tracy and later Marvin Kaplan as Alfred, a poor man's poet who lived in the apartment house. ANNOUNCER: Bob LeMond. ORCHESTRA: Irving Miller. CREATOR: Frank Galen.

Meet Millie was greeted with mixed reviews. ''Oh, no, not another *Maisie*,'' groaned *Radio Life*. The series seemed to ape too many dumb-dame forerunners, with ''intermittent outcroppings of (*My Friend*) *Irma* and perhaps a smattering of Joan Davis's wisecracking without Joan's basic wit.'' Millie's romance with Johnny Boone, her boss's son, was promoted by her mother and disdained by Boone Sr. The characters migrated to CBS-TV in October 1952. Audrey Totter's film studio refused permission for the TV show, and Totter resigned from the radio series as well. With Elena Verdugo as Millie, the radio show ended and the TV version ran until March 1956.

MEET MR. McNUTLEY, situation comedy.

BROADCAST HISTORY: Sept. 17, 1953–June 10, 1954, CBS. 30m, Thursdays at 9. General Electric. CAST: Ray Milland as Ray McNutley, English professor at the all-girl Lynnhaven College. Phyllis Avery as Peggy, his wife. Gordon Jones as Pete, McNutley's bachelor pal. Verna Felton as dean of the college. Also: Joe Kearns, Ken Christy, Mel Blanc, etc. ANNOUNCER: Del Sharbutt. DIRECTOR: Joe Rines.

This comedy aired concurrently on television, with much the same cast. The plots revolved around McNutley's relationships with his students, who thought he was a dreamboat. The TV show outlived its radio counterpart by a year, the hero's last name becoming ''McNulty'' in the fall of 1954.

MEET MR. MEEK, situation comedy.

BROADCAST HISTORY: July 10, 1940–April 1, 1942, CBS. 30m, Wednesdays at 7:30; at 8 beginning in Jan. 1942. Lever Brothers for Lifebuoy Soap. CAST: Frank Readick as the henpecked Mortimer Meek. Adelaide Klein as Agatha, his shrewish wife. Doris Dudley as Peggy, their daughter. Marjorie Davies also as Peggy. Charlie Cantor as Mr. Barker, Meek's boss. John McIntire as the "sour and cynical Mr. Apple." Ann Thomas as Lily, the maid. ANNOUNCER: Dan Seymour. MUSIC: Elliott Jacoby. DIRECTOR: Don Bernard.

Revival series—*Meet the Meeks*: Sept. 6, 1947–April 30, 1949, NBC. 30m, Saturdays at 11 A.M. Swift Packing. CAST: Forrest Lewis as Mortimer. Fran Allison as Agatha. Elmira Roessler and Beryl Vaughn as Peggy. Cliff Soubier as Uncle Louie. WRITER: Les Weinrott.

MEET MR. WEEKS, literary talk.

BROADCAST HISTORY: Nov. 7, 1939–March 11, 1941, Blue Network. 30m, Tuesdays at 9:30 until Feb. 1940; returned Nov. 12, Tuesdays at 10:30.

This series began as *The Human Side of Literature*, and was also heard as *Meet Edward Weeks*. Weeks, editor of the *Atlantic Monthly*, was lured to radio by NBC's Lewis Titterton, who considered him a fascinating speaker. He discussed diarists, books, and "poets who made the world laugh." A guest slot in the half-hour was filled by someone from theater, publishing, higher learning, or the press. Max Wylie selected one show for *Best Broadcasts of 1939–40*. The script bristles with color and wit. In an opening monologue, Weeks discusses great diarists of history, then brings on actress Ruth Gordon, who talks about her diary. Weeks wraps it up with a discussion of the diary of Arnold Bennett.

MEET THE MISSUS, audience show.

BROADCAST HISTORY: Ca. 1944–50, CBS West Coast. 15m and 30m versions, up to six a week. HOST: Jack Bailey; later Jay Stewart, Harry Mitchell, Ed East, and Harry Koplan, who also directed.

In the *House Party* formula, women were drawn from the audience, joshed, and given gifts. The show was broadcast from Earl Carroll's restaurant.

MEET THE PRESS, news talk; a press conference of the air.

BROADCAST HISTORY: Oct, 5, 1945–Aug. 18, 1950, Mutual. 30m, initially Fridays at 10:30 but heard on a partial network until Dec. 1946; Fridays at 10, 1947–49; at 9:30, 1949–50.

May 11, 1952–July 27, 1986, NBC. 30m, Sundays at 10:30, 1952–55; at 6 beginning in 1955; various weekend timeslots after 1958.

MODERATORS: Bill Slater, Albert Warner, Martha Rountree, etc. PERMANENT PANELIST: Lawrence Spivak. GUESTS: Hot newsmakers in the political arena. PRODUCER-CREATOR: Martha Rountree.

Meet the Press grew out of a partnership between Martha Rountree and Lawrence Spivak. Rountree, a freelance writer, broke into radio around 1939. She had created the witty and spontaneous panel show *Leave It to the Girls* in 1945, and now, with *American Mercury* editor Lawrence Spivak, came up with an idea for promoting Spivak's magazine. She would produce a radio show, with Spivak as the permanent panelist representing the press. They would invite top newsmakers to be put on the spot, "without preparation or oratory," and thus "find out what they stand for."

Almost from the beginning, *Meet the Press* made its own headlines, and soon it was covered as a news event by both major wire services. Joining Spivak on the panel were noted American journalists. The mix was purposely volatile: two editors known for their opposition to the guest's viewpoint, one middle-of-the-road type, and Spivak. Earl Warren, Harry Truman, Harold Stassen, Robert Oppenheimer, James Farley, and Sen. Joseph McCarthy were among those persuaded to sit in the hot seat. Often front-page headlines erupted from the show. Sen. Theodore Bilbo of Mississippi acknowledged on the air what had been common knowledge for some time—that he was a member of the Ku Klux Klan. John L. Lewis announced a coal strike even before his union membership had been informed. Gov. Thomas Dewey declared himself out of the running for the 1952 Republican nomination, and pushed the stock of Gen. Dwight D. Eisenhower, who still had not declared his own intentions. Whittaker Chambers reiterated his charges against Alger Hiss, taking himself out from under the blanket of congressional immunity and daring Hiss to sue him.

Rountree's biggest problems were longwindedness of guests, evasiveness, and the dangers of blowups on the air. When Tex McCrary asked

Fiorello La Guardia if he had ever used his position as mayor of New York to try and get reporters fired, La Guardia snapped, "That's a damned lie." It was staunch stuff for mid-1940s radio. Spivak's cardinal rule was "never take anyone who will withhold information—that's why the show makes front-page news so often." He and Rountree had reputations as news anticipators. They tried (and many times were successful) to book people who were "ripe for headlines." Then it became simply a matter of asking provocative questions.

The show was an early TV entry, going to NBC in 1947. It was a TV-radio simulcast beginning in 1952, when NBC picked up the radio half as well. The television show is still being seen.

THE MEL BLANC SHOW, situation comedy.

BROADCAST HISTORY: Sept. 3, 1946–June 24, 1947, CBS. 30m, Tuesdays at 8:30. Colgate. CAST: Mel Blanc as himself, an addled young man who ran a repair business called the Fix-It Shop. Blanc also as Zookie, his stuttering helper in the shop. Mary Jane Croft as Mel's girlfriend, Betty Colby. Joseph Kearns as Betty's grouchy father, owner of a supermarket. Hans Conried as Mr. Cushing, president of Mel's lodge, "the Loyal Order of Benevolent Zebras." Alan Reed as Mr. Potchnik, the piano teacher. Support from Hollywood's Radio Row: Bea Benaderet, Leora Thatcher, Earle Ross, etc. ORCHESTRA: Victor Miller. PRODUCER-DIRECTOR: Joe Rines. WRITERS: David Victor and Herb Little; later, Mac Benoff.

Mel Blanc, with his vast repertoire of dialects, voice characterizations, and vocal sound effects, was one of the busiest men in Hollywood. In addition to his work on many radio sitcoms (*Abbott and Costello, Jack Benny, Point Sublime, Burns and Allen*, and *Judy Canova*, to name a few), Blanc was also the voices of Bugs Bunny, Porky Pig, and other Warner Brothers cartoon characters.

He was born May 30, 1908, in San Francisco. He began collecting dialects and characterizations in his youth, first mastering a thick Yiddish borrowed from an old Jewish couple who ran a grocery store in his neighborhood. He added the sounds of Chinatown (in Portland, where his family had moved) to what was quickly becoming an act. By the time he finished high school, Blanc was an actor, doing occasional skits on local radio with his brother Henry.

In the early 1930s, he moved to California. He worked at KGO, the NBC affiliate in San Francisco, and found that city a melting pot of races and nationalities. "For a voice man intent on assimilating new dialects," he would write in his memoir, "simply walking down the street provided daily education."

He moved on to Los Angeles, got on *The Al Pearce Show*, and then got his first major national exposure as Joe Penner's duck on *The Baker's Broadcast*. By 1940, his career was in full bloom.

In his own inevitable series, Blanc played himself in his natural voice. In his Porky Pig voice, he was Zookie, his own helper. Zookie opened each broadcast with a "Hello, every-b-uh-bbb-uh-b-bbb-uh—HI!" Mel played a scatterbrain who should have been anything but a fixer of broken objects. Items always left Mel's shop in worse condition than they had been on arrival. This greatly disgusted Mr. Colby, father of Mel's girlfriend, Betty. Many of the plots dealt with Mel's efforts to impress Colby and win favor as a serious suitor for his daughter. In one show, Mel ruined Colby's radio, then tried to cover it up by hiding behind the set and creating the programs as Colby turned the dial.

Fans will remember the senseless catchphrase "Ugga-ugga-boo, ugga-boo-boo-ugga" (the password at Mel's lodge). The entire run is preserved, but unfortunately Blanc's considerable talent was better displayed in his supporting roles with Benny and others. The writing on the Blanc show now seems silly and dated. But Blanc had a unique place in radio, and the medium was vastly enriched by his presence. He died July 10, 1989.

MELODY AND MADNESS, musical variety.

BROADCAST HISTORY: Nov. 20, 1938–Nov. 14, 1939, CBS. 30m, Sundays at 10 through May 14, 1939; Blue Network, beginning May 23, Tuesdays at 9. Old Gold Cigarettes. CAST: Robert Benchley, resident wit, with various New York personnel. Warren Hull, host, as of mid-1939. ANNOUNCERS: John Fleming, Del Sharbutt. VOCALISTS: Dick Todd, Helen Forrest, and the Four Clubmen, directed by Lyn Murray. OR-

CHESTRA: Artie Shaw (Lud Gluskin on at least three shows, in Shaw's absence). DIRECTOR: Martin Gosch.

Melody and Madness, though intended as a vehicle for Robert Benchley, became a classic stand for Artie Shaw. Benchley, nationally known as a cerebral comic, was much bally-hooed in this, his first radio series. He had been a columnist for the *New Yorker* for a decade and had made 40-odd short films, and his membership in the fabled Algonquin Round Table seemed to certify his wit. But somehow he didn't quite make it on the air. He did three monologues, and Shaw played three melodies: that was the weekly format of *Melody and Madness*.

But the show caught the Shaw band on the upswing, perhaps two pieces short of greatness. When Shaw hired Georgie Auld on reeds and Buddy Rich on drums in December 1938, the orchestra bloomed into a swing giant. The band burst into 1939 with a free and happy sound: highlighted by the trumpet of Bernie Privin, the trombone of George Arus, Shaw's clarinet, and the vocals of Helen Forrest, it captured its moment as vividly as a photograph.

MELODY PUZZLES, quiz.

BROADCAST HISTORY: Nov. 2, 1937–Jan. 25, 1938, Mutual. 30m, Tuesdays at 8. Lucky Strike.
  Jan. 10–April 4, 1938, Blue Network. 30m, Mondays at 8. Lucky Strike.
QUIZMASTER: Fred Uttal. VOCALISTS: Fredda Gibson (Georgia Gibbs), Buddy Clark. ORCHESTRA: Richard Himber, 1937; Harry Salter.

Skits were performed, and contestants guessed song titles from clues therein.

MEN AGAINST DEATH, documentary drama, based on the book by Paul De Kruif.

BROADCAST HISTORY: June 30, 1938–April 29, 1939, CBS. 30m, Thursdays at 8 until Oct. 1; Saturdays at 9 until Jan. 14; then Saturdays at 2.
CAST: Unknown New York talent in anthology roles. COMPOSER-CONDUCTOR: Bernard Herrmann. PRODUCERS: CBS Radio and the Radio Division of the Federal Theater. DIRECTORS: George Zachary, Earle McGill, William N. Robson, and Brewster Morgan of the CBS staff. WRITERS: Leo Fontaine and Lawrence Bearson of the WPA; also, Harold Hartogensis.

Men Against Death followed the one-man campaign of writer Paul De Kruif against disease, hunger, and poverty. De Kruif burst on the scene with *Microbe Hunters*, which became a worldwide bestseller upon its publication in 1926. Other titles were *Hunger Fighters, Why Keep Them Alive?, The Fight for Life*, and *Men Against Death*. Though the latter book gave the series its name, the WPA writers selected liberally from all of De Kruif's books, which the author donated without royalty to the cause. The lives of scientific trailblazers (Lister, Pasteur, etc.) were dramatized; an introductory broadcast June 30, 1938, was followed by the first drama on July 7.

THE MERCURY THEATER ON THE AIR, dramatic anthology.

BROADCAST HISTORY: July 11–Dec. 4, 1938, CBS. 60m, Mondays at 9 until Sept. 11, then Sundays at 8. Became *The Campbell Playhouse* (covered under that title) as of Dec. 9, 1938.
  June 7–Sept. 13, 1946, CBS. 30m, Fridays at 10. Pabst Beer.
CAST: Orson Welles, with his celebrated repertory company from Broadway; Martin Gabel, Ray Collins, Kenny Delmar, George Coulouris, Edgar Barrier, Paul Stewart, Everett Sloane, Joseph Cotten, Hiram Sherman, Erskine Sanford, Frank Readick, Agnes Moorehead, Alice Frost, Karl Swenson, William Alland, etc. ANNOUNCER: Dan Seymour. ORCHESTRA: Bernard Herrmann. PRODUCER: John Houseman. DIRECTOR: Orson Welles. WRITERS: John Houseman, Howard Koch. ENGINEER: John Dietz. SOUND EFFECTS: James Rogan, Ray Kremer, Ora Nichols.

The Mercury Theater, wrote *Time* in a 1938 cover story, was "bounded north and south by hope, east and west by nerve." It was the culmination of an unlikely partnership between a controversial and noisy "boy wonder" of stage and radio and a former grain merchant who had indulged a passion for theater when the grain market collapsed. One would become world-famous in his youth and would never again capture the magic of those days; the other would toil in obscurity, gaining fame as an actor in his 70s. Their time together was short and ended in acrimony. The peak of it was a scant three years, 1935–38, during which Orson Welles and John Houseman created some of the most startling and talked-about theater New York had seen in decades.

Welles was born May 6, 1915, in Kenosha, Wisc. His mother was a musician, and his father an inventor of sorts, and in childhood Welles was exposed to people from many disciplines in the arts. He knew Shakespeare early: some stories have it that he had read the entire Shakespearean canon by the time he was 10. At 12, he staged a school production of *Julius Caesar*, playing three important roles himself. He learned magic, which became a lifelong hobby, but could never adequately do figures. By the end of high school, he had set his course to be an actor.

At 16, he traveled through Ireland on a donkey cart. In Dublin, he bluffed his way into an important role in the upcoming *Jew Suss* at the Gate Theater, gathering high praise. By 1934, he had returned to the United States. A chance meeting with Thornton Wilder resulted in an introduction to Alexander Woollcott, who got him introduced to Katharine Cornell. Welles joined Cornell in road productions of *Romeo and Juliet* and *Candida*, and later opened in *Romeo* in New York. In was in this production, late in 1934, that Welles was first seen by John Houseman.

Houseman, though 13 years his senior, was a late-comer to theater. Born in Bucharest Sept. 22, 1902, he had followed his father as a grain broker until the Depression sent exports into a tailspin. Houseman's first success had come only that year, when he produced Virgil Thomson's opera, *Four Saints in Three Acts*. He had obtained the rights to an Archibald MacLeish play, *Panic*, for production in 1935, and he was so impressed by the dramatic timbre of Welles's voice that he offered him the lead. The run was short—three nights—but Houseman soon became director of the newly formed WPA Negro Theater Project and again invited Welles to take part. They decided to stage *Macbeth* as a jungle melodrama, at the suggestion of Welles's wife, Virginia. It would be set in Haiti, based on the life of Henri Christophe, and would feature voodoo drums and witch doctors instead of Shakespeare's original witches. The play ran for weeks in Harlem; it was followed by *Dr. Faustus* and in 1937 by the show that was to prove pivotal in the formation of the Mercury Theater, Marc Blitzstein's *The Cradle Will Rock*.

Welles, meanwhile, had made serious inroads on New York radio. He had become a regular on *The March of Time* and was soon to assume the lead in the Mutual Network melodrama *The Shadow*. He had taken to radio instinctively, earning about $1,000 a week on the air. His days were full: in addition to his radio shows, Welles was rehearsing *The Cradle Will Rock* in a time of labor disputes and national strife. There was an uneasiness in doing the Blitzstein play, which had deep anti-capitalist themes. It gave a vivid picture of an industrial tyrant, boss of the fictional "Steeltown," and the fight of Labor against his tyranny. The WPA was already under fire for staging what some people thought were too many labor plays, and there were rumblings in Washington that its funds might be cut. The shoe fell less than three weeks before the June 16, 1937, preview—a sweeping WPA funds cut, followed by a directive prohibiting new openings until the "reorganization" caused by the cuts was implemented.

Welles flew to Washington to argue his case. Failing in that, he threatened to open the play himself. The government's response was severe: as Houseman would recall it in his memoir, on June 15 "a dozen uniformed guards took over the building in force. Project members arriving to sign in found their theater sealed and dark. The Cossacks, as they came to be known, guarded the front of the house and the box office; they hovered in the alley outside the dressing rooms with orders to see that no government property was used or removed."

The company retreated to the safety of the basement ladies' room, where they huddled with telephones for 24 hours, plotting strategy. Obviously, they would have to find a new theater. But then, on the afternoon of the opening, the union decided that its members could not perform on an alternate stage after being paid by the WPA for months of rehearsal. Houseman, addressing the actors, put his own twist on it— the wording "on stage" in the union ruling had, he believed, left them an out: the actors should be free, "as U.S. citizens," to enter "whatever theater we find" with the rest of the audience, rise from their seats on cue, and speak their lines from the aisles. But they still had no theater, and curtain time was less than three hours away.

It was almost 8 o'clock when they got their house—the Venice Theater, some 20 blocks away. By then much of the audience had gathered outside. The crowd cheered the announcement and began to move across town—audience, actors, and the press. *The Cradle Will Rock* played in the aisles, with Blitzstein playing his music on a rinky-tink piano that Houseman had secured for the night. No one had to search the theater pages to find their notices the next day. They had made all the front pages, they were famous, and they were out of jobs. Houseman was formally dismissed a month later. A few days after that, he would recall, he and Welles were talking and Welles suddenly said, "Why the hell don't we start a theater of our own?"

Its first year was charmed. The Mercury, wrote Houseman, "was conceived one summer evening after supper; its birth was formally announced ten days later and it opened on Broadway in a playhouse bearing its own name with a program of four productions, a company of 34, and a capital of ten thousand five hundred dollars." They had leased the Comedy Theater, a playhouse at Broadway and 41st Street: *Julius Caesar* would be its first show. Houseman and Welles divided the work as partners: Houseman ran the business end while Welles did the writing and tended to the plays. Houseman found the fundraising difficult: he probed his contacts on Wall Street but got dribbles, enough, said *Time*, "to keep the cast stringing along and repair the Mercury toilets." Contributions from Claire Boothe and an advance sale of $8,000 helped, but the production would still open without expensive costumes or sets. Welles turned this to advantage: they would play *Julius Caesar* as a modern allegory. It emerged on a stark stage, a statement on fascism, with Welles playing Brutus in a blue serge suit.

The press was euphoric. "The brightest moon that has arisen over Broadway in years," swooned *Time*. "Welles should feel at home in the sky, for the sky is the only limit that his ambitions recognize." *Caesar* was followed by *Shoemaker's Holiday*, then by *Heartbreak House*. The Mercury was solvent, its future apparently bright.

In June 1938, Welles was approached by CBS and offered a timeslot for a Mercury Theater of the air. This was a little frightening to Houseman, whose only exposure to radio had been as a listener to occasional newscasts. He was accustomed to weeks of rehearsal and could hardly believe his ears when when he was told that they

would go on the air in two weeks, July 11. They had no play to perform, let alone a script: their work in the theater would have to continue without letup, with performances of the current show and rehearsals for the next one consuming their days, and now they had a 60-minute *radio* show to select, write, cast, rehearse, and perform. Houseman protested, arguing that he knew nothing about radio. Welles said he'd better start learning, and he gave Houseman the job of getting a script together.

They decided on *Treasure Island* as the opening show. They would do the classics, with emphasis on adventure, under the title *First Person Singular*. All Houseman had to do, Welles assured him, was sit down with Stevenson's novel and adapt it—mainly a cutting job. Welles would be the director, narrator, and, of course, the star. The *First Person Singular* title was significant. "The 'I' is more important in radio than in any other medium," Welles told *Radio Guide*. As narrator, he would lead the audience straight into the story, where they would experience it, almost as participants. He would narrate as the grown-up Jim Hawkins and would also play Long John Silver. The plays would be geared "for the listener alone," with no studio audience and no disruptive applause. It was believed to be the first time that radio had offered a regular slot to an entire theatrical group.

Houseman was a week into his task when Welles threw him another curve. They were bumping *Treasure Island*, putting it back a week, and opening with Bram Stoker's horror classic, *Dracula*. Welles promised a script, but this consisted of a book with key passages marked for inclusion. With the deadline looming, they retired to Reuben's, a 59th Street eatery that never closed. For 17 hours they sat in the restaurant and worked on the script. "Three days later," Houseman would recall in his memoir, "*Dracula* went on the air as the opener of what was to become a legendary air series."

The show was sustained, giving CBS high prestige but no income for the Monday night hour. The network assigned Davidson Taylor as supervisor and the tempestuous Bernard Herrmann as musical director. Herrmann and Welles got along as expected: there were "screaming rows," Houseman remembered. Batons were snapped and thrown in the air, and scripts were scattered in the heat of the moment. But each week the show went smoothly on the air, listeners unaware of the frantic improvisation wrought by Welles, usually continuing to the last minute before the opening theme (Tchaikovsky's Piano Concerto Number 1 in B-flat Minor) flowed out of their radios.

The premiere set the tone. Welles played Dracula with a cutting dialect, and took on the role of Dr. Seward as well. Martin Gabel played Van Helsing; George Coulouris was Jonathan Harker; Ray Collins played the Russian captain; Karl Swenson played the mate; Agnes Moorehead was Mina Harker; Elizabeth Farrell was Lucy Westenra. The press was solid in its praise, and the *Mercury* pushed ahead with the postponed *Treasure Island* as its second show July 18. The nine-week run concluded Sept. 5, but CBS extended it into the fall. The show moved to Sundays. Houseman was still adapting all the original novels himself, and Welles kept reaching for new techniques. For *The Count of Monte Cristo*, the two actors playing the dungeon scenes did so from the floor of the restroom, where Welles had placed two dynamic microphones against the bases of the toilet seat in an effort to obtain realistic subterranean reverberation. Another mike was strung into a toilet bowl with the stopper left open. The constant flushing, Houseman recalled, "gave a faithful rendering of the waves breaking against the walls of the Chateau d'If."

The opening show of the fall season was *Julius Caesar*. Welles employed newscaster H. V. Kaltenborn as narrator, in an effort to forge modern-day immediacy. These were "the golden years of unsponsored radio," Houseman told *Harper's* magazine, years later. "We had no advertising agency to harass us, no client to cut our withers. Shows were created week after week under conditions of soul-and health-destroying pressure." Houseman was still the lone writer. He had to boil down to 60 minutes any novel that Welles decided to air, and these were usually fat Victorian monsters that had to be scripted in about three working days. *Jane Eyre*, *Sherlock Holmes*, and *Oliver Twist* followed *Caesar*. It was at about this time that Howard Koch walked in and asked for a writing job. Houseman hired him at $75 a week and gladly turned over the unrelenting job of scriptwriting. Koch had no

way of knowing that he was stepping into radio history—that in one month he would produce the working script for the most famous single radio show ever broadcast.

His first script was *Hell on Ice*, from the book by Edward Ellsberg. This in itself was a departure. The book had been published only that year, and it would be *Mercury*'s only venture into current documentary drama. Ellsberg had written an intense account of the disastrous attempt by George W. De Long to reach the North Pole in 1879. The story told how De Long's ship, the *Jeannette*, was trapped in an icepack, and how a handful of survivors endured horrendous hardships for two years. It was compelling radio on Oct. 9, 1938. Booth Tarkington's *Seventeen* and Jules Verne's *Around the World in 80 Days* then brought them to the Halloween season. Welles wanted a spook show, deciding against better judgments to dust off the 40-year-old H. G. Wells fantasy *The War of the Worlds* and air it Oct. 30. The dissenting voices were afraid that the story would be hopelessly dated, and dull on the air. But Koch had his assignment, and the date was six days away. Welles laid out some general guidelines: he wanted the story told in a series of news bulletins, with cutaways to first-person narrative. As Koch read the original work, a sense of despair set in. H. G. Wells had set his tale in England, and his writing style was long past its prime. This was no simple cutting job: as Koch would recall in his memoir, "I realized I could use very little but the author's idea of a Martian invasion and his descriptions of their appearance and machines. In short, I was being asked to write an almost entirely original play in six days."

Koch visited his family on Monday, his day off. Driving back through New Jersey, he picked up a road map at a gas station. In his New York apartment, he opened the map, closed his eyes, and dropped his pencil point. This was where the Martians would land, a village called Grovers Mill, surrounded by farmland. Koch liked the sound of it: it had "an authentic ring" to it, he would remember, and this play would need all the authenticity he could give it.

On Tuesday, he telephoned Houseman in despair. The show couldn't be done, he said: there was simply no way to make it credible to a modern listener. Houseman considered the alternatives. On short notice, he had only one, Blackmore's *Lorna Doone*, which he found a dreary prospect. He tried to reach Welles at the theater, but Welles was rehearsing *Danton's Death* and wouldn't take the call. Houseman then tried to reprimand Koch. Finally he promised to come and help get the script together.

He arrived around 2 A.M. to find Koch in better spirits. Koch was beginning to have fun "laying waste to the state of New Jersey." Koch was especially enjoying the destruction of CBS, where the last gasping announcer would be heard mournfully calling for survivors at the 40-minute break. Houseman and Koch worked through the night and all of the following day, finishing at dusk Wednesday. There was a rehearsal on Thursday, handled in Welles's continued absence by associate producer Paul Stewart. A transcription was cut of the reading, and the crew listened to it with a creeping sense of failure. Koch had been right: it was a dull, unbelievable show. Houseman felt that another rewrite was essential, that "its only chance of coming off lay in emphasizing its newscast style and eyewitness quality." They plunged in again.

"We sat up all night, spicing it with circumstantial allusions and authentic detail," Houseman recalled. Koch would remember it as "a nightmare of scenes written and rewritten" for taskmasters "who considered sleep a luxury." It ended when they ran out of time. The script was then in the hands of Welles, the gods, and the CBS censor, who received his copy on Friday.

Whatever the censor saw in the script, true fear was not part of it. The writers had gone a little too far in their attempt to be authentic, and a few real locations were replaced with fiction. The Hotel Biltmore became "the Meridian Room of the Hotel Park Plaza in downtown New York." References to CBS were changed to "Broadcasting Building." The script went up to mimeo. As far as Houseman and Koch were concerned, it was ready for the air: they called it a very long day and went to bed.

On Sunday morning, Welles—who would receive on-air credit for almost every aspect of the broadcast—had still not seen the script or attended any of the rehearsals. He made his first appearance Sunday afternoon, taking over the final rehearsals from Paul Stewart and beginning the mysterious process of making it an Orson Welles show. "A strange fever seemed to invade the studio," Houseman said in *Harper's* from a ten-year perspective. This was "part childish mischief, part professional zeal. The first to feel it were the actors." Frank Readick, who would play the soon-to-be incinerated newsman, Carl Phillips, got out transcriptions of Herb Morrison's already classic description of the *Hindenburg* disaster. Morrison had been assigned to cover the airship's landing with recording equipment: the subsequent explosion was thus preserved in a never-to-be-forgotten moment of news broadcasting as Morrison wept in his telling of it. Readick listened to these records continuously, trying to capture the essence of distress in Morrison's voice.

Welles, meanwhile, was making last-minute changes. He stretched out the early scenes that Houseman and Koch had trimmed earlier. Back into the script went the same ingredients that Houseman feared would be so tedious—the long cutaways of dance music, the weather bulletins and astronomical observations. Welles thought that the tedium of the first minutes would add credence to the next half-hour, when events too incredible to believe would pile one on top of the others at an impossible pace. Within 40 minutes, Houseman would write, "men traveled long distances, large bodies of troops were mobilized, cabinet meetings were held, savage battles were fought on land and in the air." This would be done in the "here and now," with no fictional framework to prop it up and help the listener attain the suspension of disbelief so vital to even the possibility of success. Among the most effective of these techniques came at the first blast of the Martian heat ray, when the "field transmission" went dead and the station was forced to fill the time with a "piano interlude"—an ominous playing of *Clair de Lune*.

At 8 o'clock, Welles mounted the podium, assuming the stance of both director and star, and the play began. Dan Seymour clearly announced that *The Mercury Theater on the Air* was presenting the Orson Welles production of *The War of the Worlds*, by H. G. Wells. Welles gave a short prologue, setting the tale in the near future. Then the news bulletins began. There was a weather report, then a shift to the Park Plaza Hotel for a band remote. Herrmann's musicians gave a good account of themselves as "Ramon Raquello and his orchestra," with a popular-sounding rendition of *La Cumparsita*. This was interrupted by a news bulletin, announcing "explosions of incandescent gas, occurring at regular intervals, on the planet Mars." *La Cumparsita* ended and *Star Dust* began, with applause. Another news bulletin: reporter Carl Phillips was being sent to the Princeton Observatory to interview "the noted astronomer" Professor Richard Pierson. As Pierson, Welles gave several lines of astronomical mumbo-jumbo; then it was announced that he and Phillips were racing to Grovers Mill, N.J., where a shock "of almost earthquake intensity" had just been recorded. It took them less than two minutes to travel the 11 miles. More news bulletins were read, and when Phillips returned to the air he continued the telescoping of time. Now the pace was heightened even more. A huge cylinder had fallen in the field of Farmer Wilmuth, who was quite happy to talk about it. There was more speculation by Pierson as to the extraterrestrial nature of the metal casing. Suddenly the top began to "flake off . . . rotate like a screw." A dull metallic clank, obviously the door of a space vehicle hitting the earth, was followed by what many listeners would remember as the most terrifying lines they would ever hear from a radio.

Someone was crawling out of the hollow top . . . someone or something. Two luminous discs were visible . . . might be eyes, might be a face. Now something wriggling out of the shadow like a gray snake . . . tentacles . . . another one and another one . . . and the thing's body, large as a bear, and it glistened like wet leather. And the face: the eyes black, gleaming like a serpent's, with a V-shaped mouth dripping saliva from rimless lips . . .

And with Phillips giving a full account, the monster rigged its fighting machine and brought up its heat ray. Soldiers burst into flames. The fires spread everywhere. Suddenly Phillips was cut off the air. Dead time heightened the effect.

More bulletins. Red Cross emergency workers dispatched to the scene. Bridges hopelessly clogged with frantic human traffic. Automobiles were to use Route 7 . . .

At last came the blunt announcement that defined the show. Everything else was window dressing to this bald lie. *Ladies and gentlemen, as incredible as it may seem, both the observations of science and the evidence of our own eyes lead to the inescapable assumption that those strange beings who landed in the Jersey farm-lands tonight are the vanguard of an invading army from the planet Mars.* Soon came Kenny Delmar, as a very official and gloomy "Secretary of the Interior." More news bulletins. Martian cylinders were falling all over the country, and in New York the enemy could be seen, rising high above the Palisades. Ray Collins, the last announcer, described the machines wading the Hudson, "like a man wading through a brook." The smoke crossed Fifth Avenue, came closer, and again there was a long and terrible silence. The last pathetic voice was that of a shortwave operator, breaking through from some outpost. *2X2L calling CQ, New York . . . isn't there anyone on the air? . . . isn't there anyone on the air? . . . isn't there anyone . . . ?*

At about this time, Davidson Taylor was called away from the studio. The telephone began ringing. When Taylor returned, Houseman recalled, his face was ashen.

The panic had begun in New Jersey and spread north and west. Men staggered into bars babbling about the end of the world. Bartenders tuned in just in time to hear Kenny Delmar—playing the "Secretary of the Interior" but sounding enough like Roosevelt to chill their marrow—putting faith in God and the armed forces in this national catastrophe. In Newark, traffic ran wild through the streets. People wrapped their faces in wet towels and roared past puzzled traffic cops in their haste to get out of town. One Newark hospital treated 20 people for shock. A woman in Pittsburgh was reportedly saved by her husband as she tried to swallow poison. A power shortage in a small midwestern town at the peak of the show sent people screaming into the streets. At a college campus in North Carolina, students fought over the few available telephones. In Boston, families gathered on rooftops and imagined they could see a red glow against the night sky, as New York burned.

Inside Studio One at CBS, the drama rolled to its conclusion. Taylor had heard frightening reports of affiliate reactions to the show. Casualties were mounting across the nation, he had been told: there were deaths by suicide and mob tramplings, with more coming in every minute. He returned to the booth with orders to interrupt immediately and announce that the play was fiction. But Welles had reached the 40-minute break; Dan Seymour stepped to the microphone and said, "You are listening to a CBS presentation of Orson Welles and *The Mercury Theater on the Air* in an original dramatization of *The War of the Worlds*, by H. G. Wells.''

This was followed by 20 minutes of straight drama, with Welles as Professor Richard Pierson describing the aftermath of the war. In the punchline, the Martians were killed off by simple earth bacteria. All was right with the world again. Welles closed with assurances that *The War of the Worlds* had ''no further significance than as the holiday offering it was intended to be—*The Mercury Theater*'s own radio version of dressing up in a sheet and jumping out of a bush and saying boo.'' In his New York apartment, Howard Koch turned off his radio and went to bed, satisfied that he had done his best, unaware of the havoc his play was causing across the nation.

The most frightening part of the evening, for Houseman and Welles, was just beginning. Even as the closing Tchaikovsky theme flooded the studio, police swarmed in, confiscating scripts and segregating the players. They were kept for a time in a back office, then were thrown to the press. The questions were hard and terrifying. How many deaths had they heard of? . . . implying, as Houseman later told it, ''that they knew of thousands.'' Had they heard of the fatal stampede in the Jersey hall? Were they aware of the traffic deaths and suicides? The ditches must be choked with corpses, Houseman thought. Then they were released, taken out a back exit. Houseman found it ''surprising to see life going on as usual in the midnight streets.''

In fact, there were no deaths. There were some bumps and scrapes, a broken bone or two, and a flurry of lawsuits against CBS. Princeton commissioned a study, published in 1940 by Hadley Cantril under the title *The Invasion from Mars*. Cantril found that six million people had heard the show: 1.7 million believed it to be authentic news; 1.2 million were genuinely frightened. Contributing factors were the Munich crisis, which had set people on edge and accustomed them to the interruptions of real newsmen with breaking stories, and the Edgar Bergen broadcast on NBC. Bergen then had the top-rated show in the nation. He had just finished his opening Charlie McCarthy routine as ''Carl Phillips'' and ''Professor Pierson'' arrived at Grovers Mill on CBS. Bergen introduced a Nelson Eddy song, and a sizable portion of his formidable audience

gave the dial a quick-flip . . . and never turned back.

For the record, Welles was contrite. Forty years later—removed from the threat of mob assault—he confessed only to amusement, and amazement that people could be so gullible. For three full days the fate of *The Mercury Theater on the Air* hung in the balance. No one at CBS could decide, as Houseman told it, whether they were heroes or scoundrels. Dorothy Thompson seemed to speak for the majority: after pronouncing the broadcast unbelievable from start to finish, she lauded Welles for demonstrating how vulnerable the country was in such a panic. As for Welles, he was an overnight star on the world stage. Campbell Soups stepped up with an offer to sponsor, and in December the show moved up to first-class status.

The new *Campbell Playhouse* would emphasize big-money guests, who overshadowed the rep company that the *Mercury* had brought to radio. Current bestsellers would be mixed with the classics. There was a different sound to it, a texture flavored by money. The Martian broadcast was also a turning point in the Houseman-Welles partnership. Welles was suddenly the boy genius, for the time at least untouchable. The balance of power that had always existed between the partners shifted, leaving Houseman feeling more like a Welles employee. Houseman moved on, to other work in the theater. Welles hit his peak in 1941, with the release of *Citizen Kane*. His later Hollywood projects were starcrossed and economically troubled. He came into middle age still trading on the reputation of his youth. Houseman, meanwhile, attained his own stardom in 1973, at age 71, in an Oscar-winning film performance in *The Paper Chase*. He reprised his character—Charles W. Kingsfield, professor of law—in an acclaimed television series of the same name.

Welles died Oct. 10, 1985; Houseman Oct. 31, 1988. In a tribute to both, Howard Koch termed Houseman ''the pedestal on which the statue of Orson was erected.''

Most of the *Mercury* run can be had on tape, though the quality at times leaves much to desire. *The War of the Worlds* is of course the great attraction, though it is far from the most effective show to a modern listener. Much more interesting, dramatically, is *Dracula*. Wonderful then and now was the trilogy of August 8, containing

My Little Boy (an eloquent attack on intolerance), *I'm a Fool*, and *The Open Window*. Far and away, in this writer's view, was *Hell on Ice* the best of the series. This gripping true story could hardly have been more effectively told: its power is still in full evidence, overcoming even its rough preservation on a dozen or more 78 rpm sides, with commensurate surface noise. On a happier note, the entire 1946 *Mercury Summer Theater* is available in mostly good sound. Highlights were *The Hitchhiker*, *The Moat Farm Murder*, *The Apple Tree*, and, again, *Hell on Ice*. Here Welles was reunited with old *Mercury* players Alice Frost, Agnes Moorehead, Elliott Reid, and Edgar Barrier, and received additional support from such as Lurene Tuttle, Mary Lansing, Norman Field, and John Brown. The announcer was Ken Roberts; the composer-conductor, again, was Bernard Herrmann.

MEREDITH WILLSON, musical variety.

BROADCAST HISTORY: April 22, 1935–Feb. 12, 1954. Many 30m timeslots on various networks, including:

April 22–June 3, 1935, Blue Network. Mondays at 8:30.

June 16, 1936–Aug. 4, 1937. NBC, Tuesdays at 9; Wednesdays at 10:30, Blue Network, beginning in Jan.

June 6–Aug. 29, 1946, NBC. Thursdays at 8:30. Substitute for *Burns and Allen*. Maxwell House.

Oct. 4, 1946–March 28, 1947, CBS. Fridays at 7:30. *Sparkle Time*. Canada Dry.

June 18–Sept. 24, 1947, CBS. Wednesdays at 9:30. Ford.

Oct. 6, 1948–March 30, 1949, ABC. Wednesdays at 10:30. General Foods for Jell-O.

Aug. 25–Sept. 29, 1949, NBC. Thursdays at 8. General Foods.

Aug. 8, 1951–May 28, 1952, NBC. Wednesdays at 10:30. RCA through Dec. 1951, then sustained.

June 1–Sept. 28, 1952, NBC. Sundays at 8. RCA.

Jan. 3–June 6, 1953, NBC. Saturdays at 10:30.

Dec. 16, 1953–Feb. 12, 1954, NBC. Various 15m weekday slots. Florida Citrus.

Meredith Willson, composer, conductor, and radio personality, was prominently featured on such major shows as *Good News, Maxwell House Coffee Time, Burns and Allen*, and *The Big Show*, in addition to those bearing his own name. His specialty was lush sounds—"chiffon swing," it was called at one time. His association with General Foods was strong: in addition to his shows for Maxwell House, he created a campaign for Jell-O known as "the Talking People." Five actors (Betty Allen, Maxwell Smith, Norma Zimmer, John Rarig, and Bob Hanlon) spoke the commercials in unison, "shimmering" their voices in a vocal impression of the product's texture. Willson's greatest fame, however, was as author of *The Music Man*, the biggest hit of the 1957–58 theatrical season.

THE METROPOLITAN OPERA, concert music.

BROADCAST HISTORY: Dec. 25, 1931–Nov. 30, 1940, NBC, both networks alternately or simultaneously. 185m to 230m, Saturdays, midafternoons, beginning ca. 1 to 3. Lucky Strike, 1933–34; Listerine, 1934–35.

Dec. 7, 1940–ca. 1958, Blue Network/ABC. Up to 240m, Saturdays at 2. Texaco.

1958–60, CBS. Saturdays. Texaco.

1960—present, heard along a special network of 300 stations, coordinated by a media department within the opera organization and sponsored by Texaco. Saturdays.

HOST: Milton Cross, 1931–75; Peter Allen, long-time subsequent host. **COMMENTATORS:** Deems Taylor, early broadcasts; Marcia Davenport, 1973. **CONDUCTORS:** Artur Bodanzky, Wilfred Pelletier, Erich Leinsdorf, Gennaro Papi, Ettore Panizza, Bruno Walter, all ca. 1930s–1940s. In later years, Leonard Bernstein, Fausto Cleva, Zubin Mehta, Eugene Ormandy, Fritz Reiner, George Szell, Karl Bohm, James Levine. **STARS:** Virtually all the celebrated voices of opera, from Gladys Swarthout, Helen Jepson, Bidu Sayao, Helen Traubel, Lily Pons, John Charles Thomas, Lauritz Melchior, Kirsten Flagstad, Jussi Bjoerling, Lawrence Tibbett, Elisabeth Rethberg, and Ezio Pinza in the 1930s and 1940s, to such later stars as Renata Tebaldi, Giuseppe di Stefano, Eleanor Steber, Richard Tucker, Leonard Warren, Birgit Nilsson, Joan Sutherland, Leontyne Price, Maria Callas, Victoria de los Angeles, Robert Merrill, Luciano Pavarotti, and Placido Domingo (who sometimes conducts). **OPERAS:** Characterized by director Rudolf Bing as a museum for masterpieces, with a strong resistance to the modern.

All major Verdi and Puccini operas; the principal works of Wagner, etc.; most of the great classics (*Pagliacci; Cavalleria Rusticana; The Barber of Seville; Manon*, etc.). **PRODUCER:** Herbert Liversidge. **DIRECTORS:** Giulio Gatti-Casazza until 1935; Edward Johnson until 1950; Rudolf Bing until 1972; James Levine.

The Metropolitan Opera has been along—though at times reluctantly—for almost every stage of radio broadcasting from the dimmest prenetwork days to the present. On Dec. 13, 1910, the first experimental broadcast of opera was conducted by Lee De Forest from the Metropolitan stage. Riccardo Martin, Enrico Caruso, and Emmy Destinn were aired in *Cavalleria Rusticana* and *Pagliacci*, a pioneering effort heard by almost no one and performed against the better judgment of Met general manager Giulio Gatti-Casazza. Having granted permission for this single broadcast, Gatti then erected a stone wall against further attempts and withstood every effort to change his mind for the next 21 years.

The Met was conspicuous by its absence during the time now considered radio's "first decade," but it was still a force in the 1920s. It was a constant point of speculation and controversy. There was anger, there were even threats at Gatti's "highbrow" attitude that opera and radio did not mix. Management believed that opera was not only a glorious musical experience but a visual spectacle as well, and that radio would undercut and cheapen it. There was also a fear that broadcasting would diminish the gate, perhaps disastrously. The official denial was based on two factors: that mechanical difficulties had already proved too great, and that contracts between the Met and its stars specifically prohibited broadcasting. But the press found this ludicrous.

Radio Digest, leading the crusade, mounted an unrelenting campaign in 1922 to persuade, coax, or bully the Met off its pedestal. Gatti's arguments were dismissed as trivial: the main problem, the newspaper said, was "simply getting through to management." Editorials, articles, and even petition coupons filled each issue. Readers were urged to write the Met and to complain in newspapers around the country. There was a pointed threat: *Digest* warned that "other means may be attempted" if Gatti continued to "be unreasonable," and that these proposals, if implemented, might harm the Met's gate far more than any phantom problems that management could concoct. An "opera of the air" was suggested, along with the possibility of constructing a "relay system" to transmit programs to stations in the East from Chicago, where opera was alive and well on the radio.

So the trailblazing voice of opera broadcasting in America was KYW, the Westinghouse station in Chicago. The station had begun airing productions of the Chicago Grand Opera Company (soon to be renamed the Chicago Civic Opera) in 1921. *Radio Digest* (which, perhaps not incidentally, was based in Chicago) jumped on the KYW bandwagon enthusiastically. Back-page photo layouts showed the stars at work: Edith Mason, "golden-throated songstress"; Rosa Raisa, Mary Garden, and others. Plans were announced for the airing of *Carmen, La Bohème*, and *Parsifal*. Louise Homer starred in *Il Trovatore*; Lodovico Oliviero in *Falstaff*. The headlines were uniformly positive, creating a clear contrast of wonderful cooperation in the Midwest against the hardheaded, unbending position of the Met. WOR, it was announced, would soon air two operas by the Puccini Grand Opera Company. A fan in New York had received *Carmen* "loud and clear" from Chicago. And plans were continuing for an opera network. Though the relay technology was not yet successful, *Digest* again warned that "the Met may soon have Chicago opera as its competition."

The Met was unmoved. On Nov. 11, 1922, WEAF broadcast *Aida* from Kingsbridge Armory, with a contingent of Metropolitan Opera stars including Leon Rothier and Rosa Ponselle. By 1923, WJZ was airing frequent operatic programs. But even with the formation of NBC in 1926, and the inclusion of the *Chicago Civic Opera* in its first-year schedule, the Met remained silent. It took a stock market crash and a depression to bring about what nagging and threats had not. Faced with a diminishing gate, the Met at last succumbed to the lure of network money.

A spirited competition arose between the networks. At CBS, it was pursued by William S. Paley himself, who scheduled a demonstration of sound quality for Met chairman Otto Kahn. Paley recalled (in his memoir) that Kahn was inspired as he listened. "Just imagine," he cried, "hearing that wonderful music and we don't have to look at those ugly faces!'' Paley considered the deal closed, but at the last minute NBC won the day with a slightly higher bid— $122,000 for the first season.

The premiere was Christmas Day 1931: the production was *Hansel and Gretel*; the stars Queena Mario, Dorothee Manski, Henrietta Wakefield, and Editha Fleischer. The regular Saturday schedule commenced the following day, with Rosa Ponselle in *Norma*. The press declared it well worth the wait. Critics were lavish in their praise, the only real bone of contention the Deems Taylor commentary, which was given over the music and drew criticisms ranging from ''idiotic'' to ''unnecessary.''

Milton Cross was the announcer on the first broadcast, a job he turned into a career spanning four decades. Cross came to his work well prepared. Born April 16, 1897, he was enchanted by opera as a boy. He fought for the privilege of delivering butter to Louise Homer, and he grew into what *Time* described as a ''huge, humble, bespectacled music-charmed announcer, whose cultured genuflecting voice seems to come straight from NBC's artistic soul.'' Cross was also charmed by radio, joining WJZ in 1921 as an announcer. He dreamed of a career in music, broadcasting in a tiny booth off the women's room. Soon, at $40 a week, he worked through his trial by fire. He sang and played, pumped tunes out of the station's Ampico player piano, read the funnies to children, and, of course, announced. His diction was near-flawless: his pronunciation of difficult names was accurate and sure. He had been the announcer on the NBC broadcasts of the *Chicago Civic Opera*: this was the training he brought to his coverage of the Met. He became skilled with plot summaries and descriptions of sets and cast backgrounds. He filled in the color around the music, after Taylor's commentaries were dropped in a storm of protest. For this he was paid an average of $80 a week (this was supplemented by work on such commercial ventures as *Information, Please*, where he earned another $100). He broadcast for many years from Box 44 in the Grand Tier, accompanied by engineer Charles C. Grey and producer Herbert Liversidge. His standard opening line was a simple ''Texaco presents *The Metropolitan Opera*.'' His segue from color to performance was usually ''The house lights are being dimmed . . . in a moment, the great gold curtain

will go up.'' In 43 years, Cross missed only two performances, when his wife died. He was still doing the broadcasts at the time of his own death, Jan. 3, 1975.

The opera has been on the air continuously since its premiere. The standard broadcast season is about five months, from November to April. There were a few brief sponsors, then several ''dry'' years in the 1930s, when no sponsor could be found and the series faced extinction. Then, in 1940, Texaco began one of the longest commercial associations in broadcast history, running more than 50 years. The broadcasts have reached millions of listeners who might never otherwise have experienced opera in any form. The greats of the field have performed on the air, and the recap of stars and performances at the top of this article can do little but suggest what was offered.

METROPOLITAN OPERA AUDITIONS, talent show.

BROADCAST HISTORY: Dec. 22, 1935–April 1, 1945, NBC; Red Network, 1935–37, 1940–42; Blue Network, 1937–40, 1942–45. 30m, Sunday afternoons, timeslot varying between 3 and 6:30. Sherwin Williams Paints, 1936–45.

Jan. 4, 1948–ca. 1958, ABC. 30m, Sundays at 4:30, 1947–49; Tuesdays at 10, 1950–51; at 8:30, 1951–52; Mondays at 9, 1952–55; at 8, 1955–56; then Sundays.

HOST: Edward Johnson, managing director of the Metropolitan Opera. COMMENTATOR: Milton Cross. ANNOUNCER: Howard Claney. CONDUCTOR: Wilfred Pelletier (1930s, 1940s).

Metropolitan Opera Auditions was a high-class talent series with two major benefits for its listeners. First came the excitement of hearing brilliant new performers at the dawn of genuinely promising careers: then there was an opportunity to learn about opera in an easier way than by tuning into a *Metropolitan Opera* broadcast and hoping to pick up some finer points.

Auditions was like no other talent show on the air. This was no rich man's Major Bowes, pushing the shaggy dogs of the highbrow set. ''It is a serious attempt,'' defined *Radio Guide*, ''to find the most promising singers the country has produced and to make the most of their talents.'' Some of the competitors had sung professionally, though all were unknown to the masses.

Now they were given a chance to "come within voice-range of the Met," with the opera company committing itself to contracts for the winners.

The singers came from all walks of life. But there the similarity with *Major Bowes' Original Amateur Hour* ended. The 800 applicants who applied each year were auditioned by longtime Met maestro Wilfred Pelletier, who coached them and gradually winnowed their ranks to 63. These were the competitors who would sing on the air. The performers chose their own music, selecting the pieces that best showcased their talents. Over the weeks their ranks were thinned to fourteen semi-finalists. These were cut to six, and on the final night two winners were selected for $1,000 cash awards and Metropolitan contracts.

The judges came from the ranks of the Met. The talent level was always quite high: contracts were often extended to semi-finalists as well as the winners. Eleanor Steber, Robert Merrill, Leonard Warren, and Patrice Munsel went on to operatic careers after winning *Auditions* trials. Losers and winners both found permanent and rewarding work in radio. Many of the Frank and Anne Hummert musical shows (*Waltz Time*, *American Album of Familiar Music*, and *Manhattan Merry-Go-Round*) were staffed by *Auditions* graduates (Evelyn MacGregor, Marian McManus, Thomas L. Thomas, Jean Dickenson, Felix Knight).

THE MGM THEATER OF THE AIR, dramatic anthology; film adaptations.

BROADCAST HISTORY: 60m transcribed syndication, originally heard on WMGM, New York, Oct. 14, 1949–Dec. 7, 1951.

Jan. 5–Dec. 27, 1952, Mutual. 60m, Saturdays at 8:30.

HOST: Howard Dietz, vice president of Metro Goldwyn Mayer. **CAST:** Major Hollywood film stars in leads: Ronald Reagan, Joan Bennett, Marlene Dietrich, etc. Supporting players from radio: Les Tremayne, John Gibson, Gertrude Warner, Sarah Fussell, Frank Behrens, Chuck Webster, Kermit Murdock, Carl Eastman, etc. **ANNOUNCER:** Ed Stokes. **DIRECTOR:** Marx B. Loeb.

MICHAEL AND KITTY, husband-wife mystery series.

BROADCAST HISTORY: Oct. 10, 1941–Feb. 6, 1942, Blue Network. 30m, Fridays at 9:30, for Canada Dry. Became *Michael Piper, Private Detective*, ca. Jan. 1942. **CAST:** Elizabeth Reller as Kitty. John Gibson as Doc the cabbie. Unknown actor as Michael. **MUSIC:** Lyn Murray.

MICHAEL SHAYNE, detective melodrama, based on the books by Brett Halliday.

BROADCAST HISTORY: Oct. 16, 1944–Nov. 14, 1947, Mutual–Don Lee. 30m, Mondays at 8:30 Pacific time; later Wednesdays at 7; West Coast network for two seasons, then coast-to-coast beginning Oct. 15, 1946, Tuesdays at 8. **CAST:** Wally Maher as Michael Shayne, archtypical radio private eye. Louise Arthur as his assistant, the blonde and gorgeous Phyllis (Phyl) Knight. Cathy Lewis as Phyllis by ca. spring 1945. Joe Forte as the Inspector. Also: Charlie Lung, Anne Stone, Harry Lang, GeGe Pearson, Bob Bruce, Virginia Keith, Sharon Douglas, Hal Gerard, Jack Edwards, Earle Ross, and Virginia Gregg. **PRODUCERS:** Bob Nye, Dave Taylor. **WRITERS:** Richard de Graffe, Bob Ryf.

1948–ca. 1950, 30m transcribed syndication. *The New Adventures of Michael Shayne*. **CAST:** Jeff Chandler as Shayne, "reckless red-headed Irishman." **PRODUCER:** Don W. Sharpe.

Oct. 14, 1952–July 10, 1953, ABC. 30m, Tuesdays at 8 until Nov.; Thursdays at 9:30, Nov.-Feb.; then Fridays at 8. **CAST:** Donald Curtis as Shayne until Nov.; Robert Sterling and Vinton Hayworth subsequently as Shayne.

THE MICKEY MOUSE THEATER OF THE AIR, music and talk for children.

BROADCAST HISTORY: Jan. 2–May 21, 1938, NBC. 30m, Sundays at 5:30 for Pepsodent. **CAST:** Walt Disney, host, and as the voice of Mickey Mouse. Clarence Nash as Donald Duck. Thelma Boardman as Minnie Mouse. Stuart Buchanan as Goofy. **ANNOUNCER:** John Hiestand. **MUSIC:** Felix Mills. **SOUND EFFECTS:** Hal Reese. **THEME:** *Who's Afraid of the Big Bad Wolf?*

The Mickey Mouse Theater arrived just in time to publicize the first Disney feature-length animation, *Snow White and the Seven Dwarfs*. It was broadcast from the Disney Little Theater on the RKO lot, with most of the characters from

Disney cartoons appearing at some point. The Seven Dwarfs, singly or together, were regulars. The Felix Mills music had a proper cartoon sound to it, with "Donald Duck and his Webfoot Sextet" a feature of sorts. Donald's "gadget band" consisted of such instruments as meat grinder, auto horn, a Bob Burns–style bazooka, and a "syrup-cruet hurdy gurdy." The latter was operated by maestro Mills and soundman Reese, who really could coax music out of it.

MIDSTREAM, soap opera.

BROADCAST HISTORY: 1938, WLW, Cincinnati. May 1, 1939–Sept. 27, 1940, NBC; both networks until March 1940, then Red Network. 15m, weekdays at 5, later at 5:15, Red Network; weekdays at 10:45 A.M., Blue Network. Procter & Gamble sponsor for Teel Toothpaste, both shows.
March 4–Nov. 13, 1941, Blue Network. 15m, weekdays at 2:45.

CAST: Hugh Studebaker and Betty Lou Gerson as Charles and Julia Meredith, "who have reached the halfway mark between the distant shores of birth and death." Mercedes McCambridge as their restlessly married daughter, Midge. Willard Farnum as their son, David. Lenore Kingston as David's girlfriend, Jinny. Bill Bouchey as Stanley Bartlett, a not-so-silent admirer of Julia. Connie Osgood as Ruth, Charles's faithful secretary. *1941*: Sidney Ellstrom, Fern Persons, Laurette Fillbrandt. **DIRECTOR:** Gordon Hughes. **WRITER:** Pauline Hopkins.

Midstream was the age "where the currents of life are swiftest, the problems of life are greatest, the temptations of life are strongest." The conflict was between a husband contented with the bathrobe and slippers and a wife still passionate, hungering for gaiety and glamor.

THE MIGHTY CASEY, situation comedy.

BROADCAST HISTORY: March 1–July 26, 1947, Mutual. 30m, Saturdays at 9. **CAST:** Millard Mitchell as Casey, an over-the-hill ballplayer reduced to popping out for the local team: "the private life of Mudville's most famous left-fielder." Nancy Sheridan as the Widow Gladys Breen, whose courtship by Casey included a blooming friendship between her suitor and her son, Artie. Walter Kinsella as Casey's pal Ambrose Cooney.

ANNOUNCER: Ralph Paul. **ORCHESTRA:** Emerson Buckley. **DIRECTOR:** Chick Vincent.

THE MIGHTY SHOW, serial drama with a circus backdrop.

BROADCAST HISTORY: Sept. 12, 1938–April 28, 1939, CBS. 15m, weekdays at 5:45. My-T-Fine. **CAST:** Agnes Moorehead as Ma Hutchinson. Artells Dickson as Tex. Helen Lewis as Sally of the high wire. Jay Meredith as Jean. Anne Boley as Ruth, the knife-thrower. Brad Barker, animal imitator.

MIKE MALLOY, detective drama.

BROADCAST HISTORY: July 16, 1953–April 23, 1954, ABC. 30m, Thursdays at 9 through Sept.; serialized beginning Oct. 12, 15m, weeknights at 8:45.
April 30, 1956–March 18, 1957, CBS. 30m, Mondays at 7:30.

CAST: Steve Brodie as Mike Malloy.

MILDRED BAILEY, jazz singer.

BROADCAST HISTORY: Dec. 16, 1933–Feb. 3, 1934, CBS. 15m, Saturdays at 6:15.
Oct. 1, 1934–April 19, 1935, Blue Network. 15m, three a week at 7:15. *Plantation Echoes*, with Willard Robison and his "deep-river rhythms." Vicks.
June 21–Aug. 9, 1944, CBS. 30m, Wednesdays at 9:30. Substitute for Jack Carson. Campbell Soups.
Sept. 1, 1944–Feb. 9, 1945, CBS. 30m, Fridays at 11:30. *Music till Midnight*.

THE MILLION-DOLLAR BAND, musical variety.

BROADCAST HISTORY: May 29, 1943–March 25, 1944, NBC. 30m, Saturdays at 10. Palmolive Soap. **SINGING HOST:** Barry Wood.
April 1, 1944–Jan. 6, 1945, NBC. 30m, Saturdays at 10. Series continued as *Palmolive Party*. **CAST:** Barry Wood joined by comedienne Patsy Kelly.

The Million-Dollar Band featured the nation's top musicians—a large, shifting, makeshift aggregation (34 pieces) taken from the worlds of symphony and swing. Many were sidemen who had played for Benny Goodman, Glenn Miller, or other noted leaders. Many were soloists. A guest maestro was invited to lead each week's group: Charlie Spivak was the first guest. Listeners were solicited for their musical memories, asked to tell why certain songs moved them in sentimental ways: five diamond rings from Tiffany's were awarded weekly to the writers of the most interesting letters. The format change to *Palmolive Party* in 1944 was simply an addition of Patsy Kelly, "wisecracking screen star"; Barry Wood continued as singing emcee, and the "million-dollar band" still provided the music.

MILLIONS FOR DEFENSE, War Bond variety hour, also known as *The Treasury Hour*.

BROADCAST HISTORY: July 2–Sept. 24, 1941, CBS. 60m, Wednesdays at 9. Summer replacement for Fred Allen's *Texaco Star Theater*. Texaco. **PRODUCER:** Charles Vanda.

Sept. 30–Dec. 23, 1941, Blue Network. 60m, Tuesdays at 8. *The Treasury Hour*. Bendix Aviation. **ANNOUNCER:** Graham McNamee. **MUSIC:** Tom Jones, orchestra; Ray Bloch choir.

Millions for Defense was one of the first big Treasury Department shows of the war. It predated Pearl Harbor by six months and sounded a warning call for hard times ahead. Fred Allen was opening-night master of ceremonies. Typical of these war shows, it had all of Hollywood and New York at its beck and call, all free talent. Bob Hope, Bing Crosby, and Dorothy Lamour headlined the July 9 show. Bette Davis, Lily Pons, Abbott and Costello, Tyrone Power, and Claudette Colbert were on subsequent broadcasts. The show was quite popular in the waning months of summer, and when Fred Allen reclaimed his slot in the fall, *Millions* simply shifted networks and became *The Treasury Hour*.

THE MILLS BROTHERS, vocal harmony.

BROADCAST HISTORY: Dec. 7, 1931–April 10, 1933, CBS. 15m, mostly Mondays and Thursdays, at 9 or 9:15. Procter & Gamble.

The Mills Brothers (Herbert, Harry, Donald, and John) were celebrated in the early '30s, both for their harmony and their ability to vocally imitate musical instruments. They were costars with Bing Crosby on the Woodbury broadcasts in 1933–34, had a transcribed series for Dodge in

1936, and were heard on the Blue Network (June 28–July 19) in a 1942 run of quarter-hours, Sundays at 6:45. In 1935, John died and their father, John Sr., joined the group as bass.

THE MILTON BERLE SHOW, comedy.

BROADCAST HISTORY: 1936–42: see COMMUNITY SING; STOP ME IF YOU'VE HEARD THIS ONE; and THREE-RING TIME.

March 3–May 26, 1943, CBS. 30m, Wednesdays at 9:30. Campbell Soups.

March 21, 1944–June 27, 1945. 30m, Blue Network, Tuesdays at 7 until July; at 10:30 until mid-Dec.; then CBS, Wednesdays at 10:30 as of Jan. 3, 1945. *Let Yourself Go*. Eversharp.

July 1–Aug. 19, 1946, CBS. 30m, Mondays at 9. *Kiss and Make Up*.**CREATOR-PRODUCER-WRITER:** Cy Howard.

March 11, 1947–April 13, 1948, NBC. 30m, Tuesdays at 8. Philip Morris. **CAST:** Berle, Arnold Stang, Pert Kelton, Mary Shipp, Jack Albertson, Arthur Q. Bryan, and Ed Begley. **ANNOUNCER:** Frank Gallop. **VOCALIST:** Dick Forney. **ORCHESTRA:** Ray Bloch. **WRITERS:** Hal Block, Martin Ragaway.

Sept. 22, 1948–June 15, 1949, ABC. 30m, Wednesdays at 9. *The Texaco Star Theater*. **CAST:** Berle, Stang, Kelton, Gallop, with Charles Irving, Kay Armen, and double-talk specialist Al Kelly. **WRITERS:** Nat Hiken, Aaron Ruben, brothers Danny and Neil Simon, etc.

The Milton Berle Show was one of half a dozen titles showcasing Berle in his star-crossed radio career. He was radio's best-known failure: never able to mount a decent rating despite numerous attempts in many formats over a 13-year span, Berle finally gave up the blind medium and went exclusively to TV in 1949. There, Berle could make full use of his goofy teeth and elaborate mugging in ridiculous costumes. He was the biggest success of early television.

He was born Milton Berlinger, July 12, 1908. His mother began pushing his talents when he was still a toddler: she would remain his most enthusiastic advocate throughout his career. He entertained in the streets as a boy, worked his way through the vaudeville ranks, and gravitated naturally into radio. But his act was slapstick, and few comics have ever found a way to make that work on radio. His style was not unlike Bob Hope's: he would fire off gags like a verbal machine gun, hitting targets in every direction but missing a lot as well. He would swap insults with announcers, mug for the studio audience, and use any joke (no matter how old) that had a potential for a laugh. At some point, said his entry in *Current Biography*, he came to the conclusion that jokes were public property, and over the years he collected at least 50,000 of them, committing most to memory. That many of these had been created by other comics seemed to worry him little. Walter Winchell dubbed him the "Thief of Badgags." Hope told a *Time* reporter that "when you see Berle, you're seeing the best of anybody who has ever been on Broadway. I want to get into television before he uses up all my material."

Perhaps the best example of what was wrong with Berle on radio is found in the 1944–45 series, *Let Yourself Go*. This was a half-hour of slapstick. Contestants were selected from show business and from the studio audience, invited onstage to tell Berle and announcer Ken Roberts all about their most urgent (but until now suppressed) urges and yens. Then they pushed aside all dignity and let themselves go. Some wanted to break eggs in Berle's face, or be firemen, or throw snowballs. Berle did his best to accommodate them, playing the stooge to the hysterics of the studio audience and the stony silence of people gathered around radio sets at home.

Kiss and Make Up, his 1946 show, fared no better. It was a gimmick show built around petty gripes and a mock court. Berle was the "judge"; contestants brought their "cases" before the microphones and were awarded up to $120 if they could wring favorable "verdicts" out of a "jury" drawn from the studio audience. The "stenographers" were the Murphy Sisters, a vocal trio. After much mugging, the "litigants" were required to "kiss and make up."

Then came 1947, and *The Milton Berle Show* for Philip Morris. Berle's lack of success in radio had been cited by his critics as evidence that he lacked broad popular appeal. He was so determined to break the radio jinx that he canceled lucrative nightclub appearances (a date at the Roxy alone, he said, would have paid him $25,000 a week, almost ten times what he was getting on the air) to focus his whole energy on radio. But the result was the same: a wimpy 11 points on his opening show and no appreciable ratings progress as time went on. Most important

here was the addition of Arnold Stang, who went on to work with Berle on early TV.

There was one other attempt: *The Texaco Star Theater*, a veritable copy of his Philip Morris series. Berle would remember this years later as "the best radio show I ever did . . . a hell of a funny variety show." He considered this a hedge against his possible failure on television, which Texaco had also opted to sponsor. Berle and Texaco shared an unease about the new medium: no one was sure, in the summer of 1948, if television was here to stay. Texaco had scheduled its *Star Theater* on NBC-TV beginning in June 1948, with the star's role to rotate among Henny Youngman, Peter Donald, Morey Amsterdam, and Berle.

The rest is history. Berle won the TV job on a permanent basis. His radio show bombed, and by early 1949, *Time* was reporting that the Berle TV Texaco series had reached an 80-point Hooper, highest ever in either medium.

MISCHA, THE MAGNIFICENT, comedy.

BROADCAST HISTORY: First heard as a test broadcast on the CBS audition series, *Forecast*, 1941. Then July 5–Sept. 6, 1942, CBS. 30m, Sundays at 9. **STAR:** Mischa Auer, the "sad, screwy Russian" of film fame. **PRODUCER:** Paul Pierce. **WRITERS:** Carl Hertzinger and Paul West.

The comedy framework for *Mischa, the Magnificent* was the continuing memoir of his youth. Each episode explored some new aspect of his alleged past (Mischa the lover; Mischa the opera singer; etc.): he claimed to be born under "the sign of the poet—a Burma Shave sign, and I was just a little shaver."

MISS HATTIE, serial drama.

BROADCAST HISTORY: Sept. 17, 1944–June 17, 1945, Blue Network. 30m, Sundays at 3:30. Alcoa. **CAST:** Ethel Barrymore as Miss Hattie Thompson. Eric Dressler as Mr. Thompson. Dick Van Patten and Lois Wilson as their children.

MRS. MINIVER, serial drama, based on the novel by Jan Struther.

BROADCAST HISTORY: Jan. 7–Oct. 7, 1944, CBS. 30m, Fridays at 11:30 until mid-June, then Saturdays at 7:30. **CAST:** Judith Evelyn and Karl Swenson as the Minivers, heroic family of wartime

London. Gertrude Warner and John Moore as the Minivers later in the run.

MRS. WIGGS OF THE CABBAGE PATCH,

soap opera, based on the novel by Alice Hegan Rice.

BROADCAST HISTORY: Feb. 4, 1935–Sept. 11, 1936, CBS. 15m, weekdays at 11:30 A.M. Jad Salts.

Sept. 14, 1936–Dec. 30, 1938, NBC. 15m, weekdays at 10 A.M. Hill Cough Drops, 1936–37; Old English Wax, 1937–38.

CAST: Betty Garde as Mrs. Wiggs, a dweller of the shantytown known as Cabbage Patch. Eva Condon also as Mrs. Wiggs. Robert Strauss as Pa Wiggs, her shiftless husband. Andy Donnelly as Billy Wiggs, their son. Joe Latham as Stubbins. Agnes Young as Miss Hazy, a "dithery spinster" who was Mrs. Wiggs's close friend and partner in a bakeshop. Alice Frost also as Miss Hazy. Frank Provo and Bill Johnstone as Mr. Bob, a young newspaperman who was also a friend of the heroine. PRODUCERS: Frank and Anne Hummert.

The Cabbage Patch of the Alice Hegan Rice novel was taken from a real slum in Louisville, Ky. Mrs. Wiggs was described as "a friend of every neighbor; always first to forget herself and lend a helping hand."

MR. ADAM AND MRS. EVE, male-female quiz competition.

BROADCASTING HISTORY: Oct. 3, 1942–Sept. 4, 1943, CBS. 30m, Saturdays at 8. Tums. Title change to *The Crumit and Sanderson Quiz*. STARS: Frank Crumit and Julia Sanderson.

Teams of four from each sex competed, presided over by Crumit and Sanderson, with great partisanship. The show ended suddenly after Crumit's death, Sept. 7, 1943.

MR. ALADDIN, detective melodrama.

BROADCAST HISTORY: July 7–Sept. 8, 1951, CBS. 30m, Saturdays at 9:30. CAST: Paul Frees as Robert Aladdin, a sleuth who could perform miracles as he solved crimes. ANNOUNCER: Bill Anders. MUSIC: Marlin Skiles. DIRECTOR: Elliott Lewis. WRITER: Dick Powell.

MR. AND MRS. BLANDINGS, situation comedy.

BROADCASTING HISTORY: Jan. 21–June 17, 1951, NBC. 30m, Sundays at 5:30. Trans World Airlines. CAST: Cary Grant and Betsy Drake, real-life husband and wife, as Jim and Muriel Blandings, a young city couple who took up residence in the country. Also: Gale Gordon, Sheldon Leonard, etc. PRODUCER-WRITER: Nat Wolff. DIRECTOR: Warren Lewis.

This series was based on the Eric Hodgins novel *Mr. Blandings Builds His Dream House*. But the show was troubled from the beginning, its scripts turning on misunderstandings so farfetched that critical condemnation was constant and loud. The result was backstage chaos. The Grants blamed their material, bouncing five scripts back to writer Nat Wolff. Drake herself undertook some writing, turning out two episodes under the nom de plume Matilda Winkle. This kind of bickering seldom improves morale, and the show died quickly.

MR. AND MRS. NORTH, mystery melodrama, based on the novels by Frances and Richard Lockridge.

BROADCAST HISTORY: Dec. 30, 1942–Dec. 18, 1946, NBC. 30m, Wednesdays at 8. Jergens Lotion and Woodbury Cold Cream.

July 1, 1947–April 18, 1955, CBS. 30m, Tuesdays at 8:30, 1947–54; heard in serial form, 15m, weekdays, Oct. 4–Nov. 19, 1954; then, again, 30m, Mondays at 8, beginning Nov. 29, 1954. Colgate-Palmolive for various products, including Halo Shampoo, 1947–54.

CAST: Joseph Curtin and Alice Frost as Mr. and Mrs. North (Jerry and Pam), a book publisher and his irrepressible wife. Richard Denning and Barbara Britton as Jerry and Pam later in the run. Frank Lovejoy initially as their friend, Lt. Bill Weigand of homicide. Staats Cotsworth and Francis DeSales also as Bill Weigand. Walter Kinsella as the ever-exasperated Sgt. Mullins. Betty Jane Tyler as Susan, the Norths' 14-year-old niece. Mandel Kramer as Mahatma McGloin, a talkative cab driver. ORCHESTRA: Charles Paul. PRODUCERS: S. James Andrews, John W. Loveton. SOUND EFFECTS: Al Binnie, Al Hogan (CBS); Sam Monroe (NBC). THEME: *The Way You Look Tonight*.

Mr. and Mrs. North was conceived for radio as it had begun in literature: as a light comedy. When he wrote the original stories for the *New Yorker* in the 1930s, Richard Lockridge made them light domestic misadventures. It wasn't until 1940, when Lockridge teamed with his wife, Frances, that the Norths met murder and steamrolled their way into the most successful husband-and-wife crimefighting series of the day.

An audition was transcribed in 1941, with Peggy Conklin and Carl Eastman as Pam and Jerry North. It was a humorous light romance, written by Howard Harris and Martin Gosch, with Don Voorhees on music. But nothing came of it.

The mystery version, opening a year later, was another story. *Mr. and Mrs. North* immediately moved up to challenge the mystery frontrunner, *Mr. District Attorney*, in the ratings polls. It grew steadily in popularity until, in its second year, it held an audience of 20 million a week.

Average was its byword. Mr. and Mrs. North were not detectives, but average people who might be living next door or in the apartment upstairs. They solved only average murders—the stabbings and shootings, the crimes of passion—leaving the more exotic cases to gumshoes and gangbusters on other programs. Producer S. James Andrews once turned down a script simply because it was set in a medieval museum and involved ancient devices of torture unfamiliar to the common man. Neither Pam nor Jerry was trained in the science of deduction. Jerry was an average publisher of books who just happened, each week, to stumble over a corpse. Pam was an everyday housewife who loved cats, liked to play cupid for her single friends, and talked in riddles. Somehow she usually managed to ponder her way to the killer's identity. Jerry tried to explain how she did it for *Radio Mirror* in 1943. Men think logically, from cause to effect, went the explanation. Women (and Pam North in particular) reach a conclusion first and then gather up the facts that support it. Pam had a quick wit, a sharp tongue, and lots of female intuition.

Their best friend was Lt. Bill Weigand of homicide. Weigand eventually got used to the idea that, wherever the Norths would go, murder inevitably followed. If they went on a train trip, a corpse would be stashed in the upper berth. Look in the bathroom—body in the bathtub. The Norths lived at 24 St. Anne's Flat in Greenwich Village. Their acquaintances were slightly bizarre: floaters through the underworld, neighborhood sellers of tips, and a talkative cabbie named Mahatma McGloin. There was also a teenage niece, a problem child named Susan, who stumbled over a few unsolicited bodies.

The series was heavy with extraneous interplay, helping the characters come alive for listeners. Bill Weigand was a fearless cop, but bashful with the opposite sex. Pam schemed and plotted in a constant though futile effort to get him married. Weigand appreciated women but never understood them. Nor did he understand how his bumbling right-hand man, Sergeant Aloysius Mullins, could have such a solid family life and be the father of eight children.

MR. CHAMELEON, detective melodrama.

BROADCAST HISTORY: July 14, 1948–Aug. 7, 1953, CBS. 30m, Wednesdays at 8, 1948–51; Sundays at 5:30, 1951–52; Thursdays at 9, most of 1952; Fridays at 9, 1952–53. Off the air mid-Jan. to mid-March, 1953. Returned Fridays at 8:30. Bayer Aspirin, 1948–51; General Foods and Wrigley's Gum, 1952.

CAST: Karl Swenson as Mr. Chameleon, "the man of many faces," the "famous and dreaded detective" who often used a disguise to track down a killer. Frank Butler as his sidekick, Detective Dave Arnold. New York actors in support. **ANNOUNCERS:** Roger Krupp, Howard Claney. **ORCHESTRA:** Victor Arden. **PRODUCERS:** Frank and Anne Hummert. **DIRECTOR:** Richard Leonard. **WRITER:** Marie Baumer. **THEME:** *Masquerade.*

Mr. Chameleon was painfully contrived, employing dramatic clichés seldom heard after sundown. But its creator, Frank Hummert, was a master of soap opera, utilizing in his dramatic shows the obvious devices of simplistic dialogue, heavy exposition, and constant repetition of names, so that there was never a doubt as to the speaker's identity.

Chameleon operated out of "Central Police Headquarters." A case was sometimes said to be "famous" the moment Chameleon was assigned to it. Following the pattern set by that other prime-time Hummert stalwart, *Mr. Keen*, Chameleon had a big, dumb sidekick, Dave Arnold, whose function was to ask obvious questions and be suitably perplexed until the boss revealed an outcome already deduced by much of the listening audience. About halfway through the play, Chameleon would disappear, returning in disguise. The disguises were at all times recognized by the listener, and probably would have been even had Hummert not intended it thus. In *The Perfect Maid Murder Case*, one of only two shows available on tape, even the killer saw through the disguise at once. The show had a Hummert sound, from the music to the sponsor (Bayer Aspirin, one of Hummert's best clients).

MR. DISTRICT ATTORNEY, crime drama.

BROADCAST HISTORY: April 3–June 16, 1939, NBC. 15m, weekdays at 7.

June 27–Sept. 19, 1939, NBC. 30m, Tuesdays at 10. Summer replacement for Bob Hope. Pepsodent.

Oct. 1, 1939–April 7, 1940, Blue Network. 30m, Sundays at 7:30. Pepsodent.

April 11, 1940–Sept. 19, 1951, NBC. 30m, Thursdays at 8 through June 1940, then Wednesdays at 9:30. Bristol Myers (Vitalis).

Sept. 28, 1951–June 13, 1952, ABC. 30m, Fridays at 9:30. Vitalis.

1952–53, 30m transcribed syndication, Frederick Ziv.

CAST: Dwight Weist as Mr. District Attorney (serial version, 1939), a fearless crusader for justice and truth. Raymond Edward Johnson as Mr. District Attorney, ca. 30m shows, 1939. Jay Jostyn as Mr. District Attorney ca. 1940–52. David Brian as Mr. District Attorney, 1952 Ziv syndication. Vicki Vola as the DA's secretary, Miss (Edith) Miller, 1939–52. Walter Kinsella in various police roles in the early run, then as Len Harrington, the ex-cop turned DA's investigator. Len Doyle as Harrington from ca. 1940. Eleanor Silver and Arlene Francis as Miss Rand. Maurice Franklin as the "Voice of the Law" that opened the show. Jay Jostyn also as the "Voice." Supporting players from New York radio: Frank Lovejoy, Joan Banks, Paul Stewart, etc. ORCHESTRA: Peter Van Steeden (who composed the stirring theme); also: Harry Salter. CREATOR-WRITER-DIRECTOR: Ed Byron. COCREATOR-WRITER: Phillips H. Lord. WRITERS: Jerry Devine, Finis Farr, Harry Herman, Robert J. Shaw, etc.

Mr. District Attorney was for many years the nation's best-liked crime show. It was inspired by the exploits of Thomas E. Dewey, New York's racket-busting DA of the late '30s, whose front-page war against racketeers and corruption swept him into the governor's office and culminated in two serious runs for the presidency.

The radio character was created by Ed Byron, one-time staffer at WLW, Cincinnati, who had given up law studies for a career on the air. Phillips H. Lord, venerable radio man and producer of *Gang Busters*, had coined the *Mr. District Attorney* title and had worked with Byron on a serial based on Dewey's colorful career. Byron then bought the title, agreeing to credit Lord and pay him royalties on the subsequent series. Throughout the long run, the DA remained unnamed: he answered to the title "Mister District Attorney" or, in conversation with his sidekick Harrington and his secretary Miss Miller, to "Chief" or "Boss." The show was a dynamic departure, propelled by Byron's almost uncanny instinct for scooping the news.

Some of this, he explained, was just coincidence. But Byron was a student of crime, with a library of 5,000 books on the subject, and played crime trends with a sure hand. Con games occurred most often in the spring; juvenile delinquency in the summer; husbands and wives killed each other in the fall; burglaries were most common in winter. Byron had statistics to prove this, but he went beyond dry facts. Weekly for more than ten years he donned the clothes of a working man and plunged into some of the roughest bars in town. He rubbed elbows with thieves, lackeys, and off-duty cops in his search for material. At 40, he was an expert on con games. Interviewing him, *Newsweek* found his speech roughedged, "as if he mixes with no one but gangsters." A "Gladys" to Byron was a "nice girl"; a "double-domer" was a criminal well-versed in science; "Warner Brothers" were old-fashioned machine guns, and the "Morris" was the denouement, the necessary evil of telling listeners at the end what the story had all been about.

The result was a show of startling realism for its day. It had the air of a front-page newspaper story. At first NBC was nervous over his predictions of major crime waves; then, when they came to pass, the network took pride in his accuracy. Both the network and the government were uneasy when Byron's DA began foiling Nazis. On the show of June 17, 1942, Byron ran a story about Nazi submarines dropping spies along the Atlantic coast. G-men had arrested real spies that same week and were preparing to break the news themselves. Byron got a "visit" from the FBI after his show.

But his show was continually topical. He wrote of gasoline hijackers and black marketeers. He acknowledged the government's "loose lips sink ships" campaign in *The Case of the Whispered Word*, about a young sailor who died rather than tell the Nazis what they wanted to know. His DA raided a fake sanitarium on the day of a real raid, though his script had been written weeks before. When a berserk war vet walked through the streets of Camden, N.J., shooting people, Byron had a chillingly similar piece ready for the air that night. He supplemented his pub-crawling by reading five newspapers a day.

The show won many awards for excellence, offering plays on racial intolerance and other social ills. By January 1943, *Mr. District Attorney* had built a rating of 28.3, almost unheard-of for a show of its type. It was a year-round operation. In the summers, when such comics as Jack Benny and Bob Hope were on vacation, *Mr. DA* often soared to the top of the ratings; it was seldom out of the top ten, even in midseason. As owner, Byron packaged it and collected $10,000 a week from his longtime sponsor, Bristol Myers. After expenses, he made $50,000 a year.

The opening signature was vivid and long-remembered, with a thrilling theme and a gusty "Voice of the Law" giving the hero's credo:

Mister District Attorney!
Champion of the people!
Defender of truth!
Guardian of our fundamental rights to life, liberty, and the pursuit of happiness!
ORCHESTRA: Theme, up full.
VOICE OF THE LAW (from echo chamber): . . . *and it shall be my duty as district attorney not only to prosecute to the limit of the law all persons accused of crimes perpetrated within this county but to defend with equal vigor the rights and privileges of all its citizens . . .*

MR. FEATHERS, situation comedy.

BROADCAST HISTORY: Nov. 9, 1949–Aug. 31, 1950, Mutual. 30m, Wednesdays at 9 until March 1, 1950; returned June 29, Thursdays at 8:30.
CAST: Parker Fennelly as Mr. Feathers, a homespun philosopher "not quite like any next-door

neighbor you ever had." Supporting cast from New York radio: Eleanor Phelps, Wendell Holmes, Inge Adams, etc. ANNOUNCER: Bob Emerick. MUSIC: Ben Ludlow. PRODUCER: Herbert Rice. DIRECTOR: Rocco Tito.

As Mr. Feathers, Parker Fennelly ran a drugstore in "the untroubled and quite untypical town of Pike City."

MR. KEEN, TRACER OF LOST PERSONS, detective melodrama.

BROADCAST HISTORY: Oct. 12, 1937–Oct. 22, 1942, Blue Network. 15m continuation, three a week at 7:15. Bisodol.
Oct. 28, 1942–Nov. 26, 1943, CBS. 15m continuation, three a week at 7:45. Kolynos.
Dec. 2, 1943–July 12, 1951, CBS. 30m, Thursdays at 7: 30, 1943–47; at 8:30, 1947–51. Kolynos, etc.
July 20, 1951–April 24, 1952, NBC. 30m, Fridays at 9:30 through Aug. 1951, then Thursdays at 8:30. RCA, summer 1951; Chesterfield, 1951–52; Whitehall Pharmacal; American Chicle, 1952.
May 1, 1952–Oct. 1, 1954, CBS. 30m, initially Thursday nights, then Fridays at 8 from Oct. 1952. Procter & Gamble.
May 24, 1954–Jan. 14, 1955, CBS. 15m, weeknights at 10.
Feb. 22–April 19, 1955, CBS. 30m, Tuesdays at 8:30.
CAST: Bennett Kilpack as Mr. Keen, a kind-sounding but much-feared master detective. Phil Clarke as Mr. Keen later in the run. Arthur Hughes also as Mr. Keen. Jim Kelly as Mike Clancy, Mr. Keen's strong-arm assistant. ANNOUNCERS: James Fleming, Larry Elliott, etc. ORCHESTRA: Al Rickey. PRODUCERS: Frank and Anne Hummert. DIRECTOR: Richard Leonard. WRITERS: Dialogue attributed to Frank Hummert; actually turned out under his supervision by Hummert staffers Lawrence Klee, Bob Shaw, Barbara Bates, Stedman Coles, etc. SOUND EFFECTS: Jack Amrhein, CBS. THEME: *Someday I'll Find You.*

Mr. Keen was one of radio's longest-running detective series, a prime-time mystery with serious soap opera trappings. Coming from the radio fiction factory of Frank and Anne Hummert, it employed all the stereotypes, heavy dialogue, and trite plotting of its daytime cousins. Like the later *Mr. Chameleon,* Mr.

Keen solved his murders with a minimum of logic, often through coincidence, twists of fate, slips of the tongue, and guilty knowledge expressed by the culprits.

In the beginning, Mr. Keen lived up to his billing, a sage old tracer of missing persons. But the half-hour series was strictly murder. Mr. Keen's partner, Mike Clancy, was of the dumb-Irish school. "Saints preserve us, Mr. Keen, do you mean . . . ?" Mike would ponder in case after case. And Mr. Keen, kind old investigative genius, would say, "Yes, Mike," and explain some point of business that listeners had already figured out for themselves. Keen and Clancy seemed to have no official position: they were simply called in, whenever people were murdered, to help solve the mystery. "We usually work along with the police, ma'am," Clancy might say, explaining their presence. They seemed to have vast powers of arrest: they barged into homes without search warrants, ignored official procedure, shunned due process, and cared little for the rules of evidence. Keen was charming and persuasive, but his voice took on a mean edge when confronting a killer. And in the style of Hummert soaps, the dialogue was simplistic, identifying each speaker and subject fully in each utterance:

"Before I open this door, Mr. Keen, let me tell you something. No one in this house right now had anything to do with the murder of young Donald Travers, my niece's husband.

"That remains to be proven, Miss Martha."

"My niece Jane Travers should never have sent you here."

"Jane Travers only wanted to help you prove your innocence, Miss Martha."

As such, it appealed to a lowest common denominator, and enjoyed a run of 17 years.

MR. PRESIDENT, historical drama.

BROADCAST HISTORY: June 26, 1947–Sept. 23, 1953, ABC. 30m, Thursdays at 9:30 until Jan. 1948; Sundays at 2:30, 1948–50; Wednesdays at 9:30, 1950–52; at 9, 1952–53. **CAST:** Edward Arnold as the president of the United States, a different president each week. Betty Lou Gerson as Miss Sarah, the president's generic secretary. **CREATOR:** Robert G. Jennings. **PRODUCER-DIRECTOR:** Dick Woollen. **WRITERS:** Jean Holloway, Bernard Dougall, Ira Marion, etc.

This series told stories of "Mr. President at home in the White House—the elected leader of our people, our fellow citizen and neighbor." It specialized in "little-known stories of the men who have lived in the White House—dramatic, exciting events in their lives that you and I so rarely hear." The president was never identified by name during the story: listeners were challenged to guess his identity, which was revealed in a brief epilogue. Often the background was so general that it challenged even students of American history.

In one show, reviewed by *Radio Life* in 1951, the listener is told that the president, as the play opened, is the vice-president. A close election has given none of the candidates a majority, and the election is to be thrown into the House of Representatives. The president-to-be has close friends named Smith, which helps the *Radio Life* reviewer not a bit. There is a feud brewing with Aaron Burr, a solid clue as it now sets a specific time frame. He has a daughter named Martha and is said to be "a godless man." At the end, it is revealed that he founded the University of Virginia and authored the Declaration of Independence. The listener does not need this week's epilogue to know that Mr. President is Thomas Jefferson.

To play the role, the producers wanted an actor with "the aggressiveness of Teddy Roosevelt, the warmth and humility of Abe Lincoln, and the tenacity of Andrew Jackson." Their choice, Edward Arnold, made no attempt to characterize the men he played. "They're all Edward Arnold," he said, "or else there'd be no guessing game on the show." But the problem with the show was aptly stated by the *Radio Life* critic: the novelty of the guessing game wore thin, leaving the show steeped in boredom. For Arnold it was a prestigious part, earning him the admiration of Harry Truman despite the actor's Republican nature. Arnold was a frequent guest at the White House, where Truman referred to him as "Mr. President."

THE MODERN ADVENTURES OF CASANOVA, romance thriller, "based upon an idea by and starring Errol Flynn."

BROADCAST HISTORY: Jan. 10–Dec. 25, 1952, Mutual. 30m, Thursdays at 8. Formula 9 Shampoo and a National Health Aid weight reduction plan. **CAST:** Errol Flynn as Christopher Casanova, lover and secret agent. Hollywood radio actors in support: William Conrad, Nan Boardman, Lamont Johnson, Ted Osborne, Harry Bartell, Georgia Ellis, Alan Reed, Ben Wright, Joy Terry, Peg La Centra, etc. ORCHESTRA: Walter Schumann. DIRECTOR: William N. Robson. WRITERS: Frank Hart Taussig, Les Crutchfield, Larry Roman, etc.

Modern Casanova, like *Box 13* and *Bold Venture*, was one of the new transcribed shows of the early 1950s that brought major Hollywood stars to the weekly radio soundstage. The Casanova image fit Errol Flynn's screen persona perfectly. His Casanova was "a direct descendent of the fabulous Italian diplomat, author, and soldier of fortune, whose principal fault was not that he kissed, but that he told." Though often embarrassed by the implications of his name, the modern Casanova carried it "proudly through the drawing rooms of international society." In his secret identity, he was an agent for WORLD-POL, the "World Criminal Police Commission."

THE MOLLE MYSTERY THEATER, crime drama and mystery; often heard as *Mystery Theater* and, in spinoffs, as *Mark Sabre* and as *Hearthstone of the Death Squad*.

BROADCAST HISTORY: Sept. 7, 1943–June 25, 1948, NBC. 30m, Tuesdays at 9 until July 3, 1945; resumed Oct. 5, Fridays at 10, 1945–48. Sterling Drugs, Molle Shave Cream. CAST: Bernard Lenrow as Geoffrey Barnes, crime fiction connoisseur who introduced the shows. New York radio actors in lead and supporting roles: Richard Widmark, Joseph Julian, Elspeth Eric, Frank Lovejoy, Anne Seymour, Raymond Edward Johnson, etc. ANNOUNCER: Dan Seymour. ORCHESTRA: Alexander Semmler. WRITERS: Joseph Ruscoll, etc.

June 29, 1948–June 19, 1951, CBS. 30m, Tuesdays at 8. *Mystery Theater*. Sterling Drugs for Bayer Aspirin and Phillips Milk of Magnesia. CAST: Alfred Shirley as Inspector Hearthstone of the Death Squad, with many of the same New York actors in support. PRODUCERS: Frank and Anne Hummert.

Spinoff series: *Hearthstone of the Death Squad*. Aug. 30, 1951–Sept. 17, 1952, CBS. 30m, various times.

Oct. 3, 1951–June 30, 1954, ABC. 30m,

Wednesdays at 8, 1951–53; at 9:30, 1953–54. Continuation of *Mystery Theater* for but with a new format, also known as *Mark Sabre*. Sterling Drugs. CAST: Robert Carroll as Inspector Mark Sabre. James Westerfield as Sergeant Maloney. PRODUCERS: Frank and Anne Hummert.

The original *Molle Mystery Theater* was the most notable of all the formats and spinoffs that grew out of it. It featured "the best in mystery and detective fiction," with tales running from classic (Poe) to modern (Raymond Chandler, etc.). The trademarks were high tension and twist (often shocking) endings. Then it fell into the clutches of Frank and Anne Hummert, moved to CBS, shortened its name, and sank into melodrama. The new show was linked to the old by the continued presence of the host, "Geoffrey Barnes," but in all other respects it was a new program. Like other Hummert shows, it was replete with stilted dialogue and cardboard characters.

MONITOR, news, actualities, remotes, comedy, variety.

BROADCAST HISTORY: June 12, 1955–Jan. 26, 1974, NBC. Full weekend slates heard in four-hour blocks, beginning at 8 A.M. Saturday and running until midnight Sunday. SEGMENT HOSTS: Dave Garroway, Goodman and Jane Ace, Bob Elliott and Ray Goulding, Leon Pearson, John Cameron Swayze, Clifton Fadiman, Red Barber, Allen Funt, etc. PRODUCER: James Fleming.

Monitor was a true magazine of the air, taking advantage of radio's unique ability to provide mobility and immediacy. It offered old radio stars (Bob Hope, Fibber McGee and Molly, etc.) in new skits, took segments of such TV hits as *The George Gobel Show*, staged vignettes from Broadway and movie productions, interviewed celebrities and newsmakers, and aired live horse races from Florida, California, and New York.

MOON RIVER, mood music and poetry.

BROADCAST HISTORY: Ca. 1930–1940s, WLW, Cincinnati. 15m. NARRATORS: Bob Brown from 1930; also, Harry Holcomb, Palmer Ward, Charles Woods, Don Dowd, Jay Jostyn, Jimmy Leonard, Ken Linn, Peter Grant, etc. Many vocalists including the DeVore Sisters, Doris Day, Rosemary and Betty Clooney, Lucille Norman, Ruby Wright, Anita Ellis, Phil Brito, Janette Davis, Barbara Cameron, etc. **CREATOR:** Ed Byron.

Perhaps the best-known, best-loved, best-remembered local show of the network radio era, *Moon River* was boosted to national prominence by WLW's 500,000 watts, so powerful a beacon that the show got fan mail from Europe. "Turn on a faucet and out came WLW," wrote Dick Perry in his history of the station.

Perry traces the show's origin to a meeting in 1930 between writer Ed Byron and owner Powel Crosley Jr., who ordered Byron to create a poetry show to accommodate an organ he had just bought; Byron then retired to a speakeasy and sketched out some notes while a violinist played *Caprice Viennois*. This became the show's haunting theme; *Clair de Lune* was played as a backdrop to the poetry readings. The narrator was pivotal: his was the voice of both signatures and most of the poetry contained within them. Many of the personalities went on to national careers, and Byron became a well-known writer-director in New York (see MR. DISTRICT ATTORNEY).

As for Moon River, its closing was pure radio, frozen in time.

> *Down the valley of a thousand yesterdays*
> *Flow the bright waters of Moon River*
> *On and on, forever waiting to carry you*
> *Down to the land of forgetfulness,*
> *To the kingdom of sleep,*
> *To the realm of Moon River,*
> *A lazy stream of dreams*
> *Where vain desires forget themselves*
> *In the loveliness of sleep.*
> *Moon River,*
> *Enchanted white ribbon*
> *Twined in the hair of night,*
> *Where nothing is but sleep,*
> *Dream on, sleep on,*
> *Care will not seek for thee.*
> *Float on, drift on,*
> *Moon River . . . to the sea.*

MOONSHINE AND HONEYSUCKLE, serial drama, a forerunner of radio soap operas.

BROADCAST HISTORY: 1930–33, NBC. 30m, Sundays at 2. **CAST:** Louis Mason as Clem Betts, a mountain man who lived in Lonesome Hollow, yearned to see the world beyond the hills, but lived a day-to-day life of simple pleasures and problems.

Anne Elstner as Cracker Gaddis. Claude Cooper as Pegleg Gaddis. **DIRECTOR:** Harry Simpson. **WRITER:** Lula Vollmer.

THE MOREY AMSTERDAM SHOW, comedy.

BROADCAST HISTORY: July 10, 1948–Feb. 15, 1949, CBS. 30m, Saturday at 9 until Oct., then Tuesdays at 9:30. **CAST:** Morey Amsterdam as himself, a comic who played at the fictitious Golden Goose Cafe in New York City, singing, telling jokes, playing the cello, and introducing guests. Art Carney as Charlie the doorman, who aspired to write songs and had a catchphrase, "Ya know what I mean." Jacqueline Susann (novelist-to-be) as Lola, the cigarette girl. Betty Garde as Aunt Mimi. **VOCALIST:** Bill Lawrence. **PRODUCER:** Irving Mansfield.

The Morey Amsterdam Show ran concurrently on radio and TV, two nights apart, with the same cast and setting but with different scripts. The TV show continued for more than a year after it folded on radio.

THE MORIN SISTERS, vocal trio.

BROADCAST HISTORY: 1932–35, Blue Network. Various 15m times.
   1935–37, CBS. 15m, Sundays at 7:45. *Sunset Dreams*. Fitch Shampoo.
   June–Nov. 1939, Blue Network. 15m, Saturdays at 10 A.M.

The trio—Marge, Pauline, and Evelyn—also appeared on many 1930s variety shows, and were *Breakfast Club* regulars.

MORTIMER GOOCH, comedy serial.

BROADCAST HISTORY: Nov. 13, 1936–March 26, 1937, CBS. 15m, Fridays at 7. Wrigley's Gum. **CAST:** Bob Bailey as Mortimer Gooch, a salesman in frequent difficulty over his aggressive sales technique. Louise Fitch as Betty Lou. **PRODUCER:** Louis Jackobson. **WRITERS:** John Van Cronkhite, Dan MacMillan.

MORTON DOWNEY, crooner.

BROADCAST HISTORY: 1928, BBC, London.
   1930–31, CBS. 15m, four a week at 7.
   June 1, 1931–May 28, 1932, CBS. 15m, six a week at 7:45. *The Camel Quarter-Hour*, with Tony Wons and the Jacques Renard Orchestra.

Jan. 4–March 29, 1933, Blue Network. 30m, Wednesdays at 9:30. Woodbury Soap. Costarred with sound-alike Donald Novis in "battle of tenors" format, with neither identified from song to song (Downey fans could tell, however, by his distinct whistle before each number). Leon Belasco Orchestra.

1933–34, CBS. 15m, various times.

May 1–July 3, 1934, CBS. 15m, Tuesdays at 7. Woodbury Soap.

Dec. 16, 1934–June 14, 1935, Blue Network. 30m, Sundays at 4:30 until April, then 15m, Fridays at 8:15. Sprudel Salts (30m shows).

Jan. 5–Dec. 27, 1936, Blue Network. 45m, Sundays at 9:45. *Paul Whiteman's Musical Varieties*. Woodbury Soap.

Feb. 8, 1943–June 30, 1951. Blue Network, 15m, weekdays at 3, 1943–45; Mutual, 15m, weekdays at 12:15, 1945–47; NBC, 15m, three a week at 11:15, 1948–50; CBS, 30m, Saturdays at 10:30 A.M., 1950–51. *The Coke Club*. Coca-Cola.

Tenor Morton Downey enjoyed great success on radio, but is perhaps best remembered for his long association with Coca-Cola. Known as "the Irish Thrush," "the Irish Troubador," and other such names, Downey was actually born in Connecticut in 1902. He began singing professionally as a child, at church socials and Elks Club meetings. In 1919, he was discovered by Paul Whiteman at the Sheridan Square Theater in New York. He was soon getting equal billing with the band, and in the late 1920s he made a tour of Europe and appeared in several Hollywood movies.

In 1930, he opened the Delmonico Club and began broadcasting from its bandstand. He was heard in the '30s with Mark Warnow (for Bourjois Perfume) and Eddy Duchin (Pall Mall Cigarettes), and in 1932 was selected by a newspaper poll as the nation's best male singer. By 1936, he was one of radio's top stars, earning a reported $250,000 a year. His *Coke Club* shows of the '40s were memorable for his crooning of the sponsor's distinctive theme song. He died in 1985.

MOTHER AND DAD, comedy. See also MA AND PA.

BROADCAST HISTORY: Aug. 10, 1942–Sept. 23, 1944, CBS. 15m, weekdays at 5:15 until Oct. 1943, then 30m, Saturdays at 5:30. Allegheny Steel. **CAST:** Effie Palmer and Parker Fennelly as

Mother and Dad, a folksy couple who got together with friends for hymn-singing, discussion, and poetry-reading. Charme Allen also as Mother. **PRODUCER-DIRECTOR:** Chester "Tiny" Renier.

MOTHER O' MINE, soap opera.

BROADCAST HISTORY: Sept. 30, 1940–July 4, 1941, Blue Network. 15m, weekdays at 4. Clapp's Baby Food. **CAST:** Agnes Young as Mother Morrison. Donald Cook as John. Ruth Yorke as Helen. Jackie Kelk as Pete.

THE MOYLAN SISTERS, child singers.

BROADCAST HISTORY: Oct. 15, 1939–June 18, 1944, Blue Network. 15m, Sundays at 5, 1939–43; at 12:45, 1943–44. Thrivo Dogfood, 1939–41; then sustained.

The Moylan Sisters, Marianne and Peggy Joan, came out of the *Horn and Hardart Children's Hour* to become network stars at five and seven. Their amazing ability to harmonize won them this quarter-hour, which was heavily dog-related under Thrivo Dogfood. There were dog songs, dog awards, and frequent references to the sister's dog, Rascal. The theme was *Sittin' on a Log, Pettin' My Dog*.

MURDER AND MR. MALONE, crime drama, based on the novels by Craig Rice.

BROADCAST HISTORY: Jan. 11, 1947–March 26, 1949, ABC. 30m, Saturdays at 9:30 until June 1948, then at 8:30. Guild Wines. **CAST:** Frank Lovejoy as John J. Malone, "fiction's most famous criminal lawyer." **ANNOUNCER:** Art Gilmore. **MUSIC:** John Duffy. **PRODUCER:** Bernard L. Schubert. **DIRECTOR:** Bill Rousseau. **WRITERS:** Craig Rice (Georgiana Ann Randolph), Gene Wang.

Sept. 21, 1949–Sept. 24, 1950, ABC. 30m, Wednesdays at 8 until Nov., then Sundays at 7:30. *The Amazing Mr. Malone*. **CAST:** Gene Raymond as John J. Malone.

May 25–July 13, 1951, NBC. 30m, Fridays at 9. **CAST:** George Petrie as John J. Malone. Larry Haines as Lt. Brooks. **DIRECTOR:** Richard Lewis.

Murder and Mr. Malone had a persistent identity crisis. According to *Radio Life*, by mid-May 1948, it had undergone four changes of title: from the original to *The Amazing Mr. Malone*, to *John J. Malone for the Defense*, to *Attorney John J. Malone*, and finally back to *Murder and Mr. Malone*.

MURDER AT MIDNIGHT, mystery-horror drama.

BROADCAST HISTORY: 1946, 30m, transcribed syndication; heard on WJZ, New York Sept. 16, 1946–Sept. 8, 1947. CAST: New York actors including Elspeth Eric, Mercedes McCambridge, Berry Kroeger, Betty Caine, Carl Frank, Barry Hopkins, Lawson Zerbe, Charlotte Holland, etc. NARRATOR: Raymond Morgan. MUSIC: Charles Paul, with a creepy score on organ. PRODUCER: Louis G. Cowan. DIRECTOR: Anton M. Leader. WRITERS: Robert Newman, Joseph Ruscoll, Max Ehrlich, William Morwood, etc.

Murder at Midnight offered tales of ''the witching hour, when night is darkest, our fears the strongest, our strength at its lowest ebb ... Midnight! ... when graves gape open and death *strikes*!'' The creepy voice of the opening signature (*MURRR-DERRR—A-A-AT MIID-NIIGHT!*) belonged to Raymond Morgan, a Long Island minister who gave up the cloth for the excitement of radio.

MURDER BY EXPERTS, mystery-detective drama.

BROADCAST HISTORY: June 18, 1949–Dec. 17, 1951, Mutual. 30m, Saturdays at 2:30 through July 1949, Sundays at 10 until Sept. 1949, then Mondays at 9. HOSTS: Masters of mystery, often John Dickson Carr or Brett Halliday; Alfred Hitchcock, 1951. CAST: New York radio personnel. MUSIC: Emerson Buckley. PRODUCER-DIRECTORS: Robert A. Arthur and David Kogan. SOUND EFFECTS: Mario Siletti.

Murder by Experts offered tales by the leading writers of mystery fiction, chosen by masters of the genre: highly charged plots of crime and passion that turned on emotion rather than gimmicks. The available episodes are straightforward and honest, revealing a better series than most of its counterparts.

MURDER WILL OUT, mystery-quiz.

BROADCAST HISTORY: Jan. 30, 1945–ca. June 25, 1946, ABC West Coast network. 30m, Tues-

days. Rainier Brewing. CAST: Edmund MacDonald as Inspector Burke early 1945; William Gargan thereafter. Eddie Marr as Detective Nolan. ANNOUNCER: Larry Keating. WRITER-DIRECTOR: Lew Lansworth.

Murder Will Out followed the *Ellery Queen* formula to a point—each show contained a fully dramatized mystery, followed by guesses from the audience as to the killer's identity. Unlike *Queen*, this contained no trick clues; the stories unfolded in chronological order, with the clues considered in the order found. Listeners were thus on the same plane as the police and the contestants. Four contestants (two of each sex) were drawn from the audience. Awards of $5 (in war stamps) were given for each correct answer; winners who guessed the killer *and* the correct clue won a $50 war bond and a Gold Detective Certificate, framed for display.

THE MUSIC APPRECIATION HOUR, groundbreaking musical education for children.

BROADCAST HISTORY: Oct. 26, 1928–May 1, 1942, Blue Network. Heard as the *RCA Educational Hour*, 1928–29. 60m, Fridays at 11 A.M. from late 1928–37, then Fridays at 2. HOST: Dr. Walter Damrosch, ''the dean of American music,'' famed as a conductor, composer, producer, and champion of the great symphonic composers.

The Music Appreciation Hour was the first demonstration of orchestral music for millions of American schoolchildren, and quickly became an integrated part of hundreds of classroom workshops around the country. Its host, Dr. Walter Damrosch, had been part of the American music scene for half a century.

Damrosch was born in Prussia, Jan. 30, 1862, son of conductor Leopold Damrosch. He came to the United States in 1872 and, following his father's footsteps, was assistant director and second conductor of the Metropolitan Opera and later spent more than 40 years conducting the New York Symphony Orchestra. He was always motivated to bring the best music to the largest possible number of people, and radio was his ideal tool.

His first radio demonstration aired on WEAF Oct. 23, 1923. Soon he was praising the medium as ''by far the most powerful, the greatest, and the most fascinating means of spreading the gospel of music that I have ever known.'' In 1926, he gave more experimental broadcasts and promised still more. His voice was perfectly suited to the air, and he developed a distinct manner of speaking, in short sentences with a key word at the core of each pronouncement. He proposed a musical classroom of the air, to Merlin H. Aylesworth, president of NBC, and *The Musical Appreciation Hour* was the result, a forum he headed until he was 80.

In its first year, the show was heard in 200 New York classrooms. His listenership soon grew to seven million, with entire school systems participating in the program. In rural schools without radios, teachers would huddle their classes around automobiles in the schoolyards, to pick up the *Hour* on car sets. His goal, Damrosch told *Radio Life* in 1940, was to attain a ''class'' of 12 million students. He never quite made it: with the entry of the United States into World War II and the increased demand for radio time by the major network news organizations, Damrosch was asked to cut his show to 30 minutes. He declined, and retired in May 1942. His standard greeting, ''Good morning, my dear children!,'' was remembered for years.

He died Dec. 22, 1950.

MUSIC BY GERSHWIN, piano, song, conversation.

BROADCAST HISTORY: Feb. 19–May 18, 1934, Blue Network. 15m, Mondays and Fridays at 7:30. Feen-A-Mint.

Sept. 30–Dec. 23, 1934, CBS. 30m, Sundays at 6. Feen-A-Mint.

HOST: George Gershwin, who played piano and talked about his music; guest composers. ANNOUNCER: Don Wilson. CONDUCTOR: Louis Katzman. PRODUCER: Ed Byron. WRITER: Finis Farr.

MUSICAL AMERICANA, concert-jazz mix; ''a flag-waver for native music.''

BROADCAST HISTORY: Jan. 25, 1940–Jan. 16, 1941, NBC. 30m, Blue Network, Thursdays at 8 until July, then Tuesdays at 9 until Oct.; Red Network, Thursdays at 10:30, Oct.-Jan. COMMENTATOR: Deems Taylor. ANNOUNCER: Milton Cross. ORCHESTRA: Raymond Paige and ''his 100 men of melody,'' a giant aggregation includ-

ing members of the Pittsburgh Symphony. Lively contributions by ''20 hot musicians from KDKA.''

The fare of this series ran from Friml to (Raymond) Scott. It was a total Pittsburgh product, from sponsor to location (NBC's Pittsburgh studios).

MUSICAL BOUQUET, light music.

BROADCAST HISTORY: April 22–Oct. 14, 1945, ABC. 30m, Sundays at 4. Lily of the Valley Perfume. HOST-NARRATOR: Bret Morrison. ORCHESTRA: Earle Sheldon. VOCALISTS: Paul Frenet, Louise Marlow. PRODUCER: Mildred Fenton.

Musical Bouquet was contrived to convey in music the concepts of spring and romance promoted in the perfume commercials.

THE MUSICAL STEELMAKERS, ''home talent'' musical show.

BROADCAST HISTORY: 1936, first heard on WWVA, Wheeling, W. V.

Jan. 2, 1938–June 18, 1944. 30m, Mutual, Sundays at 5, 1938–41, then Blue Network, Sundays at 5:30. Wheeling Steel.

TALENT: All workers of the Wheeling Steel Company. *Hostess* (''femcee''): Lois Mae Nolte. ''INTERLOCUTOR'': John Wincholl, ''the oldtimer.'' VOCALISTS: secretary Regina Colbert and receptionist Alma Custer. Also: Carlo Ross, who sang the theme; Ardenne White; the ''Singing Millmen'' (William Griffiths, William Stevenson, Glynn Davies, Walter Schane); the ''Steele Sisters'' (in real life the Evans Sisters, Betty Jane and Margaret, with Lois Mae Nolte and Harriet Drake). *Harpist*: Mary Bower. ORCHESTRA: Lew Davies, etc. PRODUCER-ANNOUNCER: Walter Patterson.

This show originated from Wheeling's Capitol Theater. The performers all put at least ten hours per week into rehearsal, in addition to their regular duties at the plant. Aside from the talent listed above, many other Wheeling employees were heard.

MY BEST GIRLS, comedy-drama.

BROADCAST HISTORY: Feb. 9, 1944–Jan. 10, 1945, Blue Network/ABC. 30m, Wednesdays at 8:30. CAST: Roland Winters as Russell Bartlett, a widower with three daughters. John Griggs also as Bartlett. Bartlett's daughters played by Mary Shipp (as Linda, age 17); Mary Mason (Penny, 14); Lorna Lynn (Jill, 9). **DIRECTOR:** Wesley McKee. **WRITER:** John Kelsey.

MY FAVORITE HUSBAND, situation comedy.

BROADCAST HISTORY: July 23, 1948–March 31, 1951, CBS. 30m, initially Fridays at 9; frequent time changes, with Fridays at 8:30 (1949–50) its most sustained timeslot. General Foods. **CAST:** Lucille Ball and Richard Denning as Liz and George Cooper, "two people who live together and like it." (Lee Bowman as George in the premiere episode only.) Gale Gordon as George's boss, the short-tempered banker, Rudolph Atterbury. Bea Benaderet as Iris, Atturbury's wife. Ruth Perrott as Katie, the Coopers' maid. **PRODUCER:** Jess Oppenheimer. **WRITERS:** Bob Carroll Jr. and Madelyn Pugh.

My Favorite Husband was based on the novel *Mr. and Mrs. Cugat*, by Isabel Scott Rorick. The Cugats became the Coopers (the name sounding much less ethnic), and they lived "in a little white two-story house" at 321 Bundy Lane, "in the bustling little suburb of Sheridan Falls." Lucille Ball was a zany housewife; Richard Denning was a typical addled radio husband— sometimes forgetful, sometimes lovable, always stereotypically male. There were many male-vs.-female plots, with George and his boss, Atterbury, against their wives. The best-remembered line on the show was Atterbury's catchphrase, "Ah, Liz-girl, George-boy."

MY FRIEND IRMA, situation comedy.

BROADCAST HISTORY: April 11, 1947–Aug. 23, 1954, CBS. 30m, Fridays at 10:30 until mid-June 1947; Mondays at 8:30 until Aug.; at 10, 1947–51; Sundays at 6, 1951–52; at 9:30, mid-1952; Tuesdays at 9:30, 1952–54. Lever Brothers for Pepsodent, 1947–51; Ennds Chlorophyl Tablets ("to stop Triple O—odors of body, odors of breath, odor offense"), 1951–52; Camel Cigarettes, 1952–53; various thereafter. **CAST:** Marie Wilson as Irma Peterson, the last word in "dumb blonde" radio comediennes. Cathy Lewis as her best friend and roommate, Jane Stacy. Joan Banks as Jane Stacy, ca. early 1949, while Lewis was ill.

John Brown as Irma's boyfriend, Al. Jane Morgan initially as Mrs. O'Reilly, owner of the rooming house where Irma and Jane lived. Gloria Gordon as Mrs. O'Reilly for most of the run. Hans Conried as Professor Kropotkin, who lived in the apartment upstairs. Alan Reed as Mr. Clyde, Irma's boss. Leif Erickson as Richard Rhinelander III, Jane's boss and the love of her life. Myra Marsh as Richard's mother. Mary Shipp as Kay Foster, Irma's roommate from ca. 1953. Richard Eyer as Bobby, Kay Foster's nephew. **ANNOUNCERS:** Carl Caruso, Bob LeMond, Frank Bingman, etc. **SOUND EFFECTS:** James Murphy. **ORCHESTRA:** Lud Gluskin. **CREATOR-WRITER-PRODUCER-DIRECTOR:** Cy Howard. **WRITERS:** Parke Levy, Stanley Adams, Roland MacLane. **THEME:** *Friendship*, by Cole Porter. Secondary theme and midbreak bridge: *Street Scene*, by Alfred Newman.

In October 1947, a *Time* critic described *My Friend Irma* as a follower in the "artfully stumbling footsteps of Gracie Allen, Jane Ace, and other attractive dunderheads." But Irma had neither the malapropian qualities of Ace nor the dubiously screwy logic of Allen. She was naively friendly, with a blue-eyed innocence that managed to come across through nothing more than a voice. She was dumb indeed. Only Irma would answer a question about compulsory military service by saying that "a girl shouldn't have to go out with a sailor unless she wants to." Irma was so dumb she thought flypaper was the stationery used on airlines.

She was a stenographer by trade, and heaven help her understandably crusty boss, Mr. Clyde. Her roommate, Jane Stacy, was her dyed-in-the-wool opposite—completely sane, logical, dependable in every way that Irma was not. Jane narrated the stories with weary resignation, infusing the narrative with exasperation and love. Jane carried an unrequited torch for her boss, the millionaire Richard Rhinelander III. "Wouldn't it be great," she asked Irma one night, "if I wound up being Mrs. Richard Rhinelander the third?" Without missing a beat, Irma said, "What good will that do if he's got two other wives?"

But Jane always had Irma's best interests at heart; thus she tried to discourage Irma's relationship with the Brooklyn hustler, Al. "Hi-ya, Chicken," Al would say in his weekly greeting, and the troubles of Irma Peterson would begin to magnify. Good for one walk-on per show was Professor Kropotkin, the violinist at the Paradise Burlesque, who carried on a running battle of insults with the landlady, a fierce Irish battleaxe named Mrs. O'Reilly. His entrance was always marked by a soft knock and a sheepish Russian accent: "It's only me, Professor Kropotkin."

The show was created by Cy Howard, a reformed introvert who would also produce *Life with Luigi*, a year later. Howard had worked in local radio, from KTRH, Houston to WBBM, Chicago. He arrived at CBS in 1946, with *Irma* on his mind and a sense that the casting would make or break it. He tested for the two leads but found no suitable actresses until Cathy Lewis arrived to read for Jane Stacy. Lewis was then one of radio's busiest talents, and Howard would long remember her impatience to get on to her next job. With her first words, "All right, all right, five minutes, that's all," Howard felt he had found Jane. The critical title role followed shortly, when he saw Marie Wilson in Ken Murray's *Blackouts*, doing a part so unlike Irma but packed with the precise naive bewilderment he was looking for.

Wilson, Lewis, and Gloria Gordon took their roles to television in 1952, for a CBS series that ran two seasons. Lewis resigned midway through it, and it was decided not to try recasting a role so strongly identified with one actress. Jane was written out of both the radio and TV shows, sent off to live in Panama. Irma's new roommate, Kay Foster, moved in with her 7-year-old nephew. Though the show made Marie Wilson a national figure, it typecast her beyond redemption. Far from stupid, Wilson was constantly compared to her fictitious alter ego by critics and her fellow cast members. "She has that same touching sincerity, the same steady wide-eyed gaze," said *Radio Life*. "she can keep an admirable poker face through the most idiotic conversations. . . . She loves everything and everybody, and there isn't a person in the world that she doesn't call 'honey' with sincerest regard." Howard agreed. "She's so much like Irma that I have to rewrite the things she says to make them believable."

The Hooper rating was consistently healthy, peaking at 20-plus. In 1949, *Irma* was brought to the screen by Hal Wallis. Wilson made the transition, but the film was mainly a launching pad for the careers of Dean Martin and Jerry Lewis. The radio show, meanwhile, continued on through the TV run.

MY LITTLE MARGIE, situation comedy.

BROADCAST HISTORY: Dec. 7, 1952–June 26, 1955, CBS. Transcribed in Hollywood. 30m, Sundays at 8:30. Philip Morris. **CAST:** Gale Storm as Margie Albright, a cheerful young woman who lived with her father, Verne. Charles Farrell as Verne Albright, a busy executive with Honeywell Industries. Verna Felton as Mrs. Odetts, "friend and neighbor" of the Albrights. Gil Stratton Jr. as Margie's boyfriend, Freddie. Will Wright as Verne's crusty boss, Mr. Honeywell. Based on characters created by Frank Fox. **MUSIC:** Lud Gluskin, composer-conductor. **PRODUCER-DIRECTOR:** Gordon Hughes, with Hal Roach Jr. and Roland Reed. **WRITER:** Lee Carson.

Though best remembered as an early TV sitcom, *My Little Margie* had an almost identical run on radio. Margie was a schemer in the best radio tradition: abetted in her plots to teach the boys a lesson by her friend Mrs. Odetts. Margie and her father lived "high atop New York's Fifth Avenue." This was one of the very few radio shows that originated on TV, the video series premiering almost six months earlier.

MY SON AND I, soap opera.

BROADCAST HISTORY: Oct. 9, 1939–Jan. 3, 1941, CBS. 15m, weekdays at 2:45. Swans Down Flour and Calumet Baking Powder. **CAST:** Betty Garde as Connie Vance, former vaudeville trouper whose husband had died, leaving her with a 10-year-old son. Kingsley Colton as her son, Buddy Watson. Agnes Young as Aunt Minta Owens. Gladys Thornton as Aunt Addie. John Pickard as Bruce Barrett. **MUSIC:** Charles Paul on organ. **WRITER:** Frank Provo.

My Son and I originated as two single-act plays on *The Kate Smith Hour*. These were so well received that Smith's sponsor brought them to daytime as a running serial.

MY SON JEEP, situation comedy.

BROADCAST HISTORY: Jan. 25–June 14, 1953, NBC. 30m, Sundays at 7:30 until April, then at 7.

Oct. 3, 1955–Nov. 9, 1956, CBS. 15m, weeknights at 8, later at 9.

CAST: Donald Cook as Dr. Robert Allison of Grove
Falls, a small-town doctor and widower trying to
raise his two children alone. Paul McGrath also as
Dr. Robert Allison. Martin Huston as Allison's 10-
year-old son, Jeep. Bobby Alford also as Jeep.
Joan Lazer as Jeep's sister, Peggy. Lynn Allen as
Barbara Miller, the doctor's receptionist and low-
key romantic interest. Joyce Gordon also as Barbara. Leona Powers as Mrs. Bixby, the Allison
maid.

MY TRUE STORY, romantic melodrama, from
True Story magazine.

BROADCAST HISTORY: Feb. 15, 1943–Feb. 1,
1962. Blue Network/ABC from 1943–61; Mututal,
1961–62. Mostly 30m, weekdays, with complete
stories and new casts each day. Libby Packing,
1944–49; Sterling Drugs, 1955–56. **AN-
NOUNCER:** Glenn Riggs (1940s). **MUSIC:** Rosa
Rio on organ. **PRODUCER:** Ted Lloyd.
WRITER: Margaret Sangster.

A confession magazine of the air, with stories
of people driven by "strange, selfish desire" and
all the inherent troubles found in the monthly
pulps.

MYRT AND MARGE, soap opera, also known
as *The Story of Myrt and Marge.*

BROADCAST HISTORY: Nov. 2, 1931–Jan. 1,
1937, CBS. 15m, weeknights at 7. Wrigley's Gum.
Jan. 4, 1937–March 27, 1942, CBS. 15m, weekdays at 10:15 A.M. Super Suds. Also heard on Mutual, March 27–Oct. 6, 1939, weekdays at 1:15.
1946, transcribed syndication.

CAST: Myrtle Vail as Myrtle Spear, a seasoned chorus girl in "that most glittering of all Broadway
extravaganzas, *Hayfield's Pleasures.*" Donna
Damerel as Margie Minter, a young, fresh face in
the *Hayfield* chorus. Helen Mack as Margie, 1941–
42. Vinton Hayworth as Jack Arnold, the young
lawyer who married Marge and became a crime-
fighting assistant district attorney. Karl Way and
Ed Begley as Francis Hayfield. Gene Morgan as
Rex Marvin, motion picture director and suitor of
Marge. Santos Ortega and Dick Janaver as Lee
Kirby, another Marge suitor. Betty Jane Tyler as
Baby Midgie, Marge's daughter. Edith Evanson as
Helmi, "the faithful maid who has gone through

so many of Myrt and Marge's experiences with
them" (and who sang *Yingle Bells* endlessly at
Christmas). Ray Hedge as Clarence Tiffingtuffer,
the costume designer; an effeminate character (*Radioland* put it not so kindly and termed him a "thi-
thy," though he didn't lisp) used mainly as a
worrywart, for comic relief. Cliff Arquette as
Thaddeus Cornfelder, the other comic role. Eleanor Rella as Billie Devere. Michael Fitzmaurice
as Jimmie Kent, another friend of Marge. Frances
Woodbury and Charles Webster as Mr. and Mrs.
Arnold. Alan Devitt as Brellerton White. Sunda
Love as Leota Lawrence, for a time the show's
"archvillainess." **1946 TRANSCRIPTIONS:** Alice Yourman as Myrt. Alice Goodkin as Marge.
Vinton Hayworth and Ray Hedge in their original
roles. Richard Keith as Ray Hunt. Helen Choate
as Billie Devere. Pam Manners as Gwen Rogers.

ANNOUNCERS: Harlow Wilcox, Jean Paul King,
David Ross, Tom Shirley, Andre Baruch, etc. **DI-
RECTORS:** Bobby Brown, John Gunn, Lindsay
MacHarrie, etc. **WRITER:** Myrtle Vail, with Cliff
Thomas. **THEME:** *Poor Butterfly.*

Myrt and Marge was one of the first important
dramatic serials of radio. As a nighttime drama
it was an immediate success, leaping to a CAB
rating in the mid-20s by 1932, its second year.
In 1937, it became a soap opera in fact as well
as by nature, moving to daytime for Super Suds.

It was created by Myrtle Vail, a 43-year-old
vaudevillian whose own life was the inspiration
and background. Like her fictitious Myrt, Vail
had run away from home at 15 to go onstage.
She was a back-row chorus girl in a road show,
fell in love with the tenor, and married him the
following year. With George Damerel she had
two children, Donna and George, and they traveled as a show business family throughout the
1910s and 1920s. They retired in the late '20s,
putting their money into real estate, and were
financially devastated by the market crash of
1929. Reduced again to counting pennies, Vail
decided to return to show business, in the new
medium of radio.

Chicago was then the major broadcast center.
If she could work up a scenario, she thought, she
had a chance to sell and produce it right there in
town. Legend has it that she got the idea as she
reached for a stick of gum. The Wrigley Company was Chicago-based yet nationally prominent. Checking through radio schedules, Vail

learned that Wrigley, though a heavy advertiser in the print world, had no money invested on the air. Her story would be about the theater, and two chorus girls who were actually mother and daughter. Their names would be Myrtle Spear and Margie Minter. (Get it, Mr. Wrigley?—*Spear* and *Minter!*) Wrigley got the point. Vail dashed off ten scripts in longhand. She would play Myrt, though she had never faced a microphone. Her daughter, Donna, would play Marge. Ten days later they were on the air.

It was billed as "the world of the theater and the world of life, and the story of two women who seek fame in the one and contentment in the other." Though mother and daughter, they didn't know it when they met in that first chapter as if for the first time. Fate had separated them and cast them on different paths. Now, through thinnest coincidence, young Margie Minter would wander into Hayfield's Theater, "just off Times Square," where the 24-girl precision chorus was going through its routine. These were the Chic-Chicks, the world-famous glamour girls who danced for master showman Francis Hayfield.

Leading the troupe was Myrtle Spear, seasoned veteran of the footlight wars. Margie fainted from hunger; Myrt borrowed a "five-spot" and sent out for a meal, taking her first tentative steps into the age-old story of young brilliance and the older-but-wiser voice of experience. Margie too would become a *Hayfield* headliner, joining Myrt for a series of adventures that ranged from Broadway to the theatrical boondocks, and even to South America in 1934.

The stories were filled with romance but laced with crime. Gangsters, racketeers, and bootleggers were never far from the center in the early days. It was the notable departure of its day. The *Forum* praised it as "the most advanced program of its type now on the air." The critic (though he doubted that Donna Damerel was a real name) found the two heroines easy to take, "like honey and cream." The setting was "hard and glittering," the lines swift and direct, so different from the "ponderous exchanges" of *Amos 'n' Andy* at the same time on the rival network. The gangster element was thrilling, leading to "infinite variations never before done in a serialized 15-minute period."

Marge was 16; Myrt was 32, "although you'd never know by looking at Myrt that she was old enough to have a grown-up daughter." The char-acters were allowed to age, but gracefully: Marge became a young lady in her 20s, a "sweet and pure sex interest," as she was described by that early critic, but one who could "safely be gulped down by the hinterland without asking the children to go to bed before their proper time." Myrt remained the glamorous and still-young guiding light. She married Francis Hayfield (who bore more than a coincidental resemblance to Florenz Ziegfeld); he died in 1936. Marge married Jack Arnold and in 1935 became the mother of "Babie Midgie." But the death of Hayfield resulted in the closing of the *Pleasures*; Myrt and Marge traveled through Hollywood and the Midwest, seeking out new adventures in a road company.

In 1937, returning to New York, they were captivated by plans to reopen the theater and mount a new *Pleasures* stage show. Jack Arnold had taken a position with District Attorney Dunham, setting up new situations with gangsters and racketeers. That year Jack was killed off, leaving Marge and her tiny daughter alone though far from lonely. There was never any shortage of suitors, with both heroines getting plenty of romance.

The theme, *Poor Butterfly*, was one of the most haunting and striking of the daytime air. The show launched Vail and Damerel to a position of fame and wealth. Early in the run, they made a vaudeville tour during the summer, when the show was off the air. Damerel sang and performed with her mother, and dramatic *Myrt and Marge* skits were worked into the routine. A *Myrt and Marge* movie was released in 1934. This momentum and popularity faded gradually through the decade, with the show surpassed in the ratings by competitors using techniques it had pioneered. On Feb. 14, 1941, Donna Damerel (then married to swimmer Peter Fick) died suddenly moments after the birth of her third child. She was 29. Helen Mack played Marge for the remainder of that year. The 1946 transcription effort was short-lived: it was still running on some CBS stations in September 1947. Vail had touched up the original scripts, making the bootleggers of the '30s black marketeers of the postwar era. But *Myrt and Marge* was a product of the networks' earliest days, and its day had gone.

Myrtle Vail outlived her daughter by almost four decades. She died Sept. 18, 1978, at 90.

THE MYSTERIOUS TRAVELER, dramatic anthology; stories of the strange and terrifying.

BROADCAST HISTORY: Dec. 5, 1943–Sept. 16, 1952, Mutual. 30m, sustained in many timeslots; frequently moved. **CAST:** Maurice Tarplin as the Mysterious Traveler, host and narrator for the dramas. Leads and supporting roles by New York radio personnel: Lyle Sudrow, Bryna Raeburn, Jackson Beck, Roger DeKoven, Bill Zuckert, Bill Johnstone, Lon Clark, Wendell Holmes, Jan Miner, Frank Readick, Joseph Julian, Elspeth Eric, Santos Ortega, Lawson Zerbe, Ann Shepherd, etc. **WRITERS-PRODUCERS-DIRECTORS:** Robert A. Arthur and David Kogan. **SOUND EFFECTS:** Jack Amrhein, Jim Goode, Ron Harper, Walt McDonough, Al Schaffer.

At one time or another, *The Mysterious Traveler* was heard on virtually every night of the week. There were frequent gaps between its runs, but it always seemed good for a revival. It was eternally sustained but cheap to produce: there were no major film stars to pay, and no shortage of radio actors willing to work for union scale.

Maurice Tarplin, who played the title role, conveyed good-natured menace, the kind of mischievous malevolence imparted by *The Whistler* or Raymond of *Inner Sanctum Mysteries*. Like those characters, the Traveler stood outside the stories. With a few exceptions (when he played a ''Dr. Smith''), he narrated and commented from some omniscient perch inside the soul of his protagonist. He came to his listeners in the night, riding a phantom train. The opening signature was that loneliest of sounds, the distant wail of a locomotive, fading in gradually until steel wheels could be heard, clattering on steel rails.

This is The Mysterious Traveler, inviting you to join me on another journey into the strange and terrifying. I hope you will enjoy the trip, that it will thrill you a little and chill you a little. So settle back, get a good grip on your nerves, and be comfortable—if you can!

The stories ran from wild ''end of the world'' science fiction to straight crime. A bug-hating scientist concocted a formula to destroy all insect life, but the insects got wise and came after him. A young couple was haunted by the ghost of a woman once murdered in their newly bought house in Vermont. Perhaps the classic *Mysterious Traveler* episode was *Behind the Locked Door*, much requested and rerun over the years. This story could not have been done in any other medium, as most of it takes place inside a cave, in total darkness. A pair of archaeologists trapped by a landslide find inside the cave the remnants of an old wagon train, perhaps a hundred years old. When they are attacked by strange beings, they must conclude that the descendants of those pioneers still live in this sightless world, feeding on the fish that swim through the underground stream. The ending, of course, was a shocker—most *Mysterious Traveler* endings twisted fate and tried hard for the big surprise. The final scream blended into the train's whistle, and there was the Traveler again, clacking along on his ever-rolling journey. *Oh, you have to get off here! . . . I'm sorry! . . . I'm sure we'll meet again . . . I take this same train every week at this same time . . .*

THE MYSTERY CHEF, food economy and cooking.

BROADCAST HISTORY: 1930, local Boston radio.
Oct. 6, 1931–Dec. 5, 1941, NBC, Red and Blue Networks. 15m, various times; continuity gaps.
Jan. 6, 1932–June 28, 1934, CBS. 15m, various times with gaps in continuity.
1942–ca. 1948, ABC. 15m, various timeslots.

The Mystery Chef was John MacPherson, a Scot who broadcast anonymously because his mother was ashamed of having a son dispense recipes on the air. ''Who I am doesn't matter,'' he would frequently remind his listeners; ''it's what I have to say that counts.'' He had been cooking for more than 25 years, since his arrival in America and his tenancy in a boardinghouse where the food was so bad that he was forced to cook his own. The 10,000 recipes he had collected ran from rare to common, from frugal to rich, and contained 200 special menus of the world's great men (Burbank, Edward VII, Steinmetz, etc.). He progressed from local radio to syndication to the networks. His earliest network sponsor was the Davis Baking Company. The most important ingredient of any recipe, he said, was love: ''You must go into the kitchen with love in your heart for what you are about to do, and for the people who will eat your cooking.''

MYSTERY IN THE AIR, two disparate crime series, linked only by title, aired in the summer slot for the vacationing *Abbott and Costello Show*.

BROADCAST HISTORY: July 5–Sept. 27, 1945, NBC. 30m, Thursdays at 10. Camel Cigarettes. CAST: Stephen Courtleigh as Stonewall Scott, detective. Joan Vitez as Dr. Alison. Ed Jerome as Dr. Dietrich. Geoffrey Bryant as Tex. DIRECTOR: Ken MacGregor. WRITER: Robert Newman.

July 3–Sept. 25, 1947, NBC. 30m, Thursdays at 10. Camel. CAST: Peter Lorre in dramatizations of literature's classics of mystery and suspense. Supporting roles from Hollywood radio actors: Agnes Moorehead, Peggy Webber, Russell Thorson, Barbara Eiler, John Brown, Howard Culver, Jane Morgan, Luis Van Rooten, Herb Butterfield, Ben Wright, etc. ANNOUNCER: Henry (Harry) Morgan; Michael Roy for Camel. ORCHESTRA: Paul Baron. DIRECTOR: Cal Kuhl.

No shows of the 1945 *Mystery In The Air* were available to audition at this writing. The 1947 edition, a showcase for Peter Lorre, survives in at least eight fine-sounding broadcasts. Titles included *The Telltale Heart, The Marvelous Barastro, The Lodger, The Horla, The Black Cat,* and *Crime and Punishment*.

Lorre delivered intense, supercharged performances of men tortured and driven by dark impulses. He stood alone at a center microphone, raving and wildly gesticulating, while supporting players worked at a second mike facing him. By the end of the half-hour, he was sweat-drenched and drained. Costar Peggy Webber recalled that once, in the heat of performance, Lorre threw his script into the air and watched helplessly as the pages fluttered to the stage. Some quick work by the cast and judicious ad-libbing by Lorre got them to the midway break, at which point the script was retrieved and put in order.

MYSTERY WITHOUT MURDER, mystery melodrama.

BROADCAST HISTORY: July 5–Aug. 23, 1947, NBC. 30m, Saturdays at 10. CAST: Luther Adler as Peter Gentle, a detective who followed a doctrine of nonviolence. Teri Keane as his secretary. PRODUCER: Joseph F. Mansfield. WRITER: Alfred Bester.

N

NAME THAT TUNE, musical quiz.

BROADCAST HISTORY: Dec. 20, 1952–April 10, 1953, NBC. 30m, Saturdays at 8:30 until Jan, then Fridays at 8:30. HOST: Red Benson, who quizzed contestants on melodies played by Harry Salter's Orchestra. A $500 jackpot was given for identifying three mystery tunes.

NATIONAL AMATEUR NIGHT, talent show.

BROADCAST HISTORY: Dec. 30, 1934–Feb. 16, 1936, CBS. 30m, Sundays at 6. Feen-A-Mint.

Feb. 23–Dec. 27, 1936, Mutual. 30m, Sundays at 6.

HOST: Ray Perkins. ORCHESTRA: Arnold Johnson.

National Amateur Night was the first coast-to-coast network amateur talent show, predating Major Edward Bowes and his more famous *Original Amateur Hour* by almost three months. Despite being first, *National* never generated a fraction of the power and popularity of the Bowes hour. Host Ray Perkins bluntly warned his listeners to expect the worst and delivered exactly that. Many contestants were so hapless that they were aired strictly for laughs, though they themselves may not have known it. Perkins was quick with wisecracks at the amateur's expense, and the truly atrocious were blared off by Arnold Johnson's orchestra with a fearsome blast in G major. This was the counterpart of Bowes's famed gong, and both were derived from the "hook" of vaudeville days, when wretched performers were physically yanked offstage.

But Perkins soon learned an odd fact about the unseen radio audience: it would not tolerate cruelty. "You can't make goats of amateur performers on a commercially sponsored show," he told *Radio Guide* in 1935. "Eddie Cantor, Ed Wynn, and Phil Baker can say or do anything they like to a paid stooge and get away with it. Listeners understand that that's what the stooge is getting paid for. But they demand that you play fair with the simon pures."

By 1936, Perkins was trying to project a kinder image. In one magazine report, he was depicted as the amateur's friend, giving lengthy backstage advice before the show went on. But by then the public had turned to Bowes, who at least put forth a kindly persona while setting up his amateurs for the same kind of ridicule. *National Amateur Night* was dropped abruptly at the end of 1936; the Johnson orchestra continued in the timeslot under the title *The 1937 Radio Show*.

THE NATIONAL BARN DANCE, country music entertainment.

BROADCAST HISTORY: April 19, 1924–Sept. 23, 1933, WLS, Chicago. Alka-Seltzer, from ca. 1929.

Sept. 30, 1933–Sept. 28, 1946, NBC; Blue Network until June 29, 1940, then Red. 60m, Saturday nights; 30m beginning July 4, 1942. Alka-Seltzer.

March 19, 1949–March 11, 1950, ABC. 30m, Saturdays at 10. Phillips Milk of Magnesia. (New

York dates: possibly in some markets ca. 1948.)
1950–60, WLW, Cincinnati.
1960–70, WGN, Chicago.
HOST: Hal O'Halloran (prenetwork); Joe Kelly from Sept. 30, 1933. REGULAR PERFORMERS: "Lulu Belle and Skyland Scotty" (Myrtle Cooper and Scott Wiseman); the Hoosier Hot Shots (Paul "Hezzie" Trietsch, Ken Trietsch, Gabe Ward, Frank Kettering); Luther Ossiebrink as Arkie, the Arkansas Woodchopper; Pat Barrett as Uncle Ezra P. Waters, "the old man with young ideas"; blind duo Mac and Bob (Lester McFarland and Robert Gardner), who sang and accompanied themselves on piano, guitar, and mandolin); the Cumberland Ridge Runners (Linda Parker, Karl Davis, Red Foley, Hartford Connecticut Taylor, Slim Miller, John Lair, and Hugh Cross); the Prairie Ramblers; the Maple City Four; the Tune Twisters; the Hill Toppers; Verne, Lee, and Mary (Verne and Leone Hassell and Evelyn Wood), billed as "one of the finest girl trios in radio"; the Vass Family (Emily, Sally, Virginia, Frank, and Louisa); tenor Henry Burr; dialect storyteller Malcolm Claire; Sally Foster ("little blue-eyed Sally"); Louise Massey and the Westerners (Curt Wellington, Milt Mabie, and Allen, Dot, and Louise Massey); the Dean Brothers; Lucille Long; Ted Morse and the Novelodeons; the Ranch Boys (Jack Ross, Joe Curley Bradley, and Hubert Shorty Carson); Pat Buttram, the croaky-voiced "sage of Winston County, Ala.," with tall tales; the Dinning Sisters (Jean, Ginger, and Lou), with sweet and swing tunes to contrast with the country mix; Lt. Cmdr. Eddie Peabody, the Navy's banjoist-in-residence; Joe Parsons (who sang sad numbers with his hat on); Grace Wilson, "the girl with a million friends"; Little Georgie Gobel; Bob Hastings, child singer; Connie and Jane; Tom and Don the Hayloft Harmony Boys; Captain Stubby and the Buccaneers; Bob Atcher; Bill O'Connor; Tiny Stokes; Red Blanchard; Skip Farrell; Florence Folsom; Danny Duncan; "harmonica virtuoso" Bob Ballantine; Irish singer Billy Murray; Jane Kaye; etc. AN-NOUNCER: Jack Holden. ORCHESTRA: Glenn Welty. PRODUCER: Walter Wade, with Peter Lund and Jack Frost. DIRECTOR: Bill Jones. THEME: *Hot Time in the Old Town Tonight*, sung as "Hey-hey-hey, the hayloft gang is here!"

The growth of *The National Barn Dance* in Chicago paralleled that of *Grand Ole Opry* in Nashville. Its popularity soon exceeded the ca-pacity of its studio at WLS, and in 1928 the show moved into the 1,200-seat Eighth Street Theater. It was a Saturday night mainstay: sixty minutes were aired on the network beginning in 1933, but locally the show often exceeded four hours.

It opened to the clang of cowbells and a fiddling rendition of *The Hayloft Gang Is Here*, followed by genial greetings from host Joe Kelly. "Hello, hello, hello, everybody everywhere!" Kelly would crow: "Well-well-welcome to your ole Alka-Seltzer *National Barn Dance*." The foot-stompin' country entertainment changed little over the years, generally following the pattern set in April 1924, when WLS (the call letters an oblique bit of promotion for its owner, Sears Roebuck, meaning "World's Largest Store") was in its first week on the air. The environment had changed—the performers had begun to dress for the huge audience at the Eighth Street Theater, wearing bluejeans and hayseed shirts, coveralls and pigtails—but the sounds that flooded the air continued to be genuine Americana.

For the privilege of seeing it, people paid 75 cents at the gate (35 cents for children), making *The National Barn Dance* one of the very few radio shows able to charge admission. The stage was dressed as well as the cast, the backdrop that of a barn loft with bales of hay for performers to sit on and a large haystack in the corner. The stars were people from the boondocks, players by ear, country yodelers who had learned their songs from some dimly remembered ancestry. This was not to say, all pointed out, that the talent was less than genuine. There was an 11-piece string orchestra in the mid-1930s, with two violinists from the Chicago Symphony, three violinists from the Metropolitan Opera, and a pianist, John Brown, who had played with the Chicago Civic Opera Company.

For much of its run, *The National Barn Dance* was neck-and-neck with *Grand Ole Opry* in the ratings battle for the country crown. The razor-thin point spread shifted from year to year, a safe assumption being that the same people who tuned in the *Barn Dance* at 9 o'clock stayed around for *Opry* at 10:30. The Crossley figures were impressive, showing a national audience in excess of ten million. But the numbers barely touched the shows' true strength—the plow-boys and whistle-stop people from the Deep South to the corn belt. As producer Walter Wade told

Newsweek in 1943, *The National Barn Dance* was rated like every other big network show, by surveys of metropolitan urban areas.

The good-natured personality displayed by Joe Kelly would later land him the quizmaster's job on *The Quiz Kids*. Others on hand for the network premiere were Lulu Belle and Skyland Scotty, the Hoosier Hot Shots, Luther Ossiebrink, and announcer Jack Holden. As "Arkie, the Arkansas Woodchopper," Ossiebrink called the square dances while the couples whirled on stage. There were no faked dances on *The National Barn Dance*. Lulu Belle, born Myrtle Cooper, became the show's lead female ballad singer and was voted "Queen of Radio" in a 1936 poll. Her partner in song was Scott Wiseman, born just 40 miles from her home in North Carolina. They met in Chicago, in a receptionist's office at NBC: their courtship and wedding was one of the show's early romantic high points.

The Hoosier Hot Shots was a novelty quartet: Paul "Hezzie" Trietsch was the "virtuoso of the washboard," wearing out a dozen such "instruments" during his years on the show. Comedic music was also achieved with bulb horns and a hand-pushed klaxon; but for serious business, Gabe Ward played a hot clarinet, Frank Kettering a bass, and Ken Trietsch a guitar. Pat Barrett played Uncle Ezra P. Waters in cotton chin whiskers, and became highly popular as a rustic comic; he was also heard on his own program, *Uncle Ezra's Radio Station*. Dialect comic Malcolm Claire "stormed through a lot of Negro dialogue" in 1933, according to *Radio Stars*. And Henry Burr, who had been one of the stellar singing stars for Victor records in the days of the gramophone, staged a remarkable comeback on the medium that had put him out of business, becoming on *Barn Dance* the "Bing Crosby of the grandma set."

THE NATIONAL FARM AND HOME HOUR, rustic variety.

BROADCAST HISTORY: 1928–29, KDKA, Pittsburgh.

Sept. 30, 1929–March 17, 1945, Blue Network/ABC. 60m (except: 45m the opening year and 1939–41; 30m beginning Feb. 1942), six a week, mostly at 12:30.

Sept. 15, 1945–Jan. 25, 1958, NBC. 30m, Saturdays at 1. Allis Chalmers.

HOST: Everett Mitchell. *Regulars*: "Mirandy of Persimmon Holler"; Helen Stevens Fisher, "the little lady of the house"; Jack Baus and the Cornbusters; the four singing Cadets; Raymond Edward Johnson, Don Ameche, etc., as the forest ranger in a series of Ranger dramatizations; H. R. Baukhage, news commentator. **ORCHESTRA:** Walter Blaufuss and the Homesteaders; also, Harry Kogen. **PRODUCERS:** Lloyd "Bucky" Harris; Herbert Lateau. *Director of Agriculture*: William E. Drips. **THEME:** *Stars and Stripes Forever.*

The National Farm and Home Hour was described as "the farmer's bulletin board," "a revue of rural America," and by half a dozen similar titles. It cut a broad swath, offering music, news, political discussions, farm tips and suggestions from experts, and live coverage of "the most spectacular happenings in agricultural America."

Microphones were strung at livestock expositions, harvest festivals, and country life meetings. A corn-husking became a major piece of excitement on the *Farm and Home Hour*: it "made a sport of a farm chore that previously was nothing short of drudgery." Hal Totten gave a running account, following the huskers down the field in a network mobile unit with an "ear-by-ear" description of the race. Everett Mitchell, the show's catalyst and guiding light across the decades, was stationed in a booth at the end of the field to provide color commentary. Mitchell's sunny disposition was the show's trademark: his opening catchphrase, "It's a bee-eeu-ti-ful day in Chicago!" was used for rain, snow or sunshine.

In the main, the purpose of the series was to improve the farmer's lot. Farmers were brought into personal contact with officials of the federal government, and had the opportunity to see politics firsthand. Officials came with advice from such agencies as the Crop Insurance Corporation, the Institute of American Meat Packers, the Soil Conservation Service, and the Farm Credit Administration. The show was produced in collaboration with the U.S. Department of Agriculture, with help from the 4-H Club, the American Farm Bureau, the National Grange, Future Farmers of America, and the Farmers Union.

NATURE OF THE ENEMY, wartime propaganda.

BROADCAST HISTORY: June 16–July 14, 1942, CBS. 30m, Tuesdays at 8:30. **PRODUCER-DIRECTOR:** Charles Vanda.

Nature of the Enemy, though it ran for only a month, was a staunch example of the nature of wartime broadcasting. It spotlighted each week a different Axis leader, dramatizing the record of his "cruelty and treachery." Among the subjects: Joseph Goebbels, "father of German lies," and Alfred Rosenberg, "Nazi philosopher" and proponent of "racial purity" as a German right of conquest.

NBC PRESENTS: SHORT STORY, dramatic anthology.

BROADCAST HISTORY: Feb. 21, 1951–May 30, 1952, NBC. 30m, Wednesdays at 10:30 until May 1951; Fridays at 8 until the summer break, July 13; returned Nov. 23, 1951, Fridays at 9:30. **CAST:** Hollywood radio stars: John Dehner, Georgia Ellis, Donald Woods, Lee Millar, John McGovern, Jeff Corey, Irene Tedrow, Jim Nusser, Margaret Brayton, Anne Whitfield, Isabel Jewell, Dawn Bender, Naomi Stevens, Marlene Aames, Noreen Gammill, Wally Maher, Shep Menken, Nestor Paiva, Paul Frees, Barney Phillips, etc. **ANNOUNCERS:** Don Stanley, John Wald. **WRITERS-ADAPTERS:** NBC staff writers including Claris A. Ross, George Lefferts, Vincent McConnor, and Ernest Kinoy. **DIRECTOR:** Andrew C. Love.

NBC Presents: Short Story offered modern stories by the masters of literature. It gained no real attention and no appreciable audience, coming so late in radio's history and so completely without budget or fanfare. It was a footnote in its time, but survives as a major radio accomplishment, proving conclusively that radio and the short story (though seldom united) were ideally suited to each other. Too often radio attempted the ridiculous (such as boiling down 1,000-page novels—an *Anna Karenina* or *Anthony Adverse*—into a single hour) while ignoring the 5,000-word masterpieces that packed all their power into one emotional charge.

The stories offered on this series were largely virgin territory, heard seldom before or since. It opened with *Fifty Grand*, by Hemingway, and the early run included stories by Conrad Aiken and F. Scott Fitzgerald. Shirley Jackson's *The*

Lottery was as chilling and understated as the published story, and William Faulkner's *Honor* told of a strange affair of the '20s set against the dangerous background of wingwalking by airshow daredevils. Other high spots were *Champion*, by Ring Lardner; *Leader of the People*, by John Steinbeck; *Pot of Gold*, by John Cheever; *The Wanderers*, by Kay Boyle; *The Rocket*, by Ray Bradbury; *The Hut*, by Geoffrey Household; *The Windfall*, by Erskine Caldwell; and *That Beautiful Summer at Newport*, Felicia Gizycka's look at "the jungle land of high society" through the eyes of a child.

THE NBC RADIO THEATER, dramatic anthologies: two distinct series, aired late in the history of network radio drama.

BROADCAST HISTORY: Sept. 18, 1955–March 11, 1956, NBC. 55m, Sundays at 5:05. **HOST:** Pat O'Brien, with light dramas, often romantic in nature.

April 27, 1959–Jan. 1, 1960, NBC. 55m, weekdays at 11:05 A.M. **CAST:** Rotating company of stars (Eddie Albert, Lee Bowman, Madeleine Carroll, Gloria DeHaven, and Celeste Holm) in stories of people in "climactic moments in their lives." **PRODUCER-DIRECTOR:** Himan Brown.

THE NBC UNIVERSITY THEATER, dramatic anthology; great novels, with programs for college credit.

BROADCAST HISTORY: July 30, 1948–Feb. 14, 1951, NBC. Mostly 60m with occasional 30m runs; most often heard Sundays, though frequently moved to weeknight timeslots. **CAST:** Initially well-known Hollywood stars (Beulah Bondi, Nigel Bruce, Brian Aherne, Angela Lansbury, Preston Foster, Dane Clark, Herbert Marshall, David Niven, etc.) supported by radio actors. Later, people from Radio Row in both leading and supporting roles: Paul Frees, John Dehner, Donald Morrison, Georgia Backus, John Beal, Byron Kane, Jack Edwards Jr., Sidney Miller, Rolfe Sedan, Lou Merrill, John Lake, Earl Lee, Russell Thorson, Theodore von Eltz, Alma Lawton, Lynn Allen, Gloria Ann Simpson, Noreen Gammill, Marvin Miller, William Lally, Doris Singleton, Bob Bruce, Shep Menken, Frank Gerstle, Sarajane Wells, Ramsey Hill, Robert North, Parley Baer, Don Diamond, Lou Krugman, James Nusser, Lawrence Dobkin, Jack Kruschen, Gail Bonney,

Ken Christy, Joe Forte, Lois Corbet, Jane Webb, Stanley Farrar, Whitfield Connor, Herbert Rawlinson, Alec Harford, Norma Varden, etc. **ANNOUNCER:** Don Stanley. **MUSIC:** Arranged by Albert Harris; conducted by Henry Russell. **DIRECTOR:** Andrew C. Love. **WRITERS:** (scripts prepared in New York and then sent to Hollywood): Claris A. Ross, Ernest Kinoy, George Lefferts, and Jack C. Wilson of the NBC writing staff. **SOUND EFFECTS:** Bob Holmes, Rod Sutton.

The NBC University Theater combined superb drama with college credit. Its productions were fully the equal of any commercial radio series and better than most, though it got stuck with the "education" stigma early in its run and never attained much more than its targeted academically motivated audience. It came out of the NBC Education Department, which had contacted several accredited universities with a "college by radio" plan in English and American literature. Though educators were at first skeptical, they saw merit in the idea when the early scripts were uniformly excellent.

A correspondence course was developed at the University of Louisville, the University of Tulsa, Washington State College, and others. Study guides were prepared to accompany the radio shows, and students were required to send in reports on what they had learned. This was daunting to a general public seeking nothing more than entertainment, but *University Theater* performed magnificently in that arena, offering stories not done to death elsewhere. It was critically acclaimed: "one of the most ambitious and artistically successful dramatic series on the air" was *Radio Life*'s assessment. The intermissions featured well-known authors or critics discussing the writer whose work was being performed that day—Granville Hicks, for example, speaking on Robert Penn Warren—and adding perspective to the book being dramatized. Among the speakers were James Hilton, Diana Trilling, Clifton Fadiman, Malcolm Cowley, and Dr. Harvey C. Webster of the University of Louisville.

Outstanding among the shows were *Noon Wine*, by Katherine Anne Porter; *Justice*, by John Galsworthy; *Of Human Bondage*, by W. Somerset Maugham; *The Short Happy Life of Francis Macomber*, by Ernest Hemingway; *A Passage to India*, by E. M. Forster; *After Many a Summer Dies the Swan*, by Aldous Huxley;

The Grapes of Wrath, by John Steinbeck; *The Red Badge of Courage*, by Stephen Crane; *The Age of Innocence*, by Edith Wharton; and *The Wild Palms*, by William Faulkner.

In October 1949, the word "University" was dropped for a time, in the hope that *NBC Theater* might sound less academic and lead to higher ratings. It didn't, but the show continued to be well received by its target audience. Libraries reported that dramatizations depleted their shelves of the original works, and the University of Louisville received 250 queries a day when the show was at its peak. The series is virtually complete on tape; superb sound quality ensures memorable listening almost half a century later.

THE NEBBS, situation comedy, based on the comic strip by Sol Hess.

BROADCAST HISTORY: Sept. 9, 1945–Jan. 13, 1946, Mutual. 30m, Sundays at 4:30. **CAST:** Gene and Kathleen Lockhart, with Ruth Perrott, Francis "Dink" Trout, and Dick Ryan.

NED JORDAN, SECRET AGENT, adventure melodrama.

BROADCAST HISTORY: 1938–42, WXYZ, Detroit, with a midwestern Mutual hookup from ca. 1939. 30m. **CAST:** Jack McCarthy as Ned Jordan, federal agent. Dick Osgood as Proctor, Jordan's contact in the "Federal Department" (translate: FBI). Shirley Squires as Judy. **ANNOUNCER:** Bob Hite.

The premise of *Ned Jordan* was colorful if simple. To all appearances, Jordan was a labor and accident detective for the Consolidated American Railroad. But this was a front, as he used the position to gather information on foreign agents and enemies of the government. His "office" was the "Federal Express," a modern coast-to-coast bullet of the rails, which was a haven for spies. Agent Proctor closed each case by braying, "This is an arrest! Uncle Sam wants *you!*"

NELLIE REVELL, talk and interviews.

BROADCAST HISTORY: March 9, 1934–Nov. 27, 1943, NBC. 15m, alternating at various times and under various titles (*Neighbor Nell*; *Nellie Revell Presents*; etc.) on Red and Blue Networks.

Themes: Love Thy Neighbor; Wait till the Sun Shines, Nellie.

Nellie Revell was a purveyor of optimism and hope, who became highly popular in the mid-1930s and in 1936–37 had three shows on the Blue Network (she dispensed hope on Sundays at 11:15 A.M., did interviews Tuesdays at 3; and had a variety series with the *Strolling Songsters* Fridays at 4:45).

THE NELSON EDDY SHOW, music.

BROADCAST HISTORY: Feb. 27–July 31, 1931, CBS. 30m, Fridays at 8:30. Congress Cigars.

In addition to the series bearing his name, Eddy was featured on *Inside Story of Names That Make News* (Jan. 27–June 9, 1933, CBS, 30m, Fridays at 9:30 for Socony Vacuum), with newsman Edwin C. Hill. Eddy sang, and Hill interviewed such newsmakers as Amelia Earhart, Babe Ruth, and polar explorer Richard E. Byrd. Eddy also appeared on *The Voice of Firestone* (1934–36), *Vicks Open House* (1936–37), *The Chase and Sanborn Hour* (1937–38), *The Electric Hour* (1944–46), *The Kraft Music Hall* (summers, 1947–49), and *The New Old Gold Show* (1942–43).

NELSON OLMSTED, reader and storyteller.

BROADCAST HISTORY: Many shows, often in brief runs, under many titles, including *The World's Greatest Short Stories* (NBC, 1939, 1944, 1947); *Dramas by Olmsted* (NBC, 1940–41); *Roy Shield and Company* (various NBC dates—Olmsted is known to have worked this music-variety show in 1942, and in 1951–52); *Stories by Olmsted* (NBC, 1947–48); *Story for Tonight* (NBC; summer 1947); *Story For Today* (ABC, 1948–49); and *Sleep No More*, an NBC spook show, ca. 1952–56.

Nelson Olmsted specialized in straight readings of such classic authors as Dickens and Poe, as well as some of the lesser lights. His offerings were laced with dramatic interpretation, often compared favorably with versions fully orchestrated and dramatized. He was, in short, a one-man show.

NEVER TOO OLD, interviews with senior citizens.

BROADCAST HISTORY: Feb. 5–April 27, 1945, Mutual. 15m, weekdays at 2:45. **HOST:** Art Baker.

Baker interviewed the elderly from all walks of life. Subjects were all at least 70 years old, and most were happy to tell of life in simpler times. There were veterans of the war with Spain, oldtime reporters from newspapers of the 1880s, people who were young when the century turned.

NEW FACES OF 1948, musical variety.

BROADCAST HISTORY: June 17–Sept. 23, 1948, NBC. 30m, Thursdays at 8:30. Substitution for *Burns and Allen*. General Foods. **CAST:** Eleanor Jones, Gene Martin, Jack Williams, June Carroll, Jay Presson, etc. **PRODUCER:** Leonard Sillman.

The idea of *New Faces* was to create a revue with original material and fresh performers. Producer Leonard Sillman had been trying the formula periodically on Broadway since 1934, when his *New Faces* discovered Henry Fonda and Imogene Coca. Subsequent editions were staged in 1936 and 1943, and the 1948 radio show was billed as the medium's "first real topical revue." Sillman assembled 11 relative newcomers, who became involved in all aspects of staging the show, writing original music, and then performing it on the air. A twelfth "new face" would be presented each week, someone such as Eddie Cantor's daughter Marilyn, who was not particularly well known. Sillman fancied himself a fair talent scout: it was, he said, "about the only talent I have." A new stage version a few years later may have proved the point: *New Faces of 1952* introduced Carol Lawrence and Eartha Kitt.

THE NEW OLD GOLD SHOW, comedy-variety; musical variety.

BROADCAST HISTORY: Nov. 3, 1941–April 24, 1942, Blue Network. 30m, Mondays at 7 until mid-Jan., then Fridays at 8. Old Gold Cigarettes. **HOST:** Herbert Marshall. **CAST:** Bert Wheeler and Hank Ladd, comedy duo; the Merry Macs ("three brothers and their tuneful girlfriend," Ted, Joe, and Judd McMichael, and Mary Lou Cook); Roy Chamberlain and the "Old Gold Rhythmaires"; Lucille Ball. **ANNOUNCER:** Ben Alexander. **PRODUCER:** Bob Brewster. **WRITER:** Sam Moore.

April 29, 1942–Jan. 20, 1943, CBS. 30m, Wednesdays at 8. Old Gold. **VOCALISTS:** baritone Nelson Eddy, soprano Nadine Conner. **ORCHESTRA:** Robert Armbruster.

Jan. 27, 1943–March 29, 1944, CBS. 30m, Wednesdays at 8. Old Gold. **COMIC:** Monty Woolley. **ORCHESTRA:** Sammy Kaye.

April 5–Oct. 18, 1944, CBS. 15m, Wednesdays at 8. Old Gold. **VOCALISTS:** Allan Jones, Betty Bonney. **ORCHESTRA:** Frankie Carle.

The initial *New Old Gold Hour* began as a vehicle for Herbert Marshall but developed into the earliest radio series for Lucille Ball. Marshall was considered the apex of suave sophistication and was thought to be a natural as host of a radio variety show. But Ball, who appeared twice in guest slots, stole the show and was added to the regular cast.

THE NEW THEATER, dramatic anthology.

BROADCAST HISTORY: June 3–Sept. 23, 1951, NBC. 60m, Sundays at 7:30. **HOSTESS:** Eva Le Gallienne. **CAST:** New York radio performers: Norman Rose, Wendell Holmes, Joan Alexander, etc. Some shows from California. **WRITERS:** Ernest Kinoy, etc. **DIRECTORS:** Edward King, New York; Andrew C. Love, Hollywood.

The New Theater was an attempt by NBC to revive its *University Theater*, but with an East Coast "Broadway" thrust. Its plays derived from current English and American literature and from modern classics. But the show had a stale "canned" sound to it. Hostess Eva Le Gallienne in New York introduced and commented on the plays, at least some of which were transcribed in Hollywood by Andrew C. Love and his *U-Theater* regulars. *Radio Life*, which had been charmed by the old *University* productions, was appalled at the "pretentious" nature of the revival. The show seemed to have "acquired stage yearnings" that worked to the detriment of radio, charged the critic; Le Gallienne's attempts to "cover all the finer points of plot that were not in the scripts" were "pitiful." Among the plays were Budd Schulberg's *The Disenchanted* and Aldous Huxley's *After Many a Summer Dies the Swan*.

NEWS BROADCASTS, radio journalism: often scheduled, sometimes erupting without warning; history as it happened.

The development of news broadcasting was—like the medium itself—rich with colorful pioneers, fraught with technical and political difficulty, and ultimately triumphant. Throughout the 1930s, radio wrestled for a share of a business that had long been the exclusive province of the print man. The newspapers waged a fight, short but fierce, shutting off the flow of news at the tap and driving radio to develop news-gathering capabilities of its own. This led to a thrilling new "on the spot" kind of journalism that came to full flower in the TV era, enabling vast audiences to see a war unfold, a president assassinated, and men take their first steps on the moon.

It began by most accounts Nov. 2, 1920, when KDKA signed on the air in Pittsburgh with election-day returns from the Harding-Cox presidential race. (There had been one prior newscast of note, Sept. 1, 1920, when an experimental station, later to become WWJ, Detroit, announced primary results to a city-wide audience estimated at less than 300.) The KDKA broadcast was accomplished by a four-man staff under the direction of Dr. Frank Conrad, who had been conducting shortwave experiments from his home for several years. Conrad's station, known as 8XK, was located in his garage in nearby Wilkinsburg. He had progressed to the point of airing recorded music, and was said to have coined the term "broadcasting."

Conrad was an engineer for Westinghouse, and when the company opened KDKA, he was a logical choice to run the station. His election-day broadcasts were chronicled in the national and local press, leading to a surge of interest and sales of receiving equipment. Other pioneering stations opened for business: WJZ, Newark, in 1921; WEAF, New York, in 1922. For much of the decade, "business" was defined in the creative sense, as commercial development was controversial. News broadcasting in this very early era was largely simple and localized. Announcers read headlines from newspapers, a fact that caused little worry in the print world, as radio was still considered a novelty with an uncertain future. Newspapers devoted generous space to radio as a news story in its own right, with technical developments and programming breakthroughs heralded on front pages. The first primitive network was established in late 1923, when WEAF was linked with WJAR in the distant city of Providence, R.I. This caused no notable apprehension in the newspaper world, and by 1925 newspapers were routinely printing radio schedules and logs as matters of general interest.

The honeymoon ended when proponents of public broadcasting began losing out to advocates of commercial airwaves. Radio was now a competitor as well as a news story: newspapers were in the uncomfortable (and some felt unreasonable) position of supplying their competition with product and helping with promotion as well. Radio news operations in the early network era were still barely functional. When William S. Paley took over a struggling network established in part by the Columbia Phonograph Company, his outlet had a lone teletype machine fed by United Press, one of the three major wire services that provided most national and international newspaper coverage.

But there was an excitement in the new industry that Paley would remember years later. For the first time, the voices of such presidential aspirants as Herbert Hoover and Al Smith could be sent into any living room with the apparatus to receive them. Microphones were set up for the 1928 political conventions, announcers giving running accounts of floor action. Even more impressive was the inauguration of Hoover, descriptions of the automobile trip for the swearing-in, and the inaugural ball. Radio captured all this with an immediacy that no newspaper could equal. It was clear that news was a vital part of the industry's future.

At Columbia, the first regular news broadcasts were established in 1929: five-minute summaries inserted into a half-hour morning show called *Something for Everyone*. It was still rip-and-read journalism, with United Press supplying the copy. Paley began to see that radio would never realize its rich potential unless the networks began developing an independent capability, with newsmen well rooted in journalistic principles. He hired H. V. Kaltenborn and William Wile, experienced print men, to do commentary and news of the day. Another veteran newspaperman, Cesar Saerchinger, was hired and sent to England. In December 1930, Paul White became the Columbia news editor. He too had come up through the print world, working at the *New York*

Evening Bulletin and later with United Press. Paley had made a vital decision at the outset: he would always "favor good newsmen over the pleasant speaking voice." He elevated the news operation to an equal position with entertainment and gave White the authority to interrupt regular programs, if breaking news warranted.

The Depression had settled in, and network radio was soaking up advertising dollars at a rate the newspapers found alarming. Increasing demands were imposed upon stations and networks using wire services: a strict embargo was placed on breaking news, meaning radio could not use wire bulletins until newspapers were off the presses and on the streets. Radio editors were galled. Many jumped the gun and deepened the rift with the press. In 1932, CBS ignored an embargo and broke the story of the Lindbergh baby kidnapping: the network then sent Boake Carter to the scene for live follow-up. The 1932 presidential election was also marked by widespread embargo-jumping. The results, showing Roosevelt a strong winner over Hoover, were on almost every radio station hours before newspapers could print them.

The feud became a war. "They don't speak to us and we don't answer" was the comic assessment by NBC news chief A. A. Schechter. Like his CBS counterpart, Schechter had come from a solid print background: he had been a reporter for the *Providence Journal*, the *New York World*, the Associated Press, and International News Service. He was the paragon of the never-say-can't scoop-chaser of the '20s, scoring many beats of world interest (he had once disguised himself as a waiter to get color on the wedding of Calvin Coolidge's son, after the president had strictly forbidden press coverage). In a real sense, the press had also trained its new enemy, and in Schechter and White had armed radio with two formidable soldiers.

The American Newspaper Publishers Association took up two avenues of attack: the wire services would be completely closed to radio, and radio schedules would be dropped from entertainment pages around the nation. At CBS, Paley threatened to create his own worldwide news operation if such a policy was implemented. NBC took a more cautious approach, preparing to cover the world by telephone in the event of a prolonged wire service lockout. This was to have far-reaching impact: while CBS opened bureaus and hired stringers around the globe, NBC ran up huge international telephone bills. It is no accident that most of the pictures taken of Schechter at the time catch him with a phone to his ear: he was the whole NBC news staff, and his telephone was his ticket around the world.

Schechter's biggest asset was Lowell Thomas, "a million-dollar voice" without "a nickel's worth of news." Schechter's job was to get Thomas some news to report without getting caught stealing from newspapers. Press associations had hired stenographers to monitor newscasts: in some places, radio news was airchecked, with the transcription intensely combed in the hunt for even the smallest bit of cribbing. To supplement his phone work, Schechter received by air copies of foreign newspapers. The *London Express* became a prime source, Schechter jokingly calling himself the charter member of "the Scissors-and-Pastepot Press Association." He cut, pasted, and rewrote, and each night handed Thomas a script that bore the illusion of freshness and an occasional scoop. The scoops (irony of ironies) were then cribbed by the Associated Press, to appear a day later in American newspapers. Schechter also learned to milk Thomas's vast national popularity: "I made the discovery that by saying I was talking for Lowell Thomas, I could get practically anyone on the telephone." If a court case had significant interest, Schechter called the judge, who was usually impressed. If Lowell Thomas called all the way from New York, the least a judge could do was talk to him. The judge then "became a reporter for NBC."

Meanwhile, at CBS, Paul White was building an organization that would take on an almost legendary reputation. He had been promoted to general manager of the new Columbia News Service, given Studio Nine as an operating base in New York, and charged with preparing three newscasts a day. A typical newscast, he estimated, ran five minutes and took up to four hours to compile. A brief thaw in the press-radio war, brought about by a compromise in late 1933, did little but break his stride.

After a year of intimidation, the press wanted to compromise. A meeting at the Hotel Biltmore Dec. 11, 1933, resulted in new standards between the antagonists. A Press-Radio Bureau was established to cull the wire services and feed bulletins to the networks. This came with a rigid set of rules. Radio could offer just two brief newscasts a day, at 9:30 A.M. and 9 P.M., well after newspapers were off the presses. It could sell no advertising for any "straight news" program, but was free to sell time for its analysts and commentators. No legmen with microphones would be sent to scenes of breaking news, and each newscast would end with notice that "complete details may be found in your daily newspaper." This was the last hurrah in the attempt by the press to control radio news.

Even before the Press-Radio Bureau was operational, the networks were disregarding its provisions. Radio had discovered its own capability. Microphones could now travel anywhere a man could walk. They could be attached to portable transmitters, which in effect were miniature broadcasting stations. A reporter could walk into an inferno with a microphone, if the engineer carrying the "suitcase" would go with him. These portables could transmit without wires to a mobile unit, which could then call in the nearest network affiliate. The mobile units were designed for fast-and-furious radio work. By the mid-1930s they were capable of speeds of 70 miles an hour; they had wide front seats that could hold four men, and fold-down tables that contained typewriters and microphones. The transmitting range was about 150 miles when parked and 50 miles on the road, so the network was seldom out of touch with its men in the field. Even in a foreign country, there was usually a friendly radio station nearby, which could transfer a broadcast from the field to New York. In 1936, H. V. Kaltenborn gave CBS listeners the first running account of war. Hiding in a haystack in Spain, Kaltenborn broadcast with gunfire in the background.

White had hired Edward R. Murrow in 1935; in 1937, Murrow was sent to London to direct CBS European operations. Murrow hired William L. Shirer, and Thomas Grandin was engaged as the CBS man in Paris. White established a shortwave "cue channel," a closed circuit that enabled him to talk with his reporters in London and Paris simultaneously and set up cues between reporters thousands of miles apart. In New York, CBS had Bob Trout, one of those rare talents who could talk without a script for as long as a situation demanded. Paley believed that Trout could talk for two hours, if necessary: Kaltenborn, he wrote, could do the same—"then comment on and analyze what he had just said.'' On March 13, 1938, CBS began its *European Roundup*, with Bob Trout in New York becoming, perhaps, ''the first anchorman in the profession.''

CBS was getting its ducks in a row for the biggest news story in history, World War II. NBC had continued riding on Schechter's aggressive creativity, and had had one stroke of luck that resulted in an immortal broadcast. On May 6, 1937, announcer Herb Morrison and engineer Charles Nehlsen were sent by WLS, the NBC affiliate in Chicago, to cover the arrival of the German airship *Hindenburg* at Lakehurst, N.J. They were not expected to cover the event live: they were equipped with recording equipment to test the feasibility of transcribing an event and shipping it by air to Chicago for later broadcast (it was also thought that the noises of a blimp mooring might add something to the station's sound effects department). But just as Morrison was describing a letter-perfect mooring, the *Hindenburg* exploded. ''It's burst into flames!'' he shouted suddenly. ''Get out of the way! Get this, Charley! . . . Get out of the way, please! She's bursting into flames! This is terrible! This is one of the worst catastrophes in the world! The flames are shooting five hundred feet up into the sky!'' Then, his voice breaking into sobs, Morrison described radio's first on-the-scene disaster. ''Oh, the humanity! Those passengers . . . there's not a chance that any of them could have escaped.'' But there were survivors, and that night NBC broke its rule against broadcasting prerecorded transcriptions and aired the Morrison report to the nation.

In 1939 came the *Squalus* disaster, when a submarine went down near Portsmouth, N.H., and failed to resurface. Radio broke the news and was instrumental in coordinating the rescue efforts. A breaking story could now be on the air less than 30 seconds after the wire-machine bells went off. The era of press domination slipped into history.

By late 1939, with England and Germany at war, both networks faced the job of putting together at least a dozen news reports a day. There was a grown-up sound to network radio news. Accuracy and objectivity were the professional cornerstones: fairness was another, with a clear understanding for the need to separate commentaries from hard news. Vitriol gave way to calm voices; the duty to be dependable was paramount. Radio's ability to broadcast news as it happened was fraught with pitfalls and dangers. A newspaper could retract its mistakes with a well-conceived statement, composed in the luxury of time. But ''the spoken word is impossible to confine,'' said *Radio Mirror*; ''a radio report comes straight from mouth to ear, and it can be heard only once. For some strange reason it is easier to shriek untruths over the radio, and make them sound plausible, than to print these same untruths in a newspaper.'' The passion to be first was countered by the need to be prudent. With the war just days old, the networks began informing their listeners about censorship and the need for it. What they were hearing from distant foreign capitals was news that had been cleared by the warring governments.

In September 1939, NBC was still relying heavily upon wire reports from Europe, and on Abe Schechter's magic with the telephone. Max Jordan was installed in Berlin; Fred Bate was in London; and Pierre Van Passan joined Dorothy Thompson with commentary in New York. Thompson sounded, according to *Time*, like she was ''itching to get her fingers in Hitler's hair.'' The New York *Daily News* branded her commentary ''hysterical,'' and couldn't help wishing that her 10-year-old son was 19, a transition that might help calm her rhetoric. At CBS, Murrow had hired Eric Sevareid to help cover Paris; in New York, Elmer Davis was hired to replace H. V. Kaltenborn, who left for London. Albert Warner was the CBS man in Washington, and W. R. Willis was the network's Tokyo correspondent. Mutual, though struggling with a much smaller budget than the two main networks, had John Steele in London, Sigrid Schultz in Berlin, Waverley Root in Paris, Fulton Lewis Jr. in Washington, and Raymond Gram Swing in New York.

NBC, still playing catch-up, continued getting major stories. In December 1939, when three British cruisers chased the German battleship *Graf Spee* into Uruguay, NBC correspondent James Bowen was standing on the Montevideo docks with a portable microphone and a clear shortwave channel to New York. The situation was tense and uncertain: the *Graf Spee*, which had preyed on British shipping lanes, was battered by shellfire, and the British lay in wait off the coast. Rumors of a German rescue effort were rife; speculation was high as to what neutral Uruguay might do. International law seemed to demand that the warship put to sea as soon as repairs could be made, and for three days it hung in limbo. Just before dusk on Dec. 17, Bowen informed New York on the closed circuit that the *Graf Spee* looked ready to leave. NBC replied that everything was ready—"as soon as something happens, you'll be on the air." Bowen watched as the ship moved slowly through the channel to Buenos Aires. Men seemed to be leaving, he told New York: "Something's going on, but we can't tell what yet." Then he shouted, "Give me the air, quick! She's exploded!" The Germans had blown up their ship, and NBC had a firsthand account just half a minute after the explosion.

With the coming of war, the voices of newscasters became as well known as those of Rudy Vallee and Bob Hope. The Hoosier twang of Elmer Davis contrasted with the clipped nononsense of William L. Shirer, who followed the Nazis into Paris. In London, Murrow described preparations for the expected German invasion. But Hitler opted for bombing raids, and Murrow's reports of the city beseiged became instant classics. "This—is London," he began each day, and as he took his microphone to the rooftops to capture the sounds of the Blitz, the three words were absorbed into popular American folklore. Murrow's "orchestrated hell" broadcast in December 1943 was published in newspapers and lauded as literature. He described a harrowing bombing raid on Berlin—dodging enemy searchlights, maneuvering through flack, and blasting the German capital—in the language of a poet (*the small incendiaries were going down like a fistful of rice thrown on a piece of black velvet . . . the cookies, the 4000-pound high explosives, were bursting below like great sunflowers gone mad*).

At home, Roosevelt hinted that he would (or perhaps would not) break precedent and run for a third term. Through his Fireside Chats, the president had become one of the most effective commentators on the air. He was nominated, and accepted, in July 1940, with radio microphones carrying it all. But through the summer of 1940, the focus remained on London. On Aug. 12 and 13, Sevareid described the fiercest battles yet seen in the air war—more than 100 British and German planes in combat over London. On Aug.

19, Murrow reported that all of England had become a defense area, and he told of the sometimes rustic preparations of people in the streets. The Hitler invasion was still expected: Sevareid detailed a "calm before the storm" atmosphere on Aug. 24, the air raids having slacked off and the people settled down to wait. But when it broke, the storm took the form of new air raids, as reported Aug. 26.

The RAF retaliated, penetrating to Berlin. A report by Larry Lesueur from London was dramatically heightened on *The CBS Morning News* Aug. 31, 1940, when an air raid siren went off as he was speaking. But as autumn came and the invasion failed to materialize, radio focused on other fronts: the Far East, the deserts of Africa. Defense efforts in the United States were accelerated and covered, often in new and dramatic ways. On Oct. 29, 1940, President Roosevelt opened the selective service lottery, beginning a new era of conscription. As the first number was called, a woman was clearly heard screaming on the Mutual air: the president had drawn her son's number. One of the Mutual announcers then heard his number read out. On March 7, 1941, CBS West carried a 30-minute demonstration program on a test blackout of Seattle, with microphones stationed throughout the city to capture reaction and atmosphere.

Then, on Dec. 7, 1941, CBS listeners heard John Daly interrupt regular programming to announce that the Japanese had attacked Pearl Harbor. H. V. Kaltenborn, who had left Columbia, was on the air at NBC. The next day, Roosevelt went before a joint session of Congress to ask for a declaration of war, and all networks followed the buildup, the speech, the vote, and the aftermath. The president held a pool-fed Fireside Chat Dec. 9, and the congressional declaration against Germany and Italy on Dec. 11 was handled by the networks as a brief matter of fact.

War news became a fact of life. In addition to regularly scheduled commentaries and sudden bulletins, the networks made their correspondents around the world available for five-and ten-minute newscasts at various time of the day. *The CBS World News Roundup*, begun in 1939 as an 8 A.M. daily quarter-hour, used frequent shortwave remotes from Murrow, Lesueur, Shirer, and others. In the evening, CBS had *The World Today* (6:45 P.M., 1940–46, sponsored in part by General Electic). There were *News*

Roundup shows on Mutual (8 A.M., 1939–43), NBC (8 A.M., 1940–43), and the Blue Network (8 A.M., 1941–43). The networks also ran weekly news summaries on Sundays, with live developments integrated into half-hour timeslots. CBS had *World News Today* (Sundays at 2:30, 1942–45, for Admiral Radios); NBC offered *World Front* (Sundays at noon, 1944–48, for Bunte Candy); and the Blue Network had its *Weekly War Journal* (Sundays at noon, 1943–45), which became *This Week Around the World* as the network became ABC in 1945, and ran at various times Sundays until 1954.

As D-Day approached, radio prepared to give its listeners "a fireside seat at the most tragic and biggest military show in history" (*Radio Life*). At CBS, Paul White wrote a memo to his staff, reminding everyone that the audience was made up of the "mothers, fathers, wives and sweethearts of the men participating in this story." His reporters should "always aim for their confidence, and remember that winning the war is a hell of a lot more important than covering it." Stanley Richardson headed the invasion staff at NBC. Newsrooms were placed on 24-hour schedules, and pooling arrangements were coordinated through the BBC in London. Murrow was still in England for CBS, along with Charles Collingwood, Larry Lesueur, Bill Downs, Charles Shaw, and Richard C. Hottelet. In New York were reporters Bob Trout, William L. Shirer, John Daly, Everett Holles, Quincy Howe, and Douglas Edwards. Quentin Reynolds had also joined CBS: he and Maj. George Fielding Eliot were to analyze and interpret operations as they unfolded. At NBC, William Brooks was now the news director: his front-liners in England included John MacVane, David Anderson, Merrill Mueller, Don Hollenbeck, Edwin Haaker, W. W. Chaplin, George Y. Wheeler, and John Vandercook. Max Hill was in Italy; Robert Magidoff in Russia. The NBC effort in New York was handled by Lowell Thomas, H. V. Kaltenborn, and Robert St. John; in Washington by Richard Harkness, Morgan Beatty, William McAndrew, Leif Eid, and Capt. Thomas Knode. Mutual's coverage was headed by John Steele: reporters in London were Arthur Mann, Larry Meier, Tom Wolfe, and John Thompson; in Italy, Seymour Korman; in Cairo, Leslie Nichols; in New York, Cecil Brown, Boake Carter, Henry Gladstone, Royal Arch Gunnison, Frank Sin-

giser, Gabriel Heatter, and Leo Cherne, who would cover the impact of the invasion on the home front; and in Washington, Walter Compton and Fulton Lewis Jr. On the Blue Network, G. W. Johnstone was news director; George Hicks was in London, with Arthur Feldman, Thomas Grandin, and Ted Malone; Gordon Fraser and Donald Coe were in Naples; Fred Lee was in Cairo.

Radio had come of age.

Roll Call
Newscasters or programs with regular timeslots on network radio, ca. 1930–56.

ADELA ROGERS ST. JOHNS, 1936–37, NBC. 15m, three a week (later five) at 9:45 A.M. St. Johns was primarily a novelist and magazine reporter, but did a personality-oriented commentary for one season.

ALBERT WARNER, 1949–50, ABC. 15m, Saturdays at 6. Commentary and news. Warner joined ABC after serving with CBS during World War II.

ALEX DREIER, NBC newsman and commentator, who joined the network in 1941 while covering Berlin for United Press. He encountered increasing hostility from German officials and was placed under surveillance by the Gestapo during his year in Berlin. He left the city Dec. 6, 1941, one day before the Japanese attack on Pearl Harbor drew the United States into the war. Regular timeslots:

1942–43, NBC. 15m, Saturdays at 5:45. His partner in commentary was Abo Hosiosky, a Latvian who had taught law in Berlin and had also escaped the Nazis.

1944–45, NBC. 15m, Saturdays at 10:45 A.M.

1951–56, NBC. 15m, weekdays at 8 A.M. Skelly Oil.

1953–56, NBC. 15m, weekdays at 7. Co-op sponsorship.

ALLAN JACKSON, 1950–56, CBS. 15m, weekdays at 6. Metropolitan Life.

ANN HARD, 1932–33, NBC. 15m, weekdays at 9:15 A.M.

ARTHUR GAETH, 1944–45, Mutual, 15m, weekdays at 11 A.M.; 1946–47, Mutual, 15m, weekdays at 10 A.M.; 1947–48, Mutual, 15m, Wednesdays at 7:30; 1948–49, ABC, 15m, Mondays at 10.

ARTHUR HALE, Mutual newsman and commentator, often heard under the title *Confidentially Yours.*

1939–40, Mutual. 15m, Sundays at 9:30; also twice a week at 9.

1940–47, Mutual. 15m, two and sometimes three a week at 7:30. Richfield Oil.

BEN ADAMS, 1932–33, Blue Network. 15m, Mondays at 2:30. *Next Week's News.*

BERNARDINE FLYNN, the remarkable Sade of Paul Rhymer's landmark comedy series, *Vic and Sade,* who held a *News for Women* series, 1943–45, on CBS, 15m, weekdays at 1:30. Procter & Gamble.

BILL CUNNINGHAM, 1944–56, Mutual. 15m, Sundays at 2:30, 1944–52; at 12:30, 1952–56.

BOAKE CARTER, one of the earliest and strongest commentators of network radio. Carter was born in Russia to British parents; he came to the United States in 1920 and took his citizenship 13 years later. Like most radio commentators, he came from the print world, learning the news business on newspapers in London and Philadelphia. In 1930, he was sent by WCAU radio in Philadelphia to cover a rugby game, and soon he was doing radio reports of many kinds.

His rise to national prominence began in March 1932, when CBS asked WCAU, its affiliate, to borrow a mobile unit to cover the kidnapping of the Lindbergh baby. The network got Carter in the bargain. Carter's style was distinctive: his voice was robust and British, creating an image later described as "Bond Street" and "Anthony Edenish," which Americans found fascinating. His popularity was established almost overnight. Carter did constant reports and updates until the child's body was found. This led directly to his own regular network commentary for Philco Radios. He went where angels had long feared to tread, blending news with staunch commentary that became ever more stinging. He viewed his calling as an "editorial page of the air," a revival of the "old-time, red-hot, fighting editorials" of the turn-of-the-century newspaper. He ran afoul of CBS by plugging an NBC show. He accused New Jersey politicians of "playing political checkers" with the life of Bruno Richard Hauptmann, later executed in the Lindbergh case, and was sued for libel by the governor of that state.

Carter denounced labor's CIO, which promptly threw a picket line around WCAU, still his studio of origin. Philco gave him its "unwavering support," and his tone grew harsher. He "moved from lukewarm support of the New Deal to a one-man fort from which he bombarded Washington and anything or anybody who walked into the firing zone" (*Radio Guide*). His tenure for Philco was solid through most of the 1930s. After it ended, in 1938, he went on a speaking tour. He drew huge crowds, charging that "the great white father in Washington" had pulled strings, using the influence of a White House press secretary with a CBS lobbyist to have him fired. He returned to the air in the 1940s; though he never regained the power of his best years, he remained one of the best-known voices of World War II. His salutation was usually " 'Ello, everyone," his closing a bright "Cherrio."

Jan. 2, 1933–Feb. 18, 1938, CBS. 15m, weekdays at 7:45. Philco.

Feb. 28–Aug. 26, 1938, CBS. 15m, weekdays at 6:30. Post Toasties, Huskies.

Nov. 16, 1940–Nov. 24, 1944, Mutual. 15m, three a week at 8:30 for United Air Lines, 1940–41; three a week at 4:45 for Land of Lakes, 1941–42; three a week at noon for Land of Lakes 1942–43; weekdays at noon for Chef Boyardee, 1943–44.

BOB CONSIDINE, primarily a print man but worked in radio news as early as 1932, broadcasting nightly for the *Washington Post.* Also: 1952–56, NBC. 15m, Sundays at 3:30, 1952–53; at 6, 1953–54; at 6:30, 1954–56. Mutual of Omaha.

BOB TROUT, CBS newsman and occasional commentator, said to be the most extraordinary ad-libber on the air. Trout joined WJSV, Washington, in 1931 and came to CBS Oct. 20, 1932, when his station became an affiliate. Throughout his career, Trout was one of radio's most dependable reporters. He was billed as Columbia's "presidential announcer," assigned during the first term to introduce Roosevelt's talks to the nation. Roosevelt was reportedly so taken with Trout's ability to improvise that he occasionally delayed his speech for a moment to see how Trout would cover himself.

In 1941, he relieved Edward R. Murrow for a time in the CBS London bureau. Returning home, he conducted epic vigils on D-Day (on the air 35 times in one 24-hour stint) and on V-E and V-J Days. He had the honor of speaking the most coveted line of the war—"This, ladies and gentlemen, is the end of the Second World War." Of his ability to improvise, he once wrote: "You just start talking and you keep talking until the second-hand tells you it's all over. Then you give the cue, like this—Bob Trout speaking. . . . this is the Columbia Broadcasting System."

Jan. 17–April 18, 1937, CBS. 15m, Sundays at 1:45. *History Behind the Headlines.*

Oct. 10, 1937–Dec. 25, 1938, CBS. 30m, Sundays at 10:30. *Headlines and Bylines*, with Trout, H. V. Kaltenborn, etc.

Sept. 5, 1938–May 12, 1939, CBS. 15m, weekdays at 6:30.

April 1, 1946–Sept. 19, 1947, CBS. 15m, weekdays at 6:45. *The News till Now.* Campbell Soups.

1952–53, CBS. 15m, weeknights at 10:30, with Bob Trout and Cedric Adams. Ford Motors.

CAL TINNEY, self-styled "barnyard artist," "hog editor," and dispenser of homespun humor in the form of a newscast. Tinney was sometimes compared to Will Rogers: he grew up in Oklahoma and was first heard on KVOO, Tulsa, in 1932, when he went on the air to advertise a newspaper he was editing. The paper expired, but Tinney found a new career. In New York, he gained a reputation as a talker on such shows as the Maxwell House *Show Boat* and *Vanity Fair.* He began his newscast in Tulsa in 1940; heavy mail response brought it to Mutual, which carried it on 74 outlets beginning Aug. 4, 1941. Although Tinney's humor was best remembered, his commentary was often pointed and hard. He took on Westbrook Pegler in Charlie Chaplin's defense, calling Pegler's story on Chaplin "one of the unfairest, meanest little pieces of journalism in our time."

1941–44, Mutual. 15m, three a week at 8. Often called *Sizing Up the News.* Bayuk Cigars, makers of Phillies.

1945–46, ABC. 15m, weekdays at 6:45, ending March 8, 1946.

1952–53, ABC. 25m, weekdays at 4, last heard May 29, 1953. General Mills.

CECIL BROWN, CBS correspondent during early World War II; Mutual commentator thereafter. Brown worked for various newspapers and wire services before going to Europe in 1937 to freelance. He joined CBS in January 1940, embarking on a career of high adventure.

Thrown out of Rome by the Fascists, he sub-

sequently filed reports from Yugoslavia, Turkey, Syria, Cairo, and Singapore. He was thought killed when the British battle cruiser *Repulse* was sunk, but survived to file a vivid account. His experiences were told in a book, *Suez to Singapore*, published in 1942. In June that year he was in New York, working the CBS timeslot recently vacated by Elmer Davis. On Feb. 7, 1944, he joined Mutual.

1944–56, Mutual. 15m, three a week at 8 for Bayuk Cigars (1944–45), taking over the *Sizing Up the News* slot formerly held by Cal Tinney; five a week at 11 A.M. (1945–47); five a week at 10 A.M. (1947–56) with co-op advertising. Also: 1953–54, 15m, Sundays at 6:30 for Farm Mutual.

CEDRIC FOSTER, Mutual commentator, first heard Jan. 6, 1940, and continuing for more than 15 years; 15m, five a week at 2 (1940–47) for Employers Insurance; weekdays at 1 thereafter, co-op sponsorship.

CESAR SAERCHINGER, the first CBS European reporter (1930–37) and an NBC commentator (1938–44). Billed on NBC as *Behind the Headlines*, he was heard 15m, Fridays at 10:45 in 1938–39; at 6, 1940–41; Sundays at 11:15, 1941–42; at 11, 1942–43; and Saturdays at 5:30, 1943–44.

CHARLES COLLINGWOOD, CBS war correspondent and postwar commentator. Collingwood was hired by Edward R. Murrow in March 1941; he covered North Africa for CBS, heard daily at 8 A.M. and 6:45 P.M. in 1942. He scored notable scoops by an almost uncanny ability to "catch the turn of events" just before they broke. He won a Peabody Award in 1943, had brief commentary stints in 1946 and 1948, and was heard 15m, Sundays at 1 (later at 12:45) from 1949 until 1952.

CHET HUNTLEY, newscaster and special events man for CBS beginning in the late 1930s and on through the 1940s, specializing in features and stunts (a broadcast from a town destroyed by forest fire; a man walking across a bed of coals, etc). Huntley joined ABC–Los Angeles in 1951 and NBC–New York in 1955. His *Huntley-Brinkley Report*, with newsman David Brinkley, was the most popular TV newscast of its time.

DAVID LAWRENCE, early NBC commentator, 15m, Sundays at 9, 1927–32; at 10:15, 1932–33. *Our*

Government. Also: April 1–Dec. 30, 1951, 15m, Sundays at 3:30.

DON GARDINER, ABC, long-running newscast, often aired Sundays as *Monday Morning Headlines.* 15m timeslots: 1944–47, Sundays at 7:15 for Serutan and Air Wick. Then 1947–53, Sundays at 6: 15 for Air Wick (1947–51), Seaman (1951–52), and Old Gold (1952–53). Then 1953–56, Sundays at 6 for Kent Cigarettes. Concurrent Saturday broadcasts, 1948–49, 11:30 A.M. for Air Wick, titled *Tomorrow's Headlines.*

DOROTHY THOMPSON, crusading commentator whose radio work supplemented her widely read "On the Record" newspaper column to make her one of the most controversial news personalities of two decades. She became an international celebrity in 1934 after a series of magazine articles got her thrown out of Germany by Hitler. Her tirades against Hitler grew so heated that her sponsor, Pall Mall Cigarettes, was uncomfortable, and her NBC contract was not renewed when it expired in May 1938. She was heard, in addition to the following timeslots, as commentator on Phil Spitalny's *Hour of Charm* for a season (NBC, Mondays at 9, 1938–39).

1936–38, NBC, both networks at various times; 15m, initially Mondays at 7:15 on the Blue; 1937–38, Red Network, Fridays at 10:45, heard as *People in the News* and joined by a series of the same title on the Blue Network, Tuesdays at 7:30, in early 1938. Pall Mall.

1940–41, Mutual. 15m, Sundays at 8:45.

1942–45, Blue. 15m, Sundays at various times, marked by frequent absences of weeks or months. Triamount.

1945, Mutual. Live shortwave commentaries from Europe.

DOUGLAS EDWARDS, CBS newsman, 1942–88; worked prior to network at WSB, Atlanta, and WXYZ, Detroit. Edwards was a wartime regular on *The World Today,* describing himself as an "understudy" to John Daly. He worked in London with Edward R. Murrow and in the network's Paris bureau. In 1948, he began airing newscasts within the soap opera *Wendy Warren and the News*; his 13-year tenure as anchorman on *The CBS Evening News* also began that year. He was anchorman of *The World Tonight,* again on CBS Radio, from 1966 until his retirement.

DREW PEARSON, investigative reporter, whose long career in radio was part of a longer career in newspapers. Pearson and his partner, Robert Allen, were tenacious diggers, turning up many scoops that their respective newspapers would not publish (in the early 1930s Allen was with the *Christian Science Monitor* and Pearson the *Baltimore Sun*). Convinced that American newspapers were swayed by economic greed, they published the best of their stories in a book, *Washington Merry-Go-Round.* This was issued anonymously in 1932, but its authors were revealed and fired from their jobs. Thus began their collaboration on the "Merry-Go-Round" column, syndicated by United Features, which led naturally to radio. Pearson and Allen discontinued their partnership in 1941; Allen went to war while Pearson continued his newspaper and radio work. Allen returned from the war (missing an arm) in 1945, but he and Pearson had a falling-out and never resumed their partnership.

1935–36, Mutual. Pearson and Allen, 15m, twice a week at 7: 45.

1939–40, Mutual. Pearson and Allen, 30m of music and news, Sundays at 6. *Listen, America,* first heard Oct. 22. Music by Erno Rapee.

1941–53, Blue Network/ABC. Pearson alone, 15m, Sundays at 6:30, 1941–42; at 7 as *Drew Pearson Comments,* 1942–45; at 7, 1945–47, then at 6, final broadcast March 29, 1953. Serutan, 1941–44; Nutrex, 1944–45; Lee Hats, 1945–49; Adam Hats, 1949–51; Carter Products for Serutan, 1951–53.

EARL GODWIN, dubbed "the Earl of Godwin" by President Roosevelt and given a seat near the presidential desk at White House press conferences. Godwin was so broken up at Roosevelt's death that fellow ABC newsman H. R. Baukhage had to finish his broadcast. His closing line was always "God bless you one and all."

1942–44, Blue Network. 15m, nightly at 8. *Watch the World Go By.* Ford Motors.

1944–49, ABC. Mostly weekly; 15m, Thursdays at 8 for Hastings, 1944–45; Thursdays at 8: 15 for Northwestern Insurance, 1945–46; twice a week at 10:30, 1947–48; Tuesdays at 8:30, 1948–49.

EDWARD R. MURROW, CBS war correspondent and commentator, and possibly the most famous voice of World War II. Born in 1908, Murrow had almost no journalistic experience when he joined

CBS in 1935. For two years he was "director of talks," a job much closer to public relations than to news. His voice was a great natural asset that almost everyone seemed to have overlooked—"a coppery baritone charged with authority," as the *Saturday Evening Post* would call it.

In 1937, Murrow was in New Orleans attending a National Education Association meeting when a CBS executive called to ask if he would accept a position in Europe. This, he would say, "was the most important decision of my life . . . it gave me a front-row seat for some of the greatest news events in history." Arriving in London, he hired newspaperman William L. Shirer to "cover the continent," though the job of both men continued to be in the production of CBS educational and entertainment shows.

This all changed in March 1938. Murrow was in Warsaw working up a segment for *The American School of the Air* when Shirer called him from Austria with news of Hitler's invasion. Murrow sent Shirer to broadcast the story from London while he chartered a 27-seat Lufthansa transport and flew to Vienna to cover subsequent developments himself. There on the night of March 12, 1938—after coordinating technical difficulties with Shirer in London and with CBS in New York—Murrow was heard for the first time. For ten days he broadcast from Austria, launching a career that would become synonymous with the highest ideals in the profession.

Returning to London, he was instructed to build a staff and hired Eric Sevareid, Larry Lesueur, Charles Collingwood, Howard K. Smith, Bill Downs, Winston Burdette, Farnsworth Fowle, and Cecil Brown. His own broadcasts continued without letup. He covered the British capital through most of the Blitz, returning to the United States in 1941 for a brief vacation. In England, his office was bombed three times. His reports, prefaced by the dramatic announcement "This . . . is London," were complied at great personal risk, with Murrow often stationing himself on the rooftop of the broadcasting building during the most furious German bombardment. He flew two dozen combat missions with Allied air forces, overriding the objections of CBS boss William S. Paley.

His career as a commentator began in 1942, though in the main this was straight reportage. Murrow was most at home reporting the opinions of others: when he had a point to make, his style was to highlight it in a factual framework. At this

he was the master, knowing at once where the emotional freight of a given story was to be found, understanding that the surest test of his own truth lay in the strongest opposing voice. At the end of the war he toured Buchenwald, the notorious German concentration camp. His report on the BBC was carried on the front pages of London newspapers.

In 1946, having returned to New York, he became a CBS vice president and the network's director of public affairs. But the front office did not suit him, and he returned to broadcasting with a weekday news show in 1947. In 1948, with Fred Friendly, he recorded the first of his historical albums, *I Can Hear It Now*, for Columbia Records; this led to the radio series *Hear It Now*, which led to the TV series *See It Now*. Murrow also began, on Sept. 24, 1951, a series of five-minute philosophical summaries with noted personages, titled *This I Believe*. His interview series, *Person to Person*, premiered on CBS-TV Oct. 2, 1953, and ran, with Murrow, until June 26, 1959 (another two seasons with Charles Collingwood). On radio, his nightly newscasts continued until 1959, when he left CBS for a year-long sabbatical. His radio work in the 1950s was highlighted by his stand against Communist-hunting Sen. Joseph McCarthy. In 1961, President John F. Kennedy appointed him to head the U.S. Information Agency, where he stayed until 1964.

Murrow died in 1965.

1942–44, CBS. 15m, Sundays at 6 for International Silver the first year; Sundays at 11:30, sustained, in 1943–44, a London report. Also heard almost daily on CBS news reports.

Sept. 29, 1947–June 26, 1959, CBS. 15m, weeknights at 7:45. *Edward R. Murrow and the News*. Campbell Soups, 1947–50; Amoco, 1953–54; multiple sponsorship in other years.

EDWARD TOMLINSON, Blue Network commentator on Latin American affairs. Tomlinson was tireless in his advocacy of South America's importance to the United States: his strongest message was that the United States should scrap its "superiority complex" and learn about the strengths of its neighbors.

1935–1936, Blue Network. 30m, Fridays at 10:30, premiering Dec. 6 as *The Other Americans* and running about three months.

1938, Blue. 15m, Sundays at 5:45. *What's New in South America?*, beginning Aug. 14.

1940–45, Blue/ABC. 15m, various times, usually Saturdays or Sundays.

1946–49, NBC. 15m, Saturday afternoon.

EDWIN C. HILL, popular commentator on CBS and later NBC. Hill came from a long newspaper background: he worked on journals in Indianapolis and Cincinnati, beginning in 1901, and in 1904 he moved to New York, where he quickly became the star reporter for the *Sun*. For more than 20 years, Hill covered everything from politics and murders to the sinking of the *Titanic*. He made his first radio broadcast in 1931: then, beginning in 1932, he had a regular run on the air that lasted 20 years. He was often heard under the title *The Human Side of the News*, which he also used for his King Features syndicated column. His voice was described as "big and jovial . . . pleasing and cultured." He was compared favorably to Lowell Thomas: he had the longevity, but failed to attain Thomas's stature on the air. Timeslots (all 15m):

1932–33, CBS. Three a week at 10:30.

1933–35, CBS. Weeknights at 8:15. Barbasol.

1936, NBC. Three a week at 7:30.

1936–37, NBC. Fridays at 7:30.

1937–38, CBS. Weekdays at 12:15. *Your News Parade*. Lucky Strike.

1938–39, NBC. Twice a week at 7:15. Campbell Soups.

1939–40, CBS. Six a week at 6. American Oil.

1940–41, CBS. Weekdays at 6.

1941–42, CBS. Weekdays at 6:30. American Oil.

1942–45, CBS. Tuesdays at 6:15. Johnson and Johnson.

1946–47, ABC. Weekdays at 3:30. Wesson Oil.

1950, NBC. Sundays at 4. Doubleday.

1951–52, CBS. Sundays at 4, final broadcast Feb. 10, 1952. Beltone.

EDWIN D. CANHAM, Washington bureau chief of the *Christian Science Monitor*, who began broadcasting nine-minute summaries on the CBS news series *Headlines and Bylines* in 1937. His series, *Monitor Views*, sponsored by his newspaper, ran in these 15m timeslots, all on ABC: 1945–46, Saturdays at 6:15; 1946–48, Thursdays at 8:15; 1948–50, Tuesdays at 9:30; 1950–54, Tuesdays at 9:45; 1955–56, Sundays at 10.

ELLIOTT ROOSEVELT, son of the president, who conducted a seven-month commentary on Mutual, April 3–Nov. 30, 1939; 15m, Tuesdays, Thursdays, and Saturdays at 7:15 for Emerson Radios. Roosevelt made news by loudly disagreeing with some of his father's policies: he was known as a "hell-raiser" on the air and off. He established a Texas State Network of 26 radio stations, beginning with the three he and his wife purchased and managed. These were linked with Mutual.

ELMER DAVIS, a fiction writer and newspaperman who joined CBS Aug. 23, 1939, as a substitute for H. V. Kaltenborn and became almost immediately one of the most popular news broadcasters of his day. Davis came from Indiana: in the opinion of *Radio Guide*, he had "an Oxford brain and an Indiana twang that reeked of neutrality," but also possessed "exactly the kind of homey down-to-earth manner needed in a moment of crisis."

Like so many of his colleagues, he came up through the print world. He had joined the *New York Times* in 1914, and wrote a history of the newspaper in 1921. In the 1920s and 1930s he was a successful writer of novels and short stories. He had tried radio a few times without notable success, but CBS news chief Paul White was impressed by the obvious intelligence and measured straight talk inherent in his writings. When Kaltenborn left for Europe, Davis was given his spot in New York. This meant filling a five-minute nightly newscast at 8:55, and doing a three-a-week quarter-hour (1939–40) at 6:30. Within weeks he was among radio's five most popular newsmen. Gilbert Seldes called him a "master of understatement," adding that, in Davis, "the qualities of all good news broadcasters are completely fused . . . his style, his intelligence, his integrity and his passions are not in conflict one with another."

He went to England in the spring of 1941, returning with a deep appreciation of the British character. In June 1942, he resigned from CBS to become director of the Office of War Information, remaining there until the agency was dissolved in 1945. He returned to broadcasting, joining ABC, which outbid CBS for his services. His well-remembered trademark was to involve his listeners with a question, then pause and give his reaction, beginning with a measured "Well . . ."

Timeslots after 1940, all 15m:

1940–41, CBS. Saturdays at 6:30 (in addition to other duties, described above).

1941–42, CBS. Three a week at 6:30.

1945–46, ABC. Mondays and Tuesdays at 8:15; Sundays at 3.

1946–53, ABC. Weekdays at 7:15. Various sponsors.

1953–55, ABC. Sundays at 10:15, final broadcast June 26, 1955.

ERIC SEVAREID, one of "Murrow's boys," recruited at the outset of World War II. Sevareid broadcast from Paris, leaving that conquered city just ahead of the German army. He helped Murrow cover London in the Blitz and returned to the United States in 1942, becoming chief of the CBS Washington bureau. He was given a roving assignment in the Far East, beginning in July 1943, during which he jumped by parachute from a crippled airplane into Burmese jungles inhabited by headhunters, and he covered military operations in Italy in 1944. His regular CBS newscast began Feb. 17, 1947, and was heard 15m weekdays at 6 for Metropolitan Life until 1950. Sevareid also had a 15m Sunday show at 5:45 in 1950–51.

FIORELLO H. LA GUARDIA, mayor of New York, who conducted a colorful radio commentary on the city's station, WNYC, from 1941–46, and on ABC for six months, Jan. 6–June 30, 1946, Sundays at 9:30 for *Liberty* magazine. La Guardia's New York show was called *Talk to the People*. It was described by *Time* as "the most unorthodox chatter on the air." He "left sentences dangling, mispronounced words, skipped syllables when he tantrum-well felt like it; he growled at chiselers, sang sarcastically at enemies, squeaked angrily at hecklers; he read the comics with expression and told housewives how to prepare oxtail ragout." La Guardia reviewed the war news, discussed its implications for New Yorkers, warned loansharks (sometimes by name) to get out of town, and lobbied shamelessly for public support in his efforts to get his favored bits of legislation passed. His city show ran from 1 to 1:30 on Sundays. As he left office, ABC took him on in a quarter-hour, which was a condensed version of the old show. *Liberty* magazine paid him $1,000 a week, more than twice what he had earned as mayor.

FIRESIDE CHATS, a term coined by Harry Butcher of the CBS Washington office to describe President Franklin D. Roosevelt's radio talks with the American people. This quickly became an almost folkloric title. Roosevelt was one of radio's most effective commentators: he took to the air 30 times, beginning March 12, 1933. He spoke about the banking crisis, economic affairs, agriculture, and, later, the war in Europe and the coal strike. It was the first time in history that a large segment of the population could listen directly to a chief executive, and the chats are often credited with helping keep Roosevelt's popularity high.

Roosevelt usually spoke in the Diplomatic Reception Room of the White House. The president would enter about fifteen minutes before his allotted time and greet the press, radio, and newsreel men; then he would read his speech from a black looseleaf binder. Carleton E. Smith, NBC White House announcer, officiated at the broadcasts. His introduction was simple: "Ladies and gentlemen, the president of the United States." Roosevelt usually began, "My friends," or "My fellow Americans," enhancing his image as everybody's neighbor.

FLOYD GIBBONS, the first daily newscaster on the network air. Gibbons was a colorful personality, "a professional hero," in the words of *Vanity Fair*, who swaggered across the journalistic landscape in the first three decades of the 20th century. He was inevitably compared with Richard Harding Davis, the major journalist of the previous generation.

Gibbons served on the *Minneapolis Daily News*, and arrived at the *Chicago Tribune* in time to cover the most sensational stories of the pre–World War era. He interviewed Pancho Villa, survived the sinking of the *Laconia*, and was usually to be found wherever armies of men were shooting at each other. He was decorated by the French in World War I and was wounded three times in Belleau Wood, where he lost his left eye and thus acquired the white linen eyepatch that was his trademark ever after. In later years, he went to battle fronts in Russia, Morocco, China, Ethiopia, and Spain. His life of adventure included a year in Africa, where he rode a camel across the Sahara and explored the jungles of the Niger.

His first radio broadcast came in 1925, in the Philippines. In the United States, he first broadcast on Christmas 1925, at WGN, Chicago. Gibbons described in emotional detail all the Christmases he had spent in distant and barbaric lands, huddling in trenches and passing the day with strangers in bleak French hamlets. The broadcast drew heavy mail, and Gibbons was invited to relate more of his adventures on subsequent dates. He was heard on WGN for about a month. He began his regular broadcasts in 1929, a Wednesday night

(10:30) NBC half-hour called *The Headline Hunter*. This was not a news broadcast: Gibbons was backed by an orchestra, and he told more of his adventures in a conversational but dramatic style. Gibbons was the first rapid-talker of radio; once clocked at 217 words a minute, he gloried in palsy, slangy copy packed with color. He was also heard on *The General Electric Program* (1929–30, NBC, 60m, Saturdays at 9), a symphonic series seasoned generously with Gibbons talk.

Gibbons also pioneered the use, in 1929, of a portable microphone, covering the *Graf Zeppelin*'s arrival for NBC. His brief career as a daily newscaster begin in 1930, when he was engaged by *Literary Digest* to read the news and announce a poll on the prohibition question. The magazine moved its sponsorship to Lowell Thomas after less than a year (according to columnist Ben Gross, Gibbons was canceled for "serenading" at his sponsor's home after a night out drinking in a Long Island speakeasy). Gibbons continued his weekly adventure talks into 1933. He opened a school of broadcasting, headquartered in Washington, though he himself was off to new wars. He broadcast for NBC from Ethiopia in 1935, and from Spain in 1936. He died in 1939.

Jan. 24–Sept. 26, 1930, NBC. 15m weeknights at 6:45. *Literary Digest.*

Sept. 28, 1930–Aug. 23, 1931, Blue Network. 15m, Sundays at 9:30.

Oct. 21–Dec. 23, 1932, NBC. 15m, Fridays at 10:30. *The Elgin Adventurer's Club.* Elgin Watches.

1933, NBC. Johns Manville.

FRANK SINGISER, Mutual newscaster: 1938–39, 15m, Sundays at 7:30; 1944–45, three a week at 8; 1945–46, 15m, three a week at 7:30, *The Sinclair Headliner,* for Sinclair Oil, continuing a series that had been running on WOR.

FREDERICK WILLIAM WILE, weekly Blue Network newscaster at the beginning of network broadcasting; later of CBS.

1926–29, Blue. 15m, Wednesdays at 8 until 1927, then at 7:45. *The Political Situation.*

1929–36, CBS. 15m, Thursdays at 8:15, 1929–30; Tuesdays at 7:15, 1930–31; Saturdays in early evening timeslots, generally between 6 and 7, 1932–36.

FULTON LEWIS JR., Mutual commentator whose vast popularity and influence packed a 20-year broadcasting career with color and controversy. Lewis was loved and hated with equal intensity; his life on the air was well summarized by the title of his autobiography, *Praised and Damned.*

He came from the print world: a reporter for the *Washington Herald* and Hearst's Universal News Service and, beginning in 1933, a columnist for King Features syndicate. He began broadcasting on local stations, reading headlines and his *Herald* fishing column and later, in October 1937, taking over a news slot on WOL, the Washington affiliate of the Mutual Network. In December 1937, he joined Mutual and went coast-to-coast; his series, *Top of the News from Washington,* became a 7 P.M. standby, running in the same timeslot for two decades. His method of co-op sponsorship was the strongest of its kind; Lewis was sold locally in hundreds of markets. Though his clients eventually numbered more than 500, Lewis gave them localized opening signatures, mentioned their products, and was then neatly segued into his live presentation from Washington (or, when he was traveling, from the nearest Mutual affiliate).

Lewis gathered a growing reputation as a political conservative. Though he liked Roosevelt, he was critical of the New Deal, and in his later years his support of Sen. Joseph McCarthy opened deep rifts with his fellow newsmen. He broke many stories that were considered sensational at the time, relying on his own sources and a relentless determination to dig out the truth as he saw it. He subscribed to no wire services and claimed that he seldom listened to the broadcasts of his competitors (though he could quote them quickly enough when they said something that annoyed him). He had a derisive way of putting down the "facts" of other newsmen: on Lewis's broadcasts, these were labeled "so-called facts" by "purported" commentators. This earned him the scorn of his targets (among them Edward R. Murrow and Elmer Davis) and the adulation of up to ten million people who regularly tuned him in.

Among Lewis's fans he was considered the ultimate straight-shooter who feared no one and knuckled under to no political or commercial pressure. His localized sponsorship was ideally suited to this end: if a client dropped off in Indianapolis, there were always others waiting in line to take that spot.

GABRIEL HEATTER, Mutual commentator, known by various "unhappy" nicknames because of the somber tone of his voice, but in his own opinion and in the substance of his broadcasts "the soul of optimism." In the trade, Heatter was called "the old crier," "the unhappy warrior," or the "voice of doom," yet he was usually able to comb through the bleakest news during the darkest days of World War II and proclaim to the nation, "Ah, there's good news tonight!"

Heatter had a solid background in the press, working for the *New York American*, the *Brooklyn Times*, the *New York Journal*, and the *New York Herald*. He turned to broadcasting Dec. 14, 1932, when an open letter challenging the views of socialist Norman Thomas appeared with his byline in the *Nation*. He was invited to speak on WMCA as a result; this led to a nightly commentary at $40 a week, which led to WOR and a raise to $75 per broadcast. His local broadcasts continued until 1935, when Mutual asked him to cover the kidnap-murder trial of Bruno Richard Hauptmann. The coverage had not been sold, the network explained, so Heatter would only be paid for his expenses. But the nation's interest in the Lindbergh-Hauptmann case was intense, and Heatter was heard in 15-minute timeslots three times a day. By the second day, Grove's Bromo Quinine and Tastyeast had come on as sponsors at $800 a week, and Heatter was an overnight success.

He also covered Hauptmann's execution April 13, 1936. He was assured by the governor of New Jersey that there would be no delay, and he went on the air prepared to speak for five or six minutes. Almost an hour lapsed before Hauptmann was actually executed; Heatter's ad-libbing, as described by the *New Yorker*, "left his audience limp with admiration." He discussed his hotel room; he speculated as the delay mounted that Hauptmann may have decided to confess; he wondered about the possibility of a last-minute reprieve; finally he talked about the strange emotional linkage that everyone—"you, I, judges, Mrs. Hauptmann, the mother of that dead baby"—felt with the man about to die.

The Lindbergh case launched Heatter to the top of his profession. Soon, wrote the *New Yorker*, "he was sponsored, at various moments of the day and night, by Rogers Peet, Johns Manville, Sanka, the Modern Industrial Bank, and a shirt called Big Yank." In the notoriety of the Hauptmann coverage, he became an "across-the-board" commentator—trade slang for a man who was on the air seven days a week.

He was one of Hitler's greatest enemies on radio, and thought himself doomed should Germany win the war. This he thought likely, despite the stiff upper lip presented in his broadcasts. To counter his own deep pessimism, he searched diligently for the smallest crumb of hope in the most disastrous battle reports. It annoyed other commentators, said the *Saturday Evening Post*, "to tune into Heatter at 9 P.M., long after finishing their own bleak stints, hear him open with, 'Ah, there's good news tonight!'—and then prove to his own satisfaction that there was."

Heatter broadcast from his Freeport, Long Island, home, where one room was equipped as a radio studio. His day began at 8 A.M., listening to overseas commentators by shortwave. The rest of the day he spent formulating his reaction to incoming news, writing, culling, and pruning his script. By the time he went on the air he had logged 11 hours to get his quarter-hour of news. His stock in trade was heroism, mother love, optimism, unselfishness, prayer, and the faithfulness of dogs. Heatter always loved a good dog story.

1935–36, Mutual. 15m, four a week at 8. Also: Blue Network, Sundays at 5.45.

1936–37, Mutual. 15m, Sundays at 3 and 9:30; also six a week at 5:15, and four a week at 9.

1937–49, Mutual. Varying numbers of weekday 15m slots at 9. Kreml Hair Tonic, 1940–42; various sponsors other times. Also: 1941–46, Sundays at 8:45. Barbasol.

1949–61, Mutual. 15m, weeknights at 7:30. Various sponsors.

GALEN DRAKE, CBS West Coast commentator, ca. 1942–43, and later personality on more general talk shows; sometimes heard nationally as *This Is Galen Drake*. At KNX, he aired news for the West Coast. He was associated with Fletcher Wiley, longtime commentator in San Francisco and Los Angeles. By 1943, he and Wiley were on the same air, six hours apart. The problem was, their voices were almost identical, so much so that even their secretaries had trouble telling them apart. During the war, Wiley was billed as the *Home Front Reporter*. While Drake was doing a series called *Sunrise Salute* (Monday–Saturday, 6:15 A.M. Pacific time), and was also heard weekdays at 3, Wiley aired weekdays at 1 for Campbell Soups (ca. early to mid-1940s). Neither man used scripts; both were solid ad-libbers, doing even the commercials off the cuff. Once as a prank, Wiley walked into

Drake's show and took it over, with the audience none the wiser.

This is Galen Drake, meanwhile, had a long and fruitful run, on ABC (1945–49), Mutual (1949–50), and CBS (1950–58). It was heard mostly as a weekday quarter-hour until 1950, then on Saturdays.

GEORGE FIELDING ELIOT, CBS military analyst, beginning in 1939 and heard throughout the war. A veteran of World War I, Eliot used his old rank, major, on the air. He was first featured in a 15m, twice-a-week newscast with Albert Warner (1939–40, at 6:30), and was heard extensively on major battle stories, such as the D-Day invasion, telling listeners what was probably happening, where, and why.

GEORGE HICKS, NBC special events announcer and feature reporter, and Blue Network war correspondent. Hicks spent ten years with NBC doing light feature work before the war broke out. Then came Pearl Harbor. Hicks talked the Blue Network into doing a daily series about men at war. His best broadcasts during that time (1942) were, according to *Newsweek*, about merchant seamen "at a time when our ships were going down off Hatteras like diving ducks."

Hicks longed for an overseas post, but his network had just separated from NBC and had little budget for a foreign bureau. In March 1943, he persuaded the network to open a London office, with himself its entire staff. Soon he was given an assistant, Arthur Feldman, and Hicks moved on to the battle fronts. He was the only newsman with first-hand reports on the liberation of Corsica. In November 1943, he went to Italy, describing the battles of the Fifth Army under what *Newsweek* termed "frightful weather conditions and nightmarish terrain."

But Hicks had his greatest moment on D-Day. Equipped with a film spool recorder, he gave a gripping account of an attack in progress by enemy planes upon a landing craft. This recording, edited to a ten-minute broadcast, has become a classic: it was aired on every network for days, and established Hicks as a top battle correspondent.

1944–45, Blue/ABC. 15m, twice a week at 4:45, beginning June 27; later Tuesdays and Thursdays at 10:20; by Jan., Sundays at 1:15. Script.

1947–49, ABC. 15m, weekdays at 8:45 A.M.

1949–50, NBC. 15m, weekdays at 1:30.
1953–55, ABC. 15m, weekdays at 6:45.

GEORGE F. PUTNAM, commentator for NBC and Mutual: "the greatest voice in radio," according to Walter Winchell. "Silvery, melodious and super-smooth," said *Time*. From 1941 until 1944, he shared commentator duties with Lowell Thomas on Movietone newsreels. Putnam remains active in the nineties, with a two-hour daily California TV talk show.

1943–44, NBC. 15m, four a week at 6.
1946–47, Mutual. 15m, five a week at 3:30.

GEORGE R. HOLMES, Depression-era NBC newscaster, heard under the title *Washington News*. 1933–34, 15m, Wednesdays at 6:30; 1934–36, 15m, Fridays at 11.

GEORGE SOKOLSKY, conservative ABC commentator, ca. 1948–55. Sokolsky was an ardent booster of capitalism and a frequent guest on such shows as *America's Town Meeting of the Air*. 15m, timeslots: Sundays at 10:45, 1949–50; at 10:30, 1950–52; at 6:30 1952–54; at 7:15, 1954–55.

GILBERT MARTYN, Blue/ABC newscaster, 1943–47, 15m, weekdays at 11:30 A.M. Kellogg.

H. R. BAUKHAGE, Blue/ABC commentator; began with five-minute news wrapups on *The National Home and Farm Hour* in 1932, progressed to general network commentator by the late 1930s, and covered the beginning of World War II from Berlin. Baukhage had a reputation for fairness: he was described as "friendly but gruff," and usually took a midroad position on the issues of the day. He never used his given names (Hilmar Robert) or even his initials on his broadcasts, introducing himself abruptly as "Baukhage talking."

Feb. 9, 1942–Oct. 10, 1950, Blue/ABC. 15m, weekdays at 1. Local co-op sponsorship.
1952–53, Mutual. 15m, weeknights at 11.

H. V. KALTENBORN, the "dean of American commentators," so called because his was the first radio commentary, his career was the longest, and his combination of talents was the most remarkable.

Kaltenborn was born in 1878, a native of Milwaukee and son of a German immigrant. At 15, he was writing for the local newspaper in Merrill, Wis. He wrote (from an Alabama infantry camp) of the Spanish-American War, then shipped to Europe on a cattleboat to cover his first stories as a foreign correspondent.

He joined the *Brooklyn Eagle* in 1910, rising through the ranks to become associate editor. He first spoke on the air in 1921, an experiment at WJZ, Newark. In 1922, he gave his first analytical broadcast, talking about a coal strike on WVP, a government radio station on Bedloe's Island. On Oct. 23, 1923, he was first heard on WEAF, New York: sponsored by his newspaper, Kaltenborn was both apprehensive and thrilled. He would later recall the WEAF draped studio as a "torture chamber," but the simple fact was that the man who would make thousands of broadcasts in a fabled career spanning three decades had the classic symptoms of mike fright. "Radio speaking," he would write, "is an almost indecent exposure of personality. Your audience hears you breathe, knows when you turn your head or turn a page, catches the whispered comment intended only for one ear, and gets a nervous shock from the blasting detonation of a half-suppressed cough."

Kaltenborn was also thrilled when he stepped from the studio and was handed a telegram. It said: "We're listening. Good stuff. Keep it up. Captain Cunningham, Steamship George Washington." The fact that his voice could be heard by a steamer well out to sea, and the captain's congratulations could reach the studio even before he was off the air, excited Kaltenborn about the future of the medium. But his tenure at WEAF was not smooth. He ran afoul of station management, and of government bureaucrats, with his outspoken comments. When he advocated American recognition of Soviet Russia, the station tried to cancel his contract. The *Eagle* threatened to make this a front-page censorship issue, and WEAF relented, letting the contract run its course. As early as 1925, Kaltenborn was writing that air censorship was a fact, that people were censored by exclusion. That year he was heard on WAHG of Richmond Hill, Long Island.

He had lost his fear of the microphone, but it had taken six months of regular broadcasting to put him at ease. For a time in the mid-1920s he was heard on WOR, airing a commentary called *The Kaltenborn Digest*, Mondays at 8. He moved into the networks in 1927, and in 1930 he quit the *Eagle* and joined the CBS staff. He was generally considered to be among the second tier of radio commentators: although he had been first, such hot new personalities as Edwin C. Hill, Boake Carter,

and Lowell Thomas had surpassed him in popularity and influence. In the 1930s he made frequent trips to Europe. Fluent in German, Italian, and French, he could chat easily with world leaders without cumbersome translators. He interviewed Hitler in 1932 and also spoke with Mussolini, Gandhi, and Chiang Kai-shek. He was the first to bring the sounds of battle into American homes, with his haystack broadcast in 1936, during the Spanish Civil War. He had located a house close enough to the fighting that a long wire could be strung from the telephone to the haystack, where he hid for nine hours. Twice his cable was shot to pieces, but he got through to New York at 11 P.M., with machine guns chattering in the background.

This, coupled with his coverage of the Munich crisis in September 1938, elevated him to the front ranks of his profession. For 18 days, while Hitler and Chamberlain negotiated the fate of Czechoslovakia, Kaltenborn remained at his listening post in New York, sleeping on a couch in rumpled clothes and eating onion soup that his wife brought in. During this time he made 102 broadcasts, ranging in length from two minutes to two hours. At the end of his watch, 50,000 letters of congratulation poured in.

In person Kaltenborn was lanky, with a clipped moustache and thin hair. He was described as "confident but not conceited," "pompous," "unpretentious," and by many other contradictory adjectives. His capabilities were vast. He was the only newscaster in radio who could strap on a pair of shortwave earphones, listen without translation to speeches by Hitler, Mussolini, or Daladier, go on the air immediately with only his cryptic notes as a script, and deliver a polished analysis. He was a rapid-fire commentator but spoke in simple sentences packed with one-syllable words and was easy to understand. He could read a one-line news bulletin and immediately give a quarter-hour explanation of its significance and probable consequences. He died in 1965.

Timeslots (in addition to those mentioned above): 1927–28, CBS. 30m, Tuesdays at 8:30.

1929–30, CBS. 30m, Mondays at 6:30.

1931–35, CBS. 15m, sometimes Mondays, sometimes twice a week, one year three times; generally at 6, 6:30, or 7:30. *Current Events.* Also: 1931–32, CBS. 15m, twice a week at 7:30. *Kaltenborn Edits the News.*

1935–36, CBS. 25m, Fridays at 6:35.

1936–39, CBS. 15m, Sundays at 10:45, 1936–

37; at 10:30, 1938–39.

1940–51, NBC. 15m, three a week until 1945; weeknights, 1945–48; then three a week. At 7:45, except at 7, 1950–51. Pure Oil.

1951–55, NBC. 15m, Saturdays at 6:15, final broadcast Jan. 15, 1955.

HARRISON WOOD, ABC commentator broadcasting under the title *Changing World*, 1948–50, 15m, Sundays at 3:15, later at 3, for Fruehauf Trailers. In the 1950s he worked for Mutual. A drunken newscast survives from this run, a funny bit of trivia.

HARRY W. FLANNERY, successor to William L. Shirer in the CBS coverage of Nazi Berlin, 1940–41. Returning home in October 1941, he went to CBS West Coast, where he did a daily commentary from KNX.

HELEN HIETT, Blue Network reporter; 1941–42, 15m, five a week at 10:15 A.M.

HENDRIK WILLEM VAN LOON, author and illustrator of popular books and NBC commentator beginning Dec. 22, 1936, 15m, Tuesdays at 6:45; twice a week at 7:30, 1937–38; final broadcast March 25, 1938.

HENRY J. TAYLOR, conservative political commentator, who had a long stand for General Motors on three networks, often under the title *Your Land and Mine.*

1945–48, Mutual, beginning Dec. 21, 1945. 15m, Mondays and Fridays at 10, 1945–46, then twice a week at 7:30.

1948–54, ABC. 15m, Mondays at 8:30 into 1951, then at 8.

1954–56, NBC. 15m, Mondays at 8, final broadcast Dec. 3, 1956.

HOWARD K. SMITH, CBS correspondent and later commentator; author of *Last Train from Berlin*, the story of his experiences covering the German capital in the final days before the United States entered the war. Smith was assistant to Harry W. Flannery until October 1941, when Flannery left Berlin and Smith was left to run the post alone. By December, relations with the Nazi government had deteriorated to the extent that Smith could no longer function. He applied for an exit visa and crossed into Switzerland Dec. 7, 1941—thus the title of his book. As a commentator, he was heard on CBS 15m, Sundays at 12:30 from London,

1952–56. Smith later had a distinguished career on ABC television.

HUGH S. JOHNSON, retired Army general and former head of the National Recovery Act in the early Roosevelt administration, and a Blue Network commentator beginning Sept. 27, 1937. His announced agenda included politics, agriculture, big and little business, and the New Deal. One season, 1937–38, 15m, Mondays and Thursdays at 8, and Tuesdays and Wednesdays at 10, all for Bromo Quinine.

JOHN B. HUGHES, NBC and Mutual commentator; specialist on the Orient. Hughes came out of theater; his work in a stock company led to radio, which led him into news. After a season on NBC, he joined Mutual, predicted that Japan would attack the United States, and was used extensively in Mutual's West Coast chain when that prediction materialized Dec. 7, 1941.

1937–38, NBC. 15m, five a week at 4:30. *Hughes Reel.* Borden's Milk.

1941–43, Mutual. 15m, weekdays at noon for Aspertine, 1941–42; twice a week at 10 for American Home Products, 1942–43.

JOHN B. KENNEDY, announcer and news analyst, heard at various times on each of the four networks. Kennedy had worked for many newspapers and had been at *Collier's* magazine for ten years when he first tried radio, in November 1933. He was a straight announcer as well, heard on NBC's *General Motors Concert Hour* and *The Magic Key* of RCA.

Timeslots included: 1933–34, NBC. 15m, twice a week at 11. *Looking Over the Week.*

1934–35, NBC. 15m, Sundays at 7:15.

1936–37, NBC. 15m, Thursdays at 11.

1939–40, Mutual. 15m, twice a week at 7:15.

April 1941–January 1944, WNEW, New York.

1942–43, CBS. 15m twice a week at 6. Barbasol.

Jan. 1944, joined the Blue Network; used 15m daily at 6.

1944–46, Blue/ABC. 15m, Sundays at 1. Harvel Watches and others.

1945–46, ABC. 15m, weekdays at 2.

1948–49, Mutual. 15m, Sundays at 1:15. Doubleday.

1949–50, Mutual. 5m, Saturdays at 7:55.

1950–51, ABC. 15m, four a week at 10:30; also weekdays at 2:30.

JOHN DALY, CBS reporter and correspondent, one of the network's pivotal men during and around the war years. Possessed of a rich and memorable voice, Daly announced or covered some of the biggest stories of the day. He joined CBS in 1937, signing on at WJSV, Washington. As White House correspondent, he logged 150,000 miles traveling with Roosevelt. He was used for CBS convention coverage and launched *Report to the Nation* with Brewster Morgan in December 1940. He was heard on *The Spirit of '41*, which also had a season in 1942. His voice was an integral part of *The World Today*, the CBS nightly newscast, ca. 1941–43. Daly was the man who interrupted regular CBS programming on Dec. 7, 1941, to announce that the Japanese had bombed Pearl Harbor.

He was sent to London in early 1943. From there he went to North Africa, and from there to Italy. He reported on battles at Anzio, Cassino, and Messina. In 1944, he returned to New York and another stint on *The World Today*. He was the first to broadcast the bulletin announcing the death of President Roosevelt April 12, 1945. He took part in his network's V-E Day broadcast and later covered the trial of Nazi war criminals at Nuremberg. He was a prominent voice on *CBS Is There* (see YOU ARE THERE). Though his life at CBS was rich and varied, he was known to the following generation only as the genial and mischievous host of the TV game show *What's My Line?*

JOHN GUNTHER, author and print man, writer of the popular "Inside" books (*Inside Europe*, etc.), and frequent guest on the *Information, Please* panel show. Gunther covered London for NBC in 1939 and was a commentator on the Blue Network in the 1940s: a brief stint beginning in March 1941, and another in 1943–44 (15m, twice a week at 10 for General Mills).

JOHN MACVANE, NBC news reporter throughout World War II. MacVane worked for the *Brooklyn Eagle* and the *Brooklyn Sun*, and then took assignments in London with the *Daily Express* and *Daily Mail* before the war. He was with International News Service in Paris when the Germans invaded France. In London, he joined NBC, broadcasting news of the Blitz through the summer of 1940. He later covered North Africa, D-Day at Omaha Beach, and the liberation of Paris. His memoir, *On the Air in World War II*, is a valuable document of "radio at work."

Postwar timeslots: 1945–46, NBC. 15m, Saturdays at noon.

1953–56, ABC. 15m, weekdays at 8:45. Co-op advertising.

JOHN W. VANDERCOOK, author and globetrotter, who turned a chance opportunity into a news career at NBC. In September 1940, Vandercook happened to be chatting with an NBC vice president when news broke that the United States and England had made a deal for bases in the Caribbean. The network man asked if Vandercook knew anything about the West Indies. Vandercook was something of an expert, having traveled there extensively since 1925. He was rushed to a microphone and was a network fixture for the rest of the war. In 1944, *Time* called him "the most elegant voice on the U.S. air."

1940–41, NBC, beginning Oct. 21. 15m, Wednesdays at 7:15. Remington-Rand.

1941–46, NBC. 15m, weeknights at 7:15 *News of the World*, Vandercook in New York, coordinating shortwave news from around the world. Miles Laboratories.

1945–46, NBC. 15m, Sundays at 5:30. Oldsmobile.

1953–55, ABC. 15m, weeknights at 7. CIO.

JOSEPH C. HARSCH, *Christian Science Monitor* reporter who became a CBS commentator after filling in occasionally for William L. Shirer in Germany, ca. 1940–41. His work had impressed CBS news chief Paul White, who gave him a daily five-minute commentator's slot at 6:55 P.M., beginning March 15, 1943.

Other timeslots: 1947–48, CBS. 15m, Sundays at 2:30.

1948–49, CBS. 15m, Sundays at 1.

1955–56, NBC. Twice a week, 10m, Tuesdays at 10:20 and 15m, Fridays at 6:15.

KATHRYN CRAVENS, the first female radio commentator, whose series *News Through a Woman's Eyes* ran on CBS for Pontiac from Oct. 19, 1936, until April 8, 1938.

Cravens began her career at KMOX, the CBS affiliate in St. Louis. She had been an actress, and now, on radio, she told stories, sang, and did Negro dialect by memory of her mammy in Texas. She had no news background and paid little attention to the tenets of reporting. As she told *Radio Guide*, the "five *w*'s" were less important in her stories than the big question, "how does it feel?"

... "how does it feel to be the mother of a murdered boy, of one to be executed that night? ... how does it feel to survive flood and misery? ... to be America's most notorious shoplifter? ... to be mayor of a great city, a congressional lobbyist, a famous playwright, a war-torn cripple, a flophouse bum?" This was her scope.

LARRY LESUEUR, CBS correspondent, notably in London during the Blitz and in Russia during the bleak winter of 1941–42. Lesueur served six years with United Press and came to CBS in 1939. He covered the human interest of the British in wartime, joining Edward R. Murrow and Eric Sevareid in the network's daily reports. In the fall of 1941 he was assigned to Moscow. He traveled extensively across the vast country to report on fighting fronts at Mozhaisk, Borodino, Rzhev, Klin, and the upper Volga (*Current Biography*); "he visited factories, schools, hospitals, collective farms, Red Army encampments, camps for prisoners, theaters, public gatherings and ordinary Russian homes." His book, *Twelve Months That Changed the World*, was published in 1943. That year Lesueur returned to London, where he was used extensively in subsequent war coverage, including the invasion of France in 1944. He opened a long-running CBS commentary Sept. 28, 1946, heard intermittently until 1958. In later years he worked for the Voice of America.

LARRY SMITH, NBC specialist on the Far East, heard 15m weekdays at 9:15 A.M. on the West Coast chain, 1944–45. Smith had a good record, in the fall of 1944, at predicting events just before they happened.

LELAND STOWE, 1944–45, ABC. 15m, Saturdays at 7:15. National Underwriters. Also heard on Mutual, 1947–48.

LEO CHERNE, 1943–44, Mutual. Saturdays at 10:45.

LEON HENDERSON, economist, head of the Office of Price Administration in the early 1940s; Blue Network commentator 1943–44. 15m, Saturdays at 6:45. Also a frequent panelist on *Information, Please*.

LOWELL THOMAS, longest-running daily newscaster in radio: on the air almost continuously from Sept. 29, 1930, until May 14, 1976.

Thomas was the straightest of newsmen: he was neither a commentator of the Kaltenborn school nor a pundit like Davis. As Maurice Zolotow wrote in a career-capping *Coronet* article: "He neither views with alarm like Winchell nor views with gaiety like Heatter ... he doesn't offer social messages or uplift; he never gives the impression that he has inside information like Drew Pearson, yet his rating as a newsman has consistently been either first, second, or third over the years." In the words of a colleague, "He has no opinions, and his only enemies are rattlesnakes, cannibals, Fascists, and Communists ... but even these he will rarely condemn outright."

As a young man Thomas attended four colleges, working his way through with odd jobs, including stints on two Denver newspapers. In his 20s, he organized expeditions to the Arctic. During World War I, he was assigned to compile a picture history of Allied fighting men: this took him to front lines throughout Europe, and in 1918 he went beyond the lines to cover the revolution in Germany. He went to the Holy Land to cover Gen. Edmund H. H. Allenby's campaign to oust the Turks from Palestine. This led to a meeting with T. E. Lawrence and what Zolotow called "the great adventure of his life." He traveled with Lawrence across the Arabian desert and subsequently wrote a book about this trek (*With Lawrence in Arabia*, 1924, the first of more than 40 books he would publish). For ten years he lectured on Lawrence, supplementing his talks with photos and film.

His tour of the world from 1919 through 1922 included treks through India, the bush country of Australia, and the Himalayan heights. It was this background that Thomas brought to radio in September 1930.

When William S. Paley of CBS learned that *Literary Digest* was parting company with its ace newscaster, Floyd Gibbons, on NBC, he quickly arranged an audition with Thomas in the hope of luring the sponsor to his network. The *Digest* people were impressed with Thomas but had commitments to NBC, putting Paley in the position of scouting for the enemy. CBS was given small solace, allowed to carry the show to the West Coast while Thomas was heard on the Blue Network in the East and Midwest. This lasted only about six months, and NBC emerged with the entire program in 1931. Thomas's popularity was immediate and vast: he was carrying a Crossley rating of 18.9 in 1932, while other newsmen didn't even register in the polls. His broadcast time, 15m, weekdays at 6:45 in the East, was consistent for years. In 1932, when his relations with *Literary Digest* became strained, he switched to Sun Oil, which sponsored him until 1947. On Sept. 29, 1947, he moved to CBS, and Paley reaped the benefit of his long-past effort: Procter & Gamble became the new sponsor, and the 6:45 timeslot continued as always. Later sponsors included Kaiser and General Motors. Thomas was with CBS until his radio career ended in 1976.

He was seldom absent from his broadcast. Even when traveling, he was usually able to find a microphone, and in some cases he taped his show and sent it on to New York. It was said that he only lost his temper once on the air, after a tour of the Nazi death camp at Buchenwald in 1945. He did have one celebrated attack of giggles, which is preserved on tape. At CBS, he often broadcast from his home, 100 miles upstate.

By then it was estimated that Thomas was earning $10,000 a week from Procter & Gamble. He continued writing ten articles and a book a year, and delivering 20 lectures at $2,000 each. He also provided commentary for Fox Movietone Newsreels, doing two a week for $1,500. His longtime assistant was Prosper Buranelli, who joined him on his first broadcast and, with Louis Sherwin, wrote his scripts. Among his announcers was Hugh James. Thomas's standard opening was "Good evening, everybody"; his closing, "So long until tomorrow." These became the titles of his two autobiographical works. He died in 1981 at age 89.

MARK HAWLEY, 1941–43, CBS. 15m, three a week at 4:45 and weeknights at 10:45, 1941–42; weeknights at 11, 1942–43.

MARIAN YOUNG, WOR news reporter and commentator who took over the *Martha Deane* show, a program that had been highly successful with Mary Margaret McBride and held briefly by Bessie Beatty. Young rebuilt *Martha Deane* in her own style, which still contained the interview segments favored by McBride but focused more on hard news. Young joined WOR in 1941; though heard only locally, nine states could pick up the powerful signal. *Martha Deane* aired until 1956.

MARTIN AGRONSKY, Blue Network/ABC reporter-commentator, heard on *The ABC Morning News* (8 A.M., five and sometimes six times a week), beginning July 10, 1944, and running more than a dozen years.

MORGAN BEATTY, NBC news reporter and conservative commentator. Beatty's career as the voice of *News of the World* spanned 23 years, 1944–67. 15m, timeslots: 1944–46, weekdays at 1:45; early evening thereafter, at 7:15 or 7:30. Miles Laboratories.

NED CALMER, 1943–44, CBS. 15m, four a week at 6.

PAUL HARVEY, ABC newscaster whose success was based more on personality than news. Harvey premiered Nov. 26, 1950, originally heard 15m, Sundays at 10:15 for Dixie Cup. Eventually he was heard six times a week on a co-op basis, and was still going strong in the late 1990s. The unmistakable touches of Bill Stern are evident in his style.

PAUL SCHUBERT, Mutual. 15m. 1939–40, Wednesdays at 9:15; 1943–44, weekdays at 10:30; 1944–45, weekdays at 10:15.

PAUL SULLIVAN, CBS. 15m. 1939–40, six a week at 11; 1940–41, weekdays at 6:30, both seasons for Raleigh Cigarettes. His sign-off was always "Good-night and thirty."

PAULINE FREDERICK, 1949–53, ABC 15m, weekdays at 8:45 A.M.; 1953–56, NBC, 15m, weekdays at noon, later 1:30, and finally 12:30. United Nations specialist: her series *At the UN* was heard on NBC, 1954–55, 15m, Sundays at 11:30 A.M.

PRESCOTT ROBINSON, 1942–43, Mutual. 15m, Mondays at 2:30.

QUINCY HOWE, editor turned commentator, first heard on Mutual in 1938, during the Czechoslovakian crisis. Howe was an isolationist whose humor and intellect made him a formidable debater. He was heard on WQXR, New York, in the late 1930s.

Network 15m timeslots: 1943–46, CBS. Twice a week at 6, 1943–44, then weeknights at 6, with a sixth broadcast added in 1945.

1953–57, ABC. Weeknights at 7:15.

RAY DADY, 1943–44, Mutual. 15m, weekdays at 1. Grove Laboratories.

1944–45 NBC. 15m, weekdays at 1. Grove Laboratories.

RAY PORTER, 1942–43, Blue Network. 15m, weekdays at 10:15 A.M.

RAYMOND CLAPPER, Kansas-born journalist and newspaper columnist; United Press reporter from 1923 until mid-1930s and Scripps-Howard columnist thereafter. Clapper was first heard on the air in 1931: his *Washington News Summary* ran Saturdays at 7 on CBS. But he did not take up broadcasting seriously until 1942, when he opened a 15m Monday and Thursday (at 10) commentary on Mutual for General Cigars. The show ran until 1944, when Clapper was killed in an air collision over the Marshall Islands.

RAYMOND GRAM SWING, one of America's top news analysts ca. 1939–48. As *Current History* put it: Swing "broke upon the American radio public pretty much as a man out of nowhere, yet he had been preparing for a radio career for years."

Swing had a solid news background, beginning in 1906 at the *Cleveland Press*. He worked for other newspapers in the Midwest and eventually landed at the *Chicago Daily News*, where he covered Berlin and European affairs during World War I. He later worked for the *New York Herald* and the *Wall Street Journal*. In Berlin in 1920, he married Betty Gram, a militant suffragette and hunger striker, who had several times been arrested for picketing. She was, he would recall, "on the verge of being a Lucy Stoner, that is, a feminist who retains her own name after marriage." This was a problem when they attempted to register in German hotels as a married couple, so a compromise was reached: she would take his name if he would take hers. Thus did he become Raymond Gram Swing, a name he would make world famous two decades later.

He moved on to London. For eight years he was a correspondent for the *Philadelphia Public Ledger* and the *New York Evening Post*. His first experience with a microphone came in 1930, when he interviewed a British lecturer on the BBC. In 1931 he made a special NBC broadcast from Geneva, and in 1932 he was part of the first two-way transatlantic broadcast, London to New York, on CBS. He returned to the United States, and in 1935 began airing a three-a-week commentary, via shortwave, to the BBC. He was admired in England: members of Parliament formed a "Swing Club," listening to his broadcasts Saturday nights in the parliamentary lounge. Winston Churchill sent complimentary cables. But in the United States he continued to toil in obscurity.

He had obtained a weekly spot on the CBS series *The American School of the Air*, but this was discontinued in 1936 because a network vice president did not like his voice. He went to WOR, where he was assigned one newscast a week, Fridays at 9. For three years he worked this slot, and then, quite suddenly, he "broke upon the radio public," and his vast experience in world affairs became one of the medium's prized assets. On Sept. 25, 1939, Swing went into the entire Mutual Network. He was praised by author James Street in *Radio Guide* as "more than a commentator . . . in language that farmers, cab drivers, and bartenders understand, he explains to us the strange ways of European politicians who never mean what they say." He was compared with Kaltenborn, but the comparison was weak. Swing could never, as Kaltenborn did daily, go on the air cold: he labored at length over his scripts, the result being a sharply etched picture of the day's events. "He is gentle yet forceful," wrote *Current History*, "assured but never pompous. He never raises his voice; he stresses important points simply by increasing his intensity and pace."

In the early 1950s he went to work for Murrow at CBS, writing many of Murrow's newscasts and editing the *This I Believe* series. He later broadcast for the Voice of America. His marriage to Betty Gram ended after 22 years, and he attempted to drop the Gram from his name, feeling no longer entitled to it. People paid no attention: he was Raymond Gram Swing and that was that. In England, where his fame continued, he was known simply as "Gram Swing."

1936–38, WOR. 15m, Fridays at 9, Fridays at 6:45, Tuesdays at 7:15, in the three successive years.

1939–42, Mutual. 15m, weeknights at 10. White Owl Cigars.

1942–47, Blue/ABC. 15m, weeknights at 10 for Socony Oil, 1942–45; at 7:15 thereafter, co-op sponsorship. Final broadcast Jan. 3, 1947.

1947–48, ABC. 15m, Sundays at 1:15.

RICHARD HARKNESS, NBC reporter, 1944–53: 15m, weeknights at 11, 1944–45; at 11:15 A.M., 1947–48; twice a week at 7:45, 1948–50; at 7, 1950–51; weekdays at 7, 1951–53. Pure Oil, 1948–53.

THE RICHFIELD REPORTER, NBC West, 1931–48; ABC, 1948; NBC, 1950–57. One of the earliest, longest-running of all newscasts, *Richfield* was confined to the West because of the regional nature of its sponsor, Richfield Oil. It became a listening tradition in the Pacific time zone and was known for its brisk reporting of straight news—no murders, no suicides, no editorializing, no sensationalism. For most of the run, it was written by Wayne Miller and given voice by John Wald. It opened with a trumpet fanfare and a catchphrase: "And a good, good evening, ladies and gentlemen." Chet Huntley was also a Richfield Reporter for a time.

ROBERT McCORMICK, 1947–49, NBC. 15m, weekdays at 1:30.

ROBERT MONTGOMERY, 1949–51, ABC. 15m, Thursdays at 9:45; at 10:30 in closing days. Lee Hats.

ROBERT S. ALLEN, 1948–49, Mutual. 15m, Sundays at 8:45.

ROBERT ST. JOHN, 1943–46, NBC. 15m, weekdays at 10 A.M.

SIDNEY ALBRIGHT, 1943–44, NBC. 15m, weekdays at 9:45 A.M.

SUMNER WELLES, 1944–45, Mutual. 15m, Wednesdays at 10. Waltham Watches.

TAYLOR GRANT, 1945–54, ABC. All 15m. Weeknights at 7, 1945–53; Sundays at 9:15 for Old Gold, 1952–54; four a week at 10, 1953–54. *Headline Edition.*

UPTON CLOSE, conservative NBC and Mutual commentator. Close was a nom de plume: his real name was Josef Washington Hall. His professional signature was acquired during World War I, when a tagline indicating that he was "up close" to the fighting front was mistaken for his name and used as a byline.

He was a globetrotting adventurer early in life: he was friendly with Lowell Thomas, with whom he made a broadcast as early as 1924, and for whom he occasionally substituted on the air and in Fox Movietone newsreels.

Close became part of the NBC scene around 1934: he was used sporadically until April 1941, when he was tapped as the network's expert on Asia and the Pacific. But he ran afoul of liberal groups, which threatened to boycott his sponsor, Sheaffer Pens. He was described as being anti-labor and unsympathetic to American allies in Eu-

rope. He was fired by NBC in December 1944. His charge that Communist elements had forced him out was vigorously denied by NBC chief Niles Trammel.

1941–42, NBC. 15m, Sundays at 1. Also: Blue Network. Wednesdays at 7:45.

1942–44, NBC. Sundays at 3:15, 1942–43; at 4:15, 1943–44; at 3, 1944. *World News Parade.* Sheaffer Pens. Also: 1942–44, Mutual. Sundays at 5:15, 3:15, and 6:30 in successive years. Lumberman's Casualty Insurance.

VAN DEVENTER, was Fred Van Deventer, who used only his last name on the air. He was heard on Mutual beginning in 1944 and had a regular Mutual run, 15m, Sundays at 1, 1951–53. He also created the quiz show *Twenty Questions* and appeared on this with his family.

WALTER KIERNAN, 1945–48, ABC. 15m, weekdays at 6, 1945–46; at 2, 1946–48.

WALTER WINCHELL, See WALTER WINCHELL'S JERGENS JOURNAL.

WESTBROOK VAN VOORHIS, *March of Time* "voice" who held a 15m daily 4:30 (later four a week at 4.) commentary on Blue/ABC 1943–45; sponsored in part by *Time.*

WILLIAM L. SHIRER, the first reporter hired by Edward R. Murrow in the buildup of CBS News in Europe prior to World War II. Shirer began his career as a newspaperman with the *Cedar Rapids Republican.* He went to Europe on borrowed money in 1925 and was down to his last $10 when he got a job in the *Chicago Tribune's* Paris bureau. He was soon promoted to the general European staff, was headquartered in Vienna in the early 1930s, and later traveled through Afghanistan and India, becoming friendly with Mohandas Gandhi. In 1934 he joined Universal News as its Berlin correspondent. In 1937 he was hired by Murrow and CBS.

Shirer was used extensively by CBS in its daily coverage of the buildup to war. He did a daily five-minute broadcast from Prague in 1938, and tried to cover Hitler's invasion of Austria but was ejected from the Vienna radio station at bayonet-point. At Murrow's directive, he flew to London and gave his report from there. He returned to Berlin in September 1939: his daily reports, beginning "This is Berlin," were done under strict censorship. But Shirer was able to tell much by using slang phrases that otherwise might not have been allowed. He returned to the United States in 1940, bringing the detailed diaries he had kept throughout his years in Germany. These were published in June 1941 as *Berlin Diary*, which became a bestseller.

Shirer settled with his family in Bronxville, New York, and began a regular stint as a CBS commentator Sept. 28, 1941. But he and Murrow (who by 1947 was head of CBS News) came to an unfortunate parting of ways, and Shirer went to Mutual. His final broadcast was April 10, 1949. He then entered a new career, that of contemporary historian. His history of Nazi Germany, *The Rise and Fall of the Third Reich*, was published to great acclaim and financial success in 1960. He was still producing books in his 80s.

1941–47, CBS. 15m, Sundays at 5:45. Sanka Coffee, 1941–43; J. B. Williams, 1943–47.

1947–49, Mutual. 15m, Sundays at 1. Piedmont.

WILLIAM S. HARD, NBC commentator of the early Depression, heard as *Back of the News*: 15m, 1930–31, Wednesdays at 7:45; 1931–32, Tuesdays at 7:45; 1932–33, Tuesdays at 6:45.

WYTHE WILLIAMS, 1940–41, Mutual. 15m, twice a week at 8 for American Razor, and Sundays at 7:45 for Peter Paul.

NICK CARTER, MASTER DETECTIVE, crime melodrama.

BROADCAST HISTORY: April 11, 1943–Sept. 25, 1955, Mutual. Many timeslots from 1943–46; moved every few weeks or months; mostly sustained. October 1944–April 1945, 30m, Sundays at 3 for Acme Paints and Lin-X April-Sept. 1944, 15m serial, four and five times a week, often at 9:15. April 1945–June 1946, 30m, Sundays at 6. March-Aug. 1946, Tuesdays at 8. A long stand Aug. 18, 1946–Sept. 21, 1952, Sundays at 6:30 for Old Dutch Cleanser and Cudahy Packing. Subsequently: 1952–53, Sundays at 6 for Libby Packing. 1953–55, Sundays at 4:30.

CAST: Lon Clark as Nick Carter, brilliant sleuth derived from the old Victorian dime novels. Helen Choate as Nick's assistant, the lovely Patsy Bowen, until mid-1946; Charlotte Manson as Patsy thereafter. John Kane as Scubby Wilson, "demon reporter," friend of Nick and Patsy. Ed Latimer as Sgt. Mathison (Matty to Nick) of the

police department. New York radio actors in support: Bill Johnstone, Bryna Raeburn, Raymond Edward Johnson, etc. **ANNOUNCER:** Michael Fitzmaurice. **MUSIC:** Organ by Lew White, George Wright, Hank Sylvern. **PRODUCER-DIRECTOR:** Jock MacGregor. **WRITERS:** David Kogan, Alfred Bester, Milton J. Kramer, etc.

Nick Carter was a pulp magazine story of the air. During the early days it was broadcast as *The Return of Nick Carter*, an acknowledgement of the hero's origins in the 1886 pages of *Street and Smith* weekly. The stories were in the classic tradition, the murderer revealed only after all the clues had been gathered and deciphered by Nick. Then came the epilogue, when Nick would explain what each clue meant and how irrevocably it sealed the fate of the killer.

Nick and his friends Patsy Bowen and Scubby Wilson made life miserable for Sgt. Mathison of the police department. Mathison took offense at the suggestion that his success in homicide was due to his friendship with Nick Carter, but Patsy usually reminded him anyway. The show's opening was vivid: someone knocking at the door to Carter's Brownstone office. *Bang-bang-bang-bang-bang!* No answer. *Bang-bang-bang-bang-bang!* No answer. Urgently now: *BANG-BANG-BANG-BANG-BANG!* Patsy (jerking the door open with a startled cry): "What's the matter, what is it?" *Another case for Nick Carter, Master Detective!* "Yes, it's another case for that most famous of all manhunters, the detective whose ability at solving crime is unequaled in detective fiction!" The series usually contained subtitles: thus *Death in the Pines* (the title spoken ominously by a graveled voice, just above a whisper) was also billed as *The Mystery of the Murdered Driver.*

THE NIGHT CLUB OF THE AIR, musical variety.

BROADCAST HISTORY: May 20–June 3, 1937, Blue Network. 30m, Thursdays at 11. **CAST:** Morey Amsterdam, master of ceremonies, with singers Clark Dennis and the Morin Sisters. **ANNOUNCER:** Bob Brown. **MUSIC:** Harry Kogen.

Night Club re-created a club atmosphere in a Chicago studio, with floor acts and music. Couples wrote in for tickets, and danced while the show progressed.

NIGHT EDITOR, human interest melodrama.

BROADCAST HISTORY: 1934–48, NBC West Coast. 15m, heard irregularly; known to have been on Sundays at 7:45, 1938–39; Thursdays at 8:15, 1942–43. Edwards Coffee (1940s). **STAR:** Hal Burdick as the Night Editor, who told stories of crime, war, and adventure; occasionally ghost stories (Burdick also characterized the people in his tales, switching roles with slight voice inflections). **ANNOUNCERS:** Wallace Elliot, Bill Baldwin.

The signatures of *Night Editor* were done to "the roar of the presses"; the stories were framed in a "letter to editor" format, with Burdick giving a story requested by a "reader."

NIGHT LIFE, jazz music by black artists.

BROADCAST HISTORY: June 11–July 16, 1946, CBS. 30m, Tuesdays at 10. **HOST:** Willie Bryant. **ORCHESTRA:** Teddy Wilson. **VOCALIST:** Maxine Sullivan.

NIGHT WATCH, crime documentary.

BROADCAST HISTORY: April 5, 1954–April 21, 1955, CBS. 30m, Mondays at 10 until June; Fridays at 9:30 until July 10; Saturdays at 8:30 until Oct.; then Thursdays at 8:30. **CAST:** Donn Reid, reporter, who rode in a prowl car with Sgt. Ron Perkins of the Culver City Police Department. **ANNOUNCER:** Dan Cubberly. **PRODUCER:** Sterling Tracy.

Night Watch was the inevitable result of *Dragnet*'s success, an attempt to bring the crime documentary to its peak by having a microphone present as the crime was being committed. Reporter Donn Reid rode with police during the 6 P.M. to 2 A.M. shift, wearing a hidden wire to capture the high drama of the job. Before the premiere broadcast, Reid had accumulated 100 reels of tape—criminals caught in the act, including a homicide confession and "the statement of a dope fiend." There were no actors, no sound effects, no dramatic musical bridges: everything was authentic, just as it happened. In one case, Reid was nearly shot; in another, he was stabbed but was saved by a leather jacket.

The show was produced in cooperation with Chief W. N. Hildebrande. William Froug supervised for CBS. Vernon McKenny was the engineer, and Ray Gerhardt the editor (removing all traces of real names and locales).

NIGHTBEAT, adventure drama with a newspaper background.

BROADCAST HISTORY: Feb. 6–Nov. 10, 1950; revived March 4, 1951–Sept. 25, 1952, all NBC. 30m, Mondays at 10, until Oct. 1950, then Fridays. Sundays in March-May 1951; Fridays at 8:30, May–Sept.; Fridays at 10, Oct. 1951–April 1952; Thursdays at 8 until July, then at 10. Mostly sustained; General Mills for Wheaties (mid-1950).

CAST: Frank Lovejoy as Randy Stone, who covered the "nightbeat" for the *Chicago Star*. Hollywood radio actors in support: Joan Banks, Ted de Corsia, Tony Barrett, Peter Leeds, Jeanne Bates, Lawrence Dobkin, Wilms Herbert, David Ellis, Stacy Harris, Junius Matthews, Lurene Tuttle, Ruth Perrott, Jeff Corey, Martha Wentworth, Peggy Webber, William Conrad, Jack Kruschen, Bill Johnstone, Parley Baer, Jerry Hausner, Howard McNear, Paul Frees, Charlotte Holland, etc. **MUSIC:** Frank Worth; later, Robert Armbruster. **DIRECTOR:** Warren Lewis. **WRITERS:** Larry Marcus, Russell Hughes, E. Jack Neuman, etc.

Nightbeat was a superior series that focused as much on people as predicament. Frank Lovejoy, a distinctive radio voice, played the role of a reporter who cared about the human interest angle, and about the people who suffered through life's hard knocks. In a Jan. 13, 1950, audition program, the character was named "Lucky" Stone: he prowled Chicago after sundown, looking for a story "that grabs your heart and shakes it until it hollers uncle."

He could be found "peering into blank alleys, wandering through the bright neon, listening to the sounds of the city at night . . . the whisper of footsteps, the shattering roar of an el-train, the sob of an ambulance siren." He stumbled across "the wino dreaming of a muscatel paradise in cold dark doorways . . . painted little dames defying the world with their brassy laughter . . . the homeless, the hopeless." Stone didn't try to outsmart the police, said *Radio Life*; nor did he have a sidekick. Killings were minimized, but the suspense was tense and delicious. There were crime stories, tender stories, tales of the common man in trouble, races against time. Then, having wrapped it up for another night, Stone sat at his desk, pounded out his story, and briskly called, "Copy boy!"

It opened to a bass drum fanfare; the closing invited listeners to join Randy Stone again as he "searches through the city for the strange stories waiting for him in the darkness." The series was timeless and energetic, infused with Lovejoy's unique personality. Happily, the title count now exceeds 100.

NIGHTMARE, dramatic horror anthology.

BROADCAST HISTORY: Oct. 1, 1953–Oct. 6, 1954, Mutual. 30m, Thursdays at 8:30; later Wednesdays. Transcribed in Hollywood. **HOST:** Peter Lorre, "your exciting guide to terror." **EP-IGRAPH:** "Out of the dark of night, from the shadows of the senses, comes this—the fantasy of fear."

NILES AND PRINDLE, comedy; also known as *Ice Box Follies.*

BROADCAST HISTORY: Jan. 24–June 6, 1945, Blue Network. 30m, Wednesdays at 10. Hires Root Beer. **CAST:** Wendell Niles and Don Prindle, announcer and gagwriter respectively, as friends who argued over everything. (*Radio Life*, reviewing the show, found them an amusing pair who couldn't even agree on who was playing the straight man; in a skit on sailing, they argued over who'd wear the captain's hat, then couldn't decide which way the wind was blowing.) **ANNOUNCER:** Harlow Wilcox. **VOCALISTS:** Mel Tormé and the Mel Tones.

THE 1937 RADIO SHOW, musical variety with comedy.

BROADCAST HISTORY: Jan. 3–May 16, 1937, Mutual. 30m, Sundays at 6. Aspergum. **CAST:** Raymond Knight and his Cuckoos, with Sallie Belle Cox; the Ambassadors (vocal trio comprised of Jack Smith, Ray Hall, and Marty Sperzel); Christina Lind. **ANNOUNCER:** Joe Bolton. **PRODUCER AND MUSICAL DIRECTOR:** Arnold Johnson.

The 1937 Radio Show evolved from *National Amateur Night*, assuming the latter's timeslot, with musical director Arnold Johnson the link between the shows. Johnson dropped the amateur format, though *1937* regular Christina

Lind had been one of the amateurs under her real name, Jean Peterson.

NINETY-NINE MEN AND A GIRL, musical variety.

BROADCAST HISTORY: Feb. 22–Aug. 18, 1939, CBS. 30m, Wednesdays at 10 until June, then Fridays at 9. U.S. Tires. **HOSTESS:** "The Incomparable Hildegarde" (Hildegarde Loretta Sell). **ORCHESTRA:** Raymond Paige.

Ninety-Nine Men and a Girl was the result of an idea that bandmaster Raymond Paige had been selling for a decade—that a large orchestra produces sounds like none other, and that listeners would love a program of beloved melodies (including modern hits) played by such a group. But network people believed it would be too expensive and too technically difficult, until Paige obtained the services of the WPA Symphony Orchestra and a sponsor. The show went on.

The "girl," Hildegarde, was a steamy chanteuse then reaching her peak of international appeal. She had come a long way from Milwaukee, where she had once sold hairpins in a department store, sung in Catholic choirs, and played piano in moviehouses. Now she sang such pieces as *Deep Purple* and *Why Do I Love You?*, charging them with emotional international flavor. The orchestra highlighted unusual combinations of instruments: there was an eight-voice choir, and the sound of the full group was described (after the master showman of the '20s) as "Roxy-style." Hildegarde left in June, as the show changed timeslots, and she was followed by a series of guest vocalists (Jane Pickens, Evelyn Case, Vivian Della Chiesa, etc.).

NITWIT COURT, satire.

BROADCAST HISTORY: July 4–Sept. 26, 1944, Blue Network. 30m, Tuesdays at 8:30. Substitute for *Duffy's Tavern.* Ipana Toothpaste. **CAST:** Ransom Sherman as the judge, who dispensed personal advice to any nitwit who came before the microphone. Sara Berner as Bubbles Lowbridge, Mel Blanc as Mr. Hornblower, and Arthur Q. Bryan as Mr. Willow—a "panel" that gave equally ridiculous suggestions.

Nitwit Court, said *Radio Life*, "satirizes *The Goodwill Hour* in the same way that *It Pays to*

Be Ignorant is a comic misrepresentation of *Information, Please.''*

NOAH WEBSTER SAYS, word quiz.

BROADCAST HISTORY: April 4, 1942–Feb. 20, 1943, NBC, West Coast until June 6, 1942, then full NBC Network, 30m, Saturdays at 7 in the East.

July 6–Sept. 28, 1943, Blue Network. 30m, Tuesdays at 8:30. Substitute for *Duffy's Tavern.* Ipana.

July 14–Dec. 1, 1945, NBC. 30m, Saturdays at 7:30.

1945–51, NBC West, continuity uncertain. Wesson Oil and Snowdrift, in part.

HOST - CREATOR - WRITER - PRODUCER - DIRECTOR: Haven MacQuarrie. ANNOUNCER: Doug Gourlay. JUDGE: Professor Charles Frederick Lindsley of Occidental College.

Haven MacQuarrie's lifelong interest in words was the catalyst for *Noah Webster Says.* Webster, of course, was the dictionary. Listeners sent in lists of words; the contestants had to define them. Each show went through about eight contestants: each contestant was given a list of five tough words. The contestant won $1 for defining the first word, $2 for the second, $3 for the third, $4 more for the fourth, and at that point was eligible for a go-for-broke prize of $50. Winners were given a "final exam," a written quiz to determine how to divide up the money that had been lost by the losers. "Judge" Lindsley was the final authority on whether a contestant had won or lost.

MacQuarrie's previous air credits had been *Do You Want to Be an Actor?* and *The Marriage Club.* Though it was heard regionally for most of its run, *Webster* drew letters (as many as 30,000 pieces a week) from all parts of the country. Its coast-to-coast summer run for *Duffy's Tavern* in 1943 was ironic: Archie, the manager on *Duffy's,* mangled the language as a sport. MacQuarrie was witty with words, and Noah Webster Clubs popped up around the country. In 1944, when Robert Ripley declared in a panel strip that only six words in English ended with the letters "cion," MacQuarrie promptly found a seventh.

NOBODY'S CHILDREN, interviews with and dramas about orphaned children.

BROADCAST HISTORY: July 2, 1939–Jan. 12, 1941, Mutual. 30m, various Saturday or Sunday timeslots. HOST-CREATOR: Walter White Jr. GUESTS: Celebrities including Jack Benny, Otto Kruger, Jeanette MacDonald, etc., who talked with homeless children. SERIES "MATRON": Georgia Fifield. VOCALISTS: The Robert Mitchell Boys' Choir. ANNOUNCER: Bill Kennedy.

The interest of Walter White in the problems of orphans came about when he and his wife were told, wrongly, that they might never have children of their own. As they explored orphanages, White envisioned a radio show combining Hollywood glamor with a social need. After the orphans had been interviewed by a famous film star, they would be hustled away out of earshot while White and the guest discussed the real circumstances of the case. The show centered around cases at the Children's Home Society of Los Angeles: placements from the home rose dramatically during the show's time on the air. The first guest, Barbara Stanwyck, was said to have postponed her honeymoon with Robert Taylor so she could do the show. Actress Fay Bainter burst into tears after touring the home. The series was heard later in 1941, and in 1942, on the West Coast.

NONA FROM NOWHERE, soap opera.

BROADCAST HISTORY: Jan. 9, 1950–Jan. 5, 1951, CBS. 15m, weekdays at 3. Bab-O. CAST: Toni Darnay as Nona Dutell, young lovely searching for her natural parents. Karl Weber as Vernon Dutell, her adoptive father. James Kelly as film producer Pat Brady. Florence Robinson as Gwen Parker. Mitzi Gould as Thelma Powell. ANNOUNCER: Ford Bond. PRODUCERS: Frank and Anne Hummert.

NOW HEAR THIS, Navy drama.

BROADCAST HISTORY: June 24–Nov. 4, 1951, NBC. 30m, Sundays at 5:30. CAST: Arnold Robertson as Boats, narrator of these "dramatic stories based on the personal experiences of those gallant men and women who embody the great traditions of a great service—the United States Navy." Larry Haines also as Boats. New York radio actors in support: Jack Grimes, James McCallion, Bill Quinn, Maurice Tarplin, Don Griggs, Bob Readick, Bill Zuckert, Richard Newton, Charles Smith,

Chuck Webster, Jim Boles, Bernard Lenrow, John Sylvester, Sandy Becker, Frank Behrens, Ian Martin, Lyle Sudrow, Gilbert Mack, William Redfield, Casey Allen, Leon Janney, Frank Maxwell, Clifford Carpenter, Inge Adams, etc. ANNOUNCER: Jack Costello. PRODUCERS: Chick Vincent; Sy Levine. WRITER-DIRECTOR: David Harmon. THEME: *Anchors Aweigh*.

Most of the stories on *Now Hear This* were set in World War II, "the dirty days of the early war." The experiences of sailors everywhere were related through the character known as Boats, a gruff salt with a no-nonsense attitude about the Navy. Boats told of marine landings, of underwater demolition teams, of the war in the Aleutians, and of Seabees in action. The signature was the sharp blast of the bosun's pipe, and the orders of the day: the closing signature was likewise endowed, the bosun calling the "all hands secure until 1730 next Sunday."

NOW IT CAN BE TOLD, fictionalized war drama, previously classified.

BROADCAST HISTORY: June 25–Aug. 24, 1945, Mutual. 15m, weeknights at 8:15. NARRATOR: Don Logan. PRODUCER: Dan Seymour. DIRECTOR: Anton M. Leader.

NTG AND HIS GIRLS, musical variety.

BROADCAST HISTORY: July 9, 1935–Jan. 21, 1936, NBC; Blue Network through Oct. 22, then Red. 30m, Tuesdays at 9. Bromo Seltzer. HOST: Nils T. Granlund. ORCHESTRA: Harry Salter. DIRECTOR: Herb Polesie of J. Walter Thompson. WRITER: Carroll Carroll. THEME: *Four Bars*.

NTG and His Girls capitalized, with lukewarm results, upon the dual attractions of the nightclub chorus line and the amateur show. The proprietor, Nils Thor Granlund, was a radio pioneer, restaurateur, and producer of many nightclub floor shows. He was self-promoted as "big brother of every girl in show business," and on *NTG* he proposed to pluck six or eight "girls" out of chorus lines and give them a chance to perform solo.

Granlund had done this, it was said, for many girls in his long career: Joan Crawford, Ruby Keeler, and Barbara Stanwyck were listed as graduates of his chorus lines. His roots in radio were deep: in 1922 he was at WHN, New York, where he organized amateur shows and read poetry on the air. He stood before a carbon microphone, as Ben Gross remembered it, "and with a sob recited Kipling" to the enchantment of his fans. With Harry Richman, he began what Gross believed to be the first of the trumped-up radio feuds.

In the 1920s, he became a producer of stage revues. Writer Carroll Carroll recalled his "ballroom-type cabarets" in "block-long lofts" on upper floors of buildings just off Broadway. "The rooms featured a line of 12 to 16 girls, and that's about the age Granny liked them. They wore as little as the going law allowed, danced, sang, and looked available." Carroll, who was assigned to write the *NTG* radio show as a staffer for J. Walter Thompson, was little impressed by Granlund or his show. He was a "fanny-patter," Carroll would write in his memoir, and none of the girls ever did more than one show "because none had that much talent. But the show went on and I was the midwife who delivered it."

Said *Newsweek*: "Only the lack of the gong and the girls' professional standing distinguish it from any amateur show."

O

OF MEN AND BOOKS, the book review column of the air.

BROADCAST HISTORY: May 26, 1938–Dec. 21, 1946, CBS. 15m and 30m formats, heard in various timeslots, often Saturday afternoons. Revived Jan. 15–July 22, 1948. **HOST-CRITIC:** John T. Frederick, professor of modern letters at Northwestern University's Medill School of Journalism. Later, John Mason Brown; Russell Maloney and Sterling North, 1948. **PRODUCER:** CBS Adult Education section.

Host Frederick reviewed one to three books per show: these, said *Radio Guide*, were works that "impress him as significant interpretations of American life, with particular stress on regional literature." Occasional guests were used. In one show, guest T. V. Smith debated himself on the season's newest books. Smith was a University of Chicago professor as well as a congressman from Illinois. First he considered the books as a scholar; then he tore into his own conclusions as a legislator.

OFFICIAL DETECTIVE, police melodrama.

BROADCAST HISTORY: Jan. 19, 1947–March 7, 1957, Mutual. Many weekly timeslots, including Tuesdays at 8:30 (1948 and 1949–52) and Thursdays at 8 (1953–57). 15m until Sept. 1947; then 30m. Pharmaco, 1947–48; otherwise sustained. Presented "in cooperation with *Official Detective Stories Magazine*." **CAST:** Craig McDonnell as Detective Lt. Dan Britt. Tommy Evans as Sgt. Al Bowen. **DIRECTOR:** Wynn Wright.

Official Detective was produced in New York. The cases weren't always murders: they ranged from arson to insurance scams. The hero occasionally stumbled and wasn't always right, but the same thing was done more effectively on *The Lineup* and far more effectively on *Dragnet*.

OG, SON OF FIRE, prehistoric serial drama with cave people characters.

BROADCAST HISTORY: Oct. 1, 1934–Dec. 27, 1935, CBS. 15m, three a week at 5 as part of the Libby Packing *Adventure Hour*. **CAST:** Alfred Brown as Og. Patricia Dunlap as Nad. James Andelin as Ru. **CREATOR-WRITER:** Irving Crump.

There was little difference between *Og* and *Jack Armstrong* except for the prehistoric setting, according to a *Variety* review. Soundmen Herb Johnson and Louie Wehr were cited for noisiest effects and for creativity in bringing brontosauri and other beasts to life.

THE OLD GOLD HOUR, sometimes known as *The Old Gold Program*: a commercial name for many variety series sponsored by Old Gold Cigarettes.

The titles were used for, perhaps among others, *The Paul Whiteman Hour* (CBS, 60m, Tuesdays at 9, 1929–30); *Fred Waring* (CBS, 30m, Wednesdays at 10, 1933–34); *The Old Gold*

Show, with Dick Powell, Harry Richman, Milton Berle, and the Ted Fio Rito Orchestra (CBS, 30m, Wednesdays at 10, Feb. 7–May 3, 1934); *Melody and Madness*, with Artie Shaw and Robert Benchley (CBS, 30m, Sundays at 10, 1938-39; then Blue Network, Tuesdays at 9, 1939); *The New Old Gold Show*, covered under that title; *The Frank Sinatra Show* (CBS, 30m, Wednesdays at 9, 1945–47); and *The Don Ameche Show*, with Frances Langford and Frank Morgan (CBS, 30m, Fridays at 9, 1947–48).

OLSEN AND JOHNSON, vaudeville-style comedy.

BROADCAST HISTORY: Sept. 22, 1933–March 30, 1934, CBS. 30m, Fridays at 10. Swift Packing. STARS: Ole Olsen and Chic Johnson (real names John Sigvard Olsen and Harold Ogden Johnson). Their style was simple and visual: they never made any real inroad in radio and, except for this short run, were confined to guest appearances on other shows.

OMAR, THE MYSTIC, juvenile adventure serial.

BROADCAST HISTORY: Oct. 7, 1935–July 10, 1936, Mutual. 25m, weekdays at 5:05. Tasty Bread. CAST: M. H. H. Joachim as Omar. Ethel Everett as Zaidda. A *Chandu, the Magician* offshoot.

ON STAGE, dramatic anthology; aired as *Cathy and Elliott Lewis on Stage*.

BROADCAST HISTORY: Jan. 1, 1953–Sept. 30, 1954, CBS. 30m, Thursdays at 8:30 until Sept. 1953, then Wednesdays at 9 or 10 until April 1954, then Thursdays at 9. CAST: Cathy and Elliott Lewis in dramas with strong male-female relationships. Hollywood radio actors in support: Byron Kane, Peggy Webber, Mary Jane Croft, Clayton Post, John McIntire, Jeanette Nolan, William Conrad, Howard McNear, Lou Merrill, GeGe Pearson, John Dehner, Ben Wright, Barney Phillips, Tony Barrett, Edgar Barrier, Paul Frees, Joan Danton, Jack Kruschen, Joseph Kearns, Truda Marson, Tyler McVey, Johnny McGovern, Lee Millar, Ken Christy, Bob Sweeney, Hal Gerard, Martha Wentworth, Vivi Janiss, Paula Winslowe, Sheldon Leonard, Junius Matthews, Frank Nelson, Peter Leeds, Jay Novello, Harry Bartell, etc. ANNOUNCER: George Walsh. MUSIC: Lud Gluskin, conductor; Fred Steiner, composer. PRODUCER-DIRECTOR: Elliott Lewis. WRITERS: Morton Fine and David Friedkin; also, E. Jack Neuman (who specialized in hard-hitting, controversial pieces that drew strong mail) and Shirley Gordon (who wrote sensitive stories about the mysteries of love). THEME: *The Cathy and Elliott Theme*, by Ray Noble.

On Stage was a groundbreaking dramatic series capping the radio careers of Cathy and Elliott Lewis. It came in what might have been a watershed era but was instead radio's last hurrah. The Lewises reached the crest as the ship began to sink, though in a strange way it was a time of peace. The war with television had been lost in a single season, and the big money had gone, as it always does, with the winner.

What was left on radio fell into several broad categories, none ruled by money as they had been in the old days. Agencies and producers still had radio budgets, but the tide had irrevocably turned. The end of big-time radio had for its best artists a liberating effect. "I can do things now that I wouldn't dare to do two or three years ago," said Elliott Lewis in *Newsweek* in mid-1953. As producer-director of *Suspense*, he had just aired a two-part adaptation of Shakespeare's *Othello*, which would have been unthinkable for the thrill show in 1945. Network people paid less attention, and if money was tighter, there was no lack of talent to prove it. People still wanted to work in radio: they remained because it was a dear first love, terminally ill and soon to disappear. Jack Benny and Jack Webb were still on the air; *Gunsmoke* was in its first year, and just ahead were more frugal but extremely creative shows—*X-Minus One*, *Frontier Gentleman*, and *The CBS Radio Workshop*. These were produced and enacted by people who loved what they were doing: some would mourn its final loss so deeply that they spoke of it reluctantly even two decades later. It was in this time that the Lewises produced *On Stage*, by some accounts the best radio anthology ever heard.

Elliott Lewis had as active a radio career as anyone in the industry. A native of New York, he went to Los Angeles to study law and instead began playing toughs on the air. This was in

1939, which he once described as "the beginning of the wonderful decade for radio." Business was booming: by 1940, he was doing 20 or more shows a week and had arrived at that envious plateau of being in constant demand. His brash Manhattan accent, it was discovered, could be effective in comedy, tragedy, or melodrama. He could play psychopaths, leading men, and sarcastic stooges. He went into Armed Forces Radio in World War II, emerging as a master sergeant with a career in his pocket and a new wife at his side.

Cathy Lewis was by then as active in radio as her husband. She had come to Hollywood in 1936 with the goal of becoming a singer. They were introduced by a mutual friend, who thought it might be amusing since they shared the surname. They were married April 30, 1943. Cathy had had brief flings at stage and film work, and now her unmistakable voice began appearing—often uncredited—on dozens of shows (*Suspense, The Whistler*, and many others; long runs on *The Great Gildersleeve* and the *Michael Shayne* detective series). Occasionally the Lewises crossed paths at the microphone: they were notably together on *Suspense* and *The Adventures of Sam Spade*, and it was during a 1948 episode of *The Clock* on ABC when the seeds of *On Stage* were planted. Someone suggested that they should work together regularly, perhaps in their own theater. They took this to heart, and kept it in mind for years.

The time was right in 1952, when they had reached the top in radio; known in the industry as "Mr. and Mrs. Radio," they were the busiest people on the air. In addition to producing and directing *Suspense*, Elliott was running *Broadway Is My Beat* in the same capacity. He was also playing his greatest comedy role, the hard-drinking guitar player (originally called Frankie Remley but now named Elliott Lewis) on *The Phil Harris/Alice Faye Show*. Cathy was busy as Jane Stacy on *My Friend Irma*, on radio and TV. The TV show was the time-killer, she said: it took many times the commitment of the radio series, and she was to drop it in 1953.

In late 1952, the Lewises were told by CBS to go ahead with the anthology idea, and immediately they began forming their own production company. This was called Haven Radio Productions, named for the home they occupied in Beverly Hills. Through this entity they would produce and transcribe their show. The stories would be rooted in powerful male-female situations, with two characters of equal strength the goal for each. They would use a mix of classic and original tales, cutting across all dramatic disciplines: there would be mysteries, adventures, melodramas, satires, and farcical comedies. But there wouldn't be stereotypes—no foreign agents, no newspaper reporters, no private-eye-and-his-girl pieces. The series came and went and was soon forgotten. But many transcriptions were saved, and the present is enriched by *On Stage* on tape, a vivid example of how good radio could be.

Still, a table of highlights at this writing remains sketchy, as less than half the run has thus far surfaced. Superb entertainment were *The Public Furlough* (a sad and haunting commentary by writer Antony Ellis on the shallow nature of fame); *Four Meetings* (a Henry James tale about a man who met a certain woman four times during his life); *The Party* (a near-perfect slice-of-life giving a searing picture of the two protagonists against the bleary background of a boozy party); *Call Me a Cab* (a marvelous Shirley Gordon treatise on loneliness); *Eddie* (the E. Jack Neuman story that drew such heavy mail, pro and con; perhaps the first time that the theme of a woman's vulnerability to a man who forces his way into her life was so graphically demonstrated); *Statement of Fact* (Neuman's gripping account of a ruthless district attorney and his interrogation of a female murder suspect); *Dig the Thief* (a very funny swindle plot that goes awry); and *The Bear* (Walter Brown Newman's adaptation of the Anton Chekhov comedy).

Two of the *On Stage* plays had special personal relevance for the stars. *The Anniversary* (aired on their tenth anniversary, April 30, 1953) told of the ups and downs of married life; and *Heartbreak* prefaced the heart problems that Elliott faced in later years. In that later life, he would produce a stereo radio series, *The Zero Hour*, would write a series of detective novels, and would serve as a "script doctor" on the TV show *Remington Steele*. His marriage to Cathy Lewis ended in divorce in 1958; he then married actress Mary Jane Croft, with whom he lived the rest of his life. Cathy died at 50, a lung cancer victim, on Nov. 20, 1968. Elliott died May 20, 1990, after recurring heart trouble.

ON THE TOWN, interviews and variety.

BROADCAST HISTORY: Nov. 19, 1940–Feb. 12, 1941, Mutual. 15m, twice a week at 7:15. HOST: Eddie Mayehoff. MUSIC: Tommy Dorsey.

ONE MAN'S FAMILY, the great American radio serial.

BROADCAST HISTORY: April 29, 1932–June 4, 1950, 30m weekly continuation. Initially heard Fridays at 9:30 Pacific time, in San Francisco, Los Angeles, and Seattle; became part of the full NBC West Coast network in May 1932; 9:30 Wednesdays as of Aug. 3, 1932, sponsored by Snowdrift and Wesson Oil. On May 17, 1933, *One Man's Family* went on the coast-to-coast NBC network, becoming the first West Coast show regularly heard in the East. Sponsored by Penn Tobacco Company for the new Kentucky Winner Cigarette beginning in the fall of 1934; by April 1935, Standard Brands had become the sponsor, promoting Fleischmann's Yeast, Royal Puddings and Gelatin, and Tenderleaf Tea for the next 14 years. Timeslots (all times now Eastern): 1935–39, Wednesdays at 8; Oct.–Dec. 1939, Thursdays at 8; 1940–45, Sundays at 8:30; 1945–49, Sundays at 3:30; 1949–50, Sundays at 3. Dropped by Standard Brands in Sept. 1949; sustained until June 4, 1950, when reorganized to 15m weekdays.

June 5, 1950–May 8, 1959, NBC. 15m continuation, weeknights at 7:45. Miles Laboratories for Alka-Seltzer, Bactine, and Tabcin. Episodes broadcast, 1932–59: 3,256.

CAST: J. Anthony Smythe as Henry Barbour, a stockbroker who, with his wife Fanny, lived in the Sea Cliff area of San Francisco and raised five children (in order, Paul, Hazel, twins Claudia and Clifford, and Jack): Smythe played Henry Barbour from the first broadcast to the last, 27 years. Minetta Ellen as Fanny Barbour, 1932–55; Mary Adams thereafter. Michael Raffetto as son Paul, an aviator and writer who was frequently at odds with his father; Russell Thorson as Paul Barbour from ca. mid-1955, when Raffetto left the role because of a voice affliction. Bernice Berwin as Hazel Barbour, 1932–ca. 1958. Kathleen Wilson as Claudia, 1932 until Aug. 1943, when she married and left the show; Claudia written out until Oct. 1945; Barbara Fuller as the "new" Claudia, 1945–59.

Barton Yarborough as Clifford, 1932 until Yarborough's death (of a heart attack) Dec. 19, 1951; Clifford then written out of the script. Page Gilman as Jack Barbour, beginning to end. SUPPORTING CAST: Bert Horton as Bill Herbert, Hazel's first husband, early to mid-1930s. Wally Maher as Dan Murray, Hazel's later husband; Russell Thorson, Bill Bouchey, and Ken Peters also as Dan Murray. Helen Musselman as Ann Waite, Clifford's troubled first wife. Naomi Stevens and Janet Waldo as Irene Franklin, Clifford's second wife. Frank Provo as Johnny Roberts, Claudia's first husband, early 1930s. Walter Paterson as Nicholas Lacey, Claudia's second husband, until Paterson's suicide in 1942; Nicholas then written out until 1945; Tom Collins as Nicholas from ca. 1945; Dan O'Herlihy and Ben Wright also as Nicholas in later years. Jean Rouverol as Betty Carter, Jack's wife; Virginia Gregg also as Betty. THIRD GENERATION: Winifred Wolfe as Teddy Lawton Barbour, Paul's adopted daughter; Jeanne Bates also as Teddy. Conrad Binyon, Dickie Meyers, and Bill Idleson as Hazel's son Hank (Martin Henry Herbert). Richard Svihus as Hank's twin brother, Pinky (William Barbour Herbert), Hazel's irresponsible and troublesome son; Dix Davis, Eddie Firestone Jr., Tommy Bernard, George Pirrone, and Bill Idelson also as Pinky. Dawn Bender as Hazel's daughter, Margaret. Anne Shelley and Mary Lou Harrington as Claudia's daughter Joan Roberts, the former beginning at age 4. Anne Whitfield as Claudia's daughter Penelope Lacey. Many performers as Clifford's son Andy (also known as Skippy or the Skipper), including Mary Lansing (Skippy as a child), Henry Blair, Michael Chapin, and David Frankham. Jack's children figured peripherally in the story and were crossplayed by many of the same performers: Mary Lansing, Susan Luckey, Jill Oppenheim, Marilyn Steiner, and Susan Odin as Jack's daughter Elizabeth Sharon Ann; Luckey, Odin, and Jana Leff as Jack's daughter Janie; Mary Lansing and Mary McGovern as Jack's daughter Mary Lou; Jack's triplets, Abigail, Deborah, and Constance Barbour, all played by Leone Ledoux, who specialized in baby talk. Ledoux also as Joan's son, Paul John Farnsworth, the first great-grandchild. SPOUSES OF GRANDCHILDREN, ROMANTIC INTERESTS, FRIENDS, AND NEIGHBORS: Barbara Jo Allen as Beth Holly, Paul's flame of the 1930s. Mary Jane Croft as Christine Abbott, the great love of Paul's later years. Jeanette Nolan as Paul's friend Nicolette Moore. Cy Kendall as Henry's old friend and romantic rival, Dr. Fred Thompson; Frank Cooley, Earl Lee, William Green, and Emerson Tracy also as Dr. Thompson. Charles McAllister as Henry's other old friend, Judge Glenn Hunter; George Rand, Norman Field, Lloyd Corrigan, Herb Butterfield, and Jay Novello also as Judge Hunter. Brothers Sam and Jack Edwards as Tracy Baker and Wayne Grubb, Teddy's suitors of the early war era. Vic Perrin as Ross Farnsworth, who married Claudia's daughter Joan. Tyler McVey as Elwood Giddings, who married Teddy. Bob Bailey as Raymond Borden. Marvin Miller as Roderick Stone and in many other roles. Sharon Douglas as Greta Steffanson and as Lois Holland. Jimmy McCallion as Sidney Lawrence. ANNOUNCERS: William Andrews, from the beginning; Ken Carpenter in the 1940s; Frank Barton thereafter. ORGANISTS: Paul Carson, 1932–51; Sybil Chism, 1951–54; Martha Green. CREATOR-WRITER-DIRECTOR: Carlton E. Morse. Also: Harlen Ware and Michael Raffetto, writers; Clinton Buddy Twiss, Charles Buck, George Fogle, and Michael Raffetto, directors. THEMES: *Destiny Waltz*, 1932–41; the most memorable theme, *Waltz Patrice*, or *Patricia*, composed by Paul Carson, used thereafter.

Seldom in modern entertainment has the American public taken to its heart an entire fictional family in quite the same way that people embraced the Barbours of Sea Cliff, San Francisco. Creator Carlton E. Morse loosely followed the example of John Galsworthy in *The Forsyte Saga*: a sprawling family tree with tempestuous people who loved each other but often disagreed. It went where soap opera seldom trod—into prime time, doing battle with the giants and emerging at its peak with a giant share of the audience. Its 28.7 CAB rating in 1939–40 put it well up among the top five shows in the nation. Though it couldn't hold such a lofty peak, it remained a solid favorite of more than 15 million listeners for years.

People grew up and grew old listening to the Barbours: more than that, the Barbours grew old. Never has a serial so accurately portrayed the river of life and the aging process in its characters. The patriarch, Henry Barbour, was a stern white-collar working man when the series premiered in 1932: he was a doting, fussing great-grandfather when it left the air in 1959. There

was a deep sense of permanence even when the cast and characters were struck by sudden death. The same actors played the seven major roles for many years, and two of them went the distance.

Carlton E. Morse was born June 4, 1901, in Jennings, La. He was raised on a fruit and dairy ranch in Oregon—a background he would use well in his radio work. At 17, he enrolled at the University of California at San Francisco, developing a strong affection for the city he would depict years later. In the 1920s he was a newspaperman. He married Patricia DeBall (who would lobby him vigorously on *One Man's Family* plot developments in the 1930s, and in 1942 wrote an important six-part *Radio Guide* history of the Barbours, lovingly told and accurate within its fictional context).

In 1929, Morse took a job at NBC, San Francisco, where, headquartered at KGO, he began writing and producing radio serials. Some of his titles—*The Cross-Eyed Parrot, Phantoms at Sea, House of Myths, Chinatown Squad, Split-Second Tales*, and *Jack and Ethel*—have been dimmed by time; but *City of the Dead* and *Dead Men Prowl* would serve him again, on the 1944 syndication *Adventures by Morse*. At KGO, he began putting together the framework for *One Man's Family*. Believing that the rise of juvenile delinquency had a direct relationship to the deterioration of the family after the world war, he thought of a serial that stressed family ties. *The Forsyte Saga* was his working model, and some of the young players from the university theater program might fill the roles.

Morse visioned a big family: the Forsytes were such, and so was his own family. In the beginning, there would be seven: Henry Barbour, his wife Fanny, and their children: Paul, Hazel, Claudia, Clifford, and Jack. Though Morse in later life would staunchly deny it ("the only similarity with my family is that it's conservative"), his wife had a different view. "Father Barbour is Father Morse, even to his beefing and being crazy about the girls in the family. Mother Barbour is a combination of my mother and Carlton's. Carlton may not know it himself, but he is Paul: much of the philosophy that Paul gives on the air is Carlton's. Hazel is a combination of his sisters. When the character of Claudia was first created, Carlton took the part from me, I think. All the Morse men are intensely devoted people, especially to their wives. Father and Mother Morse, who live in Sacramento, have been married for 44 years [1943], but they are still lovers. Every year the Morse family holds a reunion consisting of Carlton's mother and father, his brothers and sisters and their children—there were 68 people last year when we held the gathering at our Woodside place on the peninsula south of San Francisco. The Sky Ranch [the idyllic farm owned by Claudia and her family in the serial] is Woodside idealized. We haven't a pool at Woodside yet.''

In 1932, Morse wrote out the first three chapters, and was given permission by NBC's Don Gilman (father of the actor who would play Jack) to try it on the air. But Gilman warned that he had better write the sixth chapter with a conclusion in mind, in case it failed to catch on. On April 29, 1932, West Coast listeners heard for the first time the dedication that would be repeated weekly and sometimes daily for the next 27 years: "*One Man's Family* is dedicated to the mothers and fathers of the younger generation, and to their bewildering offspring." Somewhere in the interim, Morse had been given a longer rein, but it was still announced as a limited 13-week run.

The cast was introduced by their fictional names. Henry Barbour was "a successful San Francisco stockbroker who has reached the peak of middle life." Though Henry's history was not discussed on that opening show, Morse would fill it in as the serial grew in stature and strength. Listeners would learn that Henry came to San Francisco as a very young boy with his parents. Transplants from Ohio, they were confirmed San Franciscans from that first spring day in 1879. Henry made friends with the boys of the neighborhood, notably Glenn Hunter and Fred Thompson, who in adulthood would become a judge and doctor. Henry's good-natured rivalry with these two began in 1893, at a party in the Palace Hotel, when they all scrambled for the affections of Fanny Martin. Henry won that courtship; he and Fanny married May 10, 1896, and established a home at Sea Cliff, just below where the Golden Gate Bridge would be built 40 years later.

Henry established the brokerage house that bore his name on Montgomery Street in 1912. This prospered under his tight rein for three decades. In 1932, Henry was still years away from the retired grandfather that listeners only to the later run would remember. He was a crusty and strict father, completely dedicated to family life and the American way. He believed in corporal punishment. In the first episode, he hauled young Jack into the living room by the ear, and later shows established that he kept a "hard-soled slipper" in his bedroom. To spare the rod was to spoil the child. Henry was suspicious of anyone who failed to embrace his philosophy. The bigger the family the better, thought Henry Barbour in those long-ago days before problems with this viewpoint became obvious.

Again from the opening episode, the spotlight falls on Hazel: at 27, the eldest daughter, "and good-looking, too." Then comes "the hero of the Barbour family," Paul, age 31, an aviator who was shot down in the world war. "One of Paul's legs was badly injured—he'll use a cane for the rest of his life." The listener can hear the tapping of the cane as Paul comes forth to be introduced. Next are the twins, Claudia and Clifford: "they're just nineteen, straightforward, honest-eyed, lovable . . . they go in pairs." The youngest, Jack, is 14, still at the stage when airplane models are more exciting than girls.

Although it was sometimes said (and published in premium books) that Claudia was married in 1931, the opening script shows this not to be the case. The initial crisis was the accidental shooting by Claudia of young Johnny Roberts, her future husband. At a party, Johnny had tried to "get fresh"; a gun was present, one thing led to another, and Johnny took a flesh wound in the shoulder. Another pattern was established: it fell to Paul to set things straight. The phone call to the family home caught Paul in the first of many philosophical disputes with his father. He had returned from the war a pacifist. "I'd rot in jail before I'd fight again," he tells Henry and Judge Hunter, "and I'd rather see Cliff and Jack stood up against a wall and shot than to be sent to front-line trenches." The world war he calls "the most horrible catastrophe known to man . . . that's what your generation of thinking men did for the world." Paul, it will soon be revealed, lost his young wife, Elaine Hunter, in the flu epidemic: she was an army nurse, and they had less than a month together before Paul was assigned in France. From the first day, Paul and Henry will wage a war of attitude, of changing morals: in Henry's eyes, the right to be called the head of the family.

The serial was an immediate success. Letters to journals praised its unprecedented realism. Never, it was repeatedly stressed, had anything remotely approaching the lifelike qualities of *One Man's Family* been presented on American radio. When public outcry against tobacco sponsorship forced Kentucky Winner Cigarettes out of the show in early 1935, after only nine weeks, Morse received a letter of apology from Penn Tobacco president T. F. Flanagan, praising the show as "the finest artistic performance on the radio in the United States." People everywhere were fascinated by the Barbours: they embodied so many conflicting elements that tense situations were always at the surface. There were no heroes. Henry was stubborn and hidebound, yet he had moments of magnificent mettle. He could put on airs; he was bullheaded and overbearing and in the end something of a snob, and still he managed to be warm and even lovable. Fanny was the family peacemaker: her exasperation with Henry was frequently heard in nothing more than a sigh. She knew that buried on Henry's side of the rift with Paul was rankling jealousy: the siblings would confide in Paul secrets they would never tell their father.

Early in the run, Hazel married Paul's old war buddy, William Herbert. Herbert was solid and right-thinking, and even Henry liked him at once. This was not the case with Johnny Roberts: Henry was outraged when Claudia eloped to Reno with this irresponsible boy. But Hazel had always been her father's favorite, the one most like her mother. Claudia was tempestuous, fiery, and eager for adventure. She and Clifford would sit on the sea wall, watching ships steam away to the Orient. "Once they divided up the world between them," Fanny wrote in her *Memory Book*. "Cliff took the sky because it was quiet and peaceful. Claudia took the ocean because it was changeable, restless. I guess that describes Claudia's nature as well as anything could."

In January 1933, the first grandchildren were born, the twin sons of Hazel and William Herbert: Martin Henry and William Barbour Herbert—Hank and Pinky for short. But Claudia's marriage was doomed from the start: John Roberts was brash and thoughtless, and soon he had abandoned his wife to enlist in the National Chinese Army. Wounded in the civil war, he caught pneumonia and died. His estate was a fortune: at $350,000, enough to bring independence for the young widow and leave her forever free of parental control. But Henry would never give up his right to criticize: he believed she should refuse the estate because Johnny Roberts had not lived up to the proper code of conduct. There were many arguments, and in 1933 Claudia gave birth to Joan Roberts, the third grandchild, in an atmosphere of bickering and uncertainty.

Clifford too felt his father's stern scrutiny. Claudia's elopement had left a gulf in his life. Gone was his twin, his soulmate, and he lost himself in the pursuit of girls. Henry loudly disapproved of Clifford's reputation as a playboy. Henry had hopes that at least one of his sons would follow him in the brokerage house. Paul, obviously, would not: he had continued his career in aviation, to Henry's deep annoyance. Henry focused on Clifford, who remained a ne'er-do-well. Cliff talked of becoming an actor, yet another worthless occupation in Henry's eyes, and filled his time in the frivolous pursuit of new women. One of Cliff's girlfriends, a level-headed woman named Beth Holly, became a long-running romantic interest, her tenure spanning the decade. The romance took an unexpected twist when Cliff backed away and Paul stepped in to take his place. Although even Father Barbour would come to love her in time, Beth was viewed with chilly indifference by all in the early days of the relationship. This too was a recurring theme—the hazard of falling in love with a Barbour: Henry, and sometimes the others as well, put up such a wall of resistance that only the strongest love could survive.

Marriage was not in Paul's life plan, but he did adopt a daughter, Teddy Lawton, in 1933. She was 8 years old, and she and her sister, Lindy, were orphans. They had come to live in Sea Cliff with the Carter family. Teddy swung on the gate and chatted away as Father Barbour worked in his garden. She loved Paul desperately, and over time she found her way into his heart. When Lindy moved east to be married, Paul brought Teddy into the family: the adoption was handled by Judge Hunter, and Teddy became as much a part of the Barbours as the original five. Paul took pride in watching her grow into a fine young woman, and they took long walks and talked into the night, Paul filling the air with his philosophy and wisdom. But Teddy's love was misdirected: it was she who drove the final wedge between Paul and Beth

Holly. Beth refused to compete with a child, and the romance melted away.

Hazel and Bill Herbert had settled down the peninsula, on a dairy ranch with their sons. Clifford had given in to the stronger personality and joined his father's brokerage house. But this did not last: Soon he again considered acting, and drew Henry's fire. Claudia had left home, taking her baby on a trip to Europe, after weeks of haggling over her inheritance. At loose ends, Beth Holly went with her. On the crossing, Claudia met Capt. Nicholas Lacey, an officer with the British army in India, and accepted his invitation to the Lacey estate in Devonshire. They were married in mid-1935. Beth Holly married millionaire Philip Spencer, a union that quickly fell apart. And even young Jack was learning about love: he had become infatuated with Vivian, the "pesky little girl next door," but remained friends with Betty Carter.

Nicholas and Claudia Lacey were immediately among Sea Cliff's upper crust. They owned a home five houses down from the family estate, and in August 1936 they bought a 400-acre ranch 40 miles south of town, not far from the dairy ranch where Hazel and Bill Herbert lived. This they called the Sky Ranch: Nicky would raise fine Thoroughbred horses for sale to the government, and the family would use the ranch for outings and summer vacations. Claudia also owned the house next door to the family home: it was part of her inheritance from Johnny Roberts, and it stood empty and dark. This, she announced, would be her gift to the first of her brothers to marry.

Clifford had left the brokerage house to try acting. The bickering with his father intensified, then became ridicule when Henry learned that Clifford's role was merely "the second burglar" in a melodrama called *The City of the Dead*. Henry's relentless arguing finally pushed Cliff back to the brokerage house, but his chase after girls continued. For a time he was infatuated with Marian Galloway, daughter of the firm's treasurer, who killed himself when a mistake cost Henry a small fortune. Marian was "wise beyond her years": she accepted Cliff's ring, but this too ended badly when she decided that he was still too fond of other women.

Then Cliff met Ann Waite, a daughter of a music professor at the university. "She was like a gentle strain of music herself," Patricia Morse wrote in *Radio Guide*. "Clifford loved her madly, fiercely, but his efforts to approach her softly—to reach her plane of thought and feeling—were obviously failures from the moment they were married." Henry gave them a trip to the Orient. This was a "thrill to Cliff," Mrs. Morse wrote, "but it was one long violence to Ann," who viewed the marriage as a spiritual union and was repelled by the physical side of it. The new couple also won the house next door, Claudia's wedding gift, but never lived there. They returned from the honeymoon only to separate, Ann retreating to her father's home and Cliff moving back with the Barbours. Thereafter, Cliff was like a "lost child." His troubles culminated in two disasters—an auto accident on the Bay Bridge when Cliff driving in a daze, plowed into a maintenance truck; and Ann's death in childbirth. From the accident he would have long memory gaps and would wear a metal plate in his head; from the death of his wife he would gain a son, but one he could not bear to look at. He had not even known of Ann's pregnancy.

Now it became known that Jack had been secretly married to Betty Carter for months. The house next door thus became theirs: they would live there with their ever-growing family from then on. Hazel and Bill Herbert had produced another grandchild, Margaret, in 1936: she would become Henry's favorite, as her mother had been his favorite child. In the midst of constant turmoil with Cliff, Claudia, and Paul, Henry's relationship with Hazel was steady and sure. He was "utterly contented with the rightness of Hazel's life," wrote Mrs. Morse: but this too shattered in 1939 when Herbert began having mental trouble. It was a delayed form of shellshock from the world war, resulting in severe split personality disorders. He disappeared from home, sometimes for weeks, leaving Hazel and the children alone and heartsick. "All those years on the dairy ranch—Hazel, the children—were no longer part of his life," wrote Mrs. Morse. "It all seemed to have happened to another Bill Herbert, and the life of this other Bill Herbert left this one cold." He would listen with cool, impersonal attention, but remained untouched by anything that was said. Six months later, Herbert was killed in an auto wreck.

Hazel decided to keep the dairy ranch and hire a manager to help her run it. Applying for the job was Daniel Murray, described by Patricia Morse as "young and bookish and in his early thirties." This was a time of transition for all the characters. Henry Barbour had sold his brokerage house, despairing that Cliff would ever make anything of it. The family in 1940 numbered 17. Claudia and Nicky had two children, Penelope (1938) and little Nicky (1940). Clifford's son, born in 1938, was still unnamed: he had been taken in by Henry and Fanny and was still being called by the initials "J. D." This stood for "John Doe." Clifford said the child could choose his own name, when he got old enough to need one. But in 1940 Clifford began letting his son into his life. The boy became known as "the Skipper" and then "Skippy" (his name finally would be Andrew, some years later). Cliff went to work for Dan Murray on Hazel's dairy ranch. His relationships with the opposite sex continued to be frivolous and short-lived. His affair with the redheaded divorcee Margaret Lloyd was typical—frustrating and all for naught. On Paul's side of the family, adopted daughter Teddy was leading a thrilling life, pursued by two flying cadets, Tracy Baker and Wayne Grubb. As 1941 ended and the Japanese attack on Pearl Harbor drew the United States into the war, Paul began ferrying planes for the government. He was now a major in the Air Defense Command, his job flying planes up the coast for subsequent use in the Pacific war.

At this point in the Barbour saga, transcriptions of broadcasts begin to turn up. Listeners may now pick up shows and hear storylines for themselves, at first in fragments and then a remarkable run of more than 300 chapters, many consecutive, crossing storylines in superb sound quality, fully viable to the modern listener. The foregoing synopsis of the show's first decade is offered in such detail to supplement the actual broadcasts, so the listener may follow the story with minimal effort. The remainder of the character discussion will be an update.

In the 1940s, Henry and Fanny settled into old age. Henry became crustier and more difficult. The garden was now his greatest pleasure. Still he carped: when he took to a cause, he was relentless in his effort to ramrod it past his family. He picked and fussed until the family was on the verge of open rebellion. When things went wrong, he brooded and sulked. His suspicion of strangers was intense, especially if the

stranger wanted to marry a Barbour. But once an outsider had won him over, Henry became his staunchest ally. He resisted change with an iron will. His feelings were easily bruised, especially at the hint that Paul might supplant him as head of the house. His sermons were those of grandfathers everywhere. His flaws made him believable and human. His expression "yes, yes" became the show's trademark. This could be said in irritation or penitence. In his later years, his ire transferred from Claudia and Clifford to Claudia's daughter Joan. Fanny remained the soul of patience, salt of the earth, a Molly McGee without the humor, and she suffered in her own way, with Henry, as much as Molly suffered with Fibber.

Paul carried the scars of war, physical and mental, all his life. He never remarried, though he came close. He was the mature romantic lead: the strong male presence, ever-dependable for forceful action and wise, sound judgment. As Teddy became a woman, her infatuation with Paul colored her life. Always she compared prospective suitors to Paul; always they failed the comparison. Her feeling for Paul was largely responsible for the failure of her marriage to dentist Elwood Giddings. Paul's notable ladyfriends in the 1940s were Nicolette Moore, governess at brother Jack's house, and Christine Abbott, a widow and noted concert pianist. Paul and Nicolette remained good friends, and his romance with Christine was foredoomed by Henry's interference and the presence of a psychotic brother, Rexford Frome. Throughout the run, Paul was the philosopher. For a time, he ended each chapter with a poetic epilogue and the observation "That's how it is with the Barbours today."

Hazel married Dan Murray in 1945: he became the true father figure for the three children she had had with Bill Herbert. The Murrays moved to Sea Cliff, "three blocks down and two blocks over" from the family home. Hazel's main problem in later life was with her son Pinky, a child of postwar America who viewed all the adults as "out of touch with the times." Pinky failed at everything: he swaggered and played the bigshot's role, flunked out of Stanford, piled up debts and then tried to shirk his responsibility to repay them. His failure was more notable when compared with the straight-A achievements of his brother, Hank.

Claudia led a life of tragedy and adventure in the 1940s. Her home in Sea Cliff was five houses down from the family estate. (With Paul, now an author, living in a writer's loft in the family home, Teddy in a room off the attic, Jack next door, and Hazel a few blocks away, the family maintained its unity.) But early in the war, Claudia's husband Nicky was sent on a mission to Europe. It was decided that Claudia and her two youngest would accompany him, while Joan would remain with the family. Soon after her departure (Aug. 29, 1943), the Scandinavian liner on which they were traveling was torpedoed by the Germans, and all were presumed lost. Claudia, Nicky, and the children were written out and presumed dead by family and listeners alike. In fact, they were prisoners in a German concentration camp. Little Nicky died in his mother's arms during the train ride, but Claudia, Nicholas, and Penelope survived. In 1945 came new hope, and Paul was off to Europe on the long search, and one of the show's most memorable stories. Joan inherited her mother's rebellious, fiery traits: in the postwar years, she was a constant worry to Claudia, who saw too many of her own failings coming to play in her daughter. Joan suffered a long identity crisis—she felt left out of Claudia's life after being left with the grandparents in 1943. Eventually she married Ross Farnsworth and produced the first great-grandchild, Paul John Farnsworth. But this was a long time coming, and the road was full of growing pain.

Clifford was haunted by the memory of his delicate wife Ann. The metal plate in his head caused continuing lapses of memory and depression. But his fortunes improved in 1942 when he began a friendship with Irene Franklin, a student at Berkeley. She was ten years younger than Cliff, but gradually her relationship with the Barbours improved from "chilly indifference" to love. Her marriage to Cliff lasted four happy years, but again there was a tragic ending. A madman, cornered at the Sky Ranch, made a run in a stolen station wagon down the mountain road that connected the ranch with the main highway at Woodside. Irene, coming up the mountain, was rammed head-on and killed instantly. Cliff withdrew from life: he moved into the family home, lived off his parents, and made no effort to support himself. His moods of quiet meditation were broken by frequent quarrels

with Henry. But gradually he warmed to his son, Andrew, and began seeing women again. He dated Roberta Evans, but Andrew saw her as a threat and the romance died on the vine. In 1950, Cliff met Maudie Pemberton, a spunky young woman rooming with Teddy during Teddy's separation from Elwood Giddings. Maudie got Cliff back on the road to self-respect. This made her a champion with Henry, but it all came to nothing when Maudie refused Clifford's offer of marriage. Cliff returned to his moping ways, and in 1952 was written out of the show forever. He moved to Scotland, listeners were told, where he met and married Mary McLeod and made a successful new life for himself. The faithful were kept informed through Cliff's frequent letters home, which were always read aloud. Cliff lived happily ever after—rather a pat finish to a moody, complex, and well-liked character.

Jack was the one truly average member of *One Man's Family*. His life was marked by no deep tragedies: he served with the Navy in World War II, returned home to study law, and eventually became a junior partner in the law firm of Henry's old friend Glenn Hunter. He lived with his wife Betty in the house next door; they had six children (including a set of triplets) and fought a constant battle with the budget.

Morse wrote the show alone through the early run. He wasn't very religious, he once said, so the Barbours weren't either. "They didn't go to church much, except for weddings and funerals." Their struggles were based on morals, not religion: thus, while *One Man's Family* contained much moralizing, it was almost totally free of the partisan preaching (usually promoting a white Anglo-Saxon Protestant viewpoint) that was ruthlessly worked into other shows of American family life. Morse directed as well. During the years 1939–44, he was also writing and directing the adventure serial *I Love a Mystery*, which featured many of the same performers from his *Family* company. *One Man's Family* was almost a perfect harmony of writer and cast. To Morse went the credit for the show's creation and durability: to the cast came the job of bringing it to life. From the beginning, Morse shaped his drama to the lives of his players. This worked, sometimes uncannily, for years. He wanted people in the seven major roles who conformed as nearly as possible to the physical and temperamental characteristics of their fictional counterparts. The show's success was due in no small part to a magnificent 27-year run as Henry Barbour by J. Anthony Smythe. Henry simply could not have been more perfectly played. A bachelor, Smythe was a native San Franciscan of long stage experience. He and Minetta Ellen (Fanny) had appeared together often—many times as a married couple—on the stage of Oakland's Fulton Theater. But Fanny was the last of the major roles cast: Ellen was referred to Morse by Michael Raffetto, who had already won the role of Paul. Raffetto, Ellen, and Barton Yarborough (Clifford) had known each other from their performances together with the Berkeley Players. Raffetto and Yarborough also knew Bernice Berwin and Kathleen Wilson, university players who had appeared in early Morse serials and would become Hazel and Claudia.

This cast remained together for more than 11 years. Raffetto brought to Paul a deep-voiced aura of strength, tenderness, and intelligence. Yarborough had run away from home as a boy, hooking up with a traveling show and later playing in vaudeville. A native of Goldthwaite, Tex., his accent (which he used effectively as Doc Long on *I Love a Mystery*) was softened though by no means eliminated in his sensitive portrayal of Clifford. Bernice Berwin had begun in radio at NBC in 1928 and started with Morse the following year. She first heard the *Family* idea when she encountered Morse at Clark's market and he gave her a verbal blueprint as they walked along together. Just as she and her husband were about to embark on a trip to New York, Morse called and invited her to play Hazel. Kathleen Wilson, a fencing champion in college, had appeared in numerous Morse shows and was offered the role of Claudia without an audition. Page Gilman, at 14 already a microphone veteran, was Jack.

Morse plotted the show in part from tidbits picked up from his cast. When Bernice Berwin had a child, so did Hazel. When Page Gilman went into service in the Pacific, so did Jack. When Kathleen Wilson left to get married in 1943, Claudia was written out and presumed dead at sea. Morse was deluged with mail: some listeners were outraged; some threatened never to listen again unless the "same Claudia" was returned to the air. Morse waited until October 1945, then introduced the "new Claudia," the versatile actress Barbara Fuller.

Barton Yarborough died suddenly in 1951, and Clifford was no more. Minetta Ellen and Michael Raffetto left in mid-1955. Bernice Berwin played Hazel until the last year, when the pain of commuting to Hollywood (where the show had moved in 1937) became greater than the pleasure of doing it. Winifred Wolfe grew up playing Teddy: her marriage in 1945 was conducted at the Morse home, and for a time Teddy was written out of the story. She returned, fully mature but still troubled, in the voice of Jeanne Bates.

As Jack and Father Barbour, Page Gilman and J. Anthony Smythe stayed till the end.

This was *One Man's Family*: dismissed as sentimental and naive by some, cherished by others, it sprawled across the landscape of dramatic network radio. It was the first show to speak frankly of the Kinsey Report, and the last to make the grumblings of an old-fashioned fussbudget palatable. When Standard Brands dropped it in 1949, 75,000 letters flooded NBC in its support. Reorganized as a daily quarter-hour, it lost none of its appeal to its faithful. Although it officially ended May 8, 1959, some affiliates chopped it off two weeks earlier. It just stopped one April day, with Father Barbour brooding over the troubles of his grandson Pinky: a snuffed-out finish to a 27-year slice of life.

ONE OUT OF SEVEN, documentary drama.

BROADCAST HISTORY: Early 1946, ABC West Coast. 15m weekly. **STAR:** Jack Webb as narrator and in all character roles. **DIRECTOR:** Gil Doud. **WRITER:** James Edward Moser.

One out of Seven is notable for two reasons: it was one of Jack Webb's earliest series, and it took an uncompromising stand against racial prejudice. Aired on a partial network from San Francisco, it required a variety of dialects, from black to Jewish, and Webb brought them off in good form. The stories were taken taken from news of the past week, from "authoritative files" and wire services. "From these past seven days, the editors in our San Francisco newsroom have chosen the one story which they have judged worthy of retelling. This is one out of seven!"

The stories were often tough attacks against bigotry and hate merchants. Webb emphasized that the material came from wire reports, and the network "assumes no responsibility for the attitudes such statements reflect." But the Associated Press never arranged any story quite like this. The show of Feb. 6, 1946, for example, was a blistering attack on Mississippi senator Theodore G. Bilbo, an outspoken foe of civil rights. Bilbo's own statements were read like a damning indictment, the narrative punctuated by Webb's frequent inserts: "Senator Bilbo is an honorable man, and we do not intend to prove otherwise." Shades of Marc Antony.

ONE THOUSAND DOLLARS REWARD, quiz with drama.

BROADCAST HISTORY: June 25–Oct. 29, 1950, NBC. 30m, Sundays at 7. **HOST:** John Sylvester. **DRAMATIC CAST:** Ralph Bell, Ken Lynch, Ethel Everett, etc. **ANNOUNCER:** Ken Roberts.

A 25-minute crime play was staged without the solution. Host Sylvester then placed a call to a listener, who tried to solve the mystery for a $1,000 prize.

ONE WORLD FLIGHT, interviews and documentary.

BROADCAST HISTORY: Jan. 14–April 8, 1947, CBS. 30m, Tuesdays at 10. **WRITER-PRODUCER-HOST:** Norman Corwin.

One World Flight was the final result of a singular presidential election. How Wendell Willkie, a Democrat by nature, got nominated by Republicans to oppose a man running for an unprecedented third term is a matter of history. In 1942, President Roosevelt asked Willkie to tour the world, visit the Allies, and observe the battle fronts. Willkie's mission became a book, *One World,* in 1943, which proposed that an international organization be formed after the war to keep the peace. Willkie died in 1944: a One World Award was established in his name the following year, and one of the first winners was Norman Corwin of CBS.

Willkie's "one world" concepts were close to Corwin's heart. The prize was a round-the-world flight, which would form the background of a new series of CBS broadcasts. With engineer Lee Bland, Corwin logged more than 40,000 miles in 1946, touching 16 countries. He returned with 100 hours of recorded interviews, talks with "prince and fellah, commissar and coolie, pundit and stevedore" (*Time*). "The English transcript filled 3,700 typed pages. For three months Corwin, four recording engineers, and six typists chewed at this great bulk, finally worked it down to a hard core." Corwin himself was the series guide, and the show—despite occasional flat spots noted by both major news magazines—was given generally high critical marks. *Time* cited its "heady power" and "wonderfully perceptive, intimate sound track," while *Newsweek* termed it "the most accurate diary ever kept by a globe girdler."

It was Corwin's last major run on CBS, and one of the last shows to use recording wire for the purposes of interviewing. Corwin would remember the wire as horrendous to edit. The equipment weighed 200 pounds, and the recordings had to be cut, knotted, and fused with a lit cigarette before they could be transferred to the newly developed recording tape. But at the end of it, as Corwin told *Time*, it was "all there for history, if history is interested."

THE O'NEILL CYCLE, drama by Eugene O'Neill.

BROADCAST HISTORY: Aug. 2–23, 1937, Blue Network. Mondays at 8:30. Four 60m plays: *Beyond the Horizon* (with Helen Hayes); *The Fountain* (with Ian Keith); *Where the Cross Is Made* (with Henry Hull); and *The Straw* (with Peggy Wood).

This brief series was offered in a year when the air was full of Shakespeare. It was aired in an effort to "contrast Elizabethan with modern genius," and staged four Eugene O'Neill plays never before heard on radio. The final broadcast was followed in the same timeslot, Aug. 30, by a 75-minute condensation of George Bernard Shaw's *Back to Methuselah* (adapted by Shaw from his five-hour play). On Sept. 6 and 13 the network offered plays enacted by John and Elaine Barrymore: *The Animal Kingdom* and *Accent on Youth.* Capping off the summer on Sept. 20 was an original radio play by Maxwell Anderson, *The Feast of Ortolans.* It was a very good radio year for stage enthusiasts.

THE O'NEILLS, serial drama.

BROADCAST HISTORY: June 11–Dec. 7, 1934, Mutual. 15m, three a week at 7:30.

Dec. 10, 1934–March 27, 1942, various networks (frequently carried on two simultaneously). 15m, weekdays. 1934–35, CBS, three a week at 7:30; 1935–37, NBC Red at 3:45; 1936–37, NBC Blue at 11 A.M.; Jan.–June 1938, CBS at 2:15; 1938–41, NBC at 12:15; 1940–41, CBS at 5:15; 1941–42, CBS at 5:30. Gold Dust, 1934–35 (CBS); Ivory Soap, 1935–42.

Oct. 5, 1942–June 18, 1943, NBC. 15m, weekdays at 10:15 A.M. Standard Brands.

CAST: Kate McComb as Mother O'Neill, a widow left to her own resources in raising her children, Danny and Peggy. Jimmy Tansey as Danny O'Neill. Betty Caine and Violet Dunn as Peggy O'Neill in the 1930s; Claire Niesen as Peggy, late 1930s and early 1940s; Betty Winkler as Peggy in the final days. Chester Stratton as Monte Kayden, Peggy's husband. Jack Rubin as Morris Levy, who ran a dry goods business (later a hardware store) and was Mother O'Neill's best friend. Jane West as Trudy Bailey, meddlesome-but-lovable busybody who ran a knick-knack store, lived upstairs in the two-family house owned by the O'Neills, and loved Morris Levy. Janice Gilbert and Jimmy Donnelly as Janice and Eddie Collins, brother and sister adopted by the O'Neills after the death of their father in an accident. (Janice Gilbert at 16 was an accomplished baby mimic, and also played Peggy's three children.) Arline Blackburn as Eileen Turner, whose father employed Danny O'Neill in the late 1930s. Alfred Swenson and Effie Lawrence Palmer as Mr. and Mrs. Turner. Santos Ortega and Marjorie Anderson as Mr. and Mrs. Collins. Roy Fant as Grandpa Hubbell. Ethel Everett as Mayme Gordon. Charles Carroll as Jack Vernon. Helen Claire as Sally Scott O'Neill. Julian Noa as Judge Scott. Linda Carlon as Mrs. Scott. ANNOUNCER: Ed Herlihy, Howard Petrie. MUSIC: William Meeder, organ. CREATOR-WRITER: Jane West. DIRECTORS: Carlo De Angelo, Jack Rubin. THEME: *Londonderry Air*.

The O'Neills followed the trail blazed by *One Man's Family*. Mother O'Neill was a matriarch in the grand tradition, a 60-ish woman whose stock in trade was wisdom and understanding. Her children grew into fine citizens, though Peggy was impetuous and Danny sometimes was hot-headed and brash. Danny also sank into deep depression after his young wife Sally died in childbirth. Peggy married Monte Kayden, an ambitious young lawyer and entrepreneur whose intentions were often better than his judgment. For a time Monte pursued his goal (to make a fortune) so ruthlessly that it almost cost him his family.

Janice and Eddie Collins lived with the O'Neills: Janice was full of teenage curiosity and growing pain, which Mother O'Neill helped ease with kindness, wisdom, and clear-eyed philosophy. Mother's friend Morris Levy was her confidant and a father-figure to her children: he too was generous with sage advice to the troubled. Mrs. Trudy Bailey was ardent in her pursuit of Morris Levy, but even after they were married she continued to live upstairs from the O'Neills: she was always "fresh out" of one thing or another, and was constantly calling down the dumbwaiter to ask if Mother O'Neill had this item or that.

The action took place in Royalton, a midwestern town typical of radio soaps. *Radio Guide* described the O'Neills as "neither rich nor poor, neither devils nor angels, neither utterly unfortunate nor completely happy—just an average family." There was less jerky melodrama than listeners found in most daytime serials, though there were moments. Once Peggy's husband Monte ran away with actress Gloria Gilbert, who then turned up murdered. Peggy was suspected of the deed until the arrest of Mayme Gordon. Mayme was later released on parole and became friends with Mother O'Neill, who helped her find work as a maid for her friends the Vernons. But young Jack Vernon, struggling against his mother's domination, fell in love with her.

The show also contained incidents similar to situations on *One Man's Family*. As she grew older, Janice formed an adolescent attraction to Danny, her brother by adoption (shades of Paul and Teddy Barbour); and the death of Danny's wife left him with a son, Kenny, toward whom he initially felt only indifference (see Clifford and Andrew, *One Man's Family*). Early in the run, Danny was a construction engineer: he wrote a column, "My Town," for the local paper, and the column frequently got him in trouble with political movers and shakers. In the 1940s, Danny ran a "vital" war plant. *The O'Neills* was popular: by the late '30s, its Crossley ratings had approached double digits, unusual for a daytime serial.

THE OPEN DOOR, serial drama.

BROADCAST HISTORY: June 21, 1943–June 30, 1944, NBC. 15m, weekdays at 10:15 A.M. until Jan. 3, then CBS at 10:30 A.M. Standard Brands. **CAST:** Dr. Alfred Dorf as Dean Eric Hansen of Vernon University. Barbara Weeks as Liz Arnold; Florence Freeman also as Liz Arnold. Charlotte Holland as Corey Lehman, Hansen's secretary. Also: Joan Alexander, Martin Blaine, Alexander Scourby, Edwin Bruce. **WRITER:** Sandra Michael, with Doria Folliott.

The Open Door was author Sandra Michael's try at a second "quality" daytime serial (her first, *Against the Storm*, was the only show of its kind to win a Peabody Award). Backed by husband John Gibbs as producer, Michael fashioned a series of slow-moving, character-building vignettes around the dean of the fictitious Vernon University.

The stories involved people in the life of the dean, Eric Hansen: their problems, lives, and loves. Dean Hansen was almost a literal transplant from *Against the Storm*—he had been Pastor Hansen there—and was played by the same actor, Alfred Dorf. Michael had known Dorf since her childhood in Denmark: he had come to America to establish his church, Our Savior, in Brooklyn, and was the true inspiration for the character whose life Michael now asked him to portray. Hansen was depicted as a staunch man who cared about people and believed in being his brother's keeper.

But the agency handling the Standard Brands account (which Michael had inherited along with the timeslot just vacated by the canceled serial *The O'Neills*) didn't share Hansen's philosophy. Michael was pressured to change the show: she resisted and finally quit, staying on the high road and paying the price.

THE OPEN HOUSE, musical variety, interviews.

BROADCAST HISTORY: July 19–Aug. 30, 1941, NBC. 30m, Saturdays at 10:30. A showcase for torch singer Helen Morgan.
    Sept. 2, 1943–March 25, 1946, CBS. 30m,

Thursdays at 3, 1943; Mondays, often at 4 or 4:30, Pacific time, 1943–46. **CREATOR-HOSTESS:** Beverly Barnes, 1943–44; Ona Munson thereafter. The hostess interviewed such stars as Robert Young, Groucho Marx, Billie Burke, and Ruth Hussey: the stars were portrayed as "real people" with human interest stories. **AN-NOUNCER:** Jay Stewart. **VOCALIST:** Anita Ellis. **MUSIC:** Lud Gluskin.

THE OPEN ROAD, documentary serial.

BROADCAST HISTORY: Aug.–Sept. 1935, NBC. 15m, four a week at 10:45.

The Open Road was created by Red Quinlan, a teenager with an unusual idea. Quinlan wanted to take a cross-country freight trip and have radio dramatize his experiences. Sidney Strotz, NBC executive headquartered in Chicago, was dubious, but Quinlan embarked on the journey anyway. He rode the Rock Island rails to Hollywood and back, a 6,000-mile odyssey that made both NBC and the pages of *Newsweek*. He left Chicago with $1.50 in his pocket and returned with a dime. His show described fights with yard bulls and flights from police. Vagrancy was still very much a crime in 1934, when Quinlan's trip took place.

THE OPIE CATES SHOW, situation comedy.

BROADCAST HISTORY: Oct. 20, 1947–Feb. 2, 1948, ABC. 30m, Mondays at 8:30. **CAST:** Opie Cates, orchestra leader of many another show, as a typical radio bumbler, "a countrified Dennis Day" (*Variety*). Barbara Fuller as his girlfriend, Cathy. Also: Noreen Gammill, Fred Howard, Ruth Perrott, and Francis X. Bushman. **MUSIC:** Basil Adlam. **PRODUCER-DIRECTOR:** Glenhall Taylor. **WRITER:** Rozwell Rogers.

In this series, Opie Cates played "a boy from Clinton, Arkansas" who took up residence in Ma Buskirk's boardinghouse. Ma and Pa Buskirk were described in one review as "stereotyped characters" reminiscent of Marjorie Main and W. C. Fields.

THE ORANGE LANTERN, mystery-adventure melodrama.

BROADCAST HISTORY: Oct. 2, 1932–July 2, 1933, Blue Network. 30m, Sundays at 10:30.

CAST: Arthur Hughes as Botak, an adventurer from Java. Also: Agnes Moorehead, Johnny McGovern, Peggy Allenby.

Little is known of this early effort. The content is presumed to be similar to *Fu Manchu*, running on CBS at the same time: Oriental intrigue and the fight against evil.

ORPHANS OF DIVORCE, soap opera.

BROADCAST HISTORY: March 6–June 26, 1939, Blue Network. 30m continuation, Mondays at 7. Dr. Lyons Toothpaste. CAST: Margaret Anglin as Nora Kelly Worthington.

Sept. 25, 1939–April 17, 1942, Blue. 15m continuation, weekdays at 3. Dr. Lyons. CAST: Effie Palmer as Nora Kelly Worthington. Richard Gordon as Cyril Worthington. Madeleine Pierce (babytalk specialist) as Baby Sandy. Also: Claire Wilson, Patricia Peardon, and Warren Bryan as Juliet, Joan, and Dick Worthington. PRODUCERS: Frank and Anne Hummert.

ORSON WELLES THEATER, music, variety, drama, readings, commentary.

BROADCAST HISTORY: Sept. 15, 1941–Feb. 2, 1942, CBS. 30m, Mondays at 10. Lady Esther. CAST: Orson Welles, star and host, with many players from his old *Mercury Theater*: Agnes Moorehead, Ray Collins, Paul Stewart, Joseph Cotten, Erskine Sanford, etc. Also: Elliott Lewis, Hans Conried, Dorothy Comingore, Nancy Gates, Ruth Gordon, Gale Gordon, Rita Hayworth, Merle Oberon, Cedric Hardwicke, John Barrymore, etc. Cliff Edwards as Jiminy Cricket on many shows. MUSIC: Bernard Herrmann.

Jan. 26–July 19, 1944, CBS West. 30m, Wednesdays. *Orson Welles Almanac*. Mobil Oil. CAST: Orson Welles, star and host, with Agnes Moorehead, Hans Conried, Ray Collins, etc. Cliff Edwards as Jiminy Cricket. Major film stars as guests: Lionel Barrymore, Lucille Ball, Charles Laughton, Jimmy Durante, etc. MUSIC: Lud Gluskin.

The Orson Welles Almanac was a format that intrigued Welles throughout the early 1940s: it consisted of everything from odd facts to jazz (pianist Meade Lux Lewis was a guest in 1941 when the show was called *Orson Welles Theater*; Duke Ellington in 1944). But it was heavy with dramatized short stories, such pieces as *The Ap-* ple Tree* and *The Hitchhiker*, both of which Welles would do again on *The Mercury*. The 1944 series spotlighted readings from John Donne, Thomas Paine, and other giants of poetry and prose. But Welles had a running battle with his sponsor, Mobil Oil, and the run was short-lived.

OUR BARN, children's theater.

BROADCAST HISTORY: Jan. 28, 1936–Dec. 6, 1941, Blue Network. 30m, Saturday mornings. CAST: Many juvenile performers developed on *The Children's Hour* (also known as NBC's *Coast to Coast on a Bus*): Billy Halop, Patricia Ryan, Walter Tetley, Jimmy McCallion, Charita Bauer, etc. Also: Tommy Hughes, Virginia and Clementine Torell, Marg MacLaren, Peggy Zinke, Charles Belin, Larry Robinson, Adrian Wragge, etc. DIRECTOR: Madge Tucker. WRITER: Jean Peterson.

For a time *Our Barn* was considered the NBC equivalent to *Let's Pretend*: director Madge Tucker developed the same kind of juvenile repertory company that Nila Mack was heading at CBS. Both shows offered auditions to all comers, regardless of race or creed. *Our Barn* had status while it ran, but was no match for *Let's Pretend* in durability.

OUR DAILY FOOD, recipes, food discussion, menus.

BROADCAST HISTORY: Nov. 3, 1930–March 3, 1933, NBC. 15m, Red Network, six a week at 9:45 A.M. Concurrent Blue Network run, six a week at 8:30 A.M., later at 10:30 A.M. until Dec. 1932, then, beginning Jan. 13, 1933, Fridays at 6. A&P. HOST: George Rector, with programs on school lunches, workings of a grape juice factory, etc.

OUR GAL SUNDAY, soap opera.

BROADCAST HISTORY: March 29, 1937–Jan. 2, 1959, CBS. 15m, weekdays at 12:45. American Home Products for Anacin and Kolynos, 1937–55; Procter & Gamble, etc., at other times. CAST: Dorothy Lowell as Sunday (1937–46), an orphan from Colorado who struggled to find happiness as the wife of "a wealthy and titled Englishman." Vivian Smolen as Sunday, 1946–59. Karl Swenson as Sunday's husband, Lord Henry Brinthrope, for most of the run. Alistair Duncan also as Lord

Henry. Jay Jostyn and Robert Strauss as Jackie and Lively, miners who raised Sunday from childhood. Joe Latham and Roy Fant also as Lively. **1937 SUPPORTING CAST:** Irene Hubbard as Mrs. Segewick, Henry's aunt. Carleton Young as Bill Jenkins, Sunday's childhood friend who loved her desperately. Van Heflin as Slim Delaney, devoted friend of Sunday and Henry, and Henry's foreman at the dude ranch (the Klondike) that he owned in Colorado. Alastair Kyle and John Grinnell as Lonnie, adopted son of Sunday and Henry. **1940 SUPPORTING CAST:** Fran Carlon and Joseph Curtin as Irene and Peter Galway, a friendly couple who lived near Black Swan Hall, the Brinthrope estate, and became the Brinthropes' best friends. Ann Shepherd as Pearl Taggart, a girl from Sunday's hometown in Colorado; John Raby as St. John ("Sinjun") Harris, a temperamental artist who loved Pearl. John McQuade as Steve Lansing, a friend of Jackie's from Colorado, and an old sweetheart Pearl Taggart was running from. Venezuela Jones as Susie Robinson, owner of the country store. Ara Gerald as the Countess Florenze, arrogant and demanding. Inge Adams as her daughter, Lili Florenze, "guarded and spoiled by her mother." Also: Eustace Wyatt as Lord Percy. Santos Ortega as Oliver Drexton. Kaye Brinker as Barbara Hamilton. Joan Tompkins as Madelyn Travers. Anne Seymour as Prudence Graham. Charlotte Lawrence as Leona Kenmore. **ANNOUNCERS:** John Reed King, Art Millet, Bert Parks, John A. Wolfe, Charles Stark, James Fleming, etc. **PRODUCERS:** Frank and Anne Hummert. **DIRECTORS:** Stephen Gross, Art Hanna, etc. **WRITERS:** John DeWitt, from 1937; Helen Walpole; Jean Carroll, ca. 1945–59. **THEME:** *Red River Valley.*

Our Gal Sunday was one of the five major soap operas of Frank and Anne Hummert. It was one of the most enduring, least credible melodramas ever heard on daytime radio. It exploited the age-old story of the young beauty who marries far outside her station in life. The opening signature captured it well:

And now, Our Gal Sunday, the story of an orphan girl named Sunday, from the little mining town of Silver Creek, Colorado, who in young womanhood married England's richest, most handsome lord, Lord Henry Brinthrope—the story that asks the question, can this girl from a mining town in the West find happiness as the wife of a wealthy and titled Englishman?

Sunday found happiness, but it took 22 years of the most convoluted agony ever concocted for public consumption. These were just a few of the tortures Sunday had to endure:

—Her beloved guardian shot and wounded the brother of the man Sunday would come to love and marry. In a related crime, Sunday was then blackmailed for $10,000 by the scheming Violet Morehead.

—She was kidnapped by cattle rustlers.

—The ink was barely dry on her marriage license when another blackmailer appeared, ready to tell the world that Lord Henry was the father of an i-l-l-e-g-i-t-i-m-a-t-e child. This was false (the faithful knew it all the time), but Sunday was wracked by doubt. A serial character could be wracked by doubt for months.

—Sunday ran home to the West; Henry had a devil of a time tracking her down.

—Impostors were part of her daily life. One claimed to be Sunday's father; another—Lord Henry's identical twin—actually moved in with Sunday, who "knew in her heart" that something was wrong.

—Sunday was constantly shunned by snooty in-laws.

—She and Henry, being among the world's most desirable people, were always in danger from schemers who had fallen in love with them. Henry was always the prey of one adventuress or another; Sunday was set upon by an endless array of "brilliant, handsome" men, some of them psychos. Most notable was a crazed artist, who always painted his victims before killing them. Sunday was saved by "handsome, brilliant" attorney Kevin Bromfield, who had gone blind after defending Henry for murder, and now threw himself in front of the bullet and died in Sunday's arms.

Added to this was Generic Serial Male Syndrome, to which few male leads of daytime radio were immune. Henry joined Larry Noble of the Hummerts' *Backstage Wife* in being irresponsible and unreliable. He could be swayed by a pretty ankle; his financial judgment was often clouded, so that the Brinthrope fortune was never quite secure. But he was "handsome and brilliant," and listeners knew that, no matter how badly he strayed, in his heart he loved Sunday and no other.

The saga began on the Broadway stage in 1904, when Ethel Barrymore starred in the play *Sunday*, by Thomas Raceward. When the Hummerts gained control of the property, the fun began. The serial opened in Colorado, where a child was left at the door of a mountain cabin. Jackie and Lively, the grizzled miners who lived there, devoted themselves to her welfare from then on. She was named Sunday because she was found on that day. Her last name was later said to be Smithson. In this remote and sheltered world, she grew into lovely womanhood. Her childhood friend Bill Jenkins yearned for her passionately. But Sunday had a different hunger: there was more to life than these idyllic hills, and she wanted to see the world.

Into her life came Arthur Brinthrope, a wealthy young Englishman whose family owned a silver mine. Arthur had come to Silver Creek to inspect the holdings. Sunday was enchanted by this "brilliant, handsome" stranger whose ways were so foreign. But Arthur was a playboy: when he proposed that Sunday run away with him without benefit of clergy, the hot-tempered Jackie shot him down.

Enter Sir Henry, later a lord and soon to be Sunday's beau. Henry's roguish young brother was merely wounded, not dead. These early days were filled with western fantasy. "The principals leap from one fabulous situation to another," said *Radio Guide*: "dramatic incidents that leave listeners breathless with suspense." The characters leaped to England, then back to Colorado, where Henry had a dude ranch named the Klondike. Jackie and Lively, who had accompanied her across the sea, were never happy in the world of the Brinthropes.

Eventually Henry and Sunday settled in Virginia, at a castle-like estate named Black Swan Hall. There they raised their adopted son, Lonnie, and their two natural children, Little Davy and Caroline. But Little Davy was struck down and crushed by a hit-and-run driver, leaving him a "hopeless cripple." Sunday vowed to pull him through, with mother love and tenderness, and she did, proving that in the world of the daytime seriel, nothing was hopeless. In 1946 her happiness was threatened by the arrival of Henry's childhood friend Thelma Mayfield, who brazenly told Sunday her intention of someday being mistress at Black Swan Hall.

But as the serial ended, Sunday found her happiness, as she and Henry left Black Swan Hall for a dramatic pilgrimage to his ancestral stamping ground. It had finally come down to Ethel Barrymore's famous closing line 55 years earlier in the play that inspired it: "That's all there is, there isn't any more."

OUR MISS BROOKS, situation comedy.

BROADCAST HISTORY: July 19, 1948–July 7, 1957, CBS. 30m, Mondays at 9 until Sept. 13, 1948, then Sundays at 9 (1948–49), at 6:30 (1949–54), at 8 (1954–57). Colgate for Lustre Creme Shampoo, etc., Oct. 1948–June 1954; Toni Home Permanent and others thereafter.

CAST: Eve Arden as Connie Brooks, teacher of English at Madison High School. Gale Gordon as blustery Madison principal Osgood Conklin (initially played by Joe Forte). Jeff Chandler as Philip Boynton, the bashful biology teacher, chief object of Miss Brooks's affection. Richard Crenna as Walter Denton, a student in the Henry Aldrich mold. Jane Morgan as addled Mrs. Margaret Davis, the landlady at the house where Miss Brooks lived. Gloria McMillan as Harriet Conklin, Walter's girlfriend and daughter of the principal. Leonard Smith as Stretch Snodgrass, the dumbest student (but a whale of a basketball player) at Madison High. Mary Jane Croft as Miss Enright, chief rival for the attentions of Mr. Boynton. Maurice Marsac as the French teacher Miss Brooks charmed occasionally in her efforts to make Mr. Boynton more attentive. Gerald Mohr as Jacque Monet, a similar French teacher. ORCHESTRA: Wilbur Hatch. PRODUCER: Larry Berns. DIRECTOR-WRITER: Al Lewis. WRITER: Art Alsberg. SOUND EFFECTS: Bill Gould.

Teachers everywhere took *Our Miss Brooks* to heart from the beginning of its highly popular run. Here at last a teacher was seen as something other than a sexless tormentor of tenth-grade morons. Connie Brooks lived in middle America (*not* Madison, Wis., writer Al Lewis would insist), a town that seemed to have a piece of everywhere built into its woodwork.

Miss Brooks had a devilish streak of witty sarcasm. Her dialogue was wonderfully "feline," as critic John Crosby would note: her snappy comeback to the stuffy assertions of her boss, principal Osgood Conklin, bristled with intelligence and fun. She complained about her low pay (and how teachers identified with that!), got her boss in no end of trouble, pursued biologist Philip Boynton to no avail, and became the favorite schoolmarm of her pupils, and of all America.

The role was perfect for Eve Arden, a refugee

of B movies and the musical comedy stage. Arden was born Eunice Quedens in Mill Valley, Calif., in 1912. In her youth she joined a theatrical touring group and traveled the country in an old Ford. She was cast in Ziegfeld's *Follies* revivals in 1934 and 1936, working in the latter with Fanny Brice. She became Eve Arden when producer Lee Shubert suggested a name change: she was reading a novel with a heroine named Eve, and combined this name with the Elizabeth Arden cosmetics on her dressing room table.

As Eve Arden, she broke into films in 1937, having done a few earlier as Eunice Quedens: her supporting role in *Oh, Doctor!* was followed the same year by *Stage Door*, a film that helped push her to fame and establish the biting, cynical specialty she would achieve. She appeared in *Stage Door* wearing a live-cat furpiece, and later worked in such films as *Slightly Honorable, She Couldn't Say No*, and *She Knew All the Answers*.

She broke into radio on *The Danny Kaye Show* (1945–46), then costarred with Jack Haley (1946–47) and Jack Carson (1947–48) on *The Sealtest Village Store*. She was cast in the ego-deflating role she had always played, and her interest in radio was at a low ebb. Then she met CBS boss William Paley at a nightclub. Paley proposed that she star in a prospective comedy series, to be called *Our Miss Brooks*, but the script she received failed to convince her. The promised rewrite, by Al Lewis and Joe Quillan, was more to her liking: the character was perhaps settling around Arden's real personality by then. Lewis would later put her in a comedy league with Groucho Marx, calling her the only woman in show business capable of achieving that kind of·humor. She agreed to do the show if the eight weeks could be transcribed, allowing her to get away with her children for the summer. The network ban against transcriptions had already begun crumbling, so *Our Miss Brooks* premiered in July 1948 by transcription.

It was an instant hit. Arden projected an image that by all accounts was her own. "She is a brilliant woman," said film director Michael Curtiz as the series began. "She adds life to any cast." She had a kind heart on stage and off, say those who knew her: she was apparently incapable of temperament, but was so adept at delivering those double-edged zingers in a script. The world of Connie Brooks began at a rooming house, where she lived frugally and often sought the advice (against her better judgment) of her landlady, Mrs. Davis. This batty old woman could begin a conversation and lose it in midsentence. She fancied herself a cook, but her concoctions usually involved such mixtures as eggs, peanut butter, and pickles.

Then Walter Denton dropped by to drive Miss Brooks to school. Walter was usually a pivotal character in the evening's mischief. Perhaps it would be a campaign to have the food improved in the school cafeteria, or a push to have Miss Brooks named teacher of the year. Walter was often in trouble with Mr. Conklin, as was Miss Brooks. Conklin disdained Walter's relationship with his daughter, Harriet, and he rightly considered Miss Brooks the source of most of the spontaneous mischief that went on at Madison. He was heavy-handed, short-tempered, and windy. "At ease," he would say when Miss Brooks presented herself in his office. And usually during the half-hour, he would blow his top at least once.

Writer Lewis saw Miss Brooks as a woman without a past, with no living relatives, "not even a stray cousin or a grand-uncle. We're going to have to give her an aunt or somebody," he told *Radio Life*, "but meanwhile her only real friends are me and her landlady, Mrs. Davis." She didn't sound friendless on the air: indeed, she sounded much loved and appreciated. But her romance with Mr. Boynton never materialized, as the biology teacher had eyes only for his frog, McDougall.

By the end of the summer, the show was solid. Eve Arden would take it to television in 1952, to be seen concurrently with the rest of the eight-year radio run. She had an unforgettable voice: 20 years after *Our Miss Brooks* left the air, she would be recognized by her character name in restaurants and department stores. She received thousands of letters from real teachers frustrated with their circumstances. At least half a dozen high schools offered her jobs teaching English. By then she was making more than 20 times a teacher's salary, some $200,000 a year for being the wisecracking schoolteacher of the air. But she often addressed PTA meetings and educational associations, expressing satisfaction at having dispelled some of the stereotypes that teachers faced every day.

Her supporting cast was distinguished and funny, proving again that a ship seldom sails with a single mast. As Mr. Conklin, Gale Gordon brought to a peak all the "windbag" roles he had been playing for years. He was dry and cynical, blustery and explosive, all at once. Jeff Chandler played the bumbling Mr. Boynton perfectly, falling over words and laughing nervously, his embarrassment becoming acute at any mention, in mixed company, of his tadpoles' breeding habits. Chandler (Ira Grossel, who would die of blood poisoning following surgery in 1961) became a major film star in the 1950s, promoting such a he-man image that few would remember his notable comedy role. Richard Crenna (Walter Denton) later became a serious leading man in the movies.

In its heyday the show was broadcast live from Hollywood at 3:30, to play in the East at 6:30: the cast then did a live repeat for the west, four and a half hours later. The CBS TV show ran from Oct. 3, 1952, until Sept. 21, 1956. Most of the principal actors (Arden, Gordon, Crenna, Morgan, and McMillan) moved successfully with their roles to TV. Jeff Chandler was replaced by Robert Rockwell, who took the radio role as well when Chandler left in 1953. Eve Arden died Nov. 12, 1990.

OUR SECRET WEAPON, counterpropaganda talk.

BROADCAST HISTORY: Aug. 9, 1942–Oct. 8, 1943, CBS. 15m, Sundays at 7 through Oct. 18, then Fridays at 7:15. Philco. **CAST:** Rex Stout, debunker of Axis propaganda, with a small group of actor-impersonators for dramatic skits. Paul Luther as Hitler. Guy Repp as Mussolini. Ted Osborne as Hirohito. **CREATOR:** Sue Taylor White.

Rex Stout, creator of orchid-loving detective Nero Wolfe, achieved a new wave of popularity on this amusing series. Axis shortwave broadcasts were monitored by a staff of linguists at the CBS listening station; what were considered the most outrageous lies were then typed into a weekly log of about 30,000 words. Stout would read this, select up to 150 items he found most interesting, and give them to Sue Taylor White (who had given up a job writing soap operas to do war work) for researching. The most entertaining lies, as well as those lending themselves to what *Time* called Stout's "lunch-counter sarcasm," were used on the air. The lies were read rapid-fire by an announcer, often in mock German or Japanese accents, and were just as quickly countered by Stout. When it was claimed that all the best American baseball players were German, Stout's reply was typical: "They've got the facts, no getting away from it. Take the six leading batters in the major leagues—Williams, Gordon, Wright, Reiser, Lombardi, Medwick. Some bunch of Germans. Also the great German prizefighter, Joe Louis."

Stout, then chairman of the Writers War Board and a representative of Freedom House, wrote much of his own material. He was supported by a flood of "give it to 'em, Rex" fan mail. Jack Gerber, who headed the multilingual staff that gathered the canards from German, Italian, and Japanese broadcasts, wondered "if they'd tell enough lies in a week to keep the show interesting." Actually, he said, the quarter-hour could have been doubled with no fear of a material shortage.

OUR SECRET WORLD, dramatized love letters.

BROADCAST HISTORY: Oct. 17, 1942–Jan. 16, 1943, Mutual. 30m, Saturdays at 8:30. **CAST:** Ann Starrett and Milton Stanley as Irene and Michael, a husband and wife torn apart by war (he was a flier stationed in England; the show consisted of spoken love letters, intimate snatches of love talk that reflected the world at war and their parts in it).

OUT OF THE DEEP, adventure drama.

BROADCAST HISTORY: Dec. 1, 1945–Jan. 5, 1946, NBC. 30m, Saturdays at 7:30. **CAST:** Ted Maxwell as Gunnar Carlyle, deep-sea diver and owner-skipper of the *Blue Falcon*, a salvage ship that sailed the world in the search for fortune and adventure. **ANNOUNCER:** Don Stanley. **PRODUCER-DIRECTOR:** Homer Canfield. **WRITER:** Ted Maxwell.

P

PACIFIC STORY, documentary.

BROADCAST HISTORY: July 11, 1943–Jan. 26, 1947, NBC. 30m, Sundays at 11:30. **NARRATOR:** Gayne Whitman. **GUESTS:** Authorities on Pacific affairs—Henry Luce, Pearl S. Buck, etc. **CREATORS:** Jennings Pierce, director of public service programs at NBC West, and Inez Richardson of Stanford University. **PRODUCER-WRITER:** Arnold Marquis. **CONSULTANT:** Owen Lattimore, emissary to China in the Roosevelt administration.

The premise of the show was that with Europe in ruins, the Pacific might emerge as the center of political and social change in the world, and people should know something about it.

THE PACKARD HOUR, musical variety.

BROADCAST HISTORY: Sept. 18, 1934–March 19, 1935, Blue Network. 30m, Tuesdays at 8:30. Packard Motor Car Company. *The Packard Show*, a showcase for baritone Lawrence Tibbett. **ANNOUNCER:** John B. Kennedy. **ORCHESTRA:** Wilfred Pelletier.

Oct. 1, 1935–March 17, 1936, CBS. 30m, Tuesdays at 8:30. A continuation of the Tibbett series. **ORCHESTRA:** Don Voorhees.

Sept. 8, 1936–July 20, 1937, NBC. 60m, Tuesdays at 9:30. *The Packard Hour.* **CAST:** Fred Astaire with song and dance; Charlie Butterworth, comedian. Cliff Arquette, joining in progress as Grandpa Sneed. **VOCALISTS:** Trudy Wood and Jimmy Blair; later Francia White; also, Conrad

Thibault and Jane Rhodes. **ORCHESTRA:** Johnny Green.

Sept. 7, 1937–March 1, 1938, NBC. 60m, Tuesdays at 9:30. Now sponsored by Packard as *Mardi Gras*. **CAST:** Lanny Ross, singing star, costarring Walter O'Keefe. Rhodes, Butterworth, and Arquette returned, with singer Ruby Mercer and soprano Florence George of the Chicago City Opera. **ANNOUNCER:** Don Wilson. **ORCHESTRA:** Raymond Paige.

Although *The Packard Hour* was heard in several formats and timeslots, the 1936–37 series with Fred Astaire drew most of the critical attention. Astaire had no sooner signed a contract with Packard ("ask the man who owns one") when he began to fret. How does one *dance* on radio? He missed his own premiere, letting guests Jack Benny and Ginger Rogers carry the show. Astaire arrived for the second week. He pulled young soprano Trudy Wood out of the chorus for an on-air duet, and she went on to become the headliner when Astaire, costar Charlie Butterworth, and the rest of the company broke for the summer June 1. Rumors spread along Radio Row that Astaire and Butterworth were incompatible: Butterworth was reportedly annoyed with Astaire's habit of stepping on his laughs. For whatever reason, Astaire never returned, and when the show opened in the fall it was with Lanny Ross in the spotlight, and with a new name, *Mardi Gras*.

PADUCAH PLANTATION, country music, humor, and philosophy.

BROADCAST HISTORY: Oct. 17, 1936–April 10, 1937, NBC. 30m, Saturdays at 10:30 Oldsmobile. **CAST:** Irvin S. Cobb, humorist, journalist, and famed after-dinner speaker. John Mather, Norman Field, and guests. **VOCALISTS:** Dorothy Page and Clarence Muse. Also: The Hall Johnson Negro Choir and the Four Blackbirds Quartet. **ORCHESTRA:** Harry Jackson.

Paducah Plantation placed humorist Irvin S. Cobb in a fictionalized setting (it was aired from Hollywood) called White Hall Plantation, near Paducah, Ky. The humorous wisdoms of Cobb (whose stories of Old Judge Priest were minor classics of philosophical comedy) were interspersed with operatic and minstrel-type melodies. Cobb preached tolerance and understanding. "I'm a great believer in lying," he said, quoting Mark Twain that "the truth is so precious that it should be used sparingly." He was complimented by *Radio Guide* for his "back-porch philosophy" and the tobacco-and-racehorse plantation atmosphere. The impression that Cobb had "a mint julep right handy and a hound dog lazing in the shade" was offset by such guests as opera stars Marion Talley and Gertrude Niesen.

PAINTED DREAMS, soap opera.

BROADCAST HISTORY: 1930–ca. early 1940s, WGN, Chicago. 15m, various times; heard in Chicago in the 1940s at 1:15 Central time.

Oct. 10, 1933–Feb. 2, 1934, CBS. 15m, four a week at 1:45, Eastern time. Kellogg.

1935–36, Mutual. 15m, three a week, Midwest network. Cal-Aspirin.

April 29–Nov. 20, 1940, Blue Network. 15m, weekdays at 10 A.M.

CAST: WGN, EARLY 1930S: Irna Phillips and Ireene Wicker in many roles, Phillips notably as Mother Moynihan. *CBS run, 1933–34*: Bess Flynn as Mother Moynihan. Also, Mary Afflick, Kay Chase, Alice Hill. **LATER YEARS:** Constance Crowder as Mother Moynihan. **CREATOR-WRITER:** Irna Phillips. **WRITERS:** Bess Flynn, Kay Chase (CBS run, 1933–34).

Painted Dreams was perhaps radio's first soap opera, predating in its local version even the network's *Betty and Bob*. Equally as significant, it was the first serial of Irna Phillips, who would make a career out of daytime melodrama, who

would mount the only serious challenge to Frank and Anne Hummert as the most important figures of the matinee air, whose influence is still seen in the maze of televised soaps. The major difference between Phillips and the Hummerts (aside from the considerable differences in style) was that Phillips wrote her own material. So prodigious was her output (at her peak of two million words a year, about the equivalent of 40 novels) that she was sometimes compared with the one-man fiction factory of the previous century, Alexandre Dumas père.

Phillips arrived at WGN, Chicago, in 1930: she was asked to read Eugene Field's *Bowleg Boy*, and performed so professionally that she was offered a job. Like so many radio jobs of that time, it didn't pay, but she did appear in several sketches and plays. She became friends with Ireene Wicker (*The Singing Story Lady*) and soon began writing a quarter-hour continuation in which she, Phillips, played a character named Sue and Wicker played her friend, Irene. This was well received, and finally WGN offered her $50 a week to produce a serial that became *Painted Dreams*.

Phillips played her own lead character, kindly, sweet-hearted Mother Moynihan. The story revolved around Mother M., her grown children, and her friends. Most of it was carried through dialogue in Moynihan's home, usually between "Mother" and one other character, often played by Wicker. This would become a Phillips trademark—long expository scenes in which characters talked out their situations thoroughly. But Phillips quit in anger in 1932, when WGN refused an offer to sell the serial to a network. She sued the station, seeking the rights to the show, but the final ruling in the station's favor established the principle of "work for hire," upholding the employer's ownership to property he had commissioned and titled.

Undaunted, Phillips created a new serial, *Today's Children*, which contained the same ingredients she had conjured up for *Painted Dreams*: the heroine was named Mother Moran, and Phillips and Wicker played several of the roles. This she took to NBC, and there she established her reputation. *Painted Dreams* continued for years as a WGN feature, with the station relenting on its "no network" policy for two brief runs. A WGN newspaper ad of the early 1940s pictures Constance Crowder as a young-looking Mother indeed: she was described as "patient, gentle, and wise," one who "comforts the afflicted, counsels the worried, and mends broken hearts as she goes through life."

THE PALMOLIVE BEAUTY BOX THEATER, operetta, Broadway and film musicals.

BROADCAST HISTORY: April 8, 1934–July 30, 1935, NBC. 60m, Tuesdays at 10. Palmolive. MU-SICAL CAST: Gladys Swarthout and John Barclay, regular leads, with performances also by James Melton, Helen Jepson, etc. Francia White a regular as of 1935. DRAMATIC CAST: Georgia Backus, Peggy Allenby, Frank McIntyre, etc. AN-NOUNCER: Tiny Ruffner. ORCHESTRA: Nat Shilkret.

Aug. 9–Dec. 27, 1935, Blue Network. 60m, Fridays at 9. Palmolive. COMMENTATOR: Otto Harbach. ORCHESTRA: Al Goodman.

Jan. 11–Feb. 15, 1936, CBS. 60m, Saturdays at 8.

Jan. 13–Oct. 6, 1937, CBS, 30m, Wednesdays at 9:30. Palmolive. CAST: Jessica Dragonette, with Charles Kullman. PRODUCER: Atherton W. Hobler. ANNOUNCER: Jean Paul King. OR-CHESTRA: Al Goodman.

The initial run of *The Palmolive Beauty Box Theater* was a huge success, drawing an estimated 25 million people in its first year and tapering off sharply thereafter. The series presented some of the most celebrated "serious" singers on the American scene and spotlighted the best work of Franz Lehar, Sigmund Romberg, Oscar Straus, Georges Bizet, Victor Herbert, Rudolf Friml, and Noel Coward. It had a decidedly popular sound, making it more palatable to the masses than the *Metropolitan Opera Broadcasts*, which had begun three years earlier. The music was familiar, the arrangements thrilling, and the dramatics were clear and easy to follow. Highlights of the two-year run included *The Vagabond King, The Student Prince*, and *Rogue Song*, all with Gladys Swarthout; *Carmen*, with Swarthout and James Melton; *Sweethearts*, with Melton and Lucy Monroe; *The Bohemian Girl*, with Frank Parker; *Lady Be Good*, with Jane Froman; *Mississippi*, with Melton and Francia White; and *Maytime*, with Melton and Rose Bampton. The final broadcast, on Feb. 15, 1936, costarred Melton and Jessica Dragonette in *The Great Waltz*.

Dragonette, then the star of the *Cities Service Concerts* on NBC, was one of the most popular singers ever developed by radio. "She was the last of the great stars to be identified with one, and only one, program over a period of years," wrote *Radio Guide*. But *Cities* and Dragonette parted in acrimony. She signed with CBS and opened in a new *Beauty Box Theater* in 1937. She had been lured with a promise of a new format that would allow her to explore whatever acting talent she might have, but the show was a watered version of the old. The timeslot was cut in half, and the fare consisted of distillations from the old show: *The Student Prince, The Merry Widow, Maytime, Bittersweet*, etc. The result was a disappointment to Dragonette's many fans, and to the star herself, who was heard infrequently thereafter.

THE PALMOLIVE HOUR, concert-variety.

BROADCAST HISTORY: Dec. 1927–July 29, 1931, NBC, 60m, Fridays at 10, 1927–28, then Wednesdays at 9:30. Palmolive Soap. CAST: Frank Munn and Virginia Rea, billed, in deference to the sponsor, as Paul Oliver and Olive Palmer. Also: Elizabeth Lennox and various "name" guests, such as Fanny Brice; the Revelers (James Melton, Lewis James, Wilfred Glenn and Elliott Shaw); Frank Black, piano. ANNOUNCERS: Alois Havrilla, Phillips Carlin. ORCHESTRA: Gus Haenschen.

The Palmolive Hour was one of NBC's major prestige concert shows in the earliest days of the network, immediately hailed by critics as the foremost program of its kind. Musical selections ranged from opera to Broadway to jazz, with emphasis on old favorites and classics. The formula was simple, as described by Thomas A. DeLong in *The Mighty Music Box*: it usually opened with a Munn-Rea duet, which created "an aura of ethereal romance" around them. Then came the Revelers, a variety of musical acts, and, at the beginning of the second half, frequent duets with contralto Lennox and soprano Rea.

THE PARKER FAMILY, situation comedy.

BROADCAST HISTORY: July 7–Oct. 5, 1939, CBS. 15m, Fridays at 7:15 through Aug. 25; then Thursdays at 7:15. Woodbury Soap.

Oct. 8, 1939–April 10, 1944, Blue Network. 15m, Sundays at 9:15 for Woodbury Soap until

March 18, 1943; then Fridays at 8:15 for Bristol Myers.
CAST: Leon Janney as teenager Richard Parker, who narrated the misunderstanding of the week and was nicknamed "Richard the Great." Michael O'Day also as Richard. Jay Jostyn as Richard's father, Walter. Linda Carlon-Reid and Marjorie Anderson as Richard's mother, Helen. Mitzi Gould and Patricia Ryan, respectively, as Richard's sisters, Nancy and Elly. ANNOUNCERS: Harry Clark, Hugh James, etc. CREATOR-PRODUCER: Don Becker. DIRECTORS: Chick Vincent, Oliver Barbour, etc. THEME: *Deep Purple*.

PARTIES AT PICKFAIR, fictionalized Hollywood chatter.

BROADCAST HISTORY: Feb. 11–June 21, 1936, CBS. 30m, Tuesdays at 10; final broadcast, Sunday. Sponsored by "leading ice and refrigerator dealers of America." STAR: Mary Pickford, America's sweetheart of the screen in the silent era. Eric Snowden as Alvin the butler. Also: Bret Morrison, Mary Jane Higby, Lou Merrill, Ted Osborne, etc. MUSIC: Al Lyons. DIRECTOR: Eric Snowden.

Parties at Pickfair purported to be a series of actual party conversations at the fabulous estate where Mary Pickford and her husband, Douglas Fairbanks, entertained the giants of show business, world affairs, and royalty. It was a clever illusion, with trumped-up dialogue read by radio professionals. As actor Bret Morrison told Frank Bresee: there was an initial attempt to do a remote from Pickfair, but the musicians left cigarette burns on the white piano. From then on it was broadcast from the studio.

THE PASSING PARADE, tall tales and strange happenings.

BROADCAST HISTORY: 1937–51, many network/timeslot changes:
Feb. 1–Aug. 16, 1937, NBC. 15m, Mondays and Tuesdays at 7:45. Cream of Milk Face Cream.
Sept. 12–Dec. 5, 1937, Mutual. 15m, Sundays at 9. Duart.
July 3, 1938–Jan 1, 1939, CBS. 30m, Sundays at 7:30. Gulf Oil.
1940–41, Blue Network, West Coast.
June 29–Sept. 21, 1943, NBC. 30m, Tuesdays at 9:30. Substitute for *Fibber McGee and Molly*. Johnson's Wax.

1943–45, NBC. 30m, Sundays at 2:30 as part of the John Charles Thomas *Westinghouse Program*.
March–Oct. 1944, CBS. 15m, three a week at 7:15.
1948–49, Mutual. 15m, weekdays at 4:30 in the West.
1950–51, NBC West. 30m, weekdays at 10:30.
HOST-STORYTELLER: John Nesbitt.

The Passing Parade dealt in yarns almost too incredible to believe, though thoroughly documented by John Nesbitt and his research staff. It grew out of an earlier program produced by Nesbitt, ca. 1935, called *Headlines of the Past*.
Nesbitt had been a seaman and a janitor: he had many interests and hobbies, produced short films, and was a student of Shakespeare. The idea for *The Passing Parade* came to him when his father left him a trunk containing news clippings of strange happenings around the world. He told his stories "straight," without any sound effects or music, but slipping into dialect when the situation demanded. He usually told two tales per quarter-hour: in one series, he had a musical intermission by the Victor Young Orchestra. His stock in trade was said by *Radio Life* to be "disasters, disappearances, inventions, fanatics, swindlers, prehistoric animals, adventurers, famous fighters, treasure hunters, and men against the sky." He told of daring prison breaks, amazing coincidences, unexplained phenomena that changed people's lives. He once told of a man who lived four years in a cupboard. He had a dash of Robert Ripley, a dash of Bill Stern, and a lot of Nelson Olmsted. A fast, prolific writer, he often scripted his show in the last hour, but a staff of fourteen people aided in his research.

PASSPORT FOR ADAMS, documentary drama.

BROADCAST HISTORY: Aug. 17–Oct. 12, 1943, CBS. 30m, Tuesdays at 10. CAST: Robert Young as Douglas Adams of "Centerville, USA," a small-town newspaperman "who's been sent on a trip around the world to visit the cities and talk to the people of the United Nations." Dane Clark as his companion, photographer Perry "Quiz" Quisinberry. ORCHESTRA: Lucien Moraweck; also, Lud Gluskin. PRODUCER-DIRECTOR-WRITER: Norman Corwin. WRITER: Ranald MacDougall.

Passport for Adams grew out of a request by the Office of War Information for a "goodwill" documentary series on the fighting countries of the United Nations. CBS took up the call; Norman Corwin was asked to produce, write, and direct the first script, and Ranald MacDougall would write the rest. But MacDougall got a movie job and, after writing four shows, left the rest to Corwin.

The action followed a country editor on his mission for Consolidated Newspaper Syndicate. It was because of his small-town background that Doug Adams was chosen: "most of the people of the world are small-town people," and he was to write about "how they live, what the war's done to them," and try to answer the tougher questions: "are they pulling together or scrapping among themselves? . . . how do American boys get along with them? . . . what do our soldiers and sailors and Marines do when they're on leave? . . . are they making friends for the United States? . . . what kind of people are fighting for our side? . . . are they like us? . . . *do* they like us?"

Adams's companion, photographer Quiz Quisinberry, was pugnacious and a good foil for the show's larger purpose: Adams spent a fair part of each half-hour correcting Quisinberry's misapprehensions and in the process imparting information to the listener. Quisinberry got in a fistfight in Moscow, almost caused an international incident by flirting with natives in Marrakesh, and disappeared for a "three-day toot" in Cairo. They also visited Belem, Monrovia, Tel Aviv, and Stalingrad. Corwin's "Tel Aviv" was later repeated as part of *Columbia Presents Corwin*, with Myron McCormick and Paul Mann as Adams and Quiz. But this was done on a lower key than most of Corwin's work: the nature of the program made it impossible for Corwin to grapple with the "evils in our midst," which he often did so well.

PAT NOVAK, FOR HIRE, detective drama.

BROADCAST HISTORY: 1946–47, ABC West; produced at KGO, San Francisco, and aired on the West Coast network only. CAST: Jack Webb as Pat Novak, acid-tongued waterfront troubleshooter, until ca. spring 1947; Ben Morris as Pat Novak thereafter. Jack Lewis as Jocko Madigan, ex-doctor, "boozer," and friend of Novak. John

Galbraith as Inspector Hellman, the brutish police detective. WRITER: Richard Breen; Gil Doud after Breen and Webb departed.

Feb. 13–June 18, 1949, ABC. 30m, Sundays at 7 until April; Saturdays at 9:30 until mid-May; then Saturdays at 8. CAST: Jack Webb as Pat Novak. Tudor Owen as Jocko Madigan. Raymond Burr as Hellman. ANNOUNCER: George Fenneman. ORCHESTRA: Basil Adlam. DIRECTOR: Bill Rousseau.

Pat Novak was Jack Webb's first significant radio crime drama. It was also the vanguard of radio hard-edge, so hard-boiled as to be high camp in its own time. The show was rich with hilarious pessimism, rippling with ridiculous metaphors. "The street was as deserted as a warm bottle of beer," Novak would say. "The car started up down the street and the old man couldn't have made it with a pocketful of aces. I caught a glimpse of the license plate in a dull, surprised way, the way you grab a feather out of an angel's wing."

In two separate stands as Pat Novak, Webb was propelled to national prominence. Novak operated out of "Pier 19," a small office where "I rent boats and tell a few white lies, if the price is right." Writer Richard Breen wrote the kind of dialogue that Webb delivered better than anyone else: it was sassy, brassy, and full of pent-up anger. "I'll give you $200 to follow a woman," a client says. In a heartbeat, Novak bounces back: "How'll I spot her, read it off an ankle bracelet?" At the end of the case, the woman falls to her death, filling the air with a horrible scream as she leaps over the embankment. "Too bad her name wasn't Jill," Novak says, with only a slight hint of pity.

The series existed, in fact, simply to push the one-liners. Each story was exactly like all the others. They all opened to the same general patter. "That's what the sign out in front of my office says—Pat Novak, for hire. That's the only way to make a living down on the waterfront in San Francisco, because around here a set of morals won't cause any more stir than Mother's Day in an orphanage. And it wouldn't do any good to build a church down here, because some guy would muscle in and start cutting the wine with wood alcohol. Well, I rent boats and do anything else that'll buy a warm winter. But if anything goes wrong, your trouble comes hard and it doesn't do any good to sing the blues, because down here you're just another guy in the chorus. I found that out Wednesday afternoon . . .''

This was always the transition into the so-called story. Someone would hire Novak: if not a beautiful dame, the job would lead to a beautiful dame. Someone would get murdered, Novak would become the "patsy," and he'd get beaten up at least once by the thugs and again for good measure by his old enemy, Police Inspector Hellman. His drunken pal, Jocko Madigan ("to him the hangover is the price of being sober"), would be enlisted to help with the legwork, and all would end in glorious violence. The closing line was always the same: "Well, Hellman asked only one question . . . ,'' and this always led to Novak's wrap-up. The listener was told who had done what, to whom, and occasionally why and how. None of it made much sense, but people tuned in for the writing and delivery.

The series was such a hit in its initial West Coast run that when Webb left for Hollywood in the spring of 1947, ABC decided to recast the lead and continue the run. The role fell to Ben Morris, an almost impossible job: Morris played it straight and died trying. *Radio Life* was deluged with letters, most asking two questions: "Who is Webb?" and "Where has he gone?" In Hollywood, Webb and Breen were reunited for a coast-to-coast Mutual series, *Johnny Modero: Pier 23*. This was almost a literal *Novak* revival, the same series in everything but the name. Webb continued building his reputation with appearances on *Escape*, *The Whistler*, and other adventure shows. When *Pat Novak* resurfaced in February 1949, it was to a nationwide ABC audience, setting up his debut on *Dragnet* later in the year.

Novak remains an enormously popular and entertaining series on tape. Listeners who approach it as comedy find that it still satisfies. Even *Richard Diamond, Private Detective* took note of the hero's abrasive nature, with an episode involving a wisecracking rival named "Pat Cosak."

PAUL WHITEMAN PRESENTS, musical variety.

BROADCAST HISTORY: June 6–Aug. 29, 1943, NBC. 30m, Sundays at 8. Substitute for Edgar Bergen. Chase and Sanborn. CAST: Paul Whiteman

and his 35-piece orchestra. ANNOUNCER: Bill Goodwin. VOCALIST: Dinah Shore.

Paul Whiteman Presents was the big hit of the summer. Each week featured one major guest star (Eddie Cantor, Burns and Allen, Red Skelton, Jimmy Durante, Ed "Archie" Gardner, etc.) and a member of the "Whiteman Alumni Association": Bing Crosby and the Rhythm Boys (Harry Barris and Al Rinker); Ferde Grofé; Johnny Mercer; Matty Malneck.

Another *Paul Whiteman Presents* aired seven years later on ABC (June 27–Nov. 7, 1950, 30m, Tuesdays at 8).

THE PAUL WINCHELL–JERRY MAHONEY SHOW, comedy-ventriloquism act.

BROADCAST HISTORY: Nov. 29, 1943–July 17, 1944, Mutual. 30m, Mondays at 9:30; returned Aug. 29–Sept. 17, 1944, Tuesdays at 8:30. STAR: Paul Winchell, ventriloquist, with his dummy, Jerry Mahoney. VOCALISTS: Imogene Carpenter, Vera Barton. ORCHESTRA: Russell Bennett; later Bob Stanley. PRODUCER: Roger Bower,

Paul Winchell rode the crest of the Charlie McCarthy wave. Though Winchell was a better ventriloquist than Edgar Bergen, as TV later revealed, Bergen was funnier. More important, Bergen was on radio first.

THE PAUSE THAT REFRESHES ON THE AIR, musical variety.

BROADCAST HISTORY: Dec. 21, 1934–May 3, 1935, NBC. 30m, Fridays at 10:30. Coca-Cola. CAST: "90 musicians and singers" under the direction of Frank Black.

Dec. 1, 1940–Dec. 10, 1944, CBS. Sundays, various times, mostly at 4:30; 30m until April 1941; 45m April–June; then 30m. Coca-Cola. CAST: Andre Kostelanetz and his "shimmering" 45-piece orchestra. Violinist Albert Spalding, narrator. GUESTS: John Charles Thomas, Lawrence Tibbett, Lily Pons (Mrs. Kostelanetz), and other renowned soloists. PRODUCER: Paul Lewis. WRITER: Gilbert Seldes.

Aug. 17, 1947–Feb. 18, 1949, CBS. 30m, Sundays at 6:30 until Jan. 1949, then Fridays at 10:30. Coca-Cola. HOST: Roger Pryor. CAST: Andre Kostelanetz and his orchestra, 1947–48; Percy Faith with another large orchestra thereafter. VOCALISTS: Ginny Simms; from ca. 1948, Jane

Froman, who was returning from a valiant four-year struggle to regain her health after suffering crippling injuries and near death in a 1943 Lisbon Harbor plane crash.

The Pause That Refreshes was the slogan of Coca-Cola, and the title of three musical series sponsored by Coke. The common denominators were large orchestras and "quality" music.

THE PENNY SINGLETON SHOW, situation comedy.

BROADCAST HISTORY: May 30–Sept. 26, 1950, NBC. 30m, Tuesdays at 9:30 for Johnson's Wax as summer substitute for *Fibber McGee and Molly* until July 4; then Tuesdays at 9 for Wheaties in the Bob Hope slot. **CAST:** Penny Singleton as Penny Williamson, a window who lived in a town named Middleton and sold real estate to support her two daughters. Sheilah James and Mary Lee Robb as daughters Sue and Dorothy ("DG" for short). Jim Backus as Horace Wiggins, Penny's partner in the realty firm. Gale Gordon as crusty Judge Beshomer Grundell. Bea Benaderet as Margaret, Penny's nasally cook. **DIRECTOR:** Max Hutto.

Penny Singleton was synonymous with Blondie, having played that role on radio and in films throughout the 1940s. Her *Penny Singleton Show* was a lighthearted pitch for women's liberation, portraying Penny and her daughters as highly competent, self-sufficient females in a sea of male ineptitude. Chief bunglers, and fierce competitors for her hand, were realtor Horace Wiggins and Judge Beshomer Grundell.

THE PEOPLE ACT, documentary; community action.

BROADCAST HISTORY: Jan. 6–June 29, 1952, CBS. 25m, Sundays at 10:05. **NARRATOR:** Bob Trout. **REPORTER:** Dave Moore. **PRODUCER:** Irving Gitlin.

The People Act was a joint project of CBS and the Ford Foundation. The premise was that radio dramatization of real-life community problems could help solve those problems. Topics included juvenile delinquency in Seattle and slum conditions in Harlem. The show made broad use of newly developed tape recorders, putting an estimated 250 miles of recorded actualities and sound effects in the CBS can.

PEOPLE ARE FUNNY, audience show; human interest.

BROADCAST HISTORY: April 10, 1942–May 29, 1951, NBC. 30m, Fridays at 10, 1942–43; at 9:30, 1943–45; at 9, 1945–48; Tuesdays at 10:30, 1948–51. Wings Cigarettes, 1942–45; Kool Cigarettes; Raleigh Cigarettes and Sir Walter Raleigh Tobacco, 1945–51.

Oct. 9, 1951–March 30, 1954, CBS. 30m, Tuesdays at 8. Mars Candy.

Oct. 12, 1954–June 10, 1960, NBC. 30m, Tuesdays at 8 for Toni, 1954–55; later Wednesdays (1956–59) and Fridays (1959–60) for multiple sponsors.

HOST: Art Baker until Oct. 1, 1943; then Art Linkletter. **ANNOUNCERS:** Herb Allen, Rod O'Connor, Ted Myers. **PRODUCER-DIRECTOR:** John Guedel. **WRITERS:** John Guedel and his father, Walter; Johnny Murray, writer and idea man in the early days; Jackson Stanley for more than 13 years, beginning ca. 1943.

People Are Funny rivaled *Truth or Consequences* as radio's best-known audience stunt show. Creator John Guedel was a radio entrepreneur whose career is also discussed in the article on *House Party*.

In 1938, Guedel produced an audition record at a cost of $30 for the show that would earn millions. This contained the basic ingredients, though it was still years—and several format and title changes—away from the breezy series known as *People Are Funny*. The first attempt, in 1939, was called *Pull Over, Neighbor*: it aired on NBC and CBS outlets in Los Angeles and was later revamped under the title *All Aboard*. But the true title crystallized one day when Guedel attended a boring after-dinner speech. Watching the fidgeting audience, letting his eyes roam across each face, Guedel made a note on a napkin. "People are funny, aren't they?"

The idea was simple on paper: a stunt show, with prizes of cash and merchandise. But each stunt would be carefully contrived to reveal a humorous facet of human nature, to prove that people were funny. Guedel knew a few things about human nature: he was a jack-of-all-trades, a ditch-digger with the WPA, a traveling salesman, a writer for Hal Roach, a collector of rejection slips from slick-paper magazines. He had slept in parks and even in a graveyard in poorer times. Now, in 1942, he was in a doctor's office and happened to read in a trade magazine that a current radio show had just been canceled. He dashed off a note to the agency handling the account. A few days later, he was outlining the basics of *People Are Funny* on the telephone. The agency liked it: the show was quickly assembled and inserted into the Friday NBC schedule.

The host was vital. Guedel needed a man with great ad-lib capability. He had been impressed with a brash young mikeman named Art Linkletter, but Linkletter was employed in San Francisco. Art Baker—then one of the best-known emcees on the coast—got the job. But for the first two weeks, Linkletter was brought in as cohost, giving Guedel a look at both men in action on the same soundstage.

The show built an immediate audience. By the end of its fourth month, Baker had pushed it to the top of its class. It was rated the second most popular quiz on the Pacific coast, and it wasn't a true quiz at all. The stunt was the thing: those off-the-wall gags that lit up and revealed the contestant's real nature. Double-cross was a key part of it. The participant was drawn from the audience and sent out into the world, accompanied by assistant Irvin Atkins, with a mission to accomplish. Only after he was safely out of earshot did Baker confide to the studio audience and listeners that the deck was stacked against him. Conspirators had been planted outside to make the contestant look more ridiculous than he was. While the contestant was gone, other games would be played in-house. Then the original contestant would return, bringing back the most interesting person he had encountered, to tell how he had made out. Baker and the audience got a hearty laugh, prizes were given, and everyone went home happy.

A few 1942 stunts give an idea of content. An aircraft worker was set up on Sunset and Vine with a naked mannequin, a bolt of cloth, some pins, and a pair of scissors. His mission: clothe her. As he snipped and pinned, a crowd gathered and the wisecracks began. Contestants seeking to prove that people were funny had only to try to give away money. A man sent out with a pocketful of silver dollars could only give away three. Another contestant sent out to sell apples

at "two cents each or two for a nickel" sold many more at two for a nickel.

Sometimes the sponsor played into the stunts. One contestant was ordered to take the sponsor's mascot, a penguin named Kenny Kool (in the days before Kool Cigarettes adopted Willie the Penguin as its symbol), into Hollywood's fanciest clothing stores and have it fitted for a sports coat. Perhaps the most sensational stunt of the first season had a man attempt to register at the Knickerbocker Hotel with a trained seal as his "girlfriend."

The show changed abruptly 78 weeks into the run, when Baker was dropped and Linkletter was installed as star. Baker did not go gladly. "I gave all I had to that show," he said, and promptly filed suit. His contract, he said, could only be broken if the sponsor canceled the show. He charged that Guedel and the sponsor had conspired to cancel and then immediately re-sign with Linkletter at a lower salary. Baker never got his show back: *People Are Funny*, from that day on, was Linkletter's show. Here Linkletter rose to national prominence. He displayed an ad-lib ability that became the envy of the industry, drawing kudos from Eddie Cantor, Bing Crosby, and other headliners. Soon fans forgot that there had ever been another host.

Linkletter conveyed obvious glee as contestants got doused with water, hit with pies, and ordered to guess which of the hamburgers they had just eaten was made of horsemeat (the audience roared as the contestants blanched; then Linkletter told them that both had been all-beef hamburgers). The stunts seemed endless. Would *you* kiss a pig for five cents? Would you run out onto the field during a football game and tackle a player? Half the fun was in Linkletter's provocative interviews before the game. *Collier's* said he had a "long list of basic questions that provoke laughter no matter how they are answered." He could be naughty, especially with young, good-looking female contestants. "He ventures so close to sticky terrain in some of these quizzes and stunts that his associates are in agony waiting for him to bog down." But he never did. Among his standard questions for young brides were how they met their husbands, what they did on their first dates, and how they spent their honeymoons.

In 1945, Linkletter staged one of his most celebrated stunts, dropping 12 little boxes sealed in floating plastic balls into the Pacific and offering a $1,000 prize to the first person who found one. This was claimed two years later by a native of the Ennylageban Islands. Linkletter also gave a man $20,000 to play the stock market for a week: the stocks bought gained more than $1,000, and the contestant kept the profit.

In addition to *People Are Funny* and *House Party*, Guedel later created the Groucho Marx quiz, *You Bet Your Life*. This had its origins in the early days of *People Are Funny*: a game in which contestants would bet the sponsor's cigarettes, and big winners took home 30 or 40 cartons.

THE PEOPLE'S PLATFORM, topical affairs discussion.

BROADCAST HISTORY: July 20, 1938–Aug. 10, 1952, CBS. Various times, notably 30m, Saturdays at 7, 1942–46. **MODERATORS:** Lyman Bryson, 1938–46; Dwight Cooke thereafter. **PRODUCER-DIRECTOR:** Leon Levine.

The People's Platform was a project of the CBS Adult Education Board. Chairman Lyman Bryson (a noted educator appointed to head the CBS board the previous January) brought to the air a selected panel of four people, who debated topics of current interest with spirit and sometimes with great heat. Topics included proposals for a bigger, stronger military in light of Germany's continued military buildup; Roosevelt's foreign policy; how far the United States should go in aiding democracies faced with aggression; and the role of the United Nations in keeping the peace. The guests were served dinner before the broadcast: they ate and chatted in a room just off a CBS New York studio, with the dining table wired for sound. Opposing viewpoints and input from average citizens were keenly sought.

Among the most prominent guests were Herbert Hoover, Dorothy Thompson, Groucho Marx, Lillian Hellman, Samuel Goldwyn, Gene Tunney, Irving Berlin, Tallulah Bankhead, Sen. Robert Taft, and Harold Stassen. Host Dwight Cooke estimated that one guest in four was a "table-pounder." He saw himself as a referee, to ensure that both sides got to air their views in detail—but not too much detail.

THE PEOPLE'S RALLY, quiz, issue-oriented debate; public affairs poll.

BROADCAST HISTORY: Oct. 16, 1938–April 30, 1939, Mutual. 30m, Sundays at 3:30; at 9 in the final three weeks. Mennen Shave Cream.
QUIZMASTER: Bob Hawk. **DISCUSSION MODERATOR:** John B. Kennedy.

This was a strange mix. The quiz was a *Quixie Doodle* format of silly questions and answers: "Could a baseball game end in a 6-6 tie without a man touching first base?" *Yes, if the game was played between two girl teams*. The debate presented two opposing viewpoints on such topics as the Neutrality Act. After both speakers had had their say, the audience was polled and the "people's opinion" was announced.

PEPPER YOUNG'S FAMILY, soap opera.

BROADCAST HISTORY: Oct. 2, 1932–Jan. 22, 1933, Blue Network. 30m, Sundays at 10:30. *Red Adams*.

Sept. 23, 1933–May 24, 1935 (heard seasonally, ca. Sept.–May), Blue Network. 15m, three a week, early evening (7:30, 8, 8:45). *Red Davis*. Beech-Nut Gum.

Jan. 13–June 26, 1936, NBC. 15m, weekdays at 3. *Forever Young*.

June 29, 1936–Jan. 16, 1959, NBC. 15m, weekdays at 3 until 1938; at 3:30 until 1955; at 4:30, 1955–56; at 3:45, 1956–59. *Pepper Young's Family*. Procter & Gamble for Camay, "the soap of beautiful women."

Also heard concurrently on other networks: 1936–41, Blue Network, weekdays, late mornings; 1937–38, Mutual, weekdays at 1:30 (making it, for a time, a serial with three simultaneous network outlets); 1942–43, CBS, weekdays at 2:45.

CAST: Burgess Meredith as Red Adams/Red Davis, a high school student who was tops at football, basketball, and tennis. Elizabeth Wragge as his little sister, Betty, who would come to be Peggy when the Davis family over several early format changes became the Young family. Jack Roseleigh as their father, Sam Davis; Marion Barney as their mother. John Kane as Red's friend, Clink. Eunice Howard as Luda Barclay. Jean Sothern as Connie Rickard. **AFTER THE TRANSITION TO THE YOUNG FAMILY:** Curtis Arnall as Pepper Young, ca. 1936–early 1940s. Lawson Zerbe as Pepper until 1945. Mason Adams as Pepper, 1945–59. Elizabeth Wragge as Pepper's sister, Peggy. Jack Roseleigh as their father, Sam Young, until 1939; Bill Adams also as Sam Young; Thomas

Chalmers as Sam Young for most of two decades, 1940–59. Marion Barney as Mary Young, the mother. Alan Bunce as Ted Hart, the football coach. Eunice Howard as Pepper's girlfriend, Linda Benton. John Kane as Pepper's pal, Nick Havens. Jean Sothern as Peggy's best friend, Edie Gray. Laddie Seaman as Biff Bradley, an awkward and gangly student. Elliott Reid and Tony Barrett, later, as Biff Bradley. Greta Kvalden as Hattie the maid. Edwin Wolfe (who also directed in the late 1930s) as Curt Bradley, Sam Young's closest friend. Grace Albert as Nancy Wayne, a secretary in the office who married Curt Bradley. Many actors as Carter Trent, who married Peggy Young: Stacy Harris, Bert Brazier, James Krieger, Michael Fitzmaurice, Chester Stratton, and Bob Pollock. Arthur Vinton as Pete Nickerson, the crooked mayor. Babytalk specialist Madeleine Pierce as Baby Butch. **ANNOUNCERS:** Alan Kent, Stuart Metz, Martin Block, Richard Stark, etc. **MUSIC:** William Meeder. **CREATOR-WRITER:** Elaine Sterne Carrington. **DIRECTORS:** Edwin Wolfe, Chick Vincent, John Buckwalter, etc. **THEME:** *Au Matin*, played hauntingly on piano.

Pepper Young's Family went through four major format changes, grew into a radio institution, and had one of the longest runs in history. Its author, Elaine Carrington, rivaled Irna Phillips in the hearts of soap fans. Carrington had been a successful short story writer in the 1920s and had written a play, *Alibi*, staged in 1929. The Depression forced her to consider radio as a means of support.

Carrington approached the serial world as one who had something better to offer than what was currently on the networks. An oft-repeated story tells of her being chased into a Fifth Avenue skyscraper by a rainstorm in 1932; then, realizing that she had walked into NBC, she left one of her plays with a receptionist for consideration. She later described her actions as far more calculated. Soon she was contacted by a producer, who asked if she could write a serial. Yes, she said, but not one of those harrowing things: the serial she would do would be quieter and would deal with the relationships of a small-town family.

Thus was *Red Adams* born. Red was a high school athlete; his sister, Betty, was two years younger, beautiful and self-centered, but likable. The parents were in their 40s: the father was in

manufacturing and made a good living, around $5,000 a year, which in those days put a family solidly in a middle-income bracket. The crises faced by Red, his family, and friends were low-key: Carrington wanted to reflect life as she knew it, with people who dealt with the same problems that faced her own son and daughter. The show tapped the same "river of life" theme that Carlton E. Morse was utilizing on *One Man's Family*. The first series, *Red Adams*, went through a brief run as a nighttime show. Later that year (1933), it was picked up by Beech-Nut Gum, which insisted on the surname change (Adams was Beech-Nut's staunch competitor in the chewing gum market). In 1936, when Red Davis had finally emerged as Pepper Young, Carrington had the formula that she would work for the rest of her life.

The Youngs lived in a small town, Elmwood, and were described as Roosevelt Republicans. Sam Young owned a manufacturing plant; his wife Mary was the kindly mother figure, prone to philosophize and give advice to the young people in town. Their children were Larry "Pepper" Young and Peggy Young: himself an athletic whiz and aspirant to literature; she as lovely as a Hollywood starlet. Pepper's steady girl was Linda Benton. Peggy, described by *Radio Guide* (1937) as a "gushy girl who takes herself much too seriously," was greatly loved by Biff Bradley, a newcomer to Elmwood High. Pepper's best friend, Nick Havens, was chubby, jovial, and lazy; he usually followed wherever Pepper led. Peggy's confidante was Edie Gray, "a lovable nitwit with nothing on her mind but boys, including Pepper, who can't stand the ground she walks on." The serial opened as a coming-of-age piece, with Pepper and Peggy about to leave school and begin their lives as adults.

"Pepper is constantly exposed to new adventures," *Radio Guide* informed: "among them, girls older than he, and learning to fly." His steady romance with Linda Benton was seldom threatened, though once he "got involved with a divorcee, who toyed with him." Peggy's life was a series of "successive excruciating heart-sicknesses, outgrowths of her crushes." It didn't matter that their names had been changed twice, or that faithful listeners could easily remember their *Red Adams* days. "They are the same—the same people are playing the father, the mother, the big brother, and the sister." This was almost true: Burgess Meredith had moved on, leaving the lead to others.

Pepper Young's Family thrived at a time when the most successful serials were melodramas of preposterous scope. Sometimes the action was no more dramatic than the morning walk to school. Sam Young made this walk with his kids every morning at 8:30, parting along the way to go to his factory. He was a good-natured father who was well liked. Peggy was the apple of his eye: she could do no wrong and she knew it, counting on her father to be her ally in any family dispute. She drifted through her life, dreaming about boys and marriage, often forgetting to study. Her romance with Biff Bradley was a sometime thing: she was dating Lew Wallace in 1938, but *Radio Guide* thought "she will probably return to Biff."

Curt Bradley was Biff's father, who became friends with the Youngs, unsuccessfully courted Mary Young's sister, Meg, and went into business with Sam. Pete Nickerson was the town crook, longtime mayor until ousted by Sam Young in a spirited election. Hattie was the Youngs' maid, who joined the family after her husband Jack, a sailor, ran away and left her with a child. Her "Baby Butch" was also part of the family, with various characters taking on his welfare in the "Bigger and Better Butch Club."

Pepper became a reporter at the local newspaper, the *Free Press*. He and Linda married and settled down to raise their child, "Button." Peggy and Biff parted: in the early '40s she met Carter Trent, a Chicago transplant who sat with her under the stars and proposed, dreaming of the wonderful life they could have *if only* he could get a job making $35 a week. By then the economic status of the Youngs was tenuous. Sam's business had failed; the Youngs had lost their house; money was tight. Peggy's lot with Carter Trent was to be difficult. He had given up an inheritance to marry her, and now the reality of life set in. Late in the run, after being a leading character for more than 15 years, Carter sank into despair, ran away, and died a broken man. This came about after oil was discovered on the Young farm, where Pepper and Linda were living. The oil well caught fire, burned out half the town, and killed Sam's closest friend, Curt Bradley. Carter, asleep at the site when the fire broke out, blamed himself.

The success of *Pepper Young's Family* led Elaine Carrington into new serials in the late '30s. Like Irna Phillips, she wrote her own material, dictating about 30,000 words a week. In 1940, with both *Pepper* and *When a Girl Marries* on the networks, Carrington was working about three weeks ahead. She spent each Monday dictating from her bed. She often worked from 10 A.M. until midnight, getting the week's ten episodes roughed out. She spent Tuesday and Wednesday in revision and finished up on Thursday. She wrote *Pepper Young* until her death in 1958, and her children, Bob and Pat, wrote the final year.

PERRY MASON, crime serial, based on the novels of Erle Stanley Gardner.

BROADCAST HISTORY: Oct. 18, 1943–Dec. 30, 1955, CBS. 15m continuation, weekdays at 2:45, then at 2:30 the first two years, then at 2:15, 1945–55. Procter & Gamble for Tide and Camay, 1943–55; General Foods, mid-1955. CAST: Bartlett Robinson as Perry Mason, crime-busting lawyer. Santos Ortega and Donald Briggs as Perry Mason, ca. mid-1940s. John Larkin as Mason from 1947. Gertrude Warner as Mason's faithful secretary, Della Street. Jan Miner and Joan Alexander as Della in subsequent eras. Matt Crowley as Paul Drake, Mason's investigator. Chuck Webster also as Paul Drake. Mandel Kramer and Frank Dane as Police Lt. Tragg. MUSIC: William Meeder, organ and piano. ANNOUNCERS: Alan Kent, Richard Stark, Bob Dixon, etc. DIRECTORS: Carlo De Angelo, from 1943; also, Art Hanna, Carl Eastman, Ralph Butler, Hoyt Allen. WRITERS: Erle Stanley Gardner, Irving Vendig, Eugene Wang, Dan Shuffman, Ruth Borden.

Though it came in the guise of crime drama, *Perry Mason* arrived with all the trumped-up baggage of a soap opera. Mason, of course, was famous in fiction for unmasking killers in court. On radio, he was as much detective as lawyer, at times swapping gunfire with criminals. This was a far cry from the Raymond Burr television series (CBS, 1957–66), which enjoyed powerful ratings success and is considered a black-and-white classic.

THE PERSONAL COLUMN OF THE AIR, dramatized human interest messages.

BROADCAST HISTORY: Nov. 16, 1936–Sept. 10, 1937, NBC. 15m daily: Blue Network weekdays at 11:15 A.M.; Red Network concurrently at 2:45, four a week. Chipso. CREATOR: Octavus Roy Cohen. PRODUCER: Inez Lopez (Mrs. Cohen). THEME: *L'Amour, Toujours L'Amour*, on organ.

The Personal Column of the Air was devised in England in 1935 and brought to NBC the following year. There was a brief run in selected cities before the national premiere in November.

Octavus Roy Cohen had been fascinated by the "agony columns" in the London *Times* and thought a radio show built around the same premise would pack great human interest. Listeners were invited to send in "messages you wish broadcast to people you have lost track of— friends, relatives, and dear ones who have disappeared from your life." Producer Inez Lopez sifted through hundreds of letters to find the few to be dramatized each week. The letter-writers were all impersonated by radio actors. *Newsweek* found it a "slow-paced show, sandwiched between explanations and legal warnings, but with an extraordinary degree of human interest."

THE PET MILK SHOW, musical variety.

BROADCAST HISTORY: Oct. 2, 1948–Sept. 10, 1950, NBC. 30m, Saturdays at 7:30 until Aug. 28, 1949; returned with new personnel Oct. 24, Sundays at 10:30. HOST-NARRATOR: Warren Sweeney. CAST: Vic Damone and Kay Armen, 1948–49, with a mix of stage favorites by Cole Porter, Rodgers and Hammerstein, etc. Bob Crosby and the Bobcats, 1949–50. MUSIC: Gus Haenschen and the Emil Coté Serenaders. THEME: *You and the Night and the Music*.

This was an outgrowth of Pet Milk's long-running *Saturday Night Serenade*. Subsequently, Pet would sponsor *Fibber McGee and Molly* under the title *The Pet Milk Program*.

PETE KELLY'S BLUES, crime drama.

BROADCAST HISTORY: July 4–Sept. 19, 1951, NBC. 30m, Wednesdays at 8. CAST: Jack Webb as Pete Kelly, player of a hot cornet in a Kansas City speakeasy in the 1920s. Meredith Howard as Maggie Jackson, singer in the speakeasy. Supporting players from Hollywood's Radio Row: William Conrad, Stacy Harris, Jack Kruschen, Whitfield Connor, Vic Perrin, Herb Butterfield,

Peggy Webber, etc. Jazz players in "Pete Kelly's Big Seven": Dick Cathcart, cornet; Matty Matlock, clarinet; Elmer Schneider, trombone; Ray Schneider, piano; Bill Newman, guitar; Marty Carb, bass; Nick Fatool, drums. ANNOUNCER: George Fenneman. CREATOR: Richard Breen. WRITERS: James Moser, Jo Eisinger.

Pete Kelly's Blues arrived on radio almost two years after Jack Webb reached stardom in *Dragnet*. It was a role quite different from the stoic Sergeant Friday: the world of Pete Kelly was a smoke-filled Kansas City gin mill of the mid-1920s, where "it's still tough to get a clear gin, but a lady likes the idea of a drink to match the color of her dress." Pete played cornet and headed up a hot jazz combo at George Lupo's, at 417 Cherry Street. "We start every night about ten and play till the customers get that first frightening look at each other in the early light."

This was a step backward for Webb, back to the tempo and pitch of his hard-boiled pre-*Dragnet* shows, *Pat Novak* and *Johnny Modero*. Never again would he be quite as sassy as in *Novak*, but as Pete Kelly he made the '20s roar a little louder and produced another topnotch series whose only drawback was that it ran a mere 12 weeks. All the Webb trademarks were here: the quips, the snappy comebacks, the short-tempered realism. "Let's all play together," he would bark as his Big Seven jazz combo opened on a clinker. His world was filled with sidemen, flappers, and gangsters, with Prohibition agents lurking around the fringes. Kelly's boss was "a fat, friendly little guy who wouldn't harm a fly— there's no money in harming flies." The stories were thin, but the atmosphere was rich. Most of the shows worked the same theme: Kelly would run afoul of some hood or mob boss, and his main work over the half-hour was in trying to get out of a bad situation with his skin intact.

Much of the show's appeal was in the music: Webb was a lifelong fan of hot jazz, and when the band played, the crowd got quiet. Two full jazz numbers were featured on each broadcast, giving it an unusual sound. Thirty musicians were auditioned for Pete Kelly's musical voice. Webb chose Dick Cathcart, a cornet player he had known in the Army. "That's not why he got the job," he hastened to inform *Radio Life*. But Webb was known for loyalty to old friends: he had known blues singer Meredith Howard (who played Maggie Jackson) since his days at Belmont High, and announcer George Fenneman worked with Webb for years after "showing him around" when he first broke into radio at KGO.

This was one of Webb's best shows, and the basis of his 1955 film of the same name.

PETER PFEIFFER, situation comedy.

BROADCAST HISTORY: Feb. 13–May 22, 1935, CBS. 30m, Wednesdays at 10. Frigidaire. **CAST:** Jack Pearl as Peter Pfeiffer, middle-aged Germanic manager of a hotel and tavern whose "good nature is imposed upon by his guests to moth-eaten advantage." Also: Cliff Hall, Pearl's straight man of long standing. **MUSIC:** Freddie Rich, with orchestra and a 12-voice choir. **VOCALIST:** Patty Chapin.

Peter Pfeiffer was devised as a change of pace for dialectician Jack Pearl after Pearl's famous *Baron Munchhausen* had slipped badly in the ratings. Pfeiffer was an old musician, forced by circumstances into running a hotel, but was still able to give music lessons to a group of children who came for them. Pearl described him as "a little old man of 50 years, the epitome of Casper Milquetoast, the same kind of befuddled, genuine character that Charlie Chaplin and Marie Dressler have played for so long." But the series was short-lived, and Pearl never did regain his former glory.

PETER QUILL, detective melodrama.

BROADCAST HISTORY: April 14, 1940–March 30, 1941, Mutual. 30m, Sundays at 4. Brach Candy. **CAST:** Marvin Miller as Peter Quill, a detective who was also a scientific genius. Alice Hill as his assistant, Gail Carson. Ken Griffin as Capt. Roger Dorn.

Most notable on this series was the opening signature, a wailing *Peeeeterrrr Quilllll . . .* This was achieved, according to Frank Buxton and Bill Owen, by having Marvin Miller "wail into the strings of a piano while the sostenuto pedal was held down."

THE PHIL BAKER SHOW, comedy, with musical variety.

BROADCAST HISTORY: Dec. 6–Dec. 20, 1931, CBS. 30m, Sundays at 9. Sheaffer Pens.

March 17, 1933–July 26, 1935, Blue Network. 30m, Fridays at 9:30. *The Armour Jester.* Armour Meats.

Sept. 29, 1935–July 3, 1938, CBS. 30m, Sundays at 7:30. *The Gulf Headliner.* Gulf Oil.

Jan. 14–Oct. 4, 1939, CBS. 30m, Saturdays at 9 until July, then Wednesdays at 8. *Honolulu Bound.* Dole Pineapple.

CAST: Phil Baker, accordion-playing vaudeville comic. Harry McNaughton as his butler, Bottle. Hank Ladd as Beetle, a mysterious ghostlike voice who heckled the star. Sid Silvers and Ward Wilson also as Beetle. Supporting players ca. early 1930s: Mabel Albertson, Florence Seward, Jack Murray. Agnes Moorehead as Mrs. Sarah Heartburn, an abrasive nitwit, 1936. Elvia Allman a regular, ca. 1938. **ANNOUNCERS:** Tom Hanlon, 1938, Harry Von Zell, 1939. **VOCALISTS:** Al Garr, 1938; the Andrews Sisters, 1939. **ORCHESTRA:** Roy Shield, ca. 1933; Leon Belasco, 1935; Hal Kemp, 1936; Oscar Bradley, 1937–38; Eddie DeLange, ca. 1939. **WRITERS:** Hal Block, Arthur Phillips, Sam Perrin.

The Phil Baker Show achieved a high rating in the early 1930s, despite its scheduling on only part of a national network. Through all of his radio shows that decade, Baker's formula was little changed: he brought to the air the same kind of comedy that he had been practicing for more than 20 years in vaudeville.

His career began on the stage of a local movie house. He toured with Ben Bernie in the '20s, an accordion-and-violin act that was one of the headliners of its day. His earliest radio shows featured Baker in amusing accordion sketches and in skits with his butler, Bottle, an English chap who had a "suspended sense of humor" and liked Shirley Temple dolls. Baker had an extreme fear of the microphone, a fact that may ironically have contributed to his success. He knew his limitations, he told a magazine writer, and it terrified him: he could not establish that rapport with audience that was his on stage, and often before a broadcast his hands would tremble violently and he broke out in a rash. So he created the heckling stooge, a character who would appear from nowhere and keep things rolling by making life miserable for the star.

This was Beetle, who was never seen even by the studio audience (the actors who played the part spoke through loudspeakers, with voice effects added, and they always posed for publicity stills in masks). Beetle would interrupt the show at least a dozen times, breaking in to chide Baker's routines and rudely demand that he get off the air. This was hugely successful: it also helped Baker get past his fear of the mike, for once he was on the air his symptoms vanished. The show usually included one accordion number, and vocals by such groups as the Neill Sisters and the Seven G's.

The same basic show was heard from 1933 until 1939, through changes of support from Armour to Gulf to Dole Pineapple. The Andrews Sisters brightened an otherwise business-as-usual Dole show in 1938–39. Baker and the public tired of the format simultaneously, and he dropped out of radio in 1939. He returned Dec. 28, 1941, taking the host's job on the quiz show *Take It or Leave It*, already in progress on CBS: this he held until Sept. 7, 1947. His final series was another quiz, *Everybody Wins* (April 23– Oct. 22, 1948, CBS, Fridays at 10 for Philip Morris). His greatest contribution to radio was the heckling stooge: his writer then, Sam Perrin, would go on years later to *The Jack Benny Program* and help develop the greatest heckler of all, the bile-dipped Frank Nelson.

THE PHIL HARRIS/ALICE FAYE SHOW, situation comedy.

BROADCAST HISTORY: Sept. 29, 1946–May 23, 1948, NBC. 30m, Sundays at 7:30. *The Fitch Bandwagon*. Fitch Shampoo.

Oct. 3, 1948–June 18, 1954, NBC, Sundays at 7:30 until 1951, at 8 until 1953, then Fridays at 9. Rexall until June 4, 1950; RCA as of Feb. 1951.

CAST: Phil Harris and Alice Faye as themselves; the zany, egotistical bandleader of questionable musical ability, and his wife, glamorous film star. Elliott Lewis as Frankie Remley, the hard-drinking, sardonic guitar player in Phil's band. Walter Tetley as Julius Abbruzio, the insufferable and abrasive delivery boy from the grocery store. Jeanine Roose as Alice Jr., and Anne Whitfield as little Phyllis, the Harris daughters. Robert North as Alice's brother Willie, a deadbeat and a creampuff. John Hubbard as Willie from ca. 1953. Gale Gordon as Mr. Scott, ranking officer of the Rexall Drug Company, the harried sponsor. Supporting players often from *Jack Benny Program* regulars: Frank Nelson, Sheldon Leonard, the Sportsmen Quartet, etc.

ORCHESTRA: Walter Scharf. **PRODUCER-DIRECTOR:** Paul Phillips. **WRITERS:** Ray Singer and Dick Chevillat, ca. 1946–50; Ed James, Ray Brenner, Al Schwartz, and Frank Gold in the 1950s. **ANNOUNCER:** Bill Forman. **THEMES:** *Sunday*, main theme ca. late 1940s, with *Rose Room* (a Harris favorite in his big band days) as a secondary theme; *It's a Big Wide Wonderful World*, theme in the last days of the 1950s.

In some ways, *The Phil Harris/Alice Faye Show* was an extension of *The Jack Benny Program*, where Harris had been practicing his considerable ability as a comic since 1936. Benny's show would sometimes end with Harris saying, "So long, Jackson," as the scene then shifted to *The Fitch Bandwagon*, which immediately followed. Harris played himself on both shows— the hard-drinking, sarcastic Benny bandleader, impressed by nothing more than his own good looks, his curly hair, and his natty clothes. He was loud and brash and usually insulting. He used English like a weapon, brutalizing unfamiliar words (which usually meant everything of more than two syllables). The *Fitch* action centered on Phil's home life with his wife, Alice Faye, and their two little girls, Alice Jr. and Phyllis, and on the cast of wiseguys that Harris would meet on the way home.

By 1948 the show was well established, and the link with Benny no longer seemed quite so important. The format continued in the Benny mode: the comedy focusing on Harris in rehearsal, on sponsor dissatisfaction, or on Phil's stormy relationships with his cast. There were two musical numbers in each broadcast: he dispensed such novelty numbers as *Shadrack, The Thing*, and *The Preacher and the Bear*, while she sang songs from her movie days or current hits (*Buttons and Bows*, etc.). Harris was also known for his ballads of the South, notably the oft-mentioned but seldom sung *That's What I Like About the South*. But it was the "Phil Harris character" that carried it: his timing was exceeded by none, including Benny himself. Like Benny, Harris played a character who in real life would be intolerable. That both men projected themselves through this charade and made their characters treasures of the air was a notable feat.

Alice played herself, the movie queen who had given up a fabulous Hollywood career to be a wife and mother. She had first met Harris in

1933, when she was singing with Rudy Vallee and was still unknown as an actress. Her face was wrapped in bandages, the result of an accident, and their conversation was limited to a few polite words. At that time, Harris was leading a top novelty band, formed in the '20s, with his own showmanship its main attraction. "Without doubt he was one of the strongest personalities ever to front a dance band," wrote Leo Walker in *The Big Band Almanac*. "Because of his reputation as a wisecracking front man, it might well have been forgotten that he was an accomplished drummer, although his secret ambition was to play trombone." He was becoming a national celebrity via radio: his broadcasts from the Cocoanut Grove in Los Angeles featured the bouncy rhythms synonymous with the early Depression, and the gay duets he sang with Leah Ray enhanced the happy nonsense.

Harris and Faye met again eight years later and were married in 1941 after a brisk courtship. From the beginning, *The Phil Harris/Alice Faye Show* was one of the funniest programs on the air. The lines bristled with sarcasm: the boys in the band were masters of backtalk, and none was more keenly etched than Frankie Remley, the left-handed guitar player. This character originated on the Benny show and was drawn from life. The real Frank Remley had known Harris in the mid-1920s; he had worked the Benny show as part of the Harris band, and Benny often singled him out for critical comment. The Harris aggregation was depicted as lazy, shiftless, stupid, and alcoholic, and Remley, though never given voice in those Benny programs, became the point man for all those virtues (as Harris saw them). On the Harris show, the "Frank Remley gag" was expanded into a speaking role: Remley himself auditioned but was not good enough. Remley recommended Elliott Lewis, who played it with such deadpan wit that the character was soon one of radio's comic masterpieces.

Remley's mission in life was simple: to get Phil Harris into one mess after another. His opening line was always the same: "Hiya, Curley," he would say, sending ripples of laughter through the studio before the first jokes were told. Remley's other standard line was the weekly invitation to trouble. "I know a guy . . . ," he would venture, leading Harris to some cut-rate "expert" in the problem of the week. The expert, of course, would crystallize the problem

and make it worse. Harris and Remley got in trouble babysitting and hanging wallpaper; they became chimneysweeps, and in one memorable episode (whose predictable outcome remains unspoiled to this day) they tried to impress their sponsor, Rexall, by creating a new drug.

Harris also had to contend with Julius Abbruzio, the most caustic brat in radio. Julius turned up in the second half of the program, delighted to find Harris and Remley in hot water and eager to do his part to keep them there. Walter Tetley of *The Great Gildersleeve* was perfect as the delivery boy with the high-pitched Brooklyn accent. "Are you kiddin'?" he would snarl. "Get outta here!" Long after reaching adulthood, Tetley was still specializing in playing wiseguy kids on radio.

At home, Harris was annoyed by Alice's brother Willie, who roomed with Alice and Phil and heckled Phil all the time. Willie's opening line—"Gooooood morning, Philip!"—was timed for maximum impact. The Harris children were given their "father's" mannerisms and had some brash and funny lines. In one episode, when it seemed that Harris had lost his show, he consoled his weeping daughters by reminding them that he still had a job with Jack Benny. "Oh, you know there ain't no money connected with that job!" little Alice said.

Gale Gordon was his usual dry self as Mr. Scott of the Rexall Drug Company. The sponsor was worked into the storylines to an unusual degree, eliminating the need for the middle commercial during the Rexall years. This went far beyond the old integrated commercial concepts. Rexall let itself in for some marvelous ribbing at the hands of Harris and Remley: Frankie loudly disdained the sponsor ("What's a Rexall?" he asked in an early show), and Harris once suggested that the company could make a bundle bottling and selling the Harris charm.

The writing was razor sharp: the scripts by Ray Singer and Dick Chevillat were so raucous that four-to-five-minute cuts were often necessary to allow for audience laughter. The principle of contagious laughter was maximized in the overhead placement of audience microphones, making it one of the loudest shows on the air. Some of the brilliance went out of the scripts when Singer and Chevillat departed, but the scripting remained solid, lacking perhaps the finer touches of their former cleverness. Also in

1953, the Frankie Remley gag was phased out and Elliott Lewis began using his real name. "There was some kind of beef with the real Remley," Lewis recalled years later. The character lost much of its punch, in his opinion, when it lost the Remley name. "Elliott Lewis just isn't as funny as Frank Remley," he said.

But the biggest change came in 1949, when Benny moved his show to CBS. This created a time problem, as the networks were two blocks apart and the shows were back-to-back. This meant Harris had to be in the first half only of Benny's show: he would leave CBS by 4:15, Pacific time, cut through the parking lots between the studios and knock on the NBC back door at 4:17. Then he would step onto his own stage, warm up his own audience, and *Phil Harris/Alice Faye* was ready for the air.

It remains, on tape, one of radio's brightest lights: the passage of time has done nothing to blunt its delightful impact. The characters were bums, but the listeners knew it and didn't care. When Harris crowed, "Oh, you dawg!" a listener knew he was probably looking at himself in a mirror. The timing displayed by the star leaves a modern listener with nothing but admiration; Elliott Lewis matches him show for show, in the comedy performance of his life. Of special interest are a dozen or so shows from the RCA era that contain full audience warmup routines. These add a backstage flavor and give listeners the sense of being there.

THE PHIL SILVERS SHOW, situation comedy.

BROADCAST HISTORY: June 25–Oct. 20, 1947, ABC. 30m, Wednesdays at 10 for Philco (substituting for Bing Crosby) until Sept. 24; then Mondays at 8:30, sustained. CAST: Phil Silvers, Betty Garde, Beryl Davis, Jean Gillespie, and Danny Ocko.

Silvers played "a nearsighted, not entirely stupid, reporter on a show-business trade paper" (*Newsweek*).

THE PHILCO HOUR, musical drama and variety.

BROADCAST HISTORY: 1927–28, Blue Network. 60m, Saturdays at 9. *The Philco Hour of Theater Memories*, light operettas with music from *The Vagabond King, Naughty Marietta*, etc. NARRATOR: Henry M. Neely, known on the air as "the Old Stager." CAST: Jessica Dragonette, Doris Coe, Mary Hopple, Muriel Wilson, Colin O'More, Walter Preston, Charles Robinson, and Dan Gridley. MUSICAL DIRECTOR: Harold Sanford.

1928–29, Blue Network. 30m, Fridays at 9:30.

1929–31, CBS. 30m, Thursdays at 10, 1929–30; Tuesdays at 9:30, 1930–31. *The Philco Concert Orchestra*, a shift to symphonic offerings.

Most of what is known about *The Philco Hour* comes from Jessica Dragonette's autobiography, *Faith Is a Song*. It was the first regularly scheduled operetta of the air. Initially the producers brought in members of original casts—Donald Brian in *The Merry Widow* and Fritzi Scheff in *Madamoiselle Modiste*, for example—but by 1928 Dragonette had signed to play all lead female roles. It changed direction with the move to CBS: Dragonette was committed to NBC, where on the *Cities Service Concerts* she quickly became the major radio star of her day.

THE PHILIP MORRIS FOLLIES OF 1946, musical variety.

BROADCAST HISTORY: Jan. 22–Sept. 3, 1946, NBC. 30m, Tuesdays at 8. Philip Morris. CAST: Johnny Desmond and Margaret Whiting, singing costars, with comic Herb Shriner. ANNOUNCER: Ken Roberts. ORCHESTRA: Jerry Gray. PRODUCER: Ward Byron.

THE PHILIP MORRIS PLAYHOUSE, music, variety, and drama.

BROADCAST HISTORY: June 30, 1939–Feb. 18, 1944, CBS. 30m, Fridays at 8:30 until fall 1939, then at 9. Philip Morris. Grew out of an earlier series, *Johnny Presents*.

Nov. 5, 1948–July 29, 1949, CBS. 30m, Fridays at 10. Top stars of Hollywood in stories of suspense and murder: Vincent Price, Dan Dailey, Donald O'Connor, Marlene Dietrich, etc. ANNOUNCER: Art Ballinger. ORCHESTRA: Lud Gluskin. PRODUCER-DIRECTOR: William Spier. WRITERS: Morton Fine and David Friedkin, etc. THEME: *On the Trail*, from *Grand Canyon Suite*.

March 15, 1951–Sept. 2, 1953, CBS (NBC briefly, Sept.–Jan. 1951–52). 30m, various nights.

New York based, with increasing emphasis on Broadway adaptations. Title switch to *The Philip Morris Playhouse on Broadway* in April 1951. **PRODUCER-DIRECTOR:** Charles Martin.

The Philip Morris Playhouse had a complicated history, evolving from an earlier mix of music and drama called *Johnny Presents*. This began in 1934, so called because the Philip Morris midget, Johnny Roventini, had become the country's most famous living trademark. The original *Johnny* program, though a showcase for big band music (Leo Reisman and later Russ Morgan), also offered a dramatic segment by Charles Martin titled *Circumstantial Evidence*. In mid-1938, director Jack Johnstone was staging these under the subtitle *Jack Johnstone's Dramas*. The band and drama segments were broken into two shows on opposing networks in 1939: Johnny Green, who had replaced Russ Morgan, aired on NBC Tuesdays at 8, supplemented by regular dramatic sketches (Una Merkel was a regular in the fall of 1941). On CBS, meanwhile, *Johnny* opened a series of dramatized short stories June 30, 1939, which was showing up in some logs as *The Philip Morris Playhouse* by January 1940.

The most notable thing about the show in all its forms was the commercial. Since 1933, when the first "Calllll for Philip Mor-raisss!" spot went over the air, millions of cigarettes had been sold by a four-foot midget with an uncanny ability to hit a perfect B-flat every time. Johnny Roventini was a $15-a-week bellhop at the Hotel New Yorker when a chance encounter changed his life. Milton Biow, head of the agency handling the Philip Morris account, arrived at the hotel, saw Roventini, and had a stroke of pure advertising genius. Roventini was auditioned there in the hotel lobby: under Biow's direction, he walked through the hotel paging Philip Morris, and he was soon in show business at $20,000 a year. As the brilliance of the ads became apparent to all, he was given a lifetime contract that was still in effect decades after the last "call" for Philip Morris left the air. He was a walking public relations campaign, reminding people of the product wherever he appeared. "Johnny" ads were prominent on billboards and in magazines. Always in his red bellhop's uniform, he was "stepping out of storefronts all over America" to remind smokers that they got "no cigarette hangover" with Philip Morris. When MGM's Leo the Lion died, it was said that Roventini was the only remaining living trademark.

Philip Morris was one of the biggest advertisers on radio. In addition to its *Playhouse* and the continuing *Johnny Presents*, the company carried *Crime Doctor*, *It Pays to Be Ignorant*, and other shows. Some originated in Hollywood and some in New York. A group of understudies—"Johnny Juniors"—was recruited and trained by Roventini as fill-ins for times of transcontinental conflict. Johnny Mirkin, one of the first, was lifted from a pageboy's job in Philadelphia. Forty years after its demise, *The Philip Morris Playhouse* is primarily remembered as a forum for Johnny, accompanied by the forlorn strains of Ferde Grofé's *Grand Canyon Suite*, enticing listeners to "Calllll for Philip Mor-raisss!"

PHILO VANCE, detective melodrama, based on the novels by S. S. Van Dine.

BROADCAST HISTORY: July 5–Sept. 27, 1945, NBC. 30m, Thursdays at 7:30. Bob Burns replacement. Lifebuoy. **CAST:** José Ferrer as Philo Vance. Frances Robinson as his assistant.

1946, ABC West, series with unknown cast noted, first heard July 23.

1948–50, Frederick Ziv syndication. **CAST:** Jackson Beck as Vance. Joan Alexander as his secretary, Ellen Deering. George Petrie as District Attorney Markham.

PHONE AGAIN, FINNEGAN, situation comedy.

BROADCAST HISTORY: March 30–June 22, 1946, NBC. 30m, Saturdays at 5. Household Finance.

June 27, 1946–March 20, 1947, CBS. 30m, Thursdays at 10:30. Household Finance. Title change to *That's Finnegan*, ca. autumn 1946.

CAST: Stuart Erwin as Fairchild Finnegan, a none-too-bright nice guy who managed the Welcome Arms Apartments and had problems with residents and with his friends at Gabby O'Brien's athletic club. Frank McHugh as Finnegan as of Oct. 1946. Florence Lake as Miss Smith, the switchboard operator, whose cheery "Phone again, Finnegan" was the show's catchphrase. Harry Stewart as Longfellow Larsen, the Swedish janitor. **DIRECTOR:** Hobart Donovan.

PICK AND PAT, minstrel-style variety.

BROADCAST HISTORY: Jan. 27, 1934–May 31, 1935, NBC. 30m, Saturdays until March, then Fridays at 10:30. U.S. Tobacco on behalf of Dill's Best. **CAST:** Pick Malone and Pat Padgett, comics.

June 3, 1935–Feb. 20, 1939, CBS. 30m, Mondays at 8:30. U.S. Tobacco. **CAST:** Pick Malone and Pat Padgett with vocalists Edward Roecker, baritone, and the Landt Trio and White. **MUSIC:** Benny Krueger, Ray Bloch.

Jan. 18–July 18, 1944, Mutual. 30m, Tuesdays at 8:30. Helbros Watches. **CAST:** Pick and Pat with singers Mary Small and Diane Courtney. **AN-NOUNCERS:** Tiny Ruffner, Paul Douglas. **OR-CHESTRA:** Vincent Lopez.

July 23–Aug. 30, 1945, ABC. 15m, four a week at 8. Vacation replacement for *Lum and Abner*.

Vaudeville comics Pick Malone and Pat Padgett were Irishmen who met in 1929. They specialized in heavy blackface, creating a Negro spoof act called *Molasses and January*, which they used on the Maxwell House *Show Boat* concurrently with their own shows. They often worked without scripts, each building spontaneously upon gags and situations thrown out by the other. In 1938, their show was also called *Model Minstrels*.

THE PICKARD FAMILY, hillbilly music.

BROADCAST HISTORY: 1928–32, Blue Network. 30m, Fridays at 8 for Interwoven Socks, 1928–29; 30m, Saturdays at 8, sustained, 1929–30; 15m, Saturdays at 7:45 for Billiken Shoes, 1930–31; 15m, Thursdays at 8:30, 1931–32.

1935–36, Mutual. 30m, three a week at 9.

The Pickard Family arrived at NBC in 1928, a scene that might have inspired *The Beverly Hillbillies* more than 30 years later. May Singhi Breen recalled their arrival for *Radio Guide*. They pulled up at the NBC Fifth Avenue studio in a big touring car overflowing with clothes, bags, and household possessions and "announced calmly that they were the best musicians in their part of the country, and wanted to play on 'this here radio.' " Everyone was given an audition in those days, and Breen recalled the Pickards' as "a riot . . . they were immediately spotted as one of the greatest novelties of all time."

The Pickards were Charlie, Ruth, Bubb, Ma, and Dad. "Always musical, they had been touring the mountains of Tennessee, playing where they could. The father played the kazoo and the mouth organ, the mother played the violin and the piano, the daughter the guitar, and the son the violin. Also in the family was a child, three and one-half years old. They called her Baby Ann."

THE PICKENS SISTERS, vocal trio.

BROADCAST HISTORY: 1932–36, NBC. Various 15m timeslots. 1932–33, Red Network, Sundays at 7:30, and Blue Network, Saturdays at 10:45. 1933–34, Blue, Wednesdays at 11. 1934–35, Blue, three a week. Early 1936, NBC, Tuesdays at 8:30, with Morton Downey and the Mark Warnow Orchestra, as part of a series called *Evening in Paris*.

The Pickens Sisters—Grace, Jane, and Helen—came from Macon, Ga. Taught by their mother to harmonize from childhood, they arrived in New York with a striking sound but no experience in the style and delivery of popular music. Their specialty was the Negro spiritual. They were singing these old-fashioned songs at a party when they were discovered by Stella Karn, a radio publicity woman who later managed Mary Margaret McBride. Karn took them to maestro Vincent Lopez, who helped arrange auditions for RCA records and at NBC.

Grace disliked performing and soon dropped out of the act. She became the business manager, and her singing slot was taken by a fourth sister, Patti, who was then just 14 years old. Though never as commercially popular as the Boswell Sisters (and neither act approached the glory of the Andrews Sisters a decade later), the Pickens Sisters had marvelous harmony and helped define their era. Jane, always the most ambitious, selected their songs, worked out the arrangements, and decided matters of orchestration. By 1936, she was eagerly pursuing a career as a soloist, accepting a song-a-week job on the Texaco show. The other sisters were romantically inclined: they married and that was the end of it. Jane went on to appear in the *Ziegfeld Follies of 1936*, sang with Eddy Duchin, and was for several seasons a singer in New York's Plaza Hotel. She appeared with Ed Wynn in *Boys and Girls Together* (1940–41) and in 1949 starred as Regina in the Marc Blitzstein musical *The Little*

Foxes. Her later radio career included stints on the revived *Chamber Music Society of Lower Basin Street* (NBC, 1950) and in her own NBC show, sometimes called *Pickens Party* (1948–57, various times; some broken continuity).

PLANTATION PARTY, country music and cornpone humor.

BROADCAST HISTORY: May 7–Dec. 3, 1938, Mutual. 30m, Saturdays at 10:30, later at 10. Bugler Tobacco.

Dec. 9, 1938–Jan. 22, 1943, NBC. 30m, Blue Network, Fridays at 9 until May 1940; Red Network, Wednesdays at 8:30 until Feb. 1942, then Fridays at 9:30. Bugler Tobacco.

CAST: Whitey Ford, host, in character as "the Duke of Paducah," whose standard opening was, "Howdy, neighbors!" Red Foley, country singer, ca. 1938. Louise Massey and the Westerners (Curt Massey, Milt Mabie, Allen Massey, Larry Wellington). Tom, Dick, and Harry (Bud Vandover, Marlin Hurt, Gordon Vandover). Michael Stewart, bass singer. **ANNOUNCER:** Charlie Lyon.

THE PLAYER, mystery drama.

BROADCAST HISTORY: 1948 15m syndication. **CAST:** Paul Frees, a "one-man theater," who impersonated all the characters; as the Player, he also narrated in the same manner as the title character on *The Whistler*. **ANNOUNCER:** Gary Goodwin.

PLAYS FOR AMERICANS, topical wartime dramas.

BROADCAST HISTORY: Feb. 1–July 5, 1942, NBC. 30m, Sundays at 4:30 until April, then at 5:30. **CAST:** Major film stars in leading roles: Bette Davis, James Stewart, Robert Taylor, Olivia De Havilland, etc. Supporting players from Hollywood's Radio Row: Elliott Lewis, Mercedes McCambridge, Byron Palmer, Byron Kane, Lou Merrill, Hans Conried, Paul Dubov, Jack Zoller, Tim Graham, Thelma Hubbard, Joseph Kearns, Hank Wilbur, Irene Tedrow, Mary Lansing, Rosemary DeCamp, Jack Mather, Earle Ross, Cathy Lewis, Elisabeth Bergner, Alfred Ryder, etc. **MU-SIC:** Gordon Jenkins, composer-conductor, with some conducted by Paul Lavalle, Charles Dant, or Frank Black. **PRODUCER-DIRECTOR-WRITER:** Arch Oboler.

Plays for Americans was among playwright Arch Oboler's contributions to the war effort. Oboler had given up many lucrative writing-and-directing assignments to produce, gratis, radio plays that promoted the Allied cause. The stories were heavy with emotional appeal and political meaning. There were the usual "if we hadn't been so blind" themes—fantasies contrived to illustrate what life under the Nazis might be like, should they win the war. There were love stories wrapped in relevant messages. They were broadcast with one purpose, said C. L. Menser of NBC—"to stimulate by indirection rather than appeal." The plays were collected in a book, published by Farrar & Rinehart in 1942 and donated by Oboler for free use on any sustaining radio show for the duration of the war.

POINT SUBLIME, comedy-drama.

BROADCAST HISTORY: 1940–42, NBC Pacific Network. 30m, Mondays at 8:30 Pacific time.

1942–44, Mutual–Don Lee. Same timeslot.

Oct. 6, 1947–May 31, 1948, ABC, full network. 30m, Mondays at 8. John Hancock Insurance.

CAST: Cliff Arquette as Ben Willet, storekeeper, town philosopher, man of deep curiosity, and mayor of Point Sublime. Jane Morgan as Evelyn (Evy) Hanover, his romantic interest. Earle Ross as Howie MacBrayer, Ben's friendly rival. Mel Blanc as August Moon, the stuttering railway clerk. Verna Felton as Hattie Hirsch, the town gossip. Lou Merrill as Aaron Saul, the town jeweler (he and his wife Sadie were the community's only Jews). Fred MacKaye as Monk Rice, son of the local newsman, who worked as a reporter on his father's *Point Sublime Herald* and helped combat the low-handed competition from the unscrupulous *Vernon Sun*. **WRITER:** Robert L. Redd.

Point Sublime was a good-hearted comedy about life in a small seaport village, "located in the quiet reaches of anybody's imagination." As described by author Robert L. Redd, the town had 750 people, a golf course, one newspaper, and a general store. There was a closed lighthouse on the point, facing the Pacific, and the town itself was split by the Coast Highway, its principal thoroughfare. It was strictly a one-street town: "The street climbs up over the point and dips down into the sea, losing itself in the tumbling breakers."

The mayor, Ben Willet, owned the general

store. He also owned the adjacent motel, pumped gas, and carried on a low-key courtship of Evy Hanover. Evy had come to Point Sublime to work for a paleontologist. The scientist left, but she stayed on. Her talks with Ben led often to humor, sometimes to drama, occasionally to mystery. Ben's rival, Howie MacBrayer, was a retired millionaire cattle baron from Texas: Howie bought the Point Sublime Golf and Surf Club and became the butt of all Ben's jokes about Texas. The railway clerk, August Moon (played by Mel Blanc in his Porky Pig cartoon voice), doubled as a helper in Ben's store, and especially enjoyed a good "feel in the rice bin."

The show, billed as "the human story of a fella named Ben Willet," ran on the West Coast only for four years. In 1947, the original cast was reassembled for the coast-to-coast ABC premiere. This opened with Ben Willet returning home after many months in Europe.

POLICE WOMAN, crime drama, based on the career of NYPD cop Mary Sullivan.

BROADCAST HISTORY: May 6, 1946–June 29, 1947, ABC. 15m, Mondays at 10:45 until June 1947; then Sundays at 9:45. Carter's Pills. CAST: Betty Garde as the policewoman.

THE PONDS PLAYERS, prestige drama.

BROADCAST HISTORY: Jan. 12–March 2, 1934, NBC. 30m, Fridays at 9:30. Ponds Cold Cream. STAR: Maude Adams. ORCHESTRA: Victor Young. DIRECTOR: Herschel Williams of J. Walter Thompson. THEME: *The Babbie Waltzes*, by William Fuerst.

The Ponds Players was a 30-minute anthology, with many of the stories taken from the stage triumphs of Maude Adams. One of the most popular actresses of the 1890s, Adams was famous for her youthful appearance (which followed her into middle age), her demand for privacy, and her portrayals of James M. Barrie characters. She was in her 60s when NBC began courting her. Radio intrigued her, and she agreed to at least come and observe the process. She insisted on touring NBC incognito and was introduced to directors and control room people as "Miss Ewell." She sat quietly and watched, then agreed to try it.

With the Ponds account came director Her-

schel Williams of the J. Walter Thompson radio department, who had been handling the Civil War drama *Roses and Drums* on another network. The Adams series, he said, would be "pure theater on the air." Adams insisted on complete privacy during the broadcasts: there was no studio audience, and the doors were guarded—not even the sponsor was allowed inside. Adams did not read a script. She memorized her lines and "played" them to the microphone. Her opening show was Barrie's *The Little Minister*: she played Lady Babbie, as she had on stage.

THE PONTIAC VARSITY SHOW, variety show with college talent.

BROADCAST HISTORY: Jan. 22–May 14, 1937, NBC. 30m, Fridays at 10:30. Pontiac. CAST: Host John Held Jr. ("raccoon-clad, noisy and overgrown," said *Radio Guide*) with undergraduates from Notre Dame, Texas, Oklahoma, etc.

Oct. 1–Dec. 31, 1937, Blue. 30m, Fridays at 8, later 9. Pontiac. CAST: Held replaced by "local cheerleaders from the schools"; later, Paul Dumont as emcee. Students from Alabama, Indiana, Brigham Young.

POPEYE THE SAILOR, cartoon drama, based on the comic strip by Elzie Segar.

BROADCAST HISTORY: Sept. 10, 1935–March 27, 1936, NBC. 15m, Tuesdays, Thursdays, and Saturdays at 7:15. Wheatena. CAST: Detmar Poppen as Popeye. Olive Lamoy as his girlfriend, Olive Oyl. Charles Lawrence as Wimpy. Jackson Beck as the bully, Bluto. Mae Questel as Sweetpea, the tot left on Olive's doorstep. Jimmy Donnelly as Sonny, the young boy adopted by Popeye in the first episode and later known as Matey the newsboy. ANNOUNCER: Kelvin Keech. MUSIC: Victor Irwin's Cartoonland Band.

Aug. 31, 1936–Feb. 26, 1937, CBS. 15m, Mondays, Wednesdays, and Fridays at 7:15. Wheatena. CAST: Floyd Buckley as Popeye.

May 2–July 29, 1938, CBS. 15m, three a week at 6:15. Popsicle.

As in the King Features comic strip, Popeye was a gravel-voiced weakling who became a man of steel by eating a certain food. In the strip it was spinach; on radio, it was Wheatena, the sponsor's product. For this favor, Wheatena paid the syndicate $1,200 a week. The major problem was finding an actor who could create the croaking "whiskey baritone" that cartoon viewers knew as the hero's voice. Det Poppen got the job after an entire aggregation of Coney Island barkers was auditioned. The cartoon ambience was abetted by Victor Irwin, whose Cartoonland Band had also provided tunes for the films. Musical effects were used for everything from Popeye's bulging "mus-kles" to his "rolling walk."

Spinach was again absent from the CBS run, with Floyd Buckley in the lead. Instead of the old musical climax ("I'm strong to the finich, 'cause I eats me spinach"), listeners got this frog-voiced wrap-up:

Wheatena's me diet,
I ax ya to try it,
I'm Popeye the saiiilor man!
Beep-beep.

PORTIA FACES LIFE, soap opera.

BROADCAST HISTORY: Oct. 7, 1940–April 25, 1941, CBS. 15m, weekdays at 4. General Foods for Post Flakes and Post Bran.

April 28, 1941–March 31, 1944, NBC. 15m, weekdays at 5:15. General Foods.

April 3–Sept. 29, 1944, CBS. 15m, weekdays at 2. General Foods.

Oct. 3, 1944–June 29, 1951, NBC. 15m, weekdays at 5:15. General Foods.

CAST: Lucille Wall as Portia Blake, a young woman lawyer who battled corruption in the small town of Parkerstown. Anne Seymour and Fran Carlon as Portia during Wall's six-month illness, 1948. Myron McCormick (ca. early 1940s) as Walter Manning, the man in her life. Robert Shayne also as Walter. Bartlett Robinson as Walter for the last eight years. Raymond Ives as little Dickie Blake, Portia's son. Larry Robinson, Alastair Kyle, Skip Homeier, and Edwin Bruce heard variously as Dickie. Marjorie Anderson as Kathy Marsh, Portia's best friend. Esther Ralston, Rosaline Greene, Selena Royle, Anne Seymour, and Elizabeth Reller also as Kathy. Richard Kendrick and Les Damon as Bill Baker, the man Kathy married. Nancy Douglass and Joan Banks as the scheming Arline Harrison Manning. Lesley Woods as the neurotic, crafty, and scheming Elaine Arden. Henrietta Tedro and Doris Rich as the faithful housekeeper, Miss Daisy. Carleton Young as the devious Kirk Roder. Jack H. Hartley as the crooked Boss Con-

nelly. Walter Vaughn as Lambert, his henchman. Don Briggs as Dr. Stanley Holton. Santos Ortega as Clint Morley. Lyle Sudrow as Mark Randall. John Larkin as Walter's old friend Eric Watson. Cora B. Smith as Lili. Ginger Jones as the scheming Joan Ward. **ANNOUNCERS:** George Putnam, Ron Rawson. **PRODUCER-DIRECTORS:** Tom McDermott, Hoyt Allen, Kirby Hawkes, Beverly Smith, Paul Knight, Don Cope, Mark Goodson. **WRITERS:** Mona Kent; also, Hector Chevigny. **THEME:** *Portia*, by Lew White.

Portia Faces Life opened in crisis, and in a strong 11-year run the turmoil never ended. Portia Blake was married to handsome young attorney Richard Blake, who was waging a ruthless campaign against corruption in Parkerstown. But Richard was killed on opening day, leaving Portia to raise their son Dickie alone. Portia, also a lawyer, provided a strong guiding hand for her son and took up the fight against the corrupters in her husband's memory. This unusual combination—a truly feminine lead who faced lawbreakers in court and out—pushed *Portia* to the top of the soap heap, where it remained until the last year of its run.

Portia was "a story reflecting the courage, spirit, and integrity of American women everywhere." Later, when Portia was romantically linked to "brilliant, handsome" journalist Walter Manning (her dead husband's best friend), it was billed as "a story taken from the heart of every woman who has ever dared to love completely." Written for a decade by Mona Kent, *Portia* was based on the heroine of *The Merchant of Venice*.

Though Walter Manning was the main man in her life, he was usually absent when there was a crisis to face. First he was "tricked into marriage" by the beautiful and willful Arline Harrison, daughter of the publisher of the *Parkerstown Herald*, where Walter worked. Arline became Portia's bitterest enemy in the early years of the show. Rightly convinced that her husband still carried a torch for Portia, Arline grew selfish, cold-hearted and insanely jealous. Meanwhile, Portia—"tiny, resolute, and brave"—decided that she must forget Walter while continuing her fight against corruption. She took on a crusade against the town slums, trying to help people reach a decent standard of living. The crooked politicians, headed by Mayor

Bartlett and Boss Connelly, had their own agenda. This brought Portia into conflict with the city hall henchman, Kirk Roder, "sleek front man for the crooked politicians"; then with Lambert, top racketeer in the Connelly machine; and finally with Dr. Stanley Holton of the City Health Department, who seemed strangely sympathetic while working with the gangsters.

This investigation took Portia and her best friend, Kathy Marsh, under cover. In the heart of the slums they met Miss Daisy, kindly owner of a boardinghouse, who was to become Portia's housekeeper and longtime friend. The relationship deepened between Portia and Dr. Stanley Holton, whose true colors came out when Connelly henchmen tried to murder Portia in a fire. Saved but left in a coma, she had but one chance—a risky brain operation pioneered by the brilliant brain surgeon Clive Russell, who had dropped from sight years ago. But at the eleventh hour it was revealed that Clive Russell was none other than Dr. Holton, who had been living under an assumed name because "of the hold Boss Connelly had over him."

During all this, Walter Manning had disappeared. Having obtained his freedom from Arline, he had misunderstood Portia's silence as a refusal to marry him, given up his job, and run off to cover the war as a frontline reporter in the Far East. Later he was reported to be in Yugoslavia, where he had supposedly been caught smuggling guns and executed by a firing squad. This Portia never believed ("My heart would have told me if Walter had been killed"). Now, with Portia saved, Walter returned. Dr. Holton (Russell) had fallen in love with Portia, but again went to seed when she spurned him and rushed again into Walter's arms. In another sequence, Walter disappeared into Nazi Germany. Later accused of sympathizing with the enemy, Walter was vindicated by Portia's brilliant legal defense in court.

They married, but for a year had to keep this secret. Then came Clint Morley, candidate for state's attorney, who was determined that Portia should love him. Walter again was in a distant land, and Portia was in a family way. At the moment when Walter lay ill in a Turkish hotel—unaware that Portia was carrying his child—her condition was the talk of Parkerstown. This was daring radio fare, with the town covertly gossiping about Portia and Clint, all unaware of her

marriage. In Ankara, Walter was told that he had a fatal disease. The thought of having Portia waste her life on an invalid was more than he could bear. Only one man could save him—Dr. Peter Steinhart, long presumed dead in a Nazi concentration camp, but who at that moment was flying in from Tel Aviv on his mission of mercy . . .

This was a difficult decade for Portia. Even after the birth of her daughter Sheilah, happiness was impossible. The serial ended as it had begun, in turmoil. She was framed, convicted, and sentenced to prison. Actress Lucille Wall told writer Richard Lamparski that this downbeat ending was deliberately concocted in the hope that a public outcry would force NBC to renew the show. It didn't work, and listeners were betrayed in a dark, ironic fulfillment of the long-running title. Portia faced life.

POT O' GOLD, the nation's first big-money giveaway show.

BROADCAST HISTORY: Sept. 26, 1939–June 5, 1941, NBC. 30m, Red Network, Tuesdays at 8:30, 1939–40; then Blue Network, Thursdays at 8. Lewis-Howe for Tums. HOST: Ben Grauer; also, Rush Hughes. ANNOUNCER: Jack Costello. VOCALISTS: Don Brown, Amy Arnell, and the Le Ahn Sisters. ORCHESTRA: Horace Heidt; also, Tommy Tucker. CREATOR: Ed Byron.

Oct. 2, 1946–March 26, 1947, ABC. 25m, Wednesdays at 9:30. Lewis-Howe. HOST: Happy Felton, a singing clown. ANNOUNCER: Bob Shepard. VOCALISTS: Jimmy Carroll, Vera Holly. ORCHESTRA: Harry Salter. WRITER-DIRECTOR: Paul Dudley.

The rise of *Pot o' Gold* was a radio phenomenon. But its fall came almost as fast, and when it bowed out its credibility was shaken and its audience reduced to a fraction of what it once commanded. The lure of *Pot o' Gold* was rooted in simple human greed. Each week the sponsor gave away $1,000 to people who answered their telephones when the *Pot o' Gold* host called. There were no questions to answer; people didn't have to squirt seltzer into the host's face or stand on one foot while reciting the Gettysburg Address in iambic pentameter. They didn't even have to be listening. All they had to be was home to answer the phone: they would then be told that *Pot o' Gold* was calling from New York and that $1,000 was being sent to them at once by telegraph.

The prospect that anyone might win spread like wildfire. The odds were roughly 20 million against, based on telephones then in use, but few people considered that. Within four months, *Pot o' Gold* had peaked at 21.1 in the Crossley poll.

Three times during the show a Wheel of Fortune was spun. The first number selected by the wheel indicated the volume to be plucked from the vast library of phone books displayed on stage. The second spin revealed the page number. The third gave the line number of the person to be called. The spinnings were dragged out for maximum impact and suspense, with musical entertainment by Horace Heidt and his Musical Knights interspersed between them. When a party was reached, host Ben Grauer would shout, "Stop, Horace!" and inform the winner that his $1,000 was on its way via Western Union. Names and phone numbers were freely discussed, so that a person who missed a *Pot o' Gold* call could expect to hear about it from friends for weeks. If the "pot" was unclaimed, a $100 consolation prize was awarded to the person whose number had been called; the other $900 was added to the next week's pot.

The show was so successful in the waning months of 1939 that movie theaters played to empty houses on Tuesdays. Some theater managers soon began offering their own $1,000 jackpots to anyone who missed a *Pot o' Gold* call while attending the movie. Those theaters quickly filled again, for without the lure of big money *Pot o' Gold* was quickly reduced to an ordinary band show. Big money it was: $1,000, then, could pay off a mortgage, and in some cases jackpots reached $2,800. Early stories of big winners were full of positive feedback— every winner seemed to be needy or had some worthy project in mind for the money. A minister building a new church . . . a family fallen on hard times . . . often when Grauer asked about the economic straits of the winners, the studio audience erupted in thunderous applause as it was revealed that, yes, the money was a godsend.

Then the trouble began. *Pot o' Gold* was attacked as being in violation of the ban against radio lotteries. While this debate raged in the press (the show seemed to skirt the stigma of gambling by requiring no investment by its winners), two would-be winners were victimized by bad connections. Grauer claimed the numbers called never answered: the people at home claimed they did, and one man asked the operator to make note of the call as proof. *Radio Guide* challenged the sponsor (Lewis-Howe for Tums) with a table of questions: (1) *Who* was being called, the telephone number or the name selected by the wheel? (2) If the person listed in the book had moved and another now had that number, who got the money? (3) Who got the money if an apartment owner sublet the unit and the tenant—not the person listed in the book— answered the phone? (4) What happened if the signal was busy? (5) What if there was trouble getting through? (6) What if Grauer got connected to a wrong number? Lewis-Howe responded to these and other questions, saying that the show had operated along established guidelines from the beginning. Lewis-Howe may have understood the guidelines, but the listeners did not, and the two highly publicized incidents damaged the show's integrity. Erosion was swift, and the show dropped away after its second year. The one-season revival of 1946–47 was a weak sister of the original. Big-money giveaways were then common, and the show never generated much enthusiasm.

A PRAIRIE HOME COMPANION, live music and folklore.

BROADCAST HISTORY: July 6, 1974–June 13, 1986. Returned Nov. 1989 as *American Radio Company* from N.Y.; resumed as *PHC* from Minn. Oct. 1993—present. Minnesota Public Radio/ American Public Radio. 90m, later 120m, Saturdays, early evenings. **HOST:** Garrison Keillor, vocalist and storyteller. **VOCALISTS AND MUSICIANS:** Vern Sutton, Phillip Brunelle, Bill Hinckley, Butch Thompson, Rudy Darling, Rod Bellville, Sean Blackburn, Dakota Dave Hull, Judy Larson, Craig Ruble, etc. Also: The Powdermilk Biscuit Band (Mary Du Shane, fiddle; Adam Granger, guitar; Bob Douglas, mandolin; Dick Rees, bass, among others). **PRODUCER:** Margaret Moos (through mid-1985).

A Prairie Home Companion, heard over 300 public radio stations, has been described as the nearest thing to an oldtime radio variety show that radio has produced in decades. Host Garrison Keillor became a national personality with his tales of small-town life in Lake Wobegon, a mythical Minnesota hamlet probably inspired by several actual towns.

Keillor has acknowledged his debt to oldtime radio, notably *Grand Ole Opry, Fibber McGee and Molly*, Gene Autry's *Melody Ranch*, Smilin' Ed McConnell, Arthur Godfrey, and regional broadcaster Cedric Adams. He worked in local radio beginning in 1960, and the idea for *A Prairie Home Companion* began to develop when he was in Nashville researching an *Opry* story for the *New Yorker*. The show found its audience, at first gradually, then with an explosion of popular acclaim that made Keillor a household word.

PRESENTING CHARLES BOYER, romantic drama.

BROADCAST HISTORY: July 4–Sept. 12, 1950, NBC. 30m, Tuesdays at 9:30. Replaced *The Penny Singleton Show* in midsummer as the vacation substitute for *Fibber McGee and Molly*. Johnson's Wax. Then: Sept. 14–Oct. 26, 1950, NBC. 30m, Thursdays at 10:30. **CAST:** Charles Boyer as Michel, shameless liar, womanizer, raconteur, and rake. Hanley Stafford as Bart Conway, American writer who dramatizes Michel's romantic and sometimes farfetched tales. Herb Butterfield as Bart Conway, ca. Sept.–Oct. Supporting players from Hollywood's Radio Row: Veola Vonn, Joseph Kearns, Jeanne Bates, Tudor Owen, Betty Moran, Hy Averback, Wilms Herbert, Rolfe Sedan, Jane Morgan, Jeffrey Silver, Sheldon Leonard, Lurene Tuttle, Stanley Waxman, etc. **ANNOUNCER:** Don Stanley. **PRODUCER-DIRECTOR:** Nat Wolff. **WRITERS:** Barbara and Milton Merlin, Jerome Lawrence and Robert E. Lee, David Robson, True Boardman, Leonard St. Clair.

Charles Boyer was right in character in this lighthearted dramatic series, playing the same romantic French rogue that had made him one of the most glamorous film stars of the '30s and '40s. His Michel, said the announcer, "belongs to that royal line of adventurers whose titles are stitched on the fabric of their own imaginations but who'd willingly give up any title for a moment of romance or a spot of cash." The show opened with lively French music being played by a street accordionist while a young woman sings. Michel walks out of the early evening, his

footsteps coming close. "Bon soir, my dear," he says in passing. "Bon soir, Michel," she replies wistfully.

In the cafe, Michel meets his friend, writer Bart Conway. He always arrives broke, and Conway is always in need of a story. The story Michel tells him becomes the tale of the week. At $200 each, the tales are a bargain, as Conway sells them at big rates to slick American magazines. One week might find Michel impersonating a general in the French Foreign Legion; the next week he will take on the cause of a young artist whose work is destined to hang in the Louvre. Michel is a con man with a world of chutzpah. He impersonates an art connoisseur; then, when unmasked, pretends to be a policeman and bluffs his way out. He teases next week's tale, and when Conway demands the rest, Michel laughs and says, "Ah, but that is another story—and another $200."

PRETTY KITTY KELLY, soap opera.

BROADCAST HISTORY: March 8, 1937–Sept. 27, 1940, CBS. 15m, weekdays, at 6:45 briefly, then at 10 A.M., 1937–40. "Slow-baked Wonder Bread" and Hostess Cupcakes. **CAST:** Arline Blackburn as Kitty Kelly, "golden-haired Irish girl" trying to make her way in America. Clayton Bud Collyer as Michael Conway, the policeman who befriended her. Helen Choate as Bunny Wilson, Kitty's best friend. Bartlett Robinson as Kyron Welby, the playboy to whom Kitty was engaged in England. Ethel Intropidi and Dennis Hoey as Phyllis and Edward Welby, Kitty's distant relatives from England. Richard Kollmar as Jackie Van Orpington, Michael Conway's main rival for Kitty's attentions. Artells Dickson as Slim, reporter on the *Blade* and Bunny Wilson's boyfriend. Howard Smith as Inspector Grady, the Irish police chief who made Kitty's welfare his concern. Charme Allen as Mrs. Murger. John Pickard as Grant Thursday, another of Kitty's suitors. **NARRATOR:** Matt Crowley. **ANNOUNCER:** Andrew Stanton. **DIRECTOR:** Kenneth W. MacGregor. **WRITER:** Frank Dahm. **THEME:** *Kerry Dance.*

Pretty Kitty Kelly opened with the most overworked malady of soap opera heroines: she landed on Ellis Island with amnesia, having only a vague memory of her former life in a Dublin orphanage. On the passage she had met old Patrick Conway, brother of New York Police Inspector Michael Conway, and an unscrupulous woman known only as "Mrs. Megram." Both disappeared on arrival: Mrs. Megram then turned up dead, and when Kitty tried to find Inspector Michael Conway, he too was killed. Kitty was arrested for murder but later proven innocent. In the course of this, she became friends with young Michael Conway, the inspector's son and also a policeman. Michael later became a New York attorney and pursued Kitty through some harrowing adventures.

For a time Kitty was employed as a maidservant for the family of playboy Jack Van Orpington. Later she worked at Marks' Department Store on Fifth Avenue, where she met lowbrow shopgirl Bunny Wilson, who became her best friend. A year after her arrival in New York, it was revealed that Kitty was actually the "long-lost Countess of Glennannan," throwing her relationship with Michael (did he still have the right to love her?) into a quandary. The theme, *Kerry Dance*, belied the blood-and-thunder content, which ranged from kidnapping in the Everglades to murder in the city. "Take Grimm's *Fairy Tales*," advised *Radio Guide*, add "Horatio Alger, the best of S. S. Van Dine's detective stories, one modern Cinderella, mix well, and you have it!"

THE PRIVATE FILES OF REX SAUNDERS, detective drama.

BROADCAST HISTORY: May 2–Aug. 1, 1951, NBC. 30m, Wednesdays at 8:30. RCA. Produced in New York. CAST: Rex Harrison as Rex Saunders, a British detective strongly reminiscent of *Bulldog Drummond* (with an opening consisting of similar foghorns and footsteps). Leon Janney as Alec, his sidekick. Lesley Woods and Elspeth Eric in female lead roles. ANNOUNCER: Kenneth Banghart. PRODUCER-DIRECTOR: Hyman Brown. WRITER: Ed Adamson.

Rex Saunders attempted to cash in on the long-running popularity of *Bulldog Drummond*, employing identical theme music and resurrecting at least one script from the *Drummond* series, which had departed the air in 1949.

THE PRIVATE PRACTICE OF DR. DANA, medical drama.

BROADCAST HISTORY: 1947–48, CBS West. 30m Sunday afternoons. CAST: Jeff Chandler as Steve Dana, doctor of medicine and good-hearted philosopher. Mary Lansing as Nurse Gorcey. PRODUCER: Sterling Tracy. WRITERS: Adrian Gendot, Bob Ryf.

Initially medical horror stories (*Radio Life*), mellowing into a highly positive routine dealing with problems that Dr. Dana "leads the patient to solve for himself."

PROFESSOR QUIZ, the first true radio quiz show.

BROADCAST HISTORY: May 9, 1936–Sept. 25, 1941, CBS. Many 30m timeslots. Aired on a limited CBS hookup from Washington, D.C., for George Washington Coffee, Saturdays at 8:30 until Sept. 12. Expanded into the full network Sept. 18, 1936, Sundays at 7 from New York. Among other timeslots: 1937–38, Saturdays at 8 for Kelvinator; 1938–39, Saturdays at 8:30 for Noxzema; 1939–40, Fridays at 7:30 for Teel Soap; 1940–41, Tuesdays at 9:30 for Velvet Tobacco.

Jan. 24, 1946–July 17, 1948, ABC. 30m, Thursdays at 7:30, 1946–47; Saturdays at 10, 1947–48. American Oil.

HOST: Arthur Godfrey (ca. 1937). QUIZMASTER: Craig Earl, both 1936–41 and 1946–48 runs. ANNOUNCER: Bob Trout (CBS). DIRECTORS: Ed Fitzgerald, Lee Little. JUDGES (SCOREKEEPERS): "Mrs. Quiz" (Mrs. Earl); William Gernannt.

From this simple program of questions and answers the entire giveaway industry evolved. Its roots were sunk in an earlier kind of impromptu broadcasting, a natural outgrowth of the man-in-the-street interview. Announcer Bob Trout said the quiz movement grew in the early '30s, when he was a staff announcer at WJSV, Washington. From numerous man-on-the-street programs came the "quiz-in-the-street": opinion questions gradually gave way to questions of fact, then trick questions, and it was only a matter of time until the element of money was added. The series *Vox Pop*, already a year old when *Professor Quiz* arrived on the network, had been interviewing people and giving nominal prizes, but this was still a step away from a true quiz show.

It was hardly a fortune that *Professor Quiz* offered: 25 silver dollars to the winner and $15 to the runner-up, but a fresh element was the participation of the listening audience. Listeners were invited to send in six questions for the six contestants on each show. A listener whose questions were used was also awarded $25. The questions were simple, with contestants asked to "name a heavenly body with a tail and one with rings" (any comet and the planet Saturn) or "identify the shortest verse in the Bible" ("Jesus wept"). The identity of "Professor Quiz" was a guarded secret until *Radio Guide* in 1937 revealed him to be Craig Earl, a law school graduate and a former circus tightrope walker and magician. Earl was known as "the King Midas of radio"; the questions were drawn from an "old battered hat," and Earl paid off by dropping the silver dollars into the winner's hand at the microphone. For a short time, Arthur Godfrey—like announcer Trout, a veteran of WJSV—was host.

THE PRUDENTIAL FAMILY HOUR, concert music; and **THE PRUDENTIAL FAMILY HOUR OF STARS** Hollywood-style drama.

BROADCAST HISTORY: Aug. 31, 1941–Sept. 26, 1948, CBS. Sundays at 5 in a 45m timeslot, cut to 30m in 1945. *The Prudential Family Hour.* Prudential Insurance. STAR: Gladys Swarthout, soprano, of the Metropolitan Opera, 1941–44; later, Risë Stevens, Eileen Farrell, Patrice Munsel. SUPPORTING VOCALISTS: Ross Graham, Jack Smith, and for a time novelty singer Sterling Holloway. MUSICAL COMMENTATOR: Deems Taylor (1941–44). HOST: José Ferrer (briefly). ANNOUNCER: Frank Gallop. ORCHESTRA: Al Goodman.

Oct. 3, 1948–Feb. 26, 1950, CBS. 30m Sundays at 6. *The Prudential Family Hour of Stars.* Prudential. CAST: Six top Hollywood film stars— Gregory Peck, Bette Davis, Ginger Rogers, Humphrey Bogart, Robert Taylor, and Barbara Stanwyck—billed as the Prudential "family." ANNOUNCER: Truman Bradley. ORCHESTRA: Carmen Dragon. PRODUCER: Ken Burton. DIRECTOR: Jack Johnstone.

The Prudential Hour offered seven solid seasons of concert music, the fare well-known melodies from the operatic stage and from popular charts. The shows included short dramatic sketches on the lives of Beethoven, Schubert,

and other composers, revealing how a piece just performed had been written.

After a gradual erosion of audience, the *Family Hour of Stars* opened with no break in continuity. Unfortunately, this had much the same sound as half a dozen "Hollywood glitter" shows then on the air. Periodic bonus stars (Ray Milland, Kirk Douglas, etc.) supplemented the regular Prudential "family" for variety, and original stories were fresher than standard film fare. But the sound was the same, due to the glut of such programming on CBS and the other networks as well.

PULITZER PRIZE PLAYS, dramatic anthology.

BROADCAST HISTORY: June 2–Aug. 11, 1938, Blue Network, 60m, Thursdays at 10, later at 9.

The series was announced as an answer for the neglect that even Pulitzer winners suffer once they have closed in New York. Titles included *Anna Christie* and *Beyond the Horizon*, by Eugene O'Neill; *Icebound*, by Owen Davis, and *Men in White*, by Sidney Kingsley.

PURSUIT, suspense-detective drama.

BROADCAST HISTORY: Oct. 27, 1949–May 9, 1950, CBS. 30m initially Thursdays at 10:30, then Fridays at 10 until mid-Jan., then Tuesdays at 10:30.

Also heard in two CBS vacation slots: July 1950, 30m, Saturdays at 8 for Gene Autry and Wrigley's Gum; and July–Aug. 1951, 30m, Tuesdays at 9 for *Life with Luigi*, again Wrigley's.

Sept. 18, 1951–March 25, 1952, CBS. 30m, Tuesdays at 9:30. Molle.

CAST: Ted de Corsia as Inspector Peter Black, 1949–50. John Dehner also as Peter Black. Ben Wright as Peter Black, 1951–52. Hollywood radio actors in support: Bill Johnstone, Jeanette Nolan, Tudor Owen, Joseph Kearns, Raymond Lawrence, etc. MUSIC: Leith Stevens, orchestra, 1949–50; Eddie Dunstedter, organ, 1951–52. PRODUCER-DIRECTORS: Elliott Lewis, William N. Robson. WRITERS: Antony Ellis, E. Jack Neuman, etc.

The epigraph for *Pursuit* described the content well: *A criminal strikes, and fades back into the shadows of his own dark world . . . and then, the man from Scotland Yard, the relentless, dangerous pursuit, when man hunts man!* The hero, Inspector Black, usually closed with "*Pursuit*, and the pursuit is ended."

THE PURSUIT OF HAPPINESS, radio Americana.

BROADCAST HISTORY: Oct. 22, 1939–May 5, 1940, CBS. 30m, Sundays at 4:30. HOST: Burgess Meredith. GUESTS: Celebrities including Fredric March, Charles Laughton, Jane Froman, Bud Abbott and Lou Costello, Louis Armstrong, Clifton Fadiman, Ethel Barrymore, Frances Farmer, Huddie (Leadbelly) Ledbetter, Woody Guthrie, Gertrude Lawrence, etc. ROVING REPORTER: Carl Carmer. ORCHESTRA: Mark Warnow. PRODUCTION EXECUTIVES: W. B. Lewis, Davidson Taylor. DIRECTOR: Norman Corwin. WRITERS: George Faulkner, Erik Barnouw. THEME: *Of Thee I Sing*, by Gershwin.

In the words of Max Wylie, *The Pursuit of Happiness* was a "flag-waving show" that "had the good sense not only to admit this at the beginning but to insist upon it throughout the run." It was the first major directing job for Norman Corwin, who became by quantum leaps the medium's brightest star in an exclusive little group commonly called "triple-threat men." (Orson Welles, Arch Oboler, and Elliott Lewis are other examples of people who could write, produce, and direct, and eventually achieved billing on a par with their series titles.)

The Pursuit of Happiness was conceived by CBS vice president Edward Klauber, who wanted (again quoting Max Wylie) "a show that was thoroughly entertaining, but also rich in things American." It would inspire in a listener "an increasing respect for his own heritage by bringing him forgotten pages from the lives of his ancestors; reanimated pictures of events grown stale by repetition or bad handling; music that had a meaning and a history; authentic

scenes of Americans, living and dead, in the midst of their great moments. And it did not matter whether these moments were fiery or placid." In short, it was the great American variety show.

In one broadcast, the listener could hear Walter Huston in a scene from *The Devil and Daniel Webster*, along with a musical skit by Jimmy Durante. In January 1940, New York garment workers offered a scene from Broadway's *Pins and Needles*, while Danny Kaye gave an impression of life in Russia; *Pinocchio* came to life in a preview of the Disney cartoon, and the release of a new Washington Irving postage stamp was celebrated in a dramatic skit from one of Irving's stories. Host Burgess Meredith sometimes performed (playing George to Lon Chaney's Lennie in an excerpt from *Of Mice and Men*); Ray Middleton sang Maxwell Anderson's *How Can You Tell an American?*; Bert Lahr and Ethel Merman gave a comedy moment from *Du Barry Was a Lady*; Raymond Massey read from *Abe Lincoln in Illinois*. "Life, liberty, and most particularly the pursuit of happiness," Meredith said on one opening. "Of these we sing!"

One of the most sensational broadcasts in radio occurred with Paul Robeson's appearance Nov. 5, 1939. Robeson sang an 11-minute *Ballad for Americans*, written by a little-known troubador named Earl Robinson and embodying all the strife and hope of America—the men, machines, oppression, and grief. Backed by a husky chorus, Robeson rocked the CBS studio and at the thunderous conclusion brought the 600 people in the audience to their feet in spontaneous applause. The cheering continued through the closing credits and for 15 minutes after the show left the air. The CBS switchboard was swamped with congratulatory calls for two hours, and letters came in for weeks. As for Norman Corwin, his green years were over: his best work was straight ahead.

THE QUALITY TWINS, nonsense talk; also known as *Sisters of the Skillet*.

BROADCAST HISTORY: 1928, WGN, Chicago. Also heard on various networks in many 15m timeslots, including 1930–31, Blue Network (as *Sisters*), six a week at 2:45; 1931–32, Blue, three a week at 8:45 for Crisco; 1932–33, Blue, Fridays at 9:30 for Armour; 1933–34, NBC, various formats; 1935–37, CBS, various formats; 1937–38, CBS (as *Quality Twins*), Tuesdays and Thursdays at 11:15 A.M. for Kellogg Cereals. **CAST:** Ed East and Ralph Dumke, with parodies of "advice to the housewife." Among their continuing characters were "Gwendolyn the gorgeous dishwasher" and "Pat Plenty, love expert extraordinaire." They told women how to keep husbands from snoring, save time in the kitchen, or handle unruly children.

QUEEN FOR A DAY, audience show.

BROADCAST HISTORY: April 30, 1945–June 10, 1957, Mutual. Premiered as *Queen for Today*. 30m weekdays at 2 or 2:30, 1945–50, then at 11:30 A.M. Miles Laboratories for Alka-Seltzer, 1946–50; Old Gold, ca. 1950–51; then multiple sponsors. **HOST:** Dud Williamson from New York for about two months; Jack Bailey from Hollywood thereafter. **ANNOUNCERS:** Mark Houston, Gene Baker. **DIRECTORS:** Bud Ernst, James Morgan, Lee Bolen.

Queen for a Day was created over lunch. Dud Williamson, then the host of the quiz show *What's the Name of That Song?*, was being feted by a pair of advertising men, Raymond R. Mor-

gan and Robert Raisbeck. Morgan had long dabbled in radio, helping create *Chandu, the Magician* a dozen years earlier. It was suggested that Williamson host a new radio series, a daily show that would highlight the host's interviewing ability. Williamson recalled an interview show he had done years before: he had stationed himself on a corner and asked women to describe what was nearest to their hearts at that moment. This musing led to another question: *what would you do if you could have anything you wanted?* Morgan perked up. "That's our program. Let's give women some of their wishes and have some real fun on the air."

Each day five women would be drawn from the studio audience. Each would express her wish, the audience would (by applause) select the one most deserving, and that woman would be crowned "queen for a day." She would be decked out in a crown and robe and inundated with gifts. The first queen, Mrs. Evelyn Lane of Arcadia, Calif., was given a new outfit, then was wined and dined in New York's hottest nightspots.

Williamson was assisted by his *Name of That Song* cohort, Bob Spence, but their era was brief. Morgan moved the show to Hollywood, where it thrived with Jack Bailey at the helm. Bailey was an old vaudeville music man and a barker at two world's fairs. He knew how to work a crowd, and he made *Queen for a Day* a career, playing the devilish but sympathetic host for 12 years of radio and eight years of TV. The format changed little: before each broadcast, Bailey, producer Bud Ernst, and announcer Mark Houston canvassed the crowds at the El Capitan Theater for potential queens. Neither age nor appearance mattered: they were looking for personality. Wishes were both common and bizarre. Women wanted to have screen tests, to meet Walt Disney, to get new false teeth, to get plastic surgery on protruding ears. "My mother needs a burro," said one; "she's a prospector." Gestures of kindness toward others were usually favored by the audience, but contestants with shaggy dog stories could also win. One queen wanted to change roles with Bailey and did: she took over the host's job, and Bailey was crowned, draped, and plastered in cold cream. Among the more touching cases was that of Mrs. Rose Basch, who wanted the tattoo from her days in a German concentration camp removed.

An "out-of-town queen" was selected by the spinning of a roulette wheel marked with the names of the 48 states. One person from the "state of the day" was drawn from the audience to select the "out-of-town queen," who was sent a box of stockings. Stockings were also given to the losers. Two "jesters" were drawn from each audience and allowed to tell one joke apiece.

Fred Allen lampooned the series in an immortal skit with Jack Benny. But almost four decades after its demise, it is still remembered for its dramatic opening signature, when Bailey would cry: "Would *YOU* like to be queen for a day?"

THE QUICK AND THE DEAD, documentary on the atom.

BROADCAST HISTORY: July 6–Aug. 17, 1950, NBC. 30m, Thursdays at 8. **CAST:** Bob Hope as "Taxpayer," a devil's advocate inserted to ask the obvious questions in order to make difficult scientific material understandable to the average man. Helen Hayes as Dr. Lise Meitner, Austrian-Swedish physicist whose work contributed to the development of the atomic bomb. Paul Lukas as Dr. Albert Einstein. Also: recorded interviews with actual scientists, physicists, statesmen, and laymen. **CREATOR:** William Brooks, NBC vice president. **PRODUCER-DIRECTOR:** Fred Friendly.

This was a fast-paced, controversial show, written in common terms and making print in both major national news magazines. It ran across seven weeks with some repeats. Among those interviewed were the crew members of the *Enola Gay*, the plane that dropped the first atomic bomb.

QUICK AS A FLASH, quiz show.

BROADCAST HISTORY: July 16, 1944–Dec. 17, 1949, Mutual. 30m, Sundays at 6, 1944–46; at 5:30, 1946–49; then Saturdays at 7:30, beginning Sept. 24, 1949. Helbros Watches.

Dec. 12, 1949–June 29, 1951, ABC. 30m, three a week at 11:30 A.M., 1949–50, then weekdays. Quaker Oats, 1949–50; Toni, 1950; Block Drugs, 1950–51.

HOSTS: Ken Roberts, ca. 1944–47; Win Elliot, 1947–49; Bill Cullen on ABC, 1949–51. **ANNOUNCERS:** Frank Gallop, Cy Harrice. **ORCHESTRA:** Ray Bloch. **PRODUCER:** Bernard J. Prockter. **DIRECTOR:** Richard Lewis.

Quick as a Flash was devised to provide entertainment on several levels, in addition to its main purpose, the game. Ken Roberts, its first host, considered it the ultimate quiz show, and it quickly captured and retained a loyal following.

Six panelists were drawn from the studio audience. Each was placed at a desk containing a buzzer button connected to different-colored lights that flashed across the desk's face. When the buzzer was pressed, the question was stopped in progress and the contestant was given a chance to answer. The questions were posed as "races," each with the name of a famed racecourse (the Belmont, Jamaica, etc.). The questions measured a contestant's reaction speed, with a $10 purse going to the winner of each.

Contestants who gave wrong answers dropped out of the running for that race, and more clues were given to the others. Often the clues were elaborately dramatized or were musically illustrated by Ray Bloch's orchestra. The "first race" was a current news question, the second was musical, the third was historical, and the fourth was on literature or entertainment. The highlight was the "fifth race," the "Sponsor's Handicap." This usually featured a mystery play, fully dramatized by radio's top detective stars, in character. Jay Jostyn, star of *Mr. District Attorney*, was in the first mystery play. Lon Clark later appeared as Nick Carter (master detective); John Archer (and Bret Morrison) as the Shadow, Santos Ortega as Bulldog Drummond, Raymond Edward Johnson of *Inner Sanctum Mysteries*, and Ed Begley as Charlie Chan. *Mr. and Mrs. North, Counterspy, Crime Doctor*, and *Abbott Mysteries* were among many others represented.

QUICKSILVER, game show.

BROADCAST HISTORY: June 27, 1939–April 17, 1940, NBC. 15m, Tuesdays at 7:15 until Sept. 26; returned Oct. 11, Blue Network, 30m, Wednesdays at 8:30. Tums. **HOST:** Ransom Sherman. **ANNOUNCER:** Bob Brown.

Riddles solicited from the audience were foisted upon people on the street.

QUIET, PLEASE, outstanding dark fantasy.

BROADCAST HISTORY: June 8, 1947–Sept. 13, 1948, Mutual. 30m, Sundays at 3:30 until June 29; then, beginning July 28, 1947, there were two weekly broadcasts—Mondays at 10 in New York (out of WOR) and Wednesdays at 8:30 on Mutual. On Feb. 2, 1948, the network broadcast moved to Mondays at 9:30, resulting in a single weekly performance thereafter.
   Sept. 19, 1948–June 25, 1949, ABC. 30m, Sundays at 5:30 until May 15; then Saturdays at 9.
HOST AND STAR: Ernest Chappell. **MUSIC:** Albert Berman, with eerie piano-and-organ score. **CREATOR-WRITER-DIRECTOR:** Wyllis Cooper. **THEME:** Franck's *Symphony in D minor*.

Quiet, Please was unsung and little-heard in its day, but a few good-sounding episodes among the dozens surviving on tape in poor quality give evidence of a potent series bristling with rich imagination. Creator Wyllis Cooper was radio's best practitioner of an almost surrealistic dramatic form that sometimes read like poetry but contained all the elements of the play. Cooper had founded *Lights Out* in Chicago in 1934. He had given that series over to Arch Oboler, whose career was built upon its macabre foundation. Cooper, meanwhile, had gone on to Hollywood. He had written some films, produced a patriotic wartime series (*The Army Hour*), and toiled in obscurity while Oboler became a household name.

With *Quiet, Please*, Cooper was returning to his radio roots. His characters walked in a fuzzy dream world where the element of menace was ripe and ever-present. In Cooper's hands, a field of lilies could be deadly; a grove of trees touched with sinister implication. Little was explained or justified: the impact was the thing, and at its best *Quiet, Please* packed a terrifying punch.
   Cooper's scripts "begin as immediately and

forcefully as opening a door on a madman's monologue," said *Radio Life*. In the story *Twelve to Five*, a disc jockey was visited by a dead colleague during his overnight request show. Cooper backgrounded this with a steady stream of popular recorded music, causing the Mutual switchboard to be jammed by callers requesting their favorite songs. In *Let the Lilies Consider*, Cooper's flowers became thinking, talking beings, bursting with a chilling kind of love. These were not tales of people living happily ever after. A strange fate awaited the midget who used a magic wishing ring to become a giant. An even more bizarre twist confronted the hero of *The Thing on the Fourble Board*, a story of oil-well drillers who found their platform inhabited by an invisible creature from a stony world two miles deep. "Cooper takes liberties with stories whose payoffs are out of this world," said *Radio Life*. The result was a show that lingered with those who heard it, sometimes for decades after the episodes were heard.

Ernest Chappell told the tales, in first person, sometimes in present tense, often in flashback. Each week he played some "ordinary fellow who gets all bollixed up with the supernatural," and it didn't much matter that it was always the same voice. Cooper employed few supporting voices: mostly the stories were carried by Chappell, with one or two others. The cast was told to play it straight: Cooper's pet hate was of "acting," and he wanted it related with a deadpan sense of "here's how it happened." His other major annoyance was having his show compared with *Lights Out* by people who remembered only that Arch Oboler had written it. Cooper closed each broadcast with a teaser for the next play. These were usually done cold, with no script, and often had a grimly humorous undertone. "I've got a story next week about an explorer who explored where he shouldn't explore," he might say. The star, who also announced, had the last word: "I'm quietly yours, Ernest Chappell."

It remains a gripping and desired series, still possessing its full dramatic appeal. Cooper is known to have influenced science fiction writer Harlan Ellison, among others. *The Thing on the Fourble Board* is a classic shocker, as terrifying as anything the medium has produced: when Cecil Roy gives voice to the monster in the final moment of the play, the blood chills. A listener may be equally affected by *Whence Came You?*, the story of an archaeological dig and a frightening resurrection of hawklike gods of antiquity.

QUIXIE DOODLES, satire and nonsense; also heard as *Colonel Stoopnagle's Quixie Doodle Quiz.*

BROADCAST HISTORY: Oct. 20, 1939–April 12, 1940, Mutual. 30m, Fridays at 8. Mennen.
  Sept. 29, 1940–March 23, 1941, CBS. 30m, Sundays at 5:30. Mennen.
STAR: F. Chase Taylor as Col. Lemuel Q. Stoopnagel. ANNOUNCER: Alan Reed. WRITER-PERFORMER: Snag Werris.

Quixie Doodles came to radio soon after F. Chase Taylor dissolved his partnership with Budd Hulick. As "Stoopnagle and Budd," they had set a zany standard for early 1930s comedy. Taylor was often considered ahead of his time: his kind of humor wouldn't be seen again until Bob Elliott and Ray Goulding arrived in the late '40s. His classic line, often quoted, was "People have more fun than anybody."

He was also the author of funny definitions— "gasoline is the stuff that if you don't use good in your car, it doesn't run as well as if" and "a straw is a thing that you drink a soda through two of them" being two examples. On *Quixie Doodles*, the question was the thing: the hilarity of Stoopnagle's sometimes ingenious queries was far more important than whether the guest was able to figure the answers. *How could an egg be dropped three feet without breaking the shell?* Drop it from four feet—it will fall the first three feet without breaking, but then, what a mess! *When is it perfectly good grammar to use "I is" in a sentence?* Three possibilities: "I is the ninth letter of the alphabet" . . . "Eye is something that when you don't pay your rent, you get a sock in" . . . "Aye is what a sailor, when addressed by his captain, replied twice, sir!"

Guests won awards up to $25.

THE QUIZ KIDS, quiz show with juvenile panel.

BROADCAST HISTORY: June 28–Aug. 30, 1940, NBC. 30m, Fridays at 10:30. Summer substitute for *Alec Templeton Time.* Alka-Seltzer.
  Sept. 4, 1940–Sept. 22, 1946, Blue Network/ ABC: 30m Wednesdays at 8 until July 8, 1942, then Sundays at 7:30. Alka-Seltzer.

  Sept. 29, 1946–Sept. 23, 1951, NBC. 30m, Sundays at 4, 1946–49; Sundays at 3:30, 1949–51. Alka-Seltzer.
  Sept. 14, 1952–July 5, 1953, CBS. 30m, Sundays at 4, later at 4:40, then at 6.
HOST: Joe Kelly. NOTABLE QUIZ KIDS: Richard Williams, Gerard Darrow, Joan Bishop, Claude Brenner, Ruth Duskin, Harve Fischman, Lonny Lunde, Patrick Owen Conlon, Margaret Merrick (a polio victim who made personal appearances on crutches), Joel Kupperman, Naomi Cooks, Harvey Dytch, Smylla Brind (who as Vanessa Brown had a notable film career), George Van Dyke Tiers. ANNOUNCERS: Fort Pearson; Roger Krupp. CREATOR: Louis G. Cowan. PRODUCER-WRITER: John Lewellen. WRITER-SCOREKEEPER: Maggie O'Flaherty. RESEARCH: Eliza Hickok. DIRECTORS: Jack Callahan, Forrest Owen, Ed Simmons, Riley Jackson, Clint Stanley. BROADCAST FROM STUDIO E IN CHICAGO'S MERCHANDISE MART.

It was radio's juvenile version of *Information, Please*, with this notable exception: while the four wits on *Information* were respected intellects, the children on *The Quiz Kids* were regularly called genius. IQ tests were measured at 135–180, a few 200 and up, and, as *Radio Life* put it, the Kids routinely answered questions that "would make *Information, Please* look as elementary as a Kay Kyser musical questionnaire." Typical was this brain-buster: "Would it be cheaper to buy a coat for $300, or a second coat, if there were $40 between the prices of the second and a third coat, three-fourths the cost of the second being equal to two-thirds the cost of the third?" This had to be answered almost instantly, with a studio audience watching and millions of people listening. Eleven-year-old math wizard Richard Williams did it, then explained how to a visiting panel of University of Chicago professors who had come on the air in a good-spirited though ill-advised challenge to the Quiz Kids. The Kids trounced the professors by a score of 275–140, and later did the same to a University of Michigan panel, 420–390.

Creator Louis G. Cowan was a Chicago advertising and public relations man who had dabbled in radio since the mid-1930s. *Information, Please* had demonstrated to its doubters that such a show could overcome the "highbrow" stigma:

a panel of brilliant children seemed the next logical step, if the kids could be found. It wasn't just a matter of intellect: the kids needed poise, personality, and good microphone presence; they should be able to discuss what they knew and not just repeat words they had read. They should come across as brilliant but never brash.

Cowan found his first kids in the newspapers. A 6-year-old boy had given a lecture on birds to older students and had been written up in a news article. Little Gerard Darrow could identify more than 1,000 birds, and he was also expert on butterflies, flowers, fish, animals, reptiles, amphibians, and shells. He was the original Quiz Kid; Joan Bishop, Cynthia Cline, and Van Dyke Tiers completed the panel for the audition record. The first broadcast featured Gerard, Van Dyke, Joan, Mary Ann Anderson, and Charles Schwartz. Soon parents were writing in, certain that their prodigies would compete well with the kids who were on the air every Friday night.

But before it came to that, the show needed a quizmaster, an adult who, like Clifton Fadiman on *Information, Please*, gave it exactly the right edge. This chair was as vital to the show's success as were the young panelists. A pair of college professors auditioned: they were too impressed with themselves, giving the kids no time to talk. A candidate from the lecture circuit gave away half the answers. Among the 20-odd people who auditioned was Joe Kelly, a third-grade dropout, seasoned vaudevillian, and host of the hayseed music show *The National Barn Dance*. "His height of intellectual polish before *The Quiz Kids* was to ring a cowbell and chortle, 'I'm teakettled pink to be here,' " wrote John Lear in the *Saturday Evening Post*. Kelly was far from dumb: he had finished third grade a year ahead of schedule but at age 8 had gone into show business. He was a "stranger to every science," wrote Lear, and now he would be asked to "referee controversies on the atomic theory" and decide the answers to questions he couldn't understand. "Out of a youthful acquaintance with a dime-store dictionary, he must approve or disapprove definitions of words like 'pteridophyte.' From a history he never studied he must identify the circumstances of distant events like the Charge of the Light Brigade. He must discuss books he has not read and plays whose authors he is not sure are living or dead."

Kelly got the job through a process of sur-

vival: given the negative factors of the others, he was the only one left standing at the end. But this was hardly a Clifton Fadiman, an ideal matchup. Often as the show went on, Kelly himself would wonder what he was doing there. Each new broadcast was ripe with potential humiliation. On his first broadcast he was heard to groan, "Sakes alive, am I ever dumb!" Lear reported that Cowan wanted him off the show, but an Alka-Seltzer representative intervened. Kelly added a human element that might be impossible to replace. He brought the show down to earth.

What Kelly lacked, the producers now proposed to give him. Though the kids were never coached, Kelly was given the questions and answers well in advance. Regular meetings between Kelly and chief researcher Eliza Hickok ironed out problems with diction. A linguist was hired to be at Kelly's beck and call. And Kelly was a quick read: his recall was keen, and a phone check with the linguist usually cleared up last-minute problems. But then he was on the air, and the mikes were live, and there before him were four young intellects waiting to spotlight his ignorance. To a cute question such as "What college has no football team, no faculty, and no curriculum?" there should be just one logical answer—the electoral college. But there was this child, talking about a college in Arabia that consisted only of students reading the Koran, and the kid was probably right—they usually were. When this happened, Kelly simply fell back on his dunce demeanor and admitted he didn't know. "Well, that's a new one on me," he would say, trying to move the kid out of Arabia without calling him wrong. At once the kids would pick up the drift—the answer was wrong though probably not wrong, and they were being asked to find the "real" answer. This they did with more than 85 percent of questions asked.

Kelly cast off his jitters and took a hands-on approach to the research. He double-checked Hickok's facts until he was as comfortable as he could be with the material. He was no Clifton Fadiman and knew it: *The Quiz Kids* would never challenge *Information, Please* at the pinnacle of radio wit. Because of his interest in nature, Gerard Darrow would sometimes be called a "little John Kieran," but the kids sold wit only as a secondary commodity. Genius may spring from anywhere, but wit seldom comes without experience. *The Quiz Kids* offered a sense of wonder, amazement for listeners that sometimes bordered on disbelief. Gerard displayed such a deep and mature grasp of mythology that the network received angry letters charging that the show was a fake. This was another hurdle in the show's bid for broad public appeal. In July 1940, when *Kids* was just a month old, *Radio Life* summed it up: perhaps adults were too limited in intelligence to enjoy the show.

But it was judged best new radio program by *Radio Daily* and *Radio Guide*. It was run, said *Collier's*, like a school: "Five children sit at a table behind microphones . . . Gerard is so small that his shoulders are barely above table level, but he indignantly scorned a higher chair." The kids each received a $100 Liberty or War Bond for every appearance. Questions were sent in by listeners, and the kids were graded by a committee of "judges." The three kids with the highest scores were carried over to the following week, opening two chairs for fresh faces. The show was soon flooded with applicants; referrals came from teachers, parents, and acquaintances of bright children everywhere. Few were chosen. Early kids were Joan Alizier, Geraldine Hamburg, Mary Clare McHugh, Claude Brenner, and Richard Williams. But the panel was dominated by regulars over the 12-year run. Popular Quiz Kids became prized personalities and were given chances to reinstate themselves after being eliminated, by competing a few weeks later for one of the two vacant chairs. The encore system started early, when Gerard Darrow was eliminated after his ninth show. Listeners demanded his return, and the panel was seldom without a solid mix of old favorites.

A traveling group of Quiz Kids was established for a national tour. They visited the White House and went to Hollywood. They appeared on the air with Jack Benny and Eddie Cantor, and the term "quiz kid" entered the popular lexicon, soon designating any brilliant practitioner of any skill, and of any age. When the show celebrated its 100th broadcast, the panel was composed of Ruth Duskin, 7-year-old expert on Shakespeare; Richard Williams, 12, mathematics king; Harve Fischman, 11, a "jack of all knowledge"; Jack Lucal, 15, a whiz at political science; and special guest Reyna Cooper, who had won a *Quiz Kids* contest. At 12, Claude Brenner had such a polished microphone presence that he was asked to substitute no less than four times

for Joe Kelly as quizmaster. Joan Bishop seemed to know everything on Beethoven and Brahms. Dick Bannister was steeped in history, science, and general subjects. Mark Mullin went into such detail on the mating habits of the grouse that an embarrassed Joe Kelly had to change the subject. By October 1948, 269 kids had passed through their ranks, and local *Quiz Kids* competitions were running in 35 cities. But the regulars continued to dominate: Darrow, Lunde, Brenner, Duskin, Williams, Tiers, Fischman, Lucal, Bishop, Merrick, Conlon, Cooks. Only when they reached the "grand old age" of 16 and their eligibility expired did they leave the show.

Perhaps the most famous of all Quiz Kids was Joel Kupperman. He arrived in 1942, a junior-grade Richard Williams still shy of his sixth birthday. Joel and Richard had equal capability with math. On his first show, Joel figured a detailed equation for a drugstore bill, and did it instantly. Then, asked to multiply that number by 98, he had that answer at once. His charm, wrote Jerome Beatty, was in his delivery: he lisped, stumbled, and seemed to struggle mightily before coming up with the answer. His toughest problem Beatty described as "so complicated that you probably won't understand the question, let alone get the answer." Joel was told to imagine an eight-inch circle, put an equilateral triangle inside it, then put another circle inside the triangle and another triangle inside the circle. Joel was to give the area of the fifth circle in this progression. The question had been submitted, with the answer, by a university expert. When Joel's answer differed, the expert was found to be wrong.

Through it all they remained humble and gracious on the air. They were major celebrities by 1942. Their likenesses appeared in toy stores and in cutout books and radio premiums. But there were few petty squabbles and no apparent jealousies. On one occasion Richard Williams drew a huge cheer from the audience when he interrupted Kelly to insist that Ruth Duskin be awarded his points—Ruth had spoken first and Kelly had not heard her. These qualities were judged as carefully in the screening process as were the barometers of intelligence. "We won't take a cocky kid," said producer John Lewellen in 1948. Also eliminated were the kids of cocky parents: many were excused because the parents were so "pushy, predatory, and disruptive" that they were certain to cause trouble.

In later years, owner-creator Cowan was troubled by charges that the show had exploited the kids and robbed them of their youth. Especially troubling were the views of Gerard Darrow, who had been profiled under the alias "Bruce Fletcher" by Studs Terkel for the book *Working*. Terkel described an aging man with a string of menial jobs and long periods of unemployment. "I wish it had never happened," Darrow told Terkel of his days as a Quiz Kid. "I can't forgive those who exploited me." Joel Kupperman is believed to share this view: today he lives a private life and declines all requests for interviews. The most valuable document likely to be produced on the *Quiz Kid* experience was done by Ruth Duskin (now Feldman), who undertook the difficult dual task of tracing the most celebrated kids and examining their life experience in light of their *Quiz Kids* childhood. There was a bittersweet edge to their collected memories. Joan Bishop sang with the Chicago Opera Company but never realized her childhood ambition, to perform at the Met. Jack Lucal became a Jesuit priest. Claude Brenner was an energy consultant; Margaret Merrick an educational consultant and mother of eight. Richard Williams, the "super Quiz Kid," became U.S. consul general in Canton and first U.S. ambassador to Mongolia. Harve Fischman became Harve Bennett, producer of TV shows. Lonny Lunde was a "composer by day, lounge pianist by night." Pat Conlon was acting and directing in New York. Naomi Cooks was running a store. Harvey Dytch was a computer programmer. Joel Kupperman was teaching at the University of Connecticut. Gerard Darrow had died at 47, "a man in broken health who had spent a good portion of his final years on welfare." Ruth Duskin became a wife, mother, and journalist, still living in the Chicago area. After years of uneasiness about her own *Quiz Kids* heritage, she plunged wholeheartedly into her book. *Whatever Happened to the Quiz Kids?* (Chicago Review Press, 1982) is a wise and haunting look at "the perils and profits of growing up gifted."

QUIZ OF TWO CITIES, quiz with city rivalry.

BROADCAST HISTORY: Sept. 24, 1944–April 6, 1947, Mutual. 30m, Sundays at 3:30. Listerine. Based on an earlier show of the same name, heard on the West Coast Don Lee Network since ca. 1940, and in upstate New York, 1941. **PERSONNEL:** *Ca. 1940–44, Don Lee West Coast version*: **HOSTS:** Reid Kilpatrick in Los Angeles; Stu Wilson in Los Angeles, ca. 1944. Mark Goodson (later Hale Sparks) in San Francisco. **PRODUCER:** Jim Burton. **HOST:** (*Mutual, 1944–47*) Michael Fitzmaurice. **PRODUCER:** Dan Enright.

The original version of *Quiz of Two Cities* exploited nicely the natural rivalry between Los Angeles and San Francisco. The L.A. part of the show was produced at KHJ; the San Francisco portion at KFRC. Reid Kilpatrick opened with cutting remarks about San Francisco, then drew from his audience four contestants for the quiz. Mark Goodson asked his contestants the same questions and hurled some equally choice insults at L.A. The city with the most correct answers was declared winner of the night, and a keen sense of competition developed among listeners in both cities. The scores were usually close (in March 1942 San Francisco had 37 victories; L.A. 35). Clubs, groups, and families competed in each area: ladies of the San Francisco Jinx Club trounced a group of Hollywood stunt men; Earl Carroll glamour girls beat the San Francisco Mutual Business Club; and so on.

The Mutual run expanding the scope beyond California, never quite generated the genuine rivalry of the original. Michael Fitzmaurice was overall master of ceremonies, with additional announcers serving as partisans in the cities of the evening. On one show, Bud Collyer was partisan in New York; Holland Engle did the honors in Chicago.

QUIZZER'S BASEBALL, quiz with baseball motif.

BROADCAST HISTORY: July 2–Aug. 27, 1941, NBC. 30m, Wednesdays at 8. **CAST:** Harry Von Zell, host, or "umpire". Budd Hulick and Glenda Farrell, "opposing pitchers." **ORCHESTRA:** Peter Van Steeden.

Two teams were assembled, each with three players. "Pitchers" Hulick and Farrell fired questions; players were awarded "base hits," doubles," or "home runs," depending on how fast they answered. The jackpot was $100.

R

RADIO CITY PLAYHOUSE, dramatic anthology.

BROADCAST HISTORY: July 3, 1948–Jan. 1, 1950, NBC. 30m, various times. **CAST:** New York radio actors; Jan Miner and John Larkin in many roles: adaptations of Cornell Woolrich, Ray Bradbury, John Galsworthy, and other major writers. **ANNOUNCERS:** Bob Warren, Fred Collins. **PRODUCER:** Richard P. McDonagh. **DIRECTOR-NARRATOR:** Harry W. Junkin.

Radio City Playhouse specialized in high-octane stories of adventure, often turning on life-and-death situations with strong male-female roles. Jan Miner created a minor sensation in the play *Long Distance*, about a woman who frantically tries to stay her husband's execution by phoning in new evidence. "Not since Aggie Moorehead's tour de force in *Sorry, Wrong Number* has an actress caused such a one-role stir," said *Radio Life*.

As the show settled in, stories of all kinds were used, including such heartwarming pieces as Paul Gallico's *Twas the Night Before Christmas*.

THE RADIO GUILD, radio's first major theater of experimental drama.

BROADCAST HISTORY: 1929–1940, Blue Network. 60m, usually heard in winter months, often in late afternoon (at 3 or 4 through the mid-1930s) and at one time or another on almost every day in the week. **DIRECTOR:** Vernon Radcliffe.

There were no stars on *The Radio Guild*. Director Vernon Radcliffe tried using Broadway people in the early 1930s, but found them unable to act for the air. They didn't understand that "the ear is more important to emotional influences alone than when aided by the eye," he told *Newsweek* in 1935. But Radcliffe had a cozy little obscure hour, unnoticed and free to do almost anything. If an hour wasn't long enough for all of *Henry VI* or *Richard III*, he did them in broken installments. He used a good mix of original plays and classics: intermingled with Galsworthy's *Justice* and Shakespeare's *Midsummer Night's Dream*, listeners heard such seldom-broadcast pieces as *Clear All Wires*, by Sam and Bella Spewack, and *Chopin*, by Wilfred Rooke-Ley. The focus was usually on the experimental, with plays in verse, slices of life, and opportunities for new and unknown writers.

THE RADIO HALL OF FAME, musical variety with drama.

BROADCAST HISTORY: Dec. 5, 1943–April 28, 1946, Blue Network/ABC. 60m, 1943–45, then 30m, Sundays at 6. Philco. Produced in New York by *Variety*, the trade paper of the entertainment world. **HOST:** Deems Taylor. **CAST:** Conceived as a kind of weekly Academy Awards of radio, with those judged worthy that week invited to perform in an all-star hour of music, drama, comedy, and news: Groucho Marx, Lauritz Melchior, Fred Allen (with his entire radio company), Sophie Tucker, Paul Muni, Eddie Cantor, Bing Crosby,

George Burns and Gracie Allen, Raymond Gram Swing, the Andrews Sisters, etc. **MUSICAL DIRECTOR:** Paul Whiteman. **DIRECTOR:** Devere Joseph (Dee) Engelbach. **WRITERS:** George Faulkner, Milton Geiger. **THEME:** *The World Outside*.

The most singular thing about *The Radio Hall of Fame* was its strong production link to the trade journal *Variety*. This was seriously questioned even as it was announced. How could a newspaper whose business was reviewing show business enter it? Could such a paper honestly review its own performers? Ben Bodec, a *Variety* reporter for 15 years, quit in protest, but the show went on.

It was a glittering spectacle, with comedy opening and closing its premiere broadcast. Sandwiched between Jimmy Durante and Bob Hope were chanteuse Hildegarde, an excerpt from the Broadway play *Winged Victory*, newsman Quentin Reynolds with thoughts on the fighting fronts, and boogie-woogie pianist Maurice Rocco. In the weeks that followed, listeners heard Howard and Shelton of *It Pays to Be Ignorant*, Helen Hayes in her stage play *Harriet*, Jennifer Jones and Charles Bickford in *The Song of Bernadette* (with score and orchestration by Alfred Newman), and Agnes Moorehead in a condensed version of her celebrated *Suspense* play, *Sorry, Wrong Number*.

The production schedule was hectic, with elaborate cut-ins from Hollywood. Each Monday director Dee Engelbach met with *Variety* editors, the editors chose the talent, and a booking agency lined up the performers. A week of rehearsals and coordination followed before maestro Paul Whiteman and his 31-piece orchestra put the show on the air. In its later days the show was modified—Martha Tilton became a singing regular, and the timeslot was cut—but initially its virtues were tempered by persistent criticism of *Variety*'s role. Nonsense, retorted editor Abel Green. "Jimmy Durante may conceivably louse up the air tomorrow, and we're going to say so." This, of course, was taken with a grain of salt.

THE RADIO READER'S DIGEST, true stories adapted from *Reader's Digest*.

BROADCAST HISTORY: Sept. 13, 1942–Sept. 30, 1945, CBS. 30m, Sundays at 9. Campbell Soups.
Jan. 13, 1946–June 3, 1948, CBS. 30m, Sundays

at 2; Thursdays at 10 beginning the new season, Sept. 12, 1946. Hallmark Cards.
HOSTS: Conrad Nagel, 1942–45; Richard Kollmar, 1946–47; Les Tremayne from ca. 1947. **ORCHESTRA:** Lyn Murray; later Jack Miller. **DIRECTORS:** Robert Nolan for Campbell Soups; Marx Loeb for Hallmark.

Reader's Digest did not sponsor this show: it simply supplied the material, from its current or past issues. Conrad Nagel narrated as well as introduced the plays in its early era; the stories were often a "most unforgettable character" sketch or from some other heartwarming department of the magazine. The drama was soft and always ended on the upbeat. The Hallmark run blended without a break into the sponsor's *Hallmark Playhouse*, but it was on *The Radio Reader's Digest* that the slogan "when you care enough to send the very best" got its first major exposure.

RAFFLES, detective melodrama, based on the character of E. W. Hornung.

BROADCAST HISTORY: 1942–43, CBS West. 30m, Wednesdays at 9:15 Pacific time. **STAR:** Neil Hamilton as A. J. Raffles, reformed burglar, safecracker, and gentleman adventurer. **MUSIC:** Gaylord Carter on organ. **PRODUCER:** Ted Bliss. **WRITERS:** Paul West, John Dunkel.

Raffles, made famous in a turn-of-the-century series of mystery tales, was identified in *Tune In Yesterday* as a 1945 New York show starring Horace Braham and directed by Jock MacGregor. It now appears that this may have been an audition record that never got on the air, as no evidence of its airing has been found. The 1942 series, from the Coast, did run for at least part of a season.

THE RAILROAD HOUR, musical drama; operettas, Broadway plays, etc.

BROADCAST HISTORY: Oct. 4, 1948–Sept. 26, 1949, ABC. 45m through April 25, then 30m, Mondays at 8. Association of American Railroads.
Oct. 3, 1949–June 21, 1954, NBC. 30m, Mondays at 8. American Railroads.
CAST: Gordon MacRae in all male leads, singing and acting. Leading ladies from stage, radio, and opera: Lucille Norman, Dorothy Kirsten, and Dorothy Warenskjold most often. Also: Nadine

Conner, Risë Stevens, Marion Bell, Ginny Simms, Eileen Wilson, Irra Petina, Mimi Benzell, Anna Mary Dickey, Margaret Whiting, Gladys Swarthout, etc. ANNOUNCER: Marvin Miller. MUSICAL DIRECTOR: Carmen Dragon. CHOIR: Norman Luboff. DIRECTORS: Ken Burton, Fran Van Hartesveldt, Murray Bolen. WRITERS: Jean Holloway; later Jerome Lawrence and Robert Lee. THEME: *I've Been Working on the Railroad.*

The Railroad Hour was a lush-sounding series that switched networks to become part of NBC's "Monday night of music"—a remarkable schedule that also included *The Voice of Firestone, The Telephone Hour*, and *The Cities Service Band of America*. But a lingering weakness continued on the dramatic side. The play itself was out of kilter, *Radio Life* suggested. The talent was first-rate: Gordon MacRae was backed on the first broadcast by Dinah Shore and Jane Powell, and Carmen Dragon provided a thrilling musical score. But the spoken lines were watery, too much like a formless sketch with music.

Not that it mattered. *The Railroad Hour* was never about drama. It focused on the melodies of George Gershwin, Victor Herbert, Franz Lehar, Jerome Kern, Rodgers and Hammerstein, and Sigmund Romberg. There was time-honored music from Gilbert and Sullivan, and such famous titles as *Show Boat, The Merry Widow*, and *The Vagabond King*. Original scores were also worked in, there were special appearances (as when Margaret Truman was costarred in a 1952 offering, *Sari*), and each December the old year was reviewed in music and song.

The opening signature by Marvin Miller was always the same: "Ladies and gentlemen, *The Railroad Hour*!" accompanied by whistles and train noises and the hiss of escaping steam. "And here comes the star-studded show train!" with more train noises and the orchestra coming up full with the theme. The stories had nothing to do with trains: the title was derived from the sponsor—"the same railroads that bring you most of the food you eat, the clothes you wear, the fuel you burn, and all the other things you use in your daily life." The commercials were often political, pushing the legislative agenda that the troubled industry favored in its fight to remain competitive with the growing trucking and airline business. Each broadcast ended with MacRae and his leading lady chatting about next

week. Marvin Miller then chanted, "All aboard!" The train effects came up full with music, and *The Railroad Hour* was off for another week.

RAINBOW HOUSE, children's show.

BROADCAST HISTORY: March 8, 1941–Feb. 22, 1947, Mutual, after three years on local New York radio, 45m, Saturdays at 10:15 A.M. until Sept. 1945, then 30m at 9:30 A.M. HOST AND DIRECTOR: Bob Emery. MUSIC: Dolphe Martin.

RAISING JUNIOR, comedy strip show.

BROADCAST HISTORY: 1930–32, Blue Network. 15m, six a week at 6. Wheatena. CAST: Peter Dixon and Aline Berry (Mrs. Dixon) as the Lees. Walter Tetley as Bobby. Also: Raymond Knight. WRITERS: Peter Dixon, Raymond Knight.

Raising Junior, a domestic comedy, has as its chief claim to fame discovery of Walter Tetley as a major radio character actor. According to the legend, collaborator Ray Knight snatched Tetley, then 9, off an elevator and thrust him before the microphone when the child scheduled to play Bobby failed to arrive. Tetley, of course, went on to thousands of radio broadcasts (an estimated 2,300 appearances on 150 separate series by the late 1930s, with the bulk of his work still ahead), specializing in wiseguy kid roles on *The Fred Allen Show, Easy Aces, The Great Gildersleeve*, and *The Phil Harris/Alice Faye Show*.

RAISING YOUR PARENTS, juvenile forum.

BROADCAST HISTORY: 1936–37, Blue Network. 30m, Saturdays at 10:15 A.M. HOST: Milton Cross. CREATOR: Dan Golenpaul. PRODUCERS: Paul Wing and Alice White Benson.

Children with problems, at home or at school, would write in for advice and support. These letters were discussed by a panel of children, who then rendered a verdict. Questions ranged from simple discipline to heartbreaking stories of neglect. One little girl was continually betrayed by her mother, who promised her a bicycle for passing the seventh grade, then the eighth grade. When the child saved up her own money, the mother "borrowed" it and never paid it back.

THE RALEIGH-KOOL SHOW, musical variety.

BROADCAST HISTORY: Nov. 9, 1936–Sept. 20, 1939, NBC; Blue Network through Jan. 1938, then Red. 30m, Mondays at 9:30 until March 1937; Fridays at 10 until Oct. 1937, then at 9:30 through Jan. 1938; Wednesdays at 8:30 as of switch to Red Network Feb. 2, 1938. Raleigh Cigarettes. See: THE JACK PEARL SHOW, 1936–37; and BAND REMOTES, *Tommy Dorsey,* page 72.

The Raleigh-Kool Show began as a revival of the old *Jack Pearl Show,* with Tommy Dorsey, his orchestra, and vocalists Jack Leonard and Edythe Wright backing up the ''Baron Munchhausen'' skits of Pearl and Cliff Hall. When Pearl departed June 25, 1937, the program continued as a showcase for the Dorsey band.

A notable broadcast on tape from ca. 1939 presents an ''amateur swing contest,'' with Dick Powell on cornet, Bing Crosby on drums, Ken Murray on clarinet, Shirley Ross on piano, and Jack Benny on violin. The producers went to the trouble of setting up an applause device, then short-changed the audience by refusing to name a winner. Dick Powell seemed to have the best beat, and Ken Murray got the most applause, but Dorsey mumbled only that the meter had malfunctioned (a likely story), and the $75 pot was given to charity.

RANSOM SHERMAN PRESENTS, comedy-variety.

BROADCAST HISTORY: Feb. 1–Oct. 4, 1939, Blue Network. 30m, Wednesdays at 10.

Sherman was a creative comic whose radio shows were generally limited to brief runs. No copies of this series were available to review. Sherman was later heard on CBS (Jan. 23–June 24, 1942) under his own name and was also chief perpetrator of the shows *Grapevine Rancho, Sunbrite Smile Parade, Hap Hazard, Smile Parade,* and *Club Matinee.*

RATE YOUR MATE, quiz.

BROADCAST HISTORY: July 30, 1950–Feb. 27, 1951, and again July 7–28, 1951, CBS. 30m, various times. **HOST:** Joey Adams.

Adams questioned couples, with mates scored on their ability to predict their partners' knowledge.

REBUTTAL, talk.

BROADCAST HISTORY: Jan. 15–Feb. 26, 1950, Mutual. 15m, Sundays at 9:15. Muntz TV. **MODERATOR:** John W. Vandercook. **PRODUCERS:** John Masterson, John Nelson, John Reddy.

Rebuttal was a forum for people who believed they had been unfairly attacked in the press or on the air. Three or four guests each week were given a few minutes to make their cases. Editors from *Newsweek* selected the rebuttalists, basing their decisions on interest, timeliness, and news appeal. Moderator John W. Vandercook opened each discussion with a review of the dispute. On the opening show, Mrs. Joseph Stilwell answered a magazine attack on her late husband's China policies, and comic Henry Morgan defended radio comedy after a denouncement by Sen. Wayne Morse. The sponsor, all but forgotten now, was fleetingly famous as the home of ''Mad Man Muntz.''

RED RYDER, juvenile western adventure; characters created by Fred Harman.

BROADCAST HISTORY: 1942–51, Blue Network and Mutual, sometimes concurrently, mostly West Coast; a confusing bit of schedule-jumping as described below. Langendorf Bread. **CAST:** Reed Hadley as cowboy hero Red Ryder (1942–44). Also as Red Ryder: Carlton KaDell (ca. 1945); Brooke Temple (1946–51). Tommy Cook (from 1942) as Little Beaver, Red Ryder's Indian ward. Also as Little Beaver: Franklin Bresee (1942–46, as an alternate); Henry Blair (1944–47); Johnny McGovern (1947–50); Sammy Ogg (1950–51). Arthur Q. Bryan as Roland (Rawhide) Rolinson. Horace Murphy as Buckskin Blodgett, Red Ryder's sidekick. Also: Jim Mather with much of the Indian dialect (Little Beaver's ''You betchum, Red Ryder'' an exception). **ANNOUNCERS:** Ben Alexander, Art Gilmore, etc. **PRODUCER:** Brad Brown. **WRITER-DIRECTOR:** Paul Franklin. **WRITER:** Albert Van Antwerp. **SOUND EFFECTS:** Monty Fraser, Bob Turnbull, James Dick. **THEME:** *The Dying Cowboy.*

Red Ryder was billed as ''America's famous fighting cowboy.'' The red-haired, red-shirted hero was first seen in a series of short stories by writer-cartoonist Harman, who adapted it as a comic strip for the *Los Angeles Times* in 1938. This led to national syndication (600 newspapers and a readership estimated at 13 million), a series of movie serials, and finally to radio.

Ryder's air career, though long and successful, was largely confined to the West Coast. First heard on the Blue Network Feb. 3, 1942, it aired three times a week at 7:30 Pacific time. But from May 20 through Sept, 9, 1942, it was also heard in the East, on Mutual. This convoluted series of events began when *The Lone Ranger*, Mutual's prize melodrama for the juvenile horsey set, was wrestled away by the Blue. Stung by the loss, Mutual promptly bought *Red Ryder* (still running on the Blue in the West) for its eastern network, then programmed it in direct competition with *The Lone Ranger*, now on the Blue. The result: *Ryder* gunned down the *Ranger* in early Hooper reports and staked a strong claim to being the new king of radio cowboys. *Ryder* might have become a potent national force had the show not been sold to a regional sponsor, Langendorf Bread, and disappeared from the East after less than four months. Mutual did emerge with a plum—sole possession of *Red Ryder* for its West Coast Don Lee Network, where it ran Tuesdays, Thursdays, and Saturdays at 7:30 for Langendorf for the rest of the decade.

As in the strip, the radio Ryder was a two-fisted tornado who lived with his aunt (the "Duchess"), his sidekick Buckskin, and his ward, Little Beaver, in the western settlement of Painted Valley. For trivia buffs, Ryder rode a horse named Thunder; Little Beaver's steed was named Papoose. The organ theme (*oh, bury me not . . . on the lone prairie . . .*) was distinctive.

THE RED SKELTON SHOW, comedy.

BROADCAST HISTORY: Jan. 7–Dec. 20, 1939, NBC. 30m, Saturdays at 7 until March, then at 8:30; Wednesdays at 8:30 with the new fall season. *Avalon Time*, joined by Skelton in progress and continuing with other performers after his departure. Avalon Cigarettes. **CAST:** Red Skelton, with country singer Red Foley; Skelton's wife, Edna Stillwell Skelton, as heckler; singer Dick Todd (who joined Edna in hurling insults at Skelton); Marlin Hurt as "Madamoiselle Levy" (the *Beulah* voice without the blackface accent); "torrid song-stress" Janette Davis; Bud Vandover as a character

called Hercules (Hercky); "Professor" Tommy Mack; Curt Massey, replacing Red Foley at mid-year. **ANNOUNCER:** Del King. **ORCHESTRA:** Bob Strong.

Oct. 7, 1941–June 6, 1944, NBC. 30m, Tuesdays at 10:30. *The Raleigh Cigarette Program.* Raleigh Cigarettes. **CAST:** Red Skelton in voice variations as Clem Kadiddlehopper, Junior "the mean widdle kid," and other characters. Also: Ozzie and Harriet Nelson; Harriet as Clem's girl-friend, Daisy June, and as Junior's mother; Wonderful Smith, a Skelton antagonist, reviewed as "the Negro comedy find of the year." **AN-NOUNCER:** Truman Bradley. **VOCALIST:** Harriet Hilliard. **ORCHESTRA:** Ozzie Nelson. **PRODUCER-DIRECTOR:** Keith McLeod. **WRITER:** Edna Stillwell.

Dec. 4, 1945–May 20, 1949, NBC. 30m, Tuesdays at 10:30, 1945–48; Fridays at 9:30, 1948–49. *The Raleigh Cigarette Program.* **CAST:** Red Skelton as Clem Kadiddlehopper, Junior, Willie Lump-Lump, Cauliflower McPugg, Deadeye, and other voice characters. GeGe Pearson as Clem's new girlfriend, Sarah Dew. Pearson also as the wives of Skelton's other characters—Mrs. Willie Lump-Lump, Mrs. Bolivar Shagnasty, etc. Lurene Tuttle as Junior's mother; Verna Felton as Junior's grandmother. Also: Wonderful Smith. **AN-NOUNCERS:** Pat McGeehan, Rod O'Con-nor. **VOCALIST:** Anita Ellis. **ORCHESTRA:** David Forrester, David Rose. **PRODUCER-DIRECTOR:** Keith McLeod. **WRITERS:** Edna Stillwell, Jack Douglas, Johnny Murray, Benedict Freedman. **THEME:** *Great Day.*

Oct. 2, 1949–June 25, 1952, CBS. 30m, Sundays at 8:30 for Tide until mid-1951, then Wednesdays at 9 for Norge. Many of the same personnel.

Sept. 16, 1952–May 26, 1953, NBC. 30m, Tuesdays at 8:30. Multiple sponsorship.

Red Skelton, like Edgar Bergen, was among the least likely to succeed in radio. Both practiced visual arts (Bergen was a ventriloquist; Skelton a pantomimist), both made initial appearances on *The Rudy Vallee Show*, and both were ultimately top ten radio attractions on their own programs. It took Skelton slightly longer to catch on.

He was born Richard Bernard Skelton in Vincennes, Ind., July 18, 1913, according to most records, but Skelton himself reportedly claimed

1906 as the date. His father died before his birth, making it necessary for him to work from the age of 10. He began his career in blackface, singing and doing odd jobs for $15 a week. He would later say that he had done everything in show business except opera, giving a reporter the impression that he might even be crazy enough to give that a try. He traveled with medicine shows and worked in vaudeville, stock, and burlesque. He worked on the same circus his father had joined as a clown in the 1890s. He entertained on showboats and on the walkathon circuit. By his 17th birthday, Skelton was a battle-scarred professional.

He was playing the Pantages Theater in Kansas City in 1930 when he met Edna Stillwell. She was an undertaker's daughter, working as an usherette in the theater, and she thought his act was "terrible." The feeling was mutual, *Radio Life* would recall years later: "He thought she was a priggish snip, and the only thing smart about her was her black-and-white uniform." A return engagement found him somewhat improved in her eyes: one of his jokes, she would admit grudgingly, gave her a small laugh. A quantum leap came six months later: Skelton was playing a walkathon date at the El Torreon Ballroom, and Stillwell was the cashier. He was "trying very hard to cheer up half a hundred limp couples staggering around the huge hall," and when he told the "joke about the corn cob, Edna was convulsed." In June 1931, they were married.

Stillwell began playing his stooge in the long string of small-time engagements that followed. Soon she was writing his routines, playing her vision of life into Skelton's comedic strengths. For seven years they toiled in obscurity, living out of trunks, working tent and medicine shows, burlesque, walkathons, and riverboats. His appearance with Rudy Vallee Aug. 12, 1937, was promising: he returned by popular demand two weeks later and again in November, but the lightning didn't strike as it had with Bergen. They were in Canada in 1938 when Stillwell developed the routine that would send Skelton to the top. In a Montreal cafe, she noticed a man dunking his doughnuts. His manner was furtive, as if he feared getting caught at it. She developed this as a routine for Skelton: they used it to immediate effect, for 26 weeks in Montreal. It then turned out there was an American Dunkers Association, which named Skelton its titular president and promptly plastered his likeness on posters for restaurant display. Skelton was doing three shows a day, eating a dozen doughnuts in each. He gained 35 pounds but came to the attention of Hollywood. In 1938, he was signed to do the skit in the Ginger Rogers film *Having Wonderful Time.*

He joined the radio show *Avalon Time* in progress and quickly became its centerpiece. Edna joined him on mike in skits both simple and simply written. The comedy harkened back to vaudeville, the humor of stooges and straight men, of insults and one-liners. Many of the routines were Fred Allen–type "news from coast to coast" gimmicks. A "news item" about fighter Joe Louis would be followed by a related joke. "I used to be a fighter," Skelton would say. "Did I ever tell ya about my first fight? . . . Did I ever tell ya about my last fight? . . . Same fight." And on it went.

Avalon Time was actually a prelude to Skelton's true radio career: his *Raleigh Program* of 1941 was the first accurate measure of his worth on the air. He refined a vaudeville routine he had first used in the early '30s—he would play a child, the most obnoxiously mischievous brat on the air. His "mean widdle kid," Junior, challenged Bergen's Charlie McCarthy and Fanny Brice's Baby Snooks for the title, and the fact that the medium could not light up the act with pictures somehow enhanced it. There would be time for pictures later—as the mute hobo Freddie the Freeloader, Skelton would enlarge TV screens of another decade with brilliant skits of pure pantomimic silence, impossible for radio to achieve—but in 1941 a "mean widdle kid" could be played by a 28-year-old man for a blind audience. Junior's "I dood it again!" was national slang in the spring of 1942. "If I dood it, I gets a whipping," he would muse. Then, after the briefest pause during which he allegedly reflected on the crime and its probable punishment, he'd say, "I dood it," and the vase would break, the window would shatter, the snowball would knock the postman's hat off. And Junior would have another sore bottom.

Skelton's other major character was Clem Kadiddlehopper, the singing cab driver. The early *Raleigh Program* also benefited greatly from the presence of Ozzie and Harriet Nelson, both polished performers in light comedy. Ozzie was particularly clever with musical novelties: his song

I'm Looking for a Guy Who Plays Alto and Bar-
itone, Doubles on a Clarinet, and Wears a Size
37 Suit was the maestro's outrageous lament in
1940. Skelton's chief writer continued to be his
wife, even after they were divorced in 1943
(both would remarry two years later). "Without
her I'd still be making ten dollars a week," he
said at the time of their divorce. She remained
his business manager and an important influence:
she took custody of the massive Skelton gag file,
painstakingly compiled by a large office staff
and said to contain 180,000 jokes. But later Skelton denied her influence, and, as Arthur Marx
relates in his Skelton biography, he grew bitter
and finally denied her existence.

He was drafted in March 1944. This was questioned by some critics, who noted that he had
worked tirelessly to entertain servicemen. Eventually he was shipped overseas as a private, losing 18 months at the top of his radio career. His
Raleigh Program had been an immediate success, reaching a Hooper of 28 points in three
months and peaking at 40 in its second season.
His was among radio's top five shows, frequently challenging Bob Hope and *Fibber*
McGee and Molly for the top spot. It remained
a ratings giant until his last show, June 6, 1944.
In Italy he suffered a nervous breakdown. He
was hospitalized for three months and discharged
in September 1945. He returned to the air as if
he had never left it, on the same network, in the
same timeslot, for the same sponsor. All his old
characters were on hand, as well as some new
ones: Junior, Clem, Deadeye (the "fastest gun in
the West," who could fire without letup at a fly
on the wall, blow down the wall, and leave the
fly untouched), Willie Lump-Lump, Bolivar
Shagnasty, and J. Newton Numbskull. Clem's
girlfriend Daisy June had married and moved
away while Clem was in the service; he welcomed his new girl, Sarah Dew, with the weekly
greeting, "Well, Sarah Dew, how do you do?"
His audience returned within weeks. Skelton was
one of radio's all-time great laugh-makers: in
one study, it was estimated that he got a laugh
every 11 seconds on the air.

He was so supercharged that he couldn't do
an audience warmup—it always left his audience
limp with laughter instead of primed for the main
event. So Skelton reversed the formula and gave
his fans an aftershow. Among his peers the aftershow was considered the hottest comedy act

in town. Tickets were often gobbled up by other
comedians: they were hawked by tour guides,
recommended by columnists, and awaited hopefully by lines of people who had tried to get in
but had not bothered to write for free admission.
Often as many as 300 were turned away.

The audience witnessed two wildly diverse
acts, based on the same ingredients but distinguished by a script and precise timing on the
broadcast and impromptu insanity on the aftershow. After the broadcast, Skelton would perhaps blunder down into the audience, giving his
interpretation of a "late arrival at the movies,"
tiptoeing through the crowd in search of a seat
that was never there. Or perhaps he'd be the
"Irish tenor," a singer trying to perform with a
loose upper plate and a temperamental accompanist on piano. His "Guzzler's Gin" routine
was an aftershow favorite, when Skelton played
a TV announcer who took a nip of his sponsor's
product, got drunker by degrees, and finally fell
flat on his face. He had more than 350 routines,
from the vaudeville juggler to dying movie heroes to bathing a baby, and all changed constantly as he added new material. After the show
he was free of the mike's restrictions. All the
visual material that would follow him into television came into full play: the battered hat and
goofy teeth of Clem Kadiddlehopper; the cigar;
the thumbs in the vest pockets and the rumpled,
tattered coats of punch-drunk fighter Cauliflower
McPugg or perpetual inebriate Willie Lump-
Lump.

He also had vast success in films (more than
25 starring or costarring roles, 1938–65) and
television (an unbroken run on NBC and CBS
from Sept. 30, 1951 until Aug. 29, 1971). Skelton died Sept. 17, 1997.

RED TRAILS, adventure drama.

Broadcast history: Feb. 7–July 6, 1935, Blue
Network. 30m, Thursdays at 8:30 until April, then
Tuesdays at 9. American Tobacco. **Cast:** Victor
McLaglen as Mountie Eric Lewis of the Royal
Northwest Mounted Police. Warren Colston as Sgt.
Tim Clone. Arline Blackburn as Clone's daughter,
Genevieve. Also: Alfred Corn. **Music:** Graham
Harris with a full military band. **Writer:** Stew-
art Sterling.

Red Trails related the adventures of the
Mounted Police ca. 1875–77, during the rebel-

lion to form an independent Republic of the Northwest.

REFRESHMENT CLUB, musical variety.

BROADCAST HISTORY: ca. 1936–37, 30m, transcribed syndication for Coca-Cola. First show Nov. 23, 1936. CAST: Don McNeill and various personnel from *The Breakfast Club*; a lively, charming series filled with Depression-era music. ORCHESTRA: Walter Blaufuss.

REFRESHMENT TIME, musical variety.

BROADCAST HISTORY: Oct. 30, 1935–April 22, 1936, CBS. 30m, Wednesdays at 9:30. Coca-Cola. VOCALIST: Connie Boswell. ORCHESTRA: Ray Noble.

REG'LAR FELLERS, comedy, based on the comic strip by Gene Byrnes.

BROADCAST HISTORY: June 8–Aug. 31, 1941, NBC. 30m, Sundays at 7. Substitute for *The Jack Benny Program*. Jell-O. CAST: Dickie Van Patten and Dickie Monahan as Jimmy and Dinky Dugan. Supporting players: Joyce Van Patten, Patsy O'Shea, Skippy Homeier.

RELIGIOUS PROGRAMMING, broadcasts of religious content, from actual Sunday services to choir music, singers of spirituals, or distinguished soloists.

Religious events were part of radio from its earliest prenetwork days. Men of the cloth were quick to recognize radio's power: as early as 1923, New York's WEAF faced the problem of growing requests by religious and charitable groups for air time (which was often expected to be donated). By the time NBC was formed in 1926, religion was a fact of broadcasting life. This listing is composed of regular series broadcasts and does not include such religiously based dramas as *Family Theater* and *Light of the World* or such political figures as Father Coughlin. These have their own main entries in this volume.

THE AVE MARIA HOUR, never a network show, but by transcription reached 146 stations in 45 states by the late 1930s. It was first heard around 1930, a creation of the Brown Friars of Graymoor, and was aired twice a week from St. Christopher's Inn near Garrison, N.Y. The primary stations were WMCA and WINS, both New York, and WIP, Philadelphia. On Wednesdays at 3:30 the novena services were heard, with organ music and choir; on Sundays at 6:30 came dramatizations of the lives of the saints. Friars performed all roles; Father Patrick McCarthy directed. Still heard on WMCA in the 1970s.

THE BACK HOME HOUR, 1929–31, CBS, 60m, Sundays at 11 A.M. Rousing fire-and-brimstone evangelist Billy Sunday, whose popular attacks on sin were wrapped in colorful language. ("I'll punch it, kick it, butt it, bite it, and when I'm old and fistless and toothless I'll gum it!")

THE BACK TO GOD HOUR, Mutual, 30m, Sundays at 11 A.M., 1948–51; at 9:30 A.M., 1951–56. Christian Reformed Church.

THE BAPTIST HOUR, 1949–50, ABC, 30m, Sundays at 3:30. Southern Baptist Church.

THE CATHEDRAL HOUR, 1929–31, CBS. 60m. Choral music with orchestra and soloists.

THE CATHOLIC HOUR, 1930–1960s, NBC, 30m, Sundays at 6 until 1951, then Sundays at 2. Prominent church figures were heard as speakers and soloists. For its tenth anniversary broadcast, March 3, 1940, Archbishop Francis J. Spellman gave the apostolic benediction of Pope Pius XII, Monsignor Fulton J. Sheen was the speaker, and the soloist was Jessica Dragonette with a passage from Mendelssohn's *Hear My Prayer*. Notable on *The Catholic Hour* were performances of the Paulist Choristers, Father William Joseph Finn, director.

THE CBS CHURCH OF THE AIR, a distinguished series catering to all denominations and faiths, first heard Sept. 13, 1931, and running across three decades. Sterling Fisher supervised and Ruth J. Allen directed through the CBS Adult Education Department: this educational approach ensured that all voices would be heard and that the programs would be as much like actual church services as possible. Two broadcasts were aired each Sunday, making it possible to hear a Methodist, Baptist, or other service in the morning and a program from the Catholic, Mormon, Christian Science, or Dutch Reform Church in the afternoon. These 30m segments were aired at 10 A.M. and 1 P.M., 1931–47, after which it was consolidated into one 60m program at 10 A.M.

CHRISTIAN SCIENCE TALKS, 1949–50, Mutual, 15m, Sundays at 9:45 A.M. Also: 1954–56, Mutual, 15m, *Christian Science Healing*, Sunday afternoons.

ELDER MICHAUX BROADCASTS, Jan. 27, 1934–Jan. 12. 1935, CBS, 30m, Saturdays at 7 later at 10:30 or 11. From Georgia Avenue and U Street "on the banks of the Potomac" in Washington, D.C., came this black church broadcast. The elder was Solomon Lightfoot Michaux, who was described by *Radioland* as having "all the knack of Billy Sunday with picturesque vernacular, slang, and popular allusion." A former fish peddler, Michaux described his congregation as "God's Radio Church, God the Father president, God the Son treasurer." His theme was *Happy Am I*. He was supported by his wife Mary, who sang and also preached.

THE GOSPEL SINGER, the popular radio name for Edward MacHugh. 1933–43, Blue Network, three to five times a week and usually in a 15m slot from 10 to 11 A.M.; also, 1938–42, Red Network, 15m, most often weekdays at 9:45 A.M.; sponsored by Ivory Soap, 1936–38. MacHugh began broadcasting in Boston in 1925; he was credited by *Radio Guide* with making *The Old Rugged Cross* "truly famous."

GREENFIELD CHAPEL CHOIR, 1937–40, CBS, 30m, Wednesdays at 8:30 A.M.; also, 1940–43, 15m, Sundays at 8:45 A.M.; also, 1943–45, Blue Network, 15m, Sundays at 8 for the Ford Motor Company.

HERALD OF TRUTH, 1952 throughout the 1950s; subsequent tenure unknown; ABC, 30m, Sundays at 12:30. Church of Christ.

HOUR OF DECISION, 1950–56, ABC, 30m, Sundays at 2; at 3:30 beginning 1951. Also heard on Mutual, 30m, Sundays at 10, 1954–56. Later heard on NBC, still running in 1960. Billy Graham.

HOUR OF FAITH, 1942–50, Blue Network/ABC, 30m, Sundays at 11:30 A.M., continuing as *Christian in Action*, same timeslot, from 1950.

HYMNS OF ALL CHURCHES, a highly popular quarter-hour in the midst of the network serial schedule; heard for a dozen seasons and on each of the four networks: 1935–36, Mutual, weekdays at 9 A.M.; 1936–37, CBS, weekdays at 10:30 A.M.; 1937–38, CBS, three a week at 1:15; 1938–40,

NBC, three and four a week at 2:45; 1940–41, NBC, twice a week at 2; 1941–42, CBS, three a week at 10 A.M.; 1942–46, NBC, three to five a week at 2:45; 1945–47, ABC, weekdays at 10:30 A.M. After the first sustained season on Mutual, *Hymns* was sponsored by General Mills, which moved with the series across networks and made it the first commercially sponsored religious show. Originated by baritone Joe Emerson, it boasted a choir and an orchestra, directed by *First Nighter* maestro Eric Sagerquist in the late 1930s. William Sumner was the organist.

THE JEWISH HOUR, 1928–30, NBC, 60m, Sundays at 3. Also: *Jewish Program*, 1934–35, Blue Network, 30m, Fridays at 10:30.

THE LUTHERAN HOUR, first heard on CBS Oct. 2, 1930. This powerful radio beacon attained a worldwide audience and is still heard more than 60 years later.

It was launched and propelled through its first two decades by Walter A. Maier, a Lutheran minister who was its voice. Maier began broadcasting in an attic in 1927. At that time, he aired everything from book reviews to sermons to family problems. His 30m CBS run was heard Thursdays at 10, lasted only one season, and left the air in June 1931.

On Oct. 20, 1935, the series resumed on Mutual; heard mostly 30m on Sundays at 1:30, it ran there until 1956. ABC joined Mutual for a 3:30 broadcast, 1949–51. Since 1956, it has been carried on NBC. At its peak it was transcribed in 36 languages, reaching 1,236 stations in 55 countries.

Maier was often said to be "more evangelist than minister." His "flaming choice of words and strict religious principles wrought unswerving tirades against liquor, divorce, birth control, and sin." He held "dynamically to the absoluteness of the Scriptures," said *Radio Life*: "Before he goes on the air he whips off his coat, vest, shirt, tie, and belt, advances to the microphone in his undershirt, and preaches with flailing fists." The *Lutheran Hour* chorus was composed of ministry students and was commended by Fred Waring.

MESSAGE OF ISRAEL, Blue Network/ABC 30m series of long duration, first heard in 1935; still on through the 1950s.

THE MORMON TABERNACLE CHOIR, also known as *The Salt Lake Tabernacle Choir*. This 350-voice singing group (the largest in the world) was first heard on the Blue Network in 1929. It aired Mondays at 6; at 6:15 in 1930–31; and Fridays at 2:45 in 1931–32. In 1932 it moved to CBS, and a 30m Sunday schedule (mostly at 11 or 11:30 A.M., noon, or 12:30) that lasted more than 30 years. Anthony Lund, Spencer Cornwall, Richard P. Condie, and Jerold Ottley directed.

THE NATIONAL RADIO PULPIT, outgrowth of a pre-network series of *Men's Conference* (of the Brooklyn YMCA) broadcasts on WEAF. It began locally on Jan. 7, 1923. The speaker was Dr. S. Parkes Cadman, who brought it to NBC when the network was formed in 1926. It was heard Sundays at 4, 1926–31, in 90m timeslots trimmed to an hour in 1928. It arrived as *The National Radio Pulpit* in 1930, taking a 30m, 10 A.M. Sunday slot in 1933 and keeping it for most of the next three decades. The Rev. Ralph Sockman took over for Cadman in 1936.

NATIONAL VESPERS, began its long run as *The National Church of the Air*. It was first heard on the Blue Network in early 1927, the liberal Baptist minister Harry Emerson Fosdick presiding. Fosdick was a champion of interdenominationalism and a central figure in the Protestant squabbles over literal-vs.-spiritual Christian beliefs in the 1920s. *The National Church of the Air* became *National Vespers* in 1929. It ran under that title on the Blue/ABC, 30m, until 1954: Sundays at 5 (1929–34), at 3:30 (1934–35), at 4 (1935–43), at 2:30 (1943–48), and at 1:30 (1948–54). Retitled *Pilgrimage* in 1954, it continued on through the decade.

THE OLD-FASHIONED REVIVAL HOUR, a culmination of local religious programs conducted by the Rev. Charles E. Fuller and heard on Mutual and ABC, 1930s–1950s.

Fuller, a Baptist minister, was first asked to speak on the air while attending a Bible conference in Indianapolis in 1927. Response was so gratifying that he began thinking of radio as the primary vehicle for his Christian message. In February 1928, he initiated a series of remote broadcasts from Calvary Church in Placentia, Calif., where he was pastor. These were carried on KGER, Long Beach, and ran five years. In May 1933, he formed the Gospel Broadcasting Association to continue his radio ministry. His services were a regular part of KFI and KNX programming. His KNX, Los Angeles, series was notable, expanding to an hour and reaching into 11 states. His early broadcasts were known as *The Gospel Hour* or *The Pilgrim Hour*, a name he would use for a later series apart from *The Old-Fashioned Revival Hour*.

In January 1937 he went on Mutual's western hookup, with 13 stations reaching as far east as Gary, Ind. When this became a coast-to-coast chain in August 1937, Fuller took an enormous gamble and agreed to absorb the additional cost. It leaped to more than $4,000 a week with the first national broadcast, Oct. 3, 1937, but his radio congregation supported him. By 1940 the series was a national institution. Fuller moved to the 4,400-seat Long Beach Municipal Auditorium. The services were transcribed and aired the following Sunday, and the transcriptions were circulated worldwide. In addition to Fuller's sermons, there was a chorus and a male quartet. It was heard on Mutual Sundays at 9 A.M. until 1942; then Fuller moved it into the evening so that it would not interfere with local Sunday church services. In September 1944, Mutual initiated a policy prohibiting religious broadcasts after noon on Sundays, and *The Old-Fashioned Revival Hour* was dropped from the network, to be heard on independent stations, 1944–49.

It returned to a network, ABC, in 1949. After a season at 8 A.M., it moved into a 60m 4 P.M. slot, where it remained for more than a decade.

THE PILGRIM HOUR, the second show from the Rev. Charles E. Fuller and his Gospel Broadcasting Association. Originally heard on local stations in the early 1930s, it came to Mutual in 1942, as a supplementary broadcast to *The Old-Fashioned Revival Hour*, heard Sundays at 2. When Mutual discontinued religious broadcasting after noon on Sundays, Fuller trimmed *The Pilgrim Hour* from 60 to 30m and scheduled it at 12 o'clock. It was heard 1944–47, while the *Revival Hour* was off the network air.

RADIO BIBLE CLASS, 1940–57, Mutual, 30m, Sundays at 10 A.M.; also, 1953–56, ABC, 30m, Sundays at 8 A.M.

RELIGION IN THE NEWS, 1933–50, NBC, 15m, mostly Saturdays at 6:45, occasionally at 6:15 or 7:15. Walter W. Van Kirk, speaker.

REVEREND JOHN E. ZOLLER, 1943–46, Mutual, 30m, Sundays at 11 A.M. The Wesley League.

ST. GEORGE VESPER SERVICE, 1926–27, Blue Network, 90m, Sundays at 4.

SYNAGOGUE SERVICE, 1926–29, NBC, 30m, Wednesdays at 7.

THE VOICE OF PROPHECY, the radio ministry of the Seventh-Day Adventists, first heard on Mutual Jan. 4, 1942. Pastor H. M. S. Richards was the "voice" of this long-running series, which began broadcasting in a renovated shed near South Gate, Calif. Eventually it was offered in more than 40 languages worldwide, with a correspondence course in Bible studies. In 1946, *Voice* moved into a $250,000 building in Glendale, often called "the house that radio built." It was heard 30m, Sundays at 9:30 A.M. until 1949, then at 10:30 A.M. The Mutual run ended in 1954, but the program was later carried worldwide by syndication and on a special network.

WINGS OVER JORDAN, a Negro choir that began its air career at WGAR, Cleveland, in 1938 and was heard on CBS 1939–47, 30m, often at 9:30 A.M., with breaks in continuity. Also, 1948–49, Mutual, 30m, Saturdays at 4.

It began when the Rev. Glenn T. Settle, a Cleveland pastor, offered his church choir to WGAR program director Worth Kramer for a broadcast series. Kramer became involved in the musical arrangements and finally quit his job to help direct the *Wings* aggregation. In addition to its choir, it featured outstanding black leaders from all walks of life as speakers.

YOUNG PEOPLE'S CONFERENCE, 1926–32, NBC, 60m until 1931, then 30m, Sundays at 3. 1932–33, Blue Network, 30m, Sundays at 4:30. Bible talks with the Rev. Dan Poling.

THE REMARKABLE MISS TUTTLE, light drama.

BROADCAST HISTORY: July 5–Aug. 30, 1942, NBC. 30m, Sundays at 7. Substitute for *The Jack Benny Program.* Jell-O. **CAST:** Edna May Oliver as Miss Josephine Tuttle, possessed of a boundless desire to help people. Also: Cy Kendall, Arnold Stang, Lillian Randolph. **ORCHESTRA:** Leith Stevens.

RENFREW OF THE MOUNTED, juvenile adventure.

BROADCAST HISTORY: March 3, 1936–March 5, 1937, CBS. 15m, Tuesdays, Fridays, and Saturdays at 6:45; soon expanded to weeknights. Wonder Bread.

Dec. 24, 1938–Oct. 19, 1940, Blue Network. 30m, Saturdays at 6:30. Sustained.

CAST: House Jameson as Inspector Douglas Renfrew of the Royal Canadian Mounted Police. Supporting players: Joan Baker, Carl Eastman, Joseph Curtin, Robert Dryden, etc. **ANNOUNCERS:** Bert Parks, etc. **ANIMAL SOUNDS** (including the wolf call that opened and closed the show): Brad Barker.

Renfrew, based on the stories by Laurie York Erskine, differed little from the longer-running and better-known *Challenge of the Yukon.* The hero was a no-nonsense "always get our man" character; the background contained sparse, bleak sound effects and no music on the show auditioned by this writer. But the signature was memorable—wind, the lonely cry of a wolf, and the announcer's equally forlorn call: *Rennnnn-frewwwwww! . . . Renfrew of the Mounted!*

RENFRO VALLEY FOLKS, a hayseed show, also known as *The Renfro Valley Barn Dance.*

BROADCAST HISTORY: 1937, WLW, Cincinnati.

1938, Mutual. 30m, Saturdays. Allis Chalmers.

1940–41, NBC. 30m, Mondays at 9:30. Big Ben Clocks.

Sept.–Dec. 1941, Blue Network. 30m, Saturdays at 8:30. Brown and Williamson Tobacco.

1941–42, CBS. 15m, twice a week at 3:30.

1943–49, CBS. Various and intermittent.

1946–47, Mutual. 30m, Saturdays at 9:30 A.M.

1951, CBS. 15m, weekdays. *The Renfro Valley Country Store.* General Foods.

CAST: Whitey Ford, Red Foley, and other country stars at various times.

REPORT TO THE NATION, documentary-drama.

BROADCAST HISTORY: Dec. 7, 1940–Dec. 1, 1945, CBS. Many 30m timeslots, including Saturdays at 6, 1940–41; Tuesdays at 9:30, 1941–42; Sundays at 10:30, 1942–43; Tuesdays at 9:30, 1943–44; Saturdays at 1:30, 1944–45. Electric company co-ops, 1941–44; Continental Cans, 1945. **NARRATOR:** Albert Warner, CBS newsman, 1940–43; Quentin Reynolds, 1943–45.

FIELD MEN: CBS reporters and personalities; Eric Sevareid, Webley Edwards, etc. **PRODUCER-DIRECTOR:** Brewster Morgan; later Paul White, producer, and Earle McGill, director. **WRITERS:** Richard Hippelheuser, editor of *Fortune* magazine, and Joseph Liss of the Library of Congress; later, Bill Slocum and Peg Miller.

Report to the Nation was a mix of news remotes and re-creations, much like *The March of Time* but without the pomp and drum rolls. It was designed to describe "whatever U.S. government activity was uppermost in the news" each week. Since the United States wasn't yet in the war when the series premiered, many of the early shows dealt with domestic issues (unemployment, pending legislation, etc.); later shows took listeners overseas, on trips in flying fortresses and to battlefields in stories of dramatic rescue. There were new war songs, shortwaved reports from overseas, and continued use of dramatized skits with sound effects. It was produced in Washington. Eventually producer Brewster Morgan developed an acting company of 200 amateurs, most of whom worked for the government during the day.

REQUEST PERFORMANCE, big-star variety, by listener request.

BROADCAST HISTORY: Oct. 7, 1945–April 21, 1946, CBS. 30m, Sundays at 9. Campbell Soups. **DIRECTOR:** William N. Robson. **WRITERS:** Jerome Lawrence and Robert E. Lee.

Request Performance was the domestic answer to *Command Performance*, following the same formula. Listeners wrote in (about 1,000 letters a week) asking their favorite Hollywood stars to do offbeat routines on the air. Boris Karloff might be asked for a comedy skit; Veronica Lake would be required to play a scene as Mae West might do it; Phil Harris and Alice Faye were asked to appear together for the first time, which was such a good idea that their comedy series followed shortly. It was a true vaudeville show of the air, perhaps lacking the staying power of *Command Performance* because the war was over and the need was gone. The stars no longer worked gratis, as the sponsor soon learned, budgeting $15,000 a week for talent. Most of the requests were for Frank Sinatra, Bing Crosby, Alan Ladd, or Van Johnson.

RESULTS, INCORPORATED, mystery comedy-drama.

BROADCAST HISTORY: Oct. 7–Dec. 30, 1944, Mutual. 30m, Saturdays at 9. **CAST:** Lloyd Nolan as Johnny Strange, private detective. Claire Trevor as his secretary, "the irrepressible Theresa Travers." **CREATOR:** Lawrence E. Taylor. **PRODUCER-WRITER:** Don Sharpe.

This light series began with detective Johnny Strange placing two newspaper ads: First, *Results, Incorporated, your problem is our problem, will locate your long-lost uncle, work your crossword puzzle, hold your baby*. Then, *Secretary wanted, blonde, beautiful, between 22 and 28 years, unmarried, with the skin you love to touch and a heart you can't*. Terry Travers answered the latter, hired herself, and went to work for "25 percent commission, my hospital bills, and bail money." The first case was a museum mummy that seemed to walk at night.

THE REXALL SUMMER THEATER, a series of summer replacements for shows sponsored by Rexall on the regular network schedules.

BROADCAST HISTORY: July 6–Sept. 7, 1945, CBS. 30m, Fridays at 10 (substituting for *The Jimmy Durante–Garry Moore Show*). *The Ray Bolger Show*, comedy-variety. **CAST:** Bolger, Elvia Allman, Verna Felton, and singer Jeri Sullivan. **ANNOUNCER:** Howard Petrie. **ORCHESTRA:** Roy Bargy. **DIRECTOR:** Phil Cohan.

July 2–Sept. 24, 1947, NBC. 30m, Wednesdays at 10:30 (substituting for *The Jimmy Durante–Garry Moore Show*). *Dan Carson*, light drama. **CAST:** Pat O'Brien as Dan, a small-town drugstore proprietor, a typically wise countertop philosopher who "takes a personal interest in every one of his customers." O'Brien said the character was based on a druggist in his hometown, Milwaukee, where he, O'Brien, worked as a teenager before World War I. Lynn Bari, costar. **ANNOUNCER:** Howard Petrie. **ORCHESTRA:** Roy Bargy. **PRODUCER-DIRECTOR:** Glenhall Taylor. **WRITER:** True Boardman.

May 30–Sept. 26, 1948, NBC. 30m, Sundays at 7:30 (lead-in to *The Phil Harris/Alice Faye Show*, which Rexall premiered in Oct.). *Dan Carson*, a reprise of the 1947 show. **CAST:** Pat O'Brien as Dan. Virginia Bruce as Susan Read, his "nurse and confidante.'' O'Brien believed his role to be the first in which a druggist was the leading character (Mr. Peavey of *The Great Gildersleeve* was strictly in support).

RFD AMERICA, rural quiz.

BROADCAST HISTORY: Oct. 29, 1947–April 22, 1948, Mutual. 30m, Wednesdays at 9:30 until Nov., then Thursdays at 9:30. **QUIZMASTER:** Joe Kelly. **PRODUCER:** Louis G. Cowan.

June 6–Sept. 26, 1948, NBC. 30m, Sundays at 8:30. Substitute for vacationing Fred Allen. Ford Motors. **COUNTRY EDITOR (QUIZMASTER):** Ed Bottcher.

Jan. 8–Sept. 24, 1949, NBC. 30m, Saturdays at 2:30. **COUNTRY EDITOR:** Bob Murphy. **ANNOUNCER:** Hugh Downs.

All the contestants on *RFD America* were farmers from various states. Each show was a battle of wits between four farmers, with the winner crowned ''Master Farmer of the Week.'' The champion returned to defend his title, and repeated as long as he kept winning. Farmers' wives were also allowed to enter. Contestants were screened through local contests in their home states. Typical questions might range from ''Name two songs with farm animals mentioned and sing a few bars'' to ''What are the advantages of hybrid corn?'' Alabama farmer Ed Bottcher won eight consecutive weeks and became the quizmaster when Kelly had to resign due to conflicts with his schedule as *Quiz Kids* inquisitor.

RHAPSODY IN RHYTHM, popular music.

BROADCAST HISTORY: June 16–Sept. 15, 1946, CBS. 30m, Sundays at 10:30. Old Gold Cigarettes. **CAST:** Singer Connie Haines with the Jan Savitt Orchestra.

June 11–Sept. 17, 1947, CBS. 30m, Wednesdays at 9. Old Gold. **CAST:** Singer Peggy Lee with the Savitt orchestra. Buddy Clark and Johnny Johnston, alternating singing hosts. The Jubilaires, vocal group. Robert Maxwell, swing harpist.

RICH MAN'S DARLING, soap opera.

BROADCAST HISTORY: Feb. 17, 1936–March 26, 1937, CBS. 15m, weekdays at 12:45. Outdoor Girl Cosmetics. **CAST:** Karl Swenson and Peggy Allenby as Packy and Peggy O'Farrell. Ed Jerome as Gregory Alden. **PRODUCERS:** Frank and Anne Hummert.

This serial's claim to fame was that, on March 29, 1937, it became the enduring *Our Gal Sunday*.

RICHARD DIAMOND, PRIVATE DETECTIVE, detective drama.

BROADCAST HISTORY: April 24, 1949–Dec. 6, 1950, NBC. Various 30m timeslots, Sundays, then Saturdays, also Wednesdays. Rexall, from April 5, 1950.

Jan. 5, 1951–June 27, 1952, ABC. 30m, Fridays at 8 for Camel Cigarettes until the summer break, June 29, 1951; returned October 5, Fridays at 8 for Rexall.

May 31–Sept. 20, 1953, CBS. 30m, Sundays at 7:30. Substitute for *Amos 'n' Andy* (repeat broadcasts from an earlier season). Rexall.

CAST: Dick Powell as Richard Diamond, private detective. Virginia Gregg as his girlfriend, Helen Asher. Frances Robinson also as Helen. Ed Begley as police lieutenant Walt Levinson. Arthur Q. Bryan as Levinson later in the run. Wilms Herbert as police sergeant Otis. Wilms Herbert also as Francis, Miss Asher's butler. Supporting casts from Hollywood radio: Betty Lou Gerson, Betty Moran, Ted de Corsia, etc. **ORCHESTRA:** David Baskerville, Frank Worth. **PRODUCERS/DIRECTORS:** Don Sharpe, producer, with William P. Rousseau, director; Blake Edwards, writer, graduating to the director's booth; Jaime del Valle later producer-director. Many other directors from week to week. **WRITERS:** Blake Edwards, Harvey Easton, etc. **THEME:** *Leave It to Love*, by Henry Russell, whistled by Dick Powell.

Though a lighthearted, wisecracking detective show, *Richard Diamond* could be heavy on demand. It was the right show at the right time for Dick Powell, babyfaced singer of Hollywood musicals in the early '30s who had struggled for years to change his image. He was cast as ''an eternal juvenile'' by Warner Brothers, playing (in his words) ''the same stupid story'' over and over. In frustration he purchased his contract from Warners and moved to Paramount in the '40s, but the meaty dramatic roles he coveted were slow in coming. He wanted the lead in

Double Indemnity, but Paramount balked and Powell walked. He landed at RKO and the role of his life, playing Philip Marlowe in *Murder, My Sweet* (1945). His new career, with one film, was launched.

In quick succession he made *Cornered* and *Johnny O'Clock* in a similar vein, then moved into the detective business on radio. His portrayal of gumshoe Richard Rogue (*Rogue's Gallery*, 1945–46) and well-baked reporter Hildy Johnson (*The Front Page*, 1948) were right in step for the "new" Powell, though neither was a major series. Assigned to create a character for Powell was Blake Edwards, a young screenwriter who had never worked in radio. Edwards saw Richard Diamond as a former OSS agent, fast on his feet and even quicker with a quip. As the series went on the air, Diamond became an ex-cop whose ties to the police remained sarcastically friendly.

Diamond was a happy-go-lucky detective who answered his telephone with atrocious commercial jingles and was a master of the verbal put-down (especially with police). His relationship with frustrated Lt. Walt Levinson was abrasive but rooted in honest affection, and his special delight was ribbing the stupid desk sergeant, Otis, a stock character inserted strictly for laughs. The opening each week set up the problem and propelled the sarcasm with the cops; the ending usually found Diamond in the Park Avenue penthouse of his girlfriend, the rich redhead Helen Asher. He would sit at Helen's piano and sing a song, usually a standard from Broadway or Hollywood, sometimes a chestnut from the earlier career of the younger Dick Powell. Miss Asher's butler, Francis, always arrived at the most inopportune moment and left stammering in embarrassment.

Richard Diamond was also seen on TV (1957–60), but the role as played by David Janssen bore little resemblance to the Powell original. The most notable gimmick of the TV series was the addition of a secretary, Sam, who was seen only as a pair of gorgeous legs (which belonged to Mary Tyler Moore). The radio show was charming, though peppered with moments of genuine silliness. A solid run is available on tape. Powell, though at ease with the microphone, did tend to fluff. Once when the the answer to the mystery depended upon Diamond

realizing (by the smell of gunpowder) that the murder weapon had been fired inside the room, Powell fluffed it and said "outside." Such was life in live radio. The show was later transcribed.

RICHARD LAWLESS, adventure drama.

BROADCAST HISTORY: June 23–Sept. 22, 1946, CBS. 30m, Sundays at 8. **CAST:** Kevin McCarthy as an adventurer in England in the 1600s.

RICHARD MAXWELL, cheer and fellowship, with hymns.

BROADCAST HISTORY: Ca. 1929, local broadcasts.
   May 28, 1934–Jan. 21, 1935, Blue Network. 15m, Mondays at 2:45.
   April 21, 1936–Oct. 10, 1941, CBS. Various 15m timeslots.
   Sept. 17, 1945–May 17, 1946, Mutual. 15m, weekdays at 12:30. Serutan.

Richard Maxwell was a good Samaritan of the air; he was a hymn-singing tenor whose shows were also heard under the title *A Friend in Deed*. In December 1938, Maxwell began a Good Neighbor program that quickly spread into 18 states. More than 75 of his Good Neighbor Clubs were formed, containing 10,000 members. Maxwell received hundreds of hard-luck stories by mail: the most poignant were used on the air, and "good neighbors" were dispatched by the clubs to help on the local level.

THE RIGHT TO HAPPINESS, soap opera.

BROADCAST HISTORY: Oct. 16, 1939–Jan. 19, 1940, Blue Network. 15m, weekdays at 10:15 A.M. Procter & Gamble.
   Jan. 22, 1940–Dec. 26, 1941, CBS. 15m, weekdays at 1:30, Procter & Gamble.
   Dec. 29, 1941–June 29, 1956, NBC. 15m, weekdays at 11:15 A.M. until 1942, then at 3:45 or 4.
   July 2, 1956–Nov. 25, 1960, CBS. 15m, weekdays at 2.
CAST: Ruth Bailey as Rose Kransky, briefly the protagonist after being transplanted from *The Guiding Light*. Mignon Schreiber, Seymour Young, Bernardine Flynn, Carl Kroenke, Nancy Hurdle, Pat Murphy, Carlton KaDell, Lucille Gilman, Constance Crowder, Reese Taylor, and Art Peterson,

all Chicago players in the leading roles of the early storylines. CAST: *Later long-running roles*: Eloise Kummer as Carolyn Allen, daughter of a magazine editor, whose search for a "God-given right to happiness" would lead her through four husbands, a prison sentence, and hours of anguish at the hands of her rebellious son Skip. Claudia Morgan as Carolyn post-1942, from New York. Selena Royle as Carolyn's mother, Doris Mintern (nee Cameron). Constance Crowder, and Irene Hubbard also as mother Doris. Charles Webster, Hugh Studebaker, and Art Kohl as Fred Mintern. Reese Taylor as Bill Walker, Carolyn's first husband. Frank Behrens, Dick Wells, David Gothard, and Ed Prentiss as Dwight Kramer, the second husband. Gary Merrill and John Larkin as Miles Nelson, the third husband. Julian Noa and Leora Thatcher as Mr. and Mrs. Kramer. Violet Heming and Luise Barclay as Carolyn's best friend, Connie Wakefield, who married Dwight Kramer after his divorce from Carolyn. Ian Martin as Arnold Kirk, unscrupulous lawyer plotting to brand Carolyn an unfit mother. Peter Fernandez and others as Carolyn's son Skip. ANNOUNCERS: Michael Fitzmaurice, Hugh Conover, Ron Rawson. MUSIC: William Meeder on organ. CREATOR-WRITER: Irna Phillips. PRODUCERS: Carl Wester, Paul Martin, Kathleen Lane, Fayette Krum. DIRECTORS: Art Hanna, Frank Papp, Charles Urquhart, Gil Gibbons, etc. WRITER (NEW YORK): John M. Young. THEME: *Song of the Soul*.

The Right to Happiness began as an experiment and survived to become one of the major serials of Irna Phillips. Phillips liked to cross-plot, dropping characters from one of her soaps into another, and *Happiness* began by following troubled Rose Kransky from *The Guiding Light*. But soon it became the story of Carolyn Allen, much-married heroine of Chicago radio.

Husband Bill Walker was a self-centered man "capable of anything." Carolyn killed him with a pistol, then endured months of legal maneuvering and trial. Her union with Dwight Kramer was doomed by the fickle nature of both. Husband Miles Nelson became governor and brought political intrigue into the plot. At last Carolyn settled down with handsome lawyer Lee MacDonald. Her fight for happiness often centered upon the welfare of her son Skip, born while she was incarcerated in the state penitentiary.

Irna Phillips wrote the serial until 1942, when she sold it to Procter & Gamble outright. P&G moved it to New York, with a new lead.

RIN-TIN-TIN, dog adventure drama.

BROADCAST HISTORY: April 5, 1930–June 8, 1933, Blue Network. 15m, Saturdays at 8:15 through March 1931, then Thursdays at 8:15. Heard as *The Wonder Dog* until Sept. 1930, then *RTT*. Ken-L-Ration. Based on the *Rin-Tin-Tin* movie adventures, begun in 1923 with one or two a year produced into the early 1930s. CAST: Don Ameche and Junior McLain, with the original German shepherd wonder dog doing his own sound effects until his death ca. 1931, when his son, Rin-Tin-Tin Jr., took over both radio and film roles.

Oct. 5, 1933–May 20, 1934, CBS. 15m, Sundays at 7:45. Ken-L-Ration.

Jan. 2–Dec. 25, 1955, Mutual. 30m, Sundays at 5. National Biscuit for Shredded Wheat and Milk Bone. CAST: Lee Aaker as Rusty, boy-owner of wonder dog Rin-Tin-Tin. The only survivors of an Indian massacre, they came to live with the cavalry. James Brown as Lt. Rip Masters and Joe Sawyer as Sgt. Biff O'Hara of the 101st Cavalry.

THE RISË STEVENS SHOW, concert music.

BROADCAST HISTORY: July 2–Sept. 3, 1945, NBC. 30m, Mondays at 9:30. STAR: Risë Stevens, Metropolitan Opera mezzo-soprano, backed by a full orchestra with guest conductors. ANNOUNCER: Lou Crosby.

RISING MUSICAL STAR, talent show.

BROADCAST HISTORY: Oct. 17, 1937–April 10, 1938, NBC. 30m, Sundays at 10. Sealtest. COMMENTATOR: Richard Gordon. ORCHESTRA: Alexander Smallens with a symphony aggregation comprised of New York Philharmonic players. CHORUS: Hans Fuerst with 70 voices.

Rising Musical Star bore some resemblance to the *Metropolitan Opera Auditions*. It replaced the sponsor's ill-conceived *Saturday Night Party* and was far more focused. The highlight each week was the appearance of an "unknown professional" who had not yet graced the nation's great concert halls. The show was structured in four-week cycles, with winners of each cycle awarded $100, and $1,000 going to the grand winner. The candidates were selected by a jury of musical talents, including orchestra leader Smallens, Met prima donna Alma Gluck, and conductor Ernest Schelling of the Baltimore Symphony.

ROAD OF LIFE, soap opera.

BROADCAST HISTORY: Often heard on NBC and CBS simultaneously.

Sept. 13, 1937–June 18, 1954, NBC. 15m, weekdays at 11:45 A.M., 1938–39; 11:15 A.M., 1939–40; 11:30 A.M., 1940–41; 10:45 A.M., 1941–42; 11 A.M., 1942–45; 10:30 A.M., 1945–49; 3:15, 1945–54. Procter & Gamble (Chipso, then Duz, later Ivory Soap and Crisco).

1938–42, and again 1945–47, CBS. 15m, weekdays, usually at 1, 1:30, or 1:45. Procter & Gamble.

Dec. 29, 1952–Jan. 2, 1959, CBS, again concurrent with NBC until 1954, when CBS emerged with sole possession. 15m, weekdays at 1. Procter & Gamble until late 1958.

CAST: Matt Crowley as young Jim Brent (1937–39), who rose from common origins in the steel mill district of South Chicago to become one of the most respected surgeons in the Midwest. Ken Griffin as Jim Brent through most of the 1940s. Don MacLaughlin as Jim Brent by ca. 1948. Also as Jim Brent: David Ellis and Howard Teichmann. Peggy Allenby as Helen Gowan, supervisor of nurses at City Hospital and Jim Brent's close confidante. Also as Helen: Betty Lou Gerson, by ca. 1939; Muriel Bremner, ca. 1941; and Janet Logan. Jack Roseleigh and Percy Hemus as Dr. Winslow, the Brent family physician and wise adviser to Jim Brent in his early medical studies. Effie Palmer and Joseph Latham as Jim's mother and father. Olive Parker as Julia. Frank Dane, ca. 1939, and Lawson Zerbe, ca. 1945, as Fred, Jim Brent's brother. Vivian Fridell and Dale Burch as Mary Holt, Jim Brent's childhood sweetheart. Reese Taylor as the unscrupulous Dr. Reginald Parsons. Joan Winters, Ireene Wicker, and Lois Zarley as Sylvia Bertram, one of Dr. Parsons's wives. Harry Elders, Lee Young, and Bill Griffis as Jim's friend, Dr. Bill Evans. Lesley Woods as Carol Evans, who cut a swathe of torment across Jim's life and became his wife. Barbara Luddy, Louise Fitch, and Marion Shockley also as Carol Evans Martin Brent. Donald Kraatz as John (Butch) Brent, Jim's adopted son. Lawson Zerbe, Roland Butterfield,

Bill Lipton, and David Ellis also as Butch. Elizabeth Lawrence as Butch's wife, Francie. Julie Stevens and Helen Lewis as Maggie Lowell, left by Jim at the altar. Barbara Becker as Jocelyn McLeod, Jim's wife at the end. INTERCOM VOICE: Jeanette Dowling, Angel Casey. ANNOUNCERS: Bud Collyer, Ron Rawson, George Bryan. ORGANIST: Charles Paul. CREATOR-WRITER: Irna Phillips. PRODUCERS: Carl Wester (longtime Phillips associate); also, Kay Lane, Fayette Krum, Walt Ehrgott. DIRECTORS: Edwin Wolfe, Howard Keegan, Charles Schenck, Walter Gorman, Stanley Davis, Charles Urquhart, Gil Gibbons. WRITERS: John M. Young, Howard Teichmann, William Morwood. THEME: *Pathetique Symphony*, by Tchaikovsky.

Road of Life was the first major soap opera to be set in the world of doctors and nurses. It departed significantly from the "common hero" so favored by Frank and Anne Hummert, and launched writer Irna Phillips to the top of daytime drama.

The hero, Jim Brent, was first shown as a young intern at City Hospital: he was last heard two full decades later as a quiet, strong, and mature figure, at the top of his professional powers. He had specialized in neuropsychiatry, and had thus become secret confessor to a cavalcade of characters with emotional problems mild and bizarre. Often his battles were fought outside the hospital, though he had plenty of woes on the medical front as well.

In the early days he had a fear of marriage. His union with childhood sweetheart Mary Holt was postponed by one crisis after another. In 1938, Jim was accidentally shot by his brash and irresponsible brother, Fred—the hand wound threatened Jim's surgical career and cast doubt on his future (no soap opera hero could marry with his future in doubt). Mary's death in some ways simplified things: now Jim could develop as the hospital's rising star; he could be sympathetic and warm to women without encouraging romance. This made him intensely desirable to characters ranging from nurses to vixens.

In its first few years, the show opened to the filtered voice of a nurse: *Dr Brent . . . call surgery . . . Dr. Brent . . . call surgery*. Brent's early nemesis was Dr. Reginald Parsons, to whom he was assigned as an intern. Brent was concerned when his friend, nurse Helen Gowan, began a relationship with Parsons. Helen and Parsons married; then Parsons confirmed Brent's suspicions by putting their child out for adoption and refusing to tell Helen where the child had gone.

Brent was also a tower of strength to Carol Evans Martin, who was young and pretty and devoted. Carol was the sister of Bill Evans, a young doctor who was Brent's closest friend. She lived in the nearby community of Fair Oaks. When Brent adopted an orphan (who became John Brent, known to all as Butch), Carol's concern for the youth drew her close to them both. This part of the storyline was played out for a decade: the inevitable marriage was not happy, for Carol's head was turned by a career. Often she left her husband and their little daughter Janie for weeks, to pursue her advancement with the White Orchid Cosmetics Company. The marriage was a series of quarrels, coming to a climax when Carol's plane crashed and she was reported killed. This left Jim free to marry the woman he had come to love in Carol's absence—the sweet and lovely Maggie Lowell. But on the day of their wedding, Carol returned: Brent turned away from his true love and prepared to "do the right thing" by Carol. What none of them knew was that this was not Carol but an impostor. In reality she was Beth Lambert, a down-and-out actress hired by the sinister Ed Cochran to spy on Jim, who with son Butch was then conducting a series of secret government experiments. Beth had accomplished the hoax with "thorough training and slight facial surgery," though in his heart Jim knew there was "something different" about her. Inevitably, Beth realized what a fine man she was living with, "examined her conscience, searched her heart," and fell in love with Jim.

Most of the action took place in the town of Merrimac. Young Butch Brent studied medicine and became a pediatrician in the same Merrimac hospital where his father served. During the war, Butch met a girl named Francie in San Francisco; they were married at the war's end. Francie, a poor girl from across the tracks, became one of the show's most tempestuous and sympathetic characters. In later years, the problems of Francie and Butch took center stage, while Jim Brent became a kind of romantic elder statesman. Old Brent eventually found happiness

with another wife, Jocelyn McLeod. And so it ended.

Phillips took her title from a piece of personal philosophy—that the doctor's road is the road of life. Although NBC was considered the home network during the best years, the CBS run often drew better ratings. In its peak year, 1940–41, *Road of Life* drew a 9.2 on CBS and 7.3 on NBC; either number would have placed it in soapdom's top 12.

THE ROAD TO DANGER, adventure drama, based on a story by James Street.

BROADCAST HISTORY: Nov. 6, 1942–March 4, 1944, NBC. 30m, Fridays at 11:30 until Nov. 26, 1943, then Saturdays at 10 A.M.
CAST: Curley Bradley and Clarence Hartzell as Stumpy and Cottonseed, behind-the-lines American truck drivers, who transported anything from munitions to prisoners of war "on the unmarked highways of the world." DIRECTOR: Jack Simpson. MOST FORGETTABLE CATCHPHRASE: *Stumpy, what're we waitin' for?*
Not a durn thing, Cottonseed—let's go!

THE ROBERT MERRILL SHOW, concert music.

BROADCAST HISTORY: Dec. 2, 1945–March 24, 1946, NBC. 30m, Sundays at 12:30. RCA. STAR: Baritone Robert Merrill at the beginning of his career (he won a *Metropolitan Opera Auditions* competition and went on to a long career at the Met). ORCHESTRA: Leopold Spitalny, conductor.

THE ROBERT Q. LEWIS SHOW, comedy-variety and talk.

BROADCAST HISTORY: 1944–45, NBC; 1947–59, CBS. Many briefly held timeslots, frequently changed as partially described below.

The Robert Q. Lewis Show was by any other name the same: a sporadic comedy effort packaged in numerous formats that never really caught on. Lewis was a bright young spectacled comic who was hired to fill an early-morning NBC comedy slot. He was fired the following year for making jokes about network vice presidents (NBC had no sense of humor about this: see THE FRED ALLEN SHOW). He first turned up on NBC prime time April 7, 1945, a Saturday-at-7:30 series that ran exactly three months. Again he filled the NBC morning air, a weekday 8 o'clock slot with Jack Arthur (Aug. 6–Dec. 29, 1945). When Lewis resurfaced after his NBC stints, it was as a disc jockey on WHN. There, he was discovered by an executive with CBS.

To CBS, Lewis looked like the answer to a prayer. The network was light on comedy (it would be another two years before William S. Paley would find the true answer, and steal away NBC's prime comedy lineup in the infamous "talent raids" of 1949), and Lewis was primed for bigger things that never quite happened. His first CBS venture was called *The Little Show* (May 3–June 7, 1947, Saturdays at 7:30), a quarter-hour in which Lewis (who added the *Q* to his name as a distinguishing trademark) rambled on about movies, radio, and whatever else came to mind. He was compared, not always favorably, to Henry Morgan, who did much the same on ABC. CBS was impatient, reorganizing the show to give it more hype. Goodman Ace, the network's high-priced "doctor of scripts" assigned to *The Little Show*, was ruffled. "I give them a good, tight 15-minute comedy show and what do they do?" he asked rhetorically. "Expand it to half an hour and throw in an orchestra and an audience. Who the hell said a comedy show had to be half an hour, Marconi? Ida Cantor?" Lewis moved to Fridays at 8:30 (June 6–July 25, 1947) and subsequently dotted the CBS schedule in willy-nilly fashion.

He was an evening fixture in 1947–48, though his runs were short and irregular. He was heard Sundays at 5 in the fall of 1948, and again weekdays in the first half of 1949. He substituted for Arthur Godfrey that summer, registered well with Godfrey's corn-fed audience, then moved again into prime-time variety. The new series was *The Show Goes On* (Jan. 20–July 4, 1950, 60m, Fridays at 8). CBS continued giving him the big push, concurrently putting him in Bing Crosby's Chesterfield slot for the summer (May 31–Oct. 4, 1950, Wednesdays at 9:30) and billing him as *The ABCs of Music*. He retreated to platter-spinning: a disc-jock series called *Waxworks* (July 2, 1951–May 2, 1953, various times). He was heard Sundays at 10 in the summer of 1953. His final major radio series was an hour-long show, Saturdays at 11 A.M. (1954–59). He was heard concurrently in a weekday series,

1956–58. Perhaps he wasn't the savior of CBS comedy. But it wasn't for lack of effort, either by Lewis or the network.

THE ROBERT SHAW CHORALE, musical harmony.

BROADCAST HISTORY: June 6–Sept. 26, 1948, NBC. 30m, Sundays at 8. Substitute for vacationing Edgar Bergen.
March 19–April 9, 1950, ABC. 30m, Sundays at 7.

Using a mixed chorus of 30 voices, Shaw was praised by *Radio Life* as having "one of the most unusual shows on the air." He had worked with large singing groups since 1938, when he formed the glee club for Fred Waring's radio show, and by 1948 he had carved out "an almost exclusive domination in the sphere of choral singing."

ROBINSON CRUSOE JR., juvenile adventure serial.

BROADCAST HISTORY: Oct. 2, 1934–Feb. 2, 1935, CBS. 15m, Tuesdays, Thursdays, Fridays, and Saturdays at 5:45. **CAST:** Lester Jay as Robinson Brown Jr., one of a group of shipwrecked children. Cal Tinney as Binnacle Barnes the sailor man. Also: Billy and Bobby Mauch, Toni Gilman, Michael O'Day.

ROCKING HORSE RHYTHMS, song and talk for children by a child performer.

BROADCAST HISTORY: April 4, 1943–Dec. 15, 1945, Mutual. 15m, initially a brief run Sundays at 10:45; then, beginning June 3, 1944, 30m, Saturdays at 11:30 A.M., titled *Hookey Hall*.

Bobby Hookey of *Rocking Horse Rhythms* was said by *Newsweek* to be "the youngest star ever to have his own weekly network program." Bobby was 5, able to remember and sing most of the songs he had heard from the beginning of his life. He won an amateur show at age 2, then played on *The Horn and Hardart Children's Hour* for three seasons before Mutual gave him a national hookup. He aired live from New York ("he should be in bed," *Newsweek* scolded, taking note of his late schedule) and was sponsored in the West by Pharmaco, makers of Chooz, the chewing gum antacid. He sang while riding a rocking horse and had a repertoire of 150 songs.

ROCKY FORTUNE, adventure drama.

BROADCAST HISTORY: Oct. 6, 1953–March 30, 1954, NBC. 30m, Tuesdays at 9:30. **STAR:** Frank Sinatra as Rocky Fortune, "footloose and fancy-free young man" drifting from one hazardous job to another. **DIRECTORS:** Fred Weihe, Andrew C. Love. **WRITERS:** George Lefferts, Ernest Kinoy.

Rocky Fortune came at a low ebb for singer-actor Frank Sinatra: the bobby-soxer boom was gone forever, and the impact of his career-saving performance in *From Here to Eternity* hadn't yet been felt. As Rocky Fortune, Sinatra found adventure by chance and design. He worked in a museum and found a body in the sarcophagus. He drove a truck and hauled nitro over a bumpy road. It was an undistinguished, low-budget affair. Even Sinatra sounded bored with it.

ROCKY JORDAN, adventure-drama; resurrection of the 1945–47 CBS West serial *A Man Named Jordan*.

BROADCAST HISTORY: Oct. 31, 1948–Sept. 10, 1950, CBS, West Coast network. 30m, Sunday evenings. Del Monte Foods. **CAST:** Jack Moyles as Rocky Jordan, American owner of the Cafe Tambourine in Cairo. Jay Novello as Capt. Sam Sabaaya of the Cairo police. Supporting players from Hollywood's Radio Row. **ANNOUNCER:** Larry Thor. **MUSIC:** Richard Aurandt. **PRODUCER-DIRECTOR:** Cliff Howell. **WRITERS:** Larry Roman and Gomer Cool.

June 27–Aug. 22, 1951, CBS, full network. 30m, Wednesdays at 8. Substitute for *Mr. Chameleon*. **STAR:** George Raft as Rocky Jordan. **PRODUCER-DIRECTOR:** Cliff Howell. **MUSIC:** Richard Aurandt.

Rocky Jordan was first known to West Coast listeners as the hard-bitten restaurateur in Istanbul of *A Man Named Jordan*, one of the unsung high spots of radio continuations in 1945. *Rocky Jordan* was virtually a copy of the original: the major change was that Jordan's Cafe Tambourine was uprooted from Istanbul and plopped down in Cairo—"gateway to the ancient East, where modern adventure and intrigue unfold against the backdrop of antiquity." Jordan was a rugged hero who each week was confronted by a crime, a mystery, a beautiful woman, or a combination of the three. It was a detective show with a difference: the Oriental background was played to the hilt, giving it a sound like no other. Writers Larry Roman and Gomer Cool strove for authenticity and flavor: Rocky's Cafe Tambourine was given no street or number, but the surrounding Cairo streets were real. Most of the information came from the Army's *Pocket Guide to Egypt*, distributed to armed forces personnel about to be sent there. Roman and Cool were also aided at one point by an Egyptian writer, Anderoux Bittar, who wrote stories about Hollywood because, to him, the settings of his native land were too common.

Ideas came from newspapers. When an Egyptian dug up a relic on his property and decided to sell it on the black market, he got caught: this newspaper squib became a *Rocky Jordan* tale about black marketeers operating out of Cairo. Jordan usually got involved by happenstance. This brought him into contact with the Cairo police, in the form of Capt. Sam Sabaaya, who was often on hand to shackle the criminals at the end. The show was exceptionally scored with original Oriental-sounding music by Richard Aurandt, and Larry Thor's announcing likewise contributed to the show's grit.

The change of lead, from Jack Moyles to George Raft in 1951, did little for the character. Raft brought a glamour name, but on radio Moyles was easily his equal.

ROGER KILGORE, PUBLIC DEFENDER, crime drama.

BROADCAST HISTORY: April 27–Oct. 12, 1948, Mutual. 30m, Tuesdays at 7. **CAST:** Santos Ortega as Roger Kilgore. Raymond Edward Johnson also as Kilgore. Staats Cotsworth as Kilgore's stubborn rival, D. A. Sam Howe. New York regulars in support: Donald Buka, Bryna Raeburn, Charita Bauer, Lawson Zerbe, Bill Griffis, Bernard Grant, Robert Dryden, Bill Lipton, etc. **DIRECTOR:** Jock MacGregor. **WRITER:** Stedman Coles (scripts based on actual cases).

Roger Kilgore had the same pitch as *Mr. District Attorney*—that "justice, equal justice, is the sacred right of all people in a democracy," and that "life, liberty and the pursuit of happiness" are precious to all. The two obvious differences: Kilgore sat at the defendant's table, and *Mr. Dis-*

trict Attorney was a major series playing almost 15 years.

ROGERS OF THE GAZETTE, light drama.

BROADCAST HISTORY: July 8, 1953–Jan. 20, 1954, CBS. 30m, Wednesdays at 9:30. **CAST:** Will Rogers Jr. as Will Rogers, editor of a weekly newspaper in a small town named Illyria. Georgia Ellis as Maggie Button, his assistant. Parley Baer as Doc Clemmens, Will's friend, who often narrated the stories. Support from Hollywood regulars: Virginia Gregg, Harry Bartell, John Dehner, Mary McGovern, Vivi Janiss, Jeanette Nolan, Lawrence Dobkin, Vic Perrin, etc. **ANNOUNCER:** Roy Rowan; occasionally Bob LeMond. **MUSIC:** Rene Garriguenc, composer; Wilbur Hatch, conductor. **PRODUCER:** Norman Macdonnell. **WRITERS:** Kathleen Hite, Les Crutchfield, E. Jack Neuman, Walter Newman, etc.

Rogers of the Gazette came to radio following *The Story of Will Rogers*, a 1952 movie eulogizing America's favorite humorist and folk hero. Will Rogers Jr. had played his father on film, and now continued the legacy on the air. Although there was no serious attempt to tie the series to *the* Will Rogers, Rogers Jr. played a country role pumped full of homespun wisdom.

His neighbors were his friends; he knew everybody, and everybody knew him. It was billed as a "heartwarming story of a country newspaper and its friendly editor." Rogers was introduced by assistant Maggie Button in a prologue without fanfare. He then delivered a bit of rustic wisdom in this vein: "A feller once said that you oughta keep one eye on your children and the other on the politicians. I guess that's right, but if only one eye is workin' and you gotta make a choice, just figure that the children will probably do pretty good by themselves." The story was similarly rustic—Will helped people who had gone astray—and always ended on the upbeat. The atmosphere of the small town, with its good people and its gossip and its founders' days, was well realized. The music was striking, with a fine trumpet effect.

ROGUE'S GALLERY, detective drama.

BROADCAST HISTORY: June 24–Sept. 16, 1945, NBC. 30m, Sundays at 7:30, *Bandwagon Mysteries*. Summer substitute for *The Fitch Bandwagon*.

Sept. 27, 1945–June 20, 1946, Mutual. 30m, Thursdays at 8:30. **CAST:** Dick Powell as Richard Rogue, private detective, a continuation of the role he had also played on NBC. Peter Leeds as Eugor, Rogue's alter ego. Support from Hollywood regulars: Lou Merrill, Gloria Blondell, Gerald Mohr, Tony Barrett, Ted von Eltz, Lurene Tuttle, etc. **ANNOUNCER:** Jim Doyle. **ORCHESTRA:** Leith Stevens. **DIRECTOR:** Dee Engelbach. **WRITER:** Ray Buffum.

June 23–Sept. 22, 1946, NBC. 30m, Sundays at 7:30. *Bandwagon Mysteries*. Fitch **CAST AND CREW** mostly the same.

June 8–Sept. 28, 1947, NBC, 30m, Sundays at 7:30. *Bandwagon Mysteries*. Fitch. **CAST:** Barry Sullivan as a very different Rogue. **PRODUCER:** Charles Vanda. **WRITER:** Ray Buffum.

Nov. 29, 1950–Nov. 21, 1951, ABC. 30m, Wednesdays at 9. **CAST:** Chester Morris as Rogue; Paul Stewart also as Rogue.

In his best-known incarnation, Richard Rogue trailed lovely blondes and protected witnesses in the new tough-guy persona of Dick Powell. This was the transition series for Powell in his quest to be recognized as an actor rather than a singer. It had some of the same cute elements that would make *Richard Diamond* a high spot four years later.

The gimmick on *Rogue's Gallery* was the presence of an alter ego, "Eugor," ("Rogue" spelled backward), who arrived in the middle of the story to goad Rogue on to his final deduction. Eugor was merely a state of mind, achieved when Rogue was knocked unconscious (or given knockout drops). In his trip to "Cloud Number Eight," Eugor would appear, cackling like the host of *The Hermit's Cave* but imparting some bit of business that the hero was in danger of overlooking. Then Rogue would come "back to planet earth," awakening with a vague idea of what to do next.

ROMANCE, dramatic anthology; romance and high adventure.

BROADCAST HISTORY: April 19, 1943–Jan. 5, 1957, CBS, a 30m schedule-filler, seldom heard for more than a few weeks or months at a time. The complicated broadcast log by Ray Stanich reveals at least 20 changes of time or day, with long breaks in continuity. Thus the premiere series in 1943 resembled the final one in 1956 only by the general topic of its stories. A fine series, nothing like its title would indicate: under directors Macdonnell, MacKaye, and especially Ellis, *Romance* just bloomed, with adventure, slices of life, and touching little dramas the order of the day.

April 19, 1943–June 20, 1944. A somber affair with violin overture and HOST Frank Gallop as "your guide through the pages of all the great stories of all time—tender love stories of today, the memorable love stories of the past." Gallop, a sober-voiced announcer at best, was an undeniable talent with comedy; he gave this an almost teary presence. CAST: Alice Frost, Santos Ortega, Peter Capell, Betty Winkler, Frank Lovejoy, etc. ORCHESTRA: Charles Paul. DIRECTOR: Marx Loeb. WRITER-ADAPTER: Jean Holloway, with scripts ranging from classics and historical whimsy to original creations.

July 4, 1944–Aug. 27, 1946, Tuesdays at 8:30. *Theater of Romance*. Colgate Tooth Powder and Halo Shampoo. The only brush for this series with the Hollywood star system. HOST: Frank Graham, only slightly less morose than Gallop. CAST: Humphrey Bogart, Van Johnson, Ronald Colman, Henry Fonda, Shirley Temple, Errol Flynn, and other major film stars in famous screen stories. PRODUCER: Charles Vanda. WRITER: Jean Holloway.

Oct. 2, 1946–Feb. 5, 1949, many short runs, sometimes Mondays, often Wednesdays, occasionally Fridays or Saturdays; many breaks in continuity, but the same theme music linked all these brief runs. DIRECTOR: Albert Ward. WRITER: Charles Monroe.

June 20–Aug. 8, 1950, Tuesdays at 9 for Wrigley's Gum, substituting for *Life with Luigi*: a significant run, an early collaboration of PRODUCER-DIRECTOR Norman Macdonnell and WRITER-EDITOR John Meston, later of *Gunsmoke*. CAST: William Conrad, Georgia Ellis, John Dehner, Jeanne Bates, Peggy Webber, Lawrence Dobkin, Jack Edwards, etc. ANNOUNCER: Bob Stephenson. ORCHESTRA: Alexander Courage.

Jan. 6, 1951–Dec. 26, 1953, more hit-or-miss scheduling (in Jan. 1951 there were only two broadcasts, with nothing for months on either end); June 6–Sept. 1, 1952, Mondays as part of the *Lux Radio Theater* vacation schedule (Macdonnell and Meston again as director and writer, with Conrad, Ellis, Dobkin and other names who also appeared on *Gunsmoke*—Harry Bartell, Irene Tedrow, Ben Wright, Ted von Eltz, Joan Banks, Betty Harford,

Alec Harford, Edgar Barrier, Jay Novello and Jack Kruschen—carrying the acting chores. ANNOUNCER: Roy Rowan.

May 22, 1954–Jan. 5, 1957, Saturdays at 12:05; the most sustained run and the best stories, with more than 100 preserved on tape. CAST: The same voices as in years just past, with Lou Krugman, Bob Bailey, Herb Butterfield, Howard McNear, Sammie Hill, Hans Conried, Richard Beals, Charles Seel, Clayton Post, Michael Ann Barrett, Eleanore Tanin, Paula Winslowe, Sam Edwards, Sarah Churchill, Mary Jane Croft, Richard Crenna, Parley Baer, etc. ANNOUNCERS: Roy Rowan, Hugh Douglas; later Dan Cubberly. MUSIC: Jerry Goldsmith. DIRECTORS: Fred MacKaye, Antony Ellis. WRITERS: Les Crutchfield, Kathleen Hite, E. Jack Neuman, etc.

THE ROMANCE OF HELEN TRENT, soap opera.

BROADCAST HISTORY: Heard regionally from July 24, 1933.

Oct. 30, 1933–June 24, 1960, CBS. 15m continuation, weekdays at 2:15 until 1936, then at 12:30. American Home Products, most of 1930s until ca. 1946; Whitehall Drugs, 1946–53; various sponsors thereafter. CAST: Virginia Clark as glamorous dress designer Helen Trent, 1933–44. Julie Stevens as Helen Trent, 1944–60. On a few occasions, fill-ins were used in the leading role. David Gothard as Gil Whitney, Helen's longtime love. Marvin Miller and William Green also as Gil Whitney. David Gothard also as Philip King, Helen's early suitor. Bess McCammon through most of the run as loyal, helpful Agatha Anthony, the aging dowager who was Helen Trent's best friend. Marie Nelson and Katherine Emmet also as Agatha Anthony. Mary Jane Higby as evil Cynthia Swanson. Reese Taylor as Drew Sinclair, Hollywood mogul. Janet Logan as his unscrupulous wife, Sandra Sinclair. Kurt Kupfer as kindly Joseph Steinbloch of Consolidated Films. Bill Bouchey as Gordon Decker, the Consolidated set designer. Pat Murphy and Don MacLaughlin, respectively, as Trent suitors Reginald Travers and Dwight Swanson. Herbert Nelson as George Lawlor, a young actor madly in love with Helen. Virginia (Ginger) Jones as Alice Carroll, who stole Philip King away and later became Helen's friend. Spencer Bentley as Douglas Stanwood, brilliant film director. Marjorie Hannan as Gloria Grant,

Stanwood's sometimes neurotic wife. Bartlett Robinson as shy and deceptive Curtis Bancroft. Kenneth Daigneau as Jeff Brady, Bancroft's partner and Helen's boss at International Artists. Helene Dumas as Lydia, Brady's wife. Lauren Gilbert as Norman Hastings, Helen's shipboard romance. Ed Latimer as Bugsy O'Toole, Gil Whitney's house servant. Les Tremayne, Ed Prentiss, John Hodiak, Jay Barney, Karl Weber, Alan Hewitt, Grant Richards, Olan Soulé, and Carlton KaDell as as various suitors, sane and otherwise, of Helen Trent. Leon Janney as John Cole, who finally won her. **AN-NOUNCERS:** Don Hancock, Pierre Andre (Chicago); Fielden Farrington (New York), as of 1944. **PRODUCERS:** Frank and Anne Hummert. **DI-RECTOR-PRODUCER:** Stanley Davis, who also hummed the opening and closing signatures, accompanying himself on guitar and banjo. **DIREC-TORS:** Les Mitchel, Ernest Ricca, Richard Leonard, and Blair Walliser, who worked the show through its Chicago years—most of a decade. **WRITERS:** Margo Brooks, Ruth Borden, Marie Banner, Ronald Dawson, Michael Alexander, etc. **THEME:** *Juanita.*

Helen Trent was a daytime radio institution. Its heroine was "queen of the soaps," a Cleopatra of the air who reigned through 27 years and 7,222 chapters of unparalleled melodrama. Helen Trent never aged: she never laughed or gave in to an impure thought. She was, as *Time* put it, the "idol of the romantically-minded U.S. housewife of a certain age," and her power to draw four to eight million to their sets every day was almost magnetic. *Time* took the tally in 1956, when her days seemed short: by then she had logged 5,900 chapters, "88,508 roseate minutes," and in fact she still had four spry years of life left.

Her aggregate adventures had hardened into radio folklore, incredible even by the standards of daytime serials. No fewer than 28 serious suitors pursued her, to no avail. Something inevitably happened—she jilted them, they jilted her; one died of a heart attack just before the wedding; some came in deceit and were later unmasked; some were murdered; one plowed his airplane into a cliff. Then there were the madmen, those "if I can't have her nobody will" types who tried to have their evil ways with her. She was mesmerized by an unscrupulous hypnotist, charmed by a homicidal physician; she

was shot, poisoned, jailed for murder, and pushed toward her death at the edge of a cliff. She remained a marvel of exquisite womanhood to all who saw her: as *Life* noted as she passed into radio history, she always enjoyed perfect health of mind and body "except when recovering from murder attempts."

Who could be responsible for such unbridled carnage but Frank and Anne Hummert? *Trent* was one of the Hummerts' earliest and biggest success stories. It gathered steady momentum, peaking in double digits (11 points on the Nielsen charts as late as January 1950). Its opening is still remembered as *the* soap opera classic—a plunking banjo, a soft male voice a-humming, and the signature from announcer Fielden Farrington:

Time now for "The Romance of Helen Trent" . . .

The melody is *Juanita*. Millions who hear it will never know its name.

"The Romance of Helen Trent" . . . *the real-life drama of Helen Trent, who—when life mocks her, breaks her hopes, dashes her against the rocks of despair—fights back bravely, successfully, to prove what so many women long to prove in their own lives . . . that because a woman is 35, and more, romance in life need not be over . . . that the romance of youth can extend into middle life and even beyond . . .*

The humming fades, the banjo plunks its final note. The kitchens of America are electric with expectation and suspense.

Like *Ma Perkins, Just Plain Bill*, and other Hummert contemporaries, *Trent* worked the endless theme of good and evil. Its characters were black and white, and its listeners understood it at once. Certain characteristics were solid indicators of friends or foes. Helen, being Good, never drank, smoked, or uttered even the softest of oaths. Her Bad opposites did all these things and more. The evil gossip columnist, Daisy Parker, conclusively demonstrated her "low moral stature," said *Time*, by drinking a "martini on the rocks," and then drove the point home by adding, "and no olive." Helen was put on a pedestal and kept there. "Once she walked into the stateroom of a man she had just met on shipboard; faithful listeners were scandalized." Housewives who went through three packs a day recognized the newest "evil adventuress" immediately by the cigarette in her hand.

Helen's past was shrouded in mystery. At some point it was hinted that her husband had been lost at sea, but it didn't matter—he was never a factor. A capsule biography in a 1938 *Radio Guide* explained it another way. Helen had been married for 13 years to Martin Trent and was divorced when he fell in love with another woman. At a low ebb in her life, she vowed to make something of herself. She became a designer of fine dresses, settled near Hollywood, and found work in some of the major film studios. By 1938 she was the most famous in her field. She shared a home—a ranch in the San Fernando Valley and later a luxury apartment on Palm Avenue in Hollywood—with her best friend, aging Agatha Anthony. Drew Sinclair, Hollywood's "youngest and brightest mogul," engaged Helen to design the costumes for the make-or-break new Sentinel Pictures film, *Fashions of 1939*. Sinclair's wife, Sandra, was jealous and petty; she neglected their son, Peter, and remained with Sinclair only because of the money and social position. Joseph Steinbloch was the head of Consolidated Films, where Helen had got her start; he was a good friend who wanted to lure her back into the fold. Gordon Decker was a set designer at Consolidated who was madly in love with Helen and on one occasion proved her innocent of treachery. George Lawlor, the young British actor, was also in love with Helen, though she considered him "too young to know his own mind." Alice Carroll was an old enemy, now her friend. Douglas Stanwood was a brilliant Consolidated director, "the complete sophisticate." Gloria Grant was the former movie extra who became a star with Helen's help, later tried to commit suicide, and still later married Douglas Stanwood. These were characters of the late 1930s.

This was the tip of the iceberg. One of the earliest to love Helen was Dr. Reginald Travers, who begged for her hand two or three times a week, was rebuffed, and disappeared forever into upper-class Vienna. Philip King died; so did Dennis Fallon, the young Irishman Helen loved, whose weak heart was not up to the task. Movie mogul Drew Sinclair joined the ranks of those who loved in vain: he fired Helen when his film was sabotaged (the wrong costumes being worn in an important nightclub scene), but was contrite when the real culprit was shown to be treacherous Reggie Peabody, head of the costume department, who feared that Helen would

get his job. She did, after nightclub owner Frankie Messara helped her prove her innocence. But *Fashions of 1939* was a flop—the best things about it, said critics, were the Helen Trent costumes—and Drew Sinclair went into a financial tailspin.

There were other studios, other suitors. Curtis Bancroft was handsome but shy. He had made a fortune in Oklahoma oil and owned most of International Artists Studio, where Helen worked in 1946. His major drawback as a lover was neglect—he neglected to tell Helen he was married. Helen went to London for a job with a major studio there: on the crossing she met Norman Hastings, writer and world traveler. He was handsome, unpredictable, and mysterious. He had vanished by the time she returned to Hollywood, but reappeared as she stood on the brink of true happiness with Gil Whitney.

Gil was her on-again, off-again romantic interest for 18 tortuous years. He was perhaps the most persistent and hapless suitor in the history of radio melodrama. They met when Helen was stranded in a rainstorm on Sunset Boulevard around 1940. Soon this "brilliant and prominent attorney" became the man of her life. But trouble arrived, said *Radio Mirror*, because "Gil and Helen are both so dynamic and attractive that the pattern of their romance is constantly being interrupted by other people, who are drawn, often explosively, into their activity-filled lives." This was done in an amusing *Mirror* photo layout: amusing because the pictures revealed them to be neither stunning nor dynamic. Radio people could hold their own as actors with most movie stars, but they were seldom paragons of physical radiance, and that's why they were radio actors.

But Helen and Gil were soulmates. So it must have seemed to listeners who couldn't remember a time when they weren't part of each other's lives. An army of rival suitors flowed through their star-crossed, elixir-fed affair, and Gil was always there, waiting to be propped up, dusted off, and brought to full flame again. Gil Whitney, in almost any use of the term, was the romance of Helen Trent.

He went overseas "on a secret government mission" during the war. He returned only to be struck down and paralyzed in a train wreck. He refused to tie Helen to an invalid, and took up teaching. There he met Cynthia Carter, a young and beautiful colleague who saw through his paralysis to the brilliant, dynamic man strapped in the wheelchair. When her uncle, a brilliant and famous surgeon, arrived on the scene, Gil was cured. In a moment of gratitude, he took Cynthia into his arms. Who should walk in at that moment but Helen Trent. She rebuffed Gil and turned to another, opening the door for Cynthia to become one of the show's most memorable vixens. Cynthia married Dwight Swanson, inherited a fortune, and made life miserable for Gil Whitney from then on.

The villains shared certain traits. Almost all of them were millionaires, *Time* reported, "and the effect Helen has on them is generally deadly. She drove Brett Chapman, millionaire rancher, to exile in South America. Dwight Swanson, oilman, piloted his plane into a crash. Kelsey Spencer, motion picture tycoon, went off a cliff to his death. But Dick Waring, madman, was sane only with Helen." Mad hypnotist Karl Dorn lured her into danger at a desolate mountain cabin. And Kurt Bonine, insanely jealous, shot Gil in his wheelchair and then tried to frame Helen for the deed.

The Gil Whitney affair ended in 1958, when Gil married Helen's archenemy and disappeared forever. Writer Margo Brooks explained it this way: "I simply had to get rid of Gil. He made Helen look silly." Two years later, as the show left the air, Helen was firmly clutched in the arms of Senate candidate John Cole, who looked like a solid bet to carry her into eternity. The cast and crew favored polishing off the heroine in typically outrageous style. As *Life* reporter Peter Bunzel described it: "An assistant director wanted Helen and all her friends to be invited for dinner by Ma Perkins. That benevolent old busybody would serve roast turkey spiked with poison. The guests would successively clutch their throats and choke to death as Ma softly chuckled.

"But this was child's play compared to the finale plotted by Leon Janney, a veteran radio actor who played several of Helen's suitors including her last. Janney proposed a different agony for each of the five chief characters. During the final week of broadcasting, they would be disposed of one by one on a daily basis. On Monday there would be a plane crash, on Tuesday an amnesia seizure, on Wednesday a landslide, on Thursday a lightning bolt. The worst would come last. Friday would be saved for Helen.

"After the music fades, Helen is discovered on a high balcony, soliloquizing about the week's carnage. Suddenly, with a resounding crash, the balcony topples into a deep gorge. Silence, long and ominous. Then comes a familiar pleading voice, the voice of the man she had loved the longest and had hated to lose: *Helen! Helen!—it's Gil!—Helen!*"

ROMANCE OF THE RANCHOS, historical drama.

BROADCAST HISTORY: 1940s. First heard Sept. 7, 1941, with various runs on CBS West Coast throughout the decade; still running Sunday afternoons in 1948. **EARLY 1940s CASTS:** Frank Graham as "the wandering vaquero," who told stories of Southern California in "the days of the dons." Also, Pat McGeehan, Howard McNear, ca. 1941–42. **ANNOUNCER:** Bob LeMond. **PRODUCER:** Ted Bliss. **WRITER:** John Dunkel.

MID-1940s CAST: Pedro de Cordoba as narrator Jose Alvarado, 1945–46; Herb Butterfield later as Alvarado, with de Cordoba in various anthology roles. **CONDUCTOR:** John Leipold. **PRODUCER-DIRECTOR:** Tom Hargis. **WRITERS:** Les Farber and Ray Wilson.

Romance of the Ranchos was based on the title records of its sponsor, Title Insurance and Trust Company of Los Angeles. It was designed to give listeners a sense of changing times through changing ownership of the land: "Perhaps this is the story of the rancho on which your home is now located." The vastness of the sponsor's records was emphasized (more than 3,000 volumes), and the writer's job was "to make those dry records live and breathe." The original series told of the ranchos that once existed where Westwood, Culver City, and Azusa now stood. W. W. Robinson of Title Insurance was the researcher.

THE ROOKIES, boot camp comedy.

BROADCAST HISTORY: Aug. 17–Nov. 6, 1941, Mutual. 30m, Sundays; later Thursdays. **CAST:** Jay C. Flippen and Joey Faye as sergeant and recruit. **ORCHESTRA:** Bob Stanley. **PRODUCER:** Roger Bower.

ROOSTY OF THE AAF, music and adventure.

BROADCAST HISTORY: April 9, 1944–Jan. 20, 1945, Mutual. Various 30m timeslots. **CAST:** William Tracy as Roosty, whose bomber crew was assigned to England in World War II. Lee J. Cobb as the tailgunner. **ANNOUNCER:** Hal Gibney. Content information is sparse, with no shows unearthed at this writing.

ROSE OF MY DREAMS, soap opera.

BROADCAST HISTORY: Nov. 25, 1946–May 14, 1948, CBS. 15m, weekdays at 2:45. Sweetheart Soap. **CAST:** Mary Rolfe as Rose, the good, and Charita Bauer as Sarah, the bad, in a story of sibling rivalry.

ROSEMARY, soap opera.

BROADCAST HISTORY: Oct. 2, 1944–March 23, 1945, NBC. 15m, weekdays at 11:15 A.M. Procter & Gamble.

March 26, 1945–July 1, 1955, CBS. 15m, weekdays at 2:30 until 1946, then at 11:45 A.M. Procter & Gamble, sponsor.

CAST: Betty Winkler as Rosemary Dawson, wife of a shell-shocked war veteran. Virginia Kaye also as Rosemary. George Keane and Bob Readick as Rosemary's husband, Bill Roberts. Marion Barney as Rosemary's mother. Mary Jane Higby and Helen Choate as Joyce Miller, Rosemary's best friend. Jone Allison and Patsy Campbell as Rosemary's sister, Patti Dawson. Jone Allison again as Bill Roberts's first wife, Audrey. Lesley Woods and Joan Alexander also as Audrey. Lawson Zerbe and Sydney Smith as Peter Harvey. Bill Adams and Charles Penman as Dr. Jim Cotter. Joan Lazer as Jessica. Jackie Kelk as Tommy Tyler. James Van Dyk as Dick Phillips. **MUSIC:** Paul Taubman. **CREATOR-WRITER:** Elaine Carrington. **PRODUCER-DIRECTORS:** Tom McDermott, Carl Eastman, Theodora Yates, Ralph Butler, Leslie Harris, Charles Fisher, etc.

Rosemary was Elaine Carrington's third major serial, following *Pepper Young's Family* and *When a Girl Marries*. It was the story of Rosemary Dawson, a 20-year-old secretary when the story began, who lived with her kindly mother and teenage sister, Patti. Rosemary supported the family on her meager salary and became its chief spiritual guide as well. There was an early hint that Rosemary might become involved with handsome, brilliant lawyer Peter Harvey. But she married Bill Roberts, who suffered recurring bouts of amnesia because of wartime trauma.

It was billed on CBS as *Rosemary's* "struggle

to find happiness as the wife of a returned veteran." She and Bill lived in a small white cottage near Springdale, a generic soap opera town somewhere in the Midwest. Mother Dawson and Patti lived with them, and all might have ended happily had not Rosemary's singing of *Night and Day* jarred Bill's memory, forced him to remember his former wife Audrey and their daughter Jessica, and in the process blanked out his marriage to Rosemary. "Are you someone I should know?" Bill asked, and the story spun off into turmoil. Predictably, Audrey became the serial's "bad girl."

Carrington got generally higher marks from critics than most of her daytime competition. Though *Rosemary* was cited for its "realistic approach to life," such devices as amnesia (in fact a rare malady that seemed to infect soap opera characters almost weekly) gave it the breathless "tune in tomorrow" edge they all had.

ROSES AND DRUMS, historical drama.

BROADCAST HISTORY: April 24, 1932–March 29, 1936; CBS through June 3, 1934, then Blue Network beginning Sept. 9, 1934. 30m, Sundays at 5 for United Central Insurance on both networks. **CAST:** Stars of stage and film in historical anthology until ca. 1933. American Civil War continuation thereafter: Elizabeth Love and Helen Claire as Betty Graham of Winchester, Va.; John Griggs as Capt. Randy Claymore of the Confederacy, who loved her; Reed Brown Jr. as Capt. Gordon Wright of the Union, who also loved her; Guy Bates Post as Ulysses S. Grant; Bert Lytell as Gen. Jeb Stuart; Bill Adams as Daniel Stark. **HOST-NARRATOR:** De Wolf Hopper. **ORCHESTRA:** Wilfred Pelletier. **DIRECTOR:** Herschel Williams of J. Walter Thompson.

Roses and Drums was a major series of historical dramas, in its first year drawing material from the entire scope of the American past. The opening program starred Cecilia Loftus as Sarah Wright in a drama of the 1676 Nathaniel Bacon Rebellion. Other shows that year featured Fritz Leiber as James Madison, Henry Hull as Nathan Hale, Charles Coburn as Andrew Jackson, and Glenn Hunter in a Valley Forge play. In the fall the series dramatized *The Battle of the Alamo*, with De Wolf Hopper, who became its host thereafter.

After mid-1933, the focus was on adventurous

romance, with the central character, the fictitious Betty Graham, pursued by two young students at Virginia Military Adacemy. Randy Claymore, a Virginian, joined the South's army at the outbreak of the Civil War; Gordon Wright, who came from Ohio, fought for the North. Each continued his romantic pursuit of the charming Betty, who became a "resourceful and courageous spy" for the Rebels. Betty was drawn as part ingenue and part hellcat. Often the action took place in army camps where her beaux were stationed. Fictional characters mixed with historic personages (once Randy was directed on a flanking maneuver by Gen. Jeb Stuart, remembered by history for his love of riding around vast armies without doing much fighting).

The scripts were checked for accuracy by Professor M. W. Jernegan of the University of Chicago. Carroll Carroll of J. Walter Thompson remembered it as "one of the first dramatic shows to permit an audience to come in and watch grown men and women read from a piece of paper." The players appeared at the microphone in costume. The series ended with an episode called *Road's End*, in which the tempestuous Betty made her choice, marrying the Yankee, Gordon Wright.

ROXY AND HIS GANG, musical variety.

BROADCAST HISTORY: 1923–25, WEAF, New York.
March 7, 1927–July 27, 1931, Blue Network. 60m until 1930, then 45m, Mondays at 7:30.
Sept. 15, 1934–April 27, 1935, CBS. 45m, Saturdays at 8. Castoria. Also known as *The Roxy Revue*.
HOST: Samuel Lionel Rothafel, master showman known widely as Roxy. **SPECIAL GUESTS:** Stars of opera and symphony halls. **REGULARS:** J. W. Roddenberry (whose voice was said by Roxy to be "perfect" for radio in those days of fragile and sensitive tubes); tenors James Melton, Harold Van Duzee, and William (Wee Willy) Robyn; baritones Alva (Bomby) Bomberger and Leonard Warren; bass Peter Hanover; soprano Betsy Ayres; contralto Adelaide De Loca; pianist Julia Glass; cellist Yasha Bunchuk; dancer Patricia Bowman; and a male quartet comprised of George Reardon, Fred Thomas, Frank Miller, and John Young. **ANNOUNCERS:** Phillips Carlin; also, Milton Cross

(both NBC). **MUSICAL COACH AND ARRANGER:** Leo Russotto.

Roxy and His Gang was the first successful attempt at "group" radio performing by a "family" of regular artists, remembered 30 years later as a forerunner of Arthur Godfrey and his "friends." Roxy—Samuel L. Rothafel—was a showman on a grand scale, who was captivated by a panoramic vision of entertainment that finally destroyed him.

He was born July 9, 1882, in Stillwater, Minn., and had his greatest success as an innovator and entrepreneur in movie theaters. In Forest City, Pa., he fitted a vacant storeroom with seats and created his first film emporium. His experiments with lights, music, and color—coordinating a stage production that worked in harmony with the film being shown—were sensational at the time, and in 1913 Rothafel became director of the largest movie house in the world, the Strand on Broadway. This led to other theaters—the Rialto, the Rivoli, and finally the Capitol, where he began his broadcasting career.

He had become widely known as Roxy, a name picked up in youth, when he played in a northern Pennsylvania baseball league. His *Capitol Family Broadcasts* began Nov. 19, 1922, on WEAF. He was the first to broadcast from the stage of a theater, and soon the Capitol was outfitted with a broadcast studio as well. The productions were lavish: he had a symphony orchestra (known as the "Capitol Grand"), a choral ensemble, and concert soloists who soon became the toasts of the town. A typical *Roxy* broadcast of 1924 was split into two halves: the first, direct from the stage, consisted of music by the orchestra; the second, from the studio, featured vocal and instrumental soloists. It sprawled across two hours, 7:20 to 9:15 P.M., and was the highlight of WEAF's Sunday schedule. His closing signature—"Good night, pleasant dreams, and God bless you"—was well known in the East, and newspapers referred to him as "the high priest of cathedral entertainment."

But he was criticized in some quarters for the informality of his announcing, and in 1925 he left the Capitol and the *Family* broadcasts in the hands of Major Edward Bowes, who went on to his own great success as an organizer and manager of amateur shows. Roxy, meanwhile, opened a theater that bore his nickname. It was equipped with a broadcast studio and lines to NBC's Blue Network, where in 1927 he aired *Roxy and His Gang* over a regional hookup. His first show spotlighted sopranos Beatrice Belkin, Dorothy Miller, Gladys Rice, and Anna Robinson; contraltos Celia Branz and Florence Mulholland; baritone Douglas Stanbury; tenor Adrian da Silva; Geoffrey O'Hara; violinist Joseph Stopak; pianists Phil Ohman and Victor Arden; Jim Coombs; comedian Frank Moulan; ballerina Maria Gambarelli; a "mixed chorus of 100 voices and a complete symphony orchestra of 110 instrumentalists." There was also a studio orchestra of 60 musicians, with four conductors on hand. But Roxy himself soon snatched up the baton. Without any training, he was able to conduct by a "sense of feeling"; he had mastered other specialties in the same way.

"In the throes of production, he is a demon," said *Radio Guide* a few seasons later, "a Simon Legree dominating the slaves of the theater. But once the task of the moment is over (and it isn't over until his idea of perfection has been attained), he is the first to sit down with his harrassed musicians and literally cry with them over their worn muscles, their weary hearts and uncertain minds." On his first network show, he paced back and forth, moving his soloists at the microphone to adjust for the strength of their voices. That he was radio's pioneer of the colossal is generally conceded, though he was finally swamped by his passion for ever-bigger productions. His *Roxy* years were marked by solid successes: he was the first to bring to the air such notables as the Barrymores and Mme. Ernestine Schumann-Heink, but his real significance lay in providing a forum for young talent. Ben Gross recalled that he had a "fatherly solicitude for his performers," as did Godfrey in a later and different day. He enjoyed promoting himself as motivated only by the discovery of fresh new talent. Tenor Jan Peerce was a major Roxy discovery, though Rothafel's actual use of Peerce was minimal. Later in the '30s, when Rothafel was attempting a comeback, Peerce was asked to tour with a promotional gang of *Roxy* alumni, and did, but his resentment that Roxy had discovered and then abandoned him got into the press. Rothafel was also said to have "discovered" Jessica Dragonette, but in her memoir Dragonette had a different view of it: she had walked out on him, she said, because of his "patronizing air." Conductors Eugene Ormandy and Erno Rapee came to prominence during Rothafel's tenure at the Capitol and Roxy.

The end of the radio show in 1931 found Rothafel preparing for the biggest venture of his life, and the one that led to his downfall. He had joined a group (David Sarnoff, Merlin H. Aylesworth, Owen D. Young, and John D. Rockefeller Jr. its principals) to create the last word in rococo film cathedrals, the 6,000-seat Radio City Music Hall. Everything was done to Roxy's specifications: it was to be the biggest, most distinctive theater on earth, and Roxy was "enthroned there," as *Radioland* put it, "with all the pushbuttons, lavish technical accoutrement, and heraldry of an Oriental potentate." He was dethroned just as quickly. His opening night was a disaster: he had littered the stage with 15 acts, the show sprawling into the early morning. The result, recalled Ben Gross, was "pathetic boredom." It quickly lost money; Roxy fell into disfavor and was banished.

A reorganized Radio City rose from the ashes to become a top New York tourist attraction. Roxy alumnus Erno Rapee remained to lead the Music Hall's symphony orchestra for years in its weekly broadcasts, but Rothafel never recovered. He resurfaced in late 1934, talking of plans for a new series that would "revolutionize radio." But he sounded bitter, attacking the medium at the top (Eddie Cantor, he said, was "the worst," and Ed Wynn "never has been and never can be broken into the tempo of radio"). When it came, his new *Roxy* show was just more of the same: it struggled to fair ratings before disappearing with the tattered remains of Rothafel's radio dream. He died the following year, Jan. 13, 1936, a heart attack victim.

THE ROY ROGERS SHOW, western variety; music and drama.

BROADCAST HISTORY: Nov. 21, 1944–May 15, 1945, Mutual. 30m, Tuesdays at 8:30. Goodyear Tire and Rubber Company.

Oct. 5, 1946–March 29, 1947, NBC. 30m, Saturdays at 9. Miles Laboratories.

Aug. 29, 1948–May 13, 1951, Mutual. 30m, Sundays at 6. Quaker Oats.

Oct. 5, 1951–July 21, 1955, NBC. 30m, Fridays at 8, 1951–52; Thursdays at 8, 1952–53. Post Toasties, 1951–53; Dodge, beginning Jan. 1954.

CAST: Roy Rogers, "king of the cowboys," with various personnel over the years. *1945–46*: songstress Pat Friday and the Sons of the Pioneers with western harmony; maestro Perry Botkin and the Goodyear Orchestra; and announcer Verne Smith. *1946–48*: costar Dale Evans, with vocal harmony by Foy Willing and the Riders of the Purple Sage (Johnny Paul, Al Sloey, and Scotty Harrell); Gabby Hayes, sidekick-stooge, later Pat Brady; orchestra led by Frank Worth. *Ca. 1951*: Rogers and Evans with Forrest Lewis as sidekick Jonah Wilde, "the wisest trail scout of them all." Supporting roles by Frank Hemingway, Herb Butterfield, Stan Waxman, Pat McGeehan, Leo Curley, Ken Peters and Ralph Moody. *Ca. 1952*: Pat Brady returned in the sidekick's role; songs by the Whipporwills; music by Milton Charles; scripts by Ray Wilson; direction by Tom Hargis or Fran Van Hartesveldt. *Ca. 1953*: Ralph Rose, writer-director.

The Roy Rogers Show was never better described than by the *Christian Science Monitor* wag who wrote, "a little song, a little riding, a little shooting, and a girl to be saved from hazard." Rogers rode hard on the heels of Gene Autry into B-western stardom, then followed Autry into radio.

He was born Leonard Slye in Cincinnati, Ohio. Though he played on hundreds of radio shows in a long career, he had mike fright for years. He faced his first microphone in 1931, as part of a singing group called Uncle Tom Murray's Hollywood Hillbillies. He spent much of the early 1930s organizing and performing with similar groups (the Texas Outlaws, the Rocky Mountaineers, etc.), then joined Bob Nolan to form the Sons of the Pioneers. This was a winning formula, containing at various times singers Tim Spenser, Lloyd Perryman, Ken Dawson, and Hugh and Karl Farr. By 1935, they were appearing in bit parts for Republic Pictures. A break in 1937, when Republic's top cowboy, Autry, quit in a dispute, elevated Rogers to the front ranks of Saturday matinee horse operas.

He bought a palomino colt, named it Trigger, and taught it tricks that were guaranteed crowd-pleasers. Rogers was soon nip-and-tuck with Autry at the box office. These low-budget westerns were highly profitable, and Rogers was considered a major personality by his studio. In the mid-1940s he was among the top ten money-

makers in the entire industry. His voice, a high-pitched tenor, was used to good advantage, both on film and on the air. He projected a boyish charm but would have listeners believe he could match any badman in rough-and-tumble. He was "shy, drawling, [and] courteous" (*Radio Life*), and his first radio series, on Mutual, had an air of campfire banter. Dramatic sketches were lighter and shorter than the ones Rogers used in his later radio work. The Pioneers sang such standards as *Cool Waters* and Nolan's *Tumbling Tumbleweeds*.

Rogers's wife, Arlene, died in 1946. By then he had been teamed with singer Dale Evans on the screen, and they were married Dec. 31, 1947. Evans continued playing unattached female roles in his movies and on the air. The 1948 Rogers show was reviewed by *Radio Life* as "typical western drammer," in which Rogers and sidekick Gabby Hayes "meet villainous adversity, save Miss Evans's ranch-home, or her father, or her younger brother, and ride off in a swirl of dust." It was an early example of transcribed drama: Rogers's contractual commitments would not have allowed him to do it live. Pat Brady soon filled the sidekick's role, and the subsequent eras were largely drama, with songs worked into the storylines.

The opening theme was often *It's Roundup Time on the Double-R-Bar*, a reference to Rogers's ranch in "Paradise Valley." The closing theme was the better-known *Happy Trails*, which by 1953 became the all-around theme. That year the new sponsor, Dodge, asked for a reorganization with a more adult audience in mind. Writer-director Ralph Rose came up with a mystery format for the final season, with Evans's song usually figuring in the plot. Rogers, too, was asked to try new musical challenges, such as *Old Man River*, for this series. But his name will best be remembered for juvenile fare, with Roy, Dale, their horses Trigger and Buttermilk, dog Bullet, and sidekick Brady the heart of it. Rogers's closing signature, encompassing his Christian ideals and his belief in the Golden Rule, became a radio classic: "Goodbye, good luck, and may the good Lord take a likin' to ya."

ROY SHIELD AND COMPANY, musical variety and drama.

BROADCAST HISTORY: 1935–52, NBC, Red and Blue, many brief formats with little continuity; more than 15 series, sometimes known as *The Roy Shield Revue*, though few lasted beyond two months and some were as brief as two weeks. Nelson Olmsted was often featured in straight readings of classic stories. Shield's most notable run was on NBC from March 6, 1943, to March 11, 1945; Saturday afternoons, 1943–44; then in 1944–45, he was sponsored by Sheaffer Pens, heard Sundays at 3 as *The Sheaffer Parade*.

THE ROYAL VAGABONDS, musical variety.

BROADCAST HISTORY: Jan. 4–Dec. 30, 1932, Blue Network. 15m, three a week at 6:30 until June, then twice a week at 7:15. Standard Brands for Royal Gelatin. **CAST:** Comic impersonator Ward Wilson. Willie and Eugene Howard, comedians. **MUSIC:** Billy Artz.

Jan. 4–Dec. 27, 1933, NBC. 30m, Wednesdays at 8. Standard Brands for Royal Gelatin. **CAST:** Initially, Ken Murray, host, with Ward Wilson a transition act from the 15m show. Beginning March 15, Fanny Brice replaced Murray as the headliner, with routines and songs (*Second-Hand Rose*, etc.) from her stage repertoire. Beginning Oct. 4, Bert Lahr replaced Brice. **ORCHESTRA:** George Olsen.

In Jan. 1934, this series was discontinued, and Standard Brands inserted the new *Jack Pearl Show* into the timeslot.

RUBINOFF AND HIS VIOLIN, musical variety.

BROADCAST HISTORY: Oct. 26, 1935–April 11, 1936, NBC. 30m, Saturdays at 9. Chevrolet.

Oct. 18, 1936–July 11, 1937, CBS. 30m, Sundays at 6:30. Chevrolet.

Transcribed series, concurrent with above, heard on 394 stations around the country.

ORCHESTRA: Dave Rubinoff. **VOCALISTS:** Jan Peerce and Virginia Rea (1936–37).

For about five years in the early to mid-1930s, Russian-born violinist Dave Rubinoff was a major radio star. He rose to prominence on *The Chase and Sanborn Hour*. Though this is primarily remembered as Eddie Cantor's first starring vehicle, Cantor did not join the show until September 1931, giving Rubinoff the starring role for its first eight months. Rubinoff became

a "personality" during the Cantor run. He did not speak on the air because of his strong Russian accent, but was impersonated by stooges, who made the accent even stronger. His *Rubinoff* shows were considered "serious" music, in which his violin was promoted almost as a living entity. He was a temperamental, often fiery performer who once walked off stage in the middle of a Cleveland concert, caught a train for New York, and left his audience flat.

THE RUDY VALLEE SHOW, variety.

BROADCAST HISTORY: 1928, WABC, New York. Herbert's Blue-White Diamonds.

Oct. 24, 1929–Sept. 28, 1939, NBC. 60m, Thursdays at 8. *The Fleischmann Yeast Hour*, 1929–36; *The Royal Gelatin Hour* thereafter. Standard Brands. **CAST:** Singing host Rudy Vallee with guests from stage, screen, and radio. Regulars: Ole Olsen and Chic Johnson, 1932; Tom Howard and George Shelton, 1935. **ANNOUNCER:** Graham McNamee. **ORCHESTRA:** Rudy Vallee's Connecticut Yankees. **PACKAGED** by J. Walter Thompson with agency people as directors and writers. **DIRECTORS:** Gordon Thompson, Tony Stanford, etc. **WRITERS:** George Faulkner, Bob Colwell, Carroll Carroll, etc. **FLEISCHMANN SPOKESMAN:** Dr. R. E. Lee. **THEME:** *My Time Is Your Time.*

March 7, 1940–July 1, 1943, NBC. 30m, Thursdays at 9:30; at 10 beginning in July 1940; at 9:30 again as of Jan. 1943. Sealtest (Kraft Foods for a time in the West). **CAST:** A shift of emphasis into comedy, with Rudy Vallee surprisingly supported by regular John Barrymore. Joan Davis added ca. 1941 as a looney man-chaser. Shirley Mitchell as Shirley Anne, the "village belle." Gil Lamb as Homer Clinker, who was somewhat in love with Davis. **MUSIC:** Eliot Daniel and Joe Lilley, who adapted popular songs into show themes and wrote original music as well. **PRODUCERS:** Ed Gardner, ca. 1940; Tom McAvity. **DIRECTOR:** Dick Mack. **WRITERS:** Bill Demling, Sid Zelinka, Ray Singer and Dick Chevillat. This series became *The Sealtest Village Store* and continued with Joan Davis as star.

Sept. 9, 1944–June 27, 1946, NBC. Initially 30m, Saturdays at 8; Thursdays at 10:30 after two months. *Villa Vallee*. Drene Shampoo. **COSTAR:** Monty Woolley.

Sept. 10, 1946–March 4, 1947, NBC. 30m,

Tuesdays at 8. Philip Morris. COSTAR: Ruth Etting.

Feb. 20, 1950–April 27, 1951, WOR, New York. 30m, weekdays. Records and talk.

Feb. 27–June 19, 1955, CBS. 60m, Sundays at 9. Kraft Foods. Records and talk.

Rudy Vallee first appeared on radio in 1924, during a musical tour of London. But it was his network show of 1929 that ushered in the era of the big-time radio variety show. *The Rudy Vallee Hour* was the most important show on the air in the early to mid-1930s, so influential that a young, unknown talent could rightly consider a booking there the break of a lifetime. Vallee's discoveries of people who later joined the front ranks of the entertainment world has never been equaled.

He was the most difficult taskmaster of all. "He has no patience with stupidity or the slightest deviation from what he considers the truth," said *Radioland* in 1934. "He is the most generous of friends, willing to go out of his way to help people. But once he feels they have violated his trust, he is the bitterest of enemies." His rehearsals were notorious as the toughest in radio. He was known to do physical battle with people who offended him. His fistfights were front-page news, and seldom was it suggested that these were publicity stunts. He had a hatred of trumped-up press, disliking even photographs that were too obviously posed. He fought a reporter who wrote too explicitly of his ugly divorce from Fay Webb, and he punched a photographer who took his picture with a female companion. Hecklers learned that he would come down from the stand and accost them at their tables if they gave him cause.

"He went forth with a chip on his shoulder to prove he wasn't a sissy," wrote author James Street in *Radio Guide*. "When he hit his peak he was arrogant and unreasonable, popular with a public that didn't know him and unpopular with his hired hands." He was "perspicuous, persnickety, and cantankerous, cold as a witch's kiss." He would quibble over pennies but would support a disabled musician through years of distant and expensive tuberculosis therapy. His musicians traveled first class but resented his hard-driving tirades. Once he bounced a roll of sheet music off his pianist's head for playing off key. He saw the world in black and white but

was willing to apologize when it was proved to his own satisfaction that he had been wrong. "When I do something wrong and stupid, I ask the injured person's pardon," he told an interviewer. "I don't mind at all eating humble pie."

He was the original crooner, "the Sinatra of the '20s," as he was known to a later generation. His success was as sensational as any in radio's first years: his eye for talent beyond question. He contributed more to the ranks of radio stardom than all the amateur shows combined.

He was born Hubert Prior Vallee in Island Pont, Vt., July 28, 1901. His family moved to Maine, where he prepared to take up his father's calling in the pharmacy. He was cocky even as a child: he was kicked out of the Navy in World War I when it was learned that he had lied about his age. His interest in music grew; the attractions of the pharmacy faded. The saxophone was his instrument of choice, and he taught himself to play it, striving for the style of sax trickster Rudy Wiedoeft, whose records he studied intensely. At the University of Maine his colleagues nicknamed him Rudy, in tribute to his idol Wiedoeft. He moved to Yale and joined a group that played private engagements and vaudeville jobs.

Later he joined the Vincent Lopez orchestra, and in 1928 he formed his own group. They played New York's Heigh-Ho Club, where Vallee adopted the salutation—"Heigh-ho, everybody!"—that would become his trademark. This he carried into radio. By 1929, after a season on the New York air, NBC considered him to host a proposed variety hour. His choice was by no means unanimous: it took a woman, Bertha Brainard, to carry the day for him (only a woman, she later explained, could relate to the hypnotic power of his voice). Vallee became a national figure overnight. By 1930–31, the first year in which solid ratings figures were available, his show was second only to *Amos 'n' Andy*, with a high of 36.5 in January.

It was the first show to attain such heights without a comedian at the helm. This was pure variety. Vallee's role was to sing, introduce guests, and conduct an occasional interview. The show was leisurely and broad-based, giving guests time to enact entire sequences from celebrated stage plays. There was an opening song, something popular in the Vallee style such as *I'd Rather Lead a Band* or *I'm Putting All My Eggs in One Basket*; then came a guest skit, usually with a top personality in the field of music. Another Vallee song might be followed by an interview with someone in the news. A drama was enacted in the second half. A typical show might feature Ozzie and Harriet Nelson, comic Frank Fay, the remarkable Helen Keller (deaf and blind, who, with the aid of her companion, Anne Sullivan Macy, spoke with Vallee and his radio audience), and a play with Douglas Fairbanks Jr. and June Walker.

But almost from the beginning, Vallee's special ability as a talent scout came to the fore. He plucked Alice Faye out of the chorus in George White's *Scandals* and sent her to vocal and film stardom. He found Frances Langford singing on a small station in Florida. Beatrice Lillie, Milton Berle, and Phil Baker got their first major radio exposure on the Vallee show. Tommy Riggs introduced his little-girl character Betty Lou on a series of Royal Gelatin broadcasts. Joe Penner leaped from obscurity to fame after an appearance with Vallee. *The Aldrich Family* was first heard as a skit on Vallee's show. The most sensational discovery was Edgar Bergen, who on Dec. 17, 1936, first wisecracked on the air as Charlie McCarthy, beginning a career that soon surpassed Vallee's own and a show that was lodged for a decade among radio's ratings giants.

On the air, Vallee had a style that was somewhat pontifical. Often he played this role for the benefit of his guest, making it difficult for a listener to know where Vallee ended and the showman began. His most popular guests returned, sometimes for the bulk of a season. In 1938 he employed Irving Caesar to write and sing safety jingles for children.

By then the show was tired, sapped by swarming competition and unrejuvenated by the aggressive talent chase that Vallee had embraced a few seasons before. He had found too much talent and lost it, suggested James Street. A rival reporter, a woman obviously charmed by Vallee's personal magnetism, argued that his aim had never been to hold these people; his sole interest was to further their careers and, having accomplished this, he was happy to send them on their way. Street, far less charmed, wondered if Vallee had let his biggest discoveries escape in the supreme confidence that he could find exciting new people whenever he wished. But this was harder in the late '30s: Vallee's show, once

the only game in town, was suddenly flanked by half a dozen serious competitors. One of them was Kate Smith, directly across the dial in the Thursday-at-8 hour on CBS: Smith whisked *The Aldrich Family* away from Vallee and made it a prime feature of her show, and in 1939 she nudged ahead in the ratings.

Vallee decided to give it up. "My time has been your time for ten solid years," he said in closing, "and it will be yours once more after my time has been my time for a little while." When it came in March 1940, Vallee's new show was a striking departure. It was a much-tightened half-hour, with stage giant John Barrymore doing comedy and becoming, in his last years, a mild sensation to a new generation. Though remembered by writer Carroll Carroll as "embarrassing" (mainly because he felt Barrymore had "capitalized on his drunkenness"), the new Vallee show was a hit with the public, building its ratings into the mid-20s. Barrymore needled Vallee and mixed borderline slapstick with heavy Shakespeare. He had a few brilliant moments, notably his Shakespearean duel with guest Orson Welles (each giving a good-spirited, humorous, and undoubtedly type-cast portrayal of himself as an unbridled egomaniac). Barrymore was gracious: it was said that he even took suggestions on Shakespeare from director Dick Mack, which caused the cast to hold its collective breath. Barrymore's health was fragile all the way: often he was absent, his place taken by brother Lionel. On some occasions, his absence may have been due to drinking. But a highlight of this time was the appearance of three Barrymores—John, Lionel, and Diana—on a single show. Barrymore's final broadcast was May 14, 1942. The following Tuesday he collapsed in rehearsal and was rushed to a hospital, where he died May 29.

The show shifted into a new mode. Joan Davis, who had first appeared on the Sealtest show in the fall of 1941, was boosted into a regular role. She played a zany man-chaser, and the man she chased was Vallee. It was now typical '40s sitcom material, with Davis considered in many quarters the year's brightest new star. Then Vallee enlisted in the Coast Guard: critics, who knew the torch was being passed, wondered in print whether Davis was strong enough professionally to carry the show without a male lead. She was, as her later career proved, but the nervous client insisted on bringing in Jack Haley to cohost when Vallee stepped aside in July 1943.

Vallee spent much of the following year conducting the 11th Naval District Coast Guard Band, known as one of the best military units in the nation. He returned to civilian life, and to radio, in 1944. Neither his 1944 Drene show with Monty Woolley nor his 1946 Philip Morris series with singer Ruth Etting was successful. But radio really died when Vallee turned up as a weekday disc jockey on WOR in 1950. He seemed to mellow in his later years. In the 1980s he was easily accessible to his fans, his name listed in the Los Angeles telephone directory. One fan who called it was delighted when Vallee answered and chatted pleasantly for more than an hour. In an interview with this writer, Vallee was talkative and witty and courteous while controlling the flow of the talk, acknowledging his contributions as a talent hunter while laughing off the suggestion that posterity was at all enriched by the preservation of his old shows.

He died July 3, 1986.

S

THE SAD SACK, situation comedy, developed from George Baker's cartoon feature in *Yank*, the Army weekly newspaper.

BROADCAST HISTORY: June 12–Sept. 4, 1946, CBS. 30m, Wednesdays at 9. Summer replacement for *The Frank Sinatra Show*. Old Gold. **CAST:** Herb Vigran as the Sad Sack, the "beloved and eternal buck private" who was (as was Vigran) just returning to civilian life. Jim Backus as the Sack's roommate, the chiseling Chester Fenwick. Sandra Gould as Lucy Twitchell, the Sack's girlfriend. Ken Christy as Lucy's father. Patsy Moran as Mrs. Flanagan, the landlady. **PRODUCER-DIRECTOR:** Ted Sherdeman. **WRITERS:** Charlie Isaacs, Arthur Stander. **ANNOUNCER:** Dick Joy.

The characters of *The Sad Sack* were introduced on Frank Sinatra's season finale, June 5. Cartoonist George Baker had been turning out the *Yank* panels as an editorial feature since June 1942, but the radio show took the Sack on into civilian life. It opened with his discharge from the Army and his return to the apartment house run by crusty Mrs. Flanagan and to his prewar friends. Many of the shows were of his bumbling attempts to impress Lucy Twitchell and her unimpressible father.

THE SAINT, detective drama, based on the novels by Leslie Charteris.

BROADCAST HISTORY: Jan. 6–March 31, 1945, NBC. 30m, Saturdays at 7:30. Bromo Seltzer.

CAST: Edgar Barrier as Simon Templar, a.k.a. the Saint, "Robin Hood of modern crime."

June 20–Sept. 12, 1945, CBS. 30m, Wednesdays at 8. Summer replacement for Jack Carson. Campbell Soups. **CAST:** Brian Aherne as Simon Templar. Louise Arthur as Patricia Holm, Templar's favorite lady friend in the novels. **PRODUCER:** William N. Robson. No shows from these first two runs were available to review; thus the support crews are unknown.

July 9, 1947–June 30, 1948, CBS, West Coast network only. **CAST:** Vincent Price as Simon Templar.

July 10, 1949–May 28, 1950, Mutual. 30m, Sundays at 7:30. Ford Motors. **CAST:** Vincent Price as Simon Templar. **ANNOUNCER:** Merrill Ross.

June 11, 1950–Oct. 14, 1951, NBC. 30m, Sundays at 7:30 until Oct. 1950, then Sundays at 4:30 until July 1951, then at 4. **CAST:** Vincent Price as Simon Templar until May 20, 1951; Tom Conway thereafter. Lawrence Dobkin as Louie, the cab driver. Support from Hollywood regulars: Lurene Tuttle, Harry Bartell, Tony Barrett, Barney Phillips, Dan O'Herlihy, Peggy Webber, Ted von Eltz, Jerry Hausner, etc. **ANNOUNCER:** Don Stanley. **MUSIC:** Harry Zimmerman. **PRODUCER:** James L. Saphier. **DIRECTORS:** Helen Mack, Thomas A. McAvity. **WRITERS:** Louis Vittes; Dick Powell. **THEME:** A haunting whistle, with accompanying footsteps, suggestive of a lonely street at night.

The Saint, said actor Brian Aherne, who played the role briefly, was "a sort of superman.

He's never at a loss in any situation, and can get himself out of any scrape, and always quite legitimately.'' Following the Leslie Charteris novels and the film portrayals by suave George Sanders, the radio Saint righted wrongs and aided victims of crime when the law was rendered powerless by restrictive procedure. The Saint simply broke the law, if the result justified it. He was a dapper dresser, equally at home at the wheel of a fast car, in an airplane, or on horseback.

The Vincent Price series came in the wake of Jack Webb's *Pat Novak*, when all the detective shows were striving for the clever quip. Price was able to elevate ordinary lines and make them sing: his series was on a par with *Richard Diamond* in the clever-comeback department, though neither could touch *Novak*, whose writer, Richard Breen, excelled in outrageous dialogue. Price's Saint was a patron of the arts and a diner at superb restaurants. His all-time peeve was being interrupted while dining. The numerous interruptions inevitably led to jewel thieves, embezzlement, or murder.

In addition to the runs with Barrier, Aherne, and Price, a series is known to exist with Barry Sullivan as Templar. No other details have yet come to light.

SAN QUENTIN ON THE AIR, prison variety show.

BROADCAST HISTORY: Jan. 25, 1942, first heard on the West Coast Mutual–Don Lee Network; tenure uncertain, but still heard in 1943, Thursdays at 7:30 Pacific time. PERSONNEL: Produced, written and performed by inmates of the famed California penitentiary; broadcast directly from a makeshift stage in the prison's mess hall. REGULARS: Johnny Trudrung, tenor; ''colored singer'' Milton White. ANNOUNCER: Johnny White. COMMENTATOR: Warden Clinton T. Duffy on such topics as juvenile delinquency. CHORUS: Jack Reavis with a 30-voice glee club. ORCHESTRA: Inmate John A. Hendricks (who had been a major in World War I), with a 17-piece band. PRODUCER: Mel Venter. WRITER-ANNOUNCER: Rolph Burr.

San Quentin on the Air was quickly nicknamed ''Concerto in the Clink'' and ''Harmonies in the Hoosgow'' by witty prisoners. Its

theme, *Time on My Hands*, was also amusing, but there was real talent involved, and when it was dropped in 1942, 22,000 letters ensured its quick return. The show had a patriotic flavor, urging listeners to buy War Bonds.

SARA'S PRIVATE CAPER, detective spoof.

BROADCAST HISTORY: June 15–Aug. 24, 1950, NBC. 30m, Thursdays at 10:30. Wheaties. CAST: Sara Berner as a stenographer with ambitions to be a detective. Bob Sweeney as her hapless boyfriend. MUSIC: Robert Armbruster. DIRECTOR: Joe Parker. WRITERS: Ken Starr and Larry Klein; Morton Fine and David Friedkin.

Sara Berner was a talented dialectician: Mabel Flapsaddle and Gladys Zybisco (with Jack Benny), Ingrid Mataratza (Jimmy Durante), Mrs. Horowitz (*Life with Luigi*), and Mrs. Jacoby (Dennis Day's show) were some of her creations, and she got to use most of her wares on her own brief program. As a detective of sorts, she was frequently in disguise and had to shift dialects accordingly.

THE SATURDAY MORNING VAUDEVILLE THEATER, musical variety.

BROADCAST HISTORY: July 12, 1941–Jan. 3, 1942, NBC. 30m, Saturdays at 11:30 A.M. Lever Brothers. HOST: Jim Ameche. REGULARS: Dick Todd, baritone, with Charles Kemper, Jess Mack, Joan Shea, Anita Boyer, and the Symphonettes. ORCHESTRA: D'Artega (who used only his last name).

SATURDAY NIGHT PARTY, musical variety.

BROADCAST HISTORY: Oct. 17, 1936–Oct. 10, 1937, NBC. 60m, Saturdays at 8. Sealtest. Sundays at 10 as *Sunday Night Party* beginning May 23, 1937.

This series had trouble finding its purpose, a star, and finally even a title. It opened with Walter O'Keefe as comedian and Jane Pickens as singer. O'Keefe quit less than two months into the show, and sponsor Sealtest reconsidered the project. For a time a format of guest stars was used. In May 1937, it became *The Sunday Night Party* with tenor James Melton and comic Tom Howard. This led, as of Oct. 17, 1937, to yet another series, *Rising Musical Star*.

SATURDAY NIGHT SERENADE, popular music.

BROADCAST HISTORY: Oct. 3, 1936–Sept. 25, 1948, CBS. Saturdays, various 30m timeslots. Pet Milk. **CAST:** Mary Eastman, soprano, and Bill Perry, tenor (1936–41); Jessica Dragonette with Bill Perry (1941–46). **ANNOUNCERS:** Bill Adams (1936–41); Bob Trout, Warren Sweeney. **CHORUS:** Emil Coté with 14 mixed voices. **ORCHESTRA:** Howard Barlow (1936–37), then Gus Haenschen. **PRODUCER:** Roland Martini.

Pet Milk viewed its *Saturday Night Serenade* as a positive half-hour, even though ratings were never more than lukewarm and for its first six seasons the show was not carried in New York. There were three distinct eras. Soprano Mary Eastman was a highly popular performer but was replaced in 1941 by Jessica Dragonette, one of radio's best-loved singers; tenor Bill Perry spanned these eras. Producer Roland Martini was remembered by Dragonette as being extremely conscious of the sponsor's wholesome image (she was "shocked," she said in her autobiography, to learn that Martini had "put a detective on us" to make sure that her sister, with whom she was living, was really her sister). She left because Pet was "getting ready to cut expenses and change the format," which it did. The 1946–48 era was rather bland, with Haenschen, Sweeney, and the Coté singers and not much excitement at the top. From Oct. 2, 1948, the same basic show continued as *The Pet Milk Program*.

SAUNDERS OF THE CIRCLE X, western serial drama.

BROADCAST HISTORY: 1941–42; 30m, produced in San Francisco for Blue Network West Coast outlets beginning Oct. 2, 1941. **CAST:** John Cuthbertson as Singapore Bill Saunders, foreman of the 90,000-acre Circle X Ranch. Bert Horton as Hank Peffer, "the tireless storyteller." Lou Tobin as ranch owner Thomas Mott. Bobbie Hudson as Pinto, the happy cowboy. Jack Kirkwood as Joe Williams. **WRITER:** Sam Dickson.

Outrageously corny, with heavy organ music.

THE SCARLET PIMPERNEL, adventure, from the novel by Baroness Emmuska Orczy.

BROADCAST HISTORY: Transcribed in London in 1952 for the Towers of London, a syndicate that was then the world's top dealer in recorded radio shows; sold to NBC as a summer replacement for *The Cavalcade of America*, July 1–Aug. 19, 1952, 30m, Tuesdays at 8; then as its own series, Sept. 21, 1952–Sept. 20, 1953, 30m, Sundays at 6. **CAST:** Marius Goring as Sir Percy Blakeney, the London dandy who, in moments of crisis, became the infamous Scarlet Pimpernel and battled purveyors of terror during the French Revolution. With his companion, Lord "Tony" Dewhurst, the Pimpernel rescued unfortunates about to be guillotined during the reign of Louis XVI. **PRODUCER:** Harry A. Towers. **WRITER:** Joel Murcott (who went to London to adapt the novel).

SCATTERGOOD BAINES, serial drama/situation comedy, based on the magazine stories by Clarence Budington Kelland.

BROADCAST HISTORY: Feb. 22, 1937–June 12, 1942, CBS: West Coast only until Oct. 28, 1938, then full network; continuity gap Aug. 29–Dec. 1, 1941; 15m serial, weekdays at 11:15 A.M., 1938–39, then at 5:45. Wrigley's Gum. **CAST:** Jess Pugh as Scattergood Baines, hardware merchant and benevolent force, wise and friendly, who used psychology and the powers of persuasion to get people to do what was best for them. John Hearne as Hippocrates Brown, Scattergood's helper in the hardware store, who swept, delivered, and did as little actual work as he could manage—a genial jack of all trades known affectionately as "Hipp." Francis "Dink" Trout as Pliny Pickett, conductor on the branch line, a crusty character who distrusted anyone who'd dare travel any other way. Catherine McCune as Clara Potts, the beautiful, nagging wife of garage mechanic Ed Potts and a town activist who got involved in everything. Arnold Robertson as Ed Potts. Charles Grant as Jimmy Baines, the adopted son raised by Scattergood from infancy. Eileen Palmer as Dodie Black, Jimmy's natural mother, who turned up and claimed custody (unsuccessfully, though she gave the hero some bad moments). Boris Aplon as Harvey Fox, a double-dealer who promoted Mrs. Black's scheme to get Jimmy away from Scattergood. Forrest Lewis as J. Wellington Keats, who blew into town with a crooked carnival and stayed around to become manager of the hotel. Forrest Lewis also as Ernie Baker the barber, and as a character named Agamemnon. **PRODUCER-DIRECTOR:** Walter Preston.

Feb. 10–Oct. 26, 1949, Mutual. 30m comedy-drama, Thursdays at 8:30 until July; Saturdays at 5:30 until Sept.; then Wednesdays at 10. **CAST:** Wendell Holmes as Scattergood Baines. Parker Fennelly as Hannibal Gibbey, "bookkeeper at Jason Green's feed store." Eleanor Phelps as Tilda Gibbey. Also: Lyle Sudrow, Bryna Raeburn, Don Griggs, Robert Dryden, etc. **ORCHESTRA:** Ben Ludlow. **PRODUCER:** Herbert Rice. **WRITER:** Gerald Holland.

The two runs of *Scattergood Baines* were produced in different decades and were aimed at different audiences. It was initially produced in Hollywood but moved to Chicago in October 1938 with its pickup by the national CBS network.

The 1949 show aired from New York. It continued the setting, in the small town of Coldriver, but with different supporting characters. Now Scattergood was billed as "the shrewd and jovial hardware merchant who finds himself drawn into everything that happens around him." He was "the best-loved, most cussed-at, and by all odds the fattest man" in town. Parker Fennelly played the same Titus Moody New England type that he had brought to fame on *The Fred Allen Show*.

SCOTLAND YARD'S INSPECTOR BURKE, detective drama.

BROADCAST HISTORY: Jan. 21–Dec. 29, 1947, Mutual. 30m, Tuesdays at 8 until April, then Mondays at 8. **CAST:** Basil Rathbone as Burke. **MUSIC:** Sylvan Levin.

Basil Rathbone chose this as his starring vehicle in the wake of his long *Sherlock Holmes* stint. It differed from *Holmes* in its most vital aspect—the criminal was most often caught through his own psychological weaknesses rather than by the deductive genius of the hero. The show originated in New York. Few details are known, as no shows have yet surfaced.

SCRAMBLE, wartime aviation adventure and news for children.

BROADCAST HISTORY: July 10, 1942–April 16, 1943, Blue Network. 25m, Fridays at 7:05. A joint project of the National Aeronautic Association and the Army Air Forces to interest youngsters in avi-

ation careers. **HOST:** Robert Ripley (of *Believe It or Not*) and others. **WRITER-DIRECTOR:** Robert Monroe.

Scramble used no fiction: it dramatized the exploits of such real-life warriors as "Jap-killing brothers Frank and Chuck Freeman," and often brought them to the microphone for some post-show dialogue. A Junior Air Reserve promoted on the show enlisted 70,000 boys aged 10 to 16.

SCRAMBY AMBY, word-scrambling quiz.

BROADCAST HISTORY: 1941, WLW, Cincinnati. 1943, NBC West Coast network.

1944, Blue Network, West Coast, from KFI, Los Angeles. Sweetheart Soap.

July 26, 1944–Jan. 17, 1945, Blue Network, coast-to-coast. 30m, Wednesdays at 7 until Sept.; then at 10:30. Sweetheart Soap.

Dec. 21, 1946–May 10, 1947, Mutual. 30m, Saturdays at 8:30.

HOST: Perry Ward. **ANNOUNCER:** Larry Keating. (Ward and Keating in these roles both on the West Coast and on the Blue Network national line.) **ORCHESTRA:** Paul Martin, Charles Dant. **WRITER-PRODUCER:** Howard Blake.

Scramby Amby was a simple word game, but fascinating enough to outgrow its local origins, become a national series twice, and spawn a number of listening clubs around the country. The quiz was based on lists of scrambled words submitted by the audience. IGOLOANBIT was actually OBLIGATION; SOINVAIN was INVASION. Many of the words had war themes and made sense in their scrambled versions as well. Listeners could win $5 to $50, depending on how many clues a contestant needed to solve it. The value of the words decreased as new clues were given. Some of these were verbal hints ("Shall I *advance* a few more hints?" Ward asked on the INVASION scramble: "you're sharp as *attack*"). Some were musical (*Over There* played by the orchestra). Some were framed as "daffy definitions" ("Some say it'll be Greece, some say Norway, some say all at once; but let's not argue, it doesn't matter *where* it *starts*, just so it ends up *Unter den Linden*").

Words submitted by listeners were evaluated for adaptability to definitions and music. Announcer Keating sometimes sang the clues. In the listening clubs, players had to "feed the kitty,'' and the winner took home most of the pot.

THE SCREEN DIRECTORS' PLAYHOUSE,
Hollywood dramatic anthology.

BROADCAST HISTORY: Jan. 9, 1949–Sept. 28, 1951, NBC. Various timeslots; 30m, expanded to 60m weekly as of Nov. 9, 1950. Opened as *NBC Theater*; also known as *The Screen Directors' Guild*. Pabst Beer, July–Sept. 1949; RCA Victor, 1950; RCA, Anacin, and Chesterfield, 1950–51. CAST: Top Hollywood stars in famous film stories. ANNOUNCER: Jimmy Wallington. ORCHESTRA: Henry Russell. PRODUCER: Howard Wylie. DIRECTOR: Bill Karn. WRITERS: Dick Simmons, Milton Geiger.

When *The Screen Directors' Playhouse* arrived, late in radio's history, the air was full of similar-sounding glamour shows. This followed closely in the footsteps of the famous *Screen Guild Theater* but added the element of director participation. The directors of the films introduced the radio adaptations, and afterward reminisced with the stars on how the films had been made and what the stars and directors had done in the meantime. But more important than any of this was the writing. Creator Don Sharpe believed that ''writing is the most important single factor in a radio package,'' and it was seldom better demonstrated than here. Though the material had a familiar sound, it was made fresh.

It opened with John Wayne, Claire Trevor, and Ward Bond reliving their days making *Stagecoach* with director John Ford. Such subsequent shows as *The Sea Wolf* (Edward G. Robinson), *Champion* (Kirk Douglas), and *Miss Grant Takes Richmond* (Lucille Ball) captured their stories rather than just the high spots. The series is largely available on tape. Still fully viable are *The Night Has a Thousand Eyes* (Edward G. Robinson), *Pitfall* (Dick Powell and Jane Wyatt), and *The Spiral Staircase* (Dorothy McGuire). A gripping, powerful show was *All My Sons*, based on the Arthur Miller play and starring Edward G. Robinson with Jeff Chandler. The expansion to the hour-long format was applauded by *Radio Life*: ''It takes a full hour's time, at least, to transfer effectively a good screenplay into the medium of sound.'' The hours were powerhouse radio: among them, *Lifeboat* (Tallulah Bankhead), *Mrs. Mike* (Joseph Cotten), *The Lady Gambles* (Barbara Stanwyck), and *Jackpot* (James Stewart and Margaret Truman).

THE SCREEN GUILD THEATER, Hollywood dramatic anthology and variety.

BROADCAST HISTORY: Jan. 8, 1939–April 19, 1942, CBS. 30m, Sundays at 7:30. Initially heard as *The Gulf Screen Guild Show*, becoming *The Gulf Screen Guild Theater* in Nov. 1939. Gulf Oil.
Oct. 19, 1942–July 7, 1947, CBS. 30m, Mondays at 10. *The Lady Esther Screen Guild Theater*. Lady Esther Cosmetics.
Oct. 6, 1947–June 28, 1948, CBS. 30m, Mondays at 10:30. *The Camel Screen Guild Players*. Camel Cigarettes.
Oct. 7, 1948–June 29, 1950, NBC. 30m, Thursdays at 10, 1948–49, then at 9. Camel Cigarettes.
Sept. 7, 1950–May 31, 1951, ABC. 60m, Thursdays at 8.
1951–52: The ''Screen Guild'' formula was resurrected, with *Screen Guild Players* as a subtitle, on such series as *Stars in the Air* and *Hollywood Soundstage*.
April 6–June 29, 1952, CBS. 30m, Sundays at 9.
HOST: George Murphy, 1939; Roger Pryor for the remainder of the Gulf era. CAST: Virtually every star in Hollywood in radio adaptations of famous films; a variety format in the first year, with stars also performing stunts and comedy skits. ANNOUNCERS: John Conte for Gulf Oil; Truman Bradley for Lady Esther; Michael Roy for Camel. ORCHESTRA: Oscar Bradley for Gulf; Wilbur Hatch for Lady Esther; Basil Adlam on ABC, 1950–51. PRODUCER-DIRECTOR: Bill Lawrence. WRITERS: Bill Hampton, Harry Kronman, etc.

The Screen Guild Theater was unparalleled in its ability to draw top Hollywood film stars. Its early shows spotlighted as many as four a week from the front ranks of the entertainment world—$20,000 worth of talent on a single broadcast. Gary Cooper could be found on the same billing with Bing Crosby and Marlene Dietrich; Jimmy Cagney with George Burns and Gracie Allen. This was a show with a purpose, a charity show, and the charity was close to Hollywood's heart. All fees that would normally have gone to the stars were given to the Motion Picture Relief Fund, almost $800,000 by the summer of 1942.

This money was used to build and maintain the Motion Picture Country House, 40 bungalow units for the housing of aging and indigent film stars.

In its earliest days it was seen as the ultimate variety revue. Jack Benny, Joan Crawford, and Judy Garland appeared on the first broadcast, setting a trend that continued through the first year. Song-and-dance routines were liberally mixed with comedy and dramatic sketches. Almost everyone in Hollywood was anxious to appear and contribute to the cause. If William Powell dropped out because of illness, James Stewart, Cary Grant, James Cagney, Fred MacMurray, and Clark Gable would call and offer to step in. Shirley Temple's parents allowed the child star to appear on *Screen Guild* without pay, after turning down a reported $35,000 offer for Temple to do another commercial program. When the series was scheduled on Monday nights, immediately following *The Lux Radio Theater*, the producers agreed to stagger their heavy and light fare in a rare spirit of cooperation. When *Lux* ran a melodrama, *Screen Guild* might have Ann Sothern in a bit of fluff. The scheduling gave CBS a corner on the glamour market for 90 minutes each Monday night.

But it got off to a shaky start. There seemed to be an attitude in the first Gulf year that big names alone were enough. The material was often second-rate: the stars seemed to be marking time. The entire production in 1939 had the sound of a cut-and-paste job—a song by Mickey Rooney and Judy Garland here, a bit of Bob Hope comedy there. The job of Roger Pryor, who replaced George Murphy as host, was largely ornamental. He introduced the players and the plays and sometimes played supporting roles. He was also to be found in a lingering bit of silliness, when the stars were quizzed at the end and made to pay penalties (cackling like a rooster, singing off key, etc.). Gulf dropped the show as of April 19, 1942, citing the adverse effect of the war on the oil industry.

Efforts to sell it that summer were not successful until Lady Esther came to the rescue at the last moment. A new theme was added, and the show settled into the tried-and-true niche that was all too familiar as the '40s unfolded. Producer Bill Lawrence eagerly sought films that hadn't been worked on *Lux* or on the many copycat series that arose during the Lady Esther tenure. With writers Bill Hampton and Harry Kronman, he viewed two and three films a day in the search for material. To Hampton and Kronman fell the difficult job of capturing the film's essence in a 22-minute script.

More than 200 programs are available on tape: without doubt the major show of its kind, the leader in half-hour film fare. A table of highlights would run many pages (a few being *Bluebird*, with Shirley Temple and Nelson Eddy; *Sergeant York*, with Gary Cooper and Walter Brennan; *Yankee Doodle Dandy*, with James Cagney, Rita Hayworth, and Betty Grable; *High Sierra*, with Humphrey Bogart and Ida Lupino; and *Command Decision*, with Clark Gable, Walter Pidgeon, Van Johnson, John Hodiak, Edward Arnold, and Brian Donlevy). But to this listener, *Screen Guild* seldom matched the lesser-known and later *Screen Directors' Playhouse* in writing and staging. The stars were the same, the plays were often the same, but the difference was in the telling. *Screen Guild* always seemed like the quick economy tour, jerky and uneven, scenes knit together by thin thread and taxing a modern listener's willingness to suspend disbelief.

Unfortunately, not much has yet been seen of the 60-minute run on ABC. Based on two available programs, it does appear that *Screen Guild* benefited greatly from the additional half-hour, reaching new highs in listenability. *Champagne for Caesar* (Ronald Colman, Vincent Price, Audrey Totter, Barbara Britton, and Art Linkletter, Oct. 5, 1950) must rank among the most delightful comedies ever broadcast, and *Birth of the Blues* (Bing Crosby, Dinah Shore, and Phil Harris, Jan. 18, 1951) remains an enjoyable musical, four decades after it aired.

THE SEA HAS A STORY, dramatic anthology; also heard as *The Story of the Sea*.

BROADCAST HISTORY: July 2–Aug. 20, 1945, CBS. 30m, Mondays at 9:30. **NARRATOR:** Pat O'Brien with tales of seafarers. **ORCHESTRA:** Lud Gluskin.

THE SEA HOUND, adventure serial.

BROADCAST HISTORY: June 29, 1942–Sept. 22, 1944, Blue Network/ABC. 15m, weekdays at 5:15 until Sept. 1942; at 5, 1942–43; at 4:45, 1943–44. **CAST:** Ken Daigneau as Captain Silver of the ship *Sea Hound*, which traveled adventurous waterways from jungle ports to desert outposts. Bobby Hastings as his young mate, Jerry. **DIRECTOR:** Cyril Armbrister.

June 21–Sept. 2, 1948, ABC. 30m, variously two and three times a week at 5:30, alternating with *Sky King*. **CAST:** Barry Thomson as Silver. **DIRECTOR:** Charles Powers.

June 26–Aug. 7, 1951, ABC. 30m, Tuesdays at 8:30.

THE SEALED BOOK, mystery-terror dramatic anthology.

BROADCAST HISTORY: March 18–Sept. 9, 1945, Mutual. 30m, Sundays at 10:30. **CAST:** Philip Clarke as "the keeper of the book," a croaking, cackling hermit-type who in each show unlocked "the great padlock" that kept "the sealed book safe from prying eyes." **DIRECTOR:** Jock MacGregor. **WRITERS:** Robert A. Arthur and David Kogan.

The Sealed Book was a corny takeoff on *The Witch's Tale*—an allegedly spooky narrator with omniscient knowledge of the black arts, who told a spook story each week. Contained in the "sealed book," listeners were told, were "all the secrets and mysteries of mankind through the ages."

THE SEALEST VARIETY THEATER, musical variety.

BROADCAST HISTORY: July 6–Sept. 28, 1947, NBC. 30m, Sundays at 8:30. This early version titled *Front and Center*, was created to promote U.S. Army recruitment. **CAST:** Dorothy Lamour, singing hostess, with guest stars from screen and radio. **VOCALISTS:** The Crew Chiefs (Johnny Huddleston, Gene and Steve Steck, and Lillian Lane). **ORCHESTRA:** Henry Russell. **DIRECTOR:** Glenhall Taylor.

Sept. 9, 1948–July 7, 1949, NBC. 30m, Thursdays at 9:30. *The Sealtest Variety Theater*. Sealtest. Format and personnel unchanged from *Front and Center*. Top guests including Ronald Colman, Gregory Peck, Bob Hope, Jim and Marian Jordan (Fibber and Molly), Ed Gardner, and Harold Peary. **ANNOUNCER:** John Laing.

Although *Front and Center* and *The Sealtest Variety Theater* were a year apart, the latter was virtually a literal extension of the former. Dorothy Lamour was remembered by director Glen-

hall Taylor as warm and unpretentious, saying, at the start, "I can't sing and I can't act; it's up to you guys to make me look good."

A notorious broadcast occurred on St. Patrick's Day, March 17, 1949, when an attempt was made to do a remote from the Shamrock Hotel in Houston. As Taylor recalled, reservations were oversold, and when the doors opened, some 1,600 people "were in near-mortal combat for the possession of 1,000 seats." The bedlam extended to the booth and became critical when guests began shortcutting across the soundstage. Again, from Taylor's recollection: "One hefty matron grabbed a microphone and, before I could intervene, announced, 'I don't give a goddamn about your broadcast—I want my dinner-table seat!' " In a moment of despair, an NBC engineer uttered the most-dreaded four-letter expletive, which was carried coast-to-coast before the show was cut off the air. A transcription survives at SPERDVAC, the radio historical society of Southern California.

THE SEALTEST VILLAGE STORE, musical variety; the hand-picked successor to *The Rudy Vallee Show*, the transition complete as of July 8, 1943.

BROADCAST HISTORY: July 8, 1943–Sept. 2, 1948, NBC. 30m, Thursdays at 9:30. Sealtest.

1943 CAST: Joan Davis as proprietress of the mythical "Sealtest Village Store." Jack Haley as her "helper" in the store. Sharon Douglas as Penelope (Penny) Cartwright, Davis's main rival for Haley's attentions. Shirley Mitchell and Verna Felton continuing in supporting roles from *The Rudy Vallee Show*, Felton playing a character named Blossom Blimp. **VOCALISTS:** Dave Street and the Fountainaires Quartet. **ORCHESTRA:** Eddie Paul. **DIRECTOR:** Robert L. Redd. **WRITERS:** Ray Singer and Dick Chevillat.

FROM CA. 1945. CAST: Jean Carroll, comedienne, as the store proprietor, replacing Joan Davis for the summer, 1945 (Davis moved on to her own series and never returned). Eve Arden as the "store manager" as of Sept. 27, 1945. Jack Haley as "proprietor." Jack Carson replacing Jack Haley as of Sept. 11, 1947; Eve Arden continuing as "manager." Dave Willock, longtime Carson friend and associate, as nephew Tugwell. **ANNOUNCER:** Hy Averback. **VOCALIST:** Bob Stanton, replacing

Dave Street, ca. 1946. **ORCHESTRA:** Frank De Vol.

The Sealtest Village Store was marked by transitions: the company that took over from Rudy Vallee in 1943 was not the same as the one that finished the show five years later, and Vallee himself had been reducing musical variety content in favor of situation comedy throughout his run. When Vallee went into the Coast Guard, Joan Davis was elevated to the lead. As proprietess of the "Village Store," she chased men and pined for a steady beau. She played a "forlorn, frustrated female, as utterly devoid of glamour and allure as a cold fried egg" (*Radio Life*), and played it well enough that the studio audience was often surprised when an attractive young actress stepped up to the microphone.

With Vallee's departure, Jack Haley was signed to carry what was viewed by the sponsor as an "essential" male lead, though critics thought Davis was strong enough to handle it herself. By mid-1945, Davis had demonstrated her comedic strength: she broke away for her own show. Haley also left, in July 1947 (it was said for a summer vacation, but he never returned). Eve Arden, who had replaced Davis, ran the "store" with the supporting cast until September, when new lead Jack Carson arrived. There were some good musical moments, notably a date with Louis Armstrong and Jack Teagarden, but the comedy paled. Arden and Carson departed July 8, 1948, each to a new series (she would open in less than two weeks in the solid comedy hit *Our Miss Brooks*). The final weeks of *The Village Store*, July 15–Sept. 2, 1948, were carried by Ilene Woods and maestro Ray Noble.

THE SEARS RADIO THEATER, dramatic anthology.

BROADCAST HISTORY: Feb. 5, 1979–Feb. 11, 1980, CBS. 60m, weeknights. Original shows until Aug. 3, 1979; repeats thereafter.

Feb. 14, 1980–Dec. 19, 1981, Mutual. 60m, weeknights. *The Mutual Radio Theater.*

HOSTS: Lorne Greene with "Western Night" on Mondays; Andy Griffith with "Comedy Night," Tuesdays; Vincent Price with "Mystery Night," Wednesdays; Cicely Tyson with "Love-and-Hate Night," straight drama, Thursdays; Richard Widmark with "Adventure Night," Fridays. **CAST:** Hollywood radio performers in original dramas:

John McIntire, Tyler McVey, Daws Butler, Mary Jane Croft, Elliott Reid, Elvia Allman, Doris Singleton, Byron Kane, Virginia Gregg, Barney Phillips, Lou Krugman, Hans Conried, Parley Baer, Eve Arden, John Dehner, Howard Duff, Lurene Tuttle, Marvin Miller, Jeanette Nolan, Vic Perrin, Herb Vigran, Peggy Webber, Jim Jordan, Shirley Mitchell, Rolfe Sedan, Frank Nelson, Sam Edwards, Janet Waldo, Ben Wright, Howard Culver, etc. **ANNOUNCER:** Art Gilmore. **MUSIC:** Original theme composed and conducted by Nelson Riddle. **PRODUCER-DIRECTORS:** Elliott Lewis, Fletcher Markle. **WRITERS:** Ted Sherdeman, Shirley Gordon, William Froug, Norman Macdonnell, Michael Raffetto, etc.

The Sears Radio Theater was another attempt to revive radio as a network entertainment medium in the wake of *The CBS Radio Mystery Theater*. It had a serious budget ("several million dollars," said a spokesman), the backing of the huge Sears Roebuck department store chain, and a commitment by CBS for a year of 60-minute nightly timeslots. Many notables from radio's "golden" era were involved. Norman Corwin and Arch Oboler produced, directed, and wrote plays. But it failed to generate sufficient listener support, and ended its year on CBS with rebroadcasts. Its subsequent run on Mutual, without a sponsor, was titled *The Mutual Radio Theater*. Despite the talent involved, it succeeded only in proving the sad fact that radio's day in the sun was over.

SECOND HONEYMOON, human interest.

BROADCAST HISTORY: 1947, WAAT, Newark. 30m, weekdays at 10:30 A.M.

Sept. 20, 1948–Nov. 11, 1949, ABC. 30m, weekdays at 4, later at 2:30.

Nov. 14, 1949–Jan. 16, 1950, Mutual. 30m, weekdays at 2.

HOST: Bert Parks (beginning in Newark).

Housewives told Parks why they'd like second honeymoons. The winners, chosen by panel vote, were sent on new honeymoons and given prizes.

SECOND HUSBAND, serial drama/soap opera.

BROADCAST HISTORY: April 14–July 28, 1937, NBC, Blue Network until June, then Red. 30m continuation, Wednesdays at 8:30.

Aug. 3, 1937–April 14, 1942, CBS. 30m continuation, Tuesdays at 7:30.

April 20–July 31, 1942, Blue Network. 15m continuation, weekdays at 11 A.M.

Aug. 3, 1942–April 26, 1946, CBS. 15m continuation, weekdays at 11:30 A.M. until 1943, then at 11:15 A.M. Sterling Drugs for Bayer Aspirin and Dr. Lyons Tooth Powder, 1937–46.

CAST: Helen Menken as Brenda Cummings, a young Montana woman who lost her husband, Richard Williams, in an auto accident, married rich and influential Grant Cummings, and then— against her second husband's staunch wishes— pursued a career as a glamorous film star. Joseph Curtin as husband Grant. Janice Gilbert and Charita Bauer as Brenda's daughter, little Fran; Tommy Donnelly and Jackie Grimes as Brenda's son, little Dick. Ralph Locke as Milton Brownspun, head of KDF Studios, where Brenda became a star. Carleton Young as Bill Cummings, Grant's younger brother, rambunctious and a "gambler at heart." Joy Hathaway as Irma Wallace, a jealous, conniving young actress who resented Brenda and tried to ruin her. Jay Jostyn as Ben Porter, Brenda's faithful old friend from Montana. ANNOUNCER: Andre Baruch. PRODUCERS: Frank and Anne Hummert. WRITERS: Nancy Moore, Elizabeth Todd, Helen Walpole, etc.

Second Husband took over a Blue Network timeslot formerly occupied by *The Ethel Barrymore Theater* under the subtitle *The Famous Actors Guild*. It continued the *Famous Actors* affiliation for a while, but in fact it was a soap opera. The heroine, Brenda Cummings, tried to reconcile husband and career, and had problems getting her children to accept Grant Cummings as their father. The storylines were typical Hummert fare: scheming, jealousy, and the inevitable "is Richard still alive" plot.

THE SECOND MRS. BURTON, soap opera.

BROADCAST HISTORY: Jan. 7, 1946–Nov. 25, 1960, CBS. 15m continuation, weekdays at 2. General Foods until 1954; Armour and Company, 1954–55; then multiple sponsorship. CAST: Claire Niesen, Sharon Douglas, Patsy Campbell, Teri Keane, and Jan Miner, variously, as Terry Burton, who lived with her husband Stan in the town of Dickson. Dwight Weist as Stan Burton. Evelyn Varden and Ethel Owen as Old Mother Burton, Terry's domineering and snobbish mother-

in-law. Alice Frost as Stan's sister, Marcia. Larry Robinson as young Brad Burton, son from Stan's first marriage. Dix Davis, Karl Weber, and Ben Cooper also as Brad. Kathleen Cordell and Joan Alexander as Marian Burton Sullivan, Stan's first wife. Bob Readick as Don Cornwell, Brad Burton's best friend. Rod Hendrickson as Cornelius Van Vliet, Stan's lawyer. ANNOUNCERS: Hugh James, Harry Clark, Warren Sweeney. PRODUCER-DIRECTOR: Ira Ashley; also, Viola Burns, Beverly Smith, Stuart Buchanan. WRITERS: Martha Alexander, 1946–47; John M. Young, 1947–52; Hector Chivigny, from ca. 1952; also Priscilla Kent, and, at the end, Johanna Johnston.

The Second Mrs. Burton marked the end of an era: the last soap opera of the air. It was developed from a 1942 CBS West Coast serial, *Second Wife*. The second wife searched for happiness in a small town somewhere in America. Terry and Stan Burton lived frugally, Stan having lost his Burton Department Store in a divorce from the first Mrs. Burton, the self-centered and devious Marian Burton-now-Sullivan. Terry's problems were compounded by a boorish mother-in-law. An adolescent stepson whose affections were sought by his real mother in underhanded ways further complicated things, but the Burtons largely avoided the tragedies so common to daytime radio.

It was a family show, with character dominant over plot. Stan's sister Marcia was part of the mix, marrying her boyfriend Lew over the vigorous objections of old Mother Burton. A "family counselor" segment was initiated in April 1947, a three- or four-minute feature heard every Wednesday, wherein a guest speaker was interviewed by Terry Burton on a problem then being experienced by her radio family. Among the guests were novelist Faith Baldwin (speaking on children of divorce) and financial consultant Sylvia Porter (on living within the family income). But that year also saw the departure of writer Martha Alexander, who disagreed with the sponsor's agency over the low-key storylines. For a time, according to Raymond William Stedman, it became a "formula serial," and when Hector Chevigny took over in 1952 he inherited an "amnesia sequence." Chevigny returned it to the family cycle, filling it with moments of light comedy.

SECRET CITY, detective serial.

BROADCAST HISTORY: Nov. 3, 1941–Sept. 25, 1942, Blue Network. 15m continuation, weekdays at 5:15. **CAST:** Bill Idelson as Detective Ben Clark. Jerry Spellman as his friend, mechanic Jeff Wilson. Chicago radio actors in support: Clarence Hartzell, Sidney Ellstrom, etc.

This was described by *Variety* as a juvenile serial, with Detective Clark initially trying to solve the doings of the Stranger in the long-vacant mansion.

SECRET MISSIONS, espionage melodrama.

BROADCAST HISTORY: July 18, 1948–Oct. 31, 1949, Mutual. 30m, Sundays at 10 until May 1949, then Mondays at 9:30. Based on the book of the same name by Rear Admiral Ellis M. Zacharias, who narrated. **CAST:** New York radio actors in anthology roles, among them Luis Van Rooten, Steffan Schnabel, Raymond Edward Johnson, Alice Yourman, Ivor Francis, Peter Capell, and Bernard Lenrow. **DIRECTOR:** Roger Bower. **WRITER:** Howard Merrill.

Ellis M. Zacharias had been wartime deputy chief of the Office of Naval Intelligence, on whose records his book and the radio show were based. The stories ranged from the home front (ONI agents tracking Japanese activity on the West Coast prior to the bombing of Pearl Harbor) to germ warfare (Nazi plans to infect Paris with plague as liberating armies arrived in 1944).

THE SEIBERLING SINGERS, vocal quartet.

BROADCAST HISTORY: 1927–29, NBC. 30m, Tuesdays at 8 until 1928, then Thursdays at 9. Seiberling Tires.

The Seiberling Singers was actually the Revelers under a commercial title. James Melton was billed—at least in the first year—only as "Seiberling's own tenor," and the Seiberling Orchestra was led by Frank Black. The music was lively and sentimental; the announcements sparse. The group specialized in evergreens: *Roll On, Mississippi, Roll On; Can't You Hear Me Callin', Caroline?; I Love You Truly*; and the like.

SETH PARKER, a mix of fiction, fact, and song.

BROADCAST HISTORY: March 3, 1929–Dec. 3, 1933, NBC. 30m, Sundays at 10:45. *Sundays at Seth Parker's.*

Dec. 5, 1933–March 27, 1934, NBC. 30m, Tuesdays at 10. *The Cruise of the Seth Parker.* Frigidaire.

June 30, 1935–March 22, 1936, Blue Network. 30m, Sundays at 10.

Sept. 25, 1938–March 19, 1939, Blue. 30m, Sundays at 7:30. Vicks.

CAST: Phillips H. Lord as Seth Parker, who headed a group of rustic New Englanders in spirited renderings of spirituals and between-hymns chatter. Effie Palmer as Mother Parker. Bennett Kilpack as Cephus Peters and as Laith Pettingal. Sophia Lord (wife of the star) as Lizzie Peters. Raymond Hunter as "the ferocious and lovable Captain Bang." Joy Hathaway and Erva Giles as Jane. **CREATOR-PRODUCER-DIRECTOR-WRITER:** Phillips H. Lord.

Seth Parker was the first major creation of producer Phillips H. Lord, begun as a weekly hymn-sing. It had a cast of regulars who became as friends to the radio audience: as the *Forum* described it, *Parker* was built around "the pleasant little conceit that they are all gathered every Sunday after supper in the rural New England home of an old gentleman, Seth Parker. These quaint creatures sing old-fashioned hymns with many dear and charming halts and interruptions while they josh each other in their very nice and restrained manner. They do their best to conjure up days of long ago, when applejack and bundling were in vogue."

Seth Parker's, according to the announcement that set it up each week, was "way up on the coast of Maine, in a little old-fashioned white farmhouse sitting high upon a hill and looking out over the Bay of Fundy. Tonight we find them already in the living room," began a typical show. "A fire blazing on the hearth takes off the chill of the evening air, and everything in the little sitting room spells peace and comfort." The songs were both religious and popular: Stephen Foster was mixed with pieces extolling the virtues of mother love. The vernacular was thick. "That was real purty," Ma Parker was apt to exclaim at the end of a song. The talk was all geared to paint a picture of life on the coast.

Lord claimed that his own grandfather was the model for Seth Parker. He played the role in white chin whiskers, though he was still in his mid-20s. He had created the show in Hartford, Conn., when a local station aired a similar sketch that failed to convince him. It was a story not uncommon in radio's early days: Lord called to complain, the programmer challenged him to do better, and he did. It became one of NBC's biggest early hits, lauded by ministers and loved throughout mid-America.

Despite its status as a sustainer (NBC did not want to "sell religion"), it made Lord a wealthy man. Its success led to a new Lord serial, *The Country Doctor* (June 20, 1932—March 15, 1933, Blue Network, 15m, at 8:45, three to five a week, Listerine), wherein he played a similarly wise oldster given to philosophy and rustic observation. More than 300 *Seth Parker* clubs had formed throughout the United States and Canada, to listen to the broadcasts and practice philanthropy. The show was an energetic dispenser of premium books—hymnals and scrapbooks—and by 1933 its fans numbered 15 to 20 million people.

But Lord had grown restless. He had purchased a four-masted 186-foot schooner, named it *The Seth Parker*, and announced an around-the-world cruise of two years duration. NBC made enthusiastic plans to go along, installing a $12,000 shortwave broadcasting set and putting an engineer among the crew. The schooner's original owner, Capt. C. Flink, was engaged to sail her, and Lord invited old friends and some of his radio cast to go along. The radio show would continue: "Ma Parker" would remain in Jonesport, "just as women have always waited when their men go down to the sea." The hymns would be sung, and once a week there would be a shortwave cutaway to the schooner for an update on the voyage. This was the plan, but in fact, the entire character of the program changed.

The new half-hour, *The Cruise of the Seth Parker*, was to be sponsored by Frigidaire, whose people saw it as a perfect tie-in. The schooner was filled with modern Frigidaire appliances, which the crew would discuss in the course of things. As the show unfolded, it took on more human interest. Lord told tales of the sea and of the ports he was visiting. One week he persuaded four lost seamen, thought dead by their families, to appear on the show, setting it up with personal telegrams to each family saying only that an event of deep personal significance

would take place on his Tuesday night air. Songs were done from the ship, and authentic sounds of ships' bells and sea winds were ever-present, courtesy of phonograph records.

The schooner sailed along the eastern United States in early 1934. Almost from the beginning the new show was dogged by rumor and bad luck. There were celebrated run-ins between Lord and British officials in the West Indies. Gossip magazines printed stories of wild parties, long drinking sessions, and open rebellion among the crew. The Seth Parker image suffered, and Frigidaire did not renew its contract. The show ended in March, but Lord, undaunted, set sail for Morocco, Cairo and points east. In February 1935, the *Seth Parker* was destroyed by a South Seas gale. Lord wired urgent SOS calls, which newspapers denounced as a publicity stunt. He returned to New York, declared himself a changed man, and made plans for his return to radio.

His new *Seth Parker* series (1935–36) attracted only a fraction of its original audience. A final run for Vicks (1938–39) also lagged in the ratings, but by then Lord was deep in a new phase of his career. His *Gang Busters* was well entrenched, establishing him as a producer of hard-hitting gangster shows.

THE SHADOW, crime melodrama.

BROADCAST HISTORY: July 31, 1930–July 23, 1931, CBS. 30m, Thursdays at 9:30. *The Detective Story Hour.* Street and Smith and its *Detective Story Magazine.* CAST: James La Curto as the Shadow, a mystery man who served only to narrate an anthology of crime stories. Frank Readick as the Shadow after La Curto's departure, a few weeks into the run, to do a Broadway play. DIRECTOR: Bill Sweets.

Sept. 6, 1931–June 5, 1932, CBS. 60m, Sundays at 5:30. *The Blue Coal Radio Revue.* Blue Coal. A variety show highlighted by a half-hour *Shadow* mystery narration. CAST: Frank Readick as the Shadow. ORCHESTRA: George Earle, said by the trade press to have played the lead briefly in 1932 (Anthony Tollin, writing in *The Shadow Scrapbook*, doubts this but allows that "he may have filled in for Readick on occasion").

Oct. 1, 1931–Sept. 22, 1932, CBS. 30m, Thursdays at 9:30. *The Love Story Hour.* Street and Smith. The Shadow narrated material from the

S&S *Love Story Magazine*. **CAST:** Frank Readick as the Shadow. Elsie Hitz and Ned Wever in anthology roles.

Jan. 5–Feb. 2, 1932, CBS. 30m, Tuesdays at 10. The first series to use *The Shadow* as its title. Perfect-o-Lite. **CAST:** Frank Readick as the Shadow, still a narrator only. **ORCHESTRA:** Eugene Ormandy.

Oct. 5, 1932–April 26, 1933, NBC. 30m, Wednesdays at 8, then at 8:30. Also: Oct. 1, 1934–March 27, 1935, CBS. 30m, Mondays and Wednesdays at 6:30. Both runs sponsored by Blue Coal. A watershed series, the end of the Shadow-as-narrator and the beginning of the character's active participation in the stories. **CAST:** Frank Readick as the Shadow; James La Curto in a few 1934 episodes.

Sept. 26, 1937–March 20, 1938, Mutual. 30m, Sundays at 5:30. Blue Coal. **CAST:** Orson Welles as Lamont Cranston, who in the Orient learned to cloud men's minds so that they could not see him, and is now known as the Shadow. Agnes Moorehead as his "friend and companion, the lovely Margo Lane." Ray Collins as Commissioner Weston. **PRODUCER:** Clark Andrews. **DIRECTORS:** Martin Gabel, Bourne Ruthrauff.

1938, transcribed 30m syndication for B. F. Goodrich, aired in summer months. **CAST:** Orson Welles and Margot Stevenson as Lamont and Margo.

Sept. 25, 1938–Dec. 26, 1954, Mutual, 30m, Sundays, with seasons that generally ran from Sept. to April; at 5:30 P.M. until 1945, then at 5. Blue Coal, 1938–49; Grove Laboratories, 1949–50; U.S. Air Force, early 1951; Wildroot Cream Oil, 1952–53; various sponsors, 1953–54. **CAST:** As Lamont Cranston, the Shadow: Bill Johnstone until March 21, 1943; Bret Morrison, 1943–44; John Archer, 1944–45; Steve Courtleigh, Sept.–Oct. 1945; Bret Morrison, Oct. 1945–Dec. 26, 1954. As Margo Lane: Agnes Moorehead, 1938–39; Marjorie Anderson, 1939–44; Judith Allen opposite John Archer, 1944–45; Laura Mae Carpenter opposite Steve Courtleigh, Sept.–Oct. 1945; Lesley Woods, 1945–46; Grace Matthews, 1946–49; Gertrude Warner, 1949–54. Alan Reed, Keenan Wynn, Everett Sloane, and Mandel Kramer as Shrevvy, the talkative cab driver. Dwight Weist, Kenny Delmar, Santos Ortega, Bernard Lenrow, Ted de Corsia, and Arthur Vinton as Police Commissioner Ralph Weston. Arthur Vinton in other roles requiring "clear and resonant voices" (*Radio Guide*, 1939). Everett Sloane in voices requiring the sound of youth ("whenever you hear a newsboy, or a weak young man who is led astray," said *Radio Guide*, it was probably Sloane).

CREATOR: Walter B. Gibson. **DIRECTORS:** Harry Ingram, Dana Noyes, Chick Vincent, Bob Steel, John W. Loveton, John Cole, Wilson Tuttle, etc. "John Barclay, Blue Coal's distinguished heating expert" for the show's most consistent sponsor (the Delaware, Lackawanna and Western Coal Company, which paid the bills until the coal market collapsed in 1949), was impersonated by Tim Frawley and Paul Huber. **WRITERS:** Edith Meiser, script editor. Harry Engman Charlot, Edward Hale Bierstadt, Jerry Devine, Sidney Slon, George Lowther, Peter Barry, Alonzo Deen Cole, Max Ehrlich, Robert Arthur and David Kogan, Stedman Coles, Frank Kane, Gail Ingram, Jerry McGill, Alfred Bester, Judith and David Bublick. **ANNOUNCERS:** Ken Roberts, 1931–32 and 1935–44; David Ross, 1931–32; Arthur Whiteside, ca. 1937–38. Don Hancock, 1944–47; Andre Baruch, 1947–49; Carl Caruso, 1949–51; Sandy Becker, 1951–53; Ted Mallie, 1953–54. **SOUND EFFECTS:** Al April, Barney Beck, Walt Gustafson, Al Schaffer, Fritz Street. **ORGANISTS:** Elsie Thompson, Rosa Rio, Charles Paul. **THEME:** *Omphale's Spinning Wheel*, by Saint-Saëns, played spookily on organ.

The story of *The Shadow*, perhaps radio's most famous fictitious crimefighter, has been thoroughly documented by its creator, Walter B. Gibson, and radio historian Anthony Tollin in *The Shadow Scrapbook*. It was the epitome of radio crime drama. Today it remains one of the three or four shows cited by people as a synonym for "oldtime radio." The medium is routinely defined as "*The Shadow, Fibber McGee*, and *The Lone Ranger*." Sometimes *Inner Sanctum* or some other famous title is plugged into the mix, but *The Shadow* is a given. It makes everybody's list.

The character combined the strongest elements of rank melodrama and delivered them as truth. There may not have been a believable story in the entire 25-year run, but *The Shadow* thrived, claiming at various times audiences of more than 15 million a week. It opened a new era of pulp magazine superheroes, its print format harkening back to the days of the dime novel.

Its fans would never forget the signatures or the premise. The spooky organ theme, the eerie laugh, the electric voice: *Who knows . . . what evil . . . lllllurks . . . in the hearts of men? . . . The Shadow knows!* A Blue Coal commercial was followed by exposition. "The Shadow, Lamont Cranston, a man of wealth, a student of science, and a master of other people's minds, devotes his life to righting wrongs, protecting the innocent, and punishing the guilty. Using advanced methods that may ultimately become available to all law enforcement agencies, Cranston is known to the underworld as the Shadow—never seen, only heard, as haunting to superstitious minds as a ghost, as inevitable as a guilty conscience. . . ."

Cranston had learned "the hypnotic power to cloud men's minds so that they cannot see him." He had been taught this by a yogi priest in India, as he explained in one episode. Cranston's "friend and companion, the lovely Margo Lane, is the only person who knows to whom the voice of the invisible Shadow belongs." Together, Lamont and Margo confronted the maddest assortment of lunatics, sadists, ghosts, and werewolves ever heard on the air. Evil doctors holding lovely ladies for experiments too terrible to comprehend were standard fare: in one show, a madman intends to replace the woman's brain with that of a gorilla; in another, an evil genius captures Margo Lane and tries to replace her vocal cords with those of a dog. There were villains who wanted to poison the city's water; there were killers in opera houses and wax museums. The titles gave ample description of content: *The Laughing Corpse, Death Rides a Broomstick*, and *They Kill with a Silver Hatchet* are a few.

As creator Gibson tells it, the character evolved almost by accident. In 1930, Street and Smith—prolific producers of pulp fiction magazines—decided to try the new medium, radio, in an effort to boost circulation. Once a week a drama would be adapted from an upcoming issue of *Detective Story*. Adapter Harry Engman Charlot added the gimmick of the mysterious host, called him the Shadow, and left the link to the magazine somewhat tenuous. "Apparently," wrote Gibson in his *Shadow Scrapbook*, "some listeners didn't get this message clearly, because instead of asking about *Detective Story Magazine*, they wanted the magazine that told about the Shadow." The answer was obvious—a new magazine, with the Shadow as its nucleus.

Gibson, then a hustling freelancer whose acquaintances included magicians Houdini and Blackstone, was called in to help develop the character and get the new publication off the ground.

Readers and listeners were solicited for input. A contest, announced in *Detective Story* and promoted on the air, offered $500 cash rewards for best descriptions of the elusive host. Slender clues were given on *The Detective Story Hour* as to his appearance, habits, and tastes. The contest ran through February and March 1931, with judging by pulp writer Edgar Wallace, a New York policeman, a private detective, and others. The winner, John G. Porter, described his Shadow as "just over 40 . . . tall and strikingly slender, with slim hands and small, narrow feet, yet possessing a giant's strength . . . a tattooed cobra on his chest . . . college graduate . . . accomplished linguist"—in other words, a combination of brains and brawn.

Beginning with the first issue of *The Shadow Magazine* (April 1931), Gibson stepped onto a relentless treadmill, writing a full novel for each issue. Working under the pseudonym Maxwell Grant, he became one of the busiest practitioners of the pulp era. By 1932, buoyed by success, the magazine had become bimonthly, and Gibson was writing a novel every two weeks. Ultimately, he would do more than 280 *Shadow* books.

It was Gibson who gave the Shadow his everyday name, Lamont Cranston. Nothing was said in those early days about invisibility: Cranston was known as the Shadow because of his elusive capabilities, coupled with his habit of stepping out of the shadows to capture a culprit. Also conspicuous by her absence was Margo Lane, strictly a radio creation and still several years away. But even then the character captured the imagination: on radio, and especially in the pulps, the Shadow thrived. That chilling laugh was audio magic.

But for the first five sporadic seasons the character remained outside the stories, as a narrator of a general crime anthology. As early as 1931 Street and Smith wanted the radio Shadow to follow the pulps and take an active role in the plays. The new sponsor, Blue Coal, resisted this. In 1937, the sponsor's representatives agreed to let the Shadow become the hero on a trial basis. Margo Lane was created for romantic interest, and most of Cranston's magazine cohorts fell by the wayside. The regular supporting characters on radio were Shrevvy, the talkative cab driver, and Police Commissioner Weston. Shrevvy (often spelled Shrevie in printed accounts but Shrevvy by Gibson) was the standard comic relief: usually to be found on the perimeter of a story, squiring Lamont and Margo to some new adventure at death's doorstep and chattering inanely. Commissioner Weston was (especially in the early years) a vain and bullheaded man who refused to take even the simplest advice but was quick to accept the glory after the Shadow had wrapped up his case for him.

Margo was simply Lamont's best friend: their relationship deepened gradually from Lamont-Margo to darling-darling, though to all appearances they had a thoroughly asexual friendship. Sex was never seen, never heard, as haunting to practical minds as a ghost, as elusive as a guilty conscience. They shared extraordinary and unchaperoned adventures and somehow managed to escape the wrath of the "right-thinking people" who had threatened stations' licenses with protests over the harmless "Adam and Eve" skit on Edgar Bergen's *Chase and Sanborn Hour*.

Orson Welles, Bill Johnstone, and Bret Morrison were the best-known voices of the Shadow. Welles was a 22-year-old unknown, a regular toiling in anonymity on *The March of Time*, when he won the role in audition. His salary, $185 a week, seemed a fortune for a half-hour weekly job that required no rehearsal. His agreement with Blue Coal allowed him to go on without as much as a prior peek at his script: thus, as he told film director Peter Bogdanovich, when he was thrown into a snake pit, he didn't know how he'd get out till the show ended. He was the first Shadow to be freed of omniscient narration, and the results were dramatic. A "blizzard" of fan mail deluged the network, according to Welles biographer Frank Brady; *Shadow* fan clubs sprang up around the country, and "Orson would occasionally appear at stores and social functions, swathed in black hat, cape, and mask, for special promotions." But his laugh was then considered wrong for the role, and throughout the Welles era recordings from the earlier Frank Readick series were used for the signatures.

Blue Coal carried the show across two decades. A subsequent split sponsorship had Balm

Barr carrying the show in the South, Carey Salt in the Midwest, and the United States Air Force in the far West. Through it all the Shadow remained a cruel and unforgiving dispenser of justice. From the guilty he obtained confessions using intimidation and torture: then he cackled that electric laugh as the hapless killer was carted away to the death house. His closing line, like the opener, was memorable: *The weed of crime bears bitter fruit . . . crime does NOT pay! . . . The Shadow knows!*

It is difficult to overstate the impact that this program had on children of the 1940s. This writer vividly remembers an episode when the Shadow tracked down a murdering scarecrow. When the killer's coat was ripped off, revealing nothing but straw, the implications were so terrifying that the young writer-to-be could not sleep in an unlighted room for weeks. Today it's the highest of all high camp, scaring neither the aging collector nor his jaded children.

SHAFTER PARKER AND HIS CIRCUS, juvenile adventure serial.

BROADCAST HISTORY: 1939–40, Don Lee Network, West Coast only. 1941, Mutual, brief national hookup. **CAST:** Hal Berger as Gen. Shafter Parker, owner of a circus who, with his sister Dolly, braved the wilds of Africa to get animals for his show. Dale Nash (Mrs. Berger) as Dolly. **CREATOR-WRITER:** Hal Berger.

This grew out of an earlier show, *The In-Laws*, heard locally in Los Angeles. Hal Berger, a baseball announcer in season and one of radio's earliest sportscasters, created the title character in 1930. He played the lead when an actor failed to appear, and kept playing it through various incarnations of *The In-Laws* in the 1930s. By 1939 it was titled *The Adventures of General Shafter Parker and His Circus*. Though a thriller, violence was downplayed, and no character was ever killed on the show. Berger wrote a balance between circus and safari life and kept the comedy element high.

SHELL CHATEAU, a major variety hour; created for and covered at AL JOLSON.

BROADCAST HISTORY: April 6, 1935–June 26, 1937, NBC. 60m, Saturdays at 9:30. Shell Oil. **STARS:** Al Jolson with the Victor Young Orchestra until March 28, 1936; Wallace Beery (a frequent fill-in host) and Smith Ballew continuing the series after Jolson's departure; comedian Joe Cook the headliner at Ballew's departure, from Jan. 2, 1937.

THE SHERIFF, western drama; outgrowth of *Death Valley Days*.

BROADCAST HISTORY: Aug. 10, 1944–June 21, 1945, CBS. 30m, Thursdays at 8:30. *Death Valley Sheriff*. Pacific Borax.
  June 29, 1945–Sept. 14, 1951, ABC. 30m, Fridays at 9:30. *The Sheriff*. Borax until March 1951; Procter & Gamble, March–June 1951; then American Chicle.
CAST: Robert Haag as Sheriff Mark Chase, a progressive-minded lawman in the modern era. Don Briggs and Bob Warren also as Mark Chase. Olyn Landick as Cassandra Drinkwater, the sheriff's cousin and housekeeper. William Podmore as Professor Barnabas Thackery, a retired psychologist who assisted the sheriff in his cases. Helen Claire as Thackery's beautiful daughter, Jan. ANNOUNCER: John Reed King (original). MUSIC: Joseph Bonime (original series). DIRECTORS: Walter Scanlan, Florence Ortman, John Wilkinson. WRITERS: Ruth Cornwall Woodman, originator of *Death Valley Days*; later, Dr. Milton Lieberthal (said to be well-rooted in psychology).

This western series retained some of the trappings of its long-running parent show, *Death Valley Days*, notably the "morning bugle call" that had always been its opening. But though formerly an anthology, it now focused on Sheriff Mark Chase, "energetic ex-soldier about 38 years of age, who has currently returned from two years of fighting Japs in the Pacific." Chase was a bachelor who took his job seriously and had an eye on a possible political career. His household was run by "Cousin Cassie," a "humorous but simple lady whose heart is in the right place but whose tongue is just about everywhere." Cassie opened each broadcast with a telephone monologue: though her first love was spreading gossip, her sworn duty was protecting Sheriff Chase from the advances of amorous females.

Chase had all the modern crimefighting tools at his fingertips. Gone were pursuits on horseback: Chase patrolled the territory in a new car. Violence was out: Chase was a student of

psychology who seldom carried a gun. He was a law school graduate with a private fortune, left to him by an uncle. He used the money to help rehabilitate criminals, especially juvenile delinquents.

In a rather odd bit of casting, Cousin Cassie was played by Olyn Landick, a man who had been entertaining as a female impersonator since his days in the Navy during World War I.

SHERLOCK HOLMES, mystery-detective drama.

BROADCAST HISTORY: Oct. 20, 1930–May 26, 1935, NBC. 30m, Red Network, Mondays at 10 until the summer break in June 1931; Blue Network, Wednesdays at 9, and Red, Thursdays at 9:30, concurrent in 1931–32; Blue continuing Wednesdays at 9, 1932–33; Blue, Sundays at 4, Nov.–Dec. 1934, then Sundays at 9:45. George Washington Coffee. CAST: William Gillette as Sherlock Holmes in the opening story, *The Adventure of the Speckled Band*. Clive Brook as Holmes, 1930–31. Richard Gordon as Holmes, 1931–33. Louis Hector as Holmes, 1934–35. Leigh Lovel as Dr. Watson, 1930–35. Louis Hector also, periodically through the 1930s, as Moriarty, supervillain and Holmes's archenemy.
  Feb. 1–Sept. 26, 1936, Mutual 30m, Saturdays at 10:30 until April, then at 7:30. Household Finance. CAST: Richard Gordon as Holmes. Harry West (replacing the deceased Leigh Lovel) as Watson.
  Oct. 1–Dec. 24, 1936, NBC. 30m, Thursdays at 11:15. Household Finance. CAST: Gordon, West.
  Oct. 2, 1939–May 27, 1946, various networks. The most celebrated of all *Sherlock Holmes* offerings. CAST: Basil Rathbone as Holmes. Nigel Bruce as Watson. Pushed by the success of Rathbone and Bruce in the film series begun with *The Hound of the Baskervilles*, it ran seven seasons (with some summers off) in the following 30m timeslots: 1939–40, Blue Network, Mondays at 8:30, Bromo Quinine; 1940–41, Blue, Sundays at 8:30, Bromo Quinine; 1941–42, NBC, Sundays at 10:30, Bromo Quinine; 1943 (April–Oct.), Mutual, Fridays at 8:30, Petri Wines; 1943–46, Mutual, Mondays at 8:30, Petri Wines.
  Oct. 12, 1946–July 7, 1947, ABC. 30m, Saturdays at 9:30 until mid-Jan., then Mondays at 8:30. Semler Company. CAST: Tom Conway as Holmes. Nigel Bruce as Watson.
  Sept. 28, 1947–June 6, 1949, Mutual. 30m, Sun-

days at 7 until Jan. 1949, then Mondays at 8:30. Clipper Craft. CAST: John Stanley as Holmes. Alfred Shirley as Watson, 1947–48; Ian Martin as Watson, 1948–49.

Sept. 21, 1949–June 14, 1950, ABC. 30m, Wednesdays at 8:30 until late Jan., then at 9. Petri Wines. CAST: Ben Wright as Holmes. Eric Snowden as Watson.

Jan. 2–June 5, 1955, NBC. 30m, Sundays at 9. Also, May 1–Sept. 4, 1956, ABC. 30m, Tuesdays at 7:30. Both taken from a BBC transcribed series aired in England in 1954. CAST: John Gielgud as Holmes. Ralph Richardson as Watson. Orson Welles as Moriarty.

CREATOR: Arthur Conan Doyle, in turn-of-the-century fiction. PRODUCERS: Edna Best, etc. DIRECTORS: Joseph Bell, early 1930s; Basil Loughrane; Glenhall Taylor, mid-1940s; Tom McKnight; Glan Heisch. WRITERS-ADAPTERS: Edith Meiser, ca. 1930–1940s; Leslie Charteris, 1940s; Denis Green and Anthony Boucher, ca. 1946 and late 1940s; Max Ehrlich, Howard Merrill, and Leonard Lee, in later runs. ANNOUNCERS: Joseph Bell, Knox Manning, Owen Babbe, Herb Allen, Harry Bartell, Cy Harrice.

Sherlock Holmes, the remarkable hero of the Conan Doyle novels and stories was well suited to radio, and few characters enjoyed greater exposure at the hands of more actors. Almost everyone, it seemed, wanted a fling at *Holmes*, and many got the chance.

The idea of a *Sherlock Holmes* of the air seemed natural to Edith Meiser, but she was admittedly biased. She had loved the deductive genius from the time she was 11, when he had rescued her from boredom on a long sea voyage. Subsequently, Meiser had become an actress, a vaudevillian, and a confirmed *Holmes* addict. So certain was she of the character's radio potential that she wrote two scripts, complete with sound effects, from the master's "canon." Her initial approach to NBC was encouraging: a programmer liked her material but passed for lack of a sponsor. Meiser then began working the agencies. When she had her sponsor, the scheduling was easy.

It opened a new career for Meiser, who would write the series singlehandedly for a dozen years and with help through much of the 1940s. In the early scripts especially, she followed the Conan Doyle canon, beginning with the short stories.

The Speckled Band, A Scandal in Bohemia, The Red-Headed League, The Copper Beeches, and *The Bascombe Valley Mystery* were, in order, the first five shows. She dramatized *A Study in Scarlet* in four parts beginning Nov. 18, 1931; *The Hound of the Baskervilles* in six parts, Jan. 27, 1932; *The Sign of the Four* in six chapters beginning Oct. 26, 1932. When the series outlived original material, she created new stories, but used some character or incident in the canon as her jump-off point. So successful was she at capturing the color of the written word that she drew warm praise from Conan Doyle's widow and son. Denis Conan Doyle, watching from the sponsor's booth as Basil Rathbone and Nigel Bruce became his father's characters in a 1941 radio play, pronounced it "admirable, absolutely admirable."

The format was set at the beginning. The stories were told in retrospect by Dr. Watson, the detective's friend and assistant, coaxed out of him by a weekly visitor and lovingly etched by the perspective of time. Director Joseph Bell was the visitor in the early 1930s, invited into the study where there was always a "blazing fire and a cup of G. Washington Coffee brewing." Watson joined Bell in plugging the product, the alleged aroma eliciting zesty "aaaahhhhs" and Watson's challenge to "try and find a better cup of coffee anywhere." The stories were nicely mysterious: atmosphere was a prime ingredient. "You can almost see the fog swirling and eerie as it blankets Baker Street," wrote one critic much later in the run. This might have been written at any time. The effect was melodrama of the highest order, with the music likewise concocted to contribute. "The music is utterly frenetic," wrote a *Radio Life* reporter in 1941: maestro Lou Kosloff gave it a "turgid, deathly ghastliness." The stories relied on detail, Holmes reconstructing entire scenarios with tiny clues and scraps of evidence, his mind leaping ahead of Watson's to the latter's neverending wonder. "Simply amazing, Holmes!" Watson would exclaim, to which Holmes with quiet mirth would reply, "Elementary, Watson, elementary."

No audiences were allowed during the early broadcasts. A crowd, said *Radio Guide*, "might destroy the mad eeriness, which the cast is able to intensify in a closed broadcast room." As in the films, Watson was something of a disappointment on radio. In the mass media, Watson never achieved the intent of his creator—a man of high intellect whose brain seemed small only by comparison with Holmes's. The significance of the fragmentary clues pieced together instantly by Holmes was lost on Watson (who came off, in the end, as something of a boob on the air), and thus on the listener as well. When listeners complained that the clues were often too obscure, little could be done without reducing Holmes to the level of ordinary radio detectives and destroying him.

William Gillette, who played the lead for the first episode, was the most famous Holmes of his time. He toured with his *Holmes* stage play and also did the character on *The Lux Radio Theater*, Nov. 18, 1935. The series peaked in the ratings around 1933, when Richard Gordon was playing Holmes. The Basil Rathbone run was propelled by a continuous flow of films, 16 during the seven years that Rathbone and Nigel Bruce worked the show. Ratings were lukewarm (despite this series' continuing fame in radio's afterlife), perhaps because of the emphasis on intellect over romance. This to Rathbone was its greatest attraction, that Holmes could be so absorbed in the game of wits with a brilliant killer. It was "very proper," Rathbone asserted, that with one notable exception Holmes "never associated with women, showed no interest in them—such was his intensity on the work at hand." But faithful listeners might have been amazed, at a glimpse behind the microphone, to find in Rathbone and Bruce two ribald cutups, "delightfully humorous and frightfully unpredictable" as remembered by director Glenhall Taylor. One of Taylor's most vivid recollections was of the stars pelting the director's booth with sweet rolls, coating the glass with dripping sugar.

By mid-1946, Rathbone felt he had exhausted the character as a radio entity. Curiously, he went almost immediately into a Mutual soundalike. But as Inspector Burke of *Scotland Yard* he was far less deductive and lost the advantage of the magical name. Actor Tom Conway seemed a good replacement—he was at ease with the British accent, having played Bulldog Drummond and the Falcon in the movies—but his performance failed to excite. In some quarters the writers were blamed: they were now writing for Nigel Bruce as the ranking star, and Watson's role had expanded to intrude upon

Holmes. By the fall of 1947 both were gone, leaving the roles to John Stanley and Alfred Shirley. The tinkering continued through 1950, with Ben Wright and Eric Snowden. These were all fine talents, but few listeners would remember the shows beyond their initial impact. Even today the essence of *Sherlock Holmes* is found in that middle period. There, an aghast Nigel Bruce is forever warning an unconcerned Basil Rathbone, "Good Godfrey, Holmes, you're walking to your death!"

SHORTY BELL, drama, based on stories by Frederick Hazlitt Brennan.

BROADCAST HISTORY: March 28–June 27, 1948, CBS. 30m, Sundays at 9:30 until May, then at 10. **CAST:** Mickey Rooney as Shorty Bell, brash, combative young "circulation hustler" for a city newspaper, whose big goal in life was to be a reporter. John Hoyt as hard-boiled managing editor Don Robard. Florence Halop as Irene Brown, a waitress in Fred's Grill and a friend of Shorty's. Bert Holland as Shorty's pal Emmett, a parolee with a nose for trouble. Carol Williams as Lois, Emmett's sister. **MUSIC:** Cy Feuer. **DIRECTOR:** William N. Robson. **WRITERS:** Richard Carroll and Milton Geiger.

Shorty Bell was a high-powered newspaper adventure show, whose hero managed to be cocky, loud, and admirable. Shorty's real name was Ralph J. Bell, "but down on the streets where I grew up, a moniker like that ain't got a chance." His "old man" had been a linotype operator for the *News*, infusing in Shorty a flaming desire to become a reporter. But so far, as the series opened, all Shorty could get was a job "drivin' a truck that delivers the bundles hot off the presses."

Each episode, though self-contained, had enough continuing threads to ensure listener interest from week to week. The problem was, *Shorty* never captured much interest at the outset. It was championed by *Time* and *Radio Life*, but CBS gave it a scant three months. The storyline involved Shorty's attempt to free his pal Emmett from involvement in a gangland murder, to get the true story and thus prove his "nose for news," and to overcome his biggest obstacle— a fiery temper that made him his own worst enemy. Sensitive about his lack of education and willing to do battle over any insult ("never swing at a man's head, Emmett—push yer left into his face just to bring his hands up, then whack'm in the belly''), Shorty emerged in his brief run as one of the most memorable characters of 1948.

Unlike some Hollywood screen stars, Mickey Rooney was a superior radio talent, giving his role exactly the "stark realism" that director William N. Robson wanted. Even his few fluffs sound real. But the writing was on the wall, and after June 27, *Shorty* was replaced by a talent show, *Hollywood Showcase*, with Rooney as performing emcee.

SHOW BOAT, musical variety; also known as *The Maxwell House Show Boat*.

BROADCAST HISTORY: Oct. 6, 1932–Oct. 28, 1937, NBC. 60m, Thursdays at 9. Maxwell House Coffee. **ORIGINAL PRINCIPAL CAST:** Charles Winninger as Captain Henry, genial and robust skipper and host. Tenor Lanny Ross, singing star, and his singing sweetheart, "Mary Lou," sung by Muriel Wilson. Allyn Joslyn and Rosaline Greene as the speaking voices of Lanny Ross and "Mary Lou." **ALSO, CA. 1932: CAST:** Soprano Mabel Jackson, Jules Bledsoe, singer Annette Hanshaw, the Hall Johnson Choir, Pick Malone and Pat Padgett as blackface comics "Molasses and January." Irene Hubbard as Maria, Captain Henry's sister and Mary Lou's chaperone. Wright Kramer as Maria's husband, Walter Jamison. **AN-NOUNCER:** Tiny Ruffner. **ORCHESTRA:** Don Voorhees. **WRITER-DIRECTOR:** William A. Bacher. **CA. 1934: CAST ADDITIONS:** Mark Smith as Uria Calwalder. Conrad Thibault, baritone, who became the main rival to Lanny Ross for the attentions of Mary Lou. Ned Wever in Thibault's spoken lines, until both Thibault and Ross began handling their own. Rosaline Greene reading for Muriel Wilson and then for Lois Bennett, who sang as Mary Lou briefly in 1934. Also: Jean Sothern. **CA. 1935: CAST:** Frank McIntyre, as Captain Henry. Ross, Wilson, Hubbard, and Thibault, with Molasses and January (the "two Dixie rascals" who had burnished their faces with charcoal) and the *Show Boat* Four (a singing quartet: Scrappy Lambert, Randolph Weyant, Leonard Stokes, and Robert Moody). Also: Helen Oelheim. **ANNOUNCER:** Tiny Ruffner. **ORCHESTRA:** Gus Haenschen. **PRODUCER:** Tom Revere of Benton and Bowles. **DIRECTOR:** Kenneth

MacGregor. **WRITER:** Bernard Dougall. **CA. 1936: CAST ADDITIONS:** Winifred Cecil, now lead prima donna. Also: Lucy Monroe; singer Ross Graham; pianist Victor Arden; Louise Massey and the Westerners (Dot and Allen Massey, Larry Wellington, and Milt Mabie) with country ballads; Tommy Donnelly; blues singer Honey Dean. Adele Ronson as leading lady in speaking dramas with Lanny Ross. **ORCHESTRA:** Al Goodman. **BEGINNING JULY 8, 1937: CAST:** Charles Winninger returning as Captain Henry; baritone Thomas L. Thomas, lead male singer, replacing Lanny Ross; soprano Nadine Conner; blues singer Virginia Verrill; comic Jack Haley with stooge Patricia Wilder ("Honey Chile" from Bob Hope's earliest radio days); Alma Kruger with speaking roles; Hattie McDaniel in a "mammy" characterization. **ANNOUNCER:** Warren Hull. **MUSIC:** Meredith Willson, with a large "Maxwell House orchestra." **CHOIR:** Max Terr.

May 3, 1940–April 21, 1941, NBC. 30m, Blue Network, Fridays at 9 until Aug., then Red Network, Mondays at 9:30. Brown and Williamson Tobacco. **CAST:** Carlton Brickert as Captain Barney, with Marlin Hurt as Beulah, and singers Dick Todd and Virginia Verrill.

Show Boat was one of the giant hits of early network radio musical variety. It had glamour and color and leaped almost immediately to Crossley ratings in the mid-30s, within a year surpassing even Rudy Vallee's *Fleischmann Hour*. Its January 1934 rating of 45.9 was topped only by Eddie Cantor.

It was a pure radio fantasy of music and sound effects, concocted in the vast NBC Studio 8-H at Radio City, New York. First came the noises of an excited crowd; then the blare of a steamboat whistle, the playing of a calliope, and the swish of a paddle wheel. A vocal ensemble brought up the theme—"Here comes the show boat, here comes the show boat, puff-puff-puff-puff-puff-puffing a-long!"—and the carnival atmosphere was punctuated by announcer Tiny Ruffner describing the mooring of the riverboat. Captain Henry, skipper and host, then took over the microphone, welcoming his listeners as well as the imaginary crowds on the "docks" with a hearty "Howdy, folks, howdy!" The show gave an illusion of perpetual movement, allegedly visiting cities and towns up and down the Mississippi, and eventually broadening its base to include locations along the Atlantic seaboard. Greetings would be read from real-life mayors of these honor cities, with actors taking the roles and trying to impersonate the mayors' speech mannerisms. And though it was all audio illusion (the paddle wheels were produced in a washtub), it was one of the earliest shows to involve the radio audience on such an exciting excursion. For the first three years it reaped huge rewards.

It was conceived by an agency executive and sold to Maxwell House as a package. The idea derived from the 1927 Jerome Kern musical hit of the same name. William A. Bacher, the first director, sought out a lifelong trouper named Charles Winninger for advice. Winninger had worked on a real show boat, Captain Adams's *Blossom Time*, which had sailed the Mississippi at the turn of the century; later, Winninger had played the central role of Captain Andy in the Ziegfeld stage show. "Most people have the wrong idea about a show boat," he told *Radioland* in 1934. "It's just a theater built on a scow. A steamboat hooks on behind with a paddle wheel and acts as the pilot boat. The captain of the show boat in reality knows very little about navigation. He is simply the manager of the theatrical troupe."

Captain Henry's troupe would include a stable of singers, some of whom were launched into major careers by the show. The rags-to-riches stars were Lanny Ross and Muriel Wilson. By the end of the first year, Ross was the sensation of Radio Row, propelled into front ranks by his boyish good looks (as radio fans could see on every heartthrob magazine) and his clear tenor voice. Murial Wilson as Mary Lou was the sweet young singer with whom Ross shared so many memorable duets, as well as the fictional backstage romance. Each week, Wilson and Ross sang their love scenes, with the audience unaware that radio actors were used for the speaking roles. It was a combination variety show and minstrel act, with such headliners as Bob Hope and Jessica Dragonette brought in as guests. The fare ranged from classical to blues to popular songs, and in each broadcast was another chapter in the backstage *Show Boat* love story. By 1934, regular Annette Hanshaw had become one of the most popular vocalists in radio. According to *Radio Stars*, she spoke "shyly for herself" on the air.

So realistic was the *Show Boat* illusion that crowds would sometimes gather on the docks of cities where the "boat" was scheduled to "visit." Seventy-three people were involved in the production when a *Radio Guide* reporter visited in 1935. Even the audience was utilized: signaled to applaud by Tiny Ruffner (at six-seven the tallest announcer in radio) and to stop when he gave them the cutoff motion.

But the loss of Charles Winninger in 1935 had an immediate effect on the show's popularity, a plunge of almost 15 points. Winninger had had backstage disputes and clashes of personality with producers, though ostensibly he left to move to the West Coast. The parade of guest stars continued—Ruth Etting, George Jessel, and Amelia Earhart, who on March 4, 1937, discussed her upcoming and ill-fated world flight. But it was no longer a happy show. Frank McIntyre was criticized for the different approach he brought to the role of Captain Henry: Lanny Ross was made master of ceremonies, putting him in the uncomfortable position of announcing his own musical numbers. And three-quarters of the audience had gone elsewhere.

In a final attempt to save the show, it was decided to move to California and coax Winninger back into the lead. This was a wicked trade-off, for it meant saying goodbye to Lanny Ross, who could not be expected (as one reporter put it) to retreat to his supporting role after attaining top billing. The new *Show Boat* opened from Hollywood July 8, 1937, with Winninger flanked by a new cast. But it never regained the old momentum, and it passed from the scene in October, less than four months later.

Maxwell House moved its money to an even more elaborate variety hour, *Good News of 1938*, which floundered in misdirection and only continued the confusion over what the sponsor wanted to do with its Thursday night NBC slot. After two years on the shelf, the *Show Boat* formula was picked up by *Avalon Time*, another series in search of a nucleus, and a thin version ran on NBC for Brown and Williamson in 1940–41. This was *Show Boat* in name only.

THE SIGNAL CARNIVAL, comedy; an important forum for developing and established radio performers.

BROADCAST HISTORY: Ca. 1936–41, NBC West Coast 30m, various days. Signal Oil. **1941 CAST:** Jack Carson, master of ceremonies. Barbara Jo Allen as Vera Vague. Harold Peary as Smagooznok. Also: Dave Willock; singer Kay St. Germain. **AN-NOUNCER:** Johnny Frazer. **ORCHESTRA:** Meredith Willson, Gordon Jenkins. **DIRECTOR:** Paul Conlan.

THE SILENT MEN, dramatic intrigue.

BROADCAST HISTORY: Oct. 14, 1951–May 28, 1952, NBC. 30m, Sundays at 5:30 until mid-March, then Wednesdays at 10. Transcribed in Hollywood. **CAST:** Douglas Fairbanks Jr. in anthology roles, as a different federal agent each week. William Conrad as Fairbanks's boss, "the chief." Herb Butterfield also as "the chief." Hollywood radio players in support: Virginia Gregg, Raymond Burr, Lou Merrill, Lurene Tuttle, Paul Frees, John Dehner, etc. **ANNOUNCER:** Don Stanley. **PRODUCER-DIRECTOR:** Warren Lewis. **WRITERS:** Joel Murcott, etc.

This flashy if predictable series told of "the special agents of all branches of our federal government, who daily risk their lives to protect the lives of all of us . . . to guard our welfare and our liberties, they must remain nameless—*The Silent Men*!" Star Douglas Fairbanks Jr. played various agents from the Department of Commerce, the Postal Service, Immigration, and various governmental brotherhoods that weren't named.

THE SILVER EAGLE, juvenile adventure.

BROADCAST HISTORY: July 5, 1951–March 10, 1955, ABC. 30m, Thursdays at 7:30; later Tuesdays as well. General Mills. **CAST:** Jim Ameche as Jim West, the famed "Silver Eagle" of the Northwest Mounted Police, whose eagle-feather arrow was his trademark. Jack Lester as his sidekick, the giant Joe Bideaux. Michael Romano also as Joe Bideaux. John Barclay and Jess Pugh as Inspector Argyle. Clarence Hartzell as Doc. **AN-NOUNCERS:** Bill O'Connor, Ed Prentiss, Ed Cooper, Ken Nordine, etc. **PRODUCER:** James Jewell. **THEME:** *Winged Messenger*.

The Silver Eagle is generally considered the last of the significant juvenile radio adventures. It was cast in the image of Sergeant Preston of *Challenge of the Yukon* (producer James Jewell worked with *Challenge* owner George W. Trendle during the formative years of that classic show), and its theme enclosed a typically shrill "wild northwest" opening:

A cry of the wild!

A trail of danger!
A scarlet rider of the Northwest Mounted, serving justice with the swiftness of an arrow!
THE SILVER EAGLE!

Like Sergeant Preston, Mountie Jim West was a ruthless tracker of criminals and lawbreakers. Widely known for never giving up on a case, he was aided by a mammoth sidekick, Joe Bideaux. To a vivid 10-year-old mind, Joe Bideaux was an unwashed superman, a towering Canadian of French ancestry who could batter down doors with his fists and crush a man's neck between his fingers. He slurred words in realistic bursts of dialogue, colorfully mixing "sacre bleu" and "sonobagun" in a single sentence and constantly referring to Jim West as "mon ami." In keeping with the image, Jack Lester, who played the role, was billed as "Jacque Lestair."

THE SILVER SUMMER REVUE, musical variety; subtitled *The Raymond Paige Show* and *Musicomedy*.

BROADCAST HISTORY: June 18–Oct. 1, 1948, CBS. 30m, Fridays at 9:30. Summer replacement for *The Adventures of Ozzie and Harriet*. International Silver. **CAST:** Johnny Desmond and Julie Conway, with Kenny Bowers, Helen Carroll, and the Escorts. **ANNOUNCER:** Dan Seymour. **OR-CHESTRA:** Raymond Paige.

Music with a thin storyline, typical boy-meets-girl material, with the leads supplying their own singing intros and breaking into song at the drop of a hat. The musical fare was Broadway show tunes and popular evergreens.

SILVER THEATER, Hollywood drama.

BROADCAST HISTORY: Oct. 3, 1937–April 19, 1942, CBS. 30m, Sundays at 5 until Dec. 26, 1937; left the air temporarily, returning Oct. 2, 1938. Sundays at 6, 1938–41; Thursdays at 6, 1941–42. International Silver.

July 4, 1943–Oct. 1, 1944, CBS. 30m, Sundays at 6. International Silver.

Also: Three summer seasons, June–Aug. 1945–47, CBS. 30m, Sundays at 6. Substitute for *The Adventure of Ozzie and Harriet*. International Silver. Final broadcast: Aug. 17, 1947.

HOSTS: Conrad Nagel, John Loder. **CAST:** Major Hollywood stars in original stories, with the occasional movie adaptation. **ANNOUNCERS:** John Conte, 1930s; Dick Joy, 1940; Henry Charles,

1941; also, Roger Krupp, Jack Bailey, Harry Bartell. ORCHESTRA: Felix Mills; also, Jack Meakin. PRODUCER-DIRECTOR: Glenhall Taylor of Young & Rubicam; Edna Best, Ted Bliss, and Walter Bunker, producers, mid-1940s. WRITERS: True Boardman, Grover Jones, Joseph Russell, George Wells, etc. SOUND EFFECTS: David Light.

The Silver Theater was strongly identified with its sponsor's "1847 Rogers Brothers" silverware and was sometimes referred to on the air as *The 1847 Silver Theater*. Host Conrad Nagel, a film star from the silent era, got billing as director but was actually a "front man" à la Cecil B. DeMille of *The Lux Radio Theater*. The stories were heavy drama with intermittent comedies.

It was launched with a four-part story called *First Love*: this starred Rosalind Russell as a girl trying to get a leg up in Hollywood, and James Stewart as a fellow she met there. It was announced as a new concept in radio drama. Screen scripter Grover Jones had employed stream-of-consciousness techniques then uncommon. Stewart and Russell, moreover, were asked to learn their lines and play them at the microphone rather than simply read. Maestro Felix Mills was said to have created a three-dimensional musical score, and sound effects were integrated in an attempt to achieve ultimate clarity. The story was linked to the product, the sponsor creating a new silver line called "First Love" and declaring on the air that Russell had coined it.

Subsequent shows were equally star-laden, with Cary Grant in *Wings in the Dark*, Helen Hayes in *Stars in Their Courses*, Clark Gable in *Danger Lights*, and Ginger Rogers in *Son of the Navy* a few of the offerings. When Nagel left in the early '40s (moving to New York to do a play), John Loder became the new host, with billing as director, which he never was. Nagel returned in the three summer series, 1945–47. In the 1947 summer season, the star formula was abandoned and radio stars were used. The format allowed the stars to discuss their running radio roles and then display their versatility in dramas quite different from what their fans might expect. The first such show linked Staats Cotsworth (*Casey, Crime Photographer*), Jay Jostyn (*Mr. District Attorney*), and Mary Jane Higby (Cynthia Swanson on *The Romance of Helen Trent*).

A later broadcast had Anne Elstner (*Stella Dallas*) and Virginia Payne (*Ma Perkins*) as "two wacky old ladies in a whimsical comedy" (*Radio Life*).

THE SINCLAIR WIENER MINSTRELS, skits, gags, and harmony.

BROADCAST HISTORY: 1930, WENR, Chicago.

March 5, 1932–Jan. 4, 1937, Blue Network. 30m Saturdays, briefly, then Mondays at 9. Sinclair Oil. CAST: Gene Arnold as "Interlocutor" (host), with a singing quartet (Pat Petterson, Al Rice, Fritz Meissner, and Art Janes), a trio (Bill Childs, Fritz Clark, and Cliff Soubier), and Malcolm Claire, Negro imitator, as "Spare Ribs." Gus Van, Interlocutor, 1936. MUSIC: Harry Kogen.

April 21, 1937–April 6, 1939, Blue Network. 30m, Wednesdays at 10:30 (1937–39) and Thursdays at 10:30 (1939). *The NBC Minstrels.* CAST: Gene Arnold as Interlocutor, with singers Edward Davies, baritone, and Clark Dennis, tenor. Also: Comedy by "endmen" Jimmy Dean and Vance McCune, and a 12-voice choir, which included Harold Peary and Bill Thompson of *Fibber McGee and Molly*. MUSIC: Al Short, who died in Aug. 1937 and was replaced by guest conductors.

The Sinclair Wiener Minstrels was the most popular program of its type in the early to mid-1930s, attaining a Crossley rating of more than 25 points at its peak. Its title derived from WENR, the station of its origin, and the sponsor, Sinclair Oil. Its cancellation in January 1937 sparked a groundswell of popular demand, and it was returned in April. Now, without the sponsor and far removed from WENR, it was retitled *The NBC Minstrels*.

SING IT AGAIN, musical quiz.

BROADCAST HISTORY: May 29, 1948–June 23, 1951, CBS. 60m, Saturdays at 8 for seven months, then at 10. CAST: Dan Seymour, "the man-at-the-phone," with singers Patti Clayton, Bob Howard, Alan Dale, and "the Riddlers" (Carter Farriss, Connie Desmond, Bob Evans, Ann Seaton, Rudy Williams). ORCHESTRA: Ray Bloch. PRODUCER: Lester Gottlieb. DIRECTORS: Rocco Tito, Bruno Zirato Jr. WRITERS: Hy Zaret, Johanna Johnston.

Sing It Again came on the heels of *Stop the Music* and featured the familiar gimmicks of home audience telephone participation and a "phantom voice" revealed through singing clues. Dan Seymour called listeners from Florida to Ohio with thousands of dollars in cash and prizes for winners. A typical stumper: "Put him in a box, tie him in a jacket, and throw him in the deep blue sea." A listener who identified magician Harry Houdini could win $100 and a crack at the "phantom voice" jackpot, always worth at least $1,000.

SINGIN' SAM, songfest.

BROADCAST HISTORY: Ca. 1925–30, WLW, Cincinnati.

1930–33, CBS. Various 15m timeslots. *Singin' Sam The Barbasol Man.* Barbasol.

May–Aug. 1934, CBS. Mondays at 10:30. Atlas Beer.

1935–37, various networks: initially on Mutual in early 1935; CBS, 1935–36, 15m, Tuesdays at 7:30 until Sept., then Mondays at 7:30; Blue Network, 1936–37, 15m, Mondays at 10 (Nov.–Jan.) and Fridays at 8:15 (Sept.–May). Barbasol.

1939–42, transcribed 15m syndication for Coca-Cola. Also known as *Refreshment Time.* **ANNOUNCER:** Del Sharbutt. **ORCHESTRA:** Victor Arden.

Jan. 5–June 30, 1943, Mutual. 15m, twice a week at 8. Barbasol.

1945–late 1940s, transcribed syndication. *Reminiscin' with Singin' Sam.* Local sponsorship including Hamms Beer (Midwest) and Dr. Cowan's Translucent Tru-Bite Dental Plates (West Coast). **VOCAL SUPPORT:** The Mullen Sisters. **MUSIC:** Charlie Magnante on accordion.

Singin' Sam was the professional name of Harry Frankel, who worked vaudeville and minstrel shows in the 1920s, turned to radio, and became nationally famed as a balladeer. As a boy he sang on streetcorners in Richmond, Ind. At 17, he joined J. A. Coburn's Great Barlow Minstrels; later he played the RKO Keith Circuit. But he frequently returned to Indiana and around 1925 began broadcasting on a neighboring station, WLW, Cincinnati. In 1930 he was advertising a lawn mowing company (as *Singin' Sam the Lawnmowing Man*) when the makers of Barbasol offered to sponsor him on CBS.

His smooth bass voice was perfect for the popular ballads and semi-classical numbers that became his trademarks. His association with

Barbasol was remembered long after his death in 1948: his singing of the jingle (*Bar-ba-sol!* . . . *Bar-ba-sol!* . . . *No brush, no lather, no rub-in . . . wet your razor, then be-gin!*) was one of radio's most fondly remembered themes. He left his show in 1934, to marry and return to Indiana. But the lure of performing drew him back to CBS for a brief summer series for Atlas Beer. In 1935, Barbasol asked him to continue the old series: it would be carried on Mutual, which was not yet a national chain but did afford him the convenience of broadcasting from Cincinnati, where WLW was an hour's drive from his home. But by May it was again on CBS.

He was off the network air for more than five years, but his *Refreshment Time* transcriptions for Coca-Cola played on more than 170 stations ca. 1939–42. This to an Indiana farmer was ideal: he could fly to New York every two weeks, record ten shows, work 52 days a year, and earn up to $175,000. But it ended when James Caesar Petrillo, head of the musicians' union, banned transcriptions and the sponsor was forced to drop the show. Frankel returned briefly to Barbasol.

In 1945, he began a new series of transcriptions in the wake of union agreements. Throughout his career, he was a champion of old songs: often he claimed that, in all his years on the air, he never introduced a new tune. He didn't croon, he said: he just sang 'em. His favorites were such as *Darktown Strutters' Ball* and *Every Cloud Must Have a Silver Lining.* Frankel died June 13, 1948, but shows he had already transcribed were continued.

THE SINGING STORY LADY, children's radio.

BROADCAST HISTORY: 1931, WGN, Chicago. *The Singing Lady.*

Jan. 11, 1932–Aug. 11, 1938, Blue Network. 15m, most often at 5:30, four and sometimes five a week. Kellogg Cereals.

Dec. 25, 1936–June 25, 1937, Blue Network, Fridays at 5:15; and Oct. 3–Dec. 26, 1937, Mutual, Sundays at 5. 30m, operetta series for children (*Oberon; The Life of Goethe*; etc.). Kellogg.

Dec. 11, 1938–May 7, 1939, NBC. 30m, Sundays at 1.

Jan. 22, 1940–Sept. 26, 1941, Blue Network. 15m, four a week until fall 1940, then weekdays mostly at 5:15.

June 25–Sept. 7, 1945, ABC. 15m, weekdays at 5:45.

CAST: Ireene Wicker, "the Singing Lady," with longtime piano accompanist Milton Rettenberg. For operetta series, 1936–37: James Meighan, Florence Malone, John Brewster, and a small chorus of children. ANNOUNCERS: Bob Brown, etc.

Ireene Wicker was one of the most honored figures in juvenile radio. Her shows were simple yet effective: she told fairy tales, adapted operas for children, and dramatized the childhoods of famous people. Her stories were done to straight piano accompaniment, with Wicker taking various roles and acting out dialogue vividly and naturally.

Her first husband, Walter Charles Wicker, was a radio writer-producer-director. At the outset of her own radio career, she modified her first name on the advice of a numerologist: she had been born Irene Seaton and was told that fame and fortune would be hers on the air by adding the extra *e* to her name. She used her natural voice as narrator of her musical skits, then slipped into dialect and mood for her characters. She received many awards: she virtually owned the juvenile award based on polls of radio editors in the *New York World-Telegram*, winning it every year from 1934 on. She won similar polls in *Radio Guide, Parent's Magazine*, and the *New York Journal*, capping it all with radio's highest honor, the Peabody. Her series *When the Great Were Small* told in story and song the childhoods of Chopin, Beethoven, Michelangelo, Verdi, and others from the worlds of music and art. She avoided the blood-and-thunder of juvenile potboilers, and as a result was deeply appreciated by parents.

But in the early 1950s, congressional inquisitors tried to brand her a Communist sympathizer who had been subverting children for two decades. As usual, their evidence was simple innuendo, and she was able to fight back with partial success. She was still on local radio when visited by Richard Lamparski for a *Whatever Became Of* piece in the 1970s. She died in 1987, at 81. Her themes are preserved on brittle acetate, with more than 40 shows on tape:

Chil-dren, you who wish to hear
Songs and stories, come draw near.
Both young and old come hand-in-hand
And we'll be off to story-land.

For stories true from his-to-ry,
And fairy tales and mys-ter-y.
So come along on wings of song,
Oh, come to story-land with me.

SINGO, musical quiz.

BROADCAST HISTORY: Jan. 25–April 13, 1944, Blue Network. 15m, twice a week at 1:45. CAST: Welcome Lewis, Art Gentry.

Hostess Lewis sang the clues, song titles sent in by listeners; Gentry pitched in on duets. Contestants split a minuscule jackpot (usually $4) with a serviceman. A similar Lewis-Gentry show, *The Singing Bee*, was heard on CBS (July 5, 1940–April 5, 1941, Saturday mornings) and later on the Blue Network (Nov. 5, 1942–Nov. 19, 1943, various times).

THE SIX SHOOTER, western drama.

BROADCAST HISTORY: Sept. 20, 1953–June 24, 1954, NBC. 30m, Sundays at 8 until April 1954, then Thursdays at 8. Coleman Heaters, first few episodes only.

CAST: James Stewart as Britt Ponset, "the Texas plainsman who wandered through the western territories, leaving behind a trail of still-remembered legends." Transcribed in Hollywood with radio actors in support: Elvia Allman, Harry Bartell, B. J. Thompson, Jess Kirkpatrick, Lou Merrill, Howard McNear, Shep Menken, Frank Gerstle, Sam Edwards, Virginia Gregg, Bert Holland, Parley Baer, etc. ANNOUNCERS: Hal Gibney; later John Wald. MUSIC: Basil Adlam. DIRECTOR: Jack Johnstone. WRITER: Frank Burt. THEME: *Highland Lament*.

The Six Shooter came well past radio's best years and was an unusual and at times fetching western. The hero, Britt Ponset, was a slow-talking, easy-going gentleman, but dangerous when pushed into a gunfight. The epigraph set it up: *The man in the saddle is angular and long-legged . . . his skin is sun-dyed brown . . . the gun in his holster is gray steel and rainbow mother-of-pearl, its handle unmarked. People call them both "the Six Shooter."*

James Stewart was right in character as the maverick who blundered into other people's troubles and sometimes had to shoot his way out. He played *Hamlet* with a road company, ran for mayor and sheriff of the same town at the same time, and became involved in a western version of the Cinderella legend, complete with mean old stepmother, ugly sisters, and a shoe that didn't fit. At Christmas he told a young runaway the story of *A Christmas Carol*, substituting Dickens characters with western heavies. Ponset even fell in love, but in a cowboy-into-the-sunset finale rode forlornly away from the lovely Myra Barker on his horse, Scar.

Stewart was a superb radio actor, overcoming the drift of some scripts into folksy platitude. His narration-in-whisper of one particular climax (*The Silver Belt-Buckle*) was a gripping moment of truth, and the series as a whole just lacked the fine edge to be found in radio's two best westerns, *Gunsmoke* and *Frontier Gentleman*. In the theme, Basil Adlam provided a haunting melody, conjuring up the wandering plainsman. Despite Stewart's great prestige, the show was largely sustained. Chesterfield was interested, but Stewart declined, not wanting a cigarette company to counter his largely wholesome screen image.

THE $64,000 QUESTION, quiz.

BROADCAST HISTORY: Oct. 4–Nov. 29, 1955, CBS. 30m, Tuesdays at 10. Revlon. **HOST:** Hal March.

The $64,000 Question ushered in the era of quiz show scandals on television. But in its earliest days, no one knew that the questions were rigged and the contestants coached. The show built a vast audience soon after its June 7, 1955, TV premiere, becoming so successful so quickly that this brief radio show, a simulcast, was a natural result.

SKIPPY, juvenile serial; based on the comic strip by Percy Crosby and, more immediately, on the 1931 Jackie Cooper Paramount film.

BROADCAST HISTORY: Jan. 11–July 9, 1932, NBC. 15m, six a week at 5:15. Wheaties.

July 11, 1932–July 7, 1933, CBS. 15m, six a week at 5:30. Wheaties.

July 31, 1933–March 29, 1935, CBS. 15m, weekdays at 5, 1933–34; off for the summer; weekdays at 5:15, 1934–35. Phillips.

CAST: Franklin Adams Jr. as Skippy Skinner, a Tom Sawyer type. Francis Smith as Sooky, his pal, who lived in Shanty Town. St. John Terrell as Jim.

PRODUCERS: Frank and Anne Hummert. **DIRECTOR:** David Owen. **WRITER:** Robert Hardy Andrews.

According to writer Robert Hardy Andrews, Skippy, the hero of this serial, was a rascal, ever testing his parents' patience by figuring out honorable ways of fooling them without actually lying. "Skippy is physically strong . . . a wise and courageous leader among his fellow small boys." When confronted with adversity, Skippy "always speaks up and always shows 'em."

SKIPPY HOLLYWOOD THEATER, dramatic anthology.

BROADCAST HISTORY: 1941–49, transcribed 30m syndication. Best Foods and Skippy Peanut Butter. **CAST:** Hollywood stars in original stories: Joan Bennett, Herbert Marshall, Vincent Price, etc. **MUSIC:** Mahlon Merrick. **PRODUCER:** C. P. MacGregor. **WRITER:** True Boardman.

Dec. 1, 1949–Sept. 21, 1950, CBS. 30m, Thursdays at 10:30. Skippy. **MUSIC:** Del Castillo. **PRODUCER:** Les Mitchel.

The Skippy Hollywood Theater was one of radio's most successful syndicated shows. Producer C. P. MacGregor had been turning out radio shows on disc since 1929 but had encountered resistance to such "canned" entertainment by the Hollywood establishment. He argued that transcriptions enabled him to produce flawless shows, and losing the excitement of live performances was a small price to pay. His *Hollywood Theater* was a slick show, the equal of many network series: it was syndicated as a complete-with-commercials package and helped boost Skippy Peanut Butter to national prominence. The format followed *The Lux Radio Theater*, with MacGregor acting as host and interviewing the stars after the play, much as Cecil B. DeMille had done on *Lux*. MacGregor thus became known in radio as "the DeMille of the discs."

SKY BLAZERS, drama.

BROADCAST HISTORY: Dec. 9, 1939–Aug. 31, 1940, CBS. 30m, Saturdays at 7:30 until June, then at 8. Continental Baking and Wonder Bread. **HOST-NARRATOR:** Col. Roscoe Turner. **PRODUCER-WRITER:** Phillips H. Lord.

Each week *Sky Blazers* dramatized some piece of the aviation story, from early days of flying orange crates to modern epics of prewar America. Host Roscoe Turner was himself a World War pilot, holder of many transcontinental speed records and former operator of a flight school and flying circus. After each drama, Turner interviewed the story's real daredevil.

SKY KING, juvenile serial; adventure drama.

BROADCAST HISTORY: Oct. 28, 1946–Aug. 29, 1947, ABC. 15m, weekdays at 5:15. Swift.

Sept. 2, 1947–June 2, 1950, ABC. 30m twice and three times a week on alternate weeks, sharing the 5:30 timeslot equally with *Jack Armstrong*. Time shared with *The Sea Hound*, summer 1948. Peter Pan Peanut Butter.

Sept. 12, 1950–June 3, 1954, Mutual. 30m, twice a week at 5:30. Derby Foods for Peter Pan.

CAST: Jack Lester, Roy Engel, Earl Nightingale, and John Reed King, variously, as Schuyler (Sky) King, the flying rancher who went to extraordinary lengths to right wrongs. Beryl Vaughn and Jack Bivens as his flying companions and fellow adventurers, Penny and Clipper. Johnny Coons also as Clipper.

Sky King, "America's favorite flying cowboy," was heard for most of a year as a daily serial before ABC executives began eliminating cliffhanger breathlessness in the "kiddie hour" and turning the shows into self-contained half-hours. The hero was an Arizona rancher who zoomed down for each episode in his plane, the *Songbird.*

SMILE PARADE, comedy variety.

BROADCAST HISTORY: 1938–39, NBC. 30m, Friday mornings from Chicago. **CAST:** Ransom Sherman, Fran Allison, Ethel Owen, Wayne Van Dine, pianist Bob Trendler, and the Our Serenaders Quartet (Gale Watts, Gunther Decker, Earl Wilkie, Burton Dole). **ORCHESTRA:** Rex Maupin. The format, according to *Radio Guide,* was "wacky discourses, interviews, travelogues, household hints."

SMILE TIME, comedy.

BROADCAST HISTORY: Ca. 1945–47, West Coast Don Lee Network. 15m, weekdays at 7:15 A.M. Pacific time.

CAST: Steve Allen, Wendell Noble, and June Foray, lampooning everything "from bank robbers to Boy Scouts" (*Radio Life*). They once sang their theme with every *i* replaced by an *o*.

SMILIN' ED'S BUSTER BROWN GANG, children's potpourri.

BROADCAST HISTORY: Sept. 2, 1944–April 11, 1953, NBC. 30m, Saturdays at 11:30 A.M. Buster Brown Shoes. **CAST:** Smilin' Ed McConnell, host, and in character as "Squeeky the Mouse," "Midnight the Cat," "Grandie the Piano," and the mischievous "Froggy the Gremlin." Jerry Marin as Buster Brown, the boy who "lived in a shoe." Hollywood radio actors in dramatized tales told by Smilin' Ed: Lou Merrill, June Foray, Joe Fields, Ken Christy, Wendell Noble, Tommy Cook, Conrad Binyon, Lou Krugman, John Dehner, Tommy Bernard, Bobby Ellis, Jimmy Ogg, Billy Roy, Marvin Miller, etc. **ANNOUNCER:** Archie Presby. **MUSIC:** John Duffy on organ; Ken Cameron on piano. **PRODUCERS:** Frank Ferrin; Hobart Donovan. **SOUND EFFECTS:** Bud Tollefson, Jack Robinson, Virgil Reimer.

Smilin' Ed McConnell was a Saturday staple for children under 12 for nine years. But McConnell—a jovial, gravel-voiced fat man who liked to kid himself about his weight—was a radio pioneer with 15 years on the air before his memorable *Buster Brown* series began.

Son of an itinerant Georgia preacher, McConnell was a dishwasher and a small-time prizefighter, and an alumnus of vaudeville and chautauqua before World War I. His first air stint was May 30, 1922. He broadcast regularly on WSB, Atlanta: "I started at 10:45 P.M.," he said, "and quit when I felt like it." Sometimes he ran until 3 and 4 A.M., and the clear signal at that time of night reached all over the eastern United States. The station was above the Western Union office, and all night long he was delivered baskets of telegrams from afar. His early work was off the cuff: he sang light ballads and played piano and later indulged in homespun philosophy. His first network broadcast was Sept. 20, 1932, a quarter-hour CBS run for Acme Paints, which became his loyal sponsor throughout the decade. Acme sponsored McConnell until 1940, with his shows heard in various timeslots on CBS, NBC, and the Blue Networks. In 1937 he was billed as NBC's *Sunshine Melody Man,* singing hymns to the accompaniment of Irma Glen on piano.

Buster Brown, meanwhile, was first seen in a comic strip by R. F. Outcault. The Buster Brown Shoe Company bought the character as a commercial symbol and brought the strip to radio in an early series of CBS dramas, heard 15m Fridays at 8 in 1929–30. Buster was the "boy who lives in a shoe"; a rousing bark introduced "my dog Tige, who lives in there too." For its second season, *Buster Brown and His Dog Tige* ran on the Blue Network, Fridays at 7:45. Then it left the air, and it wasn't until 1944 when idea and personality meshed to make it one of the jolliest of all juvenile radio shows.

McConnell told stories of life on the frontier, of treks through jungles, of Robin Hood in merry England. The tales were done in quarter-hour segments within the half-hour show. In the other half, McConnell read letters from his young fans (often submitted as "Brown Jug Jingles") and chatted with his imaginary cast, Squeeky the Mouse, Midnight the Cat, Grandie the Piano, and Froggy the Gremlin. A distinctive feature was the plunking of the piano to each word emphasized by McConnell. But the star of the show was Froggy. Supposedly an invisible imp whose "magic twanger" could bring him into view, Froggy delighted in badgering such regular "guests" as "Algernon Archibald Percival Sharpfellow, the Poet," "Jim Nasium, the athletic instructor," and "Alkalai Pete, the cowboy." The guests were always long-winded types who became tongue-tied at Froggy's taunts, finally exploding in anger and running offstage to the delight of the young studio audience. Announcer Archie Presby doubled as Froggy whenever McConnell and the Gremlin sang a duet. Presby also dressed up in frog regalia and leapt out to thunderous laughter whenever McConnell would shout, "Come out from behind that curtain, Froggy, and let the kids see what you really look like!" Froggy's manner of speech was to constantly repeat himself ("Now I'll sing my song, I will, I will").

The show was loud and boisterous, from the opening bar of McConnell's Buster Brown song (*I got shoes/You got shoes/Why, everybody's got to have shoes!/And there's only one kinda shoes for me/Good ole Buster Brown Shoes!*) to the final thump of Grandie the Piano.

The show made the jump to TV in 1950.

McConnell died in 1955, and Andy Devine took over the TV series. It kept alive the McConnell characters, running on NBC as *Andy's Gang* until 1960.

SMILIN' JACK, juvenile adventure, from the comic strip by Zack Mosley.

BROADCAST HISTORY: Feb. 13–May 19, 1939, Mutual. 15m, three a week at 5:30. Tootsie Roll. CAST: Frank Readick as Smilin' Jack Martin, young aviator who fought international crime. ANNOUNCER: Tom Shirley.

One storyline found Jack and his friend Rufus in Arabia, pursuing a criminal known as "the Mad Dog." The opening was typical of aviation thrillers: the drone of a plane and a filtered voice ordering, *Clear the runway for Smilin' Jack!* Tootsie Rolls leaped right into the premium fray, offering a flying chart "just like the one Jack uses" for ten penny wrappers.

THE SMITH BROTHERS, patter and song.

BROADCAST HISTORY: 1926–33, NBC. Blue Network ca. 1928–32; Red Network otherwise. Various 15m or 30m times. Smith Brothers Cough Drops.
    1931–34, CBS. 15m, Friday or Saturday evenings. Smith Brothers Cough Drops.

The Smith Brothers was an early attempt to link a product (cough drops) with vaudeville performers (Billy Hillpot and Scrappy Lambert) and thus popularize a sponsor in the days when direct advertising was just beginning to be realized. It was also known as *Trade and Mark*, supposedly the names of the Smith brothers as taken from the caricatures on the cough drop packages. Hillpot played the role of Trade; Lambert was Mark. The fare was simple vaudeville material.

THE SMITHS OF HOLLYWOOD, situation comedy.

BROADCAST HISTORY: 1946, transcribed 30m syndication (aired in New York on WOR Jan. 10–July 11, 1947).
CAST: Harry Von Zell as attorney Bill Smith. Brenda Marshall as Nancy, his wife. Jan Ford as Shirley, their daughter, better known as "Bumps." Arthur Treacher as Sir Cecil Smythe, their stuffy British uncle, who arrived one day to stay with

them. Supporting roles by Hollywood radio regulars: Jerry Hausner, Sidney Fields, Sara Berner, etc. ANNOUNCER: Tyler McVey. MUSIC: Carl Hoff, Charles Hathaway. DIRECTORS: Vick Knight, Robert Presnell Jr. WRITERS: Dick Nasserman, Robert Presnell Jr. SOUND EFFECTS: Wayne Kenworthy.

The Smiths of Hollywood was billed as "a usual family doing average things," the exception being that this family lived in the film capital. This setting brought out numerous guest stars (Lucille Ball, William Holden, Ann Sheridan, etc.), unusual for a transcribed offering. Actress Jan Ford, who played the daughter, was in reality Helen Koford: she experimented with several stage names before settling on Terry Moore, with which she had a lukewarm film career.

SNOW VILLAGE SKETCHES, comedy in various formats.

BROADCAST HISTORY: Feb. 29, 1928–Sept. 26, 1934, NBC. 30m, Tuesdays at 7:30, 1928–30; Mondays at 8, 1931–34, Tuesday at 9:30, mid-1934. *Soconyland Sketches*. Socony Oil. CAST: Arthur Allen and Parker Fennelly as village rubes in the New Hampshire town of Snow Village. WRITER: William Ford Manley.

   Oct. 6, 1934–May 11, 1935, CBS. 30m, Saturdays at 7. Socony.

   Oct. 3, 1936–June 26, 1937, NBC. 30m, Saturdays at 9. *Snow Village Sketches*. Loose Wiles Biscuits. CAST: Arthur Allen as Dan'l Dickey and Parker Fennelly as Hiram Neville, rustic villagers. Agnes Young as Dan'l's wife Hattie. Also: John Thomas, Jean McCoy, Katharine Raht, Elsie Mae Gordon.

   Dec. 28, 1942–Nov. 11, 1943, NBC. 15m continuation, weekdays at 11:30 A.M. Procter & Gamble.

   Jan. 13–June 16, 1946, Mutual. 30m, Sundays at 10:30 A.M. until Feb., then at 11 A.M. CAST: Arthur Allen and Parker Fennelly as Dan'l Dickey and Hiram Neville. Kate McComb as Dan'l's wife Hattie. ANNOUNCER: George Hogan. MUSIC: Chet Kingsbury. DIRECTOR: Harold McGee.

Of all the incarnations of *Snow Village Sketches*, only the 1946 Mutual run is available to audition at this writing. Arthur Allen's Dan'l Dickey was the more sympathetic of the two

leads. Parker Fennelly as Hiram Neville was a punitive gentleman of old-fashioned values. They were farmers who doubled as game warden and truant officer respectively, and the skits were slices of a life that exists no more. Fennelly and Allen did many such series, playing countrified New Englanders in one situation or another. Among them: *Uncle Abe and David* (NBC, 1930–31, for Goodrich Tires); *The Stebbins Boys* (NBC, 1931–32, weekdays on the Red, then Blue, for Swift Meats); *The Simpson Boys of Sprucehead Bay* (Blue, 1935–36, various); *Four Corners USA* (CBS, 1938–39, Saturdays at 10:30); and *Gibbs and Feeney, General Delivery* (Blue, July–Oct. 1942, Sundays).

SO PROUDLY WE HAIL, dramatic anthology.

BROADCAST HISTORY: Late 1940, syndication for the War Department, to promote Army recruitment; first show released for broadcast June 1, 1946. 15m until 1948, then 30m. CAST: Major film stars in original stories with Army commercials built in: Clark Gable, Ava Gardner, William Holden, Ronald Reagan, Alan Ladd, Robert Mitchum, etc. PRODUCER: C. P. MacGregor.

SO THIS IS RADIO, biography-survey of the broadcast industry.

BROADCAST HISTORY: July 24–Sept. 29, 1939, CBS; 30m, heard sporadically, with other installments July 31, Aug. 14 and 21, and Sept. 7. An outgrowth of Norman Corwin's verse-play, *Seems Radio Is Here to Stay*, originally aired on *The Columbia Workshop*. CAST: House Jameson, Martin Gabel, John Gibson, Frank Gallop, Everett Sloane, Karl Swenson, Arnold Moss, Minerva Pious, Adelaide Klein, Sydney Smith. ORCHESTRA: Bernard Herrmann, Raymond Scott, Perry Lafferty. DIRECTOR-WRITER: Norman Corwin.

In this inquisitive series, Corwin covered his medium from the viewpoints of historian, educator, musician, and people in special events. He employed a "running footnote," a random voice that interrupted to ask the questions that a listener might ask.

SO YOU WANT TO BE, vocational education.

BROADCAST HISTORY: July 8–Dec. 21, 1938, CBS. 15m, Fridays at 5:45 until Oct., then Wednesdays at 5:15.

Aimed at children but of broad general interest, this brought to the microphone holders of colorful jobs: John William Anderson described being captain of an ocean liner; explorer Leila Roosevelt (cousin of the president) recounted treks in Africa; Irene Kuhn told about being a foreign correspondent.

SO YOU WANT TO LEAD A BAND, musical game show.

BROADCAST HISTORY: Sept. 5–Oct. 24, 1946, ABC. 30m, Thursdays at 10.

This half-hour of fun with Sammy Kaye and his orchestra had its origin during a Hotel Commodore date around 1941. A couple came to the bandstand and the man asked to lead the band. "Sure, if you'll let me dance with your girl," said Kaye. The maestro discovered that most of the dancers had harbored the same secret wish, and that was the beginning of a novel game show. Kaye would select contestants from the audience, awarding prizes (a $1,000 grand prize in 1946) for best instant maestro. The audience found some efforts riotous. Among celebrity contestants were Betty Grable, Linda Darnell, and Ethel Merman. Kaye used the idea in personal appearances long after the radio show expired.

SOLDIERS OF THE PRESS, war drama.

BROADCAST HISTORY: 1942–45, transcribed syndication; World Broadcasting System. 15m "eyewitness accounts of world news as it happens." Heard on WOR, New York, Sundays at 12:30, Feb. 28, 1943–Aug. 5, 1945. CAST: Lon Clark of New York radio in the adventures of United Press correspondents in all theaters of warfare (Marines on Tarawa, paratroopers, torpedo boats, etc.).

SOMEBODY KNOWS, real-life murder drama, with rewards.

BROADCAST HISTORY: July 6–Aug. 24, 1950, CBS. 30m, Thursdays at 9. Summer replacement for *Suspense*. ANNOUNCER: Frank Goss. NARRATOR-DIRECTOR: Jack Johnstone. PRODUCER: James L. Saphier.

Somebody Knows was based on an idea originated in the *Chicago Sun-Times*: that no murder is ever perfect and that, somewhere, someone has information that could help police crack a baffling crime. Killers were addressed directly. "You out there—you who think you have committed the perfect crime, that there are no clues, no witnesses, that your identity is unknown—listen! . . . SOMEBODY KNOWS!" The trick was to persuade that somebody to give evidence leading to the arrest and conviction of the culprit. CBS offered $5,000 rewards. Clues were to be submitted on plain sheets of paper. Instead of a signature, the tipster could write six numbers on the page, rip off a corner in a jagged tear, and write the same six numbers on the piece he would retain. When the killer was convicted, the bearer of the matching paper could walk out of CBS with the reward, no questions asked. The cases were fully dramatized: the final broadcast, available on tape, told of the famous "Black Dahlia" case. Elizabeth Short was murdered and mutilated Jan. 15, 1947. Her death is still a mystery.

THE SOMERSET MAUGHAM THEATER, dramatic anthology.

BROADCAST HISTORY: Jan. 20–July 14, 1951, CBS. 30m, Saturdays at 11: 30 A.M. Tintair.
    Oct. 27, 1951–Jan. 19, 1952, NBC. 30m, Saturdays at 11 A.M. By-Mart.
CAST: Stars of Broadway and Hollywood in stories by the prolific British author: Martha Scott, Dane Clark, Nancy Kelly, Alfred Drake, Hume Cronyn and Jessica Tandy, etc. PRODUCERS: Ann Marlowe and John Gibbs. DIRECTOR: Mitchell Grayson.

Somerset Maugham, who wrote more than two dozen novels and 100 short stories, was barely tapped in this anthology. It mixed well-known tales (*Rain*) with the little-known (*The Land of Promise*). Major novels (*The Razor's Edge*; *Of Human Bondage*) were done in two parts. The series was unusual in that it began on CBS television, Oct. 18, 1950, and then moved to radio.

A SONG IS BORN, musical human interest.

BROADCAST HISTORY: Feb. 21–Dec. 2, 1944, NBC West. 30m, various times. Langendorf Bread. CREATOR AND MUSICAL DIRECTOR: Richard Aurandt. ANNOUNCER: Larry Keating. VO-

CALISTS: Pat Kaye, Ronny Mansfield. PANEL-ISTS: Ferde Grofé, bandmaster Joe Reichman, NBC musical director Thomas Peluso. PRODUCER: Tom Hargis.

Four composers were invited each week to Radio City in Hollywood, to play, sing, and tell the stories of their works. Three of the subjects were complete unknowns; the fourth was a professional. Their stories were sometimes dramatized. Each was awarded $25, and the grand winners, as judged by the panel, had their songs published.

SONG OF LIBERTY, patriotic drama and music.

BROADCAST HISTORY: Ca. 1950 (exact tenure unknown, heard 30m, Tuesdays at 8 Pacific time as of Nov. 1950), West Coast Mutual–Don Lee Network. Farmers Insurance. CAST: Charles Coburn. PRODUCER: Bill Gordon.

Coburn, the voice of the show, gave fiery and passionate readings of Lincoln's Gettysburg Address and other historic documents. The readings were accompanied by rousing music: Irving Berlin's *This Is the Army*; Rodgers and Hammerstein's *You'll Never Walk Alone*; etc.

THE SONG SHOP, musical variety.

BROADCAST HISTORY: Sept. 10, 1937–June 3, 1938, CBS. 45m, Fridays at 10 until Jan., then mostly at 9. Coca-Cola. HOSTESS: Kitty Carlisle, 1937; Nadine Conner, 1938. MASTER OF CEREMONIES: Frank Crumit, 1937; Del Sharbutt, 1938. VOCALISTS: Reed Kennedy, baritone; Alice Cornett, rhythm singer. ORCHESTRA: Gus Haenschen, with a 47-piece group. Also: a 22-voice glee club.

SOPHIE TUCKER AND HER SHOW, musical variety.

BROADCAST HISTORY: Nov. 7, 1938–May 5, 1939, CBS. 15m, Mondays-Wednesdays-Fridays at 6:45. Roi Tan Cigars. STAR: Sophie Tucker, "the last of the red-hot mammas."

SOUTHERN CRUISE, musical variety.

BROADCAST HISTORY: July 4–Aug. 15, 1941, CBS. 30m, Fridays at 8. Titled *American Cruise* as of Aug. 1. VOCALISTS: Dick Powell and Frances Langford. ORCHESTRA: Lud Gluskin. PRODUCER-ANNOUNCER: Ken Niles.

A musical company visited Latin American ports of call on an ocean liner.

SPACE PATROL, juvenile space adventure.

BROADCAST HISTORY: Sept. 18, 1950–March 19, 1955, ABC. 30m, Mondays and Fridays at 5:30 until Jan. 8, 1951; returned Aug. 18, 1951, Saturdays at 7:30 through Sept. 29, 1951, then at 10:30 A.M. Ralston, 1951–54; Nestle, 1954–55. CAST: Ed Kemmer as Buzz Corry, commander of United Planets' Space Patrol. Lyn Osborn as his companion, Cadet Happy. Virginia Hewitt as Carol Karlyle, daughter of the secretary general of the United Planets. Ken Mayer as Maj. "Robbie" Robertson. Norman Jolley as Dr. Malingro. Nina Bara as the tempestuous Tonga. Bela Kovacs as Prince Baccarritti, etc. ANNOUNCERS: Dick Tufeld, Dick Wesson, etc. PRODUCER-DIRECTORS: Larry Robertson, Mike Moser. WRITER: Lou Huston.

Space Patrol ran concurrently on radio and television, with the same performers in key roles. The story concerned the universe-jumping exploits of Cmndr. Buzz Corry, assigned to bring law and order to the interplanetary frontier, and Cadet Happy, whose astonishment at inevitable trouble was expressed in the catchphrase "Smokin' rockets!" Archenemies of the Space Patrol were Dr. Ryland Scarno, "Mister Proteus," and Prince Baccarritti, who was known as "the Black Falcon." Nina Bara became so popular as Tonga that the producers changed her villainous nature and made her a sympathetic romantic interest. The opening signature:

High adventure in the wild, vast reaches of space!

Missions of daring in the name of interplanetary justice!

Travel into the future with Buzz Corry, commander-in-chief of the SPACE PATROL!

The series had no music: all effects were achieved with sound patterns. The Space Patrol ventured forth in their ship, the *Terra V.*

THE SPARROW AND THE HAWK, juvenile adventure serial

BROADCAST HISTORY: May 14, 1945–Sept. 27, 1946, CBS. 15m, weekdays at 5:45. CAST: Donald Buka as Barney Mallory, fictitious 16-year-old pilot, nicknamed "Sparrow" by his friends. Michael Fitzmaurice as his uncle, the famous Army Air Corps flyer Col. Spencer Mallory, known far and wide as the "Hawk." Joseph Julian as Tony. Mary Hunter as Barney's mother. Susan Douglas as Laura. ANNOUNCER: Tony Marvin. DIRECTOR: Richard Sanville. WRITERS: Carl A. Buss and Larry Menkin.

"A story of modern adventure high in the sky, wherever planes can go."

SPECIAL AGENT, adventure drama.

BROADCAST HISTORY: April 17–Aug. 28, 1948, Mutual. Produced in New York. 30m, Saturdays at 9, later at 11:30. CAST: James Meighan as Alan Drake, "the insurance detective whose company protects all comers against all perils, anywhere in the world." Lyle Sudrow as Jim Lawlor, Drake's partner.

SPECIAL INVESTIGATOR, crime drama.

BROADCAST HISTORY: May 19, 1946–June 17, 1947, Mutual. 15m, Sundays at 8 through March, then Tuesdays at 8:15. Commercial Credit. CAST: Richard Keith as Frank W. Brock, who exposed professional swindlers and was especially interested in crimes against returning servicemen (housing shortage frauds, memorial park fakes, diploma mills). MUSIC: Chet Kingsbury on organ. PRODUCER: Herbert Rice.

SPEED GIBSON OF THE INTERNATIONAL SECRET POLICE, juvenile aviation serial.

BROADCAST HISTORY: 1937–38, 15m transcribed syndication. CAST: Unknown actor as Speed Gibson. Howard McNear as Clint Barlow. John Gibson as Barney Dunlap. Also: Hanley Stafford, Elliott Lewis, Sam Edwards, etc. WRITER: Virginia Cooke.

Speed Gibson told of a 15-year-old pilot on the worldwide trail of a master criminal, "the Octopus," and his ruthless gang of henchmen. The chase, with the fate of the world at stake, led to Africa and the Orient. Speed's membership in ISP was secured by his uncle, crack agent Clint Barlow. Their semi-comical sidekick was Barney Dunlap; his interminable catchphrase

was "Suffering whangdoodles!" This trio flew to Tibet in the airship *Flying China Clipper*, to keep after the Octopus gang. The opening signature brought in the sound of a droning aircraft and the urgent voice of an air trafficker: "Ceiling zero! . . . ceiling zero! . . . ceiling zero!" The entire serial (178 chapters) is available on tape, a fine example of mid-1930s juvenile radio.

THE SPEED SHOW, music and talk; also known as *The Nash Program.*

BROADCAST HISTORY: Oct. 3, 1936–June 26, 1937, CBS. 30m, Saturdays at 9. Nash and Lafayette autos; Kelvinator appliances. CAST: Floyd Gibbons with globetrotting adventure tales in his mile-a-minute style; guests Lupe Velez, etc. Gibbons left the show in March; his replacement, as of April 3, couldn't have been more his opposite: Grace Moore of the operatic stage. ORCHESTRA: Vincent Lopez throughout.

THE SPIKE JONES SHOW, musical madness.

BROADCAST HISTORY: June 3–Aug. 26, 1945, NBC. 30m, Sundays at 8 for vacationing Edgar Bergen. *The Chase and Sanborn Show.* COSTAR: singer Frances Langford.

March 22–May 9, 1946, Mutual–Don Lee, West Coast. 15m and 30m. *Spike's at the Troc*, straight big band swing music.

Oct. 3, 1947–Dec. 24, 1948, CBS. 30m, Fridays at 10:30. *Spotlight Revue.* Coca-Cola. CAST: Spike Jones and the City Slickers, a novelty band that played hot jazz and popular songs as musical satire, to great comedic effect. Dorothy Shay, "the Park Avenue Hillbilly," as full costar. ANNOUNCERS (who advertised 24-bottle cases of Coke for a dollar): Michael Roy and Myron "Mike" Wallace. PRODUCER: Hal Fimberg. WRITERS: Jay Sommers, Eddie Brandt, Eddie Maxwell.

Jan. 2–June 25, 1949, CBS. 30m, Sundays at 6:30 through March 6, then Saturdays at 7:30. Name change to *The Spike Jones Show* with the departure of Dorothy Shay. PRODUCER: Joe Bigelow.

Spike Jones and his City Slickers turned cowbells, foghorns, and kitchen utensils into musical instruments. They clanged, hissed, honked, and chugged through radio's prime years.

Jones was one of those people who toil in obscurity for a decade and then become an overnight success. He was born Lindley Armstrong Jones, son of a railroad agent, and given his nickname by a telegraph operator who thought him skinny as a railroad spike. Jones had an early affinity for music, playing drums while still in grammar school and organizing bands while still in his teens. His first radio jobs were at KFOX and KGER, Long Beach, around 1928. His group was Spike Jones and his Five Tacks: the music they played was hot and loud, like that of a hundred other bands struggling for attention. In January 1938, he joined Victor Young's band, beginning a long and anonymous career drumming for some of the top aggregations in radio.

From 1938 until 1943 he worked in half a dozen studio orchestras with regular weekly airshots on national programs. With Young he worked the Al Jolson Lifebuoy show; he played with Dave Rubinoff, then with Henry King on *Burns and Allen*; he was successively employed with Jacques Renard, with Edgar "Cookie" Fairchild on Eddie Cantor's half-hour, and with Freddie Rich on *Tommy Riggs and Betty Lou*. He joined Oscar Bradley in 1938, for the first year of the Gulf *Screen Guild Theater*. And he was with John Scott Trotter on Bing Crosby's *Kraft Music Hall* (ca. 1937–41) and with Billy Mills on *Fibber McGee and Molly* (1940–43).

The trouble with all this work was its play-by-the-numbers predictability. Jones was bored with it: he sought refuge in a little spare-time group he had organized with clarinet-and-sax man Del Porter. They were regulars at the Jonathan Club in Los Angeles, with billing as the club's dance band. There was no clear-cut leader, and a few years later, when the band was world famous and Jones had emerged with control of it, some of its early players were unclear as to how this had come about. Jones biographer Jordan R. Young was clear enough: when the band became hot, Jones simply took it over.

The band had appeared as "Duke Daniels and his City Slickers" on the light comedy series *Point Sublime*, playing on a West Coast NBC hookup July 7, 1941. Five Bluebird records had been released, but nothing serious happened until July 28, 1942, when Jones went into the studio to record an amusing anti-Nazi war ditty, *Der Fuehrer's Face*. Originally intended for the Walt Disney cartoon, *Donald Duck in Axis Land*, this became in Jones's hands a musical riot, rocketing the group to national stardom in less than a

month. It demolished Hitler's claims to genetic superiority and established the raspberry as a respectable part of American radio.

The song was embraced by Martin Block, who plugged it twice an hour in New York on *Make-Believe Ballroom*. Within a week, Jones had signed a movie contract; he had joined a radio series, *Furlough Fun*, become part of *The Bob Burns Show* (CBS, Oct.–Dec. 1942, and NBC, 1943–44), and learned from RCA that sales of *Der Fuehrer's Face* had gone past the half-million mark.

The band at this time was variously composed of Don Anderson and Bruce Hudson, trumpets; John Stanley and King Jackson, trombones; Luther Roundtree and Perry Botkin, banjos; Joseph H. (Country) Washburne and Hank Stern, tubas; Frank Leithner and Stan Wrightsman, pianos; Del Porter, clarinet, ocarina, and vocals; and Carl Grayson, violin and vocals. There was also an alleged character named Willie Spicer, who played such bizarre instruments as the "kalaedophone," "birdaphone," "anvilaphone," and finally the "latrinophone," a toilet seat with strings. As Jordan Young disclosed, this character was "just a figment of Spike's imagination."

Their stint on *Furlough Fun* ran two seasons. Supplementing their radio work were recordings, many destined to become classics of their kind: hilarious takeoffs on *Cocktails for Two*, *Chloe*, *Holiday for Strings*, *Hawaiian War Chant*, and *Liebestraum*. The mid-1940s was a time of transition, with many original players departing and new people taking the band to greater insanity and pandemonium. Ernest "Red" Ingle came and went, leaving his mark in comic vocals on *Chloe* and *Glow Worm*. Others were Dick and Freddie Morgan, unrelated banjo players; Joe Siracusa, drummer; Dick Gardner, sax and violin; Joe Colvin, trombone; Jack Golly and Mickey Katz, clarinets; and Roger Donley, tuba. Paul Leu arranged and played piano. Purv Pullen, an incredible bird and animal imitator, was billed as "Horatio Q. Birdbath." George Rock, the 260-pound trumpet player, could sing like a child and recorded the major hit *All I Want for Christmas Is My Two Front Teeth*. And Winstead "Doodles" Weaver specialized in mixing the words of popular songs and in doing horse race routines to *The William Tell Overture* (the winner, inexplicably, was always Feetlebaum).

These were the characters who went with Jones into his major radio series, *Spotlight Revue*. Getting equal billing with the band was Dorothy Shay, "the Park Avenue Hillbilly," who sang two numbers (*Feudin' and Fightin'* perhaps the best-remembered) from her deep well of novelty tunes in each half-hour, then returned to share in the closing medley. Though the band was renowned for such "instruments" as washboards, flitguns, pop bottles, and doorbells, their music was at its heart genuine hot jazz. The act was perfected through long rehearsals and executed with meticulous timing. There were also many stage engagements, traveling "Musical Depreciation Revues," and the broadcasts were done from San Francisco, Chicago, Indianapolis, or Detroit—wherever the stage show was playing that week. The format of the radio shows was standard: a crazy Dixieland number would open it (*Charlie My Boy* was a favorite); Jones would shout his weekly salutation—"Thank you, music lovers!" (which was a surefire laugh); a guest would arrive, do a straight number, and perhaps engage the band in an insane "roundtable discussion" of some unlikely topic; Dorothy Shay would be heard, then Doodles Weaver with "Feetlebaum"; and a closing theme-related medley would feature Shay, the Slickers, and their guest. Guests included Victor Borge, Frank Sinatra, Gene Kelly, Peter Lorre, Dinah Shore, and, in a memorable spoof, Basil Rathbone reading *Peter and the Wolf*.

THE SPIRIT OF '41, documentary.

BROADCAST HISTORY: June 29, 1941–Sept. 11, 1943, CBS. 30m, Sundays at 4:30 until Oct. 1941, then at 2; Saturdays at 2:30 from Dec. 1942. Became *The Spirit of '42* in Jan. 1942, and *of '43* the following year.

Newsman John Daly was the initial "voice" of the series, which "each week takes a separate branch of the Army, Navy, or Marine Corps, explains its duties, delves into its history and development, and picks up live broadcasts from the field" (*Radio Life*). Representative broadcasts: a description of the Army Corps of Engineers (which helped the army "bridge rivers, repair roads, touch off enemy mines and fight when necessary"); a report on air corps maintenance from "somewhere in England"; and music by the U.S. Army band, with guest Kate Smith as singing hostess.

SPORTS BROADCASTS, mostly special events; see also LIBERTY BROADCASTING SYSTEM.

From the moment radio began developing remote capabilities in the early 1920s, live coverage of sports was demanded and delivered as a natural part of the business. The demand created a new kind of reporter: one who could vividly (and, in an ideal world, accurately) describe an event as it passed before him; who could react to bombshell developments a heartbeat ahead of the roar of the crowd; who could wring from an event, instantly, every drop of its drama; who required no script because none was possible; who combined the instincts of a showman with the keen eye and experience of a journalist.

This was uncharted territory in 1921. In some respects the craft and its demands were unique. Unlike the war correspondent, who might suddenly get caught up in a battle and be called upon to describe it, the sports broadcaster went to every event expecting a battle and savoring the prospect. If the affairs they covered were trivial in the grand scheme of life, they possessed the *illusion* of vast importance. It was the "golden age of sports," and the man on the street cared more about Jack Dempsey and Babe Ruth than about the fact that his government was involved in a crooked little oil deal at a place called Teapot Dome. The game, the race, the fight—these events were now in every home, and the voices that brought them were famous overnight. Analyzing it later, *Radio Guide* was "tempted to say that baseball broadcasts are more potent than music, more productive of speculation than foreign or political situations, and are more widely heard than any other daytime program in the summertime. Radio has really made baseball the national game."

Baseball and boxing were the front-burner radio sports. At the beginning of radio, baseball held the attention of the public to a degree that can barely be imagined by the pale millionaire "superstars" of today's game. Statistics were bandied by congressmen and elevator boys, and seldom was there a hint that money was more important than the Game. There had been the scandal of 1919, but the culprits had been unmasked and thrown out, and radio brought a new era when giants rode the airwaves. Fighters in all divisions (but especially the heavyweights) were ranked with heroes of folklore, and radio often made these gargantuan battles more vivid than what witnesses saw at the stadiums.

The first great radio fight, the brawling Dempsey-Firpo clash of Sept. 14, 1923, gave ample evidence. The crowd went berserk, and fans who had paid $25 saw little after the first knockdown. Many spectators had to go home and learn what had happened from their families, who had listened on the radio. Firpo went down seven times in the first round; Dempsey was knocked through the ropes and out of the ring, landing on top of assistant announcer Graham McNamee. But radio fans missed none of it: McNamee's partner, Maj. J. Andrew White, continued the broadcast while all around him newspapermen who had seen scores of ring battles "went almost insane." As for McNamee, he would recall that "my heart was thumping at my breast until I thought it would rend my ribs."

The first sports event ever broadcast is said by historian William Peck Banning to be the 1920 World Series. This was carried by a small experimental station, predecessor of WWJ, Detroit, operated by the *Detroit News*. "Returns were sent out during the games describing the plays," possibly from running wire service accounts. But clearly the first live event was carried by KDKA, Pittsburgh, when, on April 11, 1921, the nation's first licensed station broadcast a prizefight with local newspaperman Florent Gibson doing the commentary. This was followed on July 2 by the heavyweight title fight between Jack Dempsey and French champion Georges Carpentier. The latter was produced by David Sarnoff of RCA, who had to build his broadcast facility from scratch. Sarnoff borrowed a powerful transmitter from the Navy and sent Maj. White and engineers Harry Walker and J. O. Smith to New Jersey, where the fight was to be held at an arena called Boyle's Thirty Acres. The transmitting equipment was installed in a galvanized tin shack in a Hoboken trainyard. Pullman porters who used the shack for a dressing room were annoyed and threatened to tear up the equipment. Smith slept in the shed the night before the fight; he and White suffered from nerves as fight time approached. The broadcast would be done on a relay: White, announcing at ringside, would

beam his voice to Smith at the transmitting shack a few miles away; Smith would then do the actual broadcast, repeating White's words verbatim as they came through his headphones. Sarnoff booked the event into theaters and public halls, and this—when added to the growing numbers of people using storebought and homemade crystal sets—brought the listening audience to more than 200,000 people. But the first heavyweight championship of the air was heard in the voice of the engineer, not the announcer.

The first baseball game was broadcast a month later. Announcer Harold Arlin of KDKA set up shop at Forbes Field on Aug. 5, 1921, and gave an account of the Pirates-Phillies game. WJZ opened its doors in October with the announced intention of broadcasting the opening game of the World Series. This it did, duplicating Sarnoff's relay system, with announcer Thomas H. Cowan taking the in-progress account from a newspaper reporter at the Polo Grounds (where the Yankees were playing the Giants) and broadcasting it to air. In Pittsburgh, Arlin continued airing sports on KDKA: the station experimented with football that fall, as well as with tennis and other sports. WBAY (soon to become WEAF) was on the air in New York: its first night schedule, Aug. 3, 1922, contained some "baseball talk" from Frank Graham of the *New York Sun*. But WEAF was not content with chat shows. On Oct. 28, 1922, via a chain of intricately linked transmitters and amplifiers, it broadcast a football game between Princeton and the University of Chicago from Stagg Field, more than 1,000 miles away. "The announcements of plays and applause of spectators were delivered to a cable circuit extending to a toll office of the telephone company in Chicago," wrote Banning. This was connected by long-distance lines to New York so that "not only did WEAF broadcast what the Stagg Field microphones picked up, but in Park Row, New York, a truck was provided with a radio receiving set," which connected to a public address system and allowed New York street crowds to hear a show transmitted from Chicago.

It was like magic. New broadcasting vistas were opening daily. Football became part of the WEAF weekend schedules. Yale and Harvard were heard on Nov. 25, 1922. The atmosphere at the station was ripe with ambition and achievement, and on this wave of optimism Graham McNamee arrived in the summer of 1923.

McNamee was still unsettled on his future. He thought he might give radio a try for five months, to see how he liked it and how it liked him. Within a year McNamee would be the most famous man in radio—without question the most influential and hardest-worked announcer in the medium's first decade. WEAF and later NBC "scheduled him for everything," recalled Red Barber in his informal history of sportscasters. "He had to announce opera and concert stars, political conventions, prizefights, football and baseball. I don't know how he did it."

He began in trepidation. It had been decided that he would cover some prizefights. Maj. White's early broadcasts, then regarded as skillful, lacked certain touches of color. The middleweight championship fight between Harry Greb and Johnny Wilson had been scheduled for the Polo Grounds in August 1923, and this was to become McNamee's baptism of fire. He was sent to the training camps to absorb the background. He interviewed the fighters and tried to prepare for the job ahead, but on the day of the fight found himself "horribly nervous," as keyed-up as the fighters themselves. As he described it in his contemporary memoir: "I found myself thinking of the 60,000 fans that would line those stands while I was up there by the ring talking to a million more for miles around. And every once in a while I would look up at the sky, praying for rain.

"I had no supper, just some pop and a hot dog or two about seven. Then I could hear the first sounds of footsteps as people began to file into the stands, at last a regular thunder. Then the preliminary fighters came down the aisle with their handlers, and there was a touch on my shoulder—just a signal to a very frightened young man who was to broadcast his first fight, detail by detail, intelligently, to millions of people. . . . But with that touch and the words, 'You're on the air, Mac,' I started, and like the fighters, once they had shaken hands, and singers at the first note, lost all my nervousness now that the job was on.

"When I was through I was as weak as any of the beaten fighters. In the nervous reaction, I could hardly stand. However, when the manager exclaimed, 'Mac, you're a hundred per cent!' I felt pretty fine. And I experienced an even bigger thrill than in my first announcing from the studio, for here I had been absolutely on my own.

I suddenly perceived the big future of radio. The five months I had set for the trial were now up, but the World Series was coming, and all at once I decided to stick."

He was in a job with no established procedure. McNamee was the first of his calling, the first complete announcer who could do play-by-play and also handle color. In a sense he was telling a story, with the roar of the crowd his one basic sound effect. The sudden shout of 50,000 people was the guarantee to a million listeners that they could believe what he was telling them, that the base runner was at that moment sliding under the catcher's mitt in a cloud of dust. "We were getting further away from announcing and deeper into the reporter's field," he would write. The good sports broadcaster needed more than a gift of gab: he needed imagination. He did not fictionalize, but he did embellish—he made the quiet moments vivid and interesting.

But McNamee was disappointed when the World Series play-by-play was given to Grantland Rice, a newspaperman, and McNamee was assigned to assist him. Rice was not the last print man to learn of the horrors of play-by-play: by the fourth inning of the third game he had had enough of it, and McNamee took over and finished the Series. He would do the Series for the next dozen years. By the end of 1923 he was famous. His opening and closing signatures ("Good evening, ladies and gentlemen of the radio audience" and "This is Graham McNamee saying good night all") were known throughout the East. His coverage of the 1925 World Series brought an avalanche of mail: 50,000 letters addressed to McNamee by name. One fan echoed the sentiments of thousands when he wrote, "I thought I was there with you." There were also quibblers: an ornithologist chastized him for describing a flock of ducks passing over between innings, when it should have been clear from the formation he described that the birds had been geese. People complained about his mistakes on the field, often enough that he developed an acute sense of error. When he could catch himself in a mistake he would laugh about it on the air, but he never lost "the impulse to dive into the microphone and pull it back. The broadcaster's mistake, once made, has passed forever."

In time McNamee found his audiences changing. The listener of 1923 wanted color above all:

he wanted "to be brought close to the scene," and McNamee gave him that. "Given a choice between an expert who knew the fine points of boxing or football and one who had scant knowledge but infused his words with glowing drama, the listeners preferred the latter every time," wrote radio critic Ben Gross. Gross had broached the subject to NBC president Merlin H. Aylesworth in the early days of the network: "What does McNamee actually know about football?" Aylesworth replied: "Damned little, but he certainly puts on a great show."

McNamee was still at the top of his game as the networks opened and capped off the decade. He covered the first radio Rose Bowl in 1927, after phone lines carrying programs from the two coasts were joined in Denver. But the fan was changing as the new decade arrived. He was no longer enchanted by the novelty of radio. He wanted facts and details, not just color, and just that quickly McNamee was on the way out. He was yanked unceremoniously from the 1935 World Series, replaced by the young team of Red Barber and Bob Elson. But Barber never lost his high regard for McNamee: to him, McNamee was a towering figure who set in motion and shaped the entire industry, one "who first went into a new land called radio, armed with only carbon microphones." But McNamee had been "burned up in nineteen years" on a continuous treadmill. His last years in radio were spent on network variety shows—as stooge for Ed Wynn, as announcer for Rudy Vallee. He died May 9, 1942, at 53, of a brain embolism. "He'd lived a thousand years," wrote Barber.

Of the others, the most prominent was Ted Husing.

But Husing (again as Barber saw it) spent his announcing career "possessed by the greatness of McNamee." Although the *New York Herald-Tribune* lauded him in 1927 as "consistently better than the more famous Graham McNamee and Phillips Carlin," Barber maintained that "Ted was to spend his entire life trying to outdo Graham." Husing was "devious," wrote Barber; "he schemed" and was difficult to like. He arrived at WJZ in 1924 and quickly became man-of-all-work at the microphone. He opened the station at 9 A.M. and closed it at midnight: he announced most of the morning shows as well as the band remotes more than 12 hours later. He knew the basic requisites of mike presence;

one trade journal described him as a "soft talker" who maintained "terrific speed" without ever raising his voice. "You could stand right next to him as he broadcast and not hear a word he says."

In 1925 he became assistant to Maj. J. Andrew White and began to cover sports. In 1926 he invented an "identification board" as an aid in football broadcasts: operated by an assistant, it lit up the names of the players and told him instantly who had done what. He used it that year in his first play-by-play assignment, the Princeton-Navy game. In 1927 he moved to the fledgling network that was about to become CBS. Maj. White had helped organize it, and Husing came in as his assistant. When William S. Paley took over the network, he found Husing entrenched as office manager. "He had no idea how to manage an office," Paley would recall in his memoir. "He drove me crazy, giving me the wrong answers to everything." But in 1928, when White was ill and could not travel to Chicago for a football commitment, Husing was sent in his place. His announcing was poised and supremely self-assured ("I lost an impossible office manager and gained the best and most famous sportscaster in the country," Paley would recall), and from then until 1946 he was the network's top man.

He covered his first World Series in 1929 and his first Kentucky Derby the same year. Paley, listening to the CBS and NBC race broadcasts simultaneously, pronounced CBS the winner, going away. By the early 1930s, Husing had mounted a serious challenge to McNamee's long reign at the top. He suffered a setback in 1935, when he was barred from baseball coverage by Commissioner K. M. Landis (the staunch Judge Landis, who had been given almost dictatorial control of the game after the "Black Sox" scandal of 1919). The commissioner had found Husing's criticisms of umpires annoying.

Husing moved on to other sports. He began his Orange Bowl coverage in 1936, covered the America's Cup race from a Coast Guard cutter in 1937, and was regarded by a *Radio Guide* writer as "one of the ablest golf reporters working in radio or any other medium." He topped McNamee in *Guide*'s "Star of Stars" poll in 1937 and 1938: McNamee was virtually out of sports by then, and his finish in second place was a tribute to his former stature. Others in the 1938 poll, in order, were Bob Elson, Clem McCarthy, Tom Manning, Paul Douglas, Pat Flanagan, Red Barber, Hal Totten, and Bill Stern.

The radio pioneer in horse racing was Clem McCarthy. Possessed of a gravel voice and a folksy style, McCarthy had been around horses most of his life. His father had been a starter, trainer, auctioneer, and veterinary dentist. Outgrowing his youthful ambition to be a jockey, McCarthy worked for both daily racing sheets, the *Morning Telegraph* and the *Daily Racing Form*, as a handicapper. In 1925, he persuaded management at Bowie racecourse to install a loudspeaker system so that fans might be kept abreast during the running of races. McCarthy was its voice. He did this again in Chicago, when Arlington Park opened in 1927, then joined NBC and aired the first network radio Kentucky Derby in 1928. Folklore has it that Damon Runyon helped him get the Derby job after the designated announcer was eased out earlier in the day: that announcer had wagered on the first race, and his "call" consisted of wire-to-wire rooting for his bet, ending with "You son of a bitch!"

McCarthy was more professional. Soon his sawblade delivery, wrapped in the colorful catchphrase "Good afternoon, rrrrraaacing fans," was an indelible part of the scene. McCarthy also worked some of the top fights: his description of the one-round Joe Louis kayo over the German hope, Max Schmeling, on June 22, 1938, is today considered a classic. But his heart was on the turf. He was in and out of the Derby picture after Churchill Downs began assigning rights to the broadcast—when CBS had it in 1935, it was covered by Thomas Bryan George and Bob Trout—but was more often in than out. He managed to make the 1937 match race between Seabiscuit and War Admiral a breathless affair, despite Seabiscuit's easy victory. They were not all so easy to call: often the fields were bunched and crowded, making racing, in McCarthy's view, the most difficult of all sports assignments. "So much happens in so short a time," he would say; "the announcer has to know the silk colors and always be correct. No mistakes can be made—the public won't forgive a racing error."

And yet, in 1947, near the end of his career, McCarthy made that most awful of mistakes: he mixed his silks in the Preakness and described a torrid stretch duel among On Trust, Phalanx, and Derby hero Jet Pilot, calling Jet Pilot the winner. In fact, Jet Pilot had faded to fourth. The real winner, Faultless, never got a call through the whole stretch drive.

By 1926, radio sports coverage was too big to ignore. Newspapers began carrying verbatim accounts of major prizefights and even three-hour baseball games. They accomplished this by hiring three shorthand reporters to sit at radio sets and take down every word. Streetcorner arguments over the relative merits of McNamee and Maj. White were as common as those about the contests they described. Radio was cussed, praised, and resented. Fight promoter Tex Rickard blamed radio when his 1928 bout between Gene Tunney and Tom Heeney of New Zealand lost money. Others blamed the fact that Jack Dempsey was gone from the scene, retired after his defeat by decision in the controversial "long count" battle with Tunney in September 1927. Rickard announced that radio would no longer be allowed at his fights without "paying big money for the privilege." But "radio refused to be displaced," as writers Alfred Goldsmith and Austin Lescarboura noted in 1930. "The people wanted radio. The people wanted the games. It was too late to take it away." There would be continuing friction between radio and organized sports, and there was a notable ban, 1934–39, when the three New York baseball teams agreed to throw the broadcasters out of their stadiums. But these policies were short-sighted and self-destrictive, and most attempts to ban microphones never got past the talking stage.

Every town with a big-league team or a major arena had its favorite son of the air. Many of these local announcers later moved on to network special events and gained national followings. One of the earliest, recalled by Ben Gross, was Perry Charles of WHN, New York. Unlike White, McNamee, and others, Charles refused to inject color into a dull event. "These here stumble-bums ain't fighting, they're just waltzing around. What's the use of boring you with this stuff? Maybe instead you'd like to hear some jokes?" At around the same time, 1925, Fred Hoey began covering the Boston Red Sox, a team he followed more than 40 years. In Chicago, Hal Totten had been doing play-by-play since the mid-1920s; Quin Ryan began shortly thereafter. Pat Flanagan aired from WBBM beginning in 1929. Red Barber recalled the 1930 big-league lineup as follows: Hoey in Boston; Ty Tyson in Detroit; Franz Laux in St. Louis; Harry Hartman in Cincinnati; Tom Manning in Cleveland; Johnny O'Hara, Totten, Flanagan, Ryan, and Elson in Chicago. The others were on "spotty schedules," Barber wrote; "like ships that pass in the night, they came and went. There are no footprints in the air."

By 1932, Barber wrote, these ten announcers were still in place and were flanked by others: Dave Parks, John Kolbmann, Bob Hawk, Arch McDonald (who worked Washington Senators games for 22 years and was known as "the Old Pine Tree"), Ellie Vander Pyl, George Bischoff, Joe Tumelty, Russ Winnie, Jack Martin, Ed Cochrane, Earl Harper, Ed Sprague, Tony Wakeman, Bill Williams, George Sutherland, Bob Newhall, Wes McKnight, Tom Stull, Merrill Bunnell, Al Nagler, Oscar Reichow, Chuck Simpson, and Gunnar Wiig. Bill Munday was described by Barber as "a firecracker" who "exploded on the radio scene when he shared the Rose Bowl broadcast with Graham McNamee in 1929."

Then there were players, managers, and even umpires who got into broadcasting. Jack Graney, the first, worked at Cleveland. Dizzy Dean, pitcher of the old St. Louis "gashouse gang," began broadcasting in 1941 and, though colorful, was the bane of English teachers everywhere with his spontaneous and ungrammatical style ("he slud into third"). Dean covered both St. Louis teams and made little attempt to hide his partiality. There were Charley Grimm, Leo Durocher, Frankie Frisch, Mel Ott, Waite Hoyt, Pie Traynor, Dolly Stark, Larry Goetz, Russ Hodges of the Giants, Truman Bradley (who later became a top studio announcer), Fort Pearson, Ford Bond, Bob Considine, Ed Thorgerson, Bill Slater, Sam Taub, Jim Britt, Sam Balter, Stan Lomax, Bert Wilson, Jack Brickhouse, Jack Drees, Don Dunphy, Bill Corum, Joe Foss, Harry Wismer, and Mel Allen.

Allen's notable career began in the mid-1930s, in Birmingham, Ala. In 1936, he went to CBS in New York; by 1939, he was assisting Arch McDonald on baseball. He went into the Army in 1943 but continued his radio work on *The Army Hour* and other Armed Forces Radio Service shows. After the war he became well known as the voice of the New York Yankees: His well-mimicked trademark—"How about that!"—accompanied most Yankee home runs after 1949.

As for Red Barber, his career began in 1930, at the University of Florida station, WRUF. He moved to Cincinnati in 1934, working at WLW and WSAI. In 1939, with the lifting of the New York broadcast ban, he became play-by-play man for the Brooklyn Dodgers on WHN and the Mutual Network. In 1946 Barber was named director of CBS sports, replacing the departing Ted Husing. There he established a Saturday *Football Roundup*, a three-and-a-half-hour program of cut-ins and progress reports on the 20 major games of the day. He retired as a play-by-play man in 1966.

Probably the most controversial sports broadcaster in the radio years was Bill Stern (see THE COLGATE SPORTS NEWSREEL). He had a well-honed sense of drama, and it was often said that a fan sitting beside Stern at a game would not recognize the event he was watching from hearing Stern's play-by-play. Barber's verdict was blunt: "Stern didn't care what he said on the air if he thought it was provocative or controversial. He never admitted he made a mistake." But his flamboyant style took him to the top of NBC sports and to lucrative stints in newsreels. He was openly disdained by many peers. His semi-fictionalizing was perhaps excusable on his *Sports Newsreel*, which was clearly labeled "legend," hearsay," "myth." But to do this on a straight news broadcast was to other sports reporters unforgivable. When Stern called the wrong ball carrier, he would fictionalize and have him lateral to the right ball carrier. "College football never had as many single, double, and triple laterals as when Stern had the mike," wrote Barber. Stern's own penchant for error made him no more charitable to the mistakes of others. He took great delight telling and retelling of Clem McCarthy's 1947 Preakness gaff. When told of this, McCarthy said, "Well, you can't lateral a horse."

SPOTLIGHT PLAYHOUSE, dramatic anthology.

BROADCAST HISTORY: Ca. 1946, ABC West Coast. 30m. CAST: Jack Webb, Natalie Masters, etc. ORCHESTRA: Phil Bovero. PRODUCER-

WRITER: Monte Masters. **EPIGRAPH:** "The spotlight of life swings in all directions."

STAGE DOOR CANTEEN, musical variety for servicemen.

BROADCAST HISTORY: July 30, 1942–April 20, 1945, CBS. 30m, Thursdays at 9:30 until Oct. 1943, then Fridays at 10:30. Corn Products Refining Company. **HOST:** Bert Lytell. **STARS:** Jane Froman, Orson Welles, Madeleine Carroll, Connie Boswell, Mary Martin, Helen Hayes, George Burns and Gracie Allen, etc. **ORCHESTRA:** Raymond Paige. **DIRECTOR:** Earle McGill.

Stage Door Canteen was developed from a live stage show produced for servicemen during World War II at a theater near Times Square. The original *Stage Door* was formed by the American Theater Wing, an organization of entertainers from every branch of show business. It offered weekly variety entertainment to hundreds of servicemen and soon became so popular that spinoff "canteens" were established in other cities. In New York, celebrities offered their services not only for entertainment but for KP duty as well. "It is nothing to see Alfred Lunt emptying garbage pails, or Lynn Fontanne presiding at the coffeepot," wrote *Radio Life*.

The radio show aired from CBS in New York but strived for an authentic "at the canteen" flavor. MC Bert Lytell opened each broadcast with the phrase "Curtain going up—for victory!" The cast, decked out in red, white, and blue, closed each week with the national anthem. Then the servicemen lined up for autographs, which took most of the next hour.

THE STAN FREBERG SHOW, comedy.

BROADCAST HISTORY: July 14–Oct. 20, 1957, CBS. 30m, Sundays at 7:30. **CAST:** Stan Freberg, Peter Leeds, June Foray, Daws Butler. **VOCALIST:** Peggy Taylor. **MUSIC:** Billy May's orchestra and the Jud Conlon Rhythmaires. **PRODUCER-WRITERS:** Stan Freberg, Peter Barnum.

The Stan Freberg Show was 30 minutes of biting comedy and satire. Freberg rose to national prominence with a series of sketches for Capitol Records. He was a shrewd satirist whose targets were mediocrity, complacency, and stuffed shirts. He specialized in lampooning American life.

He destroyed Lawrence Welk in a skit that became known as "Wunnerful, Wunnerful": maestro Billy May coaxed from his orchestra an uncannily Welkian arrangement of *Bubbles in the Wine* while Freberg—doing a credible Welk imitation—kept yelling, "Turn off the bubble machine!" until he was drowned in the foam. Freberg "interviewed" the abominable snowman, presented a group of musical sheep, and staged a western skit, "Bang Gunley, U.S. Marshal Fields." A high spot was a skit attacking censorship, when Freberg proposed to sing Jerome Kern and Oscar Hammerstein's *Ol' Man River* but was harrassed by "Tweedley," a "citizen's committee censor," who sounded a buzzer at any line he found objectionable (no poor grammar; no allusions to the old, perspiration, or drunkenness—leading to rewriting the lyrics as "Elderly man river . . .").

THE STANDARD HOUR, concert music.

BROADCAST HISTORY: Ca. 1926–1950s, NBC, Pacific network, ultimately including Hawaii and Alaska. 60m, Sunday evenings. Standard Oil.

Though it was heard only on a partial network, *The Standard Hour* was a major musical series that spanned the entire length of network broadcasting. It began in San Francisco in 1926, when the city's symphony orchestra was threatened with bankruptcy. Standard Oil paid the debt and was given broadcast rights to that year's concerts. This became a Sunday evening tradition, running more than 30 years on the West Coast network.

The fare ranged from symphonic classics to light opera. In the 1940s the show divided its time between San Francisco and Los Angeles (featuring that city's philharmonic orchestra). Two shows a year originated in Seattle (which also boasted a symphony). By 1951 Arthur Fiedler had become the regular conductor. In addition to its full symphonic programs, the show booked such regular vocalists as Richard Tucker. Its well-remembered theme was *This Hour Is Yours*, written by Julius Haug of the San Francisco Symphony: it was simple theme music, 45 seconds long, and listeners who loved it and requested "the entire piece" were surprised when told there was no more.

Augmenting the series was *The Standard School Broadcast*, a series of musical education accepted into West Coast classrooms with the same enthusiasm that greeted *The American School of the Air* on CBS. The school series ran on NBC for a decade beginning in 1928 and on Mutual in its later days: it too stretched across three decades. *School* explored, among hundreds of topics, "the science of music," "music as drama," and non-classical musical forms (folk, jazz, and ballads). Guests ranged from Dorothy Warenskjold and Jerome Hines to Louis Armstrong, Jack Teagarden, and Huddie Ledbetter (Leadbelly).

THE STAR AND THE STORY, dramatic anthology.

BROADCAST HISTORY: Feb. 6–July 30, 1944, CBS. 30m, Sundays at 8. HOST: Walter Pidgeon.

No shows have been heard, but researcher Ray Stanich reveals a log not unlike other such series featuring Hollywood stars in film stories: *His Girl Friday*, with Rosalind Russell; *Vivacious Lady*, with Ginger Rogers; *Private Lives*, with Greer Garson; etc.

STAR FOR A NIGHT, game show.

BROADCAST HISTORY: Dec. 15, 1943–March 8, 1944, Blue Network. 30m, Wednesdays at 10:30. Adam Hats. HOST: Paul Douglas. ASSISTANT: Wendy Barrie. ANNOUNCER: Hugh James. GUESTS: Lucille Ball, Gene Kelly, etc.

Amateur contestants won prizes for their ability to act out short skits.

STARR OF SPACE, juvenile adventure drama.

BROADCAST HISTORY: June 2, 1953–May 27, 1954, ABC. 25m, Tuesdays and Thursdays at 7:30. CAST: John Larch as Captain Rocky Starr of Nova City Space Station. Jane Harlan as his comrade, Gail Archer. Tom Hubbard as Cadet Sergeant Stripes. CREATOR-WRITER: Tom Hubbard.

STARRING BORIS KARLOFF, horror anthology; also known as *Presenting Boris Karloff* and *Mystery Playhouse*.

BROADCAST HISTORY: Sept. 21–Dec. 14, 1949, ABC. 30m, Wednesdays at 9, with identical versions seen on ABC-TV on Thursdays following the radio shows. CAST: Boris Karloff, host and occasional star of well-known short stories by Cornell Woolrich, Arch Oboler, etc. MUSIC: George Henniger on organ. PRODUCER-DIRECTOR: Charles Warburton.

STARS IN THE AIR, Hollywood glamour anthology.

BROADCAST HISTORY: Dec. 13, 1951–June 30, 1952, CBS. 30m, various evening times. HOST-ANNOUNCER: John Jacobs.

Stars was merely an extension of the old *Screen Guild Theater* under a different name. Offerings included *The Yearling*, with Gregory Peck; *The Paleface*, with Bob Hope; *The House on 92nd Street*, with Humphrey Bogart; etc.

STARS OVER HOLLYWOOD, dramatic anthology.

BROADCAST HISTORY: May 31, 1941–Sept. 25, 1954, CBS. 30m, Saturdays at 12:30. Dari Rich, until 1948; Armour and Company, 1948–51; Carnation, 1951–54. CAST: Hollywood stars in light drama: Alan Ladd, Anita Louise, Mary Astor, Bonita Granville, Phil Harris, Merle Oberon, Basil Rathbone, etc. Hollywood radio actors in support: Pat McGeehan, Tom Collins, Lurene Tuttle, Janet Waldo, etc. ANNOUNCERS: Jim Bannon and Frank Goss, early 1940s; Art Gilmore thereafter. MUSIC: Ivan Ditmars. PRODUCER-DIRECTOR: Paul Pierce through mid-1940s; Les Mitchel and later visiting directors including such personalities as Hans Conried.

Stars over Hollywood broke one of radio's strongest prejudices, that Saturday daytime was the ghetto of the schedule. When Paul Pierce, CBS production superintendent on the West Coast, announced plans to launch a star-packed dramatic series on Saturday morning, few observers gave it a chance. Getting movie stars to cooperate at 9:30 A.M. (local time) would be impossible, and no one would listen anyway.

Later, with *Stars* solidly established as a hit, Pierce would point out that it was the pioneer of Saturday daytime drama. This wasn't quite true—*Lincoln Highway* had preceded him by about a year—but *Stars over Hollywood* was the one that lasted. It ran 13 years in the same timeslot, with only two changes of sponsor.

The stories were generally light comedies and fluffy romances. Occasionally a suspense play was used, but there was almost no heavy drama (that, it was felt, would be pushing luck for a Saturday morning). It was the college-boy-meets-girl yarn, the showbiz-guy-meets-girl yarn, the boy-meets-girl yarn dressed up with new twists. The set was loose and informal; the dress casual. Occasionally the stars arrived in bathrobes and pajamas. Ivan Ditmars, musical director, used three instruments (organ, harp, and violin), and sounded more like a small combo than a one-man show.

Stars over Hollywood demolished the negative theories about Saturday programming. Soon the air was full of big-time drama, from *Armstrong Theater of Today* to *Grand Central Station*.

STELLA DALLAS, soap opera, based on the novel by Olive Higgins Prouty.

BROADCAST HISTORY: Oct. 25, 1937–June 3, 1938, WEAF, New York. 15m, weekdays.

June 6, 1938–Dec. 23, 1955, NBC. 15m continuation, weekdays at 4:15. Sterling Drugs (Phillips Milk of Magnesia, Double Danderine, etc.).

CAST: Anne Elstner as Stella Dallas, middle-aged heroine who gave up her daughter, Laurel, to a marriage of wealth and society. Joy Hathaway as Laurel, late 1930s; Vivian Smolen as the long-running Laurel (a role she continued while playing the lead on *Our Gal Sunday*). Grace Valentine as Stella's true friend, Minnie Grady. Leo McCabe as Stella's husband, Stephen Dallas. Arthur Hughes and Frederick Tozere also as Stephen Dallas. Julie Benell as Helen Dallas, Stephen's later wife. Albert Aley and Warren Bryan as Bob James. Carleton Young as Laurel's husband, Dick Grosvenor. Macdonald Carey, Spencer Bentley, George Lambert, and Michael Fitzmaurice also as Dick Grosvenor. Jane Houston as Mrs. Grosvenor. Arthur Vinton as Ed Munn. Arnold Moss as Ahmed. William Smith as Philip Baxter. Helen Claire as "the wealthy but insane" Ada Dexter. ANNOUNCERS: Ford Bond, Frank Gallop, Howard Claney, Jimmy Wallington, Jack Costello, Roger Krupp. ORGANIST: Richard Leibert. PRODUCERS: Frank and Anne Hummert. DIRECTORS: Ernest Ricca, Richard Leonard, Norman Sweetser, etc. DIALOGUE: Helen Walpole, on direction from Anne Hummert. THEMES: *Memories* and *The Old Refrain* (concurrent themes ca. 1940); *How Can I Leave Thee* for most of the run.

Stella Dallas was perhaps the most excruciating melodrama on radio, certainly rivaling and some believe surpassing even the Hummerts' tortuous *Backstage Wife* and *Romance of Helen Trent* in the pain-per-minute sweepstakes. It was initially billed as "the true-to-life sequel, as written by us, to the world-famous drama of mother love and sacrifice," the "sequel" business an obvious reference to the 1937 Barbara Stanwyck film of the same name. The radio serial, it was suggested, would pick up where the film left off, but both owed their existence to the turn-of-the-century book by Olive Higgins Prouty. Prouty's tale of a gallant-hearted but disadvantaged woman of the world was as relevant to audiences of 1937 as it had been to the earlier generation. On radio, Stella blossomed into middle age: the story was eventually billed as "the later life of Stella Dallas," but the epigraph still summarized in its classic purple simplicity the whole tear-stained run:

And now, Stella Dallas, a continuation on the air of the true-to-life story of mother love and sacrifice, in which Stella Dallas saw her own beloved daughter Laurel marry into wealth and society, and, realizing the difference in their tastes and worlds, went out of Laurel's life. . . .

It was learned that Stella had been born of poor parents and had led a life of hardship. In youth she had worked in the sweatshops of Boston, as a seamstress in the garment district. There she met Minnie Grady, the sharp-tongued Irishwoman who would become her lifelong friend. Early in life she also met Stephen Dallas, a man of wealth and position who was captivated by her youthful spirit. The marriage defied great odds and lost: Stella left daughter Laurel with Stephen, believing the Dallas wealth would provide her baby with advantages that she, Stella, could not.

But Stella longed for her "Lolly-baby" with a hunger that would not be denied. Battling her way back into Laurel's life, she earned the girl's respect and then her love. But class was a powerful obstacle. When Lolly grew up and fell in love, it was with Dick Grosvenor, a young banker and son of a wealthy society matron. The shrewish Mrs. Grosvenor would never accept

Stella in her family, so Stella choked back a sob and "went out of Laurel's life."

She was never out for long, but the inherent conflict with the Grosvenors was always a factor. Add to this the usual Hummert parade of kidnappers, lunatics, and murderers, and the faithful listener got the pinnacle of melodrama with his Double Danderine. Stella was as memorable a matinee heroine as radio would produce. She clipped her *g*'s, filled the air with double negatives, and stuck with "ain't" as a proper part of speech through her entire radio career. She had keen common sense, a true heart, and an instinctive understanding of human behavior. She even became a passable amateur detective. It was a skill she would need, as Lolly's life, home, and security were often threatened by dark strangers with mysterious backgrounds, lechers who would whisk her away and have her for themselves. Early in the run, Stella chased one such, Ahmed, all the way to Egypt, becoming stuck in a tense sequence at the bottom of the Suez Canal in a submarine. In another cliffhanger, she braved the deserts and jungles of Africa. Her run-ins with "the wealthy but insane" Ada Dexter added spice to her struggles at home. Finally there was the unscrupulous adventurer Raymond Wylie, partner of Stella's husband Stephen, who tried to kill both Stella and Stephen late in the run.

Stella lived in Minnie Grady's Boston rooming house. Her true friends, like Minnie, came from the common people, ensuring their disfavor with the snooty Mrs. Grosvenor. First there was Ed Munn, described by one trade journal as "a loud, boisterous, free-spending fellow, always in search of a good time." Ed loved Stella and showered her with proposals of marriage, which she shrugged off good-naturedly. She cherished Ed's friendship but never took him seriously as a suitor. His lack of social grace embarrassed even Stella, but he remained a "fine man at heart." Another friend was Bob James—a boy, really, much younger than Stella but cut from the same poverty-stricken background, and thus an instant soulmate. Once, when Stella had made some money, she offered to send Bob through law school, but he kept getting into trouble, becoming "innocently involved in the slaying of a gangster" and then accused of murder. Stella often recovered from these emotional disasters by

resting at the Massachusetts farm owned by Minnie and her husband, Gus.

Anne Elstner was sometimes said to have won the title role because of her husky voice, vaguely reminiscent of Stanwyck's. "She auditioned along with 25 other actresses," wrote Richard Lamparski; then she played Stella for 18 years "without ever having read the book or seen either of the two movie versions. After it was over and she saw the Barbara Stanwyck picture, she left the theater sobbing." In her own career, she had found the role totally absorbing. She had been in radio since 1923, played her first notable role (as Cracker Gaddis) in the early NBC serial *Moonshine and Honeysuckle* (1930–33), and had also been heard on such New York shows as *The March of Time, The Heinz Magazine of the Air*, and *Heart Throbs of the Hills*. By nature conservative, she was one of the most vocal opponents of Communism and Communists in the acting profession during the McCarthy era. With her husband, ex–FBI man Jack Mathews, she opened a New Jersey restaurant, obtained permission to use her character's name, and for years promoted it all along the Delaware as "Stella Dallas's Restaurant." There, she could be coaxed to give her customers a bit of "Lollybaby" dialogue for old time's sake.

STEPMOTHER, soap opera.

BROADCAST HISTORY: Jan. 17, 1938–July 10, 1942, CBS. Broadcast from Chicago. 15m, weekdays at 10:45 A.M. until 1940, then at 10:30 A.M. Colgate. CAST: Sunda Love, Janet Logan, and Charlotte Manson, successively, as Kay Fairchild, stepmother. Francis X. Bushman, Bill Green, Charles Penman, and Willard Waterman as her husband, John Fairchild. Peggy Wall and Barbara Fuller as John's daughter, Peggy Fairchild. Cornelius Peeples as John's son, Bud Fairchild. Ethel Owen as Kay's best friend, Genevieve Porter. Donelda Currie and Betty Arnold also as Genevieve. Edith Davis, a white woman, as Mattie, "faithful colored servant." Guila Adams also as Mattie. Ken Christy as Leonard Clark. Cornelia Osgood as Adella Winston. Harry Elders as David Houseman. Bess McCammon as Mother Fairchild, whose presence did not make life easier. Stanley Gordon as gangster Pat Rority. Betty Hanna as Luella Hayworth. Elmira Roessler and Jane Gilbert as little

Billy Fairchild, Edith Davis (while also playing Mattie) as Mrs. Fletcher, the town gossip. **AN-NOUNCER:** Roger Krupp. **DIRECTORS:** Les Weinrott, Art Glad, Charles Penman. **WRITER:** Aline Ballard, Roy Maypole, Charles Penman.

Stepmother posed the question "Can a stepmother successfully raise another woman's children?" but concerned itself equally with the dark forces of politics, corruption, and murder. It was the story of Kay Fairchild, a young (under 30) daughter of a Chicago newspaperman who gave up her own career in journalism to marry a man a dozen years her senior.

John Fairchild was a banker in the typical midwestern town of Walnut Grove. He had been a widower for years, so his children, Peggy and Bud, had been raised by their "faithful colored servant," Mattie, from whom Kay encountered open hostility the moment she arrived. Bud soon became her ally, but her real problems were just beginning. Soon there was another woman in John's life, the scheming divorcee Adella Winston. John's infatuation with Adella cost him his job at the bank, and Kay was forced to go into business to support the family. With her best friend, Genevieve Porter, she opened a dress shop, but this drove John even further away. When an opportunity arose for John to run for mayor, Kay encouraged it, hoping that his success would draw them together again. Little did she know that John was being manipulated by the evil Leonard Clark, the town's crooked lawyer and financial power. But Kay, falling back on her skills as a reporter, exposed the plot and helped John win the election honestly.

But then the adventuress Ardella was murdered by Clark, who had mistaken her for Kay; then Clark tried to frame Kay for the deed, and throughout all this John continued to brood about Kay and the difference in their ages. He went on a yearlong tantrum in 1940: convinced that Kay was falling in love with the dashing young editor, David Houseman, he ran away and was gone for weeks. Meanwhile, Peggy was having trouble with her boyfriend, Bert Weston. John returned, Peggy married Bert and was soon expecting, Bert followed John's example and ran away, Peggy disappeared, Kay sent John away again, and Bert came back, closely followed by John. Of course there was an amnesia plot, when John

collapsed in a nervous breakdown and awoke unable to remember anything since 1938. Much of 1941 was consumed in the fight against the vicious Rority gang; 1942 saw John in yet another romantic liaison, with the scheming Luella Hayworth.

John and Kay had a son of their own, little Billy. This might have helped matters, but somehow never did.

STOOPNAGLE AND BUDD, comedy and satire.

BROADCAST HISTORY: 1930, WMAK, Buffalo. **CAST:** Frederick Chase Taylor and Budd Hulick, comics. First heard Oct. 10: a gale put the transmitter for the new CBS Network out of order, and Taylor and Hulick were pushed into the gap.

May 24–Dec. 8, 1931, CBS. 15m, an unusual Sunday-through-Wednesday schedule, at 8:45. *The Gloomchasers.*

Feb. 1–Aug. 31, 1932, CBS. 15m, Mondays and Wednesdays at 8:45. *The Ivory Soap Program.*

Dec. 29, 1932–June 22, 1933, CBS. 30m, Thursdays at 9:30. *The Pontiac Program.* **CAST:** F. Chase Taylor as Col. Lemuel Q. Stoopnagle; Budd Hulick as Budd. **ANNOUNCER:** Louis Dean. **VOCALISTS:** Jeannie Lang, a cooing singer with a giggle at the end of each number; singer William "Big Bill" O'Neal. **ORCHESTRA:** Andre Kostelanetz.

Dec. 16, 1933–Feb. 7, 1934, CBS. 15m, Wednesdays and Saturdays at 9:15. Pontiac. **ORCHESTRA:** Jacques Renard.

Feb.–June 1934, CBS. Tuesdays and Thursdays at 10, part of *The Camel Caravan.* **AN-NOUNCER:** Harry Von Zell. **VOCALIST:** Connie Boswell. **ORCHESTRA:** Glen Gray's Casa Loma Orchestra.

June 22–Sept. 7, 1934, CBS. 45m, Fridays at 10. *The Schlitz Spotlight Revue.*

Nov. 18–Dec. 16, 1934, CBS. 30m, Sundays at 9:30. *The Gulf Headliners.*

March 15–July 12, 1935, CBS. 30m, Fridays at 10:30. **ANNOUNCER:** Andre Baruch. **ORCHESTRA:** Mark Warnow. Also: May 21–July 1, 1935, 15m, Tuesdays and Thursdays at 6:45, with a final show on Monday. All for DeVoe and Reynolds Paints.

March 14–June 18, 1936, CBS. 30m, Saturdays at 9:30 until May, then Thursdays at 8:30. **VO-**

CALIST: Gogo DeLys. ORCHESTRA: Leith Stevens.

July 1–Sept. 30, 1936, NBC. 60m, Wednesdays at 9. *Town Hall Tonight*, summer substitute for Fred Allen. Bristol Myers.

Oct. 4, 1936–May 16, 1937, Blue Network. 30m, Sundays at 5:30. *The Minute Men*. Minute Tapioca. ANNOUNCER: Harry Von Zell. ORCHESTRA: Don Voorhees.

July 6–Sept. 28, 1938, NBC. 30m, Wednesdays at 9. *Town Hall Tonight*, summer substitute for Fred Allen (Taylor alone, as the partnership had dissolved). Bristol Myers.

Stoopnagle and Budd were radio's earliest true satirists. Their appearance on WMAK, Buffalo, drew huge mail, and the following year they were brought to New York for a tryout. But despite their continuing appeal to the intelligentsia, they never broke through to a mainstream radio audience to achieve the powerhouse ratings of which major broadcast careers were made. Their sponsored stints tended to run less than a year.

Frederick Chase Taylor and Wilbur Budd Hulick had drifted into broadcasting in Buffalo. Taylor had been a lumberman and a broker; Hulick had formed a small band that had recently dissolved. Both landed at the Buffalo Broadcasting Corporation, Hulick announcing and playing records on WMAK while Taylor also announced and tried to write comedy. Taylor's wit was, to say the least, unconventional. He was a master of Spoonerisms ("the pee little thrigs," "Paul Revide's rear," etc.) and an alleged genius at inventing such essentials as the "movable knothole for baseball parks." Their partnership came to life spontaneously when the station failed to receive a network program because of a line failure. Hulick, the announcer on duty, saw Taylor passing in the hall and recruited him to help fill the sudden dead air. Taylor played an organ (*I Love Coffee, I Love Tea*) while Hulick engaged him in chatter and referred to him as "Colonel Stoopnagle." This impromptu act created a local sensation, and Stoopnagle and Budd became a regular feature.

In 1931 they were summoned to New York by CBS. The network had given them a buildup to the New York press, and Taylor wanted to make a splash. They threw a press banquet, appearing (unknown to their guests) as bumbling waiters who dropped trays, bickered over details, and

spilled food on reporters who had come to meet them. But their early to mid-1930s shows were short-lived with irregular ratings, alternating between simple quarter-hour nonsense and full 30-minute variety broadcasts. Taylor emerged as an expert in doubletalk, taking the full name Lemuel Q. Stoopnagle. In sustained formats they would chant, "We want a sponsor!" but Taylor nixed a number of potential clients who, he said, wanted to change his comedy.

They began to mock radio with such skits as "No-Can-Do, the Magician" and about this time introduced "Stoopnocracy," a forum for listeners who wanted to air their peeves. These bogus letters were written by Taylor and read by Budd: they contained such suggestions as "eliminate the backward swing of hammocks" and "cut out the inside of soap bars so that, when the outside is used up, the inside won't be left for people to step on." There were weekly skits—"dray-mas" in which they played all the roles. They were among the first to do imitations of living people (Calvin Coolidge, Bing Crosby) and characters from other radio shows (*Amos 'n' Andy*). The "colonel's inventions" continued—an upside-down lighthouse for submarines; a rungless ladder for washing first-floor windows; round dice for people who prefer to play marbles. There were also bogus premiums, such as the "both sides wrong" bed: "Just tear off the top of the Empire State Building, mail it in, and it's yours."

They dissolved the partnership after the 1936–37 series, *The Minute Men*. Hulick went into the Mutual game show *What's My Name?*, while Taylor was heard on a Yankee Network comedy-variety series with Donald Dickson. As Stoopnagle, Taylor resurfaced periodically over the next decade. He was heard on the crazy quiz show *Quixie Doodles* (Mutual; CBS) and on at least six briefly held and usually sustained CBS runs ca. 1941–44. Two CBS Stoopnagle shows of note: a stint for Schutter Candy (*Stoopnagle's Stooperoos*, Jan. 10–July 4, 1943, Sundays at 1:45) and a summertime gig for *Burns and Allen* (July 6–Aug. 24, 1943, Tuesdays at 9 for Swan Soap). In 1947, he substituted for Bob Hawk; again he created a groundswell of popular approval, and this led to his booking on Vaughn Monroe's new *Camel Caravan* (CBS, Saturdays at 9:30, 1947–48).

Taylor died in 1950. As for Hulick, he followed his *What's My Name?* success with a

1939 Mutual series, *Music and Manners*, and trickled back into local radio. As a comedy team, Stoopnagle and Budd were legitimate forerunners to Bob Elliott and Ray Goulding, who brought this kind of comedy to a peak in the 1950s.

STOP ME IF YOU'VE HEARD THIS ONE, panel show with jokes.

BROADCAST HISTORY: Oct. 7, 1939–Feb. 24, 1940, NBC. 30m, Saturdays at 8:30. Quaker Oats. **HOST:** Milton Berle. **PANEL:** Harry Hershfield, "Colonel" Jay C. Flippen, and a guest chair with such visiting panelists as Cal Tinney, cartoonist Peter Arno, Lionel Stander, Harry McNaughton ("Bottle" from *The Phil Baker Show*) Ward Wilson ("Beetle" from the same series), and "Senator" Ed Ford, who replaced Harry Hershfield in February 1940. **MUSIC:** Ben Cutler, Del Courtney, Vincent Travers, etc. **DIRECTOR:** Joe Rines.

Sept. 13, 1947–Oct. 9, 1948, Mutual. 30m, Saturdays at 9, then at 8:30. **HOST:** Roger Bower. **PANEL:** Morey Amsterdam, Lew Lehr, Cal Tinney.

The first run of *Stop Me If You've Heard This One* preceded the better-known sound-alike *Can You Top This?* by more than a year. It was a panel of gagmasters, whose job was to expeditiously tell as many jokes as possible during the 30-minute timeslot. Unlike *Can You* (which asked listeners to send in jokes for the panel to top), *Stop Me* solicited jokes that the panel would interrupt and finish. The listeners were given prizes for the jokes, and small bonus awards if the panel could not complete the gag before it was read to the punchline. Panelists Ed Ford and Harry Hershfield were subsequently prominent on *Can You Top This?*

The 1947 revival was still a low-budget affair: listeners got $5 if their jokes were used, and $10 if the panel missed the payoff. If one of the panelists knew the joke, he yelled, "STOP!" and picked up Roger Bower's narration from that point. A listen to just about any 15-second segment would convince most people that they were hearing *Can You Top This?*

STOP OR GO, quiz.

BROADCAST HISTORY: March 23, 1944–March 18, 1945, Blue Network. 30m, Thursdays at 10:30 through Oct. 5, 1944, then Sundays at 8:30. McKesson & Robbins for Calox (dentifrice). **HOST-QUIZMASTER:** Joe E. Brown, **PRODUCER:** Bill Krauch. **WRITERS:** Erna Lazarus, Vic McLeod, Ben Pearson.

Stop or Go gave men in uniform the opportunity to win cash awards of $20 to $80. As reviewed by *Variety*, the show took contestants on "mythical journeys" for correct answers, with each "destination" doubling the money already won. "Interloculator" Brown, said the critic, was deeply appreciated by the audience for his "unselfish labors on behalf of the boys overseas," and the show was spiced by such name guests as Dorothy Lamour.

STOP THAT VILLAIN, quiz.

BROADCAST HISTORY: Sept. 6–Nov. 29, 1944, Mutual. 30m, Wednesdays at 8:30. **HOSTS:** Marvin Miller, the "hero," who tried to keep contestants on the right track; and Jack Bailey, the "villain," who offered confusing, misleading clues.

STOP THE MUSIC, musical quiz.

BROADCAST HISTORY: March 21, 1948–Aug. 10, 1952, ABC. 60m, Sundays at 8. Various sponsors including Old Gold Cigarettes, 1950–52. **HOST:** Bert Parks. **ANNOUNCER:** Don Hancock. **VOCALISTS:** Kay Armen, Dick Brown. **ORCHESTRA:** Harry Salter. **CREATOR:** Louis G. Cowan. **PRODUCER:** Mark Goodson.

Aug. 17, 1954–Feb. 15, 1955, CBS. 60m, later 75m, Tuesdays at 8. **HOSTS:** Bill Cullen; later Happy Felton. **VOCALISTS:** Jack Haskell, Jill Corey. **ORCHESTRA:** Ray Bloch.

Stop the Music is primarily remembered as the show that ended Fred Allen's radio career. Allen was enjoying the best ratings of his life in January 1948 (28.7). His new character, Senator Claghorn (Kenny Delmar), was a national sensation, and his half-hour timeslot, Sundays at 8:30, had a powerful lead-in show, Edgar Bergen's *Charlie McCarthy Show*. Between them, Bergen and Allen had a ratings total of more than 54 points and looked almost invincible.

But *Stop the Music* worked on the same general principle as the old *Pot o' Gold* quiz. Listeners were called at home, given a crack at a question (in this case musical), and had a chance to win huge jackpots (average value $20,000) in prizes and savings bonds. The greed factor had producers confident before the first show was aired, despite the fact that ABC had booked it for the toughest hour on the air, opposite NBC's Bergen and Allen. It was announced in *Variety* under the banner headline WHO'S AFRAID OF FRED ALLEN?, and the optimism was validated immediately.

By July, Allen had been dumped out of radio's top ten: he had plunged 17 points, to 38th on the charts. Bergen wisely called it quits, taking a year's sabbatical, but for Allen there would be no comeback. He refused to move from Sundays at 8:30, and died there.

Stop the Music, meanwhile, leaped into the top ten and got as high as number two. As early as its third week it was being called "the most talked-about participation show since Ralph Edwards thought up Miss Hush for *Truth or Consequences*" (*Radio Life*). The greed factor was rooted in a jackpot unsurpassed in radio history and in the fact that it would star "*you*, the people of America!" About ten calls were made in each broadcast. Bert Parks would interrupt maestro Harry Salter or the vocalists by shouting, "STOP THE MUSIC!" in the middle of numbers. Bells would go off, and a connection would be made to someone, somewhere in America. If the person called was listening and could identify the melody being played, he won an initial prize—usually a refrigerator, stove, or radio-phonograph. More important, it put that listener in the running for the jackpot and a veritable cornucopia of loot, from cars to trailers to trips around the world.

The initial questions were easy to the point of boredom (such then-popular tunes as *Golden Earrings* and *I'm Looking over a Four-Leaf Clover*). In the vocals, Kay Armen and Dick Brown led listeners to the edge of the titles, humming over the telltale words. But the "Mystery Melody" was tantalizing and elusive. Prizes were added each week, and in one outing the swag topped $30,000. Phone numbers were selected from a huge bank of directories, and people paid scant attention to the odds against being called— at least 25 million to one. Allen tried to promote this fact without success: his $5,000 cash bounty, offered to anyone who missed a *Stop the Music* call by listening to his show, had no effect on

his erosion in the ratings. Within a year, *The Fred Allen Show* disappeared forever.

But like *Pot o' Gold*, *Stop the Music* had a quick surge of popularity and a fast fade. By the time Edgar Bergen returned in October 1949, *Music* was on the way out. Bergen moved back into his old timeslot, now on CBS, and recaptured virtually all of his old audience. *Stop the Music* plunged into single digits and struggled to a natural death in 1952. A watery attempt to revive it on CBS in 1954 failed to register any appreciable rating.

STORIES OF THE BLACK CHAMBER, adventure serial.

BROADCAST HISTORY: Jan. 21–June 28, 1935, NBC. 15m, weekdays, later three a week, at 7:15. Forhan's Toothpaste. CAST: Jack Arthur as Bradley Drake of the Black Chamber, an American espionage outfit. Gale Gordon as Paradine, master spy. Also: Helen Claire, Paul Nugent, Rosaline Greene. WRITER: Tom Curtin; based on the experiences and book of Herbert Yardley.

THE STORY OF ELLEN RANDOLPH, soap opera.

BROADCAST HISTORY: Oct. 9, 1939–Sept. 19, 1941, NBC. 15m, weekdays at 1:15, 1939–40; at 10:30 A.M., 1940–41. Super Suds. CAST: Elsie Hitz as Ellen Randolph. Also: John McGovern, Parker Fennelly, Ethel Owen, etc. WRITERS: Vera Oldham, Margaret Sangster.

No shows heard; content unknown, but described by *Variety* as the story of a "courageous heroine fighting to save her ill and discouraged hubby from the shadows of fear and defeat."

THE STORY OF HOLLY SLOAN, soap opera.

BROADCAST HISTORY: Sept. 1, 1947–May 28, 1948, NBC. 15m, weekdays at 2:30. General Mills. CAST: Gale Page as Holly Sloan, the small-town girl who came to New York for a career as a singing star of network radio. Bob Bailey as Johnny Starr, dashing president of the station where she first found work. Vic Perrin as Clay Brown, the faithful boy from back home who followed her to New York. Georgia Backus as Holly's Aunt Keturah, blind from birth, who had raised Holly in the country. Bob Griffin as network head Wilbur Ramage. Louise Arthur as Sally, a waitress who comforted Clay in his moments of despair. Marlene Aames as Lauralee McWilliams. **PRODUCER:** Carl Wester. **DIRECTOR-WRITER:** Ted Maxwell.

Holly Sloan was developed from the Rupert Hughes novel *Static* and was built around the eternal triangle. Holly, motherless and insecure, had been raised by her kindly Aunt Keturah and had learned to sing on the old woman's porch, where she spent the summer evenings crooning. Though it ran for only a season, it got good ratings and was ideally suited to songstress Gale Page, who played the lead.

THE STORY OF JOAN AND KERMIT, serial drama.

BROADCAST HISTORY: April 17–July 10, 1938, CBS. From Chicago. 30m continuation, Sundays at 7. **CAST:** Fran Carlon as Joan Martell. Olan Soulé as Kermit Hubbard. Butler Mandeville as Dr. Bolger. Donald Gallagher as Humble Dickinson. David Gothard as Lawrence Brook. **ANNOUNCER:** Franklyn MacCormack. **WRITER:** Milton Geiger.

THE STORY OF MARY MARLIN, soap opera.

BROADCAST HISTORY: Oct. 3–Dec. 28, 1934, WMAQ, Chicago.

Jan. 1, 1935–April 12, 1945, NBC, CBS, and Blue, 15m, variously: 1935, NBC, weekdays at noon, Kleenex; 1935–36, CBS at noon, Kleenex; 1936–37, NBC at 12:15, Kleenex; 1937–41, both NBC networks, Red in midafternoon (usually at 3), Blue at 11 A.M. and later at 10:30 A.M., both Procter & Gamble (Ivory Soap); 1941–42, NBC at 11 A.M. and CBS at 5 P.M., both P&G; 1942–43, NBC at 3, P&G; 1943–45, CBS at 3, "every day, just before tea time," Standard Brands and Tenderleaf Tea.

Sept. 24, 1951–April 11, 1952, ABC. 15m, weekdays at 3:15.

CAST: Joan Blaine (ca. 1934–36) as Mary Marlin, the Iowa housewife who became a United States senator. Anne Seymour as Mary Marlin, 1937–43. Betty Lou Gerson, Muriel Kirkland, Eloise Kummer, and Linda Carlon also as Mary Marlin. Robert Griffin as Mary's husband, Joe Marlin. Carlton Brickert and Arthur Jacobson as David Post, Joe Marlin's old law partner, who secretly loved Mary. Peter Donald and Bob Jellison as Oswald Ching. Phil Lord and Fred Sullivan as Frazier Mitchell; Fran Carlon and Templeton Fox as his wife, Bunny. Rosemary Garbell as Tootie, the waif who came to stay with the Mitchells. Rupert LaBelle as Rufus Kane. June Meredith as Eve Underwood. Betty Lou Gerson as Henrietta Dorn, Mary's childhood friend from Iowa, whose husband Michael went to war and came home bitter and crippled. Harvey Hays and Francis X. Bushman as Michael. Frank Dane and William Lee as Never-Fail Hendricks, the private detective hired by Mary to find her long-missing husband. Jerry Spellman, Dolores Gillen, and Bobby Dean Maxwell as little Davey Marlin, Mary's son. Frankie Pacelli as Timothy Kent, the little blind boy entrusted to Mary by his dying mother. **ANNOUNCERS:** Truman Bradley, Nelson Case, Les Griffith, John Tillman, Tip Corning. **CREATOR-WRITER:** Jane Crusinberry. **DIRECTORS:** Gordon Hughes, Basil Loughrane, Don Cope, Ed Rice, Kirby Hawkes. **THEME:** *Clair de Lune*, by Debussy; a haunting rendition simply played by pianists Allan Grant and Joe Kahn.

Mary Marlin was a glittering soap opera of Washington politics and exotic globetrotting. Purportedly based in part on the life of writer Jane Crusinberry, it told of a young woman who filled her husband's seat in the United States Senate when he disappeared on a trip to Russia. Most of the autobiographical events took place in the brief prenetwork run.

Crusinberry had aspired to a singing career and had just returned from a trip to Europe. She was in Chicago looking for work when suddenly, as she explained to an interviewer, the Marlins rose out of her imagination and begged her to tell their story. Mary and Joe Marlin lived "in a shady home on Main Street" in Cedar Springs, Iowa. Joe, a lawyer in partnership with David Post, had disgraced himself in an affair with a secretary. Mary, disillusioned, maintained the belief that as a wife she must forgive even infidelity. So they tried again: Joe ran for the Senate, won, and their lives changed dramatically and forever.

This was the situation as *The Story of Mary*

Marlin moved to NBC. It was quite unlike anything on the daytime air and reaped top ratings for its first six years. But under all the glitter, it was still a soap opera, with jealousy, scheming women, unbridled ambition, and, truly, the father of all amnesia cases woven through its fabric.

The Marlins arrived in Washington in joy and hope. Mary had just given birth to little Davey, and Joe had a new lease on life. But Joe remained a difficult man, a temperamental idealist with streaks of instability. Again he was attracted to another woman, Bunny Mitchell, wife of a powerful cabinet member. When Bunny obviously returned his affection, a two-pronged crisis arose: the Marlins drew the wrath of once-friendly Frazier Mitchell, and again they were pushed to the brink of separation.

The situation was eased by Eve Underwood, distinguished Washington hostess and widow of a former presidential candidate. Eve pulled some strings and had Joe sent on a mission to Russia. This led to the backbone of the serial, consuming a years-long search by Mary and her operative, Never-Fail Hendricks, for some trace of her missing husband. Listeners knew that Joe's plane had crashed on a mountain slope and that he had begun a long trek across Asia, searching for his identity, for the house he envisioned on a shady street, and for the woman named Mary who haunted his dreams.

As an early return for Joe Marlin looked less likely, the necessity of filling his Senate seat became vital. Mary was appointed by the governor and was thus swept into the panorama of Washington. For years the action cut back and forth from Washington to back roads around the globe. Listeners enjoyed the Washington atmosphere, the crowded parties and political intrigue: at the same time they were fascinated by Joe, traveling the world as "Mr. Ex," facing storm-tossed seas and rubbing elbows with gurus and generalissimos. At times the two stories drew tantalizingly close, Joe once arriving in Texas with his Chinese friend, Oswald Ching. Mary by then was linked with Rufus Kane, the labor leader who (Roosevelt notwithstanding) was elected president and longed for the beautiful senator from Iowa to be his first lady.

THE STORY OF SANDRA MARTIN, soap opera.

BROADCAST HISTORY: Ca. 1945, CBS West Coast. 15m continuation. **CAST:** Mary Jane Croft as Sandra Martin, reporter for the *Los Angeles Daily Courier*, who campaigned against postwar rackets (the baby black market, real estate scams). Griff Barnett as Editor Wilson. Bob Latting as Eddie Dalton, young reporter. Howard McNear as racketeer Steve Heywood. Ivan Green as Detective Hack Taggart, Sandra's love interest. **PRODUCER:** Gordon Hughes. **WRITER:** Les Edgely.

THE STORY OF SWING, musical documentary.

BROADCAST HISTORY: April 16–July 9, 1939, WMCA, New York, and an eight-station intercity network. 30m, Sunday afternoons.

The Story of Swing was an ambitious 13-week project of the WPA Federal Radio Theater. The entire history and scope of swing music was examined, from ragtime through "today's jitter-bugs and boogie-woogie." There were musical biographies of Louis Armstrong, Duke Ellington, the Dorseys, Gene Krupa, and Benny Goodman. Cut-ins from old records were frequent, and the series was narrated by "oldtime trombonist" Dave Morton. The Intercity Network ranged from Philadelphia and Baltimore west to York, Pa., and north to Lawrence, Mass. The Federal Radio Theater was created to give out-of-work actors jobs of sorts: earlier it had staged a 16-week *Shakespearean Cycle*, and other WPA projects were *Women in the Making of America, Great American Doctors,* and *The Story of the American Businessman.*

STRAIGHT ARROW, juvenile western adventure.

BROADCAST HISTORY: May 6, 1948–June 21, 1951: initially West Coast Don Lee Network, 30m, Thursdays at 8 Pacific time. Mutual Network, coast to coast, from Feb. 7, 1949. 30m, Mondays at 8 until Jan. 30, 1950. Often augmented by early evening broadcasts, Tuesdays and Thursdays at 5, this becoming its standard time in 1950–51. Sponsor throughout: Nabisco Shredded Wheat. **CAST:** Howard Culver as Steve Adams, rancher, who in times of trouble became the Commanche warrior Straight Arrow. Fred Howard as his sidekick, grizzled ranch hand Packy McCloud. Gwen Delano as Mesquite Molly. **ANNOUNCER-NARRATOR:**

Frank Bingman. MUSIC: Milton Charles on the Hammond organ, which was also used for the arrow effect. PRODUCER-DIRECTOR: Neil Reagan briefly, then Ted Robertson. WRITER: Sheldon Stark. SOUND EFFECTS: Ray Kemper, Tom Hanley, Bill James, Dick Moblo.

Straight Arrow was the story of Steve Adams, a young man of Commanche descent who was taken in by a ranching family and raised as a white man. In early adulthood, Steve was told an Indian legend about a fabulous warrior who would someday appear to save his people. He himself was to fulfill that destiny, riding out of his secret cave astride a magnificent golden horse. The opening signature, with few changes from the first show to the last, told it all:

INDIAN DRUMBEATS. ANNOUNCER, CHANTING INDIAN-STYLE:

N-a-b-i-s-c-o
Nabisco is the name to know.
For a breakfast you can't beat,
Eat Nabisco Shredded Wheat!

MUSIC UP (INDIAN THEME).

Keen eyes fixed on a flying target!
A gleaming arrow set against a rawhide string!
A strong bow bent almost to the breaking point!
And then . . .

SOUND OF ARROW BEING SHOT (A SHIMMERING ORGAN EFFECT INDICATING FLIGHT), FOLLOWED BY THE ARROW'S IMPACT.

Straaaaaiiiiight Arrow!

MUSIC UP (DRIVING INDIAN THEME).

To friends and neighbors alike, Steve Adams appeared to be nothing more than the young owner of the Broken Bow cattle spread. But when danger threatened innocent people, and when evil-doers plotted against justice, then Steve Adams, rancher, disappeared . . . and in his place came a mysterious stalwart Indian, wearing the dress and warpaint of a Commanche, and riding the great golden palomino Fury . . . galloping out of the darkness to take up the cause of law and order throughout the West comes the legendary figure of . . .

STRAAAAAIIIIIGHT ARROW!

His true identity was known only to his sidekick, Packy McCloud. His cry to the golden stallion—*Kaneewah, Fury!*—was boomed out of an echo chamber, giving it a huge, formidable sound. The dialogue was peppered with authentic-sounding Indian phrases, notably "Manituwah" ("farewell"). Howard Culver gave a robust performance, modifying his voice as he changed from Adams to Arrow, much as Bud Collyer seemed to grow as he changed from Clark Kent to Superman. Director Ted Robertson and soundman Ray Kemper did on-site research and recording at an intertribal Indian ceremonial gathering in Gallup, N.M., in 1949. Milton Charles was able to simulate the arrow's flight on the organ with a tremolo that *Radio Life* predicted "will make shivers tingle down your spine."

The vivid nature of the show kept it alive for its fans for years after it left the air. A *Straight Arrow* newsletter was still being issued in the 1990s by William and Teresa Harper of North Augusta, S.C. It is the definitive source of *Straight Arrow* lore.

STRANGE AS IT SEEMS, weird tales, based on the cartoon panels of John Hix.

BROADCAST HISTORY: Aug. 17, 1939–Dec. 26, 1940, CBS. 30m, Thursdays at 8:30. Palmolive Shave Cream. HOST: Alois Havrilla.

1947–48, transcribed 15m. HOST: Gayne Whitman. PRODUCER-DIRECTOR: Cyril Armbrister. MUSIC: Felix Mills.

THE STRANGE DR. WEIRD, mystery melodrama; supernatural fantasy.

BROADCAST HISTORY: Nov. 7, 1944–May 15, 1945, Mutual. 15m, Tuesdays at 7:15. Adam Hats. NARRATOR: Maurice Tarplin as Dr. Weird. WRITER: Robert A. Arthur.

The Strange Dr. Weird was a poor man's *Mysterious Traveler*, enacted by the same performer and written by one of *Traveler*'s authors. Except for the shorter format and a consequent lapse in quality, the shows were almost identical. Dr. Weird narrated grisly and fantastic tales, closing in *Traveler* style as well: "Oh, you have to leave now—too bad! But perhaps you'll drop in on me again soon. I'm always home. Just look for the house on the other side of the cemetery—the house of Dr. Weird!"

THE STRANGE ROMANCE OF EVELYN WINTERS, soap opera.

BROADCAST HISTORY: Nov. 20, 1944–Nov. 12, 1948, CBS. 15m, weekdays at 10:30 A.M. Sweetheart Soap. **CAST:** Toni Darnay as Evelyn Winters, a young woman who becomes the ward of a handsome and successful playwright. Martin Blaine and then Karl Weber as the playwright, Gary Bennett. Ralph Bell as Charlie Gleason, Bennett's manager. Kate McComb as Maggie, Evelyn's "dearly adored housekeeper." Stacy Harris as Ted Blades, Evelyn's would-be suitor. Mary Mason as Evelyn's young friend, Jinny Roberts. Linda Carlon-Reid as Miss Bean, secretary to Gary and Charlie. **ANNOUNCER:** Larry Elliott. **PRODUCERS:** Frank and Anne Hummert. **DIRECTOR:** Ernest Ricca. **THEME** (with a nod at the sponsor): *Sweetheart*, on organ.

This was "the story of Gary Bennett, playwright, who suddenly and unexpectedly finds himself the guardian of lovely Evelyn Winters." Just why a "girl" of 20 needed a male guardian 15 years her senior was rather glossed over, but the inevitable romantic attraction bloomed and that was that. The show opened by throwing the question to its listeners—"Do *you* think 15 years is too great a difference for marriage?"

Gary had assumed his guardianship after the war. Her father, a buddy, had been killed, and Gary had this obligation to do right by the kid. But this was no kid: the attraction was mutual, and both did what they could to mute it in the name of propriety.

STREAMLINED SHAKESPEARE, classic drama.

BROADCAST HISTORY: June 21–July 26, 1937, Blue Network. 45m, Mondays at 9:30. **CAST:** John Barrymore with his wife, Elaine Barrie, and such guests as Walter Brennan. **MUSICAL DIRECTOR:** Will Prior. **WRITER-ADAPTER:** Forrest Barnes.

Streamlined Shakespeare set off a furious Battle of the Bard between NBC and CBS. In May 1937, CBS had elaborately announced plans for a summer Shakespeare festival, which would star "a glittering list of vowel wizards" (*Newsweek*) from stage and screen. That CBS was billing it as "the first major radio production of William Shakespeare's plays" irked NBC greatly. "Spontaneous combustion fired the publicity department" at the older network: "Dusty files

were searched, and the radio world was informed that between Sept. 8, 1929, and April 23, 1937, the National Broadcasting Company had presented 70 programs of the best-known Shakespearean dramas." Furthermore, said NBC, its Blue Network was jumping the gun on the CBS show, and offering no less a Shakespearean personage than John Barrymore to star in *its* series, which would commence at once with *Hamlet.*

CBS, caught flat-footed, fired back with big names: *its* series would star the likes of Leslie Howard, Rosalind Russell, Edward G. Robinson, Walter Huston, and Humphrey Bogart. It was a grand shootout on the highest dramatic level, "a phalanx of high-priced [CBS] voices against the lone knight of NBC" (*Newsweek*). Barrymore would "streamline" the plays to 45 minutes and modernize some of the language to make it more accessible to modern Americans. He employed long sections of narrative, with the major scenes fully dramatized. Among the plays were *The Tempest, Twelfth Night,* and *The Taming of the Shrew,* which closed the run. Immediately following *Streamlined Shakespeare* in the same timeslot was a cycle of Eugene O'Neill plays, a nice bit of counterprogramming to rival CBS, which was still offering Shakespeare.

CBS finally got its series on the air, three full weeks after Barrymore. Titled *Columbia's Shakespeare* (or *The Shakespearean Cycle*), it opened July 12 with *Hamlet,* which Barrymore had already done, and ran until August 30. Its scheduling—a full hour, Mondays at 9—was obviously devised to get a 30-minute jump on Barrymore and NBC. Among the plays: *Much Ado About Nothing* (Leslie Howard, Rosalind Russell); *Julius Caesar* (Claude Rains, Raymond Massey); *The Taming of the Shrew* (Edward G. Robinson); *Henry IV* (Walter Huston, Humphrey Bogart); and *Twelfth Night* (Cedric Hardwicke, Tallulah Bankhead, Orson Welles). The series was directed by Brewster Morgan, with Conway Tearle the narrator and Victor Bay the maestro.

It was, perhaps, the heaviest dramatic season in radio history.

THE STREET SINGER, popular music.

BROADCAST HISTORY: July 17, 1931–July 26, 1933, CBS. Various timeslots, mostly 15m, late or mid-evenings.

Feb. 5–June 27, 1935, Mutual. 15m, Tuesdays and Thursdays at 7:30.

Feb. 18–April 14, 1940, Mutual. 15m, Sundays at 11 A.M.

Jan. 5–July 3, 1942, Blue Network. 15m, three a week at 4. Ex-Lax.

The Street Singer was Arthur Tracy, who rode an air of mystery to top network stardom in 1931. Tracy grew up in Philadelphia, where he gave his first concert in his father's grape arbor. He taught himself to sing by studying the records of Caruso. He was also quick with languages and soon had a respectable repertoire of songs that he could sing in six tongues.

He first tried radio in Philadelphia in 1924. By 1930 he was at WMCA, New York, where he worked many shows and earned up to $95 a week. When the station cut back in 1931, he went to CBS: he had heard that singers were being auditioned for the many late-night quarter-hour slots then open on the network. He was given a six-week trial, to begin in July 1931. Faced with this "do-or-die" situation, he decided to give his act a novelty touch by withholding his identity.

He was advised against this by friends, who remembered how the fortunes of Joe White (the Silver-Masked Tenor) had been bound to his anonymity: once White revealed his true identity, his career was over. Tracy disregarded this advice and opened on CBS as the International Balladist. Soon he changed this to the Street Singer, and his popularity soared. Hundreds of listeners wrote, demanding his identity, which was successfully withheld for many months. His initial CBS series, heard Fridays at 9, blended into another. He joined Chesterfield's *Music That Satisfies*, a six-a-week series that ran through 1932, billing him with Ruth Etting, the Boswell Sisters, announcer Norman Brokenshire, and maestro Nat Shilkret.

But like the Silver-Masked Tenor, his popularity had peaked. He had a few more series on CBS, then sailed for England, where his popularity continued through the 1930s. He became a figure of nostalgia for writers who remembered the way radio "used to be." They remembered his theme (*Marta*), and the publicity stills showing a bright young man with an accordion and felt hat. And they remembered the late-night songfests, with David Ross announcing that " 'Round the corner and down your way comes *The Street Singer*." Tracy died Oct. 5, 1997, at 98.

STRIKE IT RICH, quiz–audience show.

BROADCAST HISTORY: June 29, 1947–April 30, 1950, CBS. 30m, Sundays at 10:30, 1947–48; at 5:30, 1948–50. Ludens Cough Drops.

May 1, 1950–Dec. 27, 1957, NBC. 30m, weekdays at 11 A.M. Colgate.

QUIZMASTER: Todd Russell, 1947–48; Warren Hull thereafter. **ANNOUNCER:** Ralph Paul. **DIRECTOR:** Walt Framer.

Strike It Rich was "radio's show with a heart," the one quiz that rewarded all comers and left little suspense over the outcome. The contestants were the downtrodden—people in need of operations, of artificial legs, of transportation to visit dying relatives. They came "to tell their own true stories," to elicit sympathy from quizzer Warren Hull, and to answer a few simple questions.

The quiz progressed through several categories, with the hapless contestant betting as much as he dared on each topic. If the contestant went broke, there was a "heartline"—a telephone onstage that took calls from listeners all over America. Service organizations, businesses, and individuals might interrupt the action with offers of $25, $50, as much as $500. Nobody walked away broke: it was a charity show masked as a quiz.

In 1954, it came under fire from the New York Welfare Department, which was being flooded with relief applications from out-of-towners who had come to the city hoping to crash the show. Welfare charged that the "heartline" made it a charity organization seeking to raise funds without a license. Owner Walt Framer adjusted the game slightly, and the show went on. It was also a successful TV series (CBS, 1951–58).

STROKE OF FATE, speculative historical drama.

BROADCAST HISTORY: Oct. 4–Dec. 20, 1953, NBC. 30m, Sundays at 9. **CAST:** Alexander Scourby, Anne Seymour, Patricia Wheel, Santos Ortega, Edgar Stehli, Ed Begley, Hal Studer, and others from New York radio in anthology roles. **ANNOUNCER:** Lionel Ricco. **PRODUCERS:** Mort and Lester Lewis. **DIRECTOR:** Fred Weihe. **WRITERS:** Mort Lewis, George H. Faulkner.

Stroke of Fate tried to one-up *You Are There* by dealing with history on a "what if" basis.

What if Alexander the Great had lived beyond the age of 32 and continued his conquest of the world? What if America's first secret weapon (a one-man submarine) had succeeded in its intended purpose during the Revolutionary War? Speculative stories were offered on Robert E. Lee, Abraham Lincoln, Julius Caesar, Benedict Arnold, and the duel between Aaron Burr and Alexander Hamilton. Produced in consultation with the Society of American Historians, the series utilized several *You Are There* trappings including the echo chamber for its announcers. In the end, however, history was far more interesting when it was real than it was when imagined.

THE STU ERWIN SHOW, comedy.

BROADCAST HISTORY: June 11–Sept. 24, 1945, CBS. 30m, Mondays at 10:30. Ballantine Ale. **CAST:** Stu Erwin, Cameron Andrews, Peggy Conklin, Pert Kelton. **ANNOUNCER:** John Reed King. **VOCALIST:** Milena Miller. **ORCHESTRA:** Jay Blackton. **DIRECTOR:** Bill Wilgus. **WRITER:** Leonard L. Levinson. No shows heard; content unknown.

STUDIO ONE, dramatic anthology.

BROADCAST HISTORY: April 29, 1947–July 27, 1948, CBS. 60m, Tuesdays at 9:30. **CAST:** Initially a rotating group of radio players—Everett Sloane, Anne Burr, Robert Dryden, Paul McGrath, Mercedes McCambridge, Hester Sondergaard, Joe DeSantis, Stefan Schnabel, etc. Top-ranked film stars more frequently in 1948: Charles Laughton, James Mason, Robert Young, Franchot Tone, Marlene Dietrich, etc. **PRODUCER:** Robert J. Landry. **DIRECTOR:** Fletcher Markle. **SCRIPT EDITOR:** Vincent McConnor.

Studio One was quickly lionized by the press as "the most ambitious new series in radio." It was slotted by CBS programmer Davidson Taylor into the toughest hour on the air, opposite *Fibber McGee and Molly* and *The Bob Hope Show*. This, coupled with the fact that for the first six months of its run it was unavailable on the West Coast, led to its demise after a single season.

Employed to make something of it was Fletcher Markle, a 26-year-old Canadian who had won his broadcasting stripes on the CBC. Markle announced that *Studio One* would not

employ major stars ("Americans have been educated to think that a program is not a major program without stars; in Canadian and British radio, there are no stars, yet every performer is a star") and would concentrate on novels and plays that had received scant air play. He would use *Studio One* as a forum for a repertory company of top New York radio actors. True to this, it opened with Malcolm Lowry's *Under the Volcano* and followed with stories that had seldom if ever been heard. Markle also installed a novel credit system, whereby the actors would step to the microphone after the show and announce the names of their characters; Markle would then give their real names, building listener identification with the performers.

Script editor Vincent McConnor was told to take few liberties with the original author's work. "If you buy a property you should stick with it," said Markle. "Most writers spend two years or more writing a book or a play—why should we scrap it and start over?" The adaptations consisted mainly of skillful cutting and trying to preserve the spirit of the work. Sometimes this resulted in too much story for an hour: only the highlights of Hervey Allen's sprawling *Anthony Adverse* could be done, resulting in a disjointed show that was difficult to follow. For the most part, *Studio One* was superior entertainment, but as ratings remained in the basement Markle did succumb to the need for bigger names.

He was "the 1947 radio genius" in the Orson Welles mode, a man who did much of the directing, writing, acting, and announcing himself. Four decades later, Markle recalled the show with fondness and disbelief. Books could be bought for a song. "We even got Hemingway, I believe, for a hundred dollars."

SUMMERFIELD BANDSTAND, comedy, musical variety.

BROADCAST HISTORY: June 11–Sept. 3, 1947, NBC. 30m, Wednesdays at 8:30. Summer replacement for *The Great Gildersleeve*. Kraft Foods.

Summerfield Bandstand was designed purely for continuity: to provide a pleasant musical show and remind listeners with a "Summerfield" format that *The Great Gildersleeve* would return in the fall. Band numbers were interspersed between songs by Ken Carson and various female guests. Gildersleeve (Harold Peary), Leroy (Walter Tetley), and other "Summerfield" residents appeared sporadically in between-numbers skits.

SUSPENSE, crime anthology; "radio's outstanding theater of thrills."

BROADCAST HISTORY (ALL CBS): July 22, 1940: On-air audition for the series *Forecast*; this single show bore scant resemblance to the subsequent series. STAR: Herbert Marshall in *The Lodger*. ORCHESTRA: Wilbur Hatch. DIRECTOR: Alfred Hitchcock.

June 17, 1942–Jan. 19, 1943, 30m, Wednesdays at 9:30 from New York; Tuesdays at 9:30 as of Oct. 27. HOST: "The Man in Black," beginning Oct. 27. PRODUCER: Charles Vanda until late July; William Spier, producer, and John Dietz, Ted Bliss, Robert L. Richards, etc., directors thereafter. WRITER: John Dickson Carr.

Jan. 26, 1943–Dec. 26, 1947, Hollywood origination; various 30m timeslots until Dec. 2, 1943; then Thursdays at 8 for Roma Wines until Nov. 20, 1947; then Fridays at 9:30, sustained. HOST: Joseph Kearns or Ted Osborne as "the Man in Black." ANNOUNCERS: Truman Bradley for Roma Wines; Ken Niles and Frank Martin ORCHESTRA: Bernard Herrmann, Lucien Moraweck, Lud Gluskin. PRODUCER: William Spier. SOUND EFFECTS: Berne Surrey, David Light, etc.

Jan. 3–May 15, 1948, 60m, Saturdays at 8. HOST: Robert Montgomery. PRODUCER-DIRECTOR: William Spier until late Jan.; William N. Robson for two broadcasts; Anton M. Leader as of Feb. 21.

July 8, 1948–June 7, 1954, 30m, Thursdays at 9, 1948–51, then Mondays at 8 beginning Aug. 27, 1951. Autolite. ANNOUNCER: Harlow Wilcox for Autolite. PRODUCER-DIRECTOR: Anton M. Leader until June 30, 1949; William Spier, producer, and Norman Macdonnell, director, 1949–50; Elliott Lewis, producer-director, as of Aug. 31, 1950.

June 15, 1954–Oct. 30, 1956, various 30m timeslots, moved frequently. Sustained. PRODUCER-DIRECTOR: Norman Macdonnell until Sept. 30, 1954, then Antony Ellis. SOUND EFFECTS: Ray Kemper, etc.

Nov. 4, 1956–Aug. 23, 1959, 30m, Sundays at 4:30, 1956–58, Sundays at 5:30 beginning Nov. 23, 1958. Multiple sponsorship. End of Hollywood run. PRODUCER-DIRECTOR: William N. Robson.

Aug. 30, 1959–Nov. 27, 1960, 30m, Sundays at 5:30 from New York. Multiple sponsorship. PRODUCER-DIRECTOR: Bruno Zirato Jr.

June 25, 1961–Sept. 30, 1962, 30m, Sundays at 6:35 from New York. DIRECTORS: Bruno Zirato Jr. until June 3, 1962, then Fred Hendrickson.

At its peak, *Suspense* was one of radio's high-profile dramatic shows. Top film stars loved it: "If I ever do any more radio work, I want to do it on *Suspense*, where I get a good chance to act," said Cary Grant in 1943, when the show was just entering what would come to be regarded as its "golden era." The reason for this enthusiasm was William Spier, who personally guided every aspect of the show, molding story, voice, sound effects, and music into audio masterpieces. "He knows *everything* about music," said composer Lucien Moraweck of Spier. "Sometimes he even knows more than the musician."

Each week Spier and Moraweck conferred over the music for the coming broadcast. Spier would plot it out, giving each small piece of score a job to perform. The same was true of sound effects: soundman Berne Surrey went through the script with Spier as if the two were plotting it themselves. The smallest details were calculated for effect, and yet Surrey, like all other artists on this prizewinning series (a Peabody in 1947, among many other awards) was free to improvise even with the show on the air and in progress. Occasionally Spier would call for an unrehearsed effect, and at times Surrey had to use his own best judgment. Once when the script called for a body to fall, the actor playing the role failed to groan upon hitting the ground. Surrey did it for him. When actor Herbert Marshall read his lines differently than he had in rehearsal, it affected the background sound, and Surrey had to adjust on the air. And in the climactic scene of the chilling *Diary of Sophronia Winters*, he achieved the sound of madman Ray Collins's head meeting Agnes Moorehead's ax by stabbing a cabbage with an icepick. In the process, he stabbed himself in the hand. Whatever the effect, he said, the soundman must become one with the actor: he must feel the emotional flow of the story and be ready to respond at once if something unexpected happened on the air.

The stars felt this as well. The play was the thing, and they knew that contributing to a superior product would enhance their reputations far more than reading some feeble film condensation. *Suspense* was one of radio's glamour showcases, but it never seemed to be trading on celebrity. People like Henry Fonda, Fredric March, and Humphrey Bogart appeared each week, but in scripts fine-tuned to their talents. Spier became known as "the Hitchcock of the airlanes." With the stars he was flexible: he required little rehearsal, just a few hours before air time. He wanted them tense at the microphone. They rewarded him with performances that were almost uniformly fine, matching the levels achieved by their underpaid supporting players, the professional radio people.

The show began in the dark days of wartime. Its opening was one of radio's best-remembered classics, used with variations throughout the run. First came the ringing of soft churchbells, intermingled with faint, tense music. The early shows had the breath of Victorian melodrama: the music had a tingling quality, of time running out or fate closing in. The narration enhanced it: . . . *the hushed voice and the prowling step . . . the stir of nerves at the ticking of the clock . . . the rescue that might be too late, or the murderer who might get away . . . we invite you to enjoy stories that keep you in . . .*

Suspense . . .

But the murderer rarely got away. It was one of Spier's all-but-unbreakable rules that evil should be brought to account. His other standards were that realism must be paramount (no supernatural or science fiction stories here), and that each play open with an immediate predicament, a situation of disaster and/or bewilderment. These were not detective stories, nor was it a horror show: *Suspense* was mainly concerned with an ordinary guy caught up in a situation that intensified and soon became unbearable. The solutions were often withheld "until the last possible moment." But these rules were occasionally flouted. The two-part Orson Welles show *Donovan's Brain* (May 18–25, 1944) was a science fiction thriller in an era when the genre was still considered nothing more than juvenile fare. *The House in Cypress Canyon* was about a couple who encountered a werewolf in their newly rented canyon home. *August Heat* propelled Ronald Colman to a date with fate and a man with a knife, a chilling sequence foretold on a tombstone. The popularity of these dark tales led Spier to try one or two a year. But usually the kicker was something as simple as an auto accident. Such an accident formed the crisis in the story *Dead Ernest*, when the victim went into a cataleptic coma resembling death: the result was a race with time against the embalmer's knife.

Easily the most famous of all *Suspense* plays was on the face of it a straight murder story by novelist Lucille Fletcher. There was nothing supernatural about *Sorry, Wrong Number*, excepting perhaps the intensity of Agnes Moorehead's performance. Moorehead played the invalid Mrs. Elbert Stevenson with such terrified realism that she sometimes collapsed across the table at the conclusion. It horrified the nation when it was first heard May 25, 1943: the effect was potent despite an actor's gaffe at the most critical moment, when the "killer" missed his cue and for many listeners left the outcome in doubt. The story begins when Mrs. Stevenson is plugged into a private telephone conversation by mistake and hears two men plotting the murder of a bedridden woman. The murder is to take place at 11:15, just as the elevated train comes roaring past the window. The woman's efforts to get help by phone are frustrated: operators are stereotypically uncaring, and the police, when she does get through, don't put much credence in her story. Her mounting hysteria (as only Moorehead could do it) adds to the problem. Too late, she realizes that the murder being planned is her own: Mrs. Elbert Stevenson's agony is lost in the wail of the train. Even in *Sorry, Wrong Number*, Spier broke one of his rules. The killers got away, the final horror in the woman's pathetic death.

Sorry transcended *Suspense* and was widely perceived to be the most effective radio show ever. In the continuing hyperbolic fallout, Orson Welles proclaimed it the greatest show of all time. It was repeated seven times over the years, the first repeat (by popular demand and because of the flawed performance in the original) coming just three months later. By its fourth airing, in 1945, the show had taken on the characteristics of an urban legend. People within the industry asked for permission to watch (neither

Spier nor his successors allowed a studio audience), and by air time the soundstage was crowded with onlookers. Moorhead was oblivious: she spent the six hours immediately before the broadcast in intense preparation, going over the script with Spier and Surrey. She would read from her original script, believing it a good luck charm: a *Radio Life* reporter, present at the broadcast, noted that her script was now "torn, tattered, and heavily marked." By then she had most of the dialogue memorized. Her reliance on Surrey and his sound wizardry was well known: he had been with her on all four performances to date. The intricate timing between them was noted by the reporter: Moorehead picked up an imaginary telephone in tandem with Surrey's sounds. "She automatically dialed when he dialed, and banged down her imaginary receiver in synchronization with his very-much-in-evidence sound effect." Her scream was rehearsed to the pitch of Surrey's train whistle, so they'd hit that same frantic note in unison.

Sorry, Wrong Number was always a high spot for listeners and a headache for the phone company, which could count on a spate of calls condemning the insensitivity of its operators. The company protested, to no avail.

Orson Welles was a favorite in starring roles: he made his *Suspense* debut Sept. 2, 1942, in *The Hitchhiker*, a powerful story of a cross-country traveler, bedeviled by the same hitchhiker day after day. In 1944 he starred in *The Marvelous Barastro*, a play about magicians that must have been close to his heart. His appearances in *Donovan's Brain*, the story by Curt Siodmak, offered another challenge for soundman Surrey: to create the sound of a brain severed from its body and kept alive artificially. Surrey experimented for three weeks before finding an oscillator–motor pump combination satisfactory. Even engineer Robert Anderson improvised special effects on the series, notably the "fog music" for the Van Johnson show, *The Singing Walls*.

Spier initiated other ideas that were continued by his successors. He reversed the obvious, casting the usually villainous Peter Lorre in a gentleman's role and giving the oft-mild Harry Carey the part of the killer. He brought in people who had seldom been associated with heavy drama or suspense: Lucille Ball in one of the best thrillers of all, *Dime a Dance*; Judy Garland in *Drive-In*, a carhop's encounter with killer El-

liott Lewis; Donald O'Connor; Henry Morgan; Ozzie and Harriet Nelson. Singers Lena Horne and Dinah Shore appeared: on these shows, the screen separating cast and orchestra was removed, so that the singer might better interact with her "band."

The arrival of Anton M. Leader as director in 1948 caused few changes. Leader discontinued the veritable rep company (Cathy Lewis, Lurene Tuttle, Joseph Kearns, Wally Maher, etc.) that Spier had used for supporting roles: now there would be open auditions. Guest performances by comedians continued and, under the later direction of Elliott Lewis, increased. Jim and Marian Jordan stepped out of character (Fibber McGee and Molly) to take a ride with a killer in *Back Seat Driver* (1949). Red Skelton pronounced himself "terrified" in anticipation of his starring role in *The Search for Isabel*, but he turned in a solid performance. Lucille Ball and Desi Arnaz were heard in *The Red-Headed Woman*; Eddie Cantor in *Double Entry*; Danny Kaye in *I Never Met the Dead Man*; Milton Berle in *Rave Notice*; Jack Benny in *Murder in G-Flat*. Lewis began using true stories: *Ordeal in Donner Pass* (1953) was a gripping show, documenting the snowbound tragedy of the Donner Party in the winter of 1846. Perhaps the most interesting departure during the Lewis years was his two-part adaptation of *Othello*, May 4–11, 1953: he used Shakespeare's original dialogue, replaced the usual thrill music with passages from Verdi, and cast it with three performers who had never played Shakespeare—himself in the title role, his wife Cathy as Desdemona, and Richard Widmark as Iago.

The big-name, big-budget film stars fell away with the last Autolite show, and from 1955 on, the leads were largely carried by radio people. *Suspense* is the happiest of stories for the confirmed audiophile. Of the 945 shows broadcast, at least 900 are available, most in superior sound, many in full fidelity. The first two years contain shows that may strike the ear of a modern listener as contrived or stilted. Things look up with the arrival of Roma Wines and a budget. The celebrated *Sorry, Wrong Number* is here in all its versions, though this listener joins those who find it rather boring: the remarkable performance by Agnes Moorehead is lost in its unbelievable premise. So much better were *The Diary of Sophronia Winters*, *The Most Dangerous Game*,

August Heat, The House in Cypress Canyon, and the marvelous *Mission Completed*, which cast James Stewart as a paralyzed war veteran driven to murder by the sight of a man who resembles his former Japanese torturer.

Under Spier, Leader, Macdonnell, Ellis, Lewis, and even Robson ("the master of mystery and adventure," who toiled under the handicaps of a shrinking timeslot, shrinking budgets, and a shrinking audience), *Suspense* lived up to its name. In later years, announcer George Walsh breathed the opening signature into the microphone in a memorable bassy tremor:

And nowwwwww . . .

. . . another tale well-calculated . . .

SWEENEY AND MARCH, comedy.

BROADCAST HISTORY: Aug. 31, 1946–Oct. 1, 1948, CBS. Various 30m timeslots (first heard on CBS West Coast network July 5, 1946). Sponsored briefly by Sanka Coffee, from late Aug. 1948.

April 1–May 11, 1951, ABC. 15m, weekdays at 2:30.

CAST: Bob Sweeney and Hal March. **ANNOUNCERS:** Bob LeMond, Hy Averback, Howard Petrie. **VOCALISTS:** Doris Day, ca. 1946; Patty Bolton later. Also: "The Sweeney and March Choral Society." **ORCHESTRA:** Wilbur Hatch; later Lud Gluskin; also, Irving Miller. **PRODUCERS:** Manny Mannheim, etc. **DIRECTORS:** Sterling Tracy, etc. **WRITERS:** Jerry Brewer, John Hayes, Mannheim, Sweeney and March, ca. 1946; later, Frank Fox, Jack Crutcher, William Davenport.

As a team, Bob Sweeney and Hal March enjoyed some success on local radio in Los Angeles in the mid-1940s: they were touted in the trade press as the most promising of the new guard. Their *Sweeney and March Show* began as a series of unrelated comedy skits. There were no regular supporting actors, since each show was made up of short bits arising from vastly different comic situations. It was gradually refined until it became straight situation comedy. Then they played a pair of frustrated radio comics who lived together in a trailer and occupied the smallest office at CBS. March played the "big guy," the alleged thinker; Sweeney was immature, the slightly addled partner who approached life with a boyish sense of wonder. Sweeney's love of the magazine *Outdoor Boy* led to many of their adventures, from hunting animals in the jungle to trekking across the South Pole in search of ice cubes.

March peaked in the 1950s, when he hosted TV's scandal-plagued *$64,000 Question*. He died in 1970, at 49. Sweeney died in 1992, at 73.

SWEET RIVER, soap opera.

BROADCAST HISTORY: Oct. 4, 1943–July 21, 1944, Blue Network. 15m, weekdays at 10 A.M. Staley, makers of Stoy, "the new 100 percent soy flour for wartime meals." **CAST:** Ed Prentiss and Betty Arnold, among others; roles unknown. **WRITER:** Charles Jackson.

Raymond William Stedman describes this as the problems of "a minister-widower raising two sons in an industrial town and trying to foster tolerance toward outsiders." By Jan. 3, 1944 (the only episode available at this writing), it was "the story of Willa McCay, who strives and endures against the heartbreaks and trials that test our lives daily throughout America in towns like Sweet River." Willa was a history teacher in the town school. Religious epigraph: *Man grows richer by his faith, even if it defeats him, and still greater if he endures.*

THE SWIFT HOUR, music and commentary.

BROADCAST HISTORY: Oct. 6, 1934–April 13, 1935, NBC. 60m, Saturdays at 8. Swift. **CAST:** Sigmund Romberg, composer of popular Viennese operettas (*The Student Prince*, etc.), led an orchestra through his works, including new melodies written for the air; literary oracle William Lyon Phelps was the speaker. This general format was continued on NBC as *Studio Party* (Sept. 17, 1935–June 15, 1936), with Romberg abetted by baritone George Britton, soprano Helen Marshall, tenor Morton Bowe, and Deems Taylor, master of ceremonies.

TAILSPIN TOMMY, juvenile aviation thriller.

BROADCAST HISTORY: Ca. 1941, CBS, regional network. 30m and 15m versions. Beginning Sept. 5 but duration and cast unknown.

The adventures of ''Tailspin'' Tommy Tompkins, flying ace from the Hal Forrest comic series, and his pals Skeeter ''Skeets'' Milligan and Betty Lou Barnes. The characters flew for Paul Smith, an airship developer, in a town called Three Point.

TAKE A CARD, quiz.

BROADCAST HISTORY: April 28–Oct. 20, 1943, Mutual. 30m, Wednesdays at 8:30. Lehn and Fink. **HOSTS:** Wally Butterworth and Margaret (Honey) Johnson with questions related to playing cards and payoffs based on the face values of the cards drawn.

TAKE A NOTE, musical comedy.

BROADCAST HISTORY: Dec. 19, 1938–Nov. 3, 1939, Mutual. 30m, Mondays at 8 as *Ernie Fiorito's Studies in Contrast*, 1938–39; Mondays at 8:30 as *Take a Note* beginning April 17, 1939; Fridays at 9:30 as of June 16. **CAST:** Comic Henry Morgan joined the Fiorito orchestra in 1939, resulting in title/format changes. **VOCALISTS:** Jimmy Shields, Josephine Huston, and, later, Benay Venuta. **DIRECTOR:** Roger Bower.

TAKE A NUMBER, quiz.

BROADCAST HISTORY: June 5, 1948–May 20, 1955, Mutual. 30m, Saturdays at 8:30, 1948–51; weekdays at 10:30 A.M., 1951–52; Saturdays at 8:30, 1952–53; then Fridays at 8:30. U.S. Tobacco, 1948–49. **QUIZMASTER:** Al ''Red'' Benson; a weekday run, 1951–52, starred Happy Felton. **PRODUCERS:** Sam Levine and Robert Monroe.

Listeners sent in questions: if they were accepted, the listener won a prize. If the contestant answered correctly, the contestant won the prize. If the contestant failed, the listener won the contestant's prize. The winning contestant selected his grand prize question by choosing a number.

TAKE IT OR LEAVE IT, quiz.

BROADCAST HISTORY: April 21, 1940–Sept. 3, 1950, CBS through July 27, 1947, then NBC. 30m, Sundays at 10. Eversharp. Continued Sept. 10, 1950–June 1, 1952, as *The $64 Question*, NBC, Sundays at 10. RCA, etc., 1950–51; Sundays at 9:30, sustained, 1951–52. **QUIZMASTERS:** Bob Hawk, 1940–41 (departed Dec. 1941 in a salary dispute with Eversharp); Phil Baker, Dec. 28, 1941–Sept. 7, 1947; Garry Moore as of Sept. 14, 1947; Eddie Cantor as of Sept. 11, 1949; Jack Paar as of June 11, 1950; Phil Baker as of March 1951; Jack Paar as of December 1951. **ANNOUNCERS:** David Ross, Ken Niles, Jay Stewart, Sandy Becker, etc. **PRODUCER-DIRECTORS:** Bruce Dodge, Harry Spears, Betty Mandeville, etc. **WRITER-RESEARCHER:** Edith Oliver.

Take It or Leave It was popular and durable, running more than a decade in the same timeslot, outlasting five masters of ceremonies, and setting the mold for the most famous of TV quizzes, The $64,000 Question. The main difference between the radio and TV series was that Take It dealt in dollars, not thousands, and took itself far less seriously. There were no isolation booths for contestants, and all the coaching was done on-stage, in full view of the studio audience.

In fact, the host could be shameless with his hints, especially during the war years when contestants were usually servicemen. Contestants were chosen at random from the studio audience. Ticket stubs were placed in three glass bowls (designated "Men," "Women," and, during the war, "Servicemen"); producer Bruce Dodge drew the numbers, and the ticket holders were brought to the stage in lots of ten. The questions were arranged by difficulty on a $1-2-4-8-16-32-64 progression. There were few embellishments: the questions were asked and answered, and that was it.

The major point of interest was the interviewing skill of the host, and the taunting cry "You'll be sorrrreeeee" from the audience when the contestant risked his money to go for more. Researcher Edith Oliver tried to increase the difficulty with each step, but it was widely believed that the $32 question was the toughest. Perhaps that's why 75 percent of contestants who got that far decided to go all the way, though only 20 percent of those won the $64. Staple categories were music, sports, science, and history. The blackboard might contain 16 additional categories ranging from "cards and games," "first names of people," "titles in literature," and "detectives" to "Britain in the war," "Alice in Wonderland," "hate," and "glamour boys past and present."

There was a jackpot, comprised of monies lost by unsuccessful contestants. In later years, perhaps in an effort to stay respectable in the rush of big-money quizzes, the jackpot was enlarged, beginning at $640 and doubling from there. But its prime years were the early 1940s, when it drew ratings up to 22 points.

A TALE OF TODAY, weekly serial drama.

BROADCAST HISTORY: July 31, 1933–April 9, 1939, NBC; 30m, Blue Network, Mondays at 9:30, as Princess Pat Players, 1933–36; Red Network, Sundays at 6:30, as A Tale of Today, 1936–39. **CAST:** (as of Sept. 1936): Joan Blaine as Joan Houston. Betty Caine and Luise Barclay also as Joan. Isabel Randolph and Ethel Owen as Harriet Brooks. Laurette Fillbrandt as Dot Houston. Frank Pacelli as Billy Houston. Harriette Widmer as Beulah. Willard Farnum as Dick Martin. Harvey Hays as Robert Houston. Robert Griffin as Dr. Frank Gardner. **DIRECTOR:** Howard Keegan. **WRITER:** Gordon St. Clair.

TALES OF FATIMA, crime melodrama.

BROADCAST HISTORY: Jan. 8–Oct. 1, 1949, CBS. 30m, Saturdays at 9:30. Fatima Cigarettes. **CAST:** Basil Rathbone as himself. Francis DeSales as Lt. Farrell. **ANNOUNCER:** Michael Fitzmaurice. **ORCHESTRA:** Jack Miller. **DIRECTOR:** Harry Ingram.

Tales of Fatima came in the wake of Basil Rathbone's celebrated stand as Sherlock Holmes and his less successful Scotland Yard. As a murder series, Fatima was a laugher. Rathbone got himself into convoluted and contrived murders and solved them with the aid of a metaphysical female who spoke to him in much the same way that the trumped-up Eugor spoke to Dick Powell in Rogue's Gallery. But this was far more offensive: the maiden Fatima was a flagrant plug for the sponsor. Her filtered voice set the tone of the plays and gave a clue that, Rathbone told listeners, "might help you solve the mystery before I do." The clue was a veiled bit of metaphorical balderdash (Time is of the essence—a fact misplaced in time conceals the truth) spoken from an echo chamber. Rathbone also read the Fatima sales pitch, leading Radio Life to complain that the distinguished star had gone commercial. Indeed, there were even references to the product planted in the stories.

TALES OF THE TEXAS RANGERS, police procedural with a western flavor.

BROADCAST HISTORY: July 8, 1950–Sept. 14, 1952, NBC. 30m, Saturdays at 9:30 until Oct. 8, 1950; Sundays at various times through Sept. 1951; then Sundays at 6. Wheaties, first two months only. **CAST:** Joel McCrea as Jace Pearson, personification of Texas Rangers everywhere.

Support from Hollywood regulars: Tony Barrett, Peggy Webber, Ed Begley, Herb Vigran, Barney Phillips, Ken Christy, Frank Martin, Reed Hadley, Wilms Herbert, Lurene Tuttle, etc. ANNOUNCER: Hal Gibney. PRODUCER-DIRECTOR: Stacy Keach. WRITER: Joel Murcott. TECHNICAL ADVISER: Capt. M. T. "Lone Wolf" Gonzaullas. SOUND EFFECTS: Monty Fraser. THEME: *The Eyes of Texas Are upon You.*

Tales of the Texas Rangers bore an unmistakable *Dragnet* influence: the stories followed the step-by-step tracking of a criminal, often a killer, by a Texas lawman well versed in modern procedure. The idea was developed by Stacy Keach, who first approached it as a motion picture possibility. The Texas Rangers is one of those legendary outfits, like the French Foreign Legion, about which perpetual intrigue and romance swirls. Established in the 1820s, the Rangers numbered only about 50 men at any given time. All of them had to demonstrate virtues of maturity (at least 30 years old), intelligence, and physical stamina.

By the time Keach obtained the cooperation of the publicity-shy Rangers, the idea had become a radio show. With writer Joel Murcott, Keach went to Texas for research. There he met Capt. M. T. "Lone Wolf" Gonzaullas, a 30-year veteran described as "the last of the old quick-draw artists." They traveled 1,500 miles, watching the Rangers in actual case investigations and getting a sense of the enormity of the land.

The show would be an anthology, though there would be a single Ranger hero. The slant would be modern: the cases would span the time from ca. 1928–48, well within the working life of a single Ranger. Pursuit would be by automobile, though the Ranger would have a horse trailer attached to his vehicle, so that at any moment he might pack off after a killer into the back country. The generic ranger, Jace Pearson, had a generic horse, Charcoal. The star was a perfect choice: Joel McCrea had been in films since the 1920s but in his later career was known mainly as a western hero.

The opening signature served it well:
Tales of the Texas Rangers, starring Joel McCrea as Ranger Pearson!

Texas! . . . More than 260,000 square miles!
And 50 men who make up the most famous and oldest law enforcement body in North America!

After each broadcast, McCrea returned with a bit of Ranger lore. Again borrowing a page from *Dragnet*, the announcer then gave the disposition of the case (*sentenced to life imprisonment at Huntsville*). "Huntsville" was synonymous with "prison," referring to the state penitentiary in that town.

TALES OF TOMORROW, science fiction anthology.

BROADCAST HISTORY: Jan. 1–April 9, 1953, ABC until Feb. 26, then CBS. 30m, Thursday at 9, both networks. HOST: Raymond Edward Johnson. CAST: John Raby, Maurice Tarplin, Rolly Bester, and other New York radio players.

Content similar to NBC's earlier *Dimension X*; story adaptations from *Galaxy* magazine, etc.

TALES OF WILLIE PIPER, situation comedy.

BROADCAST HISTORY: Oct. 20, 1946–June 29, 1947, ABC. 30m, Sundays at 6:30, later at 7.
Sept. 4, 1947–May 27, 1948, ABC. 30m, Thursday at 9. *Willie Piper.* General Electric.
CAST: Dick Nelson and Elaine Rost as Willie and Martha Piper, who lived in a two-family house (her father, Mr. Gillespie, was the other occupant) "in the city of Seaport, on the coast of New England." William Redfield also as Willie; Jean Gillespie also as Martha. Charles Irving as Mr. Gillespie. MUSIC: Ralph Norman. WRITER: Samuel Taylor.

TAPESTRIES OF LIFE, historical drama.

BROADCAST HISTORY: Mid-1940s, CBS West Coast. 30m, Tuesdays at 9:30 Pacific time as of April 1946. NARRATOR: Theodore von Eltz. WRITER: David Hanna. MUSIC: Milton Charles.

Three stories were presented in each show, covering lives ranging from Julius Caesar to Walt Whitman to Ernie Pyle.

TARZAN, juvenile jungle adventure, from the novels of Edgar Rice Burroughs.

BROADCAST HISTORY: 1932–34, transcribed syndication; released as a three-a-week 15m continuation, beginning on WOR and other stations Sept. 12, 1932. Loosely adapted from the 1914 novel, *Tarzan of the Apes*. **CAST:** James Pierce as Tarzan. Joan Burroughs, his wife and the daughter of author Edgar Rice Burroughs, as Jane. Gale Gordon as Cecil Clayton. Cy Kendall as Captain Tracy. Fred Shields as Bill Fraser. Frank Nelson as Nikolas Rokoff. Jeanette Nolan as Princess La of Opar. Hanley Stafford and Art Kane in various roles, playing three and five parts respectively. Fred Harrington and Eily Malyan as Lord and Lady Greystoke. Ralph Scott as Lt. Paul D'Arnot. **PRODUCED** on disc by Frederick C. Dahlquist of American Radio Syndicate.

1934–36, 15m transcribed syndication by Edgar Rice Burroughs, in association with son Hulbert Burroughs and Ralph Rothmund. *Tarzan and the Diamond of Asher* (released in 1934) and *Tarzan and the Fires of Tohr* (1936), two 39-chapter serials. **CAST:** Carlton KaDell as Tarzan. Ralph Scott as D'Arnot. *Supporting cast, Asher*: Karena Shields as Helen Gregory. George Turner as her father, Brian Gregory. Cy Kendall as Atan Thome. Jeanette Nolan as Magra. *Supporting cast, Tohr*: Barbara Luddy as Ahtea. Cy Kendall as Wong-Tai. **ANNOUNCER:** John McIntire. **PRODUCER:** Fred Shields. **WRITER:** Rob Thompson.

1950–51, transcribed syndication, 30m each, complete in each episode. Played on the West Coast Mutual–Don Lee Network beginning ca. Jan. 1951. Later played on CBS, March 22, 1952–June 27, 1953, Saturdays at 8:30 for General Foods and Post Toasties. **STAR:** Lamont Johnson as Tarzan. **PRODUCER:** Walter White's Commodore Productions. **WRITER:** Bud Lesser.

The original *Tarzan* radio adaptation has come to be regarded as the first major syndicated serial. It followed, with some embellishments, Edgar Rice Burroughs's story of the child raised among the apes after his parents had been marooned on an African coast and later killed. The first three chapters were introductory: Lord and Lady Greystoke were presented and their predicament explained. They were killed by the apes, and by chapter 4 Tarzan was grown and the story began.

Soon he encountered the Porter expedition and met Jane, who taught him English. The serial ran 286 episodes and was discontinued in March 1934 when—according to Burroughs historian D. Peter Ogden—Burroughs declined to renew it. But it was well received across the nation. Signal Oil sponsored it throughout California, and among scores of outlets in other cities were KDKA, Pittsburgh; WGN, Chicago; KLZ, Denver; WSM, Nashville; KMOX, St. Louis; and WLW, Cincinnati. These early shows were distinguished by robust storylines and commensurate sound effects, with Tarzan's battles against beasts of the jungle well realized.

The serial, wrote Ogden, was introduced at Hollywood's Fox Pantages Theater Sept. 10, 1932, two days before the designated premiere. The first episode was played over the sound system, and the entire cast appeared on stage. Ogden also identified the casts in all *Tarzan* shows, in a detailed log prepared in 1985.

Burroughs broke with the original syndicator, said Ogden, because the story had drifted away from his novel. With the 1934 serial, *Diamond of Asher*, he took more control over production and plot. Joan Burroughs was sidelined by pregnancy, so Jane was written out of the script; her husband, James Pierce, also declined to return.

When *Tarzan* returned to the air, 15 years later, it was again as a transcribed series, produced by the same firm that had become a national force with *Hopalong Cassidy*. It was set off by Tarzan's opening war cry—a lusty *Aaaaaahhh-o-ahhhh-o-ahhhh-o!*—and a memorable epigraph:

From the heart of the jungle comes a savage cry of victory!

This is Tarzan, lord of the jungle!

From the black core of dark Africa, land of enchantment, mystery, and violence, comes one of the most colorful figures of all time, transcribed from the immortal pen of Edgar Rice Burroughs—Tarzan, bronzed white son of the jungle!

These were tales of ivory poachers, slave traders, uranium hunters, gold thieves, hijackers, and battles with cannibalistic natives. Producers didn't want it known, but it was learned that Lamont Johnson was the lead.

TEA TIME AT MORRELL'S, variety.

BROADCAST HISTORY: Sept. 3, 1936–May 28, 1937, NBC. 30m, Thursdays at 4; later Fridays at 4. John Morrell and Company for Red Heart Dog Food. **CAST:** Largely *Breakfast Club* personnel— Don McNeill, host, with singer Gale Page and tenor Charles Sears; music by Joseph Gallicchio and his "15 boys."

THE TELEPHONE HOUR, concert music, also known as *The Bell Telephone Hour.*

BROADCAST HISTORY: April 29, 1940–June 30, 1958, NBC. 30m, Mondays at 8, 1940–42, then at 9. Bell Telephone. **SOLOISTS:** Tenor James Melton and soprano Francia White, 1940–42; guest soloists thereafter. **ORCHESTRA:** Donald Voorhees. **CHORUS:** Ken Christie. **COMMENTATOR:** Floyd Mack. **ANNOUNCERS:** Tom Shirley, 1940–42; Gayne Whitman, Dick Joy. **PRODUCER-DIRECTOR:** Wallace Magill. **THEME:** *Bell Waltz,* composed by Voorhees for the first broadcast.

The Telephone Hour was a prestigious concert series, beginning as a forum of light classical music by James Melton, Francia White, and a 57-piece symphony orchestra comprised of many musicians from the New York Philharmonic. It was described by *Tune In* as "a musical melting pot, blending the old world with the new, from Bach to Irving Berlin, from *Swanee River* to *Santa Lucia,* from Latin American folksongs to the latest in Russian opera." It leaped to immediate success and acclaim, reaching an audience estimated at eight to nine million weekly, which never wavered.

The original format, with Melton and White as soloists, was replaced after the arrival of producer Wallace Magill by a "Great Artists Series," a succession of vocal and instrumental artists from opera and the concert stage. Violinist Jascha Heifetz was the first star of the new series, April 27, 1942. For the next 16 years, listeners were enchanted by the music of Marian Anderson, Helen Traubel, Lily Pons, Grace Moore, John Charles Thomas, Oscar Levant, Nelson Eddy, pianist José Iturbi, Maggie Teyte, Blanche Thebom, Gladys Swarthout, Bidu Sayao, Jennie Tourel, Jussi Bjoerling, Gregor Piatigorsky, and many others. Violinist Fritz Kreisler ended a long holdout against radio on *The Telephone Hour,* then appeared 18 times in

eight years. Many of these performers became known to the general public through repeated performances on the program.

Heifetz had made 37 return engagements by 1949; his interpretation of Dinicu's *Hora Staccato* had become the show's most requested number. A few times a year popular fare was scheduled: Bing Crosby; Benny Goodman; *South Pacific* melodies by Ezio Pinza and Mary Martin. On Dec. 14, 1953, Fred Allen read *Peter and the Wolf* while Voorhees conducted the Prokofiev music: the same program had been offered earlier with Basil Rathbone.

The show was meticulously planned, with guests booked as much as a year in advance and programs worked out two months ahead. Magill selected the music, though naturally with artists of this caliber, there was much discussion. In 1946, *The Telephone Hour* began its annual offering of young and unknown talent, the winners of the Walter W. Naumburg Musical Foundation awards. In 1949 it won a Peabody Award, radio's highest prize. In the mid-1950s the show moved to Carnegie Hall. After it left the air, Voorhees hosted and narrated a series of *Encores from the Bell Telephone Hour* (Sept. 15, 1968–June 8, 1969, NBC, Sundays), consisting of highlights from the old shows and interviews with the stars.

TELL IT AGAIN, children's drama; classics adaptations.

BROADCAST HISTORY: Jan. 18, 1948–July 2, 1949, CBS. 30m, Sundays at 1:30 until April 1949, then Saturdays at 10:30 A.M. **CAST:** Peter Leeds, Stanley Waxman, Harry Lang, June Foray, Marion Richman, Colleen Collins, etc. **NARRATORS:** Jeff Chandler; Marvin Miller by early 1949. **ANNOUNCER:** Murray Wagner. **MUSIC:** Del Castillo on organ, with Johnny Jacobs (whose percussion equipment gave it the depth of a small group. **CREATOR-DIRECTOR:** Ralph Rose.

This series presented stories so beloved that the producer wanted to "tell it again": *Black Beauty, Moby Dick, Treasure Island,* and others in the public domain.

TENA AND TIM, soap opera.

BROADCAST HISTORY: Aug. 7, 1944–Aug. 2, 1946, CBS (after a period of transcribed syndication). 15m continuation, weekdays in midafternoon. Cudahy Packing and Old Dutch Cleanser. **CAST:** Peggy Beckmark as Tena, a maid of Scandinavian tongue who lived with a family named Hutchinson. George Cisar, James Gardner, and Frank Dane as Tim. **WRITER:** Peggy Beckmark.

Tena and Tim was allegedly in the *Lorenzo Jones* mold—a humorous soap. But Tena talked too much, and the non-humor derived from her efforts to "explain" things.

TENNESSEE JED, juvenile western adventure serial.

BROADCAST HISTORY: May 14, 1945–Nov. 7, 1947, ABC. 15m, weekdays at 5:45. Ward Baking for Tip Top Bread. **CAST:** Johnny Thomas as Tennessee Jed Sloan, squirrel-gun marksman from the Old South, anxious to forget the Civil War and start anew on the frontier. Don MacLaughlin also as Tennessee Jed. Humphrey Davis as Sheriff Jackson. Raymond Edward Johnson as Masters, the gambler. **ANNOUNCER-NARRATOR:** Court Benson. **PRODUCER:** Paul DeFur. **DIRECTOR:** Bill Hamilton. Theme: Sung by Elton Britt.

Tennessee Jed Sloan was an articulate gunman whose prowess with a rifle led to one of radio's best-remembered opening signatures:
There he goes, Tennessee! Get him!
GUNSHOT/RICOCHET.
Got him! Deeeeeeeeeeaaaaaaad center!
Even with the bounce of the bullet, Tennessee got his prey. He rode a horse named Smoky and packed two sixguns, and his show was scored by harmonica-accordion themes that suggested a Deep South origin. But Tennessee was cut from *Lone Ranger* cloth: no hillbilly slang for him; it was all proper diction and a good example for the kids.

As the series went on, Tennessee became an agent for the White House, working directly for President Grant to round up evildoers.

TERROR BY NIGHT, ghost dramas.

BROADCAST HISTORY: March 1–May 31, 1936, CBS. 30m, Sundays at 10; later at 10:30. **DIRECTOR:** Earle McGill.

The short-lived *Terror by Night* offered *The Tell-Tale Heart*, *The Phantom Rickshaw*, and such chestnuts. Often preempted, it mounted one show of note: *The Bells*, March 22, with young Orson Welles, Ray Collins, and Martha Scott.

TERRY AND THE PIRATES, juvenile adventure serial, from the comic strip by Milton Caniff.

BROADCAST HISTORY: Nov. 1, 1937–March 22, 1939, NBC. 15m, Red Network until June 1, 1938, then Blue Network beginning Sept. 26, 1938. Mondays, Tuesdays, and Wednesdays at 5:15. Dari-Rich.
　　Oct. 16, 1941–May 29, 1942, WGN Midwest. 15m, weekdays. Libby.
　　Feb. 1, 1943–June 30, 1948, Blue/ABC. 15m, weekdays at 6:15; at 5, 1944–47; at 5:15, 1947–48. Quaker Puffed Wheat or Puffed Rice.
CAST: Jackie Kelk and Cliff Carpenter as Terry Lee, young adventurer in the Orient. Owen Jordan as Terry through most of the war years. Bill Fein as Terry, postwar. Clayton Bud Collyer, Warner Anderson, Bob Griffin, and Larry Alexander, variously, as Terry's pal, Pat Ryan. Agnes Moorehead, Adelaide Klein, and Marion Sweet as Terry's enemy, the Dragon Lady. Ted de Corsia as Flip Corkin. Gerta Rozan as Eleta. Frances Chaney as Burma. Cameron Andrews as Hotshot Charlie. Cliff Norton, John Gibson, and Peter Donald as Connie the coolie. **ANNOUNCER:** Douglas Browning (war era). **DIRECTORS:** Cyril Armbrister, Wylie Adams, Marty Andrews, etc. **WRITER:** Albert Barker.

Terry was one of radio's most colorful and action-packed serials. Although nothing has yet been heard of the early series for Dari-Rich, it was known even then for its staunch anti-fascism storylines.

With its return in 1943, *Terry* plunged into the war effort with a wholehearted enthusiasm rivaled only by *Captain Midnight*. It opened to the garble of coolies jabbering in Chinese pig Latin. Cymbals and a gong helped fill in the picture of rickshaws dashing along an alley somewhere in the Orient.
Terrrrr-eeeeeee . . . and the Pirates!
Closely following the comic strip, *Terry* used the Far East as its backdrop. There Terry Lee and his pals—Pat Ryan, Flip Corkin, Connie the coolie, Hotshot Charlie, and the ladies, Burma and Elita—routed villains from Shanghai to Cal-

cutta. And in 1943, when the serial returned with a style unlike any other, the world's biggest villains were Nazis, "Japs," and fascists. After a quick intro and a brief commercial (especially brief when compared with the endless Ovaltine announcements on *Captain Midnight*), the listener was plunged into intrigue. *Monday, January 10, 1944—maybe that's just another date to a lot of people. But to Pat Ryan and Terry Lee, it's a day they'll never forget. At any moment they expect the go-ahead signal to come through from British Secret Service, and when it does, Pat and Terry are starting out on the biggest adventure of their lives—a secret two-man mission to Japan, to Tokyo!* The closing contained the hook: *Tomorrow, Pat Ryan and Terry Lee are gonna get a BIG surprise! It's news that may mean life or death!* A final word from the sponsor pushed the hard-sell catchphrases: *Quaker Puffed Wheat Sparkies, the wheat that's shot from guns! No ration points, do tell! The easy step to extra pep, and boy, the taste is swell!*

Ironically, some of Terry's most formidable enemies in the Far East were Germans, spies sent by Berlin to oversee operations in the Pacific. Once he teamed with his old enemy, the Dragon Lady (then working for the Chinese), to destroy a Japanese supply depot hidden on a Yellow River plantation under the supervision of Baron Von Krell. In 1945, Pat and Terry battled a ring of Nazis operating out of Calcutta; as late as 1946, they were still sounding the alarm over isolated pockets of enemy alleged to exist. But the war was over and so, for all practical purposes, was *Terry*. The Dragon Lady returned to her old ways, to her bandit organization of international pirates, and for another two years Terry waged intermittent war with the evil ones throughout the East. But the ratings slumped, and the show left the air in 1948.

Terry needed that swarm of wartime agents as a deadly counterforce. It was a show of its time, when announcer Douglas Browning sold his product almost as a national duty ("Uncle Sam wants you to keep strong!"). In Browning's lingo, "robistitude" was what a kid got from eating Quaker Puffed Wheat; "marvolious" was what those "shot-from-guns" cereals were. The wartime shows frequently closed with "victograms," such as this:

Paper is a mighty weapon:
Haul it in, keep smartly steppin'.

Turn in every scrap you can,
To lick the Nazis and Japan!

TEX AND JINX, talk; initially one of the three major husband-wife breakfast shows.

BROADCAST HISTORY: April 22, 1946–Feb. 27, 1959, WEAF (WNBC, WRCA), New York. Weekdays at 8:30 A.M. until 1954; at 1, 1954–55; then at 6:30 and 10:35 P.M. until July 31, 1958; then WOR at 2:15.

July 2–Sept. 24, 1947, and again June 30–Sept. 29, 1948, NBC. Wednesdays at 9. Summer substitutions for *Duffy's Tavern*. Meet Tex and Jinx. Bristol Myers for Ipana Toothpaste.

HOSTS: Tex McCrary and Jinx Falkenburg.

Although *Tex and Jinx* was seldom heard on a network, the principals were known far and wide. They were "Mr. Brains and Mrs. Beauty," as reporter Jerome Beatty put it: he was the learned Yale graduate; she the cover girl of more than 200 magazines, the actress, the tennis and swimming expert. They met when she was a film star (though never a very good one, she would admit) and he was a reporter for the *New York Daily Mirror* sent to interview her. John Reagan (Tex) McCrary and Eugenia Lincoln (Jinx) Falkenburg were married June 10, 1945, after a globehopping courtship made necessary by war (she entertained troops, and he was on duty with the Army Air Force).

The breakfast talk boom had begun around 1938 with Ed and Pegeen Fitzgerald, escalated into hostile competition with the arrival of Dorothy Kilgallen and Richard Kollmar in 1945, and now reached high gear with the Tex and Jinx show, originally called *Hi Jinx*, in 1946. Of the three, *Tex and Jinx* clearly took the high road: they didn't even pretend to eat while talking world affairs with the rich and famous. McCrary, who ran the show, resisted the prattling stream-of-insipidity that often characterized the others. "Tex refuses to sidestep a controversial issue," wrote one reporter, admiring McCrary's discussions on the Bomb, the UN, and even venereal disease. While the Fitzgeralds bickered about Pegeen's weight on WJZ and the Kollmars preened amidst the birdseed on WOR, the McCrarys were interviewing Bernard Baruch, Margaret Truman, or Ethel Waters (who revealed on their air that, at her birth, her mother had been just 12 years old). Even the fluff was consistently interesting:

they got swimsuit actress Esther Williams to describe her first screen kiss, from Clark Gable, and Williams gave an uninhibited, hyperventilating account of how it had rendered her helpless and unable to act.

McCrary built the show on the assumption that the early morning audience was not stupid, as programmers generally assumed; that people in general had fresher minds and were more open to serious topics at the beginning of the day. "Most people are liberals when they drink their morning coffee and conservatives after a hard day's work," he told Beatty. Falkenburg's lack of higher education was no factor in their professional life together. "She's the most intelligent uneducated person I know," McCrary sometimes said. She was often given the task of interviewing scholars, and in this her technique was simple: she just kept asking questions until she understood the subject, and so, presumably, did all the housewives listening at home.

McCrary's style on the air was described by *Newsweek* as "dry and monotonous," sometimes sounding "as if he dislikes the whole business." They both accepted his role as oracle and guiding force: at times he would send her into the field with recording equipment and freely criticize her technique when the recorded interviews aired the next day.

THE TEXACO STAR THEATER, a generic title, used by the sponsor for several slightly related variety shows with different headliners over the years. Texaco had been a major advertiser from the first days of the networks, sponsoring Ed Wynn (NBC, 1932–35), Jimmy Durante (NBC, 1935–36), and Eddie Cantor (CBS, 1936–38) before opening its *Star Theater* in 1938.

BROADCAST HISTORY: Oct. 5, 1938–June 26, 1940, CBS. 60m, Wednesdays at 9:30 until Jan. 1938, then at 9. HOSTS: Adolphe Menjou until Nov. 1938, John Barrymore, until mid-Jan. 1939, then Ken Murray. ANNOUNCER: Jimmy Wallington. COMICS: Una Merkel, Charlie Ruggles, Ned Sparks, Irene Noblette (Ryan). VOCALISTS: Jane Froman until Jan. 1939, then Frances Langford; also Kenny Baker. CHORUS: "The Texaco Star Chorus." ORCHESTRA: David Broekman. DIRECTOR: William A. Bacher. OPENING SIGNATURE: The fireman's siren, with bells, by

soundman Ray Erlenborn, a distinctive wailing introduction. The usual 1930s variety show. Max Reinhardt appeared each week with a 20-minute dramatic skit, headed by such film stars as Bette Davis and supported by players from Reinhardt's Hollywood acting workshop. Summer break June 28, 1939; returned Sept. 13 with Irene Noblette added as comedienne. A dramatic segment from New York, with Broadway people (John Boles, Maurice Evans, etc.) in play adaptations, replaced Reinhardt's players.

Oct. 2, 1940–June 25, 1944: see THE FRED ALLEN SHOW. Ironically, Texaco was now sponsoring the act that had been its competition in the earlier series. The wailing siren was discontinued after the events of Dec. 7, 1941, deemed too much like an air raid warning.

July 4–Dec. 5, 1943, and again July 2, 1944–Sept. 22, 1946, CBS. 30m, Wednesdays at 9:30. STARS: James Melton as the 1943 summer replacement for Fred Allen: backed by Joan Roberts and the Al Goodman Orchestra, this was billed as *The Texaco Summer Theater*. But Allen was late returning from his summer break, and tenor Melton continued *Star Theater* into the fall. Allen returned Dec. 12 but continued having health problems and retired temporarily after his June 25, 1944, show. Again Melton headed *Star Theater*, 1944–46, with popular music, light classics, operetta, and comedy. Old "Texaco Fire Chief" Ed Wynn a regular, Jan.–July 1946. GUESTS: Annamary Dickey, Virginia Haskins, etc. ANNOUNCER: John Reed King. CHORUS: Lyn Murray. ORCHESTRA: Al Goodman (1945), David Broekman (1946).

March 30, 1947–Sept. 15, 1948, ABC. 30m, Sundays at 9:30 until Dec., then Wednesdays at 10:30 or 10. CAST: Musical variety with singers Tony Martin and Evelyn Knight, comic Alan Young, the Victor Young Orchestra, and the Jeff Alexander Chorus. Tony Martin replaced by Gordon MacRae March 24, 1948.

Sept. 22, 1948–June 15, 1949: see THE MILTON BERLE SHOW. Berle took *Star Theater* into TV and became the first major personality of the new medium.

THAT BREWSTER BOY, situation comedy.

BROADCAST HISTORY: Sept. 8, 1941–March 2, 1942, NBC. 30m, Mondays at 9:30. Quaker Oats.
March 4, 1942–March 2, 1945, CBS. 30m,

Wednesdays at 7:30 until June 1942, then Fridays at 9:30. Quaker Oats.

CAST: Eddie Firestone as Joey Brewster. Arnold Stang and Dick York also as Joey. Louise Fitch and Patricia Dunlap as his sister, Nancy. Hugh Studebaker and Constance Crowder as the parents, Jim and Jane. ANNOUNCER: Marvin Miller. DIRECTOR: Owen Vinson. WRITER: Louis Scofield.

THAT HAMMER GUY, detective drama, based on the novels by Mickey Spillane.

BROADCAST HISTORY: Jan. 6, 1953–Oct. 5, 1954, Mutual. 30m, Tuesdays at 8. Also known as *Mickey Spillane Mysteries.* CAST: Larry Haines as tough private eye Mike Hammer.

THATCHER COLT MYSTERIES, detective drama, based on the novels of Anthony Abbot (Fulton Oursler).

BROADCAST HISTORY: Sept. 27, 1936–April 3, 1938, NBC. 30m, Sundays at 2:30. Packer Soap. CAST: Hanley Stafford (1936–37) and Richard Gordon (1938) as New York police commissioner Thatcher Colt.

THAT'S A GOOD IDEA, inspirational drama; human interest.

BROADCAST HISTORY: 1945, CBS West, 30m, various times. NARRATOR: David Vaile. ANNOUNCER: Jay Stewart. MUSIC: Del Castillo, organ. DIRECTOR: George Allen. WRITER: Madelyn Pugh.

Five dollars was paid to listeners who submitted workable, dramatic ideas "for the betterment of mankind." Examples: a double-hooded umbrella, so two people could walk together in the rain; a phosphorescent left-handed glove for night drivers to use in hand signals. This raw material was then dramatized.

THAT'S LIFE, audience show.

BROADCAST HISTORY: May 23, 1946–Jan. 16, 1947, CBS. Various 30m times. HOST: Jay C. Flippen. ANNOUNCER: Jay Stewart. PRODUCER: Howard Blake. DIRECTOR: Harry Koplan.

This breathless game show paraded participants rapid-fire before the microphone. "The

trouble is," said *Variety,* "the listener was left with the impression that the boys who whipped the show together couldn't quite make up their minds what to get breathless about." The result: "They threw the book at the audience," with categories ranging from little white lies, troubles with parents, and landlords with tenant problems to newlyweds' mistakes—in short, anything that encouraged laughter at another's weaknesses." Such guests as William Bendix also aired gripes.

THAT'S MY POP, situation comedy, based on the comic strip by Milt Gross.

BROADCAST HISTORY: June 17–Sept. 7, 1945, CBS. 30m, Sundays at 7:30. CAST: Hugh Herbert as Pop, "a lazy windbag whose last job was selling sunglasses during the 1929 eclipse" (*Variety*). Also: Raymond Walburn, Mary Wickes, Peggy Conklin, Ronnie Liss, Ethel Owen, Walter Kinsella. PRODUCER: Bert Prager. DIRECTOR: Marx Loeb. WRITERS: Milt Gross, Hugh Wedlock, Howard Snyder.

THAT'S RICH, situation comedy.

BROADCAST HISTORY: Jan. 8–Sept. 23, 1954, CBS. 30m, Fridays at 9:30 until May 21; returned July 15, Thursdays at 9. CAST: Stan Freberg, Peter Leeds, Frank Nelson, Martha Wentworth, Alan Reed, Daws Butler, and Hal March.

Freberg played the role of Richard E. Wilk, who worked for B. B. Hackett's Consolidated Paper Products Company in the town of Hope Springs, "that bustling little community a stone's throw from the heart of Hollywood." He was a shy bumbler who mixed schoolboy naivete with razor-sharp satirical observations ("California is the only place where you can lie under a rosebush in full bloom in the middle of the winter . . . and freeze to death").

THEATER FIVE, suspense drama, often science fiction.

BROADCAST HISTORY: Aug 3, 1964–July 30, 1965. ABC, New York; another 30m weekday attempt to revive radio drama. CAST: Paul McGrath, Guy Sorel, Ruth Yorke, Cliff Carpenter, Elliott Reid, Bryna Raeburn, Court Benson, etc. ANNOUNCER: Fred Foy. PRODUCER-DIRECTORS: Warren Somerville, Ted Bell.

THE THEATER OF FAMOUS RADIO PLAYERS, dramatic anthology.

BROADCAST HISTORY: 1945–46, 30m transcribed syndication; sold to Mutual for the West Coast Don Lee Network; airing Thursdays at 8 Pacific time in April 1946. **CAST:** A repertory company of radio's best professional actors, appearing in plays written especially for them—Lou Merrill, Sharon Douglas, Barbara Fuller, David Ellis, Peggy Webber, Cathy Lewis, Lurene Tuttle, Forrest Lewis, Jack Edwards, Joseph Kearns, Gloria Blondell, Tom Collins, Earle Ross, and Marvin Miller. **MUSIC:** Del Castillo. **PRODUCER-DIRECTOR:** Les Mitchel; recorded at Mitchel's Universal Radio Productions studio, with Mitchel narrating and playing occasional support. **WRITERS:** Ralph Rose, etc.

THEATER USA, dramatic anthology.

BROADCAST HISTORY: Nov. 11, 1948–June 30, 1949, ABC. 30m, Thursdays at 8:30. Cosponsored by the U.S. Army Air Corps Recruiting Service and (on the production end) the American National Theater and Academy (ANTA). **HOST:** ANTA president Vinton Freedley. **WRITER-PRODUCER:** Howard Teichmann.

ANTA was chartered by Congress in 1935 as a non-profit agency to help promote theater on professional and amateur levels. *Theater USA* offered scenes from major plays, often with original casts. Tallulah Bankhead, Mary Martin, and Alec Templeton appeared on the first broadcast. Donald Cook offered a scene from *Private Lives*.

THEATRE GUILD ON THE AIR, Broadway drama; also known as *The United States Steel Hour.*

BROADCAST HISTORY: Dec. 6, 1943–Feb. 29, 1944, CBS. 30m, Tuesdays at 10. *Theatre Guild Dramas,* a limited, sustained series dramatizing Theatre Guild plays but unrelated to the major series that followed.

Sept. 9, 1945–June 5, 1949, ABC. 60m, Sundays at 10, 1945–47, then Sundays at 9:30. United States Steel.

Sept. 11, 1949–June 7, 1953, NBC. 60m, Sundays at 8:30. USS.

HOST: Lawrence Langner; also, in later years, Roger Pryor, Elliott Reid. **CAST:** Major stars of Broadway and Hollywood in Theatre Guild plays

of all eras. **ANNOUNCER:** Norman Brokenshire. **COMMERCIAL ANNOUNCER** (reporting the latest developments in the steel industry): George Hicks. **MUSIC:** Composed and conducted by Harold Levey. **THEATRE GUILD SUPERVISORS:** Armina Marshall, Theresa Helburn, Lawrence Langner. **PRODUCER:** George Kondolf. **DIRECTOR:** Homer Fickett. **SOUND EFFECTS:** Keene Crockett, etc.

The Theatre Guild on the Air was to Broadway what *The Lux Radio Theater* was to Hollywood: a 60-minute package of prestige drama aimed at putting "unadulterated" theater on radio. Many critics, actors, and producers believed this had not been done prior to the *Guild*'s 1945 ABC premiere. And though it was slow to rise to its full audience potential (gathering 10 to 12 million listeners a week by 1946), it was an immediate hit with critics.

The show had a sound like no other—an air of legitimate theater that at its best forged a near-perfect alliance with radio. This was not attained without some compromise, to accommodate the sometimes clashing demands of the two disciplines; nor was the result always so unadulterated as it sounded. This was its great achievement: *Theatre Guild* kept faith with two audiences, and in its run offered a fair number of immortal broadcasts.

Perhaps its greatest asset was a hands-off sponsor, United States Steel, which carried the show all the way. "We couldn't have a better sponsor," said Guild officer Armina Marshall in 1953. "He always leaves us alone." This was true even in controversy. The April 17, 1949 show, Tennessee Williams's *Summer and Smoke,* touched off a storm of protest when it depicted a young girl turning to prostitution. "It was bad timing," Marshall conceded: it had been scheduled on Easter Sunday, and thereafter the fare on that day was confined to classics and comedies.

The Theatre Guild had begun modestly, formed in 1919 by a small group of stage-lovers. Their stated purpose was to improve theater in America by producing better plays. The guiding lights were Lawrence Langner (whose $500 contribution was its entire initial capital) and Theresa Helburn. The first meeting was held in Langner's apartment: from this grew a company that helped propel Alfred Lunt and Lynn Fontanne to stardom (in *The Guardsman*, 1924), produced Eugene O'Neill's Pulitzer play, *Strange Interlude* (1928), and in 1943 had one of the best-loved musicals of all time, *Oklahoma!*

The call to radio, when it came, was seen as a way to expand knowledge of theater from the largest urban areas to the hinterlands. But problems were immediately evident—most notably the fact that none of the Guild people knew anything about radio. The biggest problems would come in the writing—adapting a play that might run three hours on stage into a radio show that (allowing time for commercials, station breaks, and signatures) could not exceed 52 minutes. Langner and Helburn saw it as a challenge, calling for craftsmen who could "preserve the spirit of the stage play" while taking "every possible advantage of the radio medium."

Fortunately, there were such craftsmen, some of them working playwrights. First-year adapters included Arthur Miller, Paul Peters, Kenyon Nicholson, Erik Barnouw, Gerald Holland, and Arthur Arent. These people had been in radio, some writing for such prestige shows as *The Cavalcade of America*, and they understood the limitations and advantages of the medium. Now the producers discovered this as well—that sound effects and music could "intensify emotion, underline dramatic or comedic situations, or point to locale." Wrote Langner and Helburn (a sentence packed with enlightenment and surprise if ever there was one): "By the ingenious uses of a narrator, or a character who appears in the first person, it is possible to bridge the gap between the actor and the audience, and to create an intimacy not possible in the theater itself."

But there were shocks ahead, for actors and fans yet unaware of radio's demands. Writing in the 1947 *Theatre Guild* radio anthology, Arthur Miller would remember his discomfort as the Lunts read his adaptation of *The Guardsman* in first rehearsal. "A scene would go along as it was written in the original, and suddenly they would stop and glare at the script as if a louse had crawled over it. A new series of lines! A whole new scene! It was only after they had both grown rather exhausted that the very troubled look vanished from their faces. You just don't fool around with a play like *The Guardsman*, especially when the two people who stamped every line with their personalities are going to play it again."

But the play had to be changed: the radio audience would be unaware of the "facial expression, physical movement, and sheer stagecraft that had made those scenes live in the theater." Barnouw too had observed, in adapting *I Remember Mama*, the difficulty of actors familiar with the roles in adjusting to cuts and changes. Often in rehearsal "an actor would coast on with a speech not in the radio script," confusing engineers, soundmen, the director, and the cast.

The other major problem, it seemed from the beginning, would be an endless battle with censors. Theater was uninhibited and often explicit, especially compared with straitlaced radio and its unwillingness to admit even the possibility of sex. Kenyon Nicholson confronted this at once with *They Knew What They Wanted*. This was a play whose whole premise turned on "illicit love, cuckolded husbands, illegitimate babies, and such," and there was no way around it. But Nicholson's fears never materialized: the play was passed pretty much as written. A new day had dawned, and people accepted without resistance the fact that *Theatre Guild* was a show for adults. Nicholson's major surprise was how good these stripped-down plays could be. "To my chagrin as a practicing playwright, I have observed that in several instances this tightening process has actually made the play more dramatically effective than it was in its original version."

The Guild created a Radio Department, with Armina Marshall as its head: Langner and Helburn, as coadministrators of the Guild, were the other two directors in the overall sense. The director in the booth was Homer Fickett, who looked like Churchill and governed with diplomacy. "He rules by suggestion," said *Radio Life*, to which Fickett sometimes said, "A good actor never resents direction." In his first year, Fickett was directing casts of stage stars, with a sprinkling of Hollywood people. There would be no prejudice against film stars: they would be welcome in appropriate roles, "if they know how to act," said Marshall candidly.

The purpose of the series was to offer a cross-section of American plays, emphasizing but not limited to its own, of the past three decades. These would be staged with the original casts where possible. It opened with *Wings over Europe*, with Burgess Meredith, Henry Daniell, and Cecil Humphreys. *The Guardsman*, with the

Lunts, was the fourth show, Sept. 30, 1945. Announcer Norman Brokenshire quickly became the "voice" of the series. The stage was the Belasco Theater in New York, though in the best tradition of the theater, it sometimes went on the road.

At its best, *Theatre Guild* touched the pinnacle of radio; at its worst—well, even Armina Marshall admitted that the theater produced an occasional flop. But it was in a class by itself: other attempts to capture the flavor of Broadway were permeated with *First Nighter*–type hyperbole. People who think of radio as nostalgia should perhaps listen to *Street Scene* (Richard Conte, Diana Lynn, Shirley Booth, and the marvelously villainous Karl Malden). A glance at the comprehensive series log compiled by Jay Hickerson reveals many highlights. Among them: *Elizabeth the Queen* (the Lunts, Dec. 2, 1945); *Golden Boy* (Dana Andrews and June Havoc, Dec. 8, 1946); *Ah, Wilderness* (Walter Huston, Feb. 13, 1949); *Our Town* (Elizabeth Taylor and Walter Huston, March 12, 1950) and *Come Back, Little Sheba* (Gary Cooper and Shirley Booth, Feb. 4, 1951). On March 4, 1951, RCA joined USS to offer a 90-minute production of *Hamlet*, with John Gielgud, Dorothy McGuire, and Pamela Brown.

As *The United States Steel Hour*, it was also seen on early television: on ABC from 1953–55, and on CBS from 1955–63.

THERE WAS A WOMAN, dramatic anthology.

BROADCAST HISTORY: Jan. 9–Oct. 2, 1938, Blue Network. 30m, Sundays at 1:30 until April, then at 5. ANNOUNCER: Les Griffith. WRITERS: Ranald MacDougall, Les Fogely.

These were stories of "women behind the men" of history: Martha Custis Washington; Martha Jefferson Randolph (daughter of Thomas Jefferson), etc. Robert Griffin and Mercedes McCambridge played Caesar and Cleopatra in one episode.

THESE ARE OUR MEN, documentary drama.

BROADCAST HISTORY: Dec. 2, 1944–Feb. 17, 1945, NBC. 30m, Saturdays at 2. Parker Watch Company. CAST: New York radio actors—Staats Cotsworth, Bill Adams, etc.—in "authentic life stories" of major Americans in World War II;

"dramatic profiles of these men of ours who will lead us to victory." ANNOUNCER: Jack Costello. DIRECTOR: Anton M. Leader.

These Are Our Men was an appeal for war bond sales, wrapped in drama. The sponsor turned over its commercial times for the cause and enlisted major stars to deliver the sales messages. The first show-told the life of President Roosevelt, with Frank Sinatra giving the bonds message. Among the others: Gen. Dwight D. Eisenhower, with Ralph Bellamy selling bonds; Gen. Douglas MacArthur, with Ralph Edwards; Adm. Chester Nimitz, with Jack Benny; Gen. George S. Patton, with Miriam Hopkins.

THESE FOUR MEN, documentary drama.

BROADCAST HISTORY: Sept. 7–28, 1941, NBC. 30m, Sundays at 7.

"The life stories of the four men most talked about in the world today." Cedric Hardwicke starred as Winston Churchill in the opening show (script by Frank Wilson). Other shows covered Hitler, Roosevelt, and Stalin.

THEY LIVE FOREVER, war drama.

BROADCAST HISTORY: Feb. 8–Oct. 18, 1942, CBS. 30m, Sundays at 10:30; then a final show Oct. 27, Tuesday at 9:30. PRODUCED in New York by Charles Vanda.

"America not on the defensive but on the offensive . . . a pledge that Pearl Harbor, Manila, and other outrages will not only be remembered but avenged." It was judged most outstanding propaganda series of the year by the National Women's Press Club. Berry Kroeger had many roles.

THINK, experimental drama, mainly science fiction/fantasy; also known as *The ABC Radio Workshop*.

BROADCAST HISTORY: Ca. 1953, ABC. 30m. HOST: Dave Ballard, the "voice of *Think*." PRODUCERS: John Eppolito and Steve Markham.

Some of the stories, such as Ray Bradbury's *Mars Is Heaven*, were well traveled, but the focus here was changed by a new script.

THE THIRD MAN, adventure; subtitled *The Lives of Harry Lime*, based on the character created by Graham Greene and the film of the same title.

BROADCAST HISTORY: 1951–52, BBC; 30m, transcribed and syndicated to American radio in 1952. **STAR:** Orson Welles as Harry Lime. **MUSIC:** Zither by Anton Karas.

The part of Harry Lime, both in Graham Greene's novel and in the subsequent film, was small but vital. For the radio shows, Lime's escapades took center stage, his career as a prince of knaves coming into sharp focus. He was a double-dealing money-grubber who managed to remain sympathetic and at times almost admirable in his deceptions. Lime stole from the rich and gave to the poor, and Harry Lime was usually the poorest chap he knew. He flitted from continent to continent, but Europe was his favored stamping ground. He charmed ladies out of their jewelry, broke and entered, played patsies wherever they were found. But he drew the line at murder and blackmail. This, along with the fact that his victims were greedier than he, kept him likable and made his capers amusing.

But the highlight of *The Third Man* was the haunting zither theme, which the film had propelled to worldwide attention. Anton Karas (discovered by film director Carol Reed playing in a Vienna bistro) wrote it, played it, and grew rich on its royalties.

All of the 52 produced shows are available to collectors on tape.

THIS AMAZING AMERICA, quiz.

BROADCAST HISTORY: Feb. 16–June 28, 1940, Blue Network. 30m, Fridays at 8 until May, then at 9:30. Greyhound Bus Lines. **HOST:** Bob Brown. **VOCAL GROUP:** Ranch Boys Trio. **ORCHESTRA:** Roy Shield.

Variety called this show "a rubberneck lecture tour done up as a parlor game." Contestants were asked about little-known pieces of the American landscape. Listeners learned that there's a diamond mine in Arkansas and a volcano on American soil (the latter a fairly tough question when Mount St. Helens hadn't erupted in a lifetime).

THIS DAY IS OURS, soap opera.

BROADCAST HISTORY: Nov. 7, 1938–Jan. 19, 1940, CBS. 15m, weekdays at 1:45, 1938–39; at 1:30, 1939–40. Crisco.

Jan. 22–March 29, 1940, Blue Network. 15m, weekdays at 10:15 A.M. Crisco.

CAST: Templeton Fox and Joan Banks as Eleanor MacDonald. Jay Jostyn as Curt Curtis. Patricia Dunlap as Pat Curtis. Alan Devitt as Wong. Santos Ortega as General Ming. **DIRECTOR:** Chick Vincent. **WRITERS:** Don Becker and Carl Bixby.

THIS IS BROADWAY, talent-variety show.

BROADCAST HISTORY: May 18–June 29, 1949, CBS. 60m, Wednesdays at 9:30. **PANEL:** George S. Kaufman, Abe Burrows, and Clifton Fadiman, regulars, with such "name" guests as Helen Hayes, Artie Shaw, Frank Parker, etc.

The panel listened to various professional acts and advised the artists on what course to pursue in order to achieve success. On one show, Eden Ahbez, composer of *Nature Boy*, was told by Fadiman to go back to what had worked so well for him, after offering a jive number.

THIS IS JAZZ, improvisational traditional jazz music.

BROADCAST HISTORY: Jan. 18, 1947, on-air audition on the Mutual series *For Your Approval*. Then: Feb. 8–Oct. 4, 1947, Mutual, 30m, Saturdays at 2:30, with a brief Mondays-at-10 stint in late March; later Saturdays at 5. **CREATOR-WRITER-NARRATOR:** Rudi Blesh, author of *Shining Trumpets* (1946), a history and defense of traditional New Orleans jazz. **IN-HOUSE MUSICIANS:** Muggsy Spanier, cornet, replaced by Wild Bill Davison on the 11th broadcast. Georg Brunis, trombone, replaced on the 19th show by Jimmy Archey. Albert Nicholas, clarinet; Edmond Hall as of show 31, Sept. 6. Warren "Baby" Dodds, drums. George Murphy "Pops" Foster, bass. Danny Barker, guitar. Joe Sullivan or James P. Johnson, frequently, on piano. Ralph Sutton, piano, as of the 21st show, June 28. **PRODUCER-ANNOUNCER:** Don Fredericks.

This Is Jazz was "pure American jazz, improvised as you hear it by great living masters of the art." In his book *Shining Trumpets*, Rudi Blesh had been strongly critical of the current interest in the "bebop" movement (as led by Charlie Parker and John Birks "Dizzy" Gillespie) and had sought a new appreciation of ragtime and traditional New Orleans music. This sentiment was promoted in his writings (including books, articles, and newspaper columns in the *San Francisco Chronicle* and later in the *New York Herald Tribune*), in the concerts he arranged, and in local and national radio shows. His shows included *Our Singing Land, Jazz Saga*, and *Dimensions of Jazz*. The most important was *This Is Jazz*, heard for 35 weeks on the Mutual Network.

Blesh was hardly a polished announcer, but his enthusiasm for the material and guests was infectious. Many of the players who were spotlighted were even then regarded as giants: Louis Armstrong, Art Hodes, Sidney Bechet appeared, and there were special broadcasts turned over to entire groups (Edward "Kid" Ory and his Creole Jazz Band, August 9; Lu Watters, Turk Murphy and the Yerba Buena Jazz Band, August 16) or themes (Thomas "Fats" Waller Memorial, May 24). The small house band roared through traditional numbers (*St. Louis Blues; Sweet Lorraine; Big Butter and Egg Man*; etc.), and the theme each week was a hot rendition of *Way Down Yonder in New Orleans*.

The initial broadcast on *For Your Approval* contained a slightly different mix than what was heard during the regular season (Ernest "Punch" Miller, Max Kaminsky, Cyrus St. Clair, Charles Luckey Roberts, Wellman Braud and Milton "Mezz" Mezzrow performed with Nicholas, Dodds, and Brunis). Near the end of the season, Blesh took his All-Star Stompers (Davison, Hall, Archey, Sutton, Dodds, Barker, and Foster) into a radio "Battle of Jazz" with Barry Ulanov's All-Star Modern Jazz Musicians (the leading proponents of the opposite musical viewpoint— Gillespie, Parker, John LaPorta, Billy Bauer, Lennie Tristano, Max Roach, and Ray Brown). These half-hour *Bands for Bonds* shows aired on Mutual Sept. 13 and 20, 1947, with encores in 1948 and 1949.

THIS IS JUDY JONES, light drama–situation comedy.

BROADCAST HISTORY: June 17–Oct. 9, 1941, NBC. 30m, initially West Coast only, Tuesdays at 9:30 Pacific time; Blue Network, Thursdays at 8 beginning Aug. 21. **CAST:** Mercedes McCambridge as Judy Jones, model and girl Friday for the eccentric fashion designer Creighton Leighton. Wally Maher as Leighton. Ben Alexander as Junior Sheldon, the love of Judy's life. Marvel McInnes as Judy's best friend, Betz Bowman. Elliott Lewis as Mr. Peterson, the next-door neighbor in love with Judy's mother. Betty Wilbur as Judy's mom. **WRITER:** Myron Dutton.

THIS IS MY BEST, dramatic anthology.

BROADCAST HISTORY: Sept. 5, 1944–May 28, 1946, CBS. 30m, Tuesdays at 9:30. Schenley Industries (Cresta Blanca Wine). **CAST:** Various; mostly Hollywood stars. **PRODUCERS-DIRECTORS:** Homer Fickett, Dave Titus, Orson Welles, Don Clark.

This Is My Best was based on the book of the same name: edited by Whit Burnett, it was a Book-of-the-Month success and a fat larder of potential new radio material. The premise was simple: the best works of the best modern authors, chosen by the authors themselves and enacted by Hollywood's best stars. Often the authors' choices were not those best known by the public, and many of the stories had seldom been heard.

The plays were selected by producer Homer Fickett and director Dave Titus: writers Burnett and Robert Tallman adapted them to radio, and only then would a search begin for the ideal star. In its first six months, *TIMB* aired such tales as *Leader of the People* (a little-known John Steinbeck piece, with Walter Brennan), *Heaven's My Destination* (by Thornton Wilder, with Van Johnson), and *The Secret Life of Walter Mitty* (by James Thurber, with Robert Benchley). John McIntire was the announcer through the spring of 1945; music was by Bernard Katz.

On March 13, 1945, the show changed abruptly when Orson Welles took over as director, narrator, actor, and adapter of sorts. Welles initiated a shift to classics, with such stories as *Heart of Darkness* (by Joseph Conrad), *Snow White* (with Jane Powell), and *The Master of Ballantrae* (by Robert Louis Stevenson). Welles's tenure was stormy and brief. He quickly crossed swords with the network and the sponsor's agency, which felt that he had abandoned the original concept, had taken the show "highbrow," and was running over his weekly budget. He was fired April 24, charged with compromising the show for his personal agenda by scheduling the play *Don't Catch Me* (which he had been trying to develop as a film prospect) against the agency's wishes. The final five weeks of 1944 were handled by Jimmy Wallington as host of an anthology series.

When the show returned September 18, it had changed yet again, becoming a testing ground for unfilmed movie properties. Film companies tried out their literary options on the air, again resulting in fresh-sounding plays unfamiliar to the radio audience. Don Clark produced.

THIS IS MY STORY, true stories dramatized, often inspiring.

BROADCAST HISTORY: Ca. June 1944–Dec. 1945, CBS Pacific Coast Network. **JUDGES:** Barbara Stanwyck, Hedda Hopper, Leo McCarey. **PRODUCER:** Bob Hafter.

Listeners sent in stories of 500 words, which were judged for dramatic content, dramatized, and enacted by radio professionals; the three best in each 12-week period were awarded war bonds of $1,000, $250, and $100.

The most notable prizewinner on *This Is My Story* was 13-year-old Louise Applewhite, who appealed to President Roosevelt because the hospitals in her hometown were so packed with polio victims that she could not get proper treatment. Roosevelt sent a B-17 and a medical crew at once to fetch her to his Warm Springs Foundation. This show was replayed on the series in April 1945, the Saturday after Roosevelt's death.

The title, *This Is My Story*, was also used on an NBC series (Oct. 13, 1955–April 26, 1956, 30m, Thursdays at 8:30), produced by the Federation of Jewish Philanthropies.

THIS IS NEW YORK, documentary; collage of city landscape.

BROADCAST HISTORY: Dec. 11, 1938–March 19, 1939, CBS. 60m, Sundays at 8. **CHORUS:** Lyn Murray. **ORCHESTRA:** Leith Stevens. **DIRECTOR:** Ed Gardner.

Whatever its greater purpose, *This Is New York* would ever be remembered as the show that led to *Duffy's Tavern*. Ed Gardner (then one of the producer-directors in the radio department at J. Walter Thompson) had long been pondering a series that would give listeners a grasp of the real

New York. "The sidewalks of New York and the people, famous and obscure, who tread them" was the cryptic description in *Radio Guide*.

This was a time when a man like Gardner might try out an idea on the air: CBS would provide the facility and the supporting talent, and the hope of all was that a sponsor might hear the show, like it, and take it on. Ironically, the part of the broadcast that gave Gardner the most trouble was finding an actor who could speak "pure New Yorkese." At last, with air time imminent, he took to the soundstage to demonstrate. When he looked up from the microphone, he later recalled, he saw "the guys in the control room havin' hysterics." One of the "guys" was his Thompson colleague, George Faulkner, who by most accounts was the first to see a character in that voice and may have been the one who named him Archie.

New York roamed freely among celebrities and cab drivers alike. The premiere featured Thomas "Fats" Waller, noted small-group jazz artist. The show of January 29 took a look at the city's Yiddish theater with an appearance by actress Molly Picon. So it went: an interesting show that never found a sponsor but served as the launch pad of one of the major comedy hits of the following decade.

THIS IS NORA DRAKE, soap opera.

BROADCAST HISTORY: Oct. 27, 1947–Jan. 2, 1959, NBC. 15m continuation, weekdays at 11, 1947–49; CBS, concurrent in 1948–49, then CBS only, weekdays at 2:30. Toni Home Permanent, 1947–51, then multiple sponsorship. **CAST:** Charlotte Holland as Nora Drake, a nurse and later departmental supervisor on the staff of Page Memorial Hospital, in a medium-sized town. Joan Tompkins as Nora by ca. 1949; Mary Jane Higby as Nora later. Alan Hewitt as her erstwhile lover, Ken Martinson. Everett Sloane and Ralph Bell as Nora's "lost" father, Alfred Drake. Lesley Woods, Mercedes McCambridge, and Joan Alexander as Peggy King Martinson. Larry Haines as gambler Fred Molina. Roger DeKoven as Andrew King. Grant Richards as Charles Dobbs, the assistant DA who prosecuted Nora's father. Joan Lorring as Hobbs's 18-year-old ward, Suzanne Turrie, who fell in love with her guardian. Irene Hubbard as Rose Fuller. **ANNOUNCERS:** Bill Cullen (for

Toni), Ken Roberts, etc. **MUSIC:** Charles Paul on organ. **DIRECTORS:** Dee Engelbach, Art Hanna, Charles Irving, etc. **WRITERS:** Julian Funt, medical specialist, initially; also, Milton Lewis.

This Is Nora Drake was "a story seen through the window of a woman's heart." Supposedly an orphan, Nora fell in love with Dr. Ken Martinson, and he with her. But Martinson was burdened with most of the emotional instabilities of serial drama males. He dashed off and married Peg King, daughter of millionaire Andrew King and herself an impulsive creature. Soon realizing that he still loved Nora, Ken asked Peg for a divorce. In a fury, Peg confronted Nora, raced away in a careening auto, and had the predictable accident, rendering her a dependent cripple. Feeling unable now to leave his wife, Ken pined unabashedly for Nora.

Meanwhile, Nora's lost father showed up, but Alfred Drake proved to be an impulsive man of weak mind. After introducing her to the gambler Fred Molina, Drake turned a gun on Molina and wounded him. For this he was sent to prison. Nora confided all to Rose Fuller, head nurse at Page Hospital, who was the show's wise and matronly figure. Rose was ever eager to share the trouble of others, despite the fact that she herself was thought to be dying of a fatal disease.

THIS IS OUR ENEMY, dramatic propaganda.

BROADCAST HISTORY: May 24, 1942–Oct. 21, 1943, Mutual. Various 30m times. **CAST:** New York radio actors including Arnold Moss, John Gibson, Lawson Zerbe, Frank Lovejoy, etc. **PRODUCER:** Frank Telford, for the Office of War Information. **WRITER:** Bernard Schoenfeld.

The theme behind this OWI series was that "we cannot win our war or make our peace unless we understand the character of the enemy we are fighting." One show demonstrated how Nazis occupying France brainwashed a young boy into hating his father. Another dramatized the quiet resistance in Czechoslovakia. "Nazis despise the common man. To have such people resist is an affront to them. It is not in their pattern of order and obey."

THIS IS PARIS, musical variety.

BROADCAST HISTORY: March 31–Sept. 22, 1949, Mutual. 30m, Thursdays at 10. **HOST:**

Maurice Chevalier. **GUESTS:** Yves Montand, Claude Dauphin, etc. **ORCHESTRA:** Paul Baron.

THIS IS WAR!, drama and documentary.

BROADCAST HISTORY: Feb. 14–May 9, 1942, all networks. 30m, Saturdays at 7. **CAST:** Major Hollywood stars in narrative and lead roles: Robert Montgomery, Fredric March, Douglas Fairbanks Jr., Tyrone Power, James Stewart, etc. **PRODUCER:** Harold McClinton. **DIRECTOR-WRITER:** Norman Corwin. **WRITERS:** Maxwell Anderson, Stephen Vincent Benét, Ranald MacDougall, etc.

This Is War! was a 13-week anti-fascist series, unique in that it aired simultaneously on all four networks. The aim was to help Americans understand themselves and their enemies. Director Norman Corwin wrote six of the shows; others were scripted by equally distinguished writers.

The show was strong and created controversy. It was attacked in the press and by some public figures. "One of the best measures of its effectiveness," wrote Corwin, "was the fact that the most notorious reactionaries in the country condemned it." The writers had strong words for the Japanese ("clay-faced, back-stabbing dirty pygmies"), Hitler (contemptuously referenced as Schicklgrüber, his grandmother's maiden name, and heard "explaining why he would've been in Moscow six months ago except for the fact that a couple of dozen annihilated Russian armies wouldn't stay annihilated"), and Mussolini ("a jackal in a cage"). The scope ran from patriotic documentaries to informative dramas that probed and questioned American attitudes and morale.

The shows *Your Navy, Your Army,* and *Your Air Forces* promoted the idea that the armed forces belonged to the people, that the Navy, for example, was a joint venture of "130 million shipowners." The Navy show mixed narrative, propaganda, music (score by Kurt Weill; Don Voorhees, conductor), and sound effects: listeners were swept along by the plaintive call of a bosun's pipe, the chatter of sandblasters in a drydock, the lonely cry of a wind at sea. For the April 11 show, *The Enemy,* Corwin visited a school in Poland, where the German army was feeding on "the spoils of starving children," stealing their blood for plasma. *To the Young* examined the war through the eyes of a young recruit: it was the first time Corwin had worked with actor Joseph Julian, leading him to request Julian's services later that year for the important lead in *An American in England*. An excellent example of the lesson-couched-as-drama was the play *You're on Your Own*. Claude Rains starred as the head of "the Department of Peoples' Interests," headquartered in Washington. Rains flies to the town of Maplewood to visit Wilbur Jones (that most important person, the "average American"). There he finds a veritable Aldrich Family, without the craziness but complete with Ezra Stone as the teenage son. With Stone chattering and playing his horn in the background, Rains and Wilbur talk about homefront sacrifices, the dangers of loose talk, the fight against insidious rumors. When Jones, incredulous, asks, "You mean we could *lose*?" Rains replies, "That's up to you, Jonsey." The show ends with Rains walking away, whistling *The Star-Spangled Banner*.

In the final show, listeners voiced their complaints, answered by narrator Raymond Massey against a musical background by Frank Black. Robert Heller researched the series, delving into such sensitive areas as "the Negro problem" and labor disputes in wartime.

THIS IS YOUR FBI, crime drama.

BROADCAST HISTORY: April 6, 1945–Jan. 30, 1953, ABC. 30m, Fridays at 8:30. Equitable Life Assurance Society.

FROM NEW YORK, CA. **1945–47:** CAST: Mandel Kramer, Karl Swenson, Santos Ortega, Elspeth Eric, Joan Banks, Helen Lewis, etc., in anthology crime tales taken from the files of the FBI. NARRATOR: Frank Lovejoy (1945), Dean Carlton (1946–47). ANNOUNCERS: Carl Frank, Milton Cross. ORCHESTRA: Nathan Van Cleave, Frederick Steiner. PRODUCER-DIRECTOR: Jerry Devine. DIRECTOR: William Sweets. WRITERS: Frank Phares; Lawrence MacArthur.

FROM HOLLYWOOD, CA. **1948–53:** CAST: Stacy Harris as Jim Taylor, fictitious Special Agent for the FBI. Also: Michael Ann Barrett, William Conrad, Whitfield Connor, Herb Ellis, Bea Benaderet, Georgia Ellis, Carleton Young, J. C. Flippen, etc. NARRATOR: William Woodson. ANNOUNCER: Larry Keating. ORCHESTRA: Frederick Steiner. PRODUCER-DIRECTOR: Jerry Devine. WRITER: Jerry D. Lewis.

This Is Your FBI was inevitably compared to *The FBI in Peace and War* in the G-Man thriller parade. *Radio Life* concluded that both were worthy and there was little to distinguish one from the other. *This Is* was privy to official Bureau files, while *Peace and War* was mainly fiction. But *Peace and War* sounded authentic: its author, Frederick L. Collins, had received Bureau cooperation in his research, though the radio version of his subsequent book remained unsanctioned.

It hardly mattered. The heroes of both shows were agents of a rather faceless nature: Field Agent Shepherd of *Peace and War* could have filled in for Special Agent Jim Taylor of *This Is* without many complaints. Both shows were framed with bouncy march music: the original theme of *This Is* conveyed the same relentless fight against crime as Prokofiev's music (*The Love for Three Oranges*) did for *Peace and War*. In both shows the Bureau was glorified. The criminal was a rat: identified, hemmed in, and inevitably tracked down and put away.

Jerry Devine was a former comedy writer who had worked for Kate Smith and Tommy Riggs before turning to thrillers. He wrote for *Mr. District Attorney* in 1941. His FBI show was wholeheartedly endorsed by Bureau chief J. Edgar Hoover. Devine was given access to closed cases in the FBI files: he was allowed to dramatize, with names and places changed to protect the innocent. He was given a recruit's-eye tour of the Bureau, beginning with a two-week session at the FBI school in Washington.

In its first year, *This Is Your FBI* ran sensational stories of Nazi agents, of escaped German prisoners of war, of traitors and saboteurs. The heroes changed weekly from one field office to another. With the move to Hollywood, the Bureau experience was channeled through one fictitious agent, Jim Taylor, who grappled with military frauds, juvenile delinquency, hijackers, bank robbers, and embezzlers. The stories were told with a split viewpoint, alternating between the agents and the criminals.

Devine stayed current with procedure by making semi-annual trips to Washington, where he studied new lab techniques and discussed coming programs with Hoover and assistant FBI director Louis Nichols. That the show was used by the Bureau as a public relations tool was inevitable. In 1951, when the tactics of the House Committee on Un-American Activities were being increasingly questioned, *This Is* aired a story of a man cleared by the FBI of rumors that he was a Communist. The conclusion was obvious: "Your FBI operates to collect only one thing—facts—for it is a firm believer in the Biblical prophesy that 'the truth shall make you free.' " The Bureau considered *This Is Your FBI* "our show," wrote Lynn Vines in her 1981 historical overview, published in the FBI newsletter. Hoover believed it "the finest dramatic program on the air."

Announcer Larry Keating delivered the well-remembered commercial punchline: "To your FBI you look for national security, and to your Equitable Society for financial security. These two great institutions are dedicated to the protection of you, your home, and your country!"

THIS IS YOUR LIFE, human interest.

BROADCAST HISTORY: Nov. 9, 1948–May 3, 1950, NBC. 30m, Tuesdays at 8, 1948–49; Wednesdays at 8, 1949–50; four final shows on CBS, May 9–30, 1950, Tuesdays at 9:30. Philip Morris. **HOST-CREATOR:** Ralph Edwards. **ANNOUNCER:** Art Ballinger. **ORCHESTRA:** Alexander Laszlo. **PRODUCER:** Al Paschall, with Jim Chadwick and Ann James. **DIRECTOR:** Axel Gruenberg.

This Is Your Life, though mainly remembered as a long-running TV show, began on radio. Created by Ralph Edwards of *Truth or Consequences*, it grew out of two unrelated *Consequences* events. During the war, Edwards connected a wounded veteran in a Hawaiian hospital by telephone to his hometown, where family and friends tried to re-create Main Street on a Saturday night. This was so successful that a later *Consequences* show reunited a paraplegic on stage with his family, teachers, old friends, and even the doctor who had delivered him.

In October 1948, Edwards brought the idea to full bloom. *This Is Your Life* was announced as a new concept in participatory entertainment. It wasn't a quiz or a game: each week it presented "the complete life story of a living American," bringing him together with people from his past, including some thought long lost. Each show depended upon two things: the ability of Edwards's producers to find the people, and the secrecy that surrounded the identity of the subject.

Because much of the impact was derived from the subject's genuine surprise at the top of the show, elaborate deceptions were used to fool him into believing that he was there for another purpose. Some were brought across the country on the wild-goose chase, which ended in the teary reunion with old friends. In this it was more successful visually—the announcement that "this is your life" packed the same emotional freight on TV as Allen Funt's deadpan announcement that (smile!) one was on *Candid Camera*. But while it lasted, the radio show had its moments.

One flabbergasted subject, elevator operator John Sexton, was surprised by remote in his elevator, with friends and relatives getting on and off as the cage stopped on various floors. Chicago organ grinder Sam Canzona realized his dream—having his wife's sister brought from Italy. War heroes were especially favored, Edwards getting tips to their whereabouts from Gen. Omar Bradley and others. Subjects were showered with prizes, vacations, and cash. Occasionally the subject was a celebrity (Jeanette MacDonald, Fifi D'Orsay, etc.), though newsman Lowell Thomas wasn't at all amused when he was surprised on the air. The subjects were introduced by "Johnny," the sponsor's living trademark, who peppered the commercials with the never-to-be-forgotten "Call for Philip Morris" chant.

THIS LIFE IS MINE, soap opera.

BROADCAST HISTORY: March 22, 1943–Aug. 24, 1945, CBS. 15m, weekdays at 9:45 A.M.; moved to 3:45 in the fall of 1943. **CAST:** Betty Winkler as Eden Channing, a teacher whose family met "our changing world with two conflicting points of view." Michael Fitzmaurice as Capt. Bob Hastings, who tried to undercut Eden's fiancé Paul in her affections while Paul was away fighting for his country. Henry M. Neely, Raymond Ives, and Ruth McDevitt as David, Joe, and Jane Channing. Paul McGrath as Edwin Lorimer. Tony Barrett as Charlie Dyer. **DIRECTOR:** Marx Loeb. **WRITERS:** Addy Richton, Lynn Stone.

THOSE HAPPY GILMANS, serial comedy-drama.

BROADCAST HISTORY: Aug. 22, 1938–May 19, 1939, NBC; Blue Network for two months, then

Red. 15m, weekdays at 1:45. General Mills and Kix Cereal. CAST: Bill Bouchey as Gordon Gilman. Edith Adams as Ethel, his wife. John Hench and Joan Kay as their two nearly grown children, Stanley and Phyllis; Cornelius Peeples as the youngest child, Wheezy. Henrietta Tedro as Aunt Bessie, finicky but beloved by all. ANNOUNCER: Donald Thompson. PRODUCERS: Frank and Anne Hummert.

Those Happy Gilmans was a rarity—a Hummert serial without the melodrama: an attempt to bring a light hand to soap opera timeslots. There were some familiar Hummert touches: the Gilman family was "average American," the father hard-working, the mother wise in the ways of her children. But as *Radio Guide* reviewed it, it dealt largely with the children's growing pains and the family's gloomy economic picture: "the ordinary problems of a $2,000-a-year family." The father, Gordon, disliked his job but was "sunny and easy-going" away from work. Wife Ethel was appropriately self-sacrificing. The older children reflected all the pleasures and pain of late adolescence; young Wheezy was constantly in Dutch with his siblings for lack of respect, and with father for misbehaving.

It was a refreshing departure for the Hummerts, but in the end wasn't strong enough for its afternoon audience.

THOSE SENSATIONAL YEARS, documentary.

BROADCAST HISTORY: April 17–Sept. 14, 1947, ABC. 30m, various times. HOST-NARRATOR: Quin Ryan, "whose own career parallels the dramatic events of radio's crowded years." CAST: Chicago radio regulars: Harry Elders, George Cisar, Paul Barnes, Cliff Norton, Boris Aplon, Tony Parrish, Jonathan Hole, Don Gallagher, Charles Flynn, etc. ANNOUNCERS: Lee Walters, Jack Lester. MUSIC: Composed by Bruce Chase; conducted by Rex Maupin. PRODUCER-DIRECTOR: Fred Killian. WRITERS: Harrison Y. Bingham, Roy W. Winsor.

"Stories that stirred the nation" during the two decades of radio broadcasting to date were presented in dramatic reenactments. Among them: the Dempsey-Tunney fight and its "long count"; the Scopes "monkey trial"; the tragic attempts to rescue Floyd Collins from a Kentucky cave; etc.

THOSE WE LOVE, serial drama.

BROADCAST HISTORY: Many changes of network and 30m timeslots, including:

Jan. 4, 1938–March 27, 1939, Blue Network. Tuesdays at 8 through March 1938, then Mondays at 8:30. Ponds Cream.

Oct. 5, 1939–March 28, 1940, NBC. Thursdays at 8:30. Royal Gelatin.

Sept. 16, 1940–June 23, 1941, CBS. Mondays at 8. Teel dentifrice.

July 1–Sept. 23, 1942, NBC. Wednesdays at 9. Summer substitute for Eddie Cantor. Sal Hepatica.

Oct. 11, 1942–May 30, 1943, CBS. Sundays at 2. General Foods.

June 6–Oct. 3, 1943, NBC. Sundays at 7. Substitute for Jack Benny. Grape Nuts.

Oct. 10, 1943–June 22, 1944, NBC. Sundays at 2. General Foods.

June 29–Aug. 24, 1944, NBC. Thursdays at 8. Summer show for Frank Morgan's *Maxwell House Coffee Time*. General Foods.

Oct. 8, 1944–April 1, 1945, NBC. Sundays at 2. Sanka Coffee.

CAST: Nan Grey through all changes of time and network as Kathy Marshall, the heroine. Richard Cromwell as her twin brother Kit until 1942; Bill Henry as Kit Marshall thereafter. Pedro de Cordoba as John Marshall, their father. Hugh Sothern as John Marshall, ca. 1939; Oscar O'Shea as John, ca. 1941; Francis X. Bushman also as John. Alma Kruger as Aunt Emily. Virginia Sale as Martha, the maid. Donald Woods as Dr. Leslie Foster, Kathy Marshall's romantic interest. Helen Wood as Elaine Dascomb, a woman who came to town with Dr. Leslie Foster, survived a murder attempt by Foster's wife, came to love Kit Marshall, and finally became Kathy's partner in a decorating shop. Jean Rogers also as Elaine Dascomb. Priscilla Lyon and later Ann Todd as Amy, Dr. Foster's little daughter. Owen Davis Jr. as Allen McCrea, Kathy's first love. Robert Cummings (on the verge of film stardom) as David Adair. Lou Merrill as Ed Neely, who perpetrated a real estate fraud and was later suspected of shooting Kathy as revenge against her father. Anne Stone as nurse Lydia Dennison. Victor Rodman as Jerry Payne. Mary Gordon as Mrs. Emmett, the Scottish woman who kept house for Dr. Foster. Clarence Straight as "Rags the dog." **ANNOUNCER:** Dick Joy. **MUSIC:** Eddie Kay, composer-conductor. **PRODUCER-DIRECTOR:** Ted Sherdeman. **WRITERS:** Agnes Ridgway, Ruth Knight.

Those We Love might have been a big show in the *One Man's Family* tradition if the sponsors had had the good sense to leave it alone. But despite a demonstrated popularity with a loyal audience that at times became militant, this weekly half-hour continuation had an unstable run broken by as much as six months of silence. It was, complained *Tune In* in 1943, a hit that had long been mishandled, getting only "three years of air time out of a possible five."

Its Blue Network premiere in 1938 was the result of a search by the makers of Ponds Cream to find a replacement for the canceled *Husbands and Wives*. The concept was roughed out by an agency executive—"a prime-time serial that would depict the contemporary American domestic scene." One of the writers invited to submit scripts was Agnes Ridgway, who had built a reputation with her one-act plays on *The Rudy Vallee Hour*. Ridgway's scenario of a motherless family in a midsized New England town won her the job.

It was the story of the Marshall family of Westbridge, Conn., a bustling community of 15,000 people. John Marshall was a lawyer who coveted peace, quiet, and honest neighbors. His wife had died years before, leaving him with two children, twins Kathy and Kit, to raise. Kathy became the serial's central character, and the focus of its romance.

Her first love, Allen McCrea, had proved unworthy, and as the show went into its second year her interest had shifted to Dr. Leslie Foster, brilliant young surgeon with a mysterious past. Presumed a widower, Foster had moved to Westbridge seeking a new start. Kathy's brother Kit was described as a perfect sibling, always there with an open heart and a sympathetic ear. Kit had begun a legal career after a near-fatal plane crash swayed him from his first choice, aviation. The other member of the family was Aunt Emily Mayfield, who "might have married in her earlier days but accepted instead the responsibility of mothering Kathy and Kit when their mother died when they were still small children" (*Radio Guide*). There was also a "beloved" maid, Martha Newbury, who had helped raise the twins from infancy.

The serial was not without its moments of true soap opera. Dr. Foster was followed to Westbridge by his unbalanced ex-wife, who kidnapped their daughter Amy and died in an auto wreck trying to escape. Foster suddenly became a sympathetic and long-running character, his role culminating in marriage to Kathy in early 1943.

Those We Love made news in its casting, taking its lead players from Hollywood film lots. Nan Grey won the lead over 23 competitors: she was a Universal starlet who had impressed in a *Lux Radio Theater* appearance opposite Bing Crosby in 1937. She was given a five-year contract, but the show was canceled as of March 27, 1939. It was dropped from the schedule so quickly that the story was left in limbo, with the major conflicts unresolved even by suggestion. The fans felt cheated and outraged: they responded with a flood of vitriolic mail to NBC, to Ponds Cream, and to such trade journals as *Radio Guide*. Some suggested boycotting the sponsor; interest was aroused in a listener's "code of rights," to force networks and sponsors to keep faith with the audience; some listeners proposed to appeal to the Federal Communications Commission.

Nothing came of it until six months later, when the Red Network picked up the story almost as if there had been no gap at all. Soon it regained most of its old audience, but in 1940 it was again suddenly canceled, by new sponsor Royal Gelatin. The letters resumed—the threats and anger. Six months later, CBS picked it up, a solid season for Teel Soap. It was immediately retrieved by NBC and used as summertime fodder for three years running. During the regular seasons its Sundays-at-2 scheduling again played havoc with continuity, as many of its West Coast fans were churchgoers and could not listen at 11 A.M., its Pacific timeslot.

Through all this convoluted scheduling, *Those We Love* kept its storyline largely continuous, and its cast remained mostly intact. Announcer Dick Joy described it as the happiest of shows to work.

THOSE WEBSTERS, situation comedy.

BROADCAST HISTORY: March 9, 1945–Feb. 22, 1946, CBS. 30m, Fridays at 9:30, taking the spot of *That Brewster Boy*. Quaker Oats.

March 3, 1946–Aug. 22, 1948, Mutual. 30m, Sundays at 6. Quaker.

CAST: Willard Waterman and Constance Crowder as George and Jane Webster, who lived at 46 River Road in Spring City and tried to prove that "families are fun." Gil Stratton Jr. and Joan Alt as their children, Billy and Liz. Bill Idelson as Billy's friend, Emil. Jane Webb as Belinda Boyd. Also: Clarence Hartzell, Lou Krugman, Eddie Firestone, Parley Baer, etc. **ORCHESTRA:** Frank Worth. **PRODUCER-DIRECTOR:** Joe Ainley. **WRITERS:** Frank and Doris Hursley.

Bumbling, misunderstandings, the usual chaos. George Webster was a member of the Sons of the Mustangs of the Moonlight Mesas, which met in the lodgehall on Commercial Street. The show originated in New York, moved briefly to Chicago, then went on to Hollywood with most of the cast and crew intact.

THREE FOR THE MONEY, quiz.

BROADCAST HISTORY: June 26–Sept. 18, 1948, Mutual. 60m, Saturdays at 9. **HOST:** Bud Collyer. **VOCALIST:** Mary Small.

Three contestants went through a process of elimination, and the winner tried to predict audience reaction to a series of tunes. Prizes up to $5,000 were awarded.

THREE RING TIME, comedy-variety.

BROADCAST HISTORY: Sept. 12–Dec. 5, 1941, Mutual. 30m, Fridays at 9:30. Ballantine Ale.

Dec. 12, 1941–June 2, 1942, Blue Network. 30m, Fridays, later Tuesdays, at 8:30. Ballantine.

March 8–Dec. 20, 1943, CBS. 30m, Mondays at 10:30. Ballantine.

CAST: *1941–42*: Charles Laughton, Milton Berle, and singer Shirley Ross, with Bob Crosby and the Bobcats. *1943*: Poet Ogden Nash, with the Guy Lombardo Orchestra. **ANNOUNCER:** Bill Goodwin (1941–42).

Three Ring Time was the first major Mutual West Coast origination, created to make the fourth network a real competitor in transcontinental broadcasting. It was Mutual's "fair-haired child," said *Radio Guide*, the title derived from the sponsor's trademark. It was launched in great expectations, and star Charles Laughton voiced great enthusiasm to *Radio Life*. He had played enough heavies to last a lifetime: the series would "give me a chance to do what I really like to do—make people laugh."

But things went wrong from the beginning, and the show was the most prominent bust of the season. The cast was basically incompatible: Laughton was miffed when costar Milton Berle presumed to direct him in comedy; Berle was miffed when he felt Laughton was stepping on his best lines. They soon came to a point of open antagonism. "Laughton wanted to shelve the tough, hard-bitten character he had made famous on the screen and in numerous on-air sorties with Charlie McCarthy. He wanted to be a sort of lovable, good-natured and funny old duck, while the whole troupe, the producer, and the sponsor counted on his doing a Captain Bligh every week." In his autobiography, Berle dismisses the entire series in a line: Laughton, he said, "decided that playing for laughs with Berle wasn't his favorite ego massage."

By January Laughton had had enough. He asked for and was given his release, and the show was reorganized with a guest star system, Edna Mae Oliver and others being brought in to play opposite Berle. Ross, Crosby, and Goodwin continued as before. By then the sponsor had taken Mutual's "fair-haired child" and jumped to NBC. Mutual responded with a $10 million lawsuit, charging NBC with restraint of trade. Ironically, NBC was then being forced to divest itself of its Blue Network under a government anti-trust case, and it lost *Three Ring Time* to the Blue anyway. What *Radio Guide* found surprising was that, despite its internal squabbles, *Three Ring Time* "from the beginning has been an uncommonly good program."

The sponsor certainly liked the concept. But the 1943 CBS series with Ogden Nash bore scant resemblance to the original, and lasted just part of a season.

THREE SHEETS TO THE WIND, comedy-mystery.

BROADCAST HISTORY: Feb. 15–July 5, 1942, NBC. 30m, Sundays at 11:30. **CAST:** Helga

Moray as Joan Lockwood of British Intelligence. John Wayne as Dan O'Brien. Sharon Douglas and Lee Bonnell in continuing supporting roles. ANNOUNCER: Ken Carpenter. CREATOR-DIRECTOR-NARRATOR: Tay Garnett.

Movie director Tay Garnett got the idea for *Three Sheets to the Wind* in 1933, while in Greenland filming *SOS Iceberg*. Garnett was known for his epics of the sea, and in 1935 his cruise on the yawl *Athene* deepened the idea and gave it color. By 1942, he had a film script of sorts (by screenwriter Ken Englund): this he sold to NBC on the premise that radio could preview the film (which was never actually shot).

The story followed the luxury liner *Empress* as it sailed from Southampton, England, on a 180-day journey, with Alexandria, Egypt, the first port of call. The scene was set two years back in time, the cruise beginning Aug. 25, 1939, in the final days of peace. A listen to the only known scrap (half a show at this writing) reveals a plot dripping with melodrama, seven people having been strangled in London in the seven days that the *Empress* has been in port. The murders seem linked to a sultan's black diamond, its secrets wrapped in mysticism.

Agent Joan Lockwood (played by Helga Moray, a British actress who was then Garnett's wife) is determined to crack the case. Also on the case is Dan O'Brien, an American posing as a drunk—thus the double-edged title. John Wayne, who did little radio, was then just beginning his rise to fabulous screen success. But it can be safely said that playing a lush was not his forte.

THUNDER OVER PARADISE, soap opera–adventure serial.

BROADCAST HISTORY: July 24, 1939–Feb. 28, 1941, Blue Network. 15m, weekdays at 10 A.M. for Mueller Macaroni, 1939–40; at 11:45 A.M., sustained, 1940–41. CAST: Laurette Fillbrandt as a woman attempting to run a cattle ranch in Central America; Bill Crawford, Pat Murphy, Bill Idelson, Sidney Ellstrom.

THURSTON, THE MAGICIAN, thriller serial.

BROADCAST HISTORY: Nov. 3, 1932–May 25, 1933, Blue Network. 15m, twice a week at 8:45. Swift and Company.

The exploits of master magician Howard Thurston, then among the most famous conjurors in the land. Thurston hosted the series and played dramatic roles, and his sponsor issued many Thurston magic premiums.

TILLIE THE TOILER, comedy, from the comic strip by Russ Westover.

BROADCAST HISTORY: April 11–Oct. 10, 1942, CBS. 30m, Saturdays at 7:30. CAST: Caryl Smith as Tillie Jones, the hard-working stenographer who supported her "Mumsy." Billy Lynn as her friend and coworker Mac MacDougal. John Brown as their boss, Simpkins. Margaret Burlen as Tillie's mom.

TIM AND IRENE, vaudeville-style comedy.

BROADCAST HISTORY: Sept. 18, 1934–Jan. 29, 1935, Blue Network. 30m, Tuesdays at 10:30.

June 28–Sept. 27, 1936, NBC, Blue Network, then Red beginning August 30. 30m, Sundays at 7. *The Jell-O Summer Show*, for Jack Benny. CAST: Tim Ryan and Irene Noblette, with tenor Morton Bowe. ANNOUNCER: Don Wilson. ORCHESTRA: Don Voorhees.

April 18, 1937–Jan. 9, 1938, Mutual. 30m, Sundays at 6:30. *Fun in Swingtime*. Admiracion Shampoo. ORCHESTRA: Bunny Berigan.

March 11–Sept. 2, 1938, Blue Network. 30m, Fridays at 9. *The Royal Crown Revue*. Nehi Soft Drinks. CAST: Tim and Irene, with singer Fredda Gibson, actor Teddy Bergman, comic Charlie Cantor, and the Golden Gate Quartet (William Sankford, Henry Owens, Willie Johnston, and Arlandus Wilson. ANNOUNCER: Graham McNamee. ORCHESTRA: George Olsen.

Tim Ryan and his wife, Irene Noblette, were comics of the old school whose humor paled as tastes changed and the national funnybone matured. They turned to radio in 1931, as bookings in vaudeville dried up. Their first success was at KHJ, Los Angeles. They were regulars on the West Coast *Carefree Carnival* and were also featured on the Joe Cook show, *Circus Night in Silvertown* (NBC for Goodrich, March-Aug. 1935). On the air, Ryan was relatively straight; Noblette was loony and squeaky. She appeared often on *The Bob Hope Show* in the 1940s and, as Irene Ryan, was seen in a later era as Granny on the TV sitcom *The Beverly Hillbillies*.

A TIME FOR LOVE, adventure drama.

BROADCAST HISTORY: Jan. 15, 1953–May 27, 1954, CBS. 30m, Thursdays at 9, later at 9:30. Jergens Lotion. **CAST:** Marlene Dietrich as Dianne La Volta, a chanteuse who flitted around the postwar continent in stories of intrigue; an outgrowth of Dietrich's earlier series, *Cafe Istanbul.*

THE TIME OF YOUR LIFE, comedy-variety.

BROADCAST HISTORY: Oct. 3–Dec. 26, 1937, NBC. 30m, Sundays at 5:30. Gruen Watches. **CAST:** Mimic Sheila Barrett; maestro and occasional comic Joe Rines; host Graham McNamee; guest vocalists.

Sheila Barrett was said to be uncanny with both facial and verbal caricatures of famous people (both sexes): "All she has to do is see a person one time and at her next performance she'll break out a sizzling takeoff" (*Radio Guide*). Robert Taylor, Marlene Dietrich, and Eleanor Roosevelt were reportedly amused; Tallulah Bankhead wasn't.

TIME'S A WASTIN', quiz.

BROADCAST HISTORY: Oct. 6–Dec. 29, 1948, CBS. 30m, Wednesdays at 10. **HOST:** Bud Collyer. **PRODUCERS:** Mark Goodson and Bill Todman.

Contestants answered questions in a race against the clock, with each second diminishing the cash value of the question by $100. Although its run was brief, the producers revamped the formula and in 1950 arrived with *Beat the Clock*, one of the big hits of early TV game shows.

THE TIMID SOUL, comedy, based on the comic strip by H. T. Webster.

BROADCAST HISTORY: Oct. 12, 1941–March 15, 1942, Mutual. 30m, Sundays at 9:30. **CAST:** Billy Lynn as Casper Milquetoast. Cecil Roy as Madge, his wife.

T-MAN, crime drama.

BROADCAST HISTORY: July 1–Sept. 2, 1950, CBS. 30m, Saturdays at 8:30. **CAST:** Dennis O'Keefe as Steve Larson, "law enforcement agent of the Treasury Department, skilled fighter against crime, relentless enemy of the underworld." Sup-porting players from Hollywood radio ranks: Ted de Corsia, Virginia Gregg, Wally Maher, Bill Johnstone, etc. **ANNOUNCER:** Roy Rowan. **MUSIC:** Del Castillo. **PRODUCER-DIRECTOR:** William N. Robson.

TODAY AT THE DUNCANS, situation comedy.

BROADCAST HISTORY: Nov. 2, 1942–July 30, 1943, CBS. 15m, three a week at 6:15 (briefly heard Fridays only, Feb.–May). California Fruit. **CAST:** Frank Nelson and his wife, Mary Lansing, as John and Mary Duncan. Dix Davis as their 10-year-old son, Dinky.

Today at the Duncans promoted Frank and Mary Nelson as typecast: as the Duncans, they shared the problems of other wartime families— "planning meals with an eye on the ration book, driving to and from town on limited gas and rubber, and lending a hand to the war effort."

TODAY'S CHILDREN, soap opera.

BROADCAST HISTORY: Sept. 11, 1933–Dec. 31, 1937, NBC. 15m, weekdays, Blue Network at 10:30 A.M. until 1936, then Red Network at 10:45 A.M. Pillsbury. **CAST:** Irna Phillips as Mother Moran. Ireene Wicker as her daughter, Eileen. *Ca. 1936*: Fran Carlon as Patty. Fred Von Ammon as Terry Moran. Jean MacGregor as Dorothy Moran. Lucy Gilman as Lucy Moran. Walter Wicker as Bob Crane. Gene Morgan as Bill Taylor. Ted Maxwell as Ralph Santo. Seymour Young as Jack Marsh. Gale Page as Gloria Marsh. Irna Phillips as Kay Crane. Bess Johnson and Sunda Love as Frances Moran. **ANNOUNCER:** Louis Roen. **CREATOR-WRITER:** Irna Phillips.

Dec. 13, 1943–June 2, 1950, NBC. 15m, weekdays at 2:15, 1943–46; at 2, 1946–48; at 2:30, 1948–50. General Mills. **CAST:** *Chicago, 1943–46*: Virginia Payne and Murray Forbes as Mama and Papa Schultz. Patricia Dunlap, Ernie Andrews, and Ruth Rau as their children, Bertha, Otto, and Maggie (in the storyline Maggie Schultz changed her name to Marilyn Larrimore in order to become a model). Kleve Kirby as John Murray, the lawyer Maggie-Marilyn married. Laurette Fillbrandt as Jen Burton, who married Otto. Art Hern as Richard Stone, the impostor. *Hollywood, 1946–50*: Betty Lou Gerson as Marilyn. Marjorie Davies, Gale Page, and Joan Banks as Carlotta Lagorro Armour.

Laurette Fillbrandt as Jennifer. Wilms Herbert as Keith. Milt Herman as Italo. Jo Gilbert as Naomi. Jack Edwards as David Lagorro. Frank Lovejoy as Christopher Barnes. Barton Yarborough as Rusty Davidson. ANNOUNCERS: Greg Donovan, Vincent Pelletier, etc. PRODUCER: Carl Wester. DIRECTOR: Axel Gruenberg. WRITERS: Irna Phillips (plot), Virginia Cooke (dialogue).

Today's Children had two distinct lives. It was one of the earliest soaps of the prolific Irna Phillips, created in anger when her first serial was taken away from her by the station that aired it. Phillips had been writing and starring in *Painted Dreams* on WGN, Chicago, since 1930. When WGN refused to allow Phillips to take *Dreams* to a network, Phillips quit the station and mounted an eight-year court fight to retain her rights. This became the classic radio case of "work-for-hire": the court ruled that Phillips was an employee, thus not entitled to ownership of her show.

By then it was a moot point: Phillips had long since moved to NBC with a *Painted Dreams* derivative called *Today's Children*. This contained many of the same characters, thinly veiled with new names, and was announced with a heavy epigraph: . . . *and today's children with their hopes and dreams, their laughter and tears, shall be the builders of a brighter world tomorrow*. The lead character, kindly Mother Moran, was based on Phillips's own mother, who died in 1937 and left Phillips without the inspiration to continue writing it. The serial was set in Chicago's Hester Street, a melting pot of hopes and nationalities.

After a gap of six years, Phillips revived *Today's Children* in title and concept, but with new characters. By now the acknowledged "queen of soaps," she had begun an ambitious *General Mills Hour*, in which the characters of three soaps (*The Guiding Light, Woman in White*, and *Today's Children*) would interrelate and participate in crossover plots, with a General Mills host (Ed Prentiss; later Terry O'Sullivan) providing the necessary bridges between them. *Today's Children* now focused on the Schultz family of the old Hester Street setting, promoting the same themes of family love and the value of woman as homemaker. The Schultzes (played by the stars of *Ma Perkins*) had three children, and another, Joseph, had been missing for 17 years as

the story opened. In one sequence, Joseph seemed to return, but listeners knew (and so, "somehow," did Mama and daughter Bertha) that he was an impostor. In reality he was Richard Stone, Joseph's buddy in the war, who had watched the real Joseph die at Anzio. Taken into the family with a tale that his war-torn face had been repaired by plastic surgery, Richard soon found that his love for Bertha went beyond the brother-sister kind. Such was life in matinee drama.

In mid-1946, Phillips moved her serials from Chicago to Hollywood. *Guiding Light* remained in the Midwest, its place on *General Mills* eventually taken by a new serial, *Masquerade*.

TOM CORBETT, SPACE CADET, juvenile science fiction.

BROADCAST HISTORY: Jan. 1–July 3, 1952, ABC. 30m, Tuesdays and Thursdays at 5:30. Kellogg's Pep. CAST: Frankie Thomas as Tom Corbett, pilot of the spaceship *Polaris*. Jan Merlin as Roger Manning, "astrographer" (in charge of radar and navigation), an eternal wiseguy whose "Aw, go blow your jets!" became a catchphrase. Al Markim as Astro, the Venusian crewman "on the powerdeck." Margaret Garland as Dr. Joan Dale. Edward Bryce as Captain Strong, their chief. Carter Blake as Commander Arkwright, head of the Space Academy. ANNOUNCER: Jackson Beck. DIRECTOR: Drexel Hines. WRITERS: Richard Jessup, Don Hughes, Gilbert Braun, etc.

Tom Corbett, which also appeared in comic books and a newspaper strip, began its dramatic life as an early TV series: first seen on CBS Oct. 2, 1950, it followed a new wave of interest in space exploration fueled by the George Pal film epic, *Destination Moon*, and by *Captain Video* on the rival Dumont Network. Announcer Jackson Beck gave it the same urgent opening as he did those other Pep-sponsored serials, *Mark Trail* and *The Adventures of Superman*:

Kellogg's Pep, the buildup wheat cereal, invites you to rocket into the future with TOMMMM CORRRBETT, SPACE CADET!

(BUZZERS), then, TOM: Stand by to raise ship! . . . Blastoff minus five! (MUSIC STING) . . . four! (STING) . . . three! (STING) two! (STING) . . . one! (STING) . . . *Zero!*

(ROCKETS BLAST)

BECK: *Now, as roaring rockets blast off to dis-*

tant planets and far-flung stars, we take you to the age of the conquest of space, with TOM CORBETT, SPACE CADET!

Based on the Robert A. Heinlein novel *Space Cadet*, the series followed the adventures of Solar Guards trainees 400 years hence (as in the TV show, the exact correlating date was used, so the radio series was set in 2352). The crew of the *Polaris* was played by the same acting crew that worked the television series. The TV version crossed four networks (CBS, ABC, NBC, Dumont) and ended June 25, 1955.

THE TOM MIX RALSTON STRAIGHT SHOOTERS, juvenile western-adventure serial.

BROADCAST HISTORY: Sept. 25, 1933–March 26, 1937, NBC. 15m continuation, three a week at 5:30, 1933–34; at 5:15, 1934–35; at 5:30, 1935–36; then weekdays at 5:15, 1936–37. Ralston Purina.

Sept. 27, 1937–March 27, 1942, Blue Network. 15m continuation, weekdays at 5:45. Ralston.

June 5, 1944–June 24, 1949, Mutual. 15m continuation, weekdays, mostly at 5:45. Ralston.

Sept. 26, 1949–June 23, 1950, Mutual. 30m, three a week at 5:30. Aka *The Curley Bradley Show*. Ralston.

Aug. 6–Dec. 31, 1950, Mutual. 30m, Sundays at 8. *The Singing Marshal*. Ralston.

June 11–Dec. 16, 1951, Mutual. 30m, three a week at 5 until Sept. 7; returned Oct. 21, Sundays at 8. Ralston.

CAST: Artells Dickson as Tom Mix, early 1930s; Jack Holden as Tom Mix from ca. 1937; Russell Thorson as Tom Mix, early 1940s; Joe "Curley" Bradley as Tom Mix from June 5, 1944. Percy Hemus as the Old Wrangler (1930s). George Gobel (the comedian of early TV fame) as Jimmy. Andy Donnelly and Hugh Rowlands also as Jimmy. Jane Webb and Winifred Toomey as Jane. Sidney Ellstrom as Amos Q. Snood. Vance McCune and Forrest Lewis as Wash. Leo Curley as Sheriff Mike Shaw (earlier information that Harold Peary and Willard Waterman were also featured in this role was denied by Waterman in recent years, though Waterman and Peary did trade off frequently in the same roles). Joe "Curley" Bradley as Pecos Williams, early 1940s. ANNOUNCERS: Les Griffith, Franklyn Ferguson, Don Gordon, etc. DIRECTORS: Charles Claggett, Clarence Menser, etc. WRITERS: George Lowther, Charles Tazewell, Roland Martini, etc. THEME: *When the Bloom Is on the Sage.*

Tom Mix was the major rival of *Jack Armstrong* in the world of juvenile adventure serials. These two defined the era: they opened and closed it, each spanning more than 15 seasons and both drawing consistently high ratings in the wheat-and-barley hour, 5–6 P.M.

Mix was created as an advertising vehicle for the Ralston Purina Company, which sponsored it throughout. The seasons generally spanned late September to late March or April in the early years, year-round later.

It was based on the life of a real cowboy, soldier of fortune, and Hollywood screen star. Mix was born in Pennsylvania in 1880, and so much of his life was glorified by Hollywood publicity agents that he soon became enshrined as a living myth. It was said that he had "seen action" with the Rough Riders; that he had had great adventures during the Philippine Insurrection, the Boer War, and the Boxer Rebellion; that he had been the last of the oldtime lawmen in Oklahoma and had served with the Texas Rangers. Like most Hollywood myths, this was largely fiction. Mix did not serve with the Rangers, and his military record was undistinguished (including no battlefield action and highlighted by desertion in 1902), according to later biographies. He did become a champion roper and rodeo hand, winning a national championship in 1909. But it was his induction into the movies in 1910, and particularly his rise to stardom with Fox beginning in 1917, that saw the buildup of the Mix legend. Like Buffalo Bill Cody, the trumped-up hero of the previous generation, Mix became famous through showmanship. By the time radio got him, he was seldom mentioned in print without a platoon of fantastic adjectives.

The creation of the radio show was detailed by Jim Harmon, whose chapter on *Mix* in *The Great Radio Heroes* contains a solid account of what the serial was and how it affected its audience. Its format was devised by Charles Claggett, a St. Louis adman retained by Ralston in 1933. "It had the ideal hero," wrote Harmon, and the hero had a "wonder horse" named Tony—already nationally famous from the movies and Mix's personal appearances. The setting was Tom's ranch, the TM-Bar, in the Texas country near Dobie township. There Tom lived with his two young wards, Jimmy and Jane, and with an elderly sidekick known only as the "Old Wrangler."

No episodes of the earliest days have yet been heard, but Harmon provides a good example of the opening and how the drama unfolded. It began "with thundering hoofbeats and the Old Wrangler crying, 'Let's git-a-goin'!' After a pitch for Ralston, the Wrangler would return to tell the story directly to the young audience. 'Howdee, Straight Shooters! howdee!' " he would say in his recap of events. Though the characters were well established by 1934, there were flashbacks to Mix's career as a soldier in the Boer, Boxer, and Spanish American wars. New characters joined the fold. Sheriff Mike Shaw replaced the Old Wrangler as Mix's sidekick after the death of Hemus, and there was a "colored cook" and man-of-all-work named Wash. Harmon recalls Wash as a stereotype, with influences from *Amos 'n' Andy*: he might be "easily frightened" but always "fought down his fear manfully." Mix, of course, feared nothing. He faced the most incredible array of rustlers, killers, ghosts, saboteurs, invisible men, and, on one occasion, a giant. His demeanor was Texas-friendly but stern. His voice gave notice: he had ice in his veins, and no nonsense would be tolerated. Two regulars as the serial progressed were Pecos Williams, another of Tom's buddies, and miserly Amos Q. Snood, owner of the hotel in Dobie, who took pink pills and was the epitome of pettiness.

Tom was a singer as well as a fighter. The shows were marked by memorable singing commercials, especially during the war years when Don Gordon was the announcer. He came galloping in to an organ crescendo, with Tony neighing and (*Up, Tony! . . . come on, boy!*) pawing the air, and the flow of Tom's golden voice pushing Ralston right off Checkerboard Square:

> *Shre-ea-ded Ralston for your breakfast,*
> *Start the day off shinin' bright:*
> *Gives you lots of cowboy energy,*
> *With a flavor that's just right!*
> *It's delicious and nutritious,*
> *Bite-size and ready to eat.*
> *Take a tip from Tom,*
> *Go and tell your mom,*
> *Shredded Ralston can't be beat!*

The serial had emerged in 1944, after two seasons of silence, with what Harmon describes as an "air of conviction." Mix joined Jack Armstrong, Captain Midnight, Terry Lee, Hop Harri-

gan, and even Superman in the war against Nazis and "Japs." There were still many homefront mysteries, and soon it became known as "radio's biggest western-detective program." But these puzzles were often enemy-inspired. When Tom tracked the giant to its lair, he discovered it to be a trick device, employed by the "Japs" to disrupt the domestic front. The mystery element pushed the serial to new heights of popularity, in some rating books surpassing even *Armstrong*, whose murderless plots were beginning to pale. While death ran rampant, Tom tackled the mystery of a vanishing village. Later he was baffled by the origin of a mystery voice that appeared without rational explanation as integrated crosstalk on his phonograph records. And with the world hanging in the balance, he flew to Europe on a secret VE-Day mission, enemy agents snapping at his heels.

Mix was one of the great premium-givers in all radio, flooding the mails with decoders, invention facsimiles and comics for its fans. There was a "rocket parachute," a "Sheriff Mike whistling badge," and a photo album containing "highly confidential information every Straight Shooter should know." The price was a dime, with one or two boxtops, sent to Ralston, Checkerboard Square, St. Louis, Mo.

Joe "Curley" Bradley, who played Mix throughout the later run, was the actor best identified in the role. Bradley was a former Oklahoma cowboy and Hollywood stunt man who had learned to sing around ranch-house bonfires. As for the real Tom Mix, he had nothing to do with the serial beyond lending it his name and glory. His movie success in the 1920s was sensational: he was the decade's leading screen star. His career in talkies was not so successful, and he retired from films to his circus and wild west shows. He died in an automobile accident near Florence, Az., Oct. 12, 1940.

TOMMY RIGGS AND BETTY LOU, comedy.

BROADCAST HISTORY: Oct. 1, 1938–March 25, 1940, NBC. 30m, Saturdays at 8 until May 20, 1939; returned Sept. 4, Mondays at 8. *The Quaker Party.* Quaker Oats. CAST: Tommy Riggs with his fictitious little-girl character, Betty Lou. Guest stars including Zasu Pitts, John Barrymore, etc. Eddie Green, 1939–40. ANNOUNCERS: Dan

Seymour, 1938–39; David Ross, 1939–40. **OR-CHESTRA AND VOCALISTS:** Larry Clinton with his singer, Bea Wain, 1938–39; Freddie Rich Orchestra with singers Leah Ray and Shirley Howard, 1939–40.

July 7–Sept. 29, 1942, CBS. 30m, Tuesdays at 9. Summer replacement for *Burns and Allen.* Swan Soap. **CAST:** Tommy Riggs with Betty Lou. Bea Benaderet as Mrs. Wingate, the talkative neighbor. Verna Felton as Mrs. MacIntyre, Riggs's outspoken Irish housekeeper. Elvia Allman and Margaret Brayton as "the gabby gals on the telephone." Mel Blanc as the telephone repairman. Wally Maher as Wilbur, Betty Lou's goofy little adenoidal playmate. **ANNOUNCER:** Bill Goodwin. **VOCALIST:** Jimmy Cash. **ORCHESTRA:** Felix Mills. **PRODUCER-DIRECTOR:** Glenhall Taylor. **WRITERS:** Sam Perrin, Jack Douglas, Bill Danch, George Balzer, Al Lewin.

Oct. 9, 1942–Oct. 1, 1943, NBC. 30m, Fridays at 7:30 until Jan., then Fridays at 10; a continuation of the summer show. Lever Brothers. **CAST:** Felton, Benaderet, Maher, Blanc, returning; Ken Christy as Mr. Hutch, Wilbur's father. **ANNOUNCER:** Frank Graham. **ORCHESTRA:** Felix Mills.

May 10–Sept. 13, 1946, CBS. 30m, Fridays at 7:30. Summer substitute for *The Ginny Simms Show.* Borden Milk. **CAST:** Riggs, Maher (as Wilbur), Jack Douglas. **ANNOUNCER:** Don Wilson. **ORCHESTRA:** Frank De Vol.

Tommy Riggs and Betty Lou was sometimes mistaken for a ventriloquism act. But Riggs never used a dummy: he never threw his voice or tried to talk without moving his lips. Riggs had a condition that doctors at the Cornell Medical Center, after X-raying his throat, described as bi-vocalism. This meant that Riggs could talk in his own voice—a deep baritone—or could assume the voice of a 7-year-old girl. This was no hammed-up falsetto imitation of a child: it was a true likeness, so vivid that he had been fooling people with it long before he discovered radio.

Riggs christened it Betty Lou Barrie. "It" became "she," for Betty Lou became ever more a real entity to Riggs. He remembered bringing her up in a locker room at Brown University, just for the fun of watching his teammates leap for their clothes. Thereafter, "Tom and Betty Lou" were in demand at parties and fraternity gatherings.

Around 1931, Riggs joined WCAE, Pittsburgh (his hometown) as a singer-piano player. The Depression had virtually eliminated his poultry business, and his entertainments at school had given him a keen interest in taking his act to radio. One night station manager J. L. Coffin was startled to hear the voice of a little girl, "swearing like a drill sergeant" in the studio. Rushing in, he found only a laughing Riggs, who then explained about the little girl in his voice. "Let's test her for the air," said Coffin. Soon *The Tom and Betty Program* was a regular.

He later went to KDKA. His shows were usually late-night affairs, prompting the Child Labor Board to demand that "that little girl" be sent home to bed where she belonged. Riggs served a tour at WTAM, Cleveland, then arrived at WLW, Cincinnati, just in time for the Ohio Valley flood of 1937. There, his show was heard by Harry Frankel, nationally known as Singin' Sam. Frankel was so impressed that he called a radio agent in New York and urged him to come out and hear Riggs for himself. The agent arrived, Riggs was invited to audition in New York, and this led to a series of transcribed shows for Chevrolet. The Chevrolet show was heard by Rudy Vallee, and suddenly Riggs was called by his agent and told that he had two days to prepare for an appearance on Vallee's *Royal Gelatin Hour.*

This was the big time. It was lost on no one that Vallee had discovered Edgar Bergen a year earlier, and that Bergen was now, as the 1937 season began, headed for the very top of radio. What Vallee could do for one ventriloquist he could do for another. Riggs explained that he was not a ventriloquist, but that seemed a small point. His first broadcast a success, he was signed by Vallee to a 13-week contract and became, for a while, radio's hottest new star. The contract was extended: Riggs ran 49 weeks, the longest ever for a Vallee engagement.

This led naturally to his own series. His Quaker Oats show was standard variety fare, except for the novelty of Betty Lou. Riggs wrote his own material, testing each Betty Lou line with careful trial and error. Everything she said had to be true to such a child's character, and he worked the flow of it so that Betty got all the punchlines while he played straight man. Bergen had soared to mid-30s ratings with his roguish dummy, Charlie McCarthy. But Riggs was no

Bergen, and his show barely broke double figures on the Hooper charts.

Critics compared them, perhaps unfairly.
Charlie was a scamp; Betty Lou—infinitely more
believable—was just a lovable little girl. But
Charlie was funnier. Riggs went into a decline
and was not heard much until the spring of 1942,
when Ted Collins brought him east for a 13-
week run on *The Kate Smith Hour*. This again
got him the attention of a large national audience, and he was signed by Lever Brothers to
fill in for *Burns and Allen* on CBS that summer.
The format was now revised: instead of being a
girl who appeared from nowhere, Betty Lou was
built into a situational series as his niece. A team
of writers, including two major talents (Sam Perrin and George Balzer) who would soon be writing for Jack Benny, turned out the scripts. By
most accounts, Riggs benefited greatly from the
changes. Most important was the addition of
Wally Maher as Betty Lou's friend, Wilbur. This
Riggs show was so well received that Lever
Brothers decided to keep it, moving it to NBC
for the fall run.

Riggs joined the Navy when this ended. He
took Betty Lou on an entertainment swing of Allied camps in the Far East and returned 18
months later to find that the radio audience had
forgotten him. He had one more brief run, and
died in 1967.

TONY AND GUS, serial drama.

BROADCAST HISTORY: April 29–Sept. 27, 1935,
Blue Network. 15m, weekdays at 7:15. General
Foods for Post Toasties. **CAST:** Mario Chamlee
as Tony, an Italian with hopes for an operatic career. George Frame Brown as Gus, his friend, a
big Swede who had a sunny disposition and
wanted to become heavyweight champion of the
world. Charles Slattery as George, the prizefight
manager. Elsie Mae Gordon as Mrs. Grainger,
landlady at the rooming house where Tony and
Gus lived. Arthur Anderson as Buddy, a small orphan. **ANNOUNCER:** Tiny Ruffner. **MUSIC:**
Joseph Stopak with a small string orchestra; accordion by Charles Magnante. **CREATOR-
WRITER:** George Frame Brown.

Tony and Gus was one of radio's great stories
of spontaneous success. George Frame Brown
had written the earlier series *Real Folks* (1928–
32, NBC/CBS) but had run out of ideas for that

drama of Thompkins Corners. Arriving at a
houseparty given by his friend, opera tenor
Mario Chamlee, Brown cried, "Hi, you crazy
faller," in his best Swedish accent. Chamlee replied in trumped-up Italian, and the two went on
improvising, to the delight of the crowd, for 15
minutes. This was not a lowbrow gathering—
among others, it included Lawrence Tibbett,
Mary Eastman, Helen Jepson, and John Charles
Thomas—but what encouraged Chamlee was
that the impromptu skit appealed to everyone,
including the children.

After the party, he confessed to Brown that he
was tired of the pace and travel of the concert
stage and was looking for a radio vehicle that
might keep him close to home. Brown stayed
overnight and wrote out the first script. In it, he
introduced a pair of immigrants on an ocean liner
headed for America. The friendship of Tony and
Gus was immediately threatened, recapped *Radio Guide*, "when a sorceress, a rich young society girl who has heard Tony's glorious voice,
attempts to vamp him."

In New York, they met NBC announcer Tiny
Ruffner, who happened to know that General
Foods was looking for just such a serial. Ruffner
sold it for them and became their announcer. Arthur Anderson, one of the players and a steady
voice on *Let's Pretend* for years, recalled it decades later. Chamlee sang two songs per broadcast. He returned to the Met for the 1935–37
seasons. Anderson also remembered a commercial blooper by Ruffner: "Friends, do you wake
up in the morning feeling dull, loggy, and lust-
less?"

TONY WONS' SCRAPBOOK, poetry, prose,
shirtsleeve philosophy.

BROADCAST HISTORY: 1930–34, CBS, 15m, five
or six a week at 8 A.M., 1930–31; at 9:30 A.M.,
1931–32; at 9 A.M. for International Silver, 1932–
33; then at 11:30 A.M. for Johnson's Wax, 1933–
34.

1934–35, Blue Network. 15m, weekdays at
11:15 A.M.

Sept. 2, 1934–June 30, 1935, NBC. 30m, Sundays at 4:30, later at 5:30. *The House by the Side
of the Road*. Johnson's Wax. **CAST:** Tony Wons,
comics Ronnie and Van, soprano Gina Vanna, baritone Emery Darcy, and the Ulderico Marcelli orchestra.

Sept. 27, 1937–March 25, 1938, CBS. 15m, three a week at 10:30 A.M. Vicks.

Oct. 13, 1940–April 5, 1942, NBC. 15m, Sundays at 4:15; also Oct. 1, 1940–Jan 1, 1942, Tuesdays and Thursdays at 1:15. Hallmark Cards.

Tony Wons was born Anthony Snow, but for air purposes he reversed the letters of his surname and became known to millions of housewives as the top dispenser of romantic dialogue in early radio. He was self-made, forced to drop out of school at 13 to help support his widowed mother, who had lost her home. He did many odd jobs, and his program of self-improvement was relentless. He bought a set of drums, which he played at dances and in vaudeville, and read widely in the fields of history, literature, and philosophy. His method was to read a page as many times as was necessary to capture the gist of it. Thus he memorized Shakespeare, and around 1924 he mounted a campaign to get Shakespeare's plays on the air in Chicago.

At WLS, he was given 40 minutes to make his case on the air. He responded with a condensed version of *The Merchant of Venice*, playing eight roles. This drew heavy mail, resulting in Wons being offered a staff job at $25 a week. He quit his $75 job in a hardware plant and began a Shakespeare series that ran on WLS for three years. He was later heard on WLW, his intimate chats there drawing more than 100,000 pieces of fan mail one winter.

CBS beckoned in 1930, and he began the *Scrapbook* series for which he became famous. It was based on a real scrapbook, put together by Wons at the suggestion of a nurse during a long hospital convalescence. His rise at CBS was swift: women found his intimate, close-to-the-mike style irresistible. "Are yuh listenin'?" he would ask. Millions were. His philosophizing was of the rustic Will Rogers type: his most-repeated bits were "truths" that could be said in a line—"a human is the only animal that can be skinned twice" or "a man who trims himself to suit everybody will soon whittle himself away."

Wons's *Scrapbook* shows fed on themselves. He seldom contributed any original material, preferring the profundity of literary masters and the obscure, as constantly submitted by his listeners. He loved such bits as the "recipe for preserving children": "Take one large, grassy field, one half-dozen children, two or three small

dogs, a pinch of brook and some pebbles, mix the children and the dogs well and put them in the field, stirring constantly; pour the brook over the pebbles, sprinkle the field with flowers, spread over all a deep blue sky and bake in the hot sun . . . when brown, remove and set to cool in the bathtub." The best of his *Scrapbook* items were collected in a long series of books, which were widely distributed and may still be found without much difficulty in used bookstores.

Wons died July 1, 1965.

THE TOP GUY, crime drama.

BROADCAST HISTORY: Oct. 17, 1951–May 28, 1953, ABC. Various 30m timeslots. American Chicle, General Mills, and Goodyear. CAST: J. Scott Smart as the police commissioner; a virtual extension of his role as *The Fat Man*, recently canceled. Also: Jay Jostyn, Ken Lynch. DIRECTOR: Joseph Graham. WRITER: Richard Ellington.

TOP SECRET, espionage adventure.

BROADCAST HISTORY: June 12–Oct. 26, 1950, NBC. Various 30m timeslots. STAR: Ilona Massey as a Mata Hari–style operative in World War II. ORCHESTRA: Roy Shield. WRITER-DIRECTOR: Harry W. Junkin.

Top Secret was highly effective, said *Radio Life*: the role played by the Hungarian actress was "tailor-made for her sultry voice and heavy accent."

THE TOWN CRIER, literary commentary.

BROADCAST HISTORY: 1929–33, CBS. Various times. HOST: Alexander Woollcott took over a sustaining slot in Oct. 1929, was billed as *The Early Bookworm*, and for the next two years was the network's commentator on literature. Sporadic shows, 1931–33.

July 21, 1933–Jan. 6, 1938, CBS. Various 15m and 30m timeslots as *The Town Crier*; some gaps in continuity. Cream of Wheat, 1934–35; Grainger Tobacco, 1937–38.

Alexander Woollcott was a critic, storyteller, "rajah of raconteurs," and some said intellectual snob. He came up through the newspaper ranks, as a reporter and later theater critic for New York papers. He was a member of the Round Table, that famous group of literary lights who met at the Algonquin Hotel in the '20s and engaged in vicious one-upsmanship.

He had worked several CBS slots when his *Town Crier* arrived and made his reputation on the air. As reviewed by *Radioland* in 1935, he offered "stylized anecdotes about his 800 personal friends, spiced with sly dissertations on literature and topped off with his distinctive brand of yarn-spinning." He claimed to have the worst voice in radio. No one disputed that, nor mistook his rotund, cherubic countenance for glamour. "He wows them just the same," said *Radioland*, "because he knows how to tell a story." The critic praised Woollcott's "verbal prestidigitation" and noted that "any topic, any musical theme, any guest who strikes Woollcott's fancy may pop up at a moment's notice."

His trademark was the ringing of a bell, town hall style, and the cry "Hear ye, hear ye!" His house orchestra in 1935 was led by Robert Armbruster, but it was as a book reviewer—not from variety—that his power derived. His endorsement (that, to use his favorite phrase, he had gone "quietly mad" over this book or that) could send a title soaring to the top of the bestseller lists. This he did with James Hilton's *Goodbye, Mr. Chips*, singlehandedly plugging it into household-name status. He was not shy about plugging his own book, *While Rome Burned*, which was also a major seller.

His ego was vast, and it was often said that he could be petty and mean. He could dismiss a person cruelly, noted his *Current Biography* entry, with such cutting words as "You are beginning to disgust me—how about getting the hell out of here?" In 1939 he gained his greatest fame, playing a none-too-flattering caricature of himself in the George S. Kaufman–Moss Hart play *The Man Who Came to Dinner*. His death nearly occurred at the microphone: on a *People's Platform* discussion of Hitlerism, Jan. 23, 1943, he collapsed in the studio while the program continued uninterrupted. Woollcott died about four hours later, a victim of a heart attack that developed into a cerebral hemorrhage.

TRANSATLANTIC QUIZ, panel show.

BROADCAST HISTORY: April 15, 1944–Sept. 2, 1945, Blue Network/BBC. 15m, Saturdays at 11:30 A.M. until Jan., then 30m, late nights, frequent schedule changes. **HOSTS:** Alistair Cooke, U.S.; Lionel Hale and Ronny Waldman, England. **PANEL:** Christopher Morley and Russel Crouse, U.S.; David Niven and Dennis Brazan, England.

The show was set up along the lines of *Information, Please*, but the panels were split between New York and London and connected by shortwave. Listeners sent in questions, and the answers were bandied across a war-torn sea.

TREASURY AGENT, crime drama.

BROADCAST HISTORY: April 14, 1947–June 6, 1948, ABC. Various 30m timeslots. **CAST:** Raymond Edward Johnson as Joe Lincoln, composite agent for "the largest group of law enforcement agencies in the world," the United States Treasury (which had under its jurisdiction the Secret Service, U.S. Revenue Intelligence, the Bureau of Narcotics, Customs, Alcohol Tax, and the Coast Guard). Also: Ralph Bell.

Oct. 5, 1954–Nov. 26, 1957, Mutual. 30m, Tuesdays at 8. **CAST:** Larry Haines as Joe Lincoln. Lawson Zerbe as Williams. **ANNOUNCER:** Carl Warren.

TREASURY STAR PARADE, patriotic drama.

BROADCAST HISTORY: Transcribed in New York and Hollywood by the Treasury Department, beginning in April 1942, to help stimulate sales of war bonds; 15m, carried on more than 800 stations, 1942–44. **HOSTS:** Henry Hull, frequently, in New York; Paul Douglas in the West. **CAST:** Top stars of stage, screen, and radio: Alfred Lunt and Lynn Fontanne, Vincent Price, John Garfield, Lionel Barrymore, Peter Donald, Paula Winslowe, Gale Gordon, Lou Merrill, Dwight Weist (in his Hitler impersonation), Lesley Woods, Parker Fennelly, etc. **ANNOUNCER:** Larry Elliott, New York. **ORCHESTRA:** David Broekman, New York; Al Goodman, Hollywood. **DIRECTOR:** William A. Bacher. **WRITERS:** Neal Hopkins, Norman Rosten, Violet Atkins, and other top radio writers with original stories; adaptations from the works of Thomas Wolfe, Stephen Vincent Benét, Thomas Mann, etc., also used. **THEME:** *Any Bonds Today?*, by Irving Berlin.

Typical of *Treasury Star Parade* fare was Arch Oboler's *Chicago, Germany*, one of many scripts written by Oboler for the series: Bette Davis helped tell what America might expect should Hitler win the war. In another show, Edward G. Robinson played a man unconcerned by gasoline rationing, until the gas turned into blood as he pumped it into his car. As with most shows of its type, *Treasury Star Parade* had its pick of top name performers, who donated their services.

A TREE GROWS IN BROOKLYN, drama, based on the novel by Betty Smith.

BROADCAST HISTORY: July 8–Sept. 30, 1949, NBC. 30m, Fridays at 8:30. **CAST:** John Larkin as alcoholic Johnny Nolan. Anne Seymour as his daughter Francie, who narrates the story years later as an adult. Also: Bryna Raeburn, Denise Alexander. **DIRECTOR:** Ed King.

TROMAN HARPER, RUMOR DETECTIVE, propaganda.

BROADCAST HISTORY: Dec. 13, 1942–Nov. 28, 1943, Mutual. 15m, Sundays at 6:30, later at 6:45. Grove's Bromo Quinine.

Troman Harper was Mutual's debunker of Axis propaganda; his show had much the same style and content as Rex Stout's *Our Secret Weapon* on CBS. Harper would set up an Axis claim, as intercepted on shortwave, and then rip into the lie with the "true facts." His denials were always emphatic. "Pure malarkey!" he would retort. "Horse-feathers!" He admonished his listeners, "If you repeat rumors, you're one of Hitler's best soldiers." The rumors were delivered rapidly. Was it true that Churchill pulled punches with British bombs because he had financial holdings in Germany? Were American GIs being fed alfalfa? *Horse feathers!* "I'll eat a bale of sawdust for every alfalfa leaf any American soldier finds on his plate!" There is no evidence that Harper ever had to eat any sawdust.

TRUE DETECTIVE MYSTERIES, crime drama.

BROADCAST HISTORY: May 16, 1929–May 8, 1930, CBS. 30m, Thursdays at 9.

Sept. 8, 1936–Aug. 31, 1937, Mutual. 30m, Tuesdays at 9:30. *True Detective* magazine.

April 5, 1938–March 28, 1939, Mutual. 30m, then 15m as of Jan. Tuesdays at 10 Listerine.

Ca. late 1930s. 30m transcribed syndication: no data on cast or crew.

April 29, 1944–June 2, 1958, Mutual. Many 30m timeslots, including Saturdays at 10:15, April–June 1944; Sundays at 1:30, 1944–45; Sun-

days at 4:30, 1945–49; Sundays at 5:30, 1949–55; Mondays at 8, 1955–58. Oh Henry Candy, 1946–53. **HOST-NARRATOR:** Richard Keith as John Shuttleworth, editor-in-chief of *True Detective* magazine. John Griggs, in a later era, as an unnamed "editor." **ANNOUNCERS:** Hugh James, Ralph Paul, etc. **MUSIC:** Paul Taubman, organ. **WRITER-DIRECTOR:** Murray Burnett, 1940s; Peter Irving in a later era.

Though based on items from *True Detective* magazine, this series was usually sponsored by other interests. Not much is known of its earliest shows, its best-known and most durable format being the Mutual run of 1944–58. This was an anthology, with a "case history of an actual crime" offered each week. Some of the cases were more than 20 years old, but all were geared to prove that crime doesn't pay.

Mysteries they weren't. Many of the stories unfolded from the criminal's viewpoint: the show was much like *Gang Busters* in allowing the audience to witness the fatal mistakes that led to the culprit's capture. Borrowing yet another page from *Gang Busters*, the magazine offered rewards of $500 (later $1,000) for information leading to the arrest of real criminals. Clues were given after each broadcast: these were highly descriptive, focusing on scars and deformities, and the show resulted in many arrests. But one of the best gimmicks was its well-remembered commercial:

TELEPHONE RING.

MAN: Hello? . . . Hello?

WOMAN: Oh Henry?

MAN: Hold the phone! Hold the phone! It's time for Oh Henry, public energy number one!

ANNOUNCER: Yes, it's time for Oh Henry, America's famous candy bar, to present, transcribed, *True Detective Mysteries* . . .

TRUE OR FALSE, quiz.

BROADCAST HISTORY: Jan. 3–June 27, 1938, Mutual. 30m, Mondays at 10. J. B. Williams (shave cream).

July 4, 1938–June 28, 1943, Blue Network. 30m, Mondays at 10, until Aug. 7, 1939, then at 8:30. J. B. Williams.

Feb. 7, 1948–Feb. 4, 1956, Mutual. Many 30m timeslots, often Saturdays; some gaps in continuity (off the air, 1951–53). Shotwell Manufacturing, 1948–49; Anahist, 1950.

QUIZMASTERS: Dr. Harry Hagen, 1938–43; Eddie Dunn. **CREATOR-WRITER:** Harry Hagen.

The format was precisely what the title suggests. Contestants had to answer seven true or false questions, each increasing in difficulty, with winners trying for a larger jackpot at the end. Hagen got the idea from the endless questions of his young daughter Patsy: he sometimes billed it as the first quiz show, which it wasn't (it was one of the first dozen). After a format change in 1948, the "Candy Box Question" was the big prize, with up to $2,500 at stake. Contestants had to answer four of five true-false questions, usually about someone in the news. The question was named for the sponsor, Shotwell, makers of Big Mac and Hi-Yank candy bars.

THE TRUITTS, situation comedy.

BROADCAST HISTORY: June 11–Sept. 10, 1950, NBC. 30m, Sundays at 3; returned July 5–Sept. 20, 1951; Thursdays at 8. **CAST:** John Dehner and Constance Crowder as Elmer and Gert Truitt. Jane Webb, Eddie Firestone, and Dawn Bender as their children, Gladys, Clarence, and Maggi. Parley Baer as Gramps. **CREATOR-WRITERS:** Frank and Doris Hursley. **DIRECTOR:** Andrew C. Love.

The Truitt family lived in Hope Springs, "the biggest little city in the world . . . big enough to have many of the advantages of New York, small enough for the tax collector to call you by your first name."

TRUTH OR CONSEQUENCES, stunt show.

BROADCAST HISTORY: March 23–July 27, 1940, CBS. 30m, Saturdays at 9:45. Ivory Soap.
    Aug. 17, 1940–June 24, 1950, NBC. 30m, Saturdays at 8:30. Duz.
    Sept. 5, 1950–May 29, 1951, CBS. 30m, Tuesdays at 9:30: Philip Morris.
    June 17–Sept. 30, 1952, NBC. 30m, Tuesdays at 9:30. Summer show for *Fibber McGee and Molly*. Pet Milk.
    Sept. 18, 1952–April 15, 1954, NBC. 30m, Thursdays at 9 (Wednesdays at 9:30, summer of 1953). Pet Milk.
    Oct. 26, 1955–Sept. 12, 1956, NBC. 30m, Wednesdays at 8. Various sponsors.

HOST-CREATOR: Ralph Edwards. **ANNOUNCERS:** Bud Collyer, Mel Allen, Ed Herlihy, Milton Cross, Jay Stewart, Harlow Wilcox, Ken Carpenter. **DIRECTOR:** Ed Bailey. **WRITERS:** Mel Vickland, Ed Bailey, Bill Burch, Phil Davis, Mort Lewis, Carl Jampel, Esther Allen, George Jeske, Paul Edwards (Ralph's brother). **THEME:** *Merrily We Roll Along*.

Truth or Consequences was described by *Life* in the mid-1940s as "the nearest thing to insanity in radio today." Theoretically a quiz show, it was "boisterous, rowdy, and full of custard-pie humor," said *Time*: "It offers $15 for correct answers, but penalties for errors are fierce. People have been put in real doghouses, mounted on mechanical horses, compelled to imitate babies and dogs, and given consolation prizes of $5."

"The truth," wrote John Lear in the *Saturday Evening Post*, "is almost impossible to attain." Everybody wanted to pay the consequences, to learn what Ralph Edwards and his band of fiends had in store for them. A man might be required to make love to a skunk; a woman to wash an elephant. Ladies were made to propose marriage to their escorts, getting down on one knee while Edwards, the studio audience, and the nation heard every word. A soldier desperately tried to converse with his best girl by phone, while a model sat on his lap and cooed such endearments as "Watch out, honey, you're ruining my hair." Some stunts were so elaborate they ran for weeks and took months to set up. When they worked to perfection, they were so sensational that they became news events, covered by the daily press or recapped in both major national news magazines.

Ralph Edwards had served his radio apprenticeship at KROW, Oakland. He arrived in New York in 1935 after hitchhiking across the country with little money and no job prospects. But his talent was obvious, and within three weeks he was on the air. The role of a dentist on *Stoopnagle and Budd* earned him $35. He played a sailor on *Renfrew of the Mounted*, then beat out 69 competitors for a CBS announcer's job. Suddenly he was doing ten shows a week, from Major Bowes's *Original Amateur Hour* to *The Phil Baker Show*. His weekly paycheck was in four figures, but, as he later recalled, "I didn't want to be an announcer." He had heard that Ivory

Soap was looking for a show: after brainstorming with his wife, Barbara, he hit upon a simple idea: "What about Truth or Consequences?"

This was an old parlor game, encouraged in childhood by his mother when he and his friends were grounded on rainy days. Also known as Forfeit, it worked on the principle that participants, tested on their knowledge, had to pay a "forfeit" if they failed to answer.

John Lear tells what happened next. "With three days to produce a sample, Ralph and Barbara threw a party on Friday night and tried out gags on their guests. On Sunday morning, at the close of the *Horn and Hardart* hour, he asked the audience to stay and hear an experiment. The key contestant froze stiff and couldn't utter a sound until Edwards tickled him suddenly from behind. Then a terrific shriek went through the microphone. The effect was superb. The man had been asked to imitate a screaming woman. The audience applauded wildly. The sponsors, oblivious of the crucial tickle, bought the show from a recording."

It was an immediate hit, getting almost 20 Hooper points by January 1941. The questions (described as "generally tricky") were sent in by listeners, who got $10 each. In case an overzealous contestant might be tempted to blurt the answer, Edwards had the fastest buzzer in radio. Nicknamed Beulah, the buzzer was the contestant's cue that "you did not tell the truth, so you must pay the consequences." Now the fun began. The audience howled as men bayed like dogs, tried to squirm into girdles, or pushed walnuts across the stage with their noses. One contestant had to lie on a sheet and pretend to be a seal wooing a mate. This was funny, but became hilarious when Edwards led a real seal out, to see how his contestant was doing. "Aren't we devils?" he would ask mischievously. Many of the tricks had two, three, or more levels: just when a contestant thought he had safely arrived, the tables would turn and the joke would start anew. A woman was told to christen a ship while wearing a blindfold. She was driven around in circles, returned to the studio, brought in amidst the most realistic wharf effects that the NBC soundman could devise, then was given a paper sack of water and broke it—across her husband's head.

Three gags were considered masterpieces. The earliest was devised by Edwards as a demonstration to the sponsor of the show's drawing power. Mrs. Dennis Mullane, the contestant, was ordered to do something to help the Treasury Department get its pennies back in circulation. She was required to count as many pennies as the listening audience could be persuaded to send her. It was hoped that the total would be enough to buy a war bond for her son, serving in the Marines. The pennies began arriving as soon as the show left the air. By Sunday morning, children were leaving them at the studio door. By midweek, Mrs. Mullane was getting 35 bags a day, and they were filling up the basement. The final tally was 315,000, a $3,100 payday for the Mullanes.

Then there was the Rudolph J. Wickel affair. For months, Edwards asked, "Is there a Mr. Wickel in the house?" On Nov. 4, 1944, there was. Wickel had heard his name, come to the broadcast, and arrived on stage. Edwards announced that $1,000 had been left for him in a vacant lot at the corner of Walnut and Prospect streets in Holyoke, Mass. By the time Wickel arrived, the lot resembled a gold rush camp. "Within an hour," *Time* reported, "two of the diggers (neither of them Wickel) had unearthed 500 silver dollars apiece, and the lot looked as if it had been bombed." Edwards, heading off hard feelings in Holyoke, offered to turn the lot into a park, but he still had Wickel to contend with. Edwards gave him a $1,000 check, but Wickel was paid in Confederate money. Edwards then gave Wickel a 1,500-pound safe, which contained the small half of a severed $1,000 bill. He gave Wickel a parrot, which, he said, would tell where the other half was. It didn't, and the gag stretched across weeks. At last Edwards promised to send Wickel the bill between pages 12 and 13 of a book. The crowning touch: Edwards asked the audience to contribute to the cause, and Wickel got 17,000 books in the mail. Once the bill was found, the books were given to the Victory Book Campaign.

Perhaps the most sensational of all *Consequences* became known as the "Yiffniff" stunt. Edwards had booked Town Hall for the occasion and had posters printed announcing the American debut of "the great European violinist, Yiffniff." This nonsense was swallowed wholeheartedly by newspapers, whose music columnists ran it as genuine news. Even the fact that the tickets were free failed to arouse suspicion, and by Saturday night 1,500 concertgoers had arrived at Town Hall for the event. Not far away, in the NBC studio, a New Jersey housewife named Mrs. Fries had missed her question and was about to pay a frightening consequence. Her mission: take a violin (she had never even touched such an instrument), go by police escort to Town Hall, and "become" Yiffniff.

Milton Cross, "the pontiff of radio music," awaited her arrival and stood ready to give her his most solemn introduction. With trembling hands she began her concert, a scraping attempt at *Flight of the Bumblebee*. The audience sat in disbelief until it became obvious—everyone had been had. A wave of laughter swept the hall, then applause for their own consolation prize— Edwards had arranged a real concert by two talented violin students.

On Dec. 29, 1945, Edwards began what was intended as a spoof of giveaway shows but soon propelled *Truth or Consequences* itself into the top ranks of such shows. Each week a veiled mystery man, known only as "Mr. Hush," gave clues to his identity in doggerel. Edwards wanted Albert Einstein, who wasn't interested: he settled for Jack Dempsey, who recorded such clues as "Hickory, dickory dock, the clock struck ten, lights out, goodnight" and watched a jackpot build over five weeks to a total of $13,500 in merchandise. It was won by a sailor, Ensign Richard Bartholomew, who confessed that he had almost gone to a *Life of Riley* broadcast instead. A subsequent "Mrs. Hush" contest awarded $17,500 in prizes to the winner, who guessed Clara Bow. In 1947 came the third "Hush" game, when dancer Martha Graham kept listeners guessing for eight weeks before being revealed as "Miss Hush." The secret identity craze climaxed in 1948, when Jack Benny became the "Walking Man" and paid off a then-fabulous jackpot, $22,500.

The show always opened in the middle of a warmup routine, with the audience still in the throes of laughter. "Hello, there, we've been waiting for you!" the announcer would begin. "It's time to play *Truth* . . . (ORGAN GLISSANDO) . . . *or Consequences!*" Al Paschall, production man, lined up the props and was in charge of doing the impossible. Edwards also hosted the

TV series, eventually relinquishing to Jack Bailey, Steve Dunne, and Bob Barker.

THE TUESDAY NIGHT PARTY, musical variety.

BROADCAST HISTORY: March 21–July 18, 1939, CBS. 30m, Tuesdays at 8:30. Lifebuoy. Resurfaced in new format, Sept. 19–Dec. 12, 1939.

Party was a continuation of *The Lifebuoy Program* in the same timeslot, after Al Jolson abruptly left this show in the spring of 1939. Suddenly on March 21, Jolson was gone and Dick Powell was the singing host, finishing the season with Jolson's old cast—Martha Raye, Harry (Parkyakarkus) Einstein, and Lud Gluskin's orchestra. The brief revival in September featured Walter O'Keefe, host; Mary Martin, vocalist; and maestro Bobby Dolan.

THE TUNE DETECTIVE, musical enlightenment.

BROADCAST HISTORY: 1931–33, Blue Network, various 15m timeslots.

This series featured musicologist Sigmund Spaeth, who revealed how popular songs were often derived and sometimes virtually copied from earlier published works. Spaeth was frequently called as an expert witness in musical plagiarism cases. *The Tune Detective* was the first of several such Spaeth shows, others airing over various local and network outlets over a 20-year span (*Sigmund Spaeth's Musical Quiz* was heard Sundays at 1:15 on Mutual, Jan. 19–March 23, 1947).

TWELVE PLAYERS, dramatic anthology.

BROADCAST HISTORY: July 21–Nov. 3, 1945, CBS. 30m, Saturdays at 5 Pacific time.
Feb. 9–March 29, 1948, ABC. 30m, Mondays at 8:30.
CAST: Jack Moyles, Edmund MacDonald, Mary Jane Croft, Jay Novello, Howard McNear, John Lake, Herbert Rawlinson, Lurene Tuttle, Cathy Lewis, Charlie Lung, Bea Benaderet, and David Ellis. John Brown replacing Charlie Lung, 1948 run. **ANNOUNCER:** Jimmy Matthews. **ORCHESTRA:** Wilbur Hatch (1945), Basil Adlam (1948). **PRODUCER-DIRECTOR:** Ray Buffum. **WRITERS:** John Michael Hayes, Dennis Murray.

Twelve Players was conceived by producer Ray Buffum, with actors Jack Moyles and Edmund MacDonald—a repertory company of top radio professionals, each of whom, while making no claim of being the best, brought years of experience to the microphone. The entire company was required for every broadcast: the opening called for each to introduce himself, and no recordings were allowed.

TWENTY-FIRST PRECINCT, police drama.

BROADCAST HISTORY: July 7, 1953–July 26, 1956, CBS. Various 30m timeslots.

CAST: Everett Sloane, James Gregory (1955), and Les Damon (1956) as Capt. Frank Kennelly. Ken Lynch as Lt. Matt King. Harold Stone as Sgt. Waters. **ANNOUNCER:** Art Hanna. **PRODUCER:** John Ives. **WRITER-DIRECTOR:** Stanley Niss.

Twenty-First Precinct was a follower in the *Dragnet* mold, putting the listener into the drama from the opening phone call until the final report was written. The 21st was described as "just lines on a map of the city of New York. Most of the 173,000 people wedged into the nine-tenths of a square mile between Fifth Avenue and the East River wouldn't know if you asked them that they lived or worked in the 21st." The detail was made up of "160 patrolmen, eleven sergeants, and four lieutenants" under the command of one captain—Frank Kennelly.

TWENTY QUESTIONS, quiz.

BROADCAST HISTORY: Feb. 2, 1946–March 27, 1954, Mutual. 30m, Saturdays at 8. Ronson Lighters, 1946–51; Wildroot Cream Oil, 1952–53. **MODERATOR:** Bill Slater. **PANEL:** Fred Van Deventer, Florence Rinard, Bobby McGuire, Nancy Van Deventer, Herb Polesie, and one guest chair. **ANNOUNCERS:** Jack Irish, Frank Waldecker, and Bruce Elliott as the "mystery voice"; Charlotte Manson as the "Ronson Girl." **PRODUCER:** Herb Polesie.

Twenty Questions was the old animal-vegetable-mineral parlor game adapted for the air: an object must be identified by a group of players, with only the clue that it is of animal, vegetable, or mineral origin, and with only twenty yes-or-no questions permitted by the panel in the effort to narrow the possibilities. In its first summer it was drawing 10,000 to 20,000 letters a week. That such an old and simple idea could be so popular surprised even those who had suggested it.

It was brought to radio by the Van Deventer family of Princeton, N.J. Fred Van Deventer was a WOR newsman. With his wife, Florence, and their children, Bobby (then 14) and Nancy (16), he had indulged his passion for quiz-type entertainment at the dinner table. One evening when another Mutual announcer was their guest, the current state of quiz shows was discussed. The Van Deventers expressed surprise at how many were built on simple premises. The simpler the better, they were told. At that point, Nancy suggested the animal-vegetable-mineral game.

The Van Deventers themselves would be the panelists. Nancy would appear occasionally, being often away at school, but Fred, Florence, and Bobby were regulars, and producer Herb Polesie filled the fourth chair. In an effort to dispel the notion that it was a family affair (which it was), Mrs. Van Deventer took up her maiden name, Rinard; her son took the name of his maternal grandmother and became Bobby McGuire. The moderator, Bill Slater, was a Mutual sportscaster.

In the beginning it was decided to create some good-natured bickering among the male panelists in order to liven it up. This was not appreciated by the audience (especially when young Bobby sassed his elders), and it was soon dropped. Polesie, noted *Time*, provided the continuing humor with such "Oscar Levantine questions as 'Can I give it to my mother-in-law?' or 'Can I do it to my wife?'" Objects might range from Ben Hur's chariot to the Republican elephant.

By 1949, noted *Newsweek*, the questions had become "much harder than anything that is heard at home." The skills of the regulars had sharpened so that they could narrow the possibilities and guess the mystery within half a dozen questions. Two that were missed that year were "the letters that husbands forget to mail" and "the stars that you see when you bump your head." Slater had the most difficult job. Reading the questions was the least of it: he also had to provide, from his well of general knowledge, the answers. Was it mentioned in fiction before 1900? Was it processed? Did it grow east of the Great Divide? . . . west of the Missouri Compromise? He usually answered in a heartbeat: yes; no; occasionally, "some do, some don't." The listening audience was told what the object was by one of the announcers—a "mystery voice" offstage, who spoke through a filtered microphone. The studio audience was informed by placard, placed on a stand facing away from the panel.

TWENTY THOUSAND YEARS IN SING SING, crime drama.

BROADCAST HISTORY: Jan. 22, 1933–April 5, 1937, NBC. Blue Network, 30m, Sundays at 9 until May 7, 1933; Wednesdays at 9, 1933–35; at 9:30, 1935–36; then Red Network, Mondays at 9, 1936–37. Sloan's Liniment. Seasons generally Sept. or Oct. to March or April

Oct. 18, 1937–April 11, 1938, Blue Network. 30m, Mondays at 10. *Behind Prison Bars*. Sloan's Liniment.

Oct. 21. 1938–April 21, 1939, Blue, 30m, Friday at 8. *Criminal Case Histories*. Sloan's Liniment.

NARRATOR: Lewis E. Lawes, warden at Sing Sing, the famed prison at Ossining, N.Y. **INTERVIEWER:** Joseph Bell as "Mr. Stark." Also: Ned Wever, Cecil Secrest, Alice Reinheart, Tony Berger, Ralph Locke, etc. **ANNOUNCERS:** Kelvin Keech, Ben Grauer. **DIRECTOR:** Joseph Bell, Arnold Michaelis.

Twenty Thousand Years in Sing Sing was one of the pioneering crime shows of the air. Written first as a book by Warden Lewis E. Lawes of Sing Sing, it became a movie in 1932 and a radio show the following year. Lawes was a progressive criminologist who, in two decades at Sing Sing, was the nation's best-known prison chief.

He worked his way up through the system, beginning as a guard at Clinton Prison in Dannemora, N.Y., in 1906. He attended the New York School of Social Work and became superintendent of the city reformatory. He was a vigorous opponent of the death penalty.

His show probed the "silent walled city" of 2,000 people. Its title signified the number of inmates multiplied by the average sentence (ten years). The stories were as varied as any collection of 2,000 people might produce but were infused with the conflict of the prison environment. There was the tale of "Mike the Rat-Catcher," who loved animals and was able to make pets of the rodents he caught in jail: put in charge of the horses, he bloomed into a model prisoner. There was the inmate who discovered a love of opera by listening on one of the prison radios. Lawes

aired many death house stories, and cases whose endings weren't so upbeat. But his stock in trade remained those who bounced back from life's knockdowns, coped with prison, and left determined to build new lives.

Lawes donated much of his fee for the show to the prison for prisoners' radios. Each cell was equipped with earphones, and inmates could request specific shows from the guards, who controlled the dials. The prisoners were Lawes's severest critics, *Radioland* noted: the favorite show behind the walls in 1934 was *The Goldbergs*.

In 1937, with the title change to *Behind Prison Bars*, a slight change of format was made: announcer Ben Grauer read letters from listeners, who asked questions about crime. Some were personal pleas for help: Lawes replied with such advice as "go to the police" or "never compromise with a blackmailer." His daughter Cherie was raised in Sing Sing: as a child, she was mascot of the prison baseball team, and in adolescence she could truthfully say that some of her best friends were convicts.

TWO FOR THE MONEY, quiz.

BROADCAST HISTORY: Sept. 30, 1952–Sept. 22, 1953, NBC. 30m, Tuesdays at 10, taped from NBC-TV. Old Gold Cigarettes.

Oct. 3, 1953–Sept. 23, 1956, CBS. 30m, Saturdays at 9, 1953–55; Sundays at 8:30, 1955–56. Old Gold.

QUIZMASTER-COMIC: Herb Shriner. **ANNOUNCER:** Durward Kirby. **PRODUCERS:** Mark Goodson and Bill Todman.

The producers hoped this comedy-quiz would do for Herb Shriner what *You Bet Your Life* had done for Groucho Marx. The emphasis was as much on the star as on the game. Shriner offered a monologue, then quizzed three sets of contestants, with the winners trying for a jackpot prize. Fred Allen had been the original choice, but he dropped out because of illness.

TWO ON A CLUE, light detective serial melodrama.

BROADCAST HISTORY: Oct. 2, 1944–Jan. 4, 1946, CBS. 15m, weekdays at 2:15, later at 2. General Foods. **CAST:** Ned Wever and Louise Fitch as husband-wife sleuths Jeff and Debby Spencer. John Gibson as Sgt. Cornelius Trumbull.

WRITER-DIRECTOR: Harry Ingram. **AN-NOUNCER:** Alice Yourman.

TWO THOUSAND PLUS, science fiction anthology.

BROADCAST HISTORY: March 15, 1950–Jan. 2, 1952, Mutual. Various 30m timeslots. **CAST:** New York regulars Joseph Julian, Bryna Raeburn, Bill Keene, Lon Clark, Amzie Strickland, etc. **AN-NOUNCER:** Ken Marvin. **MUSIC:** Elliott Jacoby, composer; Emerson Buckley, conductor. **PRO-DUCER-DIRECTOR:** Sherman H. Dryer.

Two Thousand Plus was the first anthology of science fiction tales designed for adults, arriving a month before the landmark NBC series *Dimension X*. Many of the themes that became familiar on *D-X* and its offspring series, *X-Minus One*, were first utilized here—the idea, for example, of a Martian civilization older and wiser than we, which looked upon our savage instincts with sadness and tolerance (but for how long?). Though *Two Thousand Plus* was the legitimate pioneer in its field (the 1941 series *Latitude Zero* being a hybrid), it never had the power of *Dimension X*.

𝒰

UNCLE DON, talk and music for children.

BROADCAST HISTORY: 1928–49, WOR, New York 30m, mostly six a week at 6; also, 1939–40, Mutual, limited network run for Maltex Cereal.

Uncle Don Carney was the best-known practitioner of the "uncle show," a mostly local affair for children, characterized by the *Saturday Evening Post* as "frothy stories, simple songs, a cobwebbed joke or two, birthday announcements, sometimes the reading of newspaper funnies, and advice against misbehaving."

The first known radio "uncle" was Chris Graham, who became "Uncle Wip" on WIP, Philadelphia, in 1921. By the mid-1940s there were uncles on the the the air in Chicago, Los Angeles, Salt Lake City, Des Moines, Portland (Ore.), and other cities large enough to support a radio station. Uncle Don Carney had a leg up on them all. His 50,000-watt WOR signal routinely reached into seven states, confined for most of his career to the Northeast. But his fame, like that of New York's husband-and-wife breakfast shows, had a longer reach.

He aired five, sometimes six days a week, sandwiched among the network's blood-and-thunder serials. He also read the funnies Sunday mornings, at 8:30 or 8:45. In his weekday show, he sang and played his piano; he scolded (sometimes by name) those who weren't brushing their teeth; he pushed spinach harder than Popeye, pledged allegiance to the flag, and gave "club news" regularly. His clubs were tightly linked to sponsors' financial interests: there were a "Frankfurter Club" and an "Underwear Club," which, said the *Post*, "made its members clamor for a certain brand of two-button drawers." The "Earnest Savers Club" brought the Greenwich Savings Bank some 40,000 new accounts during a nine-year sponsorship. Full membership in the clubs was attained by sending in for tokens for every product that Uncle Don pushed. Although some parents considered him "too juvenile even for juveniles" (*Time*), he held his listeners with painstaking attention to individuals. When he couldn't name all the birthday children in a given day, he sometimes called the ones he'd had to leave out on the telephone. "After service like that," said *Time*, "the kids will do anything, even to calling Mother out of the kitchen to hear what Uncle Don has to say about Wesson Oil."

He was born Howard Rice, son of a horseshoe-nail salesman. He learned piano by ear as a child in Michigan; as a young man, he discovered an ability to play while standing on his head on a piano stool. This led to vaudeville, a billing as Don Carney, Trick Pianist. He discovered an affinity for children: his act always went over best in Saturday matinees, when the seats were full of kids.

He arrived in radio around 1925. His first radio job was at WMCA, but soon he moved to WOR, where opportunity struck. A manufacturer of teddy bears wanted a show to sponsor, and Carney was asked to come up with something on 30 minutes' notice. The distinguishing feature of the client's bears were the trademark buttons in their ears, so Carney went on cold with a story of a little bear who got lost and couldn't be found because there were no buttons in its ears. "Since that day he has gone on and on, never using a script," wrote John La Cerda in the *Saturday Evening Post*: he created characters Willipus Wallipus (senior and junior) and Suzan Beduzin and her brother Huzin; he punctuated his tales with expletives: "Gosh!" "Gee-whiz!" "Isn't that swell!" One of his best-remembered stories was of Suzan Beduzin being attacked by tartar bugs and having her teeth riddled with holes until "Old Mr. Toothbrush" routed them out. He created words—"romeroff" (a runaway kid), "scuffyheeler," "takechancer," and "leave-arounder." Wrote La Cerda: "Any youngster within WOR's seven-state listening area can tell you what these words mean."

He collaborated closely with parents and was able to announce that "little Jackie Smith" or "Susie Jones" had been good children and would find a present from Uncle Don under their pillows. On one occasion it was reported that a certain "young Johnny" was left a gift from Uncle Don behind his radio, a reward for his efforts to stop swearing. As the story went, Johnny found the present, turned to his parents, and said, "How the hell did he know that was back there?"

The show often opened with a bit of nonsense, known far and wide as the "Hibbidy-Gits" song:

Hello, nephews, nieces too,
Mothers and daddies, how are you?
This is Uncle Don all set to go,
With a meeting on the ra-di-o!
We'll start off with a little song.
To learn the words will not take long;
For they're as easy as easy can be,
So come on now and sing with me:
Hibbidy-Gits has-ha ring boree,
Sibonia skividy, hi lo de!
Honi-ko-doke with an ali-ka-zon,
Sing this song with your Uncle Don!

Carney earned more than $20,000 a year. In 1928–29, his show was named one of radio's "blue-ribbon" offerings, and he earned $75,000. But he spent most of his professional life denying a delightful though unsubstantiated story that became one of radio's classic blooper tales. Carney was supposed to have been signing off one evening and—thinking the microphone dead—said, "There! I guess that'll hold the little bas-

tards for another night!" This never happened, he vowed in every interview: he tended to blame his jealous rivals in "uncle radio" for originating the rumors. His most vocal critic, Wayne Cody—who had inherited the *Uncle Wip* show from Chris Graham and others in Philadelphia—had no comment on the affair in La Cerda's *Post* piece. Although one blooper record purports to contain an aircheck of the gaffe, the actuality is clearly a re-creation.

Carney died in 1954.

UNCLE EZRA'S RADIO STATION, cornpone variety.

BROADCAST HISTORY: Oct. 19, 1934–April 21, 1939, NBC. Various 15m evening timeslots. Alka-Seltzer. **CAST:** Pat Barrett as Uncle Ezra, who told tall tales of country life on "Station E-Z-R-A, the powerful little five-watter down in Rosedale." Nora Cuneen (Barrett's wife) as Cecilia.

Oct. 23, 1938–April 16, 1939, NBC. 30m, Sundays at 5. *Sunday Afternoons in Rosedale*. Alka-Seltzer. **SUPPORTING CAST:** Henry Burr; the Vass Family; the Hoosier Hotshots; occasionally, pianist Alec Templeton.

July 13, 1940–June 28, 1941, NBC. 30m, Saturdays at 10. Camel Cigarettes. **SUPPORTING CAST:** Cliff Soubier as Mayor Boggs; the Sons of the Pioneers; the "Rosedale Girl Trio" (Carolyn Montgomery, Betty Bennett, and Fran Allison) and such guests as Al Pearce.

Uncle Ezra was an offshoot of *The National Barn Dance*. Pat Barrett had made the Ezra character famous on earlier *Barn Dance* seasons, on *The National Farm and Home Hour*, and in local radio beginning at WTMJ, Milwaukee, in 1930. His character was so successful in Milwaukee that he was hired by WLS, Chicago, and went from there to NBC.

Barrett, a real-life Illinois farmer, came to radio from vaudeville. His series, also known as *Station E-Z-R-A*, was sponsored by longtime *Barn Dance* client Alka-Seltzer.

UNCLE JIM'S QUESTION BEE, quiz.

BROADCAST HISTORY: Sept. 26, 1936–Dec. 16, 1939, Blue Network. 30m, Saturdays at 7:30. George Washington Coffee. **HOST:** Jim Mc-Williams.

June 18–Oct. 2, 1940, CBS. 30m, Tuesdays,

later Wednesdays, at 8. Summer replacement for *Big Town*. Lever Brothers for Spry. **HOST:** Jim McWilliams.

Oct. 8, 1940–July 8, 1941, Blue Network. 30m, Tuesdays at 9, later at 8:30. Lever Brothers. **HOST:** Bill Slater.

Question Bee is generally cited as the second quiz show of the air, arriving just four months after *Professor Quiz*. Six contestants were drawn from the audience (three men, three women) to compete for a top prize of $25. Questions were solicited from listeners, and everyone (contestants and their questioners alike) received a can of the sponsor's coffee. Contestants also received Uncle Jim's Question Bee Game.

UNCLE WALTER'S DOGHOUSE, variety with situation comedy.

BROADCAST HISTORY: May 2, 1939–July 8, 1942, NBC. 30m, Tuesdays at 10:30, 1939–41; Fridays at 9:30, May–Feb. 1941–42; then Wednesdays at 8:30. Raleigh Cigarettes. **HOST:** Tom Wallace as Uncle Walter. **CAST:** *1939–40:* Music and song by Tom, Dick, and Harry (Gordon and Bud Vandover with Marlin Hurt); Phil Davis, later Bob Strong, orchestra. Skits of the Wiggins Family, with Charles Penman, Kathryn Card, and Beryl Vaughn as father, mother, and daughter. Music and variety given greater emphasis in subsequent years. *Ca. 1939–41:* Virginia Verrill, vocalist, with harmony by the "Doghouse Chorus"; Charles Lyon, announcer. *Ca. 1941–42:* Mary Ann Mercer, vocalist, with Bill Demling and Florence Gill.

UNDER ARREST, police drama.

BROADCAST HISTORY: July 28–Sept. 1, 1946; June 8–Aug. 31, 1947; June 6–Sept. 5, 1948, all Mutual. 30m, Sundays at 5 as summer fill-in for *The Shadow*.

Nov. 7, 1948–Oct. 4, 1954, Mutual. 30m, Sundays at 9, 1948–49; Sundays, mostly at 4, 1950–52; Mondays at 8:30, 1953–54.
CAST: Craig McDonnell as Police Capt. John Drake, 1946–48. Joe DeSantis as Capt. Jim Scott, the new central character, from ca. 1948. Ned Wever also as Jim Scott. **PRODUCED** in New York by Wynn Wright.

THE UNEXPECTED, terror melodrama, with surprise endings.

BROADCAST HISTORY: 1948, 15m, transcribed syndication. **CAST:** Barry Sullivan, Lurene Tuttle, Virginia Gregg, etc. **DIRECTOR:** Frank Danzig. **WRITERS:** Frank Burt, etc.

Tales of the "secret future," the "hidden destiny" that may lie just ahead, "waiting for you . . . perhaps in a moment, you too will meet the unexpected!"

UNIVERSAL RHYTHM, musical variety.

BROADCAST HISTORY: Jan. 1–April 2, 1937, Blue Network. 30m, Fridays at 9. Ford Motors. **CAST:** The Landt Trio and White until pianist Howard White died two weeks into the run; then the Landt Trio and (Curly) Mahr; orchestra by Rex Chandler.

April 17–Sept. 5, 1937, CBS. 30m, Saturdays at 7:30 until June 20; then 60m, Sundays at 9. Ford Motors. **CAST:** Baritone Richard Bonelli of the Metropolitan Opera; blind pianist Alec Templeton; singer Carolyn Urbanek, all in a program featuring "the music of many lands, seasons and moods." **HOST:** Frank Crumit, as of June 20. **ORCHESTRA:** Rex Chandler.

THE UNIVERSITY OF CHICAGO ROUND TABLE, public affairs.

BROADCAST HISTORY: 1931–33, WMAQ, Chicago; premiere Feb. 1, 1931.
Oct. 15, 1933–June 12, 1955, NBC. 30m, mostly Sundays, early afternoons.
MODERATORS: John Howe (through mid-1940s), George Probst.

Round Table, on which controversial issues of the day were debated by members of the University of Chicago faculty, grew out of arguments by professors over lunch at the faculty club. When a proposal was advanced in 1931 that the best of these discussions would make good radio, WMAQ agreed to provide the forum.

This was not the university's first experiment on the air. Itself young and frisky (founded in 1892), the university had been involved with radio as early as 1922. But *Round Table* put the school solidly on the broadcasting map, becoming the first and one of the most enduring national forums of the air. With *American Forum*, *America's Town Meeting*, and *The People's Platform*, *Round Table* hashed over society's great debates during some of its most turbulent years.

Strikes, Prohibition, war, presidential politics, Communism, and isolationism were argued. The 30-minute timeslot allowed little room for pontificating, and if the series was somewhat less boisterous than the heckling and cheering *America's Town Meeting*, there was still lots of rousing disagreement. The first broadcast set the tone, when three professors sat at a simple table in a WMAQ studio and discussed the Wickersham Report on Prohibition. The professors were rotated with each broadcast according to their interests and expertise. There were no scripts (transcripts were prepared and distributed from broadcast recordings): the participants, in consultation with the school's radio department, mapped out the general territory to be explored and divided up the items accordingly. The goal was to keep it moving and keep it conversational.

A special table was developed with these goals in mind. It was triangular, not round, putting each speaker face-to-face with the others. It had time-warning lights facing each chair and was built like a sloping pyramid, with a microphone at the top. A collapsible model was built for the times when the show traveled out of Chicago. *Round Table* was the first show of its kind to issue a weekly magazine: this contained a transcript of the previous program, biographies of the participants, a column of listener feedback, a list of suggested reading on the topic of the week, and a schedule of coming broadcasts.

It won a Peabody Award for radio excellence, and its discussion of the Harlan County (Ky.) coal crisis in 1939 earned it inclusion in Max Wylie's *Best Broadcasts* of the year. Director Sherman H. Dryer of the radio department scrapped the usual format and brought in the chief antagonists, Gov. Albert B. (Happy) Chandler and Lee Pressman of the CIO, by remote, with the three professors discussing their respective remarks at the end. There were frequent guests, from Eleanor Roosevelt to William Allen White to Drew Pearson. Pearson set off an uproar when he charged on the air that boosters for Herbert Hoover were stumping the South, trying to "buy up" delegates to the 1940 Republican National Convention. When on the following program university vice president Frederic Campbell Woodward apologized to Hoover and discounted Pearson's claims as false, Pearson threatened to sue.

In later years, topics included the constitutionality of Truman's seizure of the steel industry, "the problems of prosperity," and the continuing role of the United States in Southeast Asia.

UNLIMITED HORIZONS, science education.

BROADCAST HISTORY: Nov. 1, 1940–Feb. 14, 1941, Blue Network. 30m, Fridays at 11:30.

April 20–July 20, 1942, NBC. 30m, Mondays at 11:30.

Oct. 4, 1942–July 4, 1943, NBC. 30m, Sundays at 11:30.

CREATOR: Jennings Pierce, NBC chief of public services. **PRODUCER - WRITER - RESEARCHER:** Arnold Marquis, with cooperation of the University of California at Berkeley.

Unlimited Horizons put its listeners at the vanguard of scientific research, discussing the newest advances in astronomy, cosmic rays, and long-distance transmission of high-voltage electricity. It told of life in Grand Canyon, of monkeys whose laboratory martyrdom was helping man to a better understanding of polio, of new instruments that could X-ray the earth. In 1942, the Universities of Arizona and Nevada were added as sources because, as creator Jennings Pierce put it, they had "too much good research to pass up, especially in fields not closed to us by the war." He estimated that up to 70 percent of the research in western colleges was in such war-related fields as aviation, chemicals, meteorology, and camouflage, and was therefore off limits because of secrecy.

V

VALIANT LADY, soap opera.

BROADCAST HISTORY: March 7–May 27, 1938, CBS. 15m, weekdays at 1:45. General Mills for Gold Medal Flour.

May 30, 1938–March 16, 1942, NBC. 15m, weekdays at 2:30. General Mills for Wheaties and Bisquick.

March 17, 1942–Aug. 23, 1946, CBS. 15m, weekdays at 10 A.M. General Mills.

Oct. 8, 1951–Feb. 29, 1952, ABC. 15m, weekdays at 4.

CAST: Joan Blaine as Joan Barrett, the "valiant lady," an actress with a wide assortment of personal problems. Joan Banks and Florence Freeman as Joan, late in the run. Richard Gordon, ca. 1938, as her father, Jim Barrett. Bill Johnstone and Gene Leonard also as Jim Barrett. Charles Carroll as Dr. Truman "Tubby" Scott, Joan's childhood sweetheart, eventually her husband, and the source of much grief. Bartlett Robinson and Martin Blaine also as Tubby. Judith Lowry as Joan's close friend, Emma "Stevie" Stevens. Elspeth Eric as her "closest friend" (1942 description), Eleanor Richards. Teddy Bergman (later known professionally as Alan Reed) as villain and friend in the same 1938 storyline, as the self-centered Mr. Wright, and as Jim Barrett's best friend, Mike Hagen. Bill Adams and Parker Fennelly, later, as Mike Hagen. **SUPPORTING CAST, CA.** 1938: Santos Ortega as producer Edward Curran. Raymond Edward Johnson as would-be suitor Paul Morrison. Linda Carlon as Mrs. Agnes Westcott, the store detective at the Pine River Emporium who found the incriminating $42 in Joan's glove. Elsie Mae Gordon as Estelle Cummings, Emporium cashier. Adelaide Klein as Mildred Farrell, sob sister for a New York paper, who "turns on the tears when she writes about the Broadway girl who was almost a star." Dwight Weist as Collins, kind-hearted banker who loaned Joan $2,000 of his own money to help with her legal defense. Maurice Tarplin as Barclay, editor of the *Pine River Review*, an elderly man, longtime friend, and "a character much like the emminent William Allen White of Emporia, Kan." Albert Hayes as the lawyer, Norman Price. Bernard Lenrow as Carson, the unscrupulous real estate man. Jeanette McGrady as Grace Wilson, the Emporium salesgirl, "a homely runt whose job was saved by Joan, but who felt, instead of gratitude, only jealousy." Jerry Macy as the "stern and dignified" Judge Kruger. Sidney Slon as Trent, the prosecuting attorney, convinced of Joan's guilt. Milton Herman as Lillienthal, producer of the play that almost won stardom for Joan in New York. **SUPPORTING CAST, FROM CA.** 1941: Joan Vitez as the unscrupulous Ivy Lane. Julian Noa as Dr. Malcolm Donaldson, Tubby's friend and advocate, who came to believe he was "just a bad egg," without knowing of the brain disorder that caused his behavior. Ralph Bell as Jack Eastman, gambler. Charles Webster as Thomas R. Clark; Lawson Zerbe as his worthless but lovable son, Jeff Clark. Jean Ellyn as Margie "Cookie" Cook. A. T. Kaye as Nelson, the butler. Kate McComb as Mrs. Evans, the housekeeper. Everett Sloane as Brennan. William Shelley as Dr. Abendroth. Clifford Stork as Jolly Rogers, the ruthless insurance detective. **DIRECTORS:** Ernest Ricca, Roy Lockwood, Rikel Kent, etc. **WRITERS:** Addy Richton and Lynn Stone; also, Ruth Borden, Lawrence Klee, Howard Teichmann, etc. **THEME:** *Estrellita*, played on organ.

Valiant Lady was the story of Joan Barrett, who sacrificed a promising Broadway career for her father's sake, then married a "brilliant but unstable" surgeon. The star, Joan Blaine, was a major serial personality in the heyday of Chicago radio: she was said to have been an attorney, an educator, and a musician prior to her stardom, and was one of the very few daytime actresses to get pretitle billing (most got no billing at all).

Joan Barrett was 23 years old as the serial opened. She had been raised by her father, Jim, a poor contractor. Although her birth cost Jim Barrett his wife, father and daughter shared a devotion that grew with the passing years. Dispirited after his wife's death, Jim was reduced to doing odd jobs for small change. But he resolved to leave something for his daughter: when she was still an infant, he built them a house and put it in her name.

Joan's early interest was theater: she displayed an unusual ability in high school dramatic productions, and, as the serial began, she had journeyed to New York hoping to pursue her dream. There she met Emma Stevens, who had once been a Follies girl and was "now a plump 50-year-old stage matron." Sentimental and jolly, "Stevie" showed her the ropes and became her close friend. Joan's ability and good looks attracted the attention of Edward Curran, "world-famous theatrical producer," who promptly cast her in a leading role. But this came to naught: the play flopped. Still, Curran offered to pay her $50 a week if she would study with him and allow him to make her into a great actress.

Before this could transpire, she was drawn away by a home crisis. Her father was struck by a car and paralyzed, and Joan returned to Pine River to devote herself to his care. She was accompanied by the faithful Stevie, who moved in with the Barretts and helped with the daily chores. Money was tight, and Joan found work in the Pine River Emporium. But a scheming salesgirl, Grace Wilson, framed her in the theft of $42. This was part of a larger conspiracy, a plot by an unscrupulous realtor named Carson to keep the Barretts poor and obtain their land. Joan

was fired by Mr. Wright, manager of the Emporium and the town's stuffed shirt. With the help of her father's friend Mike Hagen, Joan secured the services of a "famous and brilliant" New York attorney, Norman Price. Price came, he saw, he fell madly in love. But in the end, Joan cleared her own name by getting a confession out of Grace Wilson.

Now came the true trouble of her life, Dr. Truman "Tubby" Scott—26, blue-eyed, blond, and her childhood sweetheart. Tubby had assumed the medical care of her still-ailing father: he believed that a "sudden shock" might cure the old man's paralysis, and in the close proximity to the Barretts he discovered that he was "as much in love with Joan as ever." Joan eventually succumbed to Tubby's charm and idealism: though he was a "brilliant plastic surgeon," he remained "dreadfully poor" because he gave his services to the needy. But Tubby's character was flawed by wild jealousy. In 1939, he brawled with Joan's artist friend, handsome and dashing Paul Morrison. There was growing scandal over the true nature of this triangular relationship. A baby was mixed up in it, and this kept the small-town tongues wagging

By 1941, Joan and Tubby were married and living a harrowing life together. Tubby had been mugged on one of his trips to the poor part of town, and a blood clot had formed on his brain, warping his personality. He lived a Jekyll-and-Hyde existence, the clot ("in whose existence he does not believe") causing him to give up philanthropy and become coarse, hard, and arrogant. He fell in with bad company, the gambler Jack Eastman and the vixen Ivy Lane, "a wealthy divorcee whose fading youth has hardly touched her beauty." But Eastman wanted only to use Tubby's social prestige to further his own schemes, and Ivy dangled the promise of a clinic before Tubby's greedy eyes so she could "entice him into a shady romance."

In 1942, Tubby descended into a mine to treat the workers for silicosis (presumably, they never came to the surface, even for medical attention) and was trapped in an underground explosion. His apparent death (no body was recovered) merely complicated Joan's life, for he had been wanted by the law for a crime he didn't commit, and she had been aiding him in his flight. They had been living in the town of Fairview as "Mr. and Mrs. Steven Hargrave," and now, with

Tubby gone, Joan resolved to keep running from the law in her desperate attempt to clear her husband's name. On she went to Chicago, and a series of new adventures with the Clark family— the father, Thomas, a newspaper magnate and "one of the wealthiest men in the United States"; his playboy son, Jeff; and Jeff's blonde and beautiful girlfriend, Margie Cook, "Cookie" to her friends.

The serial was at its peak in 1938–42. In March 1942, General Mills moved it to CBS, where it aired at 10 A.M. and lost points each year from its 7-point Hooper. An attempt to revive it in 1951 was unsuccessful, failing to attract either sponsor or audience.

VANITY FAIR, musical variety.

BROADCAST HISTORY: May 26, 1933–Jan. 5, 1934, NBC. 30m, Fridays at 9:30. Pond's Cold Cream. **CAST:** Vocalists Paul Small and Lee Wiley (who became a noted jazz-blues specialist); a continuing comedy sketch, *The Carrolls*, with Ilka Chase and Hugh O'Connell. Also: Charles Lawrence. **ORCHESTRA:** Victor Young.

This series, notable for the early Lee Wiley appearance, had no connection to a later show of the same name. That *Vanity Fair* (Sept. 20–Nov. 1, 1937, Blue Network, 30m, Mondays at 8:30 for Campana) featured Cal Tinney with movie commentator Sheilah Graham.

THE VASS FAMILY, musical variety.

BROADCAST HISTORY: Oct. 1932–Sept. 1937, NBC. 15m, Saturdays at 11:15 or 10:15.

1939–40, NBC, both networks: 15m, Sundays at 1:15 on the Blue; Saturdays at 11 A.M. on the Red.

1940–41, Blue Network. 15m, Saturdays at 6:30.

The Vass Family was a singing group that came out of the South Carolina hills in the summer of 1931 to become—singly and together— well-known figures of the network air. They included Dr. and Mrs. J. L. Vass and their seven children: Lee, Harriet, Frank, Sally, Virginia ("Jitchy"), Louisa ("Weezy"), and Emily. The father was an educator whose school had burned down, and they had traveled to Connecticut to visit their Aunt Lulu (Mrs. Curtis Burnley Rail-

ing). When Mrs. Railing heard them sing, she arranged an audition with Madge Tucker, head of children's programming at NBC. Soon they began singing on Tucker's Saturday morning kid shows. The father returned to teaching; Harriet and Lee left to pursue other interests, and for most of its show business life *The Vass Family* consisted of Frank, Weezy, Jitchy, Sally, and Emily. They were heard on Paul Whiteman's variety hour and were given singing roles in such dramas as *Death Valley Days, Roses and Drums*, and *Heart Throbs of the Hills* (NBC regional, 1933–38). Emily got a part on *The Phil Baker Show*; Jitchy appeared with Eddie Cantor.

VAUGHN DE LEATH, crooner.

BROADCAST HISTORY: 1920–26, many prenetwork shows, leading to her later billing as "the first lady of radio."

1926–27, NBC. Wrigley's Gum.

1928–29, NBC. Featured soloist on *The Voice of Firestone*.

1931–33, CBS. 15m, twice a week at 6:15; later at 6:30.

1934–35, NBC. 15m, Tuesdays at 7:45, and Wednesdays at 2:30

1935–36, NBC. 15m, six a week at 10 A.M.

1936–37, Blue Network. 15m, weekdays at 1:30.

April 2, 1938–Jan. 7, 1939, Blue. 15m, Saturdays at 11 A.M.

June 30–Sept. 22, 1939, Mutual. 15m, three a week at 1:45. Summer fill-in for *The Voice of Experience*.

Vaughn De Leath was known by such nicknames as "the original radio girl" because of the widespread belief that she was the first woman ever to sing on the air. It does seem that she missed that honor by a decade, as the Swedish concert singer Madame Eugenia Farrar sang *I Love You Truly* on a Lee De Forest experimental station in 1907, when De Leath was seven years old.

She was born Sept. 26, 1900. She may have sung on a De Forest station as early as 1916: at that time, De Forest was broadcasting from the Columbia Gramophone Building in New York, playing phonograph records and, perhaps, featuring occasional live singers. In January 1920, De Leath did make several broadcasts with De

Forest: her comment, just before singing *Old Folks at Home*, was reportedly "Well, here goes something into nothing."

Daughter of a windmill maker, she claimed to have learned to sing in tempo with spinning windmill blades. In the De Forest experiment, she created the singing style of the coming decade, a soft throaty mode that would soon be known as crooning. This she adopted of necessity, as the piercing tones of sopranos were dangerous to early transmitter tubes. Though she always disliked the term, crooning was the rage of the moment, with Russ Columbo, Bing Crosby, and Rudy Vallee pushing it to ever-greater heights.

De Leath was a highly popular, though never sensational, performer throughout radio's first decade. She was on hand for the opening of WJZ in 1921, became affiliated with WDT in 1923, and was one of the first Americans heard in Europe via transatlantic broadcasting. In 1930, she participated in one of the early major television experiments. She was sometimes compared to Kate Smith—both were full-voiced singers weighing more than 200 pounds—but her career never reached the heights attained by Smith. In 1938, she took Smith to court for Smith's attempt to usurp the title "first lady of radio," which De Leath claimed was hers by tradition. She was widely known by her theme, *Red Sails in the Sunset*, which adapted ideally to her crooning style.

She died in Buffalo May 28, 1943.

VERNON CRANE'S STORYBOOK, children's show.

BROADCAST HISTORY: May 7, 1939–March 3, 1940, NBC. 15m, Sundays at 11:45 until Nov., then at noon.

Vernon Crane was billed as "the walking, talking storybook": he wrote and enacted original fairy tales, encouraging children to write him about pet rabbits, fountains in back yards, or other enchantments from their lives that could be made into drama. His style was direct—no music and sparse sound effects—plain, old-fashioned storytelling.

VIC AND SADE, comedy vignettes; a landmark series.

BROADCAST HISTORY: June 29, 1932–Nov. 2, 1934, Blue Network. 15m, weekdays at 9:30 A.M., 1932–33; at 1:30, 1933–34.

Nov. 5, 1934–Sept. 29, 1944, NBC (except 1942–43, CBS). 15m, weekdays at 3, 1934–35; at 3:30, 1935–38; at 4:30, 1938–39, at 3:45, 1939–42; at 1:45 (CBS), 1942–43; at 11:15 A.M., 1943–44. Procter & Gamble (Crisco, etc.). *Concurrent weekday broadcasts*: Blue Network, Nov.–Dec. 1934, at 1:30; 1936–38, at 11 A.M.; 1938–39, at 11:15 A.M.; 1940–41, at 10:45 A.M. CBS, May 30–Nov. 4, 1938, at 1:15; 1941–42, at 1:30. Mutual, March 31–Sept. 26, 1941, at 8:30 A.M. All P&G. *Concurrent late-night version*: NBC Red, April 6–Sept. 21, 1937, Tuesdays at 10:45. P&G's Ivory Snow.

Aug. 21–Dec. 7, 1945, CBS. 15m, four, later five, times a week at 7:15. Procter & Gamble.

June 27–Sept. 19, 1946, Mutual. Reorganized as a 30m situation comedy, Thursdays at 8:30. Fitch Shampoo.

CAST: Art Van Harvey and Bernardine Flynn as Vic and Sade, "Mr. and Mrs. Victor Gook." Bill Idelson as Rush, their adopted son. Clarence Hartzell as Uncle Fletcher. *Supporting cast* (all post-1942): Ruth Perrott and Carl Kroenke as Chuck and Dottie Brainfeeble. David Whitehouse as Russell Miller. Leonard Smith as Russell Miller, ca. Aug.–Dec. 1945. Forrest Lewis and Norman Gottschalk as Roy Delfeeno. Cliff Soubier as Dwight Twentysixer. Hugh Studebaker as Mayor Geetcham, who got Uncle Fletcher a pass to ride on the garbage wagon. Hugh Studebaker also as Rishigan Fishigan of Sishigan, Michigan. Leonard Smith as Blue-Tooth Johnson. Art McConnell as Jack Culbertson, and as Sweet Corn McBlock. Dolly Day as Mrs. Belker and Mrs. Harris. Johnny Coons in a variety of roles including Harry Dean, Smelly Clark, Mervyn S. Sprawl, L. J. Gertner, Cracky Otto, Orville Wheeney and, a few times near the end, Russell Miller. Merrill Mael, an uncanny Clarence Hartzel soundalike, as Uncle Fletcher for a few weeks, ca. 1943, when the show moved from Chicago to Hollywood. **ANNOUNCERS:** Bob Brown, 1932–40; also, Vincent Pelletier, Ed Roberts, Ralph Edwards, Ed Herlihy, Glenn Riggs, Jack Fuller, Roger Krupp, etc. **ORGANIST:** Lou Webb. **MUSICAL COMBO (1945):** June Lyons, piano; Fred Jackie, bassoon; Elwyn Owen, organ. **CREATOR-DIRECTOR:** Paul Rhymer. **DIRECTORS:** Clarence Menser, Earl Ebi, Roy Winsor,

Charles Rinehardt; Homer Heck, director for NBC, 1943–44; Caldwell Cline for CBS. **THEME:** *Oh, You Beautiful Doll*, early 1930s; *Chanson Bohemienne* for most of the run.

Vic and Sade, "radio's home folks," was (though its scheduling would suggest otherwise) in no way a soap opera. It was not even a serial in the usual definition of the word. Its story was told in thousands of 12-minute sketches without dramatic continuity, the best of them standing alone like fine short stories. Each was a little slice of life, an American original, in a category of its own making, as inimitable as its author's fingerprint. In the words of announcer Bob Brown (and with a passing nod at the daytime competition), *Vic and Sade* immediately became "an island of delight in the sea of tears."

Vic, Sade, and their adopted son Rush lived in "the small house halfway up in the next block," in a rural town somewhere in Illinois. The town was populated by the strangest aggregation of eccentrics with the most wonderful names ever heard in fiction or fact. The strangest of these was Uncle Fletcher, who often arrived at the worst possible time, rambled on about people long dead or missing, reached no discernible point, and either left or stayed around awhile. "Harry Fedrock left Belvedere in nineteen-ought-nine," he would announce suddenly. "Moved to Albuquerque, Colorado, married a woman 28 years old, went bail for his brother-in-law that skipped the country, invented a fingernail file that run by electricity, and later died." After a few lines of polite conversation, Uncle Fletcher would promise to give Sade's regards to Mr. T. K. Hoygawper (whom she didn't know) when he arrived in Dixon, his old hometown. "Walter Hoygawper left Dixon a year or so ago," he would inform. "Moved to Richmond, North Carolina, married a woman 16 and three-quarters years old, bought a dry goods store and sold it 20 minutes later at a profit of $11, grew chin whiskers to spite his landlord, and later died."

As novelist Ray Bradbury summarized four decades later, Uncle Fletcher was "an amazing man." A listener could believe him fully capable of going through the San Francisco earthquake and immediately thereafter telling a story of a man in East Cairo, Ill., aged 97, who married a woman aged 101, adopted a son, 75, and later

died. Bradbury was one in a long line of notables who were and are fans of *Vic and Sade*. Edgar A. Guest, James Thurber, and Hendrik Willem Van Loon were outspoken in their praise. Ogden Nash compared the author, Paul Rhymer, with Mark Twain, a sentiment echoed by John O'Hara in a *Collier's* column. President Roosevelt was said to have listened when he could, and along Radio Row the skits were highly regarded by such top comics as Jim and Marian Jordan (who knew a thing or two about life in Illinois) and *Lum and Abner*'s Chet Lauck and Norris Goff. Carlton E. Morse and his *I Love a Mystery* crew (Buddy Twiss, Dresser Dahlstead, Paul Carson, and Ben Alexander) kept a *Radio Life* interviewer waiting 15 minutes, until Rhymer's show was finished for the day. *Vic and Sade* was remembered for decades by people in and out of radio. Glowing forewords were written by Bradbury and Jean Shepherd to books of Rhymer's scripts. And with the slow discovery of existing shows, enthusiasts began to gather. The Vic and Sadists in Los Angeles counted Bradbury, Stan Freberg, and Norman Corwin among its members. In 1972, the Friends of Vic and Sade was formed to share information, recollections, and recordings of the program. Its driving force, Barbara Schwarz, still issues occasional newsletters packed with new discoveries and excerpts of scripts. The latter she hand-copies from the archive at the Wisconsin Historical Society, where the author's widow, Mary Frances Rhymer, deposited it in 1969.

It began, like so many of radio's most significant programs, inauspiciously. Paul Rhymer was 24 years old when he joined the NBC continuity staff in Chicago. Born in Fulton, Ill., in 1905, he arrived in radio with a well-honed talent as a wordsmith and a fully formed sense of humor. His youth had been spent in Bloomington: there he went to high school and formed many of the impressions that would carry into his radio work. His early days at NBC were described by his wife in her introduction to his book of scripts. It was a world of glass cubicles where continuity writers pounded out copy for an endless parade of shows. "Practically every word one heard on the radio was written. Even the staff orchestra, Harry Kogen's Musical Ramblers, required copy."

This Rhymer did for the three years prior to *Vic and Sade*. He created and wrote a show called *Keystone Chronicles*, about which little is known, though the scripts are apparently stored in Wisconsin. In 1932, he was assigned by Clarence Menser, the network's program director, to develop a family skit for audition to an important client. The script would be needed Monday: the client, Procter & Gamble, was about to enter radio in a big way. Indeed, P&G would soon become one of the busiest daytime advertisers, keeping its serials in business for years.

But to Rhymer it meant he'd have to work Sunday, and he approached the job with little enthusiasm. He considered the names Vic and Sade: they seemed to fit the kind of characters he had in mind, and they were simple and easy to remember, names of the country's heartland. But the sponsor was unimpressed: P&G passed, moving on to another show. Still, Menser liked it, well enough to schedule it on a sustaining basis.

The entire action was set in the house where Mr. and Mrs. Victor Gook lived. The only characters were the two of the title, though others were alluded to in the dialogue. Vic was described by *Radio Guide* as "the type of small-town character that Norman Rockwell brings to life on *Saturday Evening Post* covers. Bluff, hearty, and good-natured, Vic is a bookkeeper for Consolidated Kitchenware Company's Plant Number Fourteen. Sade met and married Vic in her hometown, Dixon, Illinois. She's one of those rare women who make really tolerant wives." These pivotal roles were given life, from beginning to end, by a former grain salesman, Art Van Harvey, and an actress, Bernardine Flynn, who was tired of life on the road and wanted to settle into something like radio that might provide the opportunity for a home life.

Van Harvey brought to Vic an accent that sounded like Hoosier mixed with second-generation German; Flynn played Sade with a nasal twang that echoed faintly of Jane Ace. Now a remarkable thing happened: Rhymer managed to create an entire town without ever leaving the Gooks' small house. "There is never a scene that goes farther than the front porch, attic or cellar," wrote Fred E. H. Schroeder in the *Journal of Popular Culture*. "All outside occurrences, even in the alley, are reported from within. There are no place or time transitions, no signals of 'meanwhile' or 'later'; in short, *Vic and Sade* has perfect Aristotelean unities of ac-

tion, place, and time. But their midwestern world is immense, peopled with a large number of ordinary friends and acquaintances with exotic names and weirdly unique pasts and personalities."

Said *Radio Guide*: "The phone rings and the door slams, but that is about all that is ever heard in the way of sound effects. Occasionally when Vic rummages around the pantry there's the sound of falling crockery or tinware. The one really indispensable prop is the telephone, as it is the means by which the neighbors are brought into the life of the Gooks." To produce such a show for a full season might have exhausted the imaginations of most writers: Rhymer did it for more than a decade, never going stale, his humor consistently at the highest levels of radio comedy.

But the initial concept was too narrow even for him. Another voice was needed, and Rhymer thought of a son. With the show already on the air, it would be awkward to introduce a character old enough to make significant contributions to the dialogue. This was the worst year of the Depression, and the script would only be following life if a child arrived because his real mother could not take care of him. On the show of July 8, 1932, Vic and Sade discussed the plight of 9-year-old Victor Rush Meadows, son of Sade's old school friend. Rush arrived July 15. Rhymer had cribbed the name from a young friend of a little girl who had lived next door to him in his own childhood. He was adopted by Vic and Sade, and in time listeners forgot that he was anything other than their own son. The role was filled by Billy Idelson, who played it with such deadpan innocence that it worked into Rhymer's little scenario to perfection. For the next eight years, these were the only voices heard.

Vic masked his cheerful nature under a cloak of trumped-up temper. He had real moments of snappy impatience, notably when he brought work home from the office, but the listener never doubted the bond that existed in the small house halfway up in the next block. Vic was described in *Radio Guide* as "a humorist of sorts" who "calls his wife Kiddo and his son Rush by a series of zany names." Vic would ask, "Are you in a trance, Pocketwatch?" and Rush—with his usual penchant for simplicity—would reply, "I'm tryin' to figure somethin' out, Gov." Rush was variously known as "Egg-Crate," "Paperweight," "Horse-Chestnut," and by a score of equally affectionate names. Sade sometimes called him Willie.

The town consisted of a main road, which became Kelsey Street, and a few cross-streets, notably Virginia Avenue and University Street. The Gooks lived on Virginia Avenue, with the back door facing an alley and, beyond that, the back yards of the houses on University. There were two hotels: the Butler House, which was fancy, and the Bright Kentucky, which was not. The Bright Kentucky butted the railroad tracks and was often deplored by Sade's ladies' club as an eyesore and a disgrace. The town had a moviehouse, the Bijou, which most people pronounced Bye-Joe. Its features changed, but the stars never did: the Bye-Joe always offered Gloria Golden and Four-Fisted Frank Fuddleman in such titles as *You're the Cowpuncher of My Dreams, Foreman Hastings*. There was a restaurant, the little Tiny Petite Pheasant Feather Tea Shoppe, where the bill o' fare included olive runt, scalded cucumbers, rutabaga shortcake, bent grass ox butter, and, of course, beef punkles, in season.

Vic was a hard-working accountant who grumbled about his boss, J. K. Ruebush, whose name was usually pronounced "Old Rubbish." Consolidated Kitchenware had a traveling inspector, Mr. Buller, who was difficult and aggressive and was said to have pulled his own teeth. Guss Fuss was a visiting kitchenware executive from Dubuque. Vic's secretary at the plant was Miss Olive Hammersweet. Aside from work and family, Vic's energy went into his lodge, the Sacred Stars of the Milky Way; he belonged to its Drowsy Venus Chapter and was Exalted Big Dipper. The Exalted Little Dipper was Hank Gutstop, who was also Sade's main source of annoyance. Hank was the town loafer. The lodge was founded by R. J. Konk, and its membership included many of the town's leading citizens. There were Robert and Slobert Hink, who had brothers named Bertie and Dirtie and sisters named Bessie and Messie. The Hinks lived in Hoopestown and, with Vic, were members of the All-Star Marching Team, which drew its ranks from such distant points as East Brain, Oregon. The team was never able to get together, so individual members marched alone in the various parades. The Hinks did have one moment of glory, when they rode a power mower from Moline to Decatur.

Then there was Rishigan Fishigan of Sishigan, Michigan, who married Jane Bayne from Paine, Maine. They planned a honeymoon at the Bright Kentucky Hotel, only to learn that the penthouse had no stairs and they'd have to climb a rope to get in. Ike Kneesuffer had an indoor horseshoe-pitching court in his basement. Godfrey Dimlock once invented a bicycle that could say "Mama." Others were Y. Y. Flirch, Homer Q. McDancey, Charlie Razorscum, Y. I. I. Y. Skeeber, S. Quentin B. H. Labelle Jr., and Steve Chestbutter. The only woman in the lodge was Pom Pom Cordova, an honorary member, who came from the Bahamas, taught Vic to play the Caribbean dream flute, and helped E. W. Smith break his habit of stealing horses. Vic was often heard reading from the lodge credo, something that sounded faintly like Latin but always came out *in hoc spittle dum cluck nomenclature*, or some derivative thereof.

Sade too had an outside interest: the ladies' Thimble Club, which met weekly to sew and gossip. Its troublemakers were Mis' Applerot and Mis' Brighton, though there were occasional snits that had all the members on the outs. Sade's dearest friend was Ruthie Stembottom, who lived on University with her husband Fred, a foreman in a factory. Sade and Ruthie collected washrags (more then 3,000 between them) and never missed a washrag sale at Yamilton's Department Store. Fred Stembottom was to Vic what Hank Gutstop was to Sade, a constant irritant. But Sade was, first and foremost, the American housewife of her time. She would read aloud letters from her sister Bessie or her Uncle Fletcher. Bess usually wrote about the twinges in Uncle Walter's kneecap; Uncle Fletcher wrote of such assorted nutty subjects that he became, by 1938, the off-mike presence that drew the heaviest listener mail. These discussions took place in the kitchen, amidst talk of beef punkles ice cream or limberschwartz cheese. Sade's oft-heard excuse for dinner being late was "the meat's not done"; her suggestion that the Gooks visit relatives in Carberry drew from Vic a groan of genuine despair. Sade's strongest expression of disgust was her catchphrase, "Oh, ish!" She and Vic suffered the friendship of Chuck and Dottie Brainfeeble: in one episode, Vic planned to celebrate the Brainfeebles' housewarming by having Hank Gutstop sing *Would That These Pale Hands Crysanthemums Might Gather* and

Throw Me over the Grape Arbor a Single Red, Red Rose, My Love.

Rush Gook came to this environment with youth's vision of the same general nonsense. At some point his name was explained as being of his mother's family, and he resisted the suggestion in Uncle Fletcher's letters that he take "pianny lessons." One girl, Mildred Tisdel, "attracts and repels him all at once," said *Radio Guide* in 1938. His best pal was Blue-Tooth Johnson, who loved baseball and could usually be found "near third base over at Tatman's vacant lot." Rush often stopped there on his way home from the YMCA, where he liked to go to watch fat men play handball. At home he would discuss the events of his life with Vic and Sade, perhaps offering the suggestion that they go to the Bijou, where Gloria Golden and Four-Fisted Frank Fuddleman were starring in *My Heart Is in Your Hands, Master Sergeant Irwin Strohm.*

His attraction to melodrama was strong: he was addicted to a series of adventure novels starring the redoubtable Third Lt. Clinton Stanley, who once hoisted a camel by its hind feet and whaled the daylights out of a villainous Arab sheik with it. Blue-Tooth Johnson shared Rush's enthusiasm for Third Lt. Stanley, perhaps because Stanley had proven himself on the fields of sport as well, having once defeated Yale and Harvard simultaneously in a legendary gridiron battle. Another Rush friend was Smelly Clark, who had his age changed from 16 to 21, held the long-distance record for spitting, was a master at jimmying penny gum machines, and was equally adept at sneaking into the movie house. Rounding out Rush's acquaintances were Rooster and Rotten Davis, Vernon Peggles, Orville Wheeney, and a dog named Mr. Albert Johnson, who couldn't bark but emitted a hissing sound. As for Rush, *Radio Mirror* offered the opinion that, "as each year goes by, he gets wiser, which amazes him greatly."

The addition of Uncle Fletcher as a fully realized character in 1940 brought *Vic and Sade* to the pinnacle of its own grand nonsense. Fletcher was described by *Radio Life* as "one of those puzzling old men who hover between near insanity and clear lucidity." But this gave only a hint of his true personality. Uncle Fletcher was eccentric even by Paul Rhymer's standard. He talked through people, hearing little (or all) that was said; his feelings were easily bruised one moment and impenetrable the next. He rambled on about friends who had once lived in Sweet Esther, Wisconsin, moved to Dismal Seepage, Ohio, and later died. He responded to the greeting "Say, Uncle Fletcher" with "Certainly" or "Fine."

He got letters from Aunt Bess and carried them unopened for a month. Once he made his landlady, Mis' Keller, the gift of a four-foot length of railroad track, thinking she might use it for a doorstop. He talked for years about the upcoming marriage of Mis' Keller and Harry Feedburn. In the midst of an unrelated conversation, Uncle Fletcher would tell of Irma Flo Kessy, who had a habit of slapping her husband's face in public. "Irma Flo Kessy's husband would say, 'Believe it's gonna rain, Irma Flo,' and Irma Flo'd turn and hit him upside the jaw. Halfwit husband got so every time he opened his mouth he'd hide his face in his arms."

Uncle Fletcher hung out at the Bright Kentucky Hotel, where Smelly Clark's Uncle Strap was the night clerk and the trains roared past on their way from Chicago to St. Louis. Sometimes he'd drift down to the Interurban Depot and pass the time with Ernie Fatler, the passenger agent, or wander out along Route 66 to sit on the wooden bench outside Ed Kennedy's gas station and watch for out-of-state license plates. He claimed to be on speaking terms with the armed guard at the Ohio State Institute for the Incurably Shy: Ohio also had state homes for the Bald and the Agreeable, while in Missouri there was a similar institution (with armed guards) for the Tall. In one program, Uncle Fletcher identified a Vermont State Home for the Freckled, an Oklahoma State Home for the Mistaken, a Kentucky State Home for the Suspicious, and a Nebraska State Home for the Nice-Looking. His landlady alternately pleased and annoyed him. He was annoyed when she went on a week-long trip and laid out his meals in advance, all over the house. "Saturday's dinner is on the numbskull sideboard. Sunday's dinner is on a tray in the lame-brain nit-wit pantry. Monday's breakfast sits on my dresser up in my bedroom. And Monday's dinner is perched like a numbskull parrot on the doggone fathead piano stool!"

His on-mike inclusion was made necessary when Art Van Harvey had a heart attack and Vic had to be temporarily written out. Since Uncle

Fletcher had been the most intriguing of the never-heard characters, Rhymer decided to bring him on as a replacement. Auditions were scheduled, though it was assumed that the part would go to veteran character actor Sidney Ellstrom. But among those auditioning was Clarence Hartzell, a young man from Huntington, W. Va. who was destined to make a good part of his living playing old men on the air. The moment Hartzell spoke his first lines, Billy Idelson and Bernardine Flynn were his champions. Here was Uncle Fletcher in the flesh. They argued and overcame the reluctance of everyone who had been predisposed toward Ellstrom, and finally Hartzell was called in and given the job. He became instantly indispensable, blending perfectly after Van Harvey returned, and he played the role from 1940 until the show left the air in 1946. Later he took the same basic character to *Lum and Abner* under the name Ben Withers.

Uncle Fletcher's befuddled ramblings are still being catalogued by old listeners who knew him well. Dr. Richard E. Hunton of the Friends of Vic and Sade compiled a list of half-forgotten Fletcherisms. Roy Delfeeno could rub his feet together and make a flame hot enough to light a cigar. O. X. Bottleman committed suicide by jumping off a piano. Sam Clinkstrap broke his elbow winding his watch. Virgil Dejectedly had eight brothers who lived in different cities. Cliff Dirtshirt once took an automobile apart with a hairpin. Tracy Flankers had a secret place for his money that involved fastening a leather strap with wires to his wisdom teeth. George and Edna Gafby invented a reversible washrag. Ollie Hasher had a friend who painted his table every day, so he wouldn't have to dust it. Atterbury Hippins went into the salted house-paint business. George McFulper was shot in the head outside Dayton, Ohio, and never recognized his wife, Dorothy, thereafter. Luke Zaker went into the chocolate-flavored sandpaper business, and later died.

Bertha Joiner went daffy from reading dime novels, and wore only one shoe. J. J. J. J. Stunbolt was always getting hit by fast passenger trains. And there were others: Cora Bucksaddle; the Brick Mush Man; and Francis Kleek, who always forgot to remove the shoehorns from his shoes. There were Nicer Scott, Myrt and Squirt Montgomery, and L. J. Gertner, the city water inspector; Ole Chinbunny, the high school principal; Charlie Urquhart, the clerk at the Bright Kentucky Hotel; Dwight Twentysixer; Mervyn S. Sprawl, the senile old man down the street who loved "them peanuts with the chocolate smeared on the outside"; and old Mr. Gumpox, the garbage man, whose wagon was pulled through the alley between Virginia and University by a horse named Howard, which suffered from dizzy spells.

Not infrequently was Rhymer's work likened to that of Charles Dickens. His characters, wrote one journalist, "rival those of Dickens for odd names and are far more humorous."

When Procter & Gamble finally decided to sponsor the show, Rhymer quit NBC and became a freelancer. He wrote his daily episode in the morning, then went to Merchandise Mart to watch the rehearsal and broadcast. His afternoons were usually free for an outing or a trip to the races. The writing, like all good writing, was a difficult process. His initial draft went through a single rewrite on the good days and was ripped apart a dozen times when the going was tough. He was honored in his lifetime and is fondly remembered five decades later, no small achievement. His show won a poll of 600 radio editors as best radio serial, and there were many who thought it the best in all radio. His personal sense of humor was, apparently, as bizarre as what his scripts reflected. He would sit in the booth and be charmed, enchanted, and reduced to fits of laughter as Van Harvey, Flynn, Idelson, and Hartzell brought his creations to life. He was said to be an avid practical joker. Once he named a group of jailbirds after all the vice presidents at NBC. Hotel clerk Charlie Urquhart got his name from an NBC production manager; Third Lt. Clinton Stanley was likewise christened after one of the producers.

In 1938, Rhymer and his cast went to Bloomington for a "Paul Rhymer Day." Residents there had reclaimed him as their own, and many professed that *Vic and Sade* contained clearly drawn aspects of their daily lives. It was perhaps the most consistent, evenly executed show on the air. Its major upheaval was the departure of Bill Idelson for the Navy in 1942. Rhymer approached this profound loss cautiously: none of the four principals was considered replaceable, so there would be no attempt to recast. Rhymer decided to bring on Chuck and Dottie Brainfeeble. The necessity was heightened by another Art Van Harvey illness and the absence of Vic as well as Rush. The spacing of the introductions indicates the care with which Rhymer approached it. Dottie Brainfeeble was first heard (according to notes taken by Barbara Schwarz at the archive) Feb. 10, 1943; Van Harvey returned in early March, and Chuck Brainfeeble was not heard until the broadcast of March 8. The Brainfeebles continued on the show until May 4.

On June 3, Rhymer introduced a more permanent voice, bringing in a new son-figure. This was Russell Miller, who was explained as the orphaned nephew of Consolidated Kitchenware's Mr. Buller. Russell blended into Rush's old circle, and Smelly Clark and Blue-Tooth Johnson continued to live in his soliloquies. This format continued until the show's temporary departure from the air Sept. 29, 1944.

Then came a brief revival on CBS, a strange format of mid-1945 in which *Vic and Sade* skits shared the spotlight with singer Jack Smith; the package was again sponsored by Procter & Gamble, this time for Oxydol. Rhymer's earlier reluctance to clutter his air with voices seems to have been resolved: now many characters who had existed by reference and innuendo were cast and brought to the microphone. Again, judicious research by Barbara Schwarz at the archive has revealed who did what (see SUPPORTING CHARACTERS, above). Bill Idelson had returned from the Navy to resume the role of Rush, though Russell Miller was left in the cast for a time as well.

In 1946 came the greatest change: a 30-minute sitcom on Mutual that ran only four months and is believed to have been an artistic and commercial failure. The prevailing view is that Rhymer had stepped out of his element, that his real genius was best employed in those quarter-hour gems when only the four voices were heard. But a listen to the tapes soon reveals that the author had lost nothing in his execution or his sense of the absurd. In one immortal broadcast, the Gooks had to cope with the closing of the sidewalk, when every half-baked idiot in town traipsed through their living room on a detour to University Street. People wandered randomly, some thinking they had come into a department store. Mervyn S. Sprawl came and went and came again, on his way to the store to buy "some of them peanuts with the chocolate smeared on the

outside"; he'd lost his penny, then found it again—it was in his mitten all the time. A man and a woman—strangers to the Gooks—rummaged through the dresser drawers while the man explained how he'd had the shape of his skull changed (the doctor had used two bricks and it had "hurt like blazes," but it made him look handsomer, didn't she think?). Of course, Vic had chosen this of all days to bring work home from the office.

Bob Brown was the best-remembered announcer: he initiated the rustic practice of opening each show with the words "Well, sir." *Well, sir, it's late afternoon as we enter the small house halfway up in the next block, and here in the kitchen we find Mrs. Victor Gook and her son, Mr. Rush Gook.*

Two attempts were made to bring Rhymer's characters to television. The first was on NBC's *Colgate Theater* in July 1949, with Bernardine Flynn as Sade, but the roles of Vic and Rush played by Frank Dane and Dick Conan. In 1957, Flynn and Van Harvey reprised their roles on WNBQ, Chicago, for a two-month TV run. Although the town where Vic and Sade lived is now routinely known as Crooper, Illinois, Barbara Schwarz believes that the first regular use of this name might have been on the 1957 TV show.

Of the major *Vic and Sade* figures, only Bill Idelson was still alive in 1995. Paul Rhymer died in 1964; Art Van Harvey in 1957; Bernardine Flynn in 1977; Clarence Hartzell in 1988.

In the truest test of a classic, *Vic and Sade* just keeps getting better. At this writing, more than 200 shows are available, but many of these have no openings or closings, are in questionable sound quality, and remain undated. The number of fully viable broadcasts in excellent sound is pitifully small. As many as 3,000 discs were destroyed by Procter & Gamble at the end of World War II, an act of corporate stupidity that defies forgiveness. Perhaps P&G is to be commended for sponsoring the show, but to turn around and destroy it is tantamount to the dinosaur eating its young. All we can do at this late date is hope that the space formerly used to house those wonderful transcriptions made some indifferent company bureaucrat a comfortable office.

On the other hand—thanks to Rhymer's practice of saving his work and his wife's diligence in getting it placed—a huge written record is on file in Wisconsin. Maybe this is the silver lining: call it a gut feeling that, of all the old-time radio shows, *Vic and Sade* is the one that will transcend its time. Yes, the casting was perfect. No, it does not seem possible to imagine that show without those voices, but who knows what might happen? A century from now, when radio is in its renaissance and new "perfect" talents are there for the casting, *Vic and Sade* could play again.

THE VICKS OPEN HOUSE, musical variety: a title used by the Vick Chemical Company in various formats with various personnel.

BROADCAST HISTORY: Oct. 7, 1934–March 31, 1935, CBS. 30m, Sundays at 5. **HOST:** Warren Hull. **VOCALIST:** Donald Novis. Also: Vera Van. **ORCHESTRA:** Freddy Martin.

Jan. 1–March 26, 1935, Blue Network. 30m, Tuesdays at 9, concurrent with CBS run. **VOCALIST:** Grace Moore. **ORCHESTRA:** Harry Jackson.

Sept. 16, 1935–March 9, 1936, NBC. 30m, Mondays at 9:30. **VOCALIST:** Grace Moore. **ORCHESTRA:** Josef Pasternack, former Metropolitan Opera conductor, whose tenure with *Vicks* spanned several eras.

Sept. 27, 1936–March 21, 1937, CBS. 30m, Sundays at 8. **VOCALISTS:** Nelson Eddy, singing star, with Francia White and later Nadine Conner as his leading ladies. **ORCHESTRA:** Josef Pasternack.

Sept. 26, 1937–March 20, 1938, CBS. 30m, Sundays at 7. **VOCALISTS:** Jeanette MacDonald, singing star, with baritone Wilbur Evans. MacDonald, then the toast of the musical screen, had spurned other radio offers, it was said, because of mike fright; she was often absent, her starring role filled by Lily Pons, John Charles Thomas, and Nadine Conner. The Eddy and MacDonald seasons were flavored by the kind of Victor Herbert–Sigmund Romberg fare that had made them famous. **ORCHESTRA:** Josef Pasternack.

THE VICTOR BORGE SHOW, musical comedy.

BROADCAST HISTORY: March 8–July 9, 1943, Blue Network. 15m, weekdays at 7. **STAR:** Victor Borge, Danish pianist-comic, in a simple format of music and humorous commentary.

July 3–Sept. 25, 1945, NBC. 30m, Tuesdays at 9:30. Summer replacement for *Fibber McGee and Molly*. Johnson's Wax. **ANNOUNCER:** Harlow Wilcox **VOCALIST:** Pat Friday. **ORCHESTRA:** Billy Mills.

Sept. 9, 1946–June 30, 1947, NBC. 30m, Mondays at 9:30. *The Victor Borge Show*. Socony Oil. **ORCHESTRA:** Benny Goodman.

Jan. 1–June 1, 1951, Mutual. 5m, Mondays-Wednesdays-Fridays at 5:55. Kellogg. Returned on ABC, same timeslot, Oct. 1–Dec. 28, 1951.

Victor Borge had attained top success in his native Denmark, becoming by 1940 one of the best-known figures in all Scandinavia. His musicianship, though sometimes questioned by critics of the serious school, was of concert caliber, but it was as a funnyman that he made his mark.

He gave his first concert at 13 in 1922. From 1933 to 1940, his rise was steady: he was often called by Americans who caught his act a "Danish Noel Coward." But he began to lampoon the rise of Hitler, and soon his life was entangled in global politics. He was playing an engagement in Stockholm when the Nazis invaded Denmark in April 1940, and, believing himself to be on Hitler's "extermination list," he escaped to New York with his wife. He arrived in the United States with no personal belongings and ignorant of American customs and speech. Attempts by his American wife to teach him English were not successful, so Borge taught himself by going to American movies and memorizing the dialogue of as many as eight a day. At last able to adapt his Danish routines, he started from scratch in the American entertainment business.

He appeared at a benefit for Scandinavian war relief, where he was seen by Rudy Vallee. Vallee's show at that time (a comedy effort for Sealtest) did not use guest performers, but Vallee invited Borge to come to NBC and do his act as a preshow warmup. Vallee then called Cal Kuhl and Carroll Carroll of J. Walter Thompson and asked them to consider Borge for a possible slot on Bing Crosby's *Kraft Music Hall*. "If Rudy had ever been right in his life, he was right about this guy," Carroll recalled in his memoir. Borge "kept the audience in such a state of laughter it was quite obvious that nothing the show could do would top him. All he did was read a little story. But to make it clear, he included all the punctuation marks, to each of which he had assigned a sound.''

This was the first American exposure to Borge's "phonetic punctuation" routine, a sensation in the winter of 1941–42. His appearance with Crosby was such a success that he became a regular, heard on *The Kraft Music Hall* for more than a year. With his departure in 1943, he joined Nelson Eddy for a 14-week engagement on the Old Gold show. Borge's first series under his own name was unspectacular but well received, a spare quarter-hour without a sponsor. But he kept hopping along Radio Row with wartime appearances on Hildegarde's *Raleigh Room, The Kate Smith Hour, The Chesterfield Supper Club, Stage Door Canteen, The Chamber Music Society of Lower Basin Street* (on which he became a regular in 1944), and even *The National Barn Dance.*

Known as "the Unmelancholy Dane," Borge was reviewed in terms ranging from "completely hilarious" to "the height of sophistication." He was said by Paul Martin to "compose" by "pasting together scores from the masters—Wagner, Strauss, Bach, and Mozart—with a result that sounds like something super out of Tin Pan Alley."

THE VICTORY PARADE AND THE VICTORY THEATER, drama for the war cause.

BROADCAST HISTORY: June 7–Aug. 23, 1942, NBC. 30m, Sundays at 7 in the Jack Benny timeslot through June, then Sundays at 6:30 for *The Great Gildersleeve. The Victory Parade.*

July 20–Sept. 7, 1942, CBS. 30m, Mondays at 9, in part of *The Lux Radio Theater* summer timeslot. *The Victory Theater.* **HOST:** Cecil B. De-Mille.

Both *The Victory Parade* and *The Victory Theater* were concocted by the Office of Facts and Figures to promote the sale of war bonds. They gave NBC and CBS opportunities to parade their best regular-season prime-time shows with original plays in the midst of the vacation schedule. Lionel Barrymore hosted at least some of the *Victory Parade* shows. An example of the fare was the July 19 entry, when the entire cast of NBC's *Mr. District Attorney* performed a new story, *The Case of the Whispered Word.*

On *The Victory Theater*, host Cecil B. DeMille gave war bonds a hard sell in the three spots

usually reserved for commercials. Eight CBS series were showcased: on August 24, *The Amos 'n' Andy Show* (still on CBS but about to be lost to NBC) featured guests Victor Moore and Edward Arnold, announcer Del Sharbutt, and Lud Gluskin's orchestra. A week later, *The Screen Guild Theater* contributed the play *Joe Smith, American*, with Robert Young and Ruth Hussey. All talent was donated. DeMille told anecdotes of military history and freedom, with appeals from men on the front lines. He gave it a *Lux* sound, interviewing the stars and offering a closing tagline ("Remember, a bond in the hand helps the Rangers to land!").

A VOICE IN THE NIGHT, mystery drama with music.

BROADCAST HISTORY: May 3–Oct. 18, 1946, Mutual. 30m, Fridays at 8:30, later at 8.

Carl Brisson, veteran of early film talkies and silents, wandered among tables at his nightclub, the Golden Oriole, singing musical favorites requested by a shouting crowd. Brisson then dashed off to solve a murder case and got back to the club in time for a closing song. Amzie Strickland, who played his secretary, also wrote for the show, but the result was laughably corny.

THE VOICE OF BROADWAY, Broadway and Hollywood gossip.

BROADCAST HISTORY: April 5, 1941–Jan. 8, 1942, CBS. 15m, Saturdays at 11:30 A.M. Johnson & Johnson. Concurrently: Aug. 19, 1941–Sept. 22, 1942, CBS, 15m, Tuesdays at 6:15.

Sept. 10–Dec. 24, 1944, Mutual. 15m, Sundays at 2:45.

HOST: Dorothy Kilgallen with Broadway news, later dealing increasingly with the doings of Hollywood stars about whom she received the most questions from listeners in the service.

THE VOICE OF EXPERIENCE, advice.

BROADCAST HISTORY: 1932–33, WOR, New York; first heard in July 1932.

April 24, 1933–May 24, 1936, CBS. 15m, six a week at noon, 1933–34; weekdays at noon, 1934–36. Also Tuesdays at 8, 1933–34, and Sundays at 6:45, 1934–36. Louis Wasey, maker of Kre-mel and other medicinal products.

May 25, 1936–May 21, 1937, NBC. 15m, three

a week at 11:45 A.M. Also twice a week at 7:15, 1936–37.

Dec. 27, 1937–Dec. 22, 1939, Mutual. 15m, weekdays at 1:45, 1937–38, then three a week. Lydia Pinkham.

The Voice of Experience was Marion Sayle Taylor, a self-made sociologist and creator of the first major advice show of the air. Taylor was born in Kentucky in 1889, a Baptist preacher's son who learned early and well the virtues of oratory. As a young man before World War I, he went into social work. In health departments of Seattle and San Francisco, he befriended "dope addicts, pickpockets, degenerates, and fallen women"; this contact with "the seamy side of life" led him in the following decade to the new business of broadcasting and made him a millionaire.

Taylor's initial goal was medicine: surgery was his ambition, but an accident ruined his hands, and instead he became a lecturer. In 1915 he traveled the Chautauqua circuits, polishing his delivery. In 1919 he was able to challenge William Jennings Bryan in a series of debates on Christian fundamentalism. In 1925 the manager of a Spokane radio station asked him to fill a sudden gap in the day's programming. The hundreds of letters the station received showed Taylor that broadcasting was indeed a powerful platform. For seven years he continued his lecturing and used radio whenever he could, improving his microphone presence with appearances on more than 50 stations.

By 1928 he had decided to become the Voice of Experience, using the premise that every listener had problems, desired well-considered solutions, and would be equally interested in the problems of others. He had the title registered that year, and with the coming of the networks he pushed for a spot on developing schedules. He was turned down by NBC and CBS, and in 1932 settled for a spot on WOR, New York. By his third week on the air, 18,000 pieces of mail had come pouring into the station. This attracted the attention of Louis Wasey, an advertising executive who also owned a company making medicinal products. Wasey wanted Taylor to help him launch a new product. But this was not yet ready for market, and Taylor was engaged in the interim to sell older, established products for a fee plus 40 percent commission on profits above the prior year's sales. It took him only 13 weeks to break the entire year's record, and soon he was on the networks that had previously turned him down.

Taylor's show was far more important than its timeslots would indicate. It consistently drew weekly mail in the 15,000–20,000 bracket, and by 1934 Taylor had to keep a staff of more than 30 sorters and assistants. The radio show was the centerpiece of an advice empire, in which Taylor issued pamphlets, published books, appeared in short films, established a magazine and continued his lectures at handsome fees. It was estimated that these activities earned him $1 million a year, much of which he gave to charity. Among other things, he financed eyeglasses and Christmas toys for children, surgeries and blood transfusions for the poor, wheelchairs and crutches for the disabled, and college educations for promising students. Still, he lived like a king, in a ten-room penthouse surrounded by antiques and expensive paintings.

In his early career, Taylor guarded his anonymity. He broadcast only as the Voice, adding an element of mystery to a show already rich with human interest. His forceful speaking voice, coupled with his frank advice on sex and affairs of the heart, made him a romantic idol for a time. Even when it became known that he was short and balding, mash letters from women arrived constantly. The main problems he addressed, in order, were marital tangles (including infidelity, incompatability, and triangles), romance and courtship, trouble with parents and in-laws, and money. People asked for help with phobias; some wanted to find lost relatives, overcome inferiority complexes, even learn the finer points of farming. When a problem seemed particularly desperate, Taylor would dispense an investigator to the writer's address, to see if the despair could be relieved until a permanent solution could be found. He was said to have saved dozens of people from suicide, but at least nine were so despondent that they did not wait, and killed themselves before his assistant arrived.

Taylor's scripts were prepared ten days in advance. His standard opening was "Greetings, my friends, and good morning." His self-written theme was *My Guiding Star*. He died Feb. 1, 1942.

THE VOICE OF FIRESTONE, concert music.

BROADCAST HISTORY: Dec. 3, 1928–June 7, 1954, NBC. 30m, Mondays at 8 through May 26, 1930; returned Sept. 7, 1931, Mondays at 8:30. Firestone Tire and Rubber Company. Simulcast with NBC-TV from Sept. 5, 1949, one of the first such shows.

June 14, 1954–June 10, 1957, ABC. 30m, Mondays at 8:30. Firestone. Continued on ABC-TV, with some gaps, until June 16, 1963.

SOLOISTS: Vaughn De Leath and Franklyn Baur, original soloists, 1928–30; James Melton and Gladys Rice, ca. 1931; Lawrence Tibbett and Richard Crooks, alternate soloists, ca. 1932–34; Frank Chapman and Gladys Swarthout, regulars, 1934, with Crooks continuing through the decade and becoming the singer most identified with *Firestone*; Margaret Speaks a regular from ca. 1936, joining Richard Crooks in many memorable duets; Eleanor Steber and Christopher Lynch regulars, mid-1940s; Thomas L. Thomas also frequently heard after the retirement of Crooks in 1946. *Guests*: Lily Pons, John Charles Thomas, Lauritz Melchior, Rose Bampton, etc. (1930s); Risë Stevens, Dorothy Kirsten, Jerome Hines, Patrice Munsel, Ezio Pinza, Igor Gorin, etc. (1940s). **ORCHESTRA:** Hugo Mariani, 1928–31, beginning with a 17-piece aggregation that was quickly enlarged to more than 30 (eventually, after Mariani's tenure, becoming the 70-piece "Firestone Symphony Orchestra"); William Daly, 1931 until his death in 1936; Alfred Wallenstein, 1936 until he left in 1943 to direct the Los Angeles Symphony Orchestra; Howard Barlow, from 1943. **ANNOUNCER:** Hugh James. **THEMES:** *In My Garden* and *If I Could Tell You*, by Mrs. Harvey Firestone.

The Voice of Firestone began as *The Firestone Hour*, and in a 24-year run was one of the prized musical shows of the air. Initially a series of popular music, show tunes, and Americana, *Firestone* found its true voice following an ugly incident between the sponsor and star male soloist. Tenor Franklyn Baur had angered rubber magnate Harvey Firestone by demanding a $1,000 fee to sing at a Henry Ford function in Dearborn. Firestone was embarrassed before notables including Herbert Hoover and Thomas Edison, and, according to Thomas A. DeLong, Baur was dismissed "the day his contract expired."

The Firestones were intimately involved with the radio show from beginning to end. Firestone appeared on the first broadcast; his son, Harvey Jr., was a frequent speaker, giving a series of talks on "the romance and drama of the rubber industry" in 1931–32. The departure of Baur and crooner Vaughn De Leath ushered in a new era, more serious fare from operatic stages. The series reached its peak in the late 1930s, when ratings indicated that seven to eight million people listened regularly. Throughout the 1940s the ratings were respectable if not spectacular, but the show lost ground steadily after the introduction of the TV simulcast in 1949. DeLong and others suggest that the small TV tube was too confining for such magnificent music; that, as television fare, *Firestone* was slightly stuffy and sometimes boring. When NBC wanted to reschedule the show in 1954, the Firestones objected, insisting on the Monday-at-8:30 timeslot that was then a tradition. NBC dropped it, but *Firestone* continued on ABC without missing a broadcast.

It remains one of the most fondly remembered shows of its kind, the vivid themes easily called to mind. *In My Garden*, written by the sponsor's wife, was first sung on the show by Richard Crooks in 1932 and became the weekly theme in 1936. In 1941, the melody was temporarily lost in an ASCAP ban: undaunted, Mrs. Firestone wrote a new one, *If I Could Tell You*, which was the opening theme for the duration and was instantly recognized as an identifying mark of the series. *In My Garden* returned as the closing theme at the end of the composers' dispute.

VOX POP, interviews, human interest, quiz; also known as *Sidewalk Interviews* (1936) and *Voice of the People.*

BROADCAST HISTORY: 1932, KTRH, Houston.

July 7–Sept. 29, 1935, Blue Network. 30m, Sundays at 7:30. Summer replacement for Joe Penner's *Baker's Broadcast*. Standard Brands and Fleischmann's Yeast.

Oct. 13, 1935–Sept. 23, 1939, NBC. 30m, Sundays at 2:30 until Jan. 1936; Tuesdays at 9, 1936–38; Saturdays at 9, 1938–39. Molle Shave Cream, 1935–38; Kentucky Club Tobacco, 1938–39.

Oct. 5, 1939–May 20, 1947, CBS. 30m, Thursdays at 7:30 for Kentucky Club, 1939–41; Mondays at 8 for Bromo Seltzer, 1941–46; Tuesdays at 9 for Lipton Tea, 1946–47. *Concurrent broad-*

cast: Aug. 8–Sept. 26, 1941, Blue Network, Fridays at 9 for Bromo Seltzer.

Oct. 1, 1947–May 19, 1948, ABC. 30m, Wednesdays at 8:30. American Express.

HOSTS: Parks Johnson and Jerry Belcher; Belcher replaced by Wally Butterworth in Oct. 1936; Butterworth replaced by Neil O'Malley in 1942; O'Malley replaced by Warren Hull soon thereafter. ANNOUNCERS: Ben Grauer, ca. 1935; Dick Joy, Roger Krupp. DIRECTORS: Rogers Brackett, John Bates, Herb Moss, etc.

Vox Pop was derived from the term "vox populi," meaning "popular sentiment" or "voice of the people." This was the premise of the long-running radio show: impromptu interviews with random passersby on location in hotel lobbies and on streetcorners.

It was initiated at KTRH, Houston, a few days before the 1932 presidential election. Parks Johnson and Jerry Belcher, ad salesmen, took portable microphones into the street to talk to people about the Hoover-Roosevelt race. The answers they got were spontaneous, sometimes humorous, occasionally hilarious. They continued this idea after the election and developed it into a running series. This mushroomed in popularity, got on the regional Southwest Broadcasting System, and came to the attention of a J. Walter Thompson talent scout, Richard Marvin. Marvin sold the show to Standard Brands as the summer replacement for Joe Penner: Johnson and Belcher were brought to New York, and, after a successful summer, the show went into the regular schedule.

The charm of *Vox Pop* was largely due to the agile interviewing abilities of the two hosts. Both were able to converse warmly with strangers and draw from them answers that were unexpected, witty, and delightful. One young woman, asked by Johnson what she wanted for Christmas, simply replied, "You." Johnson and Belcher discovered that the public was mostly uninhibited by the microphone, that people who would come on at all would say the darndest things to an interviewer who could set the proper playful tone.

In the questioning, they drew from the subject facts about his life. Personality was deepened through a series of guessing contests (how many spots are on the average leopard? . . . how broad is Broadway?), which allowed the interviewee to laugh at himself. The street locations were changed each week, to avoid causing traffic jams.

Reports of early discord between Johnson and Belcher were scotched, but in fact Belcher's tenure was brief. In 1936, Johnson emerged with ownership of the show, and Wally Butterworth became cohost. The microphones were soon moved indoors, to hotel lobbies. Though the emphasis was still on spontaneity, guest were sometimes lined up in advance, usually just a few minutes before air time. An alarm clock was set before each broadcast: when it went off on the air, the person being interviewed was given $5. The listening audience responded well to the unplanned nature of it: no one knew what would be said, and when a college professor decided that the tables should be turned and he should ask the questions, Johnson and Butterworth went along and struggled for the answers.

Vox Pop set up at the New York World's Fair, and in 1941 Johnson and Butterworth went to Central America, broadcasting from Mexico, Puerto Rico, and Cuba. In the later era, Warren Hull was master of ceremonies. Johnson's wife, Louise, was given $750 a week to buy gifts for the guests. She always shopped with local merchants, wherever the broadcast originated, and reporters marveled at her ability to buy hard-to-find items in the days of war shortages. She never dealt with black marketeers, she emphasized: "By the cost of merchandise and the availability of certain restricted commodities, she can smell 'black market' instantly," wrote one reporter. Her method was to arrive in town a few days early, "case" the stores, and do her shopping on the day of the broadcast. By then the guest list was complete, and she shopped with real people in mind. The guest list in this late era was prepared by producers who looked for certain character traits, and local people helped fill the demand.

THE VOYAGE OF THE SCARLET QUEEN, high adventure drama.

BROADCAST HISTORY: July 3, 1947–Feb. 14, 1948. Mutual. 30m, Thursdays at 8:30 through Nov.; Wednesdays at 10, Dec. 3–24; Saturdays at 9:30 A.M. from Jan. 10. CAST: Elliott Lewis as Philip Carney, master of the ketch *Scarlet Queen*. Ed Max as Mr. Gallagher. Support from Hollywood radio actors: William Conrad, Ben Wright,

John Dehner, etc. **SCORE:** Richard Aurandt. **PRODUCER:** James Burton. **WRITERS:** Gil Doud and Robert Tallman. **SOUND EFFECTS:** Ray Kemper, Bill James, Tom Hanley.

The *Scarlet Queen*, in this adventure scenario, was "the proudest ship to plow the seas." The show opened with the rousing sounds of the sea, blending into the sharp cry of the lookout in the crow's nest. Then the story would unfold, as told by the captain's entry in the ship's log. "Log entry, the ketch *Scarlet Queen*, Philip Carney, master. Position—three degrees, seven minutes north, 104 degrees, two minutes east. Wind, fresh to moderate; sky, fair. Remarks—departed Singapore after being guest at an unsuccessful wedding. Reason for failure—*The Winchester Rifle and the Ambitious Groom*." It was a creative way to introduce the title of the week's story, and all of them had colorful titles: *The Bubble Dancer and the Buccaneer, The Barefoot Nymph in the Mother Hubbard Jacket*, and the like. The closing too was filled with sea sounds, ship creaks, and the final entry in Carney's log: "Ship secured for the night. Signed, Philip Carney, master."

WALTER WINCHELL'S JERGENS JOURNAL, news and gossip.

BROADCAST HISTORY: May 12–Aug. 4, 1930, WABC-CBS. 15m, Mondays at 7:45. *Saks on Broadway—Speaker Walter Winchell.*

Aug. 30, 1931–Jan. 5, 1932, CBS. 15m, Tuesdays at 8:45. La Gerardine hair products. **STAR:** Walter Winchell. La Gerardine overlapped with Winchell's appearance on the 60m *Lucky Strike Dance Orchestra,* a long-running NBC series (1928–34), which he joined in progress in the fall of 1931. Winchell abandoned La Gerardine in Jan. 1932 to go exclusively with Luckies, and remained with the latter until Aug. 1932. Meanwhile, fellow columnist Ed Sullivan was persuaded to take over the La Gerardine show, helping Winchell obtain his release.

Dec. 4, 1932–Dec. 26, 1948, Blue Network/ABC. 15m, Sundays at 9:30, 1932–36, then Sundays at 9. *The Jergens Journal.* Jergens Lotion. **ANNOUNCER:** Ben Grauer.

Jan. 2, 1949–June 26, 1955, ABC. 15m, Sundays at 9. Kaiser-Frazer until mid-July 1949; Richard Hudnut, 1949–52; Gruen Watches, 1952–53; various sponsors, 1953–54; American Razor, 1954–55. **ANNOUNCER:** Richard Stark for Hudnut.

Sept. 18, 1955–March 3, 1957, Mutual. 15m, Sundays at 6. Trans World Airlines.

Although Walter Winchell was on the air before and after his *Jergens Journal* run, his 18-year association with Jergens Lotion made his name virtually synonymous with the product.

During his Jergens run, Winchell became the most important and powerful reporter in the nation. His radio show was often in the top ten, peaking on the Hooper scale at 33.1 in 1941–42. This, coupled with his syndicated newspaper column, gave him an influence in national affairs that was unprecedented then and has not been seen again. When he and Jergens parted company in midseason 1949, he was still packing a 25-point Hooper punch.

Winchell made his name as a reporter, but he was first of all a showman. His newscast was an act: he was an entertainer, too sloppy and careless to be taken seriously by so-called serious journalists, but far too powerful to ignore. In the same breath he could report the doings of nations and the most piddling snatches of Hollywood pillow talk. This he did in a stream of invective, clocked at 215 words a minute and underscored by the chattering keys of a telegraph "bug," which he himself manipulated. He sat at the Blue Network microphone in the classic pose of his day, the hard-bitten reporter with his hat on, his script held out in his left hand while, with his right, he jiggled the telegraph key.

Good evening, Mr. and Mrs. North America and all the ships at sea, let's go to press!— FLASH!—NEW YORK!—The funeral of Alice Brady, the stage and screen actress, who died last midnight, will be private . . .

Winchell was enormously entertaining to the common man, his harsh and staccato voice wrapped in a fearless facade. He saw himself as a "protector of little people," wrote Dickson

Hartwell in a 1948 *Collier's* profile. "Nobody browbeats a waiter in his presence." He took on Hitler, Congress, and the president, and he wasn't afraid to lambaste by name prominent Americans he suspected of a pro-Axis attitude. At various times he heaped scorn upon Huey Long, Hamilton Fish, Charles A. Lindbergh, Martin Dies, and the Ku Klux Klan. He sometimes referred to Congress as "the House of Reprehensibles," and he got in trouble with his sponsor and network (one of many such troubles) when he characterized as "damn fools" voters who had returned isolationists to office. Winchell was once called "the best reporter in the United States" by Arthur Brisbane, though, as Hartwell had it, "by most newspaper standards he is one of the worst. His repeated mistakes would shame a $25-a-week cub."

His vanity was legendary: "His egotism is so marked that only the rugged or the subservient can stay long in his company," wrote Hartwell. "He defines boredom as 'other people's conversation.' " What he had by the bucket was "an ability to make the commonplace vivid," but his ego kept him from realizing "that many of his cherished accomplishments are really trivial."

His training was nil: he matriculated on the stages of vaudeville; his education ended in the sixth grade. Winchell was born April 7, 1897, in New York City, By 1910 he was working at the Imperial Theater, where he, Jack Weiner, and George Jessel formed a trio of singing ushers. Gus Edwards took them on as part of his "Newsboys' Sextet," an act he worked for two years. He continued in vaudeville until 1917, when he joined the Navy, and he returned to the stage when his hitch was up.

His career as a reporter began in 1922, when he was hired by the *Vaudeville News* as a reviewer. He did occasional pieces for *Billboard*, and in 1924 advanced to the *New York Graphic*, where he began building his reputation. In 1929 he joined the *New York Daily Mirror*, taking on a column that was soon syndicated, read by millions for 30 years.

During this time he developed a network of sources and contacts that kept him at the top of his game for decades. "He has more people providing him with information than any press association has reporters," Hartwell would write years later, "yet he has never paid any of them." They ranged from cab drivers to press agents,

each so anxious to curry favor that they kept his phone ringing constantly. In his earliest days he combed New York's hotspots, but as his fame grew he found this unnecessary. More stories came to him than he could ever fit into a newspaper column or a quarter-hour radio broadcast. His unofficial headquarters was a table at the Stork Club, where he could be seen in conversation with all types of tipsters and newsmakers. He became friends with J. Edgar Hoover and had his car fitted with a police radio, a siren, and a flashing red light. Sometimes he beat the police to holdup scenes.

His radio show was brisk and never lacked color. Initially seen as a gossip show, it gradually broadened its scope until Winchell the grade school dropout was routinely commenting on affairs of state. In the early '30s he got on Hitler's case, terming the Nazis "thugs, racketeers, and hoodlums." His slang expression for them was "Ratzis." Winchell gloried in slang: his show was peppered with amusing phraseology that "Mr. and Mrs. North America" had never heard but could easily decipher. Among such Winchellisms were "sexcellent," "rendezwoo," "cinemadorable," and "applaudience appeal." The word "renovate" was understood to mean a couple contemplating divorce. Winchell also described such people as "on the verge," "phfft," or "curdled," while those contemplating marriage were said to be "that way," "Adam-and-Eveing," or "on the merge." The marriage ceremony was termed getting "welded," "sealed," or "middle-aisled," and the imminent arrival of a child meant the couple was "infanticipating" or about to be "storked."

A movie was a "moom pitcher" to Winchell; Broadway was "the hardened artery." The word "passion" came out "pash," legs were "shafts," a Jew was "Joosh," and a thug was a "Chicagorilla." So influential was Winchell by 1933 that Funk & Wagnalls placed him among the top ten creators of current slang. H. L. Mencken devoted a full page to him in *The American Language*. He claimed to be the first to use the term "makin' whoopie," pointing to a piece he wrote for the *New York Graphic* in 1924. Lexicographers quibbled, but Mencken noted that the "verb-phrase, *to make whoopie*, seems to be his." An amusing aside to all this scholarly phrasemaking was the fact that Winchell got into it because of his uncertainty over spelling and proper usage. "When I'm in doubt about a word, I distort it purposely," he told *Radio Guide* in 1935. This led to such sentences as "He always wanted to be a circus pafawmer, but wound up in vaudeville, poor fellah" and the frequent use of "frinstance" and "ciggies" (cigarettes) in his column. Later, slang was used as a cover on stories that were feared to be legally troublesome. To say that a movie couple was divorcing might lead to court if it happened not to be true, but reporting that they were "on the verge" was both colorful and safer, when a knowing audience relieved him of the obligation of saying what the curdled couple was on the verge of doing.

He awarded verbal "orchids" to the "rare and precious" people of his time and "scallions" to the "annoying people" who "smell terrible and make you cry." President Roosevelt, Toscanini, Will Rogers, and Ruth Etting got orchids; scallions were issued to Hitler, "comedians who use old jokes," "sponsors who try to run the broadcast," and radio censors. Winchell battled censorship throughout his radio career. His scripts were combed by an attorney and by representatives of the sponsor and the network, who searched for libelous statements, errors, and grounds for FCC action. It was, in fact, their worry, for Winchell had a clause in his contract holding him harmless from libel.

His preshow conferences usually resulted in a "friendly fight," and sometimes in fights that weren't so friendly. "He has little patience with legal bottlenecks when he is convinced of the justice of his cause," wrote William Tusher in *Radio Mirror*. His style was to hit hard in the best tradition of crusading journalism, then beat a hasty retreat if (as was often the case) he was then proved wrong. He quoted liberally from newspapers, then couched his retractions in terms that made it appear that a newspaper was at fault. His sponsor was not amused at his "damn fools" broadcast of Jan. 31, 1943, and the agency took a harder line in preshow conferences thereafter. Winchell found his gushing praise of Roosevelt and his most caustic digs at congressmen being deleted. He cried foul and threatened to quit: the agency said it was simply protecting its client by not offending the 22 million people who voted Republican in Roosevelt's tradition-breaking third term. And the network, though reluctant to admit it, fretted that Winchell's open disdain for Congress might make lawmakers hostile to pending radio legislation.

But Winchell probably won as many of these battles as he lost. Ironically, many of the items the censors would delete were the very ingredients that boosted sales and sent the show into the heady company of Jack Benny, Bob Hope, and *Fibber McGee and Molly*.

Winchell was long remembered for vendettas real and imagined. He waged a friendly feud with Ben Bernie throughout the '30s. Al Jolson, formerly a pal, threw a punch at him after a disagreement. This did little or no damage, but he took out a permit for a gun after being roughed up by men he thought were either enemy agents or sympathizers of Bruno Richard Hauptmann. He admitted that many of the shows and books he plugged had been reviewed by his wife. ("So what?" he asked. "She hasn't been wrong yet.") He was said to be sensitive to criticism, yet he often quoted his critics on the air. His values, wrote Hartwell, "come in shades of black and white . . . his mind is happily uncomplicated by doubts."

In the '40s he took up the drumbeat against the Red menace. "Nothing is more important to him today than warning against the peril of an attack by Russia," wrote William Tusher in 1948. His admiration for Roosevelt did not extend to Harry Truman, and he became a staunch supporter of Red-hunting Sen. Joseph McCarthy. The sphere of his influence now included "Mr. and Mrs. North and South America," and his bulletins were still punctuated by furious bursts of telegraph activity. Real radio operators complained that Winchell's tappings were meaningless, but attempts to legitimize them with professional telegraphers were not successful. "They were too slow," Winchell told a reporter. "Besides, it stimulates me to do it myself."

After his retirement from radio, Winchell was active in television (a *Walter Winchell Show* on ABC, 1952–55, and on NBC in late 1956; and *The Walter Winchell File*, ABC, 1957–58 and syndicated later in 1958). He narrated *The Untouchables*, an ABC gangster melodrama, 1959–63, and died in Los Angeles, Feb. 20, 1972.

WALTZ TIME, traditional music.

BROADCAST HISTORY: Sept. 27, 1933–July 16, 1948, NBC. 30m, Wednesdays at 8:30; Fridays at

9, Dec. 1933–Oct. 1945; then Fridays at 9:30. Sterling Drugs for Phillips Milk of Magnesia. **SO-LOISTS:** Frank Munn, the "golden voice of radio," with Bernice Claire, Lucy Monroe, Vivienne Segal, Mary Eastman, Evelyn MacGregor. Lois Bennett, etc. **ORCHESTRA:** Abe Lyman. **PRO-DUCERS:** Frank and Anne Hummert.

Like the other Hummert musical offerings (*American Album of Familiar Music, Manhattan Merry-Go-Round, Hammerstein Music Hall*, etc.), *Waltz Time* had a melodious, flowing, highly traditional musical mix. The ballads were richly sentimental, with such staples as *I Love You Truly* and *Harbor Lights* filling the cards. Among the favorites sung by Frank Munn were *Rose in Her Hair, Diane*, and *Afraid to Dream*. Munn, who was heard on other Hummert shows, was paired with female vocalists from the same shows. He carried many of the *Waltz Time* broadcasts ca. 1939–41 as the lone vocalist. Later he starred with Evelyn MacGregor.

WANTED, crime documentary.

BROADCAST HISTORY: July 7–Sept. 29, 1950, NBC. 30m, Fridays at 10. **HOST-PRODUCER-DIRECTOR:** Walter McGraw. **NARRATOR:** Fred Collins. **MUSICAL DIRECTOR:** Morris Mamorsky.

Wanted attempted to one-up *Dragnet* by using real names and the actual voices of victims, friends, and relatives of the criminal. The police officers working the cases were likewise real. It was billed as "the program that brings you for the first time on the air a nationwide manhunt in action." Nothing was changed, listeners were assured: "No one is protected." But its main weakness was what had been touted as its strength: the "real life" people were too obviously reading and stammered too much.

WARNER BROTHERS ACADEMY THEATER, dramatic film adaptations.

BROADCAST HISTORY: April 3–June 26, 1938, 30m studio transcriptions, issued as a package with Gruen Watch commercials and syndicated by the TransAmerica Broadcasting System.

A showcase for developing stars enrolled in Warner's "Academy of Acting" (founded 1933). WB films were given prolific plugs, and

top stars were brought onstage after the plays to chat with such newcomers as Ronald Reagan and Carole Landis.

WAY DOWN EAST, soap opera.

BROADCAST HISTORY: 1936–37, 15m, transcribed syndication. **CAST:** Agnes Moorehead and Van Heflin.

"The sequel, as written by us, to the great stage and screen melodrama"; most directly derived from the 1935 20th Century Fox film, but with roots in the 1889 play by Lottie Blair Parker. A long run of 160-plus chapters exists, giving a good impression of 1930s production.

WAY DOWN HOME, musical drama, based on the life of James Whitcomb Riley.

BROADCAST HISTORY: Sept. 26–Nov. 14, 1937, Blue Network. 30m, Sundays at 1:30 (later at 2:30). **CAST:** Willard Farnum as James Whitcomb Riley, the child; Gene Arnold setting it in adult perspective, reading the poetry in Riley's grown-up voice. Supporting cast: Isabel Randolph, Phil Lord, Laurette Fillbrandt, Fred Sullivan. **WRITER:** Howard McKent Barnes.

July 10–Sept. 11, 1938, Blue. 30m, Sundays at 1:30. **CAST:** Willard Farnum and Gene Arnold as James Whitcomb Riley, child and adult, respectively. Betty Caine as the "feminine lead." **NAR-RATOR:** Carlton Brickert. **DIRECTOR:** Gordon Hughes. **WRITER:** Howard McKent Barnes.

Way Down Home covered the boyhood of James Whitcomb Riley and his emergence as a rustic Indiana poet, one of the best-loved voices of middle-America. The early episodes dealt with Riley's unhappiness as a child, when his father—a stern lawyer—determined that his son would enter the legal profession and not become an idle dreamer. The story followed Riley through his "one and only love affair," his journeys with medicine shows, and his early career as a writer. Notable among the readings was the story of "Tradin' Joe, the feller who don't sleep with both eyes shet."

The original series was so successful that it was returned the following summer by popular demand (it is not known at this writing if these were new stories or repeats). Both series began under the title *Back Home* and changed to *Way Down Home* after a couple of broadcasts.

WE ARE ALWAYS YOUNG, soap opera.

BROADCAST HISTORY: March 3–Nov. 21, 1941, Mutual. 15m, weekdays at 1. CAST: William Janney as Gary Haven. Joe Laurie Jr. as Sniffy. Pert Kelton as Lolita. Joseph Granby as Mead Connors. Also: Linda Watkins, Margalo Gilmore, Jessie Royce Landis. ANNOUNCER: Len Sterling. PRODUCER-DIRECTOR: Robert Shayon. WRITERS: Ashley Buck; Nicholas Cosentino.

Raymond William Stedman describes this obscure serial as the story of "a serious composer working as a cab driver" while awaiting his big break—publication.

WE CARE, dramatic anthology.

BROADCAST HISTORY: Jan. 4, 1948–Sept. 22, 1949, ABC. 15m, Sundays at 10:45; later Thursdays at 10:30; gaps in continuity. HOST: Douglas Fairbanks Jr., then chairman of the "Share Through Care Committee." CAST: Hollywood stars (Vincent Price, etc.). DIRECTOR: William P. Rousseau. PRODUCER: Don Sharpe. MUSIC: Rex Koury.

An appeal for the non-profit food agency CARE. Complete stories with a weekly plea for aid to hungry people in war-torn Europe.

WE DELIVER THE GOODS, tales of the U.S. Maritime Service in wartime.

BROADCAST HISTORY: Summer 1944, CBS, possibly regional. Sundays. HOST: Howard Culver, "your Maritime narrator." ANNOUNCER: Bosun's Mate Second Class Sam Brandt. VOCALISTS: Chief Petty Officer Ray Buell and Ship's Cook Joe Sylva. PRODUCER: Del Castillo.

Stories of maritime heroism, aired from the training station at Santa Catalina Island, with seamen filling the roles; Culver's reading of true adventure stories was the highlight, and often real heroes were brought to the microphone to tell their stories.

WE LOVE AND LEARN, soap opera, spanning 15 years in irregular runs under three titles.

BROADCAST HISTORY: 1941–42, transcribed 15m syndication titled *As the Twig Is Bent*, heard on some Mutual–Don Lee stations for a year beginning in March 1941. CAST: Barbara Terrell as Andrea Reynolds. Henry M. Neely as a philosophical janitor at Beechmont School. George Coulouris as the chairman of the school board. Effie Palmer as the difficult and unsympathetic principal.

April 6, 1942–March 31, 1944, CBS. 15m, weekdays at 2:30. *We Love and Learn*. General Foods. Also: April 3–Sept. 29, 1944, NBC, 15m, weekdays at 5:15. CAST: Joan Banks as Andrea Reynolds. Louise Fitch as Andrea as of mid-1944. Betty Worth also as Andrea. Frank Lovejoy as her husband, Bill Peters. Mitzi Gould as Andrea's friend, Taffy Grahame. Bill Podmore as Harrington the butler. Grace Keddy as Mrs. Van Cleve. Juano Hernandez as Mr. Bones.

June 28, 1948–March 23, 1951, NBC. 15m, weekdays at 11:15 A.M., 1948–49; at 11 A.M., 1949–50; at 12:45, 1950–51. *We Love and Learn*. Sweetheart Soap and Blue-White Flakes. CAST: Cliff Carpenter as Jim Carlton. Sybil Trent as Thelma, his wife. Charme Allen as Mother Carlton. Ann Thomas as the Carltons' friend Dixie.

1955–56, transcribed 15m syndication as *The Story of Ruby Valentine*: the old scripts recast and revised. CAST: Juanita Hall, Ruby Dee, Viola Dean, Earl Hyman. WRITER-PRODUCER: Don Becker.

In its original 1941 syndication (then known as *As the Twig Is Bent*), this was the story of a young teacher, Andrea Reynolds, who arrived in the town of Beechmont and found herself the subject of vicious gossip. The small-minded citizens resented her "big-town college ideas," and she became alarmed to learn that her predecessor had left in a cloud of scandal.

In the early network run, Andrea had left the small town for the hustle of New York. There she met husband-to-be Bill Peters. After a four-year absence, the 1948 run had shifted its focus to Jim and Thelma Carlton. Jim was an irresponsible mamma's boy, and mamma wanted to wreck his marriage. In its final incarnation, as *The Story of Ruby Valentine*, the setting was moved to a Harlem beauty parlor, with an all-black cast.

WE, THE ABBOTTS, soap opera.

BROADCAST HISTORY: Oct. 7, 1940–April 3, 1942. 15m, CBS, weekdays at 4:15 for Best Foods (Nucoa Margarine and Hellman's Mayonnaise) until May 30, 1941; NBC, weekdays at 5:30 for the

same sponsor beginning June 2. **CAST:** John Mc-
Intire and Betty Garde as John and Emily Abbott.
Ethel Everett also as Emily. Cliff Carpenter and
Audrey Egan as their children, twins Jack and Barbara. Betty Jane Tyler and Betty Philson as their
other daughter, Linda. Dean Harens as Arthur Anderson. Ralph Dumke as Willie Tompkins, a friend
of the Abbotts. **WRITER:** Bess Flynn.

We, The Abbotts was a typical daytime melodrama of an average family trying to make ends
meet in a small town, Middledale. John, the father, worked as an editor of a house organ, where
he sometimes got in trouble with the company
for championing workers' rights. Wife Emily
was manager of a school cafeteria, a position she
relinquished to volunteer as a defense worker.
The conflicts of 1941 involved the tightness of
money and Barbara's intention to marry Arthur
Anderson. Son Jack was a radio actor; Linda, at
10, was the "baby" of the family.

WE, THE PEOPLE, human interest.

BROADCAST HISTORY: Oct. 4, 1936–May 16,
1937, Blue Network. 30m, Sundays at 5. Calumet
Baking Soda.
   Oct. 7, 1937–Oct. 25, 1949, CBS. 30m, Thursdays at 7:30, 1937–38; Tuesdays at 9, 1938–42;
Sundays at 7:30, 1942–44; Sundays at 10:30,
1945–47; Tuesdays at 9, 1947–49. Sanka Coffee,
1937–42; Gulf Oil, 1942–49.
   Nov. 4, 1949–Jan. 25, 1951, NBC. 30m, Fridays
at 8:30, 1949–50, then Thursdays at 9:30. Gulf Oil.
HOST: Phillips H. Lord, 1936–37; Gabriel Heatter,
1937–1940s; Milo Boulton by 1944; Dwight Weist
by 1948; Dan Seymour, 1949. Also: Burgess Meredith, Eddie Dowling. **ORCHESTRA:** Oscar
Bradley (for Gulf Oil). **CREATOR:** Phillips H.
Lord.

We, the People was a singular mix of humor,
pathos, tragedy, sentiment, Hollywood glamour,
and old-fashioned melodrama. It was considered
a human interest show, but it dealt with such
bizarre occurrences that some of its stories would
have fit into Ripley's *Believe It or Not* (Ripley,
in fact, was one of its major competitors for stories).
   It began as a sketch on *The Rudy Vallee Hour*
in 1936 and became so popular that it quickly
spun into a regular series. *Time* called it "anybody's and everybody's soapbox," where the

strangest variety "of human odds and ends have
said their pieces." Subjects ranged from the wife
of slain gangster Dutch Schultz to the postmaster
of Santa Claus, Ind. There was a young girl who
wanted to overcome the restriction of her iron
lung and dance again; the parents of a 12-year-
old kidnap victim; a woman 119 years old who
recalled her days in slavery before the Civil War.
Along with the obscure came the famous: Jack
Benny and Mary Livingstone, hamming it up on
their 20th anniversary; Joe Louis discussing pre-
fight strategy; Eleanor Roosevelt and Lauritz
Melchior.
   But the best stories came from unknowns. Dr.
Harvey Warren told how he'd founded the Suicide Club, whose membership consisted of 6,000
people who had all attempted suicide. Gus Lang-
ley described his wrongful conviction, death sentence, and near-execution, his final reprieve
coming 25 minutes before he was to sit in the
electric chair. One of the most-discussed stories
was that of "Mr. X," a man of about 70 who
had been living in the Mississippi State Hospital
for about eight years with acute amnesia: his
emotional plea for help drew more than 1,000
replies, including one from his brother and sister
in Alabama. Then there was Mrs. Franklin
McCall, who told how desperate poverty had
driven her husband to kidnap a 5-year-old boy
in Florida: the boy died; the husband waited on
death row. And occasionally there was an O.
Henry twist, as in the story of the man who had
saved a woman from jumping off a bridge and
now wanted to find her because she had also
saved him—he too had come to the bridge to
jump.
   But while unknowns were the show's greatest
assets, they were also its weakest links. Their
stories were scripted, and few could read with
even a touch of competence. And on several occasions the show was hoaxed, leading the producing agency, Young and Rubicam, to install
an elaborate system of checks before allowing
anyone on the air.

WEEKDAY, interviews, features, and a "bit of
everything."

BROADCAST HISTORY: Nov. 7, 1955–July 27,
1956, NBC. Weekdays from 10:15 A.M. to 6 P.M.

Launched after the success of NBC's weekend
potpourri, *Monitor, Weekday* featured four hosts

grouped in two pairs—Margaret Truman teamed with Mike Wallace; Martha Scott together with Walter Kiernan. There were cooking tips, mini-dramas, and talk with such personalities as Goodman and Jane Ace and Jimmy Durante.

WELCOME, TRAVELERS, interviews; human interest.

BROADCAST HISTORY: June 30, 1947–July 8, 1949, ABC. 30m, weekdays at noon. Procter & Gamble.

July 11, 1949–Sept. 24, 1954, NBC. 30m, weekdays at 10 A.M. Procter & Gamble.

HOST: Tommy Bartlett. **CREATORS:** Les Lear, Tommy Bartlett. **DIRECTOR:** Bob Cunningham.

Welcome, Travelers bore a superficial resemblance to *We, The People* in that both were interview shows dealing with dramatic human interest. But *Travelers* was a far more spontaneous daytime show, and the fare was far less agonizing.

It grew out of Tommy Bartlett's contention that travelers are more prone to "open up" and talk to strangers than to people in their home towns. With a staff of scouts, Bartlett began canvassing trains coming into Chicago, searching for interesting-looking travelers. Once the show was established, the broadcast was conducted from the Hotel Sherman: the scouts continued meeting trains and buses, and some became highly skilled at spotting out-of-the-ordinary people.

The audience of about 1,000 daily was also comprised of travelers, who obtained tickets to the show at booths set up in stations and airports. The guests were mostly as uninhibited as Bartlett hoped they'd be. They told of their loves, of small-town life, of wrenching separations from loved ones, and in the end were showered with gifts. They were introduced in the style of a train barker.

WENDELL HALL, THE RED-HEADED MUSIC MAKER, novelty music.

BROADCAST HISTORY: March 1922, KYW, Chicago.

1923–27, tours of stations, including WEAF, New York.

1929–30, CBS. *The Majestic Hour.*

1930, NBC from Chicago. 26 weeks beginning in April. *The Sign of the Shell.* Shell Oil.

1931, NBC. *The Pineapple Picador.*

1933–35, NBC. 15m, Sundays at 7:45. Fitch Shampoo;

June 25, 1935–Jan 14, 1936 Blue Network. 15m, three a week at 11:15 until Oct. 1935, then Tuesdays at 10. Fitch Shampoo.

1936–37, CBS. See COMMUNITY SING, with Milton Berle.

Wendell Hall was radio's first big star. He put together the first national tour of radio stations, which took him to every significant station in America between 1923 and 1927. This had the same effect as if he had appeared on a network four or five years ahead of everyone else, and by 1924 he was nationally famous.

He began on KYW, Chicago, plugging sheet music and singing to his own xylophone accompaniment. Soon he was using the ukelele, and it was on this instrument, as the Red-Headed Music Maker, that he became best known. His KYW appearances resulted in a dramatic increase in the sales of his music, and he worked out a routine that incorporated comic patter and in 1923 wrote the song—*It Ain't Gonna Rain No Mo'*—that became his trademark. He "was the first to play radio stations the way others had played theaters," wrote F. G. Fritz. "In June 1923, driving his father's automobile with built-in sleeping quarters, he set out on his first radio tour." This reached more than 30 stations, logging 5,000 miles in four months.

He coordinated his efforts with local music stores, selling vast amounts of sheet music wherever he played. He was welcomed into stations everywhere, sometimes playing for several hours a night. He appeared on WEAF, then signed on with *The Eveready Hour* in 1924. He toured for *Eveready*'s sponsor, the National Carbon Company, extending his tours to stations far outside the reaches of the small network then linked with WEAF.

Ironically, it was the coming of national networks that caused his career to flag. Suddenly the air was full of major vaudeville acts—Eddie Cantor, Ed Wynn, Will Rogers, then Jack Benny, Fred Allen, and others who would shape radio comedy-variety—and Hall couldn't compete.

WENDY WARREN AND THE NEWS, soap opera with newscast.

BROADCAST HISTORY: June 23, 1947–Nov. 12, 1958, CBS. 15m, weekdays at noon. General Foods (Maxwell House Coffee or Jell-O), 1947–54; Procter & Gamble and others thereafter. **CAST:** Florence Freeman as Wendy Warren, a reporter for the *Manhattan Gazette* who also did a daily newscast on the radio. Lamont Johnson as Mark Douglas. Les Tremayne as Gil Kendal. Rod Hendrickson as Sam Warren. Tess Sheehan as Aunt Dorrie. Horace Braham and Jane Lauren as Charles and Adele Lang. Anne Burr as Nona Marsh. Announcer Hugh James as announcer Bill Flood. Actual CBS newscast by Douglas Edwards. **DIRECTORS:** Tom McDermott, Hoyt Allen, Don Wallace, Allan Fristoe, etc. **WRITERS:** Frank Provo and John Pickard.

Wendy Warren was a "cunning trap" set by CBS to snare listeners who might not otherwise be caught dead listening to a soap opera. Scheduled in the newsy timeslot of high noon, it opened each day with three minutes of straight news read by highly respected and well-known working CBS newsman Douglas Edwards. At the end of this stint, Edwards would ask, "Now Wendy, what's the news today for the ladies?"

The fictitious Wendy would then give her "news reports from the women's world," telling about the new "rainbow cottons" just in from St. Louis, or some such. This entire intro took less than four minutes. A commercial was then followed by a dramatized scene, as Wendy stepped out of her control booth and into the world of big-time soap opera.

Unburdened by Edwards and the news of the day, Wendy's dilemmas were the usual stuff of daytime. *Radio Life* found "two loves, a demanding career and the menacing, sheathed sarcasms of another woman." The first lover was Mark Douglas, childhood sweetheart and erstwhile fiancé. They had been separated by the war, and, though Wendy had helped him escape from behind the Iron Curtain, she was disconcerted when a Polish refugee arrived claiming to be his wife. This left an opening for the second lover, Gil Kendal, millionaire publisher, and a bit of a clod to all but Wendy. Kendall was manipulated by Nona Marsh, who swore that she alone would have him, and by the evil land developer Charles Lang. Lang's equally evil wife, Adele, was flirting with Mark, snaring him in her web.

Above it all was Wendy's father, Sam Warren, crusading editor of the *Clarion*, in the tiny Connecticut town of Elmdale, where Wendy grew up. Helping make it a home was Aunt Dorrie, Sam's selfless and devoted sister. Eventually Wendy married Gil, but the road was not smooth, before or after.

WHAT MAKES YOU TICK?, quiz.

BROADCAST HISTORY: June 6–Aug. 29, 1948, Mutual. 30m, Sundays at 5:30. Summer show for *Quick as a Flash*. Helbros Watches. **HOST:** John K. M. McCaffrey. **ANNOUNCER:** Cy Harrice. **CREATOR:** Addison Smith. **PSYCHOLOGISTS:** Dr. Leon Arons and Sydney Roslow.
　　Sept. 20–Dec. 20, 1948, ABC. 15m, weekdays at 11:45 A.M.; then, Dec. 27, 1948–July 8, 1949, CBS. 15m, weekdays at 2:45. Procter & Gamble. **HOST:** John K. M. McCaffrey.
　　Sept. 23, 1950–March 31, 1951, ABC. 30m, Saturdays at 9. **HOSTESS:** Gypsy Rose Lee.

On this show, the contestant was quizzed about that most elusive subject—himself. Guests were asked to rate themselves on jealousy, tolerance, and generosity, then submit to a public analysis by a pair of psychologists. Creator Addison Smith got the idea by asking himself the question that became the title.

WHAT WOULD YOU HAVE DONE?, game show.

BROADCAST HISTORY: Jan. 26–July 17, 1940, Blue Network. 30m, Fridays at 9:30, later Wednesdays at 8:30. Energine. **HOST:** Ben Grauer, who described a dilemma to a contestant who was asked to tell how he would have handled it. **ANNOUNCER:** Jack Costello.

WHAT'S DOIN', LADIES?, audience show.

BROADCAST HISTORY: Ca. 1943–48, Blue/ABC, West Coast. 30m. **HOST:** Art Linkletter, until 1945; Perry Ward, 1945–46; Jay Stewart from ca. 1946.

This was once described as "*Breakfast at Sardi's* without Tom Breneman." But it did have Art Linkletter, who hosted from San Francisco at the beginning of his broadcasting career. Linkletter did his early shows from Hale Brothers Department Store, browsing among customers, poking through purses, being his nosy best. Practical jokes were common; running gags were developed. There was a "smallest victory garden" contest, and on Tuesdays and Fridays the feature was Barter Day, when women could bring all kinds of useless items for trade. Once a week, *What's Doin'* originated in Hollywood, when Linkletter had to fly down for his coast-to-coast *People Are Funny* broadcasts. With the arrival of *House Party* in 1945, a change of hosts was essential.

WHAT'S MY LINE?, game show.

BROADCAST HISTORY: May 20–Aug. 27, 1952, NBC. 30m, Tuesdays at 10, later Wednesdays at 8. Philip Morris.

Sept. 3, 1952–July 1, 1953, CBS. 30m, Wednesdays at 9:30. Philip Morris, 1952; Stopette, 1952–53.

HOST: John Daly. **PANELISTS:** Arlene Francis, Dorothy Kilgallen, Bennett Cerf, Hal Block. **PRODUCERS:** Mark Goodson and Bill Todman.

What's My Line? was the guessing game of occupations, beginning as a CBS-TV series Feb. 16, 1950, and moving to radio two years later. If the contestant answered "no" ten times during questioning by the panel, he won the game and a nominal amount of cash. The radio show was brief, but on television it sprawled across two decades, expiring Sept. 3, 1967.

WHAT'S MY NAME?, game show.

BROADCAST HISTORY: March 25, 1938–March 17, 1939, Mutual. 30m, Fridays at 8. Philip Morris. **HOSTESS:** Arlene Francis. **HOST:** Budd Hulick.

July 5–Sept. 27, 1939, NBC. 30m, Wednesdays at 9. Summer substitution for Fred Allen. Bristol Myers. **HOSTESS:** Arlene Francis. **HOST:** Fred Uttal.

Nov. 4, 1939–Aug. 16, 1940, NBC. 30m, Saturdays at 7 until March 1940, then Fridays at 9:30. Oxydol. **HOSTESS:** Arlene Francis. **HOST:** Budd Hulick.

July 6–Aug. 31, 1941, NBC. 30m, Sundays at 8. Summer replacement for Edgar Bergen. Chase and Sanborn. **HOSTESS:** Arlene Francis. **HOST:** John Reed King.

Jan. 6–June 30, 1942, Mutual. 30m, Tuesdays at 8. Fleischmann's Yeast. **HOSTESS/HOST:**

Only Arlene Francis listed in *Radio Guide*; no shows have been heard.

Feb. 21–June 27, 1943, NBC. 30m, Sundays at 10:30. Lydia Grey. **HOSTESS:** Arlene Francis. **HOST:** Budd Hulick.

June 3–Nov. 27, 1948, ABC. 30m, Thursday at 9, initial broadcast; then Saturdays at 9:30. General Electric. **HOSTESS:** Arlene Francis. **HOST:** Ward Wilson; Carl Frank beginning in Aug.

Feb. 5–July 30, 1949, ABC. 30m, Saturdays at 11:30 A.M., later at 12:30.

What's My Name? was one of radio's earliest cash giveaway shows. The fact that the cash was only $10 (diminished by $1 with each wrong guess) does not pale the ominous trend—the moneyed quiz was here to stay.

Arlene Francis was the common denominator throughout its long, sporadic life. A quick-witted and sexy-sounding "femcee," she was paired with various male hosts, brightening the moment with flippant chatter. The quiz was built around prominent people, with contestants trying to guess identities from clues given by the two hosts.

The duo would often impersonate their subjects, adding to the fun even when the impersonations fell flat. The first and most frequent male opposite was Budd Hulick, who had recently dissolved his comedy partnership with F. Chase Taylor (*Stoopnagle and Budd*).

Ed Byron, who later made his reputation with crime shows, was the original producer; John Gibbs later produced across several runs. The show retained its emphasis on fun rather than cash through the war years, but the 1948 revival dispensed larger jackpots. Now the prizes were $100 for first-clue guesses; $50 for a second-clue guess; $25 for third. A jackpot question at the end was worth $500, with the prize going into the next week's pot if nobody won. The contestant was given two shots at it: if he missed the first time, he was allowed to call anyone in his "old hometown" for help. Winners split the pot with the friend back home. Among the clues was a scrambled voice of the subject in question. Shades of Miss Hush.

WHAT'S NEW?, variety.

BROADCAST HISTORY: Sept. 4, 1943–Feb. 26, 1944, Blue Network. 60m, Saturdays at 7. RCA. **HOST:** Don Ameche; Cecil B. DeMille in Ameche's absence. **GUESTS:** Herbert Marshall, Lena Horne, Dinah Shore, etc.

Ameche focused on "a kaleidoscopic word-picture of what's going on in the world today via comedy, drama, and music." It aired from Hollywood, with cut-ins from New York and by armed forces personnel on shortwave around the world. Ameche was also featured in scenes from outstanding new plays, books, and films.

WHAT'S THE NAME OF THAT SONG?, musical quiz.

BROADCAST HISTORY: 1943–44, Don Lee Network, Fridays at 8:30 Pacific time; then Sept. 24, 1944–Dec. 16, 1948, Mutual, many brief 30m timeslots, its best a full season, 1944–45, Sundays at 4:30 for Knox Gelatin. **CREATOR-QUIZMASTER:** Dud Williamson. **QUIZMASTERS:** Bob Bence, upon Williamson's sudden death in May 1948; Bill Gwinn, Aug.–Dec. 1948. **PIANISTS:** Lou Maury, Frank Leithner, etc.

Contestants tried to guess song titles when staff pianists played three numbers in quick succession. They won $30 for getting all three; $15 for two; $5 for one. Additional money was awarded to contestants who could sing the songs.

Dud Williamson developed the idea while managing a station in Seattle. The show traveled, playing in huge theaters that seated up to 3,000 people and were formerly used for vaudeville shows.

WHEN A GIRL MARRIES, soap opera.

BROADCAST HISTORY: May 29, 1939–Aug. 22, 1941, CBS. 15m, weekdays at 2:45 until Aug. 1939, then at 12:15. Prudential Insurance.

Sept. 29, 1941–June 29, 1951, NBC. 15m, weekdays at 5. General Foods.

July 2, 1951–Aug. 30, 1957, ABC. 15m, late mornings, mostly at 10:45 (1952–55). General Foods, 1951–52; Carnation, 1954–55.

CAST: Noel Mills as Joan Field, daughter of high society, who, against her mother's wishes, married struggling lawyer Harry Davis. Mary Jane Higby as Joan Field Davis, from ca. late 1939 until the end, 1957. John Raby as Harry Davis, 1939–42, and again from 1946, with his return from the Army. Robert Haag as Harry Davis, beginning ca. 1942. Whitfield Connor and Lyle Sudrow also as Harry Davis. Marion Barney as Mother Davis. Ed

Jerome and Frances Woodbury as Joan's parents, Samuel Tilden Field and Stella Field. Irene Winston as Eve Stanley, née Topping. Michael Fitzmaurice, Richard Kollmar, Staats Cotsworth, Karl Weber, and Paul McGrath as Phil Stanley. Georgia Burke, a white actress, as Lily, the good-hearted and faithful Negro maid at the Davis house. William Quinn as Harry's brother Tom, who possessed neither Harry's brains nor his luck and remained a garage mechanic on the wrong side of the tracks. Joan Tetzel, Jone Allison, and Toni Darnay as Joan's sister Sylvia. John Kane as Chick Norris, the man Sylvia married. Dolores Gillen as Little Sammy, son of Joan and Harry. Jeanette Dowling as Irma Cameron, Joan's friend on the farm. Anne Francis and Rosemary Rice as Kathy, Irma's daughter. Eunice Hill and Helene Dumas as Betty McDonald, Harry's loving secretary. Joe Latham as Irma's friend John Hackett. **ANNOUNCERS:** Frank Gallop, Dennis King, Hugh James, Dick Stark, Charles Stark, George Ansbro, Wendell Niles, Don Gardiner. **ORGANISTS:** Rosa Rio, John Winters, Richard Leibert. **DIRECTORS:** Kenneth W. MacGregor, Tom McDermott, Oliver Barbour, Theodora Yates, Maurice Lowell, Warren Somerville, Scott Farnsworth, Tom Baxter, Art Richards, Olga Druce, Charles Fisher. **WRITER:** Elaine Carrington. **THEME:** *Drigo's Serenade*.

When a Girl Marries was the second major serial written by Elaine Carrington (the others were *Pepper Young's Family* and *Rosemary*). Heard at the same time for an entire decade (5 P.M., 1940s), it climbed steadily to the top of its field. It was the highest-rated soap opera for the years 1943–44, 1944–45, and 1946–47, and was pushing the leaders for most other seasons in that time.

It was the story of Joan and Harry Davis, young marrieds from opposite sides of the tracks, who fought for happiness against family interference, social differences, and gossip in the typical little soap opera town of Stanwood. Although the serial generally followed Carrington's preference for quiet family action, there were touches of insanity, murder, and other soapy staples over the long run.

It came to be known as "the tender, human story of young married life, dedicated to everyone who has ever been in love." Harry would rise above his poverty-ridden milltown background to become a successful attorney, but in the beginning he was just another law school graduate. His romance with Joan Field began at a party given by Joan's mother, Stella, to announce Joan's engagement to wealthy young playboy Phil Stanley. Harry arrived, seeking out Joan's father—prominent lawyer Samuel Tilden Field—in the hope of getting a clerkship in the old man's law office.

Little did Harry know that the elder Fields had been divorced for some time, that Sam Field was living in an apartment. Then he met Joan, and the effect was cataclysmic. Joan begged her mother not to announce the engagement, and Phil Stanley took the bad news with growing fury.

Thus began the war between the hads and the had-nots. Sam Field, a self-made man, sympathized with Harry: his own marriage had failed because of their different stations in life. Field was an advocate: "he means to see that Joan marries the man she wants in spite of Mrs. Field's ambitions." Mrs. Field (said *Radio Guide*) was "kind and generous to her friends, but feels that no one should enter their small circle without proper credentials." Meanwhile, Joan's friend Eve Topping had always wanted Phil Stanley for herself: Eve "plays a deep game and is not to be trusted," *Guide* advised.

Complicating things was Harry's soapy nature. His attributes (young, handsome, brilliant) were offset by problems (insecure, sometimes flighty, too willing to be exploited by the "other woman"). Harry got the job with Field, but continuing strife made his situation untenable. He did what all good men of soap did in such moments: quit without notice and "went away." Harry was "in love with Joan but knows he should not marry her," *Guide* informed. The year 1940 marked a turning point in the two storylines: Eve Topping and Phil Stanley "ran over to Brickton and got married"; Harry and Joan gave in to the inevitable and did the same. As Mary Jane Higby would write in her memoir, Carrington planted the seeds of five major conflicts, "all based on Joan's marriage to Harry Davis. Any of them could be made to sprout at the writer's convenience. . . . She drew endlessly on Harry's poverty in contrast to Joan's family and friends, his resulting inferiority complex, his secretary's love for him, the jealousy of Joan's ex-fiancé, the wildness of a girl who had won

the affection of Harry's young brother, and so on. In a sequence-plotted serial, a small group of permanent characters was subject to harassment from the outside. At the end of each sequence, all the evil-doers would vanish forever and a new set of malefactors would enter."

Carrington was the boss: like Irna Phillips and few others, she alone controlled the destinies of her creations, brooking little interferance from agency or sponsor. Higby recalled "the incident of the model village" in her memoir: The agency had gone to much expense to build a complete papier-mâché model of Stanwood. This, they explained to Carrington, would minimize geographical errors in her scripts. "A few weeks later, she had Harry say to Joan, 'Darling, I'm not getting ahead here in Stanwood. Let's move.' And move they did, out of the mythical town of Stanwood to the equally mythical, but uncharted, town of Beechwood."

There they settled on Foxmeadow Lane, in a semi-rural community where they made new friends, the dearest of whom were Irma Cameron and her children. With her second husband, Steve, Irma had bought a farm and, due to the unexplained deaths of many cattle, was in the process of going bankrupt. Old conflicts were worked in: Harry continued his insecure ways, and in one sequence Joan turned detective, got the goods on a killer, and cleared Harry of a murder charge. Harry's mother, Ann Davis, was the show's stock philosopher-in-residence, a virtual requirement for soap opera fare.

WHERE HAVE YOU BEEN?, game show.

BROADCAST HISTORY: Dec. 9, 1954–April 28, 1955, NBC. 25m, Thursdays at 9:30. MODERATOR: Horace Sutton. PANELISTS: Ernie Kovacs, Peggy McKay, Marc Connelly, and Harriet Van Horne, trying to guess the geographical history of contestants.

WHICH IS WHICH?, novelty quiz.

BROADCAST HISTORY: Oct. 25, 1944–June 6, 1945, CBS. 30m, Wednesdays at 9:30. Old Gold Cigarettes. HOST: Ken Murray. ORCHESTRA: Richard Himber. PRODUCER: Mel Williamson.

People from the audience were asked to guess from voices alone whether people behind a curtain were real celebrities or impersonators. Winners received $50; losers got $5, with the other $45 donated to the national war fund. The opener featured the real Basil Rathbone, the real Ted Lewis, the real Frank Morgan, and a young lady named Judie Manners, who did such a clever impersonation of Kate Smith singing *When the Moon Comes over the Mountain* that she fooled almost everyone.

THE WHISPER MEN, international crime melodrama.

BROADCAST HISTORY: Sept. 8, 1945–Feb. 2, 1946, Mutual 30m, Saturdays at various times (late morning to late night). **CAST:** Karl Weber as Max Chandler, "famous radio commentator and reporter whose assignments bring him into constant conflict with the 'Whisper Men,' international criminals who plot in secret to further their own sinister interests." Joseph Curtin also as Chandler. Kermit Murdock as Rod Buchanan, Chandler's sidekick. Support from New York radio: Ann Shepherd, Betty Caine, etc. **ORGAN:** Chet Kingsbury. **DIRECTOR:** Anton M. Leader.

WHISPERING JACK SMITH, popular songs.

BROADCAST HISTORY: Oct. 31, 1932–March 29, 1933, CBS. 15m, Mondays and Wednesdays at 8 Musterole. **BACKED BY:** Studio orchestra and "the Humming Birds."

Sept. 11–Dec. 1, 1934, CBS. 15m, Tuesdays, Thursdays, and Saturdays at 7:30.

Jan. 15–April 13, 1935, NBC. 15m, Tuesdays, Thursdays and Saturdays at 7:15. Ironized Yeast.

Whispering Jack Smith was a popular singer of the '20s whose vocal style was well described by his nickname. His best-known song was *Me and My Shadow*. He bore little vocal resemblance to the Jack Smith of the '40s, whose style was happy and upbeat.

WHISPERING STREETS, romance drama.

BROADCAST HISTORY: March 3, 1952–Nov. 25, 1960, ABC until 1959, then CBS. 20m, weekdays at 10:25 A.M., complete in each episode for General Mills and others, 1952–56; then 15m, weekdays at various times with stories completed in each five episodes. **HOSTESS-NARRATOR:** Gertrude Warner as Hope Winslow, fictional hostess who told the tales. Also as narrator: Cathy Lewis, Bette Davis (ca. 1958), Anne Seymour,

and, again, Gertrude Warner. **PRODUCER:** Ted Lloyd. **DIRECTORS:** Gordon Hughes, early ABC; Bruno Zirato Jr., CBS. *Writer:* Margaret Sangster, 1952.

THE WHISTLER, crime melodrama.

BROADCAST HISTORY: May 16, 1942–Sept. 8, 1955, CBS, West Coast regional network for Signal Oil, 1943–54; various 30m timeslots. (The sponsor, Signal Oil, operated only in the West. Only two attempts were made to split the show, with separate sponsorship in the East: July 3–Sept. 25, 1946, CBS, Wednesdays at 8 for Campbell Soups, substituting for Jack Carson; and March 26, 1947–Sept. 29, 1948, CBS, Wednesdays at 10 for Household Finance. Signal continued West Coast sponsorship throughout these times.) **CAST:** Bill Forman as the Whistler, mysterious teller of murder stories. Gale Gordon and Joseph Kearns as the Whistler in earliest shows. Marvin Miller as the Whistler while Forman was in the Army. Bill Johnstone as the Whistler, 1948. (Everett Clarke as the Whistler in a 1947 Chicago series.) Supporting casts from Hollywood's Radio Row, players who appeared so often they were known as "Whistler's children": Cathy and Elliott Lewis, Joseph Kearns, Betty Lou Gerson, Wally Maher, John Brown, Hans Conried, Gerald Mohr, Lurene Tuttle, Donald Woods, Gloria Blondell, John McIntire, Jeanette Nolan, Frank Lovejoy, Jeff Chandler, Joan Banks, Mercedes McCambridge. **ORCHESTRA:** Wilbur Hatch, who also composed the eerie mood music, as well as the theme that was whistled at the beginning and end. **WHISTLER:** Dorothy Roberts, who weekly for 13 years whistled the 37 notes (13 at the beginning, 11 leading into the story, 13 at the end); composer Hatch estimated that only one person in 20 could whistle the exact melody. **PRODUCER-DIRECTOR:** George Allen (from ca. 1944). **WRITER-PRODUCER:** J. Donald Wilson. **WRITERS:** Many freelancers; final scripts by Harold Swanton and Joel Malone. **ENGINEER:** Robert Anderson. **SOUND EFFECTS:** Berne Surrey; also, Gene Twombly, Ross Murray.

Despite its regional status for most of its days, *The Whistler* had one of radio's best-known crime-show formats and one of the longest runs. The signature ranks with radio's greatest, playing perfectly into the host's "man of mystery" role. Like the Shadow before him and the Mysterious Traveler yet to come, the Whistler was a voice of fate, baiting the guilty with his smiling malevolence.

The show opened with echoing footsteps and a lingering whistle, destined to become one of the all-time haunting melodies. The whistle got louder, then louder, finally blending with the orchestra in a high-pitched sting. Then the Whistler spoke:

I am the Whistler, and I know many things, for I walk by night. I know many strange tales, many secrets hidden in the hearts of men and women who have stepped into the shadows. Yes, I know the nameless terrors of which they dare not speak . . .

The unstated theme that ran the distance was "this could happen to you." *The Whistler* told stories of the everyday gone haywire, of common men driven to murder and then being tripped up in a cunning double-twist. These were not mysteries: the identity of the killer was never in doubt, from the first hint that the deed must be done until the moment when the killer trapped himself. The stories were told by the Whistler from the killer's viewpoint, the narration done in the unusual second-person, present tense. In the earliest days, producer J. Donald Wilson sometimes had the Whistler engage in open dialogue with the characters, the host playing Conscience, arguing with the murderer and goading him to the inevitable doom. The final act was not played out but was summarized by the Whistler in an epilogue as, like the Shadow, he laughed and sealed the killer's fate with a few terse lines of plot twist.

One of the first changes made by George Allen when he arrived as director in 1944 was to fully dramatize that closing turnabout. This was far more satisfying. The Whistler remained the great omniscient storyteller of the air, for the Shadow had long since become his own hero, and the Mysterious Traveler never packed quite the same punch. The voice was an unforgettable tenor, the message dripping with grim irony. *It all worked out so perfectly, didn't it, Roger*, he would coo, while listeners waited for the shoe to drop. This would come in "the strange ending to tonight's story," the little epilogue when the finger of fate struck, some fatal flaw of character or deficiency in the master plan that was so obvious that everyone had overlooked it.

The classic example was the story *Brief Pause for Murder*. A newscaster had decided to kill his wife. His alibi was perfect: he had cut a recording of his 10 o'clock newscast and had blackmailed a felon working at the station into playing it on the air at the exact moment of the murder. The chief of police would be listening; Roger had made sure of that. And with his wife's body still warm on the floor, the news came on as scheduled, in his own voice. *It all worked out so perfectly, didn't it, Roger? . . .* until the needle hit a flaw, and repeated . . . and repeated . . . and repeated . . .

Allen rotated his stock company depending on the needs of his scripts. He found Joe Kearns "adept at the goodbrain-plotting-his-moves type of part." Cathy and Elliott Lewis were both full-range players: Elliott "can sound like the average guy under pressure, and he builds emotion fast and holds it at a peak; Cathy has the same qualities as Elliott, the female counterpart of the average guy in her ability to sound absolutely genuine." Betty Lou Gerson he used in "parts that convey mental superiority; she's perfect for women who have catty, fencing dialogue." Wally Maher "makes a perfect blowtop." John Brown "brings all his fine comedy technique in pacing and dialogue into play," and Hans Conried was "a marvelous straight lead with tangents, a lead with two faces, a split personality." Gerald Mohr was used in parts requiring extreme sophistication or as an out-and-out thug. Lurene Tuttle, said Allen, "can be anything: she may change her performance on the air as she finds another facet of the character; she picks out the parts of her characterization that didn't ring right in rehearsal and corrects them." In the show *Death Sees Double*, Tuttle was given the role of identical twins—murderer and victim—to be done in identical voices. At one point she had six unbroken pages of double dialogue, using two microphones and letting distance and pitch tell the listener who was Mona and who was Martha.

As for the Whistler, his identity was a loosely kept secret for a decade. In November 1951, Bill Forman was introduced as the actor who had given voice to the character for so long. His was the perfect voice for a murder show that contained little on-mike violence. What there was was "velvet violence," murder by implication.

WHITEHALL 1212, crime drama, "the most baffling cases" of Scotland Yard.

BROADCAST HISTORY: Nov. 18, 1951–Sept. 28, 1952, NBC. 30m, Sundays at 5 through Feb., then at 5:30. **CAST:** All British performers, including Horace Braham, Harvey Hayes, Winston Ross, Lester Fletcher, and Patricia Courtleigh. **WRITER-DIRECTOR:** Wyllis Cooper. **RE-SEARCHER:** Percy Hoskins of the *London Daily Express.*

The cases on *Whitehall 1212* were introduced by Chief Superintendent John Davidson, caretaker of Scotland Yard's famed "Black Museum," who used some item from the museum as a wedge into the story. It opened with an alarmed woman ringing "Whitehall 1212" on the telephone and a crisp voice answering, "This is Scotland Yard."

The stories were true, "the plain unvarnished facts, just as they occurred." But the series was too much like *The Black Museum*, the Orson Welles transcription running concurrently on Mutual. Author Wyllis Cooper, tied to a set of facts, never got to exhibit the creativity that had served him well on *Quiet, Please* or the early *Lights Out.*

WHO SAID THAT?, panel show.

BROADCAST HISTORY: July 2–Sept. 24, 1948, NBC. 30m, Fridays at 8:30.
Jan. 2–April 17, 1949, NBC. 30m, Sundays at 10:30.
July 4–Aug. 22, 1950, NBC. 30m, Tuesdays at 8.
HOST: Robert Trout. **PANEL:** John Cameron Swayze, permanent member, with three or four guests. **PRODUCER:** Fred Friendly.

The object of *Who Said That?* was to match recent quotes with the people who said them. The quotes came from figures in every part of the news—from Churchill, Truman, and Einstein to Fred Allen, George Bernard Shaw, and Mae West. The key for producer Fred Friendly was assembling interesting panels. One was made up of H. V. Kaltenborn, Milton Berle, Henry Morgan, and Madge Evans; another of George S. Kaufman, Moss Hart, and Kitty Carlisle. The show had the capacity for wit and often produced it. Novelist Robert Ruark, identifying the post-election quote "I feel as if I had just been hit by a streetcar" as coming from Earl Warren, quipped on his own, "What Warren forgot to say was that the streetcar was named Desire."

A TV version premiered on NBC Dec. 9, 1948, and ran (with a change to ABC) until July 26, 1955. The TV soundtrack was used on radio in 1950.

THE WIFE SAVER, comic household hints.

BROADCAST HISTORY: 1929–32, WABC, WINS.
1932–33, Blue Network. 15m, three a week at 8 A.M.
1933–36, NBC. various early-morning 15m timeslots.
1936–37, NBC. 15m, twice a week at 11:45 A.M. for Sweetheart Soap, and CBS, 15m, twice a week at 9:30 A.M.
1938–39, NBC. 15m, Fridays at 9:45 A.M.
1939–41, Blue Network. 15m, Fridays at 8:15 A.M.
July 14, 1941–Feb. 26, 1943, Blue Network. 30m, weekdays at 3. *Prescott Presents.* **VOCAL-ISTS:** Diane Courtney, Joan Brooks. **VOCAL QUARTET:** "Hi, Lo, Jack, and the Dame." **OR-CHESTRA:** Jimmy Lytell; later, Irving Miller.
Postnetwork: 1940s, 1950s, WJZ, New York.
HOST: Allen Prescott as the Wife Saver.

The Wife Saver, as one critic quipped, offered "chatty enthusiasm for treating the clogged pores of a gas stove, the care of shoulder straps, skinning tomatoes, and making a sticky dresser drawer behave." This earned Allen Prescott reviews as a genuine comic and set his show apart from the usual ranks of his competitors.

Prescott got into radio in 1929, when he joined fellow *New York Daily Mirror* columnists Walter Winchell and Mark Hellinger at WABC, New York. Later, on WINS, he gave household hints with humorous commentary, a practice that led to *The Wife Saver.*

WILD BILL HICKOK, juvenile western adventure.

BROADCAST HISTORY: May 27, 1951–Dec. 31, 1954, Mutual. 30m, Sundays at 7, later at 4:30, sustained, until Dec. 30, 1951, then 25m, three a week at 5:30 for Kellogg Cereals.

July 17, 1955–Feb. 12, 1956, Mutual. 25m, Sundays at 5:30. Co-op advertising.

CAST: Guy Madison as Marshal Wild Bill Hickok. Andy Devine as his gravel-voiced sidekick, Jingles B. Jones. Hollywood regulars in support: Ralph Moody, Howard McNear, Charlie Lung, Forrest Lewis, Jack Moyles, Clayton Post, Paul Frees, Will Wright, Barney Phillips, Tyler McVey, etc. ANNOUNCER: Charlie Lyon. ORGAN: Richard Aurandt. DIRECTOR: Paul Pierce.

Radio's *Wild Bill Hickok* was basically the same format that was filmed and syndicated to television, ca. 1951–56—a familiar western scenario used by producers of *Hopalong Cassidy* and *The Cisco Kid* in which a strong, fearless hero is accompanied by a comic sidekick. The plots were simple; to hear one is to hear all. Wild Bill and Jingles would encounter some generic owlhoots: there'd be some fisticuffs, some gunplay, Jingles would wield his big belly as a weapon, Wild Bill would punch it out with the ringleader, and the heroes would emerge triumphant. Then it was back on their horses (Buckshot for Wild Bill; Joker for Jingles) and out on the trail for another week.

WILDERNESS ROAD, frontier serial adventure.

BROADCAST HISTORY: June 1, 1936–April 16, 1937, CBS. 15m, weekdays at 5:45. Returned in the same timeslot with some original cast members June 19, 1944–May 11, 1945. CAST: *1936*: Ray Collins as Daniel Boone. Lon Clark as Sam Weston. Vivian Block as Ann Weston. James McCallion, Jimmy Donnelly, Anne Elstner, Chester Stratton and Bill Johnstone as David, Peter, Mary, John and Simon Weston. *1944:* Lon Clark, Anne Elstner, Michael O'Day, Michael Dreyfuss, Edwin Bruce, Janet DeGore, Paul Ford. DIRECTOR: Richard Sanville 1936, 1944.

The story of the Westons, a fictitious frontier family, and their encounters with Daniel Boone, Indians, George Washington, and the British Army.

WILL ROGERS, comedy, variety, homespun philosophy.

BROADCAST HISTORY: April 6–June 22, 1930, CBS. 30m, Sundays at 10. *The Will Rogers Program.* House of Squibb.

April 30, 1933–July 8, 1934, Blue Network. 30m, Sundays at 9. *Gulf Headliners.* Gulf Oil. VOCAL GROUP: The Revelers Quartet. ORCHESTRA: Al Goodman.

Jan. 6–June 9, 1935, CBS. 30m, Sundays at 7:30. *Gulf Headliners.* Gulf Oil. VOCAL GROUP: The Revelers. ORCHESTRA: Frank Tours. The series continued, without Rogers, until Sept. 22, 1935.

Will Rogers, America's best-known country philosopher and humorist, distrusted radio. In the beginning, he wasn't quite sure he believed in it. "It's the bunk," he said on Detroit's WWJ in 1922. "I don't think you can hear. If it isn't the bunk, let me know whether you can hear me."

Rogers got postcards from all over the Midwest. Henry Ford had heard him. "He said he'd heard me very plainly on a set he'd built himself," Rogers told *Radio Digest* in October 1922. "He had it rigged up in an old cabin on his estate at Dearborn, near Detroit. Edsel, his boy, had a ready-made set at his home, but Henry stuck to the one he made himself for a few dollars." This early experiment, though it may have convinced Rogers of radio's scientific validity, did not assure him of his own future on the air. He avoided it for years, doing an occasional "visit" to such variety shows as *The Eveready Hour*, but refusing to be pinned down to a regular series.

The problem, he would later confess, was the microphone. You told a joke but it didn't laugh. "It is no secret that Mr. Rogers went into radio with his knees trembling," wrote Homer Croy in 1934. "All his life he had worked with audiences and had talked to them directly and gauged his talk according to their responses. In vaudeville there was not another actor who watched his audience as closely as he did, and now he was to step out where there was no response at all."

It was William S. Paley who finally convinced Rogers to do a weekly show. Paley had been wooing the E. R. Squibb Company of drug manufacturers as a potential account for his new Columbia Network. Squibb had turned down several proposals when Paley suggested Will Rogers. He had no idea at that point if he could deliver Rogers, but when Squibb said yes, he had to try. Rogers threw out the old argument of "the cold microphone," Paley recalled in his memoir: "I covered that immediately with a promise; I'd provide him with a studio audience . . . and he wavered.'' Rogers's wife, Betty, urged him to try it, and he did: for a fee of $72,000 (donated to charity, Paley later learned), Rogers would speak to a Sunday night audience on Squibb's behalf for a dozen weeks.

He was in typical form for his April 6, 1930, opener. ''Tonight all I know is this—just what I read in the papers during the day,'' he began. He had read about the disarmament conference, and he had an idea. Since Europe was so warlike, why not have the countries of the world trade places? Let Germany trade places with Mexico, France move to where Canada was, England switch with Cuba, and Japan with Hawaii. ''Now just surround us with those four gorillas and see how much disarmament we start hollering about. See if we want any disarmament.''

Americans loved this kind of humor in the spring of 1930. Rogers broadcast from KHJ, the CBS affiliate in Los Angeles. On his second show he talked about Charles Lindbergh; on his third, Herbert Hoover. Pity the poor president, he said: everybody wanted prosperity. ''Millions of people never had it under nobody, and never will have it under anybody, but they all want it under Mr. Hoover.'' On May 4, he talked about the Democrats (''the Lord's chosen people—He wanted to keep them exclusive, and that is why He made so few of them'') and their vanquished colorbearer, Gov. Alfred E. Smith. He gave thanks to Henry Ford on June 1 on behalf of horses: Ford had ''converted horses from a burden of toil and made them objects of curiosity.''

He went on the road for his last two shows, broadcasting from WNAC, Boston, on June 15, and WBBM, Chicago, June 22. In Chicago he talked about the city's wave of lawlessness and pretended to describe a gunbattle in the streets between the gangs of Bugs Moran and Al Capone. ''The coffin rights alone ought to run into half a million dollars here tonight.''

This was his ''trembling'' introduction to series radio.

It was easier after that. Gulf Oil signed him for the Blue Network in 1933. Initially he agreed to only seven shows, but his *Headliners* series stretched into two irregular seasons—irregular because Rogers was often absent, and at times the program was carried by supporting people or guest stars. Again, Rogers gave his fees to charity. He wired the Red Cross: ''I am going to

preach for seven Sunday nights for the Gulf Oil Company, and I am going to turn all the oil over to you. I ain't got nothing to lose but my voice, but I haven't lost it yet. The only one who can lose is Gulf—that is, if they don't sell enough gas to pay me for my gas. Don't thank me, thank the Gulf people, or, better yet, the radio listeners—they will be the sufferers.''

When the show returned for its second season, it was on CBS. *Radioland* reported that Rogers would be ''alternating appearances monthly with *Stoopnagle and Budd*.'' Charles Winninger was noted on one broadcast, without Rogers, in February; James Melton was a later guest. In the few shows available on tape, Rogers does the typical ''all I know is what I read'' routine. Croy, in the February 1935 *Radioland*, called him ''the biggest one-man show in radio. The rest of them— Eddie Cantor, Ed Wynn, Jack Pearl and so on— have a number of people with them. All Rogers has is his alarm clock.''

The alarm clock was yet another device to get him past the terrors of radio. His vaudeville routines had all been open-ended: he talked as long as he wanted, but on radio a five-minute overrun might throw a show into bedlam. So he had an alarm clock: if it went off during the broadcast, that meant he was rambling too much. This was a ''splendid gag,'' wrote Croy: it ''not only kept him from running over, but added novelty to the act.'' On the air, Rogers was his own master. There were no rehearsals; no one at the network even knew his subject, wrote Croy, unless he announced it in advance. ''One time in Chicago it romped into his head to impersonate Amos and Andy . . . also Lightnin' and Brother Crawford, and Ben Bernie. He likes to imitate Negroes and he does it well. He has an amazing method of working up his material. He does it by talking. He knows he is going to talk about Russia. His mind is full of the subject. He talks Russia to everybody he sees, and each time he tells about Russia he thinks of a new joke or a new line, and boy! does he remember them! He talks the subject for four or five days, slowly building it up as a director does a stage play, until he has it so well in hand that when Sunday night comes he ambles up to the microphone, puts his hands in his pockets, stands on one foot, screws up his face, and shouts. He has put none of it to paper. He carries it all in his head.''

The Gulf Headliners was still in progress in

the summer of 1935. James Melton, the Revelers, comic Lew Lehr, soprano Hallie Stiles, and the Pickens Sisters were filling in for Rogers, who had gone to Alaska with his friend, pilot Wiley Post. Rogers and Post were killed in an August 15 plane crash, and the nation grieved.

WINGS OF DESTINY, adventure drama.

BROADCAST HISTORY: Oct. 11, 1940–Feb. 6, 1942, NBC. 30m, Fridays at 10. Wings Cigarettes. CAST: Carlton KaDell and John Hodiak as pilot Steve Benton. Betty Arnold as Peggy Banning. Henry Hunter as Brooklyn, the mechanic. Also: Don Gordon, Art Pierce. WRITER: Mel Williamson.

Described by *Variety* as in the *Fu Manchu* "strain of fantastic happening." It aimed at an "air-minded generation, young enough to see only the excitement, old enough to smoke."

WINNER TAKE ALL, quiz.

BROADCAST HISTORY: June 14, 1946–Feb. 1, 1952, CBS. Various 30m timeslots. HOST: Bill Cullen; Bud Collyer; Ward Wilson. PRODUCERS: Mark Goodson and Bill Todman (their first).

Two players, one with a bell, the other with a buzzer, vied for the chance to answer a question.

THE WITCH'S TALE, horror melodrama.

BROADCAST HISTORY: May 21, 1931–June 13, 1938, WOR, New York until Oct. 15, 1934, then Mutual. 30m, various days. CAST: Adelaide Fitz-Allen, 1931–35; Miriam Wolfe, and Martha Wentworth as "Old Nancy, the witch of Salem," who told the tales. WRITER-DIRECTOR: Alonzo Deen Cole. DIRECTOR: Roger Bower.

The Witch's Tale was one of radio's early horror series; the tales were of ancient curses come true, of severed hands that crawl, of spirits unable to rest. The effects were crude by later standards, and the stories were one-dimensional affairs, calculated for a single effect.

The common ingredient was the narrator, Old Nancy the witch. She came cackling and yacking with Satan, "her wise black cat," who responded with appropriate yowls. "Hunner-an'-thirteen year old I be today," Nancy would crow, just before telling people to "douse all

lights. Now draw up to the fire an' gaze into the embers . . . *gaaaaze into 'em deep!* . . . an' soon ye'll be across the seas, in th' jungle land of Africa . . . hear that chantin' and them savage drums?'' And on this cue the drums came up, the witch faded, and the story proper began.

Adelaide Fitz-Allen, the original actress in the title role, died in 1935 at age 79. Her replacement, Miriam Wolfe, was a 13-year-old regular on the juvenile fairy-tale show, *Let's Pretend.* According to her fellow "Pretender," Arthur Anderson, she auditioned for director Alonzo Deen Cole at midnight, just as one of his shows was ending on WOR. He was astounded at her ability to invoke the essence of a witch, and hired her at once.

WOMAN IN MY HOUSE, soap opera.

BROADCAST HISTORY: March 26, 1951–April 24, 1959, NBC. 15m, weekdays at 4:45. Manhattan Soap for Sweetheart, 1951–54; Miles Laboratories, 1955–57. CAST: Forrest Lewis and Janet Scott as James and Jessie Carter. Les Tremayne as their grown son, Jeff. Alice Reinheart as their daughter Virginia. Bill Idelson as their son Clay. Peggy Webber and Anne Whitfield as their daughter Sandy. Jeff Silver as the youngest son, Peter. PRODUCER: Carlton E. Morse. DIRECTOR: George Fogle. WRITER: Gil Faust.

Woman in My House told of the Carter family of Miami: a brood not unlike the characters Carlton E. Morse had created in his long-running *One Man's Family.* The parents, James and Jessie, had come of age before World War I. James was tight-laced and conservative, disapproving of the freedoms accorded modern youth. Jessie was more tolerant, frequently taking the kids' side in family disputes. And the kids were no kids at all. Jeff was a 30-year-old writer, usually at odds with his father. Virginia was 25 as the serial opened: "unmarried and unresourceful," she too failed to please her father, who fretted over her spinsterhood.

The family lived on Elm Street, their troubles again revealing Morse's fascination with the generation gap. Each chapter began with the heady quotation: *Imperious man, look in your heart and dwell on this—without the woman in my house, what would I be?*

WOMAN IN WHITE, soap opera.

BROADCAST HISTORY: Jan. 3, 1938–Sept. 27, 1940, NBC. 15m, weekdays at 10:45 A.M. Pillsbury.

Sept. 30, 1940–Sept. 25, 1942, CBS. 15m, weekdays at 1:15. Camay Soap, 1940–41; Oxydol, 1941–42.

June 5, 1944–May 28, 1948, NBC. 15m, weekdays at 2:30; at 2:15, 1946–48. General Mills.

CAST: *1938–42*: Luise Barclay as Karen Adams. Betty Ruth Smith, Betty Lou Gerson, and Peggy Knudsen also as Karen Adams. Karl Weber and Arthur Jacobson as Dr. Kirk Harding. Willard Farnum and Harry Elders as John Adams, Karen's brother; Toni Gilman and Louise Fitch as Betty, her sister. Henrietta Tedro as Aunt Helen; Finney Briggs as Uncle Bill. Ruth Bailey as Alice Day. C. Henry Nathan as Betty's suitor, Bob Banning. Irene Winston and Genelle Gibbs as Rosemary Hemingway, Betty's close friend who tried to warn her about Banning. David Gothard as the star-crossed Bryant Chandler. Frank Behrens as Roy Palmer, the young Englishman who was Chandler's friend in India. Lois Zarley as Sybella Mansfield, the half-caste in love with Chandler. Lesley Woods, Edith Perry, and Barbara Luddy as Janet Munson Adams. *1944–48*: Sarajane Wells as Eileen Holmes. Ken Griffin as Dr. Paul Burton. Harry Elders and Bob Latting as Dr. Jack Landis. Hugh Studebaker as Dr. Purdy. **CREATOR-WRITER:** Irna Phillips. **PRODUCER:** Carl Wester.

Woman in White was a companion piece to Irna Phillips's *Road of Life*, the two among the first serials to explore the world of doctors and nurses. But *Woman in White* would have two distinct runs, separated by two years and featuring different casts of characters.

The first replaced the popular Phillips serial *Today's Children*, discontinued by Phillips after the death of her mother. This was the story of Karen Adams, serious-minded and idealistic graduate of nursing school. *Radio Guide* described it at its inception as "the story of a modern-day Florence Nightingale" who devoted her life to the welfare of others. At 30, Karen had assumed responsibility for her sister Betty and her brother John, following the death of their parents "years ago." Her motto was "If there is any kindness I can show, or any good that I can do to any fellow being, let me do it now, for I shall not pass this way again." All in life was subordinated to this philosophy.

In 1938 Karen was in love with Bryant Chandler, who was in India with an incurable disease. Chandler refused to marry her and bring further hardship into her life. Karen's central problem was her sister: Betty, 20, was infatuated with wealthy man-about-town Bob Banning, a dubious liaison at best. Her brother John was a "gifted violinist" whose sole ambition was a great musical career. He and Karen had heated differences of opinion, but there was real love between them. They lived with their Aunt Helen and Uncle Bill Spalding. Alice Day was Karen's roommate and closest friend during nursing school; she too lived at the Spaldings.

Karen moved beyond the Bryant Chandler affair, eventually marrying Dr. Kirk Harding. For a time this was a happy union: then Harding got tangled up in a nasty bit of business with the young wife of Karen's brother John. They fought, they separated, they suffered. Though highly popular, with ratings in the 8-point range, *Woman in White* was discontinued by Phillips after the broadcast of Sept. 25, 1942.

It returned in name only in 1944. Now it was the story of nurse Eileen Holmes and her love interest, Dr. Paul Burton. A few characters were continued from the old storyline, but the main focus was now on Eileen and Paul. This was a time of experimentation for Phillips: she had sold a 60-minute block of serial time to General Mills, to be heard on NBC as *The General Mills Hour* and consisting of three interrelated soaps with crossover characters and a master of ceremonies to guide listeners through the labyrinth. Listeners thus heard Dr. Paul Burton of *Woman in White* appear frequently on *The Guiding Light*, with emcee Ed Prentiss providing the verbal bridges. Like the original *Woman in White*, this originated in Chicago. It moved to Hollywood in 1947.

A WOMAN OF AMERICA, soap opera with a frontier background.

BROADCAST HISTORY: Jan. 25–Sept. 24, 1943, NBC, a test on a 14-station East Coast network.

Sept. 27, 1943–June 21, 1946, NBC full network. 15m, weekdays at 3. Procter & Gamble for

Ivory Snow. **CAST:** Anne Seymour as Prudence Dane, Jan.–Sept. 1943. Florence Freeman as Prudence Dane, 1943–46. James Monks as wagonmaster Wade Douglas. Ken Lynch as Slim Stark. Larry Robinson as John Dane. Jackson Beck as Emilio Prieto. Nancy Douglass as Peg Hall.

The original format of *Woman of America* told of pioneer woman Prudence Dane, who traveled in a wagon train on the Oregon Trail in 1865. Each day the heroine's great-granddaughter Margaret told another chapter in the life of her homesteading ancestor. Both roles, modern and historical, were played by Anne Seymour.

As the long journey ended, the action shifted into a modern setting, following the life of another great-granddaughter, named Prudence after the original heroine. The modern Prudence Dane was a newspaperwoman.

WOMAN OF COURAGE, soap opera.

BROADCAST HISTORY: July 17, 1939–July 10, 1942, CBS. 15m, weekdays at 9 A.M., later at 10:45 A.M. Octagon and Crystal Soap. **CAST:** Selena Royle as Martha Jackson, whose small-town life allegedly proved that "if ye have faith, nothing shall be impossible." Alice Frost and Esther Ralston also as Martha Jackson. Albert Hecht as her husband, Jim. Larry Robinson and Joan Tetzel as their children, Tommy and Lucy. Enid Markey as Martha's sister, Lillian Burke. John Brewster as Lillian's love interest, Joseph Benedict. Claire Howard as Benedict's daughter, Susan. Tess Sheehan as Cora. Horace Braham as George Harrison, the Jackson's friend. **WRITER:** Carl Buss.

Woman of Courage was billed as "the moving story of a wife and mother who is unafraid, because she knows that if you believe you can win, nothing in life can defeat you, and that what is right will be."

But Martha Jackson's trouble-prone family included a crippled, often naive husband, and a jealous, neurotic sister. The melodrama was set in the little town of Farmington.

WOMEN IN THE MAKING OF AMERICA, documentary drama.

BROADCAST HISTORY: May 19–Aug. 11, 1939, Blue Network. 30m, Fridays at 1.

Oct. 31, 1939–June 10, 1940, Blue. 30m, Tuesdays at 2 until May; then Mondays at 10, later at

10:30. *Gallant American Women.* **CREATOR:** Eva vom Baur Hansl, women's rights advocate who had collected 17,000 articles on suffrage and women's issues. **PRODUCER:** Federal Radio Theater. **WRITER:** Jane Ashman. The program's subjects included Susan B. Anthony, Elizabeth Cady Stanton, Lucretia Mott, and others important in the 300-year struggle for women's rights.

THE WOOLWORTH HOUR, concert music.

BROADCAST HISTORY: June 5, 1955–Dec. 29, 1957, CBS. 60m, Sundays at 1. **HOST:** Donald Woods. **ANNOUNCER:** Jack Brand. **ORCHESTRA:** Percy Faith, with 36 pieces. **PRODUCER-DIRECTOR:** Bruno Zirato Jr.

The fare was traditional, with an operatic mix by such guests as Metropolitan baritone Donald Dickson.

WORDS AT WAR, war anthology; documentary and drama.

BROADCAST HISTORY: June 24, 1943–June 5, 1945, NBC. 30m, initially Thursday at 8, then at various times including Tuesdays at 11:30 in 1945. Heard in the *Truth or Consequences* summer slot July 17–Aug. 14, 1943, Saturdays at 8:30; and as the full summer replacement for *Fibber McGee and Molly*, June 27–Oct. 3, 1944, Tuesdays at 9:30 for Johnson's Wax. Broadcast from New York. **HOST,** for Johnson's Wax, summer of 1944: Carl Van Doren; later Clifton Fadiman. **CAST:** Les Damon, Sam Wanamaker, Luis Van Rooten, Joan Alexander, Fay Baker, Lon Clark, Bernard Lenrow, Stefan Schnabel, House Jameson, Alfred Shirley, Don MacLaughlin, Lawson Zerbe, Jackson Beck, Mandel Kramer, Frank Lovejoy, Santos Ortega, Sarah Burton, David Gothard, Bill Zuckert, Norman Rose, Raymond Edward Johnson, Ned Wever, Everett Sloane, Kermit Murdock, Norman Lloyd, Rolfe Sedan, Richard Widmark, Jim Boles, Karl Weber, Ed Begley, Juano Hernandez, Betty Caine, Wendell Holmes, Anne Seymour, etc. **ANNOUNCER:** Jack Costello. **ORGANIST,** from ca. 1944: William Meeder. **ORCHESTRA:** Frank Black and later Morris Mamorsky, ca. 1943, with a large symphony orchestra; many members of the NBC Symphony. **DIRECTORS:** Joseph Losey, Frank Papp, Anton M. Leader, Garnett Garrison. **WRITERS:** Gerald

Holland, Edith R. Sommer, Nora Stirling, Kenneth White, Richard McDonagh, Neal Hopkins.

Words at War was an anthology of war stories, "told by the men and women who have seen them happen." It was produced in cooperation with the Council on Books in Wartime, promising "stories of the battlefronts, of behind-the-scenes diplomacy, of underground warfare, of the home front, of action on the seas." Each show was to be "a living record of this war and the things for which we fight."

Opening in the war's most critical year, *Words at War* hit the air with a punch that no postwar "now it can be told" rehash could ever match. It was praised by *Variety* as "one of the most outstanding programs in radio"; by the *New York Times* as the "boldest, hardest-hitting program of 1944"; by *Newsweek* as "one of the best contributions to serious commercial radio in many a year." Despite its often-undesirable timeslot, *Words at War* stimulated conversation and controversy throughout its two-year run.

Though sustained, it was given a grand send-off by NBC, with a stirring musical score by Frank Black and rousing execution by the network's huge symphony orchestra. The sound patterns came rumbling like Japanese dive bombers: the growl of heavy machinery, the sudden ripping chatter of machine guns, the steady drone of an airplane as two pilots stood on a runway and spoke what might be their last thoughts. But the success of *Words* was the immediacy of its subject matter. These were dramatizations of "the most significant books to thus far come out of this great world conflict," with the war's outcome by no means assured. This atmosphere—of a country fighting for its life—gave the stories maximum impact, with no holds barred save those of government-imposed security. Stories of Nazi brutality and Japanese barbarism were given the kind of explicit treatment that the radio audience had seldom if ever heard. The show titled *The Rainbow* told of a pregnant woman made to run at bayonet point through bloodstained snow, and a 16-year-old boy sent to the gallows in the Ukraine, his body left swinging for a month.

There were stories of the free French, Marines on Tarawa, prisoners of war; epic adventures of survival and damning incidents of homefront indifference. The scope was worldwide, the stories most often taken from true accounts but including fiction as well when a point was well told and powerful. The big picture was usually boiled down to a single viewpoint, making the theme poignant and personal. *The Last Days of Sevastopol* recounted the great siege on the Crimean peninsula, with hundreds of German and Russian searchlights crisscrossing in an air duel and the final line never in doubt—"there is not one building left standing in the city." *From the Land of Silent People* told the agony of Yugoslavia. *The Ship* dramatized the C. S. Forester novel about "a glorious British vessel and the men abroad her." *Prisoner of the Japs* was the story of an American newspaperwoman who was trapped in Hong Kong when the Japanese attacked and conquered. *Dynamite Cargo* relived the experience of an American torpedo victim, picked up by a British cruiser and huddled in the dark hold with other refugees—including a young Russian woman who might be inclined to pass the time—while the enemy attacked relentlessly from the air. *Eighty-three Days* was a three-month survival epic set on an open raft at sea. *Shortcut to Tokyo* was Corey Ford's account of the war in the Aleutians, and *Here Is Your War* was the first of three shows based on the works of news correspondent Ernie Pyle: *Brave Men* was dramatized the week after Pyle was killed in action.

Among the show's best titles (all of which retain their complete potence half a century later) are *Paris Underground* (Etta Shiber's testament to a lost friend who helped smuggle shot-down British fliers out of France), *Fair Stood the Wind for France* (H. E. Bates's tale of a love affair under the iron boot), *War Below Zero* (a secret mission to Greenland and how a few men coped with "the loneliest military post on earth, the great ice cap"), *Lost Island* (James Norman Hall's short novel of an engineer who had to destroy a tropical paradise in order to build an air base), and *Apartment in Athens* (Glenway Wescott's story of a Greek family whose father opened his doors to a Nazi officer and paid a dear price).

Virtually the entire run has been transferred to tape: a superb library in excellent sound, living evidence of what America was thinking and feeling and doing in the last two years of World War II. A few of the shows were perhaps too well cooked: there is a national bravado laced through the writing that may turn a modern listener aside. But the pure power carries the day. The vast symphony orchestra was discontinued in December 1943, replaced with organ themes. This was a serious loss, though hardly fatal. The brief sponsorship of Johnson's Wax in the summer of 1944 meant real money, a return of the orchestra under the baton of Morris Mamorsky, and "name" hosts Carl Van Doren and Clifton Fadiman. But even without these advantages, *Words at War* is one of the best "forgotten shows" of its day.

THE WORLD IS YOURS, informative drama.

BROADCAST HISTORY: June 14, 1936–May 3, 1942, NBC, Blue Network initially; Red from October 1936. Various 30m timeslots, often Sunday afternoons. **CAST:** Tom Hoier as the Old Timer. Elizabeth Morgan as Mona Jackson. **THEME:** *Knowledge and the Great Doors*, by Schramm.

Produced by the Smithsonian Institution, this show told of scientific achievements and technical advances, from the development of "that heroic metal, aluminum," to the movement of fighting aircraft in World War II. Historical events were also dramatized.

THE WORLD'S GREAT NOVELS, classics dramatizations.

BROADCAST HISTORY: Oct. 14, 1944–July 23, 1948, WMAQ, Chicago, and NBC. 30m, Saturdays at 7, 1944–45, then Fridays at 11:30. **CAST:** Chicago radio players including Cliff Soubier, Ken Nordine, Geraldine Kay, Eloise Kummer, Larry Alexander, Maurice Copeland, Sherman Marks, Alma Platts, Harry Elders, Charles Flynn, Hope Summers, Ernie Andrews, Jess Pugh, Jonathan Hole, Lee Young, Bob Smith, Ken Griffin, Hilda Graham, Arthur Peterson, Johnny Coons, Jack Lester, Donald Gallagher, Everett Clarke and Sid-

ney Ellstrom. **ANNOUNCERS:** Dave Garroway, Charles Chan, John Conrad. **COMPOSER:** Emil Soderstrom. **ORCHESTRA:** Bernard Berquist. **DIRECTOR:** Homer Heck.

The World's Great Novels was the well-developed forerunner of *The NBC University Theater*, possessing the same qualities but a different sound, being produced in Chicago. After the broadcast of July 23, 1948, it became *University Theater* and moved to Hollywood.

In Chicago it was produced under the banner *The NBC University of the Air.* Its producers forged the union with the University of Louisville that led to accredited radio-assisted correspondence courses in literature. The productions were first-rate, with sound, acting, and music coordinated to keep it from sounding stuffy. Big novels (*Moby Dick, A Tale of Two Cities,* etc.) were often spread into three-and four-part programs, to ensure that justice could be done to the original works. Listeners were always encouraged to read the books: the handbook of *The World's Great Novels* was offered for a quarter.

THE WORLD'S MOST HONORED FLIGHTS, aviation drama and history.

BROADCAST HISTORY: 1946, transcribed 30m syndication for the Longines Watch Company (heard on the Mutual outlet, WOR, New York, Feb. 3–June 2, and on WOW, the NBC station in Omaha, beginning February 4). **HOST-NARRATOR:** Capt. Eddie Rickenbacker, with adventures from his life and chapters from history. Gary Merrill as young Rickenbacker. **ANNOUNCER:** Ray Morgan. **DIRECTOR:** Lester Vail.

The series opened with a two-part drama of Rickenbacker's 1942 crash in the Pacific and his 24 days adrift. Subsequent stories: the Wright Brothers, Amelia Earhart, Billy Mitchell, etc.

X

X-MINUS ONE, science fiction anthology.

BROADCAST HISTORY: April 24, 1955–Jan. 9, 1958, NBC. Various 30m timeslots; moved frequently. CAST: New York radio performers including Mason Adams, Joan Alexander, Jack Grimes, Joseph Julian, Ted Osborne, Bob Hastings, Arthur Hughes, Charles Penman, Guy Repp, Norman Rose, Bill Griffis, John Gibson, Bill Lipton, Raymond Edward Johnson, Betty Caine, Roger DeKoven, Luis Van Rooten, Wendell Holmes, Joseph Bell, John Larkin, Jill Meredith, Santos Ortega, Bill Quinn, Ralph Camargo, Leon Janney, Lawson Zerbe, Teri Keane, Kermit Murdock, Mandel Kramer, Larry Haines, Charlotte Manson, Joe DeSantis, Staats Cotsworth, etc. ANNOUNCER: Fred Collins. DIRECTORS: Fred Weihe, Daniel Sutter, George Voutsas; occasionally Kenneth MacGregor, etc. WRITERS-ADAPTERS: Ernest Kinoy and George Lefferts; based on stories mostly from *Galaxy* magazine.

X-Minus One was an extension of the NBC science fiction series *Dimension X*. Its scheduling was erratic, with stands of a few months in each timeslot. This gave it little chance to break out of its hardcore genre following and perhaps attract a broader audience. This is debatable, but what is widely agreed almost four decades later is that the most interesting dramatic radio of the 1955 season was produced by two genre series, *Gunsmoke*, a western, and this space opera.

Though *X-1* did contain some old-hat S-F moralizing (such as Graham Doar's done-to-death *Outer Limit*), it blew through NBC like a breath of fresh air. The first 15 shows were straight repeats from *Dimension X*. Then *X-1* struck out into deeper space with new adaptations from a leading S-F magazine and an occasional original to keep the mix intriguing.

The opening signatures themselves indicate this creative evolution. The show used a countdown-and-launch rocketship blastoff for its opening. The earliest examples consisted of a quick count and something that sounded like a bottle rocket. S-F advocate Bill Sabis notes three later levels of opening signatures, each gaining intensity as the rocket was personified. Soon the spaceship was infused with human voices: the countdown opens, notes Sabis, "against a rising electronic frequency," and the blastoff itself combines the roar of the rocket with a chorus of voices. A "singing sigh" climbs higher and higher "until a triple brassy cresendo is reached" and the second stage fires. Announcer Fred Collins does the honors:

Countdown for blastoff . . .
X-minus five . . . four . . . three . . . two . . .
X-minus one . . . Fire!

And as the rocket climbs it becomes a living thing: the voices join the roar with a building "aaaaaaaaahhhhhhhh," and Collins returns to set the series premise:

From the far horizons of the unknown come transcribed tales of new dimensions in time and space. These are stories of the future, adventures in which you'll live in a million could-be years on a thousand may-be worlds. The National Broadcasting Company, in cooperation with

Street and Smith—publishers of Astounding Science Fiction Magazine—present:
SIGNATURE (FROM ECHO CHAMBER).
X-X-x-x. . . .
MINUS-MINUS-minus-minus. . . .
ONE-ONE-one-one. . . .

These were not stories for children, though they could certainly listen and be fascinated. But the stories didn't all end happily: some of the most memorable episodes were those in which aliens triumphed. Who could forget the closing scene of Ray Bradbury's *Mars Is Heaven*, with the last earthman frantically trying to radio home while the Martians break into his ship and overwhelm him? *Dimension X* had explored such ground, and *X-1* transcended the parent program with some of the most creative melodrama the medium had yet heard. With its magazine affiliations (the two dozen shows from *Astounding* were followed by almost 90 from *Galaxy*) came a well of untapped talent, stories by such young writers as Isaac Asimov, Robert Bloch, Robert A. Heinlein, Poul Anderson, and Theodore Sturgeon, who became the old lions to the generation that followed them. A major asset was the NBC writing staff: the two primary adapters, Ernest Kinoy and George Lefferts, were capable not only of distilling magazine stories but of writing their own superb originals.

On June 24, 1973—16 years after its network finale—NBC brought out the transcriptions in a test run, to see if modern listeners would accept radio drama again. But the scheduling was self-defeating: it was run once a month, sometimes on Saturdays, sometimes on Sundays, and even its staunchest advocates had trouble finding it in a sea of sports events and news bites. Announcer Collins implored listeners to write their support. Not enough did, and the experiment died after a surprisingly hardy two-year run, March 22, 1975.

But the good news is very good: *X-Minus One* lives in its entirety, its shows gradually upgraded in sound quality until, today, no one will have to struggle to obtain the series in excellent fidelity. Among the best are these: *The Cold Equation* (a truly haunting tale of a young woman who playfully stows away on a spaceship only to learn that the fuel supply is critical and her weight has pushed it to the point of disaster); *The Martian Death March* (a Kinoy original in which a race of spider-beings leaves its earth-imposed reservation and undertakes the long march home); *Junkyard* (a space expedition comes upon a dumping ground on an unoccupied world, then discovers that something is sucking out its collective intelligence and there isn't even enough know-how left to run the ship); *Tunnel Under the World* (a Frederick Pohl story of a monstrous experiment concocted by the brain trust of an ad agency; pure radio, with a knockout ending); *A Pail of Air* (Fritz Leiber's story of survival on a world gone cold and airless after being ripped away from its sun); *Hallucination Orbit* (a feast of imagination, by J. T. McIntosh, about a space pioneer left alone on a rock near Pluto for so long that he can't tell if what he sees, including bosomy female rescuers, is real); and *The Seventh Victim* (a Robert Sheckley story of a future that curbs violence by allowing society's predators to legally hunt down and murder people).

YESTERDAY'S CHILDREN, classics with commentary.

BROADCAST HISTORY: Nov. 24, 1939–May 24, 1940, Blue Network. 30m, Fridays at 7:30. **HOSTESS:** Dorothy Gordon.

Famous adults of the day told how, as "yesterday's children," they were enthralled by a favored piece of literature. Among the tales were *David Copperfield, Aladdin,* and *Uncle Tom's Cabin*; among the celebrities who revealed their childhood favorites were President Roosevelt, Eddie Cantor, Fannie Hurst, and Luise Rainer.

YOU ARE THERE, informative drama.

BROADCAST HISTORY: July 7, 1947–March 19, 1950, CBS. 30m, Mondays at 9 the first month, then Sundays, at 2, 1947–48; at 2:30, 1948–49; at 4:30, 1949–50. *CBS Is There* until April 25, 1948, then *You Are There.* **REPORTERS:** Don Hollenbeck, John Daly, Richard C. Hottelet, and others of CBS News. **ANNOUNCERS, ACTORS:** Harry Marble, Guy Sorel, Ken Roberts, Jackson Beck, etc. **CREATOR:** Goodman Ace. **PRODUCER-DIRECTOR:** Robert Lewis Shayon. **WRITERS:** Irve Tunick, Joseph Liss, Michael Sklar. **SOUND EFFECTS:** Jim Rogan.

You Are There was unique in the realm of historical drama. Created by Goodman Ace for CBS, it blended its history with modern technology, taking an entire network newsroom on a time trip each week to report the great events of the past. "CBS asks you to imagine that our microphone is present at this unforgettable moment. All things are as they were then, except, when CBS is there, *YOU* are there!"

It was based on "authentic fact and quotation," a present-tense stream-of-consciousness told by newsmen allegedly witnessing great events unfolding before their eyes. On-the-spot interviews were followed by "analysis"; both were interrupted by bulletins as new "facts" came to light. Real-life newsmen with established reputations handled "remote" broadcasts while anchorman Don Hollenbeck organized field reports and summarized the unfolding drama.

The shows usually opened just before some decisive event in world history. CBS asked its audience to believe that newsman John Daly was sitting in Ford's Theater with a microphone the night Lincoln was shot. The following week, Daly was stationed outside the Bastille in 1789. Reporters were placed inside the Alamo, in the "radio room" of the U.S. Senate for the 1805 impeachment of Justice Samuel Chase, on a grassy hillside three thousand years ago for the fall of Troy.

Hollenbeck or Daly would open the show with a description of the situation "as it stands now." In a few crisp sentences, Hollenbeck would convey the tense atmosphere of Gettysburg. It was the turning point in the Civil War. Lee's forces had been pushing relentlessly northward, with an unbroken chain of victories in their wake. Unless General Meade could hold the Confederates here, Lincoln would be forced to come to terms with the South and the Union would be dissolved. Hollenbeck's voice faded. Then came the opening signature, booming out of an echo chamber: *JULY 3RD, 1863! GETTYSBURG! YOU . . . ARE THERE*!

Again Hollenbeck faded in. Soon Daly was on hand, interviewing Yankee troops. Richard C. Hottelet analyzed the breaking story from the North's viewpoint. Suddenly Confederate cannons appeared in the distance. Daly returned with a description from front lines. This was the style: empires were won and lost in 30 minutes. The last days of Pompeii; the execution of Mary, Queen of Scots; the exile of Napoleon and the assassination of Caesar—all were packaged in a CBS timeslot.

The show was generally well received, with Bernard DeVoto in his *Harper's* "easy chair" providing his typical dissenting vote. The show was a "flop," said DeVoto, because the illusion so carefully contrived "dies of overfeeding." The "lethal dose" was John Daly. "We have heard his voice vibrate with the real emotion" of actual events, "and our memory of the real simply turns the imagined to ham. And every device piled on to heighten the illusion ends by increasing that initial phoniness. The broadcaster's carefully plotted ad-libbing and clichés, the stage-business of cables and viewpoints, the cut-ins, the on-the-spot interviews—all the faked paraphernalia of the actual operates to break the dream. Radio has made its fantasy literal and so has killed it. That wasn't terror in Ford's Theater, it was a sound effect."

YOU BET YOUR LIFE, comedy-quiz.

BROADCAST HISTORY: Oct. 27, 1947–May 25, 1949, ABC. 30m, Mondays at 8; then Wednesdays at 9:30 from Dec. 31, 1947. Elgin-American bracelets, compacts, cigarette cases, and dresser sets.

Oct. 5, 1949–June 28, 1950, CBS. 30m, Wednesdays at 9. Elgin-American until Jan. 4, then DeSoto-Plymouth.

Oct. 4, 1950–Sept. 19, 1956, NBC. 30m, Wednesdays at 9. DeSoto-Plymouth.

HOST: Groucho Marx. **ANNOUNCERS:** Jack Slattery, briefly; then George Fenneman; Mike Wallace for Elgin-American. **ORCHESTRA:** Billy May with a 10-piece band; later, Jack Meakin, Jerry Fielding. **CREATOR-PRODUCER-DIRECTOR:** John Guedel. **DIRECTORS:** Bernie

Smith, Bob Dwan. **WRITERS:** Ed Tyler, Hy Freedman. **THEME:** *Hooray for Captain Spaulding*, by Bert Kalmar and Harry Ruby, from the Marx Brothers film *Animal Crackers*.

It was no circumstantial juxtaposition of words that emphasized the "comedy" in the announcer's description of *You Bet Your Life* as the "comedy-quiz show." The star, Groucho Marx, was not being paid $3,000 a week to sit on a stool, ask questions, and dispense money. This was a show of human interest and razor-sharp wit. It turned on Groucho's quips, but also on the often cunning one-upsmanship of clever contestants. "We've got to have people who have something to say and will say it," explained co-director Bernie Smith. "If they're 'characters,' so much the better." Groucho loved swapping lines with characters.

It had an inauspicious beginning, arriving on the air only through the persistence of producer John Guedel. To moderate a quiz show seemed a sad comedown for a comic talent of Groucho's stature. As one of the fabled Marx Brothers he had regaled audiences in film houses of the '30s with a madcap brand of comedy, the best of it even then considered classic. He had been a star of vaudeville but had had a strange and dismal career on the air. Four times he had been lured to the microphone for regular series appearances: four times he had failed, his shows marked by mediocre ratings and brief runs. Some radio producers were even reluctant to book him as a guest.

But on one such guest spot, Marx was paired with Bob Hope. Guedel happened to be in the studio and watched the two work. Hope dropped his script, Marx discarded his as well, and a furious session of ad-libbing began. Guedel thought Groucho was sensational. After the show, he approached and asked if he could do that all the time. Marx replied that it was almost impossible for him *not* to do it. His problem on the air was simply that he hated scripted material. "I figured he'd be great working with people out of an audience," Guedel later recalled. "When people were being funny, Groucho could be the perfect straight man; when the people played it straight, Groucho couldn't miss with his own comedy."

Guedel was then one of the up-and-coming young radio producers. He had put Art Linkletter on the game show charts with *People Are Funny* and *House Party*, and his suggestion to Ozzie Nelson that the Nelson family might make good sitcom material had resulted in *The Adventures of Ozzie and Harriet*. He had been toying with a game show idea for some time. It would be called *You Bet Your Life*: he thought of it as a weeknight quarter-hour, with a somewhat traditional host asking questions of contestants from the audience. Though he had not been able to sell it, the title remained as a catchy come-on, a quiz show waiting to happen.

But Groucho brushed it off. This would be a drastic tumble from his Marx Brothers days, he felt. Guedel persisted. In 1947, he persuaded Marx to cut an audition record. Thus armed, he went out to pitch the show to clients. It quickly sold, and the press reacted predictably, just as Marx had feared. *Newsweek* summed up the general sentiment: seeing Groucho in a quiz show was like "selling Citation to a glue factory."

The show was hardly an overnight success. The early programs were live, and there were difficult moments when the contestants and even Groucho seemed hesitant. Guedel found the answer in recording tape. Bing Crosby had broken the network ban against prerecorded material: if the Groucho show could be taped at 60 minutes and edited into a 26-minute package, listeners would be getting concentrated Marxiana. Marx himself would be more at ease, knowing that fluffs and flat spots need never be heard. This was the key: in one year, *You Bet Your Life* leaped from a sorry 92nd in the Hooper ratings into the top ten. Groucho won the 1949 Peabody Award as radio's outstanding comedian, his sagging career was revived, and his confidence as a humorist was restored.

The format was based on an old parlor game, simple to a fault. Three couples were brought onstage to be interviewed and quizzed by Groucho. The questions were asked without gimmickry. Each couple was given $20 and told to bet as much as they dared risk on four questions from a category of their choosing. The money would double with each successive step: thus it was possible for couples to win $320, go broke on the first question, or finish anywhere in between. "Only one answer between you," Groucho would caution. "Think carefully, and no help from the audience."

The couple with the largest money total got a chance at the jackpot question, which began at $1,000 (with $500 added weekly, the pot sometimes got into the $3,000 range). There was also a "secret word" each week, with bonus money ($100 to $250, depending on the year) to be divided if either person said the word while the show was on the air. The word might be "table" or "hand"—"it's a common word, something you see every day," Groucho reminded contestants. Marx and Guedel, co-owners of the show, paid secret word winners out of pocket, on the spot and in cash; the sponsor picked up the tab on other winnings. If a couple lost everything, Groucho asked a nonsense question for $25, given with the grand assurance that "nobody leaves here broke." A regular consolation query was "Who was buried in Grant's tomb?"

But money was seldom the motivating factor in luring guests. "The money really did not matter," wrote one contestant: "I just wondered if I dared talk to Groucho." Contestants could expect a sly barrage of insults. If a contestant said he sold cars for a living, Groucho was almost certain to ask, "How many times have you been indicted?" Similar questions would be asked of mayors, councilmen, or politicians on any level. Groucho might pretend to slip up, calling a "spinster" a "monster," then shrug it off with the comment that "there's not a great deal of difference." To a baseball umpire, he would ask, "Do you have any little thieves at home?" Occasionally the contestant topped him. To the question "What were people wearing when you were a baby?" an elderly woman replied, "Diapers," and brought down the house.

The producers claimed that Marx enjoyed being upbraided. But he hated "smart-alecks" who came on the air with cute routines all planned out. "A wiseguy, eh?" he would say, and the contestant would be in for a verbal battering throughout his stint. Early in the series, Marx discovered a secret, wrote George Eels in *Look* magazine: "that if he needles people, he'll keep them on their toes." Said Bernie Smith: "The idea is to find a remarkable personality and let Groucho throw rocks at him." Soon everyone took this as the act it was, and Groucho could say anything, on mike or off, without giving offense.

He quickly became a shrewd interviewer who saw at once the weaknesses and strengths of the characters confronting him. If people wanted to sing, he let them: he might join them in the chorus, and the more wretched the singing, the better the comic effect. He sought anything that could be turned to laughter. A man named Crumb was in for a rough go with Groucho. He was also ever honing his self-proclaimed prowess as a wolf. Beautiful females would get at least one guarded proposition during the course of things. When a young student said she was going to "a college for girls," Groucho said, "That's the reason I'd want to go, too." His wit was considered a formidable barrier that kept the common man at bay, but he had a warm streak that his producers insisted was genuine. He was said to have a keen sense of social responsibility, occasionally making remarks on the air that advocated racial tolerance or international understanding. And though he joshed the elderly, he knew where the lines were drawn. One 80-year-old woman threatened to walk off unless he put out his cigar. "Groucho looked stunned and stamped it out," wrote Eels. He said nothing more about it, and three explanations were offered for his silence. First, he had real respect for age. Second, he knew the audience liked seeing him squelched occasionally. "Third, and least likely, is that he couldn't think of anything to say."

Playing no small role in the show's success was the contestant selection process. This was a strange mix of chance and calculation. The ideal was to have Marx confronted by couples of interesting, articulate, and uninhibited opposites. If both were alike, said Bernie Smith, "one of them gets lost." So a bachelor would be paired with a spinster, a mother-in-law with a son-in-law, a traffic cop with a woman driver. The selections were often occupationally based: the switchboard operator paired with the house detective; the four-star general with a young recruit; a hobo with a banker's wife. The producers would decide to invite a group of plumbers to the broadcast: these people were brought onstage in the preshow warmup and interviewed before the audience, which would then select the one to go on the air.

Additionally, a staff of 13 people always watched for colorful personalities in the news, in their neighborhoods, in the letters that came in asking for interviews. About 200 perspective contestants turned up each week; 20 were interviewed by the staff; six were chosen. The contestants were not paired until the night of the broadcast. Each pair was kept offstage and out of hearing while the others were interviewed and played the game. The second and third couples thus had no advantage: no one knew how much money the others had won, how much they themselves had to win to advance to the jackpot question.

The remarkable thing was not that Groucho was so consistently witty, but that the guests were. The claim of spontaneity was often doubted, but Smith insisted that none were coached: they were told only to be themselves, to speak up and not be afraid to talk back. Marx never met the contestants until they came before him with the tape spinning. In meetings with the staff, he was told only what the occupations were and occasionally that a contestant had a truly unusual background.

Announcer George Fenneman added greatly to the merriment. He was the perfect target: a super-straight mikeman with a keen sense of humor. Groucho bullied him constantly. It was Fenneman's voice that the audience heard on the closed circuit, informing how much money the other contestants had won and what the secret word was. The announcer also kept track of contestant earnings. This could be difficult when an eccentric contestant would bet some odd figure, such as "twelve dollars and forty-seven cents." Fenneman went with the show into TV where it had a highly successful run (1950–61) on NBC.

There are more than 200 shows on tape. They are fully viable four decades later. A quick listen should convince any doubters that no one was rehearsed. The average man could never be that natural if he were following a script or trying to act.

Marx died Aug. 19, 1977; Fenneman on May 29, 1997.

YOU CAN'T TAKE IT WITH YOU, situation comedy, from the play by George S. Kaufman.

BROADCAST HISTORY: Aug. 27–Nov. 19, 1944, Mutual. 30m, Sundays at 5. Emerson Radios. CAST: Everett Sloane as Grandpa Vanderhof, with a New York radio cast. ANNOUNCER: Bob Shepard. WRITER: Nathaniel Curtis.

May 13–Nov. 16, 1951, NBC. 30m, Sundays at 6 until Oct., then Fridays at 9:30. CAST: Walter Brennan as Grandpa Vanderhof. Lois Corbet as his daughter, Penny Sycamore. Charlie Lung as Penny's husband, Paul. Barbara Eiler as granddaughter Alice. GeGe Pearson as Rheba the maid. Paul Dubov as neighbor Tony Kirby.

YOUNG DR. MALONE, soap opera.

BROADCAST HISTORY: Nov. 20, 1939–April 26, 1940, Blue Network. 15m, weekdays at 11:15 A.M. General Foods and Post Cereals.

April 29, 1940–Nov. 25, 1960, CBS. 15m, weekdays at 2, 1940–44; at 1:30, 1945–60. General Foods until 1945; Procter & Gamble, 1945–55; various thereafter.

CAST: Alan Bunce as Jerry Malone, principled and idealistic physician in the little town of Three Oaks. Carl Frank, Charles Irving (mid 1940s), and Sandy Becker (from 1947) also as Jerry Malone. Elizabeth Reller and later Barbara Weeks as Ann, his wife. Madeleine Pierce, child impersonator, as their daughter, Jill. Joan Lazer and Rosemary Rice as Jill growing up and in young adulthood. Evelyn Varden and Vera Allen as Mother Malone. Larry Haines as Carl Ward. Barry Thomson as Roger Dineen. Donna Keath and Joan Banks as Lynne Dineen. Bill Smith as Dr. Brown. Bob Readick as Dr. Mason. Berry Kroeger as Sam Williams, aggressive Three Oaks businessman, who became interested in Ann Malone while Jerry was away in New York being interested in treacherous Lucia Standish. Elspeth Eric as Lucia. Joan Alexander as Jerry's second wife, Tracy, who came along in later years and took up much of the show's focus in the 1950s. Jone Allison and Gertrude Warner also as Tracy. **ANNOUNCERS:** Ron Rawson, etc. **ORGANIST:** Charles Paul. **DIRECTORS:** Walter Gorman, Stanley Davis, Theodora Yates, Ira Ashley, etc. **WRITERS:** Medical specialist Julian Funt in the early days; David Driscoll; Charles Gussman; David Leeson.

The bulk of the action through the long *Dr. Malone* run centered on Jerry and his wife Ann, their daughter Jill, Jerry's well-intentioned but interfering mother, their friends, and Jerry's professional associates at the hospital. There were the usual stock soap situations, leading to misunderstanding, jealousy, and separations. During the war, Jerry was shot down over Germany and presumed dead. Ann took up with another man. In later sequences, Jerry faced the inevitable murder trial, and there was a crippling disease,

which he overcame after a risky blood transfusion.

Through it all were woven still longer threads: Ann's continuing insecurity, her death in the early '50s, and the struggle to establish the Three Oaks Medical Center, the clinic toward which Jerry's professional life was dedicated. This goal was realized with the help of his attorney, wealthy philanthropist Roger Dineen, whose wife, Lynne, was Ann's best friend. Another close friend was Carl Ward, owner of the local newspaper.

Jerry's daughter Jill grew up on the show and became a major character as the serial drew to a close. It ended on Jill's wedding day, "the last day of soap opera" on radio, Nov. 25, 1960.

YOUNG LOVE, situation comedy.

BROADCAST HISTORY: July 4, 1949–May 13, 1950, CBS. 30m, various days with continuity gaps. Ford Motors from Nov. **CAST:** Janet Waldo and Jimmy Lydon as a young married couple named Janet and Jimmy. Herb Butterfield as crusty Dean Ferguson of Midwestern University. Shirley Mitchell as Molly Belle, Janet's roommate. Also: Jerry Hausner, Hal March. **ANNOUNCER:** Roy Rowan. **WRITER-PRODUCERS:** Jerry Lawrence and Bob Lee.

In the *Young Love* scenario, Janet and Jerry, though secretly married, were still in college. Too poor to afford an apartment, they lived apart—he in the Delta Phi Beta fraternity house; she in the girls' dorm—and had to meet on the campus bench overlooking Marble Lake. As Molly Belle, Shirley Mitchell resurrected her Leila Ransom voice from *The Great Gildersleeve*, with such sayings as "matri-li'l-ole-mony" and "flippety-li'l-ole-flop."

YOUNG WIDDER BROWN, soap opera.

BROADCAST HISTORY: June 6, 1938–June 22, 1956, NBC. 15m, weekdays at 11:30 A.M., 1938–39; at 4:45, 1939–51; at 4:30, 1951–55; at 4:15, 1955–56. Sterling Drugs (Bayer Aspirin). **CAST:** Florence Freeman as "attractive Ellen Brown, with two fatherless children to support." Wendy Drew as Ellen Brown, 1950s; Millicent Brower as Ellen in the serial's final days. Clayton Bud Collyer as Peter Turner, an idealistic humanitarian who became established in the early story as "the man

Ellen loves.'' Ned Wever as Anthony Loring, the man Ellen truly loved, who pursued her across two decades. Marilyn Erskine and Tommy Donnelly as Ellen's children, Janey and Mark. Toni Gilman as Marjorie Williams, a college girl in an early-1940s sequence who fell in love with Anthony. Ethel Remey as Anthony's ambitious sister, Victoria Loring. Riza Royce and Kay Strozzi also as Victoria. House Jameson, Eric Dressler, and Alexander Scourby as Herbert Temple. Joan Tompkins as his wife, Norine Temple, who became one of Ellen's friends. Bennett Kilpack and Tom Hoier as Uncle Josh, Ellen's dearest old friend. Joan Tompkins and Helen Shields as Joyce Burton Turner. Bess McCammon as Olive McEvoy. **AN-NOUNCER:** George Ansbro. **ORGANIST:** John Winters. **PRODUCERS:** Frank and Anne Hummert. **DIRECTORS:** Martha Atwell, Richard Leonard, Ed Slattery, etc. **THEME:** *In The Gloaming.*

Young Widder Brown mounted a staunch challenge to Frank and Anne Hummert's pinnacles of agony—*Stella Dallas, Backstage Wife*, and *The Romance of Helen Trent*—in the daytime categories of audience, longevity, and melodramatic convolution. For 18 years it was sponsored by that most loyal of Hummert accounts, Bayer Aspirin.

In the early days it was billed as the story of "a woman as real as her friends who listen to her—the dramatic story of a very human mother's duty to her children, in conflict with the dictates of her heart." Later this was modified: "the age-old conflict between a mother's duty and a woman's heart." It came to a thunderous organ theme and was one of daytime's top-rated serials throughout its run, with Hoopers in the 8s.

Still in her early 30s, Ellen struggled to raise her children in the small-town mentality of Simpsonville, W.Va. Here lurked an inspired string of tragedies that transcended even the Hummerts' usual fare. *Newsweek* toasted a few of them as Ellen departed in 1956: there were "a false accusation of murder, amnesia, innumerable broken bones, addiction to a 'powder of forgetfulness' slipped into her drink (nonalcoholic, to be sure) by an unscrupulous painter, and blindness brought on by an allergy to chocolate cake (an affliction cured when a cake-flour cosponsor complained).''

In Simpsonville, Ellen ran a tearoom. "She is successful in making a living," advised *Radio Guide* in 1940, "but longs for companionship." But she suffered the distrust of the town, as the frustrated and unhappy Maria Hawkins spread vicious gossip and then led a boycott against the tearoom. Into Ellen's life came handsome Dr. Peter Turner. But Peter proved a weak hero when, after establishing a clinic to aid the poor people of the Smoky Ridge hill country, he was "tricked into marriage" by the wealthy and beautiful though spoiled and petulent Joyce Burton.

By the time Peter saw the light, Ellen was infatuated with handsome Dr. Anthony Loring. Anthony was to Ellen what Gil Whitney was to Helen Trent, a suitor of Herculean stamina and determination. His marriage to Ellen was on and off, with all the barriers that the Hummert scripters could throw in their path, for years. In the early Peter Turner–Anthony Loring days, Ellen also met and discarded Herbert Temple, a middle-aged admirer. The Peter dilemma was pushed toward resolution by the "mental collapse" of Peter's wife, Joyce. Doctors warned that Joyce might never recover should Peter leave her, so Ellen demanded that he remain with the woman "once so gay and brilliant, now broken in mind and body."

And this was the tip of the iceberg. In another sequence, Anthony thought Ellen had been killed in a plane crash. In fact, she had lost her memory and was being held prisoner in a lonely mountain hideaway by confused David Blake. In the early 1950s, Anthony—faced with the possibility of finding happiness at last—opted to believe a lie, cast Ellen out of his life, and turned to the evil Millicent for consolation. He too was tricked into marriage. On the rebound, Ellen agreed to marry dashing Michael Forsythe. But Anthony learned of Millicent's deceit and came crawling back to Ellen. In 1955, Millicent was murdered; Anthony was the prime suspect, though Ellen knew that he could never kill. Listeners knew that the real murderer was treacherous Ivan Mansfield, an artist hired by Millicent to break up the Ellen-Anthony romance.

Having defeated the murder charge, Ellen and Anthony faced yet one final crisis. Millicent had left a devious will, offering Ellen $250,000 if she agreed never to marry Anthony. The question lingered to the last Friday of the final week when, exhausted, they fell into each other's arms.

"Will you marry me, Ellen?"

"Yes, I will, Anthony!"

It was late afternoon, June 22, 1956.

YOUR ALL-TIME HIT PARADE, popular music.

BROADCAST HISTORY: Feb. 12, 1943–Sept. 24, 1944, NBC. 30m, Fridays at 8:30 for Lucky Strike through June 2, 1944; then Sundays at 7, summer show for Jack Benny. VOCALISTS: Jerry Wayne, Bea Wain, Ethel Smith, Marie Green, Martha Stewart. VOCAL GROUP: Lyn Murray Chorus. ORCHESTRA: Mark Warnow.

This was an offshoot of sorts of the more famous *Your Hit Parade*, which Lucky Strike was cosponsoring at the time on CBS. The idea was to present such "all-time" favorites as *Wagon Wheels, Chicago*, and *Some of These Days* with such then-current hits as *I'll Be Seeing You*. This no doubt would have been just another music show but for one factor: American Tobacco and its feisty president, George Washington Hill.

Hill's favorite selling technique was repetition. He had created a minor sensation with the interminable slogan *Lucky Strike green has gone to war*: this was repeated until Dan Golenpaul of *Information, Please* had gone to court to get Hill removed as sponsor. *Your All-Time Hit Parade* was launched with a new gimmick: it would be broadcast from Carnegie Hall, with extensive preshow publicity and, yes, another jingle. The campaign was relentless: day and night, listeners heard the rhyme *The best tunes of all have moved to Carnegie Hall.*

The wisdom of such overkill was questioned by the press, but Hill reaped reams of free publicity. Radio comics lampooned the ads almost as continuously as the commercials themselves ran. Ed Gardner on *Duffy's Tavern*: "Mr. Clark Dennis will now sing *I've Heard That Song Before*. He will sing this song very quickly, as in a few minutes it will move to Carnegie Hall." Al Jolson to Monty Woolley: "How'd you like that *April Showers*, Monty?" Woolley: "It's one of the best tunes of all, and I'd appreciate it if you'd move it to Carnegie Hall."

YOUR AMERICA, regional Americana.

BROADCAST HISTORY: Jan. 8–Sept. 30, 1944, NBC, 30m, Saturdays at 5; then, Oct. 15, 1944–Sept. 30, 1945, Mutual, 30m, Sundays at 4. Sponsored by "the 65,000 employees of Union Pacific," in observance of the railroad's 75th anniversary. Full-network broadcasts originating in Omaha, the sponsor's home city: NBC broadcasts from WOW; Mutual from KBON.

PERSONNEL: Comprised largely of Omaha radio talent; talks by governors of 11 western states. NARRATORS: Thomson Holtz and Virgil Sharpe of KOIL. ANNOUNCER: Ray Olson of WOW. VOCALIST: Soprano Grace McTernan. STORY-TELLER: Nelson Olmsted; Elden Westley, after Olmsted left for military duty. ORCHESTRA: Josef Koestner, composer-conductor, with 58 musicians and vocalists. PRODUCER: Lyle DeMoss of WOW. WRITER: David P. Lewis.

This series was created to give Americans a better understanding, through story and song, "of the romantic history and factual possibilities of the Middle and Far West." A weekly high spot was Nelson Olmsted's story of "your America at war." These tales were hard-hitting and graphic. On March 18, 1944, Olmsted related atrocities of the Bataan Death March, including this prediction: "Hitler and Mussolini, in all likelihood, will break and crawl at the last, but Hideki Tojo will never let himself be tried by 'foreign barbarians.' The only thing to do is hasten the day when he will plunge a knife into his belly, draw it across, and turn it sharply upward." It didn't turn out that way, but such was the sentiment of *Your America* in the spring of 1944.

YOUR BLIND DATE, USO-type variety.

BROADCAST HISTORY: March 5–July 6, 1942, Blue Network. 30m, initially Thursdays on the regional West Coast hookup; full network beginning April 20, Mondays at 9, later at 9:30. CREATOR-HOSTESS: Frances Scully. CAST: Brenda Frazier and Cobina Wright, vocalist Connie Haines, the Brian Sisters, Nathan Scott's Melodates, Tizzie Lish (Bill Comstock from *The Al Pearce Show* in his screwy female impersonation), an all-girl band, and glamour-girl guests from the movie lots (Martha O'Driscoll and Lucille Ball among them). PRODUCER-DIRECTOR-WRITER: Myron Dutton.

Your Blind Date was created to provide live feminine entertainment for servicemen stationed in southern California. To the men in the audience, the highlight came after the show, when the stage of Studio B at Hollywood's Radio City was transformed into a giant dance floor, a free jukebox containing the top dance hits was wheeled in, and scores of women from USO groups helped the boys while away the night. Competition for tickets to the broadcasts was keen.

YOUR FAMILY AND MINE, soap opera.

BROADCAST HISTORY: April 25, 1938–April 28, 1939, NBC. 15m, weekdays at 5:15. Sealtest.

May 1, 1939–April 26, 1940, CBS. 15m, weekdays at 2:30. Sealtest.

CAST: Bill Adams as Matthew Wilbur, head of a household in High Falls, Mt., who struggled to make ends meet during the depression. Lucille Wall as his wife, Winifred Wilbur, or Win. Joan Tompkins as their daughter Judy, "the redheaded angel." Billy Lipton as their son Ken. Parker Fennelly as Lem Stacy, the well-meaning tightwad who owned the store where Matthew Wilbur worked. Francesca Lenni as Laura Putnam, Matthew's 27-year-old married sister, who had snagged her husband on the rebound and continued to flirt shamelessly. Maurice Wells as Donald Putnam, a devoted husband whose lot in life was to live with a woman who did not love him. Joy Terry as their 6-year-old daughter, Barbara, who lived with the Wilburs because of her parents' fighting, idolized young Ken Wilbur (to his annoyance), and wanted to become a baseball player. Carl Frank as Arch Hadley, the banker's son, loved by Judy but under under the thumb of his snobbish mother. Peter Donald as Dick Burgess, the poor and struggling young man who loved Judy but got little encouragement. Arthur Maitland as Silas Drake, the "town boss," head of the Drake Water Company. **ANNOUNCER:** Ford Bond. **DIRECTORS:** Larry Hammond, Harold McGee. **WRITER:** Lillian Lauferty.

The family of this serial was a product of its time, part of the great middle class trying to survive. Matthew Wilbur had bought his home years ago when he was an accountant: he was now 50, had lost many jobs of late, and had just found work in Lem Stacy's store. He filled his time tinkering with gadgets, hoping that one of his inventions would make his fortune.

His wife Win was the family mainstay, turning an ability to bake into a business of sorts that at times supported their hand-to-mouth existence. She was younger than her husband, 39 as the story opened. Their daughter Judy was a 17-year-old bundle of impatience who tried not to resent her father's failure but hated being a "nobody" in the town. Son Ken, 12, was ambitious and solid, willing to help out by earning money on a newspaper route.

YOUR HIT PARADE, popular music.

BROADCAST HISTORY: April 20, 1935–Dec. 1, 1937, NBC. Initially 60m, Saturdays at 8; split into two broadcasts March 11, 1936, with the Saturday show supplemented by a Wednesdays-at-10 hour, which was trimmed to 30m in Nov. 1936. The Saturday show, meanwhile, moved to CBS after the April 25, 1936, broadcast. Lucky Strike. **ANNOUNCERS:** Ben Grauer, NBC; Andre Baruch, CBS. **VOCALISTS:** Gogo DeLys, Kay Thompson, Charles Carlisle, etc. **ORCHESTRA:** Lennie Hayton, originally; then, visiting orchestras on a rotating basis—Al Goodman, Freddie Rich, Carl Hoff, Ray Sinatra, Harry Salter, Harry Sosnik; Abe Lyman, 1937; Mark Warnow, 1937.

May 2, 1936–April 19, 1947, CBS. Saturdays, 30m at 10, 1936–37; 60m at 10, 1937–38; 45m at 10, 1938–39; 45m at 9, 1939–44; 30m at 9, 1943–44; 45m at 9, 1944–47. **VOCALISTS: 1930s:** Loretta Lee, Willie Morris, Stuart Allen; Margaret McCrea and Edith Dick, paired in turn with Buddy Clark, 1936–37; Len Stokes, Bob Simmons, Kay Lorraine, Patricia Norman; Fredda Gibson (Georgia Gibbs) paired with Buddy Clark, 1937–38; Lanny Ross, 1938–39; Bea Wain, two stints totaling three years, 1939–44; Barry Wood and "Wee" Bonnie Baker, 1939–40. **1940s:** Louise King, 1941; Joan Edwards, five years, beginning in late 1941; Frank Sinatra, 1943–45; Lawrence Tibbett, Jan.–July 1945; Dick Todd, 1945–46; Peggy Mann, 1946; Johnny Mercer, early 1946; Joe Dosh; Andy Russell; Beryl Davis, 1947–48. **ORCHESTRA:** Richard Himber, Leo Reisman, Peter Van Steeden, 1937–39; Mark Warnow, permanent musical director, 1939–47. **VOCAL HARMONY, MID-1930s:** The Songsmiths (tenors Randolph Weyant and Scrappy Lambert, baritone Leonard Stokes, bass Robert Moody).

COMEDY ROUTINE, 1938: W. C. Fields, with Walter Tetley as the brat who pestered him.

April 26, 1947–Jan. 16, 1953, NBC. 30m, Saturdays at 9, 1947–51; Thursdays at 10, 1951–52; Fridays at 8, 1952–53. **VOCALISTS:** Frank Sinatra, returning September 1947–May 1949; Dinah Shore, Ginny Simms, the Andrews Sisters, Martha Tilton, Dick Haymes, and Doris Day, all 1947. Eileen Wilson, 1948–51; Bill Harrington, and Jeff Clark, 1949; Sue Bennett, 1951–53; Snooky Lanson, Dorothy Collins, Gisele MacKenzie, and Russell Arms, 1950s. **ORCHESTRA:** Axel Stordahl, 1947–49; Raymond Scott, 1949–57, into the TV era; Harry Sosnik, post–1957, TV only.

Your Hit Parade was a key influence in the popular culture of its day, a Saturday night instution for most of its run. "It's not unusual to see devotees of certain songs become joyous, vindictive, or disappointed," noted *Radio Life* in 1943. Bets were often placed on the weekly survey of America's most popular music, and the dramatic countdown to the Number One Song was climaxed by a trumpet fanfare and a drumroll. "It's the one burning question that every American who can carry a tune wants answered. What's Number One on the *Hit Parade?*"

In those days before disc jockeys, *Your Hit Parade* was the final word in popular music. "Once again the voice of the people has spoken," the announcer said, introducing an early show. "You've told us by your purchases of sheet music and records, by your requests to orchestra leaders in the places you've danced, by the tunes you listen to on your favorite radio programs." People who gathered at radios and cheered on the winner winced a week later when their favorite fell from grace. Hardly anyone disputed the tabulation, except, at one point, some disgruntled tunesmiths of Tin Pan Alley.

The tabulations were compiled in the offices of the agency representing American Tobacco (originally Lord and Thomas; later, Batten, Barton, Durstine, and Osborne). The agency tried to keep its ways and means secret, releasing only the general statement that a "large staff" checked the statistics, that the system was "infallible," and that it was based mainly on readings of radio requests, sheet music sales, dance-hall favorites, and jukebox tabulations. *Radio Guide* revealed that the job of conducting "an endless popularity poll on a nationwide scale" made *Your Hit Parade* "the most complex broadcast on the air." Elaborate measures were taken to ensure secrecy: the data was even transported to Lord and Thomas by armored truck. The final results were in by 8:30 Saturday. By Monday morning the order of the top ten was known, and only then could the orchestra and cast begin rehearsing for broadcasts on Wednesday and Saturday of the same week.

It didn't matter if the hyperbole had any scientific validity: the people believed it. But the show was slow to arrive at its most natural and most suspenseful format. As John R. Williams noted in his comprehensive week-by-week history, *This Was Your Hit Parade*, it "originally consisted of the 15 top songs played in random order. Several years would pass before the well-remembered format building up to the top three tunes was established."

The formats varied from seven to fifteen songs, Williams noted, with seven being most common. Having attained the weekly list, the Lord and Thomas Radio Department (under Tom McAvity) had a script prepared, consisting mainly of continuity and commercial copy. This was sent to the orchestra leader, who then wrote the charts and plotted the three "extra" medleys that would be performed on the air. The orchestra rehearsed intensely the day before the broadcast, about eight hours for each 45-minute show. The vocalists were worked in and, in the early days, were given no on-air credit.

Your Hit Parade was a revival of sorts, with new trappings, of the old *Lucky Strike Dance Orchestra*, heard on NBC from 1928 through 1931. In this old format, maestro B. A. Rolfe would play what were said to be the most popular tunes of the hour, a pleasing 60 minutes that was also heard Saturdays at 10. American Tobacco president George Washington Hill had built his product from scratch, beginning with its introduction in 1917, by the ingenious use of advertising slogans and catchy gimmicks. The first of these Lucky Strike catchwords was "It's toasted." This was used in print ads and carried over into the earliest Lucky Strike radio shows. Hill's arrival was immediately controversial when, on the *Lucky Strike Dance Orchestra* series, he introduced the slogan "Reach for a Lucky instead of a sweet." The candy industry reacted with strong indignation, but it wasn't until the advent of *Your Hit Parade* that Hill hit his best stride, employing what came to be called the "triphammer commercial."

In his early life, Hill had spent time in the tobacco auction houses and factories of North Carolina. He became interested in the auction as a selling tool, and, on a swing through the tobacco belt, he went on a search for the fastest tobacco auctioneer in the state. He was referred to L. A. "Speed" Riggs of Goldsboro, N.C., whose salary as an auctioneer he immediately doubled. Later he added a second auctioneer, F. E. Boone of Lexington, Ky. Boone's pitch was done in monotone, a striking contrast to the singsong style of Riggs (which always ended "Sold to American!").

He paid these auctioneers $25,000 a year "just to chant one and one-half minutes of open and closing commercials," said his entry in *Current Biography*. This "triphammer" approach was responsible for some of the most memorable commercials ever aired, utilizing repetition (*Lucky Strike green has gone to war*), a clicking telegraph, the slogan "LSMFT" ("Lucky Strike means fine tobacco"), and announcers (Andre Baruch and Basil Ruysdael) whose voices were as distinctive as any in radio. Hill ran *Your Hit Parade* with an iron hand. He tried to run *Information, Please*, and came to an ugly parting with its owner, Dan Golenpaul. Ironically, he made no attempt to control *The Jack Benny Program*, yet there his "triphammer commercial" reached its peak.

Few shows ran so long with so many changes of personnel. Williams lists 52 singers or groups and 19 orchestra leaders over the 24-year run. Guest soloists augmented the regulars in the first half-decade, with such people as Mario Chamlee of the Metropolitan Opera coming to the *Hit Parade* microphone. The shows of the '40s were distinguished by longer stints and bigger names. The popularity of five-year regular Joan Edwards soared; servicemen formed a nationwide "Moan-and-Groan-for-Joan" club. Ethel Smith, redheaded and dynamic, became the *YHP* organist in 1942. Frank Sinatra roared into the show in 1943, bringing a screaming crowd of bobby-soxers. Met star Lawrence Tibbett replaced Sinatra, a radical change indeed, in January 1945. The teenage screaming ceased, but the rating jumped seven points. The screamers returned with the arrival in mid-1946 of Andy Russell:

the teenagers were now nicknamed "Russell's Sprouts," but it all sounded slightly contrived.

The show moved to Hollywood in 1947, losing Joan Edwards, who had sung through the eras of Barry Wood, Sinatra, Tibbett, Dick Todd, Johnny Mercer, and Russell. Sinatra returned in September, bringing his juvenile swooners and his own orchestra leader, his pal Axel Stordahl from his Tommy Dorsey days. Sinatra and Stordahl remained until May 1949; Mark Warnow returned, and, after his death, his brother Raymond Scott led the orchestra well past the end of the radio era, through much of its run on early TV. The series was a success on television as well, simulcast in the radio years. It began a trial run on NBC July 10, 1950, and ended on CBS April 24, 1959. The latter-day singers—especially Snooky Lanson, Dorothy Collins, and Gisele MacKenzie—were strongly identified with the early TV era.

The songs? There was no telling what might make *Your Hit Parade*. Novelty numbers, Christmas songs, rhythm and blues, even jazz. A few flashed briefly onto the charts, rising high into the top five, then dropped quickly into oblivion. Others hung in for months. Williams lists these among the most popular pre-1950 hits: *Buttons and Bows; I Hear a Rhapsody; I'll Be Seeing You; Now Is the Hour; Peg o' My Heart; Some Enchanted Evening*; and *A Tree in the Meadow. White Christmas* returned for years, predictably in winter, appearing on the list 38 times, a record.

The well-remembered themes were *Happy Days Are Here Again* (1930s) and *Lucky Day*; the closing song was likewise memorable:

> So long, for a while;
> That's all the songs, for a while;
> So long to Your Hit Parade,
> And the tunes that you picked to be played . . .
> So long . . .

YOUR HOLLYWOOD PARADE, variety.

BROADCAST HISTORY: Dec. 8, 1937–March 23, 1938, NBC. 60m, Wednesdays at 10. Lucky Strike. **HOST:** Dick Powell. **COMIC:** Bob Hope, who joined the cast in late Dec. **GUESTS:** Gary Cooper, Bette Davis, Olivia DeHavilland, etc. **VOCALIST:** Rosemary Lane; also, Mable Todd. **ORCHESTRA:** Leo Forbstein, then Al Goodman.

Your Hollywood Parade was the second major variety show linking a top film studio with a network. MGM had started the stampede five weeks earlier with *Good News of 1938*, and now Warner Brothers jumped in the swim. It was an uneasy alliance between friendly rivals, with the sponsor a third cog in the wheel. George Washington Hill, president of American Tobacco, promptly let it be known that he, not Warners, was calling the shots. The scripts would be prepared by Hill's ad agency, and Warners would be limited to making its entire studio lot and star roster available.

It was a lavish mix of music, comedy, and drama, the latter taken from current and coming WB screen hits. But the show's one claim to enduring fame was Bob Hope: it wasn't Hope's first series, but it was the one that led to everything else.

YOUR LUCKY STRIKE, talent show, also known as THE DON AMECHE SHOW.

BROADCAST HISTORY: Dec. 6, 1948–March 4, 1949, CBS. 30m weekdays at 3:30. Lucky Strike. HOST: Don Ameche. ANNOUNCER: Frank Martin. TOBACCO AUCTIONEER: L. A. "Speed" Riggs. MUSIC: Al De Crescent on organ and Bill Wardell on piano. PRODUCER: Bernard Schubert. DIRECTOR: Harlan Dunning.

Your Lucky Strike was a forum for talented unknowns, people who had had some professional experience but had not received broad popularity. Each brought to the show a human interest story as well as a performing talent. The judging was done by three random housewives, different each week, who voted via long distance telephone calls. The judges were nominated by friends in the studio audience. The decision of the housewives was final, but if they failed to reach a majority vote, the studio audience made the choice. Winners received professional engagements at Earl Carroll's, the Mocambo, or some other club.

YOUR UNSEEN FRIEND, light drama, based on problems suggested by listeners.

BROADCAST HISTORY: Oct. 4, 1936–Jan. 1, 1938, CBS. 30m, Sundays at 5 until April 1937; Tuesdays at 10:30, later at 10; later Saturdays at

8. Personal Loan. HOST: Maurice Joachim as the "unseen friend," the man who arranged the listener problems in a dramatic context that might allow the listener to solve the problem himself. DRAMATIC CAST: Peggy Allenby, Alice Reinheart, Mae Murray, Sydney Smith, etc. ORCHESTRA: Harry Salter.

Your Unseen Friend, said *Radio Guide*, never gave advice "but allows us to see what is going on in a man's heart." Host Maurice Joachim maintained that all men are driven by a "voice of conscience," and this became a subtitle in his billing.

YOURS TRULY, JOHNNY DOLLAR, detective drama.

BROADCAST HISTORY: Dec. 8, 1948, audition record prepared. CAST: Dick Powell as Johnny Dollar, freelance insurance investigator (Powell opted not to do this series, but went instead into *Richard Diamond, Private Detective*). MUSIC: Richard Aurandt. WRITERS: Paul Dudley and Gil Doud. DIRECTOR: Anton M. Leader.

Feb. 11, 1949–Jan. 14, 1950, CBS. 30m, Fridays at 10:30 through April 22; returned July 17, Sundays at 6:30; Saturdays at 7 beginning October 1. CAST: Charles Russell as Johnny Dollar (also heard in a new audition record, produced prior to the premiere date.) ORCHESTRA: Mark Warnow, early 1949; then Leith Stevens. DIRECTORS: Richard Sanville, early 1949; Norman Macdonnell beginning July 17; Gordon T. Hughes beginning November 5. WRITERS: Paul Dudley and Gil Doud.

Feb. 3, 1950–Sept. 3, 1952, CBS. Many 30m timeslots; moved frequently with some continuity gaps. Wrigley's Gum, summer 1950. CAST: Edmond O'Brien as Johnny Dollar. ANNOUNCERS: Dan Cubberly, Roy Rowan. ORCHESTRA: Leith Stevens, Wilbur Hatch. PRODUCER-DIRECTOR: Jaime del Valle. WRITERS: Dudley and Doud; E. Jack Neuman, David Ellis, John Michael Hayes.

Nov. 28, 1952–Sept. 19, 1954, CBS. Various 30m timeslots, most notably Tuesdays at 9 for Wrigley's Gum, March 10, 1953–Aug. 10, 1954, the longest continuous sponsorship the series would enjoy. CAST: John Lund as Johnny Dollar. ANNOUNCER: Dan Cubberly. MUSIC: Eddie Dunstedter on organ. PRODUCER-DIRECTOR:

Jaime del Valle. **WRITERS:** E. Jack Neuman, Blake Edwards, Joel Murcott, Les Crutchfield, Sidney Marshall, Morton Fine and David Friedkin, Gil Doud.

August 29, 1955: Log writers Terry Salomonson and Don Aston note a new audition produced this date; never aired. **CAST:** Gerald Mohr as Johnny Dollar.

Oct. 3, 1955–Nov. 2, 1956, CBS. 15m continuation, weeknights at 8:15; at 9:15 beginning April 1956. Five-part stories, with a few exceptions, that concluded within the week; 55 multi-chaptered stories broadcast. **CAST:** Bob Bailey as Johnny Dollar. **ORCHESTRA:** Amerigo Marino. **PRODUCER-DIRECTOR:** Jack Johnstone. **WRITERS:** John Dawson, Les Crutchfield, Robert Ryf, Jack Johnstone, etc.

Nov. 4, 1956–Nov. 27, 1960, CBS. 30m, Sundays, various late afternoon or early evening time-slots; Saturdays on the West Coast, 1957–58. **CAST:** Bob Bailey as Johnny Dollar. **DIRECTOR:** Jack Johnstone. **WRITERS AND ORCHESTRA:** same as for 1955–56 season.

Dec. 4, 1960–June 18, 1961, CBS. 30m, Sundays, moved from Hollywood to New York with changes of personnel. **CAST:** Bob Readick as Johnny Dollar. **ANNOUNCERS:** Art Hanna, etc. **MUSIC:** Ethel Huber. **PRODUCER-DIRECTOR:** Bruno Zirato Jr. **WRITER:** Jack Johnstone, who continued to send scripts from Hollywood.

June 25, 1961–Sept. 30, 1962, CBS. 30m, Sundays from New York. **CAST:** Mandel Kramer as Johnny Dollar; same production crew as 1960–61. Fred Hendrickson director as of June 1962.

SUPPORTING CAST: Hollywood regulars, 1949–60: Vivi Janiss, Jack Kruschen, John Dehner, Ann Morrison, Paul Dubov, Lillian Buyeff, Lawrence Dobkin, Barney Phillips, Georgia Ellis, Parley Baer, William Conrad, Ed Begley, Jeanne Bates, Irene Tedrow, Peggy Webber, Joseph Kearns, Lurene Tuttle, Howard McNear, etc. Virginia Gregg virtually a regular, mid-1950s, often as Dollar's girlfriend, Betty Lewis. New York regulars, 1960–62: Joan Lorring, Robert Dryden, Ralph Camargo, Danny Ocko, Gertrude Warner, Roger DeKoven, Bill Meader, William Redfield, Bernard Grant, Ralph Bell, Jack Grimes, Santos Ortega, Martin Blaine, Bill Adams, Vicki Vola, Jackson Beck, etc.

Yours Truly, Johnny Dollar had more lives than a cat. Despite opening to derisive reviews in 1949, *Johnny Dollar* lived to fight again … and again … and again. Including unaired audition discs, the series underwent seven changes in the title role. It spanned 14 years and was the last dramatic show on the air, closing down the art of dramatic network radio, Sept. 30, 1962.

Johnny Dollar was "America's fabulous freelance insurance investigator," the "man with the action-packed expense account." He was always ready to fly to far corners of the country for a cut of recovered goods. He had an analytical mind, a nose for trouble, and the brawn to take care of himself when the going got dirty.

He often worked for "Universal Adjustment Bureau," a clearing house for all client companies, under assignment from Universal's Pat McCracken. The assignment might be to recover stolen diamonds, art, or furs; to investigate arson; to play bodyguard to a wealthy client, insured to the hilt, whose life had been threatened. Inevitably, all led to murder.

As originally played by Charles Russell, Dollar was a free-wheeling tipper who tossed silver dollars to busboys and doormen. This early trademark soon fell away, but throughout the eras of Russell, Edmond O'Brien, and John Lund, the show was standard detective fare. O'Brien was a gruff-sounding hero; Lund much the same. The humanizing touches were few, and the power source was the same toughguy demeanor that had carried Gerald Mohr so well through *The Adventures of Philip Marlowe.*

The character made a leap in personal development with the arrival of Bob Bailey as Dollar, of Jack Johnstone as writer-director, and of various freelance writers who were not so mired in the detective genre that they considered each gumshoe case an extension of the last. Bailey walked into a serial format that, compared to the old show, had the breath of life. Each story now had 75 minutes of air time per week: people and themes barely sketched in the half-hours could be fully developed. Character became the motivating factor. This would continue to some extent throughout Bailey's tenure, but with the return to the half-hours in 1956 (half-hours that were often 25 minutes or less as the radio era wound down), a certain triteness returned. The lead was still well played: Bailey had the ability to imbue the role with an unforgettable quality not heard before or after.

His shameless padding of his expense account was now played for comic relief, usually in the pretitle dialogue between the hero and Pat McCracken (or some other agent). Dollar had a girlfriend, Betty Lewis, though he was a confirmed bachelor and grumbled frequently that the "crazy life" he led would be a detriment to marriage. Unlike others of his ilk, he respected the police (one of his pals was Randy Singer, "down at headquarters"); also in his life were tipsters and stoolies (such as arsonist-turned-informant Smoky Sullivan) and recurring eccentrics (e.g., Alvin Peabody Cartwright, whose queer notions had a way of being at least partly right).

Mostly he worked alone: he whisked away to a new locale each week—perhaps to Mexico, a ghost town in California, or a swamp in the southeast. Dollar himself was the first-person narrator. The stories all developed in terms of his expense account: "Expense account, item one," and he was off. It might be a buck-fifty (including tip) for cab fare across town, or $200 airfare across the country. At the airport he'd be met by the adjuster, who would introduce him to the people in the case. Occasionally, for variety, the claim was legitimate and the company had to pay. Once in a while, Dollar simply arrived too late. His greatest personal shortcoming, as developed by Bailey, was a streak of impatience. More than once he charged into action after hearing only part of what a person was telling him— missing the one vital point that would have allowed him to clear it up sooner. But at the end, the expense account was neatly totaled and signed—"Yours truly, Johnny Dollar."

The show had a different sound after its move to New York. The character's continuity was ensured by the Jack Johnstone scripting, but *Dollar* at this point is perhaps the best example of how different shows from the opposite coasts could be. The series as a whole is interesting in that it was the great survivor of its day. Amazing that a show with little budget and only brief periods of sponsorship could keep returning and actually be the final network broadcast of the old era. There are listeners who love it all, but this writer's admiration is largely confined to that year of the serial: those five-chapter tales captured the character as never before, Raymond William Stedman's description of them as "cliché-ridden" to the contrary. It was great radio, a role Bob Bailey was born to play. "If you know how to handle your voice in radio, it's almost impossible to destroy an illusion," Bailey said in midrole. His performance is its own best evidence.

YOUTH VS. AGE, quiz.

BROADCAST HISTORY: June 6, 1939–April 20, 1940, NBC. 30m, Red Network, Tuesdays at 7:30 until Oct.; Blue, Sundays at 8:30 until mid-Jan.; then Red, Saturdays at 9. Vince Mouthwash and Sloan's Liniment. **HOST:** Cal Tinney until late Jan.; then Paul Wing.

Young contestants were pitted against old: father against son; mother against daughter. The sponsor's product, Vince Mouthwash, was sold heavily as an aid to greater smoking pleasure.

THE ZANE GREY SHOW, western drama.

BROADCAST HISTORY: Sept. 23, 1947–Feb. 24, 1948, Mutual; moved from Hollywood to New York at some point during the run. 30m, Tuesdays at 9:30. **CAST:** Vic Perrin as Tex Thorne, big-country drifter on the wild frontier, "where strong men lived by the strong law of personal justice." Don MacLaughlin as Tex Thorne, from New York. **ORCHESTRA:** Harry Zimmerman. **PRODUCER:** Stephen Slesinger. **WRITER-DIRECTOR:** Paul Franklin. **DIRECTOR:** Emmett Paul (New York).

THE ZENITH FOUNDATION, drama with extrasensory perception experiments.

BROADCAST HISTORY: Sept. 5, 1937–March 27, 1938, Blue Network until early Dec., then CBS. 30m, Sundays at 10. Zenith Radios.

The Zenith Foundation involved the national radio audience in tests to determine if extrasensory perception exists on a mass level. Eugene F. McDonald, president of the Zenith company, had long been interested in radio as a means of telepathic testing, conducting what was believed to be the first such program in history on WJAZ, Chicago, in 1924. Now, on *The Zenith Foundation*, came the first large-scale attempt.

Listeners heard a machine in studio select at random seven colors they were told were either black or white. A panel of five men and five women in studio were told to concentrate for ten seconds on the color selected by the machine. Listeners at home were told to try to receive the messages. A week later the results were announced.

It was first admitted that selections Three and Seven were colors other than black: this was done intentionally, to weed out bias and make the tests scientifically relevant. The results: 20 percent of the audience got four numbers correct, 4 percent got all, and many were blank for Three and Seven. The series went on to more intricate experiments and staged dramas illustrating case histories of telepathic communication.

THE ZERO HOUR, mystery-adventure drama anthology; also known as HOLLYWOOD RADIO THEATER.

BROADCAST HISTORY: 1973, transcribed 30m syndication; later sold to Mutual for two runs, Sept. 10–Dec. 7, 1973, and April 29–July 26, 1974. Produced in stereo, in Hollywood. **HOST:** Rod Serling. **CAST:** Radio stars (Edgar Bergen, Richard Crenna, Howard Duff, John Dehner, Lurene Tuttle, etc.) billed with current TV favorites (George Maharis, Susan Oliver, Joseph Campanella, John Astin and Patty Duke, etc.). **MUSIC:** Theme played by pianists Ferrante and Teicher. **PRODUCER:** J. M. Kholos. **DIRECTOR:** Elliott Lewis.

The syndication of *The Zero Hour* in 1973 touched off a rush to return drama to the air. It was soon joined by *The CBS Radio Mystery Theater* and others in the only serious radio revival since the networks got out of the business in 1962.

J. M. Kholos was a Los Angeles advertising man who had bought the rights to some popular suspense novels (*The Blessing Way*, by Tony Hillerman, perhaps the most prominent) and then put together an intriguing mix of talent to make it fly. "They wanted as much [current] name value as possible to help with sales," recalled director Elliott Lewis a decade later. This was the purpose in starring young TV performers along with older radio people.

There were two problems, said Lewis. "They forgot they had to sell it. Everybody sat in their offices waiting for somebody to call them up and buy the show." The other problem was that the novels were cut into five-chapter stories, each chapter running 30 minutes and requiring consecutive play. It disrupted the stations' patterns too much, so no one bought it. The name value of the TV stars didn't help because, as Lewis said, on radio, "if you miss the opening credits, you'd have no idea that was Patty and John Astin." The show was reorganized and sold to Mutual; Lewis left, the format was changed, and the commercial load was oppressive. It died, leaving *Mystery Theater* to carry on the lost art.

THE ZIEGFELD FOLLIES OF THE AIR, musical variety.

BROADCAST HISTORY: April 3–June 26, 1932, CBS. 30m, Sundays at 8; at 10:30 as of April 24. Chrysler Motors. HOST: Eddie Dowling.

STARS: Will Rogers, Helen Morgan, Jack Pearl, Fanny Brice, etc. ORCHESTRA: Al Goodman.

Feb. 22–June 6, 1936, CBS. 60m, Saturdays at 8. STARS: Fanny Brice as Baby Snooks. Jack Arthur as Daddy. Also: James Melton, Benny Fields, Patty Chapin, etc. ORCHESTRA: Al Goodman. WRITER: Gertrude Berg.

Both brief runs of *The Ziegfeld Follies of the Air* gave the atmosphere and pace of the stage shows. Florenz Ziegfeld appeared on the 1932 broadcast, recalling his greatest *Follies* thrills: his wife, Billie Burke, was piped in from California, and both seemed awed by the new medium.

Ziegfeld died soon after the original series left the air, and the 1936 show glamorized his memory. Here Fanny Brice sang her famed torch song, *My Man*, then introduced Baby Snooks to the radio world. Encouraged by good reviews, Brice continued the Snooks skits through the spring, then went on to the Maxwell House *Good News* show, and a new career on the air. There was also a contrived backstage love drama, the fictional story of Alice Moore, a girl from nowhere who hungered for her show business break. Forced to choose between love and the stage, she cast off her man and took an usher's job in the *Follies*. Week by week, she inched closer to her goal. Would she make it? . . . become the Fanny Brice of 1940?

Anything could happen. It was joyous and heartbreaking, a difficult but exciting time to be alive. Radio made it all of those things.

Bibliography

RADIO BROADCASTS

Extensive background and credit information is derived from the author's library of 35,000 vintage radio broadcasts, touching virtually every series in every field, ca. 1926–62, and accumulated steadily since 1969.

BOOKS

Abbot, Waldo. *Handbook of Broadcasting*. Mc-Graw-Hill, NY, 1941.

Ace, Goodman. *Ladies and Gentlemen—Easy Aces*. Doubleday, Garden City, NY, 1970.

Adams, Franklin P. *Nods and Becks*. Whittlesey House, NY, 1944.

Adams, Samuel Hopkins. *A. Woollcott: His Life and His World*. Reynal & Hitchcock, NY, 1945.

Adler, Irene. *I Remember Jimmy: The Life and Times of Jimmy Durante*. Arlington House, New Rochelle, NY, 1980.

Allen, Fred. *Much Ado About Me*. Atlantic–Little, Brown, Boston, 1956.

———. *Treadmill to Oblivion*. Atlantic–Little, Brown, Boston, 1954.

American Tobacco Company. *"Sold American!"—The First Fifty Years*. 1954.

Andrews, Bart, and Ahrgus Juilliard. *Holy Mackerel! The Amos 'n' Andy Story*. Dutton, NY, 1986.

Arce, Hector. *Groucho: The Authorized Biography*. Putnam, NY, 1979.

Arden, Eve. *Three Phases of Eve*. St. Martin's, NY, 1985.

Ashley, Sally. *FPA: The Life and Times of Franklin Pierce Adams*. Beaufort, NY, 1986.

Autry, Gene. *Back in the Saddle Again*. Doubleday, Garden City, NY, 1978.

Bacher, William A., ed. *The Treasury Star Parade*. Farrar & Rinehart, NY, 1942.

Bankhead, Tallulah. *Tallulah: My Autobiography*. Harper & Bros., NY, 1952.

Banning, William Peck. *Commercial Broadcasting Pioneer: The WEAF Experiment, 1922–1926*. Harvard, Cambridge, MA, 1946.

Bannon, "Red Ryder" Jim. *The Son That Rose in the West*. Devil's Hole Printery, Plano, TX, 1975.

Barabas, SuzAnne, and Gabor Barabas. *Gunsmoke: A Complete History*. McFarland, Jefferson, NC, 1990.

Barber, Red. *The Broadcasters*. Dial, NY, 1970.

Barnes, Ken. *The Crosby Years*. St. Martin's, NY, 1980.

Barnouw, Erik. *A History of Broadcasting in the United States, 1933–53*. 3 vols.: *A Tower in Babel, The Golden Web*, and *The Image Empire*. Oxford University Press, NY, 1966–70.

———, ed. *Radio Drama in Action*. Farrar & Rinehart, NY, 1945.

Barson, Michael, ed. *Flywheel, Shyster and Flywheel: The Marx Brothers' Lost Radio Show*. Pantheon, NY, 1988.

Bellamy, Ralph. *When the Smoke Hit the Fan*. Doubleday, Garden City, NY, 1979.

Benét, Stephen Vincent. *We Stand United, and Other Radio Scripts*. Farrar & Rinehart, NY, 1945.

Benny, Joan, and Jack Benny. *Sunday Nights at Seven: The Jack Benny Story*. Warner, NY, 1990.

Benny, Mary Livingstone, and Hilliard Marks, with Marcia Borie. *Jack Benny: A Biography.* Doubleday, Garden City, NY, 1978.

Berg, Gertrude. *Molly and Me.* McGraw-Hill, NY, 1961.

———. *The Rise of the Goldbergs.* Barse, NY, 1931.

Bergen, Candice. *Knock Wood.* Linden Press, NY, 1984.

Bergreen, Laurence. *As Thousands Cheer: The Life of Irving Berlin.* Viking, NY, 1990.

———. *Look Now, Pay Later: The Rise of Network Broadcasting.* Doubleday, Garden City, NY, 1980.

Berle, Milton. *B.S. I Love You.* McGraw-Hill, NY, 1988.

———. *Milton Berle: An Autobiography.* Delacorte, NY, 1974.

Blanc, Mel. *That's Not All, Folks: My Life in the Golden Age of Cartoons and Radio.* Warner, NY, 1988.

Blythe, Cheryl, and Susan Sackett. *Say Goodnight, Gracie! The Story of Burns and Allen.* Dutton, NY, 1986.

Bogue, Merwyn. *Ish Kabibble.* Louisiana State University Press, Baton Rouge, 1989.

Bordman, Gerald. *American Musical Theatre.* Oxford University Press, NY, 1978.

Brady, Frank. *Citizen Welles.* Scribners, NY, 1989.

Brokenshire, Norman. *This Is Norman Brokenshire.* McKay, NY, 1954.

Brooks, Elston. *I've Heard Those Songs Before: The Weekly Top Ten Tunes for the Past Fifty Years.* Morrow, NY, 1981.

Brooks, John. *Telephone: The First Hundred Years.* Harper & Row, NY, 1976.

Brooks, Tim, and Earle Marsh. *The Complete Directory to Prime-Time Network TV Shows, 1946–Present.* Ballantine, NY, 1979.

Brown, Jared. *Zero Mostel: A Biography.* Atheneum, NY, 1989.

Burdick, Loraine. *The Shirley Temple Scrapbook.* Jonathan David, Middle Village, NY, 1975.

Burke, Billie. *With a Feather on My Nose.* Appleton, NY, 1949.

Burlingame, Roger. *Don't Let Them Scare You: The Life and Times of Elmer Davis.* Lippincott, NY, 1961.

Burns, George. *Gracie: A Love Story.* Putnam, NY, 1988.

———. *I Love Her, That's Why! An Autobiography.* Simon & Schuster, NY, 1955.

———. *The Third Time Around.* Putnam, NY, 1980.

Buxton, Frank, and Bill Owen. *The Big Broadcast, 1920–1950.* Viking, NY, 1972.

Cahn, William. *Good Night, Mrs. Calabash: The Secret of Jimmy Durante.* Duell, Sloan, Pearce, NY, 1963.

———. *The Laugh Makers: A Pictorial History of American Comedians.* Putnam, NY, 1957.

Campbell, Robert. *The Golden Years of Broadcasting.* Scribners, NY, 1976.

Cantor, Eddie. *My Life Is in Your Hands.* Blue Ribbon Books reprint, NY, 1932.

———. *Take My Life.* Doubleday, Garden City, NY, 1957.

Cantril, Hadley. *The Invasion from Mars: A Study in the Psychology of a Panic, with the Complete Script of the Famous Orson Welles Broadcast.* Princeton University Press, NJ, 1940.

Carey, Macdonald. *The Days of My Life.* St. Martin's, NY, 1991.

Carlile, John S. *Production and Direction of Radio Programs.* Prentice-Hall, NY, 1940.

Carr, John Dickson. *The Dead Sleep Lightly and Other Mysteries from Radio's Golden Age.* Doubleday, Garden City, NY, 1983.

Carroll, Carroll. *None of Your Business, or, My Life with J. Walter Thompson (Confessions of a Renegade Radio Writer).* Cowles, NY, 1970.

CBS. *The Sound of Your Life: A Record of Radio's First Generation.* CBS, NY, 1950.

Chandler, Charlotte. *Hello, I Must Be Going: Groucho and His Friends.* Doubleday, Garden City, NY, 1978.

Cheerio. *The Story of Cheerio.* Garden City, NY, 1936.

Collier, James Lincoln. *Benny Goodman and the Swing Era.* Oxford University Press, NY, 1989.

Collins, Frederick L. *The FBI in Peace and War.* Putnam, NY, 1962.

Colman, Juliet Benita. *Ronald Colman.* Morrow, NY, 1975.

Colonna, Jerry. *Who Threw That Coconut?* Foreword by Bob Hope. Garden City, NY, 1945.

Columbia Broadcasting System, Inc. *From D-Day Through Victory in Europe: The Eye-Witness Story as Told by War Correspondents on the Air.* CBS, NY, 1945.

Connor, D. Russell, and Warren W. Hicks. *BG on the Record: A Bio-Discography of Benny Goodman.* Arlington House, New Rochelle, NY, 1969.

Considine, Bob. *Ripley, the Modern Marco Polo: The Life and Times of the Creator of "Believe-It-or-Not."* Doubleday, Garden City, NY, 1961.

Correll, Charles and Freeman Gosden. *All About Amos 'n' Andy.* Rand McNally, NY, 1929.

Corwin, Norman. *More by Corwin: Sixteen Radio Dramas.* Holt, NY, 1944.

———. *On a Note of Triumph.* Simon & Schuster, NY, 1945.

———. *Selected Radio Plays of Norman Corwin.* Armed Services Edition, Henry Holt & Co., 1944.

———. *Thirteen by Corwin: Radio Dramas.* Holt, NY, 1945.

———. *Untitled, and Other Radio Dramas.* Holt, NY, 1947.

Costello, Chris. *Lou's on First.* St. Martin's, NY, 1981.

Cotten, Joseph. *Vanity Will Get You Somewhere: An Autobiography.* Mercury House, San Francisco, 1987.

Coulter, Douglas. *Columbia Workshop Plays.* Whittlesey House, NY, 1939.

Crabb, Richard. *Radio's Beautiful Day: An Account of the First Five Decades of Broadcasting in America Based on the Experience of Everett Mitchell.* North Plains Press, Aberdeen, SD, 1983.

Cronyn, Hume. *A Terrible Liar: A Memoir.* Morrow, NY, 1991.

Crosby, Bing, with Pete Martin. *Call Me Lucky.* Simon & Schuster, NY, 1953.

Crosby, John. *Out of the Blue.* Simon & Schuster, NY, 1952.

Damrosch, Walter. *My Musical Life.* Scribners, NY, 1930.

Delaunay, Charles. *New Hot Discography.* Criterion, NY, 1948.

DeLong, Thomas A. *The Mighty Music Box: The Golden Age of Musical Radio.* Amber Crest, Los Angeles, 1980.

———. *Pops: Paul Whiteman, King of Jazz.* New Century, Piscataway, NJ, 1983.

DeMille, Cecil B. *The Autobiography of Cecil B. DeMille.* Prentice-Hall, Englewood Cliffs, NJ, 1959.

Dizikes, John. *Opera in America: A Cultural History.* Yale University Press, New Haven, CT, 1993.

Dragonette, Jessica. *Faith Is a Song.* McKay, NY, 1951.

Dunlap, Orrin E. *The Story of Radio.* Dial, NY, 1935.

Edmondson, Madeleine, and David Rounds. *From Mary Noble to Mary Hartman: The Complete Soap Opera Book.* Stein & Day, NY, 1976.

Eels, George. *Hedda and Louella.* Putnam, NY, 1972.

Elliott, Bob, and Ray Goulding. *The Bob and Ray Show.* Atheneum, NY, 1983.

———. *Write if You Get Work: The Best of Bob and Ray.* Random House, NY, 1975.

Ely, Melvin Patrick. *The Adventures of Amos 'n' Andy.* Free Press, NY, 1991.

Ewen, David. *All the Years of American Popular Music.* Prentice-Hall, Englewood Cliffs, NJ, 1977.

———, ed. *American Popular Songs.* Random House, NY, 1966.

———, ed. *Encyclopedia of the Opera.* Hill and Wang, NY, 1955.

Fabe, Maxene. *TV Game Shows.* Doubleday, Garden City, NY, 1979.

Falkenburg, Jinx. *Jinx.* Duell, Sloan, Pearce, NY, 1951.

Fang, Irving E. *Those Radio Commentators!* Iowa State, Ames, Iowa, 1977.

Feather, Leonard. *The Encyclopedia of Jazz.* Bonanza reprint; Crown, NY, 1960.

Fedo, Michael. *The Man from Lake Wobegon: An Unauthorized Biography of Garrison Keillor.* St. Martin's, NY, 1987.

Fein, Irving. *Jack Benny: An Intimate Biography.* Putnam, NY, 1976.

Feldman, Ruth Duskin. *Whatever Happened to the Quiz Kids?* Chicago Review Press, Chicago, 1982.

Fielding, Raymond. *The March of Time, 1935–1951.* Oxford University Press, NY, 1978.

Fink, John. *WGN: A Pictorial History.* WGN, Chicago, 1961.

Firestone, Ross, ed. *The Big Radio Comedy Program.* Contemporary Books, Chicago, 1978.

Fisher, Charles. *The Columnists.* Howell-Soskin, NY, 1944.

Fitelson, H. William, ed. *Theatre Guild on the Air.* Rinehart, NY, 1947.

Flower, John. *Moonlight Serenade: A Bio-Discography of the Glenn Miller Civilian*

Band. Arlington House, New Rochelle, NY, 1972.

Ford, "Senator" Ed, with Harry Hershfield and Joe Laurie, Jr. *Can You Top This?*, 1945; also *Cream of the Crop*, 1947. Didier Publishers/ Grosset & Dunlap, NY.

Forrest, Helen. *I Had the Craziest Dream*. Coward, McCann, NY, 1982.

Fowler, Gene. *Schnozzola: The Story of Jimmy Durante*. Viking, NY, 1951.

Fox, Dixon Ryan, and Arthur M. Schlesinger, eds. *The Cavalcade of America, Series 2*. Milton Bradley, Springfield, MA, 1938.

Francis, Arlene. *Arlene Francis: A Memoir*. Simon & Schuster, NY, 1978.

Franklin, Joe. *Joe Franklin's Encyclopedia of Comedians*. Citadel, Secaucus, NJ, 1979.

Friedersdorf, Burk. *From Crystal to Color: WFBM*. WFBM, Indianapolis, 1964.

Funt, Allen. *Evesdropper at Large: Adventures in Human Nature with "Candid Mike" and "Candid Camera."* Vanguard, NY, 1952.

Gabler, Neal. *Winchell: Gossip, Power and the Culture of Celebrity*. Knopf, NY, 1994.

Gambling, John. *Rambling with Gambling*. Prentice-Hall, Englewood Cliffs, NJ, 1972.

Gargan, William. *Why Me? An Autobiography*. Doubleday, Garden City, NY, 1969.

Garnett, Tay. *Light Up Your Torches and Pull Up Your Tights*. Arlington House, New Rochelle, NY, 1973.

Gates, Gary Paul. *Air Time: The Inside Story of CBS News*. Harper & Row, NY, 1978.

Geddes, Donald Porter, ed. *Franklin Delano Roosevelt: A Memorial*. Pocket Books, NY, 1945.

Gibbons, Floyd. *And They Thought We Wouldn't Fight*. Doran, NY, 1918.

Gibson, Walter B., with Anthony Tollin. *The Shadow Scrapbook*. Harcourt Brace, NY, 1979.

Godfrey, Arthur. *Stories I Like to Tell*. Simon & Schuster, NY, 1952.

Goldman, Herbert G. *Jolson: The Legend Comes to Life*. Oxford University Press, NY, 1988.

Goldsmith, Alfred N., and Austin C. Lescarboura. *This Thing Called Broadcasting*. Holt, NY, 1930.

Goldsmith, Clifford. *What a Life*, playbook, comedy in three acts. 1939.

Goldstein, Fred, and Stan Goldstein. *Prime-Time Television*. Crown, NY, 1983.

Golenpaul, Dan, ed. *Information, Please*. Simon & Schuster, NY, 1939.

Gordon, George N., and Irving A. Falk. *On the Spot Reporting: Radio Records History*. Messner, NY, 1967.

Greene, Douglas G. *John Dickson Carr: The Man Who Explained Miracles*. Otto Penzler, NY, 1995.

Gross, Ben. *I Looked and I Listened*. Random House, NY, 1954.

Guest, Edgar A. *Edgar A. Guest Broadcasting*. Reilly & Lee, Chicago, 1935.

Gurman, Joseph, and Myron Slager. *Radio Round-Ups: Intimate Glimpses of the Radio Stars*. Lothrop, Lee & Shepard, Boston, 1932.

Hamilton, David, ed. *The Metropolitan Opera Encyclopedia*. Simon & Schuster, NY, 1987.

Harmon, Jim. *The Great Radio Comedians*. Doubleday, Garden City, NY, 1970.

———. *The Great Radio Heroes*. Doubleday, Garden City, NY, 1967.

Harris, Warren G. *Lucy and Desi*. Simon & Schuster, NY, 1991.

Hasty, Jack. *Done with Mirrors*. Washburn, NY, 1943.

Herbert, F. Hugh. *Kiss and Tell: A Comedy in Three Acts*. Coward-McCann, NY, 1943.

Hickok, Eliza Merrill. *The Quiz Kids*. Houghton Mifflin, Boston, 1947.

Higby, Mary Jane. *Tune In Tomorrow*. Cowles, NY, 1968.

Higham, Charles. *Cecil B. DeMille*. Scribners, NY, 1973.

———. *Orson Welles: The Rise and Fall of an American Genius*. St. Martin's, NY, 1985.

Hope, Bob. *Don't Shoot, It's Only Me*. Putnam, NY, 1990.

———. *Have Tux, Will Travel*. Simon & Schuster, NY, 1954.

———. *They Got Me Covered*. Hollywood, 1941.

Horn, Maurice. *The World Encyclopedia of Comics*. Chelsea House, NY, 1976.

Hoseley, David H. *As Good as Any: Foreign Correspondence on American Radio, 1930–1940*. Greenwood Press, Westport, CT, 1984.

Houseman, John. *Final Dress*. Simon & Schuster, NY, 1983.

———. *Front and Center*. Simon & Schuster, NY, 1979.

———. *Run-Through*. Simon & Schuster, NY, 1972.

Hurst, Jack. *Nashville's Grand Ole Opry*. Abrams, NY, 1975.

Husing, Ted. *My Eyes Are in My Heart*. Bernard Geis, NY, 1959.

Israel, Lee. *Kilgallen*. Delacorte, NY, 1979.

Jablonski, Edward. *Gershwin*. Doubleday, Garden City, NY, 1987.

Jessel, George. *The World I Lived In*. Regnery, Chicago, 1975.

Jewell, Derek. *Duke: A Portrait of Duke Ellington*. Norton, NY, 1977.

Josefsberg, Milt. *The Jack Benny Show*. Arlington House, New Rochelle, NY, 1977.

Julian, Joseph. *This Was Radio*. Viking, NY, 1975.

Kaltenborn, H. V. *Fifty Fabulous Years*. Putnam, NY, 1950.

―――. *I Broadcast the Crisis*. Random House, NY, 1938.

―――. *Kaltenborn Edits the War News*. Dutton, NY, 1942.

Katkov, Norman. *The Fabulous Fanny: The Story of Fanny Brice*. Knopf, NY, 1953.

Katz, Ephraim. *The Film Encyclopedia*. Crowell, NY, 1979.

Kaufman, Beatrice, and Joseph Hennessey, eds. *The Letters of Alexander Woollcott*. Viking, NY, 1944.

Kaufman, Schima. *Everybody's Music*. Crowell, NY, 1938.

Kendrick, Alexander. *Prime Time: The Life of Edward R. Murrow*. Little, Brown, Boston, 1969.

Kernfeld, Barry, ed. *The New Grove Dictionary of Jazz*. St. Martin's, NY, 1991.

Ketchum, Richard M. *Will Rogers: His Life and Times*. American Heritage, NY, 1973.

Kieran, John. *Not Under Oath*. Houghton Mifflin, Boston, 1964.

Kinkle, Roger D. *The Complete Encyclopedia of Popular Music and Jazz, 1900–1950*. 4 vols. Arlington House, New Rochelle, NY, 1974.

Kirby, Edward M., and Jack W. Harris. *Star-Spangled Radio*. Ziff-Davis, Chicago, 1948.

Koch, Howard. *As Time Goes By: Memoirs of a Writer*. Harcourt Brace, NY, 1979.

―――. *The Panic Broadcast*. Little, Brown, Boston, 1970.

Kotsilibas-Davis, James. *The Barrymores*. Crown, NY, 1981.

Kupferberg, Herbert. *Those Fabulous Philadelphians: The Life and Times of a Great Orchestra*. Scribners, NY, 1969.

LaGuardia, Robert. *From Ma Perkins to Mary Hartman: The Illustrated History of Soap Operas*. Ballantine, NY, 1977.

Lamparski, Richard. *Whatever Became Of . . . ?* Various vols. Crown, NY, 1968–78.

Landry, Robert J. *This Fascinating Radio Business*. Bobbs-Merrill, Indianapolis, 1946.

Lass, A. H., Earle L. McGill, and Donald Axelrod. *Plays from Radio*. Houghton Mifflin, Boston, 1948.

Lawes, Lewis E. *Twenty Thousand Years in Sing Sing*. New Home Library reprint, NY, 1942.

Lawrence, Jerome, ed. *Off Mike: Radio Writing by the Nation's Top Radio Writers*. Essential Books, NY, 1944.

Lawton, Sherman Paxton. *Radio Continuity Types*. Expression, Boston, 1938.

Leaming, Barbara. *Orson Welles: A Biography*. Viking, NY, 1985.

Levant, Oscar. *Memoirs of an Amnesiac*. Putnam, NY, 1965.

―――. *The Unimportance of Being Oscar*. Putnam, NY, 1968.

Lewis, Fulton, Jr. *Praised and Damned*. Duell, Sloan, Pearce, NY, 1954.

Lewis, Tom. *Empire of the Air: The Men Who Made Radio*. HarperCollins, NY, 1991.

Lichty, Lawrence W., and Malachi C. Topping. *American Broadcasting: A Source Book on the History of Radio and Television*. Hastings House, NY, 1975.

Linkletter, Art. *Confessions of a Happy Man*. Bernard Geis, NY, 1960.

―――. *I Didn't Do It Alone*. Caroline House, Ottawa, IL, 1980.

―――. *Kids Say the Darndest Things*. Prentice-Hall, Englewood Cliffs, NJ, 1957.

―――. *People Are Funny*. Doubleday, Garden City, NY, 1947.

Lissauer, Robert. *Lissauer's Encyclopedia of Popular Music in America, 1888 to the Present*. Paragon House, NY, 1991.

Lopez, Vincent. *Lopez Speaking*. Citadel, NY, 1960.

Lord, Phillips H. *Seth Parker and His Jonesport Folks*. John Winston, Philadelphia, 1932.

Lotz, Rainer E., and Ulrich Neuert. *The AFRS "Jubilee" Transcription Programs: An Exploratory Discography*. Vol. 1. Norbert Ruecker, Frankfurt, 1985.

Luckman, Charles. *Twice in a Lifetime: From Soap to Skyscrapers*. Norton, NY, 1988.

Lyons, Eugene. *David Sarnoff: A Biography.* Harper & Row, NY, 1966.

McBride, Mary Margaret. *A Long Way from Missouri.* Putnam, NY, 1959.

———. *Out of the Air.* Doubleday, NY, 1960.

McCambridge, Mercedes. *The Quality of Mercy: An Autobiography.* Times Books, NY, 1981.

McCarthy, Albert. *The Dance Band Era.* Chilton, Philadelphia, 1971.

McCarthy, Joe, ed. *Fred Allen's Letters.* Doubleday, Garden City, NY, 1965.

MacDonald, J. Fred. *Don't Touch That Dial!* Nelson-Hall, Chicago, 1979.

McGill, Earle. *Radio Directing.* McGraw-Hill, NY, 1940.

McKelway, St. Clair. *Gossip: The Life and Times of Walter Winchell.* Viking, NY, 1940.

MacLeish, Archibald. *Six Plays.* Houghton Mifflin, Boston, 1980.

McNamee, Graham. *You're on the Air.* Harper, NY, 1926.

McNeil, Alex. *Total Television: A Comprehensive Guide to Programming from 1948 to the Present.* Penguin Books, NY, 1980.

MacShane, Frank, ed. *The Letters of Raymond Chandler.* Columbia University Press, NY, 1981.

MacVane, John. *On the Air in World War II.* Morrow, NY, 1979.

Maier, Paul L. *A Man Spoke, a World Listened.* McGraw-Hill, NY, 1963.

Malone, Ted. *Mansions of Imagination Album: A Listener's Aid to "American Pilgrimage."* Columbia University Press for NBC, NY, 1940.

———. *Pack Up Your Troubles.* Garden City, NY, 1946 (originally Whittlesey House, NY, 1942)

———. *Pilgrimage of Poetry: Ted Malone's Album of Poetic Shrines, a Listener's Aid.* Columbia University Press for NBC, 1940.

———. *Should Old Acquaintance.* Bookmark, Haddonfield, NJ (originally *American Pilgrimage,* Dodd Mead, NY, 1942).

———. *Ted Malone's Scrapbook: Favorite Selections form "Between the Bookends."* Bookmark, Camden, NJ, 1941.

Marcus, Sheldon. *Father Coughlin.* Little, Brown, Boston, 1973.

Marx, Arthur. *Everybody Loves Somebody Sometime: The Story of Dean Martin and Jerry Lewis.* Hawthorn, NY, 1974.

———. *Red Skelton: An Unauthorized Biography.* Dutton, NY, 1979.

Marx, Groucho. *Groucho and Me: The Autobi-ography of Groucho Marx.* Bernard Geis, NY, 1959.

———. *The Groucho Letters.* Simon & Schuster, NY, 1967.

———. *The Groucho Phile.* Wallaby, NY, 1977.

Marx, Groucho and Hector Arce. *The Secret Word Is Groucho.* Putnam, NY, 1976.

Marx, Groucho, and Richard Anobile. *The Marx Bros. Scrapbook.* Crown, NY, 1973.

Metz, Robert. *CBS: Reflections in a Bloodshot Eye.* Playboy Press, Chicago, 1975.

Mitchell, Curtis. *Cavalcade of Broadcasting.* Follett, Chicago, 1970.

Mize, J. T. H. *Bing Crosby and the Bing Crosby Style: Crosbyana, thru Biography—Photography—Discography.* Academy of American Music, Chicago, 1948.

Morgan, Henry. *Here's Morgan! The Original Bad Boy of Broadcasting.* Barricade Books, NY, 1994.

Morella, Joe, Edward Z. Epstein and Eleanor Clark. *The Amazing Careers of Bob Hope.* Arlington House, New Rochelle, NY, 1973.

Mott, Robert L. *Radio Sound Effects.* McFarland, Jefferson, NC, 1993.

Murray, Ken. *Life on a Pogo Stick: The Autobiography of a Comedian.* Holt, Rinehart, Winston, NY, 1960.

Murrow, Edward R. *In Search of Light: The Broadcasts of Edward R. Murrow, 1938–61.* Knopf, NY, 1967.

———. *This Is London.* Simon & Schuster, NY, 1941.

Murrow, Edward R., and Fred W. Friendly, eds. *See It Now.* Simon & Schuster, NY, 1955.

Museum of Television and Radio. *Jack Benny— The Radio and Television Work.* Harper-Collins, NY, 1991.

Mystery Chef. *The Mystery Chef's Own Cookbook.* Blakiston reprint, Philadelphia, 1945.

Nathan, Robert. *The Weans.* Knopf, NY, 1960.

Nelson, Ozzie. *Ozzie.* Prentice-Hall, Englewood Cliffs, NJ, 1973.

Nevins, Francis M., Jr., and Ray Stanich. *The Sounds of Detection: Ellery Queen's Adventures in Radio.* Brownstone Books, Madison, IN, 1983.

The New York Times Directory of Film. Arno Press/Random House, NY, 1971.

The New York Times Directory of the Theater. Arno Press/Quadrangle, NY, 1973.

Oboler, Arch. *Oboler Omnibus: Radio Plays and Personalities.* Duell, Sloan, Pearce, NY, 1945.

———. *Plays for Americans*. Farrar & Rinehart, NY, 1942.

O'Brien, P. J. *Will Rogers*. Great Britain, 1935.

Osgood, Dick. *Wyxie Wonderland: An Unauthorized Fifty-Year Diary of WXYZ, Detroit*. Bowling Green University, Bowling Green, OH, 1981.

Paar, Jack. *I Kid You Not*. Little, Brown, Boston, 1960.

Paley, William S. *As It Happened: A Memoir*. Doubleday, Garden City, NY, 1979.

Paper, Lewis J. *Empire: William S. Paley and the Making of CBS*. St. Martin's, NY, 1987.

Parish, James Robert, et al. *Hollywood Character Actors*. Arlington House, New Rochelle, NY, 1978.

Parsons, Louella. *The Gay Illiterate*. Garden City, NY, 1945.

Peerce, Jan. *The Bluebird of Happiness*. Harper & Row, NY, 1976.

Perry, Dick. *Not Just a Sound: The Story of WLW*. Prentice-Hall, Englewood Cliffs, NJ, 1971.

Persico, Joseph E. *Edward R. Murrow: An American Original*. McGraw-Hill, NY, 1988.

Peters, Margot. *The House of Barrymore*. Knopf, NY, 1990.

Peyton, Father Patrick. *All for Her*. Doubleday, Garden City, NY, 1967.

Ragan, David. *Who's Who in Hollywood, 1900–1976*. Arlington House, New Rochelle, NY, 1976.

Rhymer, Paul. *The Small House Halfway Up in the Next Block*. McGraw-Hill, NY, 1972.

———. *Vic and Sade: The Best Radio Plays of Paul Rhymer*. Seabury, NY, 1976.

Rogers, Will. *Autobiography*. Houghton Mifflin, Boston, 1949.

Rolo, Charles J. *Radio Goes to War*. Putnam, NY, 1942.

Rothafel, Samuel L., and Raymond Francis Yates. *Broadcasting—Its New Day*. Century, NY, 1925.

Rothel, David. *Who Was That Masked Man? The Story of the Lone Ranger*. Barnes, Cranbury, NJ, 1976.

Rovin, Jeff. *The Encyclopedia of Super Heroes*. Facts on File, NY, 1985.

Rust, Brian. *The American Dance Band Discography, 1917–1942*. 2 vols. Arlington House, New Rochelle, NY, 1975.

———. *The Dance Bands*. Arlington House, New Rochelle, NY, 1974.

———. *Jazz Records, 1897–1942*. 2 vols. Arlington House, New Rochelle, NY, 1978.

Ryan, Milo. *History in Sound: A Descriptive Listing of the KIRO-CBS Collection of Broadcast of the World War II Years ... in the University of Washington*. University of Washington Press, Seattle, 1963.

Sachs, Harvey, *Toscanini*. Lippincott, NY, 1978.

Saerchinger, César. *Hello America! Radio Adventures in Europe*. Houghton Mifflin, Boston, 1938.

St. John, Robert. *Encyclopedia of Radio and Television Broadcasting*. Cathedral Square, Milwaukee, 1970.

Sanger, Elliott M. *Rebel in Radio: The Story of WQXR*. Hastings House, NY, 1973.

Schechter, A. A., with Edward Anthony. *I Live on Air*. Stokes, NY, 1941.

Schisgall, Oscar. *Eyes on Tomorrow: The Evolution of Procter & Gamble*. J. G. Ferguson, Chicago, 1981.

Sennett, Ted. *The Old-Time Radio Book*. Pyramid, NY, 1976.

Settel, Irving. *A Pictorial History of Radio*. Grosset & Dunlap, NY, 1967.

Sevareid, Eric. *Not So Wild a Dream*. Knopf, NY, 1946.

Shaw, Arnold. *Sinatra: Twentieth-Century Romantic*. Holt Rinehart Winston, NY, 1968.

Shepherd, Donald, and Robert F. Slatzer. *Bing Crosby: The Hollow Man*. St. Martin's, NY, 1981.

Shirer, William L. *The Nightmare Years: 1930–1940*. Little, Brown, Boston, 1984.

Shurick, E. P. J. *The First Quarter-Century of American Broadcasting*. Midland, Kansas City, 1946.

Simon, George T. *The Big Bands*. Macmillan, NY, 1967.

———. *Glenn Miller and His Orchestra*. Crowell, NY, 1974.

———. *Simon Says: The Sights and Sounds of the Swing Era, 1935–1955*. Arlington House, New Rochelle, NY, 1971.

Slater, Robert. *This Is CBS: A Chronicle of Sixty Years*. Prentice-Hall, Englewood Cliffs, NJ, 1988.

Slide, Anthony. *Great Radio Personalities in Historic Photographs*. Dover, NY, 1982.

Smith, Bruce. *The Story of Little Orphan Annie*. Ballantine, NY, 1982.

Smith, Kate. *Upon My Lips a Song*. Funk & Wagnalls, NY, 1960.

Smith, Sally Bedell. *In All His Glory: The Life of William S. Paley.* Simon & Schuster, NY, 1990.

Sperber, A. M. *Murrow: His Life and Times.* Michael Joseph, London, 1987.

Spivak, John L. *Shrine of the Silver Dollar: The Documentary Story of Father Coughlin.* Modern Age, NY, 1940.

Stars of the Radio: Art Portraits of Famous Radio Favorites with Short Biographical Sketches. Broadcast Weekly, San Francisco, 1932.

Stedman, Raymond William. *The Serials.* University of Oklahoma, Norman, 1971.

Stein, Charles W. *American Vaudeville as Seen by Its Contemporaries.* Knopf, NY, 1984.

Stern, Bill. *The Taste of Ashes.* Henry Holt, NY, 1959.

Stuart, Lyle. *The Secret Life of Walter Winchell.* Boar's Head Books, NY, 1953.

Stumpf, Charles, and Tom Price. *Heavenly Days! The Story of Fibber McGee and Molly.* World of Yesterday Publications, Waynesville, NC, 1987.

Summers, Harrison B., ed. *A Thirty-Year History of Programs Carried on National Radio Networks in the United States, 1926–1956.* Arno Press, NY, 1971.

Swing, Raymond Gram. *Good Evening: A Professional Memoir.* Harcourt Brace World, NY, 1964.

———. *How War Came.* Norton, NY, 1939.

———. *Preview of History.* Doubleday-Doran, Garden City, NY, 1943.

Taylor, F. Chase (Colonel Stoopnagle). *You Wouldn't Know Me from Adam.* Whittlesey House, NY, 1944.

Taylor, Glenhall. *Before Television: The Radio Years.* Barnes, Cranbury, NJ, 1979.

Taylor, Marion Sayle. *Stranger Than Fiction: "By the Voice of Experience."* Dodd, Mead, NY, 1934.

———. *The Voice of Experience.* Dodd, Mead, NY, 1935.

Taylor, Robert. *Fred Allen: His Life and Wit.* Little, Brown, Boston, 1989.

Tebbel, John. *An American Dynasty.* Doubleday, Garden City, NY, 1947.

Teichmann, Howard. *Smart Aleck: The Wit, World and Life of Alexander Woollcott.* Morrow, NY, 1976.

Terrace, Vincent. *Radio's Golden Years.* Barnes, San Diego, 1981.

Thomas, Bob. *Bud and Lou: The Abbott and Costello Story.* Lippincott, NY, 1977.

———. *The One and Only Bing.* Grosset & Dunlap, NY, 1977.

———. *Winchell.* Doubleday, Garden City, NY, 1971.

Thomas, Lowell. *Good Evening, Everybody.* Morrow, NY, 1976.

———. *So Long Until Tomorrow.* Morrow, NY, 1977.

Thomas, Tony. *Film Score: The View from the Podium.* Barnes, Cranbury, NJ, 1979.

Thompson, Charles. *Bing: The Authorized Biography.* McKay, NY, 1976.

Treadwell, Bill. *Head, Heart and Heel: The Story of Uncle Don Carney.* Mayfair, NY, 1958.

Tull, Charles. *Father Coughlin and the New Deal.* Syracuse University Press, Syracuse, NY, 1965.

Tunney, Kieran. *Tallulah: Darling of the Gods.* Dutton, NY, 1973.

Vallee, Rudy. *Let the Chips Fall.* Stackpole, Harrisburg, PA, 1975.

———. *My Time Is Your Time.* Obolensky, NY, 1962.

———. *Vagabond Dreams Come True.* Dutton, NY, 1930.

Van Deman, Ruth, and Fanny Walker Yeatman. *Aunt Sammy's Radio Recipes: The Great Depression Cookbook.* Universe Books, NY, 1975.

Walker, Leo. *The Big Band Almanac.* Vinewood, Hollywood, 1978.

———. *The Wonderful Era of the Great Dance Bands.* Doubleday, Garden City, NY, 1972.

Waller, Judith C. *Radio—The Fifth Estate.* Houghton Mifflin, Boston, 1946.

Ward, Louis B. *Father Charles E. Coughlin: An Authorized Biography.* Tower, Detroit, 1933.

Waring, Virginia. *Fred Waring and the Pennsylvanians.* University of Illinois Press, Urbana, 1997.

Warren, Donald. *Radio Priest: Charles Coughlin, the Father of Hate Radio.* Free Press, NY, 1996.

Weaver, John D. *Carnation: The First Seventy-five Years, 1899–1974.* Carnation Company, Los Angeles, 1974.

Webb, Jack. *The Badge.* Prentice-Hall, Englewood Cliffs, NJ, 1958.

Welles, Orson and Peter Bogdanovich. *This Is Orson Welles*. HarperCollins, NY, 1992.

Wertheim, Arthur Frank. *Radio Comedy*. Oxford University Press, NY, 1979.

Whipple, James. *How to Write for Radio*. Whittlesey House, NY, 1938.

White, Llewellyn. *The American Radio*. University of Chicago Press, 1947.

Wiley, Mason and Damien Bona. *Inside Oscar: The Unofficial History of the Academy Awards*. Ballantine Books, NY, 1986.

Williams, John R. *This Was Your Hit Parade*. Rockland, ME, 1973.

Willson, Meredith. *And There I Stood with My Piccolo*. Doubleday, Garden City, NY, 1948.

Wilson, Earl. *Sinatra: An Unauthorized Biography*. Macmillan, NY, 1976.

Winchell, Walter. *Winchell Exclusive*. Prentice-Hall, Englewood Cliffs, NJ, 1975.

Wons, Tony. *'R' You Listenin'?* Reilly & Lee, Chicago, 1931.

———. *Tony's Scrap Book*. Radio editions of 1927–29, 1931–39, 1940–43, and 1944–45, 13 vols. All Reilly & Lee, Chicago.

———. *Your Dog and My Dog: Poems from Tony Wons' Famous Radio Scrap Book*. Reilly & Lee, Chicago, 1935.

Wright, J. Elwin. *The Old-Fashioned Revival Hour and the Broadcasters*. Fellowship Press, Boston, 1940.

Wylie, Max. *Best Broadcasts, 1938–39*. Whittlesey House, NY, 1939.

———. *Best Broadcasts, 1939–40*. Whittlesey House, NY, 1940.

———. *Radio and Television Writing*. Rinehart, NY, 1950.

———. *Radio Writing*. Farrar & Rinehart, NY, 1939.

Yagoda, Ben. *Will Rogers: A Biography*. Knopf, NY, 1993.

Young, Jordan R. *Spike Jones and His City Slickers*. Disharmony Books, Beverly Hills, CA, 1984.

Zolotow, Maurice. *No People Like Show People*. Random House, NY, 1951.

NEWSPAPERS AND PERIODICALS

American Magazine. Various articles including "Married Life in a Goldfish Bowl" by Vance Packard, Feb. 1948; "Up from Peoria" (*Fibber McGee*) by J. B. Griswold, March 1942; "Molly Goes Marching On" (*Goldbergs*) by William A. H. Birnie, Nov. 1941; "High, Low, Ace and Jane" (*Easy Aces*) by Jerome Beatty, Jan. 1949; "Master Mind" (Quiz Kids) by Jerome Beatty, Feb. 1941; "Quiz Dizzy" by Jerome Beatty, June 1942; "King of the Mad Men" (Linkletter) by Jerome Beatty, May 1948; "Baby Miracle" (Quiz Kids) by Jerome Beatty, Aug. 1943; "Watch Out for Candid Mike" by Jerome Beatty, July 1948; "Want a Job at a Million Dollars" by Beverly Smith, Dec. 1945.

Atlantic Monthly. "Perennial Adolescence" by Bernard Iddings Bell, Jan. 1947.

Collier's. Various articles including "The Man Who Comes to Breakfast" by Robert Froman, May 13, 1950; "Listeners Do All My Work" by Don McNeill, Jan. 10, 1953; "Alan Young—Beloved Bumbler" by Lloyd Shearer, Oct. 6, 1951; "Amos 'n' Andy—Ain't Dat Sumpin' " by John Crosby, Oct. 16, 1948; "Radio's D.A.—And How He Grew" by Eleanor Harris, May 20, 1950; "Jack the Cost Killer" (*Mystery Chef*) by Nina Wilcox Putnam, Feb. 7, 1948; "Butch Says: Cut It Out!" (La Guardia) by Amy Porter, April 28, 1945; "The Great Larynx" (Linkletter) by Robert Southern, May 28, 1949.

Coronet. "What's the Secret of (King) Arthur Godfrey?" by Carol Hughes, Dec. 1949; "The 2,000,000 Words of Lowell Thomas" by Maurice Zolotow, June 1949.

Cosmopolitan. "Mr. Elliott (Bob) and Mr. Goulding (Ray)" by Richard Gehman, Aug. 1956.

Current Biography. 1940–59.

Erbania (Tampa, Fl). "Tarzan Radio Series." by D. Peter Ogden, Summer 1985.

Forum "What America Listens To" by Darwin L. Teilhet, May 1932.

Harper's. "The Easy Chair" by Bernard DeVoto, monthly column reviewing radio ca. 1940s to early 1950s; "The Men from Mars" by John Houseman, Dec. 1948.

Hobbies. "Jessica Dragonette" by Lou Dumont, Sept. 1977.

Journal of Popular Culture. Bowling Green State University, Ohio. "In Depth Radio," vol. 12, no. 2 (1979).

Ladies Home Journal. "The Real Parents of Henry Aldrich" by Janet Flanner, Sept, 1942.

Life Magazine. Short photo essays on various radio stars (Jack Benny, Henry Morgan, *Ma*

Perkins, etc.), various dates; "A Final Fiancé For Helen Trent" by Peter Bunzel, July 11, 1960.

Look Magazine. Various articles including "Breakfast with Blondie," Dec. 1945.

Mainliner. "Renaissance for Radio Drama" by Joel Makower, May 1980.

New York Times. Daily radio logs, 1920s–1960s.

New Yorker. Various articles including "Their Own Gravity" (Bob and Ray) by Whitney Balliett, Sept. 24, 1973; "The All-American Breakfast" by Philip Hamburger, Aug. 10, 1946; "The World on His Back" (Murrow) by Charles Wertenbaker, Dec. 26, 1953; "The Crier" (Gabriel Heatter) by Philip Hamburger, Jan. 20, 1945; "Soapland" by James Thurber, five parts, May 15, May 29, June 12, July 3, July 24, 1948.

Newsweek. Weekly radio column, 1930's–1950's.

Playboy. Interview with George Burns by Arthur Cooper, June 1978.

Radio Digest. Various issues, early 1920s.

Radio Guide. Weekly, 1933–40; also *Movie and Radio Guide*, 1940–43. Hundreds of articles on every aspect of radio broadcasting and detailed daily radio schedules.

Radio Historical Association of Colorado newsletter. *Clara, Lu and Em*, by Don Koehnemann, Nov. 1976.

Radio Life. Weekly, 1942–50; *TV-Radio Life*, 1950–55.

Radio Mirror. Various issues, 1930s–1950s; also *TV-Radio Mirror*.

Radio News. "The Eveready Hour" by Julia V. Shawell, May 1928.

Radio Stars. Scattered issues, 1930s.

Radioland. Monthly, 1934–35.

R/C Model Builder. "Air Adventures of Jimmie Allen" by Walter House, Nov./Dec. 1980.

Saturday Evening Post. Various articles including "The McGees of Wistful Vista" by Robert M. Yoder, April 9 and 16, 1949; "Eighty Hours for a Laugh" (Fred Allen) by J. Bryan III, Oct. 4, 1941; "Backstage in Allen's Alley" by George Sessions Perry, Jan. 4, 1947; "Self-Made Solomon" (John J. Anthony) by Earl Wilson, May 8, 1943; "Morgan the Maleficent" (Henry Morgan) by John Durant, Sept. 19, 1942; "Wise Guys of the Air" (*Information, Please*) by Henry F. Pringle, May 11, 1946; "Jack Benny's $400

Yaks," by Cleveland Amory, Nov. 6, 1948; "Wanna Buy a Duck?" by Joe Penner, Nov. 10, 1934; "Philosopher at Work" (Kate Smith) by Jack Alexander, Aug. 15, 1942; "Hi-Yo Silver!" by J. Bryan III, Oct. 14, 1939; "The Great Gabbo" (Heatter) by Jack Alexander, March 15, 1947; "The Magnificent Ignoramus" (Joe Kelly) by John Lear, July 18, 1944; "Quiz Queen" by Maurice Zolotow, July 27, 1946; "Washboard Weepers" by Maurice Zolotow, May 29, 1943; "Anyway, the Kids Like Them" (Uncle Don, etc.) by John La Cerda, Jan. 12, 1946.

SPERDVAC Radiogram. Monthly newsletter, 1983–95.

Time. Weekly radio column, 1930s–1950s.

Tune In. Ca. 1944–45.

Variety. Various reviews, articles, and obits, ca. 1931–50.

WOW News Tower. Monthly newsletter from WOW, Omaha, 1937–49, with news of NBC shows.

LOGS

Bright, R. G. *Escape*, ca. early 1970s.

Brooks, Barry. *This Is Jazz*, ca. early 1970s.

Brooks, Barry, with Richard Brooks. *Lux Radio Theater.* ca. early 1970s.

Drew, Bernard. *Hopalong Cassidy Rides the Airwaves of the Old West*, log and article. Attic Revivals Press, Great Barrington, MA, 1995.

Dunn, Gary A., Larry Gassman and John Gassman. *Jack Benny Radio*, June 1990.

Eidemiller, Randy, and Chris Lembesis. *Dragnet*, 1992; *Suspense: The Definitive Story and Complete Log of All 944 Broadcasts*, 1994.

Gassman, John and Chris Lembesis. *The Six Shooter*, ca. 1991.

Haefele, Dan. *Crime Classics*, compiled for SPERDVAC, no date.

Hickerson, Jay. *The Ultimate History of Network Radio Programming and Guide to All Circulating Shows*, 1992; *The New, Revised Ultimate History of Network Radio Programming and Guide to All Circulating Shows*, 1996; *Theatre Guild on the Air*, 1992; *Mercury Theater on the Air/Campbell Playhouse*, 1995; *Lux Radio Theater*, May 1994; *I Love a Mystery*, July 1993.

MacDonald, J. Fred. *Destination Freedom, 1948–1950*, log and article.

Murray, Pat. *Sherlock Holmes on the Air*, with additions by Ray Stanich, revised 1978.

Price, Tom. *Fibber McGee's Closet*, 1987; *Suspense*, 1987.

Sabis, Bill. *Adventures in Time and Space on NBC Radio's Dimension X and X Minus One*, 1978.

Salomonson, Terry. *The Lone Ranger*, 1985; *Challenge of the Yukon*, 1988; *The Green Hornet*, 1990; *Dragnet*, 1991; *The Great Gildersleeve*, 1997; *Lum and Abner*, 1997.

Salomonson, Terry, and Don Aston. *Escape*, 1992; *Yours Truly, Johnny Dollar*, 1992.

Schwarz, Barbara. *Vic and Sade*, listing in progress.

Siegel, Dave. *Night Watch*, ca. 1982; *Damon Runyon Theater*, no date.

Stanich, Ray. *Campbell Playhouse; Columbia Workshop; Curtain Time; Dr. Christian; Everything for the Boys; Good News of 1938–40; Grand Marquee; Hallmark Hall of Fame; Hallmark Playhouse; Hollywood Hotel; Hollywood in Person; Hollywood Premiere; Hollywood Showcase; Hollywood Soundstage; Hollywood Star Playhouse; Hollywood Startime; Inner Sanctum Mysteries; Lights Out Revisited; Magic Key; Mercury Theater; Murder at Midnight; Norman Corwin Programs; Philip Morris Shows; This Is My Best; U.S. Borax Presents Death Valley Days*; many others. Mostly undated, ca. 1970s and 1980s.

Wedin, David Albert. *I Love a Mystery*, no date, ca. early 1970s.

Wedin, Marion D. *One Man's Family*, 1974; *Mercury Theater*, ca. 1974.

PREMIUM BOOKS AND MISCELLANEOUS

Breneman, Tom. *200,000 for Breakfast*. Kellogg Co. premium book, 1943.

Cameron, W. J. *A Series of Talks*, given on the *Ford Sunday Evening Hour*, 1935–36. Dearborn, MI, June 1936.

CBS Radio. Hundreds of publicity releases with scheduling, program, and personality information.

Flynn, Bess. *Bachelor's Children: A Synopsis of the Radio Program*. Premium book, Old Dutch Cleanser, Chicago, 1939.

Gartlan, George, H., ed. *Great Composers: Six Radio Dramatizations Presented on "The Family Hour."* Prudential, 1942.

[Heidt, Horace]. *Horace Heidt Show: In Person*. Horace Heidt Foundation, 1952 edition.

King, Fred. *Jack Armstrong Encyclopedia*. 1986.

———. *Jack Armstrong Scrapbook: A Study in Premium Advertising*. 1979.

Langworthy, Yolanda. *Poems from Arabesque*. Walter J. Black, NY, 1930.

McNeill, Don. *Don McNeill's Favorite Poems*, premium book, 1951; *Breakfast Club Family Album*, premium book, 1942; *20 Years of Corn*, premium book, 1953; *Breakfast Club Yearbooks 1947, 1948, 1949*, Chicago.

Malone, Ted. *The American Album of Poetry*. Rodeheaver, Chicago, 1938.

Morse, Carlton E. Various premium booklets including *Jack's Camera Scrapbook*, ca. 1932–33, Wesson Oil; *One Man's Family Looks at Life*, 1938, *Fannie Barbour's Memory Book*, 1940, and *Barbour Family Scrapbook*, 1946, all Standard Brands; *The Barbour Family Album* 1951, and *Mother Barbour's Favorite Recipes*, ca. 1952, both Miles Laboratories; and *This I Give*, 1953. Various scripts including the first chapter of *One Man's Family* and complete serials of *I Love a Mystery*.

NBC. *Today's Children*. Pillsbury, Minneapolis, 1937.

Ripley, Robert. *A New Believe It or Not*. Premium book by General Household Utilities for Grunow Radios, Chicago.

Rogers, Will. *Wit and Philosophy from the Radio talks of America's Humorist*. Scripts for entire CBS series April-June 1930. E. R. Squibb & Sons, 1930.

Ruthledge, Dr. John (fictitious character name). *The Guiding Light*. Chicago, 1938.

Wicker, Ireene. *When the Great Were Small: Childhood Stories of the Great Masters*. Kellogg Co., Battle Creek, MI, 1935.

WMAQ, Chicago. *The Story of WMAQ*. 1931.

Your America. Bound scripts, 1944–45.

Index

A name or a program in **boldface** denotes a main entry for that title; A number in parentheses indicates more than one appearance by the person or subject in separate programs on the same page.